*Fourth Edition*

# The Bedford Guide for College Writers

*with Reader, Research Manual, and Handbook*

X. J. Kennedy, Dorothy M. Kennedy, and Sylvia A. Holladay

Bedford Books *of* St. Martin's Press ⧉ Boston

FOR BEDFORD BOOKS

*President and Publisher:* Charles H. Christensen
*General Manager and Associate Publisher:* Joan E. Feinberg
*Managing Editor:* Elizabeth M. Schaaf
*Developmental Editors:* Denise B. Wydra, Laura Arcari, Pam Ozaroff
*Editorial Assistants:* Adrian Harris, Mark Reimold, Verity Winship
*Production Editor:* John Amburg
*Production Assistants:* Karen S. Baart, Maureen Murray
*Copyeditor:* Barbara G. Flanagan
*Text Design:* Claire Seng-Niemoeller
*Cover Design:* Hannus Design Associates

Library of Congress Catalog Card Number: 95–80795

0   9   8   7   6

f   e   d   c   b   a


*For information, write:* St. Martin's Press, Inc.
175 Fifth Avenue, New York, NY 10010
*Editorial Offices:* Bedford Books *of* St. Martin's Press
75 Arlington Street, Boston, MA 02116

ISBN: 0–312–11557–1

## ACKNOWLEDGMENTS

*Acknowledgments and copyrights are continued at the back of the book,
which constitutes an extension of the copyright page. It is a violation of the
law to reproduce these selections by any means whatsoever without the
written permission of the copyright holder.*

Kurt Andersen. "Oprah and Jo-Jo the Dog-Faced Boy." From the
October 11, 1993 issue of *Time.* © 1993 by Time, Inc. Reprinted by
permission.

Deborah C. Andrews. From "Words About Words" in *Chemical
and Engineering News*, March 13, 1989, 67(11), pp. 45–46. Reprinted
by permission of the author.

Russell Baker. "The Art of Eating Spaghetti." Reprinted from
*Growing Up* by Russell Baker, © 1982. Used with the permission of
Congdon & Weed, Inc. and Contemporary Books, Chicago.

Judy Brady. "I Want a Wife." From *Ms.,* December 1971.
Reprinted by permission of the author.

Rachel Carson. "A Fable for Tomorrow." From *Silent Spring* by
Rachel Carson. Copyright © 1962 by Rachel L. Carson, renewed 1990
by Roger Christie. Reprinted by permission of Houghton Mifflin Co.
All rights reserved.

Stephen L. Carter. "The Black Table, the Empty Seat, and the Tie"
from *Lure and Loathing: Essays on Race, Identity, and the Ambivalence of
Assimilation* edited by Gerald Early. Copyright © 1993 by Stephen L.
Carter. Reprinted by permission of the author.

Bruce Catton. "Grant and Lee: A Study in Contrasts." From *The

American Story,* edited by Earl Schenck Miers. © 1956 by United States
Capitol Historical Society.

*Consumer Reports.* From "Is There a DAT in Your Future?" Copyright 1989 by Consumers Union of U.S., Inc., Yonkers, NY 10703-
1057. Excerpted by permission from *Consumer Reports,* January 1989.

Stephanie Coontz. "The Complexities of Assessing Family
Trends" from *The Way We Never Were* by Stephanie Coontz. Copy-
right © 1992 by BasicBooks, a division of HarperCollins Publishers,
Inc. Reprinted by permission of BasicBooks, a division of Harper-
Collins Publishers, Inc.

Norman Cousins. Excerpt from "How to Make People Smaller
Than They Are." Originally appeared in *Saturday Review*, 1978.
Reprinted by permission of Eleanor Cousins.

Harry Crews. Excerpt from "The Car." From *Florida Frenzy* by
Harry Crews. Copyright © 1982 by Harry Crews. Reprinted by permission of John Hawkins & Associates, Inc.

Frank J. Cunningham. From "Writing Philosophy: Sequential Essays and Objective Tests," College Composition and Communication, May 1985. Copyright 1985 by the National Council of Teachers
of English. Reprinted with permission.

# Preface: To the Instructor

No one ever learned to swim or to play a musical instrument by reading a book. Similarly, no one ever learned to write by reading or talking about writing. If a student is to learn to write well and confidently, practice and feedback are more valuable than theory and prescriptions. We hope the structure of *The Bedford Guide for College Writers* demonstrates this conviction.

This fourth edition of *The Bedford Guide*, like the third edition, offers four composition books in one. One compact volume offers a process-oriented rhetoric, a thematically arranged reader, a full research manual, and a comprehensive handbook — all the textbooks you and your students will need for a thorough writing course. *The Bedford Guide* is now available in two other versions as well: as a briefer textbook without a handbook, and as two books in one, a rhetoric and a reader.

The revisions for this new edition, incorporating current findings of composition research, strengthen each of the four books. Once again, the emphasis in *The Bedford Guide* is on students' writing, not just reading and talking about writing. Pressed immediately into the act of writing, students learn by doing without being burdened by a lot of preliminary advice. *The Bedford Guide* is based on our belief that writing is the lively, usually surprising, often rewarding art of thinking while working with language.

Book by book, here are the highlights of this new edition.

## BOOK ONE: A WRITER'S GUIDE

This first book is a process-oriented rhetoric which, as before, involves students immediately and repeatedly in the act of writing.

*In Parts One and Two, the chapters are structured alike.* Part One, "A Writer's Resources," focuses on five major resources that writers draw on: recall (Chapter 1), observation (Chapter 2), reading (Chapter 3), conversation (Chapter 4), and imagination (Chapter 5). Part Two, "Thinking Critically," then introduces students to six major critical strategies often used in writing:

analyzing (Chapter 6), comparing and contrasting (Chapter 7), explaining causes and effects (Chapter 8), taking a stand (Chapter 9), proposing a solution (Chapter 10), and evaluating (Chapter 11). Each of these first eleven chapters begins with "Learning from Other Writers" — two model essays, one by a professional and one by a student writer. Next, students are whisked into an assignment in "Learning by Writing." As they draw on the chapter's resource or deploy its critical strategy to write an essay, students are guided by suggestions for generating ideas, planning, drafting, developing, revising, and editing. "Learning by Writing" also features checklists for discovery, revision, and peer response, as well as tips for writing with a computer and for collaborative learning. After students learn by writing, "Applying What You Learn" links the resource or critical strategy with other courses across the curriculum and with on-the-job situations. Each chapter ends with "Making Connections" sections that point the student toward specific selections in Book Two, *A Writer's Reader.*

Several features have been extensively revised for the fourth edition. The introduction to the writing process now explicitly connects critical thinking, creativity, and composing. The emphasis on critical thinking has been strengthened throughout Part Two. Of special note are a new and expanded introduction to Part Two, "Critical Thinking Strategies for Writing," which explains how writers use critical thinking strategies and stresses the importance of supporting assertions with evidence, and the new chapter on comparison and contrast (Chapter 7).

*Part Three, "Special Writing Situations," explores three situations in which students are likely to find themselves: writing about literature, writing in class, and writing for business.*

Chapter 12, "Writing about Literature," guides students through writing an analysis of a literary work, using samples of student writing about both fiction and poetry. It also illustrates how to compare and contrast two literary selections. This chapter includes a glossary of terms for analyzing the elements of literature and a section on specific strategies for writing about literature — synopsis and paraphrase. For the fourth edition, we have added two new twentieth-century poems and two new student papers.

Chapter 13, "Writing in Class," focuses on taking essay examinations, with particular emphasis on timed competency exams.

Chapter 14, "Writing for Business," guides students in their personal and professional business writing — letters, memoranda, and résumés. For the fourth edition, this chapter has been extensively revised to provide current information and up-to-date models. It now also covers electronic mail.

*Part Four, "A Writer's Strategies," presents in a handy sequence of chapters the basics of the writing process.* It explains and exemplifies the stages of writing and provides practical tips and exercises to help students improve their writing. This part contains chapters on generating ideas (Chapter 15), planning (Chapter 16), drafting (Chapter 17), developing (Chapter 18), and revising and editing (Chapter 19). Part Four also includes strategies for working with other writers (Chapter 20) and for writing with a computer (Chapter 21).

For the fourth edition, we have added "Making Connections" sections at the ends of several chapters in Part Four. These sections refer students to specific selections in the reader that exemplify the writing strategies covered in those chapters. Chapter 21, "Writing with a Computer," has also been thoroughly revised; it now provides more closely detailed information on word processing and addresses the questions and concerns of those writing on electronic networks.

Altogether, the rhetoric includes thirty readings — twenty-two of which are new — and more guidance on planning, drafting, developing, and revising essays than ever before.

## BOOK TWO: A WRITER'S READER

*A Writer's Reader* is the only thematic reader in a book of this kind. Thirty-seven brief prose selections — 29 new — are arranged in six chapters, each focusing on a familiar theme: families (Chapter 22), men and women (Chapter 23), American diversity (Chapter 24), the world of work (Chapter 25), popular culture (Chapter 26), and the interaction of nature and technology (Chapter 27). The reader mixes writings both new and familiar by writers who are culturally and professionally diverse. Here you can find perennial favorites such as E. B. White's "Once More to the Lake," Jessica Mitford's "Behind the Formaldehyde Curtain," and Judy Brady's "I Want a Wife" alongside essays by engaging contemporary writers such as Toni Morrison, Richard Rodriguez, Stephen Jay Gould, and Amy Tan. These selections complement the models in the rhetoric. Introduced by a biographical headnote, each reading is followed by questions — on meaning, writing strategies, the writer's choices, vocabulary, and connections to other selections — and suggested writing assignments, one personal and one analytic. We trust that *A Writer's Reader* will give students plenty to write about, on topics that they care about.

In the fourth edition, *A Writer's Reader* includes more readings that directly model for students the types of writing — informational, analytic, and argumentative — they themselves will be expected to produce in college. New photographs and journal prompts at the beginning of each chapter and journal prompts following each selection will stimulate writing and discussion. We have labeled the questions following selections to make them easier to use. To engage students in a broader understanding of the rhetorical context for writing, we have added a new question after each selection asking students to analyze the writer's choices.

## BOOK THREE: A WRITER'S RESEARCH MANUAL

*A Writer's Research Manual* is the most comprehensive research guide in a combination textbook. All the major information that students involved in research need to know is here, in chapters reorganized and updated since the last edition: conducting library research (Chapter 28), conducting field research (Chapter 29), writing from sources (Chapter 30), and documenting sources (Chapter 31). It is the only research section in a combination textbook to include annotated student papers in both MLA and APA formats and such an extensive selection of documentation models — 61 MLA and 38 APA. In fact, this book within a book can hold its own against research guides offered separately.

In this fourth edition, the manual is a more useful tool than ever before. The new organization of the research manual supports a process approach, reflecting the way research is actually practiced. It includes new coverage of the Internet, databases, and other electronic sources; consolidates all of the library research coverage into a single chapter; and includes three new annotated student papers — a library research paper (MLA style), a combination field-library research paper (APA style), and a researched literary analysis (MLA style).

## BOOK FOUR: A WRITER'S HANDBOOK

With thorough coverage of all standard handbook topics, reference tabs, highlighted rules, and boxed charts, *A Writer's Handbook* looks and works like a conventional handbook. Unique editing checklists and ESL guidelines are spaced at key positions throughout. The handbook includes sixty-six exercise sets for practice in and out of class. (Answers to the first five questions in each set are provided in the back of the book so that students can check their understanding.)

For the fourth edition, one-third of the exercises have been replaced. Eleven new connected-discourse exercises — 19 total — allow students to hone their skills in a narrative context. We believe that you will find no other handbook at the back of a composition textbook so useful for student reference and practice as this one.

## ANCILLARIES

As before, *The Bedford Guide for College Writers* is accompanied by a unique two-volume instructor's manual that offers an abundance of resources and practical advice. For the first time, the fourth edition now comes complete with a full ancillary package that gives instructors a wide array of resources. Providing flexibility and support for experienced instructors and beginning instructors alike, this package includes a variety of supplements that make it easier for you to tailor your course to your students' needs.

- *Practical Suggestions*, Volume One of *Teaching with The Bedford Guide for College Writers*, by Shirley Morahan of Northeast Missouri State University, revised by Linda S. LaPointe of St. Petersburg Junior College, and revised for this edition by Sylvia A. Holladay of St. Petersburg Junior College and Phillip Sipiora of the University of South Florida, offers resources and practical advice for busy composition instructors. It includes pop quizzes, syllabi, suggestions for teaching the readings, and tips on helping students develop their own critical thinking abilities.
- *Background Readings*, Volume Two of *Teaching with The Bedford Guide for College Writers*, is an anthology of articles on composition and rhetoric,

covering theory, research, and pedagogy. Revised and updated by Shirley Morahan, *Background Readings* now includes 29 articles on composition and rhetoric, chosen to provide novice instructors with professional resources to help them get the most out of this textbook and to develop their own teaching techniques. These readings are connected to *The Bedford Guide for College Writers* and to the classroom by introductions and exercises.

NEW • *On-line with The Bedford Guide for College Writers*, by David Hartman of St. Petersburg Junior College, is a comprehensive booklet for both novice and experienced computer users. It acquaints instructors with networks and the Internet and offers concrete suggestions for using computers with students in a variety of capacities: for word processing, for collaboration, as a research tool, and for distance learning. The comprehensive appendices and glossary also make it an indispensable reference tool.

NEW • *Supplemental Exercises for The Bedford Guide for College Writers*, by Mitch Evich of Northeastern University, is an ample set of exercises for students who require practice beyond that supplied in *A Writer's Handbook*; it also includes a set of exercises for ESL students.

NEW • *Exercises for The Bedford Guide for College Writers* is a software version of the *Supplemental Exercises* by Mitch Evich. It also includes all the exercises in *The Bedford Guide* itself. This software gives immediate, on-screen feedback, allowing students to work at their own pace and instructors to monitor students' progress.

NEW • *Transparencies to Accompany The Bedford Guide for College Writers* provides supplemental examples of writing strategies, visual representations of rhetorical and grammatical concepts, and other materials useful for classroom discussion.

• *Preparing for the CLAST with The Bedford Guide for College Writers* by Barbara Sloan of Santa Fe Community College and Carolyn Christensen West of Daytona Beach Community College, a manual intended to help Florida students prepare for the essay and objective English language skills portions of the College Level Academic Skills Test, has been updated. All sections of the booklet are keyed to *A Writer's Handbook*.

NEW • *The Bedford Bibliography for Teachers of Writing*, fourth edition, by Patricia Bizzell of College of the Holy Cross and Bruce Herzberg of Bentley College, provides an annotated list of books, articles, and periodicals devoted to composition and rhetoric together with a historical overview of these fields. This booklet serves as a useful resource for any writing instructor and is an ideal supplement for graduate courses in the teaching of writing.

NEW • *The Bedford Guide for Writing Tutors*, by Leigh Ryan of the University of Maryland at College Park, features exercises that help tutors practice and discuss useful skills and a bibliography that points them to other helpful resources. This guide is full of suggestions and strategies to give new tutors the expertise and confidence they need to assist students in the writing center.

- *MicroGrade: A Teacher's Gradebook* is grade-keeping software that helps instructors establish grading parameters, post scores, provide progress reports to students, and calculate final grades.

## THANKS AND APPRECIATION

Working on the fourth edition of *The Bedford Guide for College Writers* has been a giant collaborative writing project, different only in scope from those assigned to the students for whom we write. Many individuals have contributed significantly to our project, and we extend our thanks to all of them. Three members of the Bedford staff deserve special recognition. Publisher Charles H. Christensen and Associate Publisher Joan E. Feinberg have provided unstinting encouragement and inspiration from the beginnings of the book. We deeply appreciate their creative suggestions and perceptive advice, and their faith in our work has buoyed us through long hours at the computer screen. Editor Denise Wydra patiently read and reread and cogently edited our manuscript, ferreting out the gaps and inconsistencies, spotting the problems, and coming up with sound solutions. Her wise suggestions for refinements have helped make this edition a much better book. She also coordinated all aspects of the project and kept all of us on track and on schedule. Thanks also to John Amburg, Production Editor, who oversaw the redesign of the book and shepherded the book through production.

Other members of the Bedford staff contributed greatly to the fourth edition. Laura Arcari edited the research manual and handbook and oversaw the development of the ancillaries. Pam Ozaroff judiciously edited the reader. Mark Reimold assisted with the reader and edited volume one of the instructor's manual. Joanne Diaz assisted with volume one of the instructor's manual. Andrea Goldman edited volume two of the instructor's manual. Adrian Harris edited the supplemental exercises and cleared the permissions for the book. Verity Winship edited the chapter on writing about literature. Donna Dennison, Ellen Kuhl, and Susan Pace are the promotion crew who have coordinated and produced all of the advertising and publicity for the book; they also oversaw the redesign of the cover. Karen Baart and Maureen Murray assisted with the production of the book and designed the ancillaries. Also contributing significantly were Elizabeth Schaaf, Managing Editor; Karen Henry, Executive Editor; and Karen Rose, who assisted with the ancillaries. Once again, Barbara Flanagan did an efficient job of copyediting. Claire Seng-Niemoeller created a new design for this edition. Thanks are also due to Steve Csipke, who prepared the index.

The fourth edition could not have been completed without the help of numerous other individuals. Knowledge of computers, writing, and students enabled Todd Taylor (University of South Florida) to provide invaluable assistance with the computer boxes in the rhetoric and with the chapter on writing with a computer. Charlotte Smith (Virginia Technological University) researched and wrote terse, accurate headnotes and prepared the apparatus for the reader selections. Barbara Fister (Gustavus Adolphus College) did an excellent job of refocusing, revising, and updating the library research information. Barbara Gaffney (University of New Orleans) revised and wrote ESL boxes. Owen Shows effectively revised the exercises in the handbook. Phillip Sipiora (University of South Florida), Michelle Bauer (University of South Florida), Heidi Kelchner (University of South Florida), and Shirley Morahan brought their classroom wisdom to the revision of the two volumes of the instructor's manual. David Hartman (St. Petersburg Junior College) wrote an excellent booklet explaining how the textbook can be used in the electronic environment of computers and cyberspace. Mitch Evich prepared the exercises for the supplemental booklet.

Special thanks to all the students who have challenged us over the years to find better ways to help them learn. In particular we would like to thank those who granted us permission to use their essays in the fourth edition. Focused as this textbook is on student writing, their essays are the linchpin of *A Writer's Rhetoric*. The writings of Robert Schreiner, Sandra Messina, and Jonathan Burns have been included in both the third and fourth editions. New to the fourth edition are the writings of Margaret Jellison, Betsy Buffo, Robert Parr, Brenda Devlin, Tim Chabot, Yun Yung Choi, Tania Fusco, Heather Colbenson, Geoffrey Fallon, Lionel Prokop, Maria Halloran, Linda Hackler, and Chris Robinson.

Many thanks to all of our colleagues across the country who took time and care to review the third edition, to respond to questionnaires, and to send us their suggestions gleaned from experience with students. For reviewing the third edition and making suggestions to improve the fourth, we thank Peggy Brent, Hinds Community College; Beverley Brown, Maple Woods Community College; Felicia Campbell, University of Las Vegas; Gay Lynn Crossley, Kansas State University; Ned Cummings, Commonwealth College; Michel DeBenedictus, Miami—Dade Community College; Robert Eddy, Fayetteville State University; Mitch Evich, Northeastern University; JoNell Farrar, San Jacinto College, Central Campus; Barbara Fister, Gustavus Adolphus College; Kate Gadbow, University of Montana; Barbara Gaffney, University of New Orleans; Kristine Hansen, Brigham Young University; Shirley Hauch, University of Maryland, University College; John Husband, Dodge City Community College; Grace Kehrer, Valencia Community College; Paul Kleinpoppen, Florida Community College at Jacksonville, South Campus; William Lamb, Johnson County Community College; Marcia Mani, St. Louis Community College; Harris Mosley, Rock Valley College; Patricia Murray, University of California, Northbridge; Jon Patton, University of Toledo; Vickie Sarkisian, Marist College; Owen Shows; Martha Smith, Brookhaven College; Todd Taylor, University of South Florida; Ruth Thomas, Boston University; Steve Wilhoit, University of Dayton; Anne Woodlief, Virginia Commonwealth University; and Linda Wooton, North Carolina State University.

Instructors who responded to the publisher's questionnaire about our book are Norman W. Bates, Cochise Community College; Meoghan Cronin,

St. Anselm College; R. L. Davenport, Kennedy — King College; Doug Detisch, Mankato State University; Katherine Hagstrom, Course College; Laura Hutchinson, Pasco Hernando Community College; David Jordan, Delaware Technical and Community College; Gillian Jordan, University of Maine, University College; Mary Buto Lake, Normandale Community College; Lynn A. Lee, University of Wisconsin, Platteville; Janis H. Lupton, Colby Community College; Marcia A. Mani, St. Louis Community College at Meramec; Homer Mitchell, Potsdam College; Linda C. Mix, Germanna Community College; Bernard E. Morris, Modesto Junior College; Helen Olsen, Atlantic Community College; Pratul Pathak, California University of Pennsylvania; Velvet Pearson, University of Southern California; Barbara Pitz, St. Ambrose University; Kim Riddell, Frostburg State University; Richard H. Rupp, Appalachian State University; Carol H. Leigh Ryddell, Montana State University; James T. Simmons, University of North Dakota, Lake Region; Ronald L. Stone, University of Minnesota; Jeff Wheeler, University of Southern California, Los Angeles; and Jan Worth, University of Michigan, Flint. We thank you, one and all.

We remain grateful to our mentors and colleagues in universities and colleges across the country, who prompted us to reexamine our positions and defend our assertions. We thank our friends and families for their unstinting patience, understanding, and encouragement. For the fourth edition, Sylvia Holladay sends special thanks to Florence and Eddie.

# Contents

# A WRITER'S HANDBOOK    H-1

# A Writer's Guide

# Introduction:
# A Writing Process

You are already a writer with long experience. In school you have taken notes, written book reports, essays, and term papers, answered exam questions, perhaps kept a journal. In clubs you have kept minutes, and on the job you've composed memos. You've written letters and postcards to family and friends, made shopping lists, maybe even tried your hand at writing stories and poetry. All this experience is about to pay off for you.

In college you will combine what you already know about writing with the new techniques you will learn, and you will perform writing tasks more challenging than most you have faced before. To write a psychology or economics paper, you'll find that your mind has to stretch more than it did in writing a report on the solar system or a letter of application. From now on, you will find yourself working in complex disciplines, writing reports based on information from many sources, and above all thinking critically about the information — not just reading articles and stacking up facts, but analyzing what you discover, deciding what it means, weighing its value, taking a stand, proposing solutions. College instructors will expect you to question what they say and what you read, to form your own judgments, and to put them to use.

Unlike parachute jumping, writing for a college course is something you go ahead and try without first learning all there is to know. In truth, nothing anyone can tell you about writing can help you as much as learning by doing. In this book we will suggest various writing situations and say, "Go to it!" We will also recommend specific strategies that will make your writing go smoother than in the past. In this introduction, we will give you an overview of the central issues that concern most writers, and we will point out how each section in the following chapters supports you in making decisions about one or more of these issues.

# Critical Thinking, Creativity, and Writing

Effective writing is both critical and creative. Each writing task can be viewed as a problem to solve, one that requires both *creative thinking* (making), and *critical thinking* (judging). According to Richard W. Paul, director of the Center for Critical Thinking,

> "Criticality" and "creativity" have an intimate relationship to the ability to figure things out. There is a natural marriage between them. Indeed, all thinking that is properly called "excellent" combines these two dimensions in an intimate way.[1]

When you write, you create, making something out of nothing, bringing order out of chaos. Of necessity you begin to shape the information before you know clearly what you will include or where you are going with it.

Simultaneously with your creating or making when you write, you think critically. You think purposefully and judge your ideas and your processes. As a writer you not only assess *what* you create; you also assess *how* you create *as* you create. You use criteria — models, conventions, principles, standards — to help you determine whether you are fulfilling your purpose, approaching the end you have in mind. As you compose, you monitor and evaluate what you are doing by asking yourself specific questions based on your criteria for effective written communication. Have I made my point clear? Are my ideas arranged in a logical order? Does each thought follow from and support or add to the preceding thought? Are the connections clear to the reader? Have I provided sufficient evidence or proof to make my point clear? To convince my readers? Is my tone appropriate for my readers?

Thus, thinking creatively and thinking critically are integral and interrelated parts of writing well. In large measure, learning to write well is learning what questions to ask yourself as you write. Throughout *A Writer's Guide,* we include questions and suggestions designed to help you think creatively and critically about your own writing tasks and processes. In addition, Part Two, "Thinking Critically," focuses exclusively on writing assignments that challenge you to use your critical thinking skills to the fullest.

# The Process of Writing

Writing can seem at times an overwhelming drudgery, worse than scrubbing floors; at other moments, a sport full of thrills and excitement — like whizzing downhill on skis, not knowing what you'll meet around a bend.

---

[1] Richard Paul, *Critical Thinking: What Every Person Needs to Survive in a Rapidly Changing World,* rev. 2nd ed. (Rohnert Park, CA: Foundation for Critical Thinking, 1992), 17.

Surprising and unpredictable though the writing process may seem, you can understand what happens in it. Nearly all writers do similar things:

They generate ideas.
They plan, draft, and develop their papers.
They revise and edit.

These activities aren't lockstep stages: they don't always proceed in a straight line. You can skip around, taking up parts of the process in whatever order you like, or work on several parts at a time, or circle back over what you have already done. Gathering material, you may feel an urge to play with a sentence until it clicks. Writing a draft, you may decide to go back and look for more material. You may find yourself dashing off, crossing out, leaping ahead, backtracking, correcting, adjusting, questioning, trying a fresh approach, not being satisfied, trying still another approach, breaking through, tinkering a bit more, polishing — then in the end checking unfamiliar punctuation and looking up the spellings of tricky words.

These three activities form the basis of most effective writing processes. Each chapter in Part One, "A Writer's Resources," and Part Two, "Thinking Critically," has this basis at its heart. Let's look briefly at what each activity entails and how the chapters in *A Writer's Guide* help you approach it.

## GENERATING IDEAS

The first activity in writing — finding a topic to write about and finding something to say about it — is often the most challenging and least predictable. Each chapter in Parts One and Two has a section entitled "Generating Ideas" filled with examples, questions, and checklists that will trigger ideas and associations about the specific writing assignment studied in that chapter. (For an example, see p. 23). In addition, Chapter 15, "Strategies for Generating Ideas," is a storehouse of useful discovery techniques that you can apply to this part of the writing process for any writing assignment.

Discovering What to Write About.    Finding a topic you honestly want to pursue, one about which you really have something to say, is half the task: find it, and words will flow. Although finding the topic is not always easy, often it lies near home. Judith Ortiz Cofer in "The Myth of the Latin Woman: I Just Met a Girl Named María" (p. 504) remembers a bus trip; Brent Staples in "Black Men and Public Space" (p. 518), an evening walk; Michael Dorris in "Crazy Horse Malt Liquor" (p. 522), a football game — all ordinary occurrences. In college, of course, an instructor may give you a writing assignment that seems to hold no personal interest for you. In that case, you face the challenge of making it your own by finding a slant that does interest you.

Discovering Material.    You'll need information to back up your ideas — facts and figures, reports and opinions, examples and illustrations. How do you find this material to support your ideas and make them clear and convincing to your readers? Luckily you have endless resources at your fingertips. You can *recall* your own experience and knowledge, you can go out and *observe* things around you, you can *read* what others say about your subject, you can *converse* with others who are knowledgeable on your topic, and you can *imagine* possibilities and results.

These five resources are covered in depth in Part One; the five chapters there explore each resource in turn and give you some practice in applying it.

## PLANNING, DRAFTING, AND DEVELOPING

Having discovered a burning idea to write about (or at least a smoldering one) and material to back it up with (maybe not enough yet, but some), you sort out what matters most and decide on an order for your ideas. If right away you can see one main point you want to make in your paper, you're lucky. Try to state that point in writing; try various ways of expressing it. Next, you can arrange your ideas and material in what seems a clear and sensible order that will make your one point clear. To discover that order, you might group and label the ideas you have generated, or you might analyze the main idea. But if no one main point emerges quickly, never mind: you may find one while you draft — that is, while you write an early version of your paper. At least by the time you finish the paper, you should focus everything in it on a main point.

Usually your first version of a draft will be rough and preliminary. Writing takes time: a paper usually needs several drafts and perhaps a revision of your plan, especially if your subject is unfamiliar or complicated. You may decide to throw out your first attempt and start all over because a stronger idea or a better arrangement hits you. Include explanations, definitions, illustrations, and evidence to make your ideas clear. If, as you draft, you realize you don't have enough specific evidence, work through your five resources again (recall, observe, read, converse, imagine). You can expect to keep discovering ideas, having insights, and drawing conclusions while you draft. By all means, welcome them, and work them in if they fit.

Each chapter in Parts One and Two has a section entitled "Planning, Drafting, and Developing," designed to help you through this part of the writing process for the specific writing assignment studied in that chapter. (For an example, see p. 24.) Each chapter also contains a tip called "Writing with a Computer" in this section, intended to help you find new ways of integrating computers with your writing process. (See p. 25.) Finally, three chapters in Part Four contain a wealth of general strategies appropriate to this part of the writing process: Chapter 16, "Strategies for Planning"; Chapter 17, "Strategies for Drafting"; and Chapter 18, "Strategies for Developing."

## REVISING AND EDITING

Revising — both re-seeing and rewriting — occurs throughout the process of composing, not only after you have finished. It is part of your critically monitoring *what* you are creating and *how* you are creating. In an apt comparison, Chinese-American writer Maxine Hong Kingston likens writing to gardening in Hawaii: a little time spent in planting, much more time spent in "cutting and pruning and hacking back." Novelist Ernest Hemingway, when asked what made him revise the ending of *A Farewell to Arms* thirty-nine times, replied, "Getting the words right." Usually most of your revision will occur after you have completed a draft. At that time you might think that your work is done, but very few writers can get their ideas across to others by doing only one draft. For most writers the time of revising is the time when work begins in earnest. Each chapter in Parts One and Two has a section entitled "Revising and Editing," which focuses on this part of the writing process; each section contains at least one revision checklist and one suggestion for working with a peer editor. (For examples, see pp. 26 and 27.) In Part Four, Chapter 19, "Strategies for Revising and Editing," comprises a trove of revision, editing, and proofreading techniques.

**Revising.**   Revision — the word means "see again" — is more than a matter of just revising words: you sometimes revise what you know and what you think. Such changes may take place at any time while you're writing or at any moment when you pause to reread or to think. You can then shift your plans, decide to put in or leave out, move sentences or paragraphs around, connect ideas differently, or express them better. If you put aside your draft for a few hours or a day, you can reread it with fresh eyes and a clear mind.

When you revise, as humorist Leo Rosten has said, "you have to put yourself in the position of the negative reader, the resistant reader, the reader who doesn't surrender easily, the reader who is alien to you as a type, even the reader who doesn't like what you are writing." However, you should probably sit in the seat of the scornful only when your paper is well along. When your ideas first start to flow, you want to welcome them — lure them forth, not tear them apart — or they might go back into hiding. Get something on paper before you begin major rewriting. Don't be afraid to take risks: you'll probably be surprised and pleased at what happens.

**Editing.**   Near the end of your labors, you'll *edit* what you have written: you'll correct any flaws that may stand in the way of your readers' understanding and enjoyment. Don't edit too early, though, because you may waste time on some part that you later revise out. In editing, you usually accomplish these repairs:

Get rid of unnecessary words.

Choose better words.

Rearrange words into a stronger, clearer order.

Use more subordination in sentences.

Add accurate transitions for continuity of thought.

Check usage.

Check grammar (make subjects agree with verbs, pronouns with what they stand for; make verb tenses consistent).

**Proofreading.**    A final activity in the writing process, proofreading is giving your paper one last look, with a dictionary at your elbow, checking doubtful spellings and fixing any typing mistakes.

# Audience and Purpose

A big part of learning to write well is learning what questions to ask yourself. At any moment in the writing process, two questions are worth asking: Whom do I write for? And Why?

**Writing for Readers.**    In fulfilling most of the assignments for a college composition course like this one, you'll know who your readers are — yourself, your classmates, and your instructor. Writing for these readers will give you practice that will benefit you in writing for less sympathetic audiences in other settings.

As reading specialist Frank Smith says, "The writer is always the first reader." As your own first reader, you'll want to step back from a draft and reread it as though you weren't the writer but were someone else, detached and objective — and not too easy to please. You'll have to get outside yourself and see where you need explanations, examples, and bridges between thoughts. You'll also want to comb your writing for weak spots and errors before you turn it in. That is merely to follow the Golden Rule of Writing: do unto your other readers as you trust other writers will do unto you.

In fulfilling some relatively straightforward assignments — say, recalling an experience or reporting a conversation — you won't need to keep asking, Who besides myself is reading me? If, as you write a paper, you believe it is going well, chances are that your readers will think so too. But in tackling complex writing tasks, you'll write more effectively if you consider your audience. Say you wish to persuade your readers to take a certain action — to ban (or approve) a law regulating the hiring of illegal aliens or the sale of pornography. At some point you might ask: What do my readers know already about this subject? What do they need to be told? What do they probably believe? Where are my statements likely to offend them? What objections are they likely to raise? How can I keep from alienating them? You should analyze your readers carefully and know a great deal about them (what they know and don't know, what they believe, what they value) to aim your writing toward them and hit your mark. As you write, keep the uninformed reader, the reluctant reader, and the resistant reader in mind, and write for all three. Among your classmates you'll find all three types of readers, and in responding to your writing, your instructor will assume all three roles.

Writing for a Reason.    Usually a college writing assignment has a clear-cut purpose. Every assignment in this book asks you to write for a definite reason. In Chapter 1 you'll be asked to recall a memorable experience in order to explain how it changed you; in Chapter 9, to take a stand on a controversy that interests you, to argue for the soundness of your position, and to evaluate.

Be careful not to confuse the resources and strategies you are asked to apply in these assignments with your ultimate purpose for writing. "To compare and contrast two things" is not a very interesting purpose; "to compare and contrast *in order to explain* the differences between two things" implies a real reason for writing. In most college writing, your ultimate purpose will be to explain something to your readers or to convince your readers of something.

Aware that you write for a reason, you can concentrate on your task. From the start you can ask yourself, What do I want to do? And, in revising, Did I do what I meant to do? You'll find that these are very practical questions. They'll help you cut the irrelevant that wanders into your writing, anything that hinders your paper from getting where you want it to go.

The readers you write for and the reason you write will always deserve consideration. Throughout this book we'll remind you of these two points.

## What Matters Most

In *The Bedford Guide for College Writers*, we too have a purpose. It is to help you write better, deeper, clearer, more interesting, and more satisfying papers than you have ever written before and to learn to do so by actually writing. Throughout the book we'll give you a lot of practice — in writing processes, patterns, and strategies — to help you build your confidence.

How This Book Is Built.    As you already know, writing and learning to write are complex and many-faceted tasks. Each part in *A Writer's Guide* is devoted to a different aspect of writing. We hope, though, that as you work through the chapters and become adept at using them, you will come to feel they are all parts of a seamless whole, much like the writing process itself.

*Part One, "A Writer's Resources,"* encourages you to write papers that draw on the five essential resources for generating ideas and material: recalling, observing, reading, conversing, and imagining.

*Part Two, "Thinking Critically,"* asks you to write papers using critical thinking strategies. You'll develop the skills of analyzing, comparing and contrasting, explaining causes and effects, taking a stand, proposing a solution, and evaluating.

*Part Three, "Special Writing Situations,"* leads you through three special situations that most students encounter at one point or another — writing about literature, writing in class, and writing for business.

*Part Four, "A Writer's Strategies,"* is packed with advice, tips, and exercises that you can unpack whenever you are hunting for ways to generate ideas, plan, draft, develop, revise, edit, and proofread your papers. You will also find strategies for working with other writers and for using computers for writing. Browse through these chapters at your leisure, study them as you need to, or refer to them in a pinch.

Taking It to the Hoop.    Like a hard game of basketball, writing a college paper is strenuous. Without getting in your way, we want to lend you all possible support and to provide guidance and direction for your efforts. So, no doubt, does your instructor, someone closer to you than any textbook writers. Still, like even the best coaches, instructors and textbook writers can improve your game only so far. Advice on how to write won't make you a better writer. You'll learn more and have more fun when you take a few sentences to the hoop and make points yourself. After you make a few baskets, you will increase your confidence in your ability and find the process of writing a bit easier.

As you know, other students can also help you — sometimes more than a textbook or an instructor. This book suggests opportunities for you to learn from your classmates and for them to learn from you. If your instructor asks you to exchange your work with other students, to give and receive reactions, you'll face a challenge: Just how do you go about commenting on another student's writing? Throughout the book are useful hints for ways that you and other students can help one another discover ideas as you write and rewrite your papers. In Chapter 20, "Strategies for Working with Other Writers: Collaborative Learning," you will find multiple suggestions and illustrations for collaborating with your classmates. As you respond to your classmates' papers, you will learn to judge your own writing better.

# Part One

# A Writer's
# Resources

# Introduction

As a college writer you probably wrestle with the question What should I write? You may feel you have nothing to say, or nothing worth saying. Sometimes your difficulty lies in finding a topic, sometimes in uncovering enough information about the topic you have chosen. Perhaps you, like many other college writers, have convinced yourself that professional writers are different in some way, that they have some special way of thinking or looking at the world or discovering ideas for writing. But they have no magic. In reality you already possess the major resources of a writer.

None of the resources are new to you. Already you are adept at *recalling* your own experience and knowledge and *observing* the world around you. You're accustomed to *reading* books and to *conversing* with people. And you've had experience with the richest resource of all: *imagining*. If you learn to use these five tremendous resources, you need never find yourself at a loss for words. The purpose of Part One is to explore each resource in turn and give you some practice in applying it.

At the start of each chapter, we offer illustrations of good writing by two writers — a professional and a college student — who draw on the same resource. Then we suggest a writing assignment: a broad one that leaves you room to discover a specific topic you care about. Immediately following the assignment you'll find suggestions to guide you in writing it. We pose questions that, if you like, you can ask yourself. Some of these questions will remind you of your audience and your purpose. Sometimes we report the experience of other students. We offer you guidance throughout the whole shifting, tentative, surprise-filled process of writing. But if, instead of reading our suggestions, you'd rather go ahead and write, please do. Our only aim in offering suggestions is to provide you with a trusty support system for whenever you feel the need for it. "Applying What You Learn" shows you how writers typically use the same kind of writing in other college courses and in careers. Finally, "Making Connections" points out selections in *A Writer's Reader* that use these very same resources.

13

# Chapter 1

# Writing from Recall

Writing from recall is writing from memory, the richest resource a writer has, and the handiest. Novelist William Saroyan said that a writer observes — and then remembers having observed. This is clearly the case in an English course when you are asked to write of a personal experience, a favorite place, a memorable person. But even when an instructor hands you a subject that at first glance seems to have nothing to do with you, your memory is the first place to look. Suppose you have to write a psychology paper about how advertisers play on consumers' fears. Begin with what you remember. What ads have sent chills down your back? (We recall a tire ad that showed the luckless buyer of an inferior product stuck with a blowout on a remote road on a stormy night while the Frankenstein monster bore down on him.)

You may also need to observe, read more, talk with someone, and imagine. All by itself, memory may not give you enough to write about. But whenever you need to start writing, you will rarely go wrong if you start by jotting down something remembered.

## *Learning from Other Writers*

In this chapter you will be invited to write a whole paper from recall. Here are two samples of good writing — one by a professional writer, one by a college student. We begin with an essay from columnist Russell Baker's autobiography *Growing Up*, because autobiographical writing so clearly demonstrates the uses of memory. Baker recalls what it was like to be sixteen in urban Baltimore, wondering what to do with his life.

The second essay was written by a student, Robert Schreiner, in response to an assignment asking him to recall a significant event from his childhood. As you read his essay, notice the vivid details that help bring the incident alive.

## *Russell Baker*    The Art of Eating Spaghetti

The only thing that truly interested me was writing, and I knew that sixteen-year-olds did not come out of high school and become writers. I thought of writing as something to be done only by the rich. It was so obviously not real work, not a job at which you could earn a living. Still, I had begun to think of myself as a writer. It was the only thing for which I seemed to have the smallest talent, and, silly though it sounded when I told people I'd like to be a writer, it gave me a way of thinking about myself which satisfied my need to have an identity.

The notion of becoming a writer had flickered off and on in my head since the Belleville days, but it wasn't until my third year in high school that the possibility took hold. Until then I'd been bored by everything associated with English courses. I found English grammar dull and baffling. I hated the assignments to turn out "compositions," and went at them like heavy labor, turning out leaden, lackluster paragraphs that were agonies for teachers to read and for me to write. The classics thrust on me to read seemed as deadening as chloroform.

When our class was assigned to Mr. Fleagle for third-year English I anticipated another grim year in that dreariest of subjects. Mr. Fleagle was notorious among City students for dullness and inability to inspire. He was said to be stuffy, dull, and hopelessly out of date. To me he looked to be sixty or seventy and prim to a fault. He wore primly severe eyeglasses, his wavy hair was primly cut and primly combed. He wore prim vested suits with neckties blocked primly against the collar buttons of his primly starched white shirts. He had a primly pointed jaw, a primly straight nose, and a prim manner of speaking that was so correct, so gentlemanly, that he seemed a comic antique.

I anticipated a listless, unfruitful year with Mr. Fleagle and for a long time was not disappointed. We read *Macbeth*. Mr. Fleagle loved *Macbeth* and wanted us to love it too, but he lacked the gift of infecting others with his own passion. He tried to convey the murderous ferocity of Lady Macbeth one day by reading aloud the passage that concludes

> . . . I have given suck, and know
> How tender 'tis to love the babe that milks me.
> I would, while it was smiling in my face,
> Have plucked my nipple from his boneless gums. . . .

The idea of prim Mr. Fleagle plucking his nipple from boneless gums was too much for the class. We burst into gasps of irrepressible snickering. Mr. Fleagle stopped.

"There is nothing funny, boys, about giving suck to a babe. It is the — the     5
very essence of motherhood, don't you see."

He constantly sprinkled his sentences with "don't you see." It wasn't a     6
question but an exclamation of mild surprise at our ignorance. "Your pronoun needs an antecedent, don't you see," he would say, very primly. "The
purpose of the Porter's scene, boys, is to provide comic relief from the horror,
don't you see."

Late in the year we tackled the informal essay. "The essay, don't you see,     7
is the. . . ." My mind went numb. Of all forms of writing, none seemed so boring as the essay. Naturally we would have to write informal essays. Mr.
Fleagle distributed a homework sheet offering us a choice of topics. None was
quite so simpleminded as "What I Did on My Summer Vacation," but most
seemed to be almost as dull. I took the list home and dawdled until the night
before the essay was due. Sprawled on the sofa, I finally faced up to the grim
task, took the list out of my notebook, and scanned it. The topic on which my
eye stopped was "The Art of Eating Spaghetti."

This title produced an extraordinary sequence of mental images. Surging     8
up out of the depths of memory came a vivid recollection of a night in
Belleville when all of us were seated around the supper table — Uncle Allen,
my mother, Uncle Charlie, Doris, Uncle Hal — and Aunt Pat served spaghetti
for supper. Spaghetti was an exotic treat in those days. Neither Doris nor I had
ever eaten spaghetti, and none of the adults had enough experience to be
good at it. All the good humor of Uncle Allen's house reawoke in my mind as
I recalled the laughing arguments we had that night about the socially respectable method for moving spaghetti from plate to mouth.

Suddenly I wanted to write about that, about the warmth and good feel-     9
ing of it, but I wanted to put it down simply for my own joy, not for Mr.
Fleagle. It was a moment I wanted to recapture and hold for myself. I wanted
to relive the pleasure of an evening at New Street. To write it as I wanted, however, would violate all the rules of formal composition I'd learned in school,
and Mr. Fleagle would surely give it a failing grade. Never mind. I would write
something else for Mr. Fleagle after I had written this thing for myself.

When I finished it the night was half gone and there was no time left to     10
compose a proper, respectable essay for Mr. Fleagle. There was no choice next
morning but to turn in my private reminiscence of Belleville. Two days passed
before Mr. Fleagle returned the graded papers, and he returned everyone's but
mine. I was bracing myself for a command to report to Mr. Fleagle immediately after school for discipline when I saw him lift my paper from his desk
and rap for the class's attention.

"Now, boys," he said, "I want to read you an essay. This is titled 'The Art     11
of Eating Spaghetti.' "

And he started to read. My words! He was reading *my words* out loud to     12
the entire class. What's more, the entire class was listening. Listening atten-
tively. Then somebody laughed, then the entire class was laughing, and not in
contempt and ridicule, but with openhearted enjoyment. Even Mr. Fleagle
stopped two or three times to repress a small prim smile.

I did my best to avoid showing pleasure, but what I was feeling was pure ecstasy at this startling demonstration that my words had the power to make people laugh. In the eleventh grade, at the eleventh hour as it were, I had discovered a calling. It was the happiest moment of my entire school career. When Mr. Fleagle finished he put the final seal on my happiness by saying, "Now that, boys, is an essay, don't you see. It's — don't you see — it's of the very essence of the essay, don't you see. Congratulations, Mr. Baker."      13

For the first time, light shone on a possibility. It wasn't a very heartening possibility, to be sure. Writing couldn't lead to a job after high school, and it was hardly honest work, but Mr. Fleagle had opened a door for me. After that I ranked Mr. Fleagle among the finest teachers in the school.      14

**Questions to Start You Thinking**

*Meaning*

1. In your own words, state what Baker believes he learned in the eleventh grade about the art of writing. What incidents or statements help identify this lesson for readers of the essay? Tell what lesson, if any, you learned from the essay.

2. Why do you think Baker included this event in his autobiography?

3. Have you ever changed your mind about something you had to do, as Baker did about writing? Or about a person, as he did about Mr. Fleagle?

*Writing Strategies*

4. What is the effect, in paragraph 3, of Baker's many repetitions of the words *prim* and *primly*? What other devices does Baker use to make vivid his characterization of Mr. Fleagle? Why do you think the author uses so much space to portray his teacher?

5. What does the quotation from *Macbeth* add to Baker's account? Had the quotation been omitted, what would have been lost?

6. How does Baker organize the essay? Why does he use this order?

STUDENT ESSAY

## *Robert G. Schreiner*    What Is a Hunter?

What is a hunter? This is a simple question with a relatively straightforward answer. A hunter is, according to *Webster's New Collegiate Dictionary*, a person that hunts game (game being various types of animals hunted or pursued for various reasons). However, a question that is just as simple but without such a straightforward answer is What characteristics make up a hunter? As a child, I had always considered the most important aspect of the hunter's person to be his      1

ability to use a rifle, bow, or whatever weapon was appropriate to the type of hunting being done. Having many relatives
in rural areas of Virginia and Kansas, I had been exposed to
rifles a great deal. I had done extensive target shooting and
considered myself to be quite proficient in the use of
firearms. I had never been hunting, but I had always thought
that since I could fire a rifle accurately I would make a
good hunter.

One Christmas holiday, while we were visiting our grand-     2
parents in Kansas, my grandfather asked me if I wanted to go
jackrabbit hunting with him. I eagerly accepted, anxious to
show off my prowess with a rifle. A younger cousin of mine
also wanted to come, so we all went out into the garage,
loaded two .22 caliber rifles and a 20-gauge shotgun, hopped
into the pickup truck, and drove out of town. It had snowed
the night before and to either side of the narrow road swept
six-foot-deep powdery drifts. The wind twirled the fine crys-
talline snow into whirling vortexes that bounced along the
icy road and sprayed snow into the open windows of the
pickup. As we drove, my grandfather gave us some pointers
about both spotting and shooting jackrabbits. He told us that
when it snows, jackrabbits like to dig out a hollow in the
top of a snowdrift, usually near a fencepost, and lie there
soaking up the sunshine. He told us that even though jackrabbits are a grayish brown, this coloration is excellent camouflage in the snow, for the curled-up rabbits resemble rocks.
He then pointed out a few rabbits in such positions as we
drove along, showing us how to distinguish them from exposed
rocks and dirt. He then explained that the only way to be
sure that we killed the rabbit was to shoot for the head and,
in particular, the eye, for this was on a direct line with
the rabbit's brain. Since we were using solid point bullets,
which deform into a ball upon impact, a hit anywhere but the
head would most likely only wound the rabbit.

My grandfather then slowed down the pickup and told us      3
to look out for the rabbits hidden in the snowdrifts. We
eventually spotted one about thirty feet from the road in a
snow-filled gully. My cousin wished to shoot the first one,
so he hopped out of the truck, balanced the .22 on the hood,

and fired. A spray of snow erupted about a foot to the left of the rabbit's hollow. My cousin fired again, and again, and again, the shots pockmarking the slope of the drift. He fired once more and the rabbit bounced out of its hollow, its head rocking from side to side. He was hit. My cousin eagerly gamboled into the snow to claim his quarry. He brought it back holding it by the hind legs, proudly displaying it as would a warrior the severed head of his enemy. The bullet had entered the rabbit's right shoulder and exited through the neck. In both places a thin trickle of crimson marred the gray sheen of the rabbit's pelt. It quivered slightly and its rib cage pulsed with its labored breathing. My cousin was about to toss it into the back of the pickup when my grandfather pointed out that it would be cruel to allow the rabbit to bleed slowly to death and instructed my cousin to bang its head against the side of the pickup to kill it. My cousin then proceeded to bang the rabbit's head against the yellow metal. Thump, thump, thump, thump; after a minute or so my cousin loudly proclaimed that it was dead and hopped back into the truck.

The whole episode sickened me to some degree, and at the time I did not know why. We continued to hunt throughout the afternoon, and feigning boredom, I allowed my cousin and grandfather to shoot all of the rabbits. Often, the shots didn't kill the rabbits outright so they had to be killed against the pickup. The thump, thump, thump of the rabbits' skulls against the metal began to irritate me, and I was strangely glad when we turned around and headed back toward home. We were a few miles from the city limits when my grandfather slowed the truck to a stop, then backed up a few yards. My grandfather said he spotted two huge "jacks" sitting in the sun in a field just off the road. He pointed them out and handed me the .22, saying that if I didn't shoot something the whole afternoon would have been a wasted trip for me. I hesitated, then reluctantly accepted the rifle. I stepped out onto the road, my feet crunching on the ice. The two rabbits were about seventy feet away, both sitting upright in the sun. I cocked and leveled the rifle, my elbow held almost horizontal in the military fashion I had learned

4

to employ. I brought the sights to bear upon the right eye of the first rabbit, compensated for distance, and fired. There was a harsh snap like the crack of a whip, and a small jolt to my shoulder. The first rabbit was gone, presumably knocked over the side of the snowdrift. The second rabbit hadn't moved a muscle; it just sat there staring with that black eye. I cocked the rifle once more and sighted a second time, the bead of the rifle just barely above the glassy black orb that regarded me so passively. I squeezed the trigger. Again the crack, again the jolt, and again the rabbit disappeared over the top of the drift. I handed the rifle to my cousin and began making my way toward the rabbits. I sank into powdery snow up to my waist as I clambered to the top of the drift and looked over.

On the other side of the drift was a sight that I doubt 5 I will ever forget. There was a shallow, snow-covered ditch on the leeward side of the drift and it was into this ditch that the rabbits had fallen, at least what was left of the rabbits. The entire ditch, in an area about ten feet wide, was spattered with splashes of crimson blood, pink gobbets of brain, and splintered fragments of bone. The twisted corpses of the rabbits lay in the bottom of the ditch in small pools of streaming blood. Of both the rabbits, only the bodies remained, the heads being completely gone. Stumps of vertebrae protruded obscenely from the mangled bodies, and one rabbit's hind legs twitched spasmodically. I realized that my cousin must have made a mistake and loaded the rifle with hollow-point explosive bullets instead of solid ones.

I shouted back to the pickup, explaining the situation, 6 and asked if I should bring them back anyway. My grandfather shouted back, "No, don't worry about it, just leave them there. I'm gonna toss these jacks by the side of the road anyway; jackrabbits aren't any good for eatin'."

Looking at the dead, twitching bodies I thought only of 7 the incredible waste of life that the afternoon had been, and I realized that there was much more to being a hunter than knowing how to use a rifle. I turned and walked back to the pickup, riding the rest of the way home in silence.

*Meaning*

1. Where in the essay do you first begin to suspect the nature of the writer's feelings toward hunting? What in the essay or in your experience led you to this perception?

2. How would you characterize the writer's grandfather? How would you characterize his cousin?

3. How did the writer's understanding of himself change as a result of this hunting experience?

*Writing Strategies*

4. How might the essay be strengthened or weakened if the opening paragraph were cut out? How would your understanding of the author and how he changed be different if this paragraph were not included?

5. Would Schreiner's essay be more or less effective if he explained in the last paragraph what he means by "much more to being a hunter"?

6. What are some of Schreiner's memorable images?

# *Learning by Writing*

### THE ASSIGNMENT: RECALLING A PERSONAL EXPERIENCE

Write about one specific experience that changed how you acted, thought, or felt. Use your experience as a springboard for reflection. Your purpose is not merely to tell an interesting story but to show your readers the importance that that experience has had for you. Your audience is your instructor and your classmates.

We suggest you pick an event that is not too subjective. Something that happened to you or something that you observed, an encounter with a person who greatly influenced you, a decision that you made, or a challenge or an obstacle that you faced will be easier to recall (and to make vivid for your readers) than a subjective, interior experience like a religious conversion or falling in love.

Some memorable student papers we have read have recalled experiences like those that follow — some heavy, some light:

A man recalled guitar lessons with a teacher who at first seemed harsh but who turned out to be a true friend.

A woman recalled how, as a small girl, she sneaked into a nun's room, out of curiosity stole some rosary beads, and discovered that crime does not pay.

A man recalled meeting an American Indian who taught him a deeper understanding of the natural world.

To help you fulfill this assignment, let's consider: What does writing from personal experience call for?

GENERATING IDEAS

You may find that the minute you are asked to write about a significant experience in your life, the very incident will flash to mind. Most writers, though, will need a little time to shake down their memories.

Probably what will come to you first will be recent memories, but give long-ago memories time to surface, too. Be ready for any recollections that well up unexpectedly. Often, when you are busy doing something else — observing the scene around you, talking with someone, reading about someone else's experience — the activity can trigger a recollection from the past. When a promising one surfaces, write it down. It may be the start of your paper. Perhaps, like Russell Baker, you found success only when you ignored what you thought you were supposed to do in favor of what you really wanted to do. Perhaps, like Robert Schreiner, you learned from a painful experience. If nothing much surfaces, you might want to try the following strategies for generating ideas. (For more suggestions on using each of these strategies, see Chapter 15.)

*Try brainstorming.* Brainstorming is a good way to jog your memory. When you brainstorm, you try to come up with as many ideas as you can without any thought for their form or their practical applications. You just jot down ideas for a certain amount of time and see where your thoughts lead you. You can start with a suggestive word or phrase — *disobedience, painful lesson, childhood, peer pressure* — and list under that word or phrase as many ideas as occur to you through free association. You can also try asking yourself the questions in the following discovery checklist.

**DISCOVERY CHECKLIST**

## Searching Your Memory

- Did you ever break an important rule or rebel against authority? Did you learn anything from your actions?
- Did you ever succumb to peer pressure? What were the results of going along with the crowd? What did you learn?
- Did you ever regard a person in a certain way and then have to change your opinion of him or her?
- Did you ever have to choose between two equally attractive alternatives? How might your life have been different if you had chosen differently?
- Have you ever been appalled by witnessing an act of prejudice or insensitivity? What did you do? Do you wish you had done something different?
- Did you ever, as Robert Schreiner did, have a long-held belief or assumption shattered? Can you trace the change to one event or a series of events?
- Was there ever a moment in your life when you decided to reform, to adopt a whole new outlook? How would you characterize your attempt? (Successful? Unsuccessful? Laughable? Painful?)

*Try freewriting.* If you still have difficulty recalling a meaningful experience, spend ten or fifteen minutes freewriting — simply writing without stopping whatever comes into your head. If you think you have nothing to say, write "I have nothing to say" over and over, until ideas come. They will come. Don't worry about spelling, punctuation, or coherence. When you read over what you have written, you may be surprised to find the germ of a good paper.

*Try a reporter's questions.*  Once you recall an experience you want to write about, ask the reporter's questions, "the five *W*'s and an *H*" that journalists find useful in their work:

Who was involved?
What happened?
Where did it take place?
When did it happen?
Why did it happen?
How did the events unfold?

Any one of these questions can lead to further questions — and to further discovery. Take, for instance, Who was there? If there were people besides you involved in the incident, you might also ask: What did they look like? What did the people do? What did they say? (Might their words supply a lively quotation for your paper?) What information about them would a reader have to know to appreciate their importance to you and the story? Or take the question What happened? You might also ask: What were your inmost thoughts as the event took place? At what moment did you become aware that the event was no ordinary, everyday experience? Or weren't you aware of that until later — perhaps only now that you are writing about it? (For more advice about putting these questions to work for you, see p. 342.)

*Check other sources of information.*  As we find out from psychology, the memory drops as well as retains. So it may be that you will want to check your recollections against those of anyone else who shared the experience. If possible, talk to a friend or family member who was there. Did you keep a diary or a journal at the time? If so, you might glance into it and refresh your memory. Was the experience public enough (such as a riot or a blizzard) to have been recorded in a newspaper or a magazine? If so, perhaps you can read about it in a library. In doing these things, you will probably discover details or angles that you had forgotten about — which will, in turn, open up new areas for exploring through writing.

## PLANNING, DRAFTING, AND DEVELOPING

Now, how will you tell your story? If the experience you want to write about is still fresh in your mind, you may be able to start right in and write a draft, writing and planning simultaneously, following the order of occurrence of events, shaping your story as you go along. Even if you choose not to plan as a separate stage before drafting, you'll find it reassuring to have at your elbow any jottings you made as you searched your memory. If you decide to plan before you write, here are some additional suggestions. (For more advice on planning, drafting, and developing college papers, see Chapters 16, 17, and 18.)

*Establish a chronology.* Retelling an experience is called *narration,* and the simplest way to organize the information is chronologically: relating events in the order in which they occurred. In doing so, you take the King's advice to the White Rabbit in *Alice's Adventures in Wonderland:* "Begin at the beginning, and go on till you come to the end: then stop." But sometimes because all experience flows together, you may not know just when to start or stop. If that occurs, stick to the essentials and write in chronological order.

Sometimes you can start an account of a personal experience in the middle and then, through *flashback,* fill in whatever background a reader needs to know. Richard Rodriguez, for instance, begins *Hunger of Memory,* a memoir of his bilingual childhood, with an arresting sentence:

> I remember, to start with, that day in Sacramento, in a California now nearly thirty years past — when I first entered a classroom, able to understand about fifty stray English words.

The opening hooks our attention. In the rest of his essay, Rodriguez fills us in on his family history, on the gulf he came to perceive between the public language (English) and the language of his home (Spanish).

*Show what happened.* How can you best make your recollections come alive for your readers? Look again at Russell Baker's account of Mr. Fleagle teaching *Macbeth* and at the way Robert Schreiner depicts his cousin putting the wounded rabbits out of their misery. These two writers have done what good novelists and story writers do: they have not merely told us what happened but have *shown* us, by creating scenes that we can see in our mind's eye. As you

---

**WRITING WITH A COMPUTER**

A word processor can help you set down your recollections rapidly, an advantage for this assignment. You might begin by making, as fast as you can, a simple on-screen list of the events you wish to record. This done, go back and flesh out the skeleton. Add any exact details that might make the experience real to your reader. Have you recalled a person? If so, add a sentence or two that will make him or her come alive ("a gray-haired gentleman who wore old white shirts with frayed collars, fond of consulting his gold pocket watch"). Did a certain locale shape your experience? (A shallow, snow-covered ditch is central to Schreiner's memoir; see p. 18.) What made that place so unforgettable? Keep recalling, dropping in memorable details. Before your eyes, your bare list will start becoming a meaty draft.

If your list remains bare and you need more material, save your list and create a fresh document. Ask yourself a reporter's questions (the five *W*'s and an *H*) and jot down your replies. With the power of word processing to lift the contents of one document to another, you can transfer to your draft all or any of the material you generate and work it in wherever it best fits.

You can also try out different patterns of organization to see which chronology works best with your story. Move your statement of what your story means to the end, or try a flashback to start. If you don't like the changes, with word processing you can easily move the parts back or delete them.

tell your story, include at least two or three such specific scenes. Show your readers exactly what happened, where it occurred, what was said, who said it. Use details and words that appeal to all five senses: sight, sound, touch, taste, and smell.

## REVISING AND EDITING

After you have written an early draft, put it aside for a day or two if possible (for a few hours if your deadline is looming) before revising it. Then read it over carefully. Try to see everything through the eyes of one of your readers, noting both the pleasing parts and the confusing spots. Revise to ensure that you've expressed your thoughts and feelings clearly and strongly in a way that will reach your readers; edit to ensure that no distracting weaknesses in grammar or expression remain. (For more on revising and editing, see Chapter 19.)

As you read over the essay to revise it, ask yourself: What was so important about this experience? Why is it so memorable? Ask whether that importance will be clear to your readers; if nothing else, they should be able to discern why this experience was a crucial one in your life. Ask again the question you asked yourself when you began: How has your life been different ever since? Be sure that the difference is genuine and specific. Don't ramble on insincerely about "significances" that don't reflect the incident's real impact on you. In other words, be sure that your essay is focused on a single main idea or thesis.

Also ask whether you have succeeded in making the events come alive for your readers by recalling them in sufficient concrete detail. Be specific enough that your readers can see, smell, taste, hear, and feel what you experienced. Notice again Robert Schreiner's focus in his second paragraph on the world outside his own skin: his close recall of the snow, of the pointers his grandfa-

**FOR PEER RESPONSE**

You may also find it helpful during the revising stage to call on a classmate to read and respond to your draft. Your instructor may pair you with a classmate; if not, you may choose a friend. See Chapter 20 for advice on working with other student writers and for general questions you should always ask a peer editor to address. For a paper in which you write from recall, you'll also want to ask your peer editor to answer these specific questions.

- What do you think the writer's main idea or message is? Do you understand why this experience was important to him or her?
- What emotions do the people (especially the main character) in the narration feel? How did *you* feel while reading the essay?
- Where does the essay come alive? Underline any sensory images or descriptions that seem particularly effective.
- If this were your paper, what is the one thing you would be sure to work on before handing it in?

ther offered about the habits of jackrabbits and the way to shoot them. As you draft and revise, you may well recall more and more vivid details to include.

Finally, consider whether the story you tell will be easy for readers to follow. Have you consistently followed a logical sequence of events? Have you indicated transitions clearly? Readers will follow you through your essay more readily if you give them a good idea of where they're going.

Here are some questions to ask yourself as you go over your paper to revise it.

**REVISION CHECKLIST**

- Have you fulfilled your purpose by showing why this experience was important and by demonstrating how it changed your life?
- Will readers want to keep reading? Have you paid enough attention to what is most dramatic, instructive, or revealing? Can readers see and feel what you experienced?
- Why do you begin your narration as you do? Is there another place in the draft that would make a better beginning?
- If the events are not in chronological order, is it easy to follow the organization?
- Does the ending provide a sense of finality?
- Do you stick to the point? Is everything that is included relevant to your main idea or thesis?
- Do you portray any people? If so, is their importance clear? Do you provide enough detail to make them seem real, not just shadowy figures?
- If there is dialogue, does it have the ring of real speech? Read it aloud. Try it on a friend.

Revise and rewrite until you know you've related your experience and its impact as well as you know how. Then go over your paper to edit it, looking for errors or problems you may have overlooked earlier. Check grammar, word choice, punctuation, and spelling. Check the spelling of every name, even those of people and places you know well. Also make sure that you know the proper paper format for this instructor and class. (For advice on general manuscript format, see "Using Proper Manuscript Style," p. 420.)

**FOR GROUP LEARNING**

## Learning to Be a Peer Editor

To gain dry-run practice in peer response before trying your skills on a classmate's paper, select from this book's table of contents any student-written paper and write a detailed response to it. Do this in the form of a short letter to the writer. Tell the writer what is effective and what is ineffective about the essay and explain why. Get together with others in your class who chose the same paper and compare comments. What did you notice in the paper? What did you miss that others noticed? If you have any doubts that it is worth your time to compare your responses with other people's, this activity will show you that several people can notice far more than one individual can.

When you have made all the changes you need to make, retype or print out a clean copy of your paper — and hand it in.

## OTHER ASSIGNMENTS

1. Choose a person outside your immediate family who had a marked effect on your life, either good or bad, and jot down ten details about that person that might help a reader understand what he or she was like. In searching your memory for details, consider the person's physical appearance, way of talking, and habits as well as any memorable incidents. When your list is finished, look back to "The Art of Eating Spaghetti" to identify the kinds of detail Baker uses in his portrait of Mr. Fleagle, paying particular attention to the kinds of detail you might have included in your list but didn't. Then write a paper in which you portray that person and explore the nature of his or her impact on you. Include those details that help explain the effect the person had on you.

2. Write a paper in which you remember a place you were once fond of — your grandmother's kitchen, a tree house, a library, a locker room, a clubhouse, a vacation retreat. Emphasize why this place was memorable. What made it different from every other place? Why was it important to you? What do you feel when you remember it?

3. Write a paper in which, from memory, you inform your readers about some traditional ceremony, ritual, or observation familiar to you. Such a tradition can pertain to a holiday, a rite of passage (confirmation, bar or bas mitzvah, graduation), a sporting event, a family custom. Explain the importance of the tradition to you, making use of whatever information you recall. How did the observation or custom originate? Who takes part? How has the tradition changed through the years? What does it add to the lives of those who observe it?

4. Narrate an experience in which you felt like an outsider, someone who didn't belong. Explore why you felt this way and explain what you did as a result of this feeling.

# Applying What You Learn: Some Uses of Writing from Recall

Autobiographers and writers of informal essays rely extensively on recall. All of us depend on recall in much of our informal, everyday writing — when we pen a letter to friends or family members, when we write out directions for someone who doesn't know where we live, when we make a diary entry. Recall is an important resource for the kind of paper in which you are asked to explain how to do something — train a puppy, drive a car, build a coffee table, make a speech.

Recall also plays a role in writing for classes other than English. Even when you are asked to investigate, to analyze, to explain, or to argue, you can sometimes use personal experience as support for exposition and argument. Rebecca Shriver, a student who had spent a year living and working in St. Thomas, added life and verisimilitude to her research paper analyzing cultural differences between the Virgin Islands and the United States by including not only material gathered from books and periodicals but also this telling recollection:

> Among the first things an American in the Virgin Islands will notice are the driving and the drivers. St. Thomas retains the custom, a carryover from Danish rule, of driving on the left-hand side of the road. Drivers are extremely aggressive, vocal, and heedless of others. West Indians, especially the cabdrivers, virtually own the road. They stop for minutes at a time at the bottom of steep hills to chat with friends or to pick up hordes of workers. The streets resound with honks and screams as drivers yell obscenities at each other. Hitchhikers, too, are aggressive. Often a West Indian jumps into the back of one's truck, or schoolchildren tap on one's window, soliciting a ride.
>
> The mind-set of left-hand driving surfaces in an unusual way: walking habits. Since St. Thomians are so used to driving on the left, they also walk on the left, and an American who is unused to this will bump into a lot of West Indians on the sidewalk.

The writer used this recollection to make an important point: that recognizing and understanding cultural differences provide the keys to understanding. In an article called "Sex and Size," paleontologist Stephen Jay Gould makes effective use of recollection to ease his readers into a seven-page essay on a challenging subject. (Linnaeus [1707–1778], a Swedish botanist, originated the system of classifying organisms in established categories.)

> As an eight-year-old collector of shells at Rockaway Beach, I took a functional but non-Linnaean approach to taxonomy, dividing my booty into "regular," "unusual," and "extraordinary." My favorite was the common slipper limpet, although it resided in the realm of the regular by virtue of its ubiquity. I loved its range of shapes and colors, and the pocket underneath that

served as a protective home for the animal. My appeal turned to fascination a few years later, when I both entered puberty and studied some Linnaean taxonomy at the same time. I learned its proper name, *Crepidula fornicata* — a sure spur to curiosity. Since Linnaeus himself had christened this particular species, I marveled at the unbridled libido of taxonomy's father.

When I learned about the habits of *C. fornicata,* I felt confident that I had found the key to its curious name. For the slipper limpet forms stacks, smaller piled atop larger, often reaching a dozen shells or more. The smaller animals on top are invariably male, the larger supporters underneath always female. And lest you suspect that the topmost males might be restricted to a life of obligate homosexuality by virtue of their separation from the first large female, fear not. The male's penis is longer by far than its entire body and can easily slip around a few males to reach the females. *Crepidula fornicata* indeed: a sexy congeries.

Then, to complete the disappointing story, I discovered that the name had nothing to do with sex. Linnaeus had described the species from single specimens in museum drawers; he knew nothing of their peculiar stacking behavior. *Fornix* means "arch" in Latin, and Linnaeus chose his name to recognize the shell's smoothly domed shape.

Disappointment finally yielded to renewed interest a few years later when I learned the details of *Crepidula*'s sexuality and found the story more intriguing than ever, even if the name had been a come-on. *Crepidula* is a natural sex changer, a sequential hermaphrodite in our jargon. Small juveniles mature first as males and later change to female as they grow larger. Intermediate animals in the middle of a *Crepidula* stack are usually in the process of changing from male to female.

For an academic writing assignment, you usually have to research your subject in some depth before you can write about it. You need to rely on resources other than memory. Yet even as you approach such an assignment, you can *begin* by writing down your own relevant experiences. Whether or not you use them in your finished paper, they can help direct your research. Often you *will* use them, as Shriver and Gould did, in conjunction with more academic sources. A student who has worked in a day-care center can add vigor and authority to a sociology paper on day care in the United States by including a few pertinent illustrations based on that experience. An economics paper about the recent growth of the fast-food industry could benefit immeasurably from an incident remembered from harried days behind the counter at a McDonald's. If you grew up in the inner city, your recollections might lend enormous impact to a paper arguing for or against a particular city planning proposal.

Virtually every paper, no matter what it sets out to accomplish, stands to benefit from vivid examples and illustrations. And when you plan to include such examples and illustrations in your writing, your memories can prove as valuable as hidden treasure.

# *Making Connections: Writing from Recall in* A Writer's Reader

*Recall* is probably the major resource for writers in all professions and from all walks of life. In *A Writer's Reader*, some of the writers recall and respond to events from childhood, others to events from adulthood. For example, in "Transformation" (p. 514), Lydia Minatoya recalls several episodes from her childhood as she traces the development of her cultural identity. On the other hand, Stephen L. Carter in "The Black Table, the Empty Seat, and the Tie" (p. 567) recalls episodes from adulthood as he traces the evolution of his racial and professional identity. These two writers, like Russell Baker (p. 16) and Robert G. Schreiner (p. 18), not only recall and report significant events in their lives, but also reflect on the experiences and explain how their experiences have changed their thoughts, feelings, and actions.

Some of the writers from various fields who use the resource of *recall* include essayist E. B. White, "Once More to the Lake" (p. 462); poet and screenwriter Joy Harjo, "Three Generations of Native American Women's Birth Experience" (p. 471); editor and essayist Richard Rodriguez, "Does America Still Exist?" (p. 524); professor and poet Gary Soto, "Black Hair" (p. 547); and medical doctor and anthropologist Melvin Konner, "Out of the Darkness" (p. 615). These writers look back over important events in their lives and interpret how the experiences have influenced them. As you read these essays, consider the role that recall plays in them. For each essay, answer the following questions.

1. Does the author recall events from childhood or from adulthood?
2. Is the perspective of the essay that of a child or an adult? How do you know? What does the author realize after reflecting on the events? Does the realization come soon after the experience or later, when he or she examines the events from a more mature perspective?
3. How does the realization change the individual?
4. How do you think recall is useful to the author in his or her field of work or study?

# Chapter 2

# Writing from Observation

Most writers begin to write by recalling what they know. Then they look around themselves and add what they see. A very handy resource for them — and for you as a writer — is observation.

Some writing consists almost entirely of observation: a news story by a reporter who has witnessed a fire, a clinical report by a doctor or nurse detailing a patient's condition, a scientist's account of a laboratory experiment. So does any writing — fiction or nonfiction — in which the writer describes a person, place, or thing. In other writing, observation provides supporting details to make the primary ideas clear or convincing. Indeed, we can hardly think of a kind of writing that doesn't call for a writer to describe his or her observations.

Sometimes when you sit down to write, you look around the storehouse of your brain only to find empty shelves. Not enough to write about? In such a case, use the resource of observation. Open your eyes — and your other senses. Take in not only what you can see but also what you can hear, smell, touch, and taste. Then, when you write, draw upon your sensory observations and report your experiences in concrete detail. Of course, you can't record everything your senses bring you. You must be selective. Keeping in mind your purpose in writing and your audience will help you to choose the important and relevant details. To make a football game come alive for readers of your college newspaper, you might briefly mention the overcast cold weather and the buttery smell of popcorn. But if your purpose is primarily to explain which team won and why, you might stress the muddy condition of the playing field, the most spectacular plays, and the players who scored.

# Learning from Other Writers

Let's read two essays by writers who write from observation: a professional writer and a college student. In both essays, the authors observe their surroundings, and both reflect on their observations to draw conclusions about human behavior. The first essay, "A Small Island," is by Jamaica Kincaid, a professional writer born in the West Indies. She describes in vivid detail the physical beauty of the small island Antigua and comments on the effects of this overwhelming beauty on the people of the island.

Sandy Messina, a student, submitted the second essay for an assignment in both freshman composition and environmental biology. She looks closely at the desert and its inhabitants.

## *Jamaica Kincaid*    A Small Island

Antigua is beautiful.  Antigua is too beautiful.  Sometimes the beauty of 1 it seems unreal.  Sometimes the beauty of it seems as if it were stage sets for a play, for no real sunset could look like that; no real seawater could strike that many shades of blue at once; no real sky could be that shade of blue — another shade of blue, completely different from the shades of blue seen in the sea — and no real cloud could be that white and float just that way in that blue sky; no real day could be that sort of sunny and bright, making everything seem transparent and shallow; and no real night could be that sort of black, making everything seem thick and deep and bottomless.  No real day and no real night could be that evenly divided — twelve hours of one and twelve hours of the other; no real day would begin that dramatically or end that dramatically (there is no dawn in Antigua: one minute, you are in the complete darkness of night; the next minute, the sun is overhead and it stays there until it sets with an explosion of reds on the horizon, and then the darkness of night comes again, and it is as if the open lid of a box you are inside suddenly snaps into place).  No real sand on any real shore is that fine or that white (in some places) or that pink (in other places); no real flowers could be these shades of red, purple, yellow, orange, blue, white; no real lily would bloom only at night and perfume the air with a sweetness so thick it makes you slightly sick; no real earth is that color brown; no real grass is that particular shade of dilapidated, run-down green (not enough rain); no real cows look that poorly as they feed on the unreal-looking grass in the unreal-looking pasture, and no real cows look quite that miserable as some unreal-looking white egrets sit on their backs eating insects; no real rain would fall with that much force, so that it tears up the parched earth.  No real village in any real countryside would be named Table Hill Gordon, and no real village with such a name would be so beautiful in its pauperedness, its simpleness, its one-room houses painted in unreal shades of pink and yellow and green, a dog asleep in the shade, some flies asleep in the corner of the dog's mouth. Or the market on a Saturday morning, where the colors of the fruits and vegetables and the colors of the clothes people are wearing and the color of the day itself, and the color of the nearby sea, and the color of the sky, which is just overhead and seems so close you might reach up and touch it, and the way the people there speak English (they break it up) and the way they might be angry with each other and the sound they make when they laugh, all of this is so beautiful, all of this is not real like any other real thing that there is. It is as if, then, the beauty — the beauty of the sea, the land, the air, the trees, the market, the people, the sounds they make — were a prison, and as if everything inside it were locked in and everything and everybody that is not inside it were locked out. And what might it do to ordinary people to live in this way every day? What might it do to them to live in such heightened, intense surroundings day after day? They have nothing to compare this incredible constant with, no big historical moment to compare the way they are now to the way they used to be. No Industrial Revolution, no revolution of any kind, no Age of Anything, no world wars, no decades of turbulence balanced by decades of calm. Nothing then, natural or unnatural, to leave a mark on their character. It is just a little island. The unreal way in which it is beautiful now is the unreal way in which it was always beautiful. The unreal way in which it is beautiful now that they are a free people is the unreal way in which it was beautiful when they were slaves.

Again, Antigua is a small place, a small island. It is nine miles wide by twelve miles long. It was discovered by Christopher Columbus in 1493. Not too long after, it was settled by human rubbish from Europe, who used enslaved but noble and exalted human beings from Africa (all masters of every stripe are rubbish, and all slaves of every stripe are noble and exalted; there can be no question about this) to satisfy their desire for wealth and power, to feel better about their own miserable existence, so that they could be less lonely and empty — a European disease. Eventually, the masters left, in a kind of way; eventually, the slaves were freed, in a kind of way. The people in Antigua now, the people who really think of themselves as Antiguans (and the people who would immediately come to your mind when you think about what Antiguans might be like; I mean, supposing you were to think about it), are the descendants of those noble and exalted people, the slaves. Of course, the whole thing is, once you cease to be a master, once you throw off your master's yoke, you are no longer human rubbish, you are just a human being, and all the things that adds up to. So, too, with the slaves. Once they are no longer slaves, once they are freed, they are no longer noble and exalted; they are just human beings.

2

**Questions to Start
You Thinking**

*Meaning*

1. What does Kincaid mean when she says near the end of paragraph 1, "It is as if, then, the beauty . . . were a prison"?

2. According to the author, how is the unreal beauty of the island related to the inhabitants of the island? How has it shaped them? How does it reflect them?

3. Explain the meaning of the last sentence of the essay.

*Writing Strategies*

4. How does Kincaid use color to help you visualize the beauty of Antigua? What smells does she use to help make the scene come alive? What sounds?

5. Why does she keep repeating the phrase "no real" in paragraph 1? What is the result of this repetition?

6. How does Kincaid use her vivid description of the island to build to her concluding points about the people who settled and live on Antigua? Do you think this approach is successful? Why, or why not?

STUDENT ESSAY

## *Sandy Messina*   Footprints: The Mark of Our Passing

No footprints. No tracks. No marks. The Navajo leave no footprints because their shoes have no heels to dig into the earth's womb. They have a philosophy--walk gently on mother earth; she is pregnant with life. In the spring, when the earth is ready to deliver, they wear no shoes at all.

As I walk across the desert, I look at my shoes etch the sand dune. There they are following me: the telltale prints left on the brown earth. Each footprint has a story to tell, a story of change, a story of death. Many lives are marked by our passing. Our steps can bring death to the life of a flower, the life of a forest, the life of a friendship. Some of our passages can bring death to the life of a nation.

I see my prints dug deeply into the spawning grounds of the desert lavender, the evening primrose, the desert sunflower, and the little golden gilia. Life destroyed. Birth aborted. There under each mark of my passing is death. The fetuses--seeds of desert color, spring glory, trapped just below the surface waiting parturition--crushed into lifelessness. Man walks heavily on the earth.

He tramples across America, leaving giant footprints everywhere he goes. He fills swamps, furrows hillsides, forms roads, fells trees, fashions cities. Man leaves the prints of his lifelong quest to subdue the earth, to conquer the

wilderness. He pushes and pulls and kneads the earth into a
loaf to satisfy his own appetites. He constantly tugs at the
earth, trying to regulate it. Yet man was not told to regulate, restrict, restrain the Garden of Eden but to care for
it and allow it to replenish itself.

I look at my own footprints in the sand and see nearby      5
other, gentler tracks. Here on the sandy hummock I see
prints, soft and slithery. The snake goes softly on the
earth. His willowy form causes no tyranny. He has no need to
prove his prowess: he graciously gives warning and strikes
only in self-defense. He doesn't mar the surface of the earth
by his entrance, for his home is found in the burrows of the
other animals.

The spidery prints of the roadrunner, as he escapes with    6
a lizard dangling from his beak, show that he goes mercifully
on the earth. He does not use his power of flight to feed off
wide distances but instead employs his feathers to insulate
his body from high temperatures. He takes sustenance from the
earth but does not hoard or store it.

The wood rat scrambles over the hillock to burrow be-       7
neath the Joshua tree. His clawed plantigrade feet make sensitive little marks. He is caring of the earth. He doesn't
destroy forage but browses for food and eats cactus, food no
other animal will eat. His home is a refuge of underground
runways. It even provides protection for his enemy the snake,
as well as for himself, from the heat of the day. He never
feels the compulsion to be his own person or have his own
space but lives in harmony with many other animals, under the
Joshua tree.

The Joshua tree, that prickly paragon that invades the      8
desolation of desert, welcomes to its house all who would
dwell there. Many lives depend on this odd-looking creature,
the Joshua tree. It is intimately associated with the moth,
the lizard, the wood rat, the snake, the termite, the wood-
pecker, the boring weevil, the oriole. This spiky fellow is
hospitable, tolerant, and kind on the earth. He provides a
small world for other creatures: a world of pavilion, provision, protection from the harsh desert.

Unlike the Navajo's, my prints are still there in the       9
sand, but not the ruthless furrows I once perceived. My mus-

ings over nature have made my touch upon the earth lighter,
softer, gentler.

Man too can walk gently on the earth. He must reflect on     10
his passing. Is the earth changed, bent and twisted, because
he has traveled there, or has he considered nature as a symphony he can walk with, in euphony? He need not walk heavily
on the earth, allowing the heat of adversity and the winds of
circumstance to destroy him. He can walk gently on the earth,
allowing life to grow undisturbed in seeming desert places
until it springs forth.

**Questions to Start You Thinking**

*Meaning*

1. According to Messina, how is her way of walking across the earth different from the Navajo way?
2. How has the process of observing her own footprints changed the writer's behavior? How would she change the behavior of the rest of us?

*Writing Strategies*

3. Why doesn't Messina plunge right in and immediately start to report her observations? Of what use to her essay is her first paragraph?
4. Paragraph 3 isn't observation, but what does Messina accomplish in it? With paragraphs 4, 5, and 6, the writer returns to observing — for what purpose? What is the function of paragraphs 7–8? Of 9–10?
5. What specialized words suggest that this essay was written for readers familiar with biology (her instructor and other students)? Would any of the *jargon*, or technical terminology, interfere with Messina's communication of her ideas to general readers?

# *Learning by Writing*

## THE ASSIGNMENT: OBSERVING A SCENE

Observe a place near your campus or your home or your job and the people who frequent this place. Station yourself where you can mingle with the people there. Then write a paper in which you describe the place, the people, and their actions so as to convey the spirit of the place and offer some insight into the impact of the place on the people. Write for your instructor and classmates. Fill at least two typewritten or three handwritten pages.

This assignment asks you to use observation as your primary resource for writing. It is meant to start you observing closely, so we suggest you don't write from long-ago memory. Go somewhere nearby, and open your senses — all of them. Jot down what you can immediately see and sense. Notice the atmosphere of the place and how it affects the people there. Take notes in which you describe the location, the people, and the actions and events you see. After you have set down your observations in detail, use them to form a general impression of the place and the people there. What conclusions can you draw about this place? What is your main impression of the place? Of the people there? What is the relationship of the people to the place? Remember, your purpose is not only to describe what you see but also to express thoughts and feelings connected with those sights.

Three student writers wrote about these observations:

One student, who works nights in the emergency room of a hospital, observed the scene and the community of people that abruptly forms on the arrival of an accident victim (doctors, nurses, orderlies, the patient's friends or relatives, the patient himself or herself).

Another observed a bar mitzvah celebration that reunited a family for the first time in many years.

Another observed the bleachers in a baseball stadium before, during, and after a game.

## GENERATING IDEAS

Setting down observations might seem a cut-and-dried task, not a matter of discovering anything. But to reporter and essayist Joan Didion it is true discovery. "I write," she says, "entirely to find out what I'm thinking, what I'm looking at, what I see and what it means." Here are some ways to generate the observations you'll need for your final paper.

*Do some brainstorming.* First, you need to find a subject to observe. What places interest you? Which are memorable? Get out your pencil and start brainstorming — listing rapidly and at random any ideas that come to mind. (Brainstorming is often a useful technique for getting started; for more advice about it, see p. 334.) Here are a few questions to help you start your list.

DISCOVERY
CHECKLIST

### Finding a Scene to Observe

- Where do people get together to take in some event or performance? (a stadium, a theater, an auditorium)
- Where do people get together to participate in some activity? (a church, a classroom)
- Where do people form crowds while they are obtaining something or receiving a service? (a shopping mall, a dining hall or student union, a dentist's waiting room)
- Where do people gather for recreation or relaxation? (a party, a video arcade)
- What events do people gather at? (a fire, a wedding, a graduation)

*Get out and look.* After you make your list, go over it and put a check mark next to any possible subject that appeals to you. If no subject strikes you as compelling, plunge into the world and see what you will see. You might go to a city street or a hillside in the country, a college building or a campus lawn, a furiously busy scene — a shopping mall, an airport terminal, a fast-food restaurant, a student hangout — or one in which only two or three people are idling — sunbathers, dog walkers, anglers, Frisbee throwers. Move around within a group of people, if possible. Stand off in a corner for a while and then mix in again with the throng to get different angles of view of the place and the people.

*Record your observations.* Sandy Messina's essay "Footprints" began as a journal entry. In her biology course, Sandy was asked to keep a *specialized* journal in which to record her thoughts and observations on environmental biology. When she looked back over her observations of a desert walk, a subject stood out — one deep enough for a paper that she could submit to her English course as well. As you can see from her final version, keeping such a journal or notebook, occasionally jotting down thoughts and observations, creates a trove of material ready and waiting for use in more formal writing. (For further thoughts on journal keeping, see p. 339.)

The notes you take on your subject — or tentative subject — can be taken in any old order or methodically. One experienced teacher of writing, Myra Cohn Livingston, urges her students to draw up an "observation sheet" to organize their note taking. To use one yourself, fold a sheet of paper in half lengthwise. On the left make a column (which might be called "Objective") and list exactly what you saw, in an impartial way, like a zoologist looking at a new species of moth. Then on the right make a column (called "Subjective") and list your thoughts and feelings about what you observed. An observation sheet inspired by a trip to observe people at a beach might begin this way:

| Objective | Subjective |
|---|---|
| Two kids toss a red beach ball while a spotted dog runs back and forth trying to intercept it. | Reminds me of when I was five and my beach ball rolled under a parked car. Got stuck crawling in to rescue it, cried, had to be calmed down, dragged free. Never much liked beach ball after that. |

| College couples on dates, smearing each other with suntan lotion. | Good way to get to know each other! |
| Middle-aged man eating a foot-long hot dog. Mustard drips on his paunch. "Hell! I just lost two percent!" | Guy looks like a business executive: three-piece suit type, I bet. But today he's a slob. Who cares? The beach brings out the slob in everybody. |

For this writing assignment, an observation sheet seems an especially useful device. The notes in column one will trigger more notes in column two. As your list grows, it may spill over onto a fresh sheet. Write on one side of your paper only: later you can more easily organize your notes if you can spread them out and look at them all in one glance. Even in the sample observation sheet made at the beach, some sense is starting to take shape. The second and third notes both suggest that the beach is where people come to let their hair down. That insight might turn out to be the main impression the paper conveys.

The quality of your finished paper will depend in large part on the truthfulness and accuracy of your observations. If possible, while you write keep looking at your subject. Sandy Messina is a good, exact observer of nature: the details of the snake's "soft and slithery" print in the sand, the wood rat's "clawed plantigrade feet" (a technical word: *plantigrade* means walking with both sole and heel touching the ground).

*Include a range of images.*  Have you captured not just sights, but any sounds, touches, odors? A memorable *image*, or evocation of a sense experience, can do wonders for a paper. In his memoir *Northern Farm*, naturalist Henry Beston observes a remarkable sound: "the voice of ice," the midwinter sound of a whole frozen pond settling and expanding in its bed:

> Sometimes there was a sort of hollow oboe sound, and sometimes a groan with a delicate undertone of thunder. . . . Just as I turned to go, there came from below one curious and sinister crack which ran off into a sound like the whine of a giant whip of steel lashed through the moonlit air.

Apparently Beston's purpose in this passage is to report the nature of ice from his observations of it, and yet he uses accurate language that arrests us by the power of its suggestions.

When British journalist and fiction writer G. K. Chesterton wrote of ocean waves, he was tempted at first to speak of the "rushing swiftness of a wave" — a usual phrase. But instead, as he tells us in his essay "The Two Noises," he dusted off his glasses and observed a real wave toppling:

> The horrible thing about a wave is its hideous slowness. It lifts its load of water laboriously. . . . In front of me that night the waves were not like water: they were like falling city walls. The breaker rose first as if it did not wish to attack the earth; it wished only to attack the stars. For a time it stood up in the air as naturally as a tower; then it went a little wrong in its outline, like a tower that might some day fall.

## PLANNING, DRAFTING, AND DEVELOPING

Having been writing, however roughly, all the while you've been observing, you will now have some rough stuff to organize. Spread out your notes and look them over. If you have made an observation sheet, circle whatever looks useful. Maybe you can rewrite your preliminary notes into a draft, throwing out details that don't matter, leaving those that do. Maybe you'll need some kind of plan to help you organize all the details you have gathered from observing. In either case, you'll need to employ a sensible method of organization and select details that help convey your main impression. (For more on these writing strategies, see Chapters 16 and 18.)

**WRITING
WITH A
COMPUTER**

If you find it necessary to make a second, follow-up trip to the scene, word processing will allow you to amplify your draft easily. You can simply reopen your draft on the computer to insert further details wherever they will make your paper more vivid and lifelike.

Making your observations crackle with life, by the way, isn't just a matter of trying to intensify things with adverbs such as *very*. William Allen White, author and Kansas newspaper editor, hated such modifiers, which he believed are usually unnecessary. He once instructed his reporters to change every *very* they wrote to a *damn*, then cross out all the *damn*s; they would then have stronger prose. Thanks to word processors, you can easily imitate William Allen White's technique of searching for one term and replacing it with another. Many writers benefit from keeping a list of problems they tend to make over and over. White's list includes only the word *very*, but you should put on your list any words you tend to overuse when trying to write a vivid description. You can then use the word processor's SEARCH or FIND command to locate each instance of each word on your list and replace or delete all but the most effective. (You can also use the SEARCH function to find every instance of a grammar, spelling, or punctuation problem.) This technique will help you not only to edit more thoroughly but also to focus on recurring problems so that you can eventually eliminate them altogether.

*Use a sensible method of organization.* How do you map out a series of observations? One simple way is to proceed *spatially.* You can lay out your observations graphically or in a simple scratch outline. In observing a landscape, you might move from left to right, from top to bottom, from near to far, from center to periphery. Your choice will depend on your purpose in writing.

You might instead see a reason to move *from the most prominent feature to the least prominent.* If you are writing about a sketch artist at work, the most prominent and interesting feature might be the artist's busy, confident hands. If you are describing a basketball game, you might start with the action under a basket.

Or you might move *from specific details to a general statement of an overall impression.* In describing Fisherman's Wharf in San Francisco, you might start with sellers of shrimp cups and souvenir fishnets, tour boats loading passengers, and the smell of frying fish and go on to say: "In all this commotion and commerce, a visitor senses the constant activity of the area."

Or you could move *from common, everyday features to the unusual features you want to stress.* After starting with the smell of frying fish and the cries of gulls, you might go on: "Yet this ordinary scene attracts visitors from afar: the Japanese sightseer, perhaps a fan of American prison films, making a pilgrimage by tour boat to Alcatraz."

*Consider your purpose.* Perhaps your most important planning will take place as you answer the question What main insight or impression do I want to get across? Answering this question will help you decide which details to include and which to omit. Focusing on purpose will also help you avoid writing a dry recitation of observed facts. Remember that you want to *tell* readers something about what you have seen.

## REVISING AND EDITING

Your revising, editing, and proofreading will all be easier if you have taken accurate notes on your observations. Clearly, that is what Sandy Messina did. But what if, when you look over your draft, you find that in observing you skimped and now you don't have enough detail? If you have any doubts, go back to the scene and check more closely. Do you see any details you overlooked before? Did you miss anything? Take more notes to flush out your draft. Professional journalists often make such follow-ups.

Not all writers rewrite in the same way. Some start tinkering early, perfecting little bits here and there. Even in her original version of "Footprints," a few sheets of rough notes, Sandy Messina started making small improvements. In her first draft, she had written:

Each of us must learn to walk gently on the earth. We must quit pushing and pulling and kneading it into a loaf to be our own bread.

Right away, she realized that by calling the earth "a loaf" she had already likened it to bread. So she crossed out "be our own bread" and substituted "suit our own appetites." She also crossed out verbs one at a time, as they occurred to her, until a strong verb came along.

We ~~moved~~ ~~marched~~ trooped across America, leaving our giant ~~footsteps~~ footprints.

To see what parts of your draft still need work when you rewrite, you might ask yourself these questions. (For more on revising and editing, see Chapter 19.)

**REVISION CHECKLIST**

- Have you accomplished your purpose: to convey clearly your overall impression of your subject and to share some telling insight about it?
- What can you assume your readers already know? What do they need to be told?
- Have you gathered enough observations to make your subject understandable? Have you observed with *all* your senses? (Smell isn't always useful, but it might be.)
- Do any of your observations need to be checked for accuracy?
- Is the organizational pattern you have used the most effective pattern for your subject? Would another pattern be more effective?

**FOR PEER RESPONSE**

Once you've accurately recorded your observations, you may find it useful to seek another writer's reactions to your draft. See Chapter 20 for advice on working with other student writers and for general questions you should always ask a peer editor to address. For a paper in which you write from observation, you'll also want your peer editor to answer these specific questions:

- What is the main insight or impression you carry away from this piece of writing?
- Which sense does the writer use particularly well? Are any senses neglected that could be used?
- Can you see and feel what the writer experienced? Would more details make this writing more compelling? Put check marks on the manuscript wherever you want more details.
- How well has the writer used the evidence from his or her senses to build a dominant impression? Which sensory impressions contribute most strongly to the overall picture? Which seem superfluous?
- If this were your paper, what is the one thing you would be sure to work on before handing it in?

OTHER ASSIGNMENTS

1. To develop your powers of observation, follow Sandy Messina's example. Go for a walk, recording your observations in two or three detailed paragraphs. Let your walk take you either through an unfamiliar scene or through a familiar scene perhaps worth a closer look than you normally give it (such as a supermarket, a city street, an open field). Avoid a subject so familiar that it would be difficult for you to see it from a fresh perspective (such as a dormitory corridor or a parking lot). Sum up your impression of the place, including any opinion you form by your close observations.

2. Here is a short, spontaneous writing exercise that might serve as a warmup for a long assignment. Lin Haire-Sargeant of Tufts University, whose students enjoy the exercise, calls it "You Are the Detective." She asks her students to begin the assignment immediately after the class in which it is given and to turn it in the same afternoon.

> Go to a nearby public place — burger joint, library, copy center, art gallery — and select a person who catches your eye, who somehow intrigues you. Try to choose someone who looks as if she or he will stay put for a while. Settle yourself where you can observe your subject unobtrusively. Take notes, if you can do so without being observed yourself.
>
> Now, carefully and tactfully (we don't want any fistfights or lawsuits) notice everything you can about this person. The obvious place to start would be with physical characteristics, but focus on other things too. How does the person talk? Move? What does the person's body language tell you?
>
> Write a paragraph describing the person. Pretend that the person is going to hold up a bank ten minutes from now, and the police will expect you to supply a full and accurate description of him or her.

3. The perspective of a tourist, an outsider alert to details, often reveals the distinctive character of places and people. Think of some place you have visited as an outsider or a visitor in the past year, and jot down

**FOR GROUP LEARNING**

## Reading Your Writing Aloud

Instead of soliciting written comments about your work, try reading aloud to your group the draft you have written for an assignment in this chapter. Prepare your reading beforehand and try to deliver it with some feeling. Ask others to stop you when something isn't clear. Have pencil in hand to mark any such problem. After you've finished reading aloud, ask for reactions. If these are slow in coming, ask your listeners any of the questions in the peer response checklist on page 43. Have your group's secretary record the most vital suggestions and reactions that your draft provokes.

from memory any details you noticed that you haven't been able to forget. Or spend a few minutes as a tourist right now. Go to a busy spot on or off campus and record your observations of anything you find amusing, surprising, puzzling, or intriguing. Then write an essay on the unique character of the place.

4. From among the photographs that open Chapters 22 through 27, se- lect one to observe. In a paragraph or two, capture in words its most memorable features. Does the photograph have any center that draws your attention? What main impression or insight does that picture convey to you? See if you can put a sense of the picture into the mind of a reader who hasn't seen it at all. What do you see that your class- mates missed? What do they see that you missed?

## *Applying What You Learn:*
## *Some Uses of Writing from Observation*

Many college courses designed to prepare students for a professional career involve field trips. In such courses, you are often expected to observe closely and later to write your observations in a report. A sociology or a prelaw class might visit a city police court to hear the judge trying spouse abusers, drug pushers, and streetwalkers. Criminology or anatomy students might observe an autopsy. A journalism class might visit the newsroom of a daily newspa- per to see how journalists work at deadline. History students can share their firsthand impressions of a nearby historic site. A class in early childhood ed- ucation might visit a day-care center to observe and write about children's be- havior. After a visit to the coastal wetlands, biology students may be asked to describe the various forms of marine life they have observed. For a language development course, students might be asked to report on the way in which a particular child communicates.

Practitioners in the helping professions often write case studies, some- times for publication, sometimes for reference. Here, in *A Career in Speech Pathology* (1979), C. Van Riper describes his initial observations of three se- verely deprived rural children in need of treatment.

As I watched through the screen I saw the three children huddled in a cor- ner like kittens in a cold barn, silent and not moving for almost five minutes. Then the oldest one separated from the tangle and tiptoed all around the edge of the room, listening and watching. Then he motioned the other two to come with him to the door which he found was locked. Then he spied a little blue truck which had been placed under the table (with a ball and other toys), made a dive for it, and suddenly the room was full of wild animals, fighting, snarling, making animal noises of every kind, barking, mewing, shrieking. I knocked on the door and they fled again to huddle in the corner, human again but silently frozen with terror. I sat down in a chair and played with the truck and talked to myself about what I was doing, occasionally giving them a slow smile. I held out a piece of candy but none of them would reach for it. It was an eerie first session.

Much writing in scientific and technical courses involves observation. In a report for a chemistry or biology course, students might be asked to report their observations of a laboratory experiment, in zoology to observe and report on the behavior of animals. Here is a good illustration of scientific reporting from *Gorillas in the Mist,* written by Dian Fossey, a zoologist who for many years studied mountain gorillas in Rwanda, Africa.

> The body skin color of a newly born gorilla is usually pinkish gray and may have pink concentrations of color on the ears, palms, or soles. The infant's body hair varies in color from medium brown to black and is sparsely distributed except on the dorsal surfaces of the body. The head hair is often jet black, short, and slick, and the face wizened, with a pronounced protrusion of the nasal region, giving a pig-snouted appearance. Like the nose, the ears are prominent, but the eyes are usually squinted or closed the first day following birth. The limbs are thin and spidery, and the digits typically remain tightly flexed when the baby's hands are not grasping the mother's abdominal hair. The extremities may exhibit a spastic type of involuntary thrusting movement, especially when searching for a nipple. Most of the time, however, a gorilla infant appears asleep.

# Making Connections:
# Writing from Observation in A Writer's Reader

*Observation* is a major resource for writers, one that often goes hand in hand with *recall.* Authors in *A Writer's Reader* use *observation* for a variety of purposes. Essayist E. B. White in "Once More to the Lake" (p. 462) reports his carefully juxtaposed observations of a lake in Maine as it was when he was a child and as it is when he returns as an adult. White uses observation to convey the feeling that there has been no passage of time: the place, the people, even the dragonfly seem to be the same. In "Behind the Formaldehyde Curtain" (p. 604) Jessica Mitford uses observation for quite a different purpose. In her evaluation of the American funeral industry she provides graphic details that expose the work of the embalmer to our scrutiny. Bill McKibben, in "The End of Nature" (p. 620) uses vivid descriptions of his natural surroundings to give potency to his argument that we are on the verge of changing forever our relationship with nature. These two writers, like Jamaica Kincaid (p. 33) and Sandy Messina (p. 35), not only record their observations with fresh, authentic details, but they also use observation as a method for developing a larger message.

Other writers in various fields who use observation as a resource include writer Scott Russell Sanders, "The Men We Carry in Our Minds" (p. 499); editor and essayist Richard Rodriguez, "Does America Still Exist?" (p. 524); professor Michael Dorris, "Crazy Horse Malt Liquor" (p. 522); and biologist

Carol Kaesuk Yoon, "Drugs from Bugs" (p. 628). As you read these essays, consider the role that observation plays in them. For each essay, answer the following questions.

1. Specifically, what does the author observe? People? Behavior? Nature? Things?
2. What senses does he or she rely on and appeal to? What sensory images does this author develop? Is this effective, given the subject being observed? Find some striking passages in which the author reports his or her observations. What makes these passages memorable to you?
3. Why does the author use observation? How would the essay be weakened without the reported observations?
4. What conclusion does the author draw from reflecting on his or her observations?

# Chapter 3

# Writing from Reading

"A shut book," according to a saying, "is only a block of paper." So is an open book, until a reader interacts with it. Did you ever observe someone truly involved with a book? From time to time that reader may put down the book to ponder, to dream, or to doubt, may pick it up again, jot notes, underline, highlight, leaf backward for a second glance, sigh, mutter, fidget, nod approvingly, frown, perhaps laugh aloud, or disgustedly slam the book shut. Such a reader mixes in, interacts with the printed page. Not all readers are so demonstrative. Some sit quietly, hardly moving a muscle, and yet they too may be interacting, deeply involved.

The act of reading is highly personal. Do all readers extract the same things from the same reading? Surely they don't. *The Divine Comedy*, said T. S. Eliot, has as many versions as it has readers. The point is not that a book can mean any old thing you want it to, but that each reader, like each visitor to a city, has different interests and so comes away with different responses and memories. Listening to a class discussion of an essay or a poem all have read, you may be surprised by the range of insights reported by different readers. If you missed some of those insights when you read alone, don't feel crestfallen. Other students may be equally surprised by what you see — something they missed entirely.

Like flints that strike against one another and cause sparks, readers and writers provoke one another. Sometimes you read in search of a topic to write about. Sometimes when you already have a topic, you seek more information about it. Sometimes when you have an idea, you turn to other writers to help you explain it or back it up with examples and evidence. Sometimes you read because you have ideas you want to test; sometimes reading can change your ideas. Often you look to other writers — in books or journals — to stimulate your own ideas. Often when you read, you respond, carrying on a mental conversation with the writer, agreeing or disagreeing with what you have read. Often an idea you encounter in reading acts as a springboard for ideas to write about.

# Learning from Other Writers

Let's look at two examples of writing evidently stimulated by reading. The first is by James Thurber, an American humorist. He takes off from two comments by self-help authors Dr. James Mursell and Mrs. Dorothea Brande, who urge their readers to be realists and take concrete steps toward attaining their dreams. Thurber disagrees with these two self-proclaimed authorities, sets forth his own ideas on the subject of daydreaming, and in the process lampoons the entire genre of self-help books.

Margaret K. Jellison, a student at the University of Maine, wrote her essay in response to Primo Levi's *Survival in Auschwitz*. She summarizes and comments on his ideas but goes beyond his ideas to think on her own about "subtle holocausts" today. She used his comments to stimulate further thinking of her own. "I was so deeply moved by Levi's book," she said, "I wanted to share his story with others, as well as connect with people who are suffering and forgotten in our world today."

## *James Thurber*    The Case for the Daydreamer

All the books in my extensive library on training the mind agree that realism, as against fantasy, reverie, daydreaming, and woolgathering, is a highly important thing. "Be a realist," says Dr. James L. Mursell, whose *Streamline Your Mind* I have already discussed. "Take a definite step to turn a dream into a reality," says Mrs. Dorothea Brande, the *Wake-Up-and-Live!* woman. They allow you a certain amount of reverie and daydreaming (no woolgathering), but only when it is purposeful, only when it is going to lead to realistic action and concrete achievement. In this insistence on reality I do not see as much profit as these Shapers of Success do. I have had a great deal of satisfaction and benefit out of daydreaming which never got me anywhere in their definition of getting somewhere. I am reminded, as an example, of an incident which occurred this last summer.

I have been traveling about the country attending dog shows. I was writing a series of pieces on these shows. Not being in the habit of carrying press cards, letters of introduction, or even, in some cases, the key to my car or the tickets to a show which I am on my way to attend, I had nothing by which to identify myself. I simply paid my way in, but at a certain dog show I determined to see if the officials in charge would give me a pass. I approached a large, heavy-set man who looked somewhat like Victor McLaglen. His name was Bustard. Mr. Bustard. "You'll have to see Mr. Bustard," a ticket-taker had told me. This Mr. Bustard was apparently very busy trying to find bench space for old Miss Emily Van Winkle's Pomeranians, which she had entered at the last minute, and attending to a number of other matters. He glanced at me, saw that he outweighed me some sixty pounds, and decided to make short shrift of whatever it was I wanted. I explained I was writing an article about the show and would like a pass to get in. "Why, that's impossible!" he cried. "That's ridiculous! If I gave you a pass, I'd have to give a pass to everyone who came up and asked me for a pass!" I was pretty much overwhelmed. I couldn't as is usual in these cases, think of anything to say except "I see." Mr. Bustard delivered a brief, snarling lecture on the subject of people who expect to get into dog shows free, unless they are showing dogs, and ended with "Are you showing dogs?" I tried to think of something sharp and well turned. "No, I'm not showing any dogs," I said, coldly. Mr. Bustard abruptly turned his back on me and walked away.

As soon as Mr. Bustard disappeared, I began to think of things I should **3** have said. I thought of a couple of sharp cracks on his name, the least pointed of which was Buzzard. Finely edged comebacks leaped to mind. Instead of going into the dog show — or following Mr. Bustard — I wandered up and down the streets of the town, improving on my retorts. I fancied a much more successful encounter with Mr. Bustard. In this fancied encounter, I, in fact, enraged Mr. Bustard. He lunged at me, whereupon, sidestepping agilely, I led with my left and floored him with a beautiful right to the jaw. "Try that one!" I cried aloud. "Mercy!" murmured an old lady who was passing me at the moment. I began to walk more rapidly; my heart took a definite lift. Some people, in my dream, were bending over Bustard, who was out cold. "Better take him home and let the other bustards pick his bones," I said. When I got back to the dog show, I was in high fettle.

After several months I still feel, when I think of Mr. Bustard, that I got the **4** better of him. In a triumphant daydream, it seems to me, there is felicity and not defeat. You can't just take a humiliation and dismiss it from your mind, for it will crop up in your dreams, but neither can you safely carry a dream into reality in the case of an insensitive man like Mr. Bustard who outweighs you by sixty pounds. The thing to do is to visualize a triumph over the humiliator so vividly and insistently that it becomes, in effect, an actuality. I went on with my daydreams about Mr. Bustard. All that day at the dog show I played tricks on him in my imagination, I outgeneraled him, I made him look silly, I had him on the run. I would imagine myself sitting in a living room. It was late at night. Outside it was raining heavily. The doorbell rang. I went to the door and opened it, and a man was standing there. "I wonder if you would let me use your phone?" he asked. "My car has broken down." It was, of all people, Mr. Bustard. You can imagine my jibes, my sarcasm, my repartee, my shutting the door in his face at the end. After a whole afternoon of this kind of thing, I saw Mr. Bustard on my way out of the show. I actually felt a little sorry about the tossing around I had given him. I gave him an enigmatic, triumphant smile which must have worried him a great deal. He must have wondered what I had been up to, what superior of his I had seen, what I had done to get back at him — who, after all, I was.

Now, let us figure Dr. Mursell in my place. Let us suppose that Dr. Mursell   5 went up to Mr. Bustard and asked him for a pass to the dog show on the ground that he could streamline the dog's intuition. I fancy that Mr. Bustard also outweighs Dr. Mursell by sixty pounds and is in better fighting trim; we men who write treatises on the mind are not likely to be in as good shape as men who run dog shows. Dr. Mursell, then, is rebuffed, as I was. If he tries to get back at Mr. Bustard right there and then, he will find himself saying "I see" or "Well, I didn't know" or, at best, "I just asked you." Even the streamlined mind runs into this Blockage, as the psychologists call it. Dr. Mursell, like myself, will go away and think up better things to say, but, being a realist dedicated to carrying a dream into actuality, he will perforce have to come back and tackle Mr. Bustard again. If Mr. Bustard's patience gives out, or if he is truly stung by some crack of the Doctor's he is likely to begin shoving, or snap his fingers, or say " *'Raus!*,"[1] or even tweak the Doctor's nose. Dr. Mursell, in that case, would get into no end of trouble. Realists are always getting into trouble. They miss the sweet, easy victories of the daydreamer.

I do not pretend that the daydream cannot be carried too far. If at this late   6 date, for instance, I should get myself up to look as much like Mr. Bustard as possible and then, gazing into the bathroom mirror, snarl "Bustard, you dog!," that would be carrying the daydream too far. One should never run the risk of identifying oneself with the object of one's scorn. I have no idea what complexes and neuroses might lie that way. The mental experts could tell you — or, if they couldn't, they would anyway.

Now let us turn briefly to the indomitable Mrs. Brande, eight of whose   7 precious words of advice have, the ads for her book tell us, changed the lives of 860,000 people, or maybe it is 86,000,000 — Simon & Schuster published her book. (These words are "act as if it were impossible to fail," in case your life hasn't been changed.) Discussing realistic action as against the daydream, she takes up the case of a person, any person, who dreams about going to Italy but is getting nowhere. The procedure she suggests for such a person is threefold: (1) read a current newspaper in Italian, buy some histories, phrase books, and a small grammar; (2) put aside a small coin each day; (3) do something in your spare time to make money — "if it is nothing more than to sit with children while their parents are at parties." (I have a quick picture of the parents reeling from party to party, but that is beside the point.)

I can see the newspaper and the books intensifying the dream, but I can't   8 somehow see them getting anybody to Italy. As for putting a small coin aside each day, everybody who has tried it knows that it does not work out. At the end of three weeks you usually have $2.35 in the pig bank or the cooky jar, a dollar and a half of which you have to use for something besides Italy, such as a C.O.D. package. At that rate, all that you would have in the bank or the

---

[1] *'Raus. From the German, a brusque command meaning "Get out!"

jar at the end of six years would be about $87.45. Within the next six years Italy will probably be at war, and even if you were well enough to travel after all that time, you couldn't get into the country. The disappointment of a dream nursed for six years, with a reality in view that did not eventuate, would be enough to embitter a person for life. As for this business of sitting with children while their parents are at parties, anybody who has done it knows that no trip to anywhere, even Utopia, would be worth it. Very few people can sit with children, especially children other than their own, more than an hour and a half without having their dispositions and even their characters badly mauled about. In fifteen minutes the average child whose parents are at a party can make enough flat statements of fact about one's personal appearance and ask enough pointed questions about one's private life to send one away feeling that there is little, if any, use in going on with anything at all, let alone a trip to Italy.

The long and hard mechanics of reality which these inspirationalists suggest are, it seems to me, far less satisfactory than the soft routine of a dream. The dreamer builds up for himself no such towering and uncertain structure of hope; he has no depleted cooky jar to shake his faith in himself. It is significant that the line "Oh, to be in England now that April's there," which is a definite dream line, is better known than any line the poet wrote about actually being in England. (I guess *that* will give the inspirationalists something to think about.) You can sit up with children if you want to, you can put a dime a day in an empty coffee tin, you can read the Fascist viewpoint in an Italian newspaper, but when it comes to a choice between the dream and the reality of present-day Italy, I personally shall sit in a corner by the fire and read *The Ring and the Book.*[2] And in the end it will probably be me who sends you a postcard from Italy, which you can put between the pages of the small grammar or the phrase book.

9

**Questions to Start You Thinking**

*Meaning*

1. What is Thurber's disagreement with Mursell and Brande? Do you agree with Mursell and Brande, or with Thurber? Why?

2. Can you think of other examples to support either the position of the experts on being a realist or the position of Thurber?

*Writing Strategies*

3. How do the comments of Mursell and Brande serve as a springboard for Thurber's thinking and writing?

4. How much space does Thurber devote to statement and explanation of the ideas of Mursell and Brande? How much to his own ideas? How does he integrate his ideas with theirs?

---

[2] *The Ring and the Book.* A long poem by the Victorian poet Robert Browning based on an Italian murder case from 1698.

5. How does Thurber organize the essay?
6. How does Thurber use the writer's resource of recall? Of observation? Of imagination?
7. How does Thurber develop his ideas? Is he specific enough to make his point clear?
8. What techniques make his essay amusing?

STUDENT ESSAY

## *Margaret K. Jellison*     The Nothing People

```
You who live safe
In your warm houses,
You who find, returning in the evening,
Hot food and friendly faces:
Consider if this is a man
Who works in the mud
Who does not know peace
Who fights for a scrap of bread
Who dies because of a yes or a no.
Consider if this is a woman,
Without hair and without name
With no more strength to remember,
Her eyes empty and her womb cold
Like a frog in winter.
Meditate that this came about:
I commend these words to you.
Carve them in your hearts
At home, in the street,
Going to bed, rising;
Repeat them to your children,
Or may your house fall apart,
May illness impede you,
May your children turn their faces from you.
```

     This poem is taken from the book <u>Survival in Auschwitz</u> by Primo Levi. Levi recalls the many atrocities he and many other Jews suffered at the hands of the Germans in this death camp. The only realities present in Auschwitz are those of suffering: hunger, cold, exhaustion, fear, and violence.

2

These condemned people were worked nonstop for the Third
Reich. They were reduced to guarding with their lives their
most valuable possessions--a soup bowl and a spoon--so that
they might eat their two bowls of thin soup and slice of
bread per day.

Levi asks us simply to remember what happened to the          3
Jewish people there and to tell their story. I questioned how
the killing of six million Jews could have happened. I then
realized that Hitler and his followers did not view them as
"people," but only as "pieces," "numbers," "Jews" who had to
be destroyed. They were of no value, but merely served as a
slave race.

Levi makes a powerful statement about the process of de-      4
humanization after he has been "marked" for life with the indelible number on his arm:

> Nothing belongs to us any more; they have taken away our
> clothes, our shoes, even our hair; if we speak, they
> will not listen to us, and if they listen, they will not
> understand. They will even take away our name: and if we
> want to keep it, we will have to find ourselves the
> strength to do so, to manage somehow so that behind the
> name something of us, of us as we were, still remains.

Levi goes on to say that in our world, the normal world of
the living, being deprived of these things is inconceivable--
they are as much a part of us as our arms and legs. Never being able to hear another person voice our name would be a
lonely, desolate existence that would only crush us more into
death-filled despair and isolation. The most powerful "mark"
of our own unique personhood is in our name. When another
person speaks our name, we are invited and encouraged to live
our life with meaning, value, and purpose. If we are never
called by name, how can we continue to live a worthwhile existence with honor and dignity? Levi calls this offense "the
demolition of a man."

The Jewish people were "nothing people." They no longer       5
had names, voices, homes, families, dignity. We must never
forget the persecution these people suffered, and such a
Holocaust must never happen again. We all long for identity,
recognition, home, family, food, and health. These are basic

human needs and wants. But I wonder if there are not "subtle holocausts" in our world today. Are there nothing people among us still?

I recently heard the story of a city in Ecuador named Quito. On the outskirts of Quito, another city appears where the nothing people exist. These people are not recognized by their society in the sense that they have no names, no voice in their government, no homes, no food, no dignified life. On occasion, their makeshift cities are bulldozed over by those who live in Quito. They then move hopelessly to another location outside the city and struggle for survival again. In our own city of New York lies a city of cardboard houses in Central Park, much like the city outside of Quito. There nothing people also exist. They too have no voice, no names, no food, no homes, no dignity. In this, the richest country in the world, we haven't the courage to see these people as human beings with basic human needs and do something to change their existence for the better. I am afraid nothing people still exist in this world.    6

Off our shores, the Haitian people are struggling for survival. They are nothing people who have no homes, no names, no food, no dignified life. Yet our country wants to give them "a number" and process them through a court system that would determine their future existence. The United States government says these people are fleeing poverty, not political repression--so they don't deserve asylum. Only two thousand out of eleven thousand people thus far have been granted asylum. All the others are being sent back to Haiti. One Haitian man stated, "The Americans know we're being killed in Haiti--they're sending us back anyway." We as a country are closing our eyes to this atrocity.    7

The unborn are also nothing people. My friend's daughter is pregnant and unmarried. She will get an abortion while my friend grieves for the unborn grandchild she will never hold. The unborn have no rights, no voice, no name, and yet how many will never be brought into this world because of someone else's decision that they die?    8

What about the elderly, who are viewed by society as no longer "productive"? My mother, now in her seventies and homebound, struggles on a fixed income, struggles to make    9

ends meet, and struggles for health care. She relies on the
Meals on Wheels program for her daily bread. After two
months, her meals were discontinued: she had become only "a
number" whose assistance was terminated. Eventually she was
reinstated. It didn't matter to the system that she had no
food during the interim. She only was a number. Are the elderly also nothing people who have no more voice, no more
rights, no more dignity? Are they only social security numbers? Have they lost their names?

In this society that values so many material things,     10
have we so easily forgotten the great worth and value of
every human being? The most frightening and devastating holocaust of today is the reality that children in our own communities are murdering other children. How can we allow this
holocaust to continue?

When the nothing people try to speak, will we listen,    11
and if we listen, will we understand? Maybe a greater question is What has happened to our good conscience and moral
sensitivity? Do we truly feel our connectedness with one another and treat each other with honor and dignity? Are the
needs of others as important as our own needs? Do we make the
effort to reach out with compassionate hearts, caring hands,
and unshakable convictions that promote a better life for all
persons?

Yes, today's society has its own subtle holocausts. I    12
believe the annihilation of the human spirit is the greatest
darkness we face today. A Jewish rabbi once asked his students, "When does darkness end and day begin?" When his students failed to answer, he replied, "Darkness ends and day
begins when we can look into the eyes of every man, woman,
and child and recognize that they are our brothers and sisters." Let us never forget all nothing people. Let us embrace
them as our brothers and sisters.

**Questions to Start
You Thinking**

*Meaning*

1. What does Primo Levi mean by the phrase "nothing people"?
2. What does Jellison mean by the phrase "subtle holocausts"?
3. Can you think of examples of "nothing people" and "subtle holocausts" to add to the ones that Levi and Jellison discuss?

*Writing Strategies*

4. How does Levi's book serve as a springboard for Jellison's own ideas?

5. How much space does Jellison devote to statement and explanation of Levi's ideas? How much to her own ideas stimulated by Levi's comments?

6. Does Jellison provide enough details to make her own ideas clear? To convince you to agree with her? What are the sources of her details?

# Learning by Writing

## THE ASSIGNMENT: READING FOR INSIGHT

This assignment invites you to do some reading that will expand your knowledge and to use what you have read as a springboard for your writing. It asks you to look for passages that stimulate you to think, reflect on what you read, arrive at some original insight or observation, and then write a paper in which you use what you have read as the point of departure for your own ideas.

For at least five days, keep a reading journal in which you react each day to an essay, newspaper or magazine article, or chapter of a book — perhaps a textbook — that sends your thoughts in some new and interesting direction. Then look over your journal and select the most promising entry. Develop it into a paper in which you share with your readers what you have learned as well as your fresh insights. Turn in your journal along with your paper.

Among the thoughtful papers we have seen in response to this assignment are these:

A man who had recently read about the economic law of supply and demand set out to demonstrate that law by describing the behavior of both sellers and customers at a yard sale.

A woman, having read in her sociology textbook about the changes that city neighborhoods in the United States typically undergo in the course of fifty to a hundred years, thought about the changes that had taken place in a neighborhood she knew well and concluded that the textbook's generalizations did not apply. She came up with her own theory of neighborhood change and explained it with examples from her own experience.

A man, after having read and thought about George Orwell's classic essay "Shooting an Elephant," agreed with the writer that whole governments can act unwisely to save face. He used as his main example U.S. policy toward Vietnam in the 1960s and 1970s.

A man, inspired by Gradgrind, the tyrannical and shortsighted schoolmaster in Charles Dickens's *Hard Times*, humorously insisted he had encountered as much mindlessness in the elementary school he had attended as had Dickens's characters.

## GENERATING IDEAS

How will you find ideas for this assignment? First you need to find interesting and challenging reading material, and then you need to fully engage with it. Try one of each: a classic book, a current magazine article, a memorable post on a computer bulletin board, a chapter from a textbook, the letters of a famous person, a thought-provoking short story, a book about art or music — whatever engages your interest. That way, your journal will contain a variety of possibilities from which you can choose the topic for your paper.

*Check current periodicals.* Start in the library and browse through several current magazines likely to spur you to think, such as the *Atlantic, Harper's, New Republic, Commentary, Ms., Esquire.* Or check the editorials and op-ed columns in your local newspaper or in the *New York Times* or the *Wall Street Journal.* Never mind *People, Life,* the *National Inquirer,* and other periodicals written mainly to entertain. You want good, meaty articles conducive to reflection; if they are a bit difficult to understand and need to be read twice, so much the better. Try not to start out with ideas you already have, looking only for confirmation. Instead stay open to fresh ideas that your readings may unexpectedly trigger.

*Recall something you have already read.* What have you read lately that has started you thinking and wondering? Classics like Sigmund Freud's *The Interpretation of Dreams,* Rachel Carson's *The Sea around Us,* and Henry David Thoreau's *Walden* bristle with challenging ideas. Why not draw on some reading you've been assigned for another course — a chapter in a textbook, an essay for a literature course, a book assigned for outside reading.

*Skim and sample.* As you begin your search for promising material, keep in mind that you can't afford the luxury of reading everything word for word: skim, skip, and sample ideas. Try reading just the first two and the last two paragraphs of articles. Those will probably alert you to the writers' main points. When you look into books, skim through the first chapter and the last chapter. Then, if an article or a book looks interesting, you can spend more time with it.

*Read critically.* Once you zero in on a thought-provoking chapter, article, or essay, read slowly and carefully, giving yourself plenty of time to think between the lines. Try to discern the writer's opinions, even if they are unstated. But don't just soak up opinions and information. Carry on a mental dialogue with the writer. Criticize. Question. Wonder. Argue back. Dare to differ with the author. Most printed pages aren't holy writ; you can doubt them; you can disagree with them. Opinions you don't agree with can be valuable if they set your own thoughts in motion. (For more on reading and thinking critically, see "Suggestions for Critical Reading," pp. 124–26.)

*Write while you read.* Read with pencil in hand, and react in writing. Write brief notes to yourself (if you're using library materials) or mark up the text (if you own the book or magazine or have made a photocopy of it or have printed it from your computer). Underline phrases and sentences that contain essentials. Star things you think are important. Make cross-references: "Contradicts what he said on p. 17." Jot thoughts in the margin: "Reminds me of what I saw yesterday." Besides helping you participate while you read, such notes will help you later to review what you have read.

*Make daily journal entries.* What do you put into a journal entry? First put in the title, author, and source of the material. If you come across passages you especially admire, summarize or copy them into the journal — being sure to indicate direct quotations with quotation marks. Along with summaries and direct quotations, include your own reactions. A journal entry is not just a record of what you read; it is your response to your reading. Remember to turn your reading journal in with your completed essay for this assignment. (For more suggestions about keeping a journal, see Chapter 15.)

The questions in the following checklist may help you get started with your own reading journal. If in your journal you write the answers to at least some of these questions, you'll have valuable thoughts on hand when you start drafting your paper.

**DISCOVERY CHECKLIST**

## Keeping a Reading Journal

- What does the writer take for granted? What assumptions does he or she begin with — stated or unstated?
- Do the writer's assertions rest on evidence? What kind of evidence? Statistics? Surveys? Quotations from authorities? Historical facts? Are you convinced? Can you test the writer's assertions against anything you know or can find out?
- Do you agree with what the writer has said? Do his or her ideas clash with any ideas you hold dear? Does he or she question anything you take for granted?
- From any facts the writer presents, what inferences can you draw? Might any conflicting evidence be mustered? Has the writer failed to tell you anything you wish you knew?
- Has anything you read opened your eyes to new ways of looking at the world?

Margaret Jellison kept a reading journal in preparing to write her essay. Shortly after she began reading Primo Levi's *Survival in Auschwitz*, she found herself bursting with questions and insights. Levi's comments not only cast light on the Holocaust and on the Third Reich but also made her start wondering about "subtle holocausts" in our world today. Excited, Jellison jotted her thoughts in her notebook, going beyond the ideas in the book she had read. Her written thoughts illustrate a typical, spontaneous entry in a reading journal.

> No names. Instead—
>     "Wieviel Stück?" ("How many pieces?")
>     Häftling (Prisoner)
>     Tattooed numbers
>
> The people in concentration camps were treated like nameless, faceless numbers. Made into nothing. Into nothing people. Only way they could have been eliminated so completely.
>     I want to believe that this is history, that this is past, but is it? What about political repression today? Or even the subtler ways of "eliminating" everyone we don't want to deal with: the homeless, the elderly, the disabled? Are we guilty of the same dehumanization?

## PLANNING, DRAFTING, AND DEVELOPING

*Select a promising entry from your reading journal.* Faced now with your week's worth of journal entries, how do you decide which to expand into a paper? First, ask yourself which entry most interests you. Second, ask which of your reflections would most interest your possible readers — your classmates and your instructor. Which entry most clearly seems to say something? Which arrives at or points toward a conclusion, however tentative? For which one do you clearly have some ideas of your own to add, either in agreement or disagreement? That's the one to develop. You may want to discuss your possible choices with your classmates or your instructor before you proceed.

If, before you begin writing, you feel the need for more ideas than you've recorded in your journal entry, backtrack for a while. Look over the passage you have selected and do more thinking. One of the strengths of the essays of both Thurber and Jellison is the convincing array of examples. After Jellison wrote her journal entry, she decided it looked a little skimpy. She wanted to discover other examples of current "nothing people." "I thought of the one about the Haitians because I had heard a lot about them on the news and about the people of Quito, Ecuador, because we studied about them in my sociology course," she recalled, "and the one about the unborn — I'd heard that one before. I knew there must be lots of other contradictory messages, but at first it was hard to think of any."

After one fruitless attempt at brainstorming, Jellison had a conversation with three other students. She told them of her assignment, shared her preliminary thoughts, and asked, "What other subtle holocausts have you heard of lately?" They came up with ten further examples. Some of their ideas didn't fit her specifications. It seemed easy enough to think of people who are known by numbers, such as college students or Medicare recipients or credit card holders, but it was more difficult to come up with people who were really treated as "nothing people." This conversation did help her think of the example of the elderly. As Jellison began to draft, looking over the notes from her brainstorming session and from her conversation, she discarded examples that didn't work and thought of new ones. (For more on individual brainstorming, see p. 000. For more on working with other student writers, see Chapter 20.)

*Borrow honestly.*  The first law of writing from reading is to acknowledge fully and honestly your debt to the writer from whom you borrowed anything — a quotation, information, an idea. Not to do so is to lay yourself open to the charge of **plagiarism.** In the academic and professional worlds, using someone else's words or ideas and failing to cite the source is considered a grave offense akin to theft. In school, it can be the grounds for a failing grade or even for expulsion. Identify any source of an idea or quotation right away, as soon as you write it in your notebook. And make sure you carry that acknowledgment to your first draft (and subsequent drafts). Notice how Thurber and Jellison work the citations of their sources right into the text of their essays.

You can use information from your sources in any of three ways.

*Quoting.* When an author expresses an idea in a way so incisive, so brilliant, or so memorable that you want to reproduce his or her words exactly, quote them word for word. Direct quotations add life and color and the sound of a speaking voice. If you quote, be sure to quote exactly, including punctuation and capitalization. If you leave out part of a quotation, indicate the omission with an ellipsis mark — three dots (. . .). If the ellipsis mark occurs at the beginning or end of a sentence *within* the quotation, use *four* dots. You don't need an ellipsis mark at the beginning or end of the quotation. Why leave anything out? Usually because, if left in, it would be too boring or cumbersome, or perhaps because it adds some information that mattered to the author but doesn't matter to your point. But be careful that omitting words does not distort the meaning. For example, if a reviewer calls a movie "a perfect example of poor directing and inept acting," you cannot say "perfect . . . directing and . . . acting."

*Nutshelling.* Also called *summarizing,* nutshelling is a useful way to deal with a whole paragraph or section of a work when what you're after is just the general drift. Rather than quoting word for word, and without doing violence to an idea, you put it in a nutshell: you express its main sense *in your own words* and tell where you got the idea. A summary or nutshell is generally much shorter than the original; it expresses only the most important ideas in the original. Be sure you understand the passage before you attempt to summarize it, and take care not to distort the meaning.

*Paraphrasing.* This technique involves restating an author's ideas in your own words. Unlike a nutshell or summary, a paraphrase is generally about the same length as the original; it expresses every idea in the original, but in *your* words. You have to be careful not to let the author's words slip in: the style in paraphrasing, as in nutshelling, has to be yours. If a source says, "President Wilson called an emergency meeting of his cabinet to discuss the new crisis," and you say, "The president called on his cabinet to hold an emergency meeting to discuss the new crisis," your words aren't far enough removed from the original. Your sentence looks like plagiarism. You could put quotation marks around the original sentence, although it seems not worth quoting word for word. Or, better, you could write: "Summoning his cabinet to an emergency session, Wilson laid out the challenge before them." If you think through the material you are reading and you deal carefully with it, you won't have to put quotation marks around anything in your paraphrase.

In Margaret Jellison's "The Nothing People" you'll find all three methods in action. Jellison begins her essays with a direct *quotation* set off from the rest of the text and uses other quotations in the first half of her paper. "I needed to quote Levi's words because mine seemed so inadequate," Jellison explained. In the second sentence she sums up in a *nutshell* the idea she discovered in Levi's book: "Levi recalls the many atrocities he and many other Jews suffered at the hands of the Germans in this death camp." In the middle of paragraph 4, after using another long quotation, Jellison paraphrases Levi's next point. Without borrowing his very language, she produces a new version true to his ideas. Compare the original text with her paraphrase:

ORIGINAL
These things are part of us, almost like limbs of our body; nor is it conceivable that we can be deprived of them in our world.

PARAPHRASE

```
Levi goes on to say that in our world, the normal world
of the living, being deprived of these things is incon-
ceivable--they are as much a part of us as our arms and
legs.
```

How do you paraphrase another writer's thoughts? We suggest that you do the following.

1. Read the original passage over a couple of times. Underline key parts or jot them down.
2. Without looking at the passage, try to state its gist — the main point it makes, the main sense you remember, and the major supporting points.

3. Then go back and reread the original one more time, making sure you got its gist faithfully. Revise your paraphrase as necessary.
4. Check your paraphrase to be sure that you have not slipped in a few words from the original author and that you have not paraphrased too closely to the source.

***Determine an order for your ideas.*** As you plan your essay, you must not only select the ideas to include but also begin to organize the information. You may start your draft with a quotation from your reading, as Jellison does in "The Nothing People" or with a personal account of the impact of your reading, as Thurber does in "The Case for the Daydreamer." You may decide to use a summary of your reading, a relevant anecdote, or a comment about the author to establish a basis for your own reflections and insights.

Then you must decide on an arrangement of ideas in the body of your essay. Jellison moves from a summary of what she has read on the Holocaust to her own thoughts on subtle holocausts in today's society, drawing examples from her studies, her personal experiences, her conversations, and her observations of national events. If you are not sure how to organize your ideas, try several ways. To discover a satisfactory order, you might jot down your ideas and number them, or you might write a formal outline, or you might write several drafts, each organized differently. (A computer makes this last method

**WRITING WITH A COMPUTER**

Try sitting at your word processor with the book you are reading in your lap, so you can read and take notes at the same time. If you use electronic note cards instead of paper ones, you won't have to transcribe any material more than once. You can copy portions of your notes into your paper or leave them where they are and write *around* them. Remember that immediately after transcribing a passage, you should carefully record all the information you will need to acknowledge your source in your final paper — and to find it again, if necessary.

If you have long quotations that require extended proofreading, try this. Blow up a long quotation using a large font size to give your writing a different look. If your screen displays the page as it appears coming off the printer, edit it on screen; if not, print out a copy. A long passage like this might be more fun to proofread:

> ## Benvenuto Cellini, the celebrated sculptor of the Italian Renaissance, designed for Francis I a famous saltcellar of enamel and gold, preserved in the Vienna Art Museum.

Errors in an exaggerated font size will stand out more readily. But lest you turn in a paper that looks silly, return your fonts to a standard size after you finish proofreading. (For more on changing fonts, see "Formatting Your Manuscript" on pp. 448–50 in Chapter 21.)

easy.) The strategy that works for you may not work for your classmates. The important thing is that you think and plan as you work.

Finally, you'll conclude your piece by referring to your main point, not by introducing a new idea. Look again at how both Thurber and Jellison allude to the main point in the conclusion of the essay. (For more about organizing ideas, see Chapter 16; for more on openings and conclusions, see Chapter 17.)

## REVISING AND EDITING

Perhaps, as you look over your draft, you will feel the need to read further. Would your paper be stronger if it had more facts, statistics, or other evidence? Take the trouble to do additional reading if necessary.

As you discover new information while reading or think of other conclusions or examples while drafting, you may find your views changing. If you rearranged your ideas drastically since starting to write, cosmetic changes may not be enough — you may have to revise thoroughly. To see how much your ideas have changed since you first wrote your journal entry, you might try to state (to yourself or in writing) what insight you had then and what insight you have now. This exercise will help you to focus in on your main idea for your final essay.

In looking back over your paper, you might ask the following questions. (For more on revising and editing, see Chapter 19.)

 **REVISION CHECKLIST**

- Have you given emphasis to the significant and relevant points in the work you read?
- Have you gone on to develop your own ideas and insights?
- Do you see any place where a good, lively direct quotation might break the monotony?
- Have you used any direct quotations where a nutshell or a paraphrase would serve better?
- Do you identify clearly any information or ideas you have borrowed from another source?
- Is the order of your ideas easy to follow?
- Do you have enough details and examples to clarify and back up your assertions?
- Have you checked direct quotations for accuracy?

Margaret Jellison found that the hardest part of writing her paper was making the transition from the background material she felt her readers would need (paragraphs 2, 3, and 4 of her finished essay) to the insights she had gained in reading the book. In her first draft she went on too long about the book she had read. Then she included almost all the ideas she had touched upon in her reading journal entries. As she set about revising, she realized that most of those ideas belonged later in the paper; and one or two, she finally had to admit, were too weak to be included at all. So she spent a lot of time reorganizing and deleting. Remember, you can't use everything you think; you have to be selective.

In Survival in Auschwitz, Primo Levi recalls the many ~~out-~~ *atrocities* ~~rages~~ he and many other Jews suffered at the hands of the Germans in this ~~prison~~ *death* camp. ~~The book begins when Levi was in Italy and narrates his harrowing journey to the camp and his ghastly sojourn there.~~ **(so what?)** The people there ~~not only Jews, but also Gypsies, political prisoners, and criminals~~ were worked nonstop for the Reich. ~~Their every move was monitored and restricted: "There is no why here" was a common retort when they tried to do something that was irrationally forbidden.~~ They were reduced to guarding *with their lives* their most valuable possessions--a soup bowl and a spoon--so that they might eat their two bowls of thin soup and slice of bread per day. **(better as last sentence?)** The only realities present in Auschwitz are those of ~~pain and~~ suffering: hunger, ~~blows,~~ cold, exhaustion, fear, and violence. ~~Somehow, some of these people managed to survive. Not, Levi says, because of will power or survival instincts, but because the horrors were unfathomable even to the people who were living them.~~ **(off the point)**

---

**FOR PEER RESPONSE**

Once you have a preliminary draft that you like, ask a friend or classmate to read your paper and answer the following questions before you make your final revisions. See Chapter 20 for advice on working with other student writers and for general questions you should always ask a peer editor to address. For a paper in which you write from reading, you'll also want your peer editor to answer these specific questions:

- Can you restate or quote the major insight the writer shares from his or her reading?
- Does this paper make you want to read the original source?
- How useful and how interesting are the quotations the writer uses? Does the writer introduce them smoothly enough?
- Has the writer shared enough of his or her own ideas?
- Are there parts of the essay where you're not sure whether you are reading the writer's ideas or the source's ideas? Underline any such places.
- Are there any long quotations that would be better as nutshells or paraphrases?
- At any point, do you need additional examples or explanations? Put a check by such places.
- If this were your paper, what is the one thing you would be sure to work on before handing it in?

OTHER ASSIGNMENTS

1. Write a letter to the editor of your local newspaper in which you take exception to some commentary the newspaper printed recently. By referring to the commentary you have read, make the grounds of your complaint clear enough so that even someone who hasn't read the article you're criticizing will know what you're talking about. Go beyond summarizing what you have read; include your own ideas and observations.

2. Use an idea from one of the essays in *A Writer's Reader* in this textbook as a springboard for your own thinking. Write an essay in which you first give the reader an account of what you read (through quotation, nutshell, or paraphrase) and then add your own insights and ideas.

3. Use the ideas of Thurber or of Jellison as a springboard for an essay.

4. Instead of using an idea from something you have read, use an idea you have heard in a lecture, on television, on the radio, or in conversation as a springboard for an essay.

5. Respond to one or more advertisements, posters, or announcements that you have seen on television, on billboards, at work, at school, or on an electronic bulletin board. Quote the ad or announcement, comment on it, and then add your own insights and original ideas.

6. Compare two history books' or two newspapers' accounts of a celebrated event — the writing of the Declaration of Independence, the bombing of Hiroshima, or any other event you wish to read more about. Try to find one recent source, the other at least thirty years old. Describe the differences in the two versions. How do you account for them?

**FOR GROUP LEARNING**

## Discussing Your Reading

When your instructor assigns a paper in which you are to respond to a specific reading selection, first meet outside class with your writing group. Appoint a moderator to run a discussion of everyone's reaction to the reading. To start the discussion, here are some questions you might ask each group member:

• What problems did you have with this reading? What didn't you understand that someone else might explain?
• What do you take to be the author's purpose? What main point does the author make?
• Where do you disagree with or doubt the author?
• What does the author do especially well? What do you wish the author might have done better?
• What did you find out from this reading that you didn't know before?

The goal of this discussion is to give you a better understanding and appreciation of the reading so that you might come up with more ideas for your own paper.

# Applying What You Learn: Some Uses of Writing from Reading

In college, you'll write from your reading almost daily. Many instructors, to encourage you to read and write, will ask you to keep a notebook of your reading and may ask you to turn it in for inspection. Writing about your reading on tests and examinations allows you to demonstrate your mastery of the course material. (For advice about writing essay examinations, see Chapter 13.)

For other college writing assignments, reading will be just one of your resources. An education course, for instance, might ask you to combine reading and observing: to watch a toddler for an hour a day for a week, keep a detailed record of her actions, compare them with what is average for a child her age (information you would find by reading), and then draw some conclusions about her behavior. In the field of human development, students are constantly asked to make informed judgments on current issues (abortion, day care, joint custody) by learning to understand the differing views presented in books and articles.

You may be used to reading general magazines like *Newsweek* and *National Geographic*, which most literate readers enjoy. But later in college, many of your courses will require you to read journals written and read by trained specialists. Many specialists, from physicists to zoologists, write articles for others in their field, sharing what they know. Doctors and other health professionals report on new diseases or new treatments; scientists and technicians advance new theories; literary critics make fresh ventures into literary criticism; historians enlarge on and reinterpret knowledge of the past. As part of your training in a special discipline, you may be introduced to the *Journal of Comparative Behavior, Nature, Educational Research, American Journal of Sociology, PMLA,* or *Foreign Affairs.* You will often be asked to report on an article, reading it critically, perhaps summarizing or paraphrasing its essentials, and finally adding a thoughtful comment. Doing so, you will absorb the vocabulary and habits of thought of your chosen field and make them your own. You will see how skilled writers prove, demonstrate, evaluate, explain, select useful details, assert, affirm, deny, try to convince.

Many learned articles begin with a short review of previous research, which the writer then dashes to pieces. In some professional journals, though, summary or paraphrase of other writing may be an end in itself. Attorney Peter L. Knox, who writes articles about pension tax laws for professional legal journals, says that writing for him is often a matter of reading difficult writing (such as rulings of the tax court and the *Internal Revenue Manual*) and condensing it in plainer prose — "expressing in an organized, somewhat literary form a set of complex rules." You can see how Knox's articles might greatly help taxpayers and beginning tax lawyers struggling to understand legal prose such as the following, from *Final and Temporary IRS Regulations:*

> **§ 1.401(b)-1   Certain retroactive changes in plan**   [TD 7437, filed 9-23-76].
>
> (a)   *General rule.*   Under section 401(b) a stock bonus, pension, profit-sharing, annuity, or bond purchase plan which does not satisfy the requirements of section 401(a) on any day solely as a result of a disqualifying provision (as defined in paragraph (b) of this section) shall be considered to have satisfied such requirement on such date if, on or before the last day of the remedial amendment period (as determined under paragraphs (c), (d) and (e) of this section) with respect to such disqualifying provision, all provisions of the plan which are necessary to satisfy all requirements of sections 401(a), 403(a), or 405(a) are in effect and have been made effective for all purposes for the whole of such period.

The entry goes on like that for three and a half pages of fine print. Yet thousands of a client's dollars may be riding on an attorney's ability to interpret that entry correctly. In an article explaining the passage to his fellow pension plan professionals, Knox helpfully begins, "Section 401(b) provides a way for retirement plans to be retroactively corrected" and goes on to tell how the law is generally applied. Besides being a challenging exercise in translation, Knox's brand of specialized nutshelling and paraphrasing calls for hard, even imaginative, thought.

We have been viewing books and articles as *immediately* useful sources of ideas and information. But sometimes there is a time lag: you read Melville's novel *Moby-Dick* or Thorstein Veblen's *The Theory of the Leisure Class,* and although your reading isn't useful for the paper you are writing this week, something from it remains with you — a phrase, a stray idea, a way of constructing a sentence. Perhaps months later, when you are writing another paper, it returns to the forefront of your mind. In truth, writing from reading is useful to you in ways we haven't begun to indicate. We hold this truth to be self-evident: that the better you read — the more alertly, critically, questioningly — the better you will write.

# *Making Connections:*
# *Writing from Reading in* A Writer's Reader

Some writers use *reading* as a springboard for writing; others rely on it as a source of evidence for their writing. Either way, reading is a useful resource for writers. In *A Writer's Reader,* scientist Stephen Jay Gould draws on a broad scope of reading in "The Geometer of Race" (p. 532). He cites scientists Linnaeus and Blumenbach and then analyzes and evaluates their theories and arguments; he quotes Phillis Wheatley, a Boston slave poet; and he ends with a quotation from nineteenth-century British historian and moralist Lord Acton. Each enriches Gould's writing. Emily Prager in "Our Barbies, Our selves" (p. 595) uses a point she read in the obituary of Jack Ryan in the *New York Times* as the springboard for her reflections on the significance of the Barbie doll.

Like Gould, Prager, James Thurber (p. 49), and Margaret Jellison (p. 53), writers from various backgrounds in *A Writer's Reader* use reading as a resource for writing, including science writer Nicholas Wade, "How Men and Women Think" (p. 510); journalist Susanna Rodell, "Do You Work? Are You Guilty?" (p. 545); philosopher Christina Hoff Sommers, "The Backlash Myth: The Truth about How Women Are Doing in the Workplace" (p. 560); investigative journalist Jessica Mitford, "Behind the Formaldehyde Curtain" (p. 604); and physician Melvin Konner, "Out of the Darkness" (p. 615). As you read these essays, consider the role that reading plays in them. For each essay, answer the following questions.

1. Is the information discovered in the reading a result of careful selection, or is it an unexpected discovery?
2. How is the author's reading related to her or his occupation or area of study?
3. What does the author learn from reading? How does she or he use that information in the essay?
4. What original insight does the author arrive at as a result of reflecting on what she or he has read?

# Chapter 4

# Writing from Conversation

Don't know what to write about? Go talk with someone. When you exchange facts, thoughts, and feelings with people, you both give and receive. Not only do you find out things from others that you didn't know, but you have a chance to shape and define your own ideas in words. Listen closely to an hour's discussion between students and an anthropology professor, and you may get material for a paper. Just as likely, you can get a paper's worth of information from a five-minute exchange with a mechanic who relines brakes. Both the mechanic and the professor are experts. But even people who aren't usually considered experts may provide you with material.

As this chapter suggests, you can direct a conversation by asking questions to elicit what you want to find out. You do so in that special kind of conversation called the *interview*. An interview is a conversation with a purpose: usually to help you understand the other person or to find out what the other person knows.

## *Learning from Other Writers*

Here are two essays whose writers talked to someone and reported their conversations. The first is by Melina Gerosa, the entertainment editor for *Ladies' Home Journal.* It is based on an interview with movie star Jodie Foster, but Gerosa adds her own observations and conclusions to enrich her conversation with Foster.

Betsy Buffo, a student at St. Petersburg Junior College, wrote the second essay in response to an assignment asking her to interview and report on someone representing a segment of society with which she was unfamiliar but found interesting. Buffo was originally apprehensive about interviewing a stranger, but "was surprised to find it a pleasant experience" and was pleased at her own success in capturing her subject's personality and conveying his "intensity of purpose."

## *Melina Gerosa*  Jodie Loses Her Cool

Some things you might not know about Jodie Foster: Her toenails are always painted fire-engine red. She goes to the movies to cry. She still writes letters to her first love. And she doesn't always know where she's going. 1

In fact, right now, Jodie Foster is lost. A four-letter word sails from her lips like a dart, a rare blush spreads across her cheekbones, and the actress most noted for her calm and cool jerks her station wagon into reverse. A pair of little red boxing gloves swings mockingly from the rearview mirror as Foster backs away from the dead end that has taken her totally by surprise. 2

All this, and we haven't even left the parking garage. 3

That Foster has lost her way so easily is surprising, considering that she has a reputation for knowing exactly where she's going, both in the car and in her career. At thirty-two, she's arguably the most, well, driven and focused actress in Hollywood, and her penchant for being in control is no more evident than how she handles interviews. There are some things she doesn't want to talk about. One subject that is automatically off-limits: John Hinckley, Jr. (the warped fan who became obsessed with the actress's performance in *Taxi Driver* and tried to assassinate President Reagan in 1981 to impress her). And she will *not* discuss her much-speculated-about lovelife. But the real secret about Jodie Foster is that beneath that icy exterior lurks a surprisingly vulnerable soul, at once uncertain and romantic. 4

After a few more false turns, Foster finally escapes the garage and heads toward Los Angeles's Hancock Park, where she wants to spend this morning driving around looking at the houses. Perhaps the preoccupation with homes has to do with the fact that Foster is currently homeless. Sort of, anyway. She owns a house in the San Fernando Valley, but since it's too far from her production company, she wound up moving into a hotel. 5

Foster isn't house hunting; cruising around the quiet streets is like a nostalgic trip to the childhood she never had. With its manicured lawns and family homes, the area is everything that the more bohemian section where Foster grew up, in Hollywood, isn't. As a kid, she used to be dropped off in Hancock Park to trick-or-treat on Halloween; her mother also pretended that the family lived there so that Foster, from the age of nine to eleven, could attend cotillion, the stuffy dancing and manners school tradition where she was taught decorum and the fox-trot. 6

"Now every time I go to one of those Oscar things, I'm the first one on the dance floor, because it's the only time I get to use my incredible ballroom- 7 dancing skills," says Foster, looking surprisingly kidlike in red jeans, a black top, and wire-rimmed glasses, her hair wet from her shower.

When she speaks about her mother, her tone is a mixture of humor, respect, and affection. It's clear that Brandy Foster gave her daughter a lot more than dance lessons: She gave Jodie a strong heart, an independent spirit, and a firm belief in her own talent. "When you think about what in your parenting has allowed you to achieve excellence, if winning an Oscar is about excellence," says Foster, "it's not her telling me to wear my raincoat. It was the side of her that encouraged me to *fly*. And that told me to not hesitate."                                                                          **8**

A single mom of four children, Brandy Foster did this without the help of her husband, an air force pilot, who left home before Jodie was born. And Brandy started the encouragement early. At three years old, Jodie bared her bottom as the Coppertone girl, and a star was born. Thanks to Brandy's shrewd management, Jodie was able to land enough movie parts to support her entire family over the years, literally growing up before the public's eyes.                                                                          **9**

Yet once she was old enough to choose her own roles, Foster had to make some awkward decisions about her mom. And judging by how difficult mother-daughter relationships can be under normal, everyday circumstances, this transition of Brandy from business partner to mom must have been tricky. "I always get really careful around this line of questioning because she reads these things and the inference is, 'Yeah, when she was sixteen, she didn't need her ever again.' And that's not true," says Foster, a protective edge to her voice. "She has a different capacity now in my life. There was a time when I only wanted her in the professional and I didn't want her in the personal, and now it's just the opposite."                                                                          **10**

Foster hasn't hesitated to make other tough decisions as well. "I've walked away from enormous amounts of money when no one would walk away from that. I went to college when, if I wanted to have a career, it was the stupidest thing I could have done," says Foster of her stint at Yale. "I directed [*Little Man Tate*] right when I was about to win an Academy Award, when in terms of earning power as an actress you'll never be as high." Since then she's continued to forge into uncharted terrain; *Sommersby* was her first romantic lead, *Maverick* her first comedic turn, and later this year Foster will direct Holly Hunter in the drama *Home for the Holidays*.                                                                          **11**

But *Nell*, the first offspring hatched from her company, Egg Pictures, is her riskiest role to date. In the drama, released nationwide in January, Foster plays a woman raised in the Appalachian Mountains, completely isolated from society. The actress wails, dances, and speaks an indecipherable language with such passion that she is literally unrecognizable. She is playing a part that's a 180-degree turn away from the steely characters she brought to life in *The Accused* and *The Silence of the Lambs*. "It's as bold as anyone's ever been on film," says *Nell*'s director, Michael Apted. "It's one of those performances that if you don't get it right, it's laughable. . . . And she managed to give a great performance without your ever realizing that it's Jodie Foster. She doesn't implant her fingerprints all over it."                                                                          **12**

Renée Missel, who coproduced *Nell* with Foster, admits it was a stretch to     13
cast the actress even though she is a two-time Oscar winner. "Most agents saw
someone more vulnerable [in the role]," says Missel. "But I've always seen
Jodie's pain in all of her films, the vulnerability in her eyes, and I thought, If
that could just come to the forefront."

The thought of getting that emotion to the forefront made *Nell* the most     14
terrifying role Foster has ever undertaken.

"I was scared to death because I play people that have four different lay-     15
ers, and she doesn't have any," she says. "She doesn't have any protection."
For Foster, who's used to hiding behind a cooly cerebral mask both on-screen
and off, to show what is in her heart would make her feel psychologically
nude.

Yet taking calculated chances has paid off. Considering her A-list status as     16
an actress and her clout as a producer, Foster may be the most powerful thir-
tysomething woman in Hollywood. But that only exacerbates the pressure to
reach all her goals while she's still hot. "I have a very short burst of time to be
as effective as possible," Foster says. "This is a 'What was your last gig?' industry, and I'm sure at some point I'm going to have a movie that's a complete bomb."

So far, the buzz on *Nell* is more Best Actress than bomb, and with that, of     17
course, comes another sort of pressure. Does she think she will get nominated? "I try not to think about it because I don't want to get too weirded
out," says Foster. "[The pressure isn't] necessarily coming from everyone else,
it's really coming from me. But I thrive on that, because I don't let the ball
drop."

But no one, not even Foster, can stay cool and focused all the time, so she     18
unwinds by going to the movies — not as a professional but as an unabashed
fan. "I go to cry," Foster says simply. She's seen both *The Piano* (a romantic
melodrama) and *Fearless* (a story of recovery from tragedy) four times for this
very reason.

Movies aren't the only thing that moves Foster to tears. "Every time I see     19
men and women ballroom dancing, I start weeping uncontrollably," she says.
"It's romantic, and it's about opposites and celebrating the difference."

As we drive around looking at moldings and architectural detail in Han-     20
cock Park, Foster suddenly blurts, "I *love* this song!," turns up her tape deck
and hums along with Chrissie Hynde's pop love ballad "I'll Stand by You."
When the song ends, her hand immediately hits the rewind button. "I want
to hear my *favorite* song, on my *favorite* street, in front of my *favorite* house,"
says Foster, with all the enthusiasm of a teenage girl. As we pull up to a stone
Tudor, her thin lips stretch into a smile. "It looks like it has a great mahogany
library with a big green leather chair," Foster says. She cranes her neck to get
a better view. "It looks *warm.*"

The actress's ability to fantasize about romantic ideals stretches far be-     21
yond Hancock Park: She wears the male cologne Vetiver — a momento, she
says, of a long-ago love. "My first boyfriend wore it when I was fifteen," she
says, breaking her own cardinal rule never to talk about her private life. "He

was French and in the military service when I met him at a New Year's Eve party in Tahiti. I always wonder what happened to him. Every once in a while I send a letter to his parents [to forward to him], and I look him up in the French phone book," says Foster. She admits, sheepishly, that she doesn't know if he gets the letters. "It's a funny thing; it's been so many years since I knew him, but I can still remember absolutely every way that he smiled."

But when asked if she is dating anyone these days, her sentimental mood evaporates almost instantly. "You have to ask it," she says with a forced laugh, "and I get to answer that it's none of your business." In any case, her romanticism does not include children. "There is nothing that annoys me more than all of my friends who are over forty who desperately want to have children by fifty because basically they want someone to love them," she says. "It's too desperate. If I have kids, I have them. If I don't, I don't." Once she's settled in a new home in Los Angeles, she says she would like to get a dog — "a big slobbery one." 22

In the meantime, the actress feels as if she's still growing up herself, and as we drive around the streets where she used to trick-or-treat, she sums up where she is right now. "You hit a certain age, and then you realize that you're intent on changing; I've gotten more fragile as I've gotten older. I thought it would be the opposite; I thought I'd get stronger. It has completely changed the course of my relationships because I can't be in friendships with people who are antagonistic — Oh, *damn*," says Foster. Once again, she realizes she's lost her way — except this time, we're on the freeway. 23

As Foster tries to find the right exit, she keeps talking. "I finally realized that I didn't have to act like I knew everything, and like everything was okay. It was a revelation because people didn't recoil in horror — by giving them a little bit of power, it helped me out. And I didn't get as hateful and crazy. It's an interesting change, especially with my family. We're starting to have a different relationship, with my mom especially. Parents don't realize what they're talking about any more than you do. So why do you keep getting mad at them?" 24

Given this newly tolerant perspective, it's not surprising that Foster is able to acknowledge her own shortcomings, like the fact that once again she has managed to get herself lost. So, after several trips up and down a stretch of road, Foster admits defeat, picks up her car phone, and calls for directions. Lo and behold, it turns out that she was right smack where she was supposed to be. It's just a little hard to see the address from behind the black tinted windows that shield her from the rest of the world. 25

**Questions to Start You Thinking**

*Meaning*

1. What does the title of this essay — "Jodie Loses Her Cool" — mean?
2. What is the thesis of Gerosa's article?
3. How has Jodie Foster's relationship with her mother changed?

4. After reading this article, how would you describe Jodie Foster's personality? What did you learn about Foster that is surprising?

*Writing Strategies*

5. Gerosa frames the information from her interview with Jodie Foster in a narrative of driving around Los Angeles with Foster. Why does she do this instead of setting up the information in a question-and-answer format?

6. From evidence in the essay, what proportion of the conversation with Foster would you say the author has included? Why did she select the details she included? For what reasons do you think she omitted the rest?

7. What information did Gerosa use that did not come from the conversation with Foster?

STUDENT ESSAY

## *Betsy Buffo*    Interview with an Artist

The Ovo Café in the heart of Ybor City seems like the perfect place to interview an avant-garde artist, but the nouvelle cuisine holds no interest for painter Derek Washington. He wants nothing but coffee. He tells me that this is the fuel that powers his creative activities. Often he will exist on gallons of it, and little else, while involved in his artistic endeavors.

It's obvious that I've caught him at one of those times. Although he answers my questions patiently and politely, his thoughts are elsewhere. His dark eyes look through me occasionally and my guess is that he's concentrating on the unfinished project which I called him away from. His lean body vibrates with tension and his fingers search aimlessly on the tabletop when he's not holding his cup.

If my eager questions seem inane to him, he doesn't show it. His answers are articulate, delivered in a soft, almost shy voice that belies the anger that screams from his vibrant canvases. His paintings are large, caustic, often filled with images of pornography or racism meant to shock and disturb. He hopes to make a change with his work by portraying the anxiety and frustration of an African American male in today's society.

"I want my work to make a difference," he says, strangling his coffee cup, "but I get so discouraged sometimes that I think I want to quit. I don't know if I'll ever be able to make people see, but I guess I really can't stop trying."

Experiencing his intensity, I'm surprised to learn that Derek has been painting seriously for only about five years. A casual interest in art became much more when he was laid up at home with back problems for six months. "I thought it would be a good way to pass the time." He smiles and shrugs. "Instead it's become my life's passion."    5

Now he lives with his mother to save money, his bedroom turned into a makeshift studio. The income from part-time work and from the sale of his paintings is used for only one thing--paint. "When I have paint I work every day; when I don't have it I'm trying to find ways to get it," he confides.    6

Financial necessity created a unique style that has become Derek's hallmark. He rarely works on conventional canvas but uses a wide array of material: cardboard boxes carefully opened flat; old pieces of sail; yards of burlap; old wooden boards nailed together; whatever comes to hand. Besides his precious paint, these found canvases are filled with more found objects: magazine cutouts, plastic dolls or other knickknacks, rope, cloth, paper; his medium is anything that meets his needs.    7

When he began his new career, about fifty percent of his work had a social message, but the rest was more conventional fare, still lifes and such. These were never for public consumption, simply completed for perfection of technique and individual style. Now this type of painting makes only an occasional appearance among the brash and blatant pieces which he exhibits.    8

Derek is straightforward when asked about how his work is received in the local community: "My work is outside the mainstream. Because it's controversial it's not easy for me to get exposure. I've had favorable reviews from the newspaper critics, but this area doesn't have much to offer me as an artist. I have an abrasive personality and I'm much too outspoken. My contemporaries respect my work, but the avant-garde artists are white, and we have nothing in common so-    9 cially, while local black artists are not interested in the avant-garde and so we have nothing in common artistically. Most of the people who can afford to collect art are the very ones that I castigate in my paintings, so there's not much of a market for me here."

He is considering several options for his future, all of them designed to take him far away. Since he is finishing his last class at the University of South Florida, he's investigating several scholarships or grants that could enable him to work in New York City, perhaps even Europe.    10

Presently Derek is engrossed in preparations for the opening of his first St. Petersburg exhibition, which will be held in the middle of July. Prior to this show, his work was always exhibited in Tampa, most often in Ybor City. St. Pete is not known for an appreciation of experimental or controversial artists, so it will be interesting to see the outcome. Whatever it may be, it's clear that Derek Washington will not be content. He's after something more, a chance to make a statement that will affect as many people as possible. He still intends to make a difference.    11

**Questions to Start You Thinking**

*Meaning*

1. What is the main point of this essay?

2. Summarize what you think the artist's words reveal about his values, his goals, and his outlook on life.

3. What is the writer's attitude toward the artist? How do you know?

*Writing Strategies*

4. How does Buffo interweave description of Derek Washington with information and quotations from her interview with him? What is the effect of this integration of description and dialogue?

5. What specific details of his appearance and his gestures help you to understand the artist? Does Buffo provide sufficient detail to characterize Washington clearly?

6. Besides conversing, which resources (recalling, reading, observing, imagining) does Buffo draw upon?

7. Why does Buffo organize the information on Derek Washington as she does? Is the order of ideas easy to follow? Could any of the parts be put in a different location?

8. If you were Buffo's peer editor, what suggestions would you give her to strengthen the essay?

# *Learning by Writing*

### THE ASSIGNMENT: INTERVIEWING

Write a paper about someone who interests you, a paper that depends primarily on a conversation with that person. Write about any acquaintance, friend, relative, or someone you have heard about, whose traits, interests, activities, background, or outlook on life you think will interest your readers. Your purpose is to show as thoroughly as you can this person's character and personality as revealed through his or her conversation — in other words, to bring your subject alive for your readers.

Among student papers we have read that grew out of a similar assignment were the following:

A man wrote about a high school science teacher who had quit teaching for a higher-paying job in the computer industry, only to return three years later to the classroom.

A man wrote about an acquaintance who had embraced the hippie lifestyle in the 1960s by "dropping out" of mainstream society.

A woman recorded the thoughts and feelings of a discouraged farmer she had known since childhood.

A man learned about adjustment to life in a new country by talking to a neighbor from Vietnam.

If you would prefer not to write about a person but rather would like to interview someone for information *about* something, see "Other Assignments" (p. 000).

### GENERATING IDEAS

*Brainstorm for possible subjects.* It may be that the minute you read the assignment, an image of the perfect subject flashed into your mind. If that's the case, consider yourself lucky and go at once to set up an appointment with that person. If, however, you drew a blank at first, you'll need to spend a little time casting about for a likely interview subject. Try brainstorming for a few minutes, seeing what pops into your mind. (For more advice about brainstorming, see p. 334.) As you begin examining the possibilities, you may find it helpful to consider the following questions.

**DISCOVERY CHECKLIST**

## Finding an Interview Subject

- Of the people you know, whom do you most enjoy talking with?
- Are you acquainted with anyone whose life has been unusually eventful, stressful, or successful? It does not have to be a spectacular or unusual person. Ordinary lives can make fascinating reading.

- Are you curious about why someone you know made a certain decision, or how he or she got to the point in life where he or she is now?
- Is there an expert or leader whom you admire or are puzzled by?
- Do you know someone with a job or a hobby that interests you?
- Do you know a younger person or an older person who has values and attitudes different from yours?
- Do you know an older person who can tell you what life was like thirty or even fifty years ago?
- Among the people you know, who has passionate convictions about society, politics, sex, or childrearing? A likely person may be someone actively engaged in a cause.
- Is there anyone whose background and life history you would like to know more about?
- Do you know someone whose lifestyle is utterly different from your own and from that of most people you know?
- Do you have an older relative who can tell you about your family and his or her relationship to other members of the family?

*Set up your interview.* First find out whether your prospective source will grant you an interview. Make sure that the person can talk with you at some length — an hour, say. Make sure, too, that the person has no objections to appearing in your paper. If you sense any reluctance on the person's part, probably your wisest course is to find another subject.

Don't be timid about asking for an interview. When you interview a subject, you acknowledge that person as someone with valuable things to say. Most people will be flattered by your interest in them.

Try to schedule the interview on your subject's own ground: his or her home or workplace. As you can see in Buffo's essay, an interviewer can learn a great deal from the physical surroundings of an individual, and the interview becomes more realistic and the essay more vivid because of the details the writer can observe and include.

*Prepare questions.* The interview will go better if you have prepared some questions to ask. Give these careful thought. What kinds of questions will encourage your subject to open up? Questions about the person's background, everyday tasks, favorite leisure-time activities, hopes, and aspirations are likely to bring forth answers that you'll want to record. Sometimes a question that asks your subject to do a little imagining will elicit a revealing response. (If your house were on fire, what are the first objects you'd try to save from the flames? If you were stranded on a desert island, what books would you like to have with you? If you had your life to live over, what would you do differently?)

You can't find out everything there is to know about the person you're interviewing, but you should focus on whatever aspect of that person's life you think will best reveal his or her personality. Good questions will enable you to lead the conversation where you want it to go and get it back on track when it strays too far. Such questions will also help you avoid awkward silences. Here are some of the questions Betsy Buffo scribbled down before going to see Derek Washington, a man with whom she had only a slight acquaintance:

How long have you been painting?

How did you get involved in painting?

Has your involvement/commitment to painting changed your life in any way? Has it changed where you live? How you live? What you do?

What do you hope to do in your art?

What does success mean to you? Have you had a lot of success?

What are your plans for the future?

Probably Buffo didn't have to use all those questions. One good question can get some people talking for hours. Some experts insist that four or five are enough to bring to any interview, but we believe it's better to err on the side of too many than too few. If, as you're actually talking with your subject, some of your questions strike you as no longer relevant, you can easily skip them. Some of Buffo's questions would have elicited very brief answers. Others — like "How did you get involved in painting?" — clearly inspired Washington to respond with enthusiasm.

*Be flexible and observant.* If the discussion is moving in a worthwhile direction, don't be a slave to your questions. Betsy Buffo was willing to let the conversation stray down interesting byways. Sometimes the question that takes the interview in its most rewarding direction is the one the interviewer didn't write down in advance but that simply grew out of something the subject said. Buffo allowed Washington to answer some questions she hadn't even asked, and she really *listened* to what he was saying. Melina Gerosa in the account of her conversation with Jodie Foster demonstrates both the same flexibility and the same genuine interest in her subject. Of course, if the conversation heads toward a dead end, you can always steer it back: "But to get back to what you were saying about . . . ."

During the interviews, both Gerosa and Buffo do something else that will later add vividness to their characterization: they use their eyes as well as their ears. Buffo observes what's in the café — food, coffee, an unfinished project

— and the way the artist looks while they are talking. When you conduct your interview, try to notice and ask about distinctive items in the subject's environment. Your interest may encourage your subject to reveal unexpected facets of his or her personality. Gerosa reports Foster's physical appearance: her toenails are "painted fire-engine red" (paragraph 1); "her thin lips stretch into a smile" (paragraph 19); she is "surprisingly kidlike in red jeans, a black top, and wire-rimmed glasses, her hair wet from her shower" (paragraph 7). From her observations, she also indicates Foster's emotional reactions: "the enthusiasm of a teenage girl" (paragraph 19); "her sentimental mood evaporates almost instantly" (paragraph 21). (For more on using the resource of observation, see Chapter 2.)

Sometimes a question won't interest your subject as much as you'd hoped it would. Or the person may seem reluctant to answer, especially if you're unwittingly trespassing into private territory, such as Foster's love life or John Hinckley, Jr. Don't badger. If you have the confidence to wait silently for a bit, you might be rewarded. But if the silence persists, just go on to the next question.

*Decide how to record the interview.*  Many interviewers approach their subjects with only paper and pen or pencil so that they can take notes unobtrusively as the interview proceeds. However, you won't be able to write down everything the person says as he or she is talking. It's more important to look your subject in the eye and keep the conversation lively than to scribble down everything the person says. But be sure to record on the scene whatever you want to remember in exact detail: names and dates, numbers, addresses, surroundings, physical appearance, whatever. If the person you're interviewing says anything that is so memorable that you want to record it exactly, take time to jot down the speaker's words just as he or she says them. Put quotation marks around them so that when you transcribe your notes later, you know that they are a direct quotation.

A telephone interview may sound like an easy way to work, but it is often less valuable than talking with the subject in person. You won't be able to duplicate by phone the lively interplay you can achieve in a face-to-face encounter. You'll be unable to observe the subject's possessions and environment, which so often reveal a person's personality, or see your subject's smiles, frowns, or other body language. Think of the important details that would be missing from Gerosa's article and from Buffo's paper if they had not met the individual in person. Meet with your subject if at all possible.

Many professionals advise against bringing a tape recorder to an interview because sometimes it inhibits the subject and makes the interviewer lazy about concentrating on the subject's responses. Too often, the objections go, it tempts the interviewer simply to quote the rambling conversation as it appears on the tape without shaping it into good writing. If you do bring a tape recorder to your interview, be sure that the person you're talking with has no objections. Arm yourself with a pad of paper and a pen or pencil just in case the recorder malfunctions or the tape runs out before the interview ends. And don't let your mind wander.

Perhaps the best practice is to tape-record the interview but at the same time take notes. Get the main points of the conversation down in your notes and use your tape as a backup to check or expand an idea or quotation.

As soon as the interview ends, rush to the nearest available desk or table and write down everything you remember but were unable to record during the conversation. Do this while the conversation is still fresh in your mind. The questions you took with you into the interview will guide your memory, as will any notes you took while your subject talked.

## PLANNING, DRAFTING, AND DEVELOPING

Now that you have gathered information on your subject, you are ready to start planning and writing your first draft. You probably have a good notion of what information to include, what to emphasize, what to quote directly, what to summarize. But if your notes seem a confused jumble, you may need to approach your first draft more slowly. What are you to do with the bales of material you have amassed during the interview? Inevitably, much of what you collected will be garbage, useless information. Does that mean you should have collected less? No, it means that as you plan, you have to zero in on what is most valuable and throw out the rest. How do you do this?

*Evaluate your material.*   Remember that your purpose in this assignment is to show as thoroughly as possible your subject's character and personality as revealed through his or her conversation. Start by making a list of those details you're already pretty sure you want to include. To guide you as you sift and evaluate your material, you may find it useful to ask yourself a few questions.

What part of the conversation gave you the most insight into your subject's character and circumstances?

Which of the direct quotations you wrote down reveal the most about your subject? Which are the most amusing, pithy, witty, surprising, or outrageous?

**FOR PEER RESPONSE**

## Interviewing

Share with a classmate the questions you plan to use in your interview. Ask your classmate to respond to the following points about your questions.

- Are the questions appropriate for the person to be interviewed?
- Will the questions help the writer gather the information he or she is seeking?
- Are any of the questions unclear? How would you rephrase them?
- Do any of the questions seem redundant? Irrelevant?
- Is there anything you would add to these questions?

Which of the objects that you observed in the subject's environment provide you with valuable clues about his or her interests?

What, if anything, did your subject's body language reveal? Did it give evidence of discomfort, pride, self-confidence, shyness, pomposity?

Did the tone of voice or gestures of the person tell you anything about his or her state of mind?

How can you summarize your subject's personality?

Is there one theme that runs through the material you have written down? If so, what is it?

If you have a great deal of material and if, as often happens, your subject's conversation tended to ramble, you may want to emphasize just one or two things about him or her: a personality trait, the person's views on one particular topic, the influences that shaped the views he or she holds today. If such a focus is not immediately evident, try grouping your details to help you discover a focus. (For more on grouping ideas, see Chapter 16.)

*Focus on a dominant impression.*  Most successful portraits focus on a single dominant impression of the interview subject. If you had to characterize your subject in a single sentence, how would you describe him or her? Betsy Buffo's main impression of Derek Washington is that he's an idealistic, ambitious artist who's channeling his creative energies and financial resources in a sincere attempt to make a difference; everything in her paper supports this view, even though she never states it in so many words. See if you can find a single main impression that you want to convey about your subject. Then look through your material and eliminate anything that doesn't contribute to this view.

*Bring your subject alive.*  At the beginning of your paper, can you introduce the person you interviewed in a way that will frame him or her immediately in your reader's mind? A quotation, a bit of physical description, a portrait of your subject at home or at work can bring the person instantly to life.

From time to time you'll want to quote your subject directly. Be as accurate as possible, and don't put into quotation marks something your subject didn't say. Sometimes you may want to quote a whole sentence or more, sometimes just a phrase. Throughout Gerosa's article she moves gracefully back and forth between direct quotation and summing up.

In *Reporting*, a collection of interviews, noted reporter Lillian Ross suggests that when you quote directly the person you have interviewed, you work hard to "find the quotations that get to the truth of what that person is. That does not mean that you make up quotations. Somewhere along the line, in the time you spend with your subject, you will find the quotations that are significant — that reveal the character of the person, that present as close an approximation of the truth as you can achieve." Keep evaluating and selecting until you believe you have come close to that truth. (For more on selecting and using examples and details, see Chapter 18.)

*Double-check important information.* You may find yourself unable to read your hasty handwriting, or you may discover you need some crucial bit of information that somehow escaped you when you were taking notes. In such a case, telephone the person you interviewed to check out what you need to know. Have specific questions ready so that you will not take much of your subject's time. You may also want to read back to your subject any direct quotations you intend to use in your final paper, so that he or she can confirm their accuracy.

## REVISING AND EDITING

Wait a few hours or a few days before you look again at your first draft. As you read it over, keep in mind that your purpose was to bring alive for your reader the person you interviewed. Your main task now is to make sure you have succeeded in this goal. Remember, too, that most successful papers of this kind focus on a single dominant impression and that readers will be interested in your observations and insights. This checklist may help you in reviewing your work. (For more on revising and editing, see Chapter 19.)

**FOR PEER RESPONSE**

If you find it hard to criticize your own work, ask a classmate or a friend to read your draft and suggest how to make the portrait more vivid, clear, and honest. See Chapter 20 for advice on working with other student writers and for general questions you should always ask a peer editor to address. For a paper in which you write from conversation, you'll also want your peer editor to answer these specific questions:

- What is the main insight or impression you carry away from this piece of writing?
- Look at the beginning of the essay. Did the writer make you want to get to know the person? If so, how? If not, what got in your way?
- What seems to make the person interviewed interesting to the writer? What do you understand to be the writer's dominant impression of or insight into the person?
- Does the writer tell you anything about the person that seems unconnected to his or her dominant impression or insight?
- Do the quoted words of the person interviewed "sound" real to you? Has the writer quoted anything that seems at odds with the general impression you now have of the person?
- Star the places where you have questions about the subject that aren't answered in the paper.
- Would you leave out any of the conversation the writer used? Underline anything you would omit.
- If this were your paper, what is the one thing you would be sure to work on before handing it in?

**REVISION
CHECKLIST**

- Should your paper have a stronger beginning? Is your ending satisfactory?
- Are some quotations better suited to summarizing or indirect quotations? Should some of what you summed up be given greater prominence by adding specific quotations?
- When the direct quotations are read out loud, do they sound as if they're coming out of the mouth of the person you're portraying?
- Have you included revealing details about the person's surroundings, personal appearance, or mannerisms?
- Have you put in a few of your own observations and insights?
- Are the details focused on a dominant impression you want to emphasize? Are all the details in your paper relevant to this impression?
- Do the parts of the conversation you've reported reveal the subject's personality, character, or mood? Is his or her individuality clear from the details you've selected?
- Have you included details that show what your subject cares most about?
- Does any of the material in your paper strike you now as irrelevant or uninteresting?
- Have you revealed a unique individual worth paying attention to?

**WRITING
WITH A
COMPUTER**

One problem with turning conversation into writing is that the results may not make easy reading. When people talk, their facial expressions, voice inflections, and gestures can lend interest and emphasis to their words. But sometimes the conversation of even a lively speaker, transcribed word for word, will sound dull and long-winded. And almost no one speaks in complete thoughts and sentences.

A word processor can help you counter this problem. If you used a tape recorder, transcribe the conversation (or a selected portion of it) word for word; if you took notes, transcribe the conversation as fully as you can. Then scroll through the results on your computer screen. Since you can delete with a couple of keystrokes, keeping the best material and cutting the rest will be easy. While working on screen, you can readily replace any comment that seems rambling with a terse summary; remember to use quotation marks only around words and sentences that your interviewee actually said, not around your summaries or paraphrases. You may choose to revise this transcript into grammatically correct sentences (be careful not to change the words so much that you distort the meaning or tone), or if you are trying to capture more of the personal flavor of the conversation, you can leave it exactly as it sounds.

Now read the transcript and ask yourself which parts stand out. Where does the interviewee's personality or tone shine through? Which quotations would be the most useful for supporting your overall message or point? Can you combine comments that came out at different times in the conversation but that seem to be on a common theme? Can you highlight troubling ideas by juxtaposing two conflicting statements? Once you've reworked the conversation itself, you can easily copy the best portions of it into your paper.

If you find that your portrayal still lacks life and focus, you may want to skim over your interview notes or listen again to selected parts of your tape recording for material whose significance may not have struck you earlier. Do additional details now seem worth putting in after all? Do you need to do a little reading to beef up your comments? Is there anything you now wish you had asked your interview subject? It may not be too late to find new material and add it to your paper.

Double-check your quotations. As you write your final draft, be sure that where you have omitted words from a direct quotation, you have substituted an ellipsis mark ( . . . ) — three dots that show where omissions have occurred — and that the sentence that contains the omission makes sense, given the sentences before and after it. If you quote your subject quoting someone else (a quotation within a quotation), make sure to put your subject's words in double quotation marks and the words he or she is quoting in *single* quotation marks. As you can see, quoting from conversation requires special attention to punctuation and formatting; you should check your paper carefully for mechanical errors before you hand it in.

**FOR GROUP LEARNING**

## Conducting a Collective Interview

Let your whole class or just your writing group interview someone who has some special knowledge or who represents a walk of life that you want to learn more about. Public figures such as writers, who occasionally visit schools, are used to facing the questions of a whole class. Or perhaps someone on campus will be willing to be interviewed about a problem your group is interested in.

Before your subject arrives, let your group take time to plan the discussion: What do you want to find out? What questions or lines of questioning do you wish to pursue? What topic will each student ask about? We suggest that when the interviewee is present, each questioner be allowed (as far as time permits) to ask all of his or her main questions before yielding the floor to the next questioner. This way each person can pursue a complete line of thought. Preview each student's questions before the interview so that there will be no duplication. Later students can write individual papers based on the group interview, showing what they have learned not only from their own questions but from everybody's.

An alternative plan is to collaborate on the paper, to produce one group-written paper. The group might appoint two members to act as reporters or recording secretaries and take notes. After the interview the group might meet to sift what you learned. The two reporters who took notes during the interview might show (or read aloud) their notes to the group to check the accuracy of both questions and answers. To parcel out the project fairly, designate two or three others to write what the group has learned.

OTHER ASSIGNMENTS

1. Interview someone from whom you think you can learn a lot, possibly someone in a career you are considering or someone who can help you solve a problem or make a decision. Your purpose in this paper will be to gather and communicate information, not to characterize the subject you interview.

2. Write a paper based on an interview with at least two members of your extended family about some incident that is part of your family lore. You may notice that different people's accounts of the same event don't always agree. If you can't reconcile them, combine them into one vivid account, noting that some details may be more trustworthy than others. Give credit to your sources. The paper that results might be worth saving for younger relatives.

3. Interview a mother or father about her or his reactions to a child's birth and how the child has changed the family's life.

4. After briefly questioning fifteen or twenty students on your campus to find out what careers they are preparing for, write a short essay summing up what you find out. What are their reasons for their choices? Are most students more intent on earning money than on other pursuits? How many are choosing lucrative careers because they have to pay back college loans? Provide some quotations to flesh out your survey. From the information you have gathered, characterize your classmates. Are they materialists? Idealists? Practical people?

5. Interview an older person in your family or neighborhood about what life was like when he or she was a child. Gather enough information to re-create in an essay that person's past world.

# Applying What You Learn:
# Some Uses of Writing from Conversation

Interviewing is a familiar tool for many writers in the world beyond college. Biographers who write about someone living often conduct extensive interviews with their subject to guarantee accuracy. Usually they interview friends, relatives, and other associates to round out their picture of the person. Likewise, news reporters and commentators often rely on interviews with "informed sources" to give their readers the complete story. Another familiar kind of interview is that in which an author, actor, or political figure airs his or her views on a variety of subjects. Such interviews are written by people who have talked with their subjects, usually face to face. James Dickey, the poet and novelist, has even published self-interviews to present his opinions.

Often in college writing you find yourself interviewing people not because you are interested in their personalities but because they can contribute valuable insights to what you are studying. Students of human development often interview people at various stages of the life cycle. They talk to men and women about the transition from student life to the working world, to mothers about the experience of giving birth, to older people about widowhood or retirement. In recent years historians, acknowledging that "ordinary" people matter, have shown increasing interest in gathering and publishing oral histories and in uncovering those from the past. One such collection that throws vivid light on the civil rights movement is Howell Raines's *My Soul Is Rested.* (New York: Putnam's, 1977). In the following excerpt the author records the words of Franklin McCain, who participated in the now famous sit-in at Woolworth's in Greensboro, North Carolina, on February 1, 1960.

> Once getting there . . . we did make purchases of school supplies and took the patience and time to get receipts for our purchases, and Joseph and myself went over to the counter and asked to be served coffee and doughnuts. As anticipated, the reply was, "I'm sorry, we don't serve you here." And of course we said, "We just beg to disagree with you. We've in fact already been served; you've served us already and that's just not quite true. . . . We wonder why you'd invite us in to serve us at one counter and deny service at another. If this is a private club or private concern, then we believe you ought to sell membership cards and sell only to persons who have a membership card. If we don't have a card, then we'd know pretty well that we shouldn't come in or even attempt to come in." That didn't go over too well. . . . And the only thing that an individual in her case or position could do is, of course, call the manager. [Laughs].

In professional scholarly research, dozens of interviews may be necessary. The five sociologists who wrote the much-acclaimed *Habits of the Heart: Individualism and Commitment in American Life* (Berkeley: U of California P, 1985) used as their sources not only books and periodicals but also extensive interviews with both ordinary citizens and professionals in various fields. Note how this example from a chapter written by Ann Swidler enlivens its discussion with pointed, informative quotations that read like spoken words:

> Asked why she went into therapy, a woman summed up the themes that recur again and again in accounts by therapists and their clients: "I was not able to form close relationships to people, I didn't like myself, I didn't love myself, I didn't love other people." In the therapeutic ideology, such incapacities are in turn related to a failure fully to accept, fully to love, one's self.
> As the therapist Margaret Oldham puts it, many of the professionally trained, upper-middle-class young adults who come to her, depressed and lonely, are seeking "that big relationship in the sky — the perfect person." They want "that one person who is going to stop making them feel alone." But this search for a perfect relationship cannot succeed because it comes from a self that is not full and self-sustaining. The desire for relatedness is really a reflection of incompleteness, of one's own dependent needs.

# *Making Connections:*
# *Writing from Conversation in* A Writer's Reader

Conversation is a resource used in nonfiction to make an essay realistic and interesting, similar to dialogue in fiction. Writers may use conversation as a springboard for their reflections on an idea or may report conversation within the essay to support a point. For example, in "The Men We Carry in Our Minds" (p. 499), Scott Russell Sanders, a professor of English at Indiana University, uses conversation to give his essay the ring of truth. In the introduction to his essay he uses direct conversation, but in other parts of the essay he uses indirect quotations, summarizing what he has learned from talking with other people. This technique is appropriate to his background as a literature professor. Carol Kaesuk Yoon, in "Drugs from Bugs" (p. 628), uses direct quotations and reports conversations with researchers and environmentalists working in the field to bolster her persuasive argument about conservation and biodiversity.

Just as Sanders, Yoon, Melina Gerosa (p. 71), and Betsy Buffo (p. 75) use conversation as a resource for writing, so do novelist Amy Tan in "Mother Tongue" (p. 476); professor of African American studies Gerald Early in "Black like . . . Shirley Temple?" (p. 468); psychologist Lydia Minatoya in "Transformation" (p. 514); and environmentalist Gregg Easterbrook in "Forget PCBs. Radon. Alar: The World's Greatest Environmental Dangers Are Dung Smoke and Dirty Water" (p. 636). As you read these essays, consider the role that conversation plays in them. For each essay, answer the following questions.

1. Does the writer report conversation directly or indirectly?
2. Were the reported conversations the result of recall of informal discussions or of planned interviews?
3. What do the conversations show about the personality of the individual speaking? About the author/listener?
4. Why do you think the writer draws on conversation as a resource for writing?

# Chapter 5

# Writing from Imagination

"Imagination," said Albert Einstein, "is more important than knowledge." Coming from a theoretical physicist who widened our knowledge of the universe, the remark is striking. Although "imaginative writing" usually suggests stories, poems, or plays, storytellers, poets, and playwrights have no monopoly on imagination. Scientists and economists, historians and businesspeople need imagination just as much. The astronomer Copernicus *imagined* the earth revolving around the sun; he didn't see and report it. Economist John Maynard Keynes imagined the theory of aggregate demand before he set about proving it, and engineer and architect Buckminster Fuller conceived the geodesic dome before he could build one. Freud never saw the id; he imagined it. Anyone who comes up with a theory to explain a strange event or a hypothesis to account for a mysterious phenomenon uses imagination. College students will do well to call on the resource of imagination to strengthen and enliven their writing.

In one familiar sense of the word, imagining is nothing but daydreaming — imagining yourself wafted from a cold and rainy city street to a sunny beach in the tropics. Enlarging that definition a little, the *Shorter Oxford Dictionary* calls imagination "forming a mental concept of what is not actually present to the senses."

That definition is all right as far as it goes, but imagination is a far greater resource. According to mathematician Jacob Bronowski, *"To imagine* means to make images and to move them about inside one's head in new arrangements. When you and I recall the past, we imagine it in this direct and homely sense. . . . With the same symbolic vocabulary we spell out the future — not one but many futures, which we weigh one against another." He added that imagination and reason work together, beginning in childhood:

When a child begins to play games with things that stand for other things, with chairs or chessmen, he enters the gateway to reason and imagination together. For the human reason discovers new relations between things not by deduction, but by that unpredictable blend of speculation and insight that scientists call induction, which — like other forms of imagination — cannot be formalized.

In the view of Samuel Taylor Coleridge, imagination is nothing less than a "magical power" that can reveal in familiar objects "novelty and freshness." Sometimes it brings new things into existence by combining old things that already exist. Instead of creating out of thin air, imaginative writers often build from materials they find at hand. Lewis Carroll, whose Alice books seem remote from actual life, drew the stuff of his fantastic adventures from his friendship with a real child and some of his fantastic characters from real persons in England.

Yet, as many writers have testified, imagining is often playful: a fruitful kind of fooling around. Ursula K. Le Guin, writer of science fiction, calls imagination "the free play of the mind." In her essay "Why Are Americans Afraid of Dragons?" she explains:

> By "free" I mean that the action is done without an immediate object of profit — spontaneously. That does not mean, however, that there may not be a purpose behind the free play of the mind, a goal; and the goal may be a very serious object indeed. Children's imaginative play is clearly a practicing at the acts and emotions of adulthood; a child who did not play would not become mature. As for the free play of an adult mind, its result may be *War and Peace,* or the theory of relativity.

Though the result of the free play of your imagination may not be Leo Tolstoy's classic novel or Einstein's theory, you will find that such free play with language and ideas can be valuable and productive — and fun besides.

## Learning from Other Writers

It appears that, to be a whole writer and a whole human being, each of us needs both a logical, analytical mind and what Shakespeare called "the mind's eye" — the faculty of imagining. In this chapter, we don't presume to tell you how to imagine. We only suggest how you may use your imagination. Here are two examples of imaginative writing, the first by a professional writer and the second by a student.

Rachel Carson was a scientist who through observation and research became concerned about the environment. In 1962 she wrote *Silent Spring,* a deeply moving indictment of chemical pesticides in which she set forth the position that pesticides, especially DDT, were destroying the reproductive systems of birds, wildlife, and wild vegetation and would lead to a "silent spring." This work raised the public consciousness and prompted the federal government to limit the use of pesticides. In "A Fable for Tomorrow," the introduction to this important work, Carson combines imagination and reason, imaginative fiction and scientific exposition.

The student essay was written by Robert Parr, a political science major at Tarrant County Junior College. The assignment was to write a persuasive essay about a current problem of significance to the writer. Parr knew that he wanted to explore in writing some of the issues he followed in the news and in his studies; by using imagination, he said he "was able to combine my interest in politics and world affairs with my distrust of rodents." In his final paper, Parr takes a lighthearted and somewhat satirical approach: What if squirrels instead of people were trying to arm themselves with nuclear weapons?

## *Rachel Carson*    A Fable for Tomorrow

There was once a town in the heart of America where all life seemed to live in harmony with its surroundings. The town lay in the midst of a checkerboard of prosperous farms, with fields of grain and hillsides of orchards where, in spring, white clouds of bloom drifted above the green fields. In autumn, oak and maple and birch set up a blaze of color that flamed and flickered across a backdrop of pines. Then foxes barked in the hills and deer silently crossed the fields, half hidden in the mists of the fall mornings.    1

Along the roads, laurel, viburnum and alder, great ferns and wildflowers delighted the traveler's eye through much of the year. Even in winter the roadsides were places of beauty, where countless birds came to feed on the berries and on the seed heads of the dried weeds rising above the snow. The countryside was, in fact, famous for the abundance and variety of its bird life, and when the flood of migrants was pouring through in spring and fall people traveled from great distances to observe them. Others came to fish the streams, which flowed clear and cold out of the hills and contained shady pools where trout lay. So it had been from the days many years ago when the first settlers raised their houses, sank their wells, and built their barns.    2

Then a strange blight crept over the area and everything began to change. Some evil spell had settled on the community: mysterious maladies swept the flocks of chickens; the cattle and sheep sickened and died. Everywhere was a shadow of death. The farmers spoke of much illness among their families. In the town the doctors had become more and more puzzled by new kinds of sickness appearing among their patients. There had been several sudden and unexplained deaths, not only among adults but even among children, who would be stricken suddenly while at play and die within a few hours.    3

There was a strange stillness. The birds, for example — where had they gone? Many people spoke of them, puzzled and disturbed. The feeding stations in the backyards were deserted. The few birds seen anywhere were mori-    4 bund; they trembled violently and could not fly. It was a spring without voices. On the mornings that had once throbbed with the dawn chorus of robins, catbirds, doves, jays, wrens, and scores of other bird voices there was now no sound; only silence lay over the fields and woods and marsh.

On the farms the hens brooded, but no chicks hatched. The farmers complained that they were unable to raise any pigs — the litters were small and the young survived only a few days. The apple trees were coming into bloom but no bees droned among the blossoms, so there was no pollination and there would be no fruit.    5

The roadsides, once so attractive, were now lined with browned and withered vegetation as though swept by fire. These, too, were silent, deserted by all living things. Even the streams were now lifeless. Anglers no longer visited them, for all the fish had died.    6

In the gutters under the eaves and between the shingles of the roofs, a white granular powder still showed a few patches; some weeks before it had fallen like snow upon the roofs and the lawns, the fields and streams.    7

No witchcraft, no enemy action had silenced the rebirth of new life in this stricken world. The people had done it themselves.    8

This town does not actually exist, but it might easily have a thousand counterparts in America or elsewhere in the world. I know of no community that has experienced all the misfortunes I describe. Yet every one of these disasters has actually happened somewhere, and many real communities have already suffered a substantial number of them. A grim specter has crept upon us almost unnoticed, and this imagined tragedy may easily become a stark reality we all shall know.    9

What has already silenced the voices of spring in countless towns in America? This book is an attempt to explain.    10

**Questions to Start You Thinking**

*Meaning*

1. What is a *fable?* Why do you think Carson titled this introduction to her book *Silent Spring* "A Fable for Tomorrow"? What does her title mean? Is it an appropriate title?

2. Specifically what does Carson fantasize about? On what does she base her fantasies?

3. Can you think of any substances or practices that are threatening our world today?

*Writing Strategies*

4. The eye of the scientist is evident in Carson's use of specific detail. Which of the descriptive details is particularly memorable?

5. How does Carson organize the details?

6. What is the effect of her ending with a question?

7. Aesop ended his fables with a moral. State a moral that could be used to end Carson's fable.

## *Robert Parr*    Negative Views on Nuclear Squirrels

Congress must vote "NO" to selling squirrels nuclear arms. Arming militant suburban squirrels is an extreme measure since adversaries, namely dogs and cars, possess only the most conventional of weapons. Petitions for nuclear arms come from the most extreme quarters in squirrel politics, whose motives are not to be trusted. Pentagon sources see deployment plans for squirrel-compatible nuclear weapon devices as unproven. Most important, arming squirrels in this manner would disturb the balance of power that has been painstakingly maintained for the past forty years.

For decades, dogs have traditionally controlled the grounds and backyards of suburbia while squirrels have controlled trees and power lines. This territorial division gives squirrels generous access to entire neighborhoods. Due to the dangers from cars, streets were not intended for squirrels; that is why streets have power lines above them. Giving squirrels nuclear arms will give them an unfair advantage over dogs, inviting the bushy rodents to mercilessly taunt, then fiendishly destroy the ground-based dogs.

The Senate has sided with suburban squirrel extremists in the past, as have some biased journalists who wrongly claimed that squirrels have no allies in the troubled animal kingdom. One must consider the motives behind squirrel demands. Squirrels claiming to use nuclear arms only as a defense against cars are not to be trusted since in previous treaties squirrels have pledged to stay out of car-occupied territories and have consistently failed to do so.

With regard to nuclear weapon deployment for squirrels, military experts find the systems dangerous and unreliable. In field tests of the German-designed Squirrel Mobile Power Line Deployment System (SMPLDS), even the most educated squirrels had difficulty operating the sophisticated equipment. On many occasions, test firings at drone dogs failed, resulting in broken power lines and disruption of normal telephone service.

Squirrel supporters in the Senate see giving in to    5
squirrel demands for nuclear weapons as a way to maintain
balance in the animal kingdom. This thinking is outdated
since several other animal species have recently committed
themselves to improving relations within the United States.
The opossum species recently pledged to stay out of suburban
neighborhoods if in return suburban developers would limit
the number of apartments built on land presently occupied by
opossums. Since cooperation such as this has never been offered by the squirrels, the squirrels' hard-line stance may
continue as long as old guard Senate members rally for the
squirrels' pronuclear/antidog cause.

The arming of squirrel extremists against their peaceful    6
enemies will lead to severe tensions that will inevitably
strain the United States' official policy of squirrel-dog
neutrality that has existed in suburbia since the 1950s. For
almost forty years, squirrels in suburbia have coexisted with
dogs without the benefit of nuclear arms. Occasional skir-
mishes between squirrels and dogs over territory are natural;
however, allowing squirrels to possess nuclear weapons will
only lead to increased squirrel-provoked aggressions and a
loosening of the bonds that have maintained peace in the animal kingdom for generations. The prenuclear squirrel has exposed itself as a disruptive, mean-spirited tree rat;
however, the postnuclear squirrel could expose itself as
genocidal.

**Questions to Start You Thinking**

*Meaning*

1. In what remarks does Robert Parr seem to be kidding? Which ideas does he apparently mean us to take seriously? Are any comments ironic?
2. How would arming squirrels upset the balance of nature?
3. What aspects of nuclear arms does Parr come out against?

*Writing Strategies*

4. Define *fable* and *allegory*. If Carson's essay is a *fable,* is Parr's more of a *fable* or an *allegory*? Why?
5. Define *satire* and *irony*. How does Parr use each in his essay?
6. Why does Parr use squirrels instead of people?
7. Trace the specific points in Parr's argument against nuclear arms. Does his use of satire make following his argument easier or harder?

8. Which of Parr's details are rooted in reality? Which details are strictly imaginative?

9. What is the tone of this essay? Do you think it's effective in persuading the reader to Parr's point of view? Why, or why not?

10. What other topics can you think of that might be treated in a similar manner?

# Learning by Writing

## THE ASSIGNMENT: EXPLORING THROUGH IMAGINATION

Write an essay of imaginative nonfiction, one in which you use your imagination as a resource for examining, analyzing, evaluating, or solving a current problem. It may be a social problem, an economic problem, a medical problem, an educational problem, a governmental or legal problem, or a personal problem. Your treatment of the problem may be lighthearted, but the root of your concern should be serious. You may take an ironic position as Parr did, but be sure that your attitude toward the problem is clear to your readers.

Unless your instructor encourages you to do so, don't write a story. To be sure, you could conceivably write this paper as science fiction. If you were writing about the spread of unknown viruses, you might begin: "As I walked into Montopolis in 2500 A.D., the mayor rushed up to me. 'A terrible plague of headaches has struck our city! We don't know what is causing this plague,' he shouted. Luckily, I had had some experience with tracking down mysterious viruses when I lived before in the twentieth century." Instead, write imaginative *nonfiction* in the essay form you are familiar with.

To help you start imagining, here are some topics that students generated for this assignment. Some may reveal interesting dimensions in your possible major field of study.

A single parent, concerned about the problem of budgeting time, imagined what life would be like if a day were thirty hours instead of twenty-four.

A budding scientist imagined new crops to help feed the hungry.

A pacifist imagined the next war being fought only by men over fifty.

An education major wrote a fable about an animal school.

In a research paper about future space law, a student used both existing documents and his power of imagination to propose answers to the question of who should control the natural resources of the moon and other planets.

For a paper in economics, a man looked at government aid to disadvantaged people in the inner city, thinking and writing first as a liberal (his own conviction) and then — by an act of imagination — as a conservative.

## GENERATING IDEAS

Although there are no fixed rules to follow in imagining, all of us tend to imagine in familiar ways. Being acquainted with these ways may help you fulfill your assignment. Here we first give you some suggestions to help you locate a subject through brainstorming; then we describe three forms of imagination that may already be familiar to you: shifting perspective, envisioning, and synthesizing.

*Try brainstorming.* In making your own list of possible topics, you may find it helpful to brainstorm, either by yourself or with the aid of a group. Sometimes two or three imaginations are better than one. (For helpful tips on brainstorming, see p. 334.) To help you generate, here are a few questions.

**DISCOVERY CHECKLIST**

## Imagining Possibilities

- What common assumption — something we all take for granted — might be questioned or denied? (It might be a scientific opinion, such as the widely accepted knowledge that the ultraviolet rays of the sun are harmful to the skin.)
- What present-day problem or deplorable condition do you wish to see remedied?
- What problems do you foresee as happening in the future if we don't change current policies, practices, or attitudes?
- What different paths in life might you take? What problems might occur with each path? How might your life be different with each path?

Jot down as many questions as you can think of, do some trial imagining, and then choose the topic that seems most promising. Say you pick as your topic "What if the average North American life span were to lengthen to more than a century?" You might begin by reflecting on some of the ways in which society would have to change. When ideas start to flow, start listing them. No doubt a lengthened life span would mean that a greater proportion of the populace would be old. Ask questions: How would that fact affect doctors and nurses, hospitals, and other medical facilities? How might city planners respond to the needs of so many more old people? What would the change mean for retail merchants? For television programming? For the social security system? For taxes?

*Shifting perspective.* In imagining, a writer sometimes thinks and perceives from a point of view other than the usual one. This new perspective could be a preexisting one that another person or group already has (how would you argue about an issue if you were on the opposite side?) or it could be one that you make up (what would the situation look like to a Martian?). You can also try shifting perspective by shifting the debate to a somewhat different arena: what if, instead of trying to decide whether *teenagers* should be allowed to drink alcohol, the debate were about whether *people over the age of sixty-five* should be allowed to drink? To explore the legislative debate on selling nuclear arms to other countries, Robert Parr imagined that the argument was about selling nuclear arms to squirrels — this gave him a fresh perspective on the topic.

*Envisioning.* Imagining what might be, seeing in the mind's eye and in graphic detail, is the process of envisioning or imaging. A writer might imagine a utopia or ideal state, as did Thomas More in *Utopia* (1516), or an anti-utopia, as did George Orwell in his 1949 novel of a grim future, *Nineteen Eighty-Four,* or as Rachel Carson did in *Silent Spring.* By envisioning, you can conceive of other possible alternatives: to imagine, say, a different and better way of treating illness, of electing a president.

Sometimes in envisioning, you will find a meaningful order in what had seemed a chaotic jumble. Leonardo da Vinci, in his notebooks, tells how, when starting to conceive a painting, he would gaze at an old stained wall made of various stones until he began to see "landscapes adorned with mountains, rivers, rocks, trees, plains, . . . combats and figures in quick movement, and strange expressions of faces, and outlandish costumes, and an infinite number of things." Not everyone might see that much in a wall, but da Vinci's method is familiar to writers who also have looked into a confused and random array of stuff and envisioned in it a meaningful arrangement.

*Synthesizing.* Synthesizing (generating new ideas by combining previously separate ideas) is the opposite of analyzing (breaking down into component parts). In synthesizing, a writer brings together materials, perhaps old and familiar materials, and fuses them into something new. A writer makes fresh connections. Surely Picasso achieved a synthesis when, in making a metal sculpture of a baboon and needing a skull for the animal, he clapped on the baboon's neck a child's toy car. With its windshield like a pair of eyes and its mouthlike bumper, the car didn't just look like a baboon's skull: it *became* one. German chemist Friedrich August Kekulé rightly guessed the structure of the benzene molecule when, in reverie, he imagined a snake swallowing its own tail. In a flash he realized that the elusive molecule was a ring of carbon atoms, not a chain, as earlier chemists had believed. Surely to bring together the benzene molecule and a snake was a feat of imaginative synthesis.

Some things cannot be totally reduced to rule and line, and imagination is one of them. But we hope you will accept that imagining is a practical activity of which you are fully capable. The more words you put on paper, the more often you will find that you can discover surprising ideas, original examples, unexpected relationships. The more you write, the more you involve yourself with language, that fascinating stained glass window that invites you to find fresh shapes in it.

## PLANNING, DRAFTING, AND DEVELOPING

We trust we haven't given you the impression that all imagining takes place *before* you write. On the contrary, you'll probably find yourself generating more ideas — perhaps more imaginative and startling ideas — in the act of writing.

*Find a method of organization.* Though in writing a piece of imaginative non-fiction you are freely imagining, you'll still need to lay out your ideas in a clear and orderly fashion. Some writers prefer to outline. However, you might find that in fulfilling this assignment all the outline you will need is a list of points not to forget. If in writing your paper you enjoy yourself and words flow readily, by all means let the flow carry you along. In that happy event, you may be able to plan at the same time that you write your first draft. (For more on organizing ideas and using outlines, see Chapter 16.)

*Hook readers with your opening.* To help your readers envision and share your imagined world just as vividly as you do, your essay needs an engaging (and convincing) opening. Rachel Carson's "A Fable for Tomorrow" has such a beginning. The author arrests our interest with an opening sentence reminiscent of childhood fairy tales: "There was once a town in the heart of America where all life seemed to live in harmony with its surroundings." With this basis in shared reality, we are then willing to share her fantasy as well. Parr starts his essay with a sentence familiar to us from many editorials, "Congress must vote 'NO'. . . ," thus basing his fantastic argument about squirrels in a familiar and realistic framework. (For more on openings, see Chapter 17.)

*Use interesting details.* As in any essay, you also need specific concrete details and evidence to support and clarify your assertions. Carson, in relying on concrete specifics (such as her details about the deserted feeding stations, the birds trembling violently and not being able to fly, the white powder lying on roofs and lawns), makes her description of her imaginary American town ring true. Parr also roots his imaginative argument in reality with details such as the advantage of squirrels over "ground-based dogs" and the reason power lines are above the streets. Like Carson and Parr, use your imagination to come up with specific details and concrete examples for your writing. You'll need to make your vision appear tangible, as if it really could exist. (For more on selecting and using details, see Chapter 18.)

*Carry through in your conclusion.* The endings of Carson's fable and of Parr's allegory work well. Carson pushes to a believable conclusion the details of destruction and death — "The people had done it themselves" — and turns the meaning back on the readers and alludes to their responsibility for what happens to the environment. Parr imagines the nuclear-armed squirrel, who had been only "a disruptive, mean-spirited tree rat," becoming "genocidal." Your ending should have an imaginative thrust, but it should be logically based on the details you have provided. (For more on conclusions, see Chapter 17.)

*Consider your imagery.* Often imaginative writing appeals to the mind's eye. For some accessible picture-filled writing, see the sports pages of a daily newspaper. Sports writer Bugs Baer once wrote of fireball pitcher Lefty Grove: "He could throw a lambchop past a wolf." Dan Shaughnessy in the *Boston Globe* described pitcher Roger Clemens: "Watching the Mariners try to hit Clemens was like watching a stack of waste paper dive into a shredder." Such language isn't mere decoration: it points to a truth and puts vivid pictures in the reader's "mind's eye." (For more about writing with *images* — language that evokes sense experiences, not always sight — look back through Chapter 2.)

*Be patient.* Imagination isn't a constant flame: sometimes it flickers and wavers. If in shaping your draft you get stuck and words don't flow, you may find it helpful to shift your perspective. Try imagining the past, present, or future as if you were somebody else or an alien or an animal or a plant. Perhaps you will then see fresh possibilities in your topic. Also helpful may be what all writers do now and then: take a walk, relax, do something else for a while. Then return to your draft and try to look at it with a *reader's* eyes.

**WRITING WITH A COMPUTER**

Did you ever try "invisible writing"? This is a technique to make yourself less self-conscious while you write — as you'll especially need to be when you're imagining. Turn off just the monitor so that you can't see any words appearing on your screen; either twist down the contrast control or turn off the monitor's switch if it is independent from the computer's power source. Then write. Do you feel slightly at sea? Don't worry — keep writing. Then bring the screen back up and behold what you have written. The advantage of this trick is that you won't be fussing over particular words (and spelling errors); you'll be able to devote your full attention to imagining.

**FOR PEER RESPONSE**

Ask a classmate to let you know if he or she has any doubts about what you've written. Here is a list of questions for your peer editor to answer. See Chapter 20 for advice on working with other student writers and for general questions you should always ask a peer editor to address. For a paper in which you write from imagination, you'll also want your peer editor to answer these specific questions:

- Has the writer chosen a topic that you consider significant? What point is he or she trying to make?
- What do you like best about the writer's imaginative thinking?
- What did you find hardest to follow or imagine or accept? Is it difficult because of the ideas themselves or the way the writer presents them or both? List your problems and explain why they are problems.
- Is what the writer imagines sufficiently rooted in reality to be believable? Plausible?
- Where should the writer add details, examples, description, or images to make the imagined reality seem more plausible? Star the places where the writer needs to be more specific.
- If this were your paper, what is the one thing you would be sure to work on before handing it in?

## REVISING AND EDITING

As Robert Parr reread his first draft on the screen of his computer, he thought of additional details: the official policy of squirrel-dog neutrality and the field tests of the German-designed power line deployment systems. He incorporated them into his final version. Do you need more detail in places to make your vision clear and convincing? Then make yourself comfortable and do some more imagining.

In beginning to write his essay on nuclear squirrels, Parr reported that his hardest problem was to make the "basically goofy" idea of selling nuclear arms to squirrels seem like a serious debate. He realized that he had to do it "with a straight face, as if it weren't unusual in any way," and decided to use the impersonal but impassioned tone and stance of a newspaper editorial or Senate speech. Once he had decided on this approach, he was able to go back into his paper and add appropriate details, strengthen the organization, and change the vocabulary to create the effect he wanted. It took several drafts, but he was pleased with the end result.

> *angrier tone*
>
> ~~Many people have~~ *The Senate has* supported ~~the squirrels' petitions~~ *suburban squirrel extremists* in the past, including some *biased* journalists, who have ~~said~~ *wrongly claimed* that squirrels have no allies in the troubled animal kingdom. ~~But~~ *One must consider the motives behind squirrel demands.* ~~perhaps we should consider the squirrels' motives.~~ Squirrels claiming to use nuclear arms only as a defense against cars ~~aren't~~ *are not* to be trusted. *since they have failed to follow previous treaties* ⟨Squirrels were not meant to control streets—that's why they have power lines over them.⟩  *good example, but doesn't go here*
>
> *still need a more specific example*

A minor problem in envisioning may be to keep your verb tenses straight. Often writers waffle between the future tense ("you *will notice* something strange") and the conditional ("the problem *would accelerate*"). Check the tenses in your draft.

The belief of poet William Butler Yeats that inspiration can come in rewriting as well as in writing may hold true when you write your essay drawing on the resource of imagination. As you revise, you may find fresh and imaginative ideas occurring for the first time. While you review your paper, you might consider the following points. (For more on revising and editing, see Chapter 19.)

**REVISION CHECKLIST**

- Is your vision consistent? Do all the parts of your vision agree with all the others? Or is some part discordant, needing to be cut out?
- Does your paper at any point need more information about the real world? If so, where might you find it: what can you read, whom can you talk with, what can you observe?

- Is your imaginative solution plausible? Could the solution you imagine possibly exist? What physical details, vivid description, and images can you add that will help make your vision seem real?
- Have you used any facts that need verifying, any words that need checking?
- What difficulties did you run into in writing your paper? Did you overcome them? Are any still present that bother you? If you can't come up with solutions, ask your instructor or classmates to help you.

## OTHER ASSIGNMENTS

1. Write a fable about a problem in modern life, similar to the fable by Rachel Carson. Aesop and James Thurber also wrote fables about the human condition. Check them out if you want to see how someone else uses fable.

2. Think of a law or government policy or educational practice that you think should be changed, and write an ironic argument for or against it, similar to Parr's argument against arming squirrels with nuclear weapons. A classic ironic argument is the well-known "A Modest Proposal" in which Jonathan Swift proposes solving the Irish food shortage, caused by famine, by eating babies.

3. Have you ever observed some people in a public place, perhaps on a bus or plane, and imagined who they are and why they are in that place at that time? What problems might they be facing? Have you imagined the conversation they are having? What clues do you have to what they are saying? Try this kind of fantasizing the next time you go to the airport, the mall, or a restaurant, and share your imagined situation with your classmates. (This experience could also provide information for a paper.)

4. Write an essay in answer to a question that begins "What if . . . ?" You might imagine a past that unfolded differently: What if the airplane had never been invented? What if the Equal Rights Amendment had become law? What if the South had won the Civil War? What if John F. Kennedy or Martin Luther King, Jr., had not been assassinated? You might imagine a reversal of fact: What if men had to bear children? How would life be different? What problems would result? What other problems might be solved? Or you might imagine an event in the future: What if there were no more wars? Or what if you were elected president of the United States? Envision in specific detail a world in which the supposition is true. Your purpose is to make the supposition seem credible and convincing to your readers.

5. Imagine an ideal: a person (such as a teacher or boss), place (college or theme park), or thing (automobile or computer) that to your mind would be virtually perfect. Shape this ideal to your own desires. Then

put it in writing. Perhaps this ideal might combine the best features of two or three real people, places, or things. You will have to decide whether what you imagine could exist today or in a more nearly perfect future — and how far into the future? You may be tempted to build up to a surprise ending. It might seem a great trick to reveal at the end that your ideal city is really good old Topeka or that your ideal mother is your own real-life mother after all. But it probably won't be a convincing way to write your paper. Nothing that exists is ideal. Simply to describe what exists won't take any imagining.

6. Imagine two alternative versions of your own future, say, ten years down the road: the worst possible future you could have and the best possible. Describe each in detail. If you would prefer not to limit your vision to your own future, imagine the future of your hometown or city, your region, or your country, perhaps taking one current problem, such as violence or drug abuse, to a logical conclusion.

7. Recall the way you envisioned something before you experienced it; then describe the reality you found instead. Your expectations, of course, might be good or bad; the reality might be a disappointment or a pleasant surprise. But, if possible, pick something about which your ideas changed drastically.

8. Draw a connection between two things you hadn't ever thought of connecting before. Start with something that interests you — running, moviegoing, sports cars — and try relating it to something remote from it: running to writing or cars to clothes. See what both have in common and explain their similarity in two or three paragraphs.

**FOR GROUP LEARNING**

## Brainstorming in a Group

Like Robert Parr, who brainstormed with three friends before he wrote "Negative Views on Nuclear Squirrels," try a brainstorming session with your writing group to generate ideas for an imaginative paper. When you do this as a group, appoint a recording secretary to write down the ideas as fast as they are called out. Or your instructor may choose to do this exercise with the whole class, with the ideas being written on the blackboard. Don't be surprised if this activity seems wild and chaotic; order can emerge from it. Limit your initial brainstorming session to ten or twelve minutes; then stop to discuss the results, circling any items that draw strong reactions from the group. These may be the seeds that will grow a memorable paper. If nothing much comes out of this first session, brainstorm again. (For further advice on how to brainstorm, see p. 334.)

# Applying What You Learn:
# Some Uses of Writing from Imagination

Imagination, we have suggested, is tremendously useful as a resource in many fields, not only in a creative writing course. In scholarly thinking and writing, imagination is essential. French philosopher of history Paul Veyne points out that a historian has to infer the motives of persons long dead. Understanding the past, Veyne argues, is often a matter of imaginatively "filling in" what cannot be completely documented. In the field of geography, according to Robert W. Durrenberger in *Geographical Research and Writing*, a student who wishes to do research needs most of all to develop imagination. "Admittedly, an individual cannot be taught how to be creative," Durrenberger concedes. "But he can observe those who are creative and be on the lookout for new and original approaches to the solutions of problems."

Similarly, imagination can be valuable to you as a college student. To show you how you can usefully apply the ways of imagining to your writing in college and beyond, let's consider them one at a time.

*Shifting perspective.*  The next time you are given an assignment in another course, try looking at the entire topic through someone else's eyes — someone unlike yourself. This way of imagining is often at work in specialized and professional writing. Philosophers and science writers challenge us, as Dr. Peter Saltzstein of Northeast Missouri State University puts it, to "step outside of received opinion or commonly held beliefs and examine those beliefs through the use of alternative perspectives." In the following passage from *Naked Emperors: Essays of a Taboo-Stalker*, science writer Garrett Hardin shifts perspectives. He imagines that an economist asks an ecologist, "Would you plant a redwood tree in your backyard?" When the ecologist says that he would, the economist charges him with being a fool — in economic terms.

> The economist is right, of course. The supporting economic analysis is easily carried out. A redwood tree can hardly be planted for less than a dollar. To mature [it] takes some two thousand years, by which time the tree will be about three hundred feet high. How much is the tree worth then? An economist will insist, of course, on evaluating the forest giant as lumber. Measured at a man's height above the ground, the diameter of the tree will be about ten feet, and the shape of the shaft from there upward is approximately conical. The volume of this cone is 94,248 board feet. At a "stumpage" price of 15[c] a board foot — the approximate price a lumberer must pay for a tree unfelled, unmilled, untransported — the tree would be worth some $14,000.
>
> That may sound like a large return on an investment of only one dollar, but we must not forget how long the investment took to mature: 2000 years. Using the exponential formula to calculate the rate of compound interest we find that the capital earned slightly less than one-half of 1 percent per year. Yes, a man would be an economic fool to put his money into a redwood seedling when so many profitable opportunities lie at hand.

Hardin, of course, is being unfair to economists, many of whom are undoubtedly capable of feeling awe before a giant redwood. But his momentary shift to the strict dollars-and-cents point of view enables him to conclude that, if we care for the future and for our descendants, we sometimes need to act without regard for economics.

*Envisioning.* Some challenging assignments you'll meet in a college course will set forth a problem and ask you to envision a solution. The following question, from a final examination in an economics course, asks the student to imagine a better procedure:

> As we have seen, methods of stabilizing the dollar have depended on enlisting the cooperation of large banks and foreign governments, which has not always been forthcoming. Propose a better, alternative way for our own government to follow in protecting the value of its currency from severe fluctuations.

An effective answer to that question would be based on facts that the student has learned. What the exam question tries to provide is not just practice in recalling facts but also training in envisioning — in bringing the facts together and applying them.

Students in family science courses may be asked to envision ideal situations, play devil's advocate, even take a stand opposed to their own when learning to debate issues informatively. In envisioning an ideal, a writer sets up an imagined goal and perhaps also begins thinking about how to achieve it. In his epoch-making speech in Washington, D.C., on the 1963 centennial of Lincoln's Emancipation Proclamation, Martin Luther King, Jr., set forth his vision of an unsegregated future:

> I have a dream that one day on the red hills of Georgia the sons of former slaves and the sons of former slave owners will be able to sit down together at the table of brotherhood. . . . I have a dream that my four little children will one day live in a nation where they will not be judged by the color of their skin but by the content of their character.

*Synthesizing.* Combining unlike things and drawing unexpected conclusions may result in a lively and revealing paper. But in explaining almost anything, an imaginative writer can make metaphors and draw connections. Sylvan Barnet, in *A Short Guide to Writing about Art* (Boston: Little, 1989), questions whether a period of art can be entirely "Gothic" in spirit. To make a highly abstract idea clear, he introduces a brief *analogy*, a metaphor that likens the unfamiliar thing to something familiar:

> Is there really an all-embracing style in a given period? One can be skeptical, and a simple analogy may be useful. A family often consists of radically different personalities: improvident husband, patient wife, one son an idler and the other a go-getter, one daughter wise in her choice of a career and the other daughter unwise. And yet all may have come from the same culture.

To be sure, imagining has practical applications beyond the writing of college papers and scholarly articles. Asked why World War I took place, Franz Kafka, one of the most influential writers of our century, gave a memorable explanation: the war was caused by a "monstrous lack of imagination." Evidently if we are to survive, we would do well to imagine both World War III and its alternatives — not only the consequences of the problems we now face, but also the solutions.

## *Making Connections:*
## *Writing from Imagination in* A Writer's Reader

*Imagination* can be the fount of powerful nonfiction. Various writers in *A Writer's Reader* effectively use this resource to convey their ideas and enhance their stands. In "I Want a Wife" (p. 490), Judy Brady imagines what a "wife" could do for her — the same things that the traditional wife does for her husband — and concludes, "My God, who *wouldn't* want a wife?" Science and political writer Robert Wright in "Mr. Clean Genes" (p. 611) imagines some of the possible results of genetic engineering to brace up his argument.

Besides Brady, Wright, Rachel Carson (p. 92), and Robert Parr (p. 94), other writers who use imagination in their nonfiction include professor Noel Perrin, "A Part-Time Marriage" (p. 493); journalist Susanna Rodell, "Do You Work? Are You Guilty?" (p. 545); and construction worker Steve Olson, "Year of the Blue-Collar Guy" (p. 542). As you read these essays, consider the role that imagination plays in them. For each essay, answer the following questions.

1. What "What if?" question does the author ask? What is the author's answer to the question?
2. How does the writer use imagination as a resource? What does it add to this piece of nonfiction?
3. How does the imagined world differ from the real world as presented in the essay?

# Part Two

# Thinking Critically

# Introduction:
# Critical Thinking Strategies
# for Writing

*Critic,* from the Greek word *kritikos,* means "one who can judge and discern," or one who can think critically. If college leaves you better able to judge and discern — able to determine what is more important or less important, to make distinctions and recognize differences, to generalize from specifics, to draw conclusions from evidence, to grasp involved concepts and get to the bottom of things, to judge and choose wisely — then it will have given you your money's worth. Effective thinking, the kind you will need in college and on the job, is active and purposeful, not passive and ambling. It is critical thinking. Part Two of this textbook will set you off in the right direction of critical thinking for effective writing.

Critical thinking is not new to you. You use critical strategies daily to solve problems and make decisions. For example, you may not have enough money both to pay your college tuition and to buy the car you need, so you have to decide what you are going to do about this situation. First, you *identify the causes* of your lack of funds to see if you can resolve the problem by eliminating one of the causes. Have you had a medical emergency or lost your job? Have you spent a lot of money on a fancy apartment or a trip to the Bahamas? Has tuition increased? Deciding that the cause — higher tuition — is beyond your control, you *analyze* the problem, exploring it from all angles. You realize right away there are three main options: you can do without the car you want, you can decrease the cost of tuition, or you can get more money. You then analyze further to explore each of these possibilities: Can you get a cheaper car? Can you take public transportation? Can you take fewer courses? Can you get a loan from the bank or from a family member? (If so, can you repay it without sacrificing other things you need?) Can you get another job? (If so, can you maintain your studies?) You *evaluate* each of your choices and

**109**

*compare and contrast* them so that you can choose the most feasible way to solve your problem of lack of cash. Finally you reach a conclusion and *propose a solution:* you need money for both the new car and tuition, so the most logical thing to do is to get a short-term loan from your college to pay your tuition and use the money you have to buy a car. You visit the financial aid officer and *take a stand* that you should be granted a loan, presenting your reasons to support your position. Your arguments are convincing, you receive the loan, and your problem is solved. You have used critical thinking to explore and solve your problem.

You also used critical thinking in high school writing assignments and in other courses. You analyzed causes and effects when you traced the development of labor unions in the United States on your history exam. You compared and contrasted two poems for a literature paper. You evaluated when for your science class you wrote a book report that ended with a statement like "I would recommend this book highly to anyone interested in bioengineering." For a paper in college, however, you will go more deeply into the subject, analyzing it thoroughly and providing convincing evidence for your claims.

In other words, critical thinking is not a specialized, isolated activity. It is part of a continuum of thinking strategies that thoughtful people use every day to grapple with new information and to solve problems. To explain the thinking strategies necessary for purposeful writing and reading, educational expert Benjamin Bloom[1] identified six levels of cognitive activity, each level becoming more complex and demanding higher thinking skills than the previous one: *knowledge, comprehension, application, analysis, synthesis,* and *evaluation.* The first three levels are "literal" thinking skills. When you show that you know a fact, comprehend what it means, and can apply it to a new situation, you demonstrate your mastery over information, the building blocks of thought. The other three levels — analysis, synthesis, and evaluation — are "critical" thinking skills. When you use these skills, you go beyond the literal level of thinking: you break apart the building blocks to see what makes them work, recombine them in new and useful ways, and judge their worth or significance. *Analysis* is the breaking down of information into its elements. As a writer you will often analyze events, processes, structures, and ideas to understand them more fully and to be able to explain them to readers. *Synthesis* is putting together elements and parts to form new wholes. As a researcher you will synthesize information from several sources you have read, integrate this synthesized material with your own thoughts, and convey the unique combination to others through writing. Finally, *evaluation* means judging according to standards or criteria. When you as a critic evaluate something in writing, you must both convince the readers that your standards are reasonable and convince them that the subject being evaluated either does or does not meet those standards.

[1] Benjamin S. Bloom et al., *Taxonomy of Educational Objectives, Handbook I: Cognitive Domain,* David McKay, 1956.

These three cognitive activities — analysis, synthesis, and evaluation — are the core of critical thinking. They are not new to you, but their rigorous application in college-level writing may be. The writing assignments in Part Two are designed to help you focus on each of these thinking skills in turn and give you some practice in applying them in your writing.

## Applying Critical Strategies to Writing

In Part Two, we present a sequence of writing assignments that will require you to use critical thinking strategies. The six writing assignments — analyzing, comparing and contrasting, explaining causes and effects, taking a stand, proposing a solution, and evaluating — are arranged roughly in order of increasing complexity; that is, in order according to the level of critical thinking required. The first three are basically forms of analysis, breaking something down into its components in order to understand it better. The next two — taking a stand and proposing a solution — require synthesis of information from various sources with your own ideas and conclusions. You analyze all the information, reflect on it, and present a new perspective. The last one, evaluating, is the most complex of all and often incorporates several of the other critical strategies. Let's look at these six writing tasks in more detail.

**Analyzing**   is breaking an idea, event, or item into parts in order to explain it. It is the basis of the other critical strategies. In a history class you may be asked to explain the federal government. To do so, you would analyze it — breaking it into its three branches, identifying the functions of each, and demonstrating how they work together as a whole. In an English course you may be required to parse a sentence, analyze a poem, or outline an essay to explain how each part functions within the whole. The writing task of analyzing is covered in Chapter 6.

**Comparing and contrasting**   is a form of analysis that focuses on the similarities and differences of two (or more) items or groups. First you analyze each item and then you line up the characteristics of each, side by side, to determine how they are alike and how they are different. But an effective comparison and contrast analysis goes beyond merely pointing out likenesses and differences; it has a more significant purpose. You may explain how each alternative operates, or you may determine which alternative is preferable. In a government class you may compare and contrast two or more laws; in a nursing course, treatments of a disease; in a psychology course, two people in case studies; in a literature course, two or three fictional characters. The writing task of comparing and contrasting is covered in Chapter 7.

**Explaining causes and effects**   is a form of analysis which focuses on the causes and effects of an action, event, or situation. Identifying causes means ferreting out roots and origins. Determining effects is figuring out results. Often in thinking, the two are integrated; often in writing, they are combined. In a history course, you may identify the multiple causes of World War I to help readers understand why this military struggle started and why it was so difficult to end. Or you may trace the several effects of slavery on the African American family through the last four hundred years to try to understand some of the problems of African Americans today.

Sometimes as you analyze, you will find a chain of causes and effects: a situation causes specific effects, which in turn cause other results. For example, through investigating the effects of overpopulation for an economics course, you may discover that one effect is filling and building on tidal water basins. This causes depletion of plankton and other small sea life, which in turn decreases the supply of fish in the bays and oceans. That decrease may result in fewer fish for commercial fishers to catch, less money for the families of these workers, and higher prices of seafood for all of us in grocery stores and restaurants. The writing task of explaining causes and effects is covered in Chapter 8.

Taking a stand    means arguing for one side or another of an issue. You may come to the debate with strong beliefs and opinions, or you may develop a position while looking into the matter. In either case, you need to analyze the situation and the available information, reach a firm conclusion, and present your case persuasively to your readers. To be persuasive, you must support your claims with more than personal opinion, memories, and anecdotes; you must provide solid evidence — facts, statistics, expert opinion, and direct observation. In an ethics course, you might argue that abortion should be a woman's choice, or that all abortion should be illegal, or that abortion should be allowed only in the case of rape or incest or threat to the mother's life. In a biology course, you may assert that the use of large nets for fishing needlessly destroys much sea life or that these nets are necessary for commercial anglers to make a living. The writing task of taking a stand is covered in Chapter 9.

Proposing a solution    requires not only taking a stand but also presenting a feasible solution to the problem at hand. You need to identify a problem and analyze it to determine the probable causes and possible solutions. Then you need to analyze each solution to see whether it is workable and compare and contrast all the solutions to determine which one is best. Finally you need to argue persuasively that your solution is the best one possible. A civics professor may ask you to propose a way to get more students on your college campus involved in student elections. For a biology class, you may be asked to write a paper proposing a solution to the problem of increased air pollution or setting forth a proposal to solve the problem of the depletion of the ozone layer above the earth. The writing task of proposing a solution is covered in Chapter 10.

Evaluating    is a complex task that usually requires a combination of critical thinking and writing strategies. You must propose — implicitly or explicitly — specific criteria for judging the subject, whether it is a system, an idea, or a work of art. You usually determine these criteria by studying what experts in the field have to say as well as by consulting your own personal preferences; sometimes you must take a stand and defend these criteria themselves. You must also analyze the subject to see how it works, in particular to see how well it matches the criteria you propose. Finally you must make a judgment — is the subject good or bad? effective or not? — and persuade your readers that your view is correct.

You may be asked to write a review of a book or movie for a humanities course; your criterion might be plausibility of plot and character. A psychology professor may request that you evaluate Howard Gardner's theory of multiple intelligence. You might research what experts consider necessary characteristics in a theory of intelligence, apply the ones you consider valid to Gardner's theory, and compare and contrast his theory with other theories to arrive at a conclusion about the value of Gardner's theory. The writing task of evaluating is covered in Chapter 11.

Taken together, these six forms of writing represent most of the writing you will do in the rest of your college courses and in your career. The resources that you explored in Part One are still important, of course, but in the chapters in Part Two they serve as sources of background information or as evidence rather than as the focus for an entire essay. When you approach these six writing tasks, instructors will expect you (and you should expect yourself) to do the following:

1. Think through a topic or problem critically in order to understand it thoroughly.
2. Present information and arguments that will stand up to critical scrutiny.
3. And — in order to succeed at both of these — think critically about your own thinking and writing skills.

In other words, you should learn to apply the same sort of critical scrutiny to your writing that you do to the subjects about which you are writing. This careful examination does *not* mean forever criticizing what you've written. It *does* mean analyzing your current thoughts on a topic and possible weaknesses in your position, analyzing your thinking and writing processes, analyzing your methods for drafting and developing a paper, analyzing your expression of ideas in writing, and so on, to learn what is effective and what might be changed. Richard Paul, the internationally known expert on critical thinking, described that responsibility this way: "We must continually monitor and assess how our thinking is going, whether it is plausibly on the right track, whether it is sufficiently clear, accurate, precise, consistent, relevant, deep, or broad for our purposes."[2] This self-examination is a necessary ingredient for thinking critically in writing.

# Supporting Critical Thinking with Evidence

When writers use the critical strategies we have described here, they provide sound evidence from a credible stance to convince critical readers. They use evidence to clarify, explain, and support assertions. Using clear reasoning, they weave the evidence and assertions together into a cohesive explanation or argument. These standards apply to you when you write an essay using critical strategies. You should also apply them to evaluation of the work of other writers whom you read, both when you are conducting research for a specific paper and when you are reading more widely for knowledge and information. Indeed, one of the most important ways you can apply your critical thinking skills will be to analyze and evaluate the evidence and reasoning of the materials you read for your courses and career.

## TYPES OF EVIDENCE

What is evidence? Anything that demonstrates the soundness of a claim: facts and figures, observations, opinions, illustrations. The five writers' resources presented in Part One of this book — recall, observation, conversation, reading, and imagination — are five sources of evidence, five fruitful places to look for convincing examples and details. Remember, though, that in many critical writing tasks, some kinds of evidence weigh in more heavily than others: readers might discount your memories of livestock care on the farm where you spent your summers as a child unless you can demonstrate that your memories are representative or you can establish yourself as an expert on the subject. In effective analytical and argumentative writing, writers often use personal experience or imagination to bolster their arguments but usually avoid relying on it for their sole support. The three most reliable forms of evidence are facts, expert testimony, and firsthand observation.

Facts.    Facts are statements that can be verified by objective means, such as by observing or by reading a reliable account. Of course, we take many of our facts from the testimony of others. Facts are usually agreed upon by all parties in a dispute or by all reasonable people. We believe that the Great Wall of China exists although we have never seen it with our own eyes. A fact is usually stated in an impersonal way: "Algonquin Indians still live in Old Orchard Beach"; "If you pump the air out of a five-gallon varnish can, it will collapse."

---

[2] Richard Paul, *Critical Thinking: What Every Person Needs to Survive in a Rapidly Changing World*, 2nd ed. (Foundation for Critical Thinking, 1992) 17.

Sometimes people say that *facts* are *true* statements, but what is truth? Sometimes writers confuse *truth* and *soundness of evidence*. Take care that you do not do so. Truth is an ambiguous concept. Consider the truth of the following statements.

| | |
|---|---|
| The tree in my yard is ten feet tall. | *True* because it can be verified |
| Over fifty percent of the students who enter college in the United States today take freshman composition in two-year colleges. | *True* according to statistics |
| A kilometer is 1000 meters. | *True* in the metric system of measurement |
| A football team can have eleven players on the field at one time. | *True* according to the rules of football |
| The speed limit on the highway is fifty-five miles per hour. | *True* according to law |
| Fewer fatal highway accidents have occurred since the fifty-five mph speed limit became law. | *True* according to research studies |
| I went to the football game last night. | *True* according to memory |
| My favorite food is pizza. | *True* as an opinion |
| More violent criminals should receive the death penalty. | *True* as a belief |
| Murder is wrong. | *True* according to value judgment |
| Nirvana, a divine state of release from earthly pain and desire, can be reached by right living, right thinking, and self-denial. | *True* according to Buddhist religious belief |

Some individuals would claim each of the statements in this list to be true. When you are thinking critically for writing or about reading, use the word *true* very cautiously and avoid treating statements of opinion, judgment, belief, or personal experience as true in the same sense that verifiable facts and events are true.

Statistics are facts expressed in numbers. What are the odds that an American child is on welfare? According to statistics compiled by the U.S. Department of Health and Human Services and the Census Bureau in 1991, the chances are 1 in 8. (A student cited that statistic in an essay arguing that politicians should put themselves in the shoes of single mothers before denouncing "welfare handouts.")

Most writers, without trying to be dishonest, interpret statistics to help their causes. The statement "Fifty percent of the populace have incomes above the poverty level" might be used to back the claim that the government of an African nation is doing a fine job. Putting the statement another way — "Fifty percent of the populace have incomes below the poverty level" — might use the same statistic to show that the government's efforts to aid the disadvantaged are inadequate. A writer, of course, is free to interpret a statistic; and it is only human to present a case in a favorable light. But statistics should not be used to mislead. On the wrapper of a peanut candy bar, we read that one one-ounce serving contains only 150 calories and 70 milligrams of sodium. The claim is true, but the bar weighs 1.6 ounces. Eat the whole thing, as you are more likely to do than to consume 62 percent of it, and you'll ingest 240 calories and 112 milligrams of sodium — a heftier amount than the innocent statistic on the wrapper leads you to believe.

Such abuses make some readers automatically distrust statistics. Use figures fairly, and make sure they are accurate. If you doubt a statistic or a fact, why not check it out? Compare it with facts and statistics reported by several other sources. Distrust a statistical report that differs from every other report unless it is backed by further evidence.

**Testimony of Experts.**    By *experts*, we mean people with knowledge of a particular field gained from study and experience. The test of an expert is whether his or her expertise stands up to the scrutiny of others knowledgeable in that field. An essay by basketball player Michael Jordan explaining how to play offense or by economist John Kenneth Galbraith setting forth the causes of inflation carries authority, while a piece by Galbraith on how to play basketball would not be credible. But consider whether your expert has any bias that would affect his or her reliability. Statistics on cases of lung cancer attributed to smoking might be better taken from government sources than from a representative of the tobacco industry.

**Firsthand Observation.**    Obviously, firsthand observation is persuasive. It adds life to any paper and can lend concrete reality to abstract or complex points. Perhaps in supporting the claim "The Meadowfield waste recycling plant fails to meet state safety and sanitation guidelines," you might recall your own observations of the site: "When I visited the plant last January, I was struck by the number of open waste canisters and by the lack of protective gear for the workers who handle these toxic materials daily."

As readers, most of us tend to trust the writer who declares, "I was there. This is what I saw." Sometimes that trust is misplaced, though, and you should always be wary of a writer's claim to have seen something that no other evidence supports. Ask yourself: Is this writer biased? Is he or she an expert? Is there any possibility that the writer has (intentionally or unintentionally) misinterpreted what he or she saw? Be aware, too, that your own firsthand observations will be subjected to similar scrutiny; take care to reassure your readers that your observations are unbiased and accurate.

## SELECTING EVIDENCE

As a writer you must determine what evidence is appropriate to support your main point or thesis according to your purpose, your audience, and your position as a writer; as a reader, you need to determine when writers have adequately supported their points. One way to select evidence and to judge whether it is appropriate and sufficient is to consider the type of appeal: *logical appeal, emotional appeal,* and *ethical appeal.* Most effective arguments work on all three levels, using all three types of appeals. As a writer, you will usually want to make sure that you have evidence that supports all three. As a reader, you will want to make sure that the author has not relied too heavily on any one type of appeal.

Logical Appeal.   When you use a logical appeal, you appeal to the mind or the intellect. The logical appeal relies on evidence that is factual, objective, clear, and relevant. For example, if you were arguing for term limits for legislators, you wouldn't want to base your argument on the evidence that some long-term legislators weren't reelected last term (irrelevant) or that the current system is unfair to young people who want to get into politics (not logical). Instead, you might argue that a lack of term limits encourages corruption and then use evidence of legislators becoming indebted to lobbyists or special-interest committees by taking campaign contributions from them and then siding automatically with these groups in key legislative votes. Critical readers, such as college professors, demand logical evidence to support major claims and important statements; you should, too, when you read the writing of someone who claims to be an authority on a subject.

Emotional Appeal.   When you use an emotional appeal, you appeal to the reader's heart and emotions. You choose language, facts, quotes, examples, and images that will evoke emotional responses. To be convincing, every piece of writing must hit readers in their hearts as well as their minds. A strict logical appeal may seem cold and dehumanized if not combined with an emotional appeal. If you are arguing against the hunting of seals for their fur, you might combine statistics on the factual evidence of how many seals are killed each year and how the population is decreasing with a vivid description of baby seals being slaughtered. Be aware that some writers use emotional appeals to manipulate readers, to arouse their sympathy, pity, or anger in order to bring them over to the position of the writer without any logical evidence. Such emotional appeals are couched in emotionally laden words and overly sentimental examples and images. Modern readers don't like to feel used. When writing, take care not to alienate your readers by using a dishonest emotional appeal; instead of arguing against a vote for a particular candidate on the basis of pity for ill-nourished children living in roach-infested squalor, report his or her voting record on welfare reform issues. When reading, be wary of anyone who tugs on your heartstrings without giving you some hard facts as well.

**Ethical Appeal.**   When you use an ethical appeal, you appeal to readers' sense of fairness and trust. You choose evidence and present it in a manner that will make readers trust you, respect your judgment, and believe what you have to say. The best logical argument in the world will fall flat if you can't get readers to take you seriously. To use an ethical appeal, you can establish your credentials in the field. Have you had experience, such as a job or travel, that helped you learn about the subject? Have you investigated the subject through reading and interviews? Also, you can demonstrate your knowledge of the subject by the information you generate and gather, the experts and the sources you choose to cite, and the depth of understanding of the topic that you convey in your writing. Further, you can establish a meeting of the minds with your readers by indicating values and attitudes that you share and by responding to the arguments of the opposition. Finally, you can demonstrate your credibility by using language that is precise, clear, and appropriate in tone. When reading, you'll probably find that you're most swayed by authors who have managed to do all these things successfully. Be careful, however, not to let a strong ethical appeal manipulate you into believing an author who doesn't offer any hard evidence for the claims he or she makes.

## TESTING EVIDENCE

As both a reader and a writer, you should always be thinking critically about evidence, testing it to see if it is strong enough to carry the weight of the writer's claims. When is evidence useful and trustworthy? When —

*It is accurate.* A writer assumes all responsibility for facts and figures. Are the facts and figures you have used accurate? If you doubt a piece of information, try to check it against published sources. See reports by others and facts given in reference works. Be sure to copy correctly and proofread carefully.

*It is reliable.* To decide whether you can trust it, you'll need to evaluate its source and check the credentials of the writer. Whenever possible, do some reading. Compare information given in one source with information given in another. If an important point rests on your quoting an opinion or citing information you receive from an expert, do you know that the person is respected in the field? What are his or her credentials as an authority?

*It is up to date.* Facts and statistics from ten-year-old encyclopedias, such as population figures or scientific research, are probably out of date. Take information from the latest sources, especially if you are writing about a current issue.

*It is to the point.* Your evidence must back the exact claim you're making in your paper. This point may seem too obvious to deserve mention, but you'd be surprised how many writers get hung up on an interesting fact or opinion that has nothing to do with what they're trying to demonstrate. Sometimes a writer will leap from evidence to conclusion without reason, and the result is a *non sequitur* (Latin for "it does not follow"): "Benito Mussolini made the trains run on time. He was one of the world's leading statesmen." The evidence about trains doesn't support a judgment on Mussolini's statesmanship. (For more about errors in reasoning, see the next section, "Recognizing Abuses of Reason.")

*It is representative.* Any examples you select should be typical of all the things included in your claim. If you want to support the claim that, in general, students on your campus are well informed about their legal rights, don't talk just to prelaw majors; talk to an English major, an engineering major, a biology major, and others. Probably most writers, in the heat of persuading, can't help unconsciously stacking the evidence in their own favor, but the best writers don't deliberately suppress evidence to the contrary. The writer for an airline magazine who tried to sell package tours to India by declaring "India is an attractive land of sumptuous wealth and splendor" might give for evidence the Taj Mahal and a luxury hotel while ignoring the slums of Bombay and Calcutta. The result might be effective advertising but hardly a full and faithful view and not critically sound.

*It is not oversimplified.* Some writers fall into the error of *oversimplification,* supplying a too-easy explanation for a phenomenon that may be vast and complicated: "Of course our economy is in trouble. People aren't buying American-made cars." Both statements may be true, but the second is insufficient to account for the first: obviously there is much more to the economy than the auto industry alone. More information is called for. Whenever in doubt that you've given enough evidence to convince your readers, you are probably well advised to come up with more.

*It is sufficient and strong enough to back the claim and persuade your readers.* How much evidence you use depends on your claim. It will take less evidence to claim that a downtown park needs better maintenance than to claim that the Department of the Interior needs reorganizing.

How much evidence you need may depend, too, on how much your readers already know. Who will be reading your paper? A group of readers all from Washington, D.C., and vicinity will not need much evidence to be persuaded that the city's modern Metro transit system is admirable in its efficiency, but more evidence may be needed to convince readers from out of town. As you try to comprehend another person's beliefs and feelings, you can try to imagine yourself in that person's place and anticipate questions he or she would ask. If you do, you will probably think of more ideas — points to make, objections to answer — than if you think only of presenting your own view.

Not that mere quantity is enough. One piece of vivid and significant evidence — such as the firsthand testimony of a reliable expert, given in that person's memorable words — may be more valid and persuasive than a foot-high stack of statistics.

## RECOGNIZING ABUSES OF REASON

By mistakes in thinking and by misuse of language, writers may distort evidence. Good writers avoid logical fallacies and ill-used language: although they seem persuasive on the surface, critical readers will recognize them as weaknesses in your argument.

*Fallacies.* Logical fallacies are common mistakes in thinking — often, the making of statements that lead to wrong conclusions. Here are a few of the most familiar, to help you recognize them when you see or hear them and so guard against them when you write. If when you look back over your draft you discover any of these, cut them, think again, and come up with a different argument. If you come across them in a source you are considering, you should seriously doubt the validity of the writer's case.

*Non sequitur (from the Latin, "It does not follow").* This fallacy is the error of stating a claim that doesn't follow from your first premise (the statement you begin with): "Marge should marry Jergus. Why, in high school he got all A's." Come up with stronger reasons for your recommendation — reasons that have to do with getting good grades *as a husband.*

*Oversimplification.* This fallacy is evident when a writer offers neat and easy solutions for large, complicated problems: "If we want to do away with drug abuse, let's get tough — let's sentence every drug user to life imprisonment." (Even users of aspirin?)

*Post hoc ergo propter hoc ("after this, therefore because of this").* This fallacy assumes a cause and effect relationship where there is none. We assume that when one event precedes another in time, the first is the cause of the second. Many superstitions result from *post hoc* reasoning: neither seeing a black cat nor strolling under a ladder causes misfortune. (In a way, this is another form of oversimplification: attributing huge effects to just one simple cause.)

*Allness.* The allness fallacy means stating or implying that something is true of an entire class of things. There are exceptions to every rule, and your readers are likely to find them. Instead of saying "Students enjoy studying" (which implies that *all* students enjoy *all* types of studying *all* the time), qualify: "Some students enjoy studying math." Be wary of *allness* words: *all, everyone, no one, always, never.*

*Proof by example (or too few examples).* An example illustrates or helps to clarify, but it does not prove. "Armenians are great chefs. My next-door neighbor is Armenian and, boy, can he cook!" This type of overgeneralizing is the basis of much prejudice. Be sure you have sufficient evidence — enough examples, a large enough sampling — to draw a conclusion.

*Begging the question.* The writer who sets out to prove a statement already taken for granted begs the question. For instance, the argument that rapists are menaces because they are dangerous doesn't prove a thing: "menaces" are "dangerous" people. Beggars of questions just repeat in different words what they have already stated. Sometimes this fallacy takes the form of "circular reasoning": "He is a liar because he simply isn't telling the truth." Sometimes it takes the form of defining a word in terms of itself: "Happiness is the state of being happy."

*Either/or reasoning.* This logical fallacy is a special brand of oversimplified thinking: assuming that there are only two sides to a question, that all statements are either true or false, that all questions demand either a yes or a no answer. An either/or reasoner assumes that a problem has only two possible solutions, only one of which is acceptable. "What are we going to do about acid rain? Either we shut down all the factories that cause it or we just forget about acid rain and learn to live with it. We've got no choice, right?" Realize that there are more than two choices or more than two causes.

*Argument from dubious authority.* An unidentified authority can be used unfairly to shore up a quaking argument: "According to some of the most knowing scientists in America, smoking two packs a day is as harmless as eating a couple of oatmeal cookies. So let's all smoke." A reader should also doubt an authority whose expertise lies outside the subject being considered: "TV personality Pat Sajak says this insurance policy is the lowest-priced and most comprehensive available."

*Argument ad hominem (from the Latin, "against the man").* This fallacy consists of attacking an individual's opinion by attacking his or her character. This fallacy is widespread in politics: "Sure candidate Smithers advocates this tax plan. It will put money in his pocket!" Judge the tax proposal on its merits, not on the character of its originator. Or "Carruthers may argue that we need to save the whales, but Carruthers is the kind of person who always gets excited over nothing." His characteristic of being easily excited is not relevant to the argument to save whales. Joining these two ideas implies that his attempt to save the whales is not important. A person's circumstances can also be turned against him or her: "Carruthers would have us spend millons to save whales, but I happen to know that he owns a yacht from which he selfishly enjoys watching whales." His circumstances are irrelevant to any argument he may make concerning the whales. Again, judge the proposal to save the whales on its merits, not on the proposer's character.

*Argument from ignorance.* This fallacy involves maintaining that because a claim has not been disproved, it has to be accepted: "Despite years of effort, no one has conclusively proved that ghosts don't exist; therefore, we should expect to see them at any time." Don't accept the existence of ghosts merely on the basis that their existence has not been disproved. The converse is also an error: that because a conclusion has not been proved, it should be rejected. "No one has ever shown that there is life on any other planet. Evidently the notion of other living things in the universe is unthinkable." Demand other evidence of the lack of plausibility of life on other planets.

*Argument by analogy.*   The writer who makes this mistake uses a *metaphor* (a figure of speech that points to a similarity: "Her speech was a string of fire-crackers") as though it were evidence to support a claim. In explanation, an analogy may be useful. It can set forth a complex idea in terms of something familiar and easy to imagine. For instance, shooting a spacecraft to a distant planet is like sinking a golf ball with uncanny accuracy into a hole a half mile away. But if used to convince, an analogy will be logically weak, though it may sound neat and clear. Dwelling only on similarities, a writer doesn't consider differences — since to admit them would only weaken the analogy. "People were born free as the birds. It's cruel to expect them to work." Hold on — human society and bird society have more differences than similarities. Because they are alike in one way doesn't mean they're alike in *every* way.

*Bandwagon argument.*   The writer who uses this technique tries to persuade the reader to jump on the bandwagon, appealing to the human desire to belong. The argument suggests that everyone is joining the group, and if the readers don't join also, they will be left out. Often the bandwagon technique is used in arguments related to happiness, success, or reward. An advertiser may suggest that if readers don't drive a certain car or drink a certain soda, they won't be part of the "in" crowd. If readers identify with a specific group or if they aspire to a certain group (political, social, financial, or educational), a political pamphlet may imply that a particular candidate is the choice of the people in that group. A writer may argue that any readers who disagree with the position set forth, for example, in favor of more funding for education, are misinformed and should change their opinions to jump on the bandwagon with all the other well-informed taxpayers.

Misusing Language.   The effectiveness of a writer's position may also be weakened by misuse of language, either intentional or unconscious. Pitfalls that you should avoid when writing and be sensitive to when reading are lifting words out of context, equivocation, weasel words, and doublespeak.

*Lifting words or statements out of context* changes the original meaning and is often used purposefully to distort evidence. For example, a drama critic writes, "The new play is a tremendous flop, with the only real suspense being whether the audience would stay until the end." But an advertiser selectively quotes, "According to a well-known drama critic, the new play is . . . 'tremendous' with 'real suspense,' " purposefully distorting the original review in order to sell tickets.

*Equivocating* is using a word in more than one sense in the same context. Poetry is enriched by the ambiguity of multiple meaning. Poet Robert Frost ends "The Road Not Taken" with the lines "Two roads diverged in a wood, and I — / I took the one less traveled by./ And that has made all the difference." He does not specify "all the difference," a purposefully ambiguous phrase, but leaves the interpretation to readers. Puns (plays on words) turn on ambiguity: "Try a Sound Sleeper mattress for the *rest* of your life" or "No noose is good news." However, when a conclusion is drawn by using a word whose meaning has been deliberately or inadvertently shifted in the discussion, distortion of evidence occurs: "As you can see, Johnson's statistics do not fairly represent the real situation. And if he is unfair, why should we trust his judgment?" (In the first sentence, *fair* means "accurate"; in the second sentence, it means "just.") You can avoid distortion through equivocation by carefully and consciously defining your terms.

*Weasel words* are used to evade or retreat from a direct or forthright statement or opinion. According to Paul Stevens, a writer of advertising copy, weasel words "can make you hear things that aren't being said, accept as truths things that have only been implied, and believe things that have only been suggested. . . . When *you* hear a weasel word, you automatically hear the implication. Not the real meaning, but the meaning *it* wants *you* to hear."[3] One of the most commonly used weasel words is *help*, as in "helps keep you healthy" or "helps prevent cavities." Notice that these statements don't claim anything very risky: they don't say the product *will* keep you healthy or prevent cavities, only that it will *help*, which isn't saying very much at all. (Breathing probably helps, too.) When you hear or read phrases like these, you are unaware of the word *help* and process only the strong language that follows it. Other weasel words are *like* ("these changes are like a complete overhaul of the system"); *virtual* or *virtually*, which means "in essence or effect, but not in fact" ("education is virtually a right of every American"); and *up to*, which can mean none at all ("this measure guarantees improvement for up to twenty percent of the population"). When you come across these words in your own writing or in something you are reading, stop and read the sentence again: What does the sentence *really* say?

*Doublespeak or obfuscating* is using language to hide the truth, either by using a series of meaningless generalities or by using terms and phrases unfamiliar to readers. Doublespeak is language that appears to be legitimate but is actually used purposefully to distort meaning. William Lutz in the book *Doublespeak*[4] cites as an example the Pentagon's attempt to avoid unpleasant associations by referring to bombs and artillery shells that fall on civilian targets as "incontinent ordnance" and by calling the neutron bomb a "radiation enhancement device." He also cites an incident during the investigation into the *Challenger* disaster in 1986. When Jesse Moore of NASA was asked if the performance in the shuttle program had improved, he answered:

> I think our performance in terms of the liftoff performance and in terms of the orbital performance, we knew more about the envelope we were operating under, and we have been pretty accurately staying in that. And so I would

[3] Paul Stevens, "Weasel Words: God's Little Helpers," *I Can Sell You Anything*, by Carl P. Wrighter (New York: Ballantine, 1972).

[4] William Lutz, *Doublespeak: From "Revenue Enhancement" to "Terminal Living," How Government, Business, Advertisers, and Others Use Language to Deceive You* (New York: Harper, 1989).

say the performance has not by design drastically improved. I think we have been able to characterize the performance more as a function of our launch experience as opposed to it improving as a function of time.

Take care that you do not fall victim to doublespeak, either when you are reading or when you are writing.

## Suggestions for Critical Reading

You will be reading to complete the assignments in this course and in other college courses. You need the skills not only of thinking critically about an idea or issue and using critical writing strategies, but also of approaching whatever you read in an active, questioning manner. You will think critically about sources for research papers and about the pieces of literature for essays of analysis, interpretation, and evaluation. Throughout the preceding pages, we've tried to point out how most critical thinking strategies can be applied not only to what you write but also to what you read. Here we'd like to give you some further suggestions for the process of critical reading.

You should recognize that readers read for different purposes at different times: the way you read a novel for pleasure is different from the way you read an advertisement for a product (car, bike, computer) you are interested in buying. To read critically, you need to read on at least three levels:

1. Read for the literal meaning, for what is explicitly stated.
2. Read inferentially, for what is implied between the lines.
3. Read to evaluate, to assess the soundness, accuracy, and fairness of what is written.

Many readers find that the easiest way to read on three levels is to read important texts three times, once for each level. With practice, you'll find that in most cases you can read at two or three levels at once.

Just as critical writers ask themselves questions as they compose, critical readers ask themselves questions as they read. These questions help them to stay alert to important points and to monitor their processes of reading. The following checklist includes questions designed to improve your reading on all three levels. (You can also use them as a guide to revising what you have written.)

**CRITICAL READING CHECKLIST**

- What is the author's purpose?
- Does the author fulfill his or her purpose? How effectively?
- What problems and issues does the author raise?
- What is the point of view of the author?
- What is the author assuming or taking for granted?
- What are the key concepts or ideas of the text?

- What is the author's organizational pattern?
- What evidence, information, and data are presented?
- Is the evidence sufficient to clarify? to convince?
- Is the evidence adequate to the purpose?
- Is the evidence clear? precise? accurate? relevant? logical?
- What lines of reasoning does the author follow?
- What inferences does the author make?
- Which statements are generalizations? Which are specific details?
- Which statements are fact? Which are opinion?
- Is there any bias on the part of the author?
- What is the author's tone?
- What are the relationships between paragraphs? between sentences within paragraphs?
- Are the author's arguments valid?
- Does the author use logical appeal? emotional appeal? ethical appeal?
- Does the author distort any evidence?
- Does the author use any distorted reasoning?
- Does the author misuse language in any way?
- What are the implications of the information?
- What logical inferences and conclusions can you draw from the passage?

To read critically, you need to be actively engaged with your reading material. Don't just sit there and let the words wash over you. Carry on a conversation with the passage, asking it questions, exclaiming at the unexpected, pointing out oversights or weaknesses. This conversation can take place in your own mind, or you may find, as many readers do, that making notes as you read is the best way to "get into" a text. If the book is yours (or if you're reading a photocopy), you can write in it directly, underlining key passages and making notes in the margin. If you're reading someone else's book, confine your notes to a separate sheet of paper. Here's how one student annotated her photocopy of a chapter from *The Bell Curve: Intelligence and Class Structure in American Life* by Richard Herrnstein and Charles Murray, using the critical reading checklist:

*Jobs and Intelligence* [really? what are job interviews, then? how about job descriptions?] [Yes, but is that good or bad?]
No one decreed that occupations should sort us out by our cognitive abilities, and (no one enforces the process.) It goes on beneath the surface, guided by its own invisible hand. Testers observe that job status and intelligence test scores have gone together since there were intelligence tests to give. As tests evolved and as the measurement of status was formalized, [sarcasm?] studying the relation between the jobs and intelligence became a cottage industry for social scientists. By now, the relation has [sweeping] (been confirmed __many__ times, in __many__ countries, and in __many__ approaches to the data.

*almost sounds like he's making fun of "the experts"*

This is not to say that the experts find nothing to quarrel about. The (*full of*) technical literature is [replete with] disagreement. Aside from the purely technical bones of contention, the experts argue about whether the IQ-job status connection is a by-product of a more fundamental link between educational level and job status. For example, it takes a law degree to be a lawyer, and it takes intelligence to get into and through law school, but aside from that, is there any good reason why lawyers need to have higher IQs on average than, say, bus drivers? At the height of egalitarianism in the 1970s, the received wisdom in many academic circles was no, with Christopher Jencks's *Inequality* the accepted text. A related argument, stated forcefully by James Fallows, arises over whether an IQ score is a credential for certain jobs, like a union card for a musician, or whether there is a necessary link between job status and intelligence, like a good ear. By the time we get to the end of Part I, our answers to such questions should be clear. Here we review a few of the more illuminating findings, to push the discussion beyond the (fact) that occupational status is correlated with IQ.

*hard to sort out cause & effect*

*good question*

*connotation*

*check this out*

*makes intelligence seem innate, unchangeable. distortion?*

*evidence?*

*really a fact? I'm not convinced yet*

## Chapter 6

# Analyzing

Many times in college you will be asked to understand some matter that seems complicated: an earthquake, the metabolism of a cell, the Federal Reserve Bank, the Protestant Reformation. Viewed as a whole, such a subject may look intimidating. But often you can simplify your task by *analyzing* your subject: by dividing it into its parts and then dealing with it one part at a time.

Analysis is already familiar to you. If you took high school chemistry, you probably analyzed water: you separated it into hydrogen and oxygen, its two elements. You've heard many a television commentator analyze the news. Did a riot break out in Bombay? Trying to help us understand what happened, the commentator tells us what made up the event: who the protesters were, whom they protested to, what they were protesting. Analyzing a news event may produce results less certain and clear-cut than analyzing a chemical compound, but the principle is similar: to take something apart for the purpose of understanding it better. In a college writing assignment you might analyze anything from a contemporary subculture (What social groups make up the homeless population of Los Angeles?) to an ecosystem (What animals, plants, and minerals coexist in a rainforest?) in order to explain it to readers. Whenever you analyze a subject, you'll be dividing it into its components, the more readily to make sense of it.

## *Learning from Other Writers*

Let's look first at two examples of written analyses. Meg Greenfield, columnist for *Newsweek*, writes regularly about politics, politicians, and the social and cultural impact of the political goings-on in Washington, D.C. In the lighthearted essay "Wish You Were Here," she focuses on our national fascination with presidential vacations.

The second essay is by a student at the University of Florida, Brenda Devlin. In her paper she analyzes one specific beer commercial, breaking it into its parts and explaining the various devices used to manipulate the audience.

## Meg Greenfield    Wish You Were Here

The American public is a quirky employer and never more so than when our high-class labor decides to take a vacation. Oh, *definitely*, we say to whichever president it happens to be that year, you *should* take some time off . . . everyone needs to . . . it's good for you, you know . . . blah, blah, blah. And then, in the manner of employers everywhere: Oh, you were thinking of taking it now? Isn't this kind of a bad time? Oh, no, no . . . I was only thinking that . . . never mind, it's a good idea, go ahead and don't worry about anything; we can handle it here. You just have a good time and a great rest, that's what's important. My God, you're not going to wear that bathing suit, are you?

Now, it's Clinton's turn. As ever our national ambivalence on the subject of presidential vacations turns on four questions: what they wear, where they go, how much it's going to cost, and what they actually do when they get there. Considering the intensity of our conflicting emotions on these matters, Richard Nixon was probably our best president. He regularly went on vacation, as per our national instruction, but never looked like he was having a good time. This was ideal. And, crucially, Nixon never took his business clothes off, either. He was always dressed for nuclear retaliation. "My fellow Americans, it is with a heavy heart that I come before you tonight . . ." You can't go down that particular road wearing flowered trunks, a cap promoting the locally brewed beer and a T-shirt with a picture of Mauna Kea on it.

Face it: this country doesn't run to Ralph Lauren presidents. From Harry Truman's riotous shirts to Nixon's poolside oxfords to Carter's underwearish running clothes to Clinton's eye-averter shorts there has been complaint about this, but as always, ambivalent, contradictory complaint. We don't approve of their being ordinary and Uncle Ed–like in their ghastly attire and habits. We live in dread from the moment Air Force One takes off for whatever garden spot the Chief Executive has chosen that our next view of him will be in a knit swimsuit and brand-new white sneakers with short black socks. But just let them show a little class or taste for the more expensive things and look out! For although they may look like Uncle Ed, lying there sunburned and paunchy in the sand, they also necessarily travel in approximations of royal progressions from one borrowed and/or commandeered palace to another, our very own Plantagenets and Hohenzollerns. Thus, the incoherent core question we ask over and over again concerning presidential vacations: Why do these fellows look so tacky and undistinguished and who the hell do they think they are, anyway, the Queen of England?

1

2

3

The temporarily appropriated palaces deserve a special word. They are    4
not always the only recourse of presidents without vacation havens of their
own. For even those blessed with private country getaways pretty regularly
end up encamped at some well-wisher or other's beachfront spread in Florida
or some fancy Palm Springs hilltop manse, attended by their flowerbed-de-
stroying serenity-shattering armies of Secret Service agents, functionaries, and
press. Presidents, and especially their security contingents, are known to be
killer guests, fine if you treasure the prestige that goes with their visit and
don't mind the continuous presence of large groups of expressionless men
standing on top of your dahlias.

In fact, the appropriated palatial site is an ancient prerogative of the trav-    5
eling pooh-bah and so, of course, is the consequent wreckage. We have written testimony to this over the centuries at least from the Crusades, but none
more poignant than Robert Massie's account of what Peter the Great and his
traveling party did in England to the elegant house and grounds that the essayist John Evelyn had spent forty-five years perfecting: multitudinous ink
and grease stains, battered paintwork, pried-open locks, missing tiles, ripped
featherbeds ("torn as if by wild animals"), fifty chairs apparently used for fire-
wood, and twenty paintings apparently used for — yes — target practice.

### The Proper Image

Our own most notoriously destructive presidential parties have never at-    6
tained this level of achievement, but even if they had, no one would probably feel sorry for their affluent hosts. For the lenders of these great country
places, unjust as it may be, tend to be regarded the press and public as people
seeking special favors, more to be censured than pitied, guilty of some unspecified but unsavory transaction. The concept of unfelonious, if somewhat
showy, hospitality is never admitted into these discussions at all, legitimate
though it may be. This illustrates yet another of our confusions, the one about
cost: American taxpayers, who grouse all the time about the high cost of presidential travel and trappings, do not want to pay for any of it themselves, but
interestingly do not want anyone else — especially a moneybags — to pay for
it either, fearing corruption of some kind.

There is, finally, what these poor souls do on their vacations. When they    7
say it is a working vacation, we in the press go to great lengths to prove it is
not and insinuate that because of the deteriorating situation in Lower Graus-
tark they should be back in the Oval Office. When they say they are relaxing
we make jokes about how much they are working and how they are such
weirdos they don't know how to relax. We don't like graceless, common activities, but are suspicious of patrician ones. And it all comes back to what we
regard as the proper image for a vacationing president. I could have told
George Bush that the sporty cap and the golf cart had to go. There is no way
to look dignified while driving a golf cart. I don't care if you're Marcus Aure-
lius. The whole issue of Bush's being on holiday at the wrong time could actually have been avoided if he had gone in for windswept, contemplative
beach walks, merely looking preoccupied for the camera.

That's what we want — a vacationing presidential family that is at once    8
ordinary and special, frugal and regal, there and not there, on the job and on
the beach. As Ross Perot would say, it's that simple.

**Questions to Start You Thinking**

*Meaning*

1. Explain the title of Greenfield's essay. What does it mean literally? What connotations and associations does it call to mind?

2. In this essay Greenfield analyzes the American fascination with presidential vacations. What are the four elements of this obsession that she identifies?

3. Do you agree with the first sentence: "The American public is a quirky employer"? Explain why you agree or do not agree.

4. What other aspects of the president or of our government are the American public obsessed with? Why are we obsessed with them? How could Greenfield explain our obsesssion?

*Writing Strategies*

5. The author has a purpose beyond identifying four elements of the American fascination with presidential vacations. What is the larger purpose of her essay? What point is she trying to make?

6. Why does Greenfield focus on these four particular elements of presidential vacations? Why does she present the four elements in the order she does?

7. What is the tone of the essay? Identify specific passages from the essay to support your identification of the tone. Why do you think Greenfield uses this tone?

STUDENT ESSAY

# *Brenda Devlin*    Subtle Manipulations of Men

It was a normal Sunday afternoon: my father and I were    1
sitting in front of the television set placing bets on which
team would win. "The Broncos will win," I said, "fourteen to
three, no question." "Never," Dad retorted, "I bet you a tank
of gas that the Broncos will lose twenty-one to. . . ." Then
in the middle of the conversation came a booming voice seemingly from out of nowhere. "Hey!" it said. My father apparently forgot about the bet and started to stare blankly in
the direction where the voice came from. Remembering that my
car was almost on empty and I only had five dollars in my
pocket for the next five days, I tried in vain to start up

the bet once again. When all of my attempts failed, I slowly
turned around to see what exactly it was that was completely
enthralling my Dad. It was the television set. I stared in
wonder at the television as seemingly thousands of lights,
colors, pieces of music, and words flashed across the screen.
Before I could fully take in all the images, it commanded me
to answer a question. "Which one," it interrogated, "looks
like the better beer?" That's when I came back to my senses.
I realized that this was a beer commercial, and since I'm not
a beer drinker the rest of the commercial lost my interest.
However, my father, a beer drinker, continued to stare mind-
lessly at the TV. It was then that I began to wonder what
made this particular beer commercial so captivating to him. I
decided to look more closely at how this commercial manipu-
lates the minds of its intended audience, beer-drinking men.

The first thing I noticed about the commercial was that          2
it cried out to be noticed. It begins with a black background
behind large gold letters that fill the entire screen. The
letters spell the word "HEY!" The narrator, a man, says the
same word emphatically HEY! as it is shown on the screen. One
of the easiest ways to attract attention is to show bright,
colorful images. Seeing is our first and perhaps most important way of learning about the world. As children we see and
respond to strong images before we learn what words mean; as
adults, we still respond immediately on a basic level to
bright colors and flashy images. Another common method of
grabbing attention is to use a single word as a headline,
something written larger or spoken louder than the surrounding words: "Wanted," "Help!" or, in this case, "Hey!"

Now that the commercial has its audience's attention, it       3
quickly and quietly slips in another subtle manipulation: the
color of the word "HEY!" is gold. This color seemed relatively innocent until I realized that the color of the word
and the color of the beer are the same. As Judith Williamson
notes in Decoding Advertisements: Ideology and Meaning in Advertisements, color is used in advertisements to make connections between a product (the beer) and other things,
presumably those with positive messages or associations. In
the first three seconds of the commercial, the advertising

agency has managed to slip in two very influential messages
to its audience: pay attention to this commercial, and pay
attention to this beer.

The second picture in the commercial is of a bar. The
camera is following a tray of two beers; one is noticeably
darker (more golden) than the other. The camera angle tips to
the left and to the right as it approaches an individual man
in the bar, with only the beer-filled mugs in focus and
level. The man, the bar, and everything else in the backdrop
is colored a hazy, light blue. The two beers are the only
things on the screen that retain their original color. This
color could be deceptive, of course: technicians often tinker
with a product's appearance--adding food coloring to tea or
using cream for milk, for example--to make it look "right" on
screen. We have no way of judging, though, since our sense of
normality is even further skewed by the heightened contrast
between the clear gold beer and the hazy blue surroundings.
We have no choice but to accept that the mugs full of beer
are beacons of clarity and light. We focus our attention on
them, and for the next few seconds they become the center of
our world.

The screen then changes from the beer mugs and the man
in the bar back to black screen filled with letters. This
time the letters spell out a question, "WHICH LOOKS LIKE A
BETTER BEER?" Of course, the word "BETTER" is colored gold,
establishing a connection between the gold-colored beer and
the fact that it's "better." The question itself is a clever
technique to manipulate the audience. By asking the viewer a
question, the commercial demands a response--even if we don't
answer, we are aware that we're being asked to do something.
But the advertiser's question is so simple and pointed that
we answer almost automatically. And we give exactly the answer that the advertiser wants, because that answer has already been planted in our minds: obviously, the beer that's
the same color as the word "better" (Coors Extra Gold) is the
better beer.

The next few scenes in the commercial show different
men. One man is wearing a Metallica shirt, while the others
are professionals wearing unbuttoned, collared shirts with

loose-fitting ties hanging around their necks. They appear to
be relaxing. These men have clearly been chosen for their
"ordinary" appearance--far from seeming like slick, highly
paid models, they seem like "plain folks," average-looking
and unkempt. This sends two important messages to the target
audience, beer-drinking men. First, the guys on the screen
are "just like them" and the opinions and expressions of the
people on the screen are just what theirs would be if they
were there, too. Second, the beer company itself is a bunch
of regular Joes--friendly, relaxed, and ordinary. We should
trust them.

In all the scenes showing variously dressed men, one          7
thing remains the same. The emphasis is always on the mouth.
The person being filmed may, at one time or another, have his
nose or eyes or top of his head cut off, but never his mouth.
In fact, as the commercial continues to show these different
men, less of the rest of their bodies is shown, with the camera focusing directly at the subject's mouth, until all that
is shown of one man are his nose and mouth. In the end, the
commercial tells us, nothing else matters--only the means of
drinking and enjoying beer are important.

By the time the commercial reaches its thirteenth dif-        8
ferent scene, it gives its audience a piece of important information: "Coors Extra Gold was judged best premium lager at
the Great American Beer Festival!" The words "best premium
lager," and "Great American Beer Festival," fill the screen.
This phrase serves as a "bandwagon" argument for approving of
(and buying) the beer. A bandwagon argument works like peer
pressure: it tells us that "most people" do something, so we
should, too. In this case, the message is that most people
(or at least the people who matter) have already voted and
decided Coors Extra Gold is the "best." Who are we to disagree? The commercial also implies that it would almost be
unpatriotic not to go along with the crowd: if the beer was
given an award at the "great American" beer festival, then
those who object must be un-American. Thus, the commercial in
thirty seconds has successfully moved from getting the audience's attention, to drawing the audience in, to pressuring
the audience into buying the product.

Bright colors, headlines, implicit connections, disori-    9
entation, deceptive appearance, demanding questions, and
bandwagon arguments: these are the tools that advertisers use
to manipulate us and sell us their products. Yes, some might
say, but this is only one commercial. It is only one commercial, but it is one of the thousands of commercials produced
each year. We as consumers are bombarded with these messages,
and newer, sharper ones continuously replace those that are
worn-out or ineffective. Taken together, commercials form a
persuasive body of propaganda. In a larger sense, it is this
type of propaganda that affects our ideas of who we are and
who we would like to be. In a smaller sense, it is this type
of propaganda that drew my father away from our bet (incidentally, a bet I would have won) and caused me to lose a full
tank of gas.

| | |
|---|---|
| **Questions to Start You Thinking** | *Meaning* |

*Meaning*

1. Do you agree with Brenda Devlin that commercials such as the one for Coors Extra Gold are manipulative? Do you agree that this one is aimed specifically at men?

2. Can you think of other ads that are targeted at specific groups of people?

3. What are some other devices that advertisers use to manipulate consumers?

*Writing Strategies*

4. Why do you think Devlin chose to analyze the Coors Extra Gold commercial? What is the purpose of her analysis?

5. How does Devlin organize her analysis? Can you think of other possible ways of organizing such an analysis? Would those ways be as effective as the organizational pattern Devlin uses?

6. What makes Devlin's introduction effective? Why does she refer to the bet with her father again in the conclusion?

# Learning by Writing

## THE ASSIGNMENT: ANALYZING

Write an essay analyzing a subject — a thing, an idea, or a system — that you know well or want to find out about. Make the subject clear to an audience of your classmates. You will develop a larger purpose as well, some further point that you want to make, like Devlin's purpose of demonstrating that commercials manipulate consumers. Here are instances of college writers who successfully responded to this type of assignment:

A woman who plans a career as a consultant in time and motion study divided a typical day in the life of a college student into the segments that compose it (class time, study time, feeding time, grooming time, recreation time, social time, waste time) and suggested ways for a student to make more efficient use of time.

A student of psychology divided the human brain into its parts and explained the function of each to illustrate the brain's intricate complexity.

A musician analyzed the behavior of the audience at a rap concert to demonstrate his theory that rap concerts cause various types of people to act in an uninhibited manner.

## GENERATING IDEAS

To complete this assignment, you will need to find a subject you care about, determine what you want to say about it, and devise a method for explaining it.

*Find a subject.* The paper topics just listed may help start your own ideas flowing. Do some idle, relaxed thinking, with pencil and paper at hand. Or do some fast scribbling (see "Brainstorming" and "Freewriting," pp. 334–39). Try to come up with something complicated that you understand and would really like to explain to someone else or something you would like to understand more clearly yourself.

*Determine your reason for analyzing.* You want to explain your subject, but what about it do you want to explain? For example, you might want to analyze New York City for the purpose of showing its ethnic composition, or you might want to focus on its social classes. As you develop your paper, you may also find that you have a stronger point to make: that New York City's social hierarchy is oppressive and unstable, for example. Make sure before you begin that your analysis has a purpose: that it will demonstrate something or tell your readers something they didn't know before. Have a reason for analyzing.

*Decide on a principle of division.* Right away, decide on the principle you will follow in your analysis. Just as you can slice a carrot in many ways, you can find many ways to analyze a subject. If you want to explain New York City's ethnic composition, you might divide the city geographically into neighborhoods — Harlem, Spanish Harlem, Yorkville, Chinatown, Little Italy. If you want to explain its social classes, you might start at the bottom with homeless people and work your way up to the cream of society. The way you slice your subject into pieces will depend in part on the point you want to make about it — and the point you end up making will depend in part on how you've sliced it up. In other words, expect to do some fiddling around in the early stages with coming up with the right purpose and method for your analysis. (For more on the strategy of division, see p. 394.)

**DISCOVERY CHECKLIST**

- Have you found a subject that interests you and that seems worthwhile to analyze?
- Exactly what will you be trying to achieve in your essay?
- What is the principle you will follow in your analysis?
- Is your subject clear to you, so that you can make it clear to your readers?
- Can you generate enough details about each aspect of your analysis to write an interesting, informative essay?

## PLANNING, DRAFTING, AND DEVELOPING

Many college assignments call for analysis, and a paper that analyzes a subject often turns out to be among the best essays that a college student writes. The secret is to care about what you say and to organize your essay so that it won't look (and read) like a lifeless stack of blocks. It is crucial to organize your material in some logical, easy-to-follow order. Some kind of outline — whether extremely detailed or rough — will save you time and avoid confusion.

The outline for a subject analysis might be a pielike circle with the slices labeled. If you make the sizes of the slices correspond to their relative importance, the sketch might give you some notion of how much time to spend explaining each part. The pie outline for a paper analyzing the parts of a radio station's twenty-four-hour broadcast day might look like the illustration below. Another way to plan your paper is to arrange your divisions from smallest to largest or from least important to most important — or any other order that makes sense to you. (For more on organizing and outlining, see Chapter 16.)

Pie outline of a radio station's broadcast day

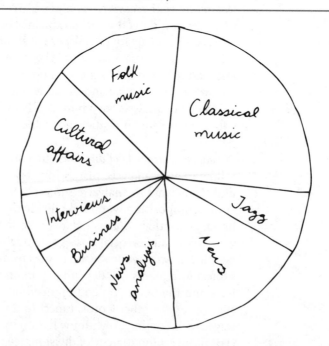

Some writers like to start a subject analysis by telling their readers the divisions into which they are going to slice their subject ("A typical political party has these components . . ." or "The federal government has three branches"). Julius Caesar opens his *Commentaries on the Gallic War* with a famous division: "All Gaul is divided into three parts." That is one clear-cut way to go. Indicate the divisions and subdivisions in your writing so that your readers won't get lost. If you haven't already done so, invent a name or label for each part you mention to distinguish it from all the others. This device will help you keep your material clearly in mind and also help your readers keep the divisions straight. As you draft your essay, provide definitions of unfamiliar words, explain anything your readers may misunderstand, and clarify with examples.

## REVISING AND EDITING

As you revise, you'll find it useful to concentrate on making sure that your essay is meaty enough. If you find places that are thin, expand them with additional details and examples. Look, for instance, at each paragraph of Greenfield's analysis to see how many details and examples from political history she has marshaled to support her points. If on rereading your paper you find any sentence that now strikes you as awkward or murky, perhaps it needs a second try, or perhaps you can do without it altogether.

How can you make sure that your readers will be able to follow your thinking as you analyze? You can make your essay as readable as possible by using transitions, those valuable words and phrases that introduce and connect ideas. Brenda Devlin, for example, begins each paragraph of her analysis with a transitional phrase or sentence that indicates where in the commercial she is: "The first thing I noticed . . . ," "The second picture in the commercial . . . ," "The screen then changes. . . ." (For more on transitions, see p. 380.)

As you revise, you should also make sure that you have applied your principle of division consistently. In other words, the parts you use in your analy-

**WRITING WITH A COMPUTER**

Analysis involves breaking a subject down into its essential parts in order to understand and explain it better. The computer itself is a good example of a subject that makes for a fairly straightforward analysis. If you were analyzing a computer you could begin by typing the name of each of the computer's major components on a different line, creating a vertical list that includes *central processing unit, monitor, disk drives, mouse,* and *keyboard*. Each of these terms could then serve as a heading for a couple of sentences or even a paragraph that describes that component in more detail.

Now try the same technique to help you analyze your subject, regardless of whether the subject is a physical object like a computer or an abstract concept like the political atmosphere of the 1990s. By using a word processor to enter headings first and then filling in description and detail, you establish a logical and methodical framework from which you can construct an analysis.

sis to explain your subject should be similar to one another and equal in importance. If in an analysis of your campus, you have used the categories *students, instructors, service staff,* and *foreign students,* you should probably consider folding *foreign students* in with the other students. You should also ask yourself whether you have left out any obvious parts that a reader might expect to find. Some readers might object to an analysis dividing pop music into rap, rock, and jazz fusion on the grounds that it has a few holes.

As you prepare to write your final draft, ask yourself the following questions. Until you can answer them all to your complete satisfaction, you probably still have more work to do on your analysis.

**REVISION
CHECKLIST**

- Does your introduction engage the reader?
- Have you explained each part completely enough that a reader will understand it?
- Have you shown how each part functions, how it relates to the whole?
- Have you made clear your basis for dividing — the principle on which you sliced?
- Is the purpose of your analysis clear?
- Does your concluding paragraph bring all the separate parts back together and affirm what your dividing has explained?

## OTHER ASSIGNMENTS

1. In an essay, analyze one of the following subjects by dividing it into its basic parts or elements and explaining the purpose and function of each part. Be sure to have a purpose beyond analyzing.

   A college
   A newspaper

**FOR PEER
RESPONSE**

Once you have a legible draft, call on the services of a trustworthy peer editor. See Chapter 20 for advice on working with other student writers and for general questions you should always ask a peer editor to address. For a paper in which you analyze, you'll also want your peer editor to answer these specific questions:

- What seems to be the writer's purpose in this essay? Is the writer successful in achieving that purpose?
- Is the logic behind the writer's principle of division clear to you? Can you make an outline or pie chart that represents the analysis?
- If the writer subdivided, has she or he clearly situated the subdivisions within the larger division? Tell the writer where he or she needs to be clearer.
- Is the paper easy to follow? Are there places where more (or better) transitions are needed?
- Did you learn something from this paper? Is there something important that the writer has left unsaid?
- If this were your paper, what is the one thing you would be sure to work on before handing it in?

A TV talk show
A symphony orchestra
A computer or other technological device
A basketball, football, baseball, or hockey team
An essay, short story, novel, or play
Education
A family
A belief or opinion

2. What point would you want to make in an analysis of each of the following? Write an informative essay analyzing one of them.

The techniques of effective teaching
The aspects of true love
One candidate's political campaign
The gap between generations
The elements of good nutrition
Things to consider in choosing an exercise plan
Excellence
Literacy
Leadership
Individualism
Civil disobedience

3. Analyze the elements of a TV commercial, a political ad, a magazine ad, or a popular device used to manipulate viewers and listeners. (See Brenda Devlin's analysis, p. 000.) What is the purpose of the manipulation?

## *Applying What You Learn: Some Uses of Analysis*

As you have no doubt seen already, many different college courses will give you an opportunity to analyze a subject. In explaining for a political science course how the power structure in Iraq works, you might divide the government into its branches, explain each branch, and then factor in the influence of religion. In a nutrition class, you might submit an essay analyzing the com-

**FOR GROUP LEARNING**

### Collaborating on an Analysis

As a group, write a paper in which you analyze one of the topics suggested in the assignments in this section. Working together, choose a subject for analysis, a purpose for the analysis, and a principle of division. Each member of the group should then take one of the parts to explain independently. Reconvene as a group to work the sections written by individuals into a single paper. As you revise and edit the final draft, consider the advantages and disadvantages of working in a group.

ponents of a healthy diet. In a paper for a course on art history, you might single out each element of a Rembrandt painting: perhaps its human figures, their clothing, the background, the light.

You won't always write papers entirely devoted to analyzing. But you may often find analysis useful in writing *part* of an explanatory paper: a paragraph or a section. In the middle of his essay "Things Unflattened by Science," Lewis Thomas pauses to divide biology into three parts.

> We can imagine three worlds of biology, corresponding roughly to the three worlds of physics: the very small world now being explored by the molecular geneticists and virologists, not yet as strange a place as quantum mechanics but well on its way to strangeness; an everyday, middle-sized world where things are as they are; and a world of the very large, which is the whole affair, the lovely conjoined biosphere, the vast embryo, the closed ecosystem in which we live as working parts, the place for which Lovelock and Margulis invented the term "Gaia" because of its extraordinary capacity to regulate itself. This world seems to me an even stranger one than the world of very small things in biology: it looks like the biggest organism I've ever heard of, and at the same time the most delicate and fragile, exactly the delicate and fragile creature it appeared to be in those first photographs taken from the surface of the moon.

Analysis helps readers understand something complex: they can more readily take in the subject in a series of bites than in one gulp. For this reason, college textbooks do a lot of analyzing: an economics book divides a labor union into its component parts, an anatomy text divides the hand into the bones, muscles, and ligaments that make it up. In *Cultural Anthropology: A Perspective on the Human Condition* (1987), authors Emily A. Schultz and Robert H. Lavenda briefly but effectively demonstrate by analysis how a metaphor like "the Lord is my shepherd" makes a difficult concept ("the Lord") easy to understand.

> The first part of a metaphor, the *metaphorical subject*, indicates the domain of experience that needs to be clarified (e.g., "the Lord"). The second part of a metaphor, the *metaphorical predicate*, suggests a domain of experience which is familiar (e.g., sheep-herding) and which may help us understand what "the Lord" is all about.

You will also find yourself from time to time being called upon to set forth an informative analysis, tracing the steps by which something takes place: the formation of a star, a mountain, or a human embryo; the fall of Rome, the awarding of child custody in a divorce case, or the election of a president. Here is an example from a professional writer of an informative analysis — a passage from *The Perceptual World of the Child* by T. G. R. Bower. The author finds it necessary to stop partway through the chapter he calls "Some Complex Effects of Simple Growth" to explain in brief the workings of the human eye.

Finally we come to the most complex sensory system, the eye and its associated neural structures. The eye is an extremely intricate and complex organ. Light enters the eye through the cornea, passes through the anterior chamber and thence through the pupil to the lens. The lens is a soft transparent tissue that can stretch out and get thinner or shorten and thicken, thus focusing the rays of light and enabling images of objects at different distances to be seen clearly. The lens focuses the light on the retina, which is the thin membrane covering the posterior surface of the eyeball. The nerve cells in the retina itself are sensitive to spots of light. Each nerve cell at the next level of analysis in the brain receives inputs from a number of these retinal nerve cells and responds best to lines or long edges in particular orientations. Numbers of these nerve cells feed into the next level, where nerve cells are sensitive to movement of lines in particular orientations in particular directions. There are other levels that seem sensitive to size, and still others that respond to specific differences in the signals from the two eyes.

As you enter the world of work, you will probably find yourself called upon any number of times to analyze — in lab reports, technical writing of all sorts, business reports and memos, case studies, nursing records, treatment histories, and a host of other kinds of writing, depending on your career. You'll find it immensely useful to know how to analyze and explain to help readers understand better.

# Making Connections:
# Analysis in A Writer's Reader

Writers often use the strategy of *analysis* to help them achieve their purposes, sometimes alone and sometimes in combination with other writing techniques. Analysis is perhaps the most frequently used critical thinking strategy, as illustrated by the authors in *A Writer's Reader*. Stephanie Coontz is a historian and women's studies specialist. In "The Way We Wish We Were: The Complexities of Assessing Family Trends" (p. 484), she analyzes popular assumptions about the American family to support her position that often our beliefs are actually erroneous, simplistic, and incomplete. In "Generation Exit" (p. 598), Alex Ross, music critic, analyzes both the factors that contributed to the career and suicide of Kurt Cobain and the impact of his music and suicide on American culture.

Similar to Meg Greenfield (p. 128), Brenda Devlin (p. 130), Coontz, and Ross, a few other writers who use analysis are poet and professor Judith Ortiz Cofer, "The Myth of the Latin Woman: I Just Met a Girl Named María" (p. 504); American Indian anthropologist and novelist Michael Dorris, "Crazy Horse Malt Liquor" (p. 522); novelist Toni Morrison, "On the Backs of Blacks" (p. 528); lawyer Stephen L. Carter, "The Black Table, the Empty Seat, and the Tie" (p. 567); columnist Ellen Goodman, "The New Hollywood

Male" (p. 577); and satirist Emily Prager, "Our Barbies, Ourselves" (p. 595). As you read these essays, consider the role that analysis plays in them. For each essay, answer the following questions.

1. What idea does the author analyze? For what purpose?
2. How is the analysis related to the writer's occupation or field of interest?
3. What devices does the writer use to make the analysis clear and easy to follow?

# Chapter 7

# Comparing and Contrasting

Which city — Dallas or Atlanta — has more advantages and more drawbacks for a young single person thinking of settling down to a career? How does the IBM personal computer stack up against a Macintosh for word processing? As songwriters, how are Bruce Springsteen and Bob Dylan similar and dissimilar? Such questions invite answers that set two subjects side by side.

When you compare, you point out similarities; when you contrast, you discuss differences. In writing assignments that ask you to deal with two complicated subjects, usually you will need both to compare *and* contrast. Taking Mozart and Bach, you might find that each has traits the other has — or lacks. In writing about the two, you wouldn't have to conclude that one is great and the other inferior. You might look at their differences and similarities and then conclude that they're two distinct composers, each with an individual style. Of course, if you have a preference for either Bach or Mozart, you'll want to voice it. In a paper whose main purpose is to judge between two subjects (as when you'd recommend that a young single person move either to Dallas or to Atlanta), you would look especially for positive and negative features, weigh the attractions of each city and its faults, and then stick your neck out and make your choice. In daily life all of us frequently compare and contrast as when we decide which menu selection to choose or which car (or other product) to buy. Though in everyday thinking we do not usually commit our reasoning to paper, comparing and contrasting are familiar habits of thought.

# Learning from Other Writers

In this chapter you will be asked to write a paper setting two subjects side by side, comparing and contrasting them. Let's see how other writers have used these familiar habits of thought in writing. First is an essay by historian Bruce Catton about two great American generals, Ulysses S. Grant and Robert E. Lee.

The second essay is by Tim Chabot, a student at the University of Virginia. Chabot compares and contrasts the sports of baseball and basketball and asks us to consider which should hold the honor of being our national pastime.

## *Bruce Catton*    Grant and Lee: A Study in Contrasts

When Ulysses S. Grant and Robert E. Lee met in the parlor of a modest house at Appomattox Court House, Virginia, on April 9, 1865, to work out the terms for the surrender of Lee's Army of Northern Virginia, a great chapter in American life came to a close, and a great new chapter began.

These men were bringing the Civil War to its virtual finish. To be sure, other armies had yet to surrender, and for a few days the fugitive Confederate government would struggle desperately and vainly, trying to find some way to go on living now that its chief support was gone. But in effect it was all over when Grant and Lee signed the papers. And the little room where they wrote out the terms was the scene of one of the poignant, dramatic contrasts in American history.

They were two strong men, these oddly different generals, and they represented the strengths of two conflicting currents that, through them, had come into final collision.

Back of Robert E. Lee was the notion that the old aristocratic concept might somehow survive and be dominant in American life.

Lee was tidewater Virginia, and in his background were family, culture, and tradition . . . the age of chivalry transplanted to a New World which was making its own legends and its own myths. He embodied a way of life that had come down through the age of knighthood and the English country squire. America was a land that was beginning all over again, dedicated to nothing much more complicated than the rather hazy belief that all men had equal rights and should have an equal chance in the world. In such a land Lee stood for the feeling that it was somehow of advantage to human society to have a pronounced inequality in the social structure. There should be a leisure class, backed by ownership of land; in turn, society itself should be keyed to the land as the chief source of wealth and influence. It would bring forth (according to this ideal) a class of men with a strong sense of obligation to the community; men who lived not to gain advantage for themselves, but to meet the solemn obligations which had been laid on them by the very fact that they were privileged. From them the country would get its leadership; to them it could look for the higher values — of thought, of conduct, of personal deportment — to give it strength and virtue.

Lee embodied the noblest elements of this aristocratic ideal. Through him, the landed nobility justified itself. For four years, the Southern states had fought a desperate war to uphold the ideals for which Lee stood. In the end, it almost seemed as if the Confederacy fought for Lee; as if he himself was the Confederacy . . . the best thing that the way of life for which the Confederacy stood could ever have to offer. He had passed into legend before Appomattox. Thousands of tired, underfed, poorly clothed Confederate soldiers, long since past the simple enthusiasm of the early days of the struggle, somehow considered Lee the symbol of everything for which they had been willing to die. But they could not quite put this feeling into words. If the Lost Cause, sanctified by so much heroism and so many deaths, had a living justification, its justification was General Lee. 6

Grant, the son of a tanner on the Western frontier, was everything Lee was not. He had come up the hard way and embodied nothing in particular except the eternal toughness and sinewy fiber of the men who grew up beyond the mountains. He was one of a body of men who owed reverence and obeisance to no one, who were self-reliant to a fault, who cared hardly anything for the past but who had a sharp eye for the future. 7

These frontier men were the precise opposites of the tidewater aristocrats. Back of them, in the great surge that had taken people over the Alleghenies and into the opening Western country, there was a deep, implicit dissatisfaction with a past that had settled into grooves. They stood for democracy, not from any reasoned conclusion about the proper ordering of human society, but simply because they had grown up in the middle of democracy and knew how it worked. Their society might have privileges, but they would be privileges each man had won for himself. Forms and patterns meant nothing. No man was born to anything, except perhaps a chance to show how far he could rise. Life was competition. 8

Yet along with this feeling had come a deep sense of belonging to a national community. The Westerner who developed a farm, opened a shop, or set up in business as a trader, could hope to prosper only as his own community prospered — and his community ran from the Atlantic to the Pacific and from Canada down to Mexico. If the land was settled, with towns and highways and accessible markets, he could better himself. He saw his fate in terms of the nation's own destiny. As its horizons expanded, so did his. He had, in other words, an acute dollars-and-cents stake in the continued growth and development of his country. 9

And that, perhaps, is where the contrast between Grant and Lee becomes most striking. The Virginia aristocrat, inevitably, saw himself in relation to his own region. He lived in a static society which could endure almost anything except change. Instinctively, his first loyalty would go to the locality in which that society existed. He would fight to the limit of endurance to defend it, because in defending it he was defending everything that gave his own life its deepest meaning. 10

The Westerner, on the other hand, would fight with an equal tenacity for    11
the broader concept of society. He fought so because everything he lived by
was tied to growth, expansion, and a constantly widening horizon. What he
lived by would survive or fall with the nation itself. He could not possibly
stand by unmoved in the face of an attempt to destroy the Union. He would
combat it with everything he had, because he could only see it as an effort to
cut the ground out from under his feet.

So Grant and Lee were in complete contrast, representing two diametri-    12
cally opposed elements in American life. Grant was the modern man emerging; beyond him, ready to come on the stage, was the great age of steel and
machinery; of crowded cities and a restless burgeoning vitality. Lee might
have ridden down from the old age of chivalry, lance in hand, silken banner
fluttering over his head. Each man was the perfect champion of his cause,
drawing both his strengths and his weaknesses from the people he led.

Yet it was not all contrast, after all. Different as they were — in back-    13
ground, in personality, in underlying aspiration — these two great soldiers
had much in common. Under everything else, they were marvelous fighters.
Furthermore, their fighting qualities were really very much alike.

Each man had, to begin with, the great virtue of utter tenacity and fidelity.    14
Grant fought his way down the Mississippi Valley in spite of acute personal
discouragement and profound military handicaps. Lee hung on in the
trenches at Petersburg after hope itself had died. In each man there was an indomitable quality . . . the born fighter's refusal to give up as long as he can
still remain on his feet and lift his two fists.

Daring and resourcefulness they had, too; the ability to think faster and    15
move faster than the enemy. These were the qualities which gave Lee the dazzling campaigns of Second Manassas and Chancellorsville and won Vicksburg
for Grant.

Lastly, and perhaps greatest of all, there was the ability, at the end, to turn    16
quickly from war to peace once the fighting was over. Out of the way these
two men behaved at Appomattox came the possibility of a peace of reconciliation. It was a possibility not wholly realized, in the years to come, but which
did, in the end, help the two sections to become one nation again . . . after a
war whose bitterness might have seemed to make such a reunion wholly impossible. No part of either man's life became him more than the part he
played in this brief meeting in the McLean house at Appomattox. Their behavior there put all succeeding generations of Americans in their debt. Two
great Americans, Grant and Lee — very different, yet under everything very
much alike. Their encounter at Appomattox was one of the great moments of
American history.

**Questions to Start**
**You Thinking**

*Meaning*

1. Catton in this essay describes two very different men. In what ways were
   Grant and Lee different? How were they similar?

2. How do the two personalities symbolize the struggle of the American Civil War?

3. Do the ways of thinking and living represented by Grant and Lee still exist today?

*Writing Strategies*

4. What techniques does Catton use to describe Grant and Lee?

5. The author ends the essay by showing how Grant and Lee were comparable. Why does he place their differences first? In your opinion, which are stronger — the similarities or the differences of the two men? Does Catton give proper proportion to both the similarities and the differences?

6. Catton compares and contrasts the two men, but he does not judge who was the better general. What, then, is his purpose in the essay, if not to say one general was better than the other?

STUDENT ESSAY

## *Tim Chabot*   Take Me Out to the Ball Game, but Which One?

For much of the twentieth century baseball has been considered the national pastime of the United States. Hank Aaron, home runs, and hot dogs seem as American as Thanksgiving. Many American presidents, from Eisenhower to Clinton, have participated in the tradition of a celebrity throwing out the first ball on opening day of a new baseball season. But in the 1990s, baseball stars are being eclipsed by the stars of another game invented in America--basketball. Michael Jordan and Shaquille O'Neal, basketball greats and household names, have become more famous than any current pitcher or home run king. In addition, the 1994-95 baseball strike has pushed the sport further out of the limelight, since the public has become disillusioned with the greed of both players and managers. The strike has raised a question in the minds of many: Should baseball continue to be considered our national pastime, or should basketball take its place?

Both sports have a wide appeal with American sports fans. Baseball has become a national treasure through its appeal to a wide, wide audience. At a Saturday afternoon game, men, women, grandparents, and kids of all ages wait to catch a fly ball. The appeal of basketball is growing, having become popular in urban and rural areas, on high school and college campuses. Both sports are played in quite a variety of locations. Baseball games occur on neighborhood sandlots as well as official diamonds. Basketball requires little space and equipment, so pickup basketball games occur in almost every neighborhood park and virtually anywhere that a hoop can be rigged up. In addition, both games attract fans of all races--white, African American, Asian American, Hispanic--and all classes, rich and poor, educated and uneducated. While baseball's popularity may be waning because of so much bad publicity and the strike, basketball's popularity is on the rise because of the increase in television coverage of college leagues as well as of the professional National Basketball Association.

Although both sports are popular with American fans, attending a baseball game is quite different from attending a basketball game. Baseball is a family-oriented spectator sport. Because of the widely diverse baseball fans with varied interests and attention spans, the experience of going to a baseball game can be compared to that of an open-air carnival, in which the game itself is only one of the many spectacles. If fans are bored with the game, they can listen to the vendors hawking ice cream, watch a fight brewing in the bleacher seats, stand in line to buy peanuts or hot dogs, participate in "the wave," or just bask in the sun. Only diehard fans keep a constant eye on the game itself since there are frequent breaks in the play.

In contrast, the central spectacle of any basketball arena is definitely the game itself because the constant motion of the sport rivets attention. Few distractions to entertain a casual fan occur, except for cheerleaders for college teams. Basketball arenas are always indoors and the games are usually at night, creating an atmosphere that is urban and adult. Attending a basketball game can be compared to an exciting night on the town, while watching a baseball game is like relaxing with the family in the backyard.

The pace of the two games is also quite different. The leisurely pace of a baseball game contributes to its popularity because it offers relaxation to harried Americans. Each batter may spend several minutes at the plate, hit a few foul balls, and reach a full count of three balls and two strikes before getting on base, hitting a routine pop fly, or striking out. While batters slow things down by stepping out of the box to practice their swing, pitchers stall the play by "holding the runners on" to prevent stolen bases. The substitution of relief pitchers suspends the game and gives spectators an opportunity to purchase junk food or memorabilia. In games in which star pitchers duel, the audience may see only a few men on base in nine innings and a very low score. Also, the tradition of the seventh-inning stretch underscores baseball's appeal to a person who wants to take it easy and relax.

On the other hand, the quick pace of basketball has contributed to its popularity in our fast-paced society. Players run down the court at sometimes exhausting speed for a "fast break," successful baskets can occur merely seconds apart, each team may score as many as one hundred points a game, and the ball changes sides hundreds of times, as opposed to every half-inning in baseball. Games can be won or lost in the few seconds before the final buzzer. Basketball players are always in motion, much like American society. The pounding excitement of basketball appeals to people who play hard as well as work hard.                                                                    6

These two sports require different athletic abilities from the players. Although baseball games are slow-paced, the sport places a premium on athletic precision and therefore showcases strategy and skill rather than brute physical strength. The choice of a pitch, the decision to bunt or to steal a base, and the order of batters are all careful strategic moves that could affect the outcome of the whole game. Baseball has been called the "thinking person's game" because of its emphasis on statistics and probabilities. Although mental strategy and dexterity are emphasized, physical strength is not unimportant to the sport. A strong arm obviously increases the power of a player's throw or of his swing, and speed is essential in running bases. But intimidating physical ability is not necessarily a required element    7 to become a major league player, and even out-of-shape players can become stars if their bats are hot. The importance of skill over brawn has contributed to baseball's popularity not merely as a spectator sport, but also as a sport in which millions of Americans participate, from Little League to neighborhood leagues for adults.

Unlike baseball, basketball emphasizes physical power, stamina, and size since jumping high, running fast, and just being tall with long legs and big hands usually contribute to a player's success. Skill and dexterity, however, are certainly necessary in executing a slam dunk or dribbling past a double team, but these skills are usually combined with physical strength. In order to be a successful rebounder, a player needs to be extremely aggressive and occasionally commit fouls. Many more injuries occur on basketball courts than on baseball fields. Perhaps the physical power and intimidation required in basketball have led to the media's focus on individual players' star qualities. Magic, Bird, Jordan, and Shaq are icons who have taken the place of baseball stars of previous generations like Joe DiMaggio, Ted Williams, and Babe Ruth. Furthermore, in the international arena of the Olympics, basketball came to be seen as a symbol of American strength and power, as the 1992 Dream Team demolished all of its opponents.

8

If the rest of the world now equates basketball with America, should we consider it to be our true national pastime? The increasing popularity of basketball seems to reflect the change in American society in the past few decades, a change to a more fast-paced and aggressive culture. But basketball doesn't yet appeal to as diverse an audience as does baseball, and thus it doesn't seem to deserve to be called a national phenomenon--yet. Until kids, women, and grandparents are as prevalent at a Lakers game as are young males, baseball will retain its title as the national pastime. But when the leisurely pace of the baseball game grinds to a halt because of players' strikes, impatient fans may turn to the exciting speed of basketball to rejuvenate their faith in American sports.

9

*Meaning*

1. In what specific ways does Chabot claim that baseball and basketball are similar? In what ways are these two sports different? Do the similarities outweigh the differences, or vice versa?

2. Can you think of other ways these two sports are similar and different?

3. As a result of comparing and contrasting baseball and basketball, what conclusion does Chabot arrive at? Does he convince you of his conclusion?

4. Would you nominate another sport, say football or ice hockey, for the national pastime? Why?

*Writing Strategies*

5. What is Chabot's thesis? Where does he state it? Why there?

6. How does Chabot organize his essay?

7. What transitional devices does Chabot use to indicate when he is comparing and when he is contrasting?

# Learning by Writing

## THE ASSIGNMENT: COMPARING AND CONTRASTING

Write a paper in which you compare and contrast two items for the general purpose of enlightening readers about both subjects. The specific points of similarity and difference will be important, but you will go beyond just comparing and contrasting to draw a conclusion from your analysis of the similarities and differences. This conclusion will be your thesis, and it will be more than "point A is different from point B" or "I prefer subject B to subject A." You will need to explain why you have drawn the conclusion you have and to provide sufficient specific supporting evidence to explain your position to your readers and to convince them of the soundness of your conclusion. You may choose two people, two kinds of people, two places, two things, two activities, or two ideas. Be sure to choose two subjects you care about. Like Bruce Catton, you might write an impartial paper that distinctly portrays both subjects, or like Tim Chabot, you might demonstrate why you favor one over the other.

Although the subjects should differ enough to throw each other into sharp relief, be sure they have enough in common to compare. A comparison of sports cars and racing cars might reveal much, but a comparison of sports cars and oil tankers would probably reveal little.

Among the most engaging and instructive recent student papers we've seen in response to similar assignments are these:

An American woman compared and contrasted her home life with that of her roommate, a student from Nigeria. Her goal was to understand more deeply Nigerian society and her own.

A man who had read some articles and books about comets contrasted the spectacular fly-by of Halley's Comet in 1910 with its less spectacular return in 1985–1986. He also compared and contrasted public responses to the comet's two twentieth-century appearances. He concluded that the comet's latest performance had not really been a flop.

For an economics course that asked for an explanation of a major idea of influential economist John Maynard Keynes, a woman compared and contrasted Keynes's views of the causes of monetary inflation with those of Karl Marx on the same subject, concluding that Keynes's theories are more relevant today.

A man compared the differences between traveling by airline and traveling by train. His purpose was to make a case for the continuation of intercontinental passenger rail service.

## GENERATING IDEAS

*Find two subjects.*  Pick subjects you can compare and contrast purposefully. An examination question may give them to you, ready-made: "Compare and contrast ancient Roman sculpture with that of the ancient Greeks" or "Discuss the main differences between the British system of higher education and the American system." But suppose you have to find your subjects for yourself. You'll need to choose things that can sensibly be compared and contrasted. Find a basis for comparison, a common element. There is probably no point in comparing and contrasting moon rocks and stars, but it will make sense to bring together Springsteen and Dylan *as songwriters,* Dallas and Atlanta *as cities to consider settling in,* or Karl Barth and Søren Kierkegaard *as religious thinkers.*

Try generating a list of what you might like to compare and contrast. Try a little *brainstorming* (see p. 334). Let your mind skitter around in search of pairs that go together. Write them down in two columns as you think of them. Consult your trusty writer's resources: Have you experienced, seen, or read anything lately that suggests a suitable subject? Have you talked to someone who reminds you of someone else or imagined a possibility that contrasts starkly with reality? You might find it useful to ask yourself the following questions.

**DISCOVERY CHECKLIST**

- Do you know two people who are strikingly different in attitude or behavior? (Perhaps your parents, or two brothers, two friends, two teachers)
- Can you think of two groups of people who are both alike and different? (Perhaps two football teams or two clubs)
- Have you taken two courses that were both valuable to you although they were quite different?
- Can you describe two places you have lived or two places you have visited? Do you prefer one over the other?
- Can you recall two events in your life that shared some similar aspects but

turned out to be quite different? (Perhaps two sporting events or two romances or the birth of two children)

- Can you compare and contrast two holidays or two family customs that you are familiar with? What would be your point in setting this pair side by side?
- Are you familiar with two writers, two artists, or two musicians who seem to have similar goals but quite different accomplishments?
- Have you studied two interesting historical figures whom you can understand better by comparing and contrasting them? (If you choose this topic for writing, you will probably have to do some review and additional reading about the two people.)
- Are you familiar with two ideas or schools of thought ("-isms") that seem strikingly different in basic principles or in effects? (Perhaps two economic theories such as capitalism and communism, two literary movements such as classicism and romanticism, or two religious groups such as Christians and Buddhists)

You can also play the game of *free association*, jotting down whatever comes to mind as you think. Write down a word, and then write down whatever comes to mind when you think of that word. What comes to mind when you write *mothers*? *Fathers* perhaps. *Democrats*? *Republicans*. *New York*? *Los Angeles*. *King Kong*? *Godzilla*. *High school*? *College*. Or whatever.

Once you have a list of pairs, go through the list and put a star by those pairs that seem promising. Ask yourself what similarities immediately come to mind. What differences? Can you think of several of each? If not, move on to another pair. As you think, write down the points of comparison for the two subjects. Then write down the points of contrast. (You may have the beginnings of a useful outline.) Review your list, and ask yourself if these are striking, significant similarities and differences. If not, keep on thinking and jotting until you discover a pair you think will work.

*Find a purpose.* You need a reason to place two subjects side by side — a reason that you and most of your readers will find compelling and worthwhile. After you have selected your pair, ask yourself if you prefer one subject in the pair over the other. And ask yourself why you have this preference. What reasons can you give for your preference? It's all right not to have a preference. Bruce Catton isn't arguing that Robert E. Lee is superior to Ulysses S. Grant, or vice versa. Instead, he shows how each throws the other into sharp relief and helps us understand both generals as well as the effects of their personalities and actions better. You may take either approach for your paper.

You also need to determine what point you want to make by your comparison and contrast of the two subjects. Bruce Catton wanted to show how the meeting of these two great men made a peace of reconciliation possible after such a bitter civil struggle between the states. Tim Chabot wanted to explore the question of whether we should continue to consider baseball our national pastime. In his freshman writing course, Eli Kavon, who had spent some time studying at an Israeli military seminary, wrote an account of his experience for the information of his instructor and classmates. In part of this account, he compared and contrasted himself (and the other American Jewish students in Israel) with Israeli students:

> We — the foreigners — had much in common with our Israeli contemporaries: a history dating back thousands of years, a belief in one God, a love of Judaism and the land of Israel. However, we would be in the country only for a year or two and would not be drafted with the Israelis, who devote two of five years in the seminary to military service. Unlike the average Israeli, none of us had grown up in a household where real weapons rested in closets and on top of refrigerators, ready for use. American teenagers know of war either as a childhood game with plastic weapons or as a memory of the battles and the body bags of a "television war." Israelis, on the other hand, have been forced to live a life of drafts, weapons, and fear. In Israel preparation for war is the norm.

As you can see from this passage, Kavon's comparing and contrasting is no meaningless exercise. It is a way to think clearly and pointedly in order to explain an idea about which the writer cares deeply.

*Limit the scope of your paper.* If you propose to write a comparison and contrast between Japanese literature and American literature in 750 words, probably you will be tackling an impossible task. To explore this topic thoroughly, you might need to write a whole book. But to cut down the size of this promising subject, you might propose to compare and contrast, say, a haiku of Basho about a snake with a short poem about a snake by Emily Dickinson. You would then be dealing with a topic you could cover adequately in 750 words. Of course, the larger and more abstract topic might be manageable — if you had much time to read and more space to develop the ideas.

*Explore each member of your pair.* Now that you have a pair of subjects and a purpose in mind and have limited your scope, you'll need to examine in depth each of your two subjects. Your goal is twofold: you want to analyze each subject using a similar approach so that you have a reasonable basis for comparison and contrast, and you want to find the details and examples that you'll need to support your points.

If you are considering writing about two events, procedures, or processes, try asking yourself a reporter's questions — the five *W*'s and an *H* that journalists use. (See p. 342). Make two columns, and write your answers to the following questions opposite each other.

Who was there?
What happened?
Where did the event take place?
When did it happen?
Why did the event occur?
How did the event or events happen?

If you are considering writing about two events from the past, try using the resource of *conversation* to generate material: discuss what happened at each event with someone else who was there. Or if you want to write about what goes on behind the scenes in the locker rooms of two professional football teams, talk to someone who has been there. When you talk to these people, go prepared with specific questions you want answers to, and ask both people the same questions so that you can compare and contrast the same points. If you don't, you will have some gaps in your information, and you may need to go back to talk to one or both at a later time. What will you do if they don't have time to talk to you again? (For more on using the resource of conversation, see Chapter 4.)

You can also try *reading*. Perhaps you can think of two possible subjects to compare and contrast, but you are not sure that the pair will work or you may not know quite enough about them to write a full essay. Go to the library and read a few articles about the subjects to test the possibility of your potential pair.

If your immediate answers to the reporter's questions are skimpy, or if you're less interested in your subjects than you thought you'd be, you may want to pick a new pair and start again. Or it may be that with a little more imagination, some reading, observing, conversing, or recalling, you'll find you've made a good choice after all.

## PLANNING, DRAFTING, AND DEVELOPING

Now that you are about to start writing your whole paper, remind yourself once more that in comparing and contrasting two subjects, you have a goal. What is it you want to demonstrate, argue, or find out?

When you write a draft, an outline isn't always necessary. If you are setting forth something you can hold clearly in mind (such as a personal experience, written from recall), you may find you work best by just taking off and letting words flow. You may find you can compare and contrast without outlining. But in comparing and contrasting, most writers find that some planning helps speed the job. For one thing, an outline — even a rough scratch outline — enables you to keep track of all the points you want to make, which so easily may be lost or confused as you glance from side to side. You can make an outline in your head, of course, but it is probably easier to keep track of things on paper. (For more on outlines, see p. 358.)

In comparing and contrasting, two ways of organizing are possible. The first way is the *opposing pattern* of *subject by subject*. You state all your observations about subject A and then do the same for subject B. The book *Educational Policies in Crisis: Japanese and American Perspectives* (New York: Praeger, 1986) is a collection of essays analyzing and evaluating the Japanese and American educational systems. In Chapter 15, "Learning from Each Other," William K. Cummings and others, the editors of the book, use the opposing pattern to compare and contrast how the two countries think about education.

More salient, however, than these structural characteristics is the way that the two nations think about education. The United States fosters a myth of limitless opportunity. Football players can earn more than corporation presidents, and the local shoe store of today has the possibility of becoming one of *Fortune*'s Top 100 in 20 years. School is but one of several routes to success. For the individual who seeks the educational route, being a late bloomer is not necessarily an obstacle to upward mobility. Thus even when they enter college, many Americans have poorly developed intellectual skills. Most Americans are also relaxed about choosing their educational institutions, believing that what happens outside school and later in life may have more influence on their chances for success than what takes place in school. In contrast with the American belief in limitless opportunity, the Japanese assign great importance to a small number of career choices in the central government bureaucracy and the top corporations. They rank other careers in descending order and assume that an individual's educational performance will determine where he or she ends up in this hierarchy. Most Japanese parents seek to manage the lives of their children, from a surprisingly young age, so that the children will have the best chances of entering the top careers. Because admission to a prestigious university is known to be essential for gaining access to these attractive careers, parents are deeply concerned with the educational performance of their children. They exert every effort to ensure that their children earn good grades and enter the best schools. The large number of parents sharing this common belief results in severe academic competition. In contrast to Americans, Japanese children develop from an early age a realistic sense of the opportunities they can expect as they grow up.

In this paragraph, following the first sentence, the editors discuss the American attitude toward education (subject A), beginning with the sentence "The United States fosters a myth of limitless opportunity." Then they explain the American attitude toward the relationship of education to career opportunities and toward choice of educational institutions. In the middle of the paragraph they announce a shift with the phrase "In contrast" and present information about the Japanese attitude toward education. Using the same order as for subject A, they discuss first the attitude toward career opportunities and then toward educational institutions. This pattern of organization is a workable method for writing a single paragraph or a short essay, but for a long essay or a more complicated subject, it has a drawback. Readers might find it difficult to remember all the separate information about subject A while reading about subject B.

There's a better way to organize most longer papers: the *alternating pattern* of *point by point*. Working by this method, you take up one point at a time, applying it first to one subject and then to the other. Both Bruce Catton and Tim Chabot use this pattern of organization. It is the more appropriate method for complicated subjects and full-blown essays. Looking at each subject before moving on to the next point, Catton leads the reader along clearly and carefully. His outline might have looked like this:

Thesis:    The encounter of Grant and Lee at Appomattox was one of the great moments of American history.

   I.  Differences in personal qualities of Lee and Grant [paragraphs 3–12]
     A.  Different ways of life
       1.  Lee's old aristocratic concept of life
         a.  His background
         b.  His view of America
       2.  Grant's new frontier concept of life
         a.  His background
         b.  His view of America
     B.  Different views of self in relation to the war
       1.  Lee
       2.  Grant
     C.  Representatives of opposing elements in American life
       1.  Grant as the man of the future
       2.  Lee as the man of the past
  II.  Similarities in leadership qualities of Lee and Grant [paragraphs 13–16]
     A.  Similarities as generals during the war
       1.  Tenacity and fidelity
         a.  Grant
         b.  Lee
       2.  Daring and resourcefulness
         a.  Lee
         b.  Grant
     B.  Ability to turn from war to peace when fighting was over

Without even outlining, you can sometimes follow the point-by-point method informally. Mystery writer Raymond Chandler, for an essay likening English people and Americans (which he left unfinished in his notebooks), wrote this opening paragraph. It probably didn't require any outline at all.

> The keynote of American civilization is a sort of warm-hearted vulgarity. The Americans have none of the irony of the English, none of their cool poise, none of their manner. But they do have friendliness. Where an Englishman would give you his card, an American would very likely give you his shirt.

In its blast-off sentence, the paragraph announces its main idea. Then Chandler proceeds to compare the English and the Americans in two ways: (1) in manner, cool or friendly, and (2) in generosity. Like all generalizations about groups of people, this one can be shot full of holes; but Chandler's paragraph states a memorable insight. A comparison and contrast can explain things neatly and intelligently, even though (like a one-paragraph description of Japanese and American literature) it might stereotype the particulars.

In developing a meaty essay that compares and contrasts, an outline, however sketchy, will be your trusty friend. Keep your outline simple, and don't be ruled by it. If excellent thoughts come to you in writing your first draft, by all means let them in.

Before you begin to draft your essay, you may need to do a bit more thinking to come up with enough details about your two subjects to write a good essay of comparison and contrast. If so, try brainstorming (p. 334) or freewriting (p. 337) again, this time specifically about the pair of subjects you have selected. Then go back over the details you have generated to eliminate any weak points (perhaps those that force the comparison or contrast) and to

**FOR PEER RESPONSE**

You may find it helpful to ask a classmate to read and respond to your draft. See Chapter 20 for advice on working with other student writers and for general questions you should always ask a peer editor to address. For a paper in which you compare and contrast, you'll also want your peer editor to answer these specific questions:

- Does the introduction make you want to read the entire essay?
- Is the point of the comparison and contrast of the two subjects clear to you? What is that point? Does the writer state it in the essay, or is it implied?
- Is the essay organized by the opposing pattern or by the alternating pattern? Would the other pattern work better for the topic, or is the pattern used the more appropriate?
- Are the same categories discussed for each item? If not, should they be?
- Are there sufficient details to allow you to understand the comparison and contrast? Put a check mark anywhere that more details or examples would be useful.
- Does the paper avoid falling into a tedious singsong pattern? Are the transitions varied and helpful?
- If this were your paper, what is the one thing you would be sure to work on before handing it in?

**WRITING WITH A COMPUTER**

In Chapter 6, on analyzing, you focused on breaking a subject down into its component parts. Comparison and contrast is a type of analysis, only now you are examining a number of things instead of just one subject — and a word processor can help immensely with this complex type of writing. Begin by writing on a word processor an analysis of one of the items you will compare. For example, to begin a comparison between surfing and badminton using this approach, first write an analysis of surfing. Describe each of the major components of surfing by using headings such as *equipment, technique, fashion, rules, environment,* and *attitude.* Add thorough descriptions beneath each of the headings, leaving lots of white space between divisions. Then go back and add descriptions of badminton under the same headings so that you generate contrasting pictures. At first, your comparison may not be balanced, and some of your original divisions may need to be rearranged or discarded if they don't produce revealing contrasts. But the beauty of word processing is that it encourages you to try different configurations and make sweeping changes.

add specifics in any sections that might be underdeveloped. You may also draw upon a writer's resources again here — recall, observation, reading, conversation, and imagination — to flesh out your ideas.

## REVISING AND EDITING

As you look over your early draft, you'll want to be sure that each comparison or contrast you include discusses similar elements. You'll only confuse your readers if, in considering the merits of two cities, you contrast New York's public transportation with Milwaukee's tree-lined streets; or if, in setting Springsteen and Dylan side by side, you deal with Springsteen's fondness for pizza and Dylan's politics. Go through your draft with a fine-tooth comb to make sure that at every point you compare or contrast, you are looking at the same feature.

If your purpose in writing is to illuminate two subjects impartially, you can ask yourself if you have given your reader a balanced view. Although you might well have more to say about one than about the other, obviously it would be unfair to set forth all the advantages of Oklahoma City and all the disadvantages of Honolulu and then conclude that Oklahoma City is superior to Honolulu on every count. If you haven't been fair, you may need to replan — perhaps make a new outline — and do some more discovering. (One useful way to tell whether you have done a thorough job of comparing and contrasting is to make an outline of your first draft and then give the outline a critical squint. See p. 155.)

Of course, if you love Oklahoma City and can't stand Honolulu, or vice versa, go ahead, don't be balanced, take a stand. Even so, you will want to include the same points about each city and to admit, in all honesty, that Oklahoma City, unlike Eden, has its faults.

Make sure, too, as you go over your draft, that you have escaped falling into a monotonous drone: A does this, B does that; A looks like this, B looks like that; A has these advantages, B has those. Comparison and contrast is a useful method, but it needn't result in a paper as symmetrical as a pair of sneakers. Revising and editing gives you a chance to add any lively details, varied transitions, interesting later thoughts, dashes of color, finishing touches that (with any luck) may occur to you.

In critiquing your draft as you rewrite, this checklist may prove handy.

**REVISION CHECKLIST**

- Have you chosen the *major* similarities and differences to write about?
- Is your reason for doing all the comparing and contrasting unmistakably clear? If not, your paper will seem an arbitrary exercise conducted in outer space. Do you need to reexamine your goal? What is it you want to demonstrate, argue for, or find out?
- Have you used the same categories for each item? In discussing each feature, do you always look at the very same thing?
- Have you come to a conclusion about the two? Do you prefer one over the other? If so, is this preference (and your reasons for it) clear?

- If you are making a judgment between your subjects, do you feel you have treated both fairly?
- Does your draft look thin for lack of evidence? If so, from which resources might you draw more?
- Have you avoided a boringly mechanical, monotonous style ("On one hand, . . . now on the other hand")?
- Have you given some attention to your introduction? Does it introduce your topic and main point clearly? Is it interesting enough to make you want to read the whole essay?

## OTHER ASSIGNMENTS

1. Choose two historical or literary figures, and write an essay in which you compare and contrast them as Catton did in his essay "Grant and Lee." Be sure to bring the two into sharp relief, and have a purpose other than merely recounting the similarities and differences.

2. Listen to two different recordings of the same piece of music as performed by two different orchestras (or groups or singers). What elements of the music does each performer stress? What contrasting attitudes toward the music do you detect? In an essay, compare and contrast these versions.

3. Write an essay in which you compare and contrast the subjects in any of the following pairs, for the purpose of throwing light on both. In a short paper, you can hope to trace only a few similarities and differences, but don't hesitate to use your own recall or observation, go to the library, or converse with a friendly expert if you need material.

   Women and men as single parents

   Living at home and living away from home

   Japanese and American workers

   The coverage of a world event on a television newscast and in a newspaper

**FOR GROUP LEARNING**

## Comparing and Contrasting Yourself with a Partner

Work with a partner to develop a single comparison and contrast essay for assignment 4 in this section. Decide together what the focus of your essay will be: Your family backgrounds? Your hobbies? Your career goals? Your study habits? Your taste in music or clothes? Your political beliefs? Then each partner should work alone to generate a detailed analysis of himself or herself, given this focus. Come together again to compare your analyses; to decide what shape the essay should take; and to draft, revise, and edit the paper.

The state of AIDS research at two moments in time: ten years ago and today

Alexander Hamilton and Thomas Jefferson: their ideas of the role of the federal government

The playing styles of two major league pitchers (or two quarterbacks or two basketball players)

Cubist painting and abstract expressionist painting

English and another language

Your college and a rival college

Two differing views of a current controversy

Classic French cooking and nouvelle cuisine

*The Odyssey* and *The Iliad* (or F. Scott Fitzgerald's *The Great Gatsby* and Earnest Hemingway's *The Sun Also Rises*, or Walt Whitman's poem "To a Locomotive in Winter" and Emily Dickinson's poem about a locomotive "I like to see it lap the Miles," or two other comparable works of literature)

Northern California and southern California (or two other regions)

The experience of watching a film on a VCR and in a theater

Euclidean and non-Euclidean geometry

Two similar works of architecture (two churches, two skyscrapers, two city halls, two museums)

4. In an essay either serious or nonserious, for the purpose of introducing yourself to other members of your class, compare and contrast yourself with someone else. You and this other person should have much in common: no sense comparing and contrasting yourself with Napoleon ("I admit to having less skill on the battlefield"). You might choose either a real person or a character in a film, a TV series, a novel, a comic strip. Choose a few points of comparison (an attitude, a habit, a way of life) and deal with each. Feel free to draw on your reading, your conversation with him or her (or with a mutual friend), your own observations, your imagination (what might it be like to be the other person?).

# Applying What You Learn: Some Uses of Comparing and Contrasting

Because comparing and contrasting shows a reader how closely writers observe and how hard they think, comparison and contrast questions are great favorites on college essay exams of many kinds. In a nursing course you might be asked to compare and contrast earlier methods of treating heart attack victims with those that prevail today. At times, the examiner won't even mention the method of comparison and contrast by name. But when you get a request such as "Evaluate the relative merits of Norman Rockwell and Andrew Wyeth as realistic painters" (for a course in American art history) or "Consider the tax consequences of doing business as a small corporation and doing business as a partnership. How are they different, or similar?" (in a course in business law), then you can bet your bottom dollar that to compare and contrast is what the examiner hopes you will do.

Sometimes, in an exam or paper, you are asked to describe a person, a thing, or a scene. One good way to approach your response is to recall the useful method of comparison and contrast and to portray your subject by setting it next to something else, something similar but a little different. If asked to describe, for instance, a Cape Cod–style house, you might most clearly reveal its distinctive features by comparing and contrasting it with a Dutch colonial. Or you might explain the protagonist of a literary selection by comparing or contrasting him or her to a contrasting foil character (for example, Othello and Iago in the Shakespearean play, or Tessie Hutchinson and Old Man Warner in "The Lottery" by Shirley Jackson; see p. 250).

Often in your college writing, when you're called on to analyze, define, or argue, you'll find it useful, as Catton does, to use comparison, contrast, or both to make a point, even though your paper's main purpose may be other than comparing and contrasting. Although Bruce Catton in his essay compares and contrasts throughout, he also has another purpose. He is trying to explain how both of these great generals contributed to American history. In an essay called "How to Make People Smaller Than They Are," Norman Cousins's purpose is to deplore "the increasing vocationalization of our colleges and universities." But in one paragraph in that essay, Cousins introduces a series of contrasts to strengthen his argument:

> The irony of the emphasis being placed on careers is that nothing is more valuable for anyone who has had a professional or vocational education than to be able to deal with abstractions or complexities, or to feel comfortable with subtleties of thought or language, or to think sequentially. The doctor who knows only disease is at a disadvantage alongside the doctor who knows at least as much about people as he does about pathological organisms. The lawyer who argues in court from a narrow legal base is no match for the lawyer who can connect legal precedents to historical experience and who employs wide-ranging intellectual resources. The business executive whose competence in general management is bolstered by an artistic ability to deal with people is of prime value to his company. For the technologist, the engineering of consent can be just as important as the engineering of moving parts. In all these respects, the liberal arts have much to offer. Just in terms of career preparation, therefore, a student is shortchanging himself by shortcutting the humanities.

In the sentence about the business executive, for variety's sake the contrast is implied rather than stated. Readers armed with the contrasts Cousins has already imagined have no difficulty inferring that this ideal business executive, like the liberally educated doctor and lawyer before him, has a less desirable counterpart: a business executive whose schooling has given him nothing more than job training.

Cousins, it would seem, directs his argument to a general audience. Let's look at two brief illustrations of comparing and contrasting found in writing more specialized and scholarly. William Broad and Nicholas Wade, in *Betrayers of the Truth: Fraud and Deceit in the Halls of Science* (New York: Simon, 1982), a book-length study of scientists who have faked evidence in order to claim fictitious discoveries, contrast two influential opinions of what it is that keeps most scientists honest.

> The renowned German sociologist Max Weber saw science as a vocation. The individual scientist's devotion to the truth, in Weber's view, is what keeps science honest. His French contemporary Emile Durkheim, on the other hand, considered that it is the community of science, not the individual, that guarantees scientific integrity. Weber's view that scientists are innately honest is still sometimes heard. "The scientists I have known . . . have been in certain respects just perceptibly more morally admirable than most other groups of intelligent men," said the scientist and novelist C. P. Snow. . . . But the opinion that scientists are somehow more honest than other people is not particularly fashionable. The prevailing view is that laid out by Robert Merton, the leading American sociologist of science, who like Durkheim attributes honesty in science to institutional mechanisms, not the personal virtue of scientists. The verifiability of results, the exacting scrutiny of fellow experts, the subjection of scientists' activities to "rigorous policing, to a degree perhaps unparalleled in any other field of activity" — these are features, says Merton, that ensure "the virtual absence of fraud in the annals of science."

Howard Gardner, in *Artful Scribbles* (New York: Basic, 1980), an inquiry into what children's drawings mean, makes a sharp contrast between the drawings of younger children and those of older children.

> When drawings made by eight- or nine-year-olds are juxtaposed to those produced by younger children, a striking contrast emerges. There is little doubt about which came from which group: works by the older children feature a kind of precision, a concern for detail, a command of geometrical form which are lacking in the attempts by younger artists. Schemas for familiar objects are readily recognized, and attempts at rendering less familiar objects can initially be decoded. And yet one hesitates to call the drawings by the older children "better" — indeed, most observers and sometimes even the youngsters themselves feel that something vital which is present at the age of six or seven has disappeared from the drawings by the older children. A certain freedom, flexibility, *joie de vivre* [zest for life], and a special fresh exploratory flavor which mark the childlike drawings of the six-year-old are gone; and instead of being replaced by adult mastery, this loss has merely been supplanted by a product that is at once more carefully wrought yet also more wooden and lifeless.

As you'll notice, Gardner, while giving the strong points of each age group of artists, apparently favors the work of the young, for all its faults.

These brief examples may suggest to you that comparing and contrasting aren't just meaningless academic calisthenics. Critical thinking strategies and explaining devices, they appeal to writers who have a passion for making things clear.

## Making Connections: Comparing and Contrasting in A Writer's Reader

Writers often use the critical thinking strategy of *comparing and contrasting* to arrive at a fuller understanding of two or more items being discussed. Various authors in *A Writer's Reader* use this strategy in their writing. Editorial writer Nicholas Wade in "How Men and Women Think" (p. 510) compares and contrasts the thinking processes of males and females to support his rather controversial position that "the test of equal opportunity, when all unfair barriers to women have fallen, will not necessarily be equal outcomes." Linguist Deborah Tannen in "Women and Men Talking on the Job" (p. 554) uses her comparison-contrast of gender differences in conversation to support and illustrate the different ways men and women make decisions.

Like Bruce Catton (p. 144), Tim Chabot (p. 147), Wade, and Tannen, other writers who use comparing and contrasting are poet Joy Harjo, "Three Generations of Native American Women's Birth Experience" (p. 471); professor of philosophy and ethics Christina Hoff Sommers, "The Backlash Myth: The Truth about How Women Are Doing in the Workplace" (p. 560); columnist Ellen Goodman, "The New Hollywood Male" (p. 577); media critic Kurt Andersen, "Oprah and Jo-Jo the Dog-Faced Boy" (p. 590); political scientist Andrew Sullivan, "Wouldn't Normally Do" (p. 592); and environmentalist Gregg Easterbrook, "Forget PCBs. Radon. Alar: The World's Greatest Environmental Dangers Are Dung Smoke and Dirty Water" (p. 636). As you read these essays, consider the role that comparison and contrast plays in them. For each essay, answer the following questions.

1. Does the writer use comparison only? Contrast only? A combination of the two? Why?
2. What two (or more) items are compared and contrasted? What does the comparison-contrast reveal about the items?
3. What is the purpose of the comparison-contrast? What idea does the information support or refute?
4. Does the writer use the opposing or alternating pattern of organization? Why?

# Chapter 8

# Explaining Causes and Effects

When a house burns down, an insurance company assigns a claims adjuster to look into the disaster and answer the question Why? He or she investigates to find the answer — the *cause* of the fire, whether it be lightning, a forgotten cigar, or a match that someone deliberately struck — and presents it in a written report. The adjuster also details the *effects* of the fire: what was destroyed or damaged, what repairs will be needed, how much they will cost.

Often for assignments and exams in college you are asked to act and think like the insurance adjuster, tracing causes or identifying effects. To do so, you have to think about a subject critically, to gather information and ideas, to marshal evidence, to analyze and evaluate the evidence logically. Effects, by the way, are usually easier to identify and demonstrate than causes. The results of a fire are apparent to an onlooker the next day, although its cause may be obscure.

Seeking causes and effects is an uncertain pursuit. In assigning you to write a paper of cause and effect, an instructor will not expect you to set forth a definitive explanation with absolute certainty. "Causality," says French philosopher of history Paul Veyne, "is always accompanied by mental reservation." However, in the process of your ferreting out, probing, and detailing causes and effects, both you and your readers learn a good deal and understand the subject more clearly.

## *Learning from Other Writers*

The following two essays explore causes and effects. The first is by David L. Evans, an engineer and college admissions officer. Evans begins his essay by commenting on a disturbing fact he has observed: black men are underrepresented in the pool of college applicants at his college. Evans asks what the causes of this situation are and explores one possibility.

Yun Yung Choi, a native of Seoul, Korea, wrote "Invisible Women" when she was a student at Harvard College. In her essay, Choi looks at one cause of women's subordinate status in Korea's traditional culture — the introduction of a new state religion — and traces the subtle but important effects of that change.

## *David L. Evans*    **The Wrong Examples**

As a college admissions officer I am alarmed at the dearth of qualified black male candidates. Often in high schools that are 90 percent black, *all* the African American students who come to my presentation are female! This gender disparity persists to college matriculation where the black male population almost never equals that of the female. 1

What is happening to these young men? Who or what is influencing them? I submit that the absence of male role models and slanted television images of black males have something to do with it. 2

More than half of black children live in homes headed by women, and almost all of the black teachers they encounter are also women. This means that most African American male children do not often meet black male role models in their daily lives. They must look beyond their immediate surroundings for exemplary black men to emulate. Lacking in-the-flesh models, many look to TV for black heroes. 3

Unfortunately, TV images of black males are not particularly diverse. Their usual roles are to display physical prowess, sing, dance, play a musical instrument, or make an audience laugh. These roles are enticing and generously rewarded. But the reality is that success comes to only a few extraordinarily gifted performers or athletes. 4

A foreigner watching American TV would probably conclude that most successful black males are either athletes or entertainers. That image represents both success and failure. Success, because the substantial presence of blacks in sports, music, and sitcoms is a milestone in the struggle begun almost 50 years ago to penetrate the racial barriers of big-league athletics and television. It is a failure because the overwhelming success of a *few* highly visible athletes, musicians, and comedians has typecast black males. Millions see these televised roles as a definition of black men. Nowhere is this more misleading than in the inner city, where young males see it as "the way out." 5

Ask a random sample of Americans to identify Michael Jordon, Bo Jackson, Magic Johnson, Hammer, Prince, Eddie Murphy, or Mike Tyson. Correct responses would probably exceed 90 percent. Then ask them to identify Colin Powell, August Wilson, Franklin Thomas, Mike Espy, Walter Massey, Earl Graves, or the late Reginald Lewis and I doubt that 10 percent would respond correctly. The second group contains the chairman of the Joint Chiefs of Staff, 6 a Pulitzer Prize–winning playwright, the president of the Ford Foundation, the secretary of agriculture, the director of the National Science Foundation, the publisher of *Black Enterprise* magazine and the former CEO of a multi-million-dollar business.

The Democratic National Convention that nominated Bill Clinton [in 1992] brought Ron Brown, Jesse Jackson, David Dinkins, Kurt Schmoke, and Bernard Shaw into living rooms as impressive role models. Their relative numbers at the convention were in noticeable contrast to the black baseball players who made up nearly half of the All-Star teams on the Tuesday night of the convention.

This powerful medium has made the glamour of millionaire boxers, ballplayers, musicians, and comedians appear so close, so tangible that, to naive young boys, it seems only a dribble or dance step away. In the hot glare of such surrealism, schoolwork and prudent personal behavior can become irrelevant.

Impressionable young black males are not the only Americans getting this potent message. *All* TV viewers are subtly told that blacks are "natural" athletes, they are "funny," and all of them have "rhythm." Such a thoroughly reinforced message doesn't lie dormant. A teacher who thinks every little black boy is a potential Bo Jackson or Eddie Murphy is likely to give his football practice a higher priority than his homework or to excuse his disruptive humor.

### Neck Jewelry

Television's influence is so pronounced that one seldom meets a young black man who isn't wearing paraphernalia normally worn by athletes and entertainers. Young white men wear similar attire but not in the same proportion. Whites have many more televised role models from which to choose. There are very few whites in comparison to the number of blacks in the NBA. Black males are 12½ percent of the American male population but constitute 75 percent of the NBA and are thereby six times overrepresented. That television presents poor role models for *all* kids doesn't wash.

These highly visible men's influence is so dominant that it has redefined the place of neck jewelry, sneakers, and sports apparel in our society. The yearning to imitate the stars has sometimes had dire consequences. Young lives have been lost over sneakers, gold chains, and jackets. I dare say that many black prison inmates are the flotsam and jetsam from dreamboats that never made it to the NBA or MTV.

Producers of TV sports, popular music, and sitcoms should acknowledge these "side effects" of the American Dream. More important are the superstars themselves. To a man, they are similar to lottery winners and their presence on TV is cruelly deceptive to their electronic protégés. Surely they can spend some of their time and resources to convince their young followers that even incredible talent doesn't assure fame or fortune. An athlete or performer must also be amazingly lucky in his quest for Mount Olympus.

A well-trained mind is a surer, although less glamorous, bet for success.   13
Arthur Ashe spent his whole life teaching precisely this message. Bill Cosby
and Jim Brown also come to mind as African American superstars who use
their substantial influence to redirect young black males. At this time, when
black men are finally making some inroads into the upper echelons of American society, we need more than ever to encourage the young to look beyond
the stereotypes of popular culture.

**Questions to Start You Thinking**

*Meaning*

1. What is Evans's thesis? Where does he state it?

2. What does the author state are the causes that so few qualified black male
   candidates apply for admission to college? Can you suggest additional causes
   that Evans has not included?

3. What does *surrealism* (paragraph 8) mean? According to Evans, in what way
   is the situation he describes surreal? Do you agree?

*Writing Strategies*

4. Is Evans trying to be exhaustive in his analysis? In other words, is he trying to
   identify every possible cause for the problem he identifies? How do you
   know?

5. Trace the chain of causes and effects that Evans sets forth in this essay. Explain how television is both a cause and an effect in this chain of causal relationships.

6. Where does Evans use specific examples? Find two examples that you think
   are especially effective. What makes them so?

7. Do you find Evans's cause and effect analysis effective? Why, or why not?

STUDENT ESSAY

## *Yun Yung Choi*   Invisible Women

For me, growing up in a small suburb on the outskirts of    1
Seoul, the adults' preference for boys seemed quite natural.
All the important people that I knew, doctors, lawyers, policemen, and soldiers, were men. On the other hand, most of
the women that I knew were either housekeepers or housewives
whose duty seemed to be to obey and please the men of the
family. When my teachers at school asked me what I wanted to
be when I grew up, I would answer, "I want to be the wife of
the President." Since all women must become wives and moth-

ers, I thought, becoming the wife of the President would be
the highest achievement for a woman. I knew that the birth of
a boy was a greatly desired and celebrated event, whereas the
birth of a girl was a disappointing one, accompanied by the
frequent words of consolation for the sad parents "A daughter
is her mother's chief help in keeping house."

These attitudes toward women, widely considered the con-           2
tinuation of an unbroken chain of tradition, are, in fact,
only a few hundred years old, a relatively short period considering Korea's long history. During the first half of the
Yi dynasty, which lasted from 1392 to 1910, and during the
Koryo period, which preceded the Yi dynasty, women were
treated almost as equals, with many privileges that were denied them during the latter half of the Yi dynasty. This
turnabout in women's place in Korean society was brought
about by one of the greatest influences that shaped the government, literature, and thoughts of the Korean people: Confucianism.

Throughout the Koryo period, which lasted form 918 to            3
1392, and throughout the first half of the Yi dynasty, according to Laurel Kendall in her book View from the Inner
Room, women were important and contributing members of the
society, and not marginal and dependent as they later became.
Women were, to a large extent, in command of their own lives.
They were permitted to own property and receive inheritances
from their fathers. Wedding ceremonies were held in the
bride's house, where the couple lived, and the wife retained
her surname. Women were also allowed freedom of movement,
that is, they were able to go outside the house without any
feelings of shame or embarrassment.

With the introduction of Confucianism, however, the             4
rights and privileges that women enjoyed were confiscated.
The government of the Yi dynasty made great efforts to incorporate into the society the Confucian ideologies, including
the principle of agnation, which, according to Kendall, made
men the important members of society and relegated women to a
dependent position. The government succeeded in its attempt
at Confucianizing the country, and the acceptance of Confucian proverbs such as the following spread: "Men are honored,

but women are abased." "A daughter is a 'robber woman' who carries household wealth away when she marries."

The unfortunate effects of this Confucianization in the lives of women were numerous. The most noticeable was the virtual confinement of women. They were forced to remain unseen in the anbang, the inner room of the house. This room was the women's domain, or, rather, the women's prison. Outside, a women was carried through the streets in a closed sedan chair. Walking outside, she had to wear a veil that covered her face and could travel abroad only after nightfall. Thus, it is no wonder that westerners traveling through Korea in the late nineteenth century expressed surprise at the apparent absence of women in the country.                     5

Women received no formal education. Their only schooling came from government textbooks. By giving instruction on the virtuous conduct of women, these books attempted to fit women into the Confucian stereotype: meek, quiet, and obedient. Thus, this Confucian society acclaimed particular women not for their talent or achievement but for the degree of perfection with which they were able to mimic the stereotype.                     6

A women even lost her identity in such a society. Once married, she became a stranger to her natal family, becoming a member of her husband's family. Her name was omitted from the family chokpo, or genealogy book, and was entered in the chokpo of her in-laws as a mere "wife" next to her husband's name.                     7

Even a desirable marriage, the ultimate hope for a woman, failed to provide financial and emotional security for her. Failure to produce a son was legal grounds for sending the wife back to her natal home, thereby subjecting the woman to the greatest humiliation and to a life of continued shame. And because the Confucian ideology stressed a wife's devotion to her husband as the greatest of womanly virtues, widows were forced to avoid social disgrace by remaining faithfully unmarried, no matter how young they were. As women lost their rights to own or inherit property, these widows, with no means to support themselves, suffered great hardships. Thus, as Sandra Martielle says in Virtues in Conflict, what the government considered "the ugly custom of remarriage" was slowly eliminated at the expense of women's happiness.                     8

This male-dominated system of Confucianism is one of the       9
surviving traditions from the Yi dynasty. Although the Constitution of the Republic of Korea proclaimed on July 17,
1948, guarantees individual freedom and sexual equality,
these ideals failed to have any immediate effect on the Korean mentality that stubbornly adheres to its belief in the
superiority of men. Women still regard marriage as their
prime objective in life, and little girls are still wishing
to become the doctor's wife, the lawyer's wife, and even the
President's wife. But as the system of Confucianism is slowly
being forced out of existence by new legal and social standards, perhaps a day will come, after all, when a little girl
will stand up in class and answer, "I want to be the President."

**Questions to Start You Thinking**

*Meaning*

1. What effect does Choi observe? What cause does she attribute it to?
2. What specific changes in Korean culture does Choi attribute to the introduction of Confucianism?
3. What evidence do you find of the writer's critically rethinking an earlier belief and then revising it? What do you think may have influenced her to change her belief?

*Writing Strategies*

4. What does Choi gain by beginning and ending with her personal experience?
5. Where does Choi use the strategy of comparing and contrasting? Do you think this is effective?
6. What resources for writing does the author draw upon?
7. Do you find Choi's cause and effect analysis persuasive? Why, or why not?

# Learning by Writing

## THE ASSIGNMENT: EXPLAINING CAUSES AND EFFECTS

Pick a disturbing fact or situation that you have observed, and seek out the causes and effects to help you and your readers understand the issue better. When you actually write your essay, you may limit your ideas to the causes *or* the effects, or you may include both but emphasize one more than the other. Yun Yung Choi uses this approach when she briefly identifies the cause of the status of Korean women (Confucianism) but spends most of her essay detailing the effects of this cause.

The situation you choose might be one that may have affected you and people you know well, such as the limited number of scholarships available for college students, the pressure to get good grades, the difficulty of working while going to school, or divorce in the family. It might have affected people in your city or region — pollution of a lake or river near you, only a small percentage of eligible voters voting in a city or county election, decaying bridge supports, or pet owners not using pooper-scoopers. It may affect society at large — the high rate of inflation in central Europe, apathy, drunk driving, or the high cost of health care. It might be gender or racial stereotypes on television, unsavory language in music lyrics, spouse abuse, teenage suicide, the difficulty of getting admitted to law school, the shortage of male elementary school teachers, the unwillingness of businesses to hire college graduates with liberal arts degrees, or the effects of using dragnets for ocean fishing.

Don't think you must choose an earthshaking topic to write a good paper. On the contrary, you will do a better job on a subject you are personally familiar with.

Write for your classmates. If you write about a situation you have observed in your own life, assume that your readers will care to know more about you. If you write about an issue in a region or in society, assume that they will want to compare their impressions of this situation with yours.

Papers written in response to this assignment have included the following.

A woman recollected her observations of the deplorable plight of Indians in rural Mexico and cited this as one cause of the recent rebellions there.

A woman analyzed the negative attitudes of men toward women in the company where she worked and the resulting tension among workers. She identified some of the effects as inefficiency and low production.

A man contended that buildings constructed in Miami are not built to withstand hurricane force winds. One reason he cited is the inadequate city inspection system.

A woman observed that popular interest in space travel has declined in the United States. She cited evidence to support this claim and then detailed causes for the decline, including decreased funding for the space program and the *Challenger* disaster.

## GENERATING IDEAS

*Find a topic.*  What situation with which you are familiar would be informative or instructive to explore? This assignment leaves you the option of writing either from personal experience or from what you know or can find out, or a combination of the two.

Begin by searching your memory. You might let your thoughts wander over the results of this undesirable situation that you have witnessed. Has the situation always been this way? Or have things changed in the last few years? Have things gotten better or worse?

The ideas in the following list may help you search your memory.

- An unpleasant situation caused by a change in your life (a new job; a fluctuation in income; personal or family upheaval following death, divorce, accident, illness, or good fortune; by starting college)
- An undesirable change in the environment (caused by air pollution, a flood or a storm, a new industry, the failure of an old industry)
- A disturbing situation caused by an invention (the automobile, the computer, the VCR, the television, the ATM)
- Employment opportunities that cause you concern (for women in management, for blacks in the military, for white males in nursing)
- A situation in your neighborhood, city, or state that is causing problems for you (traffic, pollution, population, health care)

When a few thoughts begin to percolate, reach for a pencil and brainstorm — jot down a list of likely topics that come to mind. (For more tips on brainstorming, see p. 334). Then choose the idea that you care most about and that promises to be neither too large nor too small. A paper that confined itself to the causes of a family's move from New Jersey to Montana might be only one sentence long: "My father's company transferred him." But the subsequent effects of the move on the various members of the family might form the basis of an interesting essay. So the writer might choose to focus on the effects. Unless you are writing a very long term paper, however, an exhaustive study of the effects of gangs in urban high schools is likely to prove too wide-ranging even to sketch in fewer than ten thousand words. Instead, you might consider just one unusual effect of this situation, such as gang members staking out territory in the parking lot of a local school.

*List causes and effects.* Your choice tentatively made, write for ten or fifteen minutes, identifying likely causes and effects. In looking for causes, look first for *immediate causes* — those evident and close at hand that clearly led to the situation. Then look for *remote causes* — underlying, more basic reasons for the situation, perhaps causes that came earlier. The immediate cause of unemployment in a town might be the closing of a factory. But the more remote cause might be competition from a foreign business, against which the local company couldn't survive. When looking for effects, too, consider both the *immediate* consequences of your situation and the longer-range *remote* effects it might have, even if you're not sure yet what these might be.

Whether you're looking for causes or effects, you can make separate lists of causes and effects and, next to each item on each list, insert your evidence for it. Does your evidence seem substantial? You can tell from a glance at your list exactly where you need to generate more material. Highlight (with a star or an underline) any causes and effects that stand out. A way to rate the items on your list is to ask: Is this an *essential* cause? Is it something without which the situation wouldn't exist? (Then it deserves a big star.) Or without it, might the situation have arisen nevertheless, for some other reason? (It might still matter, but less importantly.) Is this a significant effect? Has it had a resounding impact? Is it something that is necessary to include to adequately explain the results?

If you haven't figured out enough causes and effects to explain the situation to your satisfaction, you need to do some more digging. Remember, you have five major resources — recall, observation, conversation, reading, and imagination.

If your topic calls on you to account for people's behavior, consider some suggestions from Kenneth Burke (see p. 345). A literary critic and philosopher, Burke has proposed a set of questions designed to discover the deep-down causes of a person's actions. For a writer, Burke's questions often generate insights, observations, and hunches worth pursuing.

## PLANNING, DRAFTING, AND DEVELOPING

Yun Yung Choi's "Invisible Women" follows a clear plan. In the first two paragraphs Choi establishes the role of women in modern-day Korea, posits that the current attitudes toward women are relatively new, and asserts that Confucianism is the cause of this turnabout. In paragraphs 3 and 4 she contrasts the status of women before and after Confucianism. Beginning in paragraph 5 she explains the numerous adverse effects of Confucianization in the lives of women. She concludes her essay in paragraph 9 by indicating that change is again on the horizon. The essay was written from a brief scratch outline that simply lists the effects of the change:

Intro - Personal anecdote
- Tie with Korean history
- State thesis: This turnabout in women's place in Korean society was brought about by one of the greatest influences that shaped the government, literature, and thoughts of the Korean people: Confucianism.

Comparison and contrast of status of women before and after Confucianism

Effects of Confucianism on women

1) Confinement

2) Little education

3) Loss of identity in marriage

4) No property rights

Conclusion - Impact still evident in Korea today but some hints of change

The paper makes its point: it shows Confucianism as the reason for the status of Korean women and details four specific effects of Confucianism on women and Korean society. And it shows that cause and effect are closely related: Confucianism is the cause of the change in the status of Korean women, and Confucianism has had specific effects on Korean women.

You can begin planning your paper by assigning relative importance to the causal relationships: classify the causes, and then the effects, as major or minor ones. If, for example, you are writing about the reasons why more married women hold jobs now than they did twenty years ago, you might make a list that includes (1) economic necessity, (2) wanting to get out of the house, and (3) more jobs now open to women. On reflection you might decide that economic necessity — the need for both husband and wife to contribute to family expenses — is a major cause and that desire to get out of the house is a minor one. You could then plan to give the economic cause more space and place it last in your essay to emphasize it. You would organize the causes from least important to most important: (1) desire to get out of house, (2) more jobs open, (3) economic necessity.

Once you have a tentative order for the causes or effects, draft the first part of your paper: describe the situation you want to explain. Then make clear to your readers which one of the three tasks — to explain the causes of the change, to explain the effects, or to explain both — you intend to accomplish. You can do this subtly, not in a flat, mechanical fashion: "Now I am going to explain the causes of this situation." You can announce your task casually, naturally, as if you were talking to someone: "At first, I didn't realize that keeping six pet cheetahs in our back yard would bother the neighbors." Or, as one writer did in a paper about her father's sudden move to a Trappist monastery: "The real reason for Father's decision didn't become clear to me for a long while."

Using your list of causes and effects, you are now ready to draft the main part of your paper. In the first section of your paper — taking no more than

**WRITING WITH A COMPUTER**

Whether you're looking for causes or effects, word processing can simplify your job. In setting forth causes, you can make a list of them and, next to each item on the list, insert your evidence for it. In writing a paper determining effects, you can make a similar list and flesh it out with evidence. ("The lowering of the tariff on Japanese-made cars worked havoc in the automotive industry" — that statement of an effect calls for evidence: a few facts to back it up.)

Does your evidence seem substantial? You can tell from a glance at your screen exactly where you might need to generate more material. Highlight any skimpy parts with **boldface** so you won't forget these needy places when you revise. With a couple of keystrokes or mouse clicks, you can boldface a whole long passage. Later, after you've revised and strengthened the passage, you can delete the highlighting.

two or three paragraphs — describe the situation. Then show how the situation came about (the causes) or what followed as a result (the effects) or both. More than likely, the organization of your ideas will follow one of these patterns:

I. The situation
II. Its causes

I. The situation
II. Its effects

I. The situation
II. Its causes
III. Its effects

## REVISING AND EDITING

As you know by now, ascertaining causes and effects takes hard thought. You'll want to set aside an especially generous amount of time to look back over, ponder, and rewrite this paper. Yun Yung Choi wrote several drafts of "Invisible Women." As she approached the paper's final version, one of the problems she faced was making a smooth transition from recalling her own experience to probing causes.

(emphasize that
everyone thinks that) ————————————→ widely

These attitudes toward women, ~~which I once~~ believed to

, a relatively
short time,
considering
korea's long
history

be the continuation of an unbroken chain of tradition, are,

in fact, only a few hundred years old. During the first half

of the Yi dynasty, which lasted from 1392 to 1910, and during

[tell when] 

[the Koryo period] women were treated almost as equals, with

many privileges that were denied them during the latter half

of the Yi dynasty. This upheaval in women's place in Korean

society was brought about by one of the greatest influences

that shaped the government, literature, and thoughts of the

Korean people: Confucianism. Because of Confucianism, my

birth was not greeted with joy and celebration but rather

with these words of consolation: "A daughter is her mother's

chief help in keeping house." (Belongs in opening paragraph)

In revising a paper that traces causes, effects, or both, you might ask yourself some or all of the questions in the following checklist.

**REVISION CHECKLIST**

If you are tracing causes —
• Have you made it clear that you are explaining causes?
• Have you left out any essential causes?

- Have you given enough evidence to convince readers that the causal relationships are valid?
- Have you claimed remote causes you can't begin to prove? or made assertions but offered no proof?
- Have you stated the causes with swaggering certainty, when in all honesty you might admit that you're only guessing?
- Have you fallen into any logical fallacies, such as *oversimplification* (assuming that there was only one small cause for a large phenomenon) or the *post hoc* fallacy (assuming that one thing caused another just because the one preceded the other). (For more on fallacies, see p. 120.)
- Have you shown your readers your point in demonstrating causes?

If you are determining effects —

- Have you made it clear that you are explaining effects?
- What possible effects have you left out? Are any of them worth adding?
- Have you given sufficient evidence that these effects have occurred?
- Could any effect you mention have resulted not from the cause you describe but from some other cause?

 **FOR PEER RESPONSE**

Before you type a final draft, let a peer reader check over your paper and answer the questions on one of the following checklists. See Chapter 20 for advice on working with other student writers and for general questions you should always ask a peer editor to address. For a paper in which you explain causes and effects, you'll also want your peer editor to answer the following specific questions.

If the writer explains causes —

- Does he or she do more than merely list causes? Does the writer explain the causes that he or she identifies?
- Does the writer present causes that seem logical and possible?
- Did other causes occur to you that you think the writer should consider? If so, list them.

If the writer explains effects —

- Do all the effects seem to be the result of the change he or she describes?
- Has the writer overlooked some effects that should be added? List any that occurred to you as you read the paper.

For all cause and effect papers —

- What point is the writer trying to make? What is the purpose of the essay? Does the explanation of causes or effects help the writer accomplish this purpose?
- Is the order of the points in the paper clear and useful? Can you suggest a better organization?
- Are you convinced by the logic used in the paper? Do you see any logical fallacies (see p. 120)?
- Point out any causes or effects you found hard to accept.
- Does the writer give you enough detail? Enough evidence to convince you? Put stars where more evidence is needed.
- If this were your paper, what is the one thing you would be sure to work on before handing it in?

Remember, unless you are writing a paper that sets forth exact scientific findings, your instructor won't expect you to write a definitive explanation. You'll be expected only to write an explanation that is thoughtful, searching, and reasonable.

## OTHER ASSIGNMENTS

1. Pick a definite change that has taken place during your lifetime, and seek out the causes and effects to help you and your readers understand that change better. By "change" we mean a noticeable, lasting transformation produced by an event or series of events. The change might be one that has affected only you, such as as a move to another location, a decision you made that changed the course of your life, or an alteration in a strong personal opinion or belief. It might be a change that has affected not only you but also other people in your neighborhood or city (a new zoning law), in a region (the growth of high technology in the Silicon Valley of California), or in society at large (the arrival of the personal computer or the fall of communism in Europe). It might be a new invention, a medical breakthrough, or a deep-down shift in the structure or attitudes of society.

2. Explore your own motives and explain your reasons for taking some step or for doing something in a routine way. (If you need help in pinning down reasons for your own behavior, some of Kenneth Burke's suggestions on pp. 345–46 may be useful.)

3. In an introductory philosophy course at Loyola College in Maryland, Frank J. Cunningham asks his students to write, instead of a traditional research paper, a short original essay exploring their own ideas and opinions. Below is his assignment: Try it yourself.

> Over the years, in the process of growing up and growing civilized, all of us have developed certain opinions about the way things happen, about what works and what doesn't work, about how things are. We have also developed certain expectations toward our world based on these opinions.
>
> Under ordinary circumstances, we live with these opinions and expectations unquestioningly, and, on the whole, we manage quite well with our lives. But . . . in philosophy we look at things we don't normally look at, question things we normally take for granted, analyze what we accept from day to day.
>
> As preparation for this somewhat unusual (some would say perverse) activity, I would like you to think about your own opinions. Think about your views of the world, your expectations, your certainties, and decide on something of which you are absolutely certain. It may be a part of your normal life, a truth derived from your education, something that you have learned through your years of experience, something you were told, something you figured out on your own. Now write a short essay (no more than two pages) describing the one thing about which you are absolutely certain and why this thing commands such certainty.

Remember that an essay such as this requires thought as preparation. You should not expect to sit down immediately at the typewriter and produce it. Remember too that there are at least two separate thinking tasks to be performed. First you must consider your stock of truths to find one in which you have utmost confidence. This will probably take some time and effort since we are willing to let a lot of truths pass without putting them to the test. Second, you must consider the reason for your certainty. In working out this part of the essay it might be useful to pretend that you are trying to convince a very reasonable but thoroughly doubting person of the truth of your position.

4. Read one newspaper or magazine article that probes the causes of some contemporary problem: the shortage of reasonable day-care options, for instance, or the low academic scores of American students compared with those of students in other developed countries. Can you suggest additional causes that the article writer seems to have ignored? Write an essay in which you argue either that the author has done a good job of explaining the causes of this problem or that he or she has not.

## Applying What You Learn: Some Uses of Explaining Causes and Effects

Examination questions often pose a problem in causality: "Trace the causes of the decline of foreign sales of American automobiles." Equally familiar is the exam question that calls for a survey of effects: "What economic effects of the repeal of Prohibition were immediately evident in the early 1930s?" Problems of that very same sort, you'll find, will frequently turn up as paper topics. In a child development course, you might be asked to research what makes some people become child abusers. In a speech pathology course you might be called on to investigate the causes and effects of head trauma, fetal alcohol syndrome, learning disabilities, or Down's syndrome — all of which are relevant to impaired communication skills.

But in fulfilling any kind of college writing assignment, even one that doesn't ask you to look for causes or effects, you may wish to spend *part* of your paper exploring one or the other or both. In a paper that deals with any phenomenon — say, a sociology assignment to write about an increase in teenage pregnancies among middle-class suburbanites — a paragraph or two that explores the causes of that phenomenon or its effects might add depth to your paper.

In a book or article that deals with some current phenomenon, the writer may ask why — in only a paragraph or a few paragraphs. In an article titled "Propaganda Techniques in Today's Advertising," Ann McClintock analyzes the methods advertisers, corporations, and politicians use so effectively to persuade consumers to do whatever they want us to do, anything from buying a product to voting for a candidate. She exemplifies seven types of propaganda: name calling, glittering generalities, transfer, testimonial, plain folks, card stacking, and bandwagon. She concludes her article asking *why* these propaganda devices work:

> Why do these propaganda techniques work? Why do so many of us buy the products, viewpoints, and candidates urged on us by propaganda messages? They work because they appeal to our emotions, not to our minds. Often, in fact, they capitalize on our prejudices and biases. For example, if we are convinced that environmentalists are radicals who want to destroy America's record of industrial growth and progress, then we will applaud the candidate who refers to them as "treehuggers." Clear thinking requires hard work: analyzing a claim, researching the facts, examining both sides of an issue, using logic to see the flaws in an argument. Many of us would rather let the propagandists do our thinking for us.

In his article "Causation of Terror," social historian Feliks Gross seeks to explain a difficult, complex, and vitally important matter: the reasons for political assassinations and terrorism in Europe and Russia in the nineteenth and twentieth centuries. Gross recalls cases of political parties that have used terrorist tactics to overthrow moderate and democratic governments; he remembers the victims of oppressive rule who have used terrorist tactics to fight back: the Armenians and Bulgarians under Turkish rule, the Serbs under the Croatian Ustashe, the Polish underground fighters who resisted Nazi occupation. Tentatively generalizing, Gross finds that ethnic tensions and clashes of political ideology, not economic hardship, cause the victims of terrorism to respond with terrorist tactics and political assassination.

"It is of paramount significance," Gross concludes, "to understand the conditions that are conducive to political assassination." By controlling such conditions, perhaps we might even prevent terrorism. Applied to such an end, exploring causes and effects is no mere game, but a way of seeking peace and ensuring it.

**FOR GROUP LEARNING**

## Explaining the News

Together in class or in your writing group, tell aloud a two-minute story that you invent to explain the causes behind any surprising event reported in this morning's news. Either realistic explanations or tall tales are acceptable. You'll need to prepare your story carefully in advance. Invite the others to comment on it, and, with their reactions in mind, set down your story on paper to turn in at the next class. In writing it down, embellish and improve on your story as much as you desire.

Before you write *any* paper setting forth causes or effects, you will find it particularly helpful to talk over with other students what you plan to say. Ask for their comments. Invite them to add to your list of causes or effects if they can.

# Making Connections:
## Explanations of Causes and Effects in A Writer's Reader

As human beings we often try to understand why something occurs by identifying causal relationships — determining *causes* and analyzing *effects*. Writers do much the same thing; in fact, they often use the critical thinking skill of identifying and explaining causes and effects to help readers understand a person, an idea, or a process. An author's explanation of causes and effects is often interwoven with analyzing, taking a stand, investigating a problem, proposing a solution, and evaluating. Novelist Amy Tan in "Mother Tongue" (p. 476) explores the effects her mother's broken English have had upon her personal life. Bill McKibben in "The End of Nature" (p. 620) explains some of the causes of the destruction of our natural environment in his call for a change in human behavior. David Evans (p. 166) and Yun Yung Choi (p. 168) explain both causes and effects in their essays.

Some of the other writers in *A Writer's Reader* who explain causal relationships include novelist Toni Morrison, "On the Backs of Blacks" (p. 528); psychologist Brent Staples, "Black Men and Public Space" (p. 518); writer of horror fiction Stephen King, "Why We Crave Horror Movies" (p. 579); lawyer Patricia J. Williams, "Hate Radio" (p. 582); music critic Alex Ross, "Generation Exit" (p. 598); and biologist Carol Kaesuk Yoon, "Drugs from Bugs" (p. 628). As you read these essays, consider the role that explanations of cause and effect play in them. For each essay, answer the following questions.

1. Does the writer explain causes? or effects? or both? Why? Does the writer perceive and explain a chain or series of causal relationships?
2. Is the evidence sufficient to clarify the causal relationships and to provide credibilty to the essay?
3. How is the subject relevant to the writer's occupation or field of interest?

# Chapter 9

# Taking a Stand

In college, both in class and outside of class, you'll hear controversial issues discussed: the baseball strike, television talk shows, prayer in the schools, welfare reform, health care, gun control. In some fields of study, experts don't always agree, and issues remain controversies for years. That is why, in your college writing, you will soon find yourself taking up pen (or typewriter or word processor) in a cause. Taking a stand on an issue will help you understand the controversy and clarify what you believe.

Writing of this kind has a twofold purpose: to state an opinion and to win your readers' respect for it. A reader's own opinion might alter from reading what you say; then again, it might not. But at least, if you fulfill your purpose, your readers will see good reasons for your thinking the way you do. In taking a stand, you do three things:

You state what you believe.
You enlist your readers' trust.
You consider and respect what your readers probably think and feel.

## Learning from Other Writers

Let's look at two essays in which the writers take a stand effectively. Charles R. Lawrence III is a professor of law at Stanford University. In the first essay here, adapted from a speech at a conference of the American Civil Liberties Union, Lawrence sets forth a controversial opinion on First Amendment rights.

Tania Fusco wrote the second essay, "Erasing Sexism in Advertising," for her freshman writing class at Boston College. The assignment asked her to take a stand and argue one side of an issue. Fusco chose to examine the sexist stereotypes in three advertisements and to advocate eliminating such imagery.

## Charles R. Lawrence III    On Racist Speech

I have spent the better part of my life as a dissenter. As a high school stu-    1
dent, I was threatened with suspension for my refusal to participate in a civil defense drill, and I have been a conspicuous consumer of my First Amendment liberties ever since. There are very strong reasons for protecting even racist speech. Perhaps the most important of these is that such protection reinforces our society's commitment to tolerance as a value and that by protecting bad speech from government regulation, we will be forced to combat it as a community.

But I also have a deeply felt apprehension about the resurgence of racial    2
violence and the corresponding rise in the incidence of verbal and symbolic assault and harassment to which blacks and other traditionally subjugated and excluded groups are subjected. I am troubled by the way the debate has been framed in response to the recent surge of racist incidents on college and university campuses and in response to some universities' attempts to regulate harassing speech. The problem has been framed as one in which the liberty of free speech is in conflict with the elimination of racism. I believe this has placed the bigot on the moral high ground and fanned the rising flames of racism.

Above all, I am troubled that we have not listened to the real victims, that    3
we have shown so little understanding of their injury, and that we have abandoned those whose race, gender, or sexual preference continues to make them second-class citizens. It seems to me a very sad irony that the first instinct of civil libertarians has been to challenge even the smallest, most narrowly framed efforts by universities to provide black and other minority students with the protection the Constitution guarantees them.

The landmark case of *Brown v. Board of Education* is not a case that we nor-    4
mally think of as a case about speech. But *Brown* can be broadly read as articulating the principle of equal citizenship. *Brown* held that segregated schools were inherently unequal because of the *message* that segregation conveyed — that black children were an untouchable caste, unfit to go to school with white children. If we understand the necessity of eliminating the system of signs and symbols that signal the inferiority of blacks, then we should hesitate before proclaiming that all racist speech that stops short of physical violence must be defended.

University officials who have formulated policies to respond to incidents    5
of racial harassment have been characterized in the press as "thought police,"

but such policies generally do nothing more than impose sanctions against intentional face-to-face insults. When racist speech takes the form of face-to-face insults, catcalls, or other assaultive speech aimed at an individual or small group of persons, it falls directly within the "fighting words" exception to First Amendment protection. The Supreme Court has held that words which "by their very utterance inflict injury or tend to incite an immediate breach of the peace" are not protected by the First Amendment.

If the purpose of the First Amendment is to foster the greatest amount of speech, racial insults disserve that purpose. Assaultive racist speech functions as a preemptive strike. The invective is experienced as a blow, not as a proffered idea, and once the blow is struck, it is unlikely that a dialogue will follow. Racial insults are particularly undeserving of First Amendment protection because the perpetrator's intention is not to discover truth or initiate dialogue but to injure the victim. In most situations, members of minority groups realize that they are likely to lose if they respond to epithets by fighting and are forced to remain silent and submissive.     6

Courts have held that offensive speech may not be regulated in public forums such as streets where the listener may avoid the speech by moving on, but the regulation of otherwise protected speech has been permitted when the speech invades the privacy of the unwilling listener's home or when the unwilling listener cannot avoid the speech. Racist posters, fliers, and graffiti in dormitories, bathrooms, and other common living spaces would seem to clearly fall within the reasoning of these cases. Minority students should not be required to remain in their rooms in order to avoid racial assault. Minimally, they should find a safe haven in their dorms and in all other common rooms that are a part of their daily routine.     7

I would also argue that the university's responsibility for ensuring that these students receive an equal educational opportunity provides a compelling justification for regulations that ensure them safe passage in all common areas. A minority student should not have to risk becoming the target of racially assaulting speech every time he or she chooses to walk across campus. Regulating vilifying speech that cannot be anticipated or avoided would not preclude announced speeches and rallies — situations that would give minority-group members and their allies the chance to organize counter-demonstrations or avoid the speech altogether.     8

The most commonly advanced argument against the regulation of racist speech proceeds something like this: We recognize that minority groups suffer pain and injury as the result of racist speech, but we must allow this hate mongering for the benefit of society as a whole. Freedom of speech is the lifeblood of our democratic system. It is especially important for minorities because often it is their only vehicle for rallying support for the redress of their grievances. It will be impossible to formulate a prohibition so precise that it will prevent the racist speech you want to suppress without catching in the same net all kinds of speech that it would be unconscionable for a democratic society to suppress.     9

Whenever we make such arguments, we are striking a balance on the one    10
hand between our concern for the continued free flow of ideas and the democratic process dependent on that flow and, on the other, our desire to further the cause of equality. There can be no meaningful discussion of how we
should reconcile our commitment to equality and our commitment to free
speech until it is acknowledged that there is real harm inflicted by racist
speech and that this harm is far from trivial.

To engage in a debate about the First Amendment and racist speech with-    11
out a full understanding of the nature and extent of that harm is to risk making the First Amendment an instrument of domination rather than a vehicle
of liberation. We have not all known the experience of victimization by racist,
misogynist, and homophobic speech, nor do we equally share the burden of
the societal harm it inflicts. We are often quick to say that we have heard the
cry of the victims when we have not.

The *Brown* case is again instructive because it speaks directly to the psy-    12
chic injury inflicted by racist speech by noting that the symbolic message of
segregation affected "the hearts and minds" of Negro children "in a way unlikely ever to be undone." Racial epithets and harassment often cause deep
emotional scarring and feelings of anxiety and fear that pervade every aspect
of a victim's life.

*Brown* also recognized that black children did not have an equal oppor-    13
tunity to learn and participate in the school community if they bore the additional burden of being subjected to the humiliation and psychic assault
contained in the message of segregation. University students bear an analo-
gous burden when they are forced to live and work in an environment where
at any moment they may be subjected to denigrating verbal harassment and
assault. The same injury was addressed by the Supreme Court when it held
that sexual harassment that creates a hostile or abusive work environment vi-
olates the ban on sex discrimination in employment of Title VII of the Civil
Rights Act of 1964.

Carefully drafted university regulations would bar the use of words as as-    14
sault weapons and leave unregulated even the most heinous of ideas when
those ideas are presented at times and places and in manners that provide an
opportunity for reasoned rebuttal or escape from immediate injury. The history of the development of the right to free speech has been one of carefully
evaluating the importance of free expression and its effects on other important societal interests. We have drawn the line between protected and unpro-
tected speech before without dire results. (Courts have, for example,
exempted from the protection of the First Amendment obscene speech and
speech that disseminates official secrets, that defames or libels another person, or that is used to form a conspiracy or monopoly.)

Blacks and other people of color are skeptical about the argument that    15
even the most injurious speech must remain unregulated because, in an unregulated marketplace of ideas, the best ones will rise to the top and gain acceptance. Our experience tells us quite the opposite. We have seen too many

demagogues elected by appealing to America's racism. We have seen too many good liberal politicians shy away from the issues that might brand them as being too closely allied with us.

Whenever we decide that racist speech must be tolerated because of the importance of maintaining societal tolerance for all unpopular speech, we are asking blacks and other subordinated groups to bear the burden for the good of all. We must be careful that the ease with which we strike the balance against the regulation of racist speech is in no way influenced by the fact that the cost will be borne by others. We must be certain that those who will pay that price are fairly represented in our deliberations and that they are heard.    16

At the core of the argument that we should resist all government regulation of speech is the ideal that the best cure for bad speech is good, that ideas that affirm equality and the worth of all individuals will ultimately prevail. This is an empty ideal unless those of us who would fight racism are vigilant and unequivocal in that fight. We must look for ways to offer assistance and support to students whose speech and political participation are chilled in a climate of racial harassment.    17

Civil rights lawyers might consider suing on behalf of blacks whose right to an equal education is denied by a university's failure to ensure a nondiscriminatory educational climate or conditions of employment. We must embark upon the development of a First Amendment jurisprudence grounded in the reality of our history and our contemporary experience. We must think hard about how best to launch legal attacks against the most indefensible forms of hate speech. Good lawyers can create exceptions and narrow interpretations that limit the harm of hate speech without opening the floodgates of censorship.    18

Everyone concerned with these issues must find ways to engage actively in actions that resist and counter the racist ideas that we would have the First Amendment protect. If we fail in this, the victims of hate speech must rightly assume that we are on the oppressors' side.    19

**Questions to Start You Thinking**

*Meaning*

1. What is Lawrence's position? Where in the essay does his position first become clear to you?

2. What arguments against the regulation of racist speech does Lawrence set forth? Where does he stand in regard to these arguments? Does he convince you of his position?

3. Explain how the First Amendment of the Constitution can be both "an instrument of domination" and "a vehicle of liberation" (see paragraph 11).

4. Look up the Bill of Rights to the Constitution to see what other rights Americans are guaranteed. Are any of these rights threatened today?

*Writing Strategies*

5. What impression of Lawrence do you get from reading his essay? Is his argument primarily emotional or logical?

6. Why does he begin his essay as he does? Would his argument be as credible if it were written by a doctor or a musician rather than a lawyer?

7. What kinds of evidence does Lawrence use to support his argument? Is the evidence convincing to you?

8. How does he organize his argument?

9. How does Lawrence show his awareness of people with views different from his?

STUDENT ESSAY

## *Tania Fusco*   Erasing Sexism in Advertising

Why does sexism persist in our culture? What is it that influences our thoughts so deeply that we cannot get away from it, even when many of us agree that it is wrong? Surely, the many messages containing sexist images we receive through the media every day play some role. The books we read, the movies we see, and the television shows we watch all contain such stereotypes. One of the most blatant and damaging sources of sexist stereotypes is advertising.

Ever since I became aware of sexism in advertising, advertisements now convey new meaning to me. I no longer glance at them casually when I flip through my favorite magazine, but rather examine them carefully. In many of these advertisements, words are not even needed to get the product sold or the point across. Instead, ads rely on strong images, such as a man strapping on his boxing gloves or the exposed breasts of a young woman. What are these ads trying to show? What messages do they send about male and female roles in society? By looking critically at three typical advertisements--one for clothes and two for fragrances--I learned a great deal about how sexist imagery operates in this medium, and I concluded that to change our society for the better, we must work to erase sexism in advertising.

In the first advertisement, a man and woman are posing for a clothing company. The first thing that caught my attention was the positioning of the figures. The man is half standing/half leaning, while the woman is crouched below him, holding on to his leg. The positioning implies a power relationship: he is superior and has dominance over her; she is

inferior and dependent on or possessive of him. There are
also sexual overtones to the way the two figures are
arranged: her head is at an equal level with his crotch, and
the leg she is grabbing is between her own legs. Both of
these details are clearly meant to tease the imagination.

In addition to sending a message about the relationship      4
between men and women, the image also reaffirms stereotypical
notions of masculinity and femininity. The man leans against
a tire and rests his hand on his fly. His "manliness" consists of physical labor and a self-sufficient sexuality. The
fact that he's looking at his own crotch implies that his
whole world revolves around his sexual performance. Clearly,
he is in charge of both his life and his sexual prowess--he
doesn't need anything or anyone, least of all the woman. She,
on the other hand, is pictured as tugging on his leg like an
animal or small child, craving attention. Her accomplishments
or individuality are nowhere to be seen. She is simply the
embodiment of "feminine" dependency and neediness. The
woman's beauty and skimpy clothing (visual shorthand for sen-
suality) also make her appear feminine: she is transformed
into an object, on display for the viewer's gratification.

The second advertisement I examined was for a men's          5
cologne, Brut. The frank name says quite a bit right away:
being a brute is a desirable thing. The only words on the
page are the blunt statement "Men are back." In other words,
brute strength, the strength of a brute animal, is the
essence of manhood. The picture supports this formulation.
The man portrayed is unshaven, long-haired, and emotionless.
His eyes are fixed to a stare. He represents the characteristics of a sly animal as it crouches with sharp claws, preparing for some "manly" fighting action.

The third advertisement is one for Obsession perfume for     6
women. Here it is not any words that jump off the page but
rather the shocking exposure of a very young woman's breasts.
All our attention is focused on this woman's vulnerable body;
the product is not even shown on the same page. Ironically,
the intended audience for this advertisement is women: a
woman's body can sell to anyone in our culture. The bottle of
perfume is pear-shaped, a shape traditionally associated with

a woman's torso. The message of this ad is clear: this woman (and, by extension, all women) is nothing more than a beautiful body, a body that is as much a commodity as the perfume it is used to advertise.

These advertisements, and many others like them, propagate limited and stereotypical notions of femininity and masculinity. Women are sexy, sensual, and beautiful. Rarely are their individuality or accomplishments highlighted. Instead, advertisements present them as objects of desire. Men are strong, self-sufficient, and bestial, with few emotions and an overwhelming sexual appetite. Through these images, advertisers play on our worst fears and secret prejudices in order to manipulate us into buying their products.    7

None of these portrayals is very positive; none of them presents a flattering portrait of a whole and complex human being. Yet the thousands of similar advertisements we see every year send a very simple and powerful message: this is what men are like; this is what women are like. Young boys and girls are even more vulnerable to these messages, since they already hear the expression to "be a man" or "act like a lady." Where else are young boys and girls going to get their ideas of masculinity and femininity? These vivid, provocative images drown out everything else. A sexy picture that titillates and teases the imagination is far more likely to make an impression than the more reasonable but dowdy messages that young people get through their parents, teachers, and churches.    8

Many people feel that sexism in advertising isn't the real issue. Some argue that it is an effect, not a cause of the problem, while others contend that it is too trivial to worry about. I say that this is wrong. The prejudice of sexism persists in our culture because we continue to allow sexist messages to shape and pollute the minds of young people. We cannot hope to overcome sexism until we stop these messages from being spread. Advertising contains powerful sexual stereotypes, stereotypes that are made even more powerful by their presence everywhere, all the time. If we take a stand and fight to erase sexism from advertising, we can start to win the war against sexism, one battle at a time.    9

*Meaning*

1. Why does Fusco believe we should erase sexism in advertising and in other parts of our lives?

2. What evidence does Fusco present to support her claim that much advertising is sexist? Do you find this evidence persuasive?

3. Is Fusco's argument clear to you? Can you easily follow her line of reasoning? Can you think of anything that would strengthen her argument?

*Writing Strategies*

4. What impression of Fusco do you get from reading her paper? Is her argument primarily emotional or logical?

5. Does Fusco consider what her readers probably think and feel?

6. Why does Fusco spend so much space analyzing the three advertisements? Do you find this approach effective?

# *Learning by Writing*

### THE ASSIGNMENT: TAKING A STAND

Find a controversy that arouses your interest. It might be an issue currently in the news or it might be a long-standing one such as "In our public schools, does creationism, the fundamentalist explanation for the origin of species, deserve equal time with Darwin's theory of evolution?" or "Are intercollegiate sports on campus a good or a bad thing?" Your purpose in this paper isn't to try to *solve* a large social or moral problem, but just to make clear where you stand on a large or small issue of importance to you (and why) and to persuade your readers to respect your position. To do so effectively, you must first know exactly where you stand and why. As you reflect on your topic and write your paper, you may change your position, but don't shift positions in the middle of your essay. To be effective, you must also consider your readers' views and choose strategies that will enlist their support. Your readers, you can assume, are people who may be familiar with the controversy but who have not yet taken sides.

Here are brief summaries of a few good papers that take a stand, written by students at several colleges.

A woman who pays her own way through college countered the opinion that working full- or part-time during the school year provides a college student with valuable knowledge. Citing her own painful experience, she maintained that a student who can devote full time to her studies is far better off than a student who must work.

A man attacked his history textbook's portrayal of Joan of Arc on the grounds that the author had characterized Joan as "an ignorant farm girl subject to religious hysteria."

A man, citing American history and Christian doctrine, gave his reasons for preferring to keep prayer out of public school classrooms.

A woman in an education course disputed the claim of E. D. Hirsch, Jr., in his book *Cultural Literacy* that we must give schoolchildren a grounding in facts common to the majority culture, including American history, literature, mythology, science, geography, and sports. Children, she affirmed, should first study their own cultural backgrounds.

## GENERATING IDEAS

For this assignment, you will need to find an issue on which to take a stand, develop a clear position, and assemble evidence that supports your view. If you don't have a rock-solid opinion and a ready-made argument when you start out, don't worry. In fact, that's part of the challenge of an assignment like this: as you explore the topic more deeply, sifting through all the implications and information, you may find that the evidence supports a view different from one you might have started out with. Or you may find that the issue intersects with strongly held beliefs in ways you couldn't have predicted. Try to remain flexible while you are generating a topic and materials for your paper, and be prepared for a bit of backtracking when unexpected twists appear.

***Find an issue.*** The topic for this paper should be an issue or controversy that's interesting to both you and your readers. Try brainstorming a list of possible topics (see p. 334). If you can't get started, look at the headlines of a newspaper, listen to a news broadcast on television or radio, or talk with some of your friends. Consider topics that you have covered in class. Tania Fusco's paper came out of the class discussion generated by one of the readings in her freshman writing course: the points that other students made about sexism in advertising made her think about things she hadn't considered before. If you keep a journal, look over past entries to see what has perplexed or angered you in the past months.

Remember that you need to find something about which there is real debate. The question "Is sexism bad?" is probably not going to lead to a strong paper because most of your readers would agree up front that sexism is a bad thing. And what does "bad thing" really mean? That phrase is too vague to provide you with clear direction. However, the question driving Fusco's paper — "Should we fight sexism by eliminating sexist stereotypes in advertising?" — is more fruitful because it focuses on a clearly debatable topic.

Once you have a list of possible topics, go through your list and delete those that are too broad or complex for a paper to be completed in about two weeks. Strike also those that you don't know much about. Finally, weed out anything that on second thought looks as if it might not hold your interest or that of your readers. From your new, shorter list, pick one issue or controversy to write about. Choose the one for which you think you can make the strongest argument to your classmates.

*Do some preliminary exploring.* Once you have an issue in mind, you may need to do a little poking around, both to understand it better and to make sure that this is a topic you really can and want to take a stand on. Turn to some of your trusty resources. Recall how this issue has affected your own life. Observe, if you can. Converse. What do others think? Do some reading in a library. Imagine other possibilities. In gathering material, you will discover more exactly where you stand.

As she strove to discover ideas for her paper, Tania Fusco kept a free-flowing journal in which she recorded thoughts as they came to her and as she read them or heard them. Her notes reveal interesting facets of her writing process. Many of the ideas she wrote down never actually made it into her final draft. Still, when she began writing, she had more than enough material to choose from.

11/6/95

Topic: sexism in advertising

  – All the images the same, a single monolithic message

  – Women are all beautiful, sexy, reduced to nothing but bodies

  – Men are driven by instincts, no emotions

Jodie's comment in class: these aren't just ads, they're also propaganda that influences young men's and women's ideas of themselves. (Talk more to Jodie?)

11/8/95

Maybe should argue that sexism in advertising is dangerous

Simple, easy dichotomies, reducing the complexity between the sexes

Women as emotional and sensual/men as intellectual, achievement-oriented

Perfume ads

Why are these in particular so blatant?
What is it about perfume?

Connect to other stereotypes?

Movies, especially, show men as strong gun-
toting heroes, women as in need of heroes

Books: "Men Are from Mars, Women Are from
Venus"— that guy really annoyed me!

*State your position.* It will help you focus your view if you state it in a sentence: a thesis, or statement of the stand you are taking. Just as your topic had to be a debatable issue, your position needs to be one that invites continued debate. In other words, you're going to have to stick your neck out a little; if you try to play it too safe, then there isn't really any point to what you are writing. "Minority students constitute 3 percent of our school's population" isn't really a stand; it's a fact. "Minority students are underrepresented at our school" or — even better — "Our school should increase its minority population" is a strong position that can be argued.

Make your thesis narrow. For a paper due a week from now, "The city's waterfront has become a run-down disgrace" can probably be supported by your own observations. But the claim "The welfare program in this country has become a disgrace" would take much digging, perhaps the work of years. (For more advice on developing a thesis, see Chapter 16, p. 349.)

*Assemble evidence.* Your claim stated, you'll need evidence to support it. What is evidence? Anything that demonstrates the soundness of your position and the points you make in your argument: facts and figures, observations, opinions, illustrations. The five writer's resources are a good place to start: even if they don't provide you with definitive evidence, they may suggest other avenues for exploration. Ask yourself the following questions.

 **DISCOVERY CHECKLIST**

- What can you *recall* from your own life that sheds light on this issue? What has led you to have the opinions on it that you do?
- What have you *observed*, or what might you observe, that would support your stand?
- What have you *read* about this topic? What else might you read?
- What expert might you *converse* with?
- Try to *imagine* yourself as your reader — what further evidence might persuade you?

As with most critical thinking tasks, this paper will require you to assemble evidence beyond your own personal memories and beliefs. The three most important sources of evidence are these:

1. *Facts, including statistics.* Facts are statements that can be verified by objective means; statistics are facts expressed in numbers. Facts usually form the basis of a successful argument.
2. *Expert testimony.* By "experts," we mean people with knowledge of a particular field gained from study and experience.
3. *Firsthand observation.* Your own observations can be a persuasive source of evidence, if you can assure your readers that your account is accurate.

For more about each of these forms of evidence, see "Types of Evidence" on page 114.

For this assignment, you will need to assemble evidence in written form. Take notes, in a notebook or on 4-by-6-inch or 5-by-7-inch index cards or on the computer. Be sure to record where exactly each piece of information comes from. Keep the form of your notes flexible so that you can easily arrange and rearrange them as you order your thoughts in drafting your paper.

**Testing and selecting evidence.** Now that you've collected some evidence to support your position, you need to sift through it to decide which pieces of information you will use in your paper. When is evidence useful and trustworthy? When —

1. It is accurate.
2. It is reliable.
3. It is up to date.
4. It is to the point.
5. It is representative.
6. It is not oversimplified.
7. It is sufficient and strong enough to back the claim and persuade your readers.

For more on each of these criteria for testing evidence, see "Testing Evidence" on page 118.

You may find that your evidence supports a position different from the one you intended to state in your paper. Take a moment to think things through: Is it possible that you could find some facts, testimony, and observations that would support your original position after all? Is it possible that you should rethink your original position? If you need to change your approach and come at the paper from a completely different angle, this is a good time to do so.

Most effective arguments take opposing viewpoints into consideration. Do you know what the arguments on the other side of the issue are? Do you know who supports these arguments? Do you have evidence or reasons that you can use to show why these arguments are unsound? In your final paper, you will probably want to address these counterarguments and disarm them; make sure you have the necessary evidence on hand.

As you look over your evidence and begin to put together your argument, consider things from your readers' point of view. What are their attitudes, interests, and priorities? What do they already know about the topic? What do they expect you to say? Imagine your readers and ask yourself whether the evidence you now have in front of you is appropriate and sufficient to convince them.

### PLANNING, DRAFTING, AND DEVELOPING

*Reassess your position.*  Now that you have looked into the matter, what is your current position on the issue? If necessary, revise the thesis that you formulated at the beginning of this assignment. Having stated your position, summarize your reasons for holding this view. List the supporting evidence.

*Organize your material.*  Once you have clarified your position and sifted through your evidence, you will probably find your argument falling into shape. Organize your notes into the order you think you'll follow in writing your draft. You may decide to make an outline (for methods, see p. 000). One useful pattern is the classical form of argument:

1. Introduce the subject to get the readers' interest.
2. State your main point or thesis.
3. Provide evidence to support your position.

**FOR GROUP LEARNING**

### Getting a Response to Your Position

Here is a situation in which your writing group can be particularly valuable. Allow a day or two for members of the group to decide, at least tentatively, the positions they wish to take in their individual papers. Then hold a meeting at which each member takes a few minutes to set forth his or her position and to support it. Invite other members of the group to suggest useful supporting evidence or to argue with counterevidence. One tremendous advantage of this activity is that before you write, you'll probably hear some of the objections your readers are likely to raise. Ask your group's recorder to list all the objections you get so that you'll remember them when writing your paper. If you can't answer some of the counterarguments, ask other members of the group to help you generate a reply. Of course, this group discussion might cause you to alter your whole stand. If this happens, give thanks: it will be easier to revise your ideas now than to revise your paper later.

4. Refute the opposition.
5. Reaffirm your main point.

In some situations, especially when you expect readers to be hostile to your point of view, you may want to take the opposite approach: refute the opposition, build a logical chain of evidence that leads to your main point, and *then* state your position. You may want to try both ways to see which works better.

*Define your terms.* Make clear any unfamiliar or questionable terms used in your thesis. If your position is "Humanists are dangerous," give a short definition of what you mean by *humanists* and by *dangerous* early in the paper. Clearly defined terms will prevent misunderstanding and will help keep your argument on track.

*Attend to logical, emotional, and ethical appeals.* The logical appeal engages readers' intellect; the emotional appeal touches their hearts; the ethical appeal draws on their sense of fairness and reasonableness. A persuasive argument usually operates on all three levels. (For more on the three forms of appeal, see pp. 117–18.)

To use the **logical appeal,** you need to make sure that your reasoning is clear and your evidence is sound. Don't claim more than you can demonstrate, and do demonstrate everything that you claim. (Much of the advice we've given so far on testing and selecting evidence will help you construct a sound logical appeal. See pp. 117–19)

To use the **emotional appeal,** select examples and language that will have an influence on how your readers feel about the issue. In some cases, a well-chosen image can win more support than a truckload of statistics. Be careful not to overdo it though: your argument will fall flat if you tug too hard on readers' heartstrings.

To use the **ethical appeal** in a paper taking a position, you must spell out your beliefs and give attention to beliefs opposing yours. The reader who readily accepts your beliefs is probably already on your side. If you declare, "I am against eating red meat because it contains fats and chemicals known to be harmful," you assert a position and then provide evidence for it. The reader who responds, "That's right — I'm a vegetarian myself" is clearly in your camp. But even the reader who responds at first, "Oh, I don't know — a hamburger never killed anyone!" may warm to your view if you consider his or her assumptions. These might include the beliefs that a burger is delicious; that vegetables aren't; that red meat supplies needed protein; and that the chemicals haven't been proved dangerous. You should show that you are aware of these assumptions and that you have considered them seriously. You might even agree with some of them. But then you must set forth in a reasonable way your own view. By spelling out your assumptions and by imagining those of a dissenting reader, you will win respect, if not conversion to your ideas.

As part of the ethical appeal, you should establish your credentials and those of your "experts." Let your readers know who you are and why the things you say about the subject are trustworthy. If you are writing about environmental pollution, tell your readers that your allergies have been irritated by chemicals in the air. If you are writing about euthanasia, establish the fact that you have witnessed the lingering death of a grandparent. Early in "On Racist Speech," Charles Lawrence establishes himself as a convincing spokesperson on the subject of free speech. If an expert whom you quote has outstanding credentials, you may easily be able to insert a brief citation of those credentials: "Lewis Thomas, chancellor of the Memorial Sloan-Kettering Cancer Center." If you have talked to experts and are convinced of their authority, state why you believe that they can be trusted. "From conversation with Mr. Dworshak, who showed me six model wind tunnels he has built, I can testify to his extensive knowledge of aeronautics."

*Credit your sources.* As you write, make your sources of evidence clear. The simplest way to do so is to incorporate your source into the text: "According to an article in the December 10, 1995, issue of *Time*" or "When I talked with my history professor, Dr. Harry Cleghorn, he said. . . ."

## REVISING AND EDITING

When you're writing a paper taking a stand, you may be tempted to fall in love with the evidence you have gone to such trouble to collect. One of the hardest things for a writer to do is to take out information, but you must if it is irrelevant, redundant, or weak. Some of it won't help your case; some may just seem boring and likely to persuade nobody. If so, pitch it. Sometimes you can have too much evidence, and if you throw some out, a stronger argument will remain. Sometimes you can become so attached to old evidence that,

**WRITING
WITH A
COMPUTER**

If in taking your stand you'll be disputing the view of some other writer, start by creating a document into which you type those passages from the book, magazine article, newspaper column, or editorial that have provoked you to dissent. Your time will be well spent: transcribing the other writer's very words will get you looking at them closely and will probably help you respond to them. Besides, you'll have exact quotations at your fingertips. Then, on the same disk create a second document in which you'll write your paper.

When you want to cite the other writer's exact words, just use your word processor to copy the text from the first document into the document with your paper. (Different word processors have different names for "copying" — some will use COPY and PASTE; others use MOVE or INSERT.) As you incorporate the other writer's words, blend them in with your text, but avoid plagiarism by acknowledging the original source properly. (For more on copying, cutting, and pasting, see "Moving Blocks of Text" on pp. 447–48.)

when new evidence or new thoughts come along, you won't want to discard what you have on hand. But in taking a stand, as in any other writing, second thoughts often surpass first thoughts. Be willing to revise not only your words but your view.

Make sure that your main point is clear and that your paper doesn't drift away from it into a contradiction. The process of arriving at a defensible position and conveying it through writing is a complicated and sometimes ambiguous one. But the final paper should be as clear and straightforward as possible.

When you're taking a last look over your paper, proofread with care. Wherever you have given facts and figures as evidence, check for errors in names and numbers. This advice may seem trivial, but there's a considerable difference between "10,000 people" and "100,000 people."

As you revise, here are some points to consider.

**REVISION CHECKLIST**

- Does your view convince you? Or do you think you need still more evidence?
- Have you tried to keep in mind your readers and what would appeal to them? Have you answered what you think their major objections will be?
- Is your tone suitable for your readers? Do you say anything in a way that may alienate them?
- Might the points in your argument seem stronger if arranged in a different sequence?

**FOR PEER RESPONSE**

Enlist some other students to read your draft critically and tell you whether they accept your arguments.

See Chapter 20 for advice on working with other student writers and for general questions you should always ask a peer editor to address. For a paper in which you take a stand, you'll also want your peer editors to answer these specific questions:

- Can you state what you understand the writer's claim to be?
- Do you have any problems following or accepting the reasons for the writer's position? Would you make any changes in the reasoning?
- How persuasive is the writer's evidence? Do you have any questions about that evidence? Can you suggest some good evidence the writer has overlooked?
- Has the writer provided sufficient transitions to guide you through his or her argument?
- Has the writer made a good case for his or her position? Are you persuaded to his or her point of view? If not, is there any point or objection that the writer could address that would make the argument more compelling?
- If this were your paper, what is the one thing you would be sure to work on before handing it in?

- Have you unfairly omitted any evidence that would hurt your case?
- In rereading your paper, do you have any excellent, fresh thoughts? If so, make room for them.

## OTHER ASSIGNMENTS

1. Write a letter to the editor of your local newspaper or of a national newsmagazine in which you agree or disagree with the publication's editorial stand on a current question or with the recent words or actions of some public figure. Be sure to make clear your reasons for holding your view.

2. Write a short paper in which you agree or disagree with one of the following suggestions. (Or choose some other issue you have lately read about that interests you.) You need not propose an alternative action; just give your opinion of the suggestion.

   Creationism and evolution should be given equal importance in high school science courses.

   Public television should be abolished.

   To protect certain endangered species of ocean fish, fish rationing should be imposed on consumers.

   The United States should colonize Mars.

   Japan should relax its import regulations more.

3. Write a short paper in which you express your view on one of the following topics or another that comes to mind. Make clear your reasons for believing as you do.

   Bilingual education
   Nonsmokers' rights
   Date rape
   The fitness movement
   The minimum wage
   Destruction of rainforests
   Terrorism
   Prayer in public schools

4. Write a short paper in which you agree or disagree with the following quotation from Gilbert and Sullivan's musical comedy *Ruddigore*. Use examples and evidence to support your view.

   If you wish in this world to advance
   Your merits you're bound to enhance;
   You must stir it and stump it,
   And blow your own trumpet,
   Or, trust me, you haven't a chance.

# Applying What You Learn:
# Some Uses of Taking a Stand

As you may have found out by now, not only writing assignments but also college examination questions sometimes ask you to take a stand on a controversy:

> Criticize the statement "There's too much science and not enough caring in the modern practice of medicine."
>
> Respond to the view that "there's no need to be concerned about carbon dioxide heating up the earth's atmosphere because a warmer climate, by increasing farm production, would be preferable to the one we have now."

Your answers to such exam questions indicate clearly to your instructor how firm a grasp you have on the material.

In your daily life, too, you'll sometimes feel the need to advance a view in writing. You may be called on to represent the tenants of your apartment building by writing a letter of protest to a landlord who wants to raise your rent, or you may feel moved to write to a store manager complaining about the treatment you received from a salesperson. As an active citizen, you'll wish from time to time to write a letter to the editor of your local newspaper or to your senator.

When you enter the working world, you'll need to be able to state your views clearly in writing. There is hardly a professional position you can hold — lawyer, teacher, nurse, business manager, journalist — in which you won't be invited to state and support your views about some important matter, often for the benefit of others in your profession or the general public. Here is a sample of such writing, in which Mary Anne Raywid, in the *Journal of Teacher Education* (Sept.–Oct. 1978), defends professors of education against the constant charge that they use jargon when ordinary English would do:

> This is not to deny that educators speak a language of their own. Indeed they do; and it is very much a part of their specialized knowledge. These words become a way first to select out certain qualities, events, and phenomena for attention; and they expedite communication via shorthand references to particular combinations of these. To cite a familiar example, when an educationist talks about a *meaningful learning experience*, s/he is not just spouting jargon, but distinguishing out of all the events and phenomena of a given time and place, a particular set. Moreover, a substantial list of things is being asserted about what is going on — e.g., the words *learning experience* suggest that it is, or it is meant to be, an episode from which learning results. The term *meaningful* is not superfluous but does a specific job: it adds that it is likely to be or was (depending on temporal perspective) a successful exercise in learning — which not all learning experiences proffered by teachers can claim. To qualify as *meaningful* in advance — in other words, well calculated to succeed — a number of conditions must be met, ordinarily including learner comprehension, interest, motivation, capacity, and likely retention.

Scientists who do original research face the task of persuading the scientific community that their findings are valid. They write and publish accounts of their work in scientific journals for evaluation by their peers. In such articles they report new facts as well as state opinions. Some also write for general readers as well. Here, for instance, is Gerald Weissmann, in an essay called "Foucault and the Bag Lady" (*The Woods Hole Cantata: Essays on Science and Society.* Dodd, Mead, & Co., 1985), airing his views on the recent trend to deinstitutionalize the mentally ill:

> It has always seemed to me to constitute a fantastic notion that the social landscape of our large cities bears any direct relationship to that kind of stable, nurturing community which would support the fragile psyche of the mentally ill. Cast into an environment limited by the welfare hotel or park bench, lacking adequate outpatient services, prey to climatic extremes and urban criminals, the deinstitutionalized patients wind up as conscripts in an army of the homeless. Indeed, only this winter was the city of New York forced to open temporary shelters in church basements, armories, and lodging houses for thousands of half-frozen street dwellers. A psychiatrist of my acquaintance has summarized the experience of a generation in treating the mentally deranged: "In the nineteen-fifties, the mad people were warehoused in heated public hospitals with occasional access to trained professionals. In the sixties and seventies, they were released into the community and permitted to wander the streets without access to psychiatric care. In the eighties, we have made progress, however. When the mentally ill become too cold to wander the streets, we can warehouse them in heated church basements without supervision."

Weissmann's statement is a good illustration of a specialist writing for the rest of us — and forcefully taking a stand.

## *Making Connections:*
## *Taking a Stand in* A Writer's Reader

The issues of concern in our society — ranging from the significance of a particular song to our relationships with foreign nations — are debated most often in the forum of public writing. In fact, presenting one's position on an issue and giving the reasons and evidence supporting that position may be one of the most common uses of writing in our culture. Not surprisingly, *A Writer's Reader* provides a variety of examples of a writer taking a stand on an issue. Columnist Anna Quindlen in "Evan's Two Moms" (p. 481) argues the controversial position that lesbians should be allowed to adopt children. Philosopher Christina Hoff Sommers in "The Backlash Myth: The Truth about How Women Are Doing in the Workplace" (p. 560) argues that the feminist claim of discrimination against women on jobs is exaggerated. Both writers make their arguments with the aid of hard facts, personal experience and observation, and clear reasoning.

Besides Quindlen, Sommers, Charles Lawrence (p. 183), and Tania Fusco (p. 187), other writers in a variety of professions in *A Writer's Reader* take a clear, forceful stand: award-winning journalist Katha Pollitt, "The Future Is Coed" (p. 496); international journalist Susanna Rodell, "Do You Work? Are You Guilty?" (p. 545); law professor Patricia J. Williams, "Hate Radio" (p. 582); medical doctor Melvin Konner, "Out of the Darkness" (p. 615); naturalist Bill McKibben, "The End of Nature" (p. 620); and environmental writer Gregg Easterbrook, "Forget PCBs. Radon. Alar: The World's Greatest Environmental Dangers Are Dung Smoke and Dirty Water" (p. 636). As you read these essays, consider how each writer takes a stand. For each essay, answer the following questions.

1. What stand does the writer take? Is it a popular opinion, or does it break from commonly accepted beliefs?
2. Does the writer use logical appeal, emotional appeal, ethical appeal, or a combination? Is the writer's appeal appropriate to the audience and effective?
3. How does the writer support his or her position? Is the evidence sufficient to gain your respect?
4. How does the writer's occupation or expertise contribute to the credibility of his or her stand?

# Chapter 10

# Proposing a Solution

Sometimes when you learn of a problem such as acid rain, homelessness, or famine, you say to yourself, "Something should be done about that." You can do something constructive yourself: by the powerful and persuasive activity of writing. This chapter will give you some tips on how to be convincing.

Your purpose in such writing, as political leaders and advertisers well know, is to rouse your audience to action. Thomas Jefferson and his associates who wrote the Declaration of Independence accomplished as much, and even in your daily life at college you will find chances to demonstrate this effect often. Does some policy of your college administrators irk you? Would you urge students to attend a rally for a cause or a charity? You can write a letter to your college newspaper or to someone in authority and try to stir your readers to action.

The uses of such writing go far beyond these immediate applications. A college course will sometimes ask you to write a *proposal*: a recommendation that an action be taken. In Chapter 9, you took a stand and backed it up with evidence. Now go a step further. If, for instance, you have made the claim "Our national parks are in sorry condition," you might urge readers to write to their representatives in Congress or visit a national park and pick up trash. Or you might want to suggest that the Department of the Interior be given a budget increase to hire more park rangers, purchase additional park land to accommodate increased visitors, and buy more cleanup equipment. You might further suggest that the department could raise funds for this increase through sales of videos of individual parks as well as through increased revenues from visitors who come to the parks because of the videos. The first paper would be a call to immediate action on the part of your readers; the second, an attempt to forge a consensus about what needs to be done.

In making a proposal, you set forth a solution and urge action by using words like *should*, *ought*, and *must:* "This city ought to have a Bureau of Missing Persons"; "Small private aircraft should be banned from flying closer than one mile to a major commercial airport." Take care that you don't become preachy with your *should*s and *must*s. Explain the problem fully and lay out, clearly and concisely, all the reasons you can muster to persuade your readers that your proposal deserves to be implemented.

# Learning from Other Writers

The writers of the following two essays propose sensible solutions for pressing problems. One of the most controversial problems today is control of crime. What is the best treatment for criminals — punishment or rehabilitation, or a combination? And how are we going to pay for the continually increasing number of inmates in our prisons? Politicians, lawyers, and ordinary citizens have made suggestions about how to solve this major problem. One voice seldom heard in this controversy is that of the criminals themselves. The first essay is written by Wilbert Rideau, editor of the *Angolite,* the Louisiana State Penitentiary newsmagazine.

The second essay is by Heather Colbenson, who wrote the essay for a course at the University of Minnesota, where she was studying agricultural business. Her proposal addresses a problem she had encountered personally: the lack of funds to support agricultural programs in rural high schools. "I wrote about something close to my heart," states Colbenson, "and I was excited because I felt that the solutions presented could really work."

## Wilbert Rideau    Why Prisons Don't Work

I was among thirty-one murderers sent to the Louisiana State Penitentiary in 1962 to be executed or imprisoned for life. We weren't much different from those we found here, or those who had preceded us. We were unskilled, impulsive, and uneducated misfits, mostly black, who had done dumb, impulsive things — failures, rejects from the larger society. Now a generation has come of age and gone since I've been here, and everything is much the same as I found it. The faces of the prisoners are different, but behind them are the same impulsive, uneducated, unskilled minds that made dumb, impulsive choices that got them into more trouble than they ever thought existed. The vast majority of us are consigned to suffer and die here so politicians can sell the illusion that permanently exiling people to prison will make society safe.

Getting tough has always been a "silver bullet," a quick fix for the crime and violence that society fears. Each year in Louisiana — where excess is a way of life — lawmakers have tried to outdo each other in legislating harsher mandatory penalties and in reducing avenues of release. The only thing to do with criminals, they say, is get tougher. They have. In the process, the purpose of prison began to change. The state boasts one of the highest lockup rates in the country, imposes the most severe penalties in the nation, and vies to execute more criminals per capita than anywhere else. This state is so tough that last year, when prison authorities here wanted to punish an inmate in solitary confinement for an infraction, the most they could inflict on him was to deprive him of his underwear. It was all he had left.

If getting tough resulted in public safety, Louisiana citizens would be the safest in the nation. They're not. Louisiana has the highest murder rate among states. Prison, like the police and the courts, has a minimal impact on crime because it is a response after the fact, a mop-up operation. It doesn't work. The idea of punishing the few to deter the many is counterfeit because potential criminals either think they're not going to get caught or they're so emotionally desperate or psychologically distressed that they don't care about the consequences of their actions. The threatened punishment, regardless of its severity, is never a factor in the equation. But society, like the incorrigible criminal it abhors, is unable to learn from its mistakes. 3

Prison has a role in public safety, but it is not a cure-all. Its value is limited, and its use should also be limited to what it does best: isolating young criminals long enough to give them a chance to grow up and get a grip on their impulses. It is a traumatic experience, certainly, but it should be only a temporary one, not a way of life. Prisoners kept too long tend to embrace the criminal culture, its distorted values and beliefs; they have little choice — prison is their life. There are some prisoners who cannot be returned to society — serial killers, serial rapists, professional hit men, and the like — but the monsters who need to die in prison are rare exceptions in the criminal landscape. 4

Crime is a young man's game. Most of the nation's random violence is committed by young urban terrorists. But because of long, mandatory sentences, most prisoners here are much older, having spent fifteen, twenty, thirty, or more years behind bars, long past necessity. Rather than pay for new prisons, society would be well served by releasing some of its older prisoners who pose no threat and using the money to catch young street thugs. Warden John Whitley agrees that many older prisoners here could be freed tomorrow with little or no danger to society. Release, however, is governed by law or by politicians, not by penal professionals. Even murderers, those most feared by society, pose little risk. Historically, for example, the domestic staff at Louisiana's Governor's mansion has been made up of murderers, hand-picked to work among the chief-of-state and his family. Penologists have long known that murder is almost always a once-in-a-lifetime act. The most dangerous criminal is the one who has not yet killed but has a history of escalating offenses. He's the one to watch. 5

Rehabilitation can work. Everyone changes in time. The trick is to influence the direction that change takes. The problem with prisons is that they don't do more to rehabilitate those confined in them. The convict who enters prison illiterate will probably leave the same way. Most convicts want to be better than they are, but education is not a priority. This prison houses 4,600 men and offers academic training to 240, vocational training to a like num- 6 ber. Perhaps it doesn't matter. About 90 percent of the men here may never leave this prison alive.

The only effective way to curb crime is for society to work to *prevent* the    7
criminal act in the first place, to come between the perpetrator and crime. Our youngsters must be taught to respect the humanity of others and to handle disputes without violence. It is essential to educate and equip them with the skills to pursue their life ambitions in a meaningful way. As a community, we must address the adverse life circumstances that spawn criminality. These things are not quick, and they're not easy, but they're effective. Politicians think that's too hard a sell. They want to be on record for doing something now, something they can point to at reelection time. So the drumbeat goes on for more police, more prisons, more of the same failed policies.

Ever see a dog chase its tail?    8

**Questions to Start You Thinking**

*Meaning*

1. Does Rideau convince you that the belief that "permanently exiling people to prison will make society safe" is an "illusion" (paragraph 1)?
2. According to Rideau, why don't prisons work?
3. What does he propose as solutions to the problem of escalating crime? What other solutions can you think of?

*Writing Strategies*

4. How does Rideau organize his essay? Is his organization easy to follow?
5. What evidence does the author provide to support his assertion that Louisiana's "getting tough" policy has not worked? Does he provide sufficient evidence to convince you? Does he persuade you that action is necessary?
6. What evidence does Rideau give to support his proposals? Does he convince you that they would work? What would make his argument more persuasive?
7. Other than himself, what authorities does Rideau cite? Why do you think he does this?
8. Does the fact that the author is a convicted criminal strengthen or weaken his argument? Why do you think he mentions this fact in his very first sentence?

STUDENT ESSAY

# *Heather Colbenson*   Missed Opportunities

A terrible problem is occurring within some small high    1
schools in Minnesota: the agriculture classes are being reduced or even cut from the curriculum. By cutting the agriculture classes the FFA program is also cut because a student
must take an ag class to be in the FFA. At one time the FFA

stood for the Future Farmers of America; however, the organization has grown to encompass things other than farming so it is now called the National FFA Organization and it has become the largest youth organization in the United States. This is an important organization because it helps students develop leadership skills that they will use to be successful in business and in life. Therefore, the FFA programs in small schools should be saved.

Why would high schools in farming communities drop agriculture classes and the FFA program? One reason is that many colleges require that high school students take specific courses for entry into college. When funding decreases, these courses for college-bound students are seldom cut. Also, students must choose between general education college-prep courses and elective courses such as agriculture. For example, Minnesota colleges now require two years of foreign language. In small schools, like my own, the students could take either foreign language or ag classes. Most students choose the language classes to fulfill the college requirement. When the students leave the ag classes to take foreign language, the ag enrollment declines, making it easy for school administrators to cut ag classes.

The main reason that small schools are cutting ag programs is that the state has not provided significant funding for the schools to operate. When schools have to make cuts, some decide that the agriculture classes are not as important as other courses--basic education courses such as English, math, and science and college-prep courses such as foreign language, calculus, and physics. When there is not enough money, something has to go, and ag often gets cut.

If cuts have to be made, why should schools keep their ag courses and the FFA programs? If schools do cut these programs, students lose many opportunities. The FFA and ag classes are not just about cows and corn; they teach leadership, teamwork, and self motivation. The FFA provides many different ways for a student to develop skills in these areas through holding offices, competing in contests, and making friends.

The main goal of the FFA is leadership development, and one significant benefit of the FFA is the opportunity for

high school students to develop leadership skills. This opportunity is lost if ag classes and FFA organizations are cut
in the schools. Through FFA projects students learn to identify problems, to research solutions, to formulate plans to
solve problems, and to direct and guide other people in implementing the plans. Through these activities, they develop
self-confidence and self-motivation. This organization definitely helped me develop leadership and confidence. When an
FFA program is cut from a school, a major resource of leadership development is gone because students may never find out
that they can develop the ability to lead. George Bush, former president of the United States and a former member of the
FFA, praises this organization for its leadership opportunities. If FFA programs are cut, students may not have other
avenues to help them develop these skills.

Learning teamwork is another benefit of the FFA, and the    6
chance to work as a team is also lost when an ag program is
cut. Of course, students learn teamwork from sports, but what
sport has a team that consists of seventy people, as my FFA
did? When FFA programs are cut, students have fewer opportunities to learn to work cooperatively with other people.

A third advantage of FFA programs is that students dis-    7
cover that they can compete successfully against other students outside of the sports arena. The FFA has competitions
at the local, district, and state levels. If the FFA is cut,
a student may never know the pride of representing his or her
school at all these levels and might never experience the
thrill of competing with people from all over the nation at a
national contest.

A fourth advantage is that FFA offers opportunities for    8
students to explore various careers. FFA activities and competitions deal with livestock, business, sales, horticulture,
floriculture, and public speaking. Cutting the program would
result in the lost opportunity of trying different possible
career areas. I might never have found my desire to be a
business major had I not been in the FFA.

A fifth benefit from the FFA is meeting other people. If    9
I had not been in the FFA, one of the greatest losses for me
would be missing the opportunity to meet other people. I

gained friends from many different schools and states. Now
many of those same friends attend the University of Minnesota
with me. The loss of ag classes and an FFA program would result in a lot of missed opportunities for the students. I believe that there is no other student organization that can
provide the opportunities the FFA does.

With all of these benefits from FFA programs for stu-          10
dents in small high schools, these programs definitely
should be saved. But what can be done to save them? Consolidation of programs, fundraising, education, and support
are all things that can very easily keep a program going
strong. First, schools that are having financial trouble
can consolidate FFA programs. Small schools that have con-
solidated have been able to save their ag program, making
the chapter stronger and dividing the cost. A second activity that can help the financial situation is local
fundraising. This is a great way to keep an FFA program. My
chapter sells fruit and raffle tickets every year to raise
money. The school doesn't pay for any of the activities.
Third, the FFA members themselves must educate the administration, teachers, younger students, and businesspeople of
the town as to how the FFA supports and helps students beyond their increased knowledge of agriculture. If these
people realize the range of benefits that students receive
from the FFA, then they will ensure that the program remains in the local school. Fourth, FFA members must support
their own program from within. If even one FFA member says
negative things about the FFA, it will hurt the program;
people always remember negative things. Instead, members
should share their concerns with other members and work
within the group to change the situation.

I believe that ag classes and the FFA should remain          11
available for the benefit of students. Small schools do have
financial trouble and do have to make cuts, yet the FFA is
the wrong place to cut because many students would miss out
on opportunities that could very easily change their lives. I
want other students to be members of this great organization
from which I have benefited so much.

*Meaning*

1. What problem does Colbenson identify? Does she convince you that this is an important problem?
2. What solutions does she propose? Which is her strongest suggestion? Her least convincing? Can you think of any other suggestions she might have included?

*Writing Strategies*

3. What kinds of transitions does Colbenson use to lead readers through the points she makes in her paper? Do you find them effective?
4. Is her argument easy to follow? Does she provide sufficient evidence?

# Learning by Writing

## THE ASSIGNMENT: PROPOSING A SOLUTION

In this essay you're going to accomplish two things. First, you'll carefully analyze and explain a specific social, economic, political, civic, or environmental problem — a problem you care about and strongly wish to see resolved. The problem may be large or small, but it shouldn't be trivial. (No comic essays about the awful problem of ketchup that squirts from Big Macs or the problems of eating peanut butter, please.) The problem may be one that affects the whole country, or it may be one that affects mainly people in your city, campus, or classroom. Show your readers that this problem really exists and that it matters to you and to them. Write for an audience who, once made aware of the problem, may be expected to help do something about it. After setting forth the problem, you may want to include the reasons that the problem exists, similar to Colbenson's approach in her essay "Missed Opportunities."

The second thing you are to accomplish in the essay is to propose one or more ways to solve the problem or at least alleviate it. You will supply evidence that your solution is reasonable and that it can work. Remember that your purpose is to convince your readers that something should be done about the problem.

Some recent papers in which students cogently argued for actions include the following.

Using research studies and statistics, a man argued that the practice of using the scores from standardized tests such as the SAT and the ACT as criteria for college admissions or placement is a problem because it favors aggressive students from affluent families; he further argued that the practice of using the scores in this way should be abolished.

A woman argued that one solution to vacation frustration is to turn everything — planning, choosing a location, arranging transportation, reserving lodging — over to a travel agent.

A man identified the problem of nonsmokers often being exposed to a haze of cigarette smoke as they enter buildings on college campuses, and he proposed that to protect nonsmokers, outdoor smoking on college campuses be limited to restricted areas away from building entrances.

A woman argued that the best solution to the problem of her children's poor education is home schooling.

## GENERATING IDEAS

*Identify a problem.* In selecting a topic, brainstorming is a good way to begin. Write down all the possible writing topics that come to mind. Then go back over the list and star those that seem to have the most potential for your paper. (See p. 334 for more advice on this useful strategy.) Your five familiar resources may supply you with knowledge of a problem that needs to be cured. Here are a few questions to help ideas start flowing.

**DISCOVERY
CHECKLIST**

- Can you *recall* any problem you have encountered that you think needs a solution? Ask yourself what problems you meet every day or occasionally or what problems concern people near you. Can you think of a better way for your college to run course registration? A better way for your state to control dangerous drugs?
- What conditions in need of improvement have you *observed* on television or in your daily activities? What action is called for?
- What problems have you encountered in the *reading* material for your courses? If these problems are too large or remote, can you think of corresponding problems that exist in your neighborhood or community?
- What problems have you heard discussed recently in *conversation* on campus or in the classroom?
- By *imagining* yourself in the position of another person, perhaps someone of a different economic or ethnic background, can you imagine a problem of importance to that person?

Also try scanning the news. One of the most convenient sources of information about real and current problems is a daily newspaper or a newsmagazine such as *Time, Newsweek,* or *U.S. News & World Report.* In a single newspaper published on the morning we wrote these words, we found discussions of the problems of gang violence, teenage pregnancy, the high school dropout rate, overfishing in the oceans, the threat of extinction of the panda bear, overregulation by the government, the national debt, the results of floods and earthquakes in California, terrorist cults, declining academic skills of high school students, the devaluation of the American dollar, obesity, illegal Chinese aliens on a tanker off the coast of the United States, people addicted to gambling, cuts in school lunch programs, attention deficit syndrome among crack babies, the difficulty of apprehending parents suspected of child abuse, children falsely accusing parents of child abuse, traffic congestion, and the failure of a new drug to control AIDS.

*Think about solutions.*  Once you've chosen a problem, try to come up with solutions. Some problems — such as reducing international tensions — present no easy solutions. Still, give some thought to any problem that you feel seriously concerned with. You can't be expected to solve, in one college writing assignment, a problem that may have thwarted teams of experts. But sometimes a solution to a problem will reveal itself to a novice thinker. And for some problems, even a small contribution to a partial solution will be worth offering. Brainstorming — alone or with classmates — can be a valuable strategy to find solutions (see p. 334).

When thinking critically about the problem, you might try to *analyze* it, breaking it into smaller pieces — subproblems that can be solved one at a time perhaps. You should also try to develop an understanding of the *causes* of the problem and to project what some of the further *effects* will be if the problem is not solved; both of these can contribute to a persuasive paper. When you come across a promising solution, try a little *comparison and contrast* to get a sense of how effective and useful this solution would be: Has this solution been tried before? How well did it work then? Is it more or less likely to be successful now? Finally, *evaluate* how urgent this problem is. Does something need to be done about it immediately, or should you look for long-range solutions, which may take more time to implement?

*Consider your readers.*  Think of your audience — the readers you seek to persuade. For your proposal to be successful, readers need to believe that the problem is real and that your solution is feasible. Often the most difficult part is getting them to agree that you're addressing a legitimate and significant problem — one that should concern them, too. If you are addressing your classmates, maybe they haven't thought about the problem before. Try to discover any way to bring it home to them, to show that it affects them and deserves their attention. To get readers on your side, you need to consider things from their point of view. Here are some questions to ask yourself about your readers.

DISCOVERY
CHECKLIST

## Understanding Your Audience

- Who are your readers? How would you describe them?
- Why should your readers care about this problem? Why should it concern them personally? Might it affect their health, conscience, or pocketbook?
- Have they ever expressed any interest in the problem?
- Do they belong to any organization or segment of society that might make them especially susceptible to — or uninterested in — this problem?
- What attitudes relevant to the problem and your proposal do you have in common with your readers?
- Do you and your readers already agree on anything? Do they have assumptions or values different from yours that will affect how they view your proposal?

*Gather evidence.* To show that the problem really exists, you'll need evidence and examples. Draw on your five familiar resources: recall, observation, reading, conversation, and imagination. While you think, scribble notes to yourself. If you feel that further reading in the library will help you know what you're talking about, now is the time. (For more advice on assembling, testing, and selecting evidence, see pp. 114–19.)

## PLANNING, DRAFTING, AND DEVELOPING

*Start with your proposal.* A basic way to approach your paper is to state your proposal in a sentence: "A law should be passed enabling couples to divorce without having to go to court"; "The United States should secede from the United Nations." From such a statement, the rest of the argument may start to unfold. Usually a paper of this kind falls naturally into a simple two-part shape:

1. A claim that a problem exists. This part, explains the problem and supplies evidence to suggest that it is intolerable.
2. A claim that something ought to be done about it — the proposal for solution.

You can make your proposal more persuasive by including some or all of the following elements.

The knowledge or experience you have that qualifies you to propose a solution. If you are proposing changes in Little League baseball, your experience as a player or a coach can help establish your credibility as an authority.

The values, beliefs, or assumptions that have caused you to feel strongly about the need for action.

What will be required — an estimate of money, people, skills, material. This part might include a list of what is readily available now and what else will have to be obtained.

Exactly what must be done, step by step, to achieve your solution.

How long the solution is likely to take to implement.

What possible obstacles or difficulties may need to be overcome.

Why your solution is better than others that have been proposed or tried already.

What controls or quality checks might be used to make sure that your solution is proceeding as expected.

Any other evidence to show that what you suggest is practical, reasonable in cost, and likely to be effective.

Following is the informal outline that Heather Colbenson used as she was writing her essay "Missed Opportunities." Note the kinds of evidence she chose to include and the order she chose.

Thesis: FFA programs in small schools should be saved.

1. Reasons FFA programs are being cut
   - College requirements
   - Decreased funds

2. Reasons FFA programs should not be cut: benefits of FFA
   - Leadership training
   - Teamwork
   - Competition
   - Career exploration
   - Meeting people

3. Suggestions to save FFA programs
   - Consolidation
   - Fundraising
   - Education
   - Support from within

When you come to set forth your proposal, you will increase the likelihood of its acceptance if you make the first step simple and inviting. A claim that national parks need better care might begin by suggesting that readers head for such a park and personally size up the situation.

If as you go along you find you don't know enough about a certain point, don't hesitate to backtrack to the library or to one of your five resources.

*Imagine your readers' objections.* Perhaps you can think of possible objections your readers might raise: reservations about the high cost, the complexity, or the workability of your plan, for instance. It is persuasive to anticipate an objection that might occur to your readers and to lay it to rest. Jonathan Swift, in *A Modest Proposal*, is aware of this rhetorical strategy. After arguing that it will greatly help the poor of Ireland to sell their babies to rich landlords for meat (he's being ironic, savagely condemning the landlords' lack of feeling), Swift goes on:

> I can think of no one objection that will possibly be raised against this proposal, unless it should be urged that the number of people will be thereby much lessened in the kingdom. This I freely own, and it was indeed one principal design in offering it to the world.

*Cite sources carefully.* When you collect ideas and evidence from outside sources, you'll need to document your evidence; that is, tell where you got everything. Check with your instructor on the documentation method he or she wants you to use. For a short paper like the one assigned here, it will probably be enough to introduce brief lines and phrases to identify sources:

```
According to Newsweek correspondent Josie Fair . . .

As 1990 census figures indicate . . .

In his biography FDR: The New Deal Years, Kenneth S.
Davis reports . . .

While working as a Senate page in the summer of 1994, I
observed . . .
```

## REVISING AND EDITING

Revising this paper will require you truly to *re-see* or *re-vision* the problem and your proposed solution. As you revise, concentrate on a clear explanation of the problem and solid supporting evidence for the solution. Keep your purpose of convincing your readers uppermost in your thoughts. Be sure to use the necessary connections to make the parts of your essay clear for your readers.

In drafting her essay, Heather Colbenson encountered problems with organization and coherence. Following are paragraphs 2 and 3 from her first draft:

**WRITING WITH A COMPUTER**

Your word processor's ability to lift and move blocks of words is especially useful for this assignment. It gives you the power to play around, arranging the points of your argument in whatever sequence seems most effective. You might place first whatever you expect to be your readers' most powerful objection to your proposal and then answer it right away. Place the second strongest objection next, and so on. Try different sequences until you find the one that works best. Try reversing that order, putting the strongest objection last. Your most convincing point might come last — for an effective clincher. (For more on rearranging text, see "Moving Blocks of Text" on pp. 447–48.)

Why would high schools in farming communities drop agriculture classes and the FFA program? Small schools are cutting ag programs because the state has not provided significant funding for the small schools to operate. The small schools have to make cuts and some small schools are deciding that the agriculture classes are not as important as other courses. Some small schools are consolidating to receive more aid. Many of these schools have been able to save their ag program.

Many colleges are demanding that students have two years of foreign language. In small schools, like my own, the students could take either foreign language or ag classes. Therefore students choose the language classes to fill the college requirement. When the students leave the ag classes to take foreign language, the number of students declines, which makes it easier for school administrators to cut ag classes.

As she read over her draft, Colbenson realized that she was really talking about the two primary reasons FFA programs are being cut. That was clear in her mind, but she had not made it clear on paper for her readers. She decided to use transitional phrases to make her point clear and to tie her ideas together explicitly , so she added "One reason" and "The main reason." Then she decided to place the main reason, decreased funds, last for emphasis. As she worked with her draft further, she realized that her first reason was not actually college requirements, as she had stated, but it was really the competition between college-prep courses and other courses in the high school curriculum when money is limited. She further revised her second paragraph to make this point clear. As she looked at her comment about consolidation, she realized it did not fit at the end of the paragraph explaining cuts made because of inadequate funding. This point was a way to save ag programs, not a reason they were being cut. For unity, she moved the point about consolidation to the last section of her essay, which consists of suggestions to save FFA programs. She found similar problems with coherence in her section on the benefits of FFA programs. She thought through this information in a similar manner, rearranged it, and added key words for transition: "one significant benefit," "another benefit," "A third advangage," "A fourth advantage," "A fifth benefit" (see paragraphs 5–9).

With the corrections, the paper was more forcefully organized and more tightly coherent, making it easier for readers to follow and understand. The bridges between ideas in the writer's mind were now on paper. In going over her draft, Colbenson was also able to eliminate unnecessary words and, in general, improve the style. As she re-viewed her ideas for unity and coherence, she also found more precise words and more effective sentences to express her ideas. Adding those made her essay even stronger.

*Be reasonable.* Exaggerated claims for your solution will not persuade. Don't be afraid to express your own reasonable doubts that your solution will root out the problem forever. If you have ended your draft with a resounding trumpet call or a horrific vision of what will happen if your idea should go untried, ask yourself whether you have gone too far.

A temptation in writing a paper that proposes a solution is to simplify the problem so that the solution will seem all the more likely to apply. In looking back over your draft, consider whether perhaps you have fallen into *oversimplification*. (For help in recognizing this and other errors in reasoning, see p. 120.) You may need to rethink both the problem and the solution.

In looking back over your draft once more, review these points.

**REVISION CHECKLIST**

- Does your introduction invite the reader in?
- Have you made the problem clear? Have you made it of immediate concern to your readers?
- Have you made clear the steps that must be taken to solve the problem?
- Have you demonstrated the benefits of your solution?
- Have you considered other possible solutions to the problem before rejecting them in favor of your own?
- Have you anticipated the doubts readers may have about your solution?
- Do you come across as a well-meaning, reasonable writer willing to admit that you don't know everything?
- Have you avoided promising that your solution will do more than it can possibly do? Have you made believable predictions for the success of your plan, not wild ones?

### OTHER ASSIGNMENTS

1. If in Chapter 9 you followed the assignment and took a stand, now write a few additional paragraphs extending that paper, going on to propose a solution, to argue for action. You may find it helpful to brainstorm with classmates first (see p. 334).

2. Write an editorial in which you propose to your town officials an innovation you think would benefit the whole community. Here are a few suggestions to get your own thoughts working:

**FOR GROUP LEARNING**

### Exchanging Written Reactions

Here is a one-on-one activity. Exchange with some other student the papers you both have written for an assignment in this chapter. Then instead of writing the brief comments you might ordinarily write on another student's paper, write each other at least a few hundred words of reactions and suggestions. Exchange comments and then sit down together to discuss your experiences. What did you find out about proposing a solution? About writing? About peer editing?

A drug and alcohol education program in the schools

A network of bicycle paths

After-school programs for children of working parents

Getting people involved in neighborhood programs for crime prevention

A law against the dumping of hazardous wastes

Lowering college tuition

3. Write a letter to your congressional representative or senator in which you object to some government policy. End your letter with a proposal for righting the wrong that concerns you.

4. Choose from the following list a practice that seems to you to represent an inefficient, unethical, unfair, or morally wrong solution to a problem. In a few paragraphs, give reasons for your objections. Then propose a better

**FOR PEER RESPONSE**

For this type of writing in particular, it's useful to try your draft on other students. You will find your readers' feedback invaluable as you revise and edit your paper. See Chapter 20 for advice on working with other student writers and for general questions you should always ask a peer editor to address. For a paper in which you propose a solution, you'll also want your peer editor to answer these specific questions:

• What is your overall reaction to this proposal? Does it make you want to go out and do something about the problem?
• Are you convinced that the problem is of vital concern to you? If not, why don't you care?
• Are you persuaded that the writer's solution is workable?
• Restate what you understand to be the major points.

   Problem:
   Proposal:
   Explanation of proposal:
   Procedure:
   Advantages:
   Disadvantages:
   Response to other solutions:
   Recommendation:

• Has the writer argued persuasively against other solutions? List any additional solutions you think the writer should refute.
• Describe what you think makes the writer trustworthy as a proposer.
• Has the writer paid enough attention to readers?
• If this were your paper, what is the one thing you would be sure to work on before handing it in?

solution. (Or the list might prompt you to think of another wrong solution.)

> Censorship
> Corporal punishment for children
> Laboratory experiments on animals
> Surrogate motherhood
> State lotteries
> Dumping wastes in the ocean

5. What activities in your high school or your college are in jeopardy of being cut because of decreased funding, similar to Heather Colbenson's agriculture classes and the FFA in Minnesota? Music classes? Art? Foreign language? School dances? If you don't know, talk to some of your instructors to find out. What solutions can you propose to save these important activities? Write an essay in which you present a solution to this problem.

## *Applying What You Learn:*
## *Some Uses of Proposals*

In college a proposal is often a written plan submitted to someone in authority who must approve it before the proposer goes ahead with implementing a solution. Students embarking on a research project may be required to submit a proposal to an adviser or a committee in which they set forth what they intend to investigate and how they will approach their topic. Students who object to a grade can file a grievance to try to get the grade changed. Like writers of persuasive essays, they state a claim and supply evidence in support of it.

In business, too, proposals for action are often useful: for persuading a prospective customer to buy a product or service, for solving a personnel problem, for recommending a change in procedure, for suggesting a new project, or for urging a purchase of new equipment. An office manager might use a proposal as a means to achieve harmony with co-workers: first discussing with the staff a certain problem — poor morale, a conflict between smokers and nonsmokers — and then writing a proposal to outline the solution on which the group has agreed.

Every day in the world around us, we encounter proposals for solutions — on the editorial pages of newspapers and magazines, in books, in public service announcements on television, in legislative proposals and responses to proposed bills. In a 1995 "Random Access" column in *Newsweek*, Steven Levy laments the proposed legislation of Jim Exon, Democratic senator from Nebraska, to protect children by censoring information on the Internet. Exon's bill would clean up language and visuals on the Internet by levying fines and imposing jail terms on those who post obscene messages and pornographic documents on the information highway. Levy argues that censorship is not the answer and then offers his own proposal for solution:

So how do we protect our children from the pictures of naked ladies, the discussions of bestiality, and the rough language that currently characterize the Net? Even Exon has admitted that his bill probably won't stop the smut he so urgently wants to eliminate. There are high-tech dodges around anything that the simple minds of the Senate can concoct. We would have better results by implementing some newly proposed technological solutions, ranging from software that filters out possibly objectionable material to special services that present only a bowdlerized version of the Net to junior web-surfers. And then, there's always that remedy in which censorious legislators never seem to have confidence: parental guidance.

Sometimes an entire article or essay is devoted to arguing for an action. In other cases, a writer's chief purpose may be to explain something or perhaps to express an opinion and then to end with a proposal. Lewis Thomas, a distinguished physician and writer, in a 1983 article for the *New York Times Magazine*, laments the way science has been perceived as the key to understanding the universe and blames teaching from this perspective for the widespread dislike and ignorance of science. Then he proposes a drastic change in how science is taught:

> I suggest that the introductory courses in science, at all levels from grade school through college, be radically revised. Leave the fundamentals, the so-called basics, aside for a while, and concentrate the attention of all students on the things that are not known. You cannot possibly teach quantum mechanics without mathematics, to be sure, but you can describe the strangeness of the world opened up by quantum theory. Let it be known, early on, that there are deep mysteries and profound paradoxes revealed in distant outline by modern physics. Explain that these can be approached more closely and puzzled over, once the language of mathematics has been sufficiently mastered.
>
> At the outset, before any of the fundamentals, teach the still imponderable puzzles of cosmology. Describe as clearly as possible, for the youngest minds, that there are some things going on in the universe that lie still beyond comprehension, and make it plain how little is known.

Like many proposals that you will read during your college years and beyond, Thomas's is controversial. Whether Thomas persuades or fails to persuade his readers, he performs a useful service. By giving us a thoughtful proposal on this crucial issue, he challenges us to think.

In time, some calls to action that at first are controversial become generally accepted. This has certainly been true of Dr. Elisabeth Kübler-Ross's views about how dying patients and their loved ones ought to be treated. Before she wrote her landmark book *On Death and Dying* (1969), terminally ill patients in hospitals were seldom told when they were close to death, and little was done to help them die with dignity. Their families felt uncomfortable about the silences and deceptions imposed on the dying. After studying the problem, Kübler-Ross evolved a number of suggestions that would ease a patient's transition into death — easing pain for the caregivers as well as for the patient. Among them is this one:

There is a time in a patient's life when the pain ceases to be, when the mind slips off into a dreamless state, when the need for food becomes minimal and the awareness of the environment all but disappears into darkness. This is the time when the relatives walk up and down the hospital hallways, tormented by the waiting, not knowing if they should leave to attend the living or stay to be around for the moment of death. This is the time when it is too late for words, and yet the time when the relatives cry the loudest for help — with or without words. It is too late for medical interventions (and too cruel, though well meant, when they do occur), but it is also too early for a final separation from the dying. It is the hardest time for the next of kin as he either wishes to take off, to get it over with; or he desperately clings to something that he is in the process of losing forever. It is the time for the therapy of silence with the patient and availability for the relatives.

The doctor, nurse, social worker, or chaplain can be of great help during these final moments if they can understand the family's conflicts at this time and help select the one person who feels most comfortable staying with the dying patient. This person then becomes in effect the patient's therapist. Those who feel too uncomfortable can be assisted by alleviating their guilt and by the reassurance that someone will stay with the dying until his death has occurred. They can then return home knowing that the patient did not die alone, yet not feeling ashamed or guilty for having avoided this moment which for many people is so difficult to face.

At their best, like Kübler-Ross's pioneering recommendations for facing death and dying, proposals are often the advance guard that comes before useful action.

# Making Connections:
# Proposals in A Writer's Reader

Whenever we encounter a problem, we search for solutions. When we find an answer that satisfies us, we *propose a solution* to share our excitement with other people. We move from trying to convince readers of the soundness of our position to trying to get them to do something — act or change their behavior. Some writers in *A Writer's Reader* present proposals for solutions to problems. In "A Part-Time Marriage" (p. 493), professor and writer Noel Perrin, after experiencing the problems that come with divorce, proposes part-time marriages. In "Drugs from Bugs" (p. 628), biologist Carol Kaesuk Yoon proposes a radical plan — selling conservation for profit — as a solution to providing needed drugs while at the same time protecting plants and animals.

Like Perrin, Yoon, Wilbert Rideau (p. 204), and Heather Colbenson (p. 206), other writers from a variety of professions propose solutions to problems they identify: Puerto Rican poet Judith Ortiz Cofer, "The Myth of the Latin Woman: I Just Met a Girl Named María" (p. 504); journalist Susanna Rodell, "Do You Work? Are You Guilty" (p. 545); lawyer Patricia J. Williams, "Hate Radio" (p. 582); science writer Robert Wright, "Mr. Clean Genes" (p.

611); and environmentalist Gregg Easterbrook, "Forget PCBs. Radon. Alar: The World's Greatest Environmental Dangers Are Dung Smoke and Dirty Water" (p. 636). As you read these essays, consider the role that proposals play in them. For each essay, answer the following questions.

1. What problem does the writer identify? What solution does she or he propose?
2. How is the writer qualified to write on this subject?
3. What evidence for the proposed solution does the writer present? Does the writer convince you to agree with her or him? Does the writer rouse you to want to do something about the problem?

# Evaluating

Evaluating means judging. You do it when you decide what candidate to vote for, pick which camera to buy from among several on the market, watch a game and size up a team's prowess, recommend a new restaurant to your friends. All of us find ourselves passing judgments continually as we move through a day's routine.

Often in everyday situations we make snap judgments. A friend asks, "How was that movie you saw last night?" and you reply, "Terrific — don't miss it" or maybe "Pretty good, but it had too much blood and gore for me." Those off-the-cuff opinions are necessary and useful. But to *write* an evaluation calls for you to think more critically. As a writer you first decide on *criteria*, or standards for judging, and then come up with evidence to back up your judgment.

A written evaluation zeroes in on a definite subject. You inspect the subject carefully and come to a considered opinion. The subject might be a film, a book, a piece of music, a restaurant, a sports team, a group of performers, a product, a scientific theory, a body of research — the possibilities are endless.

## *Learning from Other Writers*

Here are two good evaluations, the first by a professional writer, the second by a student. Elayne Rapping is a culture critic and regular contributor to the *Progressive* magazine, where this article first appeared. In her essay Rapping evaluates the character of Roseanne, familiar to us from the television show by the same name, by placing her in the context of other female television protagonists.

Geoffrey Fallon wrote his evaluative essay "Hatred within an Illustrated Medium: Those Uncanny X-Men" for a composition class at Santa Fe Community College in Florida. Fallon enjoyed writing this paper because he was able to show how the genre of comics can be used to send important messages. "I also am proud of the way the paper sounds," he states. "It sounds very academic, even though it is discussing a comic book. I hope that helps get my point across."

## *Elayne Rapping*    In Praise of Roseanne

The other night, while flipping among the three nightly network news broadcasts, I stopped — as I often do — to check out the *Roseanne* rerun Fox cleverly schedules during that time slot in New York. And, as often happens, I found myself sticking around longer than I intended, watching the Conners wiggle their way through whatever crisis had hit their Kmart window fan that day.

On the three more respectable networks, the Dow Jones averages rise and fall; Congress and the courts hand down weighty decisions in lofty prose; the official weapons of state are deployed, around the globe and in the inner cities, to preserve democracy and the American way. But in the Conner residence, where most things are either in disrepair or not yet paid for, it is possible to glimpse — as it rarely is on the newscasts themselves — how the fallout from such headlines might actually affect those who are relatively low in the pecking order.

On CBS, NBC, ABC, and CNN, the problems of the women who make headlines are not likely to sound familiar to most of us. Zoë Baird may be struggling with the servant issue. Hillary may have misplaced her capital-gains records. The Queen of England may be embroiled in royal-family dysfunction. But Roseanne, matriarch of the shabby Conner household, will be coping with less glamorous trauma — unemployment, foreclosure, job stress, marital power struggles, unruly and unmotivated kids — in a less dignified but more realistic style.

I am a big fan of Roseanne — Barr, Arnold, Conner, whatever. So are my female and working-class students, who invariably claim her as their own and hang on to her for dear life as they climb the ladder of class and professional achievement — an effort in which their parents have so hopefully invested everything they own. But it recently occurred to me that I have never — in the many years I've regularly analyzed and commented on American popular culture — written a single word about her. Nor have I read many, outside the trashy tabloids, where her personal life and public persona are regularly recorded and described.

In the last year, I've read dozens of academic and popular articles, and two whole books, about *The Cosby Show.* Archie Bunker and *All in the Family* have been appraised and analyzed endlessly. Even *Murphy Brown* and *The*

*Mary Tyler Moore Show* are taken seriously in ever-broadening academic and journalistic circles. Not to mention the well-structured, post-structural Madonna, long the darling of feminist critics and academics.

What is it about these other media icons that makes them somehow more "respectable" subjects of intellectual analysis, more suitable to "serious" discourse? What is it about Roseanne that makes her so easy to ignore or write off, despite her (to me) obvious talent, originality, political *chutzpah*, and power? Gender and appearance are surely part of it; but I suspect that class — position as well as attitude — is the major factor. Bill Cosby's Cliff Huxtable, Mary Tyler Moore's Mary Richards, Candice Bergen's Murphy Brown are all well-turned-out, well-educated liberal professionals. And the grungy, working-class Archie Bunker, far from scoring points for his class, is always beaten down by the liberal, professional mentality of everyone else on the show. As for Madonna, while she is certainly not respectable, she makes up for it by being blond, chic, and gorgeous, which, in our culture, covers a multitude of social sins.

But Roseanne is a different story, far more unassimilable into mainstream-media iconography than any of these others. Fat, sloppy, foulmouthed, and bossy, she is just a bit too unrepentantly, combatively proud of her gender and class position and style to be easily molded into the "movin' on up" mode of American mass media. She isn't "movin' up" to anywhere. She is standing pat, week after week on her show — and a lot of the rest of the time in a lot of other places — speaking out for the dignity and the rights of those the media have set out to shame into invisibility or seduce into endless, self-hating efforts at personal transformation. With her bad hair and baggy pants and oversized shirts from the lower level of the mall, with her burned meat loaf and tuna casseroles and Mallomars, with her rough language and politically incorrect childrearing methods, with her dead-end minimum-wage jobs, Roseanne has gone further than Madonna or almost anyone else I can think of at turning the hegemonic norms of the corporate media on their heads. But few of the intellectual writing classes have seen fit to credit, much less celebrate, her for it. So I will.

To appreciate Roseanne's unlikely ascent into prime-time stardom, it's useful to place her within the generic traditions of the family sitcom. Roseanne is not a descendant of the pristine line of virginal wife/mothers who have set the norms for such characters from the days of June Cleaver to the present. No sweetly submissive smiles or politely helpful suggestions to hubby and kids for her. She is one of a rarer breed, the one invented and defined by Lucille Ball in *I Love Lucy*, in which the female protagonist is more Helpmeet from Hell than from Heaven.

The parallels between these two women are interesting, and reveal a lot about what has and hasn't changed for the women — white, working-class, and poor — who make up the female majority in this country (although you'd never know it from watching TV). Both were, and are, popular and powerful beyond the dreams of almost any woman performer of their times.

And yet both eschewed the traditional feminine, white, middle-class persona dictated by the norms of their days, preferring to present themselves as wild women, out of bounds, loud, funny, and noisy — all attributes which sexist culture beats out of most of us very early on. In a world in which females are enjoined not to take up too much space, not to make "spectacles" of ourselves, not to "disturb" but to contain "the peace," women like Roseanne and Lucy have always been frightening, repulsive, even indecent. That's why they so appall us even as, consciously or subconsciously, we are drawn to them.

I used to cringe when I watched *I Love Lucy* as a child. She filled me with embarrassment because she was so stereotypically "hysterical," so much a failure in her endless efforts to move out of the confines of traditional femininity and its many indignities (indignities otherwise kept hidden by the Stepford-like types of Donna Reed and June Cleaver). 10

I was far more comfortable, as a middle-class girl, with the persona created by Mary Tyler Moore — first as the frustrated dancer/wife in *The Dick Van Dyke Show* and later as the first real career woman in her own show. Unlike Lucy, Mary Richards was perfectly groomed and mannered. She was sweetly deferential in her apologetic efforts at assertiveness; embarrassingly grateful for every nod of respect or responsibility from her boss, "Mr. Grant." Ambitious, yes, but never forgetful of the "ladylike" way of moving up the corporate ladder, one dainty, unthreatening step at a time. Where Lucy embarrassed, Mary was soothing. No pratfalls or dumb disguises for her. 11

But through Roseanne, I've come to see the very improper Lucy differently. For her time, after all, she was a real fighter against those feminine constraints. She tried to *do* things and she tried to do them with other women, against the resistance of every man on the show. She was not well groomed, did not live in tasteful elegance, did not support and help her husband at business and social affairs — far from it. She was full of energy and rebelliousness and, yes, independence — to a point. 12

But of course she always failed, and lost, and made a fool of herself. Her show was pure slapstick fantasy, because, back then, the things she was trying to achieve were so far from imaginable that someone like her could only exist in a farcical mode. But, as Roseanne's very different way of playing this kind of woman shows, that is no longer true. 13

Like Lucy, Roseanne is loud, aggressive, messy, and ambitiously bossy. Roseanne, too, has close relationships with other women. And Roseanne, too, is larger than life, excessive, to many frightening and repulsive. But her show is no fantasy. It is the most realistic picture of gender, class, and family relations on television today. And that's because Roseanne herself is so consciously political, so gender- and class-conscious, in every detail of her show. 14

No more the harried husband rolling his eyes at his wife's antics. Where other sitcoms either ignore feminism and reproduce traditional relations or, perhaps worse, present perfectly harmonious couples — like the Huxtables — for whom gender equity comes as naturally as their good looks, Roseanne and Dan duke it out over gender and power issues as equals who seem really to love, respect, and — not least — get angry at each other. 15

Nor does Roseanne need to think up crazy schemes for achieving the impossible — a project outside the home. Roseanne, like most of us, needs to work. The jobs she is forced to take — sweeping in a hair salon, waiting tables in malls and diners, working on an assembly line — are very like the ones Lucy nabbed and then messed up, to the wild laughter of the audience. But for Roseanne the humor is different. Roseanne fights with sexist, overbearing bosses, lashes out at her kids because she's stressed out at work, moonlights to get them through the rough days when Dan is out of work. And if these things are funny to watch, they are also deeply revealing of social and emotional truths in the lives of women and working-class families today.

The most touching and impressive thing about this series — and the main reason for its popularity — is its subtle presentation of progressive "messages" in a way that is neither preachy nor condescending to audiences. Much was made of the famous episode in which Roseanne was kissed by a lesbian character. (And it is surely a tribute to Roseanne's integrity and clout that this first lesbian kiss got past Standards and Practices[1] because of her.) But the kiss itself was really no big deal. Lots of shows will be doing this kind of one minute/one scene "Wow, did you see that?" thing soon enough.

Sitcoms are, indeed, informed by liberal values, and they do, indeed, tend to preach to us about tolerance and personal freedom. Lesbianism, as an idea, an abstraction, a new entry on the now very long list of liberal tolerances to which the professional middle classes must pay lip service, was bound to hit prime time soon anyway. What made the Roseanne "lesbian episode" remarkable and radically different from the usual liberal sitcom style of tackling such issues was not the kiss itself but the startlingly honest discussions about homosexuality that followed the kiss, between Dan and his young son D.J.; and then between Dan and Roseanne, in bed.

This segment was politically audacious because it *did not* lecture the vast majority of Americans who are, yes, queasy about homosexuality. It presented them with a mirror image of their own confusion and anxiety, and led them to a position of relative comfort about it all, by sympathizing with their very real concern about radical social and sexual change.

This is how the show attacks all its difficult issues, sensational and mundane. Much has been made of Roseanne's way of yelling at her kids, even hitting them on at least one occasion. Clearly, this is not how parents, since Dr. Spock, have been told to behave, and for obvious and good reason. Nonetheless, we all do these things on occasion. (And those who don't, ever, probably have other serious parenting problems.) To pretend that parents don't do that — as most sitcoms do — is to condescend to viewers who know that this goes on everywhere, and who have, themselves, done it or at least fought the urge.

On *Roseanne*, such behavior is neither denied nor condemned; it is talked about and analyzed. After hitting her son, for example, Roseanne apologizes

16

17

18

19

20

21

---

[1]**Standards and Practices:** network censors.

and confesses, heartbreakingly, that she was herself beaten as a child and that it was wrong then and wrong now. It is this kind of honesty about negative feelings — especially when they are placed in the kind of social and economic context this show never slights — that makes the positive feelings of love and mutual respect within this battered, battling family so very believable.

Which brings me, unavoidably, to the issue of Roseanne Arnold herself, 22 as a public persona — surely the major factor in the public unease about her. There are two "Roseannes" — both media images constructed cleverly and carefully by Arnold herself. "Roseanne Conner" is, as Arnold herself says, "much nicer." She is the sitcom version of how someone overcomes personal and economic difficulty and not only survives but thrives. She comes from a long line of show-business satirists whose humor was based on social and political truth. Like the Marx Brothers and Charlie Chaplin, she is the lovable outsider sneaking into the polite world to expose its hypocrisy and phoniness.

That is the fictional "Roseanne" of sitcom fame. The other persona, 23 "Roseanne Barr Arnold" — the woman who appears in tabloids, talk shows, news shows, and comedy clubs — is far more outrageous, more dangerous. She is the ultimate bad girl, the woman who shouts out to the entire world every angry, nasty, shameful truth and emotion she feels about the lives of women, especially poor women, in America today.

Much of what Roseanne confesses to — about incest, wife abuse, mental 24 illness, obesity, prostitution, lesbianism — makes people uncomfortable. It's tacky, embarassing, improper, déclassé to discuss these issues in public. But so was much of what we Second Wave feminists and student activists and antiwar protesters and others insisted upon talking about and confessing to and doing in the 1960s. So is what Anita Hill insisted — in much classier style but to no less shock and outrage — on throwing at us from the Senate hearing rooms. So is almost every political statement and action that rocks the reactionary boats of institutionalized power and authority.

And like those other actions and statements, Roseanne's antics are inher- 25 ently political, radical, salutary. For in speaking out about her hidden demons and ghosts and scars — as a woman, a working-class person, a victim of family and institutional abuse — she speaks *for* the myriad damaged and disempowered souls, mostly still silent and invisible, who also bear the scars of such class, gender, and age abuse.

My timing, as I write this, couldn't be worse, of course. The tabloids are 26 currently ablaze with the latest, and most unfortunate, of Arnold brouhahas. Roseanne, having loudly accused her husband of infidelity and spousal abuse, filed for divorce, then almost immediately rescinded the statements and reconciled with her husband, only to file for divorce again a few weeks later.

I am neither shocked nor disillusioned by this. Every abused woman I 27 have ever known has attempted, unsuccessfully, to leave her destructive relationship many times, before finally finding the strength and support to make the break. This, after all, is the very essence of the abuse syndrome. Only Roseanne, as usual, has chosen to play it out, in all its gory details, in the spotlight.

I'm a Roseanne fan. I like her show and marvel at her compassion and intelligence, at what she manages to get away with. I like her style — even when she offends me and makes me nervous (which she often does) — because the world needs loud-mouthed unattractive women with brains, guts, a social conscience, and a sense of humor. There are few enough of them who make it through puberty with their spirits and energies intact.

28

**Questions to Start You Thinking**

*Meaning*

1. Does Rapping evaluate Roseanne Barr Arnold the real person, Roseanne Conner the television character, or *Roseanne* the television program?

2. How would Rapping respond to the charge that Roseanne the television character is crude, crass, and uncouth?

3. What does Rapping say makes *Roseanne* a good television show? What can you conclude are her criteria for good television? How would you use Rapping's criteria to evaluate one of your favorite television programs?

*Writing Strategies*

4. Does Rapping provide sufficient evidence to convince you to agree with her opinion of *Roseanne*?

5. How does the author use comparison and contrast to make her point? How does she use analysis?

6. What resources does Rapping draw upon in this essay?

7. For what audience is Rapping writing? How can you tell?

STUDENT ESSAY

*Geoffrey Fallon*    **Hatred within an Illustrated Medium: Those Uncanny X-Men**

His arms raised majestically over his head, his cape flowing behind him like an emperor's robes, the mutant called Magneto speaks to his self-proclaimed children; mutants like himself, scorned by those who fear them for being different. With fatherly undertones he defends his terrorist actions with the following address: "All my life, I have seen people slaughtered wholesale for no more reason than the deity they worshiped, or the color of their skin--or the presence in

1

their DNA of an extra, special gene. I cannot change the
world, but I can and will ensure that my race will never
again suffer for its fear and prejudice."

The year was 1976, and while the country was still re-
covering from the aftereffects of the Vietnam conflict, the
problems of civil rights and racial unrest began to rear
their heads after lying dormant for almost a decade. Activists once again began to speak out as minority groups witnessed blatant disregard for the rights their predecessors
had fought for in the mid-sixties. In the midst of this political strife, a young comic book writer named Chris Claremont decided to incorporate this unfortunate trend of
continued minority inequality into his comic book The Uncanny
X-Men. The series tells the story of a team of superheroes
who have banded together to help others like themselves, humans with a genetic quirk, an "X-Factor," that gives them su-
perhuman characteristics. These "mutants" are feared and
hated by many normal humans. In his stories Claremont is
quite deliberate in his attempt to educate readers about the
dangers and the consequences of racism. While comic books are
generally thought of as a child's medium not worth serious
attention, Claremont uses his series to speak out on a serious topic, bigotry, in a form that is accessible to a variety
of readers.

The story of the X-Men is a story of how people of diverse ethnic and racial backgrounds can come together in the
spirit of harmony but encounter widespread prejudice because
they are different. Originally, the X-Men are a team of superheroes who battle evil and use their powers to serve humanity. However, humans without an X-Factor--the genetic
quirk that makes a human exhibit mutant powers--begin to show
prejudice against mutated humans. The very people the X-Men
have sworn to protect regard the team with anger and fear.
They cry out for special laws for mutant control and set up
Human Liberation Organizations. These acts of aggression
cause other mutant groups to band together. Now, however,
their goal is not to protect the human race, but to protect
themselves from the hatred beginning to form in the normal
human population. As these new groups form, humans become

even more frightened, thinking that these mutants will someday take over the world, forcing normal humans underground.
Mutant Registration Acts are passed, forcing mutants to register with special government offices so they can be monitored. The final phase of this new trend toward slavery is
inaugurated by the creation of an entire nation, Genosha,
dedicated to the advancement of humankind and the persecution
of mutants.

The entrance of Genosha into the world market prompts an    4
ultra-powerful mutant by the name of Magneto (who possesses
control over the electromagnetic spectrum) to create a nation
of his own. Floating over Earth's atmosphere, Magneto creates
an asteroid with everything that would be needed for an entire race of mutants to make it their home. He calls it Asteroid M and invites any mutant to settle there, away from
the hate that is building on the planet below. The asteroid
is systematically destroyed by a joint task force of the most
powerful nations on Earth, who fear that the mutants will use
it as a base for terrorist actions against Earth. Magneto is
apparently killed in the explosion, while diverting all of
his vast power toward saving as many mutants as possible.
Thus, he becomes a martyr for other mutants, who vow to fight
on to reclaim their place on Earth.

The Uncanny X-Men is the best-selling comic book series    5
in the history of the industry. Tales of the mutants Cyclops,
Gamit, Rogue, Wolverine, Psylocke, Beast, Storm, Archangel,
Forge, Marvel Girl, Banshee, Ice-Man, Jubilee, Collosus, and
Professor X have propelled the Marvel Comic Series to the
front of every top ten list available. What are the messages
in this widely read story? First and foremost, there is the
utopian ideal of people of different races and backgrounds
living together in harmony. The fifteen mutants who make up
the X-Men form a loving family, with Professor X as their
parental figure. The respect and consideration they show for
one another--despite their differences--is a perfect model
for a better world. In the series, the need for harmonious
diversity is not limited to the X-Men. Almost every type of
cultural background is represented here: African, Russian,
Japanese, Canadian, Irish, and American. Different cultures

are brought together by fate and can continue to survive only through the realization that they are really all the same. In this respect, Claremont's vision corresponds to that of Martin Luther King, Jr., who spoke of a "world house" in which we must all learn to live together, because we can never again live apart.

Second, we are also introduced to the darker side of human nature--discrimination and the drive for supremacy--within the unfolding story line of Claremont's comic book. Hatred, prejudice, oppression, and the maddening spiral of ever-increasing militancy and aggression are all present. Genosha is perhaps the ultimate symbol for the supposed superiority of one race over another. Claremont quite deliberately links the fictional oppression of the mutants to similar moments in human history. Magneto's family, for instance, died in the concentration camps in Nazi Germany. The name of Nimrod, a hunter of mutants in the series, comes from Genesis 10:8-9 of the Bible; the biblical Nimrod was a mighty hunter whose skill was unparalleled. Claremont's Nimrod is similar. He is the ultimate killing machine with one primary mission: destroy mutants. The idea of complete genocide is a topic too heinous to speak about in a straightforward manner, so Claremont uses X-Men to bring it to the attention of his readers.

Claremont's third message is that activism is needed to combat this terrorism and hatred, and he provides clear models for activism. Just as is the case in the real world, there are those who try to make a difference. Magneto is portrayed as a villain, and in many cases he does indeed act like one, dealing in hatred and aggression himself. Nonetheless, Magneto makes an admirable effort to bring about change. Perhaps the real-life figure he resembles most is Malcolm X: though some may condemn his hatred for his oppressors, which motivates his actions, few can fault his passionate devotion to improving the lives of his people. It is this passion to create change that propels activists into action, and it is these activists that instill the very same passion into the people they lead.

What is to become of these powerful messages? Are they doomed to remain in the never-never land of a child's illus-

6

7

8

trated fairy tale? In actuality, comic books are much more than fantasy adventure placed in a thirty-page magazine. They have become a viable source for social commentary, and publishers both in the United States and abroad are now using the medium to express ideas for change. Pagan Kennedy makes this point in her essay "P.C. Comics" (The Nation, 19 Mar. 1990):

> Like film, comic books are far more sensual than pure language, and therefore have the potential to appeal to a large popular audience, as they do in Europe and Japan. . . . As visceral as film, as silent as a book, and as easy to produce as finding an idle photocopier, the comic book is inherently subversive.

The comic book has indeed found its way into the hands of some of the most aggressive proponents for social change. The Uncanny X-Men is one example. It sold over eight million copies in the last few months, and it is improbable that so many people are introduced to a socially correct way of thinking through any other medium each and every month. The Uncanny X-Men is a stellar forum in which to talk about the dangers of hate-mongers and supremacists. 9

Perhaps the stereotype is correct. Perhaps comic books are just for kids. If this is true, maybe it is a blessing, for children can gain enlightenment from the illustrated medium even if the minds of adults are too shrouded in prejudice and ignorance. Children, at least, have a chance to start anew with fresh dreams of equality, untainted by those who refuse to see every man and woman as equal. 10

As Asteroid M cracks in half, as its core explodes in a fiery cloud of intense heat, a regal figure floats in its midst, protected by a field of magnetic energy. With a flick of his gloved hand, the X-Men's craft is hurled toward Earth, away from danger. Magneto lowers his arm, and, looking upward to the stars, he opens his mind to Professor X, leader of the X-Men and his utter enemy, who telepathically listens to the last words of the man he has fought for so many years: 11

> I save you X-Men, because that is my task in life: to safeguard my people Homo sapiens superior-mutant

kind from those that would do us harm. And those
forces are legion. I have survived one holocaust, I
could not tolerate another. . . . Perhaps it is
best it end this way, Charles [Professor X]. Best
for my dream to end in flames and glory, here far
above Earth. . . . I give you your dream, Charles.
But I fear, in time, your heart will break, as you
realize it has ever been a fool's hope. Farewell,
my friend.

**Questions to Start You Thinking**

*Meaning*

1. What is Fallon's main point, his thesis? Do you agree with it?
2. Why does Fallon consider this comic book series worthwhile and significant? What criteria does he use in evaluating the comic book?
3. Can you think of other books, stories, or television shows considered children's entertainment that are really commentary on the adult world?

*Writing Strategies*

4. How convincing is the evidence the writer marshals to support his evaluation? What could make it more convincing?
5. How does Fallon organize his essay? How could this organization be improved?
6. What resources does Fallon draw upon in the essay? What critical strategies?
7. Fallon begins and ends his essay with descriptions of scenes from the X-Men series. Why do you think he does this?

# Learning by Writing

## THE ASSIGNMENT: WRITING AN EVALUATION

Pick a subject to evaluate, one with which you have some personal experience and which you feel reasonably competent to evaluate. This might be a movie, a TV program, a piece of music, an artwork, a new product, a government agency, or anything else you can think of. Then in a thoughtful essay, evaluate your subject. In both your preparation for writing and in the essay itself, you will need to analyze the subject before you attempt to evaluate it. You will also need to determine specific criteria for evaluation and make them clear to your readers. In writing your evaluation, you will have a twofold purpose: (1) to set forth your assessment of the quality of your subject and (2) to convince your readers that your judgment is reasonable.

Among the lively and instructive student-written evaluations we've seen recently are these:

A music major evaluated several works by American composer Aaron Copland and found Copland a trivial and imitative composer "without a tenth of the talent or inventiveness that George Gershwin or Duke Ellington had in his little finger."

A man planning a career in business management evaluated a computer firm in which he had worked one summer. His criteria were efficiency, productivity, appeal to new customers, and employee satisfaction.

A woman from Brazil, who had seen firsthand the effects of industrial development in the Amazon rainforest, evaluated the efforts of the U.S. government to protect the ozone layer, comparing them with the efforts of environmentalists in her own country.

A student of history, assigned to evaluate the long-term effects of Prohibition, found in favor of the maligned Volstead Act, passed to enforce Prohibition.

For an English course, a man evaluated *Going after Cacciato*, Tim O'Brien's novel of American soldiers in Vietnam (1978), favorably comparing it with Ernest Hemingway's World War I novel *A Farewell to Arms*.

## GENERATING IDEAS

*Find something to evaluate.* Try using *brainstorming* to find a suitable topic. List as many possible topics as you can think of that you might evaluate. Look over your list and select the ones that seem to have the most potential — the ones that you are most familiar with or that you can easily find out more about. Then combine your brainstorming with a little *freewriting*, setting down ideas about the topics as fast as they come to mind. (These strategies are discussed in detail on pp. 334 and 337.) From the results of these two techniques for generating ideas, choose one subject for your essay.

*Gather information.* You'll want to spend time finding material to help you develop a judgment. Consult your five writer's resources. You probably will *recall* (for example, a performance you have seen on television or an article you have read); you might *observe* (if you are evaluating a performance or the prowess of a sports team); you might *read* in a library, checking out reviews by other critics; or you might *converse* to see what others think.

*Establish your criteria.* In evaluating, you will find it helpful to establish and jot down criteria, standards to apply to your subject. Think of the features of the subject worth considering: in the case of a popular entertainer such as Ice-T or Michael Jackson, perhaps onstage manner, rapport with the audience, musicianship, selection of material, originality. How well does the performer score on these points? In evaluating the desirability of Atlanta as a home for a young careerist, you might ask: Does it provide an ample choice of decent-paying entry-level positions in growth firms? Any criterion you use to evaluate has to fit your subject, your audience, and your purpose. Ample entry-level

jobs might not matter to the writer of an article addressing an audience of re-
tirees. Or in a review of a new automobile for *Car & Driver,* addressed to car
buffs, a writer might use criteria such as styling and design, handling, fuel efficiency, safety features, and quality of the ride.

*Try comparing and contrasting.*    Comparing and contrasting may be useful, although they're not essential, for evaluating. (When you *compare,* you point to
similarities; when you *contrast,* you note differences.) Often you can readily
size up the worth of a thing by setting it next to another of its kind. Elayne
Rapping uses this technique effectively in her essay "In Praise of Roseanne."
To be comparable, of course, your two subjects need to have plenty in common. The quality of a Harley Davidson motorcycle might be judged by contrasting it with a Honda, but not by contrasting it with a Sherman tank.

When you decide on something that is comparable to your subject, make
a list of points you wish to compare. What similarities and differences leap to
mind? Your list might turn into a scratch outline you can use in drafting your
paper. For example, if you are writing a paper for a film history course, you
might compare and contrast the classic German horror movie *The Cabinet of
Dr. Caligari* with the classic Hollywood movie *Frankenstein,* concluding that
*Caligari* is the more artistic film. In your planning of the paper, you might
make two columns in which you list the characteristics of each film:

|  | CALIGARI | FRANKENSTEIN |
|---|---|---|
| Sets & Lighting | Dreamlike and impressionistic; | Realistic, but with heavy Gothic atmosphere; |
|  | Sets deliberately angular and distorted; | Gothic sets; |
|  | deep shadows that throw figures into relief | in climax: a night scene, torches highlighting monster's face |

And so on, point by point. By jotting down each point and each bit of evidence side by side, you can outline your comparison and contrast with great
efficiency. Once you have listed them, decide on a possible order for the
points. (For more on using comparing and contrasting, see Chapter 7.)

*Try defining your subject.*    Another technique for evaluating is to define your
subject, indicating its nature so clearly that your readers can easily distinguish
it from others of its kind. In defining, you help your readers understand your

subject: its structure, its habitat, its functions. In evaluating the television show *Roseanne*, Rapping does some *extended* defining: she discusses the nature of sitcoms over the years, their techniques, their views of women, their effects on the audience. This kind of defining isn't the same as writing a *short definition*, such as you'd find in a dictionary. (For how to do that, see "Defining," p. 392.) Your purpose is to judge. You might ask, What is the nature of my subject? Or, put differently, What qualities make my subject unique, unlike others of its sort? Scribble down any qualities that occur to you. In writing out your answer, you may find that you have written most of your paper and have formed an opinion of your subject.

*Develop a judgment.* In the end, you will have to come to a decision: Is your subject good, worthwhile, significant, exemplary, preferable — or not? Most writers find themselves coming to a judgment gradually as they explore their subjects. If you haven't developed one yet, look back over your criteria and any comparing and contrasting or defining you've done to see if a judgment becomes apparent. If not, you may have to do some more investigating.

To help you zero in on a promising subject and some likely material, you might ask yourself a few questions.

**DISCOVERY CHECKLIST**

- What criteria, if any, do you plan to use in making your evaluation? Are they clear and reasonably easy to apply?
- What evidence can you recall to back up your judgments? If not from memory, from what other resource might you draw evidence?
- Would comparing or contrasting help in evaluating your subject? If so, with what might you compare or contrast your subject?
- What specific qualities set your subject apart from all the rest of its class?

## PLANNING, DRAFTING, AND DEVELOPING

*Remember your purpose.* Reflect a moment: What is your purpose in this evaluation? What main point do you wish to make? Fallon asked himself these questions and answered them by writing a purpose statement for his project:

> In my evaluation, I plan to examine the messages about racial prejudices present in the Marvel comic book series The Uncanny X-Men. I will show how the writer Chris Claremont uses his characters to tell a compelling story of how ignorance and fear can inspire hatred. In the series, the X-Men are looked at as freaks and "gene-jokes" simply because their genetic pattern is different from the norm. This bigotry is quite apparent in all of Claremont's scripts, and the writer's purpose is to illustrate a parallel to the hate-mongers present in real life. The story line is very complex, and not the type of

```
plot you would expect in a comic book format. In the
story, the archvillain, Magneto, decides to take it upon
himself to create a world in which bigotry does not ex-
ist. He could almost be thought of as a tragic hero in
one sense. I believe it is through this particular char-
acter that Claremont explains the frustrations of op-
pressed races and cultures. In my conclusion, I plan to
prove that The Uncanny X-Men is a direct attempt to show
children the horrors of racism in a format they can re-
late to. While comic books are usually geared toward a
younger audience, I feel this particular one has some-
thing meaningful to say to any one of a number of older
generations, and through my essay I will make this point
clear.
```

Through this exploration of his early thoughts on the comic book series and his intentions in his paper, Fallon was able to focus his thinking before he began to draft his paper.

*Consider your criteria.*  Some writers like to spell out criteria to apply to whatever they're evaluating. Many find that a list of criteria gives them confidence and provokes ideas. But that isn't the only way to approach your draft. To be a good evaluator, you don't absolutely have to have foreordained criteria. T. S. Eliot said that, in criticizing literature, criteria, standards, and touchstones (great works to hold lesser works up to) don't help all that much. In a statement that sounds snobbish but isn't when you think about it, he declared that all a good critic needs is intelligence.

*Develop an organization.*  To organize your paper, you might want to make your main point at the beginning of your paper, then demonstrate it by looking at specific evidence (possibly comparison and contrast, definitely specific examples and details), and finally hark back to it in your closing lines. Organizing your paper differently, you might open by wondering, "How good a film is *Rain Man*?" or "Is Keynes's theory of inflation still valuable, or is it hopelessly out of date?" — raising a question about your subject to which your paper will reply. You then consider the evidence, one piece at a time, and conclude with your overall judgment. You might try both patterns of organization and see which works better for your subject and purpose. Or you might discover a different pattern that works better for your ideas.

Most writers find that an outline — even a rough list — facilitates writing a draft. An outline will help you keep track of points to make. Following is Fallon's scratch outline for his paper on the X-Men.

Thesis: While comic books are generally thought of as a child's medium, Claremont in the X-Men series speaks out against bigotry in any form, using the genre as a tool to make his point easily related to by a wide variety of readers.

Issue of racism in the 1970s

C.C. chose medium of comic books

Overview of story

Messages in the series

   – Possibility of peaceful coexistence

   – Reality of hatred and discrimination

   – Activism

Comics as a serious social commentary

If you intend to compare and contrast your subject with something else, one way to arrange the points is *subject by subject*. You have your say about subject A and then do the same for subject B. This method is workable for a short essay of two or three paragraphs, but for a longer essay it has drawbacks. In an essay of, say, a thousand or two thousand words, your readers might find it hard to remember all your points about subject A, ten paragraphs ago, while reading about subject B. A better way to organize a longer comparison

**WRITING WITH A COMPUTER**

This chapter opens with the declaration "Evaluating means judging." Weak evaluations are usually the result of a lack of specific support and evidence. Writing with a word processor can help strengthen your evaluation by focusing on the connections between your judgments and the evidence you use. After you have written an early draft of your evaluation, scroll through the text and highlight every *opinion* or *subjective judgment* with boldface or a different font size. Then scroll through the text again, highlighting all *facts* or *evidence* in italics or underlining. Can you identify a fairly direct correlation between your judgments and the evidence you provide? Do you need to move sentences or paragraphs around so that your support is linked more closely to your opinions? Do you need to provide additional facts or narrow the scope of your judgments?

is *point by point.* You take up one point at a time and apply it first to one subject and then to the other. (For more on organizing an essay that uses comparing and contrasting, see Chapter 7.)

Keep your outline simple, and don't be ruled by it. If, while you write your draft, good thoughts come to you, by all means let them in. (If you need a quick refresher in outlining, see p. 358.)

## REVISING AND EDITING

*Be fair.* Make your judgments reasonable, not extreme. Few things on earth are all good or all evil. A reviewer can find fault with a film and conclude that nevertheless it is worth seeing. There's nothing wrong, of course, with passing a fervent judgment ("This is the trashiest excuse for a play I have ever suffered through"), but consider your readers and their likely reactions. Read some reviews in your local newspaper or watch some movie critics on television to see how they balance their judgments.

In thinking critically about your draft, you might find this checklist handy.

**REVISION CHECKLIST**

- Is the judgment you pass on your subject unmistakably clear?
- Have you given your readers evidence to support each point you make?
- Have you been fair? If you are championing something, have you deliberately skipped over any of its disadvantages or faults? If you are condemning your subject, have you omitted any of its admirable traits?
- If you anticipate that readers will make any objections to your views, can you insert any answers to their objections?
- If you compared one thing with another, do you look consistently at the same points in both?

**FOR PEER RESPONSE**

Enlist the help of a peer editor. See Chapter 20 for advice on working with other student writers and for general questions you should always ask a peer editor to address. For a paper in which you evaluate, you'll also want your peer editor to answer these specific questions:

- What is your overall reaction to this essay? Does the writer make you agree with his or her evaluation?
- When you finish reading the essay, can you tell exactly what the writer thinks of the subject?
- Does the writer give you sufficient evidence for his or her judgment? Put stars wherever more evidence is needed.
- What audience does the writer seem to have in mind?
- Would you recommend any changes in how the essay is organized?
- If this were your paper, what is the one thing you would be sure to work on before handing it in?

OTHER ASSIGNMENTS

1. If you disagree with Elayne Rapping, write an essay setting forth your own evaluation of *Roseanne*. If you agree with Rapping, you might instead read some reviews of films, recordings, television shows, and books in recent magazines (*Time, Newsweek, Rolling Stone*, the *New Yorker*, or others) until you find a review you think quite wrongheaded. Write a reply to it, giving your own evaluation.

2. After reading Rapping's essay, write your own judgment of another television program.

3. Write an evaluation of a college course you have taken or are now taking. (So that you can be completely objective, we suggest you select some course other than your writing course.) Analyze its strengths and weaknesses. Does the instructor present the material clearly, understandably, and interestingly? Can you confer with the instructor if you need to? Is there any class discussion or other feedback? Are the assignments pointed and purposeful? Is the textbook helpful, readable, easy to use? Does this course give you your money's worth?

4. If you analyze a story, poem, or play (as we discuss in Chapter 12), you will be in a good position to evaluate it. Here are two poems on a similar theme. Read them critically, seeing what you find in them, and decide which seems to you the better poem. Then, in a brief essay, set forth your evaluation. Some criteria to apply might be the poet's choice of concrete, specific words that appeal to the senses and his awareness of his audience.

### Putting in the Seed

You come to fetch me from my work tonight
When supper's on the table, and we'll see
If I can leave off burying the white
Soft petals fallen from the apple tree
(Soft petals, yes, but not so barren quite,
Mingled with these, smooth bean and wrinkled pea),
And go along with you ere you lose sight
Of what you came for and become like me,
Slave to a springtime passion for the earth.
How Love burns through the Putting in the Seed
On through the watching for that early birth
When, just as the soil tarnishes with weed,
The sturdy seedling with arched body comes
Shouldering its way and shedding the earth crumbs.
                                    —ROBERT FROST (1874–1963)

### Between Our Folding Lips

Between our folding lips
God slips
An embryo life, and goes;
And this becomes your rose.

We love, God makes: in our sweet mirth
God spies occasion for a birth.
*Then is it His, or is it ours?*
I know not — He is fond of flowers.
                    –T. E. BROWN (1830–1897)

5.  Visit a restaurant, a museum, or a tourist attraction, and write an evaluation of it for others who might be considering a visit to the place. Be sure to specify your criteria for evaluation.

6.  Analyze and evaluate a magazine you do not often read.

7.  Analyze and evaluate one of the essays in this textbook, using the criteria for effective writing you have learned in this course.

# *Applying What You Learn: Some Uses of Evaluating*

In your college writing you'll be called on over and over to evaluate. On an art appreciation exam, you might be asked to evaluate the merits of Andrew Wyeth as a realistic painter. Speech pathology students, after considering the long-standing controversy that rages in education for the deaf, might be called on to describe and then evaluate three currently disputed teaching methods: oral/aural, signing, and a combination of the two. Students of language and linguistics might be asked to evaluate Skinner's behaviorist theory of articulation therapy: Outside of class, students on some campuses are invited to write comments for a student-run survey to evaluate their college courses.

In life beyond campus, every executive or professional needs to evaluate. An editor accepts and rejects manuscripts. A personnel director selects people to hire. A doctor evaluates a patient's symptoms. A lawyer sizes up the merits of a case and decides whether to take it. A retailer chooses the best product to sell. A speech pathologist evaluates the speech and language skills of prospective patients. You can think of endless other examples of evaluating, a kind of critical thinking we do every day of our lives. This kind of thinking is the basis of evaluative writing.

**FOR GROUP LEARNING**

## Developing a Consensus

Before you write a paper evaluating a subject, get together with your writing group. Discuss the subject you plan to evaluate and see whether the group can help you arrive at a sound judgment of it. The other group members will need to see what it is you're evaluating or hear your detailed report about it. If you are evaluating a short literary work or an idea expressed in a reading, it might be an excellent idea to read that work aloud so that the group members may become familiar with it. Ask your listeners to supply reasons for their own evaluations. Maybe they'll suggest reasons that hadn't occurred to you.

Familiar kinds of written evaluation abound. Daily newspapers and weekly or monthly magazines contain reviews of films, books, TV programs, records, and videos. Many sportswriters, columnists, and political commentators evaluate. The magazine *Consumer Reports* contains detailed evaluations of products and services, like this one from "Is There a DAT [digital audio tape] in Your Future?" (Jan. 1989).

> While prices will surely decline over time, we don't think DATs are going to make CDs obsolete anytime soon. First, while DAT players are much faster than conventional cassette decks at locating song tracks, they'll never be able to hop from track to track as quickly as a CD player.
>
> Second, digital audio tapes aren't as impervious to wear as compact discs. The tape comes into physical contact with a rotating recording head similar to a VCR's, and that will eventually degrade sound quality on the tape.
>
> Finally, recording quality might not be quite as close to perfect as DAT makers have implied — and record companies feared. When we tried out the *Sony DTC 1000 ES* DAT recorder last year, we found that it didn't match the low background noise performance of CD players. Unless that noise was a problem unique to our tested machine, DAT sound doesn't equal the quality of CD sound.
>
> For all of those reasons — price, durability, convenience, quality of sound, and the reluctance of the recording industry — we think that DAT will coexist with, rather than supplant, the compact disc in the years ahead.

Like many general magazines, professional journals contain book reviews that not only give a brief rundown of a book's contents but also indicate whether the reviewer considers the book worth reading. In *Chemical & Engineering News* (13 Mar. 1989), Deborah C. Andrews reviews the second edition of a textbook by H. J. Tichy called *Effective Writing for Engineers, Managers, Scientists*. Included in the review is an evaluation:

> What this text does well is to use words to talk about words. Pages are heavy with text, and visuals are exceedingly rare. Tichy writes within the framework of English (and French) literature as well as the literature of science, often calling upon the masters for clever phrases and telling anecdotes, some of them somewhat arcane — like a reference to an address before the French Academy by the 18th century naturalist Count Georges-Louis Leclerc de Buffon. In a section on figures of speech, she includes mention of some, like metonymy and litotes, that would stymie many English majors.

# *Making Connections:*
# *Evaluations in A Writer's Reader*

To be effective, evaluating, the highest level of critical thinking, must be based on sound comprehension and analysis. Several writers in *A Writer's Reader* successfully evaluate ideas, people, and media. They establish criteria for their evaluation and end by expressing their personal opinions based on the evaluation. Law professor Patricia J. Williams in "Hate Radio" (p. 582) evaluates what is happening on talk radio and concludes that the excesses of bigotry have gone far enough, despite claims of protection by the First Amendment. Political scientist Andrew Sullivan in "Wouldn't Normally Do" (p. 592) evaluates the movie *Philadelphia* from two perspectives, concluding that the movie is important as a vehicle to inform straight people of the fear of death that young gay men face because of AIDS.

Just as Williams, Sullivan, Elayne Rapping (p. 224), and Geoffrey Fallon (p. 229) use evaluation for writing from their individual perspectives, so do historian Stephanie Coontz, "The Way We Wish We Were: The Complexities of Assessing Family Trends" (p. 484); Native American professor Michael Dorris, "Crazy Horse Malt Liquor" (p. 522); columnist Ellen Goodman, "The New Hollywood Male" (p. 577); horror writer Stephen King, "Why We Crave Horror Movies" (p. 579); media critic Kurt Andersen, "Oprah and Jo-Jo the Dog-Faced Boy" (p. 590); and medical doctor Melvin Konner, "Out of the Darkness" (p. 615). As you read these essays, consider the role that evaluation plays in them. For each essay, answer the following questions.

1. Do you consider the writer qualified to evaluate the subject he or she chose? What biases and prejudices might the writer bring to the evaluation?
2. What criteria for evaluation does the writer establish? Are these reasonable standards for evaluating the subject?
3. Is the writer's assessment of the subject clear?
4. Does the writer provide sufficient evidence to convince you of his or her evaluation?

Part Three

# Special Writing Situations

# Introduction

Most of the writing you'll do while you are in college will fall into one of the categories covered in the preceding eleven chapters. However, three common situations that you're likely to encounter will call for specialized forms of writing: writing about literature, writing in class, and writing for business. In the next three chapters you'll find suggestions for responding to each of these special writing situations.

In college English and humanities classes you'll write papers about literature. You may need to write a personal response, a synopsis, a paraphrase, a review, or — most common in college — a literary analysis. Professors will often ask you to write literary analyses and comparison and contrast papers about literature because they reveal how well you understand the literature; how perceptively you use critical thinking skills (see Part Two); and how effectively you adapt the strategies for planning, drafting, developing, and revising (see Part Four). To write an effective analysis, you must thoroughly analyze the piece of literature, develop a coherent interpretation, and present your interpretation persuasively. You may need to write a synopsis or paraphrase as an intermediate step in one of these two complex assignments, either because the professor requires it or because you find it useful. Chapter 12 provides guidance for writing literary analyses, synopses, paraphrases, and comparison and contrast papers about literature.

Furthermore, as a student you'll often find yourself in testing situations in which you must demonstrate your knowledge of a subject as well as your proficiency in writing; more than likely, you will be constrained by a time limit. The writing in these situations usually takes the form of essay examinations, short-answer quizzes, and impromptu themes. To do this type of writing well requires you to use special skills: reading carefully, planning globally, composing quickly, and proofreading independently. Chapter 13 gives valuable tips on how not only to survive but also to thrive on in-class writings.

Finally, sometimes you'll want to respond in writing to a business situation. You may need to write a business letter to an organization with which you've had business dealings, perhaps to straighten out a bill or lodge a complaint. You may need to write memos and e-mail as part of a job that you hold while you are attending school. And you may need to write a résumé and letter of application to a company when you apply for a new position. Because time means money, business writing is concise and direct. Chapter 14 offers recommendations and samples for business writing, whether personal or corporate.

# Chapter 12

# Writing about Literature

In your college career you might take one or more literature courses: literary study has long been recognized as an essential in most college curricula. Reading and understanding a literary masterpiece offers you rewards beyond those measurable in dollars and cents.

As countless readers know, reading fiction gives pleasure and delight. Whether you are reading Dante or Danielle Steele, Stephen King or Stephen Crane, you can be swept up into an imaginative world where you can do and see things you can't in real life. You're held spellbound as you journey to distant lands and meet exotic people.

Literature also increases your understanding of life. Late-nineteenth-century American writer and editor William Dean Howells said that literature "widens the bounds of human sympathy"; contemporary novelist Ursula K. Le Guin, that it deepens "your understanding of your world, and your fellow men, and your own feelings, and your destiny." As you read, you meet characters similar to and different from yourself, and you encounter familiar as well as new ideas and ways of viewing life. By sharing the experiences of literary characters, you gain insight into your own problems and become more tolerant of others.

More often than not, a writing assignment in a literature or humanities course will require you to read a literary work (short story, novel, play, or poem) closely, divide it into its elements, explain its meaning, and support your interpretation with evidence from the work. The analysis is not an end in itself; the purpose is to illuminate the meaning of the work, to help you and others understand it better. You may also be asked to evaluate what you read and to compare and contrast individual selections with other pieces you have read.

Reading closely a work such as Shakespeare's great play *Hamlet* or Kate Chopin's classic American novel *The Awakening*, Shirley Jackson's short story "The Lottery" or Amy Lowell's poem "Patterns" will help you develop critical thinking skills useful in the academic world as well as in the job market. As you develop these skills, you will truly become a *critic* in the sense of the Greek *kritikos*, "one who can judge and discern." (See "Critical Thinking Strategies for Writers," p. 109.)

There are certain basic ways of writing about literature, each with its own purpose. We emphasize the *literary analysis*, which requires you to analyze, interpret, and evaluate what you read. We also offer an example of comparing and contrasting, another basic way of writing about literature, and examples of synopsis and paraphrase, two strategies for writing about literature. Assignments throughout the chapter give you practice with these basic forms. We also provide an introduction to literary terms.

## Literary Analysis

### LEARNING FROM ANOTHER WRITER

In a composition course, Jonathan Burns was given an assignment to write a literary analysis of "The Lottery," a short story by the American writer Shirley Jackson. "The Lottery" caused a sensation when it was published in the *New Yorker* in 1948. In this story, Shirley Jackson simultaneously conceals and reveals meaning. Students, teachers, and professional critics have offered varied interpretations of the work. Read it with care; try to figure out what it means. Then read on to see what Jonathan Burns made of it.

## *Shirley Jackson*    The Lottery

The morning of June 27th was clear and sunny, with the fresh warmth of   1
a full-summer day; the flowers were blossoming profusely and the grass was richly green. The people of the village began to gather in the square, between the post office and the bank, around ten o'clock; in some towns there were so many people that the lottery took two days and had to be started on June 26th, but in this village, where there were only about three hundred people, the whole lottery took less than two hours, so it could begin at ten o'clock in the morning and still be through in time to allow the villagers to get home for noon dinner.

The children assembled first, of course. School was recently over for the   2
summer, and the feeling of liberty sat uneasily on most of them; they tended to gather together quietly for a while before they broke into boisterous play, and their talk was still of the classroom and the teacher, of books and reprimands. Bobby Martin had already stuffed his pockets full of stones, and the

other boys soon followed his example, selecting the smoothest and roundest stones; Bobby and Harry Jones and Dickie Delacroix — the villagers pronounced his name "Dellacroy" — eventually made a great pile of stones in one corner of the square and guarded it against the raids of the other boys. The girls stood aside, talking among themselves, looking over their shoulders at the boys, and the very small children rolled in the dust or clung to the hands of their older brothers or sisters.

Soon the men began to gather, surveying their own children, speaking of planting and rain, tractors and taxes. They stood together, away from the pile of stones in the corner, and their jokes were quiet and they smiled rather than laughed. The women, wearing faded house dresses and sweaters, came shortly after their menfolk. They greeted one another and exchanged bits of gossip as they went to join their husbands. Soon the women, standing by their husbands, began to call to their children, and the children came reluctantly, having to be called four or five times. Bobby Martin ducked under his mother's grasping hand and ran, laughing, back to the pile of stones. His father spoke up sharply, and Bobby came quickly and took his place between his father and his oldest brother.

The lottery was conducted — as were the square dances, the teenage club, the Halloween program — by Mr. Summers, who had time and energy to devote to civic activities. He was a round-faced, jovial man and he ran the coal business, and people were sorry for him, because he had no children and his wife was a scold. When he arrived in the square, carrying the black wooden box, there was a murmur of conversation among the villagers, and he waved and called, "Little late today, folks." The postmaster, Mr. Graves, followed him, carrying a three-legged stool, and the stool was put in the center of the square and Mr. Summers set the black box down on it. The villagers kept their distance, leaving a space between themselves and the stool, and when Mr. Summers said, "Some of you fellows want to give me a hand?" there was a hesitation before two men, Mr. Martin and his oldest son, Baxter, came forward to hold the box steady on the stool while Mr. Summers stirred up the papers inside it.

The original paraphernalia for the lottery had been lost long ago, and the black box now resting on the stool had been put into use even before Old Man Warner, the oldest man in town, was born. Mr. Summers spoke frequently to the villagers about making a new box, but no one liked to upset even as much tradition as was represented by the black box. There was a story that the present box had been made with some pieces of the box that had preceded it, the one that had been constructed when the first people settled down to make a village here. Every year, after the lottery, Mr. Summers began talking again about a new box, but every year the subject was allowed to fade off without anything's being done. The black box grew shabbier each year; by now it was no longer completely black but splintered badly along one side to show the original wood color, and in some places faded or stained.

Mr. Martin and his oldest son, Baxter, held the black box securely on the stool until Mr. Summers had stirred the papers thoroughly with his hand. Because so much of the ritual had been forgotten or discarded, Mr. Summers had been successful in having slips of paper substituted for the chips of wood that had been used for generations. Chips of wood, Mr. Summers had argued, had been all very well when the village was tiny, but now that the population was more than three hundred and likely to keep on growing, it was necessary to use something that would fit more easily into the black box. The night before the lottery, Mr. Summers and Mr. Graves made up the slips of paper and put them in the box, and it was then taken to the safe of Mr. Summers's coal company and locked up until Mr. Summers was ready to take it to the square next morning. The rest of the year, the box was put away, sometimes one place, sometimes another; it had spent one year in Mr. Graves's barn and another year underfoot in the post office, and sometimes it was set on a shelf in the Martin grocery and left there.

There was a great deal of fussing to be done before Mr. Summers declared   7
the lottery open. There were the lists to make up — of heads of families, heads of households in each family, members of each household in each family. There was the proper swearing-in of Mr. Summers by the postmaster, as the official of the lottery; at one time, some people remembered, there had been a recital of some sort, performed by the official of the lottery, a perfunctory, tuneless chant that had been rattled off duly each year; some people believed that the official of the lottery used to stand just so when he said or sang it, others believed that he was supposed to walk among the people, but years and years ago this part of the ritual had been allowed to lapse. There had been, also, a ritual salute, which the official of the lottery had had to use in addressing each person who came up to draw from the box, but this also had changed with time, until now it was felt necessary only for the official to speak to each person approaching. Mr. Summers was very good at all this; in his clean white shirt and blue jeans, with one hand resting carelessly on the black box, he seemed very proper and important as he talked interminably to Mr. Graves and the Martins.

Just as Mr. Summers finally left off talking and turned to the assembled   8
villagers, Mrs. Hutchinson came hurriedly along the path to the square, her sweater thrown over her shoulders, and slid into place in the back of the crowd. "Clean forgot what day it was," she said to Mrs. Delacroix, who stood next to her, and they both laughed softly. "Thought my old man was out back stacking wood," Mrs. Hutchinson went on, "and then I looked out the window and the kids was gone, and then I remembered it was the twenty-seventh and came a-running." She dried her hands on her apron, and Mrs. Delacroix said, "You're in time, though. They're still talking away up there."

Mrs. Hutchinson craned her neck to see through the crowd and found her   9
husband and children standing near the front. She tapped Mrs. Delacroix on the arm as a farewell and began to make her way through the crowd. The people separated good-humoredly to let her through; two or three people said, in voices just loud enough to be heard across the crowd, "Here comes your Missus, Hutchinson," and "Bill, she made it after all." Mrs. Hutchinson reached her husband, and Mr. Summers, who had been waiting, said cheer-

fully, "Thought we were going to have to get on without you, Tessie." Mrs. Hutchinson said, grinning, "Wouldn't have me leave m'dishes in the sink, now, would you, Joe?" and soft laughter ran through the crowd as the people stirred back into position after Mrs. Hutchinson's arrival.

"Well, now," Mr. Summers said soberly, "guess we better get started, get this over with, so's we can go back to work. Anybody ain't here?"    10

"Dunbar," several people said. "Dunbar, Dunbar."    11

Mr. Summers consulted his list. "Clyde Dunbar," he said. "That's right. He's broke his leg, hasn't he? Who's drawing for him?"    12

"Me, I guess," a women said, and Mr. Summers turned to look at her. "Wife draws for her husband," Mr. Summers said. "Don't you have a grown boy to do it for you, Janey?" Although Mr. Summers and everyone else in the village knew the answer perfectly well, it was the business of the official of the lottery to ask such questions formally. Mr. Summers waited with an expression of polite interest while Mrs. Dunbar answered.    13

"Horace's not but sixteen yet," Mrs. Dunbar said regretfully. "Guess I gotta fill in for the old man this year."    14

"Right," Mr. Summers said. He made a note on the list he was holding. Then he asked, "Watson boy drawing this year?"    15

A tall boy in the crowd raised his hand. "Here," he said. "I'm drawing for m'mother and me." He blinked his eyes nervously and ducked his head as several voices in the crowd said things like "Good fellow, Jack," and "Glad to see your mother's got a man to do it."    16

"Well," Mr. Summers said, "guess that's everyone. Old Man Warner make it?"    17

"Here," a voice said, and Mr. Summers nodded.    18

A sudden hush fell on the crowd as Mr. Summers cleared his throat and looked at the list. "All ready?" he called. "Now, I'll read the names — heads of families first — and the men come up and take a paper out of the box. Keep the paper folded in your hand without looking at it until everyone has had a turn. Everything clear?"    19

The people had done it so many times that they only half listened to the directions; most of them were quiet, wetting their lips, not looking around. Then Mr. Summers raised one hand high and said, "Adams." A man disengaged himself from the crowd and came forward. "Hi, Steve," Mr. Summers said, and Mr. Adams said, "Hi, Joe." They grinned at one another humorlessly and nervously. Then Mr. Adams reached into the black box and took out a folded paper. He held it firmly by one corner as he turned and went hastily back to his place in the crowd, where he stood a little apart from his family, not looking down at his hand.    20

"Allen," Mr. Summers said. "Anderson. . . . Bentham."    21

"Seems like there's no time at all between lotteries anymore," Mrs. Delacroix said to Mrs. Graves in the back row. "Seems like we got through with the last one only last week."    22

"Time sure goes fast," Mrs. Graves said.    23

"Clark. . . . Delacroix."    24

"There goes my old man," Mrs. Delacroix said. She held her breath while    25
her husband went forward.

"Dunbar," Mr. Summers said, and Mrs. Dunbar went steadily to the box    26
while one of the women said, "Go on, Janey," and another said, "There she
goes."

"We're next," Mrs. Graves said. She watched while Mr. Graves came    27
around from the side of the box, greeted Mr. Summers gravely, and selected a
slip of paper from the box. By now, all through the crowd there were men
holding the small folded papers in their large hands, turning them over and
over nervously. Mrs. Dunbar and her two sons stood together, Mrs. Dunbar
holding the slip of paper.

"Harburt. . . . Hutchinson."    28

"Get up there, Bill," Mrs. Hutchinson said, and the people near her    29
laughed.

"Jones."    30

"They do say," Mr. Adams said to Old Man Warner, who stood next to    31
him, "that over in the north village they're talking of giving up the lottery."

Old Man Warner snorted. "Pack of crazy fools," he said. "Listening to the    32
young folks, nothing's good enough for *them.* Next thing you know, they'll be
wanting to go back to living in caves, nobody work anymore, live *that* way for
a while. Used to be a saying about 'Lottery in June, corn be heavy soon.' First
thing you know, we'd all be eating stewed chickweed and acorns. There's *always* been a lottery," he added petulantly. "Bad enough to see young Joe Summers up there joking with everybody."

"Some places have already quit lotteries," Mrs. Adams said.    33

"Nothing but trouble in *that,*" Old Man Warner said stoutly. "Pack of    34
young fools."

"Martin." And Bobby Martin watched his father go forward.    35
"Overdyke. . . . Percy."

"I wish they'd hurry," Mrs. Dunbar said to her older son. "I wish they'd    36
hurry."

"They're almost through," her son said.    37

"You get ready to run tell Dad," Mrs. Dunbar said.    38

Mr. Summers called his own name and then stepped forward precisely    39
and selected a slip from the box. Then he called, "Warner."

"Seventy-seventh year I been in the lottery," Old Man Warner said as he    40
went through the crowd. "Seventy-seventh time."

"Watson." The tall boy came awkwardly through the crowd. Someone    41
said, "Don't be nervous, Jack," and Mr. Summers said, "Take your time, son."

"Zanini."    42

After that, there was a long pause, a breathless pause, until Mr. Summers,    43
holding his slip of paper in the air, said, "All right, fellows." For a minute, no
one moved, and then all the slips of paper were opened. Suddenly, all the

women began to speak at once, saying, "Who is it?" "Who's got it?" "Is it the Dunbars?" "Is it the Watsons?" Then the voices began to say, "It's Hutchinson. It's Bill." "Bill Hutchinson's got it."

"Go tell your father," Mrs. Dunbar said to her older son.    44

People began to look around to see the Hutchinsons. Bill Hutchinson    45 was standing quiet, staring down at the paper in his hand. Suddenly, Tessie Hutchinson shouted to Mr. Summers, "You didn't give him time enough to take any paper he wanted. I saw you. It wasn't fair!"

"Be a good sport, Tessie," Mrs. Delacroix called, and Mrs. Graves said, "All    46 of us took the same chance."

"Shut up, Tessie," Bill Hutchinson said.    47

"Well, everyone," Mr. Summers said, "that was done pretty fast, and now    48 we've got to be hurrying a little more to get done in time." He consulted his next list. "Bill," he said, "you draw for the Hutchinson family. You got any other households in the Hutchinsons?"

"There's Don and Eva," Mrs. Hutchinson yelled. "Make *them* take their    49 chance!"

"Daughters draw with their husbands' families, Tessie," Mr. Summers    50 said gently. "You know that as well as anyone else."

"It wasn't *fair*," Tessie said.    51

"I guess not, Joe," Bill Hutchinson said regretfully. "My daughter draws    52 with her husband's family, that's only fair. And I've got no other family except the kids."

"Then, as far as drawing for families is concerned, it's you," Mr. Summers    53 said in explanation, "and as far as drawing for households is concerned, that's you, too. Right?"

"Right," Bill Hutchinson said.    54

"How many kids, Bill?" Mr. Summers asked formally.    55

"Three," Bill Hutchinson said. "There's Bill, Jr., and Nancy, and little    56 Dave. And Tessie and me."

"All right, then," Mr. Summers said. "Harry, you got their tickets back?"    57

Mr. Graves nodded and held up the slips of paper. "Put them in the box,    58 then," Mr. Summers directed. "Take Bill's and put it in."

"I think we ought to start over," Mrs. Hutchinson said, as quietly as she    59 could. "I tell you it wasn't *fair*. You didn't give him time enough to choose. *Every*body saw that."

Mr. Graves had selected the five slips and put them in the box, and he    60 dropped all the papers but those onto the ground, where the breeze caught them and lifted them off.

"Listen, everybody," Mrs. Hutchinson was saying to the people around    61 her.

"Ready, Bill?" Mr. Summers asked, and Bill Hutchinson, with one quick    62 glance around at his wife and children, nodded.

"Remember," Mr. Summers said, "take the slips and keep them folded    63 until each person has taken one. Harry, you help little Dave." Mr. Graves took the hand of the little boy, who came willingly with him up to the box. "Take a paper out of the box, Davy," Mr. Summers said. Davy put his hand into the box and laughed. "Take just *one* paper," Mr. Summers said. "Harry, you hold it for him." Mr. Graves took the child's hand and removed the folded paper from the tight fist and held it while little Dave stood next to him and looked up at him wonderingly.

"Nancy next," Mr. Summers said. Nancy was twelve, and her school     64
friends breathed heavily as she went forward, switching her skirt, and took a slip daintily from the box. "Bill, Jr.," Mr. Summers said, and Billy, his face red and his feet overlarge, nearly knocked the box over as he got a paper out. "Tessie," Mr. Summers said. She hesitated for a minute, looking around defiantly, and then set her lips and went up to the box. She snatched a paper out and held it behind her.

"Bill," Mr. Summers said, and Bill Hutchinson reached into the box and     65
felt around, bringing his hand out at last with the slip of paper in it.

The crowd was quiet. A girl whispered, "I hope it's not Nancy," and the     66
sound of the whisper reached the edges of the crowd.

"It's not the way it used to be," Old Man Warner said clearly. "People ain't     67
the way they used to be."

"All right," Mr. Summers said. "Open the papers. Harry, you open little     68
Dave's."

Mr. Graves opened the slip of paper and there was a general sigh through     69
the crowd as he held it up and everyone could see that it was blank. Nancy and Bill, Jr., opened theirs at the same time, and both beamed and laughed, turning around to the crowd and holding their slips of paper above their heads.

"Tessie," Mr. Summers said. There was a pause, and then Mr. Summers     70
looked at Bill Hutchinson, and Bill unfolded his paper and showed it. It was blank.

"It's Tessie," Mr. Summers said, and his voice was hushed. "Show us her     71
paper, Bill."

Bill Hutchinson went over to his wife and forced the slip of paper out of     72
her hand. It had a black spot on it, the black spot Mr. Summers had made the night before with the heavy pencil in the coal-company office. Bill Hutchinson held it up, and there was a stir in the crowd.

"All right, folks," Mr. Summers said. "Let's finish quickly."     73

Although the villagers had forgotten the ritual and lost the original black     74
box, they still remembered to use stones. The pile of stones the boys had made earlier was ready; there were stones on the ground with the blowing scraps of paper that had come out of the box. Mrs. Delacroix selected a stone so large she had to pick it up with both hands and turned to Mrs. Dunbar. "Come on," she said. "Hurry up."

Mrs. Dunbar had small stones in both hands, and she said, gasping for     75
breath, "I can't run at all. You'll have to go ahead and I'll catch up with you."

The children had stones already, and someone gave little Davy Hutchinson a few pebbles.     76

Tessie Hutchinson was in the center of a cleared space by now, and she 77
held her hands out desperately as the villagers moved in on her. "It isn't fair,"
she said. A stone hit her on the side of the head.

Old Man Warner was saying, "Come on, come on, everyone." Steve 78
Adams was in the front of the crowd of villagers, with Mrs. Graves beside him.

"It isn't fair, it isn't right," Mrs. Hutchinson screamed, and then they were 79
upon her.

| | |
|---|---|
| **Questions to Start You Thinking** | *Meaning* <br><br> 1. Where does this story take place? When? <br><br> 2. How does this lottery differ from what we usually think of as a lottery? Why would people conduct a lottery such as this? <br><br> 3. What does this story mean to you? <br><br> *Writing Strategies* <br><br> 4. Can you see and hear the people in the story? Do they seem real, or fantastic? Who is the most memorable character to you? <br><br> 5. Are the events believable? Does the ending shock you? Is it believable? <br><br> 6. Is this a realistic story, or is Jackson using these events to represent something else? |

As Jonathan Burns read "The Lottery," he was carried along quickly to the
startling ending. After the immediate impact of the story wore off, Burns
reread it, this time to savor some of the details he had missed during his first
reading. Then, knowing he had to write a literary analysis for his composition
course, he wrote a summary or *synopsis* of "The Lottery" to get a clear fix on
the literal events in the story. (We reprint his synopsis on p. 286.)

But Burns knew that he could not write a good analysis without reading
the story repeatedly and closely, marking key points in the text. Students who
read a complex work of literature only once, thinking that is enough, are mistaken. Even if you are trying to understand only the literal level — what happens in a story or what a poet says — you'll need to read the work more than
once. If your purpose is to comprehend, interpret, and evaluate, you'll find
that several close readings are necessary.

For close critical reading, read the text *at least* three times, each time for a
different reason. In all readings, read purposefully. (For more on these three
kinds of reading, see "Suggestions for Critical Reading," p. 124.)

*Read to comprehend.* Read for the literal meaning, an overall idea of what
the work contains — what happens to whom, where, when, and why. Get all
the facts straight — the setting, the events of the plot, the characters and what
they say and do. Be sure you understand all the vocabulary, especially in titles
and in poems.

*Read to interpret.* Read to understand the meaning of the story or poem
beyond the literal level. Read between the lines. Mark the sections and ana-

lyze the parts. Read with an eye for what you seek in the work: theme, character, style, symbol, form. Read with pencil in hand, and make notes. Is there an especially hard part? Try putting it into your own words. Is it a difficult piece? Try reading it aloud to yourself — that may help you make sense of it. What does the literary work mean? What does it imply? What does it help you understand about the human condition? What insights can you apply to your own life?

*Read to evaluate.* Read to assess the soundness and plausibility of what the author says. Are the words appropriate for the purpose and audience? What is the author's tone? Is it appropriate for the audience? Does the author achieve his or her purpose? Is it a worthwhile purpose? Synthesize what you have discovered from your analysis through all your readings in order to determine the effectiveness and significance of the piece of literature. As you are evaluating, be sure that you use definite criteria beyond personal or whimsical likes and dislikes.

Later, as you draft your literary analysis, you will discover, just as Jonathan Burns did, that you have to reread specific sections over and over to check your interpretations and to be sure the evidence from the story supports your claims.

Jonathan Burns knew he had to analyze the important elements in "The Lottery" to understand the story well enough to write about it. He thought about what he had learned in class about the different elements of a literary work and the terms used to describe them. (For a description of the basic elements of literature, see the glossary on pp. 263–67.) His analysis of these elements — setting, character, tone, and others — helped him think about a topic for his paper, some point on which he could focus his thoughts and comments. He immediately thought of the undertone of violence in the story but decided that the undertone was so subtle that it would be difficult to write about it. Then he considered writing about the characters in the story. Mr. Summers and Old Man Warner were especially memorable. And then there was Tessie Hutchinson; he could hear her screams as the stones hit her. But he decided not to write about the characters because he could not think of much to say about them except that they were memorable, and he knew that that was too vague a statement. He considered other elements — language and symbols, foreshadowing and ambiguity — and dismissed each in turn. All of a sudden he hit upon the surprise ending. How did Jackson manipulate all the details to generate such a shock?

To begin to focus his thinking, he brainstormed titles having to do with the ending, some serious, others flippant: Death Comes as a Surprise; The Unsuspected Finish; Patience of the Devil; An Inquiry into the Implementation of Pure Reason; The Wrath of Grapes; Bob Dylan Was Right. He chose the straightforward title "The Hidden Truth."

After reviewing his notes from his analysis of the story, Burns realized that Jackson uses characterization, symbolism, and ambiguous description to prepare readers for the ending. Writing about how the author shocks readers

at the end of the story would allow him to discuss several elements that interested him, and focusing on the techniques she uses to build up to the ending would help him unify the aspects of his interpretation.

He listed details from the story under three headings — characters, symbols, and language. Following is the informal plan he made for his paper.

Title: The Hidden Truth

Thesis: In "The Lottery" Shirley Jackson
     effectively crafts a shock ending.

1. Characterization that contributes to the
   shock ending
   - The children of the village
   - The adults of the village
   - Conversations among the villagers

2. Symbols that contribute to the shock ending
   - The stones
   - The black box

3. Language that contributes to the shock
   ending
   - The word "lottery"
   - Comments
     - "clean forgot"
     - "wish they'd hurry"
     - "It isn't fair."
   - Actions
     - Relief
     - Suspense

Then he drafted the following introduction:

Unsuspecting, the reader follows Shirley Jackson's
softly flowing tale of a rural community's timeless rit-

ual, the lottery. Awareness of what is at stake--the savage murder of one random member--comes slow, only becoming clear toward the last fraction of the story. No
sooner does the realization set in than the story is
over. It is a shock ending.

   What created so great a shock as the reader experiences after reading "The Lottery"? Shirley Jackson takes
great care in producing this effect, using elements such
as language, symbolism, and characterization to lure the
reader into not anticipating what is to come.

With his synopsis (p. 286), his plan, his copy of the story, and this beginning of a draft, he revised the introduction and wrote the following essay.

STUDENT ESSAY

*Jonathan Burns*   **The Hidden Truth: An Analysis of Shirley Jackson's
"The Lottery"**

   It is as if the first stone thrown strikes the reader as    1
well as Mrs. Hutchinson. And even though there were signs of
the stoning to come, somehow the reader is taken by surprise
at Tessie's violent death. What factors contribute to the
shock ending to "The Lottery"?  Upon closer examination of
the story, the reader finds that through all events leading
up to the ending, Shirley Jackson has used unsuspicious char-
acterizations, unobtrusive symbolism, and ambiguous descriptions to achieve so sudden an impact.

   By all appearances, the village is a normal place with    2
normal people. Children arrive at the scene first, with
school just over for the summer, talking of teachers and
books, not of the fact that someone will die today (250). And
as the adults show up, their actions are just as stereotypical: the men talk of farming and taxes, while the women gossip (251). No trace of hostility, no sense of dread in
anyone: death seems very far away here.

   The conversations between the villagers are no more omi-    3
nous. As the husbands draw slips of paper for their families,

the villagers make apparently everyday comments about the
seemingly ordinary event of the lottery. Mr. Summers is regarded as a competent and respected figure, despite the fact
that his wife is "a scold" (251). Old Man Warner brags about
how many lotteries he's seen and rambles on criticizing other
towns that have given up the tradition (254). The characters'
comments show the crowd to be more a closely knit community
than a murderous mob.

    The symbols of "The Lottery" seem equally ordinary. The          4
stones collected by the boys (250-51) are unnoticed by the
adults and thus seem a trivial detail. The reader thinks of
the "great pile" (251) as children's entertainment, like a
stack of imaginary coins rather than an arsenal. Ironically,
no stones are ever thrown during the children's play and no
violence is seen in the pile of stones.

    Similarly, Jackson describes the box and its history in          5
great detail, but there seems nothing unusual about it. It is
just another everyday object, stored away in the post office
or on a shelf in the grocery (252). Every other day of the
year, the box is in plain view but goes virtually unnoticed.
The only indication that the box has lethal consequences is
that it is painted black (251), yet this is an ambiguous detail, as a black box can also signify mystery or magic, mys-
tical forces that are sometimes thought to exist in any
lottery.

    In her ambiguous descriptions, Jackson refers regularly          6
to the village's lottery and emphasizes it as a central ritual for the people. The word lottery itself is ironic, as it
typically implies a winning of some kind, like a raffle or
sweepstakes. It is paralleled to square dances and to the
teenage club, all under the direction of Mr. Summers (251),
activities people look forward to. There is no implied difference between the occurrences of this day and the festivities of Halloween: according to Jackson, they are all merely
"civic activities" (251). Equally ambiguous are the people's
emotions: some of the villagers are casual, such as Mrs.
Hutchinson, who arrives late because she "clean forgot" what
day it is (252), and some are anxious, such as Mrs. Dunbar,
who repeats to her son, "I wish they'd hurry," without any

sign of the cause of her anxiety (254). With these descriptive details the reader finds no threat or malice in the villagers, only vague expectation and congeniality.

Even when it becomes clear that the lottery is something    7
no one wants to win, Jackson presents only a vague sense of
sadness and mild protest. The crowd is relieved that the
youngest of the Hutchinsons, Davy, doesn't draw the fatal
slip of paper (256). One girl whispers that she hopes it
isn't Nancy (256), and when the Hutchinson children discover
they aren't the winners, they beam with joy and proudly display their blank slips (256). It's like a theatrical scene,
with growing suspense and excitement apparent only when the
victim is close to being identified. And when Tessie is revealed to be the winner of the lottery (256), she merely
holds her hands out "desperately" and repeats, "It isn't
fair' " (257).

With a blend of character, symbolism, and description,    8
Shirley Jackson paints an overall portrait of a gentle-seem-
ing rural community, apparently no different from any other.
The tragic end is sudden only because there is no recognition
of violence beforehand, despite the fact that Jackson has
provided the reader with plenty of clues in the ample details
about the lottery and the people. It is a haunting discovery
that the story ends in death, even though such is the truth
in the everyday life of <u>all</u> people.

**Questions to Start You Thinking**

*Meaning*

1. What is Burns's thesis?
2. What major points does he use to support his thesis? What specific elements of the story does he include as evidence to support his interpretation?

*Writing Strategies*

3. How does this essay differ from a synopsis, a summary of the events of the plot? (For a synopsis of "The Lottery," see p. 286.)
4. Does Jonathan Burns focus on the technique of the short story or on its theme?
5. Is his introduction effective? Compare and contrast it with the first introduction he drafted (p. 259). What did he change? Which version do you prefer?
6. Why does he explain characterization first, symbolism second, and description last? Would discussing these elements in a different order have made much difference in his essay?

7. Is his conclusion effective?
8. How does he tie his ideas together as he moves from paragraph to paragraph? How does he keep the focus on idea and technique instead of plot?

## ANALYZING THE ELEMENTS OF LITERATURE: A GLOSSARY OF TERMS

Every field — scuba diving, football, gourmet cooking, engineering, business — has its own vocabulary. If you are going to play football, you should know the difference between a blitz and a quarterback sneak. Before you start cooking, you'd better know the difference between basting and shirring. Literary analysis is no different. Before you can analyze and interpret a piece of literature or write a successful literary analysis, you must be familiar with the elements of fiction, poetry, and drama and with the specialized terms critics and scholars use to talk about those elements. We list a few of the elements here — a handy glossary of terms that you can use to discuss any piece of literature.

Setting  is the time and place where events occur. The season, the weather, the atmosphere, and people in the background may be part of the setting. Jonathan Burns recognized that Shirley Jackson describes the setting in the first sentence of "The Lottery": "The morning of June 27th was clear and sunny, with the fresh warmth of a full-summer day; the flowers were blossoming profusely and the grass was richly green" (para. 1). That description is precise: Burns could almost feel the sun and smell the flowers. But he did not know the period of time — eighteenth century, nineteenth century, twentieth century? And he did not know where Jackson's village is located.

Characters  are imagined people. The author lets you know what they are like through their actions, speech, thoughts, attitudes, and background. Sometimes a writer also tells you about physical characteristics or names or relationships with other people.

Burns reread the initial description of Mr. Summers: he "had time and energy to devote to civic activities. He was a round-faced, jovial man and he ran the coal business, and people were sorry for him, because he had no children and his wife was a scold" (para. 4). These details introduce this official of the lottery. Burns also learned about him through what he says: "'Little late today, folks'" (para. 4); "'Thought we were going to have to get on without you, Tessie'" (para. 9); "'Well, now, . . . guess we better get started, get this over with, so's we can go back to work'" (para. 10). Burns decided that Mr. Summers is in charge of the situation and doesn't want any slip-ups. What does Mr. Warner's speech in "The Lottery" tell you about him?

In addition, Burns learned about the characters through what they do, as when the Watson boy "blinked his eyes nervously and ducked his head" at the lottery (para. 16) or when the villagers "only half listened to the directions; most of them were quiet, wetting their lips, not looking around" (para. 20). What does Tessie do that gives you some insight into what she is like?

Plot  is the arrangement of the events of the story — what happens to whom, where, when, and why. If the events follow each other logically and if they are in keeping with what the author tells us about the characters, the plot is **plausible,** or believable. Although the ending of "The Lottery" at first shocked Jonathan, when he looked back through the story he found **foreshadowing,** hints that the author provides to help readers understand future events or twists in the plot. Looking back, Jonathan saw numerous clues that Tessie and the other villagers are nervous and hesitant about the lottery, not the usual reaction of people who expect someone to win a desirable prize of money, a car, or a vacation. See how many of these clues you can find.

The **protagonist,** or main character, is placed in a dramatic situation of **conflict** with some other person or group of people, the **antagonist.** In "The Lottery," Burns identified Tessie Hutchinson as the protagonist, the villagers as the antagonist, and the dramatic situation as Tessie's joining the group waiting for the lottery. **Conflict** consists of two forces attempting to conquer each other or resisting being conquered. It is not merely any vaguely defined turmoil in a story. **External conflicts** are conflicts outside an individual — between two people, between a person and a group (Tessie Hutchinson versus the villagers), between two groups (those who support the lottery and those who want to do away with it), or even between a character and his or her environment. **Internal conflicts** are those within an individual, between two opposing forces or desires (such as reason versus emotion or fear versus hope in each villager as the slips of paper are drawn). The **central conflict** of a story is the primary conflict for the protagonist that propels and accounts for the action of the story. What is the central conflict for Tessie?

Events of the plot **complicate** the conflict (Tessie arrives late, Bill Hutchinson draws the slip with the black spot for his family, Tessie claims it wasn't fair) and lead to the **climax,** the moment at which the outcome is inevitable (Tessie draws the slip with the black dot). The outcome itself is the **resolution,** or conclusion (the villagers stone Tessie Hutchinson). Some contemporary stories let events unfold without any apparent plot — action and change occur inside the characters.

Point of view  is the angle from which a story is told. Who is the **narrator** — who tells the story? Through whose eyes are the events perceived? It might be the author, or it might be some character in the story. If a character, what part does he or she play, and what limits does the author place on that character's knowledge? Is the character aware of everything that is going on, or is he or she an outsider? Jonathan Burns tried to answer these questions to determine the point of view in "The Lottery." Three often-used points of view are those of a **first-person narrator** (*I*), a **third-person narrator** (*he* or *she*) who is a major participant in the action (often the protagonist), and a **third-person nar-**

**rator** who is an observer, not a participant. The point of view may be **omniscient** (told through several characters' eyes), **limited omniscient** (told through one character's eyes), or **objective** (not told through any character's eyes). Burns realized that the point of view in "The Lottery" is that of a third-person objective narrator seemingly looking on and reporting what occurs without knowing what any of the characters are thinking. Why do you think Shirley Jackson chose this point of view for "The Lottery"? How would the story be different if it were told from Tessie's point of view? From Mr. Summers's? From Old Man Warner's?

Theme  is a main idea or insight a work contains. It is the author's observations about life, society, or human nature. Sometimes you can sum up a theme in a sentence: "Honesty is the best policy," "Human beings cannot live without illusion."

In a complex work, a theme may be implied and difficult to discern. Some works have more than one theme, and they may be stated in various ways. In an analysis of "The Lottery," the critics Cleanth Brooks and Robert Penn Warren assert, "We had best not try to restrict the meaning to some simple dogmatic statement. The author herself has been rather careful to allow a good deal of flexibility in our interpretation of the meaning, yet surely a general meaning does emerge."

To state a theme, find an important subject in the story and ask yourself, What does the author say about this subject? Details from the story itself should support your statement of theme, and your theme should account for all the details in the story. Be careful not to confuse a subject or topic of a story with a theme. To find the theme, Jonathan Burns first listed some of the important subjects of "The Lottery": the unexpected, scapegoating, people's inhumanity to one another, outmoded rituals, victims of society, hostility, violence, death. What other subjects do you see in this story? Then Burns focused on Tessie's claim that the lottery wasn't fair and the reaction of the Hutchinson children and the other villagers when the children did not draw the black dot, believing these to be significant occurrences leading to Jackson's meaning. From this interpretation, he stated the theme as "People are selfish, always looking out for number one."

Images  are words or groups of words that refer to any sense experience:

*Seeing.* In his analysis of "The Lottery," Burns determined that Shirley Jackson uses many images of sight to help readers visualize what happens. The flowers bloom "profusely" and the grass is "richly green" (para. 1). Jackson describes the black box so precisely that Jonathan — and we — can see it clearly: it has grown "shabbier each year" and is "no longer completely black but splintered badly along one side to show the original wood color, and in some places faded or stained" (para. 5). When Mr. Graves drops all the slips of paper except the five for the Hutchinson family, "the breeze [catches] them and [lifts] them off" (para. 60).

*Hearing.* Burns found several images of sound in Jackson's story. The children engage in "boisterous play" (para. 2). When Mr. Summers arrives in the square, a "murmur of conversation" spreads among the villagers; a "hush" comes over the crowd when he speaks (paras. 4, 19). Nancy's friends breathe "heavily" as Nancy goes forward to draw a slip of paper (para. 64). Mrs. Dunbar is "gasping for breath" as the villagers move toward Tessie (para. 75).

*Smelling.* Although Jackson doesn't include any smells in her story, Burns himself imagined the musty smell of Mr. Summers's coal company where the black box was locked away the night before the lottery and Mr. Graves's barn where the dusty black box had been stored for a year since the last lottery.

*Tasting.* What do you think the villagers tasted when they wet their lips?

*Touching.* The stones the children gather are smooth and round (para. 2), and Tessie taps Mrs. Delacroix on the arm as she makes her way toward her husband (para. 9).

*Feeling.* Do the characters feel heat or cold, fear or joy, pain or thirst? Jonathan saw that the villagers feel "the fresh warmth of a full-summer day" (para. 1). Then he realized that because of the point of view in "The Lottery," he wasn't told much more about what the villagers feel.

Figures of speech are defined by William Thrall and Addison Hibbard as "intentional departures from the normal order, construction, or meaning of words in order to gain strength and freshness of expression" (*A Handbook to Literature*, 4th ed., Indianapolis: Bobbs-Merrill Educational Pub., 1980). Some of the most common types of figurative language are the **simile**, a comparison using *like* or *as*; the **metaphor**, an implied comparison; and **personification**, the attribution of human qualities to inanimate or non-human creatures or things. Burns found several metaphors in "The Lottery." Bobby Martin, Harry Jones, and Dickie Delacroix *guard* their pile of stones "against the *raids* of the other boys" (para. 2). Tessie *cranes* her neck to find her family (para. 9). Old Man Warner says that the young people who want to give up the lottery will next " 'be wanting to go back to living in caves' " (para. 32).

Symbols are tangible objects or visible actions or characters that hint at meanings beyond themselves. In "The Lottery," a story filled with symbols, Burns decided that the black box suggests outdated tradition, the mysteriously inexplicable, the past, resistance to change, evil, cruelty, and more. What does Old Man Warner suggest? In this story, as in others, if you can identify a central symbol and figure out what it suggests, you are well on your way to stating the theme.

Irony results from readers' sense of some discrepancy. A simple kind of irony, **sarcasm**, occurs when you say a thing but mean the opposite: "I just love scrubbing the floor" or "Of course, I don't want a Mercedes." In literature, an **ironic situation** sets up a wry contrast or incongruity. In "The Lottery," actions of evil cruelty and horror take place on a bright sunny June day in an ordinary village. **Ironic dialogue** occurs when a character says one thing but the audience or reader is aware of another meaning. When someone mentions that some people in the north village are talking of giving up the lottery, Old Man Warner snorts, " 'Next thing you know, they'll be wanting to go back to living in caves, nobody work anymore, live *that* way for a while. . . . First thing you know, we'd all be eating stewed chickweed and acorns" (para. 32). He implies that doing away with the lottery would cause the villagers to return to a more primitive way of life. His comment is ironic because the reader is aware that this lottery is a primitive ritual. A story has an **ironic point of view** when we sense a difference between the author and the character through whose eyes the story is perceived or between the author and the narrator. Burns realized that Shirley Jackson does not condone the actions of the villagers, no matter what the reason. Find some other ironic events and comments in this story.

As you read literary criticism and discuss literature in your classes, you will discover other literary terms, but the basic ones listed here give you a foundation for analyzing literature.

## LEARNING BY WRITING

**The Assignment: Analyzing a Literary Work**    A literary critic analyzes, interprets, and evaluates a work of literature. The critic sees and understands deeply not because he or she has some special inspiration or power but because he or she has studied the piece of writing very carefully. For this assignment, you are to be a critic — analyzing, interpreting, and evaluating a literary selection for your classmates. You will deepen their understanding because you will have devoted time and effort to digging out the meaning and testing it with evidence from the work itself. Even if they too have studied the work carefully, you will try to convince them that your interpretation is valid.

Write an essay interpreting one or more aspects of a literary work that intrigues you or that you think expresses a worthwhile meaning. Probably your instructor will want to approve your selection. After careful analysis of the literary work, you will become the expert critic, explaining the meaning you discern, supporting your interpretation with evidence from the work itself as well as from your own experience, and evaluating the effectiveness of the literary elements used by the author and the significance of the theme. You may draw from any of your five resources — recall, observation, reading (of the story as well as of other sources), conversation, imagination. Probably you'll use several critical thinking skills — analyzing the parts of the work; comparing and contrasting characters in the story, or comparing and contrasting the work with other works you know; identifying causal relationships in the action of the work; taking a stand on your interpretation; proposing a solution to a puzzling part of the work or to a problem posed by the author (perhaps as a theme); and evaluating the quality of the work. Refer to Parts One and Two of this book to remind yourself about these resources and critical thinking skills.

You cannot attempt to include everything about the work in your paper, so you should focus on one element (such as character, setting, or theme) or the interrelationship of two or three elements (as Jonathan Burns did when he analyzed characterization, symbolism, and ambiguity in his interpretation of the surprise ending of "The Lottery"). The purpose of your essay is to help your classmates — who have read but not studied the selection as thoroughly as you have — to understand the meaning of the work and to gain insight into their own lives just as you have through your careful study.

Your assignment is to analyze, to interpret, and to evaluate the work, not just to retell the story. Although a summary, or *synopsis*, of the plot and characterization is a good beginning point for your ideas, it is not a satisfactory literary analysis. Notice, for example, how Jonathan Burns uses details from the plot in the second and third paragraphs of his essay (260-61) but then moves beyond events of the plot to an analysis of character, symbol, and description.

Here are instances of college writers who successfully responded to this type of assignment:

A man who was a musician analyzed the credibility of Sonny as a musician in James Baldwin's "Sonny's Blues" — his attitudes, actions, struggles, relationship with his instrument and with other musicians — and concluded that Sonny is a believable character.

A woman analyzed the plot of the short story "The Necklace" by Guy de Maupassant and concluded that the change in the protagonist Mathilde Loisel at the end of the story is unrealistic.

A man demonstrated how the rhythm, rhymes, and images of Adrienne Rich's poem "Aunt Jennifer's Tigers" mesh to convey the poem's theme of tension between a woman's artistic urge and the constraints placed on her by society.

A man explained how Carson McCullers in the short story "A Tree, a Rock, a Cloud" uses characterization to reveal the theme that severe emotional hurt caused by rejection in love can predispose an individual toward emotional detachment in subsequent relationships.

A woman analyzed the reasons why the protagonist Charles Woodruff does what he does in the short story "Witness" by Ann Petry. She analyzed Woodruff's background, beliefs, and relationship to the community, the position and attitudes of the boys, and the attitudes of the community. She concluded that Woodruff's motivation is sufficient and his actions, although tragic, are plausible.

A woman majoring in psychology concluded that the relationship between Hamlet and Claudius in Shakespeare's *Hamlet* is in many ways representative of the tension, jealously, and misunderstanding between stepsons and stepfathers.

A woman explained how Walter Van Tilburg Clark uses symbols in "A Portable Phonograph" to reveal and intensify the theme of humans' inhumanity to others because of selfishness.

**Finding a Subject.**   Read several literary works until you find two or three you like. Perhaps one makes you nod your head in agreement as you read, or sends a chill up your spine when you finish, or leaves you puzzled at the end, or even makes you angry. Do you have a favorite author? A favorite short story among those you have read for this course? Any of these might make a suitable selection for your analysis.

Next, slowly and carefully reread the two or three works that tweak your interest to decide which one you want to concentrate on. Choose the one that strikes you as especially significant — realistic or universal, moving or disturbing, believable or shocking. Choose the one that seems to have a meaning that you wish to share with your classmates.

**Generating Ideas.**   Analyzing a literary work is the first step in interpreting meaning and evaluating literary quality. Your analysis of the work will give you ideas to write about and will help you find evidence in the work to support your interpretation. As you read the work you have selected, see it as divisible into its elements and analyze those elements as Jonathan Burns did in his paper on "The Lottery." Then focus on *one* significant element. When you write your interpretation, restrict your discussion to that element and possibly its relationship to other literary elements.

We provide checklists to guide you in studying different types of literature. Each analytical model is an aid to understanding; it is *not* an organizational outline for writing about literature. (See pp. 263–67 for a glossary of the literary terms used in the checklists.) The following checklist focuses on short stories and novels, but because thinking about your reaction to the work and about setting, characters, and theme is important whether you are analyzing a short story, a poem, or a play, some of the questions can help you analyze almost any kind of literary work. Checklists focusing specifically on poetry and plays follow.

**DISCOVERY CHECKLIST**

## Analyzing a Short Story or a Novel

- What is your reaction to the story? Jot it down.
- Who is the *narrator* — not the author, but the one who tells the story?
- What is the *point of view*?
- What is the *setting* (time and place)? What is the *atmosphere* or *mood*?
- How does the *plot* unfold? Write a synopsis, or summary, of the events in time order, including relationships among those events.
- What are the *characters* like? Describe their personalities and traits. Who is the *protagonist*? The *antagonist*? Do any characters change, and are the changes plausible or believable?

- How would you describe the story's *style*, or use of language? Is the style informal or conversational? Is it formal? Is there any dialect? Are there any foreign words?
- What are the *conflicts* in the story? Determine the *external conflicts* and the *internal conflicts*. What is the *central conflict*? Express the conflicts using the word *versus*, such as "dreams versus reality" or "the individual versus society."
- What is the *climax* of the story? Is there any *resolution*?
- Are there important *symbols*? What might they mean?
- What does the *title* of the story mean?
- Does the story have more than one *level of meaning*?
- What are the *themes* of the story? State your interpretation of the main theme. How is this theme related to your own life?
- What other literary works or experiences from life does the story make you think of? Jot them down.

When looking at a poem, you should consider the elements specific to poetry — for example, the importance of word choice, rhythm, and rhyme — and the elements poetry has in common with other genres. The following checklist provides both general and specific questions to ask yourself when reading a poem.

**DISCOVERY
CHECKLIST**

## Analyzing a Poem

- What is your reaction to the poem? Jot it down.
- Who is the *speaker* — not the author, but the one who tells the story?
- What is the *setting*? What is the *mood*?
- Can you put the poem into your own words — paraphrase it?
- What is striking about the language of the poem? Identify any unusual words or words used in an unusual sense. Look for *archaic* words (words no longer commonly used) and *repetition* of words. Consider the *connotations* of important words (the suggestions conjured by the words — *house* has a different connotation from *home*, although both may refer to the same place). Is the level of language colloquial or formal? What kind of figurative language is used: *imagery, metaphor, irony*?
- Is the poem *lyric* (expressing emotion) or *narrative* (telling a story)?
- What is the structure of the poem? How is it divided? Does it consist of *couplets* (two consecutive rhyming lines) or *quatrains* (units of four lines)? Notice especially how the beginning and the end relate to each other and to the poem as a whole.
- Does the poem use *rhyme* (words that sound alike)? If so, how does the rhyme contribute to the meaning?
- Does the poem have *rhythm* (regular meter or beat, patterns of accented and unaccented syllables)? How does the rhythm contribute to the meaning?
- What does the *title* of the poem mean?
- What is the major *theme* of the poem? How does this underlying idea unify the poem? How is it related to your own life?
- What other literary works or experiences from life does the poem make you think of? Jot them down.

A play is written to be seen and heard, not read. When you analyze a play, you may ask what kind of play it is and how it would appear onstage. The questions in the following checklist will help you understand a play.

**DISCOVERY CHECKLIST**

## Analyzing a Play

- What is your reaction to the play? Jot it down.
- How does the play differ from a short story or a novel? Can you visualize the action? Can you hear the words of the characters? If you were an actor, how would you interpret the stage directions and say the words? If you were the casting director, whom would you cast in the major roles of the play?
- Is the play a *tragedy* (a serious drama that arouses pity and fear in the audience and usually ends unhappily with the death or downfall of the *tragic hero* or a *comedy* (drama that aims primarily to amuse and that usually ends happily)?
- What is the *setting* of the play? What is its *mood*?
- In brief, what happens? Summarize each act of the play.
- What are the characters like? Who is the *protagonist*? What *antagonist* opposes the main character? Are there *foil characters* (those who contrast with the main character and reveal his or her traits)? Which characters are in conflict? Do any of the characters change?
- Which speeches seem especially significant?
- What is the plot? Identify the *exposition*, the background information needed to understand the story. Determine the main *external* and *internal conflicts*. What is the *central conflict*? What events *complicate* the central conflict? How are these elements of the plot spread throughout the play?
- What is the *climax* of the play? Is there a *resolution* to the action?
- What does the *title* mean?
- Can you identify any *dramatic irony*, words or actions of a character that carry meaning unperceived by the character but evident to the audience?
- What is the major *theme* of the play — a universal idea that underlies it? How is this theme related to your own life?
- What other literary works or experiences from life does the play make you think of? Jot them down.

As you write your analysis, don't worry about impressing your readers with your brilliance. Though you need a critical vocabulary, use only terms that you understand. The writer who writes "The ironic symbolism in 'The Lottery' is portrayed as highly symbolic in theme" is about as clear as corned beef hash. Assume that your readers have read the work you're analyzing but that they have not studied it as carefully as you have. This assumption will help you determine how much evidence from the story you need to include and will save you a lot of wordy summarizing ("On the next page they bring out a black box, sit it on a three-legged stool, and put slips of paper in it"). We suggest that you regard your readers as friends in whose company you are discussing something already familiar to all of you. Your purpose is to explain the deeper meaning of the story, meaning that they may not be aware of after only a cursory reading.

## Finding Ideas

- Have you known people similar to those in the literary work? Are the characters believable? Is their motivation sufficient to cause them to act as they do? How do you know what they are like (through their actions, speech, habits, and so on)?
- Have similar things happened to you? Can you use some information from your experience to explain the meaning of the work?
- Are there any significant images that help illuminate the meaning? Any important symbols? Any irony? What about the setting and the atmosphere?
- Are the characters universal (representative of all human beings)? Are they stereotypes?
- What ideas do the characters and the author consider? Do these ideas imply themes? Can you generalize about them to state some of the themes the author intends? Are the main themes in the literary work universal (applicable to all people everywhere at all times)?
- What is the main point you want to make about this work? Does the evidence that you have gathered through your close reading and analysis of the work itself support this point?
- Have you selected a major element in the work to focus on? Have you avoided focusing on a minor element simply because it strikes your fancy?

**Planning, Drafting, and Developing.**    After you have determined the element or the related elements of the work that you intend to focus on to interpret meaning, go through the work again to find all the passages that relate to your main point, marking them or taking notes as you find them. It's a good idea to put these relevant passages on note cards or in a computer file, just as you do when you are conducting library research. Remember to note the page references for the details you select, and if you use any quotations, quote them exactly.

Begin writing by trying to express the main point you want to convey in your analysis — your thesis. Suppose you start with a tentative thesis on the theme of "The Lottery" (note that the thesis statement identifies the literary work and the author):

```
In "The Lottery," Shirley Jackson reveals the theme.
```

But this statement is too vague, so you decide to rewrite it to be more precise:

```
In "The Lottery" by Shirley Jackson, the theme is tradi-
tion.
```

This thesis is better, but still unsatisfactory. The statement of the theme of the story is not yet clear or precise: In her narrative, what does Jackson imply about tradition? You try several other ways of expressing your idea.

```
In "The Lottery" by Shirley Jackson, one of the major
themes is that outmoded traditions can be harmful.
```

You used the qualifier *one of* to indicate that this theme is not the only one in the story, but the rest of the thesis is vague. What does "outmoded" mean? How are the traditions harmful?

```
In "The Lottery" by Shirley Jackson, one of the major
themes is that traditions that have lost their meaning
can cause otherwise normal people to act abnormally by
rote.
```

This is a better thesis, one you might start writing from, but keep in mind that it may change as you develop the analysis. You might decide to go beyond interpretation of Jackson's ideas to an evaluation of what she says. If so, you could write the following thesis:

```
In "The Lottery," Shirley Jackson reveals the tragic
theme that traditions that have lost their meaning can
cause otherwise normal people to act abnormally by rote.
```

In this thesis the word *tragic* reveals your evaluation of Jackson's observation of the human condition. Or you might say:

```
In "The Lottery," Shirley Jackson effectively uses sym-
bolism and irony to reveal the theme that traditions that
have lost their meaning can cause otherwise normal people
to act abnormally by rote.
```

When planning and organizing your essay, focus on ideas, not events; take care not to merely retell the story. One way you might maintain that focus is to analyze your thesis. The thesis just presented could be divided into (1) use of symbolism to reveal theme and (2) use of irony to reveal theme. If you are writing about character change, say that of Mrs. Mallard in Kate Chopin's "The Story of an Hour" (p. 289), you might divide the information into her original character traits or attitudes, the events that cause the change, and her new traits or attitudes.

To start your analysis, you might relate a personal experience that parallels that of the protagonist (for "The Story of an Hour," for instance, how you felt when someone close to you died) and tie your experience to that of the character in the work. Or you might focus on the universality of the character (pointing out that most people would feel as Tessie in "The Lottery" did and would probably shout "It isn't fair, it isn't right" if their name were drawn in the village lottery) or of the theme (discussing briefly how traditions seem to be losing their meaning in modern society). You might quote a striking line from the work ("and then they were upon her" or "'Lottery in June, corn be heavy soon'" or "'we'd all be eating stewed chickweed and acorns'"). More simply, you can start with a statement of what the work is about, or with your reaction to the work when you read it, or with a comment about a technique that the writer uses. You might begin with a "Have you ever?" question to draw the reader in to your interpretation. Be sure your beginning is tied to your main point.

As you write the body of your literary analysis, include information that supports your interpretation: descriptions of setting and character, summaries of events, quotations of important comments of the characters, and other specific evidence from the story. Cite the page numbers (for prose) or line numbers (for poetry) where details can be found in the work. (See "A Note on Documenting Sources," p. 277.) Look again at how student writer Jonathan Burns used and documented information from "The Lottery" (p. 260). Integrate details from the story with your own comments and ideas.

Use transitions to keep the focus on ideas, not events. Use transition markers that refer to character traits and personality change, not those that refer to time. Say "Although Mr. Summers was . . ."instead of "At the beginning of the story Mr. Summers was . . . ." Write "Tessie became . . ." instead of "After that Tessie was . . . ." State "The protagonist in 'The Lottery' realized . . ." or "The villagers in 'The Lottery' changed . . . ," not "On the next page . . ." or "In the following paragraph . . ." or "At the end of the story she. . . . " (See pp. 380–83 on using transitions effectively.)

Provide a conclusion for your essay; don't just stop writing. Use the same techniques you use for introductions — anecdote, personal experience, comment on technique, quotation — to provide a sense of finality and closing for the readers. Refer to or reaffirm your thesis. Often an effective conclusion ties in directly with the introduction. Notice how Jonathan Burns tied his conclusion (p. 262) to his introduction (p. 260).

In an essay for her writing class, Cindy MacDonald analyzed the change in the protagonist in a story by Meg Campbell. See how she starts and ends her essay.

INTRODUCTION

```
    All many people think about is the good old days. They
live in the past instead of living in the present. The
character of Anne in the short story "Just Saying You
Love Me Doesn't Make It So" by Meg Campbell is revealed
as a young woman who lives in the past but changes to a
person who is concerned with the present and the future.
```

CONCLUSION

> When most people are forced to take an honest look at what they think of as the good old days, they sometimes realize that the good old days were not so good after all. If they start living in the present and making the future into what they want it to be, instead of dreaming of what might have been, they will find, as Anne did, that their lives are much happier.

In an analysis of the theme in "A Tree, a Rock, a Cloud" by Carson McCullers, student Diana Ward concludes her comments:

> Carson McCullers brings out the universal capacity to be deeply hurt by rejection in a close relationship and the necessity to overcome the adverse effects of this rejection. Without exception, inherent in love is its capacity to inflict the most intense kind of pain that a human being may experience. Unless a human being is able to control this pain, the pain will control the person.

Here are some questions you can ask yourself as you shape your draft.

**REVISION CHECKLIST**

## Developing a Draft

- Are your interpretations supported by evidence from the literary work?
- Are the passages and details from the work integrated smoothly into your comments and interpretations?
- Do the transitions focus on ideas and guide your readers easily from one section or sentence to the next?
- Is the essay unified, with everything related to your main point? Do you need to refine your thesis statement to fit what you have actually written?
- Do you use words you understand? Are any sentences not clear because of your use of literary terms?
- Are any of your sentences wordy or unnecessary?
- Have you tried to share your insights into the meaning of the work with your readers, or have you slipped into trying to impress them with your profound perceptions?

You may find that you need to recast problem areas; rephrase unclear passages, using words you understand; cut out deadwood; add or change transitions. Just keep your readers in mind.

Before you write and proofread your final draft, answer the following questions about your paper. Answer them honestly, and if your evaluation of your writing indicates that the piece needs more work, take the time to make the necessary changes.

**REVISION CHECKLIST**

## Testing the Evidence

- Have you clearly identified the literary work and the author near the beginning of the analysis?
- Have you gone beyond synopsis? Have you organized your analysis according to ideas, not events? Do your transitions focus on ideas, not on plot or time sequence?
- Is your main point clear?
- Have you focused on one element or a limited number of related elements in your analysis?
- Have you used literary terms properly?
- Have you avoided lifting language and sentence structure from the work itself without properly using quotation marks and citations?
- Have you found all the details in the work that support your interpretation? Is there any additional dialogue you can use? Any action? Any description? Are the details that you use really relevant to the points of analysis, or are they just interesting sidelights?
- Have you woven the details from the work smoothly into your text? Have you cited the correct page or line numbers for the details from the work?

**FOR PEER RESPONSE**

To determine how well you have succeeded in communicating with your readers, ask one of your classmates to read your draft. See Chapter 20 for advice on working with other student writers and for general questions you should always ask a peer editor to address. For a paper in which you analyze a literary work, you'll also want your peer editor to answer these specific questions:

- What is your first reaction to the literary analysis?
- Does the analysis add to your understanding of the literary work? Add to your insights into life?
- Does the introduction make you want to read the rest of the analysis?
- Is the main point clear? Does the writer provide sufficient evidence from the work to back up that point? Put stars wherever additional evidence is needed. Is there anything in the analysis that does not belong? Put a check mark by any irrelevant information.
- Does the writer go beyond synopsis to analysis of elements, interpretation of meaning, and evaluation of literary merit?
- Is the analysis organized by ideas instead of events?
- Do the transitions guide you smoothly from one point to the next? Do the transitions focus on ideas, not on time or position in the story?
- Is the writer's use of literary terminology clear and appropriate?
- If this were your paper, what is the one thing you would be sure to work on before handing it in?

- Have you sincerely tried to add to your classmates' understanding of this work?
- If you read your introduction, would you want to read the rest of the analysis?

## A NOTE ON DOCUMENTING SOURCES

If, when writing an analysis of a literary work, you quote directly from the work or paraphrase parts of the work, you should cite your source. Correctly and systematically documenting your sources indicates your intellectual honesty. It also helps readers who want to find out more information about assertions in your paper or who want to look at one of your sources — perhaps so they can write a paper on a related topic. A documentation system provides a way to acknowledge your sources.

The style recommended by the Modern Language Association (MLA) is the style most often used when writing about literature. If you are not sure this is the style you should use for your class, check with your instructor.

If you use the MLA style, you put page or line numbers in parentheses immediately after each paraphrase of an event, detail, or description and after each direct quotation from the literary work. Referring to the precise location helps your readers find a particular detail or section in context. The following MLA-style models will help you deal with some of the most common situations.

When you use only one source in your paper, just give page or line numbers in parentheses immediately following a direct quotation from or a paraphrase of the source:

```
The reader thinks of the "great pile" (251) as children's
entertainment, like a stack of imaginary coins rather
than an arsenal.
```

When you use two or more sources in your paper, you must indicate the author's name as well as the page or line numbers. You can do this in your own sentence leading in to the quotation from or paraphrase of the source:

```
The speaker in Amy Lowell's poem "Patterns" views life
from a pleasant garden where "daffodils / Are blowing"
(2-3).
```

When the author's name does not appear in your sentence, you can give the author's name in the parentheses with the page or line numbers:

```
The speaker in the poem views life from a pleasant garden
where "daffodils / Are blowing" (Lowell 2-3).
```

> The speaker in the poem tries to ease his pain by visual-
> izing the girl with "wings" (Weigl 30).

A reader who wants more information about your source or about a particular detail or quotation can go from the in-text citation to the other part of this system of documentation: the list of works cited. On a page at the end of your paper, you list each of the sources you have used, giving information about the author, title, edition, publisher, and year of publication. (Some sources will require more complicated citations. For these, consult a research or documentation manual.) The following are two examples that might appear on a typical "Works Cited" page of a paper about literature.

When your source is a book:

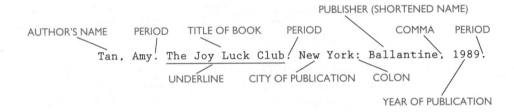

When your source is a short story or poem that appears in an anthology:

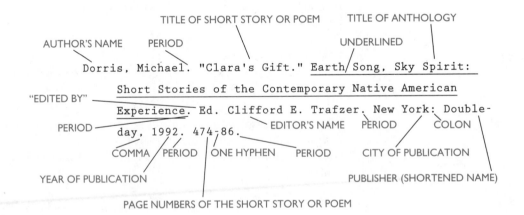

# Comparison and Contrast

### LEARNING FROM ANOTHER WRITER

One way to increase your understanding of the meaning of a piece of literature is to compare and contrast it with another work. As you identify similarities and differences, you deepen your knowledge of the technique and the meaning of both pieces. (For a complete discussion of comparison and contrast analyses, see Chapter 7.)

Lionel Prokop identified similarities and differences and thereby deepened his understanding in a comparison and contrast of two poems, "Patterns" by Amy Lowell and "Song of Napalm" by Bruce Weigl. Amy Lowell (1874–1925) was a poet and a critic from a prominent New England family. Bruce Weigl (b. 1949) is a Vietnam veteran, professor, and author of six collections of poetry. His most recent collections include *What Saves Us* (1992) and *Song of Napalm* (1988), which contains the poem Prokop analyzed. The authors of these poems come from very different times and places but, as Prokop points out in his essay, the poems have similar themes.

### Patterns

AMY LOWELL

I walk down the garden paths,
And all the daffodils
Are blowing, and the bright blue squills.
I walk down the patterned garden paths
In my stiff, brocaded gown.                                              5
With my powdered hair and jewelled fan,
I too am a rare
Pattern. As I wander down
The garden paths.

My dress is richly figured,                                             10
And the train
Makes a pink and silver stain
On the gravel, and the thrift
Of the borders.
Just a plate of current fashion,                                        15
Tripping by in high-heeled, ribboned shoes.
Not a softness anywhere about me,
Only whale-bone and brocade.
And I sink on a seat in the shade
Of a lime tree. For my passion                                          20
Wars against the stiff brocade.
The daffodils and squills
Flutter in the breeze
As they please.
And I weep;                                                             25
For the lime tree is in blossom
And one small flower has dropped upon my bosom.

And the plashing of waterdrops
In the marble fountain
Comes down the garden paths.                                            30
The dripping never stops.
Underneath my stiffened gown
Is the softness of a woman bathing in a marble basin,

A basin in the midst of hedges grown
So thick, she cannot see her lover hiding,                    35
But she guesses he is near,
And the sliding of the water
Seems the stroking of a dear
Hand upon her.
What is Summer in a fine brocaded gown!                    40
I should like to see it lying in a heap upon the ground,
All the pink and silver crumpled up on the ground.

I would be the pink and silver as I ran along the paths,
And he would stumble after                    45
Bewildered by my laughter.
I should see the sun flashing from his sword hilt and the buckles on his
    shoes.
I would choose
To lead him in a maze along the patterned paths,
A bright and laughing maze for my heavy-booted lover,                    50
Till he caught me in the shade,
And the buttons of his waistcoat bruised my body as he clasped me,
Aching, melting, unafraid,
With the shadows of the leaves and the sundrops,
And the plopping of the waterdrops,
All about us in the open afternoon —                    55
I am very like to swoon
With the weight of this brocade,
For the sun sifts through the shade.

Underneath the fallen blossom                    60
In my bosom,
Is a letter I have hid.
It was brought to me this morning by a rider from the Duke.
"Madam, we regret to inform you that Lord Hartwell
Died in action Thursday se'n-night."[1]
As I read it in the white, morning sunlight,                    65
The letters squirmed like snakes.
"Any answer, Madam," said my footman.
"No," I told him.
"See that the messenger takes some refreshment.                    70
No, no answer."
And I walked into the garden,
Up and down the patterned paths,
In my stiff, correct brocade.
The blue and yellow flowers stood up proudly in the sun
Each one.                    75
I stood upright too,
Held rigid to the pattern
By the stiffness of my gown.

---

[1] **se'n night:** a week ago (seven nights ago).

Up and down I walked,                                                      80
Up and down.

In a month he would have been my husband.
In a month, here, underneath this lime,
We would have broke the pattern;
He for me, and I for him,
He as Colonel, I as Lady,                                                  85
On this shady seat.
He had a whim
That sunlight carried blessing.
And I answered, "It shall be as you have said."
Now he is dead.                                                            90

In Summer and in Winter I shall walk
Up and down
The patterned garden paths
In my stiff, brocaded gown.
The squills and daffodils                                                  95
Will give place to pillared roses, and to asters, and to snow.
I shall go
Up and down,
In my gown.
Gorgeously arrayed,                                                        100
Boned and stayed.
And the softness of my body will be guarded from embrace
By each button, hook, and lace.

For the man who should loose me is dead,
Fighting with the Duke in Flanders,                                        105
In a pattern called a war.
Christ! What are patterns for?


## Song of Napalm

BRUCE WEIGL

*—FOR MY WIFE*

After the storm, after the rain stopped pounding,
We stood in the doorway watching horses
Walk off lazily across the pasture's hill.
We stared through the black screen,
Our vision altered by the distance                                        5
So I thought I saw a mist
Kicked up around their hooves when they faded
Like cut-out horses
Away from us.
The grass was never more blue in that light, more                         10
Scarlet; beyond the pasture
Trees scraped their voices into the wind, branches

Criss-crossed the sky like barbed wire
But you said they were only branches.

Okay. The storm stopped pounding.                              15
I am trying to say this straight: for once
I was sane enough to pause and breathe
Outside my wild plans and after the hard rain
I turned my back on the old curses. I believed
They swung finally away from me . . .                          20

But still the branches are wire
And thunder is the pounding mortar,
Still I close my eyes and see the girl
Running from her village, napalm
Stuck to her dress like jelly,                                 25
Her hands reaching for the no one
Who waits in waves of heat before her.

So I can keep on living,
So I can stay here beside you,
I try to imagine she runs down the road and wings              30
Beat inside her until she rises
Above the stinking jungle and her pain
Eases, and your pain, and mine.

But the lie swings back again.
The lie works only as long as it takes to speak                35
And the girl runs only as far
As the napalm allows
Until her burning tendons and crackling
Muscles draw her up
Into that final position                                        40
Burning bodies so perfectly assume. Nothing
Can change that; she is burned behind my eyes
And not your good love and not the rain-swept air
And not the jungle green
Pasture unfolding before us can deny it.                        45

STUDENT ESSAY

*Lionel Prokop*    # Love and War: Images of Nature in Two Poems by Bruce Weigl and Amy Lowell

Amy Lowell wrote "Patterns" during World War I from a     1
woman's viewpoint, while Bruce Weigl wrote "Song of Napalm"
about the Vietnam War from a male veteran's viewpoint. Although the poems were written approximately fifty years
apart, they still contain similar themes concerning the effects of war on people's lives.

Both poems relate experiences involving love and war. In **2**
"Song of Napalm," Weigl illustrates how a man has been unable
to forget the painful memories of war despite his desire to
love his wife and despite the seemingly peaceful setting
where he now lives. In "Patterns," Lowell explains a woman's
feelings after war took the man she was to marry. Both authors use images from nature to help express some of the in-
tricacies of love and war and to contrast with the pain both
love and war can bring.

Weigl places the Vietnam veteran and his wife in the      **3**
doorway of their home looking out into the pasture after a
storm has passed through. Although the scene depicted following the rain appears to be one of freshness and perfection,
Weigl changes the tone as he introduces branches that "Criss-
crossed the sky like barbed wire" (line 13), bringing back
the painful memories of war, the "old curses" (19). The image
of nature becomes even less peaceful as the thunder makes him
think of "pounding mortar" and "see[ing] the girl / Running
from her village" (22-24). The napalm is "Stuck to her dress
like jelly," and she reaches "for the no one / Who waits in
waves of heat before her" (25-27). The speaker in the poem
tries to ease his pain by visualizing the girl with "wings"
(30), able to rise "Above the stinking jungle and her pain"
(32-33). This is his attempt to block out the memory that
continues to return, yet he comes to realize that "Nothing /
Can change" the image because "she is burned behind my eyes"
(41-42). He concludes that neither nature--"the rain-swept
air" and "the jungle green / Pasture unfolding"--nor his
wife's "good love" has the ability to "deny" his painful memories (43-45).

The speaker in Lowell's poem views life from a pleasant   **4**
garden where "daffodils / Are blowing" (2-3) and "squills /
Flutter in the breeze" (22-23). She walks and wanders "down
the patterned garden paths" in her "stiff, brocaded gown"
(4-5) and comments that her "passion / Wars against" her restrictive dress (20-21). Perhaps she refers to the stiffness
or unfairness of life and of the events of war and how her
soul fights against what is happening. Images from nature express the sadness she feels. She sits beneath a lime tree and

weeps. The "waterdrops" that drip unceasingly in the fountain are like her tears. She relates the "sliding of the water" to the "stroking of a dear / Hand" in an image that is both sad and happy (37-39).

   The woman is brought back to reality when a small blossom drops from the lime tree, landing on her chest, where a letter is hidden. The letter informed her this morning that her lover had died in battle. She declares that her love for him will never die and that she will continue to "walk / Up and down / The patterned garden paths" (92-93). In the poem, the peaceful garden is patterned with paths and different plants, and the woman's dress is rich with patterned decoration. The woman realizes that war is a pattern too, in which people leave their loved ones, then fight, then die. The beauty of the first patterns do not make up for the pain of the second, and the woman is left asking, "What are patterns for?" (107).   5

   In both of these poems, images from nature are beautiful, but sad. Even when its images are beautiful, nature is not enough to protect the speakers in the two poems from the pain of war and loss. Walking through the many patterns of life that have come my way, I can identify with feelings of being left alone and with a broken heart. The dreams and memories that return bring with them fears of going on in this world. But because of my upbringing, I must, like the woman in "Patterns," go on with life and struggle with the memories. Like the speaker in "Song of Napalm," we all must deal with the painful realities that often overshadow love. We must not let that pain defeat us.   6

                              Works Cited

Lowell, Amy. "Patterns." Understanding Poetry. Ed. Cleanth
     Brooks and Robert Penn Warren. New York: Holt, 1950. 55-
     58.

Weigl, Bruce. "Song of Napalm." The Morrow Anthology of
     Younger American Poets. Ed. Dave Smith and David Bot-
     toms. New York: Quill, 1985. 760-61.

**Questions to Start You Thinking**

*Meaning*

1. What is the main point that Prokop makes about the two poems?

2. What memorable images does Prokop cite from the poems? How are these images related to the themes of the poems?

3. Do you think it unusual that two such different poets use nature in similar ways?

4. What other poems have you read that contain memorable images from nature?

*Writing Strategies*

5. Is Prokop's introduction effective? Is his conclusion?

6. Why does Prokop use the alternating pattern of organization for his essay of comparison and contrast? (For more on this method of organization, see Chapter 7, Comparing and Contrasting.)

7. Does he provide sufficient evidence from the poems to support and clarify his main point?

8. If you were Prokop's peer editor, what suggestions would you make to help him improve his paper?

# Strategies for Writing about Literature: Synopsis and Paraphrase

## LEARNING FROM OTHER WRITERS

Earlier in this chapter we mentioned that Jonathan Burns wrote a synopsis of "The Lottery" as part of his preparation for writing a literary analysis of the story. A *synopsis* is a summary of the plot of a work of narrative literature — a short story, a novel, a play, or a narrative poem. It describes the first level of meaning, the literal layer. It condenses the story to only the major events and the most significant details. You do not include your own interpretation in a synopsis but rather limit your comments to what the author has written. You summarize the work in your own words, taking care not to lift language or sentence structure from the work itself. Writing a synopsis is valuable to you as a writer because it requires you to get the chronology straight and to pick out the significant events and details. It also allows you to see the relationship of the parts to each other and to the themes of the work.

In your literature courses you will often be asked to write synopses of short stories and novels but to paraphrase poems. Like a synopsis, a *paraphrase* is a summary of the original piece of literature, showing understanding of meaning and relationships of the parts. Both assignments require you to dig out the literal level of the work.

In preparation for writing his literary analysis of "The Lottery" — to make sure he had the sequence of events clear — Jonathan Burns wrote the following synopsis of the story.

STUDENT EXAMPLE

## *Jonathan Burns*    A Synopsis of "The Lottery"

Around ten o'clock on a sunny June 27, the villagers                    1
gathered in the square for a lottery, expecting to be home in
time for lunch. The children came first, glad that school was
out for the summer. The boys romped and gathered stones, the
girls talked quietly in small groups, and the little ones
hovered near their brothers and sisters. Then the men came,
followed by the women. When parents called, the children came
reluctantly.

Mr. Summers, who always conducted the town lottery, ar-                 2
rived with the black wooden box and set it on the three-
legged stool that Mr. Graves had brought out. The villagers
remained at a distance from these men and didn't respond when
Mr. Summers asked for help. Finally Mr. Martin and his son
held the shabby black box as Mr. Summers mixed the papers in
it. Although the townspeople had talked about replacing the
box, they never had, but they had substituted paper slips for
the original wooden chips. To prepare for the drawing, they
listed the members of every household and swore in Mr. Summers. Although they had dropped many aspects of the original
ritual, the official still greeted each person individually.

Tessie Hutchinson rushed into the square, telling her                   3
friend Mrs. Delacroix she had almost forgotten what day it
was. Then she joined her husband and children.

When Mr. Summers asked if everyone was present, he was                  4
told that Clyde Dunbar was absent because of a broken leg but
that his wife would draw for the family. Summers noted that
the Watson boy was drawing for his mother and checked to see
if Old Man Warner had made it.

The crowd got quiet. Mr. Summers reminded everybody of                  5
what they were to do and began to call the names in alphabetical order. People in the group joked nervously as the names
were called. Mrs. Delacroix and Mrs. Graves commented on how
fast time had passed since the last lottery, and Old Man
Warner talked about how important the lottery was to the villagers. When Mr. Summers finished calling the roll, there was

a pause before the heads of households opened their slips. Everybody wondered who had the special slip of paper, who had won the lottery. They discovered it was Bill Hutchinson. When Tessie complained that the drawing hadn't been done fairly, the others told her to be a good sport.

Mr. Graves put five slips into the box, one for each member of Bill Hutchinson's family. Tessie kept charging that it wasn't fair. The children drew first, then Tessie, then Bill. The children opened their slips, smiled broadly, and held blank pieces of paper over their heads. Bill opened his and it was blank too. Tessie wouldn't open hers; Bill had to do it for her. Hers had a black spot on it.    6

Mr. Summers urged the villagers to finish quickly. They picked up stones, even little Davy Hutchinson, and started throwing them at Tessie, as she kept screaming, "It isn't fair, it isn't right." Then they stoned her.    7

**Questions to Start You Thinking**

*Meaning*

1. Does this synopsis help you understand the story better?
2. Why isn't a synopsis as interesting as a short story?
3. Can you tell from this synopsis whether Burns understands Jackson's story beyond the narrative level?

*Writing Strategies*

4. Does Burns retell the story accurately and clearly? Does he get the events in correct time order? Does he show the relationships of the events to each other and to the whole? How?
5. Does Burns select the details necessary to indicate what happened in "The Lottery"? Why do you think he omits certain details?
6. Are there any details, comments, or events that you would add to his synopsis? Why, or why not?
7. Why doesn't Burns include his own interpretation and responses to the story in this synopsis?
8. How does this synopsis differ from Burn's literary analysis (p. 260)?

In his composition course Lionel Prokop was asked to write a paraphrase of the poem "Patterns" by Amy Lowell (p. 279). His instructor wanted to know if Prokop could comprehend the poem on his own. First Prokop read the poem several times to be sure he understood it, marking important parts. He checked the definitions of words he was not sure of: *squills* (line 3), *brocaded* (line 5), *pillared* (line 96). He also looked up words that seemed familiar but were used in unfamiliar ways: *figured* (line 10), *thrift* (line 13), *stayed* (line 101). Then he divided the poem into sections and briefly summarized each in the margin of the text. Finally he drafted the paraphrase, connecting the parts of the paraphrase with transitions.

STUDENT EXAMPLE

## *Lionel Prokop*    A Paraphrase of "Patterns"

On a breezy afternoon, dressed in a brocaded gown and carrying a fan, I walk down a worn garden path lined with daffodils and blue herbs. As I walk, my long, patterned dress dusts the pebbles and the herbs along the edge of the path. I sit down in the shade of a blossoming lime tree and struggle with my feelings. I observe the freedom of the wind-blown daffodils and squills and begin to cry as a lime blossom falls on my chest. I hear the ceaseless dripping of the water in the marble fountain and yearn for my soft body to be set free from the stiffness of the gown.    1

My body is as soft as the body of a woman washing herself in a marble basin concealed behind thick hedges. She cannot see her lover, but she knows he is there. The water feels like his hand stroking her. I would like to see the dress in a pile on the ground. Laughing and naked, I would run down the path with my lover in pursuit. He would be clad in soldier's attire with a sword and boots as I would lead him in a mazelike path. He would catch me under a tree and hold me passionately against him.    2

I return to the awareness of the hot summer day and of the weight of my gown. The fallen lime blossom brings my attention back to the letter I hid in my bosom this morning. It informed me that Lord Hartwell had died in battle. As my eyes filled with tears, I returned no answer with the messenger.    3

Standing straight and tall like the bordering flowers, I continue to walk along the familiar worn path of the garden. I think about the event that had been planned: my marriage to Lord Hartwell in one month under that special lime tree. I remember when he proposed. That day the sun brought bless-    4

```
ing.  If we had married, the patterns of our lives would have
been broken.

     I vow to continue walking the path in summer and winter        5
in my fine brocaded gown as the squills and daffodils fade,
the roses and asters bloom, and the snow falls.  My dress
will protect me from any further embraces because the man who
would undo its laces has been killed in war.  War is a pat-
tern.  What is the point of all these patterns?
```

## LEARNING BY WRITING

**The Assignment: Writing a Synopsis of a Story by Kate Chopin.**   Whenever you are having trouble understanding a story or if you have a lot of stories to read and are afraid you won't remember the specifics of each one, you will benefit from writing a synopsis to refer to later. Condensing five pages to 300 words forces you to isolate the most important details in the story and allows you to see clearly the sequence of events. This focus often leads you to a statement of theme.

Kate Chopin was a nineteenth-century American writer whose female characters search for their own identity and for freedom from domination and oppression. For practice, write a synopsis of 200–300 words of Chopin's short story "The Story of an Hour."

**REVISION CHECKLIST**

### Writing a Synopsis of a Story

- Is your summary of the plot of the story true to the original? Are the details accurate? Are they in correct time order?
- Did you include only the major events and details of the story?
- Did you show the relationships of the parts without giving your opinions and interpretations?
- Did you use quotation marks to indicate any of the author's words you used?

## *Kate Chopin*  The Story of an Hour

Knowing that Mrs. Mallard was afflicted with a heart trouble, great care     1
was taken to break to her as gently as possible the news of her husband's death.

It was her sister Josephine who told her, in broken sentences, veiled hints     2
that revealed in half concealing. Her husband's friend Richards was there, too, near her. It was he who had been in the newspaper office when intelligence of the railroad disaster was received, with Brently Mallard's name leading the list of "killed." He had only taken the time to assure himself of its truth by a

second telegram, and had hastened to forestall any less careful, less tender friend in bearing the sad message.

She did not hear the story as many women have heard the same, with a paralyzed inability to accept its significance. She wept at once, with sudden, wild abandonment, in her sister's arms. When the storm of grief had spent itself she went away to her room alone. She would have no one follow her.    3

There stood, facing the open window, a comfortable, roomy armchair. Into this she sank, pressed down by a physical exhaustion that haunted her body and seemed to reach into her soul.    4

She could see in the open square before her house the tops of trees that were all aquiver with the new spring life. The delicious breath of rain was in the air. In the street below a peddler was crying his wares. The notes of a distant song which someone was singing reached her faintly, and countless sparrows were twittering in the eaves.    5

There were patches of blue sky showing here and there through the clouds that had met and piled one above the other in the west facing her window.    6

She sat with her head thrown back upon the cushion of the chair, quite motionless, except when a sob came up into her throat and shook her, as a child who has cried itself to sleep continues to sob in its dreams.    7

She was young, with a fair, calm face, whose lines bespoke repression and even a certain strength. But now there was a dull stare in her eyes, whose gaze was fixed away off yonder on one of those patches of blue sky. It was not a glance of reflection, but rather indicated a suspension of intelligent thought.    8

There was something coming to her and she was waiting for it, fearfully. What was it? She did not know; it was too subtle and elusive to name. But she felt it, creeping out of the sky, reaching toward her through the sounds, the scents, the color that filled the air.    9

Now her bosom rose and fell tumultuously. She was beginning to recognize this thing that was approaching to possess her, and she was striving to beat it back with her will — as powerless as her two white slender hands would have been.    10

When she abandoned herself a little whispered word escaped her slightly parted lips. She said it over and over under her breath: "Free, free, free!" The vacant stare and the look of terror that had followed it went from her eyes. They stayed keen and bright. Her pulses beat fast, and the coursing blood warmed and relaxed every inch of her body.    11

She did not stop to ask if it were not a monstrous joy that held her. A clear and exalted perception enabled her to dismiss the suggestion as trivial.    12

She knew that she would weep again when she saw the kind, tender hands folded in death; the face that had never looked save with love upon her, fixed and gray and dead. But she saw beyond that bitter moment a long procession of years to come that would belong to her absolutely. And she opened and spread her arms out to them in welcome.    13

There would be no one to live for during those coming years; she would live for herself. There would be no powerful will bending her in that blind    14 persistence with which men and women believe they have a right to impose a private will upon a fellow creature. A kind intention or a cruel intention made the act seem no less a crime as she looked upon it in that brief moment of illumination.

And yet she had loved him — sometimes. Often she had not. What did it matter! What could love, the unsolved mystery, count for in face of this possession of self-assertion which she suddenly recognized as the strongest impulse of her being.                                                                                      15

"Free! Body and soul free!" she kept whispering.                                          16

Josephine was kneeling before the closed door with her lips to the keyhole, imploring for admission. "Louise, open the door! I beg; open the door — you will make yourself ill. What are you doing, Louise? For heaven's sake open the door."                                                                                 17

"Go away. I am not making myself ill." No; she was drinking in a very elixir of life through that open window.                                                             18

Her fancy was running riot along those days ahead of her. Spring days, and summer days, and all sorts of days that would be her own. She breathed a quick prayer that life might be long. It was only yesterday she had thought with a shudder that life might be long.                                                                19

She arose at length and opened the door to her sister's importunities. There was a feverish triumph in her eyes, and she carried herself unwittingly like a goddess of Victory. She clasped her sister's waist, and together they descended the stairs. Richards stood waiting for them at the bottom.                      20

Someone was opening the front door with a latchkey. It was Brently Mallard who entered, a little travel-stained, composedly carrying his gripsack and umbrella. He had been far from the scene of the accident, and did not even know there had been one. He stood amazed at Josephine's piercing cry; at Richards's quick motion to screen him from the view of his wife.                           21

But Richards was too late.                                                                    22

When the doctors came they said she had died of heart disease—of joy that kills.                                                                                             23

The Assignment: Writing a Paraphrase of a Poem by Bruce Weigl.    When you study poetry, you can benefit from paraphrasing, that is, expressing the content of a poem in your own words. You may write your paraphrase in the margin of the poem or in a notebook. Writing a paraphrase forces you to divide the poem into logical sections, to figure out what the poet says in each section, and to discern the relationships of the parts.

To practice this way of writing about literature, write a paraphrase of "Song of Napalm" by Bruce Weigl (pp. 281–82).

DISCOVERY
CHECKLIST

## Writing a Paraphrase of a Poem

- How are the sections of the poem related?
- Are there any words whose meanings you don't know? Are there any words

that seem to be used in a special sense, a sense in which the usual meanings do not fit? What do those words mean in the context of the poem?

- Does the poet use any important images or pictures? Any metaphors? How do these contribute to the meaning?
- Do you leave your personal opinions out of your paraphrase?
- After you have completed the paraphrase, can you express the theme of the poem in one or two sentences?

Papers written in response to literature are often some of the most enjoyable and interesting essays you will write in college. Interpreting literature is a rewarding activity. You see yourself and your friends and family in the works you read, and the best writers provide you with insights into yourself and your relationships. As you read and analyze, solutions to problems you have struggled with may become clear, or you may just enjoy figuring out why a character does such crazy things or enjoy ferreting out the techniques an author uses to make you respond as you do. Once you understand the literary selection you are interpreting, you have the pleasure of sharing your insights with your readers and thus increasing their insights as well.

## Other Assignments for Writing about Literature

1. Use a poem, a play, or a novel instead of a short story to complete the literary assignment analysis in this chapter (p. 267).

2. Write an essay comparing and contrasting a literary element in two or three short stories or poems, as Lionel Prokop did for the poems by Amy Lowell and Bruce Weigl (p. 282).

3. Analyze and write a critical essay on a song, a movie, or a television program. Because you won't have a written text in front of you, you probably will need to hear the work or view it more than once to pull out the specific evidence necessary to support your interpretation.

4. Read the following poem by Robert Frost. Then write an essay in which you use a paraphrase of this poem as a springboard for your thoughts on a fork in the road of your life — a decision that made a big difference for you.

**The Road Not Taken**

Two roads diverged in a yellow wood,
And sorry I could not travel both
And be one traveler, long I stood
And looked down one as far as I could
To where it bent in the undergrowth;

Then took the other, as just as fair,
And having perhaps the better claim,
Because it was grassy and wanted wear;

Though as for that the passing there
Had worn them really about the same,

And both that morning equally lay
In leaves no step had trodden black.
Oh, I kept the first for another day!
Yet knowing how way leads on to way,
I doubted if I should ever come back.

I shall be telling this with a sigh
Somewhere ages and ages hence:
Two roads diverged in a wood, and I —
I took the one less traveled by,
And that has made all the difference.

5. Read the following poem by Edwin Arlington Robinson. Have you known
   and envied someone similar to Richard Cory, someone who everyone else
   thought had it all? What happened to him or her? Did you discover that
   your impression of this individual was wrong? Write a personal response
   essay in which you compare and contrast the person you knew with
   Richard Cory. This assignment requires you to analyze the poem as well
   as draw on your own experience and knowledge.

### Richard Cory

Whenever Richard Cory went down town,
We people on the pavement looked at him:
He was a gentleman from sole to crown,
Clean favored, and imperially slim.

And he was always quietly arrayed,
And he was always human when he talked;
But still he fluttered pulses when he said,
"Good-morning," and he glittered when he walked.

And he was rich — yes, richer than a king —
And admirably schooled in every grace:
In fine, we thought that he was everything
To make us wish that we were in his place.

So on we worked, and waited for the light,
And went without the meat, and cursed the bread;
And Richard Cory, one calm summer night,
Went home and put a bullet through his head.

# Chapter 13

# Writing in Class

So far, we've been considering how you write when *you* control your writing circumstances. We've assumed that in writing anything from a brief account of a remembered experience to a hefty research paper, you can write lying down or standing up, in the quiet of a library or in a clattering cafeteria. You can think, plan, draft, revise, and recopy. Although an instructor may have handed you a deadline, it is usually a week or more away, and nobody is timing you with a stopwatch.

But as you know, often in college you need to write on the spot. You face quizzes to finish in twenty minutes, final exams to complete in three or four hours, an impromptu essay to dash off in one class period. Just how do you discover, shape, and put across your ideas in a limited time?

In this chapter we discuss three types of in-class writing: the essay exam, the short-answer quiz, and the timed writing. These types of writing require thinking and composing processes different from those used for writing a paper over a period of several days or several weeks. You have probably done all three before, but the tips in this chapter will help you write better under pressure.

## *Essay Examinations*

In many courses an essay exam is the most important kind of in-class writing. Although lately multiple-choice tests, scored by computer, have been whittling down the number of essay exams that college students write, still the tradition of the essay exam endures. Instructors believe that such writing shows that you haven't just memorized a batch of material but that you understand it, have examined it critically, can see connections in it, and can make your thoughts clear to someone else.

294

## PREPARING FOR THE EXAM

The chief resource for most essay exams is your memory. What you remember may include observations, conversation, reading, and perhaps some imagination. The days before an examination offer you a chance to review what you have learned, to fill in any blank spots in your understanding, and to fix these ideas firmly in your memory. Such review enables you to think deeply about your course work, to see how its scattered parts fit together.

As you review your reading and your notes from lectures and class discussion, it's a good idea — if the exam will be closed book — to fix in memory any vitally important names, dates, and definitions. We said "vitally important" — you don't want to clutter your mind with a lot of spare parts selected at random. But preparation isn't merely a matter of decorating a vast glacier of ignorance with a few spring flowers of dates and quotations. When you review, look for the main ideas or themes in each textbook chapter. Then ask yourself: What do these main ideas have to do with each other? How might they be combined? What conclusions can I draw from all the facts?

Some instructors favor open-book exams, in which you bring your books and perhaps your notes to class for reference. In an open-book exam, ability to memorize and recall is less important than ability to reason and to select what matters most. In such a writing situation, you have more opportunity than in a closed-book exam to generate ideas and to discover material on the spot.

A good way to prepare in advance for any exam, whether the books are to be closed or open, is to imagine questions you might be asked and then plan answers. We don't mean to suggest that you should try to psyche out your instructor. You're only slightly more likely to guess all the questions in advance than you are to clean out a slot machine in Las Vegas. But by thinking up your own questions, you review much material, imaginatively bring some of it together, and gain valuable experience in shaping answers. Sometimes, to help you get ready for an exam, the instructor will supply a few questions that he or she asked in former years. If you are given such examples, you can pattern new questions after them.

As you probably don't need to be told, trying to cram at the eleventh hour, going without sleep and food, consuming gallons of coffee or cola, and reducing yourself to a wreck is no way to prepare. You can learn more in little bites than in huge gulps. Psychologists testify that if you study something for fifteen minutes a day for eight days, you'll remember far more than if you study the same material in one unbroken sprint of two hours.

## LEARNING FROM ANOTHER WRITER

To start looking at techniques of answering *any* exam question, let's take one concrete example. A final exam in developmental psychology posed this question:

What evidence indicates innate factors in perceptual organization? You might find it useful to recall any research that shows how infants perceive depth and forms.

In response, David Ian Cohn sat back in his chair for five minutes and thought over the reading he'd done for the course. What perception research had he heard about that used babies for subjects? He spent another five minutes jotting down ideas, crossed out a couple of weak ones, and drew lines connecting ideas that went together. (For an illustration of this handy technique, see "Linking," p. 355.) Then he took a deep breath and, without revising (except to cross out a few words of a sentence that seemed a false start), wrote this straightforward grade A answer:

> Research on infants is probably the best way to demonstrate that some factors in perceptual organization are innate. In the cliff box experiment, an infant will avoid what looks like a drop-off, even though its mother calls it and even though it can feel glass covering the drop-off area. The same infant will crawl to the other end of the box, which appears (and is) safe. Apparently infants do not have to be taught what a cliff looks like.
>
> Psychologists have also observed that infants are aware of size constancy. They recognize a difference in size between a 10-cm box at a distance of one meter and a 20-cm box at a distance of two meters. If this phenomenon is not innate, it is at least learned early, for the subjects of the experiment were infants of sixteen to eighteen months.
>
> When shown various patterns, infants tend to respond more noticeably to patterns that resemble the human face than to those that appear random. This seemingly innate recognition helps the infant identify people (such as its mother) from less important inanimate objects.

Infants also seem to have an innate ability to match sight with sound. When simultaneously shown two television screens, each depicting a different subject, while being played a tape that sometimes matched one screen and sometimes the other, infants looked at whichever screen matched what they heard — not always, but at least twice as often.

**Questions to Start You Thinking**

*Meaning*

1. What is the main idea of Cohn's answer?
2. If you were the psychology instructor, how could you immediately see from this answer that Cohn had thoroughly dealt with the question and only with the question?

*Writing Strategies*

3. In what places is Cohn's answer concrete and specific, not vague and general?
4. Suppose he had tacked on a concluding sentence: "Thus I have conclusively proved that there are innate factors in perceptual organization, by citing much evidence showing that infants definitely can perceive depth and forms." Would that sentence have strengthened his answer?

## GENERATING IDEAS

When, seated in the classroom, you begin your race with the clock, resist the temptation to start scribbling away frantically. First read over all the questions on the exam carefully. Notice whether you are expected to make any choices, and decide which questions to answer. Choices are luxuries: they let you ignore questions you are less prepared to answer in favor of those you can tackle with more confidence. If you are offered a choice, just X out any questions you are *not* going to answer so you don't waste time thinking about them by mistake. And if you don't understand what a question calls for, ask your instructor right away.

Few people can dash off an excellent essay exam answer without first taking time to discover a few ideas and plan an answer. So take a deep breath, get comfortable, sit back, and spend a few moments in thought. Instructors prefer answers that are concrete and specific rather than those that stay up in the clouds of generality. David Cohn's answer to the psychology question cites evidence all the way through: particular experiments in which infants were subjects. A little time taken to generate concrete examples — as Cohn did — will be time wisely spent.

Instructors also prefer answers that are organized and coherent rather than rambling. Some people have a rare talent for rapidly putting their thoughts in order. Most of us, however, need to plot some direction to follow before we begin. Your pen will move more smoothly if you have a few thoughts in mind. These thoughts don't have to be definitive — only something to start you writing. You can keep thinking and shaping and adding your thoughts as you write.

Often a question will suggest a way to start your answer. Many questions contain directive words that help you define your task: *evaluate, compare, discuss, explain, describe, summarize, trace the development of.* You can put yourself on the right track if you incorporate a form of such a word in your first sentence. For example:

QUESTION    Define romanticism, citing its major characteristics and giving examples of each.

ANSWER    Romanticism is defined as . . . .

OR

ANSWER    Romanticism is a complex concept, difficult to define. It . . . .

## PLANNING: RECOGNIZING TYPICAL EXAM QUESTIONS

Most exam questions fall into recognizable types, and if you can recognize them you will know how to organize them and begin to write. Here are examples.

**The Cause and Effect Question.**    In general, these questions usually mention *causes* and *effects.*

What were the immediate causes of the stock market crash of 1929?

Set forth the principal effects on the economy commonly noticed as a result of a low prime rate of interest.

For specific advice on writing to show cause or effect, see Chapter 8.

**The Compare or Contrast Question.**    One of the most popular types of examination questions, this calls on you to point out similarities (comparing) or discuss differences (contrasting); in the process you explain not one subject but two.

Compare and contrast *iconic memory* and *eidetic imagery.* (1) Define the two terms, indicating the ways in which they differ, and (2) state the way or ways in which they are related or alike.

After supplying a one-sentence definition of each term, a student proceeded first to contrast and then to compare, for full credit:

> <u>Iconic memory</u> is a picturelike impression that lasts for only a fraction of a second in short-term memory. <u>Eidetic imagery</u> is the ability to take a mental photograph, exact in detail, which later can be recalled and studied in detail, as though its subject were still present. But iconic memory soon disappears. Unlike an eidetic image, it does not last long enough to enter long-term memory. IM is common, EI is unusual: very few people have it. Both iconic memory and eidetic imagery are similar, however: both record visual images, and every sighted person of normal intelligence has both abilities to some degree.

A question of this kind doesn't always use the words *compare* and *contrast*. Consider this question from a midterm exam in basic astronomy:

> Signal at least three differences between Copernicus's and Kepler's models of the solar system. In what respects was Kepler's model an improvement on that of Copernicus?

That question is nothing more than good old contrasting (citing three differences and showing that Kepler's model was superior).

> Distinguish between *agnosia* and *receptive aphasia*. In what ways are the two conditions similar?

Again, without using the words *comparison* and *contrast*, the question asks for both. When you distinguish, you contrast, or point out differences; when you tell how two things are similar, you compare.

> Briefly explain the duplex theory of memory. What are the main differences between short-term memory and long-term memory?

In this two-part question, the second part calls on the student to contrast (but not compare).

> Which bryophyta resemble vascular plants? In what ways? How do these bryophyta *differ* from the vascular plants?

Writers of comparison and contrast answers sometimes fall into a trap: in this case, they might get all wound up about bryophyta and fail to give vascular plants more than a few words. When you compare and contrast two things, pay attention to both, paralleling the points you make about each, giving both equal space.

For more on comparing and contrasting, see Chapter 7.

**The Demonstration Question.**   In this kind of question, you are given a statement and asked to back it up.

> Demonstrate the truth of Freud's contention that laughter may contain elements of aggression.

In other words, you are asked to explain Freud's claim and supply evidence to support it. You might refer to crowd scenes you have experienced, perhaps quote and analyze a joke, perhaps analyze a scene in a TV show or film or use examples from your reading.

**The Discussion Question.**   A discussion question may tempt an unwary writer to shoot the breeze.

> Name and discuss three events that precipitated Lyndon B. Johnson's withdrawal from the 1968 presidential race.

This question looks like an open invitation to ramble about Johnson and Vietnam, but it isn't. Whenever a question says "discuss," you will be wise to plan your discussion. Try rewording the question to help you focus your discussion: "Why did President Johnson decide not to seek another term? Analyze the causes and explain each a little."

Sometimes a discussion question won't announce itself with the word *discuss*, but with *describe* or *explain* or *explore*.

> Describe the national experience following passage of the Eighteenth Amendment. What did most Americans learn from it?

Provided you know that the Eighteenth Amendment (Prohibition) banned the sale, manufacture, and transportation of alcoholic drinks and that it was finally repealed, you can discuss its effects — or perhaps the reasons for its repeal.

**The Divide or Classify Question.**   Sometimes you are asked to slice a subject into sections or sort things into kinds. You will analyze the idea, place, person, or process into its parts.

> Enumerate the ways in which each inhabitant of the United States uses, on the average, 1,595 gallons of water a day. How and to what degree might each person cut down on this amount?

To answer this two-part question, for a start, you would divide up water use into several parts: drinking, cooking, bathing, washing cars, and so on. Then after that division, you would give tips for water conservation and tell how effective each is.

What different genres of film did King Vidor direct? Name at least one out-standing example of each kind.

In this classification question, you sort things into categories — films into general kinds — possibly comedy, war, adventure, mystery, musical, western.
For more on division and classification, see Chapter 18.

### The Definition Question.

You'll often be asked to write an extended definition on an essay exam.

Explain the three dominant styles of parenting: *permissive, authoritarian-restrictive,* and *authoritative.*

This question calls for a trio of definitions. Illustrating each definition with an example, whether recalled or imagined, will strengthen your response.

Define the Stanislavsky method of acting, citing outstanding actors who have followed it.

Here, you would explain the meaning of the method and give examples to make your answer clear.
For more on definition, see Chapter 18.

### The Evaluation Question.

This is another favorite kind of question because it calls on students to think critically and to present an argument.

Set forth and evaluate the most widely accepted theories to account for the disappearance of the dinosaurs.

Evaluate *two* of the following suggestions, giving reasons for your judgments:

a. Cities should stop building highways to the suburbs and instead build public monorail systems.
b. Houses and public buildings should be constructed to last no longer than twenty years.
c. Freeways leading to the core of the city should have marked express lanes for buses and carpooling drivers and narrow lanes for individual commuters who drive their cars.

This last three-part question calls on you to argue for or against. Other argument questions might begin "Defend the idea of . . ." or "Show weaknesses in the concept of . . ." or otherwise call on you to take a stand. For more on taking a stand and evaluating, see Chapters 9 and 11.

### The Respond to the Comment or Quotation Question.

A question might begin, "Test the validity of this statement," and then supply a statement for close reading and evaluation.

Discuss the following statement: High-minded opposition to slavery was only one cause, and not a very important one, of the animosity between North and South that in 1861 escalated into civil war.

The question asks you to test the writer's opinion against what you know. You would begin by carefully reading that statement a couple of times and then seeing whether you can pick a fight with it. Jot down any contrary evidence you can think of. If you end up agreeing with the statement, supply evidence to support it. Sometimes the passage is the invention of the instructor, who hopes to provoke you to argument.

> Was the following passage written by Gertrude Stein, Kate Chopin, or Tillie Olsen? On what evidence do you base your answer?

> > She waited for the material pictures which she thought would gather and blaze before her imagination. She waited in vain. She saw no pictures of solitude, of hope, of longing, or of despair. But the very passions themselves were aroused within her soul, swaying it, lashing it, as the waves daily beat upon her splendid body. She trembled, she was choking, and the tears blinded her.

The passage is taken from a story by Kate Chopin. If you were familiar with Chopin, who specializes in physical and emotional descriptions of impassioned women, you would know the answer to the examination question, and you might point to language (*swaying, lashing*) that marks it as hers.

The Process Analysis Question.    Often you can spot this kind of question by the word *trace*:

> Trace the stages through which a bill becomes a federal law.

> Trace the development of the medieval Italian city-state.

Both questions want you to tell how something occurs or occurred. The other familiar type of process analysis, the "how-to" variety, is called for in this question:

> An employee has been consistently late for work, varying from fifteen minutes to a half hour daily. This employee has been on the job only five months but shows promise of learning skills that your firm needs badly. How would you deal with this situation?

For more on process analyses, see Chapter 18. In brief, you divide the process into steps and detail each step.

The Far-Out Question.    Sometimes, to invite you to use your imagination, an instructor will throw in a question that at first glance might seem bizarre. On second glance, you may see that the question reaches deep.

> Imagine yourself to be a trial lawyer in 1921, charged with defending Nicola Sacco and Bartolomeo Vanzetti, two anarchists accused of murder. Argue for their acquittal on whatever grounds you can justify.

This question calls on a prelaw student to show familiarity with a famous case (which ended with the execution of the defendants). In addition, it calls for knowledge of the law and of trial procedure. Such a question might be fun to answer; moreover, in being obliged to imagine a time, a place, and dramatic circumstances, you might learn something. The following is another far-out question, this time from a philosophy course.

> What might an ancient Roman Stoic philosopher have thought of Jean-Paul Sartre's doctrine of anguish?

In response, you might try to remember what the Stoics had to say about enduring suffering, define Sartre's view and define theirs, compare their views with Sartre's, and imagine how they would agree (or, more probably, differ) with him. For more on imagining, see Chapter 5.

## DRAFTING: THE ONLY VERSION

When the clock on the wall is ticking away, generating ideas and shaping an answer are seldom two distinct, leisurely processes: they often take place at the same time, and on scratch paper. Does your instructor hand you your own copy of the exam questions? If so, see if there's room in the margins to jot down ideas and put them in rough order. If you can do your preliminary work right on the exam sheet, you will save time: annotate questions, underline points you think important, scribble short definitions. Write reminders that you will notice while you work: TWO PARTS TO THIS QUES.! or GET IN EXAMPLE OF ABORIGINES. To make sure that you include all necessary information without padding or repetition, you might jot down a brief, informal outline before setting pen to paper. This was David Cohn's outline for his answer on his psychology exam (pp. 296–97):

Thesis: Research on infants is probably the best way to demonstrate that some factors in perceptual organization are innate

Cliff box — kid fears drop despite glass, mother, knows shallow side safe

Size constancy — learned early if not intrinsic

Shapes — infants respond more/better to face shape than nonformed

Match sound w/ sight — 2 TVs, look twice as much at right one

Budget Your Time.   When you have two or more essay questions to answer, block out your time at least roughly. Sometimes your instructor will suggest how many minutes to devote to each question or will declare that one question counts twenty points, another ten, and so on. Obviously a twenty-point question deserves twice as much time and work as a ten-pointer. If the instructor doesn't specify, then after you have read the questions, decide for yourself how much time each question is worth. Make a little schedule so that you'll know that at 10:30 it's time to wrap up question 2 and move on. Allot extra minutes to a complicated question (such as one with several parts) or to one that counts more points than the other questions. Otherwise, give every answer equal time. Then pace yourself as you write. A watch with an alarm you can set to buzz at the end of twenty or thirty minutes, alerting you that it's time to move on, might help — unless it would distract your classmates.

**Begin with the Easy Questions.**    Many students find that it helps their morale to start with the question they feel best able to answer. Unless your instructor specifies that you have to answer the questions in their given order, why not skip around? Just make sure you clearly number the questions on your answer sheet or booklet and begin each answer in such a way that the instructor will immediately recognize which question you're answering. If the task is "Compare and contrast the depression of the 1930s with the recession of the 1970s," an answer might begin:

> Compared to the paralyzing depression that began in 1929, the recession of the 1970s seems a bad case of measles.

The instructor would recognize that question, all right, whether you answered it first or last. If you have a choice of questions, label your answer to correspond to the instructor's labels or restate the question at the start of your essay so that your instructor will have no doubt which alternative you have chosen.

QUESTION

Discuss *one* of the following quotations from the writings of Voltaire:

a. "The truths of religion are never so well understood as by those who have lost the power of reasoning."
b. "All roads lead to Rome."

ANSWER

> When in September 1750, Voltaire wrote in a letter to Mme. de Fontaine, "All roads lead to Rome," his remark referred to more than the vast network of roads the ancient Romans had built — and built so well — throughout Europe. . . .

**Try Stating Your Thesis at the Start.**   Some students find it useful to make their opening sentence a thesis statement — a sentence that makes clear right away the main point they're going to make. Then they proceed in the rest of the answer to back that statement up. This method often makes good sense. With a clear thesis statement to begin with, you will be less likely to ramble into byways that carry you miles away from your main point. A clear thesis statement also lets your instructor know right away that you know what you're talking about. (See "Stating and Using a Thesis," p. 349). That's how David Cohn opens his answer to the psychology question (p. 296). An easy way to get started is to begin with the question itself. You might turn the question around, make it into a declarative statement, and transform it into the start of an answer:

QUESTION

Can adequate reasons for leasing cars and office equipment, instead of purchasing them, be cited for a two-person partnership?

ANSWER

I can cite at least four adequate reasons for a two-person partnership to lease cars and office equipment. For one thing, under present tax laws, the entire cost of a regular payment under a leasing agreement may be deducted. . . .

**Stick to the Point of the Question.**   It's a temptation to want to throw into your answer everything you have learned in the course. But to do so defeats the purpose of the examination: to put your knowledge to use, not to parade your knowledge. So when you answer an exam question cogently, you select *what matters* from what you know, at the same time shaping it.

**Answer the Whole Question.**   Often a question will have two parts. It will ask you, say, to name the most common styles of contemporary architecture and then to evaluate one of them. Or

List three differences between the landscape paintings of Monet and those of Van Gogh. Which of the two shows the greater influence of eighteenth-century neoclassicism?

When the dragon of a question has two heads, make sure you cut off both.

**Stay Specific.**   Pressed for time, some harried exam takers think, "I haven't got time to get specific here — I'll just sum up this idea in general." That's a mistake. Every time you throw in a large, general statement ("The industrial revolution was a beneficial thing for the peasant"), take time to include spe-

cific examples ("In Dusseldorf, as Taine tells us, the mortality rate from star-
vation among displaced Prussian farmworkers now dropped to nearly zero,
although once it had reached almost ten percent a year").

**Leave Room to Revise.**    It's foresighted to write on only one side of the page
in your examination booklet. Skip every other line. Then later, should you
wish to add words or sentences or even a whole paragraph, you can do so with
ease. Give yourself room for second thoughts and last-minute inspirations. As
you write and as you revise, you may well do further discovering.

## REVISING: REREADING AND PROOFING

If you have paced yourself, you'll have at least a few minutes left at the end of
your examination period when, while some around you are frantically trying
to finish, you can relax a moment and look over your work with a critical eye.

Even if you happen to stop writing with an hour to spare, it probably
won't be worth your time to recopy your whole exam. Use any time you have
left not to improve your penmanship and the appearance of the paper but to
check how clear your ideas are and how well they hang together.

Your foresight in skipping every other line will now pay off. You can add
sentences wherever you think new ones are needed. Cross out any hopelessly
garbled sentences and rewrite them in the blank lines. If you recall an important point you forgot to put in, you can add a paragraph or two on a blank
left-hand page. Just draw an arrow indicating where it goes. If you find that
you have gone off on a big digression or have thrown in knowledge merely to
show it off, boldly X out that block of wordage. Your answer may look slop-
pier, but your instructor will think the better of it.

Naturally, errors occur oftener when you write under pressure than when
you have time to edit and proofread carefully. Most instructors will take into
consideration your haste and your human fallibility. On an exam, what you
say and how forcefully you say it matter most. Still, to get the small details
right will make your answer look all the sharper. No instructor will object to
careful corrections. You can easily add words with carets:

$$\text{Israeli} \overset{\text{foreign}}{\underset{\wedge}{}} \text{policy}$$

Or you can neatly strike out a word by drawing a line through it. Some
students like to use an erasable pen for in-class writing, but most instructors
prefer cross-outs to the smears of erasable ink.

We don't expect you to memorize the following questions and carry them
like crib notes into an examination. But when you receive your paper or blue
book back and you look it over, you might learn more about writing essay exams if you ask these questions of yourself.

**DISCOVERY
CHECKLIST**

## Evaluating Your Performance

- Did you answer the whole question, not just part of it?
- Did you stick to the point, not throw in information the question didn't call for?
- Did you make your general statements clear by citing evidence or examples?
- Does your answer sprawl, or is it focused?
- Does your answer show a need for more knowledge and more ideas? Did you inflate your answer with hot air, or did you stay close to earth, giving plenty of facts, examples, and illustrations?
- Did you proofread for omissions and lack of clarity?
- On what question or questions do you feel you did a good job that satisfies you, no matter what grade you received?
- If you had to write this exam over again, how would you now go about the job?

## Short-Answer Examinations

Requiring answers much terser than those expected on an essay exam, the *short-answer exam* may call on you to identify names or phrases from your reading, in a sentence or a few words.

> Identify the following: Clemenceau, Treaty of Versailles, Maginot line, Drey-fus affair.

You might answer such a question:

> Georges Clemenceau — This French premier, nicknamed The Tiger, headed a popular coalition cabinet during World War I and at the Paris Peace Conference demanded stronger penalties against Germany.

Writing a short identification is much like writing a short definition. Be sure to mention the general class to which a thing belongs:

> Clemenceau — French premier who . . .
>
> Treaty of Versailles — pact between Germany and the Allies that . . .
>
> Maginot line — fortifications which . . .

If you do so, you won't lose points for an answer like this, which fails to make clear the nature of the thing being identified:

> Maginot line — The Germans went around it.

# Timed Writings

At some point in college you may need to prove your writing expertise on a competency exam (maybe at the end of a course or at the completion of a program). Most composition instructors, to give you experience in writing on demand, assign impromptu essays to be written in class. For such writings, your time is limited (usually forty-five minutes to an hour), the setting is controlled (usually you're sitting at a desk and you're not allowed to use a dictionary or a spell checker), and you can't choose your own subject. The purpose of timed writings is to test your writing skills, not to see how much information you can recall.

At first, this rapid-fire type of writing may cause you some anxiety — sweaty palms and a blank mind. It seems a lot different from the leisurely think-plan-draft-revise method of composing. It does require you to think and recall much faster, yet the way you write a timed essay doesn't differ greatly from the way you write anything else. Your usual methods of writing can serve you well, even though you have to use them in a hurry. With a few tips and a little practice, you can produce a top-notch piece that will please even the toughest readers.

**Budget Your Time Wisely.**   For an in-class essay, if you have forty-five minutes to write, a good rule of thumb is to spend ten minutes preparing, thirty minutes writing, and five minutes rereading and making last-minute changes. In the act of writing, you may find new ideas occurring to you and perhaps these exact proportions of time will change. Or you may know from past experience that you need longer to plan or to proofread and check what you have written. Even so, a rough schedule like that will help you to allocate your time. The worst mistake you can make is to spend so much time thinking and planning that you must rush through getting your ideas down on paper in an essay — the part you will be graded on.

**Choose Your Topic Wisely.**   For extemporaneous writing, you're given little choice of topic — usually one, two, or three. The trick is to make the topic your own. If you have a choice at all, choose the one you know the most about, not the one you think will impress your readers. They'll be most impressed by logical argument and solid evidence. If you have to write on a broad abstract subject (say, a world problem that affects many people), don't choose something you can't quickly recall much about. You'll only end up being vague and general, while your readers will be expecting specifics to back up your claims. Instead, bring it down to something personal, something you have observed or experienced. Have you witnessed traffic jams, brownouts, and condos ruining beaches? Then write about increased population. If your doctor's and dentist's fees have gone up, if your insurance rates have increased, if you have put off a medical checkup because it's so expensive, then write about the increasing costs of health care.

**Think and Plan before You Write.**    With limited time, your tendency will probably be to jump right in and start writing. However, as with all effective writing, you need to think and plan before you start putting ideas into sentences and paragraphs. You should read the instructions and the topics or questions carefully, choose your topic thoughtfully, restrict it to something you know about, form a main idea for focus, and jot down the major divisions for development. While you're thinking, if a good hook for the introduction or conclusion occurs to you, make a note of it. Just don't spend so much time on this planning part of the process that you can't finish the essay.

**Don't Try to Be Perfect.**    No one expects extemporaneous essays to be as polished as reports written over several weeks. Realize that you may not be able to do everything you would like to do in so brief a time. Turn off your internal monitor. You can't polish every sentence or remember the exact word for every spot. You may not include as many details as you would if you had more time, but do include some specifics. And never waste time recopying. A little messiness won't hurt, and you should devote your time to the more important parts of writing.

**Save Time to Proofread.**    The last few minutes you leave yourself to read over your work and correct glaring errors may be the best-spent minutes of all. Cross out and make corrections neatly. Use asterisks (*), arrows, and carets (^). (See more suggestions on how to make corrections on p. 421.) Especially check for the following:

> Omitted letters (-*ed* or -*s*)
> Added letters (develop*e*)
> Inverted letters (rec*ie*ve)
> Wrong punctuation (a comma instead of a period)
> Omitted apostrophes (*dont* instead of *don't*)
> Omitted words ("She going" instead of "She *is* going")
> Wrong words (*except* instead of *accept*)
> Misspelled words (mi*s*pelled)

## TYPES OF TOPICS

Often you can expect the same types of questions or topics for in-class writings as for essay exams. If you are familiar with those recognizable types (discussed on pp. 298–303) and know how to organize them, you can do well. Just remember to look for the key words and do what they suggest.

> What were the *causes* of World War I?
> *Compare and contrast* the theories of capitalism and socialism.
> How did the metaphysical poets of the seventeenth century *influence* the work of T. S. Eliot?
> *Define* civil rights.

Another type of topic for timed writings is a general subject on which thousands of diverse students can write. Give this type of question your own personal twist. But again, you should pay attention to key words.

A problem in education that is *difficult to solve*.
*Ways to cope* with stress.

A type of question you may be familiar with from the standardized tests is one in which you are given a short passage to read and then asked to respond to it. This type of question tests not only your writing ability but also your reading comprehension.

In one of his most famous sonnets, Wordsworth claimed, "The world is too much with us." *Explain* what he meant by that line, and *discuss* whether his assessment of the world still applies today.

Thomas Jefferson stated, "If a nation expects to be ignorant and free, in a state of civilization, it expects what never was and never will be." *How* is his comment *relevant* to education today?

**FOR GROUP LEARNING**

## Brainstorming Ideas

For practice in thinking and planning quickly, brainstorm with your classmates how you might approach writing on the sample topics provided for essay exams and timed writings in this chapter. Include in your discussions possible thesis sentences, various patterns of organization, and specific evidence you might use. Don't expect everybody to come up with the same ideas.

# Chapter 14

# Writing for Business

Most of the world's business communication takes place in writing. The reasons are easy to understand. Although a conversation or telephone message may conveniently be forgotten or ignored, a letter or memorandum is a physical thing that sits on a desk, calling for some action. Written documents also provide a permanent record of an individual's or organization's business dealings — they can be kept on file and checked for details later.

Personnel managers of large corporations, the people who do the hiring, tend to be keenly interested in applicants who can write clearly, accurately, and effectively. A survey conducted at Cornell University asked business executives to rate in importance the qualities they would like their employees to possess. Skill in writing was ranked in fourth place, ahead of managerial skill and skill in analysis. This fact is worth recalling if you ever wonder what practical good you can do your career by taking a writing course.

In this chapter, we will first outline some general guidelines for business writing and then show you four kinds of business writing likely to prove useful: letters, memoranda, electronic mail, and résumés.

## Guidelines for Business Writing

The types of writing generated in the business world are even more varied in their form and content than the types of writing you will encounter in college. Nonetheless, certain principles apply to almost all of them. Good business writing has a clear purpose and succeeds in achieving that purpose. To be effective, you need to know your purpose, remember your audience, use an appropriate tone, and present your information carefully. Perhaps most important, you need to remember that when you write to a business, your writing represents you; when you write as part of your job, your writing represents your company as well.

## KNOW YOUR PURPOSE

To write effectively for business, you first need to determine your purpose in writing. This will help you select and arrange information; it will give you a standard against which to measure your final draft. Most likely, you will want to inform your readers about something or motivate them to take a specific action. In other words, a large part of the purpose in any business writing is to create a certain response in your readers.

 DISCOVERY CHECKLIST

### Purpose in Business Writing

• Do you want to inform? (For example, do you want to make an announcement, keep your readers posted on a developing situation, explain a specialized piece of knowledge, or reply to a request?)
• Do you want to motivate some action? (For example, do you want a question answered, a wrong corrected, a certain decision to be made, or a personnel director to hire you?)
• When your readers are finished reading what you've written, what do you want them to think? What do you want them to do?
• What is your ultimate goal? What do you want to be the final outcome of writing this piece of business correspondence?

## KEEP YOUR AUDIENCE IN MIND

Consider everything in your business writing from your readers' point of view. After all, the purpose of business communication is not to express your ideas but to have your readers act on them, even if the action is simply to notice that you are well informed and on top of the situation.

Sometimes you will be acquainted with the person to whom you are writing; in such cases, you already know a great deal about that person's expertise, priorities, and attitudes. At other times, you may never have met the person. Still, if you brainstorm for a few minutes, you'll probably find that you can make some educated guesses about the person based on what you know about her or his position or company. Here are some questions to ask yourself about your readers.

 DISCOVERY CHECKLIST

### Audience in Business Writing

• What do your readers already know about the subject? Are they experts in the field? Have they been kept up to date on the situation? Avoid telling people what they already know: it will only frustrate and annoy them.
• What do your readers need to know about the subject? If your purpose is to inform, what information do they expect you to provide? If your purpose is to motivate, what information do they need before they can take action? Be sure to include this information.

- What can you assume about your readers' priorities and expectations? Are they busy executives, with stacks of mail to weed through? Are they careful, conscientious administrators who will appreciate your attention to detail? Tailor your writing to meet your readers' expectations.
- What is most likely to motivate your readers to take the action you want? Sometimes it may be acknowledging a shared interest in a social cause; sometimes it may be stating that prompt action will avoid a lawsuit. Whatever the motivating factor is, be sure to include and emphasize it.

In most business writing — especially in letters and memoranda where the purpose is to motivate — it's useful to adopt a "you" attitude. In other words, instead of focusing on what "I, the writer" would like, focus on how "you, the reader" will benefit.

| | |
|---|---|
| "I" ATTITUDE | Please send me the form so that I can process your order. |
| "YOU" ATTITUDE | So that you can receive your shipment promptly, please send me the form. |

Another technique is to picture your reader in your mind as concretely as possible. Even if you have no idea who, exactly, will be reading your writing, make someone up — and supply her or him with a personality, an office, and a wardrobe. Then imagine this reader looking over your writing and reacting to it, line by line.

## USE AN APPROPRIATE TONE

Tone is the quality of writing that reveals your attitude toward your topic and your readers. Whether or not you are aware of it, everything you write has a tone, and much of your readers' impression of you depends on the tone of your writing. If you show your readers that you respect them, their intelligence, and their feelings, they in turn are far more likely to view you and your message favorably.

Most business writing today ranges from the informal to the slightly formal. Gone are the extremely formal phrases that once dotted business correspondence: *enclosed herewith, be advised that, pursuant to the stated request.* That sort of language is considered stuffy and pompous today. At the other extreme, however, slang, overfriendliness, and any other marks of a casual style might cast doubts on your seriousness or credibility. Strive for a relaxed and conversational style, using simple sentences, familiar words, and the active voice. As you gain more experience, you may find that for certain people and certain situations a casual manner is comfortable and effective. The safest route, though, is to be somewhat more restrained.

| | |
|---|---|
| TOO CASUAL | I hear that thing with the new lackey is a definite go. |
| TOO FORMAL | This office stands informed that the administration's request for supplementary personnel has been honored. |
| APPROPRIATE | I've learned that a new office assistant has been hired. |

In all your business writing, be courteous, polite, and considerate. If you are writing to complain, remember that the person reading your letter may not be the one who caused the problem — and even if he or she is, you are more likely to win your case with courtesy than with sarcasm or insults. When delivering bad news, you might be tempted to hide behind a impersonal bureaucratic facade, but remember that your reader will probably interpret this as coldness and lack of sympathy. And try to avoid language that will make it seem as if you're avoiding responsibility; if you have made a mistake or done something wrong, acknowledge it. "Too often," notes a professor of business English, "inexperienced writers in the corporate world equate 'professional' with 'bureaucratic,' forgetting that every good writer — in or out of business — writes as one human being to another."

Having someone else read your writing to check for tone or setting it aside for a "cooling off" period is always a good idea. This will help you catch impersonal phrases such as "your claim for damaged goods is acknowledged" and transform them into the far more effective "I have received your request for a replacement part." When you reread your writing to check for tone, here are some things you can ask yourself.

 **REVISION CHECKLIST**

## Tone in Business Writing

- Have you avoided slang terms and extremely casual language?
- Have you avoided excessively formal or unnecessarily sophisticated words?
- Are your sentences of a manageable length? (Try reading a questionable sentence out loud in a single breath — if it sounds too long and complicated, it is.)
- Have you used the active voice ("I am sending it") rather than the passive voice ("It is being sent")?
- Is there anything in what you've written that might sound blaming or accusatory?
- When you read your writing, do you hear a friendly, considerate, competent person behind the words?
- Have you asked someone else to read your writing to check for tone?

## PRESENT INFORMATION CAREFULLY

In business, time is money: time wasted reading irrelevant material or trying to comprehend poorly written documents is money wasted. To be effective, the information you present in your business writing should be concise, clear, and well organized.

Concise writing shows that you respect your readers' time. In most cases, if a letter, memo, or résumé is longer than a page or two, it's too long. You might need to find a better way to present the information (long lists can be placed in separate documents, for example), or you might need to cut information or details that your readers don't really need. Go through your writing sentence by sentence and delete any wordy or unnecessary expressions.

Clear writing ensures that the correct message will reach your readers. If the readers of your business correspondence misinterpret what you've said, you may not have the chance to correct their misunderstanding. First, make sure the information you convey is accurate and complete. Then make your writing so clear and unambiguous that no possibility of misinterpretation exists. Scrutinize each word and phrase to make sure that it means exactly what you want it to mean. Avoid jargon, as it can cloud meaning. Emphasize the most important information by putting it in a prominent spot (usually at the beginning). Let your readers know exactly what you want them to do — politely, of course. If you have a question, ask it. If you want something, request it.

Well-organized writing helps readers move through it quickly and easily. Every piece of business correspondence should be written so that it can be skimmed. Although you want your readers to consider carefully what you've written, in reality many of them will glance over it quickly; if a reader spends fifteen seconds looking over what you've written, you want to be sure that she or he comes away with an accurate impression. Make sure the topic of the document is absolutely clear from the very beginning. In a letter, you should usually state your topic in the first paragraph; in a memorandum, you should put it in the subject line. Use a conventional format that your readers will expect (see Figures 14.1, 14.2, and 14.4 later in this chapter). Break information into easily processed chunks — in letters and memoranda, use paragraphs of no more than seven or eight lines. Order the chunks of information logically and consistently. Finally, use topic sentences and headings (when each is appropriate) to label each chunk of information and give your readers an overview of your document.

Crafting a concise, clear, and well-organized piece of business writing takes skill and patience — but that's true of all good writing. Take a look at the examples in the next sections to see how the principles described here can be put into action. As you work on your own business writing, here are some questions you can ask yourself.

**REVISION CHECKLIST**

## Conciseness, Clarity, and Organization in Business Writing

- Have you kept your letter, memo, or résumé to a page or two?
- Have you cut all deadwood and wordiness?
- Have you scrutinized every word and phrase to ensure that it can't be misinterpreted? Have you supplied all the background information readers need to understand your points?
- Have you emphasized the most important part of your message? Will readers know what you want them to do?
- Have you used a consistent and logical order? Have you followed a conventional format?
- If appropriate, have you included the labels and headings your readers will need to make their way through your writing quickly and easily?

# Business Letters

Knowing how to draft a good business letter is a skill that can serve you well in any job and in your personal business dealings. Organizations use business letters to correspond with outside parties — either individual people or other organizations. (Most correspondence within an organization is conveyed through memoranda; see p. 320.) Business letters are used to request and provide information, motivate action, respond to requests, and sell goods and services. Letters rather than phone calls are used for most important transactions because a letter writer has the opportunity to craft a clear, thorough statement — and a letter reader has the opportunity to review and scrutinize the facts and make a considered decision. Letters are also more convenient because a busy person can respond whenever he or she has an opportunity. Finally, letters are useful because they become part of the permanent record; they can be referred to later to determine exactly who said what and when. You should keep a copy of every letter you write; if you write on a computer, keep a printout as well as a backup on disk.

An effective business letter is straightforward, forceful (but polite and considerate), concise, neat, and legible. Letters are usually written person to person (or at least read as if they were written this way), so the tone you use is very important. A good business letter is brief — limited to one page if at all possible. It supplies whatever information the reader needs, no more. Because they are so brief, business letters are often judged on the basis of small but important details: grammar, punctuation, format, appearance, and openings and closings. In general, business letters tend to be conservative and conventional — this is not the place to try out nifty new typefaces on your word processor or experiment with stream-of-consciousness writing.

(Letters written to apply for a job are covered in "Résumés and Application Letters," see p. 324.)

## FORMAT FOR BUSINESS LETTERS

Although there are few absolute rights and wrongs, the format of business letters is fairly well established by convention. Listed here are the elements of a standard business letter followed by two examples of business letters using these elements (Figures 14.1 and 14.2). Except where noted, leave one line of extra space between elements; in very short letters, it's acceptable to leave additional space before the inside address.

*Return address.* This is your address or the address of the company for which you are writing. Use no abbreviations except the two-letter postal abbreviation for the state. (Note: You do not have to type a return address on preprinted letterhead stationery that already provides this information.)

*Date.* This goes on the first line after the return address, without an extra line of space above. Don't abbreviate the name of the month, and follow it by the day, a comma, and the year.

***Inside address.***  This is the address of the person to whom you are writing. The first name should be the full name of the person, with his or her title (*Mr., Ms., Dr., Professor*); when addressing a woman who does not have a professional title, use *Ms.* unless you know for certain that she prefers *Miss* or *Mrs.* The second line should identify the position the person holds (if any), and the third line should be the name of the organization (if you are writing to one). If you don't know the name of the person who will read your letter, it is acceptable to start with the name of the position, department, or organization. When writing the address, use no abbreviations except the two-letter postal abbreviation for the state.

***Salutation.***  Skip a line of space and then type *Dear* followed by the person's title and last name; end the line with a colon. If you don't know the name of the person who will read your letter, it is acceptable to word your salutation *Dear Editor* or *Dear Angell's Bakery*. The salutation *Gentlemen* has become too sexist for contemporary usage. You can also omit the salutation altogether.

***Body.***  This is your message. Leave one line of space between paragraphs, and begin each paragraph even with the left margin (no indentations). Paragraphs should generally be no longer than seven or eight typed lines.

***Closing.***  Leave one line of space after the last paragraph, and then use a conventional closing followed by a comma: *Sincerely, Sincerely yours, Respectfully yours, Yours truly.*

***Typed name with position.***  Leave four lines of space after the closing, and type your name in full, even if you will sign only your first name. Do not include a title before your name. If you are writing on behalf of an organization, you can include your position on the next line.

***Signature.***  After you have finished typing or printing out the letter, be sure to sign your name in the space between the closing and the typed name. Unless you have established a personal relationship with the person to whom you are writing, use both your first and last names. Do not include a title before your name.

***Abbreviations at end.***  In some cases, abbreviations after your typed name communicate additional information about the letter. If you send a copy of the letter to someone other than the person addressed, use *cc:* followed by the name of the person or organization who will receive a copy. If the letter is accompanied by another document in the same envelope, use *Enc.* or *Enclosure*. If the letter has been typed by someone other than the person who wrote and signed it, the writer's initials are given in capital letters, followed by a slash and the initials of the typist in lowercase letters: *VW/dbw*. Leave at least two lines of extra space between the typed name and any abbreviations; put each abbreviation on a separate line.

Two standard formats specify the placement of these elements on the page. To correctly align a letter using *modified block style* (see Figure 14.1), you

1453 Illinois Ave
Miami, FL 33133
January 26, 1996

Customer Service Department
Fidelity Products, Inc.
1192 Plymouth Avenue
Little Rock, AK 72210

Dear Customer Service Representative:

I recently purchased a VCR stand (Model XAR) from your company. I have been unable to assemble it because the instructions are unclear. These instructions not only are incomplete (step 6 is missing) but are accompanied by diagrams so small and dark that it is impossible to distinguish the numbers for the different pieces.

Please send me usable instructions. If I do not receive improved instructions in the next fourteen days, I will return my VCR stand to the store where I purchased it and request a full refund.

I have used your TV and video equipment for more than ten years and have been very satisfied, so I was particularly surprised and disappointed to find that you produce such an inferior item. If you continue to pay little attention to the needs of your customers, I will consider purchasing the products of other companies.

Thank you for your attention to these concerns.

Sincerely,

*James Winter, Jr.*

James Winter, Jr.

FIGURE 14.1.
Letter Using Modified Block Style

need to imagine a line running down the center of the page from top to bottom. The return address, date, closing, signature, and typed name are placed to align at the left side with this line. The *full block style* is generally used only on letterhead stationery that includes the name and address of the organization. Omit typing the return address and align all the elements at the left margin. (See Figure 14.2.)

**Fidelity Products, Inc.**

1192 Plymouth Avenue · Little Rock, AK 72210 · 501–555–0100

February 2, 1996

Mr. James Winter, Jr.
1453 Illinois Avenue
Miami, FL 33133

Dear Mr. Winter:

Thank you for your letter expressing concern about the instructions for assembling the Model XAR VCR stand. We always appreciate honest feedback from our customers. Enclosed you will find a corrected and legible copy of the instructions. You can also call one of our technicians at 1-800-555-1234 for assistance in assembling the stand. If you are still unsatisfied, we will be more than happy to refund the cost of the stand or to exchange the stand for another of our products.

We were sorry to hear that the original instructions for Model XAR were not helpful. We are working to improve them and the instructions for other products we offer. I have forwarded a copy of your letter to our director of product support, who is responsible for strengthening our instruction packages.

Thank you again for helping us improve our products. I hope you will continue to purchase and enjoy Fidelity's products. Please feel free to contact me if I can be of any further assistance.

Sincerely yours,

*Maria Solis*

Maria Solis
Customer Service Supervisor

cc: Edward Copply
Enc.

FIGURE 14.2.
Letter Using Full Block
Style

There are also two standard formats for envelopes. The U.S. Postal Service recommends a format that uses all capital letters, standard abbreviations, and no punctuation; this style makes the information on the envelope easier for the Postal Service to scan and process. However, this format may not be acceptable in all situations; it is always safe to use a conventional envelope format. See Figure 14.3 for examples of both formats.

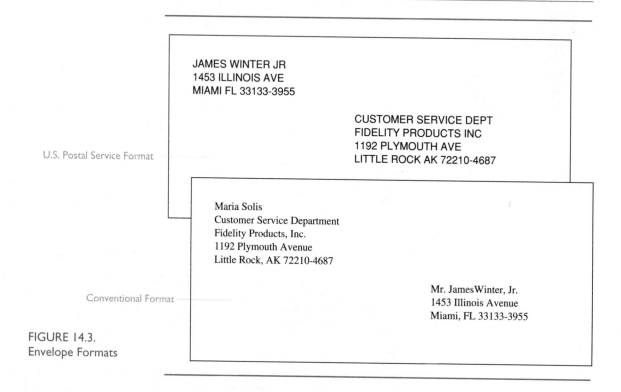

U.S. Postal Service Format

JAMES WINTER JR
1453 ILLINOIS AVE
MIAMI FL 33133-3955

CUSTOMER SERVICE DEPT
FIDELITY PRODUCTS INC
1192 PLYMOUTH AVE
LITTLE ROCK AK 72210-4687

Maria Solis
Customer Service Department
Fidelity Products, Inc.
1192 Plymouth Avenue
Little Rock, AK 72210-4687

Conventional Format

Mr. James Winter, Jr.
1453 Illinois Avenue
Miami, FL 33133-3955

FIGURE 14.3.
Envelope Formats

Finally, remember that the physical appearance of a business letter is very important. Observe these guidelines.

Use 8–1/2-by-11-inch bond paper, with matching envelopes.

If you use a typewriter, make sure the ribbon is dark and the keys are clean; if you use a word processor, use a letter-quality or laser printer.

Single-space and use an extra line of space to separate paragraphs and the different elements of the letter. Use only one side of the page.

Leave margins of at least one inch on the right and left sides; try to make the top and bottom margins fairly even, although you may have to have a larger bottom margin if your letter is very short.

Pay extremely careful attention to grammar, punctuation, and mechanics. Your readers will.

## Memoranda

A *memorandum* (*memo* for short) is a form of communication used within a company to request or exchange information, to make announcements, and to confirm what has passed in conversation. Generally, the topic is quite narrow and should be apparent to the reader in a single glance. Memos tend to be written in the first person (*I* or *we*) and can range from the very informal (if written to a peer) to the extremely formal (if written to a high-ranking superior on an important matter). Memos are frequently used to convey information to large groups — an entire team, department, or organization. Most memos are short, but the memo format can also be used to convey proposals and reports; when they are long, good memos make free use of headings, subheadings, lists, and other features that make information easy to scan.

## FORMAT FOR MEMORANDA

Every organization has its own format for memos; some organizations even have preprinted forms with spaces to fill in the appropriate information. In general, the heading consists of a series of lines with clear labels (followed by colons), each line conveying a key piece of information about the memo and its distribution.

| | |
|---|---|
| Date: | (date on which memo is sent) |
| To: | (person or persons to whom it is primarily addressed) |
| cc: | (names of anyone else who receives a copy) |
| From: | (name of the writer) |
| Subject: *or* Re: | (concise, accurate statement of the memo's topic) |

The most important line of a memo may be the subject line, as this often determines whether the memo is read or not. (The old-fashioned abbreviation *Re:* for *regarding,* is still used, but we recommend the more common *Subject.*) State the topic in very few words, but provide the details needed to make it an accurate summary ("Agenda for 12/10 meeting with Ann Kois," "Sales estimates for new product line"). Usually, instead of signing a memo, the writer simply initials it in the space after his or her name. (For an example of a memo, see Figure 14.4.)

# Electronic Mail

*Electronic mail* (*e-mail* for short) is a message sent directly from one computer to another by means of a network. E-mail is becoming more popular in business settings because it is easy (the writer needs only type a message and send it — no time is spent printing a copy, typing an envelope, putting on postage, and so on), speedy (messages usually arrive the same day they are sent), and convenient (writers can send messages at any time, and readers can read and respond to them at their convenience). E-mail combines the immediacy of a telephone conversation with the permanence of letters and memoranda. It is commonly used both within organizations and between organizations and outside parties. However, letters and memos are usually still preferred for formal, official correspondence.

Because it seems so conversational, e-mail is rarely scrutinized and polished like other written correspondence. Much of it is neither printed out before it is sent nor reviewed by anyone other than the writer. Obviously, the likelihood for errors and omissions is much higher than for letters and

## memorandum

Date:         February 8, 1996

To:           Edward Copply, Director, Product Support

cc:           Justin Blake

From:         Maria Solis, Customer Service Supervisor    *MS*

Subject:      Customer dissatisfaction with instructions for Model XAR

As I mentioned in our conversation of January 30, the Customer Service Department has recently received many letters and phone calls regarding the instructions for assembling our new VCR stand, Model XAR. Customers find these instructions confusing and often ask us to arrange a refund. (A copy of the instructions is attached.)

After examining the letters in our files, I've concluded that customers have two specific concerns. The first concern is that the written instructions skip words and entire steps. If you look at the attached copy, you will notice that there is no step 6 and that step 3 reads "Connect the to leg one." The second concern is that the drawings are too dark. Customers complain that dark shading obscures the numbers and makes it difficult to determine where one sections begins and the other ends.

The number of calls and letters we're getting suggests that these poor instructions are creating frustration and resentment among both our loyal customers and first-time buyers. In most cases, the customers who contact us are satisfied when we send them a photocopied set of the corrected instructions we've created here in Customer Service, but I feel strongly that the instructions sent out with the product should be improved.

I know that you're planning to review and revise the entire line of product information sheets and instructions, Ed. I recommend that the instructions for Model XAR be put at the top of the list.

Please let me know if I can provide further information.


Enclosure

FIGURE 14.4.
Memorandum

memos. People who correspond regularly through e-mail tend to forgive one another's spelling mistakes and infelicities; however, you should remember that your e-mail messages are a part of the official record. Remember, too, that there is no guarantee of privacy with e-mail. You may feel that you are having a confidential chat with a trusted friend or colleague, but the chat can be intercepted, recorded on other computers, and distributed either in print or over a network.

## FORMAT FOR E-MAIL

The headings for e-mail are predetermined by the systems that generate and transmit it; these almost universally use a standard memo format. The computer will prompt you to enter information in the header lines: *To:*, *cc:*, and *Subject:*, for example. Then you simply type your message. The person receiving your message sees your header information as well as a *From* line that gives your name.

E-mail is a developing and flexible form, so there are fewer conventions and a wider range of acceptable practices than with other business correspondence. Keep in mind that many e-mail messages will be read and responded to while displayed on the computer screen. If possible, keep the messages short, no more than a couple of screens. If a message is longer, make it easy to navigate by stating at the beginning what it covers and by using clear, obvious headings and visually noticeable dividers (extra space or a line of asterisks between sections, for example). If you send long messages or messages with important information, it's likely that they'll be printed out; consider what your writing will look like in this format, as well. (For an example of an e-mail message, see Figure 14.5.)

(For more about e-mail and writing with computers, see Chapter 21.)

FIGURE 14.5.
Electronic Mail

Subject: Improving Product Instructions
Date: 96-02-08 10:11:31 EST
To: JMANDALA_INTSALES (Jeannie Mandala, Institutional Sales)
From: ECOPPLY_PRODSUP (Edward Copply, Product Support)

Jeannie,
As you know, we're planning to review and revise our entire line of product info. sheets and instructions. The goal will be to make the instructions more useful and to present a consistent image for FIDELITY PRODUCTS.

Could you please fill me in on any complaints you've been receiving from our institutional customers? Let me know which products are causing difficulties, how many complaints you've received, and what the specific criticisms are.

Thanks for your help on this, Jeannie. I'll keep you posted on our plans.

Ed

# Résumés and Application Letters

The most momentous business correspondence you write may be the résumé and letter you use to apply for a job. It's wise to take great pains with both. They will enable a busy personnel manager to decide quickly whether your application deserves any follow-up. To write a good résumé and application letter, you will need to draw on many of the skills and strategies for clear and persuasive writing that you have learned about and practiced elsewhere in this book. Direct, persuasive, correct prose can help you stand out above the crowd.

## RÉSUMÉS

In a résumé, you present yourself as someone who has the qualifications needed to excel at a job, someone who will be an asset to the organization to which you are applying. You will want to consider every word and format decision carefully, revising and revising again until the finished product gleams like a jewel. Because of the time and expense spent in crafting a good résumé, job seekers often have multiple copies of a single résumé on hand to include with all their applications; any relevant information not highlighted in the résumé can be discussed in the accompanying application letter. However, if you have access to a word processor and can easily print out attractive copies, you may want to customize your résumé for each job you apply for.

A résumé is a highly formatted document, but also one that allows a wide variety of decisions about style, organization, and appearance. In this section, we describe a typical résumé, but you should know that there are many acceptable formats. Unless you have a great deal of relevant work experience, your résumé should be no longer than one page long. The standard résumé consists of a heading and labeled sections that detail your experience and qualifications in a number of areas. (For an example of a résumé, see Figure 14.6.)

*Heading.*  Put your name on the first line; street address on the second; city, state, and zip code on the third; and phone number on the fourth. The heading is generally centered on the page.

*Employment objective.*  Although this section is optional, we recommend it because it allows personnel officers to see at a glance what your priorities and goals are. Try to sound confident, ambitious, and eager, but not pompous or presumptuous.

*Education.*  This is generally the first section and is almost always included. For each postsecondary school you've attended, specify the name of the institution, your major, your date of graduation (or expected graduation), and your grade point average (if it reflects well on you). You can also mention any awards or honors or any course work that may be relevant to the job.

**Sheryl W. Fitzgerald**
266 Castrodale Ave., Apt. 4
Falmouth MA 02541
508-555-9876

| | |
|---|---|
| **Objective** | An editorial position with a publication at a nonprofit organization |
| **Education** | **Ohio State University**, Columbus, OH. Bachelor's degree in journalism, June 1995. Grade point average: 3.6. |
| | **Oakland Community College**, Bloomfield Hills, MI. Associate degree in public relations, May 1992. Course work in communications, business writing. |
| **Experience** | |
| *9/93 to 6/95* | **The Lantern** (circulation 30,000), Ohio State University's daily student newspaper. Reporter, copyeditor, layout chief. |
| *6/94 to 9/94* | **Cincinnati Enquirer** (circulation 350,000), Cincinnati, OH. General assignment reporter. |
| *6/92 to 8/93* | **Cape Cod Times** (circulation 50,000), Hyannis, MA. Business reporter. Covered local stocks, real estate, and business issues and trends. |
| *5/91 to 8/91* | **Dow Jones News Service**, New York City. Editing intern under the Dow Jones Newspaper Fund program. Edited stories from *Wall Street Journal* reporters, corporate sources, and wire services. |
| **Skills** | Word processing (WordPerfect 5.1 for DOS, Word for Windows), layout, copyediting, proofreading. |
| **Interests** | Volunteer tutor for the Cape Cod Literacy Council, 9/92 to 8/93. Founding member of the Cape and Islands News Association. |
| **References** | Available upon request. |

FIGURE 14.6.
Résumé

*Experience.* This is the most important section of the résumé. List each job separately, starting with the most recent one first. You can include both full-time and part-time jobs. For each job, give the name of the organization, your position, your responsibilities, and the dates you held the job. If you were involved in any unusual projects or were responsible for any important developments, describe them. Remember that the point of the résumé is to show your prospective employer that you are well qualified for the position you want. Highlight details that show relevant work experience and leadership ability. Minimize information about jobs or responsibilities that are unconnected to the job for which you're applying.

*Skills.* If you have special skills that your prospective employer might find attractive (data processing, technical drawing, knowledge of a foreign language) but that aren't obvious from the descriptions of your education and work experience, you can list them.

*Interests.* You can either specify professional interests and activities (*Member of Birmingham Bricklayers Association*) or personal pursuits (*skiing, hiking, needlepoint*). In either case, this section should show that you are a dedicated and well-rounded individual.

*References.* If you are answering a job advertisement that requests references, give them. Always contact your references in advance to make sure they will be willing to give you a good recommendation. For each person, give the name, his or her organization and position, and the organization's address and phone number. If references have not been requested, you can simply note "Available upon request."

Keep your résumé brief and pointed by using phrases and clauses rather than complete sentences. Use action verbs (*supervised, ordered, maintained*) and the active voice whenever possible. Highlight labels with underlining, boldface, or a larger type size. And remember that a neat, attractive, professional appearance is extremely important. Arrange information on the page so that it is pleasing to the eye, use the best paper you can, and either print your résumé on a laser printer or have it typeset.

## APPLICATION LETTERS

When writing a letter applying for a job, you should follow all the guidelines for writing other business letters (see pp. 316–20). In addition, remember that you are trying to sell yourself to your prospective employer and that your immediate objective is to obtain an interview. Remember, too, that you are competing against other candidates and that your letter and résumé are all the employer has to judge you on.

If you're responding to an advertisement, read it critically. What qualifications are listed? Ideally, you should have all the required qualifications for any job you're applying for, but if you lack one, try to find something in your background that compensates, something that gives you similar experience in a different form. What else can you tell about the organization or position from the ad? How does the organization represent itself? Creative? Prestigious? The new kid on the block? (If you're unfamiliar with the organization and you can't glean much about it from the ad, it's usually wise to do some research.) How does the ad describe the ideal candidate? A team player? A dynamic individual? If you feel that you are the person this organization is looking for, you'll want to portray yourself this way in your letter. (For an example of a job advertisement, see Figure 14.7.)

In your letter, you want to catch your readers' attention, convince them that you're a qualified and attractive candidate, and motivate them to grant you an interview. Whenever possible, address your letter to the person responsible for screening applicants and setting up interviews; you may need to call the organization to find out this person's name. In the first paragraph, you should identify the job, indicate how you heard about it, and summarize your qualifications. Try to spark some interest in your readers. In the second paragraph, you should expand on your qualifications, highlighting key information on your résumé and supplementing it with additional details, if necessary. At this point, you need to establish superiority, show your readers that you're a better candidate than the other people applying. In the third paragraph, you should restate your interest in the job, ask for an interview, and let your prospective employer know how you can be reached. (For an example of an application letter, see Figure 14.8.)

Every time you write an application letter, you'll want to draft it, ponder it, cut out unnecessary words, rephrase it, correct spelling, and check grammar and punctuation. Ask a friend to read it over for you. If you have time, set it aside for a day before printing out the final version. If you sound qualified, eager, and interesting, chances are that the prospective employer will be interested in you.

FIGURE 14.7.
Job Advertisement

# Editor
### Bloomfield College Magazine
Bloomfield College seeks an energetic, innovative, and experienced editor to join its staff. The successful candidate will join and help lead a team that promotes College interests, programs, and alumni through the *Bloomfield College Magazine*. Specific responsibilities include
- Conceptualizing themes and developing story ideas
- Writing feature articles
- Assigning writing and editing to in-house and freelance writers
- Editing copy
- Helping manage advertising and distribution

The ideal candidate will understand and enjoy working in a college atmosphere. He or she will have outstanding written and oral communication abilities as well as excellent proofreading, editing, and computer skills. Two to four years' experience in editing a magazine or other periodical is desired. Bachelor's degree or equivalent combination of education and experience is required.

Salary is commensurate with experience. Deadline is August 15, 1995. Send cover letter with résumé and three writing samples to Search Committee, *Bloomfield College Magazine*, Office of Human Resources, 101 Glengarry Ave., Bloomfield, MI 48301.

266 Castrodale Avenue, Apartment 4
Falmouth, MA 02541
August 2, 1995

Emma Kinsella
Search Committee
*Bloomfield College Magazine*
Office of Human Resources
101 Glengarry Avenue
Bloomfield, MI 48301

Dear Ms. Kinsella:

I would like to apply for the job of editor at *Bloomfield College Magazine*, which I saw advertised recently in *The Chronicle of Higher Education*. My extensive journalism experience and my recent degree in journalism, I believe, make me highly qualified for the position.

The time I spent as a reporter at *Cape Cod Times* was so rewarding that I decided to return to college to purse a degree in journalism. While at Ohio State University, I continued my work in the field of publications not only in my studies but also in the role of reporter and editor for *The Lantern*, Ohio State University's daily student newspaper. One of the most interesting of my responsibilities was to coordinate the coverage of university events with the staff of *Alumni*, the university's alumni magazine. My résumé and three writing samples are enclosed.

I believe I would be a strong addition to the team at *Bloomfield College Magazine*, and I would like to discuss my qualifications with you further in an interview. Please write to me or call me at 508-555-9876. Thank you for your consideration.

Sincerely,

*Sheryl W. Fitzgerald*

Sheryl W. Fitzgerald

Enclosures

**FIGURE 14.8.**
Application Letter

**Part Four**

# A Writer's Strategies

# Introduction

The following seven chapters constitute a manual offering in-depth advice on writing strategies. The word *strategy* may remind you of warfare: in the original Greek sense of the word, it is a way to win a battle. Writing a college paper, you'll probably agree, is a battle of a kind. In this manual you'll find an array of small weapons to use — and perhaps some heavy artillery.

Here are techniques you can learn, methods you can follow, good practices you can observe in writing effectively. The first five chapters offer a wealth of suggestions for approaching each of the stages of the writing process: generating ideas, planning, drafting, developing, and revising and editing. You're already familiar with this writing process from the chapters in Part One and Part Two. There, each stage was covered briefly for each assignment, and relevant strategies were mentioned briefly. Here, each stage of the writing process gets a full chapter, and the strategies belonging to each are explained and illustrated more fully. The last two chapters here offer advice on two writing strategies that writers may or may not choose to integrate into their writing process for a particular assignment: working collaboratively with other writers and writing on a computer.

No strategy will appeal to every writer, and no writer uses every one for every writing task. Outlining has rescued many a writer from getting lost, but we know writers who never outline except in their heads. Consider this part of the book a reference guide or instruction manual. Turn to it when you need more help, when you're curious, or when you'd like to enlarge your repertoire of writing skills. We can't tell you which of the ideas and techniques covered in these pages will work for you, but we can promise that if you try some of them out, you'll be rewarded.

# Chapter 15

# Strategies for Generating Ideas

For most writers, the hardest part of writing comes first: the moment when they confront a blank sheet of paper. Fortunately, you can do much to get ready for it. Experienced writers have many tested techniques to get moving. Many of the suggestions that follow may strike you as far-out, even silly, but all have worked for some writers — both professionals and students — and some may work for you. This chapter suggests two types of devices: methods you can try to find ideas for your writing and strategies you can use to get ready to write.

## Finding Ideas

Learning to write is learning what questions to ask yourself. When you begin to write, no matter what the source of information — recall, observation, reading, conversation, imagination — you need to start the ideas flowing. Sometimes ideas appear quickly on the paper or screen. But if at other times you find yourself staring at a blank, you needn't throw up your hands in frustration. Instead you can try one of the strategies in this chapter for getting ideas started. These strategies are useful not only when you are thinking and planning but also at any point in the writing process when you find your flow of ideas drying up or when you find that you need additional evidence. If one doesn't work for a particular writing task, try another. Seldom will you use all of them on one writing task. Think of these strategies as your arsenal of idea generators, techniques that you can call on at any point in the writing process.

### BRAINSTORMING

A *brainstorm* is a sudden insight or inspiration, and *brainstorming* is free association for stimulating a chain of ideas. When you brainstorm, you start with a word or phrase to launch your thoughts in some direction. For a set length of time, say ten or fifteen minutes, putting the conscious, analytical part of your mind on hold, you scribble a list of ideas as rapidly as possible, writing down whatever comes to mind with no editing or going back. Then you look over the often surprising results.

For a college writing assignment, you might brainstorm to find a specific topic for a paper. Or if you need to generate some material, such as an illustration or example, as you are writing your paper, you can brainstorm. If you have already written your paper, you can brainstorm to come up with a title for it.

Brainstorming can be a group activity. In the business world, brainstorming is a common strategy to fill a specific need: a name for a product, a corporate emblem, a slogan for an advertising campaign. You can try group brainstorming with a few other students or your entire class. Members of the group sit facing one another. They designate one person as the recorder to take down on paper or a blackboard whatever suggestions the others offer. If the suggestions fly too thick and fast, the secretary jots down the best one in the air at that moment. For several minutes, people call out ideas. Then they look over the recorder's list in hopes of finding useful results.

You may find solo brainstorming helpful when you need to shake an idea out of your unconscious. Here is how one student did just that. On the opening day of a writing course, Martha Calbick's instructor assigned a paper from recall: "Demonstrate that the invention of the computer has significantly changed our lives." Following the instructor's advice, Calbick went home and brainstormed. First, she wrote the key word *computer* at the top of a sheet of paper. Then she set her alarm clock to sound in fifteen minutes and began to scribble single words or phrases. The first thing she recalled was how her kid brother sits by the hour in front of a home computer playing *Wizardry*, a *Dungeons and Dragons* kind of game. The first recollection quickly led, by free association, to several more.

> Wizardry
> My kid bro. thinks computers are for kids
> Always trading games with other kids —
>     software pirates
> Mother says it's too bad kids don't play Wiffle
>     ball anymore
> In 3rd grade they teach programming
> Hackers

Some get rich

Ed's brother-in-law — wrote a program for accountants

Become a programmer? big future?

Guided missiles

Computers in subway stations—print tickets

Banks—shove in your plastic card

A man lucked out—deposited $100—computer credited him with $10,000

Sort mail—zip codes

Computers print out grades

My report card showed a D instead of a B— big fight to correct it

Are we just numbers now?

When her alarm clock rang, Calbick dropped her pencil and took a coffee break. When she returned to her desk, she was pleased to find that a few of her random thoughts suggested directions that interested her. First she went through her list with a pencil, discarding ideas that did not interest her. She didn't know much about *Wizardry* or about missiles. She circled the question "are we just numbers now?" It looked promising. Maybe some of the other ideas she had listed might express that very idea, such as the mindlessness of the computer that had credited the man with $10,000. As she looked over the list, she continued brainstorming, jotting down more thoughts, making notes on the list, and adding to it. "Dealing with computers isn't dealing with people," she wrote next to the circled question. From her rough list, an idea was beginning to emerge.

Calbick later wrote a paper on the effect of computer errors, focusing on the simple computer error in her high school office that had momentarily robbed her of a good grade. She recalled how time-consuming it had been to have that error corrected. She mentioned a few other cases of computer error, including that of the man who had struck it rich at the bank. Her conclusion was a wry complaint about computerized society: "A computer knows your name and number, but it doesn't know who you are."

You can see how brainstorming typically works and how it started one student going. It is valuable because it helps you personalize a topic and break it down into specifics. Whenever you try brainstorming, you might follow these bits of advice.

1. *Start with a key word or phrase* — one that will head your thoughts in the direction you wish to pursue. If you are trying to find a topic, begin with a general word or phrase. If you are searching for an example to fill out a paragraph in progress, use a specific word or phrase.

2. *Set a time limit.* Ten to fifteen minutes is long enough — brainstorming can be strenuous.

3. *Write rapidly.* List any words, thoughts, phrases, fragments, or short sentences that surface in connection with your key word. Keep your entries brief. Put them in a list so that you can scan over them quickly later.

4. *Don't stop.* Don't pause. While you're brainstorming, don't worry about misspelling, repetition, absurdity, or irrelevance. Write down whatever comes into your head, as fast as your pen will go. Now is not the time to analyze or to throw any suggestion away. Never mind if you come up with ideas that seem crazy or far out. Don't judge, don't arrange — just produce. If your mind goes blank, keep your pencil moving, even if you are only repeating what you've just written.

When you finish, look over your list. Circle or check anything that suggests interesting directions you may wish to pursue. If anything looks useless or uninteresting, scratch it out.

You can now do some conscious organizing. Look over your edited list. If you are brainstorming to find a topic for a paper, notice whether any of the thoughts are related. Can you group them? If so, maybe such a group of ideas will suggest a topic. (Once you have a topic, you might try another technique — *freewriting*, the next strategy we discuss.)

If you need an example or some details for a paper you've already started, you can brainstorm at any time. In writing her paper on computers, Martha Calbick couldn't think of a name for a typical computer store. She wrote down some real names she knew, and those triggered a few imaginary ones. Within three minutes, she hit on one she liked: Byte City.

Whether you brainstorm at your desk or in a classroom with your writing group, you will find this strategy calling up a rich array of thoughts from knowledge, memory, and imagination.

**EXERCISE**

## Brainstorming

From the following list, choose a subject that interests you, that you know something about, and that you'd like to learn more about — in other words, a subject that you might like to write a paper on. Then brainstorm for ten minutes.

| | | |
|---|---|---|
| travel | fear | exercise |
| dieting | dreams | automobiles |
| family | television | sports |
| advertisements | animals | education |

Now look over your brainstorming list and circle anything that looks as if it might work well as a topic for a paper. How well did this brainstorming exercise work for you? Can you think of any variations that would make it more useful?

## FREEWRITING

Like brainstorming, *freewriting* is a way to fight writer's block by tapping your unconscious. To freewrite, you simply begin writing in the hope that good ideas will surface. You write without stopping for fifteen or twenty minutes, trying to keep words pouring forth in a steady flow. In freewriting, unlike brainstorming, you write a series of sentences, not a list. The sentences don't have to be grammatical or coherent or stylish; just let them leap to the paper and keep them flowing. When you have just the beginning of an idea, freewriting can help open it up and show you what it contains. When you have an assignment that looks difficult, freewriting can get you under way.

Generally, freewriting is most productive if it has an aim. It's best to have in mind — at least roughly — a topic, a purpose, or a question you want answered. Before you begin, you write a sentence or two summing up the idea you're starting out with. Martha Calbick, who found a topic by brainstorming (p. 334), wrote her topic at the head of sheet of paper — "How life in the computer age seems impersonal" — and then, exploring some of her rough brainstorming ideas, she let words flow rapidly.

Computers – so how do they make life impersonal? You push in your plastic card and try to get some cash. Just a glassy screen. That's different – not like looking at a human teller behind a window. When the computer tells you you have no money left in your account, that's terrible, frightening. Worse than when a person won't cash your check. At least the person looks you in the face, maybe even gives you a faint smile. Computers make mistakes, don't they? That story in the paper about a man – in Utica, was it? – who deposited a hundred dollars to his account and the computer misplaced a decimal point and said he had put in $10,000.

The result, as you can see, wasn't polished prose. It was full of false starts and little asides to herself. Still, in twenty minutes she produced a paragraph that served (with much rewriting) as the basis for her finished essay.

If you want to try freewriting, here's what you do.

1. *Write a sentence or two at the top of your page or computer screen:* the idea you plan to develop by freewriting.

2. *For at least ten minutes, write steadily without stopping.* Start by expressing whatever comes to mind, even if it is only "I don't want to write a paper because I have nothing at all to say about any subject in the universe." If your mind goes blank, write, "My mind is blank, I don't know where to go next," and keep at it until some new thought floats into view.

3. *Don't censor yourself.* Don't stop to cross out false starts, misspellings, or grammatical errors. Never mind if your ideas have gaps between them. Later, when you look them over, some of the gaps may close. If you can't think of the word that perfectly expresses your meaning, put in a substitute. (You might draw a squiggly line under it to remind yourself to search for a better word or phrase later.) Keep your pencil moving.

4. *Feel free to explore.* The sentence or sentences you started with can serve as a rough guide, but they shouldn't be a straitjacket. If you find yourself straying from your original idea, a change in direction may be valuable.

5. *Prepare yourself* — if you want to. Some writers prepare for freewriting by spending a few minutes in thought. While you wait for the moment when your pencil starts racing, some of these questions may be worth asking yourself.

What interests you about this topic? What aspects of it do you most care about?

What do you recall about this topic from your own experience? What do you know about it that the next person doesn't?

What have you read about it? Observed about it? Heard about it from someone else?

**FOR GROUP LEARNING**

## Group Brainstorming

Here's another way to use the brainstorming exercise on page 336. Working with a small group of your classmates — or with the entire class — choose a subject from the list that everyone knows something about. After you've agreed on a subject, everyone in the group should brainstorm about it individually for ten minutes.

Then compare and contrast the brainstorming lists of everyone in the group. Notice especially the differences — how each individual's list reflects his or her personal experiences. Although several writers may start with the same subject, each writer's treatment will be unique because of differences in experience and perspective. What does this exercise tell you about the advantages or disadvantages of group brainstorming as a technique for generating topics for writing?

How might you feel about this topic if you were someone else (a parent, an instructor, a person from another country)?

At the very least, your freewriting session may give you something to expand and develop. You can poke at the parts that look most interesting to see if they will further unfold. In developing the ideas produced by freewriting, here are a few questions you might ask.

What do you mean by that?
If that is true, what then? So what?
What other examples or evidence does this statement call to mind?
What objections might your reader raise to this?
How might you answer them?

**EXERCISE**

## Freewriting

Edit one of your brainstorming lists by circling interesting ideas, deleting irrelevant or repetitious items, grouping related ideas. Select one significant idea you can explore further, put that idea at the top of a piece of paper or your computer screen, and freewrite about it for fifteen minutes. Are you further along in generating ideas for a paper? Share your freewriting with some of your classmates.

### KEEPING A JOURNAL

If you are already in the habit of keeping a journal, consider yourself lucky. If not, now is a good time to begin. Journal writing offers rich rewards to anyone who engages in it every day or several times a week. All you need is a notebook, a writing implement, and a few minutes for each entry; and you can write anywhere. For the faithful journal keeper, a journal is a mine studded with priceless nuggets: thoughts and observations, reactions and revelations that are yours for the taking. When you have an essay to write, a well-stocked journal is a treasure indeed. Rifle it freely — not only for writing topics, but

**WRITING WITH A COMPUTER**

## Invisible Writing

Invisible writing is a kind of freewriting done on a word processor. After typing your topic at the top of the screen, turn off your monitor so that you cannot read what's on the screen. (You can either turn down the contrast on your monitor or turn it off altogether.) Then freewrite. Not being able to see the words and the punctuation, you can relax and concentrate on the ideas. If you feel somewhat uneasy, just keep typing and let the ideas flow through your fingers. After ten minutes of invisible writing, turn the monitor back on, scroll to the beginning, and read what you have written.

for insights and material. "This book is my savings bank," wrote Ralph Waldo Emerson in his journal. "I grow richer because I have somewhere to deposit my earnings."

What do you write? The main thing to remember is that a journal is not a diary. When you make a journal entry, the emphasis is less on recording what happened than on *reflecting* about what you do or see, hear or read, learn or believe. A journal is a record of your thoughts, for an audience of one: yourself. In a journal you can explore dreams, try out ideas, vent fears and frustrations.

Poet Sylvia Plath found keeping a journal quite worthwhile. The following passage, from *The Journals of Sylvia Plath* (New York: Doubleday, 1982), was written in the early 1950s when she was a college freshman. Uncommonly sensitive and colorful, her entries exhibit the freedom and frankness of a writer who was writing for only her own eyes. In this entry Plath contrasts the happy fantasy world she inhabited as a child with the harsher realities of college life.

> After being conditioned as a child to the lovely never-never land of magic, of fairy queens and virginal maidens, of little princes and their rosebushes, of poignant bears and Eeyore-ish donkeys, of life personalized as the pagans loved it, of the magic wand, and the faultless illustrations — the beautiful dark-haired child (who was you) winging through the midnight sky on a star-path . . . of the Hobbit and the dwarves, gold-belted with blue and purple hoods, drinking ale and singing of dragons in the caverns of the valley — all this I knew, and felt, and believed. All this was my life when I was young. To go from this to the world of grown-up reality. . . . To feel the sex organs develop and call loud to the flesh; to become aware of school, exams (the very words as unlovely as the sound of chalk shrilling on the blackboard), bread and butter, marriage, sex, compatibility, war, economics, death, and self. What a pathetic blighting of the beauty and reality of childhood. Not to be sentimental, as I sound, but why the hell are we conditioned into the smooth strawberry-and-cream Mother Goose world, Alice-in-Wonderland fable, only to be broken on the wheel as we grow older and become aware of ourselves as individuals with a dull responsibility in life? To learn snide and smutty meanings of words you once loved, like "fairy." To go to college fraternity parties where a boy buries his face in your neck or tries to rape you if he isn't satisfied with burying his fingers in the flesh of your breast. To learn that there are a million girls who are beautiful and that each day more leave behind the awkward teenage stage, as you once did, and embark on the adventure of being loved. . . . To be aware that you must compete somehow, and yet that wealth and beauty are not in your realm.

Like Plath, to write a valuable journal you need only the honesty and the willingness to set down what you *genuinely think and feel*. When you first face that blank journal page, plunge boldly into your task by writing down whatever observation or reaction comes to mind. No one will criticize your spelling or punctuation, the way you organize your ideas or the way you express yourself. A journal entry can be a list or an outline, a paragraph or a full-blown essay, a poem or a letter you don't intend to send.

**Reflective Journal Writing.**    In this kind of entry, you have only to *uncover, recover, discover* what is happening both inside and outside your head. Describe a person or a place. As accurately as you can, set down a conversation you have heard, complete with slang or dialect or colloquialisms. Record any insights you have gained into your actions or those of others. Make comparisons. Record images. Make analogies. Play with language. Respond to something you have read or to something mentioned in a class. Do you agree with it? Disagree? Why? What was wrong with the last movie or television show you watched? What was good about it? Have you or has someone you know faced a moral dilemma? Was it resolved? If so, how? Perhaps you have some pet peeves. List them. What do you treasure? Have you had an interesting dream or daydream? What would the world be like if you were in charge? What are your religious convictions? What do you think about the current political scene or about this nation's priorities? Have you visited any foreign countries? Did you learn anything of worth from your travels? On days when your mind is sluggish, when you can come up with no observations or insights to record, do a stint of freewriting or of brainstorming. This may at least result in a few good thoughts to follow up in future entries.

Sometimes the opportunity to "write on anything you like" is daunting, especially to beginning journal writers; it may generate writer's block. We have provided some *reflective journal prompts* to help you get started. A *prompt* is simply a suggestion to get the wheels in your mind turning, to give you a possible direction or focus for writing. Reflective journal prompts are located at the beginning of each chapter in *A Writer's Reader*, right underneath the photograph. You can use them either when your class is focusing on the essays in the chapters or whenever you need an idea to write about. We hope you'll find them useful and interesting.

**Responsive Journal Writing.**    In this type of entry, you *respond* to something in particular — to the reading you've been doing for class or for an assignment, to classroom discussions or lectures, to a movie or television program, to a conversation or observation. This type of journal entry is more focused than the reflective entry. If your instructor assigns a journal, he or she will most likely want at least some responsive entries. Faced with a long paper to write and weeks or months to do it, you might assign *yourself* a response journal. Then when the time comes to write your paper, you will have plenty of material to quarry. In *A Writer's Reader* we have also included some *responsive journal prompts* to help you focus some of your entries. These prompts are located at the end of each selection. We hope you'll find them stimulating and thought-provoking.

**Warm-up Journal Writing.**    You can also use your journal to collect and explore your thoughts in preparation for an assignment. You can group ideas, scribble outlines, sketch beginnings, try out introductions, capture stray thoughts, record relevant material from any one of your five resources (recalling, observing, reading, conversing, imagining).

There's a fine line between responsive journal writing and warm-up journal writing: what starts out as a quick comment on one puzzling aspect of an essay you've read or a lecture you've heard may turn into the draft of a paper. Similarly, the responsive journal entries you write based on the prompts following the essays in *A Writer's Reader* can easily turn into warm-up journal entries for the writing suggestions that follow. (In fact, we hope they do.) In other words, don't let the categories and descriptions we've given discourage or straitjacket you. Remember: a journal can be just about anything you want it to be, and the best journal is the one that's most useful to *you*.

EXERCISE

## Journal Writing

Keep a journal for at least a week. Each day record your thoughts, feelings, and reactions. You may include some events, but go beyond what happens and include your reflections on what happens and your responses to what you read. Some of your entries may be free — on anything that comes to your mind. Try at least one of the reflective journal prompts at the beginnings of the chapters in *A Writer's Reader* and at least one of the responsive prompts following one of the reader selections. At the end of the week, bring your journal to class, select the entry you like best, and read it aloud to your classmates.

### ASKING A REPORTER'S QUESTIONS

Journalists, assembling facts to write the story of a news event, ask themselves six simple questions, the five *W*'s and an *H:*

> Who?
> What?
> Where?
> When?
> Why?
> How?

In the *lead*, or opening paragraph, of a good news story, where the writer tries to condense the whole story into a sentence or two, you will find simple answers to all six questions:

> The ascent of a giant homemade fire balloon [*what*] startled residents of Costa Mesa [*where*] last night [*when*] as Ambrose Barker, 79, [*who*] in an attempt to set a new altitude record [*why*], zigzagged across the sky at a speed of nearly 300 miles per hour. [*how*]

Later in the news story, the reporter will relate the details of the event, using the six basic questions to generate more information about what happened and why.

For your college writing you can use these six questions in a similar manner to generate specific details for your essays. Your topic in a college writing assignment may not be the spectacular narrative of a fire balloon's ascent, but you will find these questions just as helpful as the reporter does. The five *W*'s and an *H* can help you get started exploring the significance of an experience from childhood, analyzing what happened at some moment in history, or investigating a problem on campus or in your neighborhood.

The six basic questions can help you not only discover what to write about but also generate specific details to use as evidence in your essays. These questions can lead to further questions, providing you more to write about than space and time will allow. If you are using the five *W*'s and an *H* to explore a topic that is not based on your personal experience, you'll find that you have to do some research — reading or interviewing — to answer some of the questions. Take, for example, the topic of the assassination of John F. Kennedy.

*Who* was John F. Kennedy? What kind of person was he? What was his background? What kind of president was he? What were his goals? Who else was with him when he was killed? Who do most people believe shot him? What kind of person was the killer? Who was nearby?

*What* happened to Kennedy — exactly? What was he doing? What was his purpose in being where he was? What led up to the assassination? Describe the assassination itself. Describe his wounds. Was anyone else hurt? What happened immediately after the shots to Kennedy? What did the people around him do? How did his wife react? What did the police do? What did the Secret Service agents do? What did the media representatives do?

---

**WRITING WITH A COMPUTER**

## Keeping a Journal on a Word Processor

Consider keeping your journal on a computer. If you're more comfortable writing at a keyboard than with pen and paper or if you already do most of your writing with a word processor, it will be quite easy for you. If you don't already use word processing, keeping a personal journal will be a good way to practice using a word processor.

Keeping a journal on a computer allows you to explore topics easily and to expand ideas by inserting material at any point. Later you'll be able to move text from your journal to your papers (and vice versa) quickly and easily. Sometimes the word processor's ability to search comes in handy. For example, if you're assigned a paper on the homeless, you might want to search through your journal entries for the terms *homeless, shelters, street people,* and so on to see if you've already done some preliminary thinking and writing on the topic.

There will still be times when you want to use means other than a computer for your journal entries. Notebooks and pens are perfectly portable and unobtrusive, making them ideal for jotting down sudden inspirations whenever and wherever they occur, whether in the dining hall or at the bus stop. If you have to wait until you get back to your computer to record your fleeting insights, many of them may never get recorded at all.

What did everyone across the country do? What happened in the next forty-eight hours? Ask someone who remembers this event what he or she did upon hearing about the assassination.

*Where* was Kennedy assassinated? The city? The street? From where to where was he going? Did he follow the planned route? Was the route announced beforehand? What kind of vehicle was Kennedy riding in? Where was he sitting? Where were the other passengers in the vehicle sitting? Where did the shots likely come from? What path did they likely follow? Where did the shots hit Kennedy? Where did Kennedy die? How did he get there?

*When* was he assassinated — the day, month, year, time? When did Kennedy decide to go to this city? When — precisely — were the shots fired? When did he die? When was a suspect arrested?

*Why* was Kennedy assassinated? What are some of the theories of the assassination? What solid evidence is available to explain the assassination? Why was a suspect arrested so soon? Why has his assassination caused so much controversy? Why are most of the records related to his assassination still sealed?

*How* was Kennedy assassinated? What kind of weapon was used? How many shots were fired? How did he die? Specifically what caused his death? How can we get at the truth of how and why he was assassinated?

Don't worry if some of the questions lead nowhere or don't seem relevant or if some lead to repetitious answers. Just jot down any thoughts and information that come to you. You are trying to gather ideas and material. Later, before you start to write, you'll want to weed out the frivolous and irrelevant ones, keeping only those that look promising for your topic.

EXERCISE

## Asking a Reporter's Questions

Choose one of the following topics, or use one of your own.

a memorable event in history
an unforgettable event in your life
a concert that you have seen
an accomplishment on campus
an occurrence in your city
an important speech
a proposal for change
a questionable stand someone has taken

Answer the six reporter's questions about the topic. Then write a thesis in which you synthesize the answers to the six questions into one sentence. Incorporate that thesis sentence into an introductory paragraph for an essay that you might write later.

## SEEKING MOTIVES

In a surprisingly large part of your college writing, you will try to explain human behavior. In a paper for history, you might show why Lyndon Baines Johnson decided not to seek a second full term as president. In a report for a psychology course, you might try to explain the behavior of people in an experimental situation. In a literature course, you might analyze the motives of Hester Prynne in *The Scarlet Letter*. Because people, including characters in fiction, are so complex, this task is challenging. But here is a strategy useful in seeking out human motives.

If you want to understand any human act, according to philosopher-critic Kenneth Burke, you can break it down into five basic components and ask questions about each one.

1. The *act:* What was done?
2. The *actor:* Who did it?
3. The *agency:* What means did the person use to make it happen?
4. The *scene:* Where and when did the act happen and in what circumstances?
5. The *purpose or motive* for acting: What could have made the person do it?

As you can see, Burke's *pentad,* or set of five components, covers much the same ground as the reporter's questions. But Burke's method differs in that it can show how the components of a human act affect one another. This line of thought can take you deeper into the motives for human behavior than most reporters' investigations ever go.

How might you apply the method? Say you are writing a paper on Lyndon Johnson's decision not to run for a second term. The five components might be these:

*Act:* Announcing the decision to leave office without standing for reelection.

*Actor:* President Johnson.

*Agency:* A televised address to the nation.

*Scene* (including circumstances at the time): Washington, D.C., March 31, 1968. Protesters against the nation's involvement in Vietnam were gaining in numbers and influence. The press was increasing its criticism of the president's escalation of the war. Senator Eugene McCarthy, an antiwar candidate for president, had made a strong showing against Johnson in the New Hampshire primary election.

*Purpose:* Possible purposes might include to avoid a probable defeat, to escape further personal attacks, to spare his family, to make it easier for his successor to pull the country out of the war, and to ease bitter dissent among Americans.

To further apply Burke's method, you can begin fruitful lines of inquiry by asking questions that pair the five components:

| | | |
|---|---|---|
| actor to act | act to scene | scene to agency |
| actor to scene | act to agency | scene to purpose |
| actor to agency | act to purpose | agency to purpose |
| actor to purpose | | |

For the paper about Lyndon Johnson, you might ask, "What did the actor [Johnson] have to do with the agency [his televised address]?" Your answer might be something like "Commanding the attention of a vast audience, Johnson must have felt he was in control — even though his ability to control the situation in Vietnam was slipping."

The value of Burke's questions is that they can start you writing. Not all the questions will prove fruitful, and some may not even apply. But one or two individual questions or pairs might reveal valuable answers.

EXERCISE

### Seeking Motives

Choose an action that puzzles you. It may be one of the following.

Something you have done
An action of a family member or a friend
A decision of a historical or current political figure
Something in a movie or television program
An occurrence in a literary selection

Then apply Burke's pentad to this action to try to determine the individual's motives. If Burke's five basic categories do not go far enough to help you understand the human act, team up the components (see p. 345) to perceive deeper relationships. When you believe you understand the individual's motivation, write a paragraph explaining the action, and share it with your classmates.

# Getting Ready

Once you have generated a suitable topic and some ideas related to that topic, you are ready to get down to the job of actually writing. Sometimes at this point, your mind goes blank or you just don't know what to do next. Here are some suggestions that we hope will help you.

## SETTING UP CIRCUMSTANCES

Get Comfortable.   We don't just mean turn on a bright light because it's good for your eyes. Why not create an environment? If you can write only with your shoes off or with a can of Orange Crush, set yourself up that way. Some writers need a radio blaring heavy metal; others need quiet. Circumstances that put you in the mood for writing can encourage you.

Devote One Special Place to Writing.   When you go to your special place, your mind and body will be ready to settle in and get to work. Your place may be a desk in your bedroom, the dining room table, or a lap board on a den sofa. It may be a quiet cubicle in a corner of the library. It should be a place where no one will bother you when you are working. It should have good lighting and plenty of space to spread out. If it's at home or in your dorm, try to make it a place where you can leave projects you are working on, where you can keep your pens, paper, typewriter or word processor, dictionary, and other reference materials.

**Establish a Ritual.**   Many writers follow certain routines to get themselves in the mood for writing. You might get a drink, turn the radio on (or off), sharpen your pencils, turn on the computer, check your paper supply, and straighten the things on your desk. Some writers find that following a writing ritual relaxes them enough to think clearly and write effectively.

**Relocate.**   If you're not getting anywhere with your writing, change places. If you usually write in the college library, try writing at home. If you usually write at a desk in the den, relocate to your bedroom. Try writing in an unfamiliar place: a bowling alley, a restaurant, an airport, a mall. The noises around you and the curiosity of passersby might cause you to concentrate hard on your writing.

**Reduce Distractions.**   Most of us can't prevent interruptions when we are trying to concentrate, but we can reduce them. If you are expecting your boyfriend to call, call him before you start writing. If you have small children, write when they are asleep or at school. Turn on the answering machine for the telephone. Do all you can to let people around you know you are serious about writing and allow yourself to give your full attention to it.

**Exhaust Your Excuses.**   Most writers are born experts at coming up with reasons not to write; if you are one of those writers, you might find that it helps to run out of reasons. Is your room annoyingly jumbled? Straighten it. Drink that can of soda, sharpen those pencils, throw out that trash, and make that phone call. Then, your room, your desk, and your mind swept clean, you can sit down and write.

**Yield to Inspiration.**   Classical Greek and Roman critics held that a goddess called a Muse would gently touch a poet and leave him inspired. Whether or not you believe in divine inspiration, sometimes ideas, images, metaphors, or vague but powerful urges to write will arrive like sudden miracles. When they come, even if you are taking a shower or getting ready to go to a movie, yield to impulse and write. At these times you will probably find that words will flow with little exertion. If going to that movie is irresistible, jot down enough notes beforehand to rekindle your ideas later when you can go back to writing.

**Write at the Time Best for You.**   Some people think best early in the morning, others in the afternoon or late at night. Try writing in the small hours when the world is still. Before you are wholly awake, your stern self-critic might not be awake yet either. (When you edit and proofread, though, you want to be fully awake.) Or take a nap in the afternoon and write from 10:00 P.M. until 2:00 or 3:00 A.M. Writing at dawn or the wee hours, you also will have fewer distractions from other people.

**Write on a Schedule.**   Many writers find that it helps to have a certain predictable time of day to write. This method won't work for all, but it worked marvels for English novelist Anthony Trollope. Each day Trollope would start at 5:30 A.M., write 2,500 words before 8:30 A.M., and then go to his job at the General Post Office. (He wrote more than sixty books.) Even if you can't write at the same time every day, it may help to decide, "Today from four to five, I'll sit down and write."

**Defy a Schedule.**   If you write on a schedule and your work isn't going well, break out of your usual time frame. If you are an afternoon writer, write at night, and vice versa.

## PREPARING YOUR MIND

**Discuss Your Plans.**   Collar any nearby listener: roommate, student down the hall, spouse, parent, friend. Tell the other person why you want to write this particular paper, what you're going to put into it, how you're going to lay out your material. If the other person says, "That sounds good," you'll be encouraged; but even if the reaction is a yawn, at least you will have set your own thinking in motion.

**Keep a Notebook Handy.**   Always have some paper in your pocket or purse or on the night table to write down those good ideas whenever they pop into your mind. Imagination may strike in the checkout lane of the supermarket, in the doctor's waiting room, or during a lull on the job. Take advantage of those calm times, and write down your ideas so that you won't forget them.

**Keep a Daily Journal.**   Use a journal to record your experiences as a writer. Scribbling in a journal for fifteen minutes a day can nourish your writing. You might note writing problems you run into (and overcome), ideas for things you'd like to write, reactions to your writing from other people, writing strategies that work well. You can record your reading and your reactions to it, track your progress in any course, or save stray thoughts. (For more detailed suggestions about journals, see p. 339.)

**Read.**   The step from reading to writing is a short one. Read whatever you feel like reading. Read for fun. Even when you're just reading for kicks, you start to involve yourself with words. Who knows, you might also hit upon something useful for your paper. Or read purposefully. If you have a specific topic or a general notion for one, set out to read and take notes.

# Chapter 16

# Strategies for Planning

Starting to write often seems a chaotic activity, but to reduce the chaos and create order you can use the strategies in this chapter. For most papers you write — and certainly for all papers that rely on critical thinking — you will want to focus your writing around a central point. For help with this, see the first section in this chapter, "Stating and Using a Thesis." In nearly any kind of writing task, you can make better use of your material if it is sensibly arranged. For more help with this, see "Organizing Your Ideas" (p. 710), which includes advice on grouping ideas and on outlining.

## Stating and Using a Thesis

Most pieces of effective writing make one main point. All ideas in an essay or article are unified around that point; that is, all the subpoints and details are relevant to the point. In "What Is a Hunter?" (p. 18), student Robert G. Schreiner maintains that there is more to being a hunter than knowing how to use a rifle. In "The Myth of the Latin Woman: I Just Met a Girl Named María" (p. 504), Judith Ortiz Cofer claims that Latinas cannot escape the misconceptions about the Latin woman. After you have read such an essay, you can sum up the writer's main point in a sentence, even if the author has not stated it explicitly. We call this summary statement a *thesis*.

Often the thesis — the writer's main point — will be *explicit*, plainly stated, in the piece of writing itself. Ortiz Cofer states her thesis in the last sentence of the first paragraph of her essay — "You can leave the Island, master the English language, and travel as far as you can, but if you are a Latina, especially one like me who so obviously belongs to Rita Moreno's gene pool, the Island travels with you" — and rephrases it in paragraph 14: "For them [most Latin women] life is a struggle against the misconceptions perpetuated by the myth of the Latina as whore, domestic or criminal." Such clear statements strategically placed as well as her title help readers see her main point unmistakably.

In some writing, a thesis may be *implicit*, implied rather than directly stated. In "Once More to the Lake," E. B. White (p. 462) clearly focuses on the realization of his own mortality. All the descriptive and narrative details from the past and the present, the references to time, and the allusions to his relationships with his father and his son culminate in the final sentence: "As he [the son] buckled the swollen belt, suddenly my groin felt the chill of death." Although White does not state his main point in one concise sentence, after you have read his essay you know that he is keenly aware that one generation is quickly and inevitably replaced by the next.

The purpose of most academic and business writing is to inform, to explain, or to convince, and to achieve any of these purposes you must make your main point crystal clear. A thesis sentence will help you clarify your main idea in your own mind, and it will help you stay on track as you write. If your thesis is clear in your final paper, it will also help your readers readily see your point and follow your discussion. Sometimes you may want to imply your thesis as E. B. White does in his essay, but for most of your writing you will communicate more effectively with your readers if you state your thesis explicitly so that readers cannot miss it. In either case, for almost every essay you write, discovering and stating a thesis is a useful planning strategy.

## DISCOVERING YOUR THESIS

Don't be dismayed if your thesis does not come to you early in the writing process. In fact, it's rare for a writer to develop a clear thesis statement early in the process and then write an effective essay that fits it exactly. What you should aim for is a *working thesis* — a statement that can guide you in your writing but that you will ultimately refocus and refine. Trying to discover and state a working thesis is far less intimidating (and less likely to cause writer's block) than trying to find the perfect sentence before you've even written a first draft.

**FOR GROUP LEARNING**

## Identifying Theses

Working in a small group, select five essays from Part One and Part Two of this book to analyze (or your instructor may choose the essays for your group). Then, individually, write out the thesis for each essay. Some thesis sentences are stated outright (explicit), but others are implied (implicit). Compare and contrast the thesis statements that you identified with the statements of your classmates and discuss the similarities and differences. How can you account for the differences? Try to agree on a thesis statement for each essay.

Look back over your notes or your brainstorming or freewriting results and see if you can generalize from them. Write several tentative thesis sentences. Try some of the strategies for generating ideas or for getting started. Brainstorm titles — the title is usually a shortened form of the thesis. Freewrite the introduction or conclusion. Write a one-paragraph summary of your paper. Often during the interplay among a writer's mind, the English language, and a piece of paper or a computer screen, an insight will occur. Talk your ideas over with a friend, or tape-record your rambling thoughts about your topic. Whenever such a discovery appears to you, set it down and try it out on your peer group or your instructor.

A useful thesis contains not only the *topic* you're writing about but also the *point* you want to make or the *attitude* you intend to take. If you decide to write on the topic "the decline of old-fashioned formal courtesy toward women," you've indicated the area to be explored, but that topic doesn't tell you the point of your paper. If you say, "Old-fashioned formal courtesy toward women is a thing of the past," you are talking in circles. But a *working thesis* might be "As the roles of men and women have changed in our society, old-fashioned formal courtesy toward women has declined." Then you could focus on how changing attitudes in society have caused many men to stop exercising the old-fashioned courtesies toward women. What other thesis sentences might you come up with for this topic?

In some college writing it's easy to let the formal requirements of the assignment distract you from the purpose of writing and the point you should be making in the paper. For example, when you write a comparison and contrast paper, don't fall into the trap of thinking that the point of your paper is to compare and contrast. If you are going to compare and contrast two local newspapers in their coverage of a Senate election, ask yourself what is the point of that comparison and contrast. A suitable thesis would *not* be "The coverage of the Senate elections by the *Herald* was different from that of the *Courier*." A more satisfactory thesis sentence might be "The *Herald*'s coverage of the Senate elections was more thorough than the *Courier*'s."

**EXERCISE**

## Discovering a Thesis

Generalize about each of the following groups of details to find a working thesis for each group. Then compare and contrast your theses with those of your classmates. What other information would you need to write a good paper on each of these topics? How might the thesis statement change as you write the paper?

1. Cigarettes are expensive.
   Cigarettes can cause fires.
   Cigarettes cause unpleasant odors.
   Cigarettes can cause health problems to the smoker.
   Secondhand smoke from cigarettes can cause health problems.
2. Clinger College has a highly qualified faculty.
   Clinger College has an excellent curriculum in my field.

Clinger College has a beautiful campus.
Clinger College is expensive.
Clinger College has offered me a scholarship.

3. Crisis centers report that date rape is increasing.
Most date rape is not reported to the police.
Often the victim of date rape is not believed.
Sometimes the victim of date rape is blamed.
Sometimes the victim of date rape blames herself.
The effects of date rape stay with a woman for years.

## HOW TO STATE A THESIS

Once you have a notion of what your thesis might be, you should try to state it in a way that will be useful to you as you plan and draft the essay. Here are four suggestions for writing a workable thesis statement.

1. *State the thesis sentence exactly.* Use concise, detailed, and down-to-earth language. The statement "There are a lot of troubles with chemical wastes" is too general. Are you going to deal with all chemical wastes, through all of history, all over the world? Are you going to list all the troubles they can cause? Make the statement more specific: "Careless dumping of leftover paint is to blame for a recent skin rash in Atlanta." Now you have a concise, restricted statement that you can use as the basis for a brief essay.

2. *State just one central idea in the thesis sentence.* If your paper is to focus on one point, your thesis should state only one main idea. This statement has one idea too many: "Careless dumping of leftover paint has caused a serious problem in Atlanta, and a new kind of biodegradable paint now looks promising." Either the first half or the second half of the statement would suffice and lead you to a unified essay.

3. *State your thesis positively.* You can usually find evidence to support a positive statement, but you can't prove a negative one. Write "The causes of breast cancer remain a challenge for medical scientists" instead of "Medical scientists do not know what causes breast cancer." The former statement might lead to a paper about an exciting quest. But the latter statement seems to reflect a halfhearted attitude by the writer. Besides, to demonstrate that some medical scientists are still working on the problem would be relatively easy: you could show that after an hour of research in a library. To prove that not one medical scientist knows the answer would be a very difficult task.

4. *Limit your thesis sentence to a statement that is possible to demonstrate.* A thesis sentence should stake out enough territory for you to cover thoroughly within the assigned word length and the time available, and no more. To maintain throughout a 700-word paper the thesis "My favorite piece of music is Beethoven's Fifth Symphony" would be a difficult task because you would need to explain how and why it is your favorite and contrast it with *all* the other musical compositions you know. The statement "For centuries, popular music has been indicative of vital trends in Western society" wouldn't

do for a 700-word paper either: that thesis would be enough to inform a whole encyclopedia of music. "In the past two years, a rise in the number of preteenagers has resulted in a comeback for heavy metal on our local concert scene" — now that thesis idea sounds much more likely. You could cover it in a brief 500-to-800-word essay.

Let's try a few more examples of thesis sentences:

"Indian blankets are very beautiful." That statement is too vague and hard to demonstrate for a usual college writing assignment of 500 to 800 words.

"American Indians have adapted to modern civilization." That sounds too large, too unrestricted, unless you plan to write a 5,000-word paper in sociology.

"Members of the Apache tribe are skilled workers in high-rise construction." You could probably find support for that thesis by spending a couple of hours in a library.

EXERCISE

## Examining Thesis Statements

Discuss each of the following thesis sentences with your classmates. Answer these questions for each:

Is the thesis stated exactly?
Does the thesis state just one idea?
Is the thesis stated positively?
Is the thesis sufficiently limited for 500 to 800 words?
How might the thesis be improved?

1. Teenagers should not get married.
2. Cutting classes is like a disease.
3. Going to college prepares a person for the future, and it is increasingly expensive.
4. Students have developed a variety of techniques to conceal inadequate study from their instructors.
5. Older people often imitate teenagers.
6. There are many different types of students in college today.
7. Violence on television can be harmful to children.
8. Teachers have influenced my life.
9. I don't know how to change the oil in my car.
10. My hobbies are scuba diving, playing the guitar, and motocross racing.

## HOW TO USE A THESIS

Often a good, clear statement of a thesis will suggest an organization for your ideas. Say you plan to write a paper with the thesis "Despite the several disadvantages of living in a downtown business district, I wouldn't live anywhere else." That thesis sentence suggests how to organize your essay. You could start with several paragraphs discussing disadvantages of living in the business district, move on to a few paragraphs discussing the advantages, and then close with an affirmation of your fondness for downtown city life. (For more on using a thesis to develop an outline, see "Outlining," p. 358.)

A clear statement of the main idea in your thesis will also help keep you on track as you write. Just putting your trial thesis into words can help you stake out the territory you need to know better. You can refer to it as you select details and as you make connections between sections of the essay.

As you write, however, you don't have to cling to a thesis for dear life. If some facts or notions don't seem to fit, you can change your thesis as you write. You might think that you want to write a paper on the thesis "Because wolves are a menace to people and farm animals, they ought to be exterminated." If further investigation doesn't support that statement, your thesis isn't chiseled in marble. You can change it to "The wolf, a relatively peaceful animal useful in nature's scheme of things, ought to be protected," if that is the idea your investigation has led you to. The purpose of a thesis statement is to guide you on a quest, not to limit your ideas and put your thinking in a straitjacket. You can restate it at any time: as you write, as you revise, as you revise again.

## Organizing Your Ideas

After you have generated and gathered ideas on your topic by using the five resources of a writer — recall, observation, conversation, reading, and imagination — and employing the strategies for generating ideas (see Chapter 15), and after you have focused your ideas by stating a working thesis, you next need to plan an order for the ideas, determine how you might organize the information. Each of the chapters in Part One and Part Two of this book discusses possible organizational patterns for the particular assignment, but the following sections give you some general advice on organizing and discuss two strategies to help you — grouping ideas and outlining.

When you organize the information in an essay, you select an order for the parts that makes sense and shows your readers how the ideas are connected. If describing a place, you might use spatial organization, moving from left to right or bottom to top. You want to choose an order for the details that will make it easy for readers to visualize. Mark Twain describes a scene on the Mississippi River by beginning with the dock and moving to the steamboat coming into the landing, over the broad expanse of the river to the shore on the other side, and finally up through the trees to the clouds in the sky. If narrating an event or explaining the steps in a procedure, you would use chronological or time order — what happens first and next and next until the end. Gary Soto in "Black Hair" (p. 547) uses chronological order to tell what happened to him on his first job. If explaining an idea or trying to persuade readers, you would use some variation of logical order — for example, general to specific, specific to general, least important to most important, cause to effect, or problem to solution. In writing an essay on the results of the 1995 earthquake in Japan, you might select four major effects and arrange them in ascending order, placing the most important one last for emphasis. Following are some techniques to help you select an order for your ideas.

## GROUPING YOUR IDEAS

In the scribblings you have made while exploring a topic, you will usually find a few ideas that seem to belong together — two facts on New York traffic jams, four actions of New York drivers, three problems with New York streets. But similar ideas are seldom together in your list because you did not discover them all at the same time. As you look over your preliminary notes, indicate to yourself any connections you find among your materials. You'll need to sort your notes into groups, arrange them in sequences. Here are six common ways to work.

1. *Rainbow connections.* List on a sheet of paper all the main points you're going to express. Don't recopy all the material — just list each main point briefly, not worrying about order. Then, taking colored pencils, circle with the same color any points that go together. When you write, follow the color code and deal with similar ideas at the same time.

2. *Linking.* Start by making a list of major points, and then draw lines that link related ideas. Number each linked group to remember in what sequence to deal with the ideas. Figure 16.1 is an illustration of a linked list pro-

FIGURE 16.1.    The Linking Method for Grouping Ideas

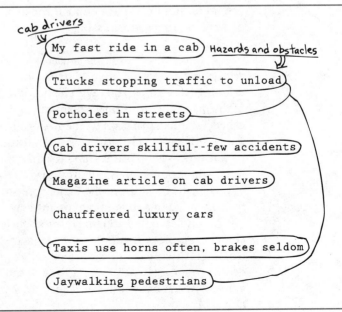

duced by one writer in a brainstorming session for an essay to be called "Manhattan Driving." The writer has drawn lines connecting points that go together and has supplied each linked group with a heading. When he writes his draft, each heading will probably inspire a topic sentence or a few lines to introduce each major division of his essay. One point failed to relate to any other: "Chauffeured luxury cars." In the finished paper, he will leave it out.

3. *Solitaire.* Collect notes and ideas on roomy (5-by-8-inch) file cards. To organize, spread out the cards and arrange and rearrange them, as in a game of solitaire. When the order looks worth keeping, when each idea seems to lead to the next, gather all the cards into a deck once more. Then when you write, deal yourself a card at a time and translate its contents into sentences. This technique is particularly helpful when you write about literature or when you write from research.

4. *Scissors and tape.* Lay out your rough notes and group the ones that refer to the same point and that probably belong in the same vicinity. With scissors, separate items that don't belong together. Shuffle the pieces around, trying for the most promising order. After throwing out any ideas that don't belong anywhere, lock up the material into a structure and join all the parts with tape. If you find places in the grand design where ideas and information are lacking, make a note of what's missing and tape that note into place. This taped-together construction of cards or slips of paper serves as a workable outline.

You may use this strategy for planning and drafting simultaneously. Tape together not just notes but separate passages you have written. Write whatever part you want to write first, then the next most tempting part, and so on until you have enough rough stuff to arrange into a whole piece of writing. Then add missing parts and supply transitions (discussed on pp. 380–83).

5. *Clustering.* Clustering is useful for coming up with ideas, but it is just as valuable as a visual method of grouping those ideas. For clustering, in the middle of a piece of paper write your topic in a word or a phrase. Then think of the major divisions into which this topic might be organized. For an essay called "Manhattan Drivers," the major divisions might be the *types* of Manhattan drivers: (1) taxi drivers, (2) bus drivers, (3) truck drivers, (4) drivers of private cars — New Yorkers, and (5) drivers of private cars — out-of-town visitors. Arrange these divisions around your topic on your page and circle them too. Draw lines out from the major topic to the subdivisions. You now have the beginning of a rough plan for an essay.

Around each division, make another cluster of points you're going to include: examples, illustrations, facts, statistics, bits of evidence, opinions, whatever. Circle each specific item and connect it to the appropriate type of driver. When you write your paper, you can expand the details into one paragraph for each type of driver. Figure 16.2 presents a cluster for "Manhattan Drivers."

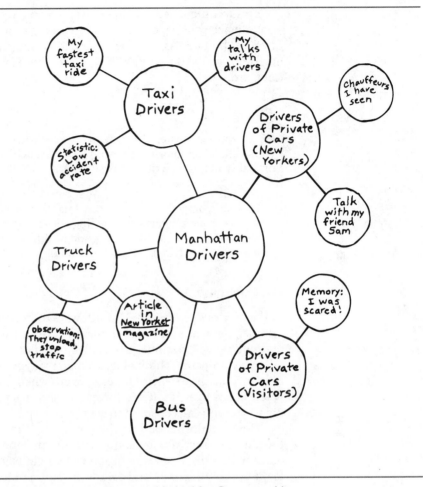

FIGURE 16.2.   The Clustering Method for Generating Ideas

**WRITING
WITH A
COMPUTER**

## Arranging Ideas On-Screen

Many writers arrange their rough notes into groups right on the computer screen, moving items from place to place until they like the resulting plan. Cutting and pasting is quicker and easier with a word processor than with scissors and tape, and the word processor's ability to create and store multiple versions makes it possible for you to try out different schemes of organizing before deciding on any one of them. Using a word processor, you can also move smoothly from grouping ideas to creating an outline without having to rewrite your notes. (For more on rearranging text, see "Moving Blocks of Text" on pp. 447–48.)

This technique lets you know where you have enough specific information to make your paper clear and interesting — and where you don't. If one of your subtopics has no small circles around it (such as "bus drivers" in Figure 16.2), you should think of some specific examples to expand it; if you can't, drop it.

EXERCISE

## Clustering

Generate idea clusters for three of the following topics. Share them with your classmates or writing group. Discuss which one of the three would probably help you write the best paper.

| | |
|---|---|
| teachers | U.S. presidents |
| television programs | civil rights |
| my favorite restaurants | drug abuse |
| fast food | good health |
| leisure-time activities | technology |

### OUTLINING

In the previous section, we set forth ways to bring related thoughts together. Another, perhaps more familiar means to organize ideas is to outline. A written outline, whether brief or detailed, shouldn't say *everything* you plan to write in your paper. Think of it as a map that you make before setting out on a journey. It shows where to leave from, where to stop along the way, and where at last to arrive. If you forget where you are going or what you are trying to say, you can consult it to get back on track.

How detailed an outline will you need? The answer depends in part on the kind of writer you are and in part on the kind of writing you are doing. Some writers like to lay out the job very carefully in advance; others prefer to lay it out more loosely and follow an outline more casually. Often college writers find an *informal outline* — perhaps just a list of points to make — is enough. If you are working with familiar material, such a brief outline will probably be sufficient. If you are dealing with complex, unfamiliar information, you'll probably need a more detailed *formal outline* to keep from getting lost. Do people tell you your writing isn't well organized and that they can't follow you? Then probably you would benefit from using a more detailed plan. Do they tell you your writing sounds mechanical? Maybe your outline is constricting you. Once you complete your essay, your outline and the essay should go hand in hand. Often instructors require that you turn in an outline with the final essay so that readers can have a skeletal summary of what your essay contains in the order you have arranged the information.

**Informal Outlines.**   For in-class writing and for brief essays, often a *short* or *informal outline*, also called a *scratch outline*, will serve your needs. It is just a brief list of points to make, in the order you plan to make them. The short outline is only for your eyes. When the writing job is done, you pitch the outline along with your preliminary drafts into the trash basket.

The following is an informal outline for a 600-word paper contrasting city drivers with small-town drivers. Its thesis sentence is "City drivers are quite different from small-town drivers." One obvious way to proceed is to think of and list the specific areas of contrast (perhaps physical fitness, skill, and consideration). Then, for each quality, the writer would discuss first city drivers and then small-town drivers — how they do or don't exhibit the characteristic. The writer could put this plan in scratch form like this:

Introduction: Different driving habits

1. Physical fitness

   - City drivers: little time and space in which to exercise

   - Small-town drivers: lifestyle conducive to physical ease

2. Skill at the wheel

   - City drivers: small, crowded streets

   - Small-town drivers: narrow streets

3. Consideration for others

   - City drivers: tendency to vent their aggressions at the wheel

   - Small-town drivers: laid-back attitude toward life reflected in driving habits

Conclusion: I'd rather drive in a small town

A simple outline like that could easily fall into a five-paragraph essay. If you have a great deal to say, though, the essay might well run longer — perhaps to eight paragraphs: introduction, conclusion, and three pairs of paragraphs in between. You probably won't know until you write the paper exactly how many paragraphs you'll need.

An informal outline can be even briefer than the preceding one. If you were writing an in-class essay, an answer to an examination question, or a very short paper, your outline might be no more than an *outer plan* — three or four phrases jotted down in a list.

Physical fitness

Skill

Consideration for others

Often a clear thesis statement (see p. 352) will suggest a way to outline. If the thesis contains a plural word (such as *benefits* or *advantages* or *teenagers*), you can make a list of outline headings related to the plural word. If one part of the thesis sentence is subordinate to another (beginning with *because* or *since* or *although*, for instance), you can analyze according to the parts of the sentence. Let's say you are assigned, for an anthropology course, a paper on the people of Melanesia. You decide to focus on the following idea:

Thesis: Although the Melanesian pattern of family life may look strange to westerners, it fosters a degree of independence that rivals our own.

Laying out ideas in the same order as they follow in that thesis statement, you might make a short, simple outline like this:

1. Features that appear strange to westerners
   - A woman supported by her brother, not her husband
   - Trial marriages usual
   - Divorce from her children possible for any mother

2. Admirable results of system
   - Wives not dependent on husbands for support
   - Divorce between mates uncommon
   - Greater freedom for parents and children

This informal outline might result in an essay that naturally falls into two parts: features that seem strange and admirable results of the system. In writing and thinking further, you will need to flesh out that outline with more details.

Say you plan to write a "how-to" essay analyzing the process of buying a used car. Your thesis statement might read:

Thesis: Despite traps that lie in wait for the unwary, you can get a good deal in a used car if you prepare yourself before you shop.

The key word in this sentence is *prepare,* and you ask yourself *how* the buyer should prepare himself or herself. What should he or she do before shopping for a used car? You think of several things, and you analyze the key word *prepare* into those parts:

- Read car magazine and <u>Consumer Reports</u>
- Check ads in the newspapers
- Make phone calls to several dealers
- Talk to friends who have bought used cars
- Know what to look and listen for when you test drive
- Have a mechanic check it out

Follow this sequence of ideas in your paper. You can start your paper with some horror stories about people who got taken by car sharks and then proceed to list and discuss, point by point, your bits of advice. Of course, you can always change the sequence, add an idea or take one out, or revise your thesis sentence if you find it makes sense to do so as you go along.

Formal Outlines.    A *formal outline* is an elaborate job built with time and care. It is probably more than you need for brief writings. As a guide for long, complex papers, it can help you express your ideas in an orderly manner.

In college, a formal outline is usually used for ambitious projects. Because long reports, research papers, and honors theses require so much work, some academic professors and departments ask a writer to submit a formal outline at an early stage of the project before proceeding and to include it in the final draft.

A formal outline offers the greatest amount of guidance that an outline can give. In a clear, logical way, it spells out where you are going. It shows how ideas relate one to another. It shows which ideas are equal and important (*coordinate*) and which are less important (*subordinate*).

When you make a formal outline, you place your thesis sentence at the beginning. Then you list your major points and label them with roman numerals: I, II, III. These points support and develop the main idea of your whole paper. Then you break down these points into divisions with capital letters, indenting them: A, B, C. You subdivide those into divisions with arabic numbers — 1, 2, 3 — indenting further, and then subdivide those into divisions with small letters — a, b, c — indenting yet again. Align like-numbered or -lettered headings under one another. As indentations go farther in, ideas become more specific.

```
Thesis:

    I.
        A.
            1.
                a.
                b.
            2.
                a.
                b.
        B.
            1.
            2.
    II.
```

The outline would continue until fully developed. If you have so much material that you have to subdivide still further, arabic numerals and small letters in parentheses are commonly used, but only hugely complicated writing projects need that much subdivision. Be sure to cast all headings in parallel grammatical form: phrases or sentences, but not both in the same outline.

A *formal topic outline* for a long paper about city and small-town drivers might be constructed as follows. Notice that the writer decided to drop the subdivision "physical fitness" because it is not directly related to the subject of driving habits.

```
               Drivers in Cities and Small Towns

Thesis: Different lifestyles cause city drivers to be more
aggressive than small-town drivers.
    I. Lifestyles of drivers
        A. Fast-paced, stress-filled lifestyle of city drivers
            1. Aggressive
            2. Impatient
```

        3. Tense

        4. Often frustrated

    B. Slow-paced lifestyle of small-town drivers

        1. Laid back

        2. Patient

        3. Relaxed

        4. Not easily upset

II. Resulting behavior as drivers

    A. City drivers

        1. Little consideration for other drivers

            a. Horn blowing

            b. Shouting

            c. Not using proper signals

                (1) Turning across lanes

                (2) Stopping without warning

        2. Disregard for pedestrians

        3. Speeding

            a. Running red lights

            b. Having many accidents

    B. Small-town drivers

        1. Considerate of other drivers

            a. Driving defensively

            b. Less yelling

            c. Signaling

                (1) For turning

                (2) For stopping

        2. Regard for pedestrians

        3. Driving within speed limits

            a. Observing traffic lights

            b. Fewer accidents

If a topic outline is not thorough enough to help you know what you want to say or how to say it or to indicate to you how ideas relate, you should consider a *sentence outline*, using complete sentences for the topic headings. Some people use a topic outline as a step in developing a full-blown sentence outline. The following is a sentence outline on types of drivers. When the headings are changed to sentences, relationships between ideas are clearer and changes in wording are needed, even in the thesis. Truly, the sentence outline can be a step in clarifying what you intend to say in the essay, but you cannot be sure how the ideas will fit together until you write the draft itself. Although you may not need to use a sentence outline for all of the papers you write in college, knowing how to construct such a complete outline will prove valuable for long, complex papers.

### Drivers in Cities and Small Towns

Thesis: Because of more stressful lives, city drivers are more aggressive drivers than small-town drivers.

I. The lives of city drivers are more stress-filled than are the lives of small-town drivers.
   A. City drivers are always in a hurry.
      1. They are impatient.
      2. They are often frustrated.
   B. Small-town drivers live slower-paced lives.
      1. They are relaxed.
      2. They are seldom frustrated on the streets.

II. As a result of the tension they live with constantly, city drivers are more aggressive than are small-town drivers.
   A. City drivers are aggressive.
      1. They show little consideration for other drivers.
         a. They blow their horns often.
         b. They shout at other drivers frequently.
      2. They show little respect for pedestrians.
      3. They do not obey traffic laws.
         a. They do not use proper signals.
         b. They turn across lanes.
         c. They stop without warning.
         d. They speed.
      4. They have many accidents.
   B. Small-town drivers are laid back.
      1. They are considerate of other drivers.
         a. They drive carefully.
         b. They rarely yell or honk at other drivers.
      2. They show concern for pedestrians.
      3. They obey traffic laws.
         a. They use proper signals.
         b. They turn properly.
         c. They stop slowly.

```
                    d. They speed less.
            4. They have fewer accidents.
```

Caution.    Some readers and instructors grow wrathful if you write only one lonesome item as a subcategory, thinking that you can't divide anything into one part (and that's what an outline does — divide or analyze ideas). Let's say that in an outline on earthquakes you write:

```
      D. Probable results of an earthquake
            1. Houses stripped of their paint
```

If you tell your reader — and yourself — that you are going to discuss the *probable results* of an earthquake, logically you need to include more than one result. If that one point is all you have to say, then why not just combine your categories:

```
      D. Houses stripped of paint during an earthquake
```

More likely, your use of only one subpoint indicates that you need to do more thinking, to discover more evidence. With a little more thought or reading, you might write:

```
      D. Probable results of an earthquake
            1. Houses stripped of their paint
            2. Cracks in foundations
            3. Gaps in road surfaces
            4. Collapsed bridges
            5. Broken water mains
```

Not only have you now come up with more points, but you have also arranged them in an order of increasing importance, placing the most im-

---

 **FOR GROUP LEARNING**

## Outlining

Discuss the formal topic outline on pages 362–63 with some of your classmates or the entire class. Answer the following questions.

1. Would this outline guide a student writer in organizing an essay? Is the organization logical? Is it easy to follow? Try to think of other possible arrangements for the ideas.
2. Does this outline indicate sufficient details to develop a paper? About how many words would an essay developed from this outline be?
3. What possible pitfalls would the writer using this outline need to avoid?

portant last for emphasis. This careful planning will save you some decisions when you write ("Now, which of these results do I deal with first?").

EXERCISE

## Outlining

1. Select one of your groups of ideas from the exercises in Chapter 15. Using those ideas, construct a formal topic outline that might serve as a guide for an essay.
2. Now turn that topic outline into a formal sentence outline.
3. Discuss both outlines with your classmates and your instructor, bringing up any difficulties you encountered. If you get any better notions for organizing your ideas, change the outline.
4. Write an essay based on your outline.

# *Making Connections:*
# *Strategies for Planning Evident in* A Writer's Reader

Experienced writers actually use the strategies for planning that we have suggested for you in this chapter. They work from statements of main idea — *thesis statements* — to focus and unify their writings, and they purposefully select an organizational pattern for each piece, often constructing an outline to guide them. The results of these techniques are evident in the selections in *A Writer's Reader*.

Explicit thesis sentences are clear in every essay in which the writer takes a stand or proposes a solution, such as Anna Quindlen, "Evan's Two Moms" (in last paragraph, p. 482), and Gregg Easterbrook, "Forget PCBs. Radon. Alar: The World's Greatest Environmental Dangers Are Dung Smoke and Dirty Water" (end of paragraph 1, p. 636). Writers of other types of essays also include explicit theses, such as Michael Dorris in his analytical evaluation "Crazy Horse Malt Liquor" (end of paragraph 3, p. 522), and Nicholas Wade in the comparison and contrast essay "How Men and Women Think" (last sentence in paragraph 11, p. 511). Other writers imply the thesis: Gerald Early, "Black like . . . Shirley Temple?" (p. 468), Lydia Minatoya, "Transformation" (p. 514), and Richard Rodriguez, "Does America Still Exist?" (p. 524).

## Chapter 17

# Strategies for Drafting

Learning to write well involves learning what questions to ask yourself. Some key questions are How can I get going on this draft? What shall I do if I get stuck? How can I flesh out the bones of my paper? How can I begin and end my paper effectively? How can I keep my readers with me? In this chapter we offer advice to get you going and keep you going on your draft, from the first paragraph to the last.

## Making a Start Enjoyable

Some writers find that if they can just make the art of writing start out playfully, like a game, they will be hard at work before they know it.

**Time Yourself.**   Try setting your watch, alarm clock, or egg timer and vow to finish a page of your draft before the buzzer sounds. Don't stop for anything. If you find yourself writing drivel, just push on. You can cross out later.

**Slow to a Crawl.**   If speed quotas don't work for you, time yourself to write with exaggerated laziness, completing, say, not a page but a sentence every fifteen minutes.

**Begin Badly — on Purpose.**   For fun, begin by writing a deliberately crummy sentence, full of mistakes and misspellings and fuzzy-headedness. Then cross it out and write another, better sentence. This technique may help you clear out the false starts all at once.

**Begin on Scrap Paper.**    Some writers feel reluctant to mess up a blank white sheet of paper that may have cost two or three cents. John Legget, novelist, biographer, and former director of the Writer's Workshop at the University of Iowa, uses the back of an old envelope or other scrap paper to get started, so he avoids feeling guilty about "spoiling a nice piece of paper with my thoughts."

**Begin Writing the Part You Find Most Appetizing.**    Start in the middle or at the end. Novelist Bill Downey points out that writing is different from childhood, "when we were forced to eat our vegetables first and then get our dessert. Writers are allowed to have their dessert first." When you begin a draft, try skipping the tough-looking steak and start with the brownie. Set down first the thoughts that come most easily to mind.

**State Your Purpose.**    In a sentence or a few lines, set forth what you want your paper to achieve. Are you trying to tell a story? To explain something? To win a reader over to your way of thinking? (For more about stating your purpose, see "Stating and Using a Thesis," p. 349.)

**Nutshell It.**    Write a very terse summary of the paper you want to write. Condense all your ideas into one small, tight paragraph. Later you can go back and expand each sentence until the meaning is clear and all points are adequately supported.

**Shrink Your Immediate Job.**    Break the writing task into several smaller parts and do only the first one. Writing a 750-word paper, you might get going faster if you vow to turn out, say, just the first two paragraphs.

**Seek a Provocative Title.**    Write down ten or twenty possible titles for your paper and then decide if any one sounds strikingly good. You can't let such a promising title go to waste, can you?

**Tape-Record Yourself.**    Talk a first draft of your paper into a tape recorder. Then play it back. Then write. You may find it hard to transcribe your spoken words, but this technique may set your mind in motion.

**Imagine You're Giving a Speech.**    On your feet, in front of an imaginary cheering crowd, spontaneously utter an opening paragraph. Then — quick! — write it down. Or tape it so you can get it down exactly.

**Write in a Role.**    Pretend you are someone else and write in that person's voice. Or invent an imaginary character and write as that character would.

**Try the Great Chef Method.**    According to legend, the great French chef Escoffier, by smelling a dish of food, could analyze its ingredients and then duplicate it in his kitchen. Analyze a paragraph you admire by another writer and cook up a new paragraph of your own from its ingredients. Take care to avoid plagiarism.

**Write with Excessive Simple-Mindedness.**   Do a whole paragraph or a whole draft the way a six-year-old talks: in plain, short, simple sentences. Karin Mack and Eric Skjei, in *Overcoming Writing Blocks*, (L.A.: J.P. Tarcher, 1979) call this technique "Dick-and-Janing," from those first-grade readers featuring Dick and Jane doing simple things in simple sentences. Of course, you won't want to turn in a paper written like that; but for the first draft you have something down on paper that you can retool.

# Restarting

When you have to write a long or demanding essay that you can't finish at one sitting, you may return to it only to find yourself stalled. You tromp your starter and nothing happens. Your engine seems reluctant to turn over. Try the following suggestions for getting back on the road.

**Take Regular Short Breaks.**   Even if you don't feel tired, take a regular break every half hour or so. Get up, walk around the room, stretch, get a drink of water, or refill your coffee cup. Two or three minutes should be enough to refresh your mind.

**Change Activities.**   When words won't come, do something quite different from writing for a while. Run, take your dog for a walk, or work out at the gym. Sometimes it helps to eat lunch, cook your favorite meal, take in a movie, listen to music, or take a nap. Or reward yourself — after you arrive at some predetermined point in your labors — with a trip to the vending machine, a phone call to a friend, or a TV show. Even while you're not thinking about your writing task, your unconscious mind will be working on it.

**Switch Instruments.**   Change the way your writing feels, looks, and sounds when it hits paper. Are you a typist? Try writing in longhand. If you are a pen user, type for a change. Try writing on note cards or on colored paper. Try composing directly on a computer screen. Perhaps you'll hit upon a new medium you'll enjoy much more.

**Reread What You Have Written.**   When you return to work, spend a few minutes rereading what you have already written. This method was a favorite of Ernest Hemingway, who, even when writing a novel, would begin a day's work by rereading his manuscript from page 1. (Just don't let rereading become a way to evade the writing itself.)

**Try Snowplowing.**    *Snowplowing* is the term invented by Jacqueline Jackson in her book *Turn Not Pale, Beloved Snail.* When you reach a point that stops you cold — an obstinate passage or paragraph that won't come right — you imitate a snowplow and charge ahead through the difficulty:

> The plow gets to the bank and can't push it any farther. Then it goes back, revs up, comes barreling along the plowed snow, hits the bank and goes through — or at least a little farther.
>
> I reread the earlier paragraphs . . . and approach the impasse pretending it isn't there. I want to take it by surprise. Then when I'm suddenly upon it, I swerve. I don't reread it, for this would keep me in the same old rut. Instead I start writing madly, on the strength of the new thrust. This often gets me a few sentences farther, sometimes right through the bank.

**Pause in Midstream.**    End a writing session by breaking off in mid-sentence or mid-paragraph. Just leave a sentence trailing off into space, even if you know what its closing words should be. When you return to your task, you can sit down and start writing again immediately.

**Leave Yourself Hints for How to Continue.**    If you're ready to quit, but your head still holds some ideas you have not yet expressed, jot them down briefly. Tell yourself what you think might come next or write the first sentence of the next section. When you come back to work, you will face not a blank wall but some rich and suggestive graffiti.

# Paragraphing

An essay is written not in large, indigestible lumps, but in *paragraphs* — small units, each more or less self-contained, each contributing some new idea in support of the thesis or main point of the essay. Writers dwell on one idea at a time, stating it, developing it, illustrating it with one or more examples or with a few facts. Paragraphing effectively means taking your readers by the hand and not only telling but also *showing* them, with plenty of detailed evidence, exactly what you mean. It means providing signposts to guide your readers through what you say.

Finished with one idea, you indent and start making a further point in a fresh paragraph. A paragraph indentation signifies a pause, as if you are taking a breath before moving on to another point. Readers assume that when you begin a new paragraph, you're moving on to a new idea, a new aspect of your thesis — and that you're going to ask them to think only about that idea for the rest of that paragraph.

Paragraphs can be as short as one sentence or as long as a page. Sometimes the length is governed by the audience for whom the paragraph is written, sometimes by the purpose of the writing, sometimes by the medium in which the paragraph appears. News writers, for instance, tend to write in brief, one- or two-sentence paragraphs. Newspaper readers, consuming facts like popcorn, find that the short paragraphing allows them to skim an article quickly. College writers, in contrast, should assume some willingness on the part of their readers to read through well-developed paragraphs.

The following sections give you some advice on using topic sentences to focus and control *body paragraphs* within an essay. You will also find advice on paragraphs that do special jobs — *opening paragraphs* that draw the reader in and *concluding paragraphs* that wrap up the discussion. You can use much of the advice on writing topic sentences for paragraphs when you are writing thesis sentences for essays. For more on filling out the main ideas within paragraphs, see Chapter 18, "Strategies for Developing."

## USING TOPIC SENTENCES

A *topic sentence* spells out the main idea of a paragraph in the body of an essay. When you read clear prose, especially writing that explains or argues, you can easily pick out the topic sentence of a body paragraph, and you know what to expect next. When you write, you should provide topic sentences to guide you in your writing and to help direct readers through your prose.

One tried-and-true way to write an effectively focused paragraph is to write a topic sentence first. It then becomes the foundation on which to build the rest of the paragraph. If you have written a sentence outline for your essay, you can convert the heading for each major subdivision (marked with roman numerals in a formal outline) into the topic sentence of a body paragraph in your essay. Even if you've written a topic outline, you may be able to expand each major subdivision heading into a topic sentence. (For more on topic outlines and sentence outlines, see pp. 362–65.)

Good topic sentences hook readers and give them a way to interpret the rest of the paragraph. An effective topic sentence is *interesting, accurate,* and *limited.* The more pointed and lively your topic sentence is, the more *interesting* it will be to your readers. "There are many things wrong with television" is dull and vague, but it's a start. Zero in on one specific flaw, and your topic sentence might become "Of all television's faults, the one I dislike most is melodramatizing the news." You can then illustrate your point with two or three melodramatic newscasts that you remember. A topic sentence should be *accurate* because it serves as a guide to the rest of the paragraph: if, after reading the topic sentence, readers think you mean one thing but then think you mean something else after reading the rest of the paragraph, you've got a problem. A topic sentence should be *limited* for the same reason — you don't want to mislead readers about what you intend to cover in a paragraph. If you start off by saying "Seven factors have contributed to the increasing obesity of the average American" but then introduce only one or two of them, you're going to frustrate your readers.

Once you have a topic sentence for a body paragraph in mind, there are four basic ways to include it in your paragraph: at the beginning, near the beginning, at the end, or implicitly.

**Topic Sentence as First Sentence.**    Usually, as in the following example from James David Barber's *The Presidential Character: Predicting Performance in the White House*, 3rd ed., (Englewood Cliffs: Prentice Hall, 1985), the topic sentence appears first in the paragraph, followed by sentences that clarify, illustrate, and support what it says. (In all the following examples, we have put the topic sentences in *italics*.)

> *The first baseline in defining Presidential types is activity-passivity.* How much energy does the man invest in his Presidency? Lyndon Johnson went at his day like a human cyclone, coming to rest long after the sun went down. Calvin Coolidge often slept eleven hours a night and still needed a nap in the middle of the day. In between, the Presidents array themselves on the high or low side of the activity line.

This paragraph moves from the general to the specific. The topic sentence clearly states at the outset what the paragraph is to be about. The second sentence defines *activity-passivity*. The third and fourth sentences, by citing extremes at either end of the baseline, supply illustrations: active Johnson, passive Coolidge. The final sentence makes a generalization that reinforces the central point.

**Topic Sentence near the Beginning of Paragraph.**    Sometimes the first sentence of a new paragraph functions as a transition, linking what is to come with what has gone before. In such a paragraph the *second* sentence might be the topic sentence. The paragraph quoted here, from "On Societies as Organisms" by science writer and physician Lewis Thomas, follows one about insects that ends "and we violate science when we try to read human meanings in their arrangements." The first sentence is transition, and the second is the topic sentence.

> It is hard for a bystander not to do so. *Ants are so much like human beings as to be an embarrassment.* They farm fungi, raise aphids as livestock, launch armies into wars, use chemical sprays to alarm and confuse enemies, capture slaves. The families of weaver ants engage in child labor, holding their larvae like shuttles to spin out the thread that sews the leaves together for their fungus gardens. They exchange information ceaselessly. They do everything but watch television.

**Topic Sentence at End of Paragraph.**    Occasionally a writer, especially one attempting to persuade the reader to agree, piles detail upon detail throughout a paragraph. Then, with a dramatic flourish, the writer *concludes* with the topic sentence. You can see this technique in the following paragraph, from student Heidi Kessler's paper giving an opinion about a contemporary social problem.

> A fourteen-year-old writes to an advice columnist in my hometown newspaper that she has "done it" lots of times and sex is "no big deal." At the neighborhood clinic where my aunt works, a hardened sixteen-year-old re-

quests her third abortion. A girl-child I know has two children of her own, but no husband. A college student in my dorm now finds herself sterile from a "social disease" picked up during casual sexual encounters. Multiply these examples by thousands. *It seems clear to me that women, who fought so hard for sexual freedom equal to that of men, have emerged from the battle not as joyous free spirits but as the sexual revolution's walking wounded.*

This paragraph moves from the particular to the general: from four examples about individuals to one large statement about American women at the end. By the time you come to the general statement at the end of the paragraph, you might be ready to accept the conclusion in the topic sentence.

**Topic Sentence Implied.**   It is also possible to find a perfectly unified, well-organized paragraph that has no topic sentence at all, like the following from "New York" by Gay Talese.

> Each afternoon in New York a rather seedy saxophone player, his cheeks blown out like a spinnaker, stands on the sidewalk playing "Danny Boy" in such a sad, sensitive way that he soon has half the neighborhood peeking out of windows tossing nickels, dimes, and quarters at his feet. Some of the coins roll under parked cars, but most of them are caught in his outstretched hand. The saxophone player is a street musician named Joe Gabler; for the past thirty years he has serenaded every block in New York and has sometimes been tossed as much as $100 a day in coins. He is also hit with buckets of water, empty beer cans and eggs, and chased by wild dogs. He is believed to be the last of New York's ancient street musicians.

No one sentence neatly sums up the writer's idea. Like most effective paragraphs that lack a topic sentence, Talese's paragraph contains something just as good: a *topic idea*. The author doesn't allow his paragraph to wander aimlessly. He knows exactly what he wants to achieve: a description of how Joe Gabler, a famous New York street musician, plies his trade. Because Talese succeeds in keeping this main purpose firmly in mind, the main point — that Gabler meets both reward and abuse — is clear to the reader as well.

**Question to Answer.**   Not all topic sentences are statements. Sometimes a question can be effective — you can alert your reader to the topic of the paragraph without giving away the punchline. Here, for example, is such a paragraph by psychoanalyst Erik Erikson.

> Is the sense of identity conscious? At times, of course, it seems only too conscious. For between the double prongs of vital inner need and inexorable outer demand, the as yet experimenting individual may become the victim of a transitory extreme identity consciousness, which is the common core of the many forms of "self-consciousness" typical for youth. Where the processes of identity formation are prolonged (a factor which can bring creative gain), such preoccupation with the "self-image" also prevails. We are thus most aware of our identity when we are just about to gain it and when we (with that startle which motion pictures call a "double take") are somewhat sur-

prised to make its acquaintance; or, again, when we are just about to enter a crisis and feel the encroachment of identity confusion.

For more specific suggestions on developing your ideas in paragraphs and essays, see Chapter 18, "Strategies for Developing."

EXERCISE

## Topic Sentences

Discuss each of the following topic sentences with your peer group, answering these questions:

Will it catch readers' attention?
Is it accurate?
Is it limited?
How might you develop the idea in the rest of the paragraph?
Can you improve it?

1. Television commercials stereotype people.
2. Teenagers face many problems growing up.
3. Living away from home for the first time is hard.
4. Violence in movies can be harmful.
5. I have been influenced by teachers.
6. It's good for a child to have a pet.
7. A flea market is a good place to buy jewelry.
8. Pollution should be controlled.
9. Everybody should recycle wastes.
10. *Casablanca* is my favorite movie.

## WRITING AN OPENING

Even writers with something to say find it hard occasionally to begin. Often they are so intent on writing a brilliant opening paragraph that they freeze, unable to write anything at all. When you sit down to draft an essay, you can ease your way into the job by simply deciding to set words — any words — on paper, without trying at all for an arresting or witty opening.

A time-honored approach to the opening paragraph is to write it *last*, after you have written the body of your essay and know exactly in what direction it is headed. Some writers like to write a long, meandering beginning in the first draft and then in rewriting cut it down to the most dramatic, exciting, or interesting essentials. Others use the introduction as a summary guide for themselves and their readers. At whatever point in the writing process you fashion an opening paragraph, remember that your chief aim is to persuade your readers to lay aside their preoccupations and enter the world set forth in your essay.

Begin with a Story.    Often a simple anecdote can capture your readers' interest and thus serve as a good beginning. Here is how writer Harry Crews opens his essay "The Car" in *Florida Frenzy* 1982:

The other day, there arrived in the mail a clipping sent by a friend of mine. It had been cut from a Long Beach, California, newspaper and dealt with a young man who had eluded police for fifty-five minutes while he raced over freeways and through city streets at speeds up to 130 miles per hour. During the entire time, he ripped his clothes off and threw them out the window bit by bit. It finally took twenty-five patrol cars and a helicopter to catch him. When they did, he said that God had given him the car and that he had "found God."

Most of us, reading such an anecdote, want to read on. What will the writer say next? What has the anecdote to do with the essay as a whole? Crews has aroused our curiosity.

**Introduce Your Subject and Comment on It.**    In some essays, the writer introduces a subject and then expands on it, bringing in vital details, as in this opening paragraph by David Morris, from an article entitled "Rootlessness":

Americans are a rootless people. Each year one in six of us changes residences; one in four changes jobs. We see nothing troubling in these statistics. For most of us, they merely reflect the restless energy that made America great. A nation of immigrants, unsurprisingly, celebrates those willing to pick up stakes and move on: the frontiersman, the cowboy, the entrepreneur, the corporate raider.

After first stating his point baldly, Morris goes on to supply some interesting statistics that back up his contention and offer a partial explanation of the phenomenon he focuses on.

**Ask a Question.**    A well-written essay can begin with a question and answer, as writer James H. Austin begins "Four Kinds of Chance":

What is chance? Dictionaries define it as something fortuitous that happens unpredictably without discernible human intention. Chance is unintentional and capricious, but we needn't conclude that chance is immune from human intervention. Indeed, chance plays several distinct roles when humans react creatively with one another and with their environment.

Beginning to answer the question in the first paragraph leads readers to expect the rest of the essay to continue the answer.

**State an Opinion.**    To challenge readers, a writer may begin with a controversial opinion, as writer Wade Thompson did:

Unlike any other sport, football is played solely for the benefit of the spectator. If you take the spectator away from any other game, the game could still survive on its own. Thus tennis players love tennis, whether or not anyone is watching. Golfers are almost churlish in their dedication to their game. Ping-Pong players never look around. Basketball players can dribble and shoot for hours without hearing a single cheer. Even baseball might survive the deprivation, despite the lack of parks. Softball surely would. But if you took away the spectators, if you demolished the grandstands and boarded up the stadium, it is inconceivable to think that any football would be played in the eerie privacy of the field itself. No football team ever plays another team just for the fun of playing football. Army plays Navy, Michigan plays Purdue, P.S. 123 plays P.S. 124, only with the prospect of a loud crowd on hand.

After his first, startling remark, Thompson generalizes about games unlike football, backing up his generalization with examples of such games. Finally he returns to his original point, emphasizing the direction his essay will take.

**End with the Thesis Sentence.**   An effective opening paragraph can end with a statement of the essay's main point. After first capturing your readers' attention with an anecdote or with gripping details or examples, you take your readers by the hand and lead them in exactly the direction your essay is to go. Such a thesis statement can be brief, as in this powerful opening of an essay by educator George B. Leonard called "No School?":

The most obvious barrier between our children and the kind of education that can free their enormous potential seems to be the educational system itself: a vast, suffocating web of people, practices and presumptions, kindly in intent, ponderous in response. Now, when true educational alternatives are at last becoming clear, we may overlook the simplest: no school.

If you find writing an opening paragraph difficult, don't worry *too* hard about capturing and transfixing your readers; just introduce your idea. Keep it simple. Open with an anecdote, a description, a comparison, a definition, a quotation, a question, or some vital background. Be sure that what you say is relevant to your main point. And don't forget to set forth your thesis (as discussed on p. 349).

## WRITING A CONCLUSION

The final paragraphs of an essay linger longest in readers' minds. E. B. White's conclusion to "Once More to the Lake" (p. 462) certainly does so. In the essay, White describes his return with his young son to a vacation spot he had known and loved as a child. At the end of the essay, in an unforgettable image, he remembers how old he really is and realizes the inevitable passing of generations.

When the others went swimming my son said he was going in, too. He pulled his dripping trunks from the line where they had hung all through the shower and wrung them out. Languidly, and with no thought of going in, I watched him, his hard little body, skinny and bare, saw him wince slightly as he pulled up around his vitals the small, soggy, icy garment. As he buckled the swollen belt, suddenly my groin felt the chill of death.

White's concluding paragraph is a classic example of an effective ending. It begins with a sentence that points back to the previous paragraph and at the same time looks ahead. Then White leads us quickly to his final, chilling insight. And then he stops.

It's easy to suggest what *not* to do at the end of an essay: Don't leave your readers suspended in midair, half expecting you to go on. Don't restate everything you've already said. Don't introduce a brand-new topic that leads away from the point of your essay. And don't feel you have to introduce your final paragraph with an obvious signal that the end is near. Avoid ending an essay with words and phrases like "In conclusion," "As I have said," or "So, as we see." In a long, complicated paper, a terse summation of your main points right before your concluding sentences may help your reader grasp your ideas; but a short paper usually requires either no summary at all or little more than a single sentence or two.

"How *do* you write an ending, then?" you might well ask.

**End with a Quotation.**   An apt quotation can neatly round out an essay, as literary critic Malcolm Cowley demonstrates at the end of an essay in *The View from Eighty* (New York: Viking Press, 1980), his discussion of the pitfalls and compensations of old age.

> "Eighty years old!" the great Catholic poet Paul Claudel wrote in his journal. "No eyes left, no ears, no teeth, no legs, no wind! And when all is said and done, how astonishingly well one does without them!"

**State or Restate Your Thesis.**   In a sharp criticism of American schools, humorist Russell Baker in "School vs. Education" ends by stating his main point, that schools do not educate.

> Afterward, the former student's destiny fulfilled, his life rich with Oriental carpets, rare porcelain, and full bank accounts, he may one day find himself with the leisure and the inclination to open a book with a curious mind, and start to become educated.

**End with a Brief Emphatic Sentence.**   For an essay that traces causes or effects, analyzes, evaluates, or argues, a deft concluding thought can reinforce your main idea. Notice the definite click with which former heavyweight champion Gene Tunney closes the door on "The Long Count," an analysis of his two victorious fights with Jack Dempsey, whose boxing style differed markedly from Tunney's own.

> Jack Dempsey was a great fighter — possibly the greatest that ever entered a ring. Looking back objectively, one has to conclude that he was more valuable to the sport or "The Game" than any prizefighter of his time. Whether you consider it from his worth as a gladiator or from the point of view of the box office, he was tops. His name in his most glorious days was magic among his people, and today, twenty years after, the name Jack Dempsey is still magic. This tells a volume in itself. As one who has always had pride in his profession as well as his professional theories, and possessing a fair share of Celtic romanticism, I wish that we could have met when we

were both at our unquestionable best. We could have decided many questions, to me the most important of which is whether "a good boxer can always lick a good fighter."

I still say yes.

**Introduce Some Ideas Implied by Your Essay.**    You don't want to introduce new topics at the end of your essay, but you might mention a few new *implications* concerning the topic you have covered. As you draw to a close, ask yourself, "What now?" "What is the significance of what I have said?" Leave your readers with one or two provocative thoughts to ponder. Obstreperous 1920s debunker H. L. Mencken uses this technique in "The Libido for the Ugly," an essay about the ugliness of American cities and towns.

> Here is something that the psychologists have so far neglected: the love of ugliness for its own sake, the lust to make the world intolerable. Its habitat is the United States. Out of the melting pot emerges a race which hates beauty as it hates truth. The etiology of this madness deserves a great deal more study than it has got. There must be causes behind it; it arises and flourishes in obedience to biological laws, and not as a mere act of God. What, precisely, are the terms of those laws? And why do they run stronger in America than elsewhere? Let some honest *Privat Dozent*[1] in pathological sociology apply himself to the problem.

**Stop When the Story Is Over.**    Even a quiet ending can be effective, as long as it signals clearly that the essay is finished. Sometimes the best way to conclude a story, for instance, is simply to stop when the story is over. This is what journalist Martin Gansberg does in his true account of the fatal beating of a young woman, Kitty Genovese, in full view of residents of a Queens, New York, apartment house. The residents, unwilling to become involved, did nothing to interfere. Here is the last paragraph of his account, "38 Who Saw Murder Didn't Call Police":

> It was 4:25 A.M. when the ambulance arrived to take the body of Miss Genovese. It drove off. "Then," a solemn police detective said, "the people came out."

EXERCISE

## Openings and Conclusions

Openings and conclusions frame an essay, contributing to the unity of the whole. The opening sets up the subject and the main idea; the conclusion reaffirms the thesis and rounds off the ideas. Discuss the following with your classmates.

I. Here are two possible beginning paragraphs from a student essay on the importance of children learning how to swim.

   1. Which introduction is more effective? Why?

[1] *Privat Dozent.* A lecturer at a German university.

2. What would the body of this essay consist of? What kinds of evidence would be included?

3. Write a suitable conclusion for this essay.

A. Humans inhabit a world made up of over 70 percent water. In addition to these great bodies of water, we have built millions of swimming pools for sports and leisure activities. At one time or another most people will be faced with either the danger of drowning or the challenge of aquatic recreation. For these reasons, it is essential that we learn to swim. Being a competitive swimmer and a swimming instructor, I fully realize the importance of knowing how to swim.

B. Four-year-old Carl, curious like most children, last spring ventured out onto his pool patio. He fell into the pool and, not knowing how to swim, helplessly sank to the bottom. Minutes later his uncle found the child and brought him to the surface. Since Carl had no pulse, his uncle immediately administered CPR on him until the paramedics arrived. Eventually he was revived. During his stay in the hospital, his mother signed him up for beginning swimming classes. Carl was a lucky one. Unlike thousands of other children and adults, he got a second chance.

II. If you were to read each of the following introductions from professional essays, would you want to read the entire essay? Why?

A. During my ninth hour underground, as I scrambled up a slanting tunnel through the powdered gypsum, Rick Bridges turned to me and said, "You know, this whole area was just discovered Tuesday." (David Roberts, "Caving Comes into Its Golden Age: A New Mexico Marvel," *Smithsonian* Nov. 1988: 52)

B. From the batting average on the back of a George Brett baseball card to the interest rate fluctuations that determine whether the economy grows or stagnates, Americans are fascinated by statistics. (Stephen E. Nordlinger, "By the Numbers," *St. Petersburg Times* 6 Nov. 1988: 11)

C. "What does it look like under there?"
It was always this question back then, always the same pattern of hello and what's your name, what happened to your eye and what's under there. (Natalie Kusz, "Waiting for a Glass Eye," *Road Song* [Farrar, 1990], rpt. in *Harper's* Nov. 1990)

III. Evaluate the effectiveness of each of the following introductions from student essays.

A. On June 4, 1985, Los Angeles police arrested Jerald Curtis Johns. Police believe he may have raped as many as 100 women, ranging in age from 24 to 71, living in a ten block radius (*Time* 5 Sept. 1985). But of those 100 women, only 13 reported rape. This situation is commonplace: most rapes are not reported.

B. Is it possible for a young girl of twelve or so who has been sexually and mentally abused to recover her self-worth and have a productive and happy life? The movie *The Color Purple* attempts to answer that question.

IV. How effective are the following introductions and conclusions from student essays? Could they be improved? If so, how? If they are satisfactory, explain why. What would be an eye-catching yet informative title for each essay?

A. Recently a friend down from New York astonished me with stories of several people infected — some with AIDS — by stepping on needles washed up on the New Jersey beaches. This is just one incident of pollution, a devastating problem in our society today. Pollution is increasing in our world because of greed, apathy, and Congress's inability to control this problem. . . .

Wouldn't it be nice to have a pollution-free world without medical wastes floating in the water and washing up on our beaches? Without garbage scattered on the streets? With every corporation abiding by the laws set by Congress? In the future we can have a pollution-free world, but it is going to take the cooperation of everyone, including Congress, to ensure our survival on this Planet Earth.

B. The divorce rate has risen 700 percent in this century and continues to rise. More than one out of every two couples who are married end up in divorce. Over one million children a year are affected by divorce in the family. From these statistics it is clear that one of the greatest problems concerning the family today is divorce and the adverse effects it has on our society. . . .

Divorce causes problems that change people for life. The number of divorces will continue to exceed the 700 percent figure unless married couples learn to communicate, to accept their mates unconditionally, and to sacrificially give of themselves.

V. Choose one of the topics from your brainstorming or freewriting in Chapter 15, and write several — at least three — different introductions with conclusions. Ask your classmates which is the most effective.

## Achieving Coherence

Effective writing is well organized. It proceeds in some sensible order, each sentence following naturally from the one before it. Yet even well-organized prose can be hard to read unless it is *coherent*. To make your writing coherent, you can use various devices that tie together words in a sentence, sentences in a paragraph, paragraphs in an essay.

Transitional Words and Sentences.   You already use transitions every day, in both your writing and your speech. Instinctively you realize that certain words and phrases help your readers and listeners follow your train of thought. But some writers, in a rush to get through what they have to say, omit important links between thoughts. Mistakenly, they assume that because a connection is clear to them it will automatically be clear to their readers. Often just a word, phrase, or sentence of transition inserted in the right place will transform a seemingly disconnected passage into a coherent one.

Time markers are transitions that make clear *when* one thing happens in relation to another. Time markers include words and phrases like *then, soon, the following day,* and *in a little while.*

Not all transitions mark time. The English language contains many words and phrases that make clear other connections between or within sentences. Consider choosing one of the following commonly used *transitional markers* to fit your purpose. They are grouped here by purpose or the kind of relation or connection they establish.

| | |
|---|---|
| TO MARK TIME | then, soon, first, second, next, recently, the following day, in a little while, meanwhile, after, later, in the past |
| TO MARK PLACE OR DIRECTION | in the distance, close by, near, far away, above, below, to the right, on the other side, opposite, to the west, next door |
| TO SUMMARIZE OR RESTATE | in other words, to put it another way, in brief, in simpler terms, on the whole, in fact, in a word, to sum up, in short, in conclusion, to conclude, finally, therefore |
| TO RELATE CAUSE AND EFFECT OR RESULT | therefore, accordingly, hence, thus, for, so, consequently, as a result, because of |
| TO ADD OR AMPLIFY OR LIST | and, also, too, besides, as well, moreover, in addition, furthermore, in effect, second, in the second place, again, next |
| TO COMPARE | similarly, likewise, in like manner |
| TO CONCEDE | whereas, on the other hand, with that in mind, still, and yet, even so, in spite of, despite, at least |
| TO CONTRAST | on the other hand, but, or, however, unlike, nevertheless, on the contrary, conversely, in contrast, instead |
| TO INDICATE PURPOSE | to this end, for this purpose, with this objective |
| TO EXPRESS CONDITION | although, though |
| TO GIVE EXAMPLES OR SPECIFY | for example, for instance, in this case, in particular, to illustrate |

| | |
|---|---|
| TO QUALIFY | for the most part, by and large, with few exceptions, mainly, in most cases, some, sometimes |
| TO EMPHASIZE | it is true, truly, indeed, of course, to be sure, obviously, without doubt, evidently, clearly, understandably |

Occasionally a whole sentence serves as a transition. Often, but not always, it is the first sentence of a new paragraph. When the transitional sentence appears in that position, it harks back to the contents of the previous paragraph while simultaneously hinting at the direction the new paragraph is to take. Here is a sample, excerpted from an essay by Marsha Traugot about adopting older and handicapped children, in which the transitional sentence (in *italics*) begins a new paragraph.

> . . . Some exchanges hold monthly meetings where placement workers looking for a match can discuss waiting children or families, and they also sponsor parties where children, workers, and prospective parents meet informally.
> *And if a match still cannot be made?* Exchanges and other child welfare organizations now employ media blitzes as aggressive as those of commercial advertising. . . .

By repeating the key word *match* in her transitional sentence and by inserting the word *still,* Traugot makes clear that in what follows she will build on what has gone before. At the same time, by making the transitional sentence a rhetorical question, Traugot promises that the new paragraph will introduce fresh material, in this case answering the question.

**Transition Paragraphs.**    Transitions may be even longer than sentences. When you write an essay, especially one that is long and complicated, you'll find that to move clearly from one idea to the next will sometimes require an entire paragraph of transition:

```
     So far, we have been dwelling on the physical and
psychological effects of driving nonstop for more than
two hundred miles. Now let's reflect on causes. Why do
people become addicted to their steering wheels?
```

Usually, such a paragraph will be shorter than other body paragraphs, but you'll want to allow it whatever space it may require. Often, as in the preceding example, it makes a comment on the structure of the essay, looking back and pointing forward.

A transition paragraph can come to your aid when you go off on one branch of argument and then return to your main trunk. Here's an example from a masterly writer, Lewis Thomas, in an essay, "Things Unflattened by Science." A medical doctor, Thomas has been complaining in his essay that biologists keep expecting medical researchers to come up with quick answers to intractable problems: cancer, schizophrenia, stress. He takes most of a paragraph to explain why he doesn't think medical science can solve the problem of stress: "Stress is simply the condition of being human." Now, to turn again to the main idea of his essay — what biological problems he would like to see solved — Thomas inserts a transition paragraph:

> But I digress. What I wish to get at is an imaginary situation in which I am allowed three or four questions to ask the world of biomedical science to settle for me by research, as soon as possible. Can I make a short list of top-priority puzzles, things I am more puzzled by than anything else? I can.

In a new paragraph, he continues: "First, I want to know what goes on in the mind of a honeybee." He wonders if a bee is just a sort of programmed robot or if it can think and imagine, even a little bit. Neatly and effectively, the transition paragraph has led to this speculation and to several further paragraphs that will come.

Use a transition paragraph only when you sense that your readers might get lost if you don't patiently lead them by the hand. If you can do without transition paragraphs, do. If the essay is short, one question or statement at the beginning of a new paragraph will be enough.

**Repetitions.**    As we see in Traugot's passage about adoption, another way to make clear the relationship between two sentences, two paragraphs, or two ideas is to *repeat* a key word or phrase. Such repetition, purposefully done, almost guarantees that readers will understand how all the parts of even a complicated passage fit together. Note the repetition of the word *anger* in the following paragraph (italics ours) from *Of Woman Born* (New York: Norton, 1976) by poet Adrienne Rich, in which the writer explores her relationship with her mother. The repetition holds all the parts of this complex paragraph together and makes clear the unity and coherence of its ideas.

> And I know there must be deep reservoirs of *anger* in her; every mother has known overwhelming, unacceptable *anger* at her children. When I think of the conditions under which my mother became a mother, the impossible expectations, my father's distaste for pregnant women, his hatred of all that he could not control, my *anger* at her dissolves into grief and *anger for* her, and then dissolves back again into *anger* at her: the ancient, unpurged *anger* of the child.

**Pronouns.**    Because they always refer back to nouns or other pronouns, pronouns serve as transitions by making readers refer back as well. Note how certain pronouns (indicated by *italics*) hold together the following paragraph by columnist Ellen Goodman.

> I have two friends who moved in together many years ago. *He* looked upon this step as a trial marriage. *She* looked upon it as, well, moving in together. *He* was sure that in a matter of time, after *they* had built up trust and

confidence, *she* would agree that marriage was the next logical step. *She*, on the other hand, was thrilled that here at last was a man *who* would never push *her* back to the altar.

Goodman's paragraph contains transitions other than pronouns, too: time markers like *many years ago, in a matter of time,* and *after;* the transitional marker *on the other hand,* which indicates that what follows will contrast with what has gone before; and repetition of synonyms like *trial marriage, marriage,* and *the altar.* All serve the main purpose of transitions: keeping readers on track.

EXERCISE

## Identifying Transitions

Go over one of the papers you have already written for this course, and circle all the transitional devices you can detect. Then share your paper with a classmate. Can the classmate find additional transitions? Does the classmate think you need transitions where you don't have any?

# *Making Connections:*
# *Strategies for Drafting Evident in* A Writer's Reader

Experienced writers use the techniques we have discussed in this chapter to strengthen their drafts as they write. Evidence of the techniques are clearly visible in many of the essays in *A Writer's Reader.* Here is a small sampling of examples you might find useful.

Topic Sentences.   When constructing their paragraphs, professional authors place their topic sentences in a variety of positions.

AS FIRST SENTENCE OF PARAGRAPH

Stephanie Coontz, "The Way We Wish We Were: The Complexities of Assessing Family Trends" (p. 484), paragraphs 1–3

Stephen King, "Why We Crave Horror Movies" (p. 579), paragraphs 8–12

NEAR BEGINNING OF PARAGRAPH

Patricia J. Williams, "Hate Radio" (p. 582), paragraphs 9, 24, 25

Kurt Andersen, "Oprah and Jo-Jo the Dog-Faced Boy" (p. 590), paragraph 2

AT END OF PARAGRAPH

Melvin Konner, "Out of the Darkness" (p. 615), paragraph 20

Carol Kaesuk Yoon, "Drugs from Bugs" (p. 628), paragraph 3

IMPLICIT

Bill McKibben, "The End of Nature" (p. 620), paragraph 1

Gregg Easterbrook, "Forget PCBs. Radon. Alar: The World's Greatest Environmental Dangers Are Dung Smoke and Dirty Water" (p. 636), paragraphs 3, 5

AS A QUESTION

Stephanie Coontz, "The Way We Wish We Were: The Complexities of Assessing Family Trends" (p. 484), paragraph 5

Katha Pollitt, "The Future Is Coed" (p. 496), paragraph 2

Can you find another example of each of the five types of topic sentences in other essays in *A Writer's Reader*?

**Openings.**   Some authors use the strategies for opening essays that are discussed in this chapter. Deborah Tannen in "Women and Men Talking on the Job" (p. 554) begins with a story. Stephen L. Carter in "The Black Table, the Empty Seat, and the Tie" (p. 567) introduces the subject and comments on it. Joy Harjo in "Three Generations of Native American Women's Birth Experience" (p. 471) asks a question. Judith Ortiz Cofer in "The Myth of the Latin Woman: I Just Met a Girl Named María" (p. 504) ends her introduction with the thesis statement for her essay. Can you find other examples in *A Writer's Reader* of these five types of openings for essays?

**Conclusions.**   Authors also use the strategies suggested in this chapter to close their essays. Stephen J. Gould in "The Geometer of Race" (p. 532) ends with a quotation. Steve Olson in "Year of the Blue-Collar Guy" (p. 542) restates his thesis. Judy Brady in "I Want a Wife" (p. 490) ends with a pithy statement. Nicholas Wade concludes "How Men and Women Think" (p. 510) with a brief discussion of some of the ideas implied by his essay. Lydia Minatoya simply stops "Transformation" (p. 514) when the story is over. Can you find other examples in *A Writer's Reader* of each of the five types of conclusions?

**Coherence.**   The devices for coherence discussed in this chapter are evident in professional writing. For example, Gerald Early uses transitions denoting time in "Black like . . . Shirley Temple?" (p. 468), and E. B. White uses transitions denoting place or direction in "Once More to the Lake" (p. 462). Andrew Sullivan in "Wouldn't Normally Do" (p. 592) and Scott Russell Sanders in "The Men We Carry in Our Minds" (p. 499) use clear transitional words and sentences, repetition, and pronouns throughout their essays. Jessica Mitford uses paragraph 4 in "Behind the Formaldehyde Curtain" (p. 604) as a transitional paragraph. Can you identify all of the types of transitions used by Robert Wright in "Mr. Clean Genes" (p. 611) and by Bill McKibben in "The End of Nature" (p. 620)?

# Chapter 18

# Strategies for Developing

In Parts One and Two of this book, you learned a lot about writing, you had a lot of practice, and we hope you improved your writing. In those sections, you saw specifically how a writer can use resources that are always available (such as recall and conversation) and critical thinking strategies (such as analyzing and evaluating) to focus and develop an entire essay. In this chapter you will look at methods for supporting and clarifying your ideas in individual paragraphs and parts of essays. Some of these methods are the same as the writer's resources and critical thinking strategies you've already seen. Others, such as defining, have not been discussed in this book before — although you've no doubt already used them in your writing, perhaps without even knowing it.

In this chapter we cover giving examples, providing details, defining, dividing and classifying, analyzing a process, comparing and contrasting, and showing cause and effect. You'll find these eight methods of development to be indispensable, whether your purpose in a particular essay is to relate a personal experience, to explain, or to persuade. Although you may choose to use only one method within a single paragraph, a strong essay will almost always require a combination of developmental strategies.

Here are some questions to ask yourself when looking for places in your essay to develop your ideas more fully.

**DISCOVERY CHECKLIST**

## Developing Ideas

- Are any paragraphs in your essay only one or two sentences long? Could these paragraphs benefit from being developed more fully?
- Are your longer paragraphs solid and stout, meaty and interesting to read? Or are they just filled with generalizations, mindless repetitions, and wordy phrasings?

386

- Is there any point in your essay where you think your readers might have difficulty following you or understanding your meaning? Would more evidence help?
- If you've shown your draft to a peer editor, has he or she pointed out ideas that need to be developed more fully?

## Giving Examples

An example — the word comes from the Latin *exemplum,* meaning "one thing chosen from among many" — is a typical instance that illustrates a whole type or kind. Giving examples to support a generalization is probably the most often used means of development. Here's an example, from *In Search of Excellence* by Thomas J. Peters and Robert H. Waterman, Jr., explaining why America's top corporations are so successful.

> Although he's not a company, our favorite illustration of closeness to the customer is car salesman Joe Girard. He sold more new cars and trucks, each year, for eleven years running, than any other human being. In fact, in a typical year, Joe sold more than twice as many units as whoever was in second place. In explaining his secret of success, Joe said: "I sent out over thirteen thousand cards every month."
>
> Why start with Joe? Because his magic is the magic of IBM and many of the rest of the excellent companies. It is simply service, overpowering service, especially after-sales service. Joe noted, "There's one thing that I do that a lot of salesmen don't, and that's believe the sale really begins *after* the sale — not before. . . . The customer ain't out the door, and my son has made up a thank-you note." Joe would intercede personally, a year later, with the service manager on behalf of his customer. Meanwhile he would keep the communications flowing.

Notice how Peters and Waterman focus on the specific, Joe Girard. They don't write *corporation employees* or even *car salespeople,* but zero right in on one particular man to make the point come alive.

America's top corporations
corporation employees
car salespeople
Joe Girard

This ladder of abstraction moves from the general — America's top corporations — to a specific person — Joe Girard. Peters and Waterman's use of the specific example of Joe Girard makes their point about the importance of closeness to the customer *concrete* to readers: he is someone readers can relate to.

Another instance of a writer moving from a broad generalization to recognizable individual examples is found on page 372, where James David Barber discusses presidential types. Barber illustrates the main idea of his paragraph (that presidents can be located on an "activity-passivity" spectrum) with two examples: the drowsy Coolidge and the energetic Johnson. Like Peters and Waterman, Barber moves several levels down the ladder of abstraction to make his idea specific.

presidents of the United States
    presidential types
        active presidents
            Lyndon Johnson
        passive presidents
            Calvin Coolidge

To check the level of specification in one of your paragraphs or outlines, draw a ladder of abstraction for it. If you haven't gone down to the fourth or fifth level, you are probably being too general and need to add examples. This strategy is also a way for you to restrict a broad subject to a topic manageable in a short essay.

An example doesn't always have to be a specific individual. Sometimes you can create a picture in your readers' minds of something that they have never encountered before (and that may not actually exist), or you can make an abstraction come alive by giving it a recognizable personality and identity. Using this strategy, writer Jonathan Kozol makes real the plight of illiterate people in our bureaucratized health care system.

> Illiterates live, in more than literal ways, an uninsured existence. They cannot understand the written details on a health insurance form. They cannot read waivers that they sign preceding surgical procedures. Several women I have known in Boston have entered a slum hospital with the intention of obtaining a tubal ligation and have emerged a few days later after having been subjected to a hysterectomy. Unaware of their rights, incognizant of jargon, intimidated by the unfamiliar air of fear and atmosphere of ether that so many of us find oppressive in the confines even of the most attractive and expensive medical facilities, they have signed their names to documents they could not read and which nobody, in the hectic situation that prevails so often in those overcrowded hospitals that serve the urban poor, had ever bothered to explain.

Examples aren't trivial doodads you add to a paragraph for decoration; they are what holds your readers' attention and shows them that your writing makes sense. By using examples, you make your ideas more concrete and tangible. To give plenty of examples is one of the writer's chief tasks. We can't stress this truth enough.

You may generate examples at any point in the writing process. To find your own examples, do a little brainstorming or thinking. Begin with your own experience, with whatever is near you, even if you're working with a topic about which you think you know nothing. With such a topic — say the psychology of gift giving — think it over slowly. Did you ever know a person who gave large gifts people didn't want and felt uncomfortable accepting? Why do you suppose the gift giver behaved that way? Was he or she looking for gratitude? A feeling of importance? Power over the recipients?

Draw on your other resources as well. With any topic, you might discover examples from conversing with others, from reading, from digging in the library. You can observe examples for your writing all around you. If you are writing a paper on bumper stickers, take a stroll through any parking lot, pen and notepad in hand. After you have gathered a few examples on your topic, share them with your classmates or writing group, and they'll probably think of some to add to your list.

Here are some questions to ask yourself when you use examples in your writing.

**DISCOVERY CHECKLIST**

## Using Examples to Develop Ideas

- Are your examples relevant to the point you are making?
- Are your examples the best ones you can think of?
- Are your examples really specific? Or do they just repeat generalities?
- From each paragraph, can you draw a ladder of abstraction to at least the fourth level?

**EXERCISE**

## Giving Examples

To help you get in the habit of thinking specifically, fill in a ladder of abstraction for five of the following general subjects. Then share your ladders with your classmates or writing group and compare and contrast your specifics with theirs. Examples:

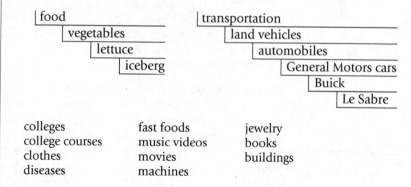

| colleges | fast foods | jewelry |
| college courses | music videos | books |
| clothes | movies | buildings |
| diseases | machines | |

# *Providing Details*

In addition to giving examples, you can make your generalizations in your writing more convincing by providing details. A *detail* is any specific, concrete bit of information. Writers usually use details to make the scenes and images they're creating more realistic and vivid for their readers or to convince their readers that they have the facts they need to make broad assertions with authority. Often details and examples work together. Besides pointing to the example of President Coolidge, James David Barber (p. 372) gives a little evidence or specific detail to show that Coolidge was sleepy: the report that he slept eleven hours a night and then took a nap in midday besides. To back up your general statements, you need to supply such statements of fact, bits of historical record, or your own observations.

Mary Harris "Mother" Jones in old age published the story of her life as a labor organizer, *The Autobiography of Mother Jones* (Chicago: C.H. Kerr Pub. Co., 1980). In this view of a Pennsylvania coal miner's lot at the turn of the century, she makes a general statement and then lends conviction to her words with ample evidence from her own experience.

> Mining at its best is wretched work, and the life and surroundings of the miner are hard and ugly. His work is down in the black depths of the earth. He works alone in a drift. There can be little friendly companionship as there is in the factory; as there is among men who build bridges and houses, working together in groups. The work is dirty. Coal dust grinds itself into the skin, never to be removed. The miner must stoop as he works in the drift. He becomes bent like a gnome.
>
> His work is utterly fatiguing. Muscles and bones ache. His lungs breathe coal dust and the strange, damp air of places that are never filled with sunlight. His house is a poor makeshift and there is little to encourage him to make it attractive. The company owns the ground it stands on, and the miner feels the precariousness of his hold. Around his house is mud and slush. Great mounds of culm [the refuse left after coal is screened], black and sullen, surround him. His children are perpetually grimy from playing on the culm mounds. The wife struggles with dirt, with inadequate water supply, with small wages, with overcrowded shacks.
>
> The miner's wife, who in the majority of cases worked from childhood in the nearby silk mills, is overburdened with childbearing. She ages young. She knows much illness. Many a time I have been in a home where the poor wife was sick in bed, the children crawling over her, quarreling and playing in the room, often the only warm room in the house.

Mother Jones, who was not a learned writer, wrote these memoirs in her mid-nineties. Her style may be heavy with short, simple sentences ("She ages young. She knows much illness."), but her writing is clear and powerful because of the specific details she uses. She knows the strength of a well-chosen verb: "Coal dust *grinds* itself into the skin." Notice how she opens her description by making two general statements: (1) "Mining is wretched work" and (2) the miner's life and surroundings are "hard and ugly." Then she supports these generalizations with an overwhelming barrage of factual evidence from her own experience. The result is a moving, convincingly detailed portrait of the miner and his family.

Writer M. Scott Momaday uses many interesting details to describe the scene of the Kiowa celebration of the Gourd Dance on the Fourth of July at Carnegie, Oklahoma:

> The celebration is on the north side. We turn down into a dark depression, a large hollow among trees. It is full of camps and cars and people. At

first there are children. According to some centrifugal social force, children function on the periphery. They run about, making festival noises. Firecrackers are snapping all around. We park and I make ready; the girls help me with my regalia. I am already wearing white trousers and moccasins. Now I tie the black velvet sash around my waist, placing the beaded tassels at my right leg. The bandoleer of red beans, which was my grandfather's, goes over my left shoulder, the V at my right hip. I decide to carry the blanket over my arm until I join the dancers; no sense in wrapping up in this heat. There is deep, brick-red dust on the ground. The grass is pale and brittle here and there. We make our way through the camps, stepping carefully to avoid the pegs and guy lines that reach about the tents. Old people, imperturbable, are lying down on cots and benches in the shadows. Smoke hangs in the air. We smell hamburgers, popcorn, gunpowder. Later there will be fried bread, boiled meat, Indian corn.

Momaday arranges his vivid details both spatially and chronologically. Notice his spatial transitions: *on the north side, turn down, on the periphery, all around, on the ground, here and there, through the camps, in the shadows, in the air.* Look also at the time markers: *At first, Now, until, Later.* These transitions guide readers through the experience.

Quite different from Momaday's personal details are Paula Gunn Allen's hard facts and objective statistics. She heaps statistic upon statistic to convince readers that ever since American Indians began making pacts with the U.S. government, their survival has been threatened.

> Some researchers put our pre-contact population at more than 45 million, while others put it at around 20 million. The U.S. government long put it at 450,000 — a comforting if imaginary figure, though at one point it was put at around 270,000. If our current population is around one million; if, as some researchers estimate, around 25 percent of Indian women and 10 percent of Indian men in the United States have been sterilized without informed consent; if our average life expectancy is, as the best-informed research presently says, 55 years; if our infant mortality rate continues at well above national standards; if our average unemployment for all segments of our population — male, female, young, adult, and middle-aged is between 60 and 90 percent; if the U.S. government continues its policy of termination, relocation, removal, and assimilation along with the destruction of wilderness, reservation land, and its resources, and severe curtailment of hunting, fishing, timber harvesting and water-use rights — then existing tribes are facing the threat of extinction which for several hundred tribal groups has already become fact in the past five hundred years.

Providing details is one of the simplest yet most effective ways of developing ideas. All it takes on your part is close observation and attention, then precise words to communicate the details to readers. Begin with the senses (combined with a bit of imagination, if you can't actually observe firsthand). If readers were on the scene or encountering your example themselves, what would be the first thing they'd see? What would they hear, smell, or feel? Would there be any tastes involved? If you're explaining a historical account, think about which small details were most meaningful to you in your reading — your readers will probably find them interesting, too. If you haven't encountered any details that make the point as strongly as you'd like, you may need to do a bit of research to find just the right fact or statistic. Remember that effective details have a specific purpose: they must help make your images more evocative or your point more convincing. In your final draft, you'll want to make sure that every detail supports — in some way — the main idea of your paragraph.

Here are some questions to ask yourself when you use details in your writing.

**DISCOVERY CHECKLIST**

## Using Details to Develop Ideas

- Do all your details support your point of view or main idea?
- Do you have details of sights? Sounds? Tastes? Touch? Smells?
- Have you included enough details to make your writing clear? To make it interesting?
- Have you arranged your details in an order that is easy to follow?

**EXERCISE**

## Providing Details

To practice generating and using specific details, brainstorm with your group or alone on one of the following subjects. Be sure to include details that appeal to all five senses. Group the details in your list (see p. 355), and write a paragraph or two using your specific details. Start off with a statement of main idea that conveys an interesting message about the subject you choose (not "My grandmother's house was in Topeka, Kansas" but "My grandmother's house was my childhood haven").

| | |
|---|---|
| the things in my room | an unforgettable game |
| my grandmother's house | an unusual person |
| the haunted house | my favorite pet |
| my graduation | a hospital room |
| my old car | a high school dance |

# Defining

Often in a paper that calls for critical thinking, you'll need to do some defining. *Define*, from the Latin, means "to set bounds to." You define a thing, a word, or a concept by describing it in such a way that it is distinguished from all similar things.

If writers and thinkers don't agree on the meaning of a word or an idea, they can't share knowledge. Scientists in particular take special care to define their terms precisely and accurately. In his article "A Chemist's Definition of pH," Gessner G. Hawley makes his subject clear to readers who can follow him. Though he goes on to write an extended definition, he begins with a brief definition:

pH is a value taken to represent the acidity or alkalinity of an aqueous solution; it is defined as the logarithm of the reciprocal of the hydrogen-ion concentration of a solution:

$$pH = 1n\frac{1}{[H^+]}$$

If you use a word in a special sense or if you coin a word, you have to explain it or your readers won't know what you're talking about. Prolific word coiner and social prophet Alvin Toffler in *The Third Wave* (New York: Morrow, 1980) invents (among many others) the word *techno-sphere*, which he defines as follows:

> All societies — primitive, agricultural, or industrial — use energy; they make things; they distribute things. In all societies the energy system, the production system, and the distribution system are interrelated parts of something larger. This larger system is the *techno-sphere*.

In his later book *PowerShift*, Toffler picks up the word *screenie* from Jeffrey Moritz, president of National College Television, and adds his own boundaries to this coined term:

> Moritz uses the term *screenie* to describe this video-drenched generation, which has digested thousands of hours of television, imbibing its "video-logic." To that must be added, for many of them, more hours of interactive video games and, even more important, of work on their own personal computers. They not only follow a different logic, but are accustomed to make the screen do things, thus making them good prospects for the interactive services and products soon to hit the market. Above all, they are accustomed to choice.

Sometimes in writing you stop to define a standard word not often used, to save your readers a trip to the dictionary. Or you may define a concept that is familiar but often misunderstood. What is equality, intelligence, socialism, HMO, minimum wage, a holding corporation? Whenever in your writing you need to indicate the nature of an idea, a thing, a movement, a phenomenon, an organization, you'll find defining a helpful strategy. The more complex or ambiguous the subject, the longer the definition you need to clarify the term for your readers.

Here are some questions you can ask yourself when you use definitions in your writing.

**DISCOVERY
CHECKLIST**

## Using Definitions to Develop Ideas

- Have you used definitions to help your readers understand the subject matter, not to show off your knowledge?
- Have you tailored your definition to the needs of your audience?
- Is your definition specific, clear, and accurate?
- Would your definition benefit from an example or from details?

EXERCISE

## Defining

Write an extended definition (a paragraph or so in length) of one of the following words. Begin with a one-sentence definition of the word. Then, to expand and clarify your ideas, use some of the strategies discussed in this chapter — examples, details, division and classification, process analysis, comparison and contrast, and identifying causes or effects. You may also use *negation* (explaining what something is by stating what it is not). Don't get most of your definition from a dictionary or textbook. Then share your definition with your classmates or writing group.

| | | | |
|---|---|---|---|
| education | abuse | exercise | literacy |
| privacy | jazz | dieting | success |
| taboo | rock music | gossip | fear |
| prejudice | AIDS | ecology | gender |

# Dividing and Classifying

To divide is to break something down into its components. It's far easier to take in a subject, especially a complex subject, one piece at a time. The thing divided may be as concrete and definite as Manhattan (which a writer might divide into neighborhoods) or as abstract as a person's knowledge of art (which the writer might divide into knowledge of sculpture, painting, drawing, and other forms). To classify is to make sense of a complicated and potentially bewildering array of things — works of literature, this year's movies — by sorting them into categories (*types* or *classes*) that you can deal with one at a time. Literature is customarily arranged by genre or class: novels, stories, poems, plays. A discussion about movies might sort them by audience (children's movies, movies for teenagers, movies for mature audiences).

These two methods of development are like two sides of the same coin. In theory, any broad subject can be *divided* into components, which can then be *classified* into categories. In practice, it's often difficult to tell where division stops and classification begins. And if you think the definitions of division and classification we've just given sound familiar, you're not imagining things: *analyzing,* the critical thinking task we discuss in Chapter 6, requires the writer to first break an item down into its component parts (and perhaps organize them into categories) to better understand, explain, or evaluate it.

In the following paragraph from his college textbook *Wildlife Management* (San Francisco: Freeman, 1978), Robert H. Giles, Jr., uses division to simplify an especially large, abstract subject: the management of forest wildlife in America. To explain which professional environmentalists in America assume which duties and responsibilities, Giles divides forest wildlife management into six levels or areas of concern, arranged roughly from large to small. To a nonspecialist, this subject may seem head-stoppingly complicated. But see how neatly Giles divides it and explains it in a paragraph of less than 175 words.

There are six scales of forest wildlife management: (1) national, (2) regional, (3) state or industrial, (4) county or parish, (5) intra-state region, management unit, or watershed, and (6) forest. Each is different. At the national and regional levels, management includes decisions on timber harvest quotas, grazing policy in forested lands, official stance on forest taxation bills, cutting policy relative to threatened and endangered species, management coordination of migratory species, and research fund allocation. At the state or industrial level, decision types include land acquisition, sale, or trade; season setting; and permit systems and fees. At the county level, plans are made, seasons set, and special fees levied. At the intra-state level, decisions include what seasons to recommend, what stances to take on bills not affecting local conditions, the sequence in which to attempt land acquisition, and the placement of facilities. At the forest level, decisions may include some of those of the larger management unit but typically are those of maintenance schedules, planting stock, cutting rotations, personnel employment and supervision, road closures, equipment use, practices to be attempted or used, and boundaries to be marked.

In a textbook lesson on how babies develop, Kurt W. Fischer and Arlyne Lazerson (writing in *Human Development* [New York: Freeman, 1984]) take a paragraph to describe a research project that classified individual babies into three types according to temperament.

The researchers also found that certain of these temperamental qualities tended to occur together. These clusters of characteristics generally fell into three types — the easy baby, the difficult baby, and the baby who was slow to warm up. The *easy infant* has regular patterns of eating and sleeping, readily approaches new objects and people, adapts easily to changes in the environment, generally reacts with low or moderate intensity, and typically is in a cheerful mood. The *difficult infant* usually shows irregular patterns of eating and sleeping, withdraws from new objects or people, adapts slowly to changes, reacts with great intensity, and is frequently cranky. The *slow-to-warm-up infant* typically has a low activity level, tends to withdraw when presented with an unfamiliar object, reacts with a low level of intensity, and adapts slowly to changes in the environment. Fortunately for parents, most healthy infants — 40 percent or more — have an easy temperament. Only about 10 percent have a difficult temperament, and about 15 percent are slow to warm up. The remaining 35 percent do not easily fit one of the three types but show some other pattern.

When you divide and classify, your point is to make order out of a complex or overwhelming jumble of stuff. Take care that your divisions and classifications really do make the jumble easier for you and your readers to understand. Make sure the components and categories you identify are sensible, given the purpose of your paragraph or essay. Use the same principle of classification of analysis for all categories. For example, if you're trying to discuss campus relations, it makes sense to divide the school population into *instructors*, *students*, and *support staff*; it would make less sense to divide it into *people from the South*, *people from the rest of the U.S.*, and *people from overseas*.

Also, try to set apples beside apples, not beside oranges. In other words, make sure all the components or categories you use are roughly equivalent. For example, if you're classifying television shows and you've come up with *sitcoms*, *dramas*, *talk shows*, *children's shows*, *news*, and *cartoons*, then you've got a problem: the last category is probably part of *children's shows*. Finally, check that your final division or classification system is simple and easy for your readers to understand. Most people can handle only about seven things at once. If you've got more than six or seven components in your division, perhaps you need to use classification to assemble the individual components into groups. If you've got more than six or seven categories in your classification, perhaps you need to combine or eliminate some.

Here are some questions to ask yourself when you use division or classification in your writing.

**DISCOVERY CHECKLIST**

## Using Division and Classification to Develop Ideas

- Do you use the most logical principle of division or classification for your purpose?
- Do you stick to one principle throughout?
- Have you identified components or categories that are comparable?
- Have you used the best order for your components or categories?
- Have you given specific examples for each of your components or categories?
- Have you succeeded in making a complex subject more accessible to your readers?

**EXERCISE**

## Dividing and Classifying

To practice dividing and classifying, choose one or two of the following subjects and brainstorm for five minutes on each, trying to come up with as many components as you can. Then compare your lists with those of your classmates. For each subject, create one large list by combining items from all students who chose that subject. Working as a group, take the largest list and try to classify the items on it into logical categories. Feel free to add or change components or categories if you find you've overlooked something.

| | | | |
|---|---|---|---|
| students | customers | sports | families |
| teachers | automobiles | vacations | drivers |

# Analyzing a Process

Analyzing a process is one of the most useful kinds of writing: telling step by step how something is or was done or how to do something. An entire essay can be built on analysis of a process, but here we will look at ways process analysis can be used in paragraphs to develop an idea within an essay.

You can analyze an action or a phenomenon: how a skyscraper is built, how a political revolution begins, how sunspots form on the sun's surface.

This strategy will be familiar if you have ever followed directions in a cookbook, but it can also explain large, long-ago happenings that a writer couldn't possibly have witnessed. Here, for instance, is a paragraph by a team of botanists, Peter H. Raven, Ray F. Evert, and Helena Curtis (from their college textbook *Biology of Plants* [New York: Worth, 1992]), analyzing the process of continental drift.

> About 127 million years ago — when angiosperm pollen first appears in the fossil record — Africa and South America were directly linked with one another and with Antarctica, India, and Australia in a great southern supercontinent called Gondwanaland. Africa and South America began to separate at about this time, forming the southern Atlantic Ocean, but they did not move completely apart in the tropical regions until about 90 million years ago. India began to move northward at about the same time, colliding with Asia about 45 million years ago and thrusting up the Himalayas in the process. Australia began to separate from Antarctica about 55 million years ago, but their separation did not become complete until about 40 million years ago.

Notice the writers' use of time markers — *about 127 million years ago, at about this time, until about 90 million years ago.* This paragraph illustrates the kind of process analysis that sets forth how something happens: an *informative* process analysis.

Another familiar kind is the *directive* or "how-to" process analysis, which instructs readers how to do something — how to box, invest for retirement, clean a painting — or how to make something — how to draw a map, blaze a trail, put together a simple computer. In the following example (from *The Little Windows Book, 3.1 Edition* [Berkeley: Peachpit Press, 1992]), technical writer Kay Yarborough Nelson uses a directive process description to teach her readers how to use a computer mouse.

> You can use the mouse in three basic ways: by clicking, double-clicking, and dragging.
>
> To select an item on the screen, you can move the mouse pointer to it and click once with the left mouse button. (If you're left-handed, you can change it to the right mouse button, as you'll see in the chapter on customizing Windows.) Selecting an item makes it active, so that you can work with it. For example, you might click on a document's icon so that you could copy or move it.
>
> You can also double-click on an item to make it active and actually start it. To double-click, quickly click twice with the left mouse button. For example, double-clicking on a program's icon will open a window and start the program. . . .
>
> A third way of using the mouse is dragging. To drag, put the mouse pointer on what you want to drag, press and hold the left mouse button down, and then move the mouse.

Notice the care Nelson takes to make each step seem as simple and logical as possible. Her clear divisions (*three basic ways*), unambiguous commands (*move . . . , click . . . , put . . .*), concrete examples (*For example . . .*), and helpful transitions (*a third way, and then*) help guide readers through an unfamiliar process step by step.

A process analysis is a wonderful way to show your readers the inside workings of an event or system, even if they're never going to participate directly in it themselves. Process analyses can be difficult to follow, though, so make sure you do everything possible to guide your readers along the way. Be sure to divide the process into logical steps or stages and to put the steps in a sensible chronological order. Add details or examples wherever your description may become too ambiguous or abstract, and use transitions to mark the end of one step and the beginning of the next.

Here are some questions to ask yourself when you use process analysis in your writing.

DISCOVERY
CHECKLIST

### Using Process Analysis to Develop Ideas

- Do you thoroughly understand the process you are analyzing?
- Do you have a good reason to use process analysis at this point in your essay?
- Have you broken the process down into logical and useful steps?
- Is the order in which you present these steps the best one possible?
- Have you used transitions to guide your readers from one step to the next?

EXERCISE

### Analyzing a Process

Analyze one of the following processes or procedures and use your analysis as the basis of a paragraph or short essay. Then share your analysis with your peer group. Can members of your group follow your analysis easily? Do they spot anything you left out?

registration for college classes        falling in love
studying for a test                     buying a used car
influenza (or another disease)          cloud formation

## *Comparing and Contrasting*

Often you can develop a paragraph effectively by setting a pair of subjects side by side and comparing and contrasting them. When you compare, you point out similarities; when you contrast, you discuss differences. Working together, these twin strategies use one subject to clarify another. The dual method works well for a pair of things similar in nature: two cities, two films, the theories of two economists. It can show that a writer has clearly observed and thoroughly understood both. For this reason, college instructors will often ask you on exams to compare and contrast ("Discuss the chief similarities and differences between nineteenth-century French and English colonial policies in West Africa").

An entire essay can be focused around a central comparison and contrast. This type of assignment is covered in Chapter 7. Here we will look at ways comparing and contrasting — or either one of them used alone — can be used to develop an idea within an essay.

In daily life, all of us frequently compare and contrast: we decide which menu selection to choose, which car (or other product) to buy, which magazine to read in a waiting room, which college course to sign up for. A comparison and contrast can lead to a final evaluation and a decision about which thing under consideration is better (as in these cases), but it doesn't have to. In a travel essay, "Venezuela for Visitors" from *Hugging the Shore* (New York: Knopf, 1983), written for the readers of the *New Yorker*, novelist John Updike sees Venezuelan society as polarized: it consists of rich people and Indians. In the following paragraph, Updike compares and contrasts the two classes without choosing between them:

> Missionaries, many of them United States citizens, move among the Indians. They claim that since Western civilization, with all its diseases and detritus, must come, it had best come through them. Nevertheless, Marxist anthropologists inveigh against them. Foreign experts, many of them United States citizens, move among the rich. They claim they are just helping out, and that anyway the oil industry was nationalized five years ago. Nevertheless, Marxist anthropologists are not mollified. The feet of the Indians are very broad in front, their toes spread wide for climbing avocado trees. The feet of the rich are very narrow in front, their toes compressed by pointed Italian shoes. The Indians seek relief from tension in the use of *ebene*, or *yopo*, a mind-altering drug distilled from the bark of the ebene tree and blown into the user's nose through a hollow cane by a colleague. The rich take cocaine through the nose, and frequent mind-altering discotheques, but more customarily imbibe cognac, *vino blanco*, and Scotch, in association with colleagues.

Updike simply sets the two side by side: the feet of the poor, the feet of the rich; how the poor get high, how the rich do. By doing so, he throws the two groups of people into sharp relief.

You can use two basic methods of organization for comparison and contrast: the opposing pattern and the alternating pattern. Using the *opposing pattern*, you discuss all of the characteristics or subdivisions of the first subject in the first half of the paragraph or essay and then discuss all the characteristics of the other subject. Using the *alternating pattern*, you move back and forth between the two subjects. This pattern places the specifics close together for immediate comparison and contrast. For example, a writer using the opposing pattern to compare and contrast the brothers Jim and Jack would discuss Jim's physical appearance, his personality traits, and his interests and would then discuss Jack's appearance, his personality, and his interests — discussing in both parts the same characteristics in the same order. A writer using the alternating pattern would discuss Jim's physical appearance, then Jack's physical appearance; Jim's personality, then Jack's; Jim's interests, then Jack's.

Whichever pattern of order you choose, be sure to cover the same subpoints under each item and do so in the same order in all parts.

In the paragraph above about Venezuelan society, John Updike uses the alternating pattern to compare and contrast rich people and Indians. In the following paragraph, Jacquelyn Wonder and Priscilla Donovan, management consultants, use the opposing pattern of organization to explain the differences in the brains of females and males.

> At birth there are basic differences between male and female brains. The female cortex is more fully developed. The sound of the human voice elicits more left-brain activity in infant girls than in infant boys, accounting in part for the earlier development in females of language. Baby girls have larger connectors between the brain's hemispheres and thus integrate information more skillfully. This flexibility bestows greater verbal and intuitive skills. Male infants lack this ready communication between the brain's lobes; therefore, messages are routed and rerouted to the right brain, producing larger right hemispheres. The size advantage accounts for males having greater spatial and physical abilities and explains why they may become more highly lateralized and skilled in specific areas.

After the topic sentence, "At birth there are basic differences between male and female brains," the authors first explain the development of the female brain and how it accounts for specific thinking styles in females, and then in the last part of the paragraph they explain the development of the male brain and the effects on males' abilities.

These brief examples may suggest that comparing and contrasting aren't just meaningless academic calisthenics. They are explaining devices that appeal to writers who have a passion for making things clear.

Here are some questions to ask yourself when you use comparison and contrast in your writing.

DISCOVERY
CHECKLIST

## Using Comparison and Contrast to Develop Ideas

- Is your reason for comparing and contrasting unmistakably clear?
- Have you chosen the *major* similarities and differences to write about?
- Have you used the same categories for each item? In discussing each feature, do you always compare or contrast like things?
- Have you used the best possible arrangement, given your subject and the point you're trying to make?
- If you are making a judgment between your subjects, have you treated both fairly?
- Have you avoided a boringly mechanical, monotonous style ("On one hand, . . . now on the other hand")?

## Comparing and Contrasting

Write a paragraph or two in which you compare and contrast the subjects in one of the following pairs. Use your own recall or observation, go to the library, or converse with an expert if you need material.

baseball and football (or basketball)

living in an apartment and living in a house

two cities or towns you are familiar with

two musicians

two poems

watching a sports event on television and in person

# Identifying Causes and Effects

From the time we are children, we ask why. Why can't I go out and play? Why is the sky blue? Why do pickles taste sour? Why did my goldfish die? Our seeking causes and effects continues into adulthood. We try to understand our often puzzling world by searching for causes and identifying effects. So it's natural that explaining causal relationships is one of the most used methods of development in writing.

To use cause and effect successfully, you must think about the subject critically, gather evidence, draw judicious conclusions, and show relationships clearly. Chapter 8 gives you detailed information about how to write a complete essay identifying causes and/or effects, but let's look at a couple of brief examples of how this technique for development can be used in one paragraph of a longer essay.

Thomas McKeown, in a chapter called "The Diseases of Affluence" in his book *The Origins of Human Disease* (New York: Blackwell, 1988) speculates on the *causes* of the attention that ill effects of smoking have received:

> There is probably no other hazard whose ill effects on health have been, or perhaps could be, charted as meticulously as those of tobacco. There are several reasons why it has received so much attention. First, it has been under investigation for almost exactly the period — the last four decades — in which the origins of non-communicable diseases have been seriously considered; until the end of the Second World War interest in the relation of behavior and environment to disease was almost confined to the infections. Second, the large increase in the frequency of smoking has occurred in the present century, when evidence from national statistics and other sources was much better than that available for diet and reproduction, in which some of the major changes occurred in the nineteenth century. And third, the effects of smoking on health are so large and so obvious that they are accepted even by people who dismiss other features of behavior as scarcely worth attention.

Notice how McKeown clearly marks his *reasons: First, Second, And third.*

Instead of focusing on causes *or* effects, often writers trace a *chain* of cause and effect relationships, as Charles C. Mann and Mark L. Plummer do in "The Butterfly Problem" (*The Atlantic* Jan. 1992):

> More generally, the web of species around us helps generate soil, regulate freshwater supplies, dispose of waste, and maintain the quality of the atmosphere. Pillaging nature to the point where it cannot perform these functions is dangerously foolish. Simple self-protection is thus a second motive for preserving biodiversity. When DDT was sprayed in Borneo, the biologists Paul and Anne Ehrlich relate in their book *Extinction* (1981), it killed all the houseflies. The gecko lizards that preyed on the flies ate their pesticide-filled corpses and died. House cats consumed the dying lizards; they died too. Rats descended on the villages, bringing bubonic plague. Incredibly, the housefly in this case was part of an intricate system that controlled human disease. To make up for its absence, the government was forced to parachute cats into the area.

As these examples show, an effective use of cause and effect can help you present a complex situation or chain of events to your readers.

Here are some questions to ask youself when you identify causes and effects in your writing.

DISCOVERY
CHECKLIST

## Using Cause and Effect to Develop Ideas

- Is your use of cause and effect clearly tied to the overall message or point you're trying to make?
- Are the causes you have identified actual causes? Can you find evidence to support them?
- Are the effects you have identified actual effects, or are they merely conjecture? If conjecture, are they logical results? Can you find evidence to support them?
- Have you judiciously drawn conclusions concerning causes and effects? Have you avoided fallacies of thinking, such as hasty generalization and stereotyping (see p. 120)?
- Have you presented things clearly and logically, so that your readers can follow and understand them easily?

EXERCISE

## Identifying Causes and Effects

1. Identify some of the *causes* of *five* of the following. Discuss possible causes with your classmates.

| | | |
|---|---|---|
| failing an exam | stage fright | losing a job |
| an automobile accident | losing or winning a game | losing weight |
| poor health | stress | going to college |
| good health | getting a job | getting a scholarship |

2. Identify some of the *effects* of *five* of the following. Discuss possible effects with your classmates.

| | |
|---|---|
| an insult | dieting |
| a compliment | speeding |

| | |
|---|---|
| poor attendance in class | drinking while driving |
| a child's running away from home | divorce |
| smoking cigarettes | increase in taxes |

3. Identify some of the *causes and effects* of *one* of the following. You may need to do a little research in the library or in a textbook to identify the chain of causes and effects for the event. How might you use what you have discovered as part of an essay? Discuss your findings with your classmates.

| | |
|---|---|
| the Civil War | the AIDS virus |
| the Vietnam War | recycling |
| Bill Clinton's tenure as president | smoking crack cocaine |
| the discovery of atomic energy | the uses of solar energy |
| a U.S. Supreme Court decision | the hole in the ozone layer |
|    on abortion | racial tension |

# *Making Connections:*
# *Strategies for Developing Evident in* A Writer's Reader

Professional writers use the same strategies to develop their ideas in writing that you have just studied in this chapter. Here we list a few clear examples that you can use to see these strategies at work in the essays in *A Writer's Reader.*

In "Mother Tongue" (p. 476), Amy Tan uses *examples* to illustrate her points (see especially paragraphs 3, 5, and 6), as does E. B. White in "Once More to the Lake" (p. 462). Jessica Mitford throughout "Behind the Formaldehyde Curtain" (p. 604) uses specific *details* (see paragraph 8), and Christina Hoff Sommers in "The Backlash Myth: The Truth about How Women Are Doing in the Workplace" (p. 560) uses *statistics and facts.* Robert Wright *defines eugenics* in paragraphs 10–11 in "Mr. Clean Genes" (p. 611), and Melvin Konner defines *placebo effect* in paragraph 4 of "Out of the Darkness" (p. 615). Christina Hoff Sommers *divides and classifies* types of feminists in "The Backlash Myth: The Truth about How Women Are Doing in the Workplace" (p. 560), and Ellen Goodman classifies the types of Hollywood stars in "The New Hollywood Male" (p. 577). Jessica Mitford *analyzes the process* of embalming in "Behind the Formaldehyde Curtain" (p. 604). In "Oprah and Jo-Jo the Dog-Faced Boy" (p. 590), Kurt Andersen *compares and contrasts* various types of television talk shows, as Scott Russell Sanders compares and contrasts types of men in his essay "The Men We Carry in Our Minds" (p. 499). In "Black Men and Public Space" (p. 518), Brent Staples identifies a chain of *causes and effects,* as Toni Morrison does in "On the Backs of Blacks" (p. 528). As you read the essays in *A Writer's Reader*, identify the strategies the authors use to develop their paragraphs and essays.

# Chapter 19

# Strategies for Revising and Editing

Good writing is rewriting. When Ernest Hemingway was asked why he rewrote the last page of the novel *A Farewell to Arms* thirty-nine times, he replied, "Getting the words right." His comment reflects the care that serious writers take in revising their work. You will do well to follow Hemingway's lead and take care with your revising.

In this chapter we provide strategies for revising and editing what you write. We suggest ways to rethink muddy ideas and emphasize important ideas, to rephrase obscure passages and restructure garbled sentences. Our advice applies not only to reseeing and rewriting whole essays but also to rewriting sentences and paragraphs. In addition, we give you tips for proofreading and editing.

## Re-viewing, Re-vising, and Editing

Revision is much more than mere correction of grammar and spelling. *Revision* actually means "seeing again" — discovering again, conceiving again, shaping again. It is not something you do only after you complete a paper. Rather, it is an integral aspect of the total writing process; it may occur at any and all stages of the process.

Most writers do a lot of rewriting. Sometimes it's general — reordering ideas or finding additional information to develop an idea. Other times it's more particular, just tinkering with sentence structure or playing around with word choice. You will be doing both types of revision. *Macro revising* is making large, global, or fundamental changes that affect the overall direction or impact of writing. Macro revising involves the rhetorical aspects of writing: purpose, voice, audience, unity, organization, development, coherence, clarity. We'll focus on techniques for revising for purpose, organization, development, and audience. *Micro revising* is paying attention to the details. It involves the language aspects of writing: sentences, words, punctuation, grammar. We'll focus on techniques for creating emphasis and eliminating wordiness. We'll also provide techniques for editing, rewriting to make the use of language more effective, and for proofreading, checking the correctness of spelling, grammar, and mechanics.

In the "Revising and Editing" sections of previous chapters, you found specific advice for making decisions about revising. Here now are some general guidelines for revising, accompanied by three *general* checklists of questions you might ask yourself as you reread and revise. You can use these questions for almost every writing task, but they will prove useful only if you allow time to give your work a thorough going-over. Allow your ideas to incubate. When you have time to spare, these questions will guide you to make not just slight, cosmetic touch-ups, but major improvements.

## REVISING FOR PURPOSE

When you revise for purpose, you make sure that your writing really accomplishes whatever it is that you want it to do. If your goal is to create an interesting profile of a person you know, have you done that? If you want to persuade your readers to take a certain course of action, have you succeeded? If you want to voice your opinion of recent legislative acts, have you done so? To revise for purpose, you'll have to take a step back from your writing and try to see it as other readers will see it. Concentrate on what's actually in your paper.

Remember that the purpose of your final essay may be different from the purpose you had in mind when you began writing. Such a change may be especially true for long, complex writing projects that usually evolve over time or for writing assignments that you begin without a clear direction.

At this point you'll probably want to review and revise your working thesis statement (if you've developed one) or create a thesis sentence (if you haven't). (See "Stating and Using a Thesis," p. 349.) Scrutinize your tentative statement of main idea, considering whether each part of the essay is directly related to it, whether each part develops and supports it, and whether everything promised in the working thesis is carried out in the essay. If you find passages that are not related to the thesis, or if you find contradictions between your thesis and the information in the essay, or if you find gaps between your thesis and the information in the essay, you have two options: revise the thesis or revise the essay. As an exercise, develop a comprehensive, detailed, and precise thesis statement that covers every major point in your essay. Then ask yourself if that thesis really makes sense. Even if you don't include the detailed thesis in your essay — and it's quite likely that you won't — it will help you to see where your essay works effectively to fulfill your purpose and where it doesn't.

Here are some questions you can ask yourself when revising for purpose.

**REVISION
CHECKLIST**

## Achieving Your Purpose

- Do you know exactly what you want your essay to accomplish? Can you express it clearly to yourself? Can you put it in one sentence: "In this paper I want to . . . ."
- Is your thesis stated outright anywhere in the essay? If not, are there enough clues that your readers will know precisely what it is?
- Does every part of the essay work to achieve the same goal?
- Have you tried to take in too much territory, with the result that your coverage of your topic seems too thin? If so, how might you reduce the scope of your essay?
- Does your essay say everything that needs to be said? Is everything — ideas, connections between ideas, supporting evidence — on paper, not just in your head?
- Do you still believe everything you say? In writing the essay, have you changed your mind, rethought your assumptions, made a discovery? Do any of your interpretations or statements of opinion now need to be recast?
- Do you have enough evidence? Is every point developed fully enough to be clear? To be convincing? If not, try recalling, observing, conversing, reading, and imagining. Try some of the strategies for generating ideas (Chapter 15) or for developing paragraphs (Chapter 18).

### REVISING FOR STRUCTURE

When revising for structure, you make sure that the order of your ideas and the arrangement of material is as effective as possible. You may have put down on paper all the ingredients of a successful essay — but in a hugely jumbled, confusing mess. What you want to do now is make sure that you've set up your essay in a way that your readers can easily follow where you want to lead them and end up at the destination you have in mind.

In a well-structured essay each paragraph, sentence, and phrase fulfills a clear function. Scrutinize opening and closing paragraphs to ensure that they are relevant, concise, and interesting. Look at each paragraph to make sure everything in it is on the same topic and that all ideas are adequately developed. Consider the paragraphs as a group to decide whether they're in the best possible order; have a reason for putting them in the order you select. Finally, review each place where you lead readers from one idea to the next to be absolutely certain that the transition is clear and painless. (For more on paragraphs, topic sentences, and transition, see Chapter 17, "Strategies for Drafting.")

An outline can be useful to diagnose a draft that you suspect doesn't quite make sense. You may have already used outlining as a planning technique (see p. 358); now you want to create an outline that shows what you've succeeded in getting down on paper. If you can't easily make an outline of what you have written, then probably your readers will have a hard time following your writing. Start by finding the topic sentence of each paragraph in your draft (or creating one, if necessary) and listing them in order. Label the sentences *I., II., A., B.,* and so on, according to logical patterns of coordination and subordination to indicate the relationships of ideas in your essay. Do the same with the supporting details under each topic sentence, labeling them also with letters and numbers and indenting appropriately. Now look at the outline. Does it make sense on its own, without the essay to explain it? Would any different order or arrangement be more effective? Is there any section that looks thin, where more evidence might be needed? Maybe the sequence of ideas needs rearranging. Maybe the connections between parts are in your head but not on paper. Maybe too many ideas are jammed into too few paragraphs. Maybe you don't have as many specific details and examples as you need. It is often easier and quicker to operate on your outline than on your ailing draft because the outline includes only the main points. Work on the outline until you get it into strong shape and then rewrite the essay to follow it.

Here are some questions to ask yourself when you are revising for structure.

REVISION
CHECKLIST

## Testing Structure

- Does the introduction set up the whole essay? Does it both grab readers' attention and hint at what is to follow? (See p. 374.)
- Does the essay fulfill all the promises that you make in your opening?
- Is there any passage later in the essay that would make a better beginning?
- Is the thesis clear early in the essay? If explicit, is it given a position of emphasis?
- Do the paragraph breaks seem logical? Does each paragraph begin a new idea? (See p. 370.)
- Is the main idea of each paragraph clear? Have you used a topic sentence in every paragraph? (See p. 371.) If not, try putting one in every paragraph to try to strengthen clarity and coherence.
- Is the main idea of each paragraph fully developed? Can you see any places where you might need more details or evidence to be convincing? (See p. 389.)
- Within each paragraph, is each detail or piece of evidence relevant to the topic sentence? If you find a stray bit, should you omit it altogether or move it to another paragraph?
- Are all the ideas directly relevant to the main point of the essay?
- Would any paragraphs make more sense or follow better if arranged in a different order?
- Does everything follow clearly? Does one point smoothly lead to the next? If connections aren't clear, would transitions help? (See p. 380.)
- Does the conclusion follow from what has gone before? Does it avoid seeming arbitrarily tacked on? (See p. 376.)

### REVISING FOR AUDIENCE

An essay is successful only if it succeeds with its particular audience, and what works with one audience of readers can fall flat with another. Take the time to think about who your readers are and to reread your essay with your intended readers in mind. Visualize one of your readers poring over the essay, sentence by sentence, reacting to what you have written. What expressions do you see on his or her face? Where does he or she have trouble understanding? Where have you hit the mark? Your organization, your selection of details, your word choice, and your tone all affect your readers, so you should pay special attention to these aspects of your writing.

Of course, there's no substitute for having another person go over your writing. Most college assignments ask you to write for an audience of your classmates, but even if your essay is written for a different group (the town council or readers of the *New Yorker*, for example), having a classmate read over your essay is a worthwhile revision technique. (See Chapter 20, "Strategies for Working with Other Writers: Collaborative Learning.")

Here are some questions you can ask yourself when you are revising with your audience in mind.

**REVISION CHECKLIST**

## Considering Your Audience

- Who will read this essay?
- Does the essay tell them what they will want to know? Or does it tell them only what they probably know already?
- Are there any places where readers might go to sleep? If so, can such passages be shortened or deleted or livened up?
- Does the opening of the essay mislead your readers by promising anything that the essay never delivers?
- Do you take ample time and space to unfold each idea in enough detail to make it both clear and interesting? Would more detailed evidence help? (See p. 389.)
- Have you anticipated questions the readers might ask?
- Are there any long-winded explanations or examples that really don't contribute to your main point?
- Are there places where readers might raise serious objections? How might you anticipate these objections and answer them?
- Have you used any specialized or technical language that your readers might not understand? Have you used any familiar words in a technical sense? If so, work in brief definitions.
- What attitude toward your readers do you seem to take? Are you chummy, angry, superior, apologetic, condescending, preachy? Should you revise to improve your attitude? Ask your peers for an opinion.
- From your conclusion and from your essay as a whole, will your readers be convinced that you have told them something worth knowing?

# Stressing What Counts

A boring writer writes as though every idea is no more important than any other. An effective writer cares what matters, decides what matters most, and shines a bright light on it. You can't emphasize merely by <u>underlining</u> things, by putting them in "quotation marks," or by throwing them into CAPITAL LETTERS. Such devices soon grow monotonous, and a writer who works them hard ends up stressing nothing at all. This section offers suggestions for how to emphasize things that count.

## STATING FIRST OR LAST

The most emphatic positions in an essay, in a paragraph, or in a single sentence are the beginning and the end. Let's consider each.

**Stating First.**   In an essay, you might state in your opening paragraph what matters most. Writing a paper for an economics course in which students had been assigned to explain the consequences of import quotas (such as a limit on the number of foreign cars allowed into a country), Donna Waite began by summing up her findings:

> Although an import quota has many effects, both for the nation imposing the quota and for the nation whose industries must suffer from it, I believe that the most important effect is generally felt at home. A native industry gains a chance to thrive in a marketplace of lessened competition.

Waite's paper goes on to illustrate her general observation with evidence. Summing up the most important point right at the start is a good strategy for answering a question in an essay examination. It immediately shows the instructor that you know the answer.

A paper that takes a stand or makes a proposal might open with a statement of what the writer believes.

> Our state's antiquated system of justices of the peace is inefficient.

> For urgent reasons, I recommend that the United States place a human observer in temporary orbit around the planet Mars.

The body of the paper would set forth the writer's reasons for holding the view, and probably the writer would hammer the claim or thesis again at the end.

That advice refers to whole essays. Now let's see how in a single sentence you can stress things at the start. Consider the following unemphatic sentence:

```
When Congress debates the Hall-Hayes Act removing
existing legal protections for endangered species, as now
seems likely to occur on May 12, it will be a consider-
able misfortune if this bill should pass, since the ex-
tinction of many rare birds and animals would certainly
be the result.
```

The coming debate and its probable date take up the start of the sentence. The writer might have made better use of this emphatic position.

```
The extinction of many rare birds and animals would
follow passage of the Hall-Hayes Act.
```

Now the writer stresses what he most fears: dire consequences. (In a further sentence, he might add the date of the coming debate in Congress and his opinion that passage of the legislation would be a misfortune.)
Consider these further examples:

DRAFT   It may be argued that the best way to choose software for a small business is to call in a professional consultant, who is likely to be familiar with the many systems available and can give helpful advice.

REVISED   The best way to choose software for a small business is to call in a professional consultant.

Notice that in the revision, the two most important ingredients of the idea are placed first and last. *Best way* is placed up front, and *professional consultant,* standing last in the sentence, is also emphasized.

Stating Last.   To place an idea last can throw weight on it. One way to assemble your ideas in an emphatic order is to proceed from least important to most important. This order is dramatic: it builds up and up.

Not all writing assignments call for drama, of course. In the papers on import quotas and justices of the peace, any attempt at a big dramatic buildup might look artificial and contrived. Still, this strategy is worth considering. Perhaps in an essay on how city parks lure shoppers to the city, the thesis sentence — summing up the whole point of the essay — might stand at the very end: "For the inner city, to improve city parks will bring about a new era of prosperity." Giving all the evidence first and leading up to the thesis at the end is particularly effective in editorials and informal persuasive essays. Ask yourself: Just where in my essay have I made my one main point, the point I most want to make? Once you find it, see if you can place it last by cutting or shifting what comes after it.

This climactic order works not only in essays but also in sentences. A sentence that suspends its main point until the end is a *periodic* sentence. Waiting for someone to finish readying for a trip, you might say, "Now that you've packed your toothbrush and a change of clothing, let's roll!" By placing "let's roll" at the end of the sentence, you emphasize it. Notice how novelist Julian Green builds to his point of emphasis:

> Amid chaos of illusions into which we are cast headlong, there is one thing that stands out as true, and that is — love.

### REPEATING

In general, it's economical to say a thing once. But at times repetition can be valuable. One such time is when repetition serves as a transition: it recalls something said earlier. (We discuss such repetition on p. 383.)

Repetition can be valuable, too, when it lends emphasis. When Robert Frost ends his poem "Stopping by Woods on a Snowy Evening" by repeating a line, he does so deliberately:

> The woods are lovely, dark and deep,
> But I have promises to keep,
> And miles to go before I sleep,
> And miles to go before I sleep.

The device of repeating the words that matter most is more often heard in a speech than found in writing. Recall Lincoln's Gettysburg Address, with its promise that "government of the people, by the people, and for the people" will endure; and Martin Luther King's famous speech with the insistent refrain "I have a dream." This is a powerful device for emphasis. Break it out only when an occasion calls for it.

## Cutting and Whittling

Like pea pickers who throw out dirt and pebbles, good writers remove needless words that clog their prose. One of the chief joys of revising is to watch 200 paunchy words shrink to a svelte 150. To see how saving words helps, let's first look at some wordiness. In what she imagined to be a gracious, Oriental style, a New York socialite once sent this dinner invitation to Hu Shi, the Chinese ambassador:

> O learned sage and distinguished representative of the numerous Chinese nation, pray deign to honor my humble abode with your noble presence at a pouring of libations, to be followed by a modest evening repast, on the forthcoming Friday, June Eighteenth, in this Year of the Pig, at the approximate

hour of eight o'clock, Eastern Standard Time. Kindly be assured furthermore, O most illustrious sire, that a favorable reply at your earliest convenience will be received most humbly and gratefully by the undersigned unworthy suppliant.

In reply, the witty diplomat sent this telegram:

CAN DO. HU SHI.

Hu Shi's reply disputes a common assumption: that the more words an idea takes, the more impressive it will seem. Most good contemporary writers know that the more succinctly they can state an idea, the clearer and more forceful it will be.

Some writers may begin by writing a long first draft, putting in every scrap of material, spelling out their every thought in detail. To them, it is easier to trim away the surplus than to add missing essentials. In their revising habits, such writers may be like sculptor Auguste Rodin, who when an admirer asked, "Oh, Monsieur Rodin, is sculpture difficult?" answered lightly, "Not at all! I merely behold the statue in the block of stone. Then I chip away everything else." Let us see how writers chip away.

**Cut the Fanfare.**   Why bother to announce that you're going to say something? Cut the fanfare. We aren't, by the way, attacking the usefulness of transitions that lead readers along (see p. 380).

WORDY    As far as getting ready for winter is concerned, I put antifreeze in my car.

REVISED    To get ready for winter, I put antifreeze in my car.

WORDY    The point should be made that . . .
I might hasten to add that . . .
Let me make it perfectly clear that . . .
In this paper I intend to . . .
In conclusion I would like to say that . . .

**Be Direct.**    The phrases *on the subject of, in regard to, in terms of, as far as . . . is concerned,* and their ilk often lead to wind.

WORDY    He is more or less a pretty outstanding person in regard to good looks.

REVISED    He is strikingly handsome.

Here's an especially grim example of corporate prose (before cutting and after):

WORDY    Regarding trainees' personal life in relation to domestic status, it is not the intention of the management to object to the marriage of any of its trainees at their own individual discretions.

> REVISED   Trainees may marry if they like.

Words can also tend to abound after *There is* or *There are*.

> WORDY   There are many people who dislike flying.
>
> REVISED   Many people dislike flying.
>
> WORDY   There is a lack of a sense of beauty in Wallace.
>
> REVISED   Wallace lacks a sense of beauty.
> Wallace is insensitive to beauty.

**Use Strong Verbs.**   Forms of the verb *be* (*am, is, are, was, were*) can make a statement wordy when a noun or an adjective follows it. Such weak verbs can almost always be replaced by active verbs.

> WORDY   The Akron game was a disappointment to the fans.
>
> REVISED   The Akron game disappointed the fans.

**Use Relative Pronouns with Caution.**   Often, when a clause begins with a relative pronoun (*who, which, that*), you can whittle it to a phrase.

> WORDY   Venus, which is the second planet of the solar system, is called the evening star.
>
> REVISED   Venus, the second planet of the solar system, is called the evening star.
>
> WORDY   Bert, who is a prize-winning violist, played a work of Brahms.
>
> REVISED   Bert, a prize-winning violist, played a work of Brahms.

**Cut Out Deadwood.**   The more you revise, the more shortcuts you'll discover. The following sentences have words that can just be cut (indicated in *italics*). Try reading each sentence without them.

Howell spoke for the sophomores and Janet *also spoke* for the seniors.

Professor Lombardi is *one of the most* amazing *men.*

He is *something of* a clown, but *sort of the* lovable *type.*

As a major in *the field of* economics, I plan to concentrate on *the area of* international banking.

*The decision as to* whether *or not* to go is up to you.

**Cut Descriptors.**   Adjectives and adverbs are often dispensable. Consider the difference between these two versions:

> WORDY   Johnson's extremely significant research led to highly important major discoveries.
>
> REVISED   Johnson's research led to major discoveries.

**Be Short, Not Long.**    While sometimes a long word conveys a shade of meaning that a shorter synonym doesn't, in general it's a good idea to shun a long word or phrase when you can pick a short one. Instead of *the remainder*, write *the rest*; instead of *activate*, *start* or *begin*; instead of *expedite*, *rush*; instead of *adequate* or *sufficient*, *enough*. Long-windedness, to be sure, doesn't always come from slinging overlarge words. Sometimes it comes from not knowing a right word — one that wraps an idea in a smaller package. The cumbersome expression *persons who are new to the sport of skiing* could be replaced by *novice skiers*. Consider these two remarks about a boxer:

WORDY    Andy has a left fist that has a lot of power in it.

REVISED    Andy has a potent left.

By the way, it pays to read. From reading, you absorb words like *potent* and *novice* and set them to work for you.

Here is a list of questions to use in slimming your writing.

REVISION
CHECKLIST

## Cutting and Whittling

- Are you direct and straightforward?
- Do you announce an idea before you utter it? If so, consider chopping out the announcement.
- Can you recast any sentence that begins *There is* or *There are*?
- Can you substitute an active verb wherever you use a form of the verb *be* (*is, was, were*)?
- Can you reduce to a phrase any clause beginning with *which*, *who*, or *that*?
- Have you used too many adjectives and adverbs?
- Do you see any long word where a short word would do?

WRITING
WITH A
COMPUTER

## Revising and Editing with a Word Processor

The tasks of revising and editing are usually more fruitful — and more fun — if you view them as opportunities to explore new options and to tinker with words and phrases. Computers are ideally suited to such exploration. The word processor can't think for you or tell you how to revise and edit, but it can make turning your thoughts into reality a bit easier. Locating, moving, and changing specific bits and pieces of text — key processes in revising and editing — are all immensely easier on a word processor than with pen and paper. And because you can save multiple versions of your work, you can try out a new introduction or rewrite a troublesome sentence without sacrificing the old one. (For more on using computers for revision and editing, see Chapter 21, "Strategies for Writing with a Computer.")

John Martin, a business administration major, wrote the following economics paper to fulfill the assignment "Set forth and briefly discuss a current problem in international trade. Venture an opinion or propose a solution." You can see the thoughtful cuts and condensations that Martin made with the help of his English instructor and his peer editor. Following the edited draft you'll find the paper as he resubmitted it — in fewer words.

### FIRST DRAFT

Japan's Closed Doors: Should the U.S. Retaliate?

~~There is currently~~ A serious problem *is* brewing in ~~the world of~~ international trade; ~~which may turn out to be a real tempest in a teapot, so to speak.~~ [*a cliche to cut*] According to the latest National Trade Estimates report, several ~~of the countries that the~~ U.S. *trading partners* ~~has been doing business with~~ deserve to be condemned for ~~what the report has characterized as~~ "unfair trade practices." The government has said it will use the report to single out ~~specific~~ countries ~~which it is then going to go ahead and~~ *to* punish under the Super 301 provisions of the trade law.

The Super 301 section ~~of the trade law~~ requires Carla Hills, ~~who is~~ the U.S. trade representative, to ~~try to get rid of~~ *attack* what she ~~has officially designated to be~~ *calls* "priority unfair practices." She will ~~be~~ slash~~ing~~ at the ~~whole~~ web of impediments ~~and obstacles~~ [*same as impediments*] that have ~~slowed down or~~ denied ~~the various products of the many United States~~ *American* firms ~~much~~ *fast* access to Japanese markets.

~~It is important for the reader to note here that for a long time, longer than anyone can remember,~~ Japan has *long* been the leading prime candidate for a dose of Super 301. Over the past decade, ~~there have been many years of negotiations and battering by different~~ industry groups *have battered* at the unyielding doors of ~~the~~ Japanese markets, ~~which have yielded~~ *with* some success~~es~~, but ~~have pretty much~~ failed ~~miserably~~ to ~~dent the invisible trade barriers that stand looming between us and the Japanese markets, preventing the free access of U.S. goods to~~ *make them swing wide.*

~~Japanese consumers. As far as~~ ⌐The U.S. trade deficit with Japan, ~~is concerned, it was somewhat~~ more than $50 billion last year, ~~and it~~ shows ~~very~~ little sign of ~~getting signifi-~~ improving ~~cantly much better~~ this year.

Some American businesspeople would ~~like to~~ take aim at Japan immediately. However, Clyde Prestowitz, ~~who is~~ a former Commerce Department official, ~~seriously~~ doubts that ~~in the~~ wise to ~~last analysis~~ it would be ~~a good idea to come out and~~ name Japan ~~to feel the terrible effects of~~ for retaliation under Super 301; ~~in view of the fact that in his opinion~~, "It's hard to negotiate with guys you are calling cheats." No doubt ~~there are~~ may other observers ~~who~~ share his view.

~~Evidently it is the task of~~ ⌐The admininstration has to try help to ~~pave the way for~~ U.S. exports ~~to~~ wedge their way into ~~the~~ protected Japanese markets while keeping ~~it firmly~~ in mind nations that the interests of both ~~the United States and Japan~~ call stronger for ~~strengthening of the~~ economic and military ties. ~~that bind both countries into a sphere of friendly relationship. It is my personal conclusion that~~ If the administration goes ahead, ~~with this~~, it will ~~certainly~~ need to plan ~~ahead for the future~~ carefully.


REVISED VERSION

Japan's Closed Doors: Should the U.S. Retaliate?

A serious problem is brewing in international trade. According to the latest National Trade Estimates report, several U.S. trading partners deserve to be condemned for "unfair trade practices." The government has said it will use the report to single out countries to punish under the Super 301 provisions of the trade law.

The Super 301 section requires Carla Hills, the U.S. trade representative, to attack what she calls "priority unfair practices." She will slash at the web of impediments that have denied American firms fast access to Japanese markets.

Japan has long been the prime candidate for a dose of Super 301. Over the past decade, industry groups have battered at the doors of Japanese markets, with some success, but failed to make them swing wide. The U.S. trade deficit with Japan, more than $50 billion last year, shows little sign of improving this year.

Some American businesspeople would take aim at Japan immediately. However, Clyde Prestowitz, a former Commerce Department official, doubts that it would be wise to name Japan for retaliation under Super 301: "It's hard to negotiate with guys you are calling cheats." No doubt many other observers share his view.

The administration has to try to help U.S. exports wedge their way into protected Japanese markets while keeping in mind that the interests of both nations call for stronger economic and military ties. If the administration goes ahead, it will need to plan carefully.

# Proofreading

Proofreading is checking for correctness of grammar, spelling, and punctuation and fixing typographical errors. In college, good proofreading can make the difference between a C and an A. On the job, it may help you get a promotion. Readers, teachers, and bosses like careful writers who take time to proofread.

Don't proofread too soon. In your early drafting, don't fret over the correct spelling of an unfamiliar word; the word may be revised or edited out in a later version. If the word stays in, you'll have time to check it later. Turn your internal monitor or editor off until you have the ideas right.

Most errors in writing occur unconsciously. Some result from faulty information in your memory. If you have never learned the difference between *its* and *it's,* you'll probably misuse these words without realizing you're making a mistake. If you have never looked closely at the spelling of *environment,* you may have never seen the second *n* and so you'll habitually spell it *enviroment.* Such errors easily become habits and reinforce themselves every time you write them.

Split-second inattention or a break in concentration can also cause errors. Because the mind works faster than the pen or the pencil (or the typewriter or word processor), when you are distracted by someone's voice or a telephone ring, you may omit a letter or a whole word or you may put in the wrong punctuation.

The very way our eyes work leads to errors. When you read normally, you usually see only the shells of words — the first and last letters. You fix your eyes on the print only three or four times per line or less. To proofread effectively, you must look at the individual letters in each word and the punctuation marks between words and not slide over the individual symbols. Proofreading requires time and patience.

The skill of proofreading does not come naturally, but it is a skill you can develop. It is your responsibility as a writer to break old habits and develop this skill. It will pay off in the long run.

Tips for Proofreading

1. Turn off your internal monitor until you get the ideas right.
2. Realize that *all* writers make mistakes in their haste to get ideas on paper and must proofread to find and correct their errors.
3. Realize that you are human and you will make mistakes. Develop a healthy sense of doubt because mistakes are so easy to make. There is nothing bad about making mistakes, only about not taking time to find and correct them.
4. Budget enough time to proofread thoroughly.
5. Let a paper "get cold." Let it sit several days, or overnight, or at least a few hours before proofreading it.
6. Learn the grammar conventions you don't understand so you can spot and eliminate problems in your own writing. Practice until you easily recognize major errors, such as fragments and comma splices. Learn how to correct your own common problems. Ask for assistance from a peer editor or a tutor in the writing center if your campus has one.
7. Read what you have written very slowly, looking at every word and every letter.
8. Read your paper aloud. Speaking forces you to slow down and see more, and sometimes you will hear a mistake you haven't seen.
9. Read what you have actually written, not what you think is there. Don't let your mind play tricks on you. Developing the objectivity to see what is really on the page or screen is one of the most difficult aspects of proofreading.

WRITING
WITH A
COMPUTER

## Proofreading

Most grammar checkers aren't very reliable or useful, but computerized spell checkers are handy tools. Remember, though, that they aren't foolproof. They can't tell you that you've used *you're* when you meant to write *your* or *affect* when you meant *effect*. For more on spell checkers and on other computer techniques for proofreading, see p. 450.

10. Use a dictionary or a spell checker whenever you can. (But be aware that a spell checker is not foolproof. It will not know if you've typed *own* when you meant to type *won*, for instance.)
11. Double-check for habitual errors (such as leaving off -*s* or -*ed* or putting in unnecessary commas).
12. Read the essay backward. This will force you to look at each word because you won't get caught up in the flow of ideas.
13. Read the essay several times, focusing each time on a specific area of difficulty (once for spelling, once for punctuation, once for a problem you know is recurrent in your writing).
14. Ask someone else to read your paper and tell you if it is free of errors. But *don't* let someone else do your work for you.
15. Take pride in your work.

**REVISION CHECKLIST**

# Proofreading

- Have you omitted any words? Any letters? -*s* or -*ed* at the ends of words? Any necessary marks of punctuation?
- Have you transposed any letters? Have you misplaced any punctuation marks?
- Have you added any unnecessary letters or punctuation?
- Have you checked your grammar? Look especially at verb tense, subject-verb agreement, pronoun agreement, pronoun case, and pronoun reference.
- Have you checked the spellings of the words you're unsure of? Of words you habitually miss?
- Have you in haste used the wrong word (*lay* for *lie*, *its* for *it's*, *advice* for *advise*)?
- Have you slowed your mind down and focused your eyes on each word, each letter in each word, each punctuation mark?

**EXERCISE**

# Proofreading and Editing

Proofread the following passage carefully. Assume that the organization of the paragraph is satisfactory. You are to look for mistakes in sentence structure, grammar, spelling, punctuation, and capitalization and correct them. There are ten errors in the paragraph. After you have completed your editing of the passage, discuss with your classmates the changes you have made and your reasons for making those changes.

> Robert Frost, one of the most popular American poets. He was born in San Francisco in 1874, and died in Boston in 1963. His family moved to new England when his father died in 1885. There he completed highschool and attended colledge but never graduate. Poverty and problems filled his life. He worked in a woolen mill, on a newspaper, and on varous odd jobs. Because of ill health he settled on a farm and began to teach school to support his wife and children. Throughout his life he dedicated himself to writing poetry, by 1915 he was in demand for public readings and speaking engagements. He was awarded the Pulitzer Prize for poetry four times — in

1924, 1931, 1937, and 1943. The popularity of his poetry rests in his use of common themes and images, expressed in everyday language. Everyone can relate to his universal poems, such as "Swinging on Birches" and "Stopping by Woods on a Snowy Evening." Students read his poetry in school from seventh grade through graduate school, so almost everyone recognize lines from his best-loved poems. America is proud of it's son, the homespun poet Robert Frost.

# Using Proper Manuscript Style

Some instructors are sticklers in specifying how your paper ought to look; others maintain a benign indifference to such commonplaces. In writing for an instructor of either stripe, you would do well to turn in a paper easy to read and to comment on.

In case you have received no particular instructions for the form of your paper, here are some general, all-purpose specifications.

## GENERAL MANUSCRIPT STYLE FOR ESSAYS, ARTICLES, AND REPORTS

1. If you handwrite your paper, make sure your handwriting is legible. If you type, keep your typewriter keys clean or make sure you have a fresh ribbon or toner in your printer. If you use a word processor, don't format your paper entirely in italics or extra-fine characters. Pick a conventional, easy-to-read typeface such as Courier, Times Roman, Helvetica, or Palatino.

2. Use dark blue or black ink if you write, a black ribbon or ink if you type or use a computer.

3. Write, type, or print on just one side of standard letter-size paper ($8\frac{1}{2}$ by 11 inches).

4. If you handwrite your paper, use $8\frac{1}{2}$-by-11-inch paper with smooth edges (not torn from a spiral-bound notebook). If you type or use a computer, use a smooth bond paper. Erasable typing paper, however helpful to a mistake-prone typist, may be irksome to an instructor who needs to write comments. The paper is easily smeared, and it won't take certain kinds of ink.

5. For a paper without a separate title page, place your name, together with your instructor's name, the number and section of the course, and the date in the upper left or right corner of the first page, each item on a new line. (Check to see if your instructor has a preference for which side.) Double-space and center your title. Don't underline the title; don't put it in quotation marks or type the title in all capital letters; and don't put a period after it. Capitalize the first and last words, the first word after a colon or semicolon, and all other words except prepositions, coordinating conjunctions, and articles. Double-space between the title and the first line of your text. (Most instructors do not require a title page for short college papers. If your instructor does request one but doesn't give you any guidelines, see number 1 under "Additional Suggestions for Research Papers" on the following page.)

6. Number your pages consecutively, including the first page. For a paper of two or more pages, put your last name in the upper right corner of each sheet along with the page number. Do not type the word *page* or the letter *p* before the number, and do not follow the number with a period or parenthesis.

7. Leave ample margins — at least an inch — left and right, top and bottom.

8. If you type or use a word processor, double-space your manuscript; if you handwrite, use wide-ruled paper or skip every other line.

9. Indent each new paragraph five spaces or one-half inch.

10. Long quotations should be double-spaced like the rest of your paper but indented from the left margin — ten spaces (one inch) if you're following MLA (Modern Language Association) guidelines, five if you're using APA (American Psychological Association) guidelines. Citations appear in parentheses immediately after the final punctuation mark of the block quotation. (For more about citing sources, consult a style manual.)

11. Place a comma or period inside closed quotation marks.

12. Try not to break words at the ends of lines. If you must break a word, divide it between syllables. If you're uncertain about where a syllable ends, check a dictionary.

13. Label all illustrations, and make sure they are bound securely to the paper.

14. Staple the paper in the top left corner. Don't use any other method to secure the pages.

15. For safety's sake and peace of mind, make a copy of your paper.

## ADDITIONAL SUGGESTIONS FOR RESEARCH PAPERS

For research papers, the format is the same as recommended in the previous section, with the following additional specifications.

1. Type a title page, with the title of your paper centered and double-spaced about a third of the way down the page. Then go down two to four more spaces and type your name, then the instructor's name, the number and section of the course, and the date, each on a separate line, double-spaced.

2. Do not number your title page; number your outline, if you submit one with your paper, with small roman numerals (ii, iii, and so on). Number consecutively all subsequent pages in the essay, including your works cited or references pages, using arabic numerals (1, 2, 3, and so on) in the upper right corner of the page.

3. Double-space your list of works cited or references list, if you have one.

## HOW TO MAKE A CORRECTION

Although you will want to make any large changes in your rough draft before you produce your final copy, don't be afraid to make small corrections in pen when you give your paper a last once-over. No writer is error-free; neither is any typist. In making such corrections, you may find it handy to use certain symbols used by printers and proofreaders.

A transposition mark (∿) reverses the positions of two words or two letters:

```
The nearby star Tau Ceti closely resmebles our sun.
```

Close-up marks (⌒) bring together the parts of a word accidentally split. A separation mark (⌐) inserts a space where one is needed:

```
The nearby star Tau Ceti closely re sembles oursun.
```

To delete a letter or a punctuation mark, draw a slanted line through it:

```
The nearby star Tau Ceti closely ressembles our sun.
```

When you insert a word or letter, use a caret (∧) to indicate where the insertion belongs:

```
                                   s
The nearby star Tau Ceti closely reembles our sun.
                                  ∧
```

The symbol ¶ before a word or a line means "start a new paragraph":

```
But lately, astronomers have slackened their efforts to study
              ¶
dark nebulae. That other solar systems may support life as we
know it makes for still another fascinating speculation.
```

You can always cross out a word neatly, with a single horizontal line, and write a better one over it (*never* type a correction right over a mistake).

```
                         closely
The nearby star Tau Ceti somewhat resembles our sun.
```

Finally, if a page has many errors on it, type or write it over again.

# Chapter 20

# Strategies for Working with Other Writers: Collaborative Learning

Some people imagine the writer all alone in an ivory tower, toiling in perfect solitude. But in the real world, writing is often a collaborative effort. In business firms, reports are sometimes written by teams and revised by committees before being submitted to top-level managers. People sit around a table throwing out ideas, which a secretary transcribes and someone else writes up. A crucial letter, an advertisement, or a company's annual report embodies the thinking and writing of many. Research scientists and social scientists often work in teams of two or more and collaborate on articles for professional journals. Even this book is the result of collaborative writing.

Student writers are often pleasantly surprised to find how genuinely helpful other students can be. When you are the writer, working with your classmates and friends gives you a very real sense of having a living, breathing, supportive audience. Asked to read an early draft, peers can respond to a paper, signal strengths in it, and offer constructive suggestions. Asked to read a later draft, they can help pinpoint problems with word choice and let you know where you need more evidence. Many instructors today encourage students to form groups and write essays collaboratively. That is why, throughout this book, we include peer response checklists and suggest activities for group learning.

If your instructor does not require peer editing or collaborative writing, you can arrange it on your own. Enlist one or more classmates or friends to read your work and comment on it. You can provide the same service in return. Before you show a draft to a friend, take a few minutes to write down two or three questions you'd like him or her to answer. If you are reading a classmate's work, ask the writer to give you a few specific questions.

If you don't know someone who is willing to respond to your writing for you, go to the writing center on campus. Here you can get help from special instructors and work with trained, experienced peer tutors. The lab staff will not do your work — planning, drafting, revising, proofreading — for you but will help you fulfill your assigned task.

## Serving as a Reader

What does it take to be a helpful, supportive peer editor? Here are a few tips for you.

Look at the Big Picture.    Your job isn't merely to notice misspelled words or misused semicolons (although it can't hurt to signal any that you see). Bend your mind to deeper matters: to what the writer is driving at, to the sequence of ideas, to the apparent truth or falsity of the observations, to the quantity and quality of the evidence, to the coherence or unity of the paper as a whole.

Be Specific.    Vague blame or praise won't help the writer. Don't say, "It's an interesting paper" or "I liked this essay a lot because I can relate to it." Such a response might make the writer feel good, but statements like "That example in paragraph 9 clarified the whole point of the paper for me" will make the writer feel good for good reason.

Be Tactful.    Approach the work in a friendly way. Remember, you aren't out to pass godlike judgment on your peer's effort. Your purpose as a reader is to give honest, intelligent comments — to help make the other writer aware of what he or she has written right, not only what he or she has written wrong. When you find fault, you can do so by making impartial observations — statements nobody can deny. A judgmental way to criticize might be "This paper is confused. It keeps saying the same thing over and over again." But a more useful comment might be more specific: "Paragraph 5 makes the same point as paragraphs 2 and 3," suggesting that two of the three paragraphs might be eliminated.

Answer Any Questions the Writer Has Asked You.    If the writer has indicated that he or she has questions about a specific spot or issue in the paper, take the time to address his or her concerns.

Ask Yourself Questions.    For help in looking for worthwhile, specific, tactful responses, skim the following checklist of readers' questions. Not all these points will apply to every paper.

FIRST QUESTIONS

What is your first reaction to this paper?

What is this writer trying to tell you? What does he or she most want you to learn?

What are this paper's greatest strengths?

Does it have any major weaknesses?

### QUESTIONS ON MEANING

Do you understand everything? Is there any information missing from this draft that you still need to know?

Is what this paper tells you worth saying, or does it only belabor the obvious? Does it tell you anything you didn't know before?

Is the writer trying to cover too much territory? Too little?

Does any point need to be more fully explained or illustrated?

When you come to the end, do you find that the paper hasn't delivered something it promised?

Could this paper use a down-to-the-ground revision? Would it be better on a different topic altogether — one the writer perhaps touches but doesn't deal with in this paper?

### QUESTIONS ON ORGANIZATION

Has the writer begun in a way that grabs your interest? Are you quickly drawn into the paper's main idea? Or can you find, at some point later in the paper, a better possible beginning?

Does the paper have one main idea, or does it struggle to handle more than one? Would the main idea stand out better if anything were removed?

Might the ideas in the paper be more effectively rearranged in a different order? Do any ideas belong together that now seem too far apart?

Does the writer keep to one point of view — one angle of seeing?

Does the ending seem deliberate, as if the writer meant to conclude at this point? Or does the writer seem merely to have run out of gas? If so, what can the writer do to write a stronger conclusion?

### QUESTIONS ON LANGUAGE AND WRITING STRATEGIES

Do you feel that this paper addresses you personally?

At any point in the paper, do you find yourself disliking or objecting to a statement the writer makes, to a word or a phrase with which you're not in sympathy? What is the problem here? Is it the writer's tone? Does the writer provide inadequate support to clarify or convince you? Should the writer keep this part, or should he or she change it?

Does the draft contain anything that distracts you, that seems unnecessary, that might be struck?

Do you get bored at any point and want to tune out? What might the writer do to make you want to keep reading?

Can you follow the writer's ideas easily? Does the paper need transitions? If so, at what places?

Does the language of this paper stay up in the clouds of generality? If so, where and how might the writer come down to earth and get specific?

Do you understand all the words the writer uses, or are there any specialized words whose meaning needs to be made clearer?

LAST QUESTION

Now that you have spent some time with this paper and looked at it closely, how well does it work for you?

**Write Comments.**    To show the writer just where you had a reaction, write notations in the margins of the paper. Then at the end write an overall comment, making major, general suggestions. Sum up the paper's strong and weak points — it can hardly be all good or all bad.

Here is a helpful comment by Maria Mendez on a draft of a paper by Jill Walker that ended up being titled "Euthanasia and the Law":

Jill—

The topic of this paper interested me a lot, because we had a case of euthanasia in our neighborhood. I didn't realize at first what your topic was—maybe the title "Life and Death" didn't say it to me. Your paper is full of good ideas and fact—like the Hemlock Society to help mercy-killing. I got lost when you start talking about advances in modern medicine (paragraph 6) but don't finish the idea. To go into modern medicine thoroughly would take a lot more room. Maybe euthanasia is enough to cover in five pages. Also, I don't know everything you're mentioning ("traditional attitudes toward life and death"). I could have used an explanation there—I'm from a different tradition. On the whole, your paper is solid and is going to make us agree with you.

Maria

## Learning as a Writer

You, the writer whose work is in the spotlight, will probably find that you can't just sit back and enjoy your fans' reactions. To extract all the usefulness from the process of peer reviewing, you'll need to play an active part in discussing your work.

*Ask Your Readers Questions.*    Probably your readers will give you more helpful specific reactions if you provide them with questions such as those in the previous section. As the writer however you may already suspect that something is wrong with your early draft, so you should add your own questions. Direct the peer readers' attention to places in your paper where you especially want insights. Express any doubts you have. Point out parts you found difficult to write. Ask what your readers would do about any weak spots.

Ask pointed questions like these *in writing* for your readers to think about:

> When you read my conclusion, are you convinced that I'm arguing for the one right solution to this problem? Can you imagine any better solution?
>
> Paragraph 4 looks skimpy—only two short sentences. What could I do to make it longer?
>
> How clear is my purpose? Can you sum up what I'm trying to say? What steps can I take to make my point hit home to you?

Throughout Parts One and Two of this book, we have provided brief checklists that writers can give to their peer editors to help them focus on the most important elements in that specific type of writing.

**WRITING WITH A COMPUTER**

## Peer Editing on Screen

If the writer wrote with a word processor, ask to work with an electronic copy of the draft in addition to a paper copy. The easiest way for you to enter your comments and suggestions is to turn on the CAPS LOCK feature (the CAPS LOCK button is usually on the left side of the keyboard). You can then type away at whatever places in the draft you would like. Your comments, now in all capital letters, will remain clearly distinguishable from the original text. The writer should make backup copies (both electronic and paper) of this file before turning it over to you — computer accidents can happen too easily. Here's an example of what a brief passage might look like:

> Harry S. Truman had a folksy way of expressing himself, which makes us remember many of his sayings. CAN YOU GIVE AN EXAMPLE? He was a folksy speaker CUT THIS REPETITION and developed his style in the rough-and-tumble of Mississippi politics. MISSOURI?

**Encourage Your Readers to be Sympathetic but Tough.**    Ask your peer editors not to be too easy on you. Let them know that you are willing to make deep structural changes in what you have written, not merely cosmetic repairs.

**Be Open to New Ideas.**    You might get completely new ideas — for focus, for organization, for details — from the readers' reactions. They may also have some tips about where to find more, and more valuable, relevant material.

**Take What's Helpful.**    Occasionally students worry that asking another student, no wiser or brighter or more experienced than they, to criticize their work is a risk not worth taking. You have to accept such help judiciously. You want to be wary about following all the suggestions you receive. While some of them may help, others may lead to a dead end.

**Realize You're the Boss.**    The important thing in taking advice and suggestions is to listen to your readers but not be a slave to them. Trust yourself. Let your instincts operate. Make a list of the suggestions you receive. Do any of them cancel out others? Does any suggestion seem worth trying? If so, give it a try, but drop it if it doesn't work.

It takes self-confidence to sift through criticism with profit. The final decision about whether or not to act on the advice you get from your fellow students is solely up to you. If you feel that one person's suggestions have not helped at all, you would be wise to get a second opinion, and maybe a third. When several of your readers disagree, only you can decide what direction to follow.

**Learn to Evaluate Your Own Writing.**    As your writing skills continue to develop, you will find yourself relying less on your peers and more on your own ability to analyze and revise your early drafts. You can ask yourself the very

**WRITING WITH A COMPUTER**

## Using E-Mail to Collaborate

E-mail offers another way for writers and readers to work together, since drafts and comments can be sent back and forth quickly and easily from almost anywhere, at almost any time. If you find it difficult to arrange a meeting between writer and reader, have the writer send the reader a copy of the draft over e-mail. The draft will sit in the reader's electronic mailbox until he or she has time to respond to it. Most e-mail can be easily answered with the REPLY command, and the original draft (or passages from it) can be incorporated into this reply.

Some writers find e-mail exchanges particularly helpful in getting started. The conversational, personal nature of e-mail helps some writers to relax and to direct their writing to a tangible audience. (For more on e-mail, see p. 321.)

same questions you use in evaluating other writers' papers. And when you learn to answer those questions searchingly, you'll become your own most valuable reader.

## Peer Editors in Action

The following brief histories point out how effectively classmates can help a revision. First, consider this early draft of an opening paragraph for the essay "Why Don't More People Donate Their Bodies to Science?" by Dana Falk, written in a tandem course in English and sociology.

> The question of why more organs and body parts are not donated "to science"--that is, for the use of organ transplants, medical research, and college education--is a puzzling one. As I have learned through my research, it is also a multidetermined one. There are a plethora of reasons that prevent there from being enough organs to go around, and in this paper I shall examine a number of the reasons I have uncovered, trying to evaluate the effectiveness of efforts to alleviate the shortage and suggest possible alternate approaches myself. Primarily, though, we will simply look at the factors that prevent health professionals from being able to supply body parts each and every time a donor is needed.

Falk showed the paper to a classmate, Pamela Kong, who commented first on the opening sentence. "This could be rephrased as a question," she suggested, and she wrote "AWKWARD" next to the sentence that begins "There are a plethora of reasons . . . ." "That sentence was pretty bad!" Falk later realized. Kong zeroed in on the stilted word *multidetermined* (apparently meaning "having several causes") and called for a clearer announcement of where the paper was going. After reading Kong's comments and doing some hard thinking, Falk recast the opening paragraph:

> The gap between the demand for human organs and their current supply is ever-widening. Although the success rate of transplants is way up because of the introduction of cyclosporine, an immunosuppressant, many potential donors and their families resist giving away their body parts, creating an acute shortage. Why is it

that people so fear giving their bodies to science? Let's
examine the causes of the shortage of transplantable organs and review some possible solutions.

In the second version Falk's language becomes more concrete and definite with the use of two figures of speech. Now we have an "ever-widening
gap" and a "bright spot" that is "clouded." The added detail about the newly
successful drug lends the paper fresh authority. Kong's suggestion to turn the
question into an actual one (with a question mark) lends life to the sentence
that now begins "Why is it that people so fear . . . ." The announced plan for
the rest of the paper, now placed at the end of the paragraph, points toward
everything that will follow.

Now let's see how a peer editor helped another student strengthen an entire paper. Kevin Deters wrote the following short essay for an English composition course. The assignment asked for a reflective essay in response to his
own reading. Even in this early draft, you'll find, Deters's paper treats a challenging subject, and it comes to a thoughtful conclusion. But as the paper
stands, what does it lack? For practice, try to critique the paper yourself before
you look at the peer editor's comments.

FIRST DRAFT

Where Few Men Have Gone Before

Kevin Deters

Space: the final frontier. This is the subject addressed    1
by the renowned writer Isaac Asimov in "Into Space: The Next
Giant Step," a short piece published in the St. Louis Post-
Dispatch. Asimov, the author of over four hundred science and
science fiction books, writes about the space station that
will be built in orbit around the earth in the near future.
He examines the advantages and numerous possibilities of
space travel that such a station would allow. This space station will give people the opportunity to be explorers, help
conserve resources on earth, and unite the nations of the
world as they forge the common goal of discovering knowledge
of outer space.

"It is absolutely necessary that we build a base other    2
than earth for our ventures into space. . . . The logical beginning is with a space station," Asimov says. The space station would serve as a stepping-stone to future permanent
bases on the moon and Mars. Adventurous settlers would pave

the spaceways just as Daniel Boone and his followers blazed trails through the Kentucky wilderness. It is these space travelers "who will be the Phoenicians, the Vikings, the Polynesians of the future, making their way into the 21st century through a space-ocean far vaster than the water-ocean traversed by their predecessors."

These spacefarers will also find ways to help conserve valuable energy on earth. Asimov suggests that, using the space station as a base, lunar materials could be excavated from the moon to construct power stations to direct solar energy toward the earth. Thus, energy and money are saved, and this conservation could serve as a deterrent to the use of nuclear energy. 3

With this new surplus of energy, nuclear energy and all its applications such as power plants and missiles would become unnecessary. A major threat to world safety would be removed. The sun's never-ending supply of solar energy could be harnessed to become the chief energy source on earth, and dangerous forms of energy could be done away with. 4

As a result, expensive heating bills and the like would be unheard of. Energy costs would plummet as earth's populace took advantage of the sun's plentiful rays. The price decrease would snowball, affecting other aspects of life, eventually resulting in a cheaper cost of living. 5

The construction of such a space station could also help unify the countries of the world. A massive project like this enterprise would cost billions of dollars and take a massive amount of time and hard work. Asimov suggests that if the United States and Russia were to work together, costs and time could be considerably lessened. Such joint U.S./Russia missions are not unheard of. The Apollo-Soyuz venture and the space shuttle-Mir hookup, projects that linked a spacecraft from each nation, were successful examples of cooperation. 6

This joint effort could help promote global togetherness as well. If the world's nations could unite to explore space, surely problems back home on earth could be easily solved. Such quibbles as the nuclear arms race and foreign trading disputes seem trivial and inconsequential when compared to the grandeur of space exploration. 7

And so, this space station will serve as a valuable tool    8
for humanity. Man must now reach for the heavens above him,
because if the earth's population keeps increasing, the
planet will soon be too small to accommodate everyone. Space
exploration is the only logical answer. Space is indeed the
final frontier that lies before us. We only have to take advantage of it.

Kevin Deters's classmate Jennifer Balsavias read his reflective essay and
filled out a peer editing questionnaire. Here are the questions and her responses to them.

PEER RESPONSE CHECKLIST

1. First, sit on your hands and read the essay through.  Then
describe your first reaction.

This was a well-written report. The only time
I really noticed any reflection on the reading
was in the last paragraph.

2. What is "reflective" about this essay? What is the purpose
of the essay and the major reflection?

The purpose of the essay was to show the
importance of space to humans and their
expansion into that final frontier. In the last
paragraph, he lets us know his feelings on the
information given. He doesn't reflect about the
reading throughout the paper.

3. How skillfully has the writer used reading?  Look at the
way quotations or paraphrases are inserted.  Is it clear when
the writer is using reading and when the ideas are the
writer's?  Comment on any areas that were problematic to you.

He uses quotes and information from the
reading very well. (By the way, where's the
second quote in the second paragraph from?)
The writer is definitely using the reading and
adds only a few thoughts of his own. Needs
to reflect more!

4. Is the paper informed enough by reading?  Where could the paper improve by more careful or detailed use of "secondary" (not personal) materials?

> It's not very personal. His own feelings and reflections should be involved. There is enough about the reading. Maybe he shouldn't expand so much on the subject. Maybe stop after the first or second paragraph and REFLECT!

5. Who is the essay written to?  Describe the audience.

> I feel it is written to those interested in space and the new space programs. I found it interesting.

6. List any terms or phrases that are too technical or specialized or any words that need further definition.

> None

7. If you were handing the essay in for a grade, what would you be sure to revise?

> I'd put some of my own reflections in, not just facts.

8. Circle on the manuscript any problems with spelling, punctuation, grammar, or usage.

> He should correct his sexist usage— for example, in the title and in paragraph 8, where "man" is used to mean "people."

In reading Jennifer Balsavias's evaluation, Deters was struck by her main criticism: "The only time I really noticed any reflection on the reading was in the last paragraph." "Needs to reflect *more!*" Deters's paper seemed more like a report on an article than an essay analyzing the article with some original thinking. It was difficult for the reader to tell Isaac Asimov's opinions from Deters's own. Perhaps Deters needed to express his views more clearly and not shun the first-person *I*. He reworked his draft, trying to set forth his own opinions, trying also to tighten and sharpen his prose. His revised essay follows.

REVISED VERSION

Where Few Have Gone Before

Kevin Deters

Space: the final frontier. The renowned writer Isaac
Asimov addresses this subject in "Into Space: The Next Giant
Step," a short piece published in the St. Louis Post-
Dispatch. Asimov, the author of over four hundred science and
science fiction books, writes about the space station that
will be built in orbit around the earth in the near future.
He examines the advantages and numerous possibilities of
space travel that such a station would allow. From this article, I gathered that this space station will give people the
opportunity to be explorers, help conserve resources on
earth, and unite the nations of the world as they forge the
common goal of discovering knowledge of outer space. I'm intrigued by each of these possibilities.

"It is absolutely necessary that we build a base other
than earth for our ventures into space," Asimov tells us.
"The logical beginning is with a space station." A space station would serve as a stepping-stone to future permanent
bases on the moon and Mars. I can imagine adventurous settlers who would pave the spaceways just as Daniel Boone and
his followers blazed trails through the Kentucky wilderness.
These space travelers Asimov describes as "the Phoenicians,
the Vikings, the Polynesians of the future, making their way
into the 21st century through a space-ocean far vaster than
the water-ocean traversed by their predecessors."

The spacefarers will also find ways to help conserve
valuable energy on earth. Asimov suggests that, with the
space station as a base, they could construct power stations
to direct solar energy toward the earth. Thus, lessening our
use of fossil fuels, conserving energy and saving money. I
believe that this conservation could also serve as a deterrent to the use of nuclear energy. With a new surplus of energy, nuclear energy and all its applications such as power
plants and missiles would become unnecessary. The sun's
never-ending supply of solar energy could be harnessed to be-

come the chief energy source on earth, and dangerous forms of energy could be done away with.

As a result, I suggest that expensive heating bills and the like would be unheard of. Energy costs would plummet as earth's populace would take advantage of the sun's plentiful rays. The price decrease would snowball, affecting other aspects of life, eventually resulting in a cheaper cost of living.     4

The construction of the space station that Asimov discusses could also help unify the countries of the world. A project like this would cost billions of dollars and take a massive amount of time and hard work. No one country could afford the project. Asimov suggests that if the United States and Russia were to work together, costs and time could be considerably lessened. I believe that this joint effort could help promote global togetherness as well. Joint missions of the United States and other countries have been conducted. For example, the Apollo-Soyuz venture linked spacecrafts from the two nations. If the world's nations can unite to explore space, surely problems back home could be easily solved. Such quibbles as the nuclear arms race and foreign trading disputes seem trivial when compared to the grandeur of space exploration.     5

Asimov suggests that the space station will serve as a valuable tool for humanity. I concur, for I believe that the human race must now reach for the heavens. Space is indeed the final frontier that lies before us. We can all be Daniel Boones.     6

You'll notice that, as Jennifer Balsavias suggested, Deters seems to reflect harder in his revised version. And by speaking out in his own voice, he makes clear (as he didn't do in the earlier version) that many of his thoughts are his own, not Asimov's. Notice, too, Deters's smaller but effective alterations. At the end, he returns to his earlier, original comparison between pioneers in space and Daniel Boone. All his changes produce a more concise, readable, and absorbing paper, one that goes a little deeper — thanks in part to the services of an honest, helpful peer editor.

# Chapter 21

# Strategies for Writing with a Computer

"I love being a writer," declares novelist Peter De Vries. "What I can't stand is the paperwork."

If you have ever felt this way, you can appreciate the modern miracle of the word processor — a computer with the software necessary for writing. Some writers think word processing is the greatest thing since Gutenberg invented movable type. Others bristle at the thought of using such complicated and sometimes intimidating machines when pencils, pens, and typewriters seem to work just fine. But those who object to computer-assisted writing sometimes misunderstand technology: they may think of computers as tools for scientists, mathematicians, and programmers, but not writers. The fact is, word processing is by far the most commonly used computer application, and in many ways the personal computer *is primarily a writing machine*.

Even though you may eventually decide against integrating computers into your writing process, to do so without giving them a serious try is unwise. Many more people are using a computer to write today than even twenty-four hours ago, much less last year. You may find yourself at a serious disadvantage not only when you write college papers but also when you apply for jobs if you don't develop computer writing skills. And you may not have another opportunity in an environment as supportive as your college.

Have you not yet tried word processing and want to know more about it? On most college campuses you will find open-access labs where you can use a computer and a variety of programs. Some of these facilities are staffed with people who can help you get started. Asking for help from a friend who knows about word processing is another great way to learn. In addition, this chapter contains advice and practical tips for new computer users (see especially the first two sections, pp. 437–51). If you are a practiced veteran who already writes with a computer, you can skip over to page 451 for some hints that can make word processing work more effectively for you. You may also find some useful advice in "Formatting Your Manuscript" (p. 448).

This chapter also discusses some recent developments in the world of computer-assisted writing, particularly those made possible by electronic networks such as the Internet (see p. 455). Finally, you've probably already noticed the suggestions for completing specific assignments in the "Writing with a Computer" boxes placed throughout the chapters of the book. (For a complete list, see the index.)

## *What Word Processing Can and Cannot Do*

At first, for a writer accustomed to typing or pushing a pen, word processing may seem unnerving. You don't place marks directly on paper, where they stay put until you erase, cross out, white out, and rewrite or retype. You arrange words on a screen in easily altered structures.

Most beginners need someone to help them learn how to use word processing but others just pick up an instruction manual and ferret out the directions for themselves, finding what works by trial and error. A combination of personal advice and going it alone is probably best. Do whatever feels more comfortable for you, but prepare yourself for obstacles and frustrations. Computers have been oversold as "miracle machines"; as a result, new users often expect too much. You must approach learning word processing with patience, flexibility, and a positive attitude. Computers can eventually save you enormous amounts of time, but you will almost certainly not realize these savings on your first project — maybe not even on your second or third.

Don't be intimidated. Computer programs are increasingly "user friendly," meaning easy to learn and easy to use. Remember, though, that user friendliness goes only so far. A word processor does not really think on its own or do things for you. It performs only as it is told. So if you are to use a word processor effectively, you must understand its advantages and disadvantages, its features and limitations. No computer has yet been developed that can write an essay for you or accurately check your grammar, although some programs claim to have such power. The writer is still in control; a word processor is merely a powerful writing tool.

### ADVANTAGES

By enabling your work-in-progress to take shape on screen instead of on paper and by storing what you write, word processing helps do away with much of the mechanical work of rewriting. No more typing and retyping draft after draft. Word processing lets you do all the following:

rearrange swiftly
insert short sentences or long sections

delete unwanted words, sentences, or passages
search for and replace a word or phrase
correct mistakes easily
format and reformat quickly
check your spelling
number pages automatically
put headings on each page
print multiple copies
store several hundred pages on a small disk

Supplemental programs can provide still greater assistance. Sometimes their features are built right into the word processing program; sometimes you can get them as separate programs. Such programs can do the following:

feed you questions or prompts to generate ideas
help you organize material
help you choose better words
review grammar rules
help you edit
help you proofread
detect clichés
count the number of words
correctly format endnotes and bibliographies
produce tables and graphs

Most items on the previous lists are accomplished through instructions you give the computer in the form of "commands." For example, the command SAVE helps you *store your work on a small disk* and PRINT allows you to *print multiple copies*. These features of word processing can free your mind for more essential considerations about composing.

But writers have also discovered some additional advantages to using a word processor, benefits that don't necessarily correspond to specific commands or features that the manufacturers included in their software packages. Here are a few.

**Ease of Drafting.**   With word processing, you can throw down thoughts in whatever order they come to mind. Then you can move them around and arrange them as seems best. Of course, you can do this kind of thinking and revising with paper and scissors, too, but word processors encourage it and make it easy. Computers enable you to write an outline and flesh it out on the screen, shaping it into a finished essay. Computers let you start with seemingly chaotic writing — messy freewrites, brainstormed lists, meandering journal entries — and build them bit by bit into solid chunks for your final paper. Unlike people who type on typewriters, writers who write with word processors may become more willing to draft quickly, less fearful of making mistakes.

**Ease of Revising.**   Earlier we wrote that "the personal computer *is primarily a writing machine.*" To be more specific, it is primarily a *revision* machine. A willingness to undergo a number of revisions is often the key to successful writing, and as a revision machine a word processor can be tremendously helpful. No more recopying a page because it is not legible or retyping a paragraph just because you wish to switch the order of two sentences. You can make changes neatly, right on the screen, before the document is printed out, or use a series of revised printouts to help you edit. You can lift out words, sentences, and paragraphs and set them down somewhere else. You can readily add material or take it out — most word processors have an UNDO command that will reverse the last change you made if you don't like it. You can play around with the sequence of ideas, rearranging them into any order you like. Try three different versions of a short paper or of a section of an essay (such as the introduction or the conclusion), starting a separate document for each. Then combine the best parts from all three versions.

**Ease of Formatting.**   Writers sometimes complain that they don't want to use a computer because they are lousy typists. But the poorer your typing skills, the more you should *want* to use a computer. Numbering pages, placing headers, centering text, indenting block quotations, and underlining titles can be very difficult on a typewriter, especially for the hunt-and-peck typist. Personal computers are now sophisticated enough to create advanced magazine-quality page designs; the typical college paper is well within their capabilities. With a word processor you can also do things that you can't do on a typewriter, such as use boldface, select a specific font and type size, and integrate sophisticated tables and graphs. A word processor used in combination with a high-resolution printer, such as a laser printer, can produce crisp, attractive papers that will both increase readability and instill in you a sense of pride. (See "Formatting Your Manuscript," p. 448).

## DISADVANTAGES

Just as word processors offer some advantages that software manufacturers did not intentionally design, these programs can also cause some problems, which we would be remiss not to mention.

**No Substitute for the Human Mind.**   The so-called mind of a computer remains relatively simple compared with the human mind. In reality, the computer has no mind, no power to originate thought, no imagination at all — even though we call its spacious capacity a "memory." Computer applications such as word processors can only *help* you with the mechanical aspects of writing, allowing you to focus more on generating ideas and crafting language. These machines cannot actually *write.* Some programs claim to check your spelling, word choice, clichés, or style for you, but they actually have serious limitations. In fact, it's questionable whether you should use any checker other than one for spelling. English grammar is far too complicated to be checked accurately by any software, despite what some programs promise. (For more on spell checkers, see p. 450.)

**Possible Loss of Data.**   If you use a computer to write, you will almost certainly lose some of your data accidentally at some point — a very aggravating experience. If, say, your roommate plugs in a hair dryer and blows a fuse or there is a power surge in the computer lab while you are word processing — Poof! — there goes your term paper. But power outages and surges are less likely to cause trouble than people are. The most common way to lose data is to mismanage your files. You can easily delete, lose, or miscopy your files and you can also easily damage or misplace your storage disks. Believe it or not, the best safety measure is to print out hard (paper) copy. (For more on file management and making backup copies, see p. 452.)

**Alienation and Discomfort.**   Since almost all of us learned to write and read with ink and paper, doing so with a keyboard and a monitor can seem disorienting and unnatural. Some writers miss the action of the typewriter or the feel of the pen and paper. According to author William Zinsser, others miss the satisfaction of being able to rip a page out of the typewriter and "crumble it in a fit of frustration or rage." Computers can also be physically uncomfortable. Staring at a monitor will fatigue your eyes faster than reading from paper. Most screens display only about twenty-four lines at a time, some as few as sixteen; so scrolling through text on screen can be tedious, compared with flipping back and forth through a stack of paper.

**Lack of Access.**   Whereas you can carry a pen and paper with you anywhere, you can't easily carry a computer around with you in your pocket. Computers are certainly more expensive to own and operate than conventional writing tools, and many writers will have trouble gaining access to one easily.

**Information Overload.**   Computers have the potential to present incredible amounts of information to the writer, and this glut of information may be overwhelming. If you use a computer to gather information off the Internet, CD-ROMs, or electronic library databases, you can become stymied by the oceans of information at your fingertips. A word processor might also free you to compose volumes of your own material — a generally beneficial feature. But you may then be faced with a new problem: having to sort through piles of your own writing.

## An Introduction to Word Processing

Maybe you have heard of the "information age" or the "computer revolution" and wondered what these sweeping labels might mean to you personally. You might wonder whether you will be left behind by what seems to be a rapidly advancing world. But, at the same time, you can deduce that revolutions cannot take place unless huge numbers of people get behind a particular trend.

In other words, you should comfort yourself with the fact that the fast-paced world of advanced technology is made up of people who, just like you, started out not knowing a mouse from a monitor.

We all have to learn. And computer and software manufacturers want *everyone* to learn so that the revolution can keep growing. The invention of the computer mouse is one of the more obvious attempts to make computers easy for almost anybody to use. Word processors, in particular, have become very easy to operate. Most recent versions of major word processing software employ a common set of user-friendly commands and principles. Once you learn some of them you should be able to transfer your knowledge easily from one program to another.

The purpose of this introduction to word processing is threefold: (1) to explain the on-screen appearance of most word processors, (2) to introduce the basic operations of word processors, and (3) to describe how these operations can be used to format a college paper. Within the space of this textbook, it is impossible to provide all the information necessary to get you going on all word processors on the market today. But it *is* possible to describe those things that most word processors have in common. Again, the best way to get started is to ask someone to guide you while you are actually sitting with your hands on a computer. This section will help you make the most of such tutoring sessions and will certainly be of great help if you can't find anyone to lend assistance.

**Note:** Please keep in mind that this section describes word processors in general; your program is certain to be slightly different. Nonetheless, you should be able to apply these descriptions to most word processors.

## ON-SCREEN APPEARANCE

When you turn on a word processor and see for the first time the image that it projects on screen, you might seriously doubt that it is "user friendly" at all. Two of the most common first reactions are "This thing doesn't look like anything from my planet" and "There's not enough information here — where do I begin?" Before you can begin anything, you need to know what the word processor is trying to tell you through its interface. *Interface* is a term for something that allows one thing to communicate with another. Your actual face is a type of interface: the expressions you use — smiles, frowns, winks, smirks — all communicate your thoughts to other people. The keyboard is an interface; through it you talk to the computer. Word processors also have interfaces; that is, when you first start a word processing program, it projects on the screen an interface through which you can tell the computer what you want it to do. There are two basic types of word processing interfaces in use today: the pull-down and the graphic.

The Pull-down Interface.    The pull-down interface has three main parts: the menu bar, the text field, and the cursor. Locate each of these parts in Figure 21.1.

*Menu bar.*   In the menu bar on the figure are the words *File, Edit, Search, Mark, Layout, Tools, Graphics, Font* and *Help*. Each word represents a different pull-

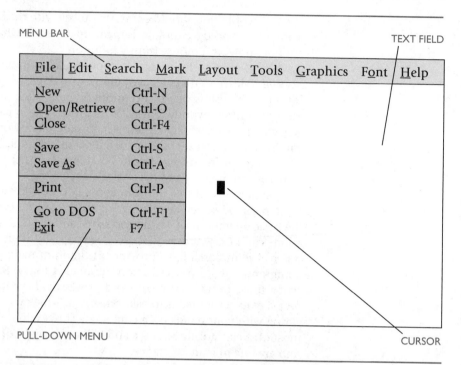

FIGURE 21.1.    The Pull-down Interface

down menu, which can be "pulled down" (opened) through different means. Sometimes holding down the ALT key on your keyboard while pressing the letter in the word that is underlined or in a different color will activate these menus. Sometimes clicking once with the mouse on the word that represents the menu you want also works. For example, in the figure, the menu for *File* has been pulled down. Once a menu is pulled down, you can select any of the choices on that menu.

*Text field.* Below the menu bar you will find the text field, the area in which you enter and manipulate your writing.

*Cursor.* The cursor is the flashing vertical line or small rectangle located in the text field. A cursor is like the tip of a pen or pencil; it is the point at which the letters will emerge as you type.

**The Graphic Interface.**    The graphic interface might appear complicated at first, but it is actually designed to be easier to use than a pull-down interface. A graphic interface almost always requires the use of a mouse to operate all of its features. A mouse works by "pointing" and "clicking." To *point,* move the mouse across the tabletop; this will cause a corresponding movement of the pointer on the computer screen. To *click,* depress and then release one of the buttons on top of the mouse; *double-clicking* means clicking this twice in rapid succession. (If your mouse has more than one button, you will generally need to use only the left button.)

Graphic interfaces also have pull-down menus, but graphic interfaces have additional user-friendly features that a simple pull-down menu interface doesn't have. The major components of the graphic interface are the open/close box, the title bar, the icon button bar, the ruler bar, the scroll bar, the text field, the cursor, and the pointer. Locate each of these parts in Figure 21.2.

*Open/close box.* This small box is located in the upper left-hand corner of the interface. It is usually gray. Double-clicking on this box should exit or close the word processor — like turning off a power tool and putting it away in its case.

*Title bar.* The title bar runs horizontally across the top of the screen. It usually displays the name of the word processing program and the name of the document that the writer is working on — the "opened" document in computer terminology. In some word processors, the title bar changes to describe the function of a particular icon button (see next section) if the pointer is placed on top of the button but the mouse is not clicked.

*Icon button bar.* Known variously as the *button bar, icon bar,* or *power bar* (depending on the word processor), the icon button bar is a horizontal series of icons (little pictures) that represent the program's major commands or functions. You can activate a function by clicking on its icon. For example, the first icon in the figure resembles a sheet of paper with a corner folded down; if you click on it, you command the computer to create a new document.

*Ruler bar.* The ruler bar looks like a ruler. It helps you see where your margins and tabs are set. A ruler bar may be turned on or off, at the writer's choice.

*Scroll bar.* The scroll bar runs vertically along the right side of the screen. It is used to tell you roughly where you are in a document and to scroll (move) through the text. A small up arrow, box, or minus sign (–) is typically located at the top of the scroll bar, representing the beginning of the document. If you click the mouse on this spot, you will move closer to the start of the document. Clicking on the down arrow, box, or plus sign (+) at the bottom of the bar will do the opposite. Between the top and bottom of the scroll bar is a rectangle or box that moves up and down to show how far into the document you are. For example, if the screen is displaying the third page of a five-page document, the box would be halfway down the scroll bar.

*Text field.* This is the area in which you enter and manipulate your writing. You often have the option of displaying only the area of the document that contains the text or the entire width of the page, including margins.

*Cursor.* The cursor is the flashing vertical line or small rectangle located in the text field. A cursor is like the tip of a pen or pencil; it is the point at which

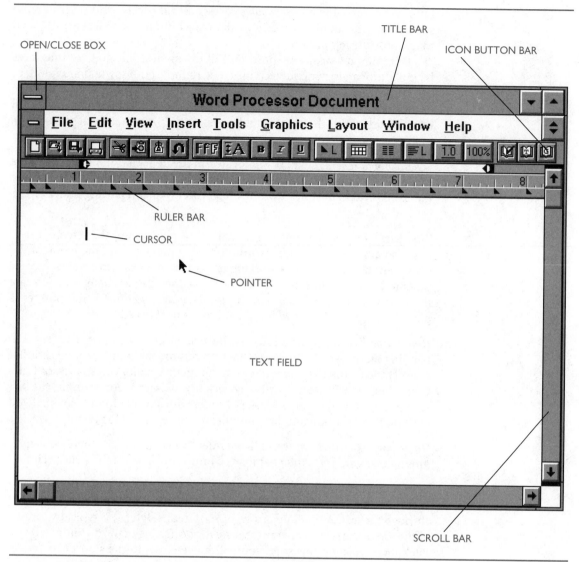

FIGURE 21.2.   The Graphic Interface

the letters will emerge as you type. Do not confuse the cursor on a graphic interface with the pointer (see next section).

*Pointer.* The pointer is the object that glides across the screen as you move the mouse across the tabletop. The pointer changes appearance depending on where it is on the screen. When the pointer is placed on top of an icon button or the name of a pull-down menu, it looks like the white arrow in the figure (or sometimes a hand with the index finger extended). In this form, the pointer works in combination with the mouse to activate buttons, icons, and pull-down menus. When the pointer moves over the text field, it changes into a text tool, which resembles a tall, thin capital letter "I." In this form, the pointer allows you to move the cursor around the text field and to select blocks of text.

## BASIC WORD PROCESSING CONCEPTS AND OPERATIONS

Word processors operate according to instructions known as "commands." Some of these commands are named in association with typewriter operations. For instance, tabs, margins, single spacing, and double spacing — terms associated primarily with typewriters — are still used in word processing programs. But just because the computer's keyboard resembles a typewriter's, you shouldn't make the mistake of thinking that you can treat the computer like a glorified typewriter. Doing so will only cause problems. For example, to center text horizontally with a typewriter, you would use the tab key or space bar until you reached the middle of the page. But imitating this technique on a word processor could cause problems; you should use the CENTER command instead.

In other words, word processors have a terminology and a logic all their own. The following list explains each of the major terms, concepts, and operations that you need to produce a college paper on a word processor. Most items also include an icon that corresponds to what you may find if your word processor uses a graphic interface. Keep in mind that your program may differ slightly in both the terminology and appearance — but such differences should be slight. Also be aware that word processors have many more features than you need to produce most college papers; explore these other features when you find the time and are feeling adventurous.

**Understanding Computers.**     The five things listed here are fundamental definitions that you need to understand to operate a computer.

*Disk.* A *disk* is any flat, circular object used to record and store data. *Floppy disks* are the small, portable disks used in floppy drives; a *hard disk* is the larger disk inside a hard drive (see next section). The 3½-inch microfloppy disk is currently the most popular computer disk. It comes in a square hard plastic case designed to protect the disk inside. The 5¼-inch floppy disk is also fairly common, although it is being phased out.

*Floppy drive.* On the front of most computers, you will find at least one narrow slot into which you can insert floppy disks. This device, which reads information from the disks, is known as a *floppy drive.* It works much like a phonograph; a stylus of sort floats along the surface of a rotating disk to read what's recorded there. Most floppy drives are labeled "A." If a computer has two floppy drives, usually one is the "A" drive and the other is the "B" drive.

*Hard drive.* A *hard drive* is a device similar to a floppy drive, except that you cannot insert and remove its disk. A hard disk is, therefore, a more secure and permanent place to store information than a floppy disk — and it usually has a far larger storage capacity. Most hard drives are labeled "C."

*Program/application/software.* A *program* is more or less an extensive set of instructions that tell the computer what to do. An *application* is a computer program designed to do a certain job, like word processing. Applications are also known as *software.* (In contrast, the physical objects that make up a computer — keyboard, central unit, monitor, mouse, and cables — constitute its *hardware.*)

*File/document.* In terms of word processing, a *file* is generally any text or manuscript that exists electronically instead of on paper. A file is a tiny packet of information stored under a particular name. For example, the file "research.doc" might hold the entire contents of your twenty-page research paper. Some word processing programs refer to files as *documents* because this sounds a little more like something from the world of writing than computing; the two words can be used almost interchangeably.

Creating, Managing, and Printing Files.    The following six commands are the ones you need to set up and print out the files that contain your writing.

We have provided sample icons for many of the commands in the next few sections to give you a general idea of what the icons on your graphical interface may look like; the details will vary. Of course, you can also access and execute these commands through pull-down menus.

NEW. Every time you give the computer the NEW command, it will create a new file. Some programs will allow you to have more than one file open at a time; check the title bar to see which file you are working on if you are not sure. As soon as you create a new document, you should use SAVE (see p. 447) to give it a name.

OPEN *or* RETRIEVE. The OPEN or RETRIEVE command "opens" (brings up on the screen) a document that was previously created and saved. When you first open a document, its name will usually appear in the title bar. You can make changes to a file only if it is open. It is usually possible to have more than one file open at a time.

CLOSE. The CLOSE command shuts down a file that is open. Before closing, be sure to use SAVE to store any changes that you made while working on a file.

In some word processors CLOSE shuts down the application, so be sure you know the difference between closing a file and closing an entire application.

 **SAVE.** The SAVE command stores your work electronically on a disk. You should save new files as soon as you create them and save all files periodically as you work on them. The first time you save a new file, you will be asked to name it. You should also make sure the file is being stored on the disk or drive you want; usually this will be on the hard drive if you have your own computer, or on the floppy drive if you are using someone else's. Every time you save a file that already has a name, it will replace the file as it previously existed. If you want to save your recent work but do not want to replace older drafts, use the SAVE AS function to give your file a new name (see next item).

**SAVE AS.** The SAVE AS command stores a copy of a currently open file in a different way. You can use SAVE AS to change the name of an open file so that you do not replace an older version of the document. Or you can use it to save a copy of the file in a different location or disk.

 **PRINT.** The PRINT command sends your document to the printer. When you give the computer this command, you will often first see a *dialog box* that will require responses from you before printing can begin. Choosing PRINT or OK from the print dialog box will usually start the printing.

**Moving Blocks of Text.**   The following six commands will allow you to move text — whether words or entire passages — from one part of your paper to another and from file to file.

*Select.*   To cut, copy, move, paste, or delete a particular block of text, you must first select it so that the computer knows which text to perform its operation on. A block of text can include something as small as a single character or something as large as an entire paper. The methods for selecting text vary from one word processor to the next, so we're not going to describe them here; take a moment to figure out how to use this feature with your program.

 **CUT.** The CUT command removes writing from the text field and stores it in the computer's temporary memory (known as a *buffer* or *clipboard*). First select the text you want to cut and then give the CUT command. Cutting can be used to delete writing altogether or to move it from one place to another. To move it to another location, you will also need to use PASTE (see p. 448). Each time you cut text you will automatically replace whatever was last stored in temporary memory.

 **COPY.** The COPY command saves selected text in temporary memory but — unlike CUT — leaves the original block intact. First select the text you want to copy and then give the COPY command. This function is useful for moving text from one place to another if you do not want to delete it from the original location. Each time you copy text you will automatically replace whatever was last stored in temporary memory

**PASTE.** The PASTE command will take whatever text is located in temporary memory — whatever text you've most recently told the computer to CUT or COPY — and put a copy of it where the cursor is located.

**MOVE.** Some word processors use the MOVE command instead of cutting and pasting. First select the text you want to move; then give the MOVE command. The method for indicating where to move the text block will depend on your word processor; a common method is placing the cursor at the new location and hitting the ENTER key.

**UNDO/REDO.** If you make a mistake, particularly while cutting, moving, or pasting, UNDO or REDO can bail you out of trouble. This command reverses the last action you've taken. So if you make a mistake, freeze. The UNDO command usually can change only the last thing you did.

Formatting Your Manuscript.    The following nine operations are invaluable for creating attractive, effective papers. See Figure 21.3 for a visual representation of each important term discussed here.

*Fonts.*  A *font* is a particular style of print. Fonts come in all sizes and shapes; some are flowery, and others look like what you would get from a typewriter. For college papers you should use conventional fonts. Courier is the name of the most widely accepted font. Helvetica, Times, Roman, and Palatino are some other fonts that will give your paper a serious academic appearance. College papers are also generally not the place to play around with different type sizes: 12-point type is the standard, although some instructors accept the smaller 10-point type.

*Italics.*  Italic type looks *like this*. To italicize, turn the italics function on, type, and turn the function off. Or you can type first, select the text you want to italicize, and then select the italics function. In general, italics and underlining accomplish the same tasks in college writing; use one or the other, but not both.

*Underline.*  Underlined type looks <u>like this</u>. The procedure for underlining is almost identical to that for italicizing, except that you select the *underline* function. Underlining evolved as a way to format manuscripts when typists were unable to produce italics. Therefore, italicizing is generally preferable to underlining if you have the choice.

*Bold.*  Bold (or boldface) type looks **like this**. The procedure for boldfacing is almost identical to that used for italicizing, except that you select the *bold* function. College papers do not usually require bold type — headings and subheadings are the only widely accepted uses of boldface.

*Line spacing.*  This refers to the amount of space between lines of type. College papers almost always require double spacing. Make sure a document is set to double line spacing before you begin entering text. You can also select a block of text and set the line spacing for that particular block only.

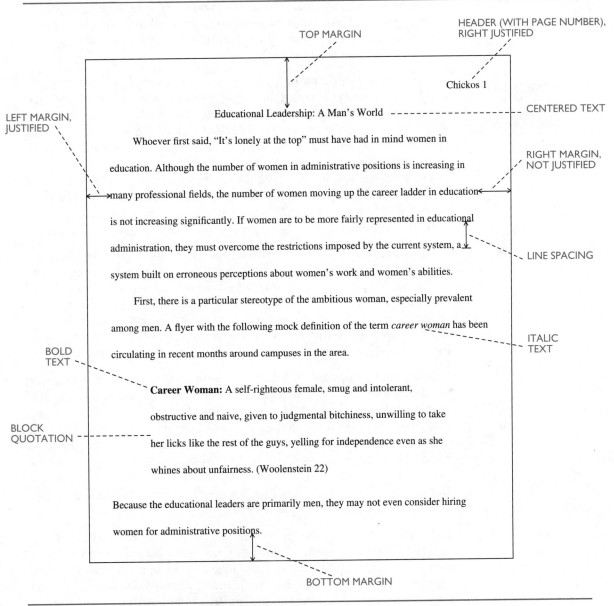

TOP MARGIN

HEADER (WITH PAGE NUMBER), RIGHT JUSTIFIED

Chickos 1

Educational Leadership: A Man's World    — — — — — — — — — CENTERED TEXT

LEFT MARGIN, JUSTIFIED

RIGHT MARGIN, NOT JUSTIFIED

Whoever first said, "It's lonely at the top" must have had in mind women in education. Although the number of women in administrative positions is increasing in many professional fields, the number of women moving up the career ladder in education is not increasing significantly. If women are to be more fairly represented in educational administration, they must overcome the restrictions imposed by the current system, a system built on erroneous perceptions about women's work and women's abilities.

LINE SPACING

First, there is a particular stereotype of the ambitious woman, especially prevalent among men. A flyer with the following mock definition of the term *career woman* has been circulating in recent months around campuses in the area.

ITALIC TEXT

BOLD TEXT

**Career Woman:** A self-righteous female, smug and intolerant, obstructive and naive, given to judgmental bitchiness, unwilling to take her licks like the rest of the guys, yelling for independence even as she whines about unfairness. (Woolenstein 22)

BLOCK QUOTATION

Because the educational leaders are primarily men, they may not even consider hiring women for administrative positions.

BOTTOM MARGIN

FIGURE 21.3.    Format Concepts for Word Processing

***Page numbers, headers, footers.***  Almost all word processors will automatically number pages for you. If you need to place your last name or a brief title adjacent to the page number, you should use a header or a footer. A *header* is writing that is preset to appear at the top of every page in a document. A *footer* is similar — only it goes at the bottom of every page. Automatic page numbers, headers, and footers can be tricky if you don't want them to appear on the first page, or if you want the first page numbered to be something other than 1. Using these functions can require a little practice, so don't try to figure them out at the last minute.

*Centering and justification.* If you want text centered horizontally in the middle of your page (as on a title page), use the CENTER function. You may either turn the CENTER function on and then type or select already typed text and then center it. Normal text is *left justified*, that is, aligned so that it is even with the left margin. Page numbers and headers are usually the only things that require alignment with the right margin. *Full justification* stretches lines of text so that each line touches both the left and right margins, like the text in this book and most books. It's probably not a good idea to use full justification on word-processed papers because it can result in awkward spacing between letters and words.

*Margins and tabs.* Each word processor handles margins and tabs differently, and they can be difficult to manage. Top and bottom margins are usually preset to 1 inch. Different instructors have different standards for left and right margins, but 1 to 1½ inches is typical. If you have very specific guidelines for your papers, be sure to practice setting margins well before your deadline. College papers generally require only a tab that indents five spaces (or one-half inch), which is where the first tab on most word processors is set.

*Creating block quotations.* If you need to format an indented block quotation for your paper, don't use tabs (as you would on a typewriter). Some word processors have commands that can automatically set block quotations for you. In general, use the following three steps: first, type the quotation as a separate paragraph; second, select the quote; third, change the left margin for this block of text only.

Getting Help.   The following two features are invaluable resources to have while you are working with a word processor.

*Help.* Word processors usually contain on-line information that can help you solve problems while sitting at the computer. Some help programs are better than others, but all are valuable. Help programs are especially useful for finding commands and features that you know your word processor has but that you can't locate — a common problem. The help function is organized according to the names of these commands and features; the descriptions and definitions that you have just read about should give you a better sense of what to look for when using help.

*Spell checker.* A spell checker locates a word it thinks is misspelled; it will highlight the word and prompt you for a response. You may retype the word yourself, select a substitution from the suggestions that the checker provides, or skip the word all together. Spell checkers can be tricky; be sure you understand yours before relying on it. The spell checker works by matching what you type against words in a dictionary stored electronically in the computer's memory. Unfortunately, none of these programs is a substitute for human proofreading. Even the cleverest spell checker won't point out certain errors. For example, if you accidentally type *her* instead of *here*, the program won't see it as a mistake, because in its dictionary *her* is a perfectly good word. Spell checking should be the very last thing you do before printing your document.

# A Few Practical Tips

Even after you have become familiar with a word processor, one of the most valuable things you can do is to try to learn from mistakes that others have made. The following is a list of practical tips that can help you avoid some of the classic pitfalls of word processing.

Count to Five.    Before quitting, closing, exiting, or deleting, pause for a count of five and make sure you're not about to make a mistake. Use this technique before you leave your workstation, especially if it is an open-use, on-campus computer. Did you save everything? Did you make the necessary printouts? Did you eject your disk and the leave the station in proper order? Taking five before leaving your computer is especially important if you use an e-mail account; you *must* be sure that you are completely disconnected so that others cannot access your account.

Create "Master Documents."    You will know ahead of time how your instructor wants you to format your papers. Manuscripts are usually double-spaced and left-justified with a 12-point standard font (such as Courier) and with 1 to 1½-inch margins top, bottom, left, and right. Go ahead and format a document according to your instructor's specifications. Save it under the name "template" or "master" so that every time you need a document with the same formatting, you can simply make a copy of the master document and give it a new name.

Don't Get Carried Away.    Word processors offer amazing features these days: you can import graphics, create tables, and incorporate dozens of fancy fonts in different sizes and even twisted shapes. Use advanced design features whenever they help clarify your writing. However, strange fonts, full justification, or an abundance of text styles tend to distract readers of academic work. You should resist the temptation to make your document look like a three-ring circus. A laser printer will produce crisp, black copy and can enhance the readability of what you write — if you have access to one, your document won't really need anything fancy to create an exceptionally attractive manuscript.

**Plan for Glitches.**　　Computer systems are more complicated than pens, pencils, or typewriters; therefore, you face a much greater chance of something going wrong. If you rely on computers and you flirt with deadlines, eventually you're going to get burned. The old excuse "the dog ate my homework" has been replaced with "the computer ate my file." Instructors have, by now, heard this new excuse so many times that they are less sympathetic than ever. Glitches are simply part of the territory; prepare for them.

**Practice Careful File Management.**　　Name your files in consistent patterns, and use numbers and dates in your filenames to keep track of which versions are most recent. Make backup copies of everything. You should have one working disk and one backup disk, which you should update weekly; if you want to be extra careful, keep one backup disk with you or at school and another one at home. Label your disks carefully and buy a plastic case to store them in. Don't let the disks melt or be exposed to something that might demagnetize them (such as a strong magnet or an airport security device). In addition to electronic backups, you should make hard copy (paper) backups. You can always retype from paper, but a damaged disk, deleted file, or broken computer can leave you with nothing to work with. A good rule of thumb is that if you spent thirty solid minutes or more working on a document, print out that work before quitting for the day. Print or photocopy two copies of a file that you absolutely can't afford to lose. (If you are printing out something just for security, you can use single spacing and a small font to save paper.) Put the date on the printout so that you can separate one version from another.

**Don't Fall into the Twilight Zone.**　　Some writers become so absorbed with writing on a computer that they lose track of time. You also want to avoid CRT fatigue — staring at a monitor for extended periods of time is more of a strain on your eyes than reading print on paper. Adjust the angle of your monitor and also its level of brightness for reading comfort. Take breaks now and then for stretching, exercise, and light refreshments. Do not allow your wrists and back to become strained either.

**Keep Reference Materials Within Reach.**　　If these resources aren't nearby, you probably won't use them when you really need to. There's an impolite term among computer users for people who don't at least sometimes try to figure things out for themselves, but we won't repeat it here. It amounts to "Why don't you read the manual?"

**Try Revising, Editing, and Proofreading on Hard (Paper) Copy.**　　Because your screen will probably display only about twenty-four lines at a time, you may find it hard to hold in mind an entire piece of writing while working online. In a long composition, large changes that involve several paragraphs may be harder to envision on screen than if you spread out pages across a table where you can glance over them in a flash. But more important, one of the secrets to editing is looking at a paper from a different perspective. If you composed on-line, editing and proofreading from paper makes mistakes stand out.

**Change the Look of Your Text.**     Changing the look of your text is one of the best ways to get a fresh perspective on it so that mistakes are easier to notice. Blowing up your text using a huge, bold, or stylish font is one good way to shake things up. Or try inserting a number of returns after each sentence, so that each one is surrounded by white space. This last technique is especially effective if you then scroll backward from the end of the document to read and edit one sentence at a time. Save a backup copy of your file before trying either of these techniques — you'll want to be sure that you can restore the document to its proper formatting after you have finished editing.

**Don't Think of a Word Processor as a Typewriter.**     Word processors are radically different from typewriters, but many users treat the two the same. For example, on a word processor you should use CENTER and TAB instead of the space bar to move text away from the left margin. You should not use the RETURN or ENTER key at the end of every line of text; almost all word processors have a function known as *word wrap* or *line wrap* that will break your lines properly. If you've been using a typewriter for a long time, it may be hard to break these habits, but you must. Otherwise, you'll probably end up with some very odd-looking printouts. More important, if you impose the rigid framework of typewriting conventions on the fluid text stored in a computer, you won't be able to take advantage of the full power and flexibility of word processing, which allows you to make sweeping changes and minor revisions with a few simple keystrokes.

## *Writing on Computer Networks*

Even if you have never touched a computer in your life, you have probably heard something recently about either the Internet, the "information super-highway," or the World Wide Web. These three projects and others like them are part of a dramatic revolution in communications that has already begun to redefine our world. It is important that you know something about these changes, especially since most of what's happening out there is text-based — that is, almost all of the action on the Internet takes place through writing.

A computer network is simply a connection of two or more computers so that they can communicate with each other. Networks come in different sizes and varying degrees of complexity. One of the simplest computer networks is known as a LAN, or local-area network. More and more writing courses are being taught in computer labs and computer classrooms, and most of these facilities link their computers through a LAN so that the computers in the room can communicate.

Computers can also be linked through networks much larger than a LAN. In fact, a small network of computers within a lab can easily be connected to a larger network of computers throughout an entire school. And your school-wide network can then be connected to other schoolwide networks. In fact, schools that are externally networked form an important segment of the Internet.

The Internet is almost exactly what it sounds like: an "international network" of computers. It is literally a network of networks organized according to "domains," or groups with common interests (like the educational institutions we have just mentioned). Aside from educational networks, the other major domains in this country are commercial networks and government networks. Through the Internet, each domain connects to other domains throughout the world. Just imagine, if the tiny workstation you use in a campus computer lab is connected to the Internet, and you have an account to access the Internet, you have the power to send messages to almost anyone else in the world who also has an account. In a matter of minutes, through your keyboard, you could send a message to the White House or to Japan.

Thus the Internet is a worldwide web of cables and satellite relays that can connect a single computer to a local network, which is in turn connected to an institutional network, connected to a domain of networks, connected to the Internet, and then possibly back down to another computer on the other side of the planet.

Here we describe briefly some issues regarding the revolution taking place in writing as a result of computer networks, particularly the Internet. Regardless of whether you write on a LAN or on the World Wide Web, you must be aware of the following point: *Any writing that you send out over a computer network should be considered public discourse, as if you were reading your words aloud in a crowded hallway.* Do not be misled into thinking that just because you wrote something in the seemingly quiet, private space of your computer workstation, others will not read and react to what you have said. You are legally and ethically responsible for what you post to a network; you can very easily be expelled from school and even arrested for the things you write. And any information you get off the Internet should be documented just as you document evidence from books, periodicals, and interviews. Sending and receiving information through a global network of computers gives the writer awesome powers, but also awesome responsibilities.

## WRITING ON A LAN

More and more, writing students are getting the opportunity to meet in classrooms equipped with computers. Through LANs, students can write to others in their class in "real time;" that is, as soon as they send their words into the network, classmates can read what they have written. Unlike many class discussions in which the instructor or one or two students do all of the talking, real-time interchanges allow for everyone in the class to participate on a more even basis. If you feel nervous about speaking publicly, or you would prefer a few moments to fine-tune what you have to say, you may enjoy such a computer-mediated discussion.

If your class participates in real-time interchanges, you should be aware of a couple of things. First, instructors can and often do print transcripts of these conversations. You are, therefore, *more* accountable for what you say than in most conventional class discussions. Some people can be misled into thinking that computers are toys for playing games, but classroom discussions are generally serious business, requiring a mature attitude. A second point is flaming. *Flaming* is rude, hostile, or impolite writing that is exchanged over a computer network. Flaming occurs when writers erroneously feel protected from being responsible for their words because of the illusion of anonymity that the computer provides. You should certainly express your viewpoints, but you should continue to consider how others in the class might react to what you say. Be respectful and courteous.

## WRITING ON THE INTERNET

The same principles of behavior apply to writing on the Internet as on LANs. In fact, there's even a new word that describes these principles: *netiquette.* The primary difference between a LAN and the Internet is one of size. Whereas a LAN connects a very small group of people, the Internet links together *the entire world*. The Internet also offers a much wider variety of ways for you to write and read information.

E-mail serves as the most basic form of writing on the Internet. E-mail works like conventional mail in that you can write letters or messages and send them to other people if you know their addresses. But instead of street addresses that correspond to actual physical locations, e-mail addresses represent electronic storage places on computers. (For more on using e-mail, see p. 321 in Chapter 14.)

But writing on the Internet can involve much more than just sending letters back and forth to one correspondent at a time. You can join Internet discussion groups in the form of listservs, newsgroups, and bulletin boards. As a member of a discussion group, when you send a message to a particular e-mail address, your message will in turn be distributed to everyone else who subscribes to the group. And they can do the same.

You can also participate in conversations that take place almost as fast as you can input your words. MOOs, MUDs, and IRCs are three of the most common Internet programs that allow people to join in imaginary conference rooms to conduct real-time interchanges. These real-time programs are somewhat controversial because they are often misused as ways to goof off. But you might like to know that a couple of these imaginary rooms have been set up to serve as on-line writing centers, staffed with instructors who will help you with your writing.

The Internet can also support advanced forms of writing such as hypertext and multimedia. If you have Internet access and software such as Mosaic,

Netscape, or Lynx, you can see some incredible things on the Internet. The monumental expansion of the Internet that began in the mid-1990s is likely to bring about sweeping changes in the ways we think about writing and the opportunities we have as writers. It's an exciting time to be studying the craft of writing.

# A Writer's Reader

# Introduction: Reading to Write

*A Writer's Reader* is a collection of professional essays that you will find worthwhile. We have carefully selected these thirty-seven essays for specific reasons. We hope, first of all, that you will read these pieces simply for the sake of reading — enjoying, comprehending, responding to the ideas presented. Good writers read widely, and in doing so, they increase their knowledge of the English language and of the craft of writing. Second, we hope you will actively study these essays as solid examples of the resources and strategies explored in *A Writer's Guide* and of effective writing in general. The authors represented in this reader, experts from varied fields, have faced the same problems and choices you do when you write. You can learn from studying their decisions, structures, and techniques. Finally, we hope that you will find the content of the essays intriguing and that the information presented in the selections and the questions posed at the ends of the essays will give you some ideas to write about.

Each chapter in *A Writer's Reader* concentrates on a broad theme that will be familiar and interesting to you: families, men and women, American diversity, the world of work, popular culture, and nature and technology. Within each chapter you'll find a variety of voices and perspectives. In some essays the writers focus on the inner world and write of personal experience and opinion. In others the authors turn their attention to the outer world and write informational, analytical, and persuasive essays. Some of the writers — Stephen King and Amy Tan, for example — may already be familiar to you. Many of the others we hope will become new friends. Some of the messages and arguments presented here will have you nodding in agreement, some will have you strongly disagreeing, and perhaps others will lead you to pause and reconsider long-held beliefs.

Each section in the reader begins with a picture and a journal prompt, both intended to stimulate you to begin to think and write. Each essay is preceded by biographical information about the author, placing him or her — and the essay itself — into a cultural and informational context. Following each essay is a set of discussion questions and writing suggestions. The five "Questions to Start You Thinking" cover the same ground for every selection: meaning, writing strategies, writer's choices, vocabulary, and comparison or contrast of this selection with one or more of the other selections in *A Writer's Reader*. After these questions come a couple of journal prompts designed to get your writing juices flowing (for more about journal writing, see p. 339) and two possible composition assignments designed with specific suggestions for writing. The first assignment is directed toward your inner world, asking you to draw generally on your personal experience and your understanding of the essay. The second is outer-directed, asking you to look outside yourself and write an analytical or argumentative paper, one that may require further reading or research.

*A Writer's Reader*, an integral part of *The Bedford Guide for College Writers*, is directly connected to *A Writer's Guide*. The essays in the reader illustrate various uses of the five resources of writers from Part One — recall, observation, reading, conversation, and imagination. They exemplify the critical thinking skills for writing from Part Two — analyzing, comparing and contrasting, explaining causes and effects, taking a stand, proposing a solution, and evaluating. They illustrate many of the writing strategies explained in Part Four. In addition, at the end of each chapter in Part One, Part Two, and Part Four, you will find "Making Connections," a brief passage that draws your attention to essays in the reader that use the resource, the critical thinking skill, or the strategies explained in the chapter.

# Chapter 22

# Families

**Journal Prompt**

What are the most important lessons you have learned from your family? Who taught you, and at what stage in your life? If you have or plan to have children, will you pass these same lessons on to them?

E. B. (Elwyn Brooks) White *(1899–1985) was born in Mount Vernon, New York. After serving in the army, he graduated from Cornell University and moved to Seattle to work as a reporter. His career led him back to the East Coast, where he joined the staff of the recently established* New Yorker *magazine in 1927. For half a century his satires, poems, and essays helped define that magazine's distinctive style of elegant wit and social comment. He moved to Maine in 1933, and his widely read books for children,* Stuart Little *(1945),* Charlotte's Web *(1952), and* The Trumpet of the Swan *(1970), draw on his life in the country to celebrate life's blend of sadness, happiness, love, and loss. In the following essay, White reflects on the experience of returning with his son to a favorite scene from his own childhood.*

## *E. B. White*   Once More to the Lake

**August 1941**

One summer, along about 1904, my father rented a camp on a lake in Maine and took us all there for the month of August. We all got ringworm from some kittens and had to rub Pond's Extract on our arms and legs night and morning, and my father rolled over in a canoe with all his clothes on; but outside of that the vacation was a success and from then on none of us ever thought there was any place in the world like that lake in Maine. We returned summer after summer — always on August 1 for one month. I have since become a salt-water man, but sometimes in summer there are days when the restlessness of the tides and the fearful cold of the sea water and the incessant wind that blows across the afternoon and into the evening make me wish for the placidity of a lake in the woods. A few weeks ago this feeling got so strong I bought myself a couple of bass hooks and a spinner and returned to the lake where we used to go, for a week's fishing and to revisit old haunts.

I took along my son, who had never had any fresh water up his nose and who had seen lily pads only from train windows. On the journey over to the lake I began to wonder what it would be like. I wondered how time would have marred this unique, this holy spot — the coves and streams, the hills that the sun set behind, the camps and the paths behind the camps. I was sure that the tarred road would have found it out, and I wondered in what other ways it would be desolated. It is strange how much you can remember about places like that once you allow your mind to return into the grooves that lead back. You remember one thing, and that suddenly reminds you of another thing. I guess I remembered clearest of all the early mornings, when the lake was cool and motionless, remembered how the bedroom smelled of the lumber it was made of and of the wet woods whose scent entered through the screen. The partitions in the camp were thin and did not extend clear to the top of the rooms, and as I was always the first up I would dress softly so as not to wake the others, and sneak out into the sweet outdoors and start out in the canoe, keeping close along the shore in the long shadows of the pines. I remembered being very careful never to rub my paddle against the gunwale for fear of disturbing the stillness of the cathedral.

The lake had never been what you would call a wild lake. There were cottages sprinkled around the shores, and it was in farming country although the shores of the lake were quite heavily wooded. Some of the cottages were owned by nearby farmers, and you would live at the shore and eat your meals at the farmhouse. That's what our family did. But although it wasn't wild, it was a fairly large and undisturbed lake and there were places in it that, to a child at least, seemed infinitely remote and primeval.

I was right about the tar: It led to within half a mile of the shore. But when I got back there, with my boy, and we settled into a camp near a farmhouse and into the kind of summertime I had known, I could tell that it was going to be pretty much the same as it had been before — I knew it, lying in bed the first morning smelling the bedroom and hearing the boy sneak quietly out and go off along the shore in a boat. I began to sustain the illusion that he was I, and therefore, by simple transposition, that I was my father. This sensation persisted, kept cropping up all the time we were there. It was not an entirely new feeling, but in this setting it grew much stronger. I seemed to be living a dual existence. I would be in the middle of some simple act, I would be picking up a bait box or laying down a table fork, or I would be saying something and suddenly it would be not I but my father who was saying the words or making the gesture. It gave me a creepy sensation.

We went fishing the first morning. I felt the same damp moss covering the worms in the bait can, and saw the dragonfly alight on the tip of my rod as it hovered a few inches from the surface of the water. It was the arrival of this fly that convinced me beyond any doubt that everything was as it always had been, that the years were a mirage, and that there had been no years. The small waves were the same, chucking the rowboat under the chin as we fished at anchor, and the boat was the same boat, the same color green and the ribs broken in the same places, and under the floorboards the same fresh water leavings and debris — the dead hellgrammite, the wisps of moss, the rusty discarded fishhook, the dried blood from yesterday's catch. We stared silently at the tips of our rods, at the dragonflies that came and went. I lowered the tip of mine into the water, tentatively, pensively dislodging the fly, which darted two feet away, poised, darted two feet back, and came to rest again a little farther up the rod. There had been no years between the ducking of this dragonfly and the other one — the one that was part of memory. I looked at the boy, who was silently watching his fly, and it was my hands that held his rod, my eyes watching. I felt dizzy and didn't know which rod I was at the end of.

We caught two bass, hauling them in briskly as though they were mackerel, pulling them over the side of the boat in a businesslike manner without any landing net, and stunning them with a blow on the back of the head. When we got back for a swim before lunch, the lake was exactly where we had left it, the same number of inches from the dock, and there was only the merest suggestion of a breeze. This seemed an utterly enchanted sea, this lake you could leave to its own devices for a few hours and come back to, and find that it had not stirred, this constant and trustworthy body of water. In the shallows, the dark, watersoaked sticks and twigs, smooth and old, were undulating in clusters on the bottom against the clean ribbed sand, and the track of the mussel was plain. A school of minnows swam by, each minnow with its small individual shadow, doubling the attendance, so clear and sharp in the sunlight. Some of the other campers were in swimming, along the shore, one of them with a cake of soap, and the water felt thin and clear and unsubstantial. Over the years there had been this person with the cake of soap, this cultist, and here he was. There had been no years.

Up to the farmhouse to dinner through the teeming dusty field, the road    7
under our sneakers was only a two-track road. The middle track was missing, the one with the marks of the hooves and the splotches of dried, flaky manure. There had always been three tracks to choose from in choosing which track to walk in; now the choice was narrowed down to two. For a moment I missed terribly the middle alternative. But the way led past the tennis court, and something about the way it lay there in the sun reassured me; the tape had loosened along the backline, the alleys were green with plantains and other weeds, and the net (installed in June and removed in September) sagged in the dry noon, and the whole place steamed with midday heat and hunger and emptiness. There was a choice of pie for dessert, and one was blueberry and one was apple, and the waitresses were the same country girls, there having been no passage of time, only the illusion of it as in a dropped curtain — the waitresses were still fifteen; their hair had been washed, that was the only difference — they had been to the movies and seen the pretty girls with the clean hair.

Summertime, oh, summertime, pattern of life indelible with fade-proof    8
lake, the wood unshatterable, the pasture with the sweetfern and the juniper forever and ever, summer without end; this was the background, and the life along the shore was the design, the cottages with their innocent and tranquil design, their tiny docks with the flagpole and the American flag floating against the white clouds in the blue sky, the little paths over the roots of the trees leading from camp to camp and the paths leading back to the outhouses and the can of lime for sprinkling, and at the souvenir counters at the store the miniature birchbark canoes and the postcards that showed things looking a little better than they looked. This was the American family at play, escaping the city heat, wondering whether the newcomers in the camp at the head of the cove were "common" or "nice," wondering whether it was true that the people who drove up for Sunday dinner at the farmhouse were turned away because there wasn't enough chicken.

It seemed to me, as I kept remembering all this, that those times and    9
those summers had been infinitely precious and worth saving. There had been jollity and peace and goodness. The arriving (at the beginning of Au-

gust) had been so big a business in itself, at the railway station the farm wagon drawn up, the first smell of the pine-laden air, the first glimpse of the smiling farmer, and the great importance of the trunks and your father's enormous authority in such matters, and the feel of the wagon under you for the long ten-mile haul, and at the top of the last long hill catching the first view of the lake after eleven months of not seeing this cherished body of water. The shouts and cries of the other campers when they saw you, and the trunks to be unpacked, to give up their rich burden. (Arriving was less exciting nowadays, when you sneaked up in your car and parked it under a tree near the camp and took out the bags and in five minutes it was all over, no fuss, no loud wonderful fuss about trunks.)

Peace and goodness and jollity. The only thing that was wrong now, really, was the sound of the place, an unfamiliar nervous sound of the outboard motors. This was the note that jarred, the one thing that would sometimes break the illusion and set the years moving. In those other summertimes all motors were inboard; and when they were at a little distance, the noise they made was a sedative, an ingredient of summer sleep. They were one-cylinder and two-cylinder engines, and some were make-and-break and some were jump-spark, but they all made a sleepy sound across the lake. The one-lungers throbbed and fluttered, and the twin-cylinder ones purred and purred, and that was a quiet sound, too. But now the campers all had outboards. In the daytime, in the hot mornings, these motors made a petulant, irritable sound; at night in the still evening when the afterglow lit the water, they whined about one's ears like mosquitoes. My boy loved our rented outboard, and his great desire was to achieve single-handed mastery over it, and authority, and he soon learned the trick of choking it a little (but not too much), and the adjustment of the needle valve. Watching him I would remember the things you could do with the old one-cylinder engine with the heavy flywheel, how you could have it eating out of your hand if you got really close to it spiritually. Motorboats in those days didn't have clutches, and you would make a landing by shutting off the motor at the proper time and coasting in with a dead rudder. But there was a way of reversing them, if you learned the trick, by cutting the switch and putting it on again exactly on the final dying revolution of the flywheel, so that it would kick back against compression and begin reversing. Approaching a dock in a strong following breeze, it was difficult to slow up sufficiently by the ordinary coasting method, and if a boy felt he had complete mastery over his motor, he was tempted to keep it running beyond its time and then reverse it a few feet from the dock. It took a cool nerve, because if you threw the switch a twentieth of a second too soon you would catch the flywheel when it still had speed enough to go up past center, and the boat would leap ahead, charging bull-fashion at the dock.

We had a good week at the camp. The bass were biting well and the sun shone endlessly, day after day. We would be tired at night and lie down in the accumulated heat of the little bedrooms after the long hot day and the breeze would stir almost imperceptibly outside and the smell of the swamp drift in

10

11

through the rusty screens. Sleep would come easily and in the morning the red squirrel would be on the roof, tapping out his gay routine. I kept remembering everything, lying in bed in the mornings — the small steamboat that had a long rounded stern like the lip of a Ubangi, and how quietly she ran on the moonlight sails, when the older boys played their mandolins and the girls sang and we ate doughnuts dipped in sugar, and how sweet the music was on the water in the shining night, and what it had felt like to think about girls then. After breakfast we would go up to the store and the things were in the same place — the minnows in a bottle, the plugs and spinners disarranged and pawed over by the youngsters from the boys' camp, the Fig Newtons and the Beeman's gum. Outside, the road was tarred and cars stood in front of the store. Inside, all was just as it had always been, except there was more Coca-Cola and not so much Moxie and root beer and birch beer and sarsaparilla. We would walk out with the bottle of pop apiece and sometimes the pop would backfire up our noses and hurt. We explored the streams, quietly, where the turtles slid off the sunny logs and dug their way into the soft bottom; and we lay on the town wharf and fed worms to the tame bass. Everywhere we went I had trouble making out which was I, the one walking at my side, the one walking in my pants.

One afternoon while we were at that lake a thunderstorm came up. It was    12
the revival of an old melodrama that I had seen long ago with childish awe. The second-act climax of the drama of the electrical disturbance over a lake in America had not changed in any important respect. This was the big scene. The whole thing was so familiar, the first feeling of oppression and heat and a general air around camp of not wanting to go very far away. In midafternoon (it was all the same) a curious darkening of the sky, and a lull in everything that had made life tick; and then the way the boats suddenly swung the other way at their moorings with the coming of a breeze out of the new quarter, and the premonitory rumble. Then the kettle drum, then the snare, then the bass drum and cymbals, then crackling light against the dark, and the gods grinning and licking their chops in the hills. Afterward the calm, the rain steadily rustling in the calm lake, the return of light and hope and spirits, and the campers running out in joy and relief to go swimming in the rain, their bright cries perpetuating the deathless joke about how they were getting simply drenched, and the children screaming with delight at the new sensation of bathing in the rain, and the joke about getting drenched linking the generations in a strong indestructible chain. And the comedian who waded in carrying an umbrella.

When the others went swimming my son said he was going in, too. He    13
pulled his dripping trunks from the line where they had hung all through the shower and wrung them out. Languidly, and with no thought of going in, I watched him, his hard little body, skinny and bare, saw him wince slightly as he pulled up around his vitals the small, soggy, icy garment. As he buckled the swollen belt, suddenly my groin felt the chill of death.

**Questions to Start You Thinking**

1. CONSIDERING MEANING: How have the lake and the surrounding community, as White depicts them, changed since he was a boy?

2. IDENTIFYING WRITING STRATEGIES: Notice the details White uses to describe life at the lake. How many different sense experiences do his images evoke? Identify and then analyze at least four memorable images from the essay, explaining what makes each memorable.

3. ANALYZING THE WRITER'S CHOICES: Using examples, explain how White compares and contrasts past with present to show that "there had been no years" since his childhood at the lake (paragraph 5). How does he use comparison to break the reader's expectations in the final paragraphs?

4. EXPANDING VOCABULARY: Define *primeval* (paragraph 3), *transposition* (paragraph 4), *hellgrammite* (paragraph 5), *undulating, cultist* (paragraph 6), and *petulant* (paragraph 10). What is White's purpose in using adult words rather than a child's words to look back on his childhood experience?

5. MAKING CONNECTIONS: Both White and Gerald Early in "Black like . . . Shirley Temple?" (p. 468) describe their efforts to please and to draw closer to their children. Whose attempt seems more successful? Why?

**Journal Prompts**

1. Describe a place that has special meaning for you. Why is it special?

2. Use White's description of a thunderstorm (paragraph 12) as a model to describe a natural event that you have witnessed.

**Suggestions for Writing**

1. Think of a place you were familiar with as a child and then visited again as an adult. Write an essay explaining how the place had changed and not changed. Use observation and recall to make the place as memorable for your readers as it was for you.

2. How do you think nostalgia, the desire to return to an important and pleasant time in the past, influences the way we remember our own experiences? Use examples from White's essay and from your experience to illustrate your explanation.

**Gerald Early**, *born in 1952 in Philadelphia, attended the University of Pennsylvania and earned his M.A. and Ph.D. at Cornell University. He now teaches English and directs the African and Afro-American Studies Program at Washington University in St. Louis. Early writes prolifically about various aspects of American culture, from literature to family to sports. Some of his many books include* Tuxedo Junction: Essays on American Culture *(1989);* The Culture of Bruising: Essays on Prizefighting *(1991);* Daughters: On Family and Fatherhood *(1994); and the autobiographical* How the War in the Street Is Won: A Black Poet's Journey into Himself *(1995). He also edited* Lure and Loathing: Essays on Race, Identity, and the Ambivalence of Assimilation *(1993). In this excerpt from an essay entitled "Life with Daughters, or the Cakewalk with Shirley Temple," which was first published in the Winter 91–92 issue of* Hungry Mind Review, *Early describes a dilemma he faced when his attempt to influence his daughters backfired.*

# *Gerald Early*    Black like . . . Shirley Temple?

It was two years ago, the summer that my daughters gave up their Afros   1
and had their hair straightened, that I decided to watch every Shirley Temple
film available on video with them. This included nineteen Twentieth Cen-
tury-Fox films that were made during her heyday — 1934 to 1938 — and several short Baby Burlesks.

I am not quite sure why I did this. I do not like Shirley Temple movies. I   2
did not like them much as a child. But my daughters — Linnet, then age ten,
and Rosalind, then age seven — after having seen a colorized version of *Our
Little Girl*, a perfectly wretched Temple vehicle (even Temple herself admits
this in her autobiography), on the Disney channel one evening, very much
wanted to do this summer project. We watched each of the films at least three
times. The project appealed to me because I felt I could share something with
my children while exercising parental control. I would seem to be a kid while
retaining my status and authority as father.

Perhaps I associate my children's change in hairstyle with our Shirley   3
Temple phase because so much was made of Temple's hair, her curls, during
her years of stardom. My daughters liked Temple's hair very much.

During the summer that we watched these films together, my relation-   4
ship with my daughters changed. At first I saw the films merely as vehicles for
parental instruction — black parental instruction, I should say, for I had prepared to give a history of black actors in Hollywood in the 1930s and provide
information on the lives of the black dancer Bill "Bojangles" Robinson, the
actress Hattie McDaniel, and some of the other blacks who appeared in
Temple films. I was never given much of an opportunity.

"I don't want to hear your old lectures, Daddy," Linnet said. "We want to   5
watch the movies. This isn't school. You make being black seem like a lesson."

When they laughed uproariously at some graceless thing that Stepin   6
Fetchit or Willie Best did, Rosalind turned to me, knowing that I was aghast,
and said:

"Don't worry, we know they aren't real black people."   7

"But do you know what you're laughing at?" I asked, chagrined.   8

"Yeah," Rosalind said, "clowns, not black people."   9

Eventually, I was told that if all I wanted to do was talk about the movies   10
or analyze them, then I would not be permitted to watch. Besides, they were
more than capable of judging the films themselves. So I grew quiet as the
summer went on. I did not want to be banished.

It was during this summer that they abandoned their Afro hairstyles for   11
good. They had had a hard time of it in school the previous year; their hair
had been the subject of jokes and taunts from both black and white children.
Moreover, I suppose they wanted straightened hair like their mother.

When they both burst through the door that evening with their hair   12
newly straightened, beaming, looking for all the world like young ladies, I

was so taken aback in a kind of horror that I could only mutter in astonishment when they asked, "How do you like it?" It was as if my children were no longer mine, as if a culture that had convinced them they were ugly had taken them from me. I momentarily looked at my wife as if to say, "This is your doing. If only you would wear your hair as you did when we first met, this would not have happened."

My wife's response was, "They wanted their hair straightened and they thought they were old enough for it. Besides, there is no virtue in wearing an Afro. I don't believe in politically correct hair. Who was the last white woman you saw who didn't have something done to her hair? Most white women don't wear their hair the way God put it on their heads. It's been dyed, moussed, permed, teased, spiked, shagged, curled, and coiffed. What do you think, Shirley Temple was born with those curls? I've got news for you. Her mom had to work like heck to get those curls set just right. I want the same privilege to do to my hair what white women can do to theirs. It's my right to self-expression." [13]

Right after this happened, late in the summer, I began to find excuses not to watch the Shirley Temple movies. After about two or three weeks, Linnet, who was particularly upset by my lack of approval, asked me why I would not watch the movies with them anymore. I said that I thought the films were for children, not adults; that I was, in effect, intruding. Besides, I had work to do. Eventually, we got around to her new hairstyle. [14]

"I like my hair like this," she said. "This is the way I want to wear it." [15]

"Do you care if I like it?" I asked. [16]

She paused for a moment. "No," she said, bravely. "I want to wear my hair the way I like." [17]

"To get the approval of other people?" I asked unkindly. [18]

"Well," she said, "a little. I don't like to be called dumb. I don't like to be called ugly. I want to be like everybody else. I wear my hair some for me and some for other people. I don't think I'm Shirley Temple or a white girl, but I want to look like a girl, not like a boy. When you write, Daddy, don't you want approval from other people, too?" [19]

Before the discussion ended, she said, "I wish you would watch the movies with us. It's more fun when you watch, too." [20]

About two weeks later, the weekend before the start of school, I received in the mail a Shirley Temple video we hadn't seen, some early shorts that mimicked adult-genre movies, in which she and the other children went around dressed in diapers. I thought this might make a good truce, and so I brought it to my daughters' room and offered to watch it with them. Just before the video started I made a gesture that surprised even me: I stood above Linnet, bent over, and smelled her hair. It had just been washed and freshly straightened ("touched up," my wife said), and it smelled a bit like shampoo, a bit like pressing oil, and very slightly burned, much like, during my childhood, my mother's, my sisters', my aunts' hair smelled. It was a smell that I had, in some odd way, become fond of because, I suppose, it was so familiar, so distressingly familiar, like home. [21]

**Questions to Start You Thinking**

1. CONSIDERING MEANING: Why does Early's wife object to "politically correct hair" (paragraph 13)?

2. IDENTIFYING WRITING STRATEGIES: Where in the essay does Early use comparison and contrast? How does the essay's final comparison reveal the author's feelings of ambiguity?

3. ANALYZING THE WRITER'S CHOICES: Reread the selection, paying special attention to each place where Early integrates dialogue with his children into his narrative. Why do you think he decided to use conversation to show how his relationship with his children changed? Where else does he use conversation in the essay, and to what effect?

4. EXPANDING VOCABULARY: What is your definition of *politically correct* (paragraph 13)? Do you think that something like hair can be politically correct or incorrect?

5. MAKING CONNECTIONS: In what ways do both Early and Joy Harjo ("Three Generations of Native American Women's Birth Experiences," p. 471) feel powerless to shape their children's lives? Where in each essay does the narrator realize that part of his or her family's history is being repeated?

**Journal Prompts**

1. Describe some of the hairstyles you have had. What or who influenced those styles?

2. What do you think your current hairstyle "says" about you?

**Suggestions for Writing**

1. Write an essay narrating a time when you rebelled against your parents with a style of dress or hair. What was the nature of your rebellion? How did your parents react? Was your rebellion "successful"? What is your opinion now of that style?

2. Were you ever influenced by a movie or television show to change your appearance or behavior? Tell the story of this change, and then use examples from your own experience to defend or rebut the notion that movies and television shows have too much influence over viewers.

**Joy Harjo** *was born in 1951 in Tulsa, Oklahoma, and is of Creek (Muscogee) descent. She studied at the Institute of American Indian Arts, the University of New Mexico, and the Iowa Writers' Workshop, where she earned an M.A. in 1978. Harjo now teaches at the University of New Mexico. A poet, essayist, and screenwriter, she writes primarily about social and spiritual themes in Native American life, especially as they relate to Native American women. Her poems and essays often blend myth with current issues, as in her books* She Had Some Horses *(1983),* Secrets from the Center of the World *(1989),* In Mad Love and War *(1990), and* The Woman Who Fell from the Sky *(1994). In the following essay, which was first published in the July–August 1991 issue of* Ms., *Harjo compares her own experiences giving birth with those of her mother and daughter, using these stories to argue for a return to a birth experience shaped by traditional Native American values.*

# *Joy Harjo*    Three Generations of Native American Women's Birth Experience

It was still dark when I awakened in the stuffed back-room of my mother-in-law's small rented house with what felt like hard cramps. At seventeen years of age I had read everything I could from the Tahlequah Public Library about pregnancy and giving birth. But nothing prepared me for what was coming. I awakened my child's father and then ironed him a shirt before we walked the four blocks to the Indian hospital because we had no car and no money for a taxi. He had been working with another Cherokee artist silk-screening signs for specials at the supermarket and making $5 a day, and had to leave me alone at the hospital because he had to go to work. We didn't awaken his mother. She had to get up soon enough to fix breakfast for her daughter and granddaughter before leaving for her job at the nursing home. I knew my life was balanced at the edge of great, precarious change and I felt alone and cheated. Where was the circle of women to acknowledge and honor this birth?

It was still dark as we walked through the cold morning, under oaks that symbolized the stubbornness and endurance of the Cherokee people who had made Tahlequah their capital in the new lands. I looked for handholds in the misty gray sky, for a voice announcing this impending miracle. I wanted to change everything; I wanted to go back to a place before childhood, before our tribe's removal to Oklahoma. What kind of life was I bringing this child into? I was a poor, mixed-blood woman heavy with a child who would suffer the struggle of poverty, the legacy of loss. For the second time in my life I felt the sharp tug of my own birth cord, still connected to my mother. I believe it never pulls away, until death, and even then it becomes a streak in the sky symbolizing that most important warrior road. In my teens I had fought my mother's weaknesses with all my might, and here I was at seventeen, becoming as my mother, who was in Tulsa, cooking breakfasts and preparing for the lunch shift at a factory cafeteria as I walked to the hospital to give birth. I should be with her; instead, I was far from her house, in the house of a mother-in-law who later would try to use witchcraft to destroy me.

After my son's father left me I was prepped for birth. This meant my pubic area was shaved completely and then I endured the humiliation of an enema, all at the hands of strangers. I was left alone in a room painted government green. An overwhelming antiseptic smell emphasized the sterility of the hospital, a hospital built because of the U.S. government's treaty and responsibility to provide health care to Indian people.

I intellectually understood the stages of labor, the place of transition, of birth — but it was difficult to bear the actuality of it, and to bear it alone. Yet in some ways I wasn't alone, for history surrounded me. It is with the birth of children that history is given form and voice. Birth is one of the most sacred acts we take part in and witness in our lives. But sacredness seemed to be far from my lonely labor room in the Indian hospital. I heard a woman screaming in the next room with her pain, and I wanted to comfort her. The nurse used her as a bad example to the rest of us who were struggling to keep our suffering silent.

The doctor was a military man who had signed on this watch not for the love of healing or out of awe at the miracle of birth, but to fulfill a contract for medical school payments. I was another statistic to him; he touched me as if he were moving equipment from one place to another. During my last visit I was given the option of being sterilized. He explained to me that the moment of birth was the best time to do it. I was handed the form but chose not to sign it, and am amazed now that I didn't think too much of it at the time. Later I would learn that many Indian women who weren't fluent in English signed, thinking it was a form giving consent for the doctor to deliver their babies. Others were sterilized without even the formality of signing. My light skin had probably saved me from such a fate. It wouldn't be the first time in my life.

When my son was finally born I had been deadened with a needle in my spine. He was shown to me — the incredible miracle nothing prepared me for — then taken from me in the name of medical progress. I fell asleep with the weight of chemicals and awoke yearning for the child I had suffered for, had anticipated in the months proceeding from his unexpected genesis when I was still sixteen and a student at Indian school. I was not allowed to sit up or walk because of the possibility of paralysis (one of the drug's side effects), and when I finally got to hold him, the nurse stood guard as if I would hurt him. I felt enmeshed in a system in which the wisdom that had carried my people from generation to generation was ignored. In that place I felt ashamed I was an Indian woman. But I was also proud of what my body had accomplished despite the rape by the bureaucracy's machinery, and I got us out of there as soon as possible. My son would flourish on beans and fry bread, and on the dreams and stories we fed him.

My daughter was born four years later, while I was an art student at the University of New Mexico. Since my son's birth I had waitressed, cleaned hospital rooms, filled cars with gas (while wearing a miniskirt), worked as a nursing assistant, and led dance classes at a health spa. I knew I didn't want to cook and waitress all my life, as my mother had done. I had watched the varicose veins grow branches on her legs, and as they grew, her zest for dancing and sports dissolved into utter tiredness. She had been born with a caul over her face, the sign of a gifted visionary.

My earliest memories are of my mother writing songs on an ancient Underwood typewriter after she had washed and waxed the kitchen floor on her hands and knees. She too had wanted something different for her life. She had left an impoverished existence at age seventeen, bound for the big city of Tulsa. She was shamed in a time in which to be even part Indian was to be an outcast in the great U.S. system. Half her relatives were Cherokee full-bloods from near Jay, Oklahoma, who for the most part had nothing to do with white people. The other half were musically inclined "white trash" addicted to country-western music and Holy Roller fervor. She thought she could disappear in the city; no one would know her family, where she came from. She had dreams of singing and had once been offered a job singing on the radio but turned it down because she was shy. Later one of her songs would be stolen before she could copyright it and would make someone else rich. She would quit writing songs. She and my father would divorce and she would be forced to work for money to feed and clothe four children, all born within two years of each other.

As a child growing up in Oklahoma, I liked to be told the story of my 9 birth. I would beg for it while my mother cleaned and ironed. "You almost killed me," she would say. "We almost died." That I could kill my mother filled me with remorse and shame. And I imagined the push-pull of my life, which is a legacy I deal with even now when I am twice as old as my mother was at my birth. I loved to hear the story of my warrior fight for my breath. The way it was told, it had been my decision to live. When I got older, I realized we were both nearly casualties of the system, the same system flourishing in the Indian hospital where later my son Phil would be born.

My parents felt lucky to have insurance, to be able to have their children 10 in the hospital. My father came from a fairly prominent Muscogee Creek family. *His* mother was a full-blood who in the early 1920s got her degree in art. She was a painter. She gave birth to him in a private hospital in Oklahoma City; at least that's what I think he told me before he died at age fifty-three. It was something of which they were proud.

This experience was much different from my mother's own birth. She and 11 five of her six brothers were born at home, with no medical assistance. The only time a doctor was called was when someone was dying. When she was born her mother named her Wynema, a Cherokee name my mother says means beautiful woman, and Jewell, for a can of shortening stored in the room where she was born.

I wanted something different for my life, for my son, and for my daughter, who later was born in a university hospital in Albuquerque. It was a bright summer morning when she was ready to begin her journey. I still had no car, but I had enough money saved for a taxi for a ride to the hospital. She was born "naturally," without drugs. I could look out of the hospital window while I was in labor at the bluest sky in the world. I had support. Her father was present in the delivery room — though after her birth he disappeared on a drinking binge. I understood his despair, but did not agree with the painful means to describe it. A few days later Rainy Dawn was presented to the sun at her father's pueblo and given a name so that she will always be recognized as a part of the people, as a child of the sun.

That's not to say that my experience in the hospital reached perfection. 13 The clang of metal against metal in the delivery room had the effect of a tuning fork reverberating fear in my pelvis. After giving birth I held my daughter, but they took her from me for "processing." I refused to lie down to be wheeled to my room after giving birth; I wanted to walk out of there to find my daughter. We reached a compromise and I rode in a wheelchair. When we reached the room I stood up and walked to the nursery and demanded my daughter. I knew she needed me. That began my war with the nursery staff, who deemed me unknowledgeable because I was Indian and poor. Once again I felt the brushfire of shame, but I'd learned to put it out much more quickly, and I demanded early release so I could take care of my baby without the judgment of strangers.

I wanted something different for Rainy, and as she grew up I worked hard to prove that I could make "something" of my life. I obtained two degrees as a single mother. I wrote poetry, screenplays, became a professor, and tried to live a life that would be a positive influence for both of my children. My work in this life has to do with reclaiming the memory stolen from our peoples when we were dispossessed from our lands east of the Mississippi; it has to do with restoring us. I am proud of our history, a history so powerful that it both destroyed my father and guarded him. It's a history that claims my mother as she lives not far from the place her mother was born, names her as she cooks in the cafeteria of a small college in Oklahoma. 14

When my daughter told me she was pregnant, I wasn't surprised. I had known it before she did, or at least before she would admit it to me. I felt despair, as if nothing had changed or ever would. She had run away from Indian school with her boyfriend and they had been living in the streets of Gallup, a border town notorious for the suicides and deaths of Indian peoples. I brought her and her boyfriend with me because it was the only way I could bring her home. At age sixteen, she was fighting me just as I had so fiercely fought my mother. She was making the same mistakes. I felt as if everything I had accomplished had been in vain. Yet I felt strangely empowered, too, at this repetition of history, this continuance, by a new possibility of life and love, and I steadfastly stood by my daughter. 15

I had a university job, so I had insurance that covered my daughter. She saw an obstetrician in town who was reputed to be one of the best. She had the choice of a birthing room. She had the finest care. Despite this, I once again battled with a system in which physicians are taught the art of healing by dissecting cadavers. My daughter went into labor a month early. We both knew intuitively the baby was ready, but how to explain that to a system in which numbers and statistics provide the base of understanding? My daughter would have her labor interrupted; her blood pressure would rise because of the drug given to her to stop the labor. She would be given an unneeded amniocentesis and would have her labor induced — after having it artificially stopped! I was warned that if I took her out of the hospital so her labor could occur naturally my insurance would cover nothing. 16

My daughter's induced labor was unnatural and difficult, monitored by machines, not by touch. I was shocked. I felt as if I'd come full circle, as if I were watching my mother's labor and the struggle of my own birth. But I was there in the hospital room with her, as neither my mother had been for me, nor her mother for her. My daughter and I went through the labor and birth together. 17

And when Krista Rae was born she was born to her family. Her father was there for her, as were both her grandmothers and my friend who had flown in to be with us. Her paternal great-grandparents and aunts and uncles had also arrived from the Navajo Reservation to honor her. Something *had* changed. 18

Four days later, I took my granddaughter to the Saguaro forest before    19
dawn and gave her the name I had dreamed for her just before her birth. Her
name looks like clouds of mist settling around a sacred mountain as it begins
to speak. A female ancestor approaches on a horse. We are all together.

**Questions to Start You Thinking**

1. CONSIDERING MEANING: Summarize Harjo's complaints about her first birth experience. How does she feel that her traditional cultural values are damaged by the type of treatment she received at the hospital? How does she regain those values?

2. IDENTIFYING WRITING STRATEGIES: Harjo judges the dominant culture's medical system by contrasting it with the traditions of her Native American heritage. To you, what were the most striking contrasts? Does she convince you that her judgment is correct?

3. ANALYZING THE WRITER'S CHOICES: Consider the intended audience for this article, which originally appeared in the feminist magazine *Ms.* Do you think Harjo's comparison of her own childbirth experience to a "rape" (paragraph 6) is an effective way for her to make her point? Where else in the essay and to what effect does Harjo use language and imagery to evoke an emotional response from her readers?

4. EXPANDING VOCABULARY: Harjo tells us that her mother "had been born with a caul over her face, the sign of a gifted visionary" (paragraph 7). Define *caul* and *visionary*. Why do you think Harjo provides this detail about her mother?

5. MAKING CONNECTIONS: What traditions of their families' pasts do Harjo and E. B. White ("Once More to the Lake," p. 462) hope to hand down to their children?

**Journal Prompts**

1. Describe some of the traditions of your family. Which traditions are part of a larger culture and which are unique to your family?

2. Do you know what your name means? If so, do you think it fits you? If not, can you think of another name for yourself that might better match your personality or identity?

**Suggestions for Writing**

1. Write an essay describing the cultural traditions of your family. In what ways are you either continuing or breaking these traditions?

2. Harjo says that her "work in this life has to do with reclaiming the memory stolen from our peoples" (paragraph 14). Think of a person you know whose work in life you admire or respect. Drawing examples from reading, observation, or conversation, write an essay in which you describe and analyze this person's lifework. Who benefits from this person's work, and in what way?

**Amy Tan** *was born in 1952 in Oakland, California, a few years after her parents immigrated to the United States from China. After receiving a B.A. in English and linguistics and an M.A. in linguistics from San Jose State University, Tan worked as a specialist in language development for five years before becoming a freelance business writer in 1981. Tan wrote her first short story in 1985; it became the basis for* *her first novel,* The Joy Luck Club *(1990), which was a phenomenal best-seller and was made into a movie. Tan's second novel,* The Kitchen God's Wife *(1991), was equally popular. She has also written children's books,* The Moon Lady *(1992) and* The Chinese Siamese Cat *(1994). "Mother Tongue" first appeared in* Threepenny Review *in 1990; in this essay, Tan explores the effect her mother's "broken" English — the language Tan grew up with — has had on her life and writing.*

## *Amy Tan*   Mother Tongue

I am not a scholar of English or literature. I cannot give you much more   1
than personal opinions on the English language and its variations in this country or others.

I am a writer. And by that definition, I am someone who has always loved   2
language. I am fascinated by language in daily life. I spend a great deal of my time thinking about the power of language — the way it can evoke an emotion, a visual image, a complex idea, or a simple truth. Language is the tool of my trade. And I use them all — all the Englishes I grew up with.

Recently, I was made keenly aware of the different Englishes I do use. I   3
was giving a talk to a large group of people, the same talk I had already given to half a dozen other groups. The nature of the talk was about my writing, my life, and my book, *The Joy Luck Club.* The talk was going along well enough, until I remembered one major difference that made the whole talk sound wrong. My mother was in the room. And it was perhaps the first time she had heard me give a lengthy speech, using the kind of English I have never used with her. I was saying things like, "The intersection of memory upon imagination" and "There is an aspect of my fiction that relates to thus-and-thus" — a speech filled with carefully wrought grammatical phrases, burdened, it suddenly seemed to me, with nominalized forms, past perfect tenses, conditional phrases, all the forms of Standard English that I had learned in school and through books, the forms of English I did not use at home with my mother.

Just last week, I was walking down the street with my mother, and I again   4
found myself conscious of the English I was using, and the English I do use with her. We were talking about the price of new and used furniture and I heard myself saying this: "Not waste money that way." My husband was with us as well, and he didn't notice any switch in my English. And then I realized why. It's because over the twenty years we've been together I've often used that same kind of English with him, and sometimes he even uses it with me. It has become our language of intimacy, a different sort of English that relates to family talk, the language I grew up with.

So you'll have some idea of what this family talk I heard sounds like, I'll   5
quote what my mother said during a recent conversation which I videotaped and then transcribed. During this conversation, my mother was talking about a political gangster in Shanghai who had the same last name as her family's, Du, and how the gangster in his early years wanted to be adopted by her family, which was rich by comparison. Later, the gangster became more power-

ful, far richer than my mother's family, and one day showed up at my mother's wedding to pay his respects. Here's what she said in part:

"Du Yusong having business like fruit stand. Like off the street kind. He is like Du Zong — but not Tsung-ming Island people. The local people call putong, the river east side, he belong to that side local people. That man want to ask Du Zong father take him in like become own family. Du Zong father wasn't look down on him, but didn't take seriously, until that man big like become a mafia. Now important person, very hard to inviting him. Chinese way, came only to show respect, don't stay for dinner. Respect for making big celebration, he shows up. Mean gives lots of respect. Chinese custom. Chinese social life that way. If too important won't have to stay too long. He come to my wedding. I didn't see, I heard it. I gone to boy's side, they have YMCA dinner. Chinese age I was nineteen."

You should know that my mother's expressive command of English belies how much she actually understands. She reads the *Forbes* report, listens to *Wall Street Week*, converses daily with her stockbroker, reads all of Shirley MacLaine's books with ease — all kinds of things I can't begin to understand. Yet some of my friends tell me they understand fifty percent of what my mother says. Some say they understand eighty to ninety percent. Some say they understand none of it, as if she were speaking pure Chinese. But to me, my mother's English is perfectly clear, perfectly natural. It's my mother tongue. Her language, as I hear it, is vivid, direct, full of observation and imagery. That was the language that helped shape the way I saw things, expressed things, made sense of the world.

Lately, I've been giving more thought to the kind of English my mother speaks. Like others, I have described it to people as "broken" or "fractured" English. But I wince when I say that. It has always bothered me that I can think of no way to describe it other than "broken," as if it were damaged and needed to be fixed, as if it lacked a certain wholeness and soundness. I've heard other terms used, "limited English," for example. But they seem just as bad, as if everything is limited, including people's perceptions of the limited English speaker.

I know this for a fact, because when I was growing up, my mother's "limited" English limited *my* perception of her. I was ashamed of her English. I believed that her English reflected the quality of what she had to say. That is, because she expressed them imperfectly her thoughts were imperfect. And I had plenty of empirical evidence to support me: the fact that people in department stores, at banks, and at restaurants did not take her seriously, did not give her good service, pretended not to understand her, or even acted as if they did not hear her.

My mother has long realized the limitations of her English as well. When I was fifteen, she used to have me call people on the phone to pretend I was she. In this guise, I was forced to ask for information or even to complain and yell at people who had been rude to her. One time it was a call to her stockbroker in New York. She had cashed out her small portfolio and it just so happened we were going to go to New York the next week, our very first trip outside California. I had to get on the phone and say in an adolescent voice that was not very convincing, "This is Mrs. Tan."

And my mother was standing in the back whispering loudly, "Why he don't send me check, already two weeks late. So mad he lie to me, losing me money." **11**

And then I said in perfect English, "Yes, I'm getting rather concerned. You had agreed to send the check two weeks ago, but it hasn't arrived." **12**

Then she began to talk more loudly. "What he want, I come to New York tell him front of his boss, you cheating me?" And I was trying to calm her down, make her be quiet, while telling the stockbroker, "I can't tolerate any more excuses. If I don't receive the check immediately, I am going to have to speak to your manager when I'm in New York next week." And sure enough, the following week there we were in front of this astonished stockbroker, and I was sitting there red-faced and quiet, and my mother, the real Mrs. Tan, was shouting at his boss in her impeccable broken English. **13**

We used a similar routine just five days ago, for a situation that was far less humorous. My mother had gone to the hospital for an appointment, to find out about a benign brain tumor a CAT scan had revealed a month ago. She said she had spoken very good English, her best English, no mistakes. Still, she said, the hospital did not apologize when they said they had lost the CAT scan and she had come for nothing. She said they did not seem to have any sympathy when she told them she was anxious to know the exact diagnosis, since her husband and son had both died of brain tumors. She said they would not give her any more information until the next time and she would have to make another appointment for that. So she said she would not leave until the doctor called her daughter. She wouldn't budge. And when the doctor finally called her daughter, me, who spoke in perfect English — lo and behold — we had assurances the CAT scan would be found, promises that a conference call on Monday would be held, and apologies for any suffering my mother had gone through for a most regrettable mistake. **14**

I think my mother's English almost had an effect on limiting my possibilities in life as well. Sociologists and linguists probably will tell you that a person's developing language skills are more influenced by peers. But I think that the language spoken in the family, especially in immigrant families which are more insular, plays a large role in shaping the language of the child. And I believe that it affected my results on achievement tests, IQ tests, and the SAT. While my English skills were never judged as poor, compared to math, English could not be considered my strong suit. In grade school I did moderately well, getting perhaps B's, sometimes B-pluses, in English and scoring perhaps in the sixtieth or seventieth percentile on achievement tests. But those scores were not good enough to override the opinion that my true abilities lay in math and science, because in those areas I achieved A's and scored in the ninetieth percentile or higher. **15**

This was understandable. Math is precise; there is only one correct answer. Whereas, for me at least, the answers on English tests were always a judgment call, a matter of opinion and personal experience. Those tests were constructed around items like fill-in-the-blank sentence completion, such as, **16**

"Even though Tom was _____ , Mary thought he was _____ ." And the correct answer always seemed to be the most bland combinations of thoughts, for example, "Even though Tom was shy, Mary thought he was charming," with the grammatical structure "even though" limiting the correct answer to some sort of semantic opposites, so you wouldn't get answers like, "Even though Tom was foolish, Mary thought he was ridiculous." Well, according to my mother, there were very few limitations as to what Tom could have been and what Mary might have thought of him. So I never did well on tests like that.

The same was true with word analogies, pairs of words in which you were supposed to find some sort of logical, semantic relationship — for example, "*Sunset* is to *nightfall* as _____ is to _____ ." And here you would be presented with a list of four possible pairs, one of which showed the same kind of relationship: *red* is to *stoplight, bus* is to *arrival, chills* is to *fever, yawn* is to *boring*. Well, I could never think that way. I knew what the tests were asking, but I could not block out of my mind the images already created by the first pair, "*sunset* is to *nightfall*" — and I would see a burst of colors against a darkening sky, the moon rising, the lowering of a curtain of stars. And all the other pairs of words — red, bus, stoplight, boring — just threw up a mass of confusing images, making it impossible for me to sort out something as logical as saying: "A sunset precedes nightfall" is the same as "a chill precedes a fever." The only way I would have gotten that answer right would have been to imagine an associative situation, for example, my being disobedient and staying out past sunset, catching a chill at night, which turns into feverish pneumonia as punishment, which indeed did happen to me.

I have been thinking about all this lately, about my mother's English, about achievement tests. Because lately I've been asked, as a writer, why there are not more Asian Americans enrolled in creative writing programs? Why do so many Chinese students go into engineering? Well, these are broad sociological questions I can't begin to answer. But I have noticed in surveys — in fact, just last week — that Asian students, as a whole, always do significantly better on math achievement tests than in English. And this makes me think that there are other Asian-American students whose English spoken in the home might also be described as "broken" or "limited." And perhaps they also have teachers who are steering them away from writing and into math and science, which is what happened to me.

Fortunately, I happen to be rebellious in nature and enjoy the challenge of disproving assumptions made about me. I became an English major my first year in college, after being enrolled as pre-med. I started writing nonfiction as a freelancer the week after I was told by my former boss that writing was my worst skill and I should hone my talents toward account management.

But it wasn't until 1985 that I finally began to write fiction. And at first I wrote using what I thought to be wittily crafted sentences, sentences that would finally prove I had mastery over the English language. Here's an example from the first draft of a story that later made its way into *The Joy Luck Club*, but without this line: "That was my mental quandary in its nascent state." A terrible line, which I can barely pronounce.

Fortunately, for reasons I won't get into today, I later decided I should en- 21
vision a reader for the stories I would write. And the reader I decided upon
was my mother, because these were stories about mothers. So with this reader
in mind — and in fact she did read my early drafts — I began to write stories
using all the Englishes I grew up with: the English I spoke to my mother,
which for lack of a better term might be described as "simple"; the English she
used with me, which for lack of a better term might be described as "broken";
my translation of her Chinese, which could certainly be described as "watered
down"; and what I imagined to be her translation of her Chinese if she could
speak in perfect English, her internal language, and for that I sought to preserve the essence, but neither an English nor a Chinese structure. I wanted to
capture what language ability tests can never reveal: her intent, her passion,
her imagery, the rhythms of her speech and the nature of her thoughts.

Apart from what any critic had to say about my writing, I knew I had succeeded where it counted when my mother finished reading my book and gave
me her verdict: "So easy to read."

**Questions to Start You Thinking**

1. CONSIDERING MEANING:  What are the Englishes that Tan grew up with? What other Englishes has she used in her life? What does each English have that gives it an advantage over the other Englishes in certain situations?

2. IDENTIFYING WRITING STRATEGIES:  What examples does Tan use to analyze the various Englishes she uses? How has Tan been able to successfully synthesize her Englishes into her present style of writing fiction?

3. ANALYZING THE WRITER'S CHOICES:  In this essay, Tan reveals that when she writes fiction she envisions her mother as the reader. Why her mother? What does she hope to convey to all of her readers by writing in a voice her mother finds "so easy to read" (paragraph 22)? In what way might that voice differ from the one she uses to address her audience when writing nonfiction, such as this piece?

4. EXPANDING VOCABULARY:  In paragraph 9, Tan writes that she had "plenty of empirical evidence" that her mother's "broken" English meant that her mother's thoughts were broken as well. Define *empirical*. What does Tan's use of this word tell us about her present attitude toward the way she judged her mother when she was growing up?

5. MAKING CONNECTIONS:  What cultural barriers faced by Tan and her mother are shared by Joy Harjo ("Three Generations of Native American Women's Birth Experiences," p. 471) and her mother? How is language a factor in both cases?

**Journal Prompts**

1. Describe one of the Englishes you use to communicate. When do you use it, and when do you avoid using it?

2. In what ways are you a "translator," if not of language, then of current events and fashions, for your parents or other members of your family?

**Suggestions for Writing**

1. In a personal essay explain an important event in your family's history, using your family's various Englishes or other languages.

2. Take note of and, if possible, transcribe one conversation you have had with      22
a parent or other family member, one with a teacher, and one with a close
friend. Write an essay comparing and contrasting the "languages" of the three
conversations. How do the languages differ? How do you account for these
differences? What do you think would happen if someone used "teacher language" to talk to a friend or used "friend language" in a class discussion or
paper?

**Anna Quindlen** *was born in 1953 in Philadelphia. After graduating from Barnard
College in 1974, she worked briefly as a reporter for the* New York Post *before moving to the* New York Times, *where she wrote the "About New York" column. From
1986 to 1989 Quindlen wrote the syndicated column "Life in the 30s," which drew
on her experiences with her family and neighborhood; until 1994, when she left the*
Times, *she wrote the syndicated column "Public and Private," which explored more
political issues. Quindlen won the Pulitzer Prize for commentary in 1992 for her articles on abortion, the Clarence Thomas hearings, and the Persian Gulf War. In addition to her two collections of columns,* Living Out Loud *(1986) and* Thinking
Out Loud *(1993), Quindlen has also written two best-selling novels,* Object
Lessons *(1991) and* One True Thing *(1994). In "Evan's Two Moms," from* Living Out Loud, *Quindlen emphatically argues that gay marriage should be legalized.*

## *Anna Quindlen*    Evan's Two Moms

Evan has two moms. This is no big thing. Evan has always had two moms      1
— in his school file, on his emergency forms, with his friends. "Ooooh, Evan,
you're lucky," they sometimes say. "You have two moms." It sounds like a sitcom, but until last week it was emotional truth without legal bulwark. That
was when a judge in New York approved the adoption of a six-year-old boy
by his biological mother's lesbian partner. Evan. Evan's mom. Evan's other
mom. A kid, a psychologist, a pediatrician. A family.

The matter of Evan's two moms is one in a series of events over the last      2
year that lead to certain conclusions. A Minnesota appeals court granted
guardianship of a woman left a quadriplegic in a car accident to her lesbian
lover, the culmination of a seven-year battle in which the injured woman's
parents did everything possible to negate the partnership between the two. A
lawyer in Georgia had her job offer withdrawn after the state attorney general
found out that she and her lesbian lover were planning a marriage ceremony;
she's brought suit. The computer company Lotus announced that the gay
partners of employees would be eligible for the same benefits as spouses.

Add to these public events the private struggles, the couples who go from      3
lawyer to lawyer to approximate legal protections their straight counterparts

take for granted, the AIDS survivors who find themselves shut out of their partners' dying days by biological family members and shut out of their apartments by leases with a single name on the dotted line, and one solution is obvious.

Gay marriage is a radical notion for straight people and a conservative notion for gay ones. After years of being sledgehammered by society, some gay men and lesbian women are deeply suspicious of participating in an institution that seems to have "straight world" written all over it. **4**

But the rads of twenty years ago, straight and gay alike, have other things on their minds today. Family is one, and the linchpin of family has commonly been a loving commitment between two adults. When same-sex couples set out to make that commitment, they discover that they are at a disadvantage: No joint tax returns. No health insurance coverage for an uninsured partner. No survivor's benefits from Social Security. None of the automatic rights, privileges, and responsibilities society attaches to a marriage contract. In Madison, Wisconsin, a couple who applied at the Y with their kids for a family membership were turned down because both were women. It's one of those small things that can make you feel small. **5**

Some took marriage statutes that refer to "two persons" at their word and applied for a license. The results were court decisions that quoted the Bible and embraced circular argument: marriage is by definition the union of a man and a woman because that is how we've defined it. **6**

No religion should be forced to marry anyone in violation of its tenets, although ironically it is now only in religious ceremonies that gay people can marry, performed by clergy who find the blessing of two who love each other no sin. But there is no secular reason that we should take a patchwork approach of corporate, governmental, and legal steps to guarantee what can be done simply, economically, conclusively, and inclusively with the words "I do." **7**

"Fran and I chose to get married for the same reasons that any two people do," said the lawyer who was fired in Georgia. "We fell in love; we wanted to spend our lives together." Pretty simple. **8**

Consider the case of *Loving v. Virginia*, aptly named. At the time, sixteen states had laws that barred interracial marriage, relying on natural law, that amorphous grab bag for justifying prejudice. Sounding a little like God throwing Adam and Eve out of paradise, the trial judge suspended the one-year sentence of Richard Loving, who was white, and his wife, Mildred, who was black, provided they got out of the State of Virginia. **9**

In 1967 the Supreme Court found such laws to be unconstitutional. Only twenty-five years ago and it was a crime for a black woman to marry a white man. Perhaps twenty-five years from now we will find it just as incredible that two people of the same sex were not entitled to legally commit themselves to each other. Love and commitment are rare enough; it seems absurd to thwart them in any guise. **10**

**Questions to Start You Thinking**

1. CONSIDERING MEANING:  What are the main points Quindlen makes in arguing that gay marriage should be legalized?

2. IDENTIFYING WRITING STRATEGIES:  Quindlen ends her essay with a comparison of gay marriage and interracial marriage (paragraphs 9 and 10). How does she use this comparison to support her argument? Do you think it is a valid comparison?

3. ANALYZING THE WRITER'S CHOICES:  Quindlen's argument is short and blunt. Do you think she oversimplifies her case at any point? Would her essay be more effective if she had given more attention to the opposition's beliefs? Why or why not?

4. EXPANDING VOCABULARY:  Define *marriage* as Quindlen would define it. How does her definition of the term differ from the one in the dictionary?

5. MAKING CONNECTIONS:  What privileges of the majority culture are gay families, Native American families (Harjo, "Three Generations of Native American Women's Birth Experiences," p. 471), and Asian-American families (Tan, "Mother Tongue," p. 476) sometimes denied?

**Journal Prompts**

1. In your opinion, is the dictionary definition of *marriage* no longer adequate? If so, how do you think it should be revised? If you think the dictionary definition is fine, defend it against attack.

2. Imagine that you have the power to design and create the perfect parents. What would they be like? What criteria would they have to meet to live up to your vision of ideal parents?

**Suggestions for Writing**

1. Describe the most unconventional family you know. How is this family different from other families? How is it the same?

2. In your opinion, would two people of the same gender help or hurt a child's development? Write an essay comparing and contrasting the possible benefits and disadvantages of this type of family. Use specific examples — hypothetical or gathered from your own observation or reading — to illustrate your argument.

**Stephanie Coontz** *was born in 1944 in Seattle. She attended the University of California at Berkeley and the University of Washington at Seattle and has taught history and women's studies at Evergreen State College in Olympia, Washington, since 1975. Coontz has explored gender roles and the American family in her three books,* Women's Work, Men's Property *(with Peta Henderson, 1986);* The Social Origins of Private Life: A History of American Families 1600–1990 *(1988); and* The Way We Never Were: American Families and the Nostalgia Trap *(1992), from which the following excerpt is taken. In this selection Coontz, herself a single mother, builds her case by citing studies and statistics that undermine our usual assumptions about the state of the American family.*

*Stephanie Coontz*   The Way We Wish We Were: The Complexities of Assessing Family Trends

It is hard . . . to make global judgments about how families have changed   1
and whether they are getting better or worse. Some generalizations about the
past are pure myth. Whatever the merit of recurring complaints about the
"rootlessness" of modern life, for instance, families are *not* more mobile and
transient than they used to be. In most nineteenth-century cities, both large
and small, more than 50 percent — and often up to 75 percent — of the residents in any given year were no longer there ten years later. People born in
the twentieth century are much more likely to live near their birthplace than
were people born in the nineteenth century.[1]

This is not to say, of course, that mobility did not have different effects   2
then than it does now. In the nineteenth century, claims historian Thomas
Bender, people moved from community to community, taking advantage . . .
of nonfamilial networks and institutions that integrated them into new work
and social relations. In the late twentieth century, people move from job to
job, following a career path that shuffles them from one single-family home
to another and does not link them to neighborly networks beyond the family. But this change is in our community ties, not in our family ones.[2]

A related myth is that modern Americans have lost touch with extended-   3
kinship networks or have let parent-child bonds lapse. In fact, more Americans than ever before have grandparents alive, and there is good evidence that
ties between grandparents and grandchildren have become stronger over the
past fifty years. In the late 1970s, researchers returned to the "Middletown"
studied by sociologists Robert and Helen Lynd in the 1920s and found that
most people there maintained closer extended-family networks than in earlier times. There had been some decline in the family's control over the daily
lives of youth, especially females, but "the expressive/emotional function of
the family" was "more important for Middletown students of 1977 than it
was in 1924." More recent research shows that visits with relatives did *not* decline between the 1950s and the late 1980s.[3]

Today 54 percent of adults see a parent, and 68 percent talk on the phone   4
with a parent, at least once a week. Fully 90 percent of Americans describe
their relationship with their mother as close, and 78 percent say their relationship with their grandparents is close. And for all the family disruption of
divorce, most modern children live with at least *one* parent. As late as 1940,
10 percent of American children did not live with either parent, compared to
only one in twenty-five today.[4]

What about the supposed eclipse of marriage? Neither the rising age of   5
those who marry nor the frequency of divorce necessarily means that marriage is becoming a less prominent institution than it was in earlier days.
Ninety percent of men and women eventually marry, more than 70 percent
of divorced men and women remarry, and fewer people remain single for
their entire lives today than at the turn of the century. One author even sug-

gests that the availability of divorce in the second half of the twentieth century has allowed some women to try marriage who would formerly have remained single all their lives. Others argue that the rate of hidden marital separation in the late nineteenth century was not much less than the rate of visible separation today.[5]

Studies of marital satisfaction reveal that more couples reported their 6 marriages to be happy in the late 1970s than did so in 1957, while couples in their second marriages believe them to be much happier than their first ones. Some commentators conclude that marriage is becoming less permanent but more satisfying. Others wonder, however, whether there is a vicious circle in our country, where no one even tries to sustain a relationship. Between the late 1970s and late 1980s, moreover, reported marital happiness did decline slightly in the United States. Some authors see this as reflecting our decreasing appreciation of marriage, although others suggest that it reflects unrealistically high expectations of love in a culture that denies people safe, culturally approved ways of getting used to marriage or cultivating other relationships to meet some of the needs that we currently load onto the couple alone.[6]

Part of the problem in making simple generalizations about what is happening to marriage is that there has been a polarization of experiences. Marriages are much more likely to be ended by divorce today, but marriages that do last are described by their participants as happier than those in the past and are far more likely to confer such happiness over many years. It is important to remember that the 50 percent divorce rate estimates are calculated in terms of a forty-year period and that many marriages in the past were terminated well before that date by the death of one partner. Historian Lawrence Stone suggests that divorce has become "a functional substitute for death" in the modern world. At the end of the 1970s, the rise in divorce rates seemed to overtake the fall in death rates, but the slight decline in divorce rates since then means that "a couple marrying today is more likely to celebrate a fortieth wedding anniversary than were couples around the turn of the century."[7]

A similar polarization allows some observers to argue that fathers are deserting their children, while others celebrate the new commitment of fathers to childbearing. Both viewpoints are right. Sociologist Frank Furstenberg comments on the emergence of a "good dad–bad dad complex": Many fathers spend more time with their children than ever before and feel more free to be affectionate with them; others, however, feel more free simply to walk out on their families. According to 1981 statistics, 42 percent of the children whose father had left the marriage had not seen him in the past year. Yet studies show steadily increasing involvement of fathers with their children as long as they are in the home.[8]

These kinds of ambiguities should make us leery of hard-and-fast pronouncements about what's happening to the American family. In many cases, we simply don't know precisely what our figures actually mean. For example, the proportion of youngsters receiving psychological assistance rose by 80 percent between 1981 and 1988. Does that mean they are getting more sick or receiving more help, or is it some complex combination of the two? Child abuse reports increased by 225 percent between 1976 and 1987. Does this represent an actual increase in the rates of abuse or a heightened consciousness about the problem? During the same period, parents' self-reports about very severe violence toward their children declined 47 percent. Does this represent a real improvement in their behavior or a decreasing willingness to admit to such acts?[9]

Assessing the direction of family change is further complicated because    10
many contemporary trends represent a reversal of developments that were themselves rather recent. The expectation that the family should be the main source of personal fulfillment, for example, was not traditional in the eighteenth and nineteenth centuries. . . . Prior to the 1900s, the family festivities that now fill us with such nostalgia for "the good old days" (and cause such heartbreak when they go poorly) were "relatively undeveloped." Civic festivals and Fourth of July parades were more important occasions for celebration and strong emotion than family holidays, such as Thanksgiving. Christmas "seems to have been more a time for attending parties and dances than for celebrating family solidarity." Only in the twentieth century did the family come to be the center of festive attention and emotional intensity.[10]

Today, such emotional investment in the family may be waning again.    11
This could be interpreted as a reestablishment of balance between family life and other social ties; on the other hand, such a trend may have different results today than in earlier times, because in many cases the extrafamilial institutions and customs that used to socialize individuals and provide them with a range of emotional alternatives to family life no longer exist.

In other cases, close analysis of statistics showing a deterioration in family    12
ily well-being supposedly caused by abandonment of tradition suggests a more complicated train of events. Children's health, for example, improved dramatically in the 1960s and 1970s, a period of extensive family transformation. It ceased to improve, and even slid backward, in the 1980s, when innovative social programs designed to relieve families of some "traditional" responsibilities were repealed. While infant mortality rates fell by 4.7 percent a year during the 1970s, the rate of decline decreased in the 1980s, and in both 1988 and 1989, infant mortality rates did not show a statistically significant decline. Similarly, the proportion of low-birth-weight babies fell during the 1970s but stayed steady during the 1980s and had even increased slightly as of 1988. Child-poverty is lower today than it was in the "traditional" 1950s but much higher than it was in the nontraditional 1960s.[11]

*Notes*

1. Rudy Ray Seward, *The American Family: A Demographic History* (Beverly Hills: Sage, 1978); Kenneth Winkle, *The Politics of Community: Migration and Politics in Antebellum Ohio* (New York: Cambridge University Press, 1988); Michael Weber, *Social Change in an Industrial Town: Patterns of Progress in Warren, Pennsylvania, from the Civil War to World War I* (University Park: Pennsylvania State University Press, 1976), pp. 138–48; Stephen Thernstrom, *Poverty and Progress* (Cambridge: Harvard University Press, 1964).

2. Thomas Bender, *Community and Social Change in America* (New Brunswick: Rutgers University Press, 1978).

3. Edward Kain, *The Myth of Family Decline: Understanding Families in a World of Rapid Social Change* (Lexington, Mass.: D. C. Heath, 1990), pp. 10, 37; Theodore Caplow, "The Sociological Myth of Family Decline," *The Tocqueville Review* 3 (1981): 366; Howard Bahr, "Changes in Family Life in Middletown, 1924–77," *Public Opinion Quarterly* 44 (1980): 51.

4. *American Demographics*, February 1990; Dennis Orthner, "The Family in Transition," in *Rebuilding the Nest: A New Commitment to the American Family*, eds. David Blankenhorn, Steven Bayme, and Jean Bethke Elshtain (Milwaukee: Family Service America, 1990), pp. 95–97; Sar Levitan and Richard Belous, *What's Happening to the American Family?* (Baltimore: Johns Hopkins University Press, 1981), p. 63.

5. Daniel Kallgren, "Women out of Marriage: Work and Residence Patterns of Never Married American Women, 1900–1980" (Paper presented at Social Science History Association Conference, Minneapolis, Minn., October 1990), p. 8; Richard Sennett, *Families against the City: Middle Class Homes in Industrial Chicago, 1872–1890* (Cambridge: Harvard University Press, 1984), pp. 114–15.

6. Mary Jo Bane, *Here to Stay: American Families in the Twentieth Century* (New York: Basic Books, 1976); Stephen Nock, *Sociology of the Family* (Englewood Cliffs, N.J.: Prentice Hall, 1987); Kain, *Myth of Family Decline*, pp. 71, 74–75; Joseph Veroff, Elizabeth Douvan, and Richard Kulka, *The Inner American: A Self-Portrait from 1957 to 1976* (New York: Basic Books, 1981); Norval Glenn, "The Recent Trend in Marital Success in the United States," *Journal of Marriage and the Family* 53 (1991); Tracy Cabot, *Marrying Later, Marrying Smarter* (New York: McGraw-Hill, 1990); Judith Brown, *Sanctions and Sanctuary: Cultural Perspective on the Beating of Wives* (Boulder, Colo.: Westview Press, 1991); Maxine Baca Zinn and Stanley Eitzen, *Diversity in American Families* (New York: Harper & Row, 1987).

7. Dorrian Apple Sweetser, "Broken Homes: Stable Risk, Changing Reason, Changing Forms," *Journal of Marriage and the Family* (August 1985); Lawrence Stone, "The Road to Polygamy," *New York Review of Books*, 2 March 1989, p. 13; Arlene Skolnick, *Embattled Paradise: The American Family in an Age of Uncertainty* (New York: Basic Books, 1991), p. 156.

8. Frank Furstenberg, Jr., "Good Dads–Bad Dads: Two Faces of Fatherhood," in *The Changing American Family and Public Policy*, ed. Andrew Cherlin (Washington, D.C.: Urban Institute Press, 1988); Joseph Pleck, "The Contemporary Man," in *Handbook of Counseling and Psychotherapy*, ed. Murray Scher et al. (Beverly Hills: Sage, 1987).

9. National Commission on Children, *Beyond Rhetoric: A New Agenda for Children and Families* (Washington, D.C.: GPO, 1991), p. 34; Richard Gelles and Jon Conte, "Domestic Violence and Sexual Abuse of Children," in *Contemporary Familes: Looking Forward, Looking Back*, ed. Alan Booth (Minneapolis: National Council on Family Relations, 1991), p. 328.

10. Arlene Skolnick, "The American Family: The Paradox of Perfection," *The Wilson Quarterly* (Summer 1980); Barbara Laslett, "Family Membership: Past and Present," *Social Problems* 25 (1978); Theodore Caplow et al., *Middletown Families: Fifty Years of Change and Continuity* (Minneapolis: University of Minnesota Press, 1982), p. 225.

11. *The State of America's Children, 1991* (Washington, D.C.: Children's Defense Fund, 1991), pp. 55–63; *Seattle Post-Intelligencer*, 19 April 1991: National

Commissions on Children, *Beyond Rhetoric*, p. 32: *Washington Post National Weekly Edition*, 13–19 May 1991; James Wetzel, *American Youth: A Statistical Snapshot* (Washington, D.C.: William T. Grant Foundation, August 1989), pp. 12–14.

**Questions to Start You Thinking**

1. CONSIDERING MEANING: Identify two or three generalizations about families that Coontz attempts to discredit as myths. What are some of her objections to these generalizations?

2. IDENTIFYING WRITING STRATEGIES: Identify some of the examples Coontz uses to support her assertion that "some generalizations about the past are pure myth" (paragraph 1). Do you find her evidence convincing?

3. ANALYZING THE WRITER'S CHOICES: In what way does Coontz use statistics to challenge the validity of popular assumptions about family life in America's past? Do you think these statistics effectively support her interpretation of family trends today? Could any of her statistics be interpreted differently from how she has interpreted them? Explain.

4. EXPANDING VOCABULARY: Define *polarization* (paragraph 7). In Coontz's opinion, how does the "polarization of experiences" complicate the issue of interpreting family trends?

5. MAKING CONNECTIONS: How might the situations presented by Anna Quindlen ("Evan's Two Moms," p. 481) factor into the trends Coontz discusses?

**Journal Prompts**

1. Which of Coontz's points most surprised you? Why?

2. What "family festivities" (paragraph 10) does your family regularly celebrate? How do they help build "family solidarity"?

**Suggestions for Writing**

1. What activities, values, or institutions are changing the traditional family? Would you label your own family as traditional or nontraditional? What changes have happened in your own family's history? Write an essay based on your own observation and experience in which you identify the changes to the traditional family.

2. Do you think the family as an institution is deteriorating or not? Write an argument for either side. Support your argument with statistics from Coontz's piece and other sources, and illustrate your essay with examples drawn from your own observation.

# Chapter 23

# Men and Women

**Journal Prompt** | Describe the behavior that you feel is expected of you as a man or as a woman. To what extent are you comfortable with these expectations?

**Judy Brady** *was born in 1937 in San Francisco, where she now makes her home. A graduate of the University of Iowa, Brady has contributed to various publications and has traveled to Cuba to study class relationships and education. More recently, she edited the book* 1 in 3: Women with Cancer Confront an Epidemic *(1991), drawing on her own struggle with the disease. In the following piece, which has been reprinted frequently since its appearance in* Ms. *magazine in December 1971, Brady considers the role of the American housewife. While she has said that she is "not a 'writer,'" this essay shows Brady to be a satirist adept at taking a stand and provoking attention.*

## *Judy Brady*    I Want a Wife

I belong to that classification of people known as wives. I am A Wife. And, not altogether incidentally, I am a mother.

Not too long ago a male friend of mine appeared on the scene fresh from a recent divorce. He had one child, who is, of course, with his ex-wife. He is looking for another wife. As I thought about him while I was ironing one evening, it suddenly occurred to me that I, too, would like to have a wife. Why do I want a wife?

I would like to go back to school so that I can become economically independent, support myself, and, if need be, support those dependent upon me. I want a wife who will work and send me to school. And while I am going to school I want a wife to take care of my children. I want a wife to keep track of the children's doctor and dentist appointments. And to keep track of mine, too. I want a wife to make sure my children eat properly and are kept clean. I want a wife who will wash the children's clothes and keep them mended. I want a wife who is a good nurturant attendant to my children, who arranges for their schooling, makes sure that they have an adequate social life with their peers, takes them to the park, the zoo, etc. I want a wife who takes care of the children when they are sick, a wife who arranges to be around when the children need special care, because, of course, I cannot miss classes at school. My wife must arrange to lose time at work and not lose the job. It may mean a small cut in my wife's income from time to time, but I guess I can tolerate that. Needless to say, my wife will arrange and pay for the care of the children while my wife is working.

I want a wife who will take care of *my* physical needs. I want a wife who will keep my house clean. A wife who will pick up after my children, a wife who will pick up after me. I want a wife who will keep my clothes clean, ironed, mended, replaced when need be, and who will see to it that my personal things are kept in their proper place so that I can find what I need the minute I need it. I want a wife who cooks the meals, a wife who is a *good* cook. I want a wife who will plan the menus, do the necessary grocery shopping, prepare the meals, serve them pleasantly, and then do the cleaning up while I do my studying. I want a wife who will care for me when I am sick and sympathize with my pain and loss of time from school. I want a wife to go along when our family takes a vacation so that someone can continue to care for me and my children when I need a rest and change of scene.

I want a wife who will not bother me with rambling complaints about     5
a wife's duties. But I want a wife who will listen to me when I feel the need to explain a rather difficult point I have come across in my course of studies.

I want a wife who will take care of the details of my social life. When my     6
wife and I are invited out by my friends, I want a wife who will take care of the babysitting arrangements. When I meet people at school that I like and want to entertain, I want a wife who will have the house clean, will prepare a special meal, serve it to me and my friends, and not interrupt when I talk about things that interest me and my friends. I want a wife who will have arranged that the children are fed and ready for bed before my guests arrive so that the children do not bother us. I want a wife who takes care of the needs of my guests so that they feel comfortable, who makes sure that they have an ashtray, that they are passed the hors d'oeuvres, that they are offered a second helping of the food, that their wine glasses are replenished when necessary, that their coffee is served to them as they like it. And I want a wife who knows that sometimes I need a night out by myself.

I want a wife who is sensitive to my sexual needs, a wife who makes love     7
passionately and eagerly when I feel like it, a wife who makes sure that I am satisfied. And, of course, I want a wife who will not demand sexual attention when I am not in the mood for it. I want a wife who assumes the complete responsibility for birth control, because I do not want more children. I want a wife who will remain sexually faithful to me so that I do not have to clutter up my intellectual life with jealousies. And I want a wife who understands that *my* sexual needs may entail more than strict adherence to monogamy. I must, after all, be able to relate to people as fully as possible.

If, by chance, I find another person more suitable as a wife than the wife     8
I already have, I want the liberty to replace my present wife with another one. Naturally, I will expect a fresh, new life; my wife will take the children and be solely responsible for them so that I am left free.

When I am through with school and have a job, I want my wife to quit     9
working and remain at home so that my wife can more fully and completely take care of a wife's duties.

My God, who *wouldn't* want a wife?     10

**Questions to Start You Thinking**

1. CONSIDERING MEANING: How does Brady define the traditional role of the wife? Does she think that a wife should perform all of the duties she outlines? How can you tell?

2. IDENTIFYING WRITING STRATEGIES: How does Brady use observation to support her stand? What other resources does she use?

3. ANALYZING THE WRITER'S CHOICES: What is the tone of this essay? How does Brady establish it? Considering the fact that she was writing for a predominantly female — and feminist — audience, do you think Brady's tone is appropriate? Defend your answer.

4. EXPANDING VOCABULARY: Why does Brady use such simple language in this essay? What is the effect of her use of such phrases as *of course* (paragraph 2), *Needless to say* (paragraph 3), and *Naturally* (paragraph 8)?

5. MAKING CONNECTIONS: Compare Brady's explanation of the role of wife with Scott Russell Sanders's discussion of the women he observed while growing up ("The Men We Carry in Our Minds," p. 499). What would the women Sanders met at college think of the kind of wife Brady discusses?

**Journal Prompts**

1. Exert your wishful thinking — describe your ideal mate.

2. Begin with a stereotype of a husband, wife, boyfriend, girlfriend, father, or mother, and write a satirical description of that stereotype.

**Suggestions for Writing**

1. In a short personal essay, explain what you want or expect in a wife, husband, or life partner. Do your hopes and expectations differ from social and cultural norms? If so, in what way(s)? How has your parents' relationship shaped your attitudes and ideals?

2. How has the role of a wife changed since this essay was written? Write an essay comparing and contrasting the wife of the 1990s with the kind of wife Judy Brady claims she wants.

**Noel Perrin** *was born in 1927 in New York City. He earned degrees at Williams College, Duke University, and Cambridge University and since 1959 has taught English and environmental studies at Dartmouth College. For all his academic credentials, much of his fame as a writer comes from three volumes of essays on part-time farming:* Second Person Rural *(1980),* Third Person Rural *(1983), and* Last Person Rural *(1991). Perrin's most recent book,* Solo *(1992), describes his travels in his electric car. In the following essay, first published in the* New York Times Magazine *on September 9, 1984, Perrin satirizes the postdivorce behavior of many middle-class couples and proposes a somewhat unorthodox solution to the problems that plague modern marriages.*

# *Noel Perrin*   A Part-Time Marriage

When my wife told me she wanted a divorce, I responded like any normal college professor. I hurried to the college library. I wanted to get hold of some books on divorce and find out what was happening to me.

Over the next week (my wife meanwhile having left), I read or skimmed about twenty. Nineteen of them were no help at all. They offered advice on financial settlements. They told me my wife and I should have been in counseling. A bit late for *that* advice.

What I sought was insight. I especially wanted to understand what was wrong with me that my wife had left, and not even for someone else, but just to be rid of *me*. College professors think they can learn that sort of thing from books.

As it turned out, I could. Or at least I got a start. The twentieth book was a collection of essays by various sociologists, and one of the pieces took my breath away. It was like reading my own horoscope.

The two authors had studied a large group of divorced people much like my wife and me. That is, they focused on middle-class Americans of the straight-arrow persuasion. Serious types, believers in marriage for life. Likely to be parents — and, on the whole, good parents. Likely to have pillar-of-the-community potential. But, nevertheless, all divorced.

Naturally there were many different reasons why all these people had divorced, and many different ways they behaved after the divorce. But there was a dominant pattern, and I instantly recognized myself in it. Recognized my wife, too. Reading the essay told me not only what was wrong with me, but also with her. It was the same flaw in both of us. It even gave me a hint as to what my postdivorce behavior was likely to be, and how I might find happiness in the future.

This is the story the essay told me. Or, rather, this is the story the essay hinted at, and that I have since pieced together with much observation, a number of embarrassingly personal questions put to divorced friends, and to some extent from my own life.

Somewhere in some suburb or town or small city, a middle-class couple separate. They are probably between thirty and forty years old. They own a house and have children. The conscious or official reason for their separation is quite different from what it would have been in their parents' generation. Then, it would have been a man leaving his wife for another, and usually younger, woman. Now it's a woman leaving her husband in order to find herself.

When they separate, the wife normally stays in the house they occupied as a married couple. Neither wants to uproot the children. The husband moves to an apartment, which is nearly always going to be closer to his place of employment than his house was. The ex-wife will almost certainly never see that apartment. The husband, however, sees his former house all the time. Not only is he coming by to pick up the children for visits; if he and his ex-wife are on reasonably good terms, he is apt to visit them right there, while she makes use of the time to do errands or to see a friend.

Back when these two were married, they had an informal labor division. 10 She did inside work, he did outside. Naturally there were exceptions: She gardened, and he did his share of the dishes, maybe even baked bread. But mostly he mowed the lawn and fixed the lawn mower; she put up any new curtains, often enough ones she had made herself.

One Saturday, six months or a year after they separated, he comes to see 11 the kids. He plans also to mow the lawn. Before she leaves, she says, "That damn overhead garage door you got is off the track again. Do you think you'd have time to fix it?" Apartment life makes him restless. He jumps at the chance.

She, just as honorable and straight-arrow as he, has no idea of asking for 12 this as a favor. She invites him to stay for an early dinner. She may put it indirectly — "Michael and Sally want their daddy to have supper with them" — but he is clear that the invitation also proceeds from her.

Provided neither of them has met a really attractive other person yet, they 13 now move into a routine. He comes regularly to do the outside chores, and always stays for dinner. If the children are young enough, he may read to them before bedtime. She may wash his shirts.

One such evening, they both happen to be stirred not only by physical 14 desire but by loneliness. "Oh, you might as well come upstairs," she says with a certain self-contempt. He needs no second invitation; they are upstairs in a flash. It is a delightful end to the evening. More delightful than anything they remember from their marriage, or at least from the later part of it.

That, too, now becomes part of the pattern. He never stays the full night, 15 because, good parents that they are, they don't want the children to get any false hopes up — as they would, seeing their father at breakfast.

Such a relationship may go on for several years, may even be interrupted 16 by a romance on one side or the other and then resume. It may even grow to the point where she's mending as well as washing his shirts, and he is advising her on her tax returns and fixing her car.

What they have achieved postdivorce is what their marriage should have 17 been like in the first place. Part-time. Seven days a week of marriage was too much. One afternoon and two evenings is just right.

Although our society is even now witnessing de facto part-time arrange- 18 ments, such as the couple who work in different cities and meet only on weekends, we have no theory of part-time marriage, at least no theory that has reached the general public. The romantic notion still dominates that if you love someone, you obviously want to be with them all the time.

To me it's clear we need such a theory. There are certainly people who 19 thrive on seven-day-a-week marriages. They have a high level of intimacy and they may be better, warmer people than the rest of us. But there are millions and millions of us with medium or low levels of intimacy. We find full-time family memberships a strain. If we could enter marriage with more realistic expectations of what closeness means for us, I suspect the divorce rate might permanently turn downward. It's too bad there isn't a sort of glucose tolerance test for intimacy.

As for me personally, I still do want to get married again. About four days   20
a week.

**Questions to Start You Thinking**

1. CONSIDERING MEANING:  How did Perrin's divorce affect him?

2. IDENTIFYING WRITING STRATEGIES:  How does Perrin use cause and effect to support the solution he proposes?

3. ANALYZING THE WRITER'S CHOICES:  Although he has read numerous books on the subject, Perrin uses imagination to bring the postdivorce scenario to life. Why do you suppose he took this approach toward developing his argument in favor of a "part-time marriage"? What advantages does this creative treatment of the subject have over a fact-laden, statistical approach?

4. EXPANDING VOCABULARY:  Define *straight-arrow, pillar-of-the-community* (paragraph 5), *dominant* (paragraph 6), *self-contempt* (paragraph 14), *de facto* (paragraph 18), and *glucose tolerance test* (paragraph 19). Would you say that Perrin's vocabulary is typical of the "normal" college professor? Give some specific examples to support your answer.

5. MAKING CONNECTIONS:  Compare Perrin's view of marriage with Judy Brady's in "I Want a Wife" (p. 490). In what ways do both writers react against traditional attitudes?

**Journal Prompt**

1. Would you prefer a full- or a part-time marriage? Why?

2. Sketch out a theory or a plan for part-time marriage. What elements or rules would be needed to make it successful?

**Suggestions for Writing**

1. Write an essay explaining how divorce has affected you or those around you.

2. Take a stand on the solution Perrin proposes. In a short essay, agree or disagree with the idea of part-time marriage. Is it a constructive response to problems of marital incompatibility? Why or why not?

**Katha Pollitt**, *born in New York City in 1949, graduated from Radcliffe College in 1972 and went on to become a freelance writer and journalist. Pollitt contributes to a wide range of journals, including the* New Yorker, *the* Atlantic Monthly, *the* Nation, Mother Jones, *and the* New Republic. *She has also written a book of poems,* Antarctic Traveler *(1982), which won the Book Critics Circle Award for best poetry in 1983, and* Reasonable Creatures: Feminism and Society in American Culture at the End of the Twentieth Century *(1994). In "The Future Is Coed," which first appeared in the* Nation *on August 22, 1994, Pollitt uses humor and well-chosen examples from both her personal life and the public arena to examine the debate over single-sex education.*

## *Katha Pollitt*    The Future Is Coed

Being a feminist can take you to some pretty strange places. Consider the past few weeks: In my capacity as tooth fairy, I bought my six-year-old, Sophie, a baseball glove; I got a warm feeling (this is embarrassing) reading an article about a reunion of the first Episcopalian women priests; and I let out a *Yesss!* when the court ruled in favor of Shannon Faulkner, the determined young woman who wants to attend the all-male-though-publicly-funded Citadel military college. Sports, religion, and war, the three banes of human existence — if this coeducation thing keeps going, we won't be able to blame them on men anymore.

Isn't it strange, though, how the more similar the lives of men and women become, the more we hear about the supposed benefits of keeping the sexes apart? Recently the case for single-sex education has mostly been made by feminists, who, rightly, note the many ways girls can get pushed to the margins of the coed classroom and who, more questionably, attribute the achievements of single-sex female grads to the single-sex factor. But as we saw in the Citadel case, two can play this game. The Citadel's arguments included such anomalies as citations from Carol Gilligan[1] and expert testimony from Harvard sociologist David Riesman,[2] who argued that the absence of women allows the Citadel's students to express their "gentler side," and write "very contemplative poetry of high aesthetic sensibility." (Gilligan herself filed an affidavit on behalf of Shannon Faulkner; Elizabeth Fox-Genovese,[3] usually to be found railing against the supposed separatism of women's studies programs, weighed in on the side of the Citadel.)

Leaving aside the question of whether we want to break out the champagne because women will now be able to get degrees in ritual humiliation and bombing Baghdad, when it comes to the merits of single-sex versus coeducation in general, I find I can argue both sides without quite persuading myself. I don't think my nine years of boyless private school did a thing for me in the math, science, leadership, or self-esteem department, but this was back in the bad old prefeminist days; surely *now* girls' schools aren't run by men like Dr. Shafer, who let me drop trigonometry because, and I quote, "I've always thought women only needed enough math to do their grocery lists." On the other hand, I note that at Sophie's coed public school, the kids are

---

[1] **Carol Gilligan** (b. 1936): Noted feminist educator and psychologist whose landmark 1982 book *In a Different Voice: Psychological Theories of Women's and Men's Development* explores the notion of gender difference in moral development. According to Gilligan, female morality is more concerned with human connectedness and personal responsibility, while male morality is more concerned with justice and rights.

[2] **David Riesman** (b. 1909): A professor of social sciences at Harvard University since 1958, he is perhaps best-known for his book *The Lonely Crowd: A Study of the Changing American Character* (1950). His later work has been on the sociology of higher education.

[3] **Elizabeth Fox-Genovese** (b. 1941): Women's historian, controversial for attacking other feminists.

pretty much permitted to sex-type themselves: no girls in the chess club, a solitary boy in the glee club. The efforts of the most outspoken feminist mom (not me) to call attention to this and other instances of stereotyping were, to put it mildly, not appreciated by the female head of the school.

A look at the research doesn't clear things up much. True, a number of studies show that single-sex education benefits girls (there's much less evidence that it helps boys, and some that it hurts them). The trouble is, since coed and single-sex schools have so many differences, it's hard to know what, exactly, is being measured. Choosing single-sex is a pretty dramatic decision, with complicated class and social ramifications that go way beyond income levels and the other things researchers use as controls. Perhaps those positive research results reflect not the school itself but what kind of students — and parents — the school attracts. Maybe, for instance, parents who choose single-sex are more ambitious for their daughters, care less about producing a "popular" teenager, take a bigger hand in their children's education. Interestingly, researchers who compared coed and single-sex comprehensive (nonselective, neighborhood, public) schools in England, where single-sex education is commonplace, found no differences in outcome for girls.

What I suspect is mostly being measured is the degree of attention kids get. The public-school experiments now in vogue — all-girl math classes, inner-city "academics" for black males — have energetic teachers who believe in what they're doing, new instructional materials and methods, a sense of mission, excitement, and commitment to success. You don't need a Ph.D. in sociology to see why kids who languished in regular classes would perk up. But if single-sex programs were to become routine, they would more and more resemble the regular classroom — perhaps even down to the sexism. As we sometimes tend to forget, women have played quite a large role in enforcing on one another those damaging stereotypes all-female classrooms are supposed to correct.

Changing coeducation to meet the needs of both sexes will take work, but will it really be so difficult as all that? If, as students in one all-girl math class told the *New York Times*, they had been mocked, teased, belittled, and interrupted by boys in coed classes, why can't the grown-ups read those boys the riot act? Why should girls be segregated because of what boys do? Similarly, it shouldn't take a barbaric regimen of military drill to get a teenage boy to write a poem — and in fact, it doesn't, as a glance at any campus lit mag shows.

At bottom, single-sex education is the counsel of despair. It says that the sexes can't be friends and colleagues and do serious work together — although the adult world (even the Army!) increasingly requires this — and can only "be themselves" in the absence of the other. In her Citadel testimony, Fox-Genovese argued that single-sex education separates "the story of mating and dating" from "education." Leaving aside the question of whether head-shaving, will-breaking, insults, and the rest further education — it sounds more like *The Story of O*[4] than Matthew Arnold[5] to me — Prof. F-G's argument is reminiscent of the one misogynists of an earlier day used to keep women out of the Ivy League, and, I wouldn't be surprised, out of the University of Bologna in the thirteenth century.

No, for better or worse the future is coed. As Shannon Faulkner advised her detractors, "Wake up and smell the '90s." And that goes for both sexes.          8

**Questions to Start You Thinking**

1. CONSIDERING MEANING:  Why must the future be coed, as Pollitt asserts in the title and in her last paragraph? What reasons does she give to support her position?

2. IDENTIFYING WRITING STRATEGIES:  How does Pollitt use comparison and contrast to evaluate the strengths and weaknesses of coed and single-sex education? What are some of the criteria, or standards, she sets for judging whether or not an educational environment is a positive one?

3. ANALYZING THE WRITER'S CHOICES:  Does Pollitt's use of a casual, even humorous tone work for or against her attempt to take a serious stand on the issue of coeducation? Why do you think she used this tone to make her point? Explain, providing examples to support your position.

4. EXPANDING VOCABULARY:  Define *anomalies* and *citations* (paragraph 2). According to Pollitt, why are the Citadel's citations from Carol Gilligan's writing an anomaly?

5. MAKING CONNECTIONS:  Pollitt acknowledges that "women have played quite a large role in enforcing on one another . . . damaging stereotypes" (paragraph 5). How might the same be true for the men Sanders describes as "toilers and warriors" in "The Men We Carry in Our Minds" (p. 499)?

**Journal Prompts**

1. Have you ever felt as though the gender makeup of a particular course you've taken put you at a disadvantage? Explain.

2. Do you agree with Pollitt that sports is one of the "three banes of human existence" (paragraph 1)? Why or why not? How did her statement affect your response to the rest of her essay?

**Suggestions for Writing**

1. Do you think students learn more at a coed or a single-sex school? Why? Compare and contrast the positive and negative aspects of a coed school, drawing from your own experience.

2. What is your opinion of the Citadel case? Defend or refute Pollitt's points using examples from your experiences, observations at your own school, and additional reading about the case.

---

[4] *The Story of O:* Controversial French erotic novel published pseudonymously in 1965; recently revealed to have been written by Dominique Aury, a prominent French journalist and translator.

[5] **Matthew Arnold** (1822–1888): English poet and critic, best known for his poem "Dover Beach."

*Scott Russell Sanders* *was born in 1945 in Memphis, Tennessee. A graduate of Brown University and Cambridge University, Sanders has taught English at Indiana University since 1971. His numerous publications include the short-story collection* Fetching the Dead *(1984), the children's book* The Floating House *(1995), and the essay collections* Paradise of Bombs *(1991) and* Staying Put: Making a Home in a Restless World *(1993). Sanders has described his writing as "driven by a deep regard for particular places and voices . . . a regard compounded of grief, curiosity, and love." In the following essay, which first appeared in* Milkweed Chronicle *in 1984, Sanders explains how the experience of growing up in a working-class community made it difficult for him to understand the grievances of women from more privileged backgrounds.*

## *Scott Russell Sanders*    The Men We Carry in Our Minds

"This must be a hard time for women," I say to my friend Anneke. "They have so many paths to choose from, and so many voices calling them." 1

"I think it's a lot harder for men," she replies. 2

"How do you figure that?" 3

"The women I know feel excited, innocent, like crusaders in a just cause. The men I know are eaten up with guilt." 4

We are sitting at the kitchen table drinking sassafras tea, our hands wrapped around the mugs because this April morning is cool and drizzly. "Like a Dutch morning," Anneke told me earlier. She is Dutch herself, a writer and midwife and peacemaker, with the round face and sad eyes of a woman in a Vermeer painting who might be waiting for the rain to stop, for a door to open. She leans over to sniff a sprig of lilac, pale lavender, that rises from a vase of cobalt blue. 5

"Women feel such pressure to be everything, do everything," I say. "Career, kids, art, politics. Have their babies and get back to the office a week later. It's as if they're trying to overcome a million years' worth of evolution in one lifetime." 6

"But we help one another. We don't try to lumber on alone, like so many wounded grizzly bears, the way men do." Anneke sips her tea. I gave her the mug with owls on it, for wisdom. "And we have this deep-down sense that we're in the *right* — we've been held back, passed over, used — while men feel they're in the wrong. Men are the ones who've been discredited, who have to search their souls." 7

I search my soul. I discover guilty feelings aplenty — toward the poor, the Vietnamese, Native Americans, the whales, an endless list of debts — a guilt in each case that is as bright and unambiguous as a neon sign. But toward women I feel something more confused, a snarl of shame, envy, wary tenderness, and amazement. This muddle troubles me. To hide my unease I say, "You're right, it's tough being a man these days." 8

"Don't laugh." Anneke frowns at me, mournful-eyed, through the sas-    9
safras steam. "I wouldn't be a man for anything. It's much easier being the victim. All the victim has to do is break free. The persecutor has to live with his
past."

How deep is this past? I find myself wondering after Anneke has left. How    10
much of an inheritance do I have to throw off? Is it just the beliefs I breathed
in as a child. Do I have to scour memory back through father and grandfather? Through St. Paul? Beyond Stonehenge and into the twilit caves? I'm convinced the past we must contend with is deeper even than speech. When I
think back on my childhood, on how I learned to see men and women, I have
a sense of ancient, dizzying depths. The back roads of Tennessee and Ohio
where I grew up were probably closer, in their sexual patterns, to the camp-
sites of Stone Age hunters than to the genderless cities of the future into which
we are rushing.

The first men, besides my father, I remember seeing were black convicts    11
and white guards, in the cottonfield across the road from our farm on the outskirts of Memphis. I must have been three or four. The prisoners wore dingy
gray-and-black zebra suits, heavy as canvas, sodden with sweat. Hatless,
stooped, they chopped weeds in the fierce heat, row after row, breathing the
acrid dust of boll-weevil poison. The overseers wore dazzling white shirts and
broad shadowy hats. The oiled barrels of their shotguns flashed in the sunlight. Their faces in memory are utterly blank. Of course those men, white and
black, have become for me an emblem of racial hatred. But they have also
come to stand for the twin poles of my early vision of manhood — the brute
toiling animal and the boss.

When I was a boy, the men I knew labored with their bodies. They were    12
marginal farmers, just scraping by, or welders, steelworkers, carpenters; they
swept floors, dug ditches, mined coal, or drove trucks, their forearms ropy
with muscle; they trained horses, stoked furnaces, built tires, stood on assembly lines wrestling parts onto cars and refrigerators. They got up before
light, worked all day long whatever the weather, and when they came home
at night they looked as though somebody had been whipping them. In the
evenings and on weekends they worked on their own places, tilling gardens
that were lumpy with clay, fixing broken-down cars, hammering on houses
that were always too drafty, too leaky, too small.

The bodies of the men I knew were twisted and maimed in ways visible    13
and invisible. The nails of their hands were black and split, the hands tattooed
with scars. Some had lost fingers. Heavy lifting had given many of them
finicky backs and guts weak from hernias. Racing against conveyor belts had
given them ulcers. Their ankles and knees ached from years of standing on
concrete. Anyone who had worked for long around machines was hard of
hearing. They squinted, and the skin of their faces was creased like the leather
of old work gloves. There were times, studying them, when I dreaded growing up. Most of them coughed, from dust or cigarettes, and most of them
drank cheap wine or whiskey, so their eyes looked bloodshot and bruised.
The fathers of my friends always seemed older than the mothers. Men wore
out sooner. Only women lived into old age.

As a boy I also knew another sort of men, who did not sweat and break    14
down like mules. They were soldiers, and so far as I could tell they scarcely
worked at all. During my early school years we lived on a military base, an arsenal in Ohio, and every day I saw GIs in the guardshacks, on the stoops of
barracks, at the wheels of olive drab Chevrolets. The chief fact of their lives
was boredom. Long after I left the arsenal I came to recognize the sour smell
the soldiers gave off as that of souls in limbo. They were all waiting — for
wars, for transfers, for leaves, for promotions, for the end of their hitch — like
so many braves waiting for the hunt to begin. Unlike the warriors of older
tribes, however, they would have no say about when the battle would start or
how it would be waged. Their waiting was broken only when they practiced
for war. They fired guns at targets, drove tanks across the churned-up fields of
the military reservation, set off bombs in the wrecks of old fighter planes. I
knew this was all play. But I also felt certain that when the hour for killing arrived, they would kill. When the real shooting started, many of them would
die. This was what soldiers were *for*, just as a hammer was for driving nails.

Warriors and toilers: those seemed, in my boyhood vision, to be the chief    15
destinies for men. They weren't the only destinies, as I learned from having a
few male teachers, from reading books, and from watching television. But the
men on television — the politicians, the astronauts, the generals, the savvy
lawyers, the philosophical doctors, the bosses who gave orders to both soldiers and laborers — seemed as remote and unreal to me as the figures in ta-
pestries. I could no more imagine growing up to become one of these cool,
potent creatures than I could imagine becoming a prince.

A nearer and more hopeful example was that of my father, who had es-    16
caped from a red-dirt farm to a tire factory, and from the assembly line to the
front office. Eventually he dressed in a white shirt and tie. He carried himself
as if he had been born to work with his mind. But his body, remembering the
early years of slogging work, began to give out on him in his fifties, and it quit
on him entirely before he turned sixty-five. Even such a partial escape from
man's fate as he had accomplished did not seem possible for most of the boys
I knew. They joined the army, stood in line for jobs in the smoky plants,
helped build highways. They were bound to work as their fathers had worked,
killing themselves or preparing to kill others.

A scholarship enabled me not only to attend college, a rare enough feat    17
in my circle, but even to study in a university meant for children of the rich.
Here I met for the first time young men who had assumed from birth that they
would lead lives of comfort and power. And for the first time I met women
who told me that men were guilty of having kept all the joys and privileges of
the earth for themselves. I was baffled. What privileges? What joys? I thought
about the maimed dismal lives of most of the men back home. What had they
stolen from their wives and daughters? The right to go five days a week, twelve
months a year, for thirty or forty years to a steel mill or a coal mine? The right
to drop bombs and die in war? The right to feel every leak in the roof, every
gap in the fence, every cough in the engine, as a wound they must mend? The

right to feel, when the lay-off comes or the plant shuts down, not only afraid but ashamed?

I was slow to understand the deep grievances of women. This was be-　18 cause, as a boy, I had envied them. Before college, the only people I had ever known who were interested in art or music or literature, the only ones who read books, the only ones who ever seemed to enjoy a sense of ease and grace were the mothers and daughters. Like the menfolk, they fretted about money, they scrimped and made-do. But, when the pay stopped coming in, they were not the ones who had failed. Nor did they have to go to war, and that seemed to me a blessed fact. By comparison with the narrow, ironclad days of fathers, there was an expansiveness, I thought, in the days of mothers. They went to see neighbors, to shop in town, to run errands at school, at the library, at church. No doubt, had I looked harder at their lives, I would have envied them less. It was not my fate to become a woman, so it was easier for me to see the graces. Few of them held jobs outside the home, and those who did filled thankless roles as clerks and waitresses. I didn't see, then, what a prison a house could be, since houses seemed to me brighter, handsomer places than any factory. I did not realize — because such things were never spoken of — how often women suffered from men's bullying. I did learn about the wretchedness of abandoned wives, single mothers, widows; but I also learned about the wretchedness of lone men. Even then I could see how exhausting it was for a mother to cater all day to the needs of young children. But if I had been asked, as a boy, to choose between tending a baby and tending a machine, I think I would have chosen the baby. (Having now tended both, I know I would choose the baby.)

So I was baffled when the women at college accused me and my sex of　19 having cornered the world's pleasure. I think something like my bafflement has been felt by other boys (and by girls as well) who grew up in dirt-poor farm country, in mining country, in black ghettos, in Hispanic barrios, in the shadows of factories, in third world nations — any place where the fate of men is as grim and bleak as the fate of women. Toilers and warriors. I realize now how ancient these identities are, how deep the tug they exert on men, the undertow of a thousand generations. The miseries I saw, as a boy, in the lives of nearly all men I continue to see in the lives of many — the body-breaking toil, the tedium, the call to be tough, the humiliating powerlessness, the battle for a living and for territory.

When the women I met at college thought about the joys and privileges　20 of men, they did not carry in their minds the sort of men I had known in my childhood. They thought of their fathers, who were bankers, physicians, architects, stockbrokers, the big wheels of the big cities. These fathers rode the train to work or drove cars that cost more than any of my childhood houses. They were attended from morning to night by female helpers, wives and nurses and secretaries. They were never laid off, never short of cash at month's end, never lined up for welfare. These fathers made decisions that mattered. They ran the world.

The daughters of such men wanted to share in this power, this glory. So 21
did I. They yearned for a say over their future, for jobs worthy of their abilities, for the right to live at peace, unmolested, whole. Yes, I thought, yes yes.
The difference between me and these daughters was that they saw me, because
of my sex, as destined from birth to become like their fathers, and therefore
an enemy to their desires. But I knew better. I wasn't an enemy, in fact or in
feeling. I was an ally. If I had known, then, how to tell them so, would they
have believed me? Would they now?

**Questions to Start You Thinking**

1. CONSIDERING MEANING: Why does Sanders call himself an "ally" (paragraph 21) of the women he met in college? Do you agree that he was their ally? Explain.

2. IDENTIFYING WRITING STRATEGIES: Sanders uses recall as a resource in this piece. How does he use the experiences he recalls to support the stand he takes?

3. ANALYZING THE WRITER'S CHOICES: Sanders divides the men he recalls from his youth into two types — warriors and toilers. How do these men differ from those that the women he met in college "carried in their minds"? Why does Sanders draw this contrast?

4. EXPANDING VOCABULARY: Sanders writes that when he was a boy "warriors and toilers" seemed to him to be the chief destinies for men (paragraph 15). What qualities do you associate with "warriors" and with "toilers"? Are the connotations of these terms primarily positive or negative?

5. MAKING CONNECTIONS: How do the images of men that Sanders acquired in his childhood differ from the images of women that Judith Ortiz Cofer ("The Myth of the Latin Woman," p. 504) acquired in hers?

**Journal Prompts**

1. Reflect on some of the men and women you knew as a child. Do any of them resemble the men and women Sanders remembers from his youth?

2. Do you agree that "it's tough being a man these days" (paragraph 8)? Why or why not? Role-play — if you are female, take a man's point of view; if you are male, take a woman's point of view.

**Suggestions for Writing**

1. Using recall as a resource, explain the qualities of an important man you "carry in your mind." Who is this man? How did he help shape your views of what masculinity is?

2. Write an essay explaining whether men's or women's roles are more difficult in today's society. Use examples from your own experience as well as from your knowledge of current events.

**Judith Ortiz Cofer** *was born in 1952 in Hormigueros, Puerto Rico, and immigrated to the United States in 1956. She studied at Augusta College, Florida Atlantic
University, and Oxford University and now teaches at the University of Georgia. Her
books include the poetry collections* Terms of Survival *(1988) and* Reaching for

the Mainland *(1995), the novel* The Line of the Sun *(1989), and the essay collection* Silent Dancing *(1990).* The Latin Deli *(1993), from which the following essay was taken, includes poetry, fiction, and nonfiction. In the essay Ortiz Cofer blends autobiography with analysis to show how Latin American women are misread within white culture.*

## *Judith Ortiz Cofer*    The Myth of the Latin Woman: I Just Met a Girl Named María

On a bus trip to London from Oxford University where I was earning    1
some graduate credits one summer, a young man, obviously fresh from a pub, spotted me and as if struck by inspiration went down on his knees in the aisle. With both hands over this heart he broke into an Irish tenor's rendition of "María" from *West Side Story*. My politely amused fellow passengers gave his lovely voice the round of gentle applause it deserved. Though I was not quite as amused, I managed my version of an English smile: no show of teeth, no extreme contortions of the facial muscles — I was at this time of my life practicing reserve and cool. Oh, that British control, how I coveted it. But María had followed me to London, reminding me of a prime fact of my life: you can leave the Island, master the English language, and travel as far as you can, but if you are a Latina, especially one like me who so obviously belongs to Rita Moreno's[1] gene pool, the Island travels with you.

This is sometimes a very good thing — it may win you that extra minute    2
of someone's attention. But with some people, the same things can make *you* an island — not so much a tropical paradise as an Alcatraz,[2] a place nobody wants to visit. As a Puerto Rican girl growing up in the United States and wanting like most children to "belong," I resented the stereotype that my Hispanic appearance called forth from many people I met.

Our family lived in a large urban center in New Jersey during the sixties,    3
where life was designed as a microcosm of my parent's casas on the island. We spoke in Spanish, we ate Puerto Rican food bought at the bodega,[3] and we practiced strict Catholicism complete with Saturday confession and Sunday mass at a church where our parents were accommodated into a one-hour Spanish mass slot, performed by a Chinese priest trained as a missionary for Latin America.

As a girl I was kept under strict surveillance, since virtue and modesty    4
were, by cultural equation, the same as family honor. As a teenager I was instructed on how to behave as a proper señorita. But it was a conflicting message girls got, since the Puerto Rican mothers also encouraged their daughters

[1] **Rita Moreno** (b. 1931): Latina actress who played Maria's friend in the movie version of the Broadway musical *West Side Story*.
[2] **Alcatraz:** Federal prison used from 1933–1963, located on a rocky island in San Francisco Bay.
[3] **bodega:** Latino grocery store.

to look and act like women and to dress in clothes our Anglo friends and their mothers found too "mature" for our age. It was, and is, cultural, yet I often felt humiliated when I appeared at an American friend's party wearing a dress more suitable to a semiformal than to a playroom birthday celebration. At Puerto Rican festivities, neither the music nor the colors we wore could be too loud. I still experience a vague sense of letdown when I'm invited to a "party" and it turns out to be a marathon conversation in hushed tones rather than a fiesta with salsa, laughter, and dancing — the kind of celebration I remember from my childhood.

I remember Career Day in our high school, when teachers told us to come    5 dressed as if for a job interview. It quickly became obvious that to the barrio[4] girls, "dressing up" sometimes meant wearing ornate jewelry and clothing that would be more appropriate (by mainstream standards) for the company Christmas party than as daily office attire. That morning I had agonized in front of my closet, trying to figure out what a "career girl" would wear because, essentially, except for Marlo Thomas[5] on TV, I had no models on which to base my decision. I knew how to dress for school: at the Catholic school I attended we all wore uniforms; I knew how to dress for Sunday mass, and knew what dresses to wear for parties at my relatives' homes. Though I do not recall the precise details of my Career Day outfit, it must have been a composite of the above choices. But I remember a comment my friend (an Italian-American) made in later years that coalesced my impressions of that day. She said that at the business school she was attending the Puerto Rican girls always stood out for wearing "everything at once." She meant, of course, too much jewelry, too many accessories. On that day at school, we were simply made the negative models by the nuns who were themselves not credible fashion experts to any of us. But it was painfully obvious to me that to the others, in their tailored skirts and silk blouses, we must have seemed "hopeless" and "vulgar." Though I now know that most adolescents feel out of step much of the time, I also know that for the Puerto Rican girls of my generation that sense was intensified. The way our teachers and classmates looked at us that day in school was just a taste of the culture clash that awaited us in the real world, where prospective employers and men on the street would often misinterpret our tight skirts and jingling bracelets as a come-on.

Mixed cultural signals have perpetuated certain stereotypes — for exam-    6 ple, that of the Hispanic woman as the "Hot Tamale" or sexual firebrand. It is a one-dimensional view that the media have found easy to promote. In their special vocabulary, advertisers have designated not only the foods but also the women of Latin America. From conversations in my house I recall hearing about the harassment that Puerto Rican women endured in factories where the "boss men" talked to them as if sexual innuendo was all they understood and, worse, often gave them the choice of submitting to advances or being fired.

[4] **barrio:** Latino neighborhood.
[5] **Marlo Thomas** (b. 1943): Actress who starred in the TV show *That Girl* (1965–71), about an aspiring actress and model.

It is custom, however, not chromosomes, that leads us to choose scarlet    7
over pale pink. As young girls, we were influenced in our decisions about
clothes and color by the women — older sisters and mothers who had grown
up on a tropical island where the natural environment was a riot of primary
colors, where showing your skin was one way to keep cool as well as to look
sexy. Most important of all, on the island, women perhaps felt freer to dress
and move more provocatively, since, in most cases, they were protected by the
traditions, mores, and laws of a Spanish/Catholic system of morality and
machismo whose main rule was: *You may look at my sister, but if you touch her
I will kill you.* The extended family and church structure could provide a young
woman with a circle of safety in her small pueblo on the island; if a man
"wronged" a girl, everyone would close in to save her family honor.

This is what I have gleaned from my discussions as an adult with older    8
Puerto Rican women. They have told me about dressing in their best party
clothes on Saturday nights and going to the town's plaza to promenade with
their girlfriends in front of the boys they liked. The males were thus given an
opportunity to admire the women and to express their admiration in the
form of *piropos*: erotically charged street poems they composed on the spot. I
have been subjected to a few piropos while visiting the island, and they can
be outrageous, although custom dictates that they must never cross into obscenity. This ritual, as I understand it, also entails a show of studied indifference on the woman's part; if she is "decent," she must not acknowledge the
man's impassioned words. So I do understand how things can be lost in translation. When a Puerto Rican girl dressed in her idea of what is attractive meets
a man from the mainstream culture who has been trained to react to certain
types of clothing as a sexual signal, a clash is likely to take place. The line I first
heard based on the aspect of the myth happened when the boy who took me
to my first formal dance leaned over to plant a sloppy overeager kiss painfully
on my mouth, and when I didn't respond with sufficient passion said in a re-
sentful tone: "I thought you Latin girls were supposed to mature early" — my
first instance of being thought of as a fruit or vegetable — I was supposed to
*ripen,* not just grow into womanhood like other girls.

It is surprising to some of my professional friends that some people, in-    9
cluding those who should know better, still put others "in their place."
Though rarer, these incidents are still commonplace in my life. It happened
to me most recently during a stay at a very classy metropolitan hotel favored
by young professional couples for their weddings. Late one evening after the
theater, as I walked toward my room with my new colleague (a woman with
whom I was coordinating an arts program), a middle-aged man in a tuxedo,
a young girl in satin and lace on his arm, stepped directly into our path. With
his champagne glass extended toward me, he exclaimed, "Evita!"[6]

Our way blocked, my companion and I listened as the man half-recited,    10
half-bellowed "Don't Cry for Me, Argentina." When he finished, the young

[6] **Evita:** Eva Perón (1919–1952), known as Evita, was the wife of Juan Perón
(1895–1974), the fascist leader of Argentina from 1946 to 1955. The song "Don't Cry for
Me, Argentina" is from the Broadway musical *Evita,* based on her life.

girl said: "How about a round of applause for my daddy?" We complied, hoping this would bring the silly spectacle to a close. I was becoming aware that our little group was attracting the attention of the other guests. "Daddy" must have perceived this too, and he once more barred the way as we tried to walk past him. He began to shout-sing a ditty to the tune of "La Bamba" — except the lyrics were about a girl named María whose exploits all rhymed with her name and gonorrhea. The girl kept saying "Oh, Daddy" and looking at me with pleading eyes. She wanted me to laugh along with the others. My companion and I stood silently waiting for the man to end his offensive song. When he finished, I looked not at him but at his daughter. I advised her calmly never to ask her father what he had done in the army. Then I walked between them and to my room. My friend complimented me on my cool handling of the situation. I confessed to her that I really had wanted to push the jerk into the swimming pool. I knew this same man — probably a corporate executive, well educated, even worldly by most standards — would not have been likely to regale a white woman with a dirty song in public. He would perhaps have checked his impulse by assuming that she could be somebody's wife or mother, or at least *somebody* who might take offense. But to him, I was just an Evita or a María: merely a character in his cartoon-populated universe.

Because of my education and my proficiency with the English language, 11 I have acquired many mechanisms for dealing with the anger I experience. This was not true for my parents, nor is it true for the many Latin women working at menial jobs who must put up with stereotypes about our ethnic group such as "They make good domestics." This is another facet of the myth of the Latin woman in the United States. Its origin is simple to deduce. Work as domestics, waitressing, and factory jobs are all that's available to women with little English and few skills. The myth of the Hispanic menial has been sustained by the same media phenomenon that made "Mammy" from *Gone with the Wind* America's idea of the black woman for generations; María, the housemaid or counter girl, is now indelibly etched into the national psyche. The big and the little screens have presented us with the picture of the funny Hispanic maid, mispronouncing words and cooking up a spicy storm in a shiny California kitchen.

This media-engendered image of the Latina in the United States has been 12 documented by feminist Hispanic scholars, who claim that such portrayals are partially responsible for the denial of opportunities for upward mobility among Latinas in the professions. I have a Chicana friend working on a Ph.D. in philosophy at a major university. She says her doctor still shakes his head in puzzled amazement at all the "big words" she uses. Since I do not wear my diplomas around my neck for all to see, I too have on occasion been sent to that "kitchen," where some think I obviously belong.

One such incident that has stayed with me, though I recognize it as a mi- 13 nor offense, happened on the day of my first public poetry reading. It took place in Miami in a boat-restaurant where we were having lunch before the event. I was nervous and excited as I walked in with my notebook in my hand.

An older woman motioned me to her table. Thinking (foolish me) that she wanted me to autograph a copy of my brand new slender volume of verse, I went over. She ordered a cup of coffee from me, assuming that I was the waitress. Easy enough to mistake my poems for menus, I suppose. I know that it wasn't an intentional act of cruelty, yet of all the good things that happened that day, I remember that scene most clearly, because it reminded me of what I had to overcome before anyone would take me seriously. In retrospect I understand that my anger gave my reading fire, that I have almost always taken doubts in my abilities as a challenge — and that the result is, most times, a feeling of satisfaction at having won a convert, when I see the cold, appraising eyes warm to my words, the body language change, the smile that indicates that I have opened some avenue for communication. That day I read to that woman and her lowered eyes told me that she was embarrassed at her little faux pas, and when I willed her to look up at me, it was my victory, and she graciously allowed me to punish her with my full attention. We shook hands at the end of the reading, and I never saw her again. She has probably forgotten the whole thing but maybe not.

Yet I am one of the lucky ones. My parents made it possible for me to acquire a stronger footing in the mainstream culture by giving me the chance at an education. And books and art have saved me from the harsher forms of ethnic and racial prejudice that many of my Hispanic *compañeras* have had to endure. I travel a lot around the United States, reading from my books of poetry and my novel, and the reception I most often receive is one of positive interest by people who want to know more about my culture. There are, however, thousands of Latinas without the privilege of an education or the entrée into society that I have. For them life is a struggle against the misconceptions perpetuated by the myth of the Latina as whore, domestic, or criminal. We cannot change this by legislating the way people look at us. The transformation, as I see it, has to occur at a much more individual level. My personal goal in my public life is to try to replace the old pervasive stereotypes and myths about Latinas with a much more interesting set of realities. Every time I give a reading, I hope the stories I tell, the dreams and fears I examine in my work, can achieve some universal truth which will get my audience past the particulars of my skin color, my accent, or my clothes.

I once wrote a poem in which I called us Latinas "God's brown daughters." This poem is really a prayer of sorts, offered upward, but also, through the human-to-human channel of art, outward. It is a prayer for communication, and for respect. In it, Latin women pray "in Spanish to an Anglo God / with a Jewish heritage," and they are "fervently hoping / that if not omnipotent, / at least He be bilingual."

**Questions to Start You Thinking**

1. CONSIDERING MEANING: What are some of the myths of the Latin woman addressed in this essay? What cultural background and other information does Ortiz Cofer provide to shatter these myths?

2. IDENTIFYING WRITING STRATEGIES: What examples does Ortiz Cofer use to compare and contrast how Latinas are seen by their own and by other cultures?

3. ANALYZING THE WRITER'S CHOICES:  Ortiz Cofer states that her goal is to "try to replace the old pervasive stereotypes and myths about Latinas with a much more interesting set of realities" (paragraph 14). To accomplish that goal in this essay, why do you think she relies so heavily on recalling her own experiences as a victim of stereotyping? Is she successful? Why or why not?

4. EXPANDING VOCABULARY:  Define *indelibly* and *psyche* (paragraph 11). According to Ortiz Cofer, how has the stereotype of the Hispanic domestic servant been "indelibly etched into the national psyche"?

5. MAKING CONNECTIONS:  Ortiz Cofer and Judy Brady ("I Want a Wife," p. 490) both seek to expose stereotypes of women. Compare and contrast Ortiz Cofer's tone with Brady's. Whose approach do you find more effective and why?

**Journal Prompts**

1. In what ways do the clothes you wear reflect your culture's expectations for men or women?

2. Have you or has someone you know ever been wrongfully stereotyped or prejudged? How did you react?

**Suggestions for Writing**

1. Recall a time when you first became aware of a stereotype. What was the stereotype, and what incident triggered your awareness of it? Narrate the incident and your reaction to it.

2. Write an essay analyzing one or two episodes of a television sitcom that you think bases its humor on the use of stereotypes. What are those stereotypes and how does the show present them? In your opinion, are these stereotypes harmless or destructive? Defend your response.

**Nicholas Wade** *was born in 1942 in England. Educated at Cambridge, Wade wrote for* Nature *magazine in London before coming to the United States in 1971. He began his U.S. career writing for* Science *magazine before joining the* New York Times *as an editorial writer. Wade is currently the editor of the* New York Times's *Science section and author of the "Method and Madness" column for the* New York Times Magazine. *His several books include* The Ultimate Experiment *(1977),* The Nobel Duel *(1981), and* A World beyond Healing *(1987). He also coedited* The Environment from Your Backyard to the Ocean Floor *(vol. 2 of* The New York Times Book of Science Literacy, *1994). In "How Men and Women Think," which was first published in the* New York Times Magazine *on June 12, 1994, Wade asks whether biological differences between men and women actually do exist — and if so, to what extent they might cause behavioral differences.*

# Nicholas Wade   How Men and Women Think

The human brain, according to an emerging new body of scientific re-   1
search, comes in two different varieties, maybe as different as the accompanying physique. Men, when they are lost, instinctually fall back on their
in-built navigational skills, honed from far-off days of tracking large prey
miles from home. Women, by contrast, tend to find their way by the simpler
methods of remembering local landmarks or even asking help from strangers.

Men excel on psychological tests that require the imaginary twisting in   2
space of a three-dimensional object. The skill seems to help with higher math,
where the topmost ranks are thronged with male minds like Andrew Wiles of
Princeton, who proclaimed almost a year ago that he had proved Fermat's
Last Theorem and will surely get around to publishing the proof almost any
day now.

Some feminist ideologues assert that all minds are created equal and   3
women would be just as good at math if they weren't discouraged in school.
But Camilla Benbow, a psychologist at Iowa State University has spent years
assessing biases like male math teachers or parents who favor boys. She concludes that boys' superiority at math is mostly innate.

But women, the new studies assert, have the edge in most other ways, like   4
perceptual speed, verbal fluency, and communications skills. They also have
sharper hearing than men, and excel in taste, smell, and touch, and in fine coordination of hand and eye. If Martians arrived and gave job interviews, it
seems likely they would direct men to competitive sports and manual labor
and staff most professions, diplomacy, and government with women.

The measurement of intellectual differences is a field with a long and   5
mostly disgraceful past. IQ tests have been regularly misused, sometimes even
concocted, in support of prevailing prejudices. Distinguished male
anatomists used to argue that women were less intelligent because their
brains weighed less, neglecting to correct for the strong influence of body
weight on brain weight.

The present studies of sex differences are venturing on ground where self-   6
deception and prejudice are constant dangers. The science is difficult and the
results prone to misinterpretation. Still, the budding science seems free so far
of obvious error. For one thing, many of the field's leading practitioners happen to be women, perhaps because male academics in this controversial field
have had their lives made miserable by militant feminists.

For another, the study of brain sex differences does not depend on just   7
one kind of subvertible measure but draws on several different disciplines, including biology and anatomy. As is described in a new book, *Eve's Rib*, by
Robert Pool, and the earlier *Brain Sex* by Anne Moir and David Jessel, the
foundations of the field have been carefully laid in animal research. Experiments with rats show that exposure in the womb to testosterone indelibly im-
prints a male pattern of behavior; without testosterone, the rat's brain is
female.

In human fetuses, too, the sex hormones seem to mold a male and female **8** version of the brain, each subtly different in organization and behavior. The best evidence comes from girls with a rare genetic anomaly who are exposed in the womb to more testosterone than normal; they grow up doing better than their unaffected sisters on the tests that boys are typically good at. There's also some evidence, not yet confirmed, that male and female brains may be somewhat differently structured, with the two cerebral hemispheres being more specialized and less well interconnected in men than in women.

If the human brain exists in male and female versions, as modulated in **9** the womb, that would explain what every parent knows, that boys and girls prefer different patterns of play regardless of well-meaning efforts to impose unisex toys on both.

The human mind being very versatile, however, any genetic propensities **10** are far from decisive. In math, for example, the average girl is pretty much as good as the average boy. Only among the few students at the peak of math ability do boys predominate. Within the loose framework set by the genes, education makes an enormous difference. In Japan, boys exceed girls on the mental rotation tests, just as in America. But the Japanese girls outscore American boys. Maybe Japanese kids are just smarter or, more likely, just better taught, Japan being a country where education is taken seriously and parents and teachers consistently push children to excel.

There are some obvious cautions to draw about the social and political **11** implications that might one day flow from brain sex research. One is that differences between individuals of the same sex often far exceed the slight differences between the sexes as two population groups: "If I were going into combat, I would prefer to have Martina Navratilova at my side than Robert Reich," says Patricia Ireland, president of the National Organization for Women. Even if men in general excel in math, an individual woman could still be better than most men.

On the other hand, if the brains of men and women really are organized **12** differently, it's possible the sexes both prefer and excel at different occupations, perhaps those with more or less competition or social interaction. "In a world of scrupulous gender equality, equal numbers of girls and boys would be educated and trained for . . . all the professions. . . . [Hiring would proceed] until half of every workplace was made up of men and half, women," says Judith Lorber in *Paradoxes of Gender,* a new work of feminist theory. That premise does not hold if there are real intellectual differences between the sexes; the test of equal opportunity, when all unfair barriers to women have fallen, will not necessarily be equal outcomes.

Greek mythology tells that Tiresias, having lived both as a man and a **13** woman for some complicated reason, was asked to settle a dispute between Zeus and Hera as to which sex enjoyed sex more. He replied that there was no contest — it was ten times better for women. Whereupon Hera struck him blind for his insolence and Zeus in compensation gave him the gift of foresight. Like Tiresias, the brain sex researchers are uncovering some impolitic truths, potent enough to shake Mount Olympus some day.

**Questions to Start You Thinking**

1. CONSIDERING MEANING:  According to Wade, why it is difficult to do valid, reliable studies of sex differences?

2. IDENTIFYING WRITING STRATEGIES:  Wade devotes much of the article to summarizing studies on sex differences. Identify the passages where he summarizes others' research as evidence to support his position.

3. ANALYZING THE WRITER'S CHOICES:  Note the various points in the essay where Wade's tone and examples are humorous. Given the socially and politically sensitive nature of brain sex research, why do you think Wade integrates humor into his writing? Do you think it is an effective device? Explain your response.

4. EXPANDING VOCABULARY:  Define *ideologues* (paragraph 3), *anomaly* (paragraph 8), *modulated* (paragraph 9), *propensities* (paragraph 10), and *scrupulous* (paragraph 12). Why are the truths that brain sex researchers are uncovering both *impolitic* and *potent* (paragraph 13)?

5. MAKING CONNECTIONS:  Wade suggests that significant differences in the way men and women think might eventually be scientifically proven. If so, how could these differences be used by institutions such as the Citadel (discussed in Katha Pollitt's "The Future Is Coed," (p. 496), to argue for single-sex education? Explain your answer.

**Journal Prompts**

1. Do you have any personality traits or intellectual qualities that you feel are typically associated with the opposite sex? How do you feel about these traits?

2. Drawing on your own experience and observations, do you believe there are significant differences in the way men and women think? If so, do you think these differences are innate or the result of socialization? Explain.

**Suggestions for Writing**

1. Recall your own experience taking aptitude tests. In your opinion, did these tests accurately measure your abilities — or were they unfair because of gender bias? Write an essay explaining your responses to these tests, offering evidence to support your assessment of their fairness and accuracy.

2. According to Wade, "every parent knows . . . that boys and girls prefer different patterns of play regardless of well-meaning efforts to impose unisex toys on both" (paragraph 9). To test this assertion, spend some time observing young children at play and remembering your own childhood games. If possible, spend at least one session observing adult interaction with children at play. Do you notice or recall any gender differences in these games? If so, are there any factors other than biology that might account for the differences? Be specific.

# Chapter 24

# American Diversity

**Journal Prompt** Do you think it's possible to assimilate into American society while still maintaining a strong sense of one's ethnic, racial, or cultural heritage? Why or why not?

*Lydia Minatoya was born in 1950 in Albany, New York, to parents who had emigrated from Japan. After earning a Ph.D. in psychology from the University of Maryland in 1981, she taught at a university in Boston but left that job in 1983 to teach and travel in Japan, China, and Nepal. She currently works as a counselor at a community college in Seattle. In her book-length memoir,* Talking to High Monks in the Snow: An Asian-American Odyssey *(1992), which won the 1991 PEN/ Jerard Fund Award, Minatoya explores her cultural identity, beginning with her childhood in upstate New York and ending with her return to the United States from Asia. In the following chapter from her memoir, Minatoya recounts her childhood struggle to embrace the American dream of "Opportunity, Will, Transformation."*

## *Lydia Minatoya*    Transformation

Perhaps it begins with my naming. During her pregnancy, my mother 1 was reading Dr. Spock. "Children need to belong," he cautioned. "An unusual name can make them the subject of ridicule." My father frowned when he heard this. He stole a worried glance at my sister. Burdened by her Japanese name, Misa played unsuspectingly on the kitchen floor.

The Japanese know full well the dangers of conspicuousness. "The nail 2 that sticks out gets pounded down," cautions an old maxim. In America, Relocation was all the proof they needed.

And so it was, with great earnestness, my parents searched for a conven- 3 tional name. They wanted me to have the full true promise of America.

"I will ask my colleague Froilan," said my father. "He is the smartest man 4 I know."

"And he has poetic soul," said my mother, who cared about such things. 5

In due course, Father consulted Froilan. He gave Froilan his conditions 6 for suitability.

"First, if possible, the full name should be alliterative," said my father. 7 "Like Misa Minatoya." He closed his eyes and sang my sister's name. "Second, if not an alliteration, at least the name should have assonantal rhyme."

"Like Misa Minatoya?" said Froilan with a teasing grin. 8

"Exactly," my father intoned. He gave an emphatic nod. "Finally, most 9 importantly, the name must be readily recognizable as conventional." He peered at Froilan with hope. "Do you have any suggestions or ideas?"

Froilan, whose own American child was named Ricardito, thought 10 awhile.

"We already have selected the name for a boy," offered my Father. "Eu- 11 gene."

"Eugene?" wondered Froilan. "But it meets none of your conditions!" 12

"Eugene is a special case," said my father, "after Eugene, Oregon, and Eu- 13 gene O'Neill. The beauty of the Pacific Northwest, the power of a great writer."

"I see," said Froilan, who did not but who realized that this naming business would be more complex than he had anticipated. "How about Maria?"

"Too common," said my father. "We want a *conventional* name, not a common one."

"Hmmm," said Froilan, wondering what the distinction was. He thought some more and then brightened. "Lydia!" he declared. He rhymed the name with media. "Lydia for *la bonita infanta!*"

And so I received my uncommon conventional name. It really did not provide the camouflage my parents had anticipated. I remained unalterably alien. For Dr. Spock had been addressing *American* families, and in those days, everyone knew all real American families were white.

Call it denial, but many Japanese Americans never quite understood that the promise of America was not truly meant for them. They lived in horse stalls at the Santa Anita racetrack and said the Pledge of Allegiance daily. They rode to Relocation Camps under armed guard, labeled with numbered tags, and sang "The Star-Spangled Banner." They lived in deserts or swamps, ludicrously imprisoned — where would they run if they ever escaped — and formed garden clubs, and yearbook staffs, and citizen town meetings. They even elected beauty queens.

My mother practiced her okoto[1] and was featured in a recital. She taught classes in fashion design and her students mounted a show. Into exile she had carried an okoto and a sewing machine. They were her past and her future. She believed in Art and Technology.

My mother's camp was the third most populous city in the entire state of Wyoming. Across the barren lands, behind barbed wire, bloomed these little oases of democracy. The older generation bore the humiliation with pride. "*Kodomo no tame ni,*" they said. For the sake of the children. They thought that if their dignity was great, then their children would be spared. Call it valor. Call it bathos. Perhaps it was closer to slapstick: a sweet and bitter lunacy.

Call it adaptive behavior. Coming from a land swept by savage typhoons, ravaged by earthquakes and volcanoes, the Japanese have evolved a view of the world: a cooperative, stoic, almost magical way of thinking. Get along, work hard, and never quite see the things that can bring you pain. Against the tyranny of nature, of feudal lords, of wartime hysteria, the charm works equally well.

And so my parents gave me an American name and hoped that I could pass. They nourished me with the American dream: Opportunity, Will, Transformation.

When I was four and my sister was eight, Misa regularly used me as a comic foil. She would bring her playmates home from school and query me as I sat amidst the milk bottles on the front steps.

[1]**okota:** A thirteen stringed musical instrument, about two meters in length, played with fingers and a pick.

"What do you want to be when you grow up?" she would say. She would  24
nudge her audience into attentiveness.

"A mother kitty cat!" I would enthuse. Our cat had just delivered her first  25
litter of kittens and I was enchanted by the rasping tongue and soft mewings
of motherhood.

"And what makes you think you can become a cat?" Misa would prompt,  26
gesturing to her howling friends — wait for this; it gets better yet.

"This is America," I stoutly would declare. "I can grow up to be anything  27
that I want!"

My faith was unshakable. I believed. Opportunity. Will. Transformation.  28

When we lived in Albany, I always was the teachers' pet. "So tiny, so preco-  29
cious, so prettily dressed!" They thought I was a living doll and this was fine
with me.

My father knew that the effusive praise would die. He had been through  30
this with my sister. After five years of being a perfect darling, Misa had reached
the age where students were tracked by ability. Then, the anger started. Misa
had tested into the advanced track. It was impossible, the community declared. Misa was forbidden entry into advanced classes as long as there were
white children being placed below her. In her defense, before an angry
rabble, my father made a presentation to the Board of Education.

But I was too young to know of this. I knew only that my teachers praised  31
and petted me. They took me to other classes as an example. "Watch now, as
Lydia demonstrates attentive behavior," they would croon as I was led to an
empty desk at the head of the class. I had a routine. I would sit carefully,
spreading my petticoated skirt neatly beneath me. I would pull my chair close
to the desk, crossing my swinging legs at my snowy white anklets. I would
fold my hands carefully on the desk before me and stare pensively at the
blackboard.

This routine won me few friends. The sixth-grade boys threw rocks at me.  32
They danced around me in a tight circle, pulling at the corners of their eyes.
"Ching Chong Chinaman," they chanted. But teachers loved me. When I was
in first grade, a third-grade teacher went weeping to the principal. She begged
to have me skipped. She was leaving to get married and wanted her turn with
the dolly.

When we moved, the greatest shock was the knowledge that I had lost my  33
charm. From the first, my teacher failed to notice me. But to me, it did not
matter. I was in love. I watched her moods, her needs, her small vanities. I was
determined to ingratiate.

Miss Hempstead was a shimmering vision with a small upturned nose  34
and eyes that were kewpie doll blue. Slender as a sylph, she tripped around
the classroom, all saucy in her high-heeled shoes. Whenever I looked at Miss
Hempstead, I pitied the Albany teachers whom, formerly, I had adored. Poor
old Miss Rosenberg. With a shiver of distaste, I recalled her loose fleshy arms,
her mottled hands, the scent of lavender as she crushed me to her heavy
breasts.

Miss Hempstead had a pet of her own. Her name was Linda Sherlock. I    35
watched Linda closely and plotted Miss Hempstead's courtship. The key was
the piano. Miss Hempstead played the piano. She fancied herself a musical
star. She sang songs from Broadway revues and shaped her students' reactions. "Getting to know you," she would sing. We would smile at her in a
staged manner and position ourselves obediently at her feet.

Miss Hempstead was famous for her ability to soothe. Each day at rest    36
time, she played the piano and sang soporific songs. Linda Sherlock was the
only child who succumbed. Routinely, Linda's head would bend and nod until she crumpled gracefully onto her folded arms. A tousled strand of blonde
hair would fall across her forehead. Miss Hempstead would end her song,
would gently lower the keyboard cover. She would turn toward the restive
eyes of the class. "Isn't she sweetness itself!" Miss Hempstead would declare.
It made me want to vomit.

I was growning weary. My studiousness, my attentiveness, my fastidious    37
grooming and pert poise: all were failing me. I changed my tactics. I became
a problem. Miss Hempstead sent me home with nasty notes in sealed envelopes: Lydia is a slow child, a noisy child, her presence is disruptive. My
mother looked at me with surprise, "*Nani desu ka*? Are you having problems
with your teacher?" But I was tenacious. I pushed harder and harder, firmly
caught in the obsessive need of the scorned.

One day I snapped. As Miss Hempstead began to sing her wretched lulla-    38
bies, my head dropped to the desk with a powerful CRACK! It lolled there,
briefly, then rolled toward the edge with a momentum that sent my entire
body catapulting to the floor. Miss Hempstead's spine stretched slightly, like
a cat that senses danger. Otherwise, she paid no heed. The linoleum floor was
smooth and cool. It emitted a faint pleasant odor: a mixture of chalk dust and
wax.

I began to snore heavily. The class sat electrified. There would be no    39
drowsing today. The music went on and on. Finally, one boy could not stand
it. "Miss Hempstead," he probed plaintively, "Lydia has fallen asleep on the
floor!" Miss Hempstead did not turn. Her playing grew slightly strident but
she did not falter.

I lay on the floor through rest time. I lay on the floor through math drill.    40
I lay on the floor while my classmates scraped around me, pushing their
sturdy little wooden desks into the configuration for reading circle. It was not
until penmanship practice that I finally stretched and stirred. I rose like Sleeping Beauty and slipped back to my seat. I smiled enigmatically. A spell had
been broken. I never again had a crush on a teacher.

**Questions to Start**     1.  CONSIDERING MEANING:  What transformation did Minatoya experience? What
**You Thinking**                 prompted that transformation?

                           2.  IDENTIFYING WRITING STRATEGIES:  Where in the essay does Minatoya use humor
                                in her recollection of a fairly painful period of her life?

3. ANALYZING THE WRITER'S CHOICES: Minatoya characterizes the images of the Japanese who were "ludicrously imprisoned" (paragraph 18) in relocation camps as "slapstick" (paragraph 20). Why do you think she chooses to take an ironic view of such serious episodes of racism from her and her family's past? How effective do you find this approach?

4. EXPANDING VOCABULARY: Define *precocious* (paragraph 29), *effusive* (paragraph 30), *pensively* (paragraph 31), and *ingratiate* (paragraph 33). How are the words *fastidious*, *tenacious*, and *obsessive* (paragraph 37) related to Minatoya's transformation?

5. MAKING CONNECTIONS: What importance do both Minatoya and Joy Harjo ("Three Generations of Native American Women's Birth Experience," p. 471) place on the names given to children? From what they hint at in their essays, what cultural values are reflected in names?

**Journal Prompts**

1. Have you or anyone you know ever been teased or cruelly treated by others because of the name your parents gave you? Explain.

2. Have you ever wished you could transform yourself? Describe the transformation you desired. Did you achieve it? If not, do you still want to?

**Suggestions for Writing**

1. Recall an event or episode from elementary school that helped form your character. Use humor, if appropriate, to tell what happened, and explain how it helped shape who you are today or who you once were.

2. Research the Japanese internment during World War II. Do you think such a thing could ever happen again in this country? Write an essay explaining why or why not?

**Brent Staples,** *born in 1951 in Chester, Pennsylvania, earned a Ph.D. in psychology from the University of Chicago and worked for the* Chicago Sun Times *and* Down Beat *magazine before joining the* New York Times *in 1985. A member of the* Times *editorial board, he has contributed to many publications and is the author of the memoir* Parallel Time: Growing Up in Black and White *(1994). In the following essay, published in a slightly different version in* Ms. *magazine in September 1986, Staples reflects on the anxiety his presence arouses in nighttime pedestrians.*

## *Brent Staples*    **Black Men and Public Space**

My first victim was a woman — white, well dressed, probably in her late twenties. I came upon her late one evening on a deserted street in Hyde Park, a relatively affluent neighborhood in an otherwise mean, impoverished section of Chicago. As I swung onto the avenue behind her, there seemed to be a discreet, uninflammatory distance between us. Not so. She cast back a worried glance. To her, the youngish black man — a broad six feet two inches with a beard and billowing hair, both hands shoved into the pockets of a bulky military jacket — seemed menacingly close. After a few more quick glimpses, she picked up her pace and was soon running in earnest. Within seconds, she disappeared into a cross street.

That was more than a decade ago. I was twenty-two years old, a graduate student newly arrived at the University of Chicago. It was in the echo of that terrified woman's footfalls that I first began to know the unwieldy inheritance I'd come into — the ability to alter public space in ugly ways. It was clear that she thought herself the quarry of a mugger, a rapist, or worse. Suffering a bout of insomnia, however, I was stalking sleep, not defenseless wayfarers. As a softy who is scarcely able to take a knife to a raw chicken — let alone hold one to a person's throat — I was surprised, embarrassed, and dismayed all at once. Her flight made me feel like an accomplice in tyranny. It also made it clear that I was indistinguishable from the muggers who occasionally seeped into the area from the surrounding ghetto. The first encounter, and those that followed, signified that a vast, unnerving gulf lay between nighttime pedestrians — particularly women — and me. And I soon gathered that being perceived as dangerous is a hazard in itself. I only needed to turn a corner into a dicey situation, or crowd some frightened, armed person in a foyer somewhere, or make an errant move after being pulled over by a policeman. Where fear and weapons meet — and they often do in urban America — there is always the possibility of death.

In that first year, my first away from my hometown, I was to become thoroughly familiar with the language of fear. At dark, shadowy intersections, I could cross in front of a car stopped at a traffic light and elicit the *thunk, thunk, thunk, thunk* of the driver — black, white, male, or female — hammering down the door locks. On less traveled streets after dark, I grew accustomed to but never comfortable with people crossing to the other side of the street rather than pass me. Then there were the standard unpleasantries with policemen, doormen, bouncers, cabdrivers, and others whose business it is to screen out troublesome individuals *before* there is any nastiness.

I moved to New York nearly two years ago and I have remained an avid night walker. In central Manhattan, the near-constant crowd cover minimizes tense one-on-one street encounters. Elsewhere — in SoHo, for example, where sidewalks are narrow and tightly spaced buildings shut out the sky — things can get very taut indeed.

After dark, on the warrenlike streets of Brooklyn where I live, I often see women who fear the worst from me. They seem to have set their faces on neutral, and with their purse straps strung across their chests bandolier-style, they forge ahead as though bracing themselves against being tackled. I understand, of course, that the danger they perceive is not a hallucination. Women are particularly vulnerable to street violence, and young black males are drastically overrepresented among the perpetrators of that violence. Yet these truths are no solace against the kind of alienation that comes of being ever the suspect, a fearsome entity with whom pedestrians avoid making eye contact.

It is not altogether clear to me how I reached the ripe old age of twenty-two without being conscious of the lethality nighttime pedestrians attributed to me. Perhaps it was because in Chester, Pennsylvania, the small, angry industrial town where I came of age in the 1960s, I was scarcely noticeable against a backdrop of gang warfare, street knifings, and murders. I grew up one of the good boys, had perhaps a half-dozen fistfights. In retrospect, my shyness of combat has clear sources.

As a boy, I saw countless tough guys locked away; I have since buried several, too. They were babies, really — a teenage cousin, a brother of twenty-two, a childhood friend in his mid-twenties — all gone down in episodes of bravado played out in the streets. I came to doubt the virtues of intimidation early on. I chose, perhaps unconsciously, to remain a shadow — timid, but a survivor. 7

The fearsomeness mistakenly attributed to me in public places often has a perilous flavor. The most frightening of these confusions occurred in the late 1970s and early 1980s, when I worked as a journalist in Chicago. One day, rushing into the office of a magazine I was writing for with a deadline story in hand, I was mistaken for a burglar. The office manager called security and, with an ad hoc posse, pursued me through the labyrinthine halls, nearly to my editor's door. I had no way of proving who I was. I could only move briskly toward the company of someone who knew me. 8

Another time I was on assignment for a local paper and killing time before an interview. I entered a jewelry store on the city's affluent Near North Side. The proprietor excused himself and returned with an enormous red Doberman pinscher straining at the end of a leash. She stood, the dog extended toward me, silent to my questions, her eyes bulging nearly out of her head. I took a cursory look around, nodded, and bade her good night. 9

Relatively speaking, however, I never fared as badly as another black male journalist. He went to nearby Waukegan, Illinois, a couple of summers ago to work on a story about a murderer who was born there. Mistaking the reporter for the killer, police officers hauled him from his car at gunpoint and but for his press credentials would probably have tried to book him. Such episodes are not uncommon. Black men trade tales like this all the time. 10

Over the years, I learned to smother the rage I felt at so often being taken for a criminal. Not to do so would surely have led to madness. I now take precautions to make myself less threatening. I move about with care, particularly late in the evening. I give a wide berth to nervous people on subway platforms during the wee hours, particularly when I have exchanged business clothes for jeans. If I happen to be entering a building behind some people who appear skittish, I may walk by, letting them clear the lobby before I return, so as not to seem to be following them. I have been calm and extremely congenial on those rare occasions when I've been pulled over by the police. 11

And on late-evening constitutionals I employ what has proved to be an excellent tension-reducing measure: I whistle melodies from Beethoven and Vivaldi and the more popular classical composers. Even steely New Yorkers hunching toward nighttime destinations seem to relax, and occasionally they even join in the tune. Virtually everybody seems to sense that a mugger wouldn't be warbling bright, sunny selections from Vivaldi's *Four Seasons*. It 12 is my equivalent of the cowbell that hikers wear when they know they are in bear country.

**Questions to Start You Thinking**

1. CONSIDERING MEANING:  How does Staples react to other people's misconceptions about him? What does he feel causes such misconceptions?

2. IDENTIFYING WRITING STRATEGIES:  At the end of the essay, how does Staples use comparison to explain his behavior?

3. ANALYZING THE WRITER'S CHOICES:  Why do you think this essay first appeared in *Ms.*, a magazine with a feminist readership? Where does Staples acknowledge and indicate that he respects the views of his audience? Do you think this approach contributes to or detracts from the impact of his essay?

4. EXPANDING VOCABULARY: Define *affluent, uninflammatory* (paragraph 1), *unwieldy, quarry, errant* (paragraph 2), *bandolier, solace* (paragraph 5), *lethality* (paragraph 6), and *bravado* (paragraph 7). Why do you think Staples uses such formal language in this essay?

5. MAKING CONNECTIONS:  Staples attempts to counter stereotypes of African American men by whistling "melodies from . . . the more popular classical composers" (paragraph 12). Compare and contrast this response to stereotyping with the one described by Gerald Early in "Black like . . . Shirley Temple?" (p. 468).

**Journal Prompts**

1. Recall a time when a person or group of people made you feel uncomfortable or afraid in a particular setting. Why were you afraid? How did you deal with your fear?

2. Recall a time when you attempted to intimidate or scare someone else. Why did you do it? How did the other person respond?

**Suggestions for Writing**

1. Staples describes his feelings about being the object of racial fear. Have you ever been the object of such a fear or of other misconceptions based on prejudice or stereotypes? Write a short personal essay discussing the causes and effects of your experience. What preconceptions were you the victim of? How did you respond?

2. How are African American men stereotyped in our society? How accurate are these stereotypes? Write an essay evaluating the typical view of the African American man in the United States. Use examples from Staples's essay and your own experiences as the basis for your evaluation.

**Michael Dorris,** *born in 1945 in Dayton, Washington, has been deeply influenced by his background as an American Indian and by his decision to become an adoptive single father. With degrees from Georgetown and Yale Universities, Dorris has taught Native American studies and anthropology at Dartmouth College since 1972. His writings, many of which have won awards, include the novel* A Yellow Raft in Blue Water *(1987); the novel* The Crown of Columbus *(1991), coauthored with his wife, Louise Erdrich; the short-story collection* Working Men *(1993); and sev-*

*eral children's books. His autobiographical work* The Broken Cord *(1989) focuses on his relationship with his son Adam, who suffered the aftereffects of fetal alcohol syndrome. In the following selection, taken from the essay collection* Paper Trail *(1994), Dorris criticizes the way the image of American Indians is used in popular culture.*

## *Michael Dorris*    Crazy Horse Malt Liquor

People of proclaimed good will have the oddest ways of honoring American Indians. Sometimes they dress themselves up in turkey feathers and paint to boogie on fifty-yard lines. Sometimes otherwise impeccably credentialed liberals get so swept up into honoring that they beat fake tom-toms or fashion their forearms and hands in to facsimiles of axes European traders used for barter and attempt, unsuccessfully, to chop their way to victory. Presumably they hope that this exuberant if ethnographically questionable display will do their teams more good against opponents than those rituals they imitate and mock did for nineteenth-century Cheyenne or Nez Percé men and women who tried, with desperation and ultimate futility, to defend their homelands from invasion.

Everywhere you look such respects are paid: the street names in woodsy, affluent subdivisions, mumbo jumbo in ersatz male-bonding weekends and Boy Scout jamborees, geometric fashion statements, weepy antilittering public service announcements. In the ever popular noble/savage spectrum, red is the hot, safe color.

For five hundred years flesh and blood Indians have been assigned the role of a popular culture metaphor. Today, they evoke fuzzy images of Nature, The Past, Plight, or Summer Camp. War-bonneted apparitions pasted to football helmets or baseball caps act as opaque, impermeable curtains, solid walls of white noise that for many citizens block or distort all vision of the nearly two million contemporary Native Americans. And why not? Such honoring relegates Indians to the long ago and thus makes them magically disappear from public consciousness and conscience. What do the three hundred federally recognized tribes — with their various complicated treaties governing land rights and protections, their crippling unemployment, infant mortality, and teenage suicide rates, their often chronic poverty, their manifold health problems — have in common with jolly (or menacing) cartoon caricatures, wistful braves, or raven-tressed Mazola girls?

Perhaps we should ask the Hornell Brewing Company of Baltimore, manufactures of The Original Crazy Horse Malt Liquor, a product currently distributed in New York with packaging inspired by, according to the text on the back, "the Black Hills of Dakota, *steeped* [my italics] in the History of the American West, home of Proud Indian Nations, a land where imagination conjures up images of blue clad Pony Soldiers and magnificent Native American Warriors."

Whose imagination? Were these the same blue-clad lads who perpetrated ⁵ the 1890 massacre of two hundred captured, freezing Lakota at Wounded Knee? Are Pine Ridge and Rosebud, the two reservations closest to the Black Hills and, coincidentally, the two counties in the United States with the lowest per capita incomes, the Proud Nations? Is the "steeping" a bald allusion to the fact that alcohol has long constituted the number one health hazard to Indians? Virtually every other social ill plaguing Native Americans — from disproportionately frequent traffic fatalities to arrest statistics — is related in some tragic respect to ethanol, and many tribes, from Alaska to New Mexico, record the highest percentage in the world of babies born disabled by fetal alcohol syndrome and fetal alcohol effect. One need look no further than the warning label to pregnant women printed in capital letters on every Crazy Horse label to make the connection.

The facts of history are not hard to ascertain: the Black Hills, the *paha* ⁶ *sapa*, the traditional holy place of the Lakota, were illegally seized by the U.S. government, systematically stripped of their mineral wealth — and have still not been returned to their owners. Crazy Horse, in addition to being a patriot to his people, was a mystic and a religious leader murdered after he voluntarily gave himself up in 1887 to Pony Soldiers at Fort Robinson, Nebraska. What, then, is the pairing of his name with forty ounces of malt liquor supposed to signify?

The Hornell brewers helpfully supply a clue. The detail of the logo is focused on the headdress and not the face; it's pomp without circumstance, ⁷ form without content. Wear the hat, the illustration seems to offer, and in the process fantasize yourself more interesting (or potent or tough or noble) than you are. Play at being a "warrior" from the "land that truly speaks of the spirit that is America."

And if some humorless Indians object, just set them straight. Remind ⁸ them what an honor it is to be used.

<table>
<tr><td>

**Questions to Start You Thinking**

</td><td>

1. CONSIDERING MEANING:  Identify the reasons Dorris feels that pairing the name Crazy Horse with a forty-ounce bottle of malt liquor is inappropriate.

2. IDENTIFYING WRITING STRATEGIES:  Where does Dorris use comparison and contrast to evaluate popular culture images of Native Americans?

3. ANALYZING THE WRITER'S CHOICES:  Do you think Dorris's sarcastic tone strengthens or weakens his argument? Why do you think he chose this approach in addressing his readers, many of whom may have previously been comfortable with the popular Native American images he is denouncing?

4. EXPANDING VOCABULARY:  What are *apparitions* (paragraph 3), and how do they create "solid walls of *white noise*" (paragraph 3)? How are these walls *impermeable* (paragraph 3)?

5. MAKING CONNECTIONS:  Compare and contrast this essay with Toni Morrison's ("On the Backs of Blacks," p. 528). What point does each writer make about racial identity and the dominant culture?

</td></tr>
<tr><td>

**Journal Prompts**

</td><td>

1. List as many uses of a Native American word or custom that you can think of. In your opinion why are these words and customs popular?

</td></tr>
</table>

2. Growing up, did you ever play or observe others playing the make-believe game of "cowboys and Indians"? How was the role of Indian played? In your observation or experiences, do children today play the game the same way?

**Suggestions for Writing**

1. As a child, what images did you have of a racial or ethnic group with which you were unfamiliar? What effect did images from popular culture have on your perceptions of that group? Have your views changed over time? If so, what do you think caused the change?

2. Do you think it is right for sports teams to name themselves after Native American tribes and to use the rituals of these tribes in cheers and halftime activities? Take a stand on this issue and write an argumentative essay clearly presenting your opinion.

**Richard Rodriguez,** *born in 1944 in San Francisco, could speak only fifty words of English when his parents enrolled him in a Catholic grammar school in Sacramento, California. But Rodriguez proceeded to earn a B.A. at Stanford University in 1967 and an M.A. in philosophy at Columbia University as well as a Ph.D. in English Renaissance literature from the University of California at Berkeley. He now works as an editor at Pacific News Service in San Francisco, as an essayist on* The MacNeil-Lehrer News Hour, *and as a contributing editor for* Harper's *magazine and for the Opinion section of the* Los Angeles Times. *In his best-known work,* Hunger of Memory: The Education of Richard Rodriguez *(1982), Rodriguez uses his own experience to support his opposition to bilingual education. His book of essays* Days of Obligation: An Argument with My Mexican Father *(1993) was nominated for the Pulitzer Prize in nonfiction. In the following essay, which appeared in* Harper's *in March 1984, Rodriguez uses examples from his experience as a child of immigrant parents to evaluate the importance of assimilation and diversity to American culture and to answer the question "Does America still exist?"*

## *Richard Rodriguez*    **Does America Still Exist?**

For the children of immigrant parents the knowledge comes easier. America exists everywhere in the city — on billboards, frankly in the smell of French fries and popcorn. It exists in the pace: traffic lights, the assertions of neon, the mysterious bong-bong-bong through the atriums of department stores. America exists as the voice of the crowd, a menacing sound — the high nasal accent of American English.

When I was a boy in Sacramento (California, the fifties), people would ask me, "Where you from?" I was born in this country, but I knew the question meant to decipher my darkness, my looks.

My mother once instructed me to say, "I am an American of Mexican descent." By the time I was nine or ten, I wanted to say, but dared not reply, "I am an American."

Immigrants come to America and, against hostility or mere loneliness, they re-create a homeland in the parlor, tacking up postcards or calendars of some impossible blue — lake or sea or sky. Children of immigrant parents are supposed to perch on a hyphen between two countries. Relatives assume the achievement as much as anyone. Relatives are, in any case, surprised when the child begins losing old ways. One day at the family picnic the boy wanders away from their spiced food and faceless stories to watch other boys play baseball in the distance.

There is sorrow in the American memory, guilty sorrow for having left something behind — Portugal, China, Norway. The American story is the story of immigrant children and of their children — children no longer able to speak to grandparents. The memory of exile becomes inarticulate as it passes from generation to generation, along with wedding rings and pocket watches — like some mute stone in a wad of old lace. Europe. Asia. Eden.

But, it needs to be said, if this is a country where one stops being Vietnamese or Italian, this is a country where one begins to be an American. America exists as a culture and a grin, a faith and a shrug. It is clasped in a handshake, called by a first name.

As much as the country is joined in a common culture, however, Americans are reluctant to celebrate the process of assimilation. We pledge allegiance to diversity. America was born Protestant and bred Puritan, and the notion of community we share is derived from a seventeenth-century faith. Presidents and the pages of ninth-grade civics readers yet proclaim the orthodoxy: We are gathered together — but as individuals, with separate pasts, distinct destinies. Our society is as paradoxical as a Puritan congregation: We stand together, alone.

Americans have traditionally defined themselves by what they refused to include. As often, however, Americans have struggled, turned in good conscience at last to assert the great Protestant virtue of tolerance. Despite outbreaks of nativist frenzy, America has remained an immigrant country, open and true to itself.

Against pious emblems of rural America — soda fountain, Elks hall, Protestant church, and now shopping mall — stands the cold-hearted city, crowded with races and ambitions, curious laughter, much that is odd. Nevertheless, it is the city that has most truly represented America. In the city, however, the millions of singular lives have had no richer notion of wholeness to describe them than the idea of pluralism.

*"Where you from?" the American asks the immigrant child. "Mexico," the boy learns to say.*

Mexico, the country of my blood ancestors, offers formal contrast to the American achievement. If the United States was formed by Protestant individualism, Mexico was shaped by a medieval Catholic dream of one world. The Spanish journeyed to Mexico to plunder, and they may have gone, in God's name, with an arrogance peculiar to those who intend to convert. But through the conversion, the Indian converted the Spaniard. A new race was born, the *mestizo*, wedding European to Indian. José Vasconcelos, the Mexican philosopher, has celebrated this New World creation, proclaiming it the "cosmic race."

Centuries later, in a San Francisco restaurant, a Mexican-American lawyer of my acquaintance says, in English, over *salade niçoise,* that he does not intend to assimilate into gringo society. His claim is echoed by a chorus of others (Italian-Americans, Greeks, Asians) in this era of ethnic pride. The melting pot has been retired, clanking, into the museum of quaint disgrace, alongside Aunt Jemima and the Katzenjammer Kids.[1] But resistance to assimilation is characteristically American. It only makes clear how inevitable the process of assimilation actually is.

For generations, this has been the pattern. Immigrant parents have sent their children to school (simply, they thought) to acquire the "skills" to survive in the city. The child returned home with a voice his parents barely recognized or understood, couldn't trust, and didn't like.

In eastern cities — Philadelphia, New York, Boston, Baltimore — class after class gathered immigrant children to women (usually women) who stood in front of rooms full of children, changing children. So also for me in the 1950s. Irish-Catholic nuns, California. The old story. The hyphen tipped to the right, away from Mexico and toward a confusing but true American identity.

I speak now in the chromium American accent of my grammar school classmates — Billy Reckers, Mike Bradley, Carol Schmidt, Kathy O'Grady. . . . I believe I became like my classmates, became German, Polish, and (like my teachers) Irish. And because assimilation is always reciprocal, my classmates got something of me. (I mean sad eyes; belief in the Indian Virgin; a taste for sugar skulls on the Feast of the Dead.) In the blending, we became what our parents could never have been, and we carried America one revolution further.

"Does America still exist?" Americans have been asking the question for so long that to ask it again only proves our continuous link. But perhaps the question deserves to be asked with urgency now. Since the black civil rights movement of the 1960s, our tenuous notion of a shared public life has deteriorated notably.

The struggle of black men and women did not eradicate racism, but it became the great moment in the life of America's conscience. Water hoses, bulldogs, blood — the images, rendered black, white, rectangular, passed into living rooms.

It is hard to look at a photograph of a crowd taken, say in 1890 or in 1930 and not notice the absence of blacks. (It becomes an impertinence to wonder if America *still* exists.)

In the sixties, other groups of Americans learned to champion their rights by analogy to the black civil rights movement. But the heroic vision faded. Dr. Martin Luther King, Jr., had spoken with Pauline eloquence[2] of a nation that would unite Christian and Jew, old and young, rich and poor. Within a

---

[1] **Katzenjammer Kids:** Early comic strip and silent film series about German children.
[2] **Pauline eloquence:** Refers to Saint Paul's rhetorical powers.

decade, the struggles of the 1960s were reduced to a bureaucratic competition for little more than pieces of a representational pie. The quest for a portion of power became an end in itself. The metaphor for the American city of the 1970s was a committee: one black, one woman, one person under thirty . . .

If the small town had sinned against America by too neatly defining who        20
could be an American, the city's sin was a romantic secession. One noticed the romanticism in the antiwar movement — certain demonstrators who demonstrated a lack of tact or desire to persuade and seemed content to play secular protestants. One noticed the romanticism in the competition among members of "minority groups" to claim the status of Primary Victim. To Americans unconfident of their common identity, minority standing became a way of asserting individuality. Middle-class Americans — men and women clearly not the primary victims of social oppression — brandished their suffering with exuberance.

The dream of a single society probably died with *The Ed Sullivan Show.*      21
The reality of America persists. Teenagers pass through big-city high schools banded in racial groups, their collars turned up to a uniform shrug. But then they graduate to jobs at the phone company or in banks, where they end up working alongside people unlike themselves. Typists and tellers walk out together at lunchtime.

It is easier for us as Americans to believe the obvious fact of our separate-   22
ness — easier to imagine the black and white Americas prophesied by the Kerner report[3] (broken glass, street fires) — than to recognize the reality of a city street at lunchtime. Americans are wedded by proximity to a common culture. The panhandler at one corner is related to the pamphleteer at the next who is related to the banker who is kin to the Chinese old man wearing an MIT sweatshirt. In any true national history, Thomas Jefferson begets Martin Luther King, Jr., who begets the Gray Panthers.[4] It is because we lack a vision of ourselves entire — the city street is crowded and we are each preoccupied with finding our own way home — that we lack an appropriate hymn.

Under my window now passes a little white girl softly rehearsing to her-       23
self a Motown obbligato.

**Questions to Start You Thinking**

1. CONSIDERING MEANING:  Is Rodriguez's answer to the title question yes or no? Briefly explain why. What does he mean by *America*?

2. IDENTIFYING WRITING STRATEGIES:  How does Rodriguez use specific examples and sensory details to support his analysis of American culture?

3. ANALYZING THE WRITER'S CHOICES:  Why does Rodriguez use so many different examples of national origins, heritages, and names? How do these examples support his thesis about assimilation and cultural diversity?

4. EXPANDING VOCABULARY:  Look up the dictionary definitions of *nativist* (para-

[3] **Kerner report:** A 1968 report on racial unrest in America by the President's National Advisory Commission on Civil Disorders.
[4] **Gray Panthers:** A national organization that promotes the rights and welfare of senior citizens.

graph 8), *pluralism* (paragraph 9), *assimilation* (paragraph 12), and *secession* (paragraph 20). What do these words mean in the context of Rodriguez's essay?

5. MAKING CONNECTIONS: Compare and contrast Rodriguez's attitude toward American identity with that of Toni Morrison ("On the Backs of Blacks," p. 528).

**Journal Prompts**

1. List and describe the images that come to mind when you think of "America."

2. Do you consider the city, the town, or the country most "American"? Compare and contrast the characteristics that make each one American.

**Suggestions for Writing**

1. Write a brief personal essay explaining how your family's heritage has shaped your experiences of America.

2. Using Rodriguez's ideas as a springboard, write a response to the question "Does America still exist?" How do you define *America*? What, in your opinion, are the most important factors in American culture today? How important are people's national or cultural origins to their participation in American culture?

**Toni Morrison,** *born Chloe Anthony Wofford in 1931 in Lorain, Ohio, received a B.A. from Howard University in 1953 and an M.A. from Cornell University. She has held teaching positions at Rutgers, Howard, and Yale Universities and is currently a professor at Princeton University. Morrison has written six novels:* The Bluest Eye *(1970),* Sula *(1973),* Song of Solomon *(1977),* Tar Baby *(1981),* Beloved *(1986), and* Jazz *(1992). She is also the author of* Playing in the Dark: Whiteness and the Literary Imagination *(1992) and the editor of* Race-ing Justice, Engendering Power *(1992), two collections of essays. Among Morrison's numerous awards are the 1988 Pulitzer Prize for* Beloved *and the 1993 Nobel Prize for literature. In the following article, published in a special Fall 1993 issue of* Time *magazine, Morrison argues that learning contempt for blacks is a fundamental though deplorable part of the immigrant's experience of becoming an American.*

## *Toni Morrison*   On the Backs of Blacks

Fresh from Ellis Island, Stavros gets a job shining shoes at Grand Central Terminal. It is the last scene of Elia Kazan's film *America, America,* the story of a young Greek's fierce determination to immigrate to America. Quickly, but as casually as an afterthought, a young black man, also a shoe shiner, enters and tries to solicit a customer. He is run off the screen — "Get out of here! We're doing business here!" — and silently disappears.

This interloper into Stavros's workplace is crucial in the mix of signs that make up the movie's happy-ending immigrant story: a job, a straw hat, an infectious smile — and a scorned black. It is the act of racial contempt that transforms this charming Greek into an entitled white. Without it, Stavros's future as an American is not at all assured.

This is race talk, the explicit insertion into everyday life of racial signs and symbols that have no meaning other than pressing African Americans to the lowest level of the racial hierarchy. Popular culture, shaped by film, theater, advertising, the press, television, and literature, is heavily engaged in race talk. It participates freely in this most enduring and efficient rite of passage into American culture: negative appraisals of the native-born black population. Only when the lesson of racial estrangement is learned is assimilation complete. Whatever the lived experience of immigrants with African Americans — pleasant, beneficial, or bruising — the rhetorical experience renders blacks as noncitizens, already discredited outlaws.

All immigrants fight for jobs and space, and who is there to fight but those who have both? As in the fishing ground struggle between Texas and Vietnamese shrimpers, they displace what and whom they can. Although U.S. history is awash in labor battles, political fights, and property wars among all religious and ethnic groups, their struggles are persistently framed as struggles between recent arrivals and blacks. In race talk the move into mainstream America always means buying into the notion of American blacks as the real aliens. Whatever the ethnicity or nationality of the immigrant, his nemesis is understood to be African American.

Current attention to immigration has reached levels of panic not seen since the turn of the century. To whip up this panic, modern race talk must be revised downward into obscurity and nonsense if antiblack hostility is to remain the drug of choice, giving headlines their kick. PATTERNS OF IMMIGRATION FOLLOWED BY WHITE FLIGHT, screams the *Star-Ledger* in Newark. The message we are meant to get is that disorderly newcomers are dangerous to stable (white) residents. Stability is white. Disorder is black. Nowhere do we learn what stable middle-class blacks think or do to cope with the "breaking waves of immigration." The overwhelming majority of African Americans, hardworking and stable, are out of the loop, disappeared except in their less than covert function of defining whites as the "true" Americans.

So addictive is this ploy that the fact of blackness has been abandoned for the theory of blackness. It doesn't matter anymore what shade the newcomer's skin is. A hostile posture toward resident blacks must be struck at the Americanizing door before it will open. The public is asked to accept American blacks as the common denominator in each conflict between an immigrant and a job or between a wannabe and status. It hardly matters what complexities, contexts, and misinformation accompany these conflicts. They can all be subsumed as the equation of brand X vs. blacks.

But more than a job is at stake in this surrender to whiteness, more even than what the black intellectual W. E. B. Du Bois called the "psychological wage" — the bonus of whiteness. Racist strategies unify. Savvy politicians always include in the opening salvos of their campaigns a quick clarification of their position on race. It is a mistake to think that Bush's Willie Horton or

Clinton's Sister Souljah[1] was anything but a candidate's obligatory response to the demands of a contentious electorate unable to understand itself in any terms other than race. Warring interests, nationalities, and classes can be merged with the greatest economy under that racial banner.

Race talk as bonding mechanism is powerfully on display in American literature. When Nick in F. Scott Fitzgerald's *The Great Gatsby* leaves West Egg to dine in fashionable East Egg, his host conducts a kind of class audition into WASP-dom by soliciting Nick's support for the "science" of racism. "If we don't look out the white race will be . . . utterly submerged," he says. "It's all scientific stuff; it's been proved." It makes Nick uneasy, but he does not question or refute his host's convictions.    8

The best clue to what the country might be like without race as the nail upon which American identity is hung comes from Pap, in Mark Twain's *Huckleberry Finn*, who upon learning a Negro could vote in Ohio, "drawed out. I says I'll never vote ag'in." Without his glowing white mask he is not American; he is Faulkner's character Wash, in *Absalom, Absalom!*, who, stripped of the mask and treated like a "nigger," drives a scythe into the heart of the rich white man he has loved and served so completely.    9

For Pap, for Wash, the possibility that race talk might signify nothing was frightening. Which may be why the harder it is to speak race talk convincingly, the more people seem to need it. As American blacks occupy more and more groups no longer formed along racial lines, the pressure accelerates to figure out what white interests really are. The enlisted military is almost one-quarter black; police forces are blackening in large urban areas. But welfare is nearly two-thirds white; affirmative-action beneficiaries are overwhelmingly white women; dysfunctional white families jam the talk shows and court TV.    10

The old stereotypes fail to connote, and race talk is forced to invent new, increasingly mindless ones. There is virtually no movement up — for blacks or whites, established classes or arrivistes — that is not accompanied by race talk. Refusing, negotiating, or fulfilling this demand is the real stuff, the organizing principle of becoming an American. Star spangled. Race strangled.    11

**Questions to Start You Thinking**

1. CONSIDERING MEANING:  What is "race talk" (paragraphs 3, 4, 5, 8, 10, and 11)? According to Morrison, how is race talk part of the "rite of passage into American culture" (paragraph 3)?

2. IDENTIFYING WRITING STRATEGIES:  How does Morrison use cause and effect in this essay?

3. ANALYZING THE WRITER'S CHOICES:  How does Morrison use her reading of Amer-

[1] **Willie Horton . . . Sister Souljah:** During the 1988 presidential race, George Bush's campaign was accused of racism when it tried to portray Michael Dukakis as "soft on crime" by prominently featuring Willie Horton in a TV ad. Horton was a convicted African American murderer who raped a woman and stabbed a man while released on Massachusetts's controversial prison furlough program. During the 1992 Democratic presidential primary campaign, Bill Clinton criticized rap singer Sister Souljah for making comments that endorsed the Los Angeles riots as revenge for racial injustice. African American Democratic opponent Jesse Jackson took issue with Clinton's comments.

ican literature to show how important "race talk" is to the American identity? Considering the intended audience for this essay, which appeared in *Time*, a relatively conservative newsmagazine, why do you think Morrison cites examples from three white authors in the American literary canon?

4. EXPANDING VOCABULARY: What is *racial estrangement, assimilation, lived experience,* and *rhetorical experience* (paragraph 3)? According to Morrison, how are these terms related to one another?

5. MAKING CONNECTIONS: Compare and contrast the views of Morrison and Michael Dorris ("Crazy Horse Malt Liquor," p. 522) on the idea that popular culture creates racial estrangement.

**Journal Prompts**

1. In your opinion how does an individual become an American? Describe the process, drawing from your observation or experience.

2. What films and television shows do you think best represent "the overwhelming majority of African Americans" (paragraph 5)?

**Suggestions for Writing**

1. Write a personal response to Morrison's essay. Support or refute her key points, drawing examples from your own experience, observations, and reading.

2. In paragraphs 8 and 9 Morrison refers to several literary works to illustrate the relationship between race and American identity. Continue her analysis, discussing how any of the works she mentions or other relevant literary works relates race to American identity.

**Stephen Jay Gould,** *born in 1941 in New York City, may be the most creative and widely read scientist of our times. An evolutionary biologist, Gould was trained in geology and paleontology at Antioch College and at Columbia University. Since 1967 he has taught at Harvard University and has written prolifically for a general audience. Gould's gift for making science and the history of science entertaining and accessible to all readers is evident in his many critically acclaimed books, which include* Ever since Darwin *(1977),* The Mismeasure of Man *(1981),* Bully for Brontosaurus *(1992),* Eight Little Piggies *(1993), and his latest essay collection,* Finders, Keepers: Treasures and Oddities of Natural History Collectors *(1994). In* "The Geometer of Race," *published in the November 1994 issue of* Discover *magazine, Gould traces the history of our current racial classification system, which he identifies as one of the most destructive misuses of science in human history.*

## Stephen Jay Gould    The Geometer of Race

Interesting stories often lie encoded in names that seem either capricious 1
or misconstrued. Why, for example, are political radicals called "left" and
their conservative counterparts "right"? In many European legislatures, the
most distinguished members sat at the chairman's right, following a custom
of courtesy as old as our prejudices for favoring the dominant hand of most
people. (These biases run deep, extending well beyond can openers and scissors to language itself, where *dexterous* stems from the Latin for "right," and
*sinister* from the word for "left.") Since these distinguished nobles and moguls
tended to espouse conservative views, the right and left wings of the legisla-
ture came to define a geometry of political views.

Among such apparently capricious names in my own field of biology and 2
evolution, none seems more curious, and none elicits more questions after
lectures, than the official designation of light-skinned people in Europe,
western Asia, and North Africa as Caucasian. Why should the most common
racial group of the Western world be named for a mountain range that
straddles Russia and Georgia? Johann Friedrich Blumenbach (1752–1840),
the German anatomist and naturalist who established the most influential of
all racial classifications, invented this name in 1795, in the third edition of his
seminal work, *De Generis Humani Varietate Nativa* (On the Natural Variety of
Mankind). Blumenbach's definition cites two reasons for his choice — the
maximal beauty of people from this small region, and the probability that humans were first created in this area.

> Caucasian variety. I have taken the name of this variety from Mount Cauca-
> sus, both because its neighborhood, and especially its southern slope, pro-
> duces the most beautiful race of men, I mean the Georgian; and because . . .
> in that region, if anywhere, it seems we ought with the greatest probability to
> place the autochthones [original forms] of mankind.

Blumenbach, one of the greatest and most honored scientists of the En- 3
lightenment,[1] spent his entire career as a professor at the University of Göttingen in Germany. He first presented *De Generis Humani Varietate Nativa* as
a doctoral dissertation to the medical faculty of Göttingen in 1775, as the
Minutemen of Lexington and Concord began the American Revolution. He
then republished the text for general distribution in 1776, as a fateful meeting in Philadelphia proclaimed our independence. The coincidence of three
great documents in 1776 — Jefferson's Declaration of Independence (on the
politics of liberty), Adam Smith's *Wealth of Nations* (on the economics of individualism), and Blumenbach's treatise on racial classification (on the science of human diversity) — records the social ferment of these decades and
sets the wider context that makes Blumenbach's taxonomy, and his subse-

[1] **Enlightenment:** Term applied to the main current of intellectual thought in eighteenth-century Europe and America, characterized by an emphasis on rationalism and
progress.

quent decision to call the European race Caucasian, so important for our history and current concerns.

The solution to big puzzles often hinges upon tiny curiosities, easy to miss or to pass over. I suggest that the key to understanding Blumenbach's classification, the foundation of much that continues to influence and disturb us today, lies in the peculiar criterion he used to name the European race Caucasian — the supposed superior beauty of people from this region. Why, first of all, should a scientist attach such importance to an evidently subjective assessment; and why, secondly, should an aesthetic criterion become the basis of a scientific judgment about place of origin? To answer these questions, we must compare Blumenbach's original 1775 text with the later edition of 1795, when Caucasians received their name.

Blumenbach's final taxonomy of 1795 divided all humans into five groups, defined both by geography and appearance — in his order, the Caucasian variety, for the light-skinned people of Europe and adjacent parts of Asia and Africa; the Mongolian variety, for most other inhabitants of Asia, including China and Japan; the Ethiopian variety, for the dark-skinned people of Africa; the American variety, for most native populations of the New World, and the Malay variety, for the Polynesians and Melanesians of the Pacific and for the aborigines of Australia. But Blumenbach's original classification of 1775 recognized only the first four of these five, and united members of the Malay variety with the other people of Asia whom Blumenbach came to name Mongolian.

We now encounter the paradox of Blumenbach's reputation as the inventor of modern racial classification. The original four-race system, as I shall illustrate in a moment, did not arise from Blumenbach's observations but only represents, as Blumenbach readily admits, the classification promoted by his guru Carolus Linnaeus in the founding document of taxonomy, the *Systema Naturae* of 1758. Therefore, Blumenbach's only original contribution to racial classification lies in the later addition of a Malay variety for some Pacific peoples first included in a broader Asian group.

This change seems so minor. Why, then, do we credit Blumenbach, rather than Linnaeus, as the founder of racial classification? (One might prefer to say "discredit," as the enterprise does not, for good reason, enjoy high repute these days.) But Blumenbach's apparently small change actually records a theoretical shift that could not have been broader, or more portentous, in scope. This change has been missed or misconstrued because later scientists have not grasped the vital historical and philosophical principle that theories are models subject to visual representation, usually in clearly definable geometric terms.

By moving from the Linnaean four-race system to his own five-race scheme, Blumenbach radically changed the geometry of human order from a geographically based model without explicit ranking to a hierarchy of worth, oddly based upon perceived beauty, and fanning out in two directions from a Caucasian ideal. The addition of a Malay category was crucial to this geometric reformulation — and therefore becomes the key to the conceptual transformation rather than a simple refinement of factual information within an old scheme. (For the insight that scientific revolutions embody such geometric shifts, I am grateful to my friend Rhonda Roland Shearer, who portrays these themes in her book *The Flatland Hypothesis*.)

Blumenbach idolized his teacher Linnaeus and acknowledged him as the source of his original fourfold racial classification: "I have followed Linnaeus in the number, but have defined my varieties by other boundaries" (1775 edition). Later, in adding his Malay variety, Blumenbach identified his change as a departure from his old mentor in the most respectful terms: "It became very clear that the Linnaean division of mankind could no longer be adhered to; for which reason I, in this little work, ceased like others to follow that illustrious man." 9

Linnaeus divided the species *Homo sapiens* into four basic varieties, defined primarily by geography and, interestingly, not in the ranked order favored by most Europeans in the racist tradition — *Americanus, Europaeus, Asiaticus*, and *Afer*, or African. (He also alluded to two other fanciful categories: *ferus* for "wild boys," occasionally discovered in the woods and possibly raised by animals — most turned out to be retarded or mentally ill youngsters abandoned by their parents — and *monstrosus* for hairy men with tails, and other travelers' confabulations.) In so doing, Linnaeus presented nothing original; he merely mapped humans onto the four geographic regions of conventional cartography. 10

Linnaeus then characterized each of these groups by noting color, humor, and posture, in that order. Again, none of these categories explicitly implies ranking by worth. Once again, Linnaeus was simply bowing to classical taxonomic theories in making these decisions. For example, his use of the four humors reflects the ancient and medieval theory that a person's temperament arises from a balance of four fluids (*humor* is Latin for "moisture") — blood, phlegm, choler (yellow bile), and melancholy (black bile). Depending on which of the four substances dominated, a person would be sanguine (the cheerful realm of blood), phlegmatic (sluggish), choleric (prone to anger), or melancholic (sad). Four geographic regions, four humors, four races. 11

For the American variety, Linnaeus wrote "*rufus, cholericus, rectus*" (red, choleric, upright); for the European, "*albus, sanguineus, torosus*" (white, sanguine, muscular); for the Asian, "*luridus, melancholicus, rigidus*" (pale, yellow, melancholy, stiff); and for the African, "*niger, phlegmaticus, laxus*" (black, phlegmatic, relaxed). 12

I don't mean to deny that Linnaeus held conventional beliefs about the superiority of his own European variety over others. Being a sanguine, muscular European surely sounds better than being a melancholy, stiff Asian. Indeed, Linnaeus ended each group's description with a more overtly racist label, an attempt to epitomize behavior in just two words. Thus the American was *regitur consuetudine* (ruled by habit); the European, *regitur ritibus* (ruled by custom); the Asian, *regitur opinionibus* (ruled by belief); and the African, *regitur arbitrio* (ruled by caprice). Surely regulation by established and considered custom beats the unthinking rule of habit or belief, and all of these are supe- 13 rior to caprice — thus leading to the implied and conventional racist ranking of Europeans first, Asians and Americans in the middle, and Africans at the bottom.

Nonetheless, and despite these implications, the overt geometry of Linnaeus's model is not linear or hierarchical. When we visualize his scheme as an essential picture in our mind, we see a map of the world divided into four regions, with the people in each region characterized by a list of different traits. In short, Linnaeus's primary ordering principle is cartographic; if he had wished to push hierarchy as the essential picture of human variety, he would surely have listed Europeans first and Africans last, but he started with native Americans instead.

The shift from a geographic to a hierarchical ordering of human diversity must stand as one of the most fateful transitions in the history of Western science — for what, short of railroads and nuclear bombs, has had more practical impact, in this case almost entirely negative, upon our collective lives? Ironically, Blumenbach is the focus of this shift, for his five-race scheme became canonical and changed the geometry of human order from Linnaean cartography to linear ranking — in short, to a system based on putative worth.

I say ironic because Blumenbach was the least racist and most genial of all Enlightenment thinkers. How peculiar that the man most committed to human unity, and to inconsequential moral and intellectual differences among groups, should have changed the mental geometry of human order to a scheme that has served racism ever since. Yet on second thought, this situation is really not so odd — for most scientists have been quite unaware of the mental machinery, and particularly of the visual or geometric implications, lying behind all their theorizing.

An old tradition in science proclaims that changes in theory must be driven by observation. Since most scientists believe this simplistic formula, they assume that their own shifts in interpretation record only their better understanding of newly discovered facts. Scientists therefore tend to be unaware of their own mental impositions upon the world's messy and ambiguous factuality. Such mental impositions arise from a variety of sources, including psychological predisposition and social context. Blumenbach lived in an age when ideas of progress, and the cultural superiority of European ways, dominated political and social life. Implicit, loosely formulated, or even unconscious notions of racial ranking fit well with such a worldview — indeed, almost any other organizational scheme would have seemed anomalous. I doubt that Blumenbach was actively encouraging racism by redrawing the mental diagram of human groups. He was only, and largely passively, recording the social view of his time. But ideas have consequences, whatever the motives or intentions of their promoters.

Blumenbach certainly thought that his switch from the Linnaean four-race system to his own five-race scheme arose only from his improved understanding of nature's factuality. He said as much when he announced his change in the second (1781) edition of his treatise: "Formerly in the first edition of this work, I divided all mankind into four varieties; but after I had more actively investigated the different nations of Eastern Asia and America, and, so to speak, looked at them more closely, I was compelled to give up that division, and to place in its stead the following five varieties, as more consonant to nature." And in the preface to the third edition, of 1795, Blumenbach states that he gave up the Linnaean scheme in order to arrange "the varieties of man according to the truth of nature." When scientists adopt the myth that theories arise solely from observation, and do not grasp the personal and social influences acting on their thinking, they not only miss the causes of their changed opinions; they may even fail to comprehend the deep mental shift encoded by the new theory.

Blumenbach strongly upheld the unity of the human species against an     19
alternative view, then growing in popularity (and surely more conducive to conventional forms of racism), that each major race had been separately created. He ended his third edition by writing: "No doubt can any longer remain but that we are with great probability right in referring all . . . varieties of man . . . to one and the same species."

As his major argument for unity, Blumenbach noted that all supposed racial     20
characteristics grade continuously from one people to another and cannot define any separate and bounded group. "For although there seems to be so great a difference between widely separate nations, that you might easily take the inhabitants of the Cape of Good Hope, the Greenlanders, and the Circassians for so many different species of man, yet when the matter is thoroughly considered, you see that all do so run into one another, and that one variety of mankind does so sensibly pass into the other, that you cannot mark out the limits between them." He particularly refuted the common racist claim that black Africans bore unique features of their inferiority: "There is no single character so peculiar and so universal among the Ethiopians, but what it may be observed on the one hand everywhere in other varieties of men."

Blumenbach, writing eighty years before Darwin, believed that *Homo sapiens* had been created in a single region and had then spread over the globe. Our     21
racial diversity, he then argued, arose as a result of this spread to other climates and topographies, and to our adoption of different modes of life in these various regions. Following the terminology of his time, Blumenbach referred to these changes as "degenerations" — not intending the modern sense of deterioration, but the literal meaning of departure from an intial form of humanity at the creation (*de* means "from," and *genus* refers to our original stock).

Most of these degenerations, Blumenbach argued, arose directly from differences in climate and habitat — ranging from such broad patterns as the     22
correlation of dark skin with tropical environments, to more particular (and fanciful) attributions, including a speculation that the narrow eye slits of some Australian aborigines may have arisen in response to "constant clouds of gnats . . . contracting the natural face of the inhabitants." Other changes, he maintained, arose as a consequence of customs adopted in different regions. For example, nations that compressed the heads of babies by swaddling boards or papoose carriers ended up with relatively long skulls. Blumenbach held that "almost all the diversity of the form of the head in different nations is to be attributed to the mode of life and to art."

Blumenbach believed that such changes, promoted over many genera-    23
tions, could eventually become hereditary. "With the progress of time," Blumenbach wrote, "art may degenerate into a second nature." But he also
argued that most racial variations, as superficial impositions of climate and
custom, could be easily altered or reversed by moving to a new region or by
adopting new behavior. White Europeans living for generations in the tropics
could become dark-skinned, while Africans transported as slaves to high lati-
tudes could eventually become white: "Color, whatever be its cause, be it bile,
or the influence of the sun, the air, or the climate, is at all events, an adventi-
tious and easily changeable thing, and can never constitute a diversity of
species," he wrote.

Convinced of the superficiality of racial variation, Blumenbach defended    24
the mental and moral unity of all peoples. He held particularly strong opinions on the equal status of black Africans and white Europeans. He may have
been patronizing in praising "the good disposition and faculties of these our
black brethren," but better paternalism than malign contempt. He cam-
paigned for the abolition of slavery and asserted the moral superiority of
slaves to their captors, speaking of a "natural tenderness of heart, which has
never been benumbed or extirpated on board the transport vessels or on the
West India sugar plantations by the brutality of their white executioners."

Blumenbach established a special library in his house devoted exclusively    25
to black authors, singling out for special praise the poetry of Phillis Wheatley,
a Boston slave whose writings have only recently been rediscovered: "I possess English, Dutch, and Latin poems by several [black authors], amongst
which however above all, those of Phillis Wheatley of Boston, who is justly
famous for them, deserves mention here." Finally, Blumenbach noted that
many Caucasian nations could not boast so fine a set of authors and scholars
as black Africa has produced under the most depressing circumstances of prejudice and slavery: "It would not be difficult to mention entire well-known
provinces of Europe, from out of which you would not easily expect to obtain
off-hand such good authors, poets, philosophers, and correspondents of the
Paris Academy."

Nonetheless, when Blumenbach presented his mental picture of human    26
diversity in his fateful shift away from Linnaean geography, he singled out a
particular group as closest to the created ideal and then characterized all other
groups by relative degrees of departure from this archetypal standard. He
ended up with a system that placed a single race at the pinnacle, and then envisioned two symmetrical lines of departure away from this ideal toward
greater and greater degeneration.

We may now return to the riddle of the name Caucasian, and to the signifi-    27
cance of Blumenbach's addition of a fifth race, the Malay variety. Blumenbach
chose to regard his own European variety as closest to the created ideal and
then searched for the subset of Europeans with greatest perfection — the
highest of the high, so to speak. As we have seen, he identified the people
around Mount Caucasus as the closet embodiments of the original ideal and
proceeded to name the entire European race for its finest representatives.

But Blumenbach now faced a dilemma. He had already affirmed the    28
mental and moral equality of all peoples. He therefore could not use these
conventional criteria of racist ranking to establish degrees of relative departure from the Caucasian ideal. Instead, and however subjective (and even ris-
ible) we view the criterion today, Blumenbach chose physical beauty as his
guide to ranking. He simply affirmed that Europeans were most beautiful,
with Caucasians as the most comely of all. This explains why Blumenbach, in
the first quote cited in this article, linked the maximal beauty of the Caucasians to the place of human origin. Blumenbach viewed all subsequent variation as departures from the originally created ideal — therefore, the most
beautiful people must live closest to our primal home.

Blumenbach's descriptions are pervaded by his subjective sense of rela-    29
tive beauty, presented as though he were discussing an objective and quan-
tifiable property, not subject to doubt or disagreement. He describes a
Georgian female skull (found close to Mount Caucasus) as "really the most
beautiful form of skull which . . . always of itself attracts every eye, however
little observant." He then defends his European standard on aesthetic
grounds: "In the first place, that stock displays . . . the most beautiful form of
the skull, from which, as from a mean and primeval type, the others diverge
by most easy gradations . . . Besides, it is white in color, which we may fairly
assume to have been the primitive color of mankind, since . . . it is very easy
for that to degenerate into brown, but very much more difficult for dark to become white."

Blumenbach then presented all human variety on two lines of successive    30
departure from this Caucasian ideal, ending in the two most degenerate (least
attractive, not least morally unworthy or mentally obtuse) forms of humanity — Asians on one side, and Africans on the other. But Blumenbach also
wanted to designate intermediary forms between ideal and most degenerate,
especially since even gradation formed his primary argument for human
unity. In his original four-race system, he could identify native Americans as
intermediary between Europeans and Asians, but who would serve as the
transitional form between Europeans and Africans?

The four-race system contained no appropriate group. But inventing a    31
fifth racial category as an intermediary between Europeans and Africans
would complete the new symmetrical geometry. Blumenbach therefore
added the Malay race, not as a minor, factual refinement but as a device for
reformulating an entire theory of human diversity. With this one stroke, he
produced the geometric transformation from Linnaeus's unranked geographic model to the conventional hierarchy of implied worth that has fos-
tered so much social grief ever since.

> I have allotted the first place to the Caucasian . . . which makes me esteem it
> the primeval one. This diverges in both directions into two, most remote and
> very different from each other; on the one side, namely, into the Ethiopian,
> and on the other into the Mongolian. The remaining two occupy the inter-
> mediate positions between the primeval one and these two extreme varieties;
> that is, the American between the Caucasian and Mongolian; the Malay be-

tween the same Caucasian and Ethiopian. [From Blumenbach's third edition.]

Scholars often think that academic ideas must remain at worst, harmless, and at best, mildly amusing or even instructive. But ideas do not reside in the ivory tower of our usual metaphor about academic irrelevance. We are, as Pascal[2] said, a thinking reed, and ideas motivate human history. Where would Hitler have been without racism, Jefferson without liberty? Blumenbach lived as a cloistered professor all his life, but his ideas have reverberated in ways that he never could have anticipated, through our wars, our social upheavals, our sufferings, and our hopes.

I therefore end by returning once more to the extraordinary coincidences of 1776 — as Jefferson wrote the Declaration of Independence while Blumenbach was publishing the first edition of his treatise in Latin. We should remember the words of the nineteenth-century British historian and moralist Lord Acton, on the power of ideas to propel history:

> It was from America that . . . ideas long locked in the breast of solitary thinkers, and hidden among Latin folios, burst forth like a conqueror upon the world they were destined to transform, under the title of the Rights of Man.

**Questions to Start You Thinking**

1. CONSIDERING MEANING:  According to Gould, what were Blumenbach's reasons for adding a fifth racial category to the original four-race system proposed by Carolus Linnaeus? What was the effect of this addition?

2. IDENTIFYING WRITING STRATEGIES:  Gould asserts that "theories are models subject to visual representation, usually in clearly definable geometric terms" (paragraph 7). How does he analyze Blumenbach's classification of human diversity in these terms? Reread paragraphs 30 and 31, and then draw a figure representing both Blumenbach's original and revised models of human variety.

3. ANALYZING THE WRITER'S CHOICES:  Gould closes his essay by emphasizing "the power of ideas to propel history," using the Declaration of Independence as an example. Why do you think he compares Blumenbach's 1776 writing on racial classification to the publication of documents by Thomas Jefferson and Adam Smith in that same year (paragraph 3)? How does this comparison support Gould's larger argument about the social and political impact of scientific theorizing?

4. EXPANDING VOCABULARY:  Define *canonical, cartography, linear ranking,* and *putative* (paragraph 15). How do these words help explain the shift from one way of visualizing race to another?

5. MAKING CONNECTIONS:  Compare and contrast how Gould and Toni Morrison ("On the Backs of Blacks," p. 528) argue that language creates racial identity.

**Journal Prompts**

1. In your opinion, is racial classification necessary or useful? How would your identity change if such classification were eliminated from our culture's way of thinking? What would be gained, and what would be lost?

[2] **Pascal:** Blaise Pascal (1623–1662), French scientist and religious philosopher.

2. Imagine a world in which there are no racial categories. How would it differ from our world?

**Suggestions for Writing**

1. What scientific event or theory of the last thirty years (for instance, the moon landing, global warming, genetic research) has made an important impact on you? Describe the event or theory, and then explain how it has changed your way of thinking or even your life.

2. Reread Gould's essay, noting his main points. Then write an essay in which you analyze these points in terms of the theme of this chapter, "American diversity." How does Gould's essay help you to understand American diversity?

# Chapter 25

# The World of Work

**Journal Prompt**

Describe the jobs you have had. Which were the most satisfying? Which were the least satisfying? Why?

541

**Steve Olson** was born in 1946 in Rice Lake, Wisconsin. Unaccompanied by the usual list of degrees, awards, and publications, Olson identified himself simply as "a construction worker" when asked for biographical information. Claiming that he writes "mostly for [him]self," he seems to be speaking for the average American. In the following piece, which appeared as a "My Turn" essay in *Newsweek* on November 6, 1989, Olson strives to honor the dialect and ethic of a group of Americans who are often stereotyped but rarely heard from.

## *Steve Olson*  Year of the Blue-Collar Guy

While the learned are attaching appropriate labels to the 1980s and speculating on what the 1990s will bring, I would like to steal 1989 for my own much maligned group and declare it "the year of the blue-collar guy (BCG)." BCGs have been portrayed as beer-drinking, big-bellied, bigoted rednecks who dress badly. Wearing a suit to a cement-finishing job wouldn't be too bright. Watching my tie go around a motor shaft followed by my neck is not the last thing I want to see in this world. But, more to the point, our necks are too big and our arms and shoulders are too awesome to fit suits well without expensive tailoring. Suits are made for white-collar guys.

But we need big bellies as ballast to stay on the bar stool while we're drinking beer. And our necks are red from the sun and we are somewhat bigoted. But aren't we all? At least our bigotry is open and honest and worn out front like a tattoo. White-collar people are bigoted, too. But it's disguised as the pat on the back that holds you back: "You're not good enough so you need affirmative action." BCGs aren't smart enough to be that cynical. I never met a BCG who didn't respect an honest day's work and a job well done — no matter who did it.

True enough, BCGs aren't perfect. But, I believe this: we are America's last true romantic heroes. When some twenty-first-century Louis L'Amour[1] writes about this era he won't eulogize the greedy Wall Street insider. He won't commend the narrow-shouldered, wide-hipped lawyers with six-digit unearned incomes doing the same work women can do. His wide-shouldered heroes will be plucked from the ranks of the blue-collar guy. They are the last vestige of the manly world where strength, skill, and hard work are still valued.

To some extent our negative ratings are our own fault. While we were building the world we live in, white-collar types were sitting on their ever-widening butts redefining the values we live by. One symbol of America's opulent wealth is the number of people who can sit and ponder and comment

[1] **Louis L'Amour** (1908–1988): Best-selling author of Westerns.

and write without producing a usable product or skill. Hey, get a real job —
make something — then talk. These talkers are the guys we drove from the
playgrounds into the libraries when we were young and now for twenty years
or more we have endured the revenge of the nerds.

BCGs fidgeted our way out of the classroom and into jobs where, it      5
seemed, the only limit to our income was the limit of our physical strength
and energy. A co-worker described a BCG as "a guy who is always doing things
that end in the letter 'n' — you know huntin', fishin', workin' . . ." My wise
friend is talking energy! I have seen men on the job hand-nail 20 square of
shingles (that's 6,480 nails) or more a day, day after day, for weeks. At the
same time, they were remodeling their houses, raising children, and coaching
Little League. I've seen crews frame entire houses in a day — day after day. I've
seen guys finish concrete until 11 P.M., go out on a date, then get up at 6 A.M.
and do it all over again the next day.

These are amazing feats of strength. There should be stadiums full of      6
screaming fans for these guys. I saw a forty-year-old man neatly fold a 350-
pound piece of rubber roofing, put it on his shoulder and, alone, carry it up
a ladder and deposit it on a roof. Nobody acknowledged it because the event
was too common. One day at noon this same fellow wrestled a twenty-two-
year-old college summer worker. In the prime of his life, the college kid was
a 6-foot-3, 190-pound body-builder and he was out of his league. He was on
his back to stay in ninety seconds flat.

### Great Skilled Work Force

Mondays are tough on any job. But in our world this pain is eased by stories      7
of weekend adventure. While white-collar types are debating the value of
reading over watching TV, BCGs are doing stuff. I have honest to God heard
these things on Monday mornings about BCG weekends: "I tore out a wall
and added a room," "I built a garage," "I went walleye fishing Saturday and
pheasant hunting Sunday," "I played touch football both days" (in January),
"I went skydiving," "I went to the sports show and wrestled the bear." Pack a
good novel into these weekends.

My purpose is not so much to put down white-collar people as to stress      8
the importance of blue-collar people to this country. Lawyers, politicians, and
bureaucrats are necessary parts of the process, but this great skilled workforce
is so taken for granted it is rarely seen as the luxury it truly is. Our plumbing
works, our phones work, and repairs are made as quickly as humanly possible. I don't think this is true in all parts of the world. But this blue-collar resource is becoming endangered. Being a tradesman is viewed with such disdain these days that most young people I know treat the trades like a
temporary summer job. I've seen young guys take minimum-wage jobs just so
they can wear suits. It is as if any job without a dress code is a dead-end job.
This is partly our own fault. We even tell our own sons, "Don't be like me, get
a job people respect." Blue-collar guys ought to brag more, even swagger a

little. We should drive our families past the latest job site and say, "That house was a piece of junk, and now it's the best one on the block. I did that." Nobody will respect us if we don't respect ourselves.

Our work is hard, hot, wet, cold, and always dirty. It is also often very sat-    9
isfying. Entailing the use of both brain and body there is a product — a physical result of which to be proud. We have fallen from your roofs, died under heavy equipment, and been entombed in your dams. We have done honest, dangerous work. Our skills and energy and strength have transformed lines on paper into physical reality. We are this century's Renaissance men. America could do worse than to honor us. We still do things the old-fashioned way, and we have earned the honor.

**Questions to Start You Thinking**

1. CONSIDERING MEANING: Why does Olson feel there should be a "Year of the Blue-Collar Guy"? What would be the purpose of such a year?

2. IDENTIFYING WRITING STRATEGIES: How does Olson support his stand by comparing and contrasting the "blue-collar guy" with "white-collar types"?

3. ANALYZING THE WRITER'S CHOICES: What is Olson's tone in this essay? Do you think his tone strengthens or weakens his purpose, as stated in paragraph 8?

4. EXPANDING VOCABULARY: Define *ballast* (paragraph 2), *eulogize* (paragraph 3), *opulent* (paragraph 4), *disdain* (paragraph 8), and *Renaissance men* (paragraph 9). Is Olson's choice of vocabulary sometimes surprising for a self-professed "blue-collar guy"?

5. MAKING CONNECTIONS: Compare and contrast this essay with Gary Soto's "Black Hair" (p. 547). How does Olson's "blue-collar guy" compare with Soto's tire factory workers?

**Journal Prompts**

1. Analyze one of the jobs you have had. Would you consider it "blue-collar," "white-collar," or something else?

2. Does "blue-collar" describe only men? Using observation or imagination as a resource, describe the appearance and identify the leisure activities of a "blue-collar woman."

**Suggestions for Writing**

1. Identify a group you belong to that you think should have a year of its own (for example, college students, secretaries, parents), and write an essay taking a stand on why your group deserves such an honor.

2. In an essay, analyze images of blue-collar workers that you have encountered in television, film, music, or literature. In your opinion how accurate are these images?

**Susanna Rodell** *was born in 1948 in Los Angeles, California. Soon after receiving her B.A. in East Asian studies from Harvard University in 1979, Rodell moved to Australia, where she worked as a journalist until returning to the United States in 1990. She has been an editorial writer on the staff of the* New York Times *since 1993 and is also the author of a children's book entitled* Dear Fred *(1995), inspired* *by the letters her children wrote from Australia to their cousins in the United States. The following essay, one of her* New York Times *editorials, ran on Mother's Day in 1994. In it Rodell urges readers to look at working mothers more positively and to reconsider what constitutes good parenting.*

## Susanna Rodell    Do You Work? Are You Guilty?

One of my favorite movies is a French film from 1978 called *Dear Inspector.* It starred the marvelous Annie Girardot as a high-ranking police detective. Ms. Girardot is teamed with a more traditional male partner, and their methods are at odds throughout the film. At one point, in frustration, Ms. Girardot's character quits her job.

This is where the movie got interesting — to me, anyway. The Girardot character was, you see, a mother as well. And she had not been home for more than a few days before her daughter was pleading: "Mother! Will you *please* go back to work?" (Or the equivalent, in French, of course.) The energetic police detective, with nowhere to put her energy except into her household, was making herself a thorough pain to her family.

I thought of this movie while reading the latest book by Penelope Leach, the British child-care guru, called *Children First.* This woman is one of the most widely read authors on child development in the world. And here she is, in 1994, trotting out all the old scare stories. Every possible form of child care, except that provided by a parent (read mother) has overwhelming deficiencies — not just for infants but for toddlers as well. A child's "special adult" is the only one he or she can really trust, the only one with the motivation to respond correctly to a child's unique needs.

Let me make my bias clear. I have four children. For most of their early childhoods, I was either a full-time student or in the workforce. For each of them I cobbled together what seemed to be happy arrangements at the time: sometimes individual care by a babysitter, but most often care in a variety of day-care centers.

Each child had joyful, trusting relationships with caregivers. When they went to day care, they got up each morning eager to see their friends and teachers. I noticed they often formed friendships more easily than kids who spent all day at home; they were more outgoing and more confident about negotiating with the world.

Indeed, the most damage I did to any of my kids was during a period, shortly after graduating from college, when I was briefly swayed by the Leach Theory and stayed at home for some months with my first daughter. She was (of course) a bright child; she became my Project. I bombarded her with flash-cards, organized activities for her, and was generally so obnoxious that, after learning to read at three, she subsequently refused to read for nearly five years. (She's eighteen now; she still can't spell.)

Why are there no studies of the damage done to children by high-energy women who have no business staying at home? I have now seen plenty of these children. They are all their mothers' Projects. Their needs are obsessed over, their emotional and intellectual development so carefully overseen that they all assume the universe revolves solely around them. They have little capacity to amuse themselves, to play cooperatively with other children, to share or — in extreme instances — be in a room by themselves for more than five minutes. 7

I sent my three younger children off to child care guilt-free. I'm prejudiced, I know, but I think they are pretty likable, well-balanced kids. Many of my female colleagues do the same thing — but they still suffer from a horrible sense of guilt. (Their husbands, of course, have no such feelings.) 8

Unlike many women my age, I had a working mother. She was a music teacher, often at the schools I attended. I saw her at work and I saw her at home. I watched her whip choirs into shape, facing down sullen adolescent males who towered over her, demanding perfection, making us all sweat to reach one sweet, perfect chord. 9

In retrospect, imagining this woman at home full time is a bit frightening. I know I would not have enjoyed being the object of all that energy, that drive, that need for perfection. Watching her, I learned the value of work, and pride in doing something well. At home, she left me the time and solitude to find my own way (a need Ms. Leach does not discuss). I think she was a better mother *because* she worked. I think I am too. 10

**Questions to Start You Thinking**

1. CONSIDERING MEANING: What is the "Leach Theory" (paragraph 3), and what is Rodell's reaction to it?

2. IDENTIFYING WRITING STRATEGIES: How does Rodell use reading and recall as resources for comparing and contrasting her ideas with those of Penelope Leach?

3. ANALYZING THE WRITER'S CHOICES: As implied by the title of this essay, what audience does Rodell seem to be addressing? How do you think she intends this audience to respond to her statement in paragraph 4 that she is biased because of her personal experience with raising four children while working?

4. EXPANDING VOCABULARY: How does Rodell's description of Penelope Leach as a "child-care *guru*" (paragraph 3) tip the reader off to her opinion of Leach? What child-care *deficiencies* (paragraph 3) might Leach find in Rodell's use of day-care centers for her children?

5. MAKING CONNECTIONS: Compare and contrast what Rodell and Gerald Early ("Black like . . . Shirley Temple?," p. 468) believe that good parenting consists of.

**Journal Prompts**

1. Who took care of you when you were a child? Was your primary caregiver a parent or someone else?

2. Do you agree with Penelope Leach that every child needs to be cared for by one "special adult" (paragraph 3)? Why or why not?

**Suggestions for Writing**

1. What do you think is the best way for families to balance work and childcare responsibilities? Write an essay from your own family experience — as a child, as a parent, or both. If you are not yet a parent but are thinking about becoming one someday, you may also speculate on how you plan to juggle these two responsibilities later on.

2. Do you agree with Rodell that there are "high-energy women who have no business staying at home" to care for their children (paragraph 7)? Do you agree that a woman can be a better mother *because* she works (paragraph 10)? Write an essay defending or refuting Rodell's point of view.

**Gary Soto** *was born in Fresno, California, in 1952 and grew up in a Mexican-American neighborhood there. He studied at California State University at Fresno and at the University of California at Irvine; he now teaches Chicano studies and English at the University of California at Berkeley. Soto's many books of poetry include* Black Hair *(1985),* Who Will Know Us? *(1990), and* Home Course in Religion *(1991). Soto's essays, often based on recollections of his childhood, are collected in* Living up the Street: Narrative Recollections *(1985),* Small Faces *(1986), and* A Summer Life *(1990). He has also published several books for children and edited* Pieces of the Heart: New Chicano Fiction *(1993). In "Black Hair," taken from* Living up the Street, *Soto tells the story of a horrible job he had as a teenager, an experience that was shaped by his ethnic identity.*

# *Gary Soto*   **Black Hair**

There are two kinds of work: One uses the mind and the other uses muscle. As a kid I found out about the latter. I'm thinking of the summer of 1969 when I was a seventeen-year-old runaway who ended up in Glendale, California, to work for Valley Tire Factory. To answer an ad in the newspaper I walked miles in the afternoon sun, my stomach slowly knotting on a doughnut that was breakfast, my teeth like bright candles gone yellow.

I walked in the door sweating and feeling ugly because my hair was still stiff from a swim at the Santa Monica beach the day before. Jules, the accountant and part owner, looked droopily through his bifocals at my application and then at me. He tipped his cigar in the ashtray, asked my age as if he didn't believe I was seventeen, but finally after a moment of silence, said, "Come back tomorrow. Eight-thirty."

I thanked him, left the office, and went around to the chain link fence to watch the workers heave tires into a bin; others carted uneven stacks of tires on hand trucks. Their faces were black from tire dust and when they talked — or cussed — their mouths showed a bright pink.

From there I walked up a commercial street, past a cleaners, a motorcycle shop, and a gas station where I washed my face and hands; before leaving I took a bottle that hung on the side of the Coke machine, filled it with water, and stopped it with a scrap of paper and rubber band.

The next morning I arrived early at work. The assistant foreman, a pot-bellied Hungarian, showed me a time card and how to punch in. He showed me the Coke machine, the locker room with its slimy shower, and also pointed out the places where I shouldn't go: the ovens where the tires were re-capped and the customer service area, which had a slashed couch, a coffee table with greasy magazines, and an ashtray. He introduced me to Tully, a fat man with one ear, who worked the buffers that resurfaced the whitewalls. I was handed an apron and a face mask and shown how to use the buffer: Lift the tire and center, inflate it with a foot pedal, press the buffer against the whiteband until cleaned, and then deflate and blow off the tire with an air hose.

With a paint brush he stirred a can of industrial preserver. "Then slap this blue stuff on." While he was talking a co-worker came up quietly from behind him and goosed him with the air hose. Tully jumped as if he had been struck by a bullet and then turned around cussing and cupping his genitals in his hands as the other worker walked away calling out foul names. When Tully turned to me smiling his gray teeth, I lifted my mouth into a smile because I wanted to get along. He has to be on my side, I thought. He's the one who'll tell the foreman how I'm doing.

I worked carefully that day, setting the tires on the machine as if they were babies, since it was easy to catch a finger in the rim that expanded to inflate the tire. At the day's end we swept up the tire dust and emptied the trash into bins.

At five the workers scattered for their cars and motorcycles while I crossed the street to wash at a burger stand. My hair was stiff with dust and my mouth showed pink against the backdrop of my dirty face. I then ordered a hot dog and walked slowly in the direction of the abandoned house where I had stayed the night before. I lay under the trees and within minutes was asleep. When I woke my shoulders were sore and my eyes burned when I squeezed the lids together.

From the backyard I walked dully through a residential street, and as evening came on, the TV glare in the living rooms and the headlights of pass-ing cars showed against the blue drift of dusk. I saw two children coming up the street with snow cones, their tongues darting at the packed ice. I saw a boy with a peach and wanted to stop him, but felt embarrassed by my hunger. I walked for an hour only to return and discover the house lit brightly. Behind the fence I heard voices and saw a flashlight poking at the garage door. A man on the back steps mumbled something about the refrigerator to the one with the flashlight.

I waited for them to leave, but had the feeling they wouldn't because there was the commotion of furniture being moved. Tired, even more des-perate, I started walking again with a great urge to kick things and tear the day from my life. I felt weak and my mind kept drifting because of hunger. I crossed the street to a gas station where I sipped at the water fountain and searched the Coke machine for change. I started walking again, first up a commercial street, then into a residential area where I lay down on someone's lawn and replayed a scene at home — my mother crying at the kitchen table, my stepfather yelling with food in his mouth. They're cruel, I thought, and warned myself that I should never forgive them. How could they do this to me.

When I got up from the lawn it was late. I searched out a place to sleep and found an unlocked car that seemed safe. In the backseat, with my shoes off, I fell asleep but woke up startled about four in the morning when the owner, a nurse on her way to work, opened the door. She got in and was about to start the engine when I raised my head up from the backseat to explain my presence. She screamed so loudly when I said "I'm sorry" that I sprinted from the car with my shoes in hand. Her screams faded, then stopped altogether, as I ran down the block where I hid behind a trash bin and waited for a police siren to sound. Nothing. I crossed the street to a church where I slept stiffly on cardboard in the balcony.

I woke up feeling tired and greasy. It was early and a few streetlights were still lit, the east growing pink with dawn. I washed myself from a garden hose and returned to the church to break into what looked like a kitchen. Paper cups, plastic spoons, a coffeepot littered on a table. I found a box of Nabisco crackers which I ate until I was full.

At work I spent the morning at the buffer, but was then told to help Iggy, an old Mexican, who was responsible for choosing tires that could be recapped without the risk of exploding at high speeds. Every morning a truck would deliver used tires, and after I unloaded them Iggy would step among the tires to inspect them for punctures and rips on the sidewalls.

With a yellow chalk he marked circles and Xs to indicate damage and called out "junk." For those tires that could be recapped, he said "goody" and I placed them on my hand truck. When I had a stack of eight I kicked the truck at an angle and balanced them to another work area where Iggy again inspected the tires, scratching Xs and calling out "junk."

Iggy worked only until three in the afternoon, at which time he went to the locker room to wash and shave and to dress in a two-piece suit. When he came out he glowed with a bracelet, watch, rings, and a shiny fountain pen in his breast pocket. His shoes sounded against the asphalt. He was the image of a banker stepping into sunlight with millions on his mind. He said a few low words to workers with whom he was friendly and none to people like me.

I was seventeen, stupid because I couldn't figure out the difference between an F 78 14 and 750 14 at sight. Iggy shook his head when I brought him the wrong tires, especially since I had expressed interest in being his understudy. "Mexican, how can you be so stupid?" he would yell at me, slapping the tire from my hands. But within weeks I learned a lot about tires, from sizes and makes to how they are molded in iron forms to how Valley stole from other companies. Now and then we received a truckload of tires, most of them new or nearly new, and they were taken to our warehouse in the back where the serial numbers were ground off with a sander. On those days the foreman handed out Cokes and joked with us as we worked to get the numbers off.

Most of the workers were Mexican or black, though a few redneck whites    17
worked there. The base pay was a dollar sixty-five, but the average was three dollars. Of the black workers, I knew Sugar Daddy the best. His body carried two hundred and fifty pounds, armfuls of scars, and a long knife that made me jump when be brought it out from his boot without warning. At one time he had been a singer, and had cut a record in 1967 called *Love's Chance,* which broke into the R and B charts. But nothing came of it. No big contract, no club dates, no tours. He made very little from the sales, only enough for an operation to pull a steering wheel from his gut when, drunk and mad at a lady friend, he slammed his Mustang into a row of parked cars.

"Touch it," he smiled at me one afternoon as he raised his shirt, his black    18
belly kinked with hair. Scared, I traced the scar that ran from his chest to the left of his belly button, and I was repelled but hid my disgust.

Among the Mexicans I had few friends because I was different, a *pocho*[1]    19
who spoke bad Spanish. At lunch they sat in tires and laughed over burritos, looking up at me to laugh even harder. I also sat in tires while nursing a Coke and felt dirty and sticky because I was still living on the street and had not had a real bath in over a week. Nevertheless, when the border patrol came to round up the nationals, I ran with them as they scrambled for the fence or hid among the tires behind the warehouse. The foreman, who thought I was an undocumented worker, yelled at me to run, to get away. I did just that. At the time it seemed fun because there was no risk, only a good-hearted feeling of hide-and-seek, and besides it meant an hour away from work on company time. When the police left we came back and some of the nationals made up stories of how they were almost caught — how they outraced the police. Some of the stories were so convoluted and unconvincing that everyone laughed *mentiras,*[2] especially when one described how he overpowered a policeman, took his gun away, and sold the patrol car. We laughed and he laughed, happy to be there to make up a story.

If work was difficult, so were the nights. I still had not gathered enough    20
money to rent a room, so I spent the nights sleeping in parked cars or in the balcony of a church. After a week I found a newspaper ad for room for rent, phoned, and was given directions. Finished with work, I walked the five miles down Mission Road looking back into the traffic with my thumb out. No rides. After eight hours of handling tires I was frightening, I suppose, to drivers since they seldom looked at me; if they did, it was a quick glance. For the next six weeks I would try to hitchhike, but the only person to stop was a Mexican woman who gave me two dollars to take the bus. I told her it was too much and that no bus ran from Mission Road to where I lived, but she insisted that I keep the money and trotted back to her idling car. It must have

[1] *pocho:* Mexican slang for "outsider."
[2] *mentiras:* Spanish for "lies."

hurt her to see me day after day walking in the heat and looking very much the dirty Mexican to the many minds that didn't know what it meant to work at hard labor. That woman knew. Her eyes met mine as she opened the car door, and there was a tenderness that was surprisingly true — one for which you wait for years but when it comes it doesn't help. Nothing changes. You continue on in rags, with the sun still above you.

I rented a room from a middle-aged couple whose lives were a mess. She was a schoolteacher and he was a fireman. A perfect setup, I thought. But during my stay there they would argue with one another for hours in their bedroom.  21

When I rang at the front door both Mr. and Mrs. Van Deusen answered and didn't bother to disguise their shock at how awful I looked. But they let me in all the same. Mrs. Van Deusen showed me around the house, from the kitchen and bathroom to the living room with its grand piano. On her fingers she counted out the house rules as she walked me to my room. It was a girl's room with lace curtains, scenic wallpaper of a Victorian couple enjoying a stroll, canopied bed, and stuffed animals in a corner. Leaving, she turned and asked if she could do laundry for me and, feeling shy and hurt, I told her no; perhaps the next day. She left and I undressed to take a bath, exhausted as I sat on the edge of the bed probing my aches and my bruised places. With a towel around my waist I hurried down the hallway to the bathroom where Mrs. Van Deusen had set out an additional towel with a tube of shampoo. I ran the water in the tub and sat on the toilet, lid down, watching the steam curl toward the ceiling. When I lowered myself into the tub I felt my body sting. I soaped a washcloth and scrubbed my arms until they lightened, even glowed pink, but still I looked unwashed around my neck and face no matter how hard I rubbed. Back in the room I sat in bed reading a magazine, happy and thinking of no better luxury than a girl's sheets, especially after nearly two weeks of sleeping on cardboard at the church.  22

I was too tired to sleep, so I sat at the window watching the neighbors move about in pajamas, and, curious about the room, looked through the bureau drawers to search out personal things — snapshots, a messy diary, and a high school yearbook. I looked up the Van Deusen's daughter, Barbara, and studied her face as if I recognized her from my own school — a face that said "promise," "college," "nice clothes in the closet." She was a skater and a member of the German Club; her greatest ambition was to sing at the Hollywood Bowl.  23

After a while I got into bed and as I drifted toward sleep I thought about her. In my mind I played a love scene again and again and altered it slightly each time. She comes home from college and at first is indifferent to my presence in her home, but finally I overwhelm her with deep pity when I come home hurt from work, with blood on my shirt. Then there was another version: Home from college she is immediately taken with me, in spite of my work-darkened face, and invites me into the family car for a milkshake across town. Later, back at the house we sit in the living room talking about school  24 until we're so close I'm holding her hand. The truth of the matter was that Barbara did come home for a week, but was bitter toward her parents for taking in boarders (two others besides me). During that time she spoke to me only twice: Once, while searching the refrigerator, she asked if we had any mustard; the other time she asked if I had seen her car keys.

But it was a place to stay. Work had become more and more difficult. I    25
not only worked with Iggy, but also with the assistant foreman who was in charge of unloading trucks. After they backed in I hopped on top to pass the tires down by bouncing them on the tailgate to give them an extra spring so they would be less difficult to handle on the other end. Each truck was weighed down with more than two hundred tires, each averaging twenty pounds, so that by the time the truck was emptied and swept clean I glistened with sweat and my T-shirt stuck to my body. I blew snot threaded with tire dust onto the asphalt, indifferent to the customers who watched from the waiting room.

The days were dull. I did what there was to do from morning until the bell    26
sounded at five; I tugged, pulled, and cussed at tires until I was listless and my mind drifted and caught on small things, from cold sodas to shoes to stupid talk about what we would do with a million dollars. I remember unloading a truck with Hamp, a black man.

"What's better than a sharp lady?" he asked me as I stood sweaty on a pile    27
of junked tires. "Water. With ice," I said.

He laughed with his mouth open wide. With his fingers he pinched the    28
sweat from his chin and flicked at me. "You be too young, boy. A woman can make you a god."

As a kid I had chopped cotton and picked grapes, so I knew work. I knew    29
the fatigue and the boredom and the feeling that there was a good possibility you might have to do such work for years, if not for a lifetime. If fact, as a kid I imagined a dark fate: to marry Mexican poor, work Mexican hours, and in the end die a Mexican death, broke and in despair.

But this job at Valley Tire Company confirmed that there was something    30
worse than field work, and I was doing it. We were all doing it, from foreman to the newcomers like me, and what I felt heaving tires for eight hours a day was felt by everyone — black, Mexican, redneck. We all despised those hours but didn't know what else to do. The workers were unskilled, some undocumented and fearful of deportation, and all stuck with an uncertainty at what to do with their lives. Although every one bitched about work, no one left. Some had worked there for as long as twelve years; some had sons working there. Few quit; no one was ever fired. It amazed me that no one gave up when the border patrol jumped from their vans, baton in hand, because I couldn't imagine any work that could be worse—or any life. What was out there, in the world, that made men run for the fence in fear?

Iggy was the only worker who seemed sure of himself. After five hours of    31
"junking," he brushed himself off, cleaned up in the washroom, and came out gleaming with an elegance that humbled the rest of us. Few would look him straight in the eye or talk to him in our usual stupid way because he was

so much better. He carried himself as a man should — with that old world "dignity" — while the rest of us muffed our jobs and talked dully about dull things as we worked. From where he worked in his open shed he would now and then watch us with his hands on his hips. He would shake his head and click his tongue in disgust.

The rest of us lived dismally. I often wondered what the others' homes were like; I couldn't imagine that they were much better than our workplace. No one indicated that his outside life was interesting or intriguing. We all looked defeated and comtemptible in our filth at the day's end. I imagined the average welcome at home: Rafael, a Mexican national who had worked at Valley for five years, returned to a beaten house of kids who were dressed in mismatched clothes and playing kick-the-can. As for Sugar Daddy, he returned home to a stuffy room where he would read and reread old magazines. He ate potato chips, drank beer, and watched TV. There was no grace in dipping socks into a washbasin where later he would wash his cup and plate.   32

There was no grace at work. It was all ridicule. The assistant foreman drank Cokes in front of the newcomers as they laced tires in the afternoon sun. Knowing that I had a long walk home, Rudy, the college student, passed me waving and yelling "Hello," as I started down Mission Road on the way home to eat out of cans. Even our plump secretary got into the act by wearing short skirts and flaunting her milky legs. . . .   33

How we arrived at such a place is a mystery to me. Why anyone would stay for years is even a deeper concern. You showed up, but from where? What broken life? What ugly past? The foreman showed you the Coke machine, the washroom, and the yard where you'd work. When you picked up a tire you were amazed at the black it could give off.   34

**Questions to Start You Thinking**

1. CONSIDERING MEANING: To Soto, what does it mean "to work at hard labor" (paragraph 20), and why does he see so little dignity and "grace" (paragraph 33) in it?

2. IDENTIFYING WRITING STRATEGIES: How does Soto use comparison and contrast to evaluate the quality of his life while working at the tire company?

3. ANALYZING THE WRITER'S CHOICES: Although this essay is written as a personal narrative, Soto is also implicitly taking a stand. What is he trying to persuade his readers to believe or understand? What do you think are the advantages of using personal narrative to make an argument? What are the disadvantages?

4. EXPANDING VOCABULARY: Soto places special emphasis on the words *dignity* and *grace* (paragraphs 31–33). How would you say he defines these words? Why are they so important to him?

5. MAKING CONNECTIONS: Compare and contrast how Soto and Steve Olson ("Year of the Blue-Collar Guy," p. 542) depict manual labor. How do you think Soto would respond to Olson's notion that blue-collar guys are "America's last true romantic heroes" (paragraph 3)?

**Journal Prompts**

1. Write a conversation that Soto might have had with Iggy or another of his co-workers.

2. Explain how you felt, both physically and mentally, after the first day of your first job.

**Suggestions for Writing**

1. Tell the story of a turning point in your life, a time when you had a sudden realization about your identity or relation to the world outside your home. Explain what you learned about yourself.

2. Write an essay comparing and contrasting the two kinds of work Soto identifies in his opening paragraph: the kind that "uses the mind" and the kind that "uses muscle." What has been your experience with each? What is society's attitude to these two kinds of work?

**Deborah Tannen,** *born in 1945 in Brooklyn, New York, received her Ph.D. from the University of California at Berkeley in 1979 and is now a professor of linguistics at Georgetown University. Tannen believes that it is her "mission" to make academic linguistic research accessible and interesting, as she has done in her many books for the general public about the way people talk to each other. Her books include* Conversational Style: Analyzing Talk among Friends *(1984),* That's Not What I Meant!: How Conversational Style Makes or Breaks Your Relations with Others *(1986), and* You Just Don't Understand: Women and Men in Conversation *(1990). The following selection is an excerpt from her most recent book,* Talking from 9 to 5: How Women's and Men's Conversational Styles Affect Who Gets Heard, Who Gets Credit, and What Gets Done at Work *(1994). Here Tannen focuses on both the causes and effects of some key differences in the way men and women negotiate, present their ideas, and express leadership on the job.*

## *Deborah Tannen*    Women and Men Talking on the Job

*Negotiating Styles*

The managers of a medium-size company got the go-ahead to hire a human-resources coordinator, and two managers who worked well together were assigned to make the choice. As it turned out Maureen and Harold favored different applicants, and both felt strongly about their preferences. Maureen argued with assurance and vigor that the person she wanted to hire was the most creative and innovative, and that he had the most appropriate experience. Harold argued with equal conviction that the applicant he favored had a vision of management that fit with the company's, whereas her candidate might be a thorn in their side. They traded arguments for some time, neither convincing the other. Then Harold said that hiring the applicant Maureen wanted would make him so uncomfortable that he would have to consider resigning. Maureen respected Harold. What's more, she liked and considered him a friend. So she felt that his admission of such strong feelings had to be taken into account. She said what seemed to her the only thing she could say under the circumstances: "Well, I certainly don't want you to feel uncomfortable here; you're one of the pillars of the place. If you feel that strongly about it, I can't argue with that." Harold's choice was hired.

In this case, the decision-making power went not to the manager who had the highest rank in the firm (their positions were parallel) and not necessarily to the one whose judgement was best, but to the one whose arguing strategies were most effective in the negotiation. Maureen was an ardent and persuasive advocate for her view, but she assumed that she and Harold would have to come to an agreement in order to make a decision, and that she had to take his feelings into account. Since Harold would not back down, she did. Most important, when he argued that he would have to quit if she got her way, she felt she had no option but to yield.

What was crucial was not Maureen's and Harold's individual styles in isolation but how their styles interacted — how they played in concert with the other's style. Harold's threat to quit ensures his triumph — when used with someone who would not call his bluff. If he had been arguing with someone who regarded this threat as simply another move in the negotiation rather than as a nonnegotiable expression of deep feelings that had to be respected, the result might have been different. For example, had she said, "That's ridiculous; of course you're not going to quit!" or "If that's how shallow your commitment to this firm is, then we'd be better off without you," the decision might well have gone the other way.

When you talk to someone whose style is similar to yours, you can fairly well predict the response you are going to get. But when you talk to someone whose style is different, you can't predict, and often can't make sense of, the response. Hearing the reaction you get, if it's not the one you expected, often makes you regret what you said. Harold later told Maureen that he was sorry he had used the argument he did. In retrospect he was embarrassed, even a bit ashamed of himself. His retrospective chagrin was like what you feel if you slam down something in anger and are surprised and regretful to see that it breaks. You wanted to make a gesture, but you didn't expect it to come out with such force. Harold regretted what he said precisely because it caused Maureen to back down so completely. He'd known he was upping the ante — he felt he had to do something to get them out of the loop of recycling arguments they were in — but he had not expected it to end the negotiation summarily; he expected Maureen to meet his move with a balancing move of her own. He did not predict the impact that personalizing his argument would have on her. For her part, Maureen did not think of Harold's threat as just another move in a negotiable argument; she heard is as a personal plea that she could not reject. Their different approaches to negotiation put her at a disadvantage in negotiating with him.

### "How Certain Are You Of That?"

Negotiating is only one kind of activity that is accomplished through talk at work. Other kinds of decision making are also based as much on ways of talking as on the content of the arguments. The CEO of a corporation explained to me that he regularly has to make decisions based on insufficient information — and making decisions is a large part of his work life. Much of his day is spent hearing brief presentations following which he must either approve or reject a course of action. He has to make a judgement in five minutes about issues the presenters have worked on for months. "I decide," he explained, "based on how confident they seem. If they seem very confident, I call it a go. If they seem unsure, I figure it's too risky and nix it."

Here is where the rule of competence and the role of communication go    6
hand in hand. Confidence, after all, is an internal feeling. How can you judge others' confidence? The only evidence you have to go on is circumstantial — how they talk about what they know. You judge by a range of signs, including facial expression and body posture, but most of all, speech. Do they hesitate? Do they speak or swallow half their words? Is their tone of voice declamatory of halting? Do they make bald statements ("This is a winner! We've got to go for it!") or hedge ("Um . . . from what I can tell, I think it'll work, but we'll never know for sure until we try")? This seems simple enough. Surely, you can tell how confident people are by paying attention to how they speak, just as you can tell when someone is lying.

Well, maybe not. Psychologist Paul Ekman has spent years studying lying, and he has found that most people are very sure they can tell when others are lying. The only trouble is, most can't. With a few thus-far inexplicable exceptions, people who tell him they are absolutely sure they can tell if someone is lying are as likely to be wrong as to be right — and he has found this to be as true for judges as for the rest of us.

In the same way, our ability to determine how confident others are is    8
probably quite limited. The CEO who does not take into account the individual styles of the people who make presentations to him will find it difficult, if not impossible, to make the best judgement. Different people will talk very differently, not because of the absolute level of their confidence or lack of it, but because of their habitual ways of speaking. There are those who sound sure of themselves even when inside they're not sure at all, and others who sound tentative even when they're very sure indeed. So being aware of differences in ways of speaking is a prerequisite for making good decisions as well as good presentations.

### Feasting On Humble Pie

Although these factors affecting decision making are the same for men and    9
women, and every individual has his or her own style, it seems that women are more likely to downplay their certainty, men more likely to downplay their doubts. From childhood, girls learn to temper what they say so as not to sound too aggressive — which means too certain. From the time they are little, most girls learn that sounding too sure of themselves will make them unpopular with their peers. Groups of girls, as researchers who have studied girls at play have found, will penalize and even ostracize a girl who seems too

sure she's right. Anthropologist Marjorie Harness Goodwin found that girls criticize other girls who stand out by saying, "See thinks she's cute," or "She thinks she's something." Talking in ways that display self-confidence are not approved for girls. . . .

The expectation that women should not display their own accomplish-    10
ments brings us back to the matter of negotiating that is so important in the workplace. A man who owned a medium-sized company remarked that women who came to ask him for raises often supported their requests by pointing to a fellow worker on the same level who earned more. He considered this a weak bargaining strategy because he could always identify a different co-worker at that level who earned less. They would do better, he felt, to argue for a raise on the basis of how valuable their own work is to the company. Yet it is likely that many women would be less comfortable "blowing their own horn" than making a claim based on fairness.

### Follow the Leader

Similar expectations constrain how girls express leadership. Being a leader of-    11
ten involves giving directions to others, but girls who tell other girls what to do are called "bossy." It is not that girls do not exert influence on their group — of course they do — but, as anthropologists like Marjorie Harness Goodwin have found, many girls discover they get better results if they phrase their ideas as suggestions rather than orders, and if they give reasons for their suggestions in terms of the good of the group. But while these ways of talking make girls — and, later, women — more likable, they make women seem less competent and self-assured in the world of work. And women who do seem competent and self-assured are as much in danger of being negatively labeled as are girls. After her retirement, Margaret Thatcher was described in the press as "bossy." Whereas girls are ready to stick this label on each other because they don't think any girls should boss the others around, it seems odd to apply it to Thatcher, who, after all, was the boss. And this is the rub: Standards of behavior applied to women are based on roles that do not include being boss.

Boys are expected to play by different rules, since the social organization    12
of boys is different. Boys' groups tend to be more obviously hierarchical: Someone is one-up, and someone is one-down. Boys don't typically accuse each other of being "bossy" because the high-status boys are expected to give orders and push the low-status boys around. Daniel Maltz and Ruth Borker summarize research by many scholars showing that boys tend to jockey for center stage, challenge those who get it, and deflect challenges. Giving orders and telling the others what to do are ways of getting and keeping the high-status role. Another way of getting high status is taking center stage by telling stories, jokes, and information. Along with this, many boys learn to state their opinions in the strongest possible terms and find out if they're wrong by seeing if others challenge them. These ways of talking translate into an impression of confidence.

The styles typical of women and men both make sense given the context    13
in which they were learned, but they have very different consequences in the
workplace. In order to avoid being put in the one-down position, many men
have developed strategies for making sure they get the one-up position instead, and this results in ways of talking that serve them well when it comes
to hiring and promotion. In relation to the examples I have given, women are
more likely to speak in the styles that are less effective in getting recognized
and promoted. But if they speak in the styles that are effective when used by
men — being assertive, sounding sure of themselves, talking up what they
have done to make sure they get credit for it — they run the risk that everyone
runs if they do not fit their culture's expectations for appropriate behavior:
They will not be liked and may even be seen as having psychological problems.

Both women and men pay a price if they do not behave in ways expected    14
of their gender: Men who are not very aggressive are called "wimps," whereas
women who are not very aggressive are called "feminine." Men who are aggressive are called "go-getters," though if they go too far, from the point of
view of the viewer, they may be called "arrogant." This can hurt them, but not
nearly as much as the innumerable labels for women who are thought to be
too aggressive — starting with the most hurtful one: bitch.

Even the compliments that we receive are revealing. One woman who    15
had designed and implemented a number of innovative programs was
praised by someone who said, "You have such a gentle way of bringing about
radical change that people don't realize what's happening — or don't get
threatened by it." This was a compliment, but it also hinted at the downside
of the woman's gentle touch: Although it made it possible for her to be effective in instituting the changes she envisioned, her unobtrusive style ensured
a lack of recognition. If people don't realize what's happening, they won't give
her credit for what she has accomplished.

Not only advancement and recognition, but hiring is affected by ways of    16
speaking. A woman who supervised three computer programmers mentioned
that her best employee was another woman who she had hired over the objections of her own boss. Her boss had preferred a male candidate, because he
felt the man would be better able to step into her supervisory role if needed.
But she had taken a dislike to the male candidate. For one thing, she had felt
he was inappropriately flirtatious with her. But most important, she had
found him arrogant, because he spoke as if he already had the job, using the
pronoun "we" to refer to the group that had not yet hired him.

I have no way of knowing whether the woman hired was indeed the bet-    17
ter of these two candidates, or whether either she or the man was well suited
to assume the supervisory role, but I am intrigued that the male boss was impressed with the male candidate's take-charge self-presentation, while the
women supervisor was put off by it. And it seems quite likely that whatever it
was about his way of talking that struck her as arrogant was exactly what led
her boss to conclude that this man would be better able to take over her job
if needed.

**Questions to Start You Thinking**

1. CONSIDERING MEANING: According to Tannen, what are the key differences in the way men and women communicate at work? What are the major consequences of these differences?

2. IDENTIFYING WRITING STRATEGIES: Where does Tannen identify the causes and the effects of each gender's style of speech in the workplace? How does she use this cause and effect strategy to make her argument that women are at a cultural disadvantage in the workplace?

3. ANALYZING THE WRITER'S CHOICES: To support her argument, Tannen draws on the studies of a psychologist, an anthropologist, and other scholars. Why do you think she includes this expert testimony? How effective would her case be without it?

4. EXPANDING VOCABULARY: Define *chagrin*, *ante* (paragraph 4), *ostracize* (paragraph 9), and *hierarchical* (paragraph 12). Why does a *declamatory* or *halting* tone provide *circumstantial* (paragraph 6) evidence about a person's level of confidence?

5. MAKING CONNECTIONS: Compare and contrast Tannen's analysis of how men and women talk with Nicholas Wade's discussion in "How Men and Women Think" (p. 510).

**Journal Prompts**

1. Analyze your own talking or presentation style at work or in the classroom. Does it conform to Tannen's analysis of how men and women talk?

2. What style of verbal presentation is one expected to use at a job interview? If this expectation did not exist, would you choose a different manner of presenting yourself? Explain.

**Suggestions for Writing**

1. Analyze the way your boss, co-workers, teachers, or classmates talk to you at work or school. How does their way of talking compare with how Tannen suggests they talk?

2. Observe the way women and men at work or school present themselves in their various styles of speech. Using your observations as evidence, formulate an argument that supports or rebuts Tannen's analysis of "how women's and men's conversational styles affect who gets heard, who gets credit, and what gets done at work" (her book's subtitle).

**Christina Hoff Sommers,** *born in 1950 in Petaluma, California, earned a B.A. at New York University and a Ph.D. in philosophy at Brandeis University. She is a professor in the Philosophy Department at Clark University, the author of several books about ethics, and a contributor to the* Wall Street Journal, *the* Washington Post, *and* USA Today. *The publication of her controversial* Who Stole Feminism? How Women Have Betrayed Women *(1994), from which the following selection is excerpted, gained Sommers sudden fame and several appearances on television talk shows. This book has evoked strong reactions: one reviewer praised Sommers for exposing "some embarrassing exaggerations in feminist literature, along with much po-*

*litical correctness silliness," while some critics charged that she oversimplified the issues. In this excerpt, Sommers uses statistics to argue that the position and pay of American women in the workforce is much better than many feminists have claimed.*

## *Christina Hoff Sommers*   The Backlash Myth: The Truth about How Women Are Doing in the Workplace

How a feminist reacts to data about gender gaps in salaries and economic   1
opportunities is an excellent indication of the kind of feminist she is. In general, the equity feminist points with pride to the many gains women have made toward achieving parity in the workplace. By contrast, the gender feminist makes it a point to disparage these gains and to speak of backlash. It disturbs her that the public may be lulled into thinking that women are doing well and that men are allowing it. The gender feminist insists that any so-called progress is illusory.

I felt the force of this insistence two years ago when my stepson, Tamler,   2
was a junior at the University of Pennsylvania. He had written a term paper on *Jane Eyre* in which he made the "insensitive" observation that vocational opportunities for women are wider than they were for Jane Eyre. "No!" wrote his instructor in the margin. "Even today women only make 59 percent of what men make!" The next semester, in another course and for another English professor, Tamler "erred" again by saying of one female character that she had a more satisfying job than her husband did. Again, his teacher expressed her irritation in the margin: "How would you rationalize women earning 49 percent of men's salaries in *all* fields?" As monitored by Pennsylvania's English department, the condition of women seemed to have grown appreciably worse in less than a year!

We have all seen these angry figures. But there is not much truth in them.   3
By most measures, the eighties were a time of rather spectacular gains by American women — in education, in wages, and in such traditionally male professions as business, law, and medicine. The gender feminist will have none of this. According to Susan Faludi, the eighties were the backlash decade, in which men successfully retracted many of the gains wrested from them in preceding decades. This view, inconveniently, does not square with the facts.

Since any criticism of Faludi's claim of a wages backlash is apt to be con-   4
strued as just more backlashing, one must be grateful to the editors of the *New York Times* business section for braving the wrath of feminist ideologues by presenting an objective account of the economic picture as it affects women. Surveying several reports by women economists on women's gains in the 1980s, *New York Times* business writer Sylvia Nasar rejected Faludi's thesis. She pointed to masses of empirical data showing that "far from losing ground, women gained more in the 1980s than in the entire postwar era before that. And almost as much as between 1890 and 1980."[1]

Today more than ever, economic position is a function of education. In   5
1970, 41 percent of college students were women; in 1979, 50 percent were
women; and in 1992, 55 percent were women. In 1970, 5 percent of law degrees were granted to women. In 1989, the figure was 41 percent; by 1991 it
was 43 percent, and it has since gone up. In 1970, women earned 8 percent
of medical degrees. This rose to 33 percent in 1989; by 1991 it was 36 percent.
The giant strides in education are reflected in accelerated progress in the professions and business. Diane Ravitch, a fellow at the Brookings Institution, reports that women have made great advancements toward full equality in
every professional field, and "in some, such as pharmacy and veterinary medicine, women have become the majority in what was previously a male-dominated profession."[2]

The *New York Times* article summarized the research as follows:   6

A fresh body of research — mostly by a new generation of female economists
who've mined a mountain of unexplored data — shows compellingly that
women were big economic winners in the 1980s expansion and that their
gains are likely to keep coming in the 1990s regardless of who is in the White
House. . . . Conventional wisdom — enshrined in the best-selling book [by
Susan Faludi] *Backlash: The Undeclared War against American Women*, among
other places — has it that women made no progress in the past decade. In
fact, women were stuck earning around 60 cents to the men's dollar from
1960 through 1980, but started catching up fast as the economy expanded
during the 1980s.[3]

The *Times* reports that the proportion women earn of each dollar of men's   7
wages rose to a record 72 cents by 1990. But the *Times* points out that even
this figure is misleadingly pessimistic, because it includes older women who
are only marginally in the work force, such as "the mother who graduated
from high school, left the work force at twenty and returned to a minimum
wage at a local store." Younger women, says the *Times*, "now earn 80 cents for
every dollar earned by men of the same age, up from 69 cents in 1980."

It might be supposed that it was not so much that women did well but   8
that men did poorly in the recent recession. However, Baruch College economics professor June O'Neill, director of the Center for Study of Business
and Government, showed that even in areas where men did well, women did
better: "At the upper end, where men did very well, women went through the
roof." According to Francine Blau, a University of Illinois economist cited in
the *Times* story, the eighties were years in which "everything started to come
together for women."

None of these facts has made the slightest impression on the backlash   9
mongers. For years, feminist activists have been wearing buttons claiming
women earn "59 cents to a man's dollar." Some journalists have questioned
this figure: Faludi calls them "spokesmen" for the backlash.[4] According to
Faludi, "By 1988, women with a college diploma could still wear the famous
59-cent buttons. They were still making 59 cents to their male counterpart's
dollar. In fact, the pay gap for them was now a bit worse than five years earlier."[5]

The sources Faludi cites do not sustain her figure. The actual figure for    10
1988 is 68 cents, both for all women and for women with a college diploma.
This is substantially higher, not lower, than it was five years earlier. The most
recent figures, for 1992, are considerably higher yet, the highest they have ever
been: 71 cents for all women and 73 cents for women with a college
diploma.[6]

The figure of 59 cents may be a useful rallying cry for gender feminist ac-    11
tivists, but like many slogans it is highly misleading and now egregiously out
of date. The following diagram shows the dramatic rise of the female-to-male,
year-round, full-time earnings ratio, from about 59 cents throughout the
1970s to 71 cents in 1992.[7] Evidently the 59 cent figure is chosen for its propaganda value rather than for true insights into any remaining discrimination.

**Female-to-Male YRFT Earnings Ratio**

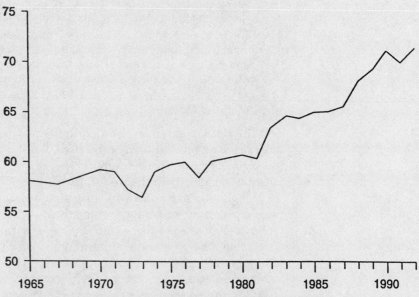

Source: U.S. Bureau of the Census, Current Population Reports, Series P-60.

What of the remaining gap between male and female earnings? For the    12
gender feminists, the answer is simple: the wage gap is the result of discrimination against women. But in fact, serious economics scholars who are
trained to interpret these data (including many eminent female economists)
point out that most of the differences in earnings reflect such prosaic matters
as shorter work weeks and lesser workplace experience. For example, the average work week for full-time, year-round females is shorter than for males.
When economists compare men's and women's *hourly* earnings instead of
their *yearly* earnings, the wage gap narrows even more.[8]

Economists differ on exactly how much, if any, of the remaining gap is      13
discrimination. Most economists agree that much of it simply represents the
fact that, on average, women have accrued less workplace experience than
men of the same age. One recent scholarly estimate shows that as of 1987, females who were currently working full-time and year-round had, on average,
one-quarter fewer years of work experience than comparable males.[9] Moreover, a year of average female work experience generally represents fewer
hours than a year of average male work experience, because of women's
shorter average work week.

The experience gap is particularly important in explaining the earnings       14
gap between older women and men, which is considerably wider than that
for younger workers (67 cents for ages fifty-five through sixty-four vs. 82 cents
for ages twenty-five through thirty-four). For older women, the experience
gap is wider than one-quarter, and adds up over time to a sizable gap in years
of experience and an even wider gap in hours of experience.

These data are important in understanding the oft-cited claim of a "glass     15
ceiling" for women. Promotion in high-powered professional jobs often goes
to those who have put in long hours in evenings and on weekends. Husbands
may be more likely to do so than wives, for a variety of reasons, including unequal division of responsibilities at home, in which case the source of the difficulty is at home, not in the marketplace.[10]

Obviously, the experience gap also reflects the fact that many women        16
choose to move into and out of the work force during childbearing and childrearing years. This reduces the amount of experience they acquire in the workplace and naturally results in lower earnings, quite apart from any possible
discrimination. Some evidence of this is provided by data on childless workers, for whom the experience gap should be much narrower, resulting in a
narrower earnings gap. This, in fact, is the case: the female-to-male ratio of
hourly earnings for childless white workers aged twenty to forty-four was
86–91 percent, as of 1987.[11]

The bottom line is that although economists still differ on how much dis-    17
crimination remains, virtually all of them would agree that the 59 cent figure
is highly misleading. For example, June O'Neill finds that "differences in
earnings attributable solely to gender are likely to be much smaller than is
commonly believed, probably less than 10 percent."[12] This contrasts rather
starkly with the 41 percent figure claimed by Faludi.

This is not to say that there is no room for improvement. An obvious case    18
in point is the modern university's failure to adjust its tenure system to the
growing number of females entering academic careers. Since all new professors are required to "publish or perish" in the first six years of their career, the
tenure clock ticks away at exactly the same rate as young women's biological
clocks.[13] Adjustments are called for since this state of affairs seriously affects
equality of opportunity. It is important to note, however, that the slow adjustment of the universities to changed circumstances is at least in part *because*
they are public or nonprofit institutions that are somewhat insulated from the
market. The private sector, arguably, has been more creative with respect to

flextime, on-site day care, and home office options, and is likely to evolve further, out of economic imperative, rather than through the kind of government intrusion favored by many of the gender warriors.[14]

The generally sober economics profession has a few of its own gender     19
feminists, too. One of its more prominent exponents is American University's professor of economics Barbara Bergmann, who claims "widespread, severe, ongoing discrimination by employers and fellow workers."[15] Professor Bergmann recently surprised some of her fellow feminist (and nonfeminist) economists by opposing a long-standing proposal to include the value of nonmarket activity, such as housework and child care, in the official gross domestic product figures. Her reason was revealing: "Part of the motive [of the proposal] is to lend some dignity to the position of housewives. What I think feminism is about is getting women off of the housewife track."[16] Professor Bergmann has proposed that all candidates for office in the American Economic Association be questioned regarding "their memberships in feminist and antifeminist organizations."[17] She did not specify which "antifeminist" memberships she was targeting, but the tone of her proposal is particularly disturbing because she had recently served as president of the American Association of University Professors.

As Ms. Nasar reminds us, women have not yet achieved parity. Neverthe-     20
less, the glass is at least three-quarters full and getting fuller. Someone ought to inform the University of Pennsylvania English department about this — and, more crucially, the many *Backlash* readers who may have been discouraged by misleading statistics.

*Notes*

1. Sylvia Nasar, "Women's Progress Stalled? Just Not So," *New York Times*, October 18, 1992, sec. 3, p. 1.
2. Diane Ravitch, *Youth Policy*, June–July 1992, p. 12.
3. Nasar, "Women's Progress Stalled?" The article summarizes the recent findings of three prominent women economists, *Understanding the Gender Gap*, by Claudia Goldin (Harvard University); *The Economics of Men, Women, and Work*, by Francine Blau and Marianne Ferber (University of Illinois); and June O'Neill (Baruch College), "Women and Wages," *The American Enterprise*, November/December 1990, pp. 25–33.
4. Susan Faludi, *Backlash: The Undeclared War Against American Women* (New York: Crown, 1991), p. 364.
5. Ibid.
6. These ratios are for median earnings — i.e., the earnings of the male or female in the middle of the pack (one-half earn more, one-half earn less). Source: Bureau of Census, Current Population Reports, Consumer Income Series P60-184, *Money Income of Households, Families, and Persons in the United States: 1992*, September 1993.
7. If gender "backlash" is to be inferred from the earnings ratio, it could only have happened back in the 1950s and early 1960s: that is the last period in which the earnings ratio fell.

8. See O'Neill, "Women and Wages," p. 29. Faludi inexplicably objects to such a straightforward correction for difference in work weeks, referring to this as "spurious data fudging" resulting in an "artificially inflated earnings" ratio.

9. June O'Neill and Solomon Polachek, "Why the Gender Gap in Wages Narrowed in the 1980s," *Journal of Labor Economics* 11, no. 1 (January 1993), part 1: 205–28. Some economists argue that the anticipation of spending less time in market activities than men leads many women to focus their education and training in less remunerative areas, both in secondary and post-secondary education, academic and vocational (see, for example, Claudia Goldin and Solomon Polachek, "Residual Differences by Sex: Perspectives on the Gender Gap in Earnings," *American Economic Review* 77, no. 2 [May 1987]: 143–51).

10. This is a theme stressed by Stanford economist Victor Fuchs, *Women's Quest for Equality* (Cambridge, Mass.: Harvard University Press, 1988). A recent study of 1972–75 graduates of the University of Michigan Law School, fifteen years after graduation, found that one-quarter of the women had at some point worked part-time to care for their children, as compared to 0.5 percent of the men. It also found that this had a very large effect on subsequent earnings, even after returning to work full-time. One of the major reasons appeared to be that such women were far less likely to become partners in large law firms: "Fewer than one-fifth [of mothers] with extensive part-time work had made partner in their firms 15 years after graduation, while more than four-fifths of the mothers with little or no part-time work had made partner" (Robert G. Wood, Mary E. Corcoran, and Paul N. Courant, "Pay Differences among the Highly Paid: The Male-Female Earnings Gap in Lawyers' Salaries," *Journal of Labor Economics* 11, no. 3 (1993): 417–41).

11. O'Neill, "Women and Wages," p. 32. The 86 percent figure standardizes for age and region only; the 91 percent figure also standardizes for additional factors. This article summarizes for noneconomists such scientific work as O'Neill and Polachek, "Why the Gender Gap in Wages Narrowed in the 1980s," and Claudia Goldin, *Understanding the Gender Gap.*

12. O'Neill, "Women and Wages."

13. See Shirley M. Tilghman, "Science vs. Women — A Radical Solution," *New York Times*, January 26, 1993, p. A23.

14. There is a good discussion of the problem of women, family, and the workplace in *Women and Work/Family Dilemma* by Deborah Swiss and Judith Walker (New York: Wiley, 1993).

15. "Does the Market for Women's Labor Need Fixing?" *Journal of Economic Perspectives*, 3, no. 1 (Winter 1989): 43–60.

16. *Chronicle of Higher Education*, December 1, 1993, p. A9.

17. American Economic Association's Committee on the Status of Women in the Economic Profession, *Newsletter*, October 1991.

**Questions to Start You Thinking**

1. CONSIDERING MEANING: According to Sommers, what is an "equity feminist" and what is a "gender feminist"? How far does each type of feminist feel women have come with respect to equality in the workplace?

2. IDENTIFYING WRITING STRATEGIES: How does Sommers use statistics to refute the claims of gender feminists?

3. ANALYZING THE WRITER'S CHOICES: In paragraphs 17 and 18, Sommers hints that there may be some common ground between equity and gender feminists. In her comparison of the two groups' views of women in the workplace, why do you think Sommers chooses to ignore what the two groups may have in common, opting instead to emphasize the differences? Does that choice strengthen or weaken her argument?

4. EXPANDING VOCABULARY: What are *ideologues* (paragraph 4) and "backlash *mongers*" (paragraph 9)? What is their relationship to *propaganda* (paragraph 11)?

5. MAKING CONNECTIONS: Both Sommers and Stephanie Coontz ("The Way We Wish We Were," p. 484) are attempting to deflate a popular myth. Compare and contrast their strategies and arguments. Whose analysis do you find more convincing, and why?

**Journal Prompts**

1. Economics professor Barbara Bergmann says that what she thinks "feminism is about is getting women off of the housewife track" (paragraph 19). What do you think feminism is about?

2. Observe the gender makeup of the classes you are currently taking. Do your observations reflect Sommers's statistics about the percentage of women enrolled in college? To what do you attribute any discrepancy?

**Suggestions for Writing**

1. Do you side with the equity or the gender feminists on the issue of the wage gap? Defend your answer with examples drawn from your observation or personal experience.

2. Read Chapter 13 of Susan Faludi's *Backlash*, the book Sommers cites in this selection. Write an essay comparing and contrasting Sommers's and Faludi's arguments, stating which position you find more convincing, and why.

**Stephen L. Carter** *was born in 1954 in Washington, D.C., and raised in Ithaca, New York. After earning a B.A. at Stanford University in 1976 and a law degree at Yale University in 1979, Carter worked in Washington, D.C., first as a law clerk, including a year with Supreme Court Justice Thurgood Marshall, and then as a practicing lawyer. Since 1982 Carter has been a professor of law at Yale, specializing in constitutional law. Recently he has risen to national prominence as the author of three books:* Reflections of an Affirmative Action Baby *(1991),* The Culture of Disbelief: How American Law and Politics Trivialize Religious Devotion *(1993), and* The Confirmation Mess: Cleaning Up the Federal Appointments Process *(1994). The following selection is excerpted from an essay that originally appeared in* Lure and Loathing: Essays on Race, Identity, and the Ambivalence of Assimilation *(1993), an essay collection edited by Gerald Early. In this excerpt Carter explores the complex relationship between his professional and racial identities.*

# Stephen L. Carter   The Black Table, the Empty Seat, and the Tie

Once or twice, when I was in law school, the "black table" (as we called [1] our solidaritied corner of the dining hall) was torn by a debate, passionate but friendly, over the question of how we should think of ourselves: as black people who happened to be Yale students? or as Yale students who happened to be black?

The black table itself was a statement of need, and of difference. We were [2] law students, but we were not like everyone else, or at least we didn't think we were. We were as grimly enthusiastic and as secretly ambitious and as ready to work hard as anyone else; we all felt the tug of professional attainment. But there were other pulls. The gray corridors and cavernous classrooms of the Yale Law School were familiar but never home. To become a law student, black or white or any other color, is to be on edge, and also on display. All law students need outlets for frustrations, irritations, fears — and joys too. As black law students, we had other needs, as well, needs that seemed to us, at least, not exactly the same as the needs of other students. The need to escape, for example. The need to seek support from each other. The need to be together. And the need to figure out exactly what we were doing there, what our *purpose* was, led us into the fierce but friendly debate over just who we were.

Our argument, never authoritatively resolved, served to remind us of two [3] important truths. The first was that we liked to argue. The second — the more important — was that something was happening to us, something like a coming change in status, as though we were caught in transit, balancing somehow between our origins and our destinations, not fully secure in either. We were all of us children of the civil rights movement: the nation had changed its laws and, in some respects, its ways during our childhoods and adolescences. We were living the opportunities for which generations of black folk had fought and died. Walking paths wet with the blood of our martyrs, we felt an uneasy fear that taking advantage of those opportunities was changing us.

As a law professor at Yale, I look back on those days with a gentle affec- [4] tion, perhaps a wistfulness for the ease with which we bantered. Our heartfelt discussions were themselves happiness of a sort; our enthusiasm was an expression of solidarity, a kind of truth. We were in it together, united by the awareness that our shared skin color made possible and the eagerness to know what was right, and no matter how vehement our political differences, the black table remained an axis around which our small worlds revolved. The ease of it all — I miss the ease.

The passage of time has left me in some ways happier, in others much [5] more pensive. Our community seems more divided now, but that perception might represent the fresh perspective that comes when, at last, one must leave the table behind. The *need*, however, is as deep and nagging as ever. Racism was real to me then, in my early twenties, a brooding enemy one could almost touch; nowadays, something over a decade later, its presence is somehow more sinister, as though it has hidden itself but not really gone away. We are lawyers now, my classmates and I, with professional success behind us and ahead, too. Affirmative action? Who cares? Look at us now! Look at what we have done with the opportunities —

And yet there is this unsettling sense, this mistrust of the world out there. **6** Time has passed, we have moved on, but we cannot honestly say — I can't, anyway — that racism has moved into the past. It is harder to point to it now, people are more careful in what they say and maybe in what they think, too. And yet one senses it there, in the shadows, lurking perhaps around the next brightly lighted corner as one walks the corridor of one's office. We are where we are, we obviously belong, that was settled long ago, and yet — and yet —

The racism. Not so much something to blame for our setbacks as some- **7** thing about which we might often wonder when we think of what we will do next. And yet, the truth is that there is no time to worry, no time and no space, not for the professional. We are too busy being busy to let racism slow us down. We are lawyers now, as I said, nearly all of us, and we have moved on in our profession, a profession defined and dominated by generations of white folk, mostly men, mostly dead, many of whose sour portraits line the corridors and classrooms of Yale and of other leading law schools. (The portraits: Once, when I was in law school, a group of students organized a conference around the theme of sexism in the legal system. Those of us who attended were divided into groups, and one of the assignments was to work out what the law school would be like were the force of sexism less apparent. One of the groups brought a hush, then loud applause, when it reported its solution: *More portraits of dead women on the walls.* Chilling, but precisely right. History is itself a message.) The profession has rules and standards and expectations, and to move upward is to swim in a sea of white people's making. The profession is more integrated than it once was, but the rewards, and most of the punishments, are still distributed by people who are white. Black lawyers in the United States of America number something above twenty-five thousand, a very impressive number indeed, until one realizes that the total number of lawyers is well over seven hundred thousand. There are people of color who deny the right of white folk to shape the profession and insist that other voices be heard . . . and one can but wish them well, even if one wonders which they suppose to be the voices that matter. Law itself remains a conservative force, even thought lawyers themselves are more progressive than they once were and, in opinion surveys, are more liberal than the nation as a whole on almost every issue. In the meantime, the profession remains what it is, and the same question we argued over the table, yet unanswered, sits more heavily as one grows older. Who exactly are we, dark-skinned lawyers in a white-skinned profession? What have we gained by our choices? And what have we cast aside? Yes, we are black. . . . but *how* are we black?

### Differentiating

Let me begin with an uneasy truth: I scare people. I write these words as I sit **8** on an Amtrak train hurrying south along the Northeast Corridor, a six-foot-three-inch male in a sober navy suit, blue oxford shirt, and conservative tie, bent over a laptop computer, the very image, one might suppose, of the seamless dull gray professional. But a professional, of course, with a difference, one that is brought home to me as I watch with mixed feelings the stream of fellow business travelers, the white ones, anyway, treating the seat next to me as though it is already occupied. Of white women this is particularly true: to sit next to a black man, even a well-attired one, is a choice to be made only when no other seat is available, and even then to be avoided if possible, occasionally by standing.

Few of us who are black and professional are unfamiliar with this circumstance. And in our irritation (although it is nice, in the abstract, to have the elbow room of two seats for the price of one), many of us readily describe the attitude of the white people so reluctant to sit next to us as racism. This description makes for an awkward and threatening world: since most white people pass the empty seat and leave it as they found it, most white people must be racist. As I sit here, waiting for the seat to be filled (and now, at last, it has been by a person nether white nor male — the other seats, I note in passing, are all taken), I wonder whether my friends who so readily call the reluctance racism can possibly be right. 9

To be a professional is to be spared the worst ravages of racism, but the many small daily slights that are the price of living here add up to a miasma of racial exclusion. It is almost a cliché that if you are black you can't get a taxi in a major city, and it isn't quite true — but it isn't quite false, either. Even in a business suit, it can be difficult; if one is dressed more casually, it can prove impossible. When in New York, for example, if I am traveling with a white person, I frequently swallow my pride and allow my companion to summon the taxi as I hang back — for to stand up for my rights and raise the arm myself would buy only a tired arm and no ride. For a black male, blue jeans in New York are a guarantee of ill-treatment. There are the jewelry-store buzzers that will not ring, the counter clerks who will not say "Sir," the men's departments with no staff to be found. I shop mostly at Brooks Brothers, but I always dress for it, recalling, from my childhood, a complicated tale involving my paternal grandmother, a rude shopkeeper, an expensive fur, and a change of tune. 10

Ah, I sometimes think, to be able to hit them over the head with my résumé! In my mind's eye, I can see the paper slamming down, as I await the grimace, the shout of pain, then the recognition and apology. Oddly, that might even do some good. Social psychologists who study racial stereotyping report that even white people who indulge in a great deal of stereotyping will alter their opinions of black people who possess a variety of identifiable status attainments, such as advanced degrees. This will not alter by a single iota, however, their judgments on other black people, about whom they know less, which means that even in the act of dressing to shop I am putting a distance between myself and my people. So there, already, is a division among us, a tax that racism imposes on success: Yes, we will treat you differently from the 11 way we treat your brethren and sistren, but only if you first mark yourself as different. If I am willing to divide myself from the whole, even symbolically, I earn a reward for it. How terrifying!

Still, I do not insist that the taxi drivers who will not stop unless I am    12
dressed as they prefer — unless I send the right signal of my difference from those they fear — are racists in the same sense that members of the Ku Klux Klan are racists. People are more complicated than that, and I have little doubt that some of the same people who will not open the doors of their jewelry stores when I am in my blue jeans will send large contributions to the Southern Poverty Law Center to do the good work of keeping the Klan at bay. For doing so, I charge them with neither insincerity nor hypocrisy — simply with normal human complexity. Similarly, I do not insist that my colleagues are racist when their evaluations of the work of a person of color differ from mine; or that law firms are racist when their record on hiring people of color is less impressive than I might like. To choose "racism" as a category to capture all of that complexity is much like suggesting that those who opposed the Persian Gulf War were not supporting America or that those who think the First Amendment protects exploitative pornography support the oppression of women. Each is a clever rhetorical point that drains the principal horror — racism, treason, sexism — of most of its normative content. Yes, of course, there is racism in the legal profession, but we must not be so blinded by our search for the covert kind that we miss the overt kind. There are people out there, people with power — fewer, I think, than some fear, but clearly too many — people with power who hate us. A white collar is no insulation against either side of *that* relationship. And dressing to shop, or to work, will change the relationship marginally, but one must not make the mistake of thinking (or desiring) that his cosmetic change also works a change in morphology sufficiently dramatic that there is a sudden and sharp discontinuity in one's life situation. There is a better job and more pay (and more white friends if that is what one desires); but there is also the lingering question, from the days of the black table, about what else one puts on when one puts on a tie.

Which brings us back to the train. Where I do wear a tie, always as care-    13
ful in dressing for travel as in dressing to shop. I am not a different person with a tie than without one, even though some people's perceptions of me will change with my clothes. Even my fellow passengers, reluctant as they are to take the seat next to mine, probably look at me *a little bit* differently than they would were I in my jeans. They do not want to sit next to me, but they are not rushing to the conductor to demand that I be tossed off the train. And besides — not to put too fine a point on it — in the end, who cares about them anyway? Beyond a certain point, reached very early in my dialogue with myself, I lose interest in their opinions of me, or even in whether they are racists or not.

Not long ago, I published a book entitled *Reflections of an Affirmative Ac-*    14
*tion Baby*, in which I urged those of us who are in the professions to quit worrying about what our white colleagues feel, to meet the "qualification

question" — *Did you get here because of affirmative action?* — with a studied *Yes, so what?* I also argued that the best way to frustrate our detractors is to overachieve, to shape ourselves into a generation of black professionals too good to ignore.

Some black professionals were angered by what I wrote. I was told that I was naive, that there was more racism in the professions than I evidently supposed, so that hard work alone would not be enough to get ahead. Others took me to task for worrying too much about what white people think. And some suggested that the call for overachievement was unfair and ill conceived, suggesting that I was the shade of Booker Washington[1] come back to life, urging us to cast down our buckets where we are, to work hard to please the white man.

I had thought that I answered all of these points in the book, but perhaps I did not write as clearly as I should have. The objection that I was worried too much about what white people think particularly rankled, however; it was my intention to argue the other way around, that we who are black worry too much about what white people think, and that our obsession with their good opinions — the same obsession, incidentally, that in the minds of some black people transforms affirmative action into a stigma — has got to stop.

Still, back on Amtrak, still heading south,[2] I cannot quite succeed in the pretense that the white people who will not sit next to me do not actually exist. I know they are there and I know they are avoiding me — how could I not? And while their behavior does not make me think less of myself, it does seem to me to demand a bit of analysis as one works through the matter of one's professional identity, and of why one wears a tie. As I have noted, the usual explanation for their refusal to sit next to black people is racism. I see little point, however, in being so harsh on my fellow passengers, or indeed, for marking them as particularly culpable. All they are doing, really, is thinking in racial terms. They are using race as shorthand for other characteristics that they find unpleasant: a tendency toward criminality, perhaps. Before one rushes to say that this is precisely what is meant by the word *racism*, let me caution that using race as a shorthand for other characteristics is precisely

---

[1] **Booker [T.] Washington** (1856–1915): Influential and controversial African American educator and thinker who was often at odds with other black leaders. He founded Tuskegee Institute in Alabama in 1881 to carry out his "accommodationist" ideas — that is, his belief that the primary goal of African Americans should be economic self-determination rather than the immediate attainment of social and political equality with whites. In a famous speech in Atlanta in 1895, Washington includes a parable about a ship lost at sea. Spotting another vessel, the ship repeatedly signaled, "Water, water; we die of thirst!" The other ship kept answering, "Cast down your bucket where you are," until the captain of the distressed ship finally did so. The bucket came up with fresh water from the mouth of the Amazon River. Washington used this parable to urge blacks to cultivate friendly relations with whites: "I could say: 'cast down your bucket where you are' — cast it down in making friends . . . of the people of all races by whom we are surrounded."

[2] This part of the description of the train ride was *not* written while on board. [Carter's note]

what affirmative action (to take the most obvious example) necessarily does. People of color who are swept, willingly or not, into the swirling maelstrom of racial preferences are presumed to share a common history or a common perspective or a common disadvantage or a common need or whatever the most persuasive justification might be. And although their motivations and results obviously differ, there is no *logical* distinction between the assumptions about race underlying affirmative action programs and the assumptions about race underlying the empty seat. Using race as a "bad" shorthand is, of course, far worse than using race as a "good" shorthand, and sometimes doing the second is important. Still, in both cases, the person of color who is the subject of the assumptions is treated as a representative of the people — it is simply that the white people who refuse to sit down, like the black people who pronounce upon the attitudes that one must hold to be truly black, are arrogating to themselves the right to decide what aspects of the people the one that they are looking at represents.

So the problem of the empty seat is not quite like the problem of being    18
the last kid picked when choosing up sides for softball or football back in grade school, for the judgment has nothing to do with skill. Indeed, the fact that it has nothing to do with skill — that none of those who pass the seat know or care whether I am good at my job — makes it much like the forms of exclusion that often cut at the professional soul. One of the reasons that it often makes sense to use affirmative action to lever open the doors is that they are closed for reasons other than a racist desire to oppress; they are closed, rather, because of the prevailing racialist stereotypes that render black people beneath the notice of white people. Affirmative action can force white people to take notice, and, if they are not truly or deeply racist, once they take notice, quality will out. For it is their ignorance as much as their hatred that keeps the barriers up — the same reason that I sit alone on the train. There are times when, sitting thus, I long for some instrument of coercive authority, a means to force one or more of the passersby not only to sit but to talk, and to listen. But only brief times. The honest truth is that the good opinion of the people passing by matters to me less and less, both on the train and professionally; what I find I like is the elbow room.

## Claiming

So let me begin to explore the question of professional identity at a slightly    19
different place; not with the vision of blackness imposed from without, whether by people who are white or by people who are black, but with the vision of blackness selected from within. For prior to one's professional identity can be, should be, a *personal* identity. One selects it: that's easy, delightfully so, for I'm black and would not be anything else if I could. Yes, I work in a mostly white profession, and, yes, I work at a mostly white law school. But that is not all there is of me and need not even be most of me. My ties with the black community, with black people, are richer and stronger than my bonds to the white. I have no generalized view that white people are

racist or insensitive; still, I must confess, the good opinions of black people, to put it simply, matter to me more. That is my choice, and I cannot imagine ever making another.

The choice is partly cultural, partly social, and partly political, but it is mostly affectional. One selects a milieu. It is a choice not about where one lives or how one votes but whom one loves. And the issue is less romantic love (although my wife is black, I recognize that there is such a thing as genuine affection across racial lines) than a sufficient love of one's own identity so that it extends in a special way to the group. I have white friends too, and care for some of them deeply, but that is beside the point. Just as in the days of the black table, simply being around black people — among black people — having that respite, that trust, that common need fulfilled, that *being together* — is something I cherish and something my wife and I are determined to preserve for our children. Which is why, as a black couple living as we do in a mostly white neighborhood, we are not content to trust our social lives to chance, but are constantly on the lookout for new black acquaintances, associates, friends — with children if possible.          20

Identifying as black is in this sense a decision. Biology plays a role, but not a complete one, and the pressure of our racialist society to treat skin color as destiny is one that some prefer to resist. The pressure *is* oppressive, but resisting it does not require pushing in the other direction; rather, one can, in the manner of the martial artist, use the opponent's strength to go where one wants to go anyway. I realize that there are black people, especially among the professionally successful, for whom connections with people who are white become more important than connections with people who are black, and I feel sorry for them, for what they have lost. Still, that is their choice, and I wish them well of it; mine, however, goes in another direction.          21

But as for the rest, one's *professional* identity, all that one can do is try on the words, and see which fit. . . .          22

A law professor.          23

A black law professor.          24

A black person who is a law professor.          25

A law professor who is black.          26

The transpositions of words, like the ones we batted back and forth in the dining hall, are subtle, but important. A few years ago, I watched a television interview in which a black man who is prominent in the conservative movement was asked whether he preferred to be called "black" or "African American." Without a moment's hesitation, he replied, "I'm an American. That's what I want to be called."          27

Fair enough: I'm happy to call him what he wants to be called. But I am not happy to think of myself that way. I need the adjective that he seemed content, almost determined, to drop. Oh, yes, I am an American, and I certainly want to be that. I take as much pride in that, I am sure, as anyone. But I am not, in my mind or in my soul, I cannot be, *just* an American, anymore than I am, in my mind or in my soul, or can be, *just* a law professor.          28

To be a black professional is to lead a dual existence, but that existence   29
need not be uncomfortable. There are some intellectuals — Shelby Steele and
Richard Rodriguez[3] perhaps foremost among them — who have suggested
that the fact of moving ahead in a predominantly white profession creates a
necessary distance between oneself and one's ethnic community. They have
argued, in effect, that the new environment slowly destroys the old, that it is
inevitable and perhaps even desirable to be thought of as (or to think of oneself as), say, a professor who happens to be black, rather than a black person
who happens to be a professor. And while I have always appreciated the logical force of the argument, it seems to me to be dangerously wrong. My wife,
for example, was the first in her family to attend college. By the Steele-
Rodriguez argument, I should feel, automatically, a distance from her relatives. But the reverse is true. Slipping warmly and comfortably into the
embrace of her family is the most natural feeling in the world.

There are sour moments — I admit it — when I stride the halls of Yale   30
Law School bitterly, angry at a world that insists on seeing me as a black person who is also a law professor instead of a law professor who is also black.
But the moments are few, for most of the time the first of these is my image
of myself as well. In that sense, I have resolved that after-dinner argument of
so many years ago, and I am what I want to be: a black law professor? Okay.
A law professor who is black? Yes, that too. But, better, a law professor who
loves black people.

Racial solidarity, in the sense of self-love, is the key to our survival in a   31
frustratingly segregated integrated professional world, just as it is the key to
our survival in a frustratingly oppressive nation. Oh, the professions are all integrated now. There are black people in them, fewer than we would like, but
more than our detractors would like. Affirmative action, whatever its flaws,
has forever changed the face of professional America, and that is all to the
good. But so have hard work and perseverance, the willingness to be less concerned with the fairness of the obstacles in one's path than with finding the
best way over, around, or through them. Affirmative action can open doors;
but running (never walking) through them is our job.

But as we run and run and run, rushing toward professional success be-   32
fore the tiny trapdoor in the glass ceiling slams shut, there remains the uneasy
question from the black table, the question of whether in running toward one
thing we are also running from another. I might explain my decision to wear
a tie on the train, and elsewhere too, on the ground that the tie is demanded
by the profession I have chosen to follow. The question is whether my willingness to wear the tie, or perhaps my insistence upon it, is itself an acceptance of the distinction that my longing for solidarity wants most to deny. If
I will vary my plumage to please creatures more powerful than myself, what
does that say about my relationship with the flock?

[3] **Shelby Steele** (b. 1946): African American writer and professor of English at San
Jose State University in California, known for his essays on race relations and his attacks
on affirmative action. **Richard Rodriguez:** See "Does America Still Exist?" p. 524.

THE WORLD OF WORK

Perhaps it says nothing. Consider the words of Mario Baeza, a black man who is a member of New York's legal elite: "I'm integrated, but I've never tried to be white. That's not what I aspire to in life." Very well, one accepts rules of dress as one accepts rules of grammar, in order to get ahead. That requires a certain ambition, but ambition is not inconsistent with a love of one's people. Solidarity can be the bridge between our roots and our destinations. Claiming one's people gives one an identity. Selecting a destination gives one a profession. The question, then is whether there is any reason one cannot have both.    33

**Questions to Start You Thinking**

1. CONSIDERING MEANING: What did the "black table" represent for Carter as a student, and what does it represent for him now as a professional?

2. IDENTIFYING WRITING STRATEGIES: How does Carter use recall to show how his feelings on racial and professional identity have evolved over the years?

3. ANALYZING THE WRITER'S CHOICES: Note Carter's frequent use of the pronouns *we* and *us*. What audience does Carter seem to be addressing? Where does Carter state or imply that he feels connected to his readers, and what effect does this assertion have on Carter's plea for "racial solidarity" (paragraphs 31–33)?

4. EXPANDING VOCABULARY: Define *solidarity, segregated,* and *integrated* (paragraph 31)? According to Carter, how is "racial solidarity" the key to black professionals' survival? What does Carter mean by the phrase "a frustratingly segregated integrated professional world" (paragraph 31)?

5. MAKING CONNECTIONS: Compare and contrast the reactions Carter and Brent Staples ("Black Men and Public Space," p. 518) have to the way their clothes and skin color affect those around them.

**Journal Prompts**

1. As a student, do you feel the "tug of professional attainment" (paragraph 2)? Explain.

2. From your observations, do you agree with Carter that the professional world is both segregated and integrated (paragraph 31)? What about the academic world?

**Suggestions for Writing**

1. In a personal essay, reflect on what you anticipate your professional identity will be. Do you think it will be affected in any way by your racial, ethnic, or cultural identity? Explain.

2. What are the similarities and differences between racism and affirmative action as Carter sees them? Write an essay in which you take a stand on affirmative action, supporting or refuting Carter's position.

# Chapter 26

# Popular Culture

**Journal Prompt**

What television shows or movies do you remember most clearly from your childhood? What vision of the world did they create for you? How did they influence you?

**Ellen Goodman,** *born in 1941 in Newton, Massachusetts, writes a nationally syndicated column on contemporary American life for the* Boston Globe, *where she is also an associate editor. Before joining the* Globe, *Goodman worked as a researcher, reporter, and feature writer for* Newsweek *and the* Detroit Free Press. *Goodman's collections of newspaper columns include* Close to Home *(1979),* Keeping in Touch *(1985),* Making Sense *(1989), and* Value Judgments *(1993). She won a Pulitzer Prize for commentary in 1980. In the following article, first published in the* Globe *on July 17, 1994, Goodman blends playfulness and seriousness in her analysis of male characters in current American movies.*

## *Ellen Goodman*    The New Hollywood Male

1   Somewhere in the middle of the movie, Forrest Gump finally proposes to the woman he's loved since first grade. "Will you marry me?" he asks. "I'd make a good husband, Jenny."

2   At that point, anyone worth the price of the popcorn wants to stand up in the theater and tell Jenny to grab him. Never mind that Forrest has an IQ of 75. In the words of countless generations of mothers, "A good man is hard to find."

3   Indeed the bottom line of the movie that's become the surprise hit of the summer is exactly how few and far between good men are.

4   In *Forrest Gump,* Tom Hanks acts as a baby boomer's tour guide through three decades of male roles and man-made disasters. Through the wonders of computer-generated imagery, he is seen next to every flawed male icon from Elvis Presley to Richard Nixon.

5   He's innocently drafted into everyman's questionable role from football star to soldier to entrepreneur. He's picked on by the good ol' boys when he's young and sent to war by the best and brightest men when he's grown up.

6   The males in Jenny's life are an even more dubious lot. They're dysfunctional poster boys. The movie's catalog of Mr. Wrongs includes a father who abused her, sleazy strip joint customers who heckle her, and an antiwar lefty who slugs her.

7   Compared to them, Forrest looks pretty, um, good.

8   Does anybody remember when the great American hero was a Jimmy Stewart character from a small town? Today, the last American hero is a Tom Hanks character with a small IQ.

9   Is there a message here? If he's good, is it because he doesn't have the brains to be bad or bitter?

10  Several years ago, Tom Hanks played another appealing New Sensitive Male of the era. His character in *Big* was actually a twelve-year-old boy magically transformed into a grown-up man's body. He was one guy in touch with his inner child.

577

Not long after that, Mike Nichols directed a movie about the male psyche    11
that offered the hope of male consciousness-raising through consciousness-
shattering. In *Regarding Henry*, a master-of-the-universe type became a model
husband and father by getting shot in the head.

Now Hanks is back as *Forrest Gump* and Nichols is back with *Wolf*. Will,    12
the main male of *Wolf*, is too benign, even passive. He is a middle-aged literary editor being eaten alive by yet another set of bad guys in the corporate
jungle.

When he's bitten on the hand, Will gets a shot of that old animal spirit.    13
The hero in this movie is a werewolf. What was in that saliva? Testosterone?

So there we have it. Once a man had to choose between the lady and the    14
tiger. Now a woman at the movies can choose between the slow-witted and
the werewolf.

Oh, but I almost forgot the lion. The third movie of this seasonal troika    15
of male images is *The Lion King*. Disney offers an animated paean to patri-
archy. All is well in the world only when the princes like Simba are willing to
take their rightful place on the throne.

Do you get the idea that Hollywood is having trouble with heroes? With    16
changing scripts?

If I read what's going on here — and reading is hard in a dark theater —    17
there's as much ambivalence about defining a good man as finding one.

Men today are handed any number of mixed cultural messages about    18
who they should be. A good man is expected to be egalitarian and protective.
He's supposed to turn away from the violence and to be able to defend himself.

We want to raise boys who are strong but not silent, sensitive but sur-    19
vivors. We want our sons to be the men we'd want our daughters to marry.
But we're afraid they'll get clobbered by the alpha males in the playground.

The real world, like Hollywood, is still full of bad guys. So we end up with    20
a small, disparate lot of good guys:

Simba, the king of nostalgic fantasies for the old "natural order."    21

Will, the modern man who needs sharper fangs to survive.    22

And Forrest, the only man allowed to utter the simple verities on the    23
screen — "A promise is a promise" and "I'm not a smart man but I know what
love is" — because he is a simpleton.

OK, OK, a good man is hard to find. But it's a whole lot harder to find    24
him at the movies.

<table>
<tr><td>Questions to Start<br>You Thinking</td><td>1. CONSIDERING MEANING: What is the new Hollywood male like, as Goodman describes him? What does Goodman think is the problem with him?<br><br>2. IDENTIFYING WRITING STRATEGIES: How does Goodman use comparison and contrast to evaluate the changing images of "good men" in the movies?<br><br>3. ANALYZING THE WRITER'S CHOICES: Goodman makes the claim that "men today are handed any number of mixed cultural messages about who they should</td></tr>
</table>

be" (paragraph 18). How does she use examples from the movies to support this claim? In your opinion, is her presumption that art imitates life valid? Why or why not?

4. EXPANDING VOCABULARY: Define *egalitarian* (paragraph 18). Why are "good men" expected to be *egalitarian*? According to Goodman, why might these good men get "clobbered by the alpha males" (paragraph 19)?

5. MAKING CONNECTIONS: Compare and contrast the "New Sensitive Male" (paragraph 10) in Goodman's essay with the men Scott Russell Sanders describes in "The Men We Carry in Our Minds" (p. 499).

**Journal Prompts**

1. Write your own definition of a "good man." Would a "good woman" have any of the same characteristics?

2. Who is your favorite male hero from a recent movie? Why do you admire him?

**Suggestions for Writing**

1. Recall a movie you have seen recently that featured a male hero. Explain your reaction to the hero. To what extent does he fit your definition of a "good man"? If he does not, explain how he would need to change to meet your standards.

2. To what extent have female protagonists changed over the years? Analyze the women characters in a few recent movies, contrasting them with women from older movies. If you notice significant differences, explain why you think these changes have occurred. If you feel that the women in the recent movies are the same as they've always been, provide evidence to support your point of view.

**Stephen King** *was born in 1947 in Portland, Maine, attended the University of Maine at Orono, and now lives in Bangor, Maine, where he writes his best-selling horror novels, many of which have been made into popular movies. The prolific King is also the author of screenplays, teleplays, short fiction, essays, and (under the pseudonym Richard Bachman) novels. His well-known horror novels include* Carrie *(1974),* The Shining *(1977),* Firestarter *(1980),* Pet Sematary *(1983),* Misery *(1987), and* Insomnia *(1994). In the following essay, first published in* Playboy *in December 1981, King draws on his extensive experience with horror to explain the human craving to be frightened.*

## *Stephen King*   **Why We Crave Horror Movies**

I think that we're all mentally ill; those of us outside the asylums only hide it a little better — and maybe not all that much better, after all. We've all known people who talk to themselves, people who sometimes squinch their faces into horrible grimaces when they believe no one is watching, people who have some hysterical fear — of snakes, the dark, the tight place, the long drop . . . and, of course, those final worms and grubs that are waiting so patiently underground.

When we pay our four or five bucks and seat ourselves at tenth-row center in a theater showing a horror movie, we are daring the nightmare.   2

Why? Some of the reasons are simple and obvious. To show that we can,   3
that we are not afraid, that we can ride this roller coaster. Which is not to say that a really good horror movie may not surprise a scream out of us at some point, the way we may scream when the roller coaster twists through a complete 360 or plows through a lake at the bottom of the drop. And horror movies, like roller coasters, have always been the special province of the young; by the time one turns forty or fifty, one's appetite for double twists or 360-degree loops may be considerably depleted.

We also go to reestablish our feelings of essential normality; the horror   4
movie is innately conservative, even reactionary. Freda Jackson as the horrible melting woman in *Die, Monster, Die!* confirms for us that no matter how far we may be removed from the beauty of a Robert Redford or a Diana Ross, we are still light-years from true ugliness.

And we go to have fun.   5

Ah, but this is where the ground starts to slope away, isn't it? Because this   6
is a very peculiar sort of fun indeed. The fun comes from seeing others menaced — sometimes killed. One critic suggested that if pro football has become the voyeur's version of combat, then the horror film has become the modern version of the public lynching.

It is true that the mythic, "fairy-tale" horror film intends to take away the   7
shades of gray. . . . It urges us to put away our more civilized and adult penchant for analysis and to become children again, seeing things in pure blacks and whites. It may be that horror movies provide psychic relief on this level because this invitation to lapse into simplicity, irrationality, and even outright madness is extended so rarely. We are told we may allow our emotions a free rein . . . or no rein at all.

If we are all insane, then sanity becomes a matter of degree. If your in-   8
sanity leads you to carve up women like Jack the Ripper or the Cleveland Torso Murderer, we clap you away in the funny farm (but neither of those two amateur-night surgeons was ever caught, heh-heh-heh); if, on the other hand, your insanity leads you only to talk to yourself when you're under stress or to pick your nose on your morning bus, then you are left alone to go about your business . . . though it is doubtful that you will ever be invited to the best parties.

The potential lyncher is in almost all of us (excluding saints, past and pre-   9
sent; but then, most saints have been crazy in their own ways), and every now and then, he has to be let loose to scream and roll around in the grass. Our emotions and our fears form their own body, and we recognize that it demands its own exercise to maintain proper muscle tone. Certain of these emotional muscles are accepted — even exalted — in civilized society; they are, of course, the emotions that tend to maintain the status quo of civilization itself. Love, friendship, loyalty, kindness — these are all the emotions that we ap-

plaud, emotions that have been immortalized in the couplets of Hallmark cards and in the verses (I don't dare call it poetry) of Leonard Nimoy.

When we exhibit these emotions, society showers us with positive rein-    10
forcement; we learn this even before we get out of diapers. When, as children, we hug our rotten little puke of a sister and give her a kiss, all the aunts and uncles smile and twit and cry, "Isn't he the sweetest little thing?" Such coveted treats as chocolate-covered graham crackers often follow. But if we deliberately slam the rotten little puke of a sister's fingers in the door, sanctions follow — angry remonstrance from parents, aunts, and uncles; instead of a chocolate-covered graham cracker, a spanking.

But anticivilization emotions don't go away, and they demand periodic    11
exercise. We have such "sick" jokes as "What's the difference between a truck-load of bowling balls and a truckload of dead babies" (You can't unload the truckload of bowling balls with a pitchfork . . . a joke, by the way, that I heard originally from a ten-year-old.) Such a joke may surprise a laugh or a grin out of us even as we recoil, a possibility that confirms the thesis: If we share a brotherhood of man, then we also share an insanity of man. None of which is intended as a defense of either the sick joke or insanity but merely as an explanation of the best horror films, like the best fairy tales, manage to be reactionary, anarchistic, and revolutionary all at the same time.

The mythic horror movie, like the sick joke, has a dirty job to do. It de-    12
liberately appeals to all that is worst in us. It is morbidity unchained, our most base instincts let free, our nastiest fantasies realized . . . and it all happens, fittingly enough in the dark. For those reasons, good liberals often shy away from horror films. For myself, I like to see the most aggressive of them — *Dawn of the Dead*, for instance — as lifting a trapdoor in the civilized forebrain and throwing a basket of raw meat to the hungry alligators swimming around in that subterranean river beneath.

Why bother? Because it keeps them from getting out, man, it keeps them    13
down there and me up here. It was Lennon and McCartney who said that all you need is love, and I would agree with that.

As long as you keep the gators fed.    14

---

**Questions to Start You Thinking**

1. CONSIDERING MEANING: According to King, why do we "crave" horror movies — what need do they fulfill?

2. IDENTIFYING WRITING STRATEGIES: How does King use humor to make his case?

3. ANALYZING THE WRITER'S CHOICES: What assumptions does King make about his audience? Why do you think he makes a point of showing the reader, through personal example and the frequent use of the inclusive pronoun *we*, that these assumptions apply to himself as much as anyone?

4. EXPANDING VOCABULARY: Why are horror movies "*innately* conservative" (paragraph 4), *reactionary*, *anarchistic*, and *revolutionary* (paragraph 11)?

5. MAKING CONNECTIONS: How is the craving for horror films like the attraction to daytime talk shows as described by Kurt Andersen ("Oprah and Jo-Jo the Dog-Faced Boy," p. 590)?

1. Recall a movie that exercised your "anticivilization emotions" (paragraph 11). Describe your state of mind before, during, and after the movie.

2. Do you agree with King that "we're all mentally ill" (paragraph 1)? Explain your answer.

1. What genre of movie do you prefer to watch, and why? What cravings does this type of movie satisfy?

2. Do you agree that "the horror film has become the modern version of the public lynching" (paragraph 6)? Write an argument in which you defend or refute this suggestion, citing examples from King's essay and from your own moviegoing experience to support your position.

**Patricia J. Williams** *was born in 1951 in Boston and grew up in Boston and New York City. A graduate of Harvard Law School, Williams has been a professor of law at Columbia University since 1992. Her articles have appeared in many publications, including* Ms. *magazine and the* Village Voice. *She is also the author of* The Alchemy of Race and Rights: Diary of a Law Professor *(1991), in which she blends autobiography and reflections about the law, especially as it relates to race. Her ability to weave personal anecdotes and perspectives into an argument is evident in "Hate Radio," which was first published in the March–April 1994 issue of* Ms.

## *Patricia J. Williams*    Hate Radio

Three years ago I stood at my sink, washing the dishes and listening to the radio. I was tuned to the rock and roll so I could avoid thinking about the big news from the day before — George Bush has just nominated Clarence Thomas to replace Thurgood Marshall on the Supreme Court. I was squeezing a dot of lemon Joy into each of the wineglasses when I realized that two smoothly radio-cultured voices, a man's and a woman's, had replaced the music.    1

"I think it's a stroke of genius on the president's part," said the female voice.    2

"Yeah," said the male voice. "Then those blacks, those African Americans, those Negroes — hey "Negro" is good enough for Thurgood Marshall—whatever, they can't make up their minds [what] they want to be called. I'm gonna call them Blafricans. Black Africans. Yeah, I like it. Blafricans. Then they can get all upset because now the president appointed a Blafrican."    3

"Yeah, well, that's the way those liberals think. It's just crazy."    4

"And then after they turn down his nomination the president can say he tried to please 'em, and then he can appoint someone with some intelligence."    5

Back then, this conversation seemed so horrendously unusual, so singu-   6
larly hateful, that I picked up a pencil and wrote it down. I was certain that a
firestorm of protest was going to engulf the station and purge those foul radio mouths with the good clean soap of social outrage.

I am so naive. When I finally turned on the radio and rolled my dial to   7
where everyone else had been tuned while I was busy watching Cosby reruns,
it took me a while to understand that there's a firestorm all right, but not of
protest. In the two and a half years since Thomas has assumed his post on the
Supreme Court, the underlying assumptions of the conversation I heard as
uniquely outrageous have become commonplace, popularly expressed, and
louder in volume. I hear the style of that snide polemicism everywhere,
among acquaintances, on the street, on television in toned-down versions. It
is a crude demagoguery that makes me heartsick. I feel more and more surrounded by that point of view, the assumptions of being without intelligence,
the coded epithets, the "Blafrican"-like stand-ins for "nigger," the mocking
angry glee, the endless tirades filled with nonspecific, nonempircally based
slurs against "these people" or "those minorities" or "feminazis" or "liberals"
or "scumbags" or "pansies" or "jerks" or "sleazeballs" or "loonies" or "animals" or "foreigners."

At the same time I am not so naive as to suppose that this is something   8
new. In clearheaded moments I realize I am not listening to the radio anymore, I am listening to a large segment of white America think aloud in ever
louder resurgent thoughts that have generations of historical precedent. It's as
though the radio has split open like an egg, Morton Downey, Jr.'s clones and
Joe McCarthy's ghost spilling out, broken yolks, a great collective of sometimes clever, sometimes small, but uniformly threatened brains — they have
all come gushing out. Just as they were about to pass into oblivion, Jack and
his humble black sidekick Rochester get resurrected in the ungainly bodies of
Howard Stern and his faithful black henchwoman, Robin Quivers. The culture of Amos and Andy has been revived and reassembled in Bob Grant's radio minstrelry and radio newcomer Daryl Gate's sanctimonious imprecations
on behalf of decent white people. And in striking imitation of Jesse Helm's
nearly forgotten days as a radio host, the far Right has found its undisputed
king in the personage of Rush Limbaugh — a polished demagogue with a
weekly radio audience of at least 20 million, a television show that vies for
ratings with the likes of Jay Leno, a newsletter with a circulation of 380,000
and two best-selling books whose combined sales are closing in on six million copies.

From Churchill to Hitler to the old Soviet Union, it's clear that radio and   9
television have the power to change the course of history, to proselytize, and
to coalesce not merely the good and the noble, but the very worst in human
nature as well. Likewise, when Orson Welles made his famous radio broadcast "witnessing" the landing of a spaceship full of hostile Martians, the
United States ought to have learned a lesson about the power of radio to appeal to mass instincts and incite mass hysteria. Radio remains a peculiarly
powerful medium even today, its visual emptiness in a world of six trillion

flashing images allowing one of the few remaining playgrounds for the aural subconscious. Perhaps its power is attributable to our need for an oral tradition after all, some conveying of stories, feelings, myths of ancestors, epics of alienation, and the need to rejoin ancestral roots, even ignorant bigoted roots. Perhaps the visual quiescence of radio is related to the popularity of E-mail or electronic networking. Only the voice is made manifest, unmasking worlds that cannot — or dare not? — be seen. Just yet. Nostalgia crystallizing into a dangerous future. The preconscious voice erupting into the expressed, the prime time.

What comes out of the modern radio mouth could be the *Iliad,* the *Rubáiyát,* the griot's song of our times. If indeed radio is a vessel for the American "Song of Songs,"[1] then what does it mean that a manic, adolescent Howard Stern is so popular among radio listeners, that Rush Limbaugh's wittily smooth sadism has gone the way of prime-time television, and that both vie for the number one slot on all the best-selling book lists? What to make of the stories being told by our modern radio evangelists and their tragic unloved chorus of callers? Is it really just a collapsing economy that spawns this drama of grown people sitting around scaring themselves to death with fantasies of black feminist Mexican able-bodied gay soldiers earning $100,000 a year on welfare who are so criminally depraved that Hillary Clinton or the Antichrist-of-the-moment had no choice but to invite them onto the government payroll so they can run the country? The panicky exaggeration reminds me of a child's fear. . . . *And then, and then, a huge lion jumped out of the shadows and was about to gobble me up, and I can't ever sleep again for a whole week.* 10

As I spin the dial on my radio, I can't help thinking that this stuff must be related to that most poignant of fiber-optic phenomena, phone sex. Aural Sex. Radio Racism with a touch of S & M. High-priest hosts with the power and run-amok ego to discipline listeners, to smack with the verbal back of the hand, to smash the button that shuts you up once and for all. "Idiot!" shouts New York City radio demagogue Bob Grant and then the sound of droning telephone emptiness, the voice of dissent dumped out some trapdoor in aural space. 11

As I listened to a range of such programs what struck me as the most unifying theme was not merely the specific intolerance on such hot topics as race and gender, but a much more general contempt for the world, a verbal stoning of anything different. It is like some unusually violent game of "Simon Says," this mockery and shouting down of callers, this roar of incantations, then insistence on agreement. 12

But, ah, if you *will* but only agree, what sweet and safe reward, what soft enfolding by a stern and angry radio god. And as an added bonus, the invis- 13

[1] *Iliad:* Ancient Greek epic poem about the Trojan War, attributed to Homer. *Rubáiyát:* Book of epigrammatic quatrains by the Persian poet Omar Khayyám (1048–1122). Edward FitzGerald (1808–1882) published a loose English translation in 1859. *Song of Songs:* Book of love poems in the Hebrew Bible, traditionally attributed to King Solomon and also known as the Song of Solomon or Canticles.

ible shield of an AM community, a family of fans who are Exactly Like You, to whom you can express, in anonymity, all the filthy stuff you imagine "them" doing to you. The comfort and relief of being able to ejaculate, to those who understand about the dark imagined excess overtaking, robbing, needing to be held down and taught a good lesson, needing to put it in its place before the ravenous demon enervates all that is true and good and pure in this life.

The audience for this genre of radio flagellation is mostly young, white, and male. Two thirds of Rush Limbaugh's audience is male. According to *Time* magazine, 75 percent of Howard Stern's listeners are white men. Most of the callers have spent their lives walling themselves off from any real experience with blacks, feminists, lesbians, or gays. In this regard, it is probably true, as former Secretary of Education William Bennett says, that Rush Limbaugh "tells his audience that what you believe inside, you can talk about in the marketplace." Unfortunately, what's "inside" is then mistaken for what's outside, treated as empirical and political reality. The *National Review* extols Limbaugh's conservative leadership no less than that of Ronald Reagan, and the Republican Party provides Limbaugh with books to discuss, stories, angles, and public support. "People were afraid of censure by gay activists, feminists, environmentalists — now they are not because Rush takes them on," says Bennett.    14

U.S. history has been marked by cycles in which brands of this or that hatred come into fashion and go out, are unleashed and then restrained. If racism, homophobia, jingoism, and woman-hating have been features of national life in pretty much all of modern history, it rather begs the question to spend a lot of time wondering if right-wing radio is a symptom or a cause. For at least four hundred years, prevailing attitudes in the West have considered African Americans less intelligent. Recent statistics show that 53 percent of people in the U.S. agree that blacks and Latinos are less intelligent than whites, and a majority believe that blacks are lazy, violent, welfare-dependent, and unpatriotic.    15

I think that what has made life more or less tolerable for "out" groups have been those moments in history when those "inside" feelings were relatively restrained. In fact, if I could believe that right-wing radio were only about idiosyncratic, singular, rough-hewn individuals thinking those inside thoughts, I'd be much more inclined to agree with Columbia University's media expert Everette Dennis, who says that Stern's and Limbaugh's popularity represents the "triumph of the individual" or with *Time* magazine's bottom line that "the fact that either is seriously considered a threat . . . is more worrisome than Stern or Limbaugh will ever be." If what I were hearing had even a tad more to do with real oppressions, with real white *and* black levels of joblessness and homelessness, or with the real problems of real white men, then I wouldn't have bothered to slog my way through hours of Howard Stern's miserable obsessions.    16

Yet at the heart of my anxiety is the worry that Stern, Limbaugh, Grant, et al. represent the very antithesis of individualism's triumph. As the *National*    17

*Review* said of Limbaugh's ascent, "It was a feat not only of the loudest voice but also of a keen political brain to round up, as Rush did, the media herd and drive them into the conservative corral." When asked about his political aspirations, Bob Grant gloated to the *Washington Post*, "I think I would make rather a good dictator."

The polemics of right-wing radio are putting nothing less than hate onto the airwaves, into the marketplace, electing it to office, teaching it in schools, and exalting it as freedom. What worries me is the increasing-to-constant commerce of retribution, control, and lashing out, fed not by fact but fantasy. What worries me is the reemergence, more powerfully than at any time since the institutions of Jim Crow,[2] of a socio-centered self that excludes "the likes of," well, me for example, from the civic circle, and that would rob me of my worth and claim and identity as a citizen. As the *Economist* rightly observes, "Mr. Limbaugh takes a mass market — white, mainly male, middle-class, ordinary America — and talks to it as an endangered minority." [18]

I worry about this identity whose external reference is a set of beliefs, ethics, and practices that excludes, restricts, and acts in the world on me, or mine, as the perceived if not real enemy. I am acutely aware of losing *my* mythic individualism to the surface shapes of my mythic group fearsomeness as black, as female, as left wing. "I" merge not fluidly but irretrievably into a category of "them." I become a suspect self, a moving target of loathsome properties, not merely different but dangerous. And that worries me a lot. [19]

What happens in my life with all this translated license, this permission to be uncivil? What happens to the social space that was supposedly at the sweet mountaintop of the civil rights movement's trail? Can I get a seat on the bus without having to be reminded that I *should* be standing? Did the civil rights movement guarantee us nothing more than to use public accommodations while surrounded by raving lunatic bigots? "They didn't beat this idiot [Rodney King] enough," says Howard Stern. [20]

Not long ago I had the misfortune to hail a taxicab in which the driver was listening to Howard Stern undress some woman. After some blocks, I had to get out. I was, frankly, afraid to ask the driver to turn it off — not because I was afraid of "censoring" him, which seems to be the only thing people will talk about anymore, but because the driver was stripping me too, as he leered through the rearview mirror. "Something the matter?" he demanded, as I asked him to pull over and let me out well short of my destination. (I'll spare you the full story of what happened from there — trying to get another cab, as the cabbies stopped for all the white businessmen who so much as scratched their heads near the curb; a nice young white man, seeing my plight, giving me his cab, having to thank him, he hero, me saved-but-humiliated, cabdriver pissed and surly. I fight my way to my destination, finally arriving in a bad mood, militant black woman, cranky feminazi.) [21]

---

[2] **Jim Crow:** System of discriminatory laws passed in the South beginning in the 1880s that legalized segregation betweeen blacks and whites. The name is thought to derive from a character in a popular minstrel show.

When Yeltsin blared rock music at his opponents holed up in the parlia-  22
ment building in Moscow, in imitation of the U.S. Marines trying to torture
Mañuel Noriega in Panama, all I could think of was that it must be like being
trapped in a crowded subway car when all the portable stereos are tuned to
Bob Grant or Howard Stern. With Howard Stern's voice a tinny, screeching
backdrop, with all the faces growing dreamily mean as though some soporif-
ically evil hallucinogen were gushing into their bloodstreams, I'd start begging to surrender.

Surrender to what? Surrender to the laissez-faire resegregation that is the  23
metaphoric significance of the hundreds of "Rush rooms" that have cropped
up in restaurants around the country; rooms broadcasting Limbaugh's words,
rooms for your listening pleasure, rooms where bigots can capture the purity
of a Rush-only lunch counter, rooms where all those unpleasant others just
"choose" not to eat? Surrender to the naughty luxury of a room in which a Ku
Klux Klan meeting could take place in orderly, First Amendment fashion?
Everyone's "free" to come in (and a few of you outsiders do), but mostly the
undesirable nonconformists are gently repulsed away. It's a high-tech world
of enhanced choice. Whites choose mostly to sit in the Rush room. Feminists,
blacks, lesbians, and gays "choose" to sit elsewhere. No need to buy black
votes, you just pay them not to vote; no need to insist on white-only schools,
you just sell the desirability of black-only schools. Just sit back and watch it
work, like those invisible shock shields that keep dogs cowering in their own
backyards.

How real is the driving perception behind all the Sturm und Drang[3] of  24
this genre of radio-harangue — the perception that white men are an op-
pressed minority, with no power and no opportunity in the land that they
made great? While it is true that power and opportunity are shrinking for all
but the very wealthy in this country (and would that Limbaugh would take
that issue on), the fact remains that white men are still this country's most
privileged citizens and market actors. To give just a small example, according
to the *Wall Street Journal*, blacks were the only racial group to suffer a net job
loss during the 1990–91 economic downturn at the companies reporting to
the Equal Employment Opportunity Commissions. Whites, Latinos, and
Asians, meanwhile, gained thousands of jobs. While whites gained 71,144
jobs at these companies, Latinos gained 60,040, Asians gained 55,104, and
blacks lost 59,479. If every black were hired in the United States tomorrow,
the numbers would not be sufficient to account for white men's expanding
balloon of fear that they have been specifically dispossessed by African Americans.

Given deep patterns of social segregation and general ignorance of his-  25
tory, particularly racial history, media remain the principal source of most
Americans' knowledge of each other. Media can provoke violence or induce
passivity. In San Francisco, for example, a radio show on KMEL called "Street
Soldiers" has taken this power as a responsibility with great consequence:

---

[3] **Sturm und Drang:** German, literally "storm and stress."

"Unquestionably," writes Ken Auletta in the *New Yorker,* "the show has helped avert violence. When a Samoan teenager was slain, apparently by Filipino gang members, in a drive-by shooting, the phones lit up with calls from Samoans wanting to tell [the hosts] they would not rest until they had exacted revenge. Threats filled the air for a couple of weeks. Then the dead Samoan's father called in, and, in a poignant exchange, the father said he couldn't tolerate the thought of more young men senselessly slaughtered. There would be no retaliation, he vowed. And there was none." In contrast, we must wonder at the phenomenon of the very powerful leadership of the Republican Party, from Ronald Reagan to Robert Dole to William Bennett, giving advice, counsel, and friendship with Rush Limbaugh's passionate divisiveness.

The outright denial of the material crisis at every level of U.S. society, most urgently in black inner-city neighborhoods but facing us all, is a kind of political circus, dissembling as it feeds the frustrations of the moment. We as a nation can no longer afford to deal with such crises by *imagining* an excess of bodies, of babies, of job-stealers, of welfare mothers, of overreaching immigrants, of too-powerful (Jewish, in whispers) liberal Hollywood, of lesbians and gays, of gang members ("gangsters" remain white, and no matter what the atrocity, less vilified than "gang members" who are black), of Arab terrorists, and uppity women. The reality of our social poverty far exceeds these scapegoats. This right-wing backlash resembles, in form if not substance, phenomena like anti-Semitism in Poland: there aren't but a handful of Jews left in that whole country, but the giant balloon of heated anti-Semitism flourishes apace, Jews blamed for the world's evils.

The overwhelming response to right-wing excesses in the United States has been to seek an odd sort of comfort in the fact that the First Amendment is working so well that you can't suppress this sort of thing. Look what's happened in Eastern Europe. Granted. So let's not talk about censorship or the First Amendment for the next ten minutes. But in Western Europe, where fascism is rising at an appalling rate, suppression is hardly the problem. In Eastern and Western Europe as well as the United States, we must begin to think just a little bit about the fiercely coalescing power of media to spark mistrust, to fan it into forest fires of fear and revenge. We must begin to think about the levels of national and social complacence in the face of such resolute ignorance. We must ask ourselves what the expected result is, not of censorship or suppression, but of so much encouragement, so much support, so much investment in the fashionability of hate. What future is it that we are designing with the devotion of such tremendous resources to the disgraceful propaganda of bigotry?

**Questions to Start You Thinking**

1. CONSIDERING MEANING: Why does Williams disagree with *Time* magazine's view that talk radio is not a threat (paragraph 16)?

2. IDENTIFYING WRITING STRATEGIES: How does Williams use direct quotations from various radio talk-show hosts to support her argument against "hate radio"?

3. ANALYZING THE WRITER'S CHOICES: Why do you think Williams chose to open her essay by quoting a radio conversation that struck her as "so horrendously unusual, so singularly hateful" that she was sure it would elicit "a firestorm of protest"(paragraph 6)? What is the effect of her using this example, along with other quotations from actual radio conversations, to develop her argument?

4. EXPANDING VOCABULARY: Define *polemicism*, *demagoguery* (paragraph 7), *antithesis*, and *individualism* (paragraph 17). According to Williams, how is the "polemicism" of "hate radio" a form of "demagoguery" and the "antithesis of individualism's triumph"?

5. MAKING CONNECTIONS: Compare and contrast Toni Morrison's analysis of "race talk" ("On the Backs of Blacks," p. 528) with Williams's analysis of "hate radio."

**Journal Prompts**

1. Explain your emotional reaction to one of Rush Limbaugh's, Howard Stern's, Bob Grant's, or another radio host's broadcasts. Is your reaction similar or dissimilar to Williams's reaction? Explain.

2. On your college campus, are there any official rules censoring or regulating "hate speech"? If so, do you approve of these rules?

**Suggestions for Writing**

1. Analyze your emotional and intellectual reaction to a radio or television show that irritated you, explaining why you reacted as you did.

2. Working from Williams's stance against such radio programs as Limbaugh's and Stern's, propose a solution that would allow these programs to retain their First Amendment rights while curbing their potential for creating racial unrest.

**Kurt Andersen** *was born in 1954 in Omaha, Nebraska. Since graduating from Harvard University, where he was the editor of the* Harvard Lampoon, *Andersen has worked as a writer for NBC; a writer, editor, and architecture critic at* Time *magazine; a coeditor of the satirical magazine* Spy; *and currently as the editor in chief of* New York *magazine. Andersen has also written and produced television shows and regularly contributes to such magazines as the* New York Times Magazine, Vanity Fair, *the* Atlantic Monthly, *and* Architectural Digest. *He is the author of* The Real Thing *(1980) and* Laughing Matters *(1987), an anthology of humorous works coedited with movie critic Gene Shalit. Andersen brings his experience with television and comedy to the following essay, a satirical analysis of daytime talk shows that first appeared as a column in* Time *on October 11, 1993.*

Back in the good old days of America's adolescence — that robust, heed- 1
less century between the gold rush and World War II — an important sector
of show business centered on freaks. Tom Thumb, Koo-Koo the Bird Girl,
Clicko the Bushman, Charles Tripp the Armless Photographer, Jo-Jo the Dog-
Faced Boy, and scores of anonymous wretches abased themselves grotesquely
for the amusement and astonishment of paying customers at circuses, carni-
vals and storefront "dime museums." However, as the modern forms of popular entertainment arose — radio, television, Madonna — freak shows grew
scarce. Geeks disappeared altogether. Show business became sanitized, ano-
dyne. Niceness prevailed.

But no more. This is the new Age of the Geek, postmodern iteration. 2
These days it has become standard for all sorts of people to flaunt not just
their physical oddities but their stupidity, vulgarity, or sinfulness as well. They
volunteer, in exchange for attention or a few bucks, to suffer sneers and outright ridicule, so long as the medium — syndicated talk show, music-video
program, film comedy — is sufficiently mass. There are various ways to become momentarily famous, but public mortification has become the easiest
by far.

Starting in the 1950s and '60s, TV game shows (*Truth or Consequences*, 3
*Queen for a Day*) and later, talk shows were the pioneering venues, where ritual gawking at the predicaments of strangers was turned into mass-market entertainment. Don Rickles, huge twenty-five years ago, based his novel act on
the ferocious, face-to-face ridicule of unlucky (but willing) members of his
audience who happened to have a salient distinguishing feature — dark skin,
an accent, some physical anomaly. The seminally abusive *Joe Pyne Show* appeared at the same time. "I have no respect for anyone who would come on
my show," Pyne once said. Why did they? And why would people agree to be
humiliated on the *Newlywed Game* and the *Gong Show*? Because shame was becoming anachronistic. Because people took Warhol's fifteen-minutes-of-fame
line literally.[1] Because show business was reverting atavistically to its
sideshow origins.

Today the syndicated daytime talk show is the straight-line mainstream 4
descendant of the odditoriums and dunk-the-fool attractions of a century
ago. The glut of programs — *Jane Whitney, Montel Williams, Bertice Berry,
Richard Bey, Ricki Lake, Jenny Jones, Maury Povich, Sally Jessy Raphael, Geraldo,
Donahue, Oprah* — constitutes an ad hoc underbelly network, a virtual round-
the-neck pageant of geeks inviting the contempt of viewers without even the

---

[1] **Warhol's . . . fame:** Artist and filmmaker Andy Warhol (1928–1987) said, "In the future everyone will be famous for fifteen minutes." He first made the statement during the
1960s, and it has been widely quoted and reprinted.

old quiz-show promises of kitchen ranges or living-room furniture. A veneer of infotainment earnestness is generally obligatory; if Jo-Jo the Dog-Faced Boy were still around, they'd book him on *Donahue*, but Phil would ask him about his struggle for self-esteem. And for those with neither the spare time nor the stomach to witness the spectacle in real time, there is *Talk Soup* on cable TV's E! channel, an arch digest of the talk shows' over-the-top moments; it permits us to go slumming and still respect ourselves in the morning. And the talk shows' stars and producers cooperate in their own lampooning, supplying whatever appalling clips the *Talk Soup* hipsters request. "They're getting a lot of promotion," says Fran Shea of the E! channel. "They understand they may be poked fun at. They get it."

Self-mortification played for laughs has become so unremarkable that now actual celebrities volunteer for abuse. Howard Stern teases Dick Cavett about his electroshock treatment for depression and Richard Simmons about his poofterishness, but Cavett and Simmons go along. There is now a whole caste of faded performers who find that by playing along with young people's fond, campy crypto-contempt for them, they can have a kind of celebrity after-burn, a part-time career collaborating with their own snide deconstruction. That explains Robert Goulet's casting in Bill Murray's *Scrooged*, Wayne Newton's appearance on a *Spy* magazine TV special and Joe Franklin's semi-witting self-parody on *Late Night with Conan O'Brien* last week.

The just-spell-my-name-right mutation of fame pursuit has become operative even at big companies. On *Beavis and Butt-head*, MTV's most popular and most excellent show, the cartoon antiheroes relentlessly dismiss videos and performers, usually with a curt "This sucks." Still, record companies are eager to have their videos rated by Beavis and Butt-head — themselves ghastly freaks presented for our amusement — because the show is hot, and attention is attention. "Bands are perfectly willing to let the characters riff on the videos, even negatively," says Judy McGrath, MTV's creative director. "In fact, it's probably cooler if they think you suck." On a David Letterman *Late Show* last week, Beavis and Butt-head were brought on to make it clear they think Letterman sucks. And he loved it.

**Questions to Start You Thinking**

1. CONSIDERING MEANING: According to Andersen, how has popular entertainment reverted to its "sideshow origins" (paragraph 3)? What reasons does he give for this change?

2. IDENTIFYING WRITING STRATEGIES: How does Andersen use humor to reveal his attitude toward popular entertainment today?

3. ANALYZING THE WRITER'S CHOICES: Why do you think Andersen uses sarcasm in his evaluation of daytime talk shows? Do you think his essay would have been more effective if he had used a different tone? Why or why not?

4. EXPANDING VOCABULARY: Define *anachronistic* and *atavistically* (paragraph 3). What does Andersen mean by calling shame "anachronistic" and show business "atavistic"?

5. MAKING CONNECTIONS:  Compare and contrast daytime talk shows as described by Andersen and talk radio as described by Patricia J. Williams ("Hate Radio," p. 582)?

**Journal Prompts**

1. Explain why you either watch or don't watch daytime talk shows.
2. Parody a typical exchange between guests on a daytime television talk show. Why is it so easy to make fun of these shows?

**Suggestions for Writing**

1. Write a personal essay identifying a time when you felt publicly mortified or ridiculed. Did you in any way invite or facilitate humiliation?
2. In your opinion, why is "public mortification" (paragraph 2) such an easy way to become famous? Write an essay in which you analyze the possible social and cultural reasons for this trend in popular entertainment.

**Andrew Sullivan,** *born in England in 1963, studied modern history and modern languages at Oxford University and then won a fellowship to study in the United States. He earned his Ph.D. in political science at Harvard University and is now editor of the* New Republic *and a columnist for the* London Sunday Times. *Openly gay, he often writes about gay issues in his essays and occasional satirical pieces. In "Wouldn't Normally Do," first published in the February 21, 1994, issue of the* New Republic*, Sullivan contrasts his reactions to two viewings of the movie* Philadelphia, *the first viewing with gay friends and the second with a straight female friend.*

## *Andrew Sullivan*    Wouldn't Normally Do

I went to see *Philadelphia* twice, and, in retrospect, I'm glad I did. The first   1
time, I went with a bunch of gay friends — a bevy of professional and mainly closeted people who are not usually given to holding back criticism. We all cried at the apposite points, of course. The movie is a tear-jerker even if you haven't seen a large proportion of your friends go down various parts of the HIV slide in their twenties and thirties. But we all agreed over margaritas later that the film was essentially a disappointing made-for-television special, with cartoon characters and cartoon morality. We winced at the sanitization of the main character's relationship; at the way the movie glibly divided humanity into those who were good, those who were bad, and those who were on their way from being bad to being good; at the excruciating moralizing of the courtroom and family scenes. It didn't capture our experience of the plague, its evocation of a common mortality, its descents into comedy, its nagging constancy, its gray-shaded dignity and indignity. It was a film in garish primary colors, directed at "them," and, we generally agreed, good for "them."

As we experienced it, however, it crammed complicated thoughts into crude parables; explained medical facts that had become numbingly familiar; teetered unnecessarily around every gay activist sensitivity (giving a few of them bit parts to buy them off); and mollified every squeamish heterosexual as well. The result was a strangely distant communiqué of moral and social uplift, in which the people involved (insofar as the characters were at all recognizable as people) were mere ciphers in an elaborate attempt at enlightenment directed at "them."

The second time I went to the movie, I went with one of "them," a straight woman friend of mine, who had had little direct experience of HIV and who had known a few gay men, but mostly through me. I have to say that, despite my best efforts, I experienced the movie very differently. My defenses, I suppose, were down. I was acutely aware throughout of what she might be thinking and feeling, of which scenes were distortive of my and others' lives, of which were not, of how she would see and interpret things that had become so familiar they had ceased even to be visible to me. For a couple of hours, I was given the chance to see the movie as if I had not somehow already acted in it; and it reminded me of the shock we had now absorbed, of the fear we had grown inured to, of the human noise that in our lives had turned increasingly white.

But *Philadelphia*, on further reflection, did more than this. Despite (and sometimes because of) its Hollywood banality, it was surprisingly true. From its soundtrack on, it insisted on the commonality of the gay and straight experience. Bruce Springsteen's elegiac title song, "Streets of Philadelphia," is the first popular song ever, I think, to be sung by a straight man in the voice of a gay man. The movie also portrayed a homosexual emphatically as a member of a heterosexual family. This is a truth that is extremely hard to convey in words, but that the film, more than any before it, placed at its center. It succinctly showed that gay people are not so much a problem for straight families; they *are* straight families. The movie conveyed this by a simple film-school cliché: we saw some scenes through the lens of a hand-held camera operated by Miguel, Andrew Beckett's lover; and in the final sentimental minutes, we watched old home movies of Beckett as a child. Sure, the moments could have been culled from "America's Saddest Home Videos." But the second time I saw the movie, I realized that the medium itself in those scenes had conveyed something subliminally that is almost impossible to persuade people of explicitly. It had made the family context normal.

Second, this movie about AIDS was directed at black America. From its black co-star, Denzel Washington, to its hype in the black press, to a number of critical black-on-black scenes, it was an aggressively black, middle-class film. (In downtown Washington, it was shown in the theater usually reserved for blaxploitation movies.) Moreover, it didn't talk of the disease as a heterosexual issue, as Magic Johnson and virtually every other black leader has done. It brazenly took a black, straight movie icon and made him grapple with a gay man. Denzel Washington's role for this reason took far more social bravery than Hank's. Homosexuality is more stigmatized in black America than even in white America, which is why attempts at a coalition between gays and blacks have so far proved futile. But in the theater, I could overhear a straight, black couple sitting behind me become completely involved in the fate of a white homosexual. And the movie's most visceral portrayal of a straight man's panic around a gay man was in a scene where two handsome, intelligent black men — one gay, one straight — clash in a drugstore. The point about sexuality in this interchange was somewhat labored. But the message about race had already been made.

*Philadelphia*, in short, is a work of translation, not creation; and for that    5
reason more than any others, it is unsettling. To those who simply don't want to know, it's an irritation; to those who know too much, it's an affront. But translation has to start somewhere; and it is infinitely preferable to a silent separatism. It is also needed. The truth is that in the last few years, after a period of remarkable convergence, the gay world and the straight world may be diverging again. Now, however, the issue is not sexuality, it's mortality. To enter young adulthood as a gay man today is to be initiated into a different world than that of your straight peers. It is to be forced to confront perishability in a manner that most heterosexuals are spared until their seventies and eighties. Death of course is no stranger to straight people; and it's a dangerous illusion to believe that gay death, or young death, or HIV death is somehow different from any other kind; and blinkered, too, to believe that straight people are not involved in this event as well. But the sheer extent of it for gay men, its seamlessness, its oppressiveness, its insistence, its ubiquity, have surely changed them for good. Whether this experience is a horror or a privilege, an intensification of life or a diversion from it, is an interesting question. But the experience is certainly a different one; and the difference may well be greater than that of sexuality. The wider the gulf becomes, of course, the harder it is to translate; but the wider it becomes, the more important it is to translate. *Philadelphia* is a beginning to that process; and we should be glad of it. The present is a foreign country for many of us now. Increasingly, we need correspondents.

<table>
<tr><td>Questions to Start<br>You Thinking</td><td>

1. CONSIDERING MEANING: What are Sullivan's two reactions to the movie *Philadelphia*? How does he account for his different responses?

2. IDENTIFYING WRITING STRATEGIES: How does Sullivan use recall and observation in his evaluation of the movie?

3. ANALYZING THE WRITER'S CHOICES: How is this essay different from a more conventional movie review? Why do you think Sullivan chose to base his evaluation of *Philadelphia* largely on his observations of the different reactions the film elicited from different audiences?

4. EXPANDING VOCABULARY: Define *cartoon characters* and *cartoon morality* (paragraph 1) from the context of Sullivan's essay, and explain how these terms are a cause or an effect of Hollywood *banality* (paragraph 3).

</td></tr>
</table>

5. MAKING CONNECTIONS: From her analysis in "The New Hollywood Male" (p. 577), how do you think Ellen Goodman would react to the main male characters in *Philadelphia*, either as Sullivan describes them or as you remember them (if you've seen the movie)?

**Journal Prompts**

1. Explain your reaction to *Philadelphia* or to another controversial film.

2. In your opinion, is the knowledge of early death from AIDS "a horror or a privilege, an intensification of life or a diversion from it" (paragraph 5)?

**Suggestions for Writing**

1. If you could make a movie on a controversial issue, what issue would you choose? How would you use the medium of film to explore the issue? Drawing on the resource of imagination, describe the movie you would make. What would be the plot? What would be the key scenes? Who would you cast as the main characters?

2. Is film an effective medium for tackling controversial issues? Defend your position, analyzing at least three cinematic examples as evidence.

**Emily Prager,** *born in 1952, writes fiction featuring a surreal and coldly humorous blend of pop culture slogans and classical allusions. Her novel* Clea and Zeus Divorce *(1987) has been called "a music video in the form of a novel." She is also the author of the novels* A Visit from the Footbinder *(1986) and* Eve's Tattoo *(1991). A former contributing editor to the* National Lampoon, *she has published essays in the* Village Voice *and writes a political and social satire column for* Penthouse *magazine. In the following essay, published in* Interview *magazine in December 1991, Prager analyzes what American culture's infatuation with Barbie tells us about ourselves.*

# *Emily Prager*   Our Barbies, Ourselves

*Major Barbie*

I read an astounding obituary in the *New York Times* not too long ago. It      1
concerned the death of one Jack Ryan. A former husband of Zsa Zsa Gabor, it said, Mr. Ryan had been an inventor and designer during his lifetime. A man of eclectic creativity, he designed Sparrow and Hawk missiles when he worked for the Raytheon Company, and, the notice said, when he consulted for Mattel he designed Barbie.

If Barbie was designed by a man, suddenly a lot of things made sense to      2
me, things I'd wondered about for years. I used to look at Barbie and wonder, What's wrong with this picture? What kind of woman designed this doll? Let's be honest: Barbie looks like someone who got her start at the Playboy Mansion. She could be a regular guest on *The Howard Stern Show.* It is a fact of Barbie's design that her breasts are so out of proportion to the rest of her body that if she were a human woman, she'd fall flat on her face.

If it's true that a woman didn't design Barbie, you don't know how much    3
saner that makes me feel. Of course, that doesn't ameliorate the damage.
There are millions of women who are subliminally sure that a thirty-nine-
inch bust and a twenty-three-inch waist are the epitome of lovability. Could
this account for the popularity of breast implant surgery?

I don't mean to step on anyone's toes here. I loved my Barbie. Secretly, I    4
still believe that neon pink and turquoise blue are the only colors in which to
decorate a duplex condo. And like many others of my generation, I've never
married, simply because I cannot find a man who looks as good in clam dig-
gers as Ken.

The question that comes to mind is, of course, Did Mr. Ryan design Bar-    5
bie as a weapon? Because it *is* odd that Barbie appeared about the same time
in my consciousness as the feminist movement — a time when women
sought equality and small breasts were king. Or is Barbie the dream date of
weapons designers? Or perhaps it's simpler than that: perhaps Barbie is Zsa
Zsa if she were eleven inches tall. No matter what, my discovery of Jack Ryan
confirms what I have always felt: there is something indescribably masculine
about Barbie — dare I say it, phallic. For all her giant breasts and high-heeled
feet, she lacks a certain softness. If you asked a little girl what kind of doll she
wanted for Christmas, I just don't think she'd reply, "Please, Santa, I want a
hard-body."

On the other hand, you could say that Barbie, in feminist terms, is defi-    6
nitely her own person. With her condos and fashion plazas and pools and
beauty salons, she is definitely a liberated woman, a gal on the move. And she
has always been sexual, even totemic. Before Barbie, American dolls were flat-
footed and breastless, and ineffably dignified. They were created in the image
of little girls or babies. Madame Alexander was the queen of doll makers in
the '50s, and her dollies looked like Elizabeth Taylor in *National Velvet.* They
represented the kind of girls who looked perfect in jodhpurs, whose hair was
never out of place, who grew up to be Jackie Kennedy — before she married
Onassis. Her dolls' boyfriends were figments of the imagination, figments
with large portfolios and three-piece suits and presidential aspirations, figments who could keep dolly in the style to which little girls of the '50s were
programmed to become accustomed, a style that spasm-ed with the '60s and
the appearance of Barbie. And perhaps what accounts for Barbie's vast popularity is that she was also a '60s woman: into free love and fun colors, anti-
class, and possessed of a real, molded boyfriend, Ken, with whom she could
chant a mantra.

But there were problems with Ken. I always felt weird about him. He had    7
no genitals, and, even at age ten, I found that ominous. I mean, here was Barbie with these humongous breasts, and that was O.K. with the toy company.
And then, there was Ken with that truncated, unidentifiable lump at his groin.
I sensed injustice at work. Why, I wondered, was Barbie designed with such
obvious sexual equipment and Ken not? Why was his treated as if it were
more mysterious than hers? Did the fact that it was treated as such indicate

that somehow his equipment, his essential maleness, was considered more powerful than hers, more worthy of the dignity of concealment? And if the issue in the mind of the toy company was obscenity and its possible damage to children, I still object. How do they think I felt, knowing that no matter how many water beds they slept in, or hot tubs they romped in, or swimming pools they lounged by under the stars, Barbie and Ken could never make love? No matter how much sexuality Barbie possessed, she would never turn Ken on. He would be forever withholding, forever detached. There was a loneliness about Barbie's situation that was always disturbing. And twenty-five years later, movies and videos are still filled with topless women and covered men. As if we're all trapped in Barbie's world and can never escape.

God, it certainly has cheered me up to think that Barbie was designed by Jack Ryan. There's only one thing that could make me happier, and that's if Gorbachev would come over here and run for president on the Democratic ticket. If they don't want him in Russia, fine. We've got the capitalist system in place, ready to go; all we need is someone to run it.                8

Gorbachev for president and Barbie designed by a man. A blissful end to 1991.                9

|  |  |
|---|---|
| **Questions to Start You Thinking** | 1. CONSIDERING MEANING: What is Prager's main point in this piece? What does she mean when she says that "if Barbie was designed by a man, suddenly a lot of things made sense to me" (paragraph 2)? |
|  | 2. IDENTIFYING WRITING STRATEGIES: How does Prager use the resource of imagination in this essay? |
|  | 3. ANALYZING THE WRITER'S CHOICES: Why do you think Prager uses humor in her analysis of Barbie's impact on young girls? Do you think a more serious tone would have strengthened her position? Why or why not? |
|  | 4. EXPANDING VOCABULARY: Define *eclectic* (paragraph 1), *ameliorate, subliminally, epitome* (paragraph 3), *phallic* (paragraph 5), and *truncated* (paragraph 7). Prager's language is a parody of formal academic speech. Is this diction appropriate to her article? Explain why or why not. |
|  | 5. MAKING CONNECTIONS: To what extent do both Prager and Deborah Tannen ("Women and Men Talking on the Job," p. 554) believe that society's expectations of women, instilled in girlhood, can be damaging? Explain. |
| **Journal Prompts** | 1. List the ways in which women are expected to look like Barbie dolls. |
|  | 2. Do you agree with Prager that in some ways we are "trapped in Barbie's world" (paragraph 7)? What exactly does she mean? |
| **Suggestions for Writing** | 1. In a brief personal essay, explain how a childhood toy affected the way you learned to view the world and yourself. How did it encourage you to see yourself? |
|  | 2. Write a counterpart to Prager's essay, analyzing the Ken doll or the G.I. Joe doll as a cultural icon. What problems equivalent to those of Barbie do Ken and G.I. Joe expose about American culture? |

**Alex Ross** *was born in 1968 in Washington, D.C. He received his bachelor's degree in English from Harvard University and now writes on classical music for the* New York Times. *He also writes music reviews and essays on popular culture for the* New Republic, *the* New Yorker, Spin, *and other magazines. In "Generation Exit," first published in the* New Yorker *on April 25, 1994, Ross explores the relationship between twenty-somethings and the media while analyzing the impact of Kurt Cobain's music and suicide on American culture.*

## *Alex Ross*    Generation Exit

When Kurt Cobain, the lead singer of the band Nirvana, killed himself  1
with a shotgun blast to the head, the major media outlets gave the story wide
play and warmed to its significance. Dan Rather led off hesitantly, his face full
of dim amazement as he read aloud phrases like "the Seattle sound" and
"Smells like Teen Spirit." But ABC ventured bravely into interpretation, explaining the grunge phenomenon to "people over thirty" and obtaining one
man-in-the-street reaction. "When you reach that kind of fame and you're still
miserable, there's something wrong," a long-haired stoner-looking dude observed. And NBC's correspondent ambitiously invoked "the violence, the
drugs, and the diminished opportunities of an entire generation," with Tom
Brokaw appending a regretful smirk. This was only the evening of the first day;
the newsstands were soon heavy with fresh musing on the latest lost generation, the twilit twenty-somethings, the new unhappiness.

From the outset of his career, the desperately individualistic Cobain was  2
caught in a great media babble about grunge style and twenty-something discontent. His intensely personal songs became exhibits in the nation's ongoing symposium on generational identity — a fruitless project blending the
principles of sociology and astrology. Those of us at the receiving end of Generation X theories find them infuriating enough; Cobain, hounded with titles
like "crown prince of Generation X," buckled under them. He was loudly and
publicly tormented by his notoriety, his influence, his importance. Everything
written about him and his wife, Courtney Love, seemed to wound him in
some way. "I do not want what I have got," he sang on his last album, yearning for oblivion of one kind or another.

And yet he chose a way of death guaranteed to bring down a hailstorm of  3
analytical blather far in excess of anything he had experienced while he was
alive. This is the paradoxical allure of suicide: to leave the chattering world behind and yet to stage-manage the exit so that one is talked about in the right
way. This was also the paradox of Cobain's bizarre pop-star career — his
choice both to abandon everyday life and to try to cast some larger spell over
it. He thought he could appropriate blank categories like "Generation X" and

"alternative culture" and fill them with the earnest ideals of the punk-rock subculture he came from. He thought he could take the road less traveled and then persuade everyone to follow him. It's amazing he got as far as he did.

"Alternative": A breathtakingly meaningless word, the emptiest cultural category imaginable. It proposes that the establishment is reprehensible but that our substitute establishment can somehow blissfully coexist with it, on the same commercial playing field. It differs from sixties notions of counterculture in that no one took "alternative culture" seriously even at the beginning; it sold out as a matter or principle. MTV, the video clubhouse that brought Nirvanamania to fever pitch, seized on the "alternative" label as a way to laterally diversify its offerings, much as soft-drink companies seek to invent new flavors. The aesthetic microscope has not been invented that could find a really significant difference between an alternative band like Pearl Jam and the regular-guy rock that it supposedly replaces.

Alternative music in the nineties claims descent from the punk-rock movement that traversed American in the seventies and eighties. The claim is weakened by the fact that punk in its pure form disavowed mass-market success, a disavowal that united an otherwise motley array of youth subcultures: high-school misfits of all kinds, skate-board kids, hardcore skinheads, doped-out postcollegiate slackers. Punk's peculiar obsession was musical autonomy—independent labels, clubs installed in suburban garages and warehouses, flyers and fanzines photocopied after hours. Some of the music was vulgar and dumb, some of it brilliantly inventive; rock finally had a viable avant-garde. In the eighties, this do-it-yourself network solidified into independent, or indie, rock, anchored in the myriad college-rock stations and alternative newspapers. Dumbness persisted, but there were always scattered bands picking out weird, rich chords and giving no thought to a major-label future.

Nirvana, which enjoyed local celebrity on the indie-rock scenes of Aberdeen, Olympia, and Seattle, Washington, before blundering into the mainstream, was perfectly poised between the margin and the center of rock. The band didn't have to dilute itself to make the transition, because its brand of grunge rock already drew more on the thunderous tread of hard rock and heavy metal than on the clean, fast, matter-of-fact attack of punk or hardcore. Where punk and indie bands generally made vocals secondary to the disordered clamor of guitars, Nirvana depended on Cobain's resonantly snarling voice, an instrument full of commercial potential from the start. But the singer was resolutely punk in spirit. He undermined his own publicity campaigns, and used his commercial clout to support lesser-known bands; he was planning to start his own label, Exploitation Records, and distribute the records himself while he was on tour.

The songs on Nirvana's breakthrough second album, *Nevermind*, walked a difficult line between punk form and pop content. For the most part, they triumphed, and, more than that, they struck a nerve, not only with trend-seeking kids but with people in their twenties or older who recognized the mixture of components that went into the music. Dave Grohl, the dead-on drummer who kept Nirvana on an even keel, has a pragmatic view of the album's appeal: "The songs were catchy and they were simple, just like an ABC song when you were a kid." Cobain was a close, direct presence, everyone's friendless friend. The songs, despite their sometimes messy roar, were cunningly fashioned. They had a seductive way of switching in midstream from plaintive meditation to all-out frenzy. If people still listen to Nirvana ten years from now, it will be on the strength of the music, not of Cobain's nascent martyr legend.

It was in the fall of 1991 that Nirvana mysteriously took hold of the nation's youth consciousness and began selling records in the millions. It's best not to analyze this sudden popularity all that closely; as Michael Azerrad points out in his book on the group, *Come As You Are*, the kind of instantaneous word-of-mouth sensation that lifted the band to the top of the charts also buoyed the careers of such differently talented personalities as Peter Frampton and Vanilla Ice. Adolescents are an omnipotent commercial force precisely because their tastes are so mercurial. In the deep dusk of the Bush Administration, some segments of the nation's youth undoubtedly identified with Cobain's punkish worldview, his sympathies and discontents, and, yes, the diminished opportunities of an entire generation. Others just got off on the crushing power of the sound. 8

Cobain was at once irritated and intrigued by the randomness of his new audience. He lashed out at the "jock numbskulls, frat boys, and metal kids" (in Azerrad's words) who jammed clubs and arenas for his post-*Nevermind* tours. But he also liked the idea of bending their minds toward his own punk ideals and left-leaning politics: "I wanted to fool people at first. I wanted people to think that we were no different than Guns n' Roses. Because that way they would listen to the music first, accept us, and then maybe start listening to a few things that we had to say." After the initial period of fame, he let loose with social messages, not as heavy-handed or as earnest as R.E.M.'s, but carefully aimed. He was happy to discover that high schools were divided between Nirvana kids and Guns n' Roses kids. 9

The zeal for subversion was well meant but naive. By condemning racists, sexists, and homophobes in his audiences, he may have promoted the cause of politically correct language in certain high-school cliques, but he did not and could not attack the deep-seated prejudices smoldering beneath that language. When he declared himself "gay in spirit," as he did in an interview with the gay magazine *The Advocate*, he made a political toy out of fragile identity. And his disavowals of masculine culture rang false alongside a stage show that dealt in sonic aggression and equipment-smashing mayhem. Who was he kidding? 10

The attempt to carry out social engineering through rock lyrics is an impossible one. Rock and roll has never been and will never be a vehicle for social amelioration, despite many fond hopes. Music is robbed of its intentions 11 and associations as it goes out into the great wide open; like a rumor passes through a crowd, it emerges utterly changed. Pop songs become the property of their fans and are marked with the circumstances of their consumption, not of their creation. An unsought listenership can brand the music indelibly, as the Beatles discovered with "Helter Skelter."[1] Or as Cobain discovered when a recording of "Smells like Teen Spirit" was played at a Guns n' Roses show in Madison Square Garden while women in the audience were ogled on giant video screens.

In his suicide note Cobain gestured toward all these crises, his lack of passion, and his disconnectedness from the broad rock audience. The story underneath is probably simpler and sadder: he was trying to get off drugs and found himself helpless without their support. He leaned on drugs long before he became famous — the malevolent media circus of his last few years cannot be easily blamed. Even when he started out, he looked tired and haggard. The rest of the story lies between him and his dealer. It's easy to make too much of these inevitable chemical tragedies; witness the overexamined case of River Phoenix, whom some of us necrologized last November. Next time, it will not shock me when a vulnerable, talented misfit about my age infiltrates celebrity cultures, then dies playing the abusive games of rebellion. But it will make me just as sad.

Killing himself as and when he did, Cobain at least managed to deliver a final jolt to the rock world he loved and loathed. Rock stars are glamorized for dying young, but they aren't supposed to kill themselves on purpose. Greil Marcus's invaluable compendium *Rock Death in the 1970s* records — among a hundred and sixteen untimely demises — dozens of drug mishaps and only a handful of suicides. A transcendent drug-induced descent is the preferred exit. Certainly the shotgun blast casts a different light on Cobain's career; the lyrics all sound like suicide notes now. ("What else could I write / I don't have the right / What else should I be / All apologies.") He made his death unrhapsodizable.

The rage we feel at suicides may be motivated by love, but it is the love that comes of possession, not compassion. It is the urge of the crowd to take control of the defective individual. The most mordant words on the subject are still John Donne's, in defense of righteous suicide: "No detestation nor dehortation against this sin of desperation (when it is a sin) can be too earnest. But yet since it may be without infidelity, it cannot be greater than that." This sin cannot be greater than our own urge to rationalize and allegorize the recently dead, especially those who were somehow faithful to themselves.

---

[1] **"Helter Skelter":** A Beatles song that became associated with murderer Charles Manson. In 1969 Manson and his hippie "family" of cult members murdered pregnant actress Sharon Tate and several others at her Beverly Hills home. The words "Helter Skelter" were written in blood at the murder site and were used as the title of a book about Manson by Vincent Bugliosi.

**Questions to Start
You Thinking**

1. CONSIDERING MEANING: Paraphrase Ross's conclusion (paragraph 14). What does he mean by the idea that fans feel possession of, rather than compassion for, Cobain?

2. IDENTIFYING WRITING STRATEGIES: How does Ross use cause and effect in his explanation of Cobain's sudden fame and eventual suicide?

3. ANALYZING THE WRITER'S CHOICES: How does Ross compare and contrast the reality of Cobain's musical career and untimely death with the typical expectations we have of "rock stars"? Why might he have chosen this approach toward analyzing Cobain's death, rather than succumbing to "the urge to rationalize and allegorize" (paragraph 14) as others have?

4. EXPANDING VOCABULARY: Define *nascent* and *martyr* (paragraph 7). What is "Cobain's nascent martyr legend"?

5. MAKING CONNECTIONS: How do the media create and sometimes destroy people, according to Ross and Kurt Andersen ("Oprah and Jo-Jo the Dog-Faced Boy," p. 590)?

**Journal Prompts**

1. Write your own definition of "alternative." Is it really a "breathtakingly meaningless word, the emptiest cultural category imaginable" (paragraph 4)?

2. What is your opinion of Ross's statement that "rock and roll has never been and will never be a vehicle for social amelioration, despite many fond hopes" (paragraph 11)?

**Suggestions for
Writing**

1. In a personal essay, describe your own taste in music and explain why you enjoy this kind of music. Who are some of your favorite musicians? How would you classify the kind of music they create and perform? How are these musicians either breaking away from or conforming to the musical establishment?

2. Write your own analysis of the career and self-destruction of a popular culture icon (such as Elvis Presley, Janis Joplin, Jim Morrison, John Belushi, River Phoenix). Be sure to identify the causes and effects of this person's rise to fame and eventual death.

# Chapter 27

# Nature and Technology

**Journal Prompt** In general, do you think technology is something to be welcomed or something to be feared? Why?

*Jessica Mitford was born in 1917 in rural England, the daughter of an English peer. After her first husband, a nephew of Winston Churchill, died in World War II, Mitford remarried, moved to the United States, and began her career as an investigative journalist. Mitford has mercilessly exposed the absurdities of American traditions in her books* The American Way of Death *(1963),* Poison Penmanship: The Gentle Art of Muckraking *(1979), and* The American Way of Birth *(1992). In the following essay, excerpted from* The American Way of Death, *an exposé of the American funeral industry, Mitford provides a graphic account of the work performed by the embalmer.*

## Jessica Mitford   Behind the Formaldehyde Curtain

The drama begins to unfold with the arrival of the corpse at the mortuary. 1

Alas, poor Yorick![1] How surprised he would be to see how his counter- 2
part of today is whisked off to a funeral parlor and is in short order sprayed,
sliced, pierced, pickled, trussed, trimmed, creamed, waxed, painted, rouged,
and neatly dressed — transformed from a common corpse into a Beautiful
Memory Picture. This process is known in the trade as embalming and
restorative art, and is so universally employed in the United States and
Canada that the funeral director does it routinely, without consulting corpse
or kin. He regards as eccentric those few who are hardy enough to suggest that
it might be dispensed with. Yet no law requires embalming, no religious doctrine commends it, nor is it dictated by considerations of health, sanitation,
or even of personal daintiness. In no part of the world but in Northern America is it widely used. The purpose of embalming is to make the corpse presentable for viewing in a suitably costly container; and here too the funeral
director routinely, without first consulting the family, prepares the body for
public display.

Is all this legal? The processes to which a dead body may be subjected are 3
after all to some extent circumscribed by law. In most states, for instance, the
signature of next of kin must be obtained before an autopsy may be performed, before the deceased may be cremated, before the body may be turned
over to a medical school for research purposes; or such provision must be
made in the decedent's will. In the case of embalming, no such permission is
required nor is it ever sought. A textbook, *The Principles and Practices of Embalming*, comments on this: "There is some question regarding the legality of
much that is done within the preparation room." The author points out that
it would be most unusual for a responsible member of a bereaved family to

[1] **Alas, poor Yorick!:** Mitford echoes Hamlet's line as he examines the skull of his old friend, the court jester, who was buried without a coffin in a common grave (Shakespeare, *Hamlet* V.i.184).

instruct the mortician, in so many words, to *"embalm"* the body of a deceased relative. The very term "embalming" is so seldom used that the mortician must rely upon custom in the matter. The author concludes that unless the family specifies otherwise, the act of entrusting the body to the care of a funeral establishment carries with it an implied permission to go ahead and embalm.

Embalming is indeed a most extraordinary procedure, and one must wonder at the docility of Americans who each year pay hundreds of millions of dollars for its perpetuation, blissfully ignorant of what it is all about, what is done, how it is done. Not one in ten thousand has any idea of what actually takes place. Books on the subject are extremely hard to come by. They are not to be found in most libraries or bookshops.

In an era when huge television audiences watch surgical operations in the comfort of their living rooms, when, thanks to the animated cartoon, the geography of the digestive system has become familiar territory even to the nursery school set, in a land where the satisfaction of curiosity about almost all matters is a national pastime, the secrecy surrounding embalming can, surely, hardly be attributed to the inherent gruesomeness of the subject. Custom in this regard has within this century suffered a complete reversal. In the early days of American embalming, when it was performed in the home of the deceased, it was almost mandatory for some relative to stay by the embalmer's side and witness the procedure. Today, family members who might wish to be in attendance would certainly be dissuaded by the funeral director. All others, except apprentices, are excluded by law from the preparation room.

A close look at what does actually take place may explain in large measure the undertaker's intractable reticence concerning a procedure that has become his major *raison d'être.* Is it possible he fears that public information about embalming might lead patrons to wonder if they really want this service? If the funeral men are loath to discuss the subject outside the trade, the reader may, understandably, be equally loath to go on reading at this point. For those who have the stomach for it, let us part the formaldehyde curtain. . . .

The body is first laid out in the undertaker's morgue — or rather, Mr. Jones is reposing in the preparation room — to be readied to bid the world farewell.

The preparation room in any of the better funeral establishments has the tiled and sterile look of a surgery, and indeed the embalmer-restorative artist who does his chores there is beginning to adopt the term "derma-surgeon" (appropriately corrupted by some mortician-writers as "demi-surgeon") to describe his calling. His equipment, consisting of scalpels, scissors, augers, forceps, clamps, needles, pumps, tubes, bowls, and basins, is crudely imitative of the surgeon's, as is his technique, acquired in a nine- or twelve-month post–high school course in an embalming school. He is supplied by an advanced chemical industry with a bewildering array of fluids, sprays, pastes, oils, powders, creams, to fix or soften tissue, shrink or distend it as needed, dry it here, restore the moisture there. There are cosmetics, waxes, and paints to fill and cover features, even plaster of Paris to replace entire limbs. There are ingenious aids to prop and stabilize the cadaver: a Vari-Pose Head Rest, the Edwards Arm and Hand Positioner, the Repose Block (to support the shoulders during the embalming), and the Throop Foot Positioner, which resembles an old-fashioned stocks.

Mr. John H. Eckels, president of the Eckels College of Mortuary Science, thus describes the first part of the embalming procedure: "In the hands of a skilled practitioner, this work may be done in a comparatively short time and without mutilating the body other than by slight incision — so slight that it scarcely would cause serious inconvenience if made upon a living person. It is necessary to remove the blood, and doing this not only helps in the disinfecting, but removes the principal cause of disfigurements due to discoloration."    9

Another textbook discusses the all-important time element: "The earlier this is done, the better, for every hour that elapses between death and embalming will add to the problems and complications encountered. . . ." Just how soon should one get going on the embalming? The author tells us, "On the basis of such scanty information made available to this profession through its rudimentary and haphazard system of technical research, we must conclude that the best results are to be obtained if the subject is embalmed before life is completely extinct — that is, before cellular death has occurred. In the average case, this would mean within an hour after somatic death." For those who feel that there is something a little rudimentary, not to say haphazard, about this advice, a comforting thought is offered by another writer. Speaking of fears entertained in early days of premature burial, he points out, "One of the effects of embalming by chemical injection, however, has been to dispel fears of live burial." How true; once the blood is removed, chances of live burial are indeed remote.    10

To return to Mr. Jones, the blood is drained out through the veins and replaced by embalming fluid pumped in through the arteries. As noted in *The Principles and Practices of Embalming*, "every operator has a favorite injection and drainage point — a fact which becomes a handicap only if he fails or refuses to forsake his favorites when conditions demand it." Typical favorites are the carotid artery, femoral artery, jugular vein, subclavian vein. There are various choices of embalming fluid. If Flextone is used, it will produce a "mild, flexible rigidity. The skin retains a velvety softness, the tissues are rubbery and pliable. Ideal for women and children." It may be blended with B. and G. Products Company's Lyf-Lyk tint, which is guaranteed to reproduce "nature's own skin texture . . . the velvety appearance of living tissue." Suntone comes in three separate tints: Suntan; Special Cosmetic Tint, a pink shade "especially indicated for female subjects"; and Regular Cosmetic Tint, moderately pink.    11

About three to six gallons of a dyed and perfumed solution of formaldehyde, glycerin, borax, phenol, alcohol, and water is soon circulating through    12

Mr. Jones, whose mouth has been sewn together with a "needle directed upward between the upper lip and gum and brought out through the left nostril," with the corners raised slightly "for a more pleasant expression." If he should be bucktoothed, his teeth are cleaned with Bon Ami and coated with colorless nail polish. His eyes, meanwhile, are closed with flesh-tinted eye caps and eye cement.

The next step is to have at Mr. Jones with a thing called a trocar. This is a     13
long, hollow needle attached to a tube. It is jabbed into the abdomen, poked around the entrails and chest cavity, the contents of which are pumped out and replaced with "cavity fluid." This done, and the hole in the abdomen sewn up, Mr. Jones's face is heavily creamed (to protect the skin from burns which may be caused by leakage of the chemicals), and he is covered with a sheet and left unmolested for a while. But not for long — there is more, much more, in store for him. He has been embalmed, but not yet restored, and the best time to start the restorative work is eight to ten hours after embalming, when the tissues have become firm and dry.

The object of all this attention to the corpse, it must be remembered, is to     14
make it presentable for viewing in an attitude of healthy repose. "Our customs require the presentation of our dead in the semblance of normality . . . unmarred by the ravages of illness, disease, or mutilation," says Mr. J. Sheridan Mayer in his *Restorative Art*. This is rather a large order since few people die in the full bloom of health, unravaged by illness and unmarked by some disfigurement. The funeral industry is equal to the challenge: "In some cases the gruesome appearance of a mutilated or disease-ridden subject may be quite discouraging. The task of restoration may seem impossible and shake the confidence of the embalmer. This is the time for intestinal fortitude and determination. Once the formative work is begun and affected tissues are cleaned or removed, all doubts of success vanish. It is surprising and gratifying to discover the results which may be obtained."

The embalmer, having allowed an appropriate interval to elapse, returns     15
to the attack, but now he brings into play the skill and equipment of sculptor and cosmetician. Is a hand missing? Casting one in plaster of Paris is a simple matter. "For replacement purposes, only a cast of the back of the hand is necessary; this is within the ability of the average operator and is quite adequate." If a lip or two, a nose or an ear should be missing, the embalmer has at hand a variety of restorative waxes with which to model replacements. Pores and skin texture are simulated by stippling with a little brush, and over this cosmetics are laid on. Head off? Decapitation cases are rather routinely handled. Ragged edges are trimmed, and head joined to torso with a series of splints, wires, and sutures. It is a good idea to have a little something at the neck — a scarf or a high collar — when time for viewing comes. Swollen mouth? Cut out tissue as needed from inside the lips. If too much is removed, the surface contour can easily be restored by padding with cotton. Swollen necks and cheeks are reduced by removing tissue through vertical incisions made down each side of the neck. "When the deceased is casketed, the pillow will hide the suture incisions . . . as an extra precaution against leakage, the suture may be painted with liquid sealer."

The opposite condition is more likely to present itself — that of emacia-    16
tion. His hypodermic syringe now loaded with massage cream, the embalmer
seeks out and fills the hollowed and sunken areas by injection. In this procedure the backs of the hands and fingers and the under-chin area should not
be neglected.

Positioning the lips is a problem that recurrently challenges the ingenu-    17
ity of the embalmer. Closed too tightly, they tend to give a stern, even disap-
proving expression. Ideally, embalmers feel, the lips should give the
impression of being ever so slightly parted, the upper lip protruding slightly
for a more youthful appearance. This takes some engineering, however, as the
lips tend to drift apart. Lip drift can sometimes be remedied by pushing one
or two straight pins through the inner margin of the lower lip and then inserting them between the two front upper teeth. If Mr. Jones happens to have
no teeth, the pins can just as easily be anchored in his Armstrong Face Former
and Denture Replacer. Another method to maintain lip closure is to dislocate
the lower jaw, which is then held in its new position by a wire run through
holes which have been drilled through the upper and lower jaws at the mid-
line. As the French are fond of saying, *il faut souffrir pour être belle.*[2]

If Mr. Jones has died of jaundice, the embalming fluid will very likely turn    18
him green. Does this deter the embalmer? Not if he has intestinal fortitude.
Masking pastes and cosmetics are heavily laid on, burial garments and casket
interiors are color-correlated with particular care, and Jones is displayed beneath rose-colored lights. Friends will say "How *well* he looks." Death by carbon monoxide, on the other hand, can be rather a good thing from the
embalmer's viewpoint: "One advantage is the fact that this type of discoloration is an exaggerated form of a natural pink coloration." This is nice because the healthy glow is already present and needs but little attention.

The patching and filling completed, Mr. Jones is now shaved, washed,    19
and dressed. Cream-based cosmetic, available in pink, flesh, suntan, brunette,
and blond, is applied to his hands and face, his hair is shampooed and
combed (and, in the case of Mrs. Jones, set), his hands manicured. For the
horny-handed son of toil special care must be taken; cream should be applied
to remove ingrained grime, and the nails cleaned. "If he were not in the habit
of having them manicured in life, trimming and shaping is advised for better
appearance — never questioned by kin."

Jones is now ready for casketing (this is the present participle of the verb    20
"to casket"). In this operation his right shoulder should be depressed slightly
"to turn the body a bit to the right and soften the appearance of lying flat on
the back." Positioning the hands is a matter of importance, and special rubber positioning blocks may be used. The hands should be cupped slightly for
a more lifelike, relaxed appearance. Proper placement of the body requires a
delicate sense of balance. It should lie as high as possible in the casket, yet not
so high that the lid, when lowered, will hit the nose. On the other hand, we

---

[2] *il faut . . . belle*: One must suffer to be beautiful.

are cautioned, placing the body too low "creates the impression that the body is in a box."

Jones is next wheeled in the appointed slumber room where a few last       21
touches may be added — his favorite pipe placed in his hand or, if he was a great reader, a book propped into position. (In the case of little Master Jones a Teddy bear may be clutched.) Here he will hold open house for a few days, visiting hours 10 A.M. to 9 P.M.

All now being in readiness, the funeral director calls a staff conference to       22
make sure that each assistant knows his precise duties. Mr. Wilber Kriege writes: "This makes your staff feel that they are a part of the team, with a definite assignment that must be properly carried out if the whole plan is to succeed. You never heard of a football coach who failed to talk to his entire team before they go on the field. They have drilled on the plays they are to execute for hours and days, and yet the successful coach knows the importance of making even the bench-warming third-string substitute feel that he is important if the game is to be won." The winning of *this* game is predicated upon glass-smooth handling of the logistics. The funeral director has notified the pallbearers whose names were furnished by the family, has arranged for the presence of clergyman, organist, and soloist, has provided transportation for everybody, has organized and listed the flowers sent by friends. In *Psychology of Funeral Service* Mr. Edward A. Martin points out: "He may not always do as much as the family thinks he is doing, but it is his helpful guidance that they appreciate in knowing they are proceeding as they should. . . . The important thing is how well his services can be used to make the family believe they are giving unlimited expression to their own sentiment."

The religious service may be held in a church or in the chapel of the fu-       23
neral home; the funeral director vastly prefers the latter arrangement, for not only is it more convenient for him but it affords him the opportunity to show off his beautiful facilities to the gathered mourners. After the clergyman has had his say, the mourners queue up to file past the casket for a last look at the deceased. The family is *never* asked whether they want an open-casket ceremony; in the absence of their instruction to the contrary, this is taken for granted. Consequently well over 90 percent of all American funerals feature the open casket — a custom unknown in other parts of the world. Foreigners are astonished by it. An English woman living in San Francisco described her reaction in a letter to the writer:

> I myself have attended only one funeral here — that of an elderly fellow worker of mine. After the service I could not understand why everyone was walking towards the coffin (sorry, I mean casket), but thought I had better follow the crowd. It shook me rigid to get there and find the casket open and poor old Oscar lying there in his brown tweed suit, wearing a suntan makeup and just the wrong shade of lipstick. If I had not been extremely fond of the old boy, I have a horrible feeling that I might have giggled. Then and there I decided that I could never face another American funeral — even dead.

The casket (which has been resting throughout the service on a Classic    24
Beauty Ultra Metal Casket Bier) is now transferred by a hydraulically operated
device called Porto-Lift to a balloon-tired, Glide Easy casket carriage which
will wheel it to yet another conveyance, the Cadillac Funeral Coach. This may
be lavender, cream, light green — anything but black. Interiors, of course, are
color-correlated, "for the man who cannot stop short of perfection."

At graveside, the casket is lowered into the earth. This office, once the pre-    25
rogative of friends of the deceased, is now performed by a patented mechanical lowering device. A "Lifetime Green" artificial grass mat is at the ready to
conceal the sere earth, and overhead, to conceal the sky, is a portable Sterile
Chapel Tent ("resists the intense heat and humidity of summer and the terrific storms of winter . . . available in Silver Grey, Rose or Evergreen"). Now is
the time for the ritual scattering of earth over the coffin, as the solemn words
"earth to earth, ashes to ashes, dust to dust" are pronounced by the officiat-
ing cleric. This can today be accomplished "with a mere flick of the wrist with
the Gordon Leak-Proof Earth Dispenser. No grasping of a handful of dirt, no
soiled fingers. Simple, dignified, beautiful, reverent! The modern way!" The
Gordon Earth Dispenser (at $5) is of nickel-plated brass construction. It is not
only "attractive to the eye and long wearing"; it is also "one of the 'tools' for
building better public relations" if presented as "an appropriate noncom-
mercial gift" to the clergyman. It is shaped something like a saltshaker.

Untouched by human hand, the coffin and the earth are now united.    26

It is in the function of directing the participants through this maze of gad-    27
getry that the funeral director has assigned to himself his relatively new role
of "grief therapist." He has relieved the family of every detail, he has re-
vamped the corpse to look like a living doll, he has arranged for it to nap for
a few days in a slumber room, he has put on a well-oiled performance in
which the concept of *death* has played no part whatsoever — unless it was in-
considerately mentioned by the clergyman who conducted the religious service. He has done everything in his power to make the funeral a real pleasure
for everybody concerned. He and his team have given their all to score an upset victory over death.

**Questions to Start
You Thinking**

1. CONSIDERING MEANING:  Why is Mitford so critical of the American funeral industry? What is her main objection to the embalming procedure?

2. IDENTIFYING WRITING STRATEGIES:  Where does Mitford simply explain the
   process of embalming and where does she actually evaluate the funeral industry and its attitudes?

3. ANALYZING THE WRITER'S CHOICES:  Mitford uses reading as a key resource in this
   essay. Why does she sometimes choose to summarize what she has read,
   while at other times she chooses to quote directly from such sources as *The
   Principles and Practices of Embalming* and *Restorative Art*? How does each use
   of her reading support her criticism of the American practice of embalming?

4. EXPANDING VOCABULARY: In this essay, Mitford juxtaposes blunt, descriptive language with the jargon of the funeral industry. Identify and define three examples of each type of language. What effect does this juxtaposition create?

5. MAKING CONNECTIONS: Compare and contrast the ways in which Mitford and Joy Harjo ("Three Generations of Native American Women's Birth Experience," p. 471) evaluate the uses of technology.

**Journal Prompts**

1. Using Mitford's style as a model, write a paragraph or two satirizing another elaborate custom, such as high school graduation, school proms, or weddings.

2. Explain your feelings about procedures in which technology plays a major but perhaps controversial role: for example, childbirth, in vitro fertilization, prenatal testing, or the medical treatment of the terminally ill.

**Suggestions for Writing**

1. Write an essay explaining the rituals of death as you have experienced them. What is their function? How have they made you feel? How would you change them?

2. Using Mitford's selection as a model, research and report on the way another culture treats death. In your report, include both straightforward description of the culture's customs and your own feelings about their "way of death."

**Robert Wright** *was born in 1957 in Lawton, Oklahoma. Educated at Princeton University, he was a senior editor at* The Sciences *magazine from 1984 to 1987 and is now senior editor at the* New Republic. *He is also the author of* Three Scientists and Their Gods: Looking for Meaning in an Age of Information *(1988), which won the National Book Critics Circle Award for biography and autobiography in 1988, and* The Moral Animal *(1994). The following essay first appeared in the* New Republic *on October 24, 1994. In it Wright explores some difficult but necessary questions about genetic engineering and the "new eugenics."*

## *Robert Wright*   Mr. Clean Genes

Suppose you are a young married woman and have just found out that you carry BRCA1 — the gene that brings an 85 percent chance of getting breast cancer. You already wanted to have children, and now, feeling suddenly mortal, your're especially eager. But you don't want to pass the gene on to them, and you realize there's a way to avoid that. Using in vitro fertilization, you can create several test-tube embryos, each consisting of only a few cells. Then you can screen the embryos for the gene and reimplant those that pass the test.

Should you do it? The answer depends, for one thing, on whether you've got $10,000 to spare. This may sound like a mundane question compared to all the moral imponderables one could ponder here, but in it lies much of the political significance of the recently discovered, much-discussed breast cancer gene. Along with other pathological genes just coming to light, it will make a new kind of argument for universal health care — and, if the argument prevails, will draw the government into the business of eugenics. In the process, the ideological character of eugenics will be redefined.

It will be a year or two before doctors can easily screen people, and thus     3
embryos, for the breast cancer gene. But once these tests exist, they will no doubt be used eugenically. The precedent was set in 1992 by a British woman carrying a gene for cystic fibrosis. Eight embryos were screened for the gene, two were reimplanted, and one survived to birth — a baby girl with healthy lungs.

There are two reasons few women have followed this precedent. First, dis-     4
covery of the cystic fibrosis gene has led to a nasal-spray treatment for the disease, dampening the eugenic incentive; no such therapy is likely anytime soon for breast cancer. Second, there are only about 1,000 new cases of cystic fibrosis in America each year. Ten times that many women contract breast cancer because of BRCA1, and a like number because of BRCA2, a gene scientists are close to locating. And then there's MSH2, the gene that gives you an 80 percent chance of getting colon cancer. It was discovered last year, and a test for it should arrive before long.

And so on. More and more genes will tempt more and more people to     5
clean up their little corner of the gene pool. Barring government intervention, the pool will get clearer around the affluent but not around the poor. Of course, there's nothing new about health care options being open mainly to the upper socioeconomic classes. You seldom run into a homeless person at a brain-scan clinic. But surely there's something uniquely, intolerably grotesque about creating a genetic underclass, letting a broad range of hereditary diseases settle at the bottom of the social hierarchy.

If you agree, you're left with two choices: either ban eugenic intervention,     6
ensuring that, say, cancer remains an equal-opportunity attacker; or provide money for people who want eugenics but can't afford it. I vote for the latter. And if you vote for the former, you can have the job of telling women with the breast cancer gene that they're not allowed to spend their hard-earned money to spare their daughters the same fate.

Once you start subsidizing eugenics, lines get hard to draw. Mark Skol-     7
nick, head of the team that found BRCA1, suffers from "Syndrome X," a genetic defect that encourages heart disease and often kills men in their forties and fifties. At forty-eight, he sticks to a no-fat diet and hopes for the best. Presumably he'd like any future offspring to live less precariously, and presumably that option will be open once the X gene is found. But what about genes that less dramatically incline us toward heart disease? Skolnick cofounded Myriad Genetics, the company that patented (yes, patented) the BRCA1 gene and will develop a test for it. The company has observed: "The market for testing for the genetic predisposition to cancer, heart disease, and other significant diseases potentially includes the entire population."

Indeed. Bringing test-tube eugenics under the rubric of health care will   8
drive home with new force the fact that providing universal coverage isn't
cheap. It will also drive home the usually unspoken corollary: providing universal and *comprehensive* coverage is impossible. Hence, more vivid than before, the case for rationing, for discouraging, high-cost, low-benefit treatment.
Given fiscal reality, we may face a choice between (a) keeping a cancer patient
alive for an extra week and (b) sparing an unborn child from eventual cancer.
To me, (b) seems the clear winner. On the other hand, when you change (b)
to "sparing an unborn child from a slightly elevated risk of heart disease," the
issue gets trickier.

Test-tube eugenics eventually will touch temperament and intelligence.   9
And though a gene strongly inclining one toward manic-depressive illness or
mental retardation might be an easy call, other genes won't be. The geneticist
Robert Plomin is studying children with low and high I.Q.s, trying to find a
cluster of genes that together appreciably influence intelligence. He says he's
getting closer. Should the government support *this* sort of eugenics? And if
not, are we willing to see only the affluent use it? (Just what rich people need:
expanded educational opportunities.) We could try to ban such uses altogether, but such a ban will be politically hard to sustain if wily international
competitors — German, Japanese, Chinese — start permitting this sort of intellectual enrichment.

Eugenics used to connote coercion, the selective *restraint* of reproductive   10
opportunities. The famous 1927 Supreme Court ruling that "three generations of imbeciles are enough" came in support of a state law dictating invol-
untary sterilization of the "feebleminded" in public institutions. And
sometimes, to make matters worse, the grounds for selection were ethnic, as
with immigration laws. These racist overtones are one thing that dried up the
surprisingly strong early liberal support for old-style eugenics and turned it
into a right-wing enterprise.

The new eugenics, in contrast, will *expand* reproductive options and do so   11
in order to keep them level across socioeconomic and ethnic lines. It will
draw most of its support from the left, both because of this expensive egalitarianism and because the religious right will blanch at the moral issues raised
(though they're in some ways less troubling than those raised by amniocentesis and abortion).

The old eugenics, by its nature, could happen only if the government   12
stepped in and orchestrated it. The new eugenics will start happening unless
the government steps in and stops it. It is the political difficulty of stopping it
— of saying no to that mother with the breast cancer gene — that will lead the
government to accept and regulate it. A large amount of good can result from
government involvement, as well as a large amount of creepiness.

| | |
|---|---|
| **Questions to Start You Thinking** | 1.  CONSIDERING MEANING:  According to Wright, what problems and benefits will government-supported eugenics cause? |

2. IDENTIFYING WRITING STRATEGIES: How does Wright divide his analysis into parts to simplify the complex moral and scientific issues surrounding eugenics?

3. ANALYZING THE WRITER'S CHOICES: Notice the various points in the essay where Wright presents the reader with either a choice or a question. Do these questions and choices seem "loaded" to you? What response might Wright hope to evoke from the reader by taking this approach?

4. EXPANDING VOCABULARY: Define *in vitro fertilization* (paragraph 1), *pathological, eugenics* (paragraph 2), and *gene pool*. What is the etymology of these scientific words?

5. MAKING CONNECTIONS: In his essay Wright analyzes some of the ways in which the misuse of science could create "a genetic underclass . . . at the bottom of the social hierarchy" (paragraph 5). Compare and contrast his position with that of Stephan Jay Gould ("The Geometer of Race," p. 532), who also makes an argument about the misuse of science: "The shift from a geographic to a hierarchical ordering of human diversity must stand as one of the most fateful transitions in the history of Western science . . . ." (paragraph 15).

**Journal Prompts**

1. Do you agree with Wright that there is "a large amount of creepiness" (paragraph 12) to the notion that government may be forced to regulate eugenics? Why or why not?

2. Imagine that the gene for acne, hay fever, or migraine headaches is discovered. In your opinion, should eugenic intervention — at a price only the rich can afford — be allowed? Should the government regulate this type of eugenics? How could this technology be made available to everyone?

**Suggestions for Writing**

1. Imagine that you are in the hypothetical situation described by Wright at the opening of his essay and that money is not a problem. Would you create and screen test-tube embryos? Explain and then justify the action you would take.

2. What is your opinion of eugenics, especially the "new eugenics" that Wright describes? Write an essay in which you argue that eugenics will primarily benefit humankind or will primarily harm humankind.

**Melvin Konner,** *born in 1946 in Brooklyn, New York, trained as a medical doctor and anthropologist at Harvard University. He now teaches anthropology at Emory University in Georgia. In his writing he not only informs his general readership of discoveries and trends in medicine but also reflects on human nature and the human spirit. His many books include* Becoming a Doctor: A Journey of Initiation in Medical School *(1987),* Why the Reckless Survive: And Other Secrets of Human Nature *(1990),* Dear America: A Concerned Doctor Who Wants You to Know the Truth about Health Reform *(1993), and* Medicine at the Crossroads: The Crisis in Health Care *(1993). In the following essay, which was originally published in the the* New York Times Magazine *on October 2, 1994, Konner draws on medical studies and personal experience to argue that the benefits of antidepressants outweigh their detriments.*

Some kind of new prescription mind-soother seems to have pervaded all   1
walks of American life. Everywhere you go, everyone you know now seems to
be listening to Prozac or to one of its new chemical cousins. Have we, one
wonders, already reached Aldous Huxley's brave new world, where soma the
wonder drug is starting to make everyone feel good?

Actually, it was back in the late '80s when the gifted young psychiatrist   2
Peter D. Kramer first began to write about a newly developed antidepressant
for the trade newspaper *Psychiatric Times.* He seemed to be writing, well, from
his heart as much as his head. He told of people who benefited from this new
drug, Prozac, in more than just the classic sense, of relief from deep emotional
depression. He saw them as essentially healthy people who were now moving through life in a new way. Again and again they said things like, "I was
never really myself before."

Kramer came out and said what others were thinking: Some normal peo-   3
ple were having their personalities changed by the new drugs, and most of
them liked the change very much. He went on to describe these people and
their experiences in greater detail in his phenomenally popular book, *Listening to Prozac.* The book was not an unabashed brief for the drug. It expressed
obvious doubts about long-term effects, and some less obvious, more philo-
sophic ones as well. But Kramer did have quite a good-news announcement:
Here was the prospect of help for many people who had no psychiatric disorder but who might, say, have not uncommon social fears or limiting inhi-
bitions or a lack of self-confidence. And some readers inferred from this the
potential for personality change through chemistry.

The news was not universally cheered. Critics expressed fears that the   4
drugs would replace needed psychotherapy, or friendship, or learning, or
even ethical reflection. Sherwin B. Nuland, a distinguished Yale surgeon and
author of *How We Die,* decried *Listening to Prozac* as simplistic and conjec-
tural, an instance of overweening ambition. In a column, the *New Yorker*
joked about *Listening to Bourbon.* Peter R. Breggin, a psychiatrist who has made
a career of criticizing his colleagues, and Ginger Rose Breggin wrote a book
called *Talking Back to Prozac,* which capitalized on Kramer's success much as
Kramer had capitalized on Prozac's.

Some of the Breggins' complaints were sleight of hand. They found weak-   5
nesses in the Food and Drug Administration's approval process for Prozac,
but ignored many studies since. They exaggerated the placebo effect, the effect
even a sugar pill may have. In fact, in eighteen studies of more than two thousand depressed patients, the three most widely prescribed of the new antidepressants proved much better than a placebo, with two-thirds of patients
typically benefiting from the drugs. The probability that these effects were due
to chance, as the Breggins claim, is less than one's chance, on an average day,
of being struck by lightning.

**615**

Still, Kramer's critics have correctly pointed to past psychiatric drug fads,    6
warning that this may be just another. At times, too many people have taken
prescription stimulants such as amphetamines, and certainly many have been
kept on Librium or Valium too long and become needlessly dependent. But
the Breggins' notion that these drugs work the same way amphetamines do is
just plain wrong. As for Librium and Valium, they blunt anxiety; they do not
dispel depression or brighten a darkened mind.

A little physiology: If you were to run a thread from the nape of your neck to    7
exit high on your forehead — don't try this at home — the line would cross
your brain stem first. Parts of the stem tap out the rhythms of breathing and
heartbeat. A little further along are the sources of two brain chemicals with
far-reaching effects: noradrenaline, related to the natural stuff risk-takers say
they get high on, and serotonin. Both are chemical messengers that shape
moods.

The older antidepressants kept them in the synapses, or gaps, between    8
nerve cells long enough to have a positive effect. Scientists wanted drugs that
would target specific chemicals — the more specific, or "cleaner," a drug's actions, the fewer its side effects — but no one was really prepared for the impact. Prozac, it turned out, kept serotonin hanging around the gap with great
effect, yet it allowed other chemical messengers to be absorbed at the usual
rate. Within a few years, millions had tried Prozac, the first of the new serotonin reuptake inhibitors; Zoloft and Paxil followed.

Depressed people are frequently troubled by anxiety as well as depres-    9
sion. The new drugs often work against both, making them a twin blessing.
Patients with an obsessional aspect to their depressions were also seen to benefit, and soon the new agents began to be prescribed for people with obses-
sive-compulsive disorders. They helped indirectly in the treatment of
alcoholism and other addictions, because many depressed patients attempted
to self-medicate with these substances in an effort to relieve their depression
or anxiety. Even emotional illnesses triggered by having a baby — not just the
jolt of becoming a mother, but disabling mental disorders — improved with
the drugs. Then the new category appeared: patients who were not mentally
ill but who were getting prescriptions anyway and having their lives improved.

The new drugs do have side effects. Not every person who takes them has    10
more gains than losses. There is no such thing as a perfect drug. Evolution did
not design the body or brain in anticipation of future chemical break-
throughs; it made a molecular patchwork, and intruders like pharmaceutical
agents never have just one effect. But so far the risks amount to a small fraction of the benefits. That is why millions of people are taking the new drugs;
not because they cannot do without them but because they see no good reason why they should.

Medical science does have much more to learn about these drugs. Pre-    11
liminary research showing that Prozac hastened tumor growth in rats is wor-

risome and must be followed up. Meanwhile, a formerly suicidal elderly man takes real pleasure in every day; a young mother who became obsessively afraid to leave her home within weeks after her baby was born is freed from mental prison; an addict is able to stop using cocaine. New effects of the drugs are reported so frequently one hesitates to mention them for fear of sounding like a hawker of snake oil. A recent *Runner's World* reported testimony from runners who claim to have improved their time after taking Prozac or Zoloft. It is likely that most were depressed, which can hurt any performance. Alberto Salazar, a world-class marathoner who had been suffering from listlessness and various minor symptoms, began taking Prozac and made a world-class comeback. He later said, "I didn't really care how fast I ran. . . . The only thing that's important to me is that Prozac has helped me lead a normal life again." Finally, veterinarians at the University of Pennsylvania began putting high-strung or down-in-the-dumps pooches on Prozac. Carrie Dolan of the *Wall Street Journal* had great fun with the research, reporting on the paper's front page that the dog "Sparky (not her real name) suffered from 'profound anxiety' " and "interdog aggression," but was greatly helped by the drug. Vets and dog owners, however, are serious about its benefits.

Among psychotherapists, even those of the traditional talk-through-everything-without-stooping-to-pharmacology school — the psychoanalysts — are succumbing. Steven Roose, a Columbia University psychoanalyst, has shown that a majority of certified analysts now have patients on psychiatric drugs. Today, along with many other psychotherapists, psychoanalysts are finding that drugs can facilitate their work, and that the prescription may be only the start of a long process of learning and personal change.    12

My own experience suggests that this is so. I grappled with lifelong depression through years of psychotherapy. I learned; I changed; I believe in it. Yet until I began taking antidepressant drugs in my mid-forties, I don't think I understood quite how depressed I had often been. When the pain began to interfere seriously with my functioning, I began taking Prozac — unsuccessfully. I then tried a "classic" antidepressant, desipramine. Within two months, I felt enormously better. But I was reminded, not just from day to day but from moment to moment, that I was on a powerful drug; the physical symptoms were tolerable, but they did not let me forget. I felt better, but I did not feel "myself."    13

So when I thought I could, I got off desipramine, and was fine for a while. But a year or so later I needed it again. This is a common pattern with antidepressants, and recent research by Ellen Frank and her colleagues at the University of Pittsburgh has cast serious doubt on the standard practice of trying to get people off these drugs as soon as possible. For me, the cycle repeated; unpleasant side effects led me to stop the drug, and when I did I was well for many months.    14

This time, when my depression became serious, my doctor suggested Zoloft, which was then new and slightly different from Prozac. This one    15 worked beautifully. It lifted my depression as well as desipramine had, but with a fraction of the side effects. I was aware of the drug when I took it, and there were some minor physical symptoms, but mostly I just felt like myself.

Was I? Am I now, nearly two years later? Here we come to a debate about the new drugs that sheds more heat than light: Do they or do they not change personality? When I was depressed, which was often, I used to think of what Oliver Wendell Holmes Jr. once said about FDR: that he had a second-class mind, but a first-class temperament. I liked to joke that I was just the reverse, a first-class mind with a second-class temperament.    16

Now I am not so sure; my temperament seems pretty darn good. Psychologists like to distinguish "state" from "trait," and some would say that I had a friendly, cheerful temperament (trait) hidden by a depressed, dour state much of the time. But what is temperament anyway, if not the thread on which our states, day by day, are strung like so many beads? Surely state becomes trait if it lasts long enough. And here, I think, turns the debate between Kramer and his critics. It is meaningless to try to define a percentage of people who will have their personalities changed, rather than just their depressions lifted. No one knows how to draw a line between the two.    17

For me the medicine became a platform on which I could function in a very different way. I noticed the difference many times a day, in the way I interacted with friends and strangers, the way I fell asleep and woke up, the way my children's complaints affected me, the way I responded to telephone calls. I had to forget many things I thought I knew about myself, and move forward on the platform the drug had built. I stayed in psychotherapy, and learned a great deal there. I had few physical reminders that I was medicated, so I still felt like "me." And yet I was becoming a new version of me, through a process of personal growth, reflection, and plain old learning, all made possible by an impressive little molecule.    18

My life is still full of external problems of a sort that no one can control; few people who know me well would want to change places with me. Yet I now know that there is a difference between depression and even the most severe life stress. People sometimes kill themselves because of life stresses, but more often they do it because of internal pain. No one who has not experienced this pain can understand it. Paradoxically, some who have experienced it but have not had it relieved may not understand it either — how totally different they might feel when they are not in such constant pain, or how different those around them might feel.    19

One time of day I am reminded of the medicine is when I first wake up and stumble out on the driveway to pick up the newspaper. I remember the dense fog I used to have to fight through at that moment, the hurt in the center of my chest, the constant questions about the simplest tasks: "Why am I doing this, why am I doing anything?" Now I amble sleepily down the drive, see the familiar blue plastic bag, and think of Pat Conroy's felicitous phrase about newspapers; the daily gift of words. I am as troubled as ever by the news, but I am more likely to do something, like call a senator or send a few    20 dollars to Rwanda. I still engage in ethical reflection; I am just not paralyzed by it. I even indulge in the consolation of philosophy, but now I get more from what I read.

Critics would have us believe that it is good for us to feel the pain, the existential dread, to work it through with friends or therapists or pastors. I tried, for too many years. One *should* try before taking medicine, but not for a quarter century — especially not now that we have medicines as good as these. Critics caution that if we blunt the pain we may fail to deal with the internal and external problems that are causing it. This is a noble sentiment. But why limit it to depression or obsession? Why not let asthmatics wheeze instead of giving them bronchodilators, so they'll feel motivated to do something about the allergens in their environment? Why give acetaminophen or aspirin to the tens of millions of sufferers of chronic arthritis pain? Their pain is only natural, signaling them to slow down, and these drugs can certainly be harmful. One could go on, but the point is very clear: It is only because we so belittle and devalue psychic pain that such critics even have a hearing.    21

In his affecting memoir, *Darkness Visible*, William Styron writes of this as few have done before, comparing recovery to Dante's emergence from the infernal regions: "For those who have dwelt in depression's dark wood," says Styron, "and known its inexplicable agony, their return from the abyss is not unlike the ascent of the poet, trudging upward and upward out of hell's black depths and at last emerging into what he saw as 'the shining world.' " Dante and Styron both conclude, "And so we came forth, and once again beheld the stars." Those of us who have emerged at last, with the help of modern medicine, from years marked too often by despair, weakness, darkness, and pain, look back at those past travels and shudder before sighing in immense relief. We learned something, no doubt, on our infernal journey, but once is enough, and there is little likelihood that we will ever be persuaded to go back.    22

**Questions to Start You Thinking**

1. CONSIDERING MEANING: According to Konner, what are the pros and cons of Prozac and other antidepressant drugs? Why does he feel the pros outweigh the cons?

2. IDENTIFYING WRITING STRATEGIES: How does Konner use reading to take a stand? What sources does he quote? Which sources seem most believable?

3. ANALYZING THE WRITER'S CHOICES: Konner chooses not to inform the reader about the specific side effects of the various antidepressant drugs, instead opting to make the generalization that "there is no such thing as a perfect drug" (paragraph 10). Why does Konner use his own experience with antidepressant drugs, along with the experiences of others he knows or has heard about, as the primary evidence for his claim that the drugs' "risks amount to a small fraction of the benefits" (paragraph 10)?

4. EXPANDING VOCABULARY: Look up *state* (as in "psychological state") and *trait* (paragraph 17) in a standard dictionary or a dictionary of medical terms.

What is the distinction between them? How is each a component of an individual's personality?

5.. MAKING CONNECTIONS: How might Konner feel about the use of eugenic intervention, as described by Robert Wright in "Mr. Clean Genes" (p. 611), to control the mental health of offspring? Explain your answer.

**Journal Prompts**

1. What is your usual state of mind and your usual temperament? Are they ever in conflict?

2. What is your opinion of the growing use of antidepressants? Has Konner's essay influenced your opinion in any way? If so, how?

**Suggestions for Writing**

1. Do you agree with Konner that as a society we "belittle and devalue psychic pain" (paragraph 21)? Write an essay exploring this question based on your own experience and observations.

2. Read an account of mental illness, such as William Styron's *Darkness Visible,* Elizabeth Wurtzel's *Prozac Nation,* or Susanna Kaysen's *Girl, Interrupted.* Compare and contrast the author's illness and treatment with Konner's.

**Bill McKibben,** *born in 1960 in Palo Alto, California, began his career at the* New Yorker *as a staff writer and editor soon after graduating from Harvard University in 1982. McKibben has published hundreds of pieces in the* New Yorker *as well as articles on environmental and related issues in the* New York Times, Rolling Stone *(where he was a contributing editor), and many other publications. He is the author of* The End of Nature *(1989),* The Age of Missing Information *(1992), and* The Comforting Whirlwind *(1994). A freelance writer since 1987, McKibben now lives in the Adirondack Mountains in New York. In this selection, taken from* The End of Nature, *McKibben argues that global warming not only damages the environment but also means the end of nature as we understand it.*

## *Bill McKibben*  The End of Nature

Almost every day, I hike up the hill out my back door. Within a hundred yards the woods swallows me up, and there is nothing to remind me of human society — no trash, no stumps, no fence, not even a real path. Looking out from the high places, you can't see road or house; it is a world apart from man. But once in a while someone will be cutting wood farther down the valley, and the snarl of a chain saw will fill the woods. It is harder on those days to get caught up in the timeless meaning of the forest, for man is nearby. The sound of the chain saw doesn't blot out all the noises of the forest or drive animals away, but it does drive away the feeling that you are in another, separate, timeless, wild sphere.

Now that we have changed the most basic forces around us, the noise of that chain saw will always be in the woods. We have changed the atmosphere, and that will change the weather. The temperature and rainfall are no longer to be entirely the work of some separate, uncivilizable force, but instead in part a product of our habits, our economies, our ways of life. Even in the most remote wilderness, where the strictest laws forbid the felling of a single tree, the sound of that saw will be clear, and a walk in the woods will be changed — tainted — by its whine. The world outdoors will mean much the same thing as the world indoors, the hill the same thing as the house.

An idea, a relationship, can go extinct, just like an animal or a plant. The idea in this case is "nature," the separate and wild province, the world apart from man to which he adapted, under whose rules he was born and died. In the past, we spoiled and polluted parts of that nature, inflicted environmental "damage." But that was like stabbing a man with toothpicks: though it hurt, annoyed, degraded, it did not touch vital organs, block the path of the lymph or blood. We never thought that we had wrecked nature. Deep down, we never really thought we could: it was too big and too old; its forces — the wind, the rain, the sun — were too strong, too elemental.

But, quite by accident, it turned out that the carbon dioxide and other gases we were producing in our pursuit of a better life — in pursuit of warm houses and eternal economic growth and of agriculture so productive it would free most of us from farming — *could* alter the power of the sun, could increase its heat. And that increase *could* change the patterns of moisture and dryness, breed storms in new places, breed deserts. Those things may or may not have yet begun to happen, but it is too late to altogether prevent them from happening. We have produced the carbon dioxide — we are ending nature.

We have not ended rainfall or sunlight; in fact, rainfall and sunlight may become more important forces in our lives. It is too early to tell exactly how much harder the wind will blow, how much hotter the sun will shine. That is for the future. But the *meaning* of the wind, the sun, the rain — of nature — has already changed. Yes, the wind still blows — but no longer from some other sphere, some inhuman place. . . .

. . . Most of the day, the sky above my mountain is simply sky, not "airspace." Standing in the middle of a grimy English mill town, George Orwell records this "encouraging" thought: "In spite of hard trying, man has yet succeeded in doing his dirt everywhere. The earth is so vast and still so empty that even in the filthy heart of civilization you find fields where the grass is green instead of grey; perhaps if you looked for them you might even finds streams with live fish in them instead of salmon tins." When Rachel Carson wrote *Silent Spring* [1962], she was able to find some parts of the Arctic still untouched — no DDT in the fish, the beaver, the beluga, the caribou, the moose, the polar bear, the walrus. The cranberries, the strawberries, and the wild rhubarb all tested clean, though two snowy owls, probably as a result of their migrations, carried small amounts of the pesticide, as did the livers of two Eskimos who had been away to the hospital in Anchorage.

In other words, as pervasive a problem as DDT was and is, one could, and can, always imagine that *somewhere* a place existed free of its taint. (And largely as a result of Carson's book there are more and more such places.) As pervasive and growing as the problem of acid rain surely is, at the moment places still exist with a rainfall of an acceptable, "normal" pH. And if we wished to stop acid rain we could; experimenters have placed tents over groves of trees to demonstrate that if the acid bath ceases, a forest will return to normal. Even the radiation from an event as nearly universal as the explosion at the Chernobyl plant has begun to fade, and Scandinavians can once more eat their vegetables.     7

We can, in other words, still plausibly imagine wild nature — or, at least, the possibility of wild nature in the future — in all sorts of places.     8

This idea of nature is hardy. Our ability to shut the destroyed areas from our minds, to see beauty around man's degradation, is considerable. A few years ago I spent some days driving around Arizona in a van with a man named Lyn Jacobs, one of a small number of environmentalists fighting a difficult battle to restrict the grazing of cattle on public lands in the West. The cows, which range over 70 percent of the federal land in the American West under a leasing program that does not pay for itself and each year requires tax subsidies, produce about 3 percent of America's beef. And by their constant grazing, the cattle convert the rangelands into barren pastures. Where there are streams they cave in the banks; where there are wildfowl they trample their nests. In their wake they leave stands of cheatgrass and thistle in place of the natural long-stemmed grasses. But the West has been a pasture so long that practically no one notices. People just assume that grass there can't grow more than a foot high. One morning, Jacobs and I drove along a ranch road that ran just parallel to the Grand Canyon about fifteen miles from the south rim. It was a glorious day, the sky a polarized blue, and though you couldn't see the canyon you knew with heart-stopping precision where it was, for the clouds dropped over its edge, their bottoms obscured like icebergs. "That's the problem," Jacobs said, stopping the van. "When you look at Western panoramas, you don't look down — your eye is trained to think this desert is normal. You tend to look at the mountains and the blue sky above them, and the clouds."     9

The idea of wildness, in other words, can survive most of the "normal" destruction of nature. Wildness can survive in our minds once the land has been discovered and mapped and even chewed up. It can survive all sorts of pollution, even the ceaseless munching of a million cows. If the ground is dusty and trodden, we look at the sky; if the sky is smoggy, we travel someplace where it's clear; if we can't travel to someplace where it's clear, we *imagine* ourselves in Alaska or Australia or some place where it is, and that works nearly as well. Nature, while often fragile in reality, is durable in our imaginations. Wildness, the idea of wildness, has outlasted the exploration of the     10 entire globe. It has endured the pesticides and the pollution. When the nature around us is degraded, we picture it fresh and untainted elsewhere. When elsewhere, too, it rains acid or DDT, we can still imagine that someday soon it will be better, that we will stop polluting and despoiling and instead "restore" nature. (And, indeed, people have begun to do just this sort of work; here in the Adirondacks, helicopters drop huge quantities of lime into lakes in order to reduce their acidity.) In our midst, nature suffers from a terrible case of acne, or even skin cancer — but our faith in its essential strength remains, for the damage always seems local.

But now the basis of that faith is lost. The idea of nature will not survive the new global pollution — the carbon dioxide and the CFCs and the like. This new rupture with nature is different not only in scope but also in kind from salmon tins in an English stream. We have changed the atmosphere, and thus we are changing the weather. By changing the weather, we make every spot on earth man-made and artificial. We have deprived nature of its independence, and that is fatal to its meaning. Nature's independence *is* its meaning; without it there is nothing but us.

If you travel by plane and dog team and snowshoe to the farthest corner of the Arctic and it is a mild summer day, you will not know whether the temperature is what it is "supposed" to be, or whether, thanks to the extra carbon dioxide, you are standing in the equivalent of a heated room. If it is twenty below and the wind is howling — perhaps absent man it would be forty below. Since most of us get to the North Pole only in our minds, the real situation is more like this: if in July there's a heat wave in London, it won't be a natural phenomenon. It will be a man-made phenomenon — an amplification of what nature intended or a total invention. Or, at the very least, it *might* be a man-made phenomenon, which amounts to the same thing. The storm that might have snapped the hot spell may never form, or may veer off in some other direction, not by the laws of nature but by the laws of nature as they have been rewritten, blindly, crudely, but effectively, by man. If the sun is beating down on you, you will not have the comfort of saying, "Well, that's nature." Or if the sun feels sweet on the back of your neck, that's fine, but it isn't nature. A child born now will never know a natural summer, a natural autumn, winter, or spring. Summer is going extinct, replaced by something else that will be called "summer." This new summer will retain some of its relative characteristics — it will be hotter than the rest of the year, for instance, and the time of year when crops grow — but it will not be summer, just as even the best prosthesis is not a leg.

And, of course, climate determines an enormous amount of the rest of nature — where the forests stop and the prairies or the tundra begins, where the rain falls and where the arid deserts squat, where the wind blows strong and steady, where the glaciers form, how fast the lakes evaporate, where the seas rise. As John Hoffman, of the Environmental Protection Agency, noted in the *Journal of Forestry*, "trees planted today will be entering their period of greatest growth when the climate has already changed." A child born today might swim in a stream free of toxic waste, but he won't ever see a natural stream. If the waves crash up against the beach, eroding dunes and destroying homes, it is not the awesome power of Mother Nature. It is the awesome power of Mother Nature as altered by the awesome power of man, who has overpowered in a century the processes that have been slowly evolving and changing of their own accord since the earth was born.

Those "record highs" and "record lows" that the weathermen are always    14
talking about — they're meaningless now. It's like comparing pole vaults between athletes using bamboo and those using fiberglass poles, or dash times between athletes who've been chewing steroids and those who've stuck to Wheaties. They imply a connection between the past and the present which doesn't exist. The comparison is like hanging Rembrandts next to Warhols; we live in a postnatural world. Thoreau once said he could walk for half an hour and come to "some portion of the earth's surface where man does not stand from one year's end to another, and there, consequently, politics are not, for they are but the cigar-smoke of a man." Now you could walk half a year and not reach such a spot. Politics — our particular way of life, our ideas about how we should live — now blows its smoke over every inch of the globe. . . .

And even as it dawns on us what we have done, there will be plenty of op-    15
portunity to forget, at least for a while, that anything has changed. For it isn't natural *beauty* that is ended; in fact, in the same way that the smog breeds spectacular sunsets, there may appear new, unimagined beauties. What will change is the meaning that beauty carries, for when we look at a sunset, we see, or we think we see, many things beyond a particular arrangement of orange and purple and rose.

It is also true that this is not the first huge rupture in the globe's history. Per-    16
haps thirty times since the earth formed, planetesimals up to ten miles in diameter and traveling at sixty times the speed of sound have crashed into the earth, releasing, according to [British scientist] James Lovelock, perhaps a thousand times as much energy as would be liberated by the explosion of all present stocks of nuclear weapons. Such events, some scientists say, may have destroyed 90 percent of all living organisms. On an even larger scale, the sun has steadily increased its brightness; it has grown nearly 30 percent more luminous since life on earth began, forcing that life to keep forever scrambling to stay ahead — a race it will eventually lose, though perhaps not for some billions of years. Or consider an example more closely resembling the sharp divide we have now crossed. About two billion years ago, the microbiologist Lynn Margulis writes, the spread of certain sorts of bacteria caused, in short order, an increase in atmospheric oxygen from one part in a million to one part in just five — from 0.0001 percent to 21 percent. Compared to that, the increase in carbon dioxide from 280 to 560 parts per million is as the hill behind my house to Annapurna.[1] "this was by far the greatest pollution crisis the earth has ever endured," Margulis writes. Oxygen poisoned most micro-

---

[1] **Annapurna:** Peak in the Himalayas, 26,000 feet.

bial life, which "had no defense against this cataclysm except the standard way of DNA replication and duplication, gene transfer and mutation." And, indeed, these produced the successful oxygen-synthesizing life forms that now dominate the earth.

But each of these examples is different from what we now experience, for    17
they were "natural," as opposed to man-made. A pint-sized planet cracks into the earth; the ice advances; the sun, by the immutable laws of stars, burns brighter till its inevitable explosion; genetic mutation sets certain bacteria to spewing out oxygen and soon they dominate the planet, a "strictly natural" pollution.

One can, of course, argue that the current crisis, too, is "natural," because    18
man is part of nature. This echoes the views of the earliest Greek philosophers, who saw no difference between matter and consciousness — nature included everything. James Lovelock wrote some years ago that "our species with its technology is simply an inevitable part of the natural scene," nothing more than mechanically advanced beavers. In this view, to say that we "ended" nature, or even damaged nature, makes no sense, since we *are* nature, and nothing we can do is "unnatural." This view can be, and is, carried to even greater lengths; Lynn Margulis, for instance, ponders the question of whether robots can be said to be living creatures, since any "invention of human beings is ultimately based on a variety of processes including that of DNA replication, no matter the separation in space or time of that replication from the invention."

But one can argue this forever and still not really feel it. It is a debator's    19
point, a semantic argument. When I say that we have ended nature, I don't mean, obviously, that natural processes have ceased — there is still sunshine and still wind, still growth, still decay. Photosynthesis continues, as does respiration. *But we have ended the thing that has, at least in modern times, defined nature for us — its separation from human society.*

That separation is quite real. It is fine to argue, as certain poets and biol-    20
ogists have, that we must learn to fit in with nature, to recognize that we are but one species among many, and so on. But none of us, on the inside, quite believe it. . . .

The invention of nuclear weapons may actually have marked the beginning    21
of the end of nature: we possessed, finally, the capacity to overmaster nature, to leave an indelible imprint everywhere all at once. "The nuclear peril is usually seen in isolation from the threats to other forms of life and their ecosystems, but in fact it should be seen at the very center of the ecological crisis, as the cloud-covered Everest of which the more immediate, visible kinds of harm to the environment are the mere foothills," wrote Jonathan Schell in *The Fate of the Earth*. And he was correct, for at the time he was writing (less than a decade ago!) it was hard to conceive of any threats of the same magnitude. Global warming was one obscure theory among many. Nuclear weapons were unique (and they remain so, if only for the speed with which they work). But the nuclear dilemma is at least open to human reason — we

can decide not to drop the weapons, and indeed to reduce and perhaps eliminate them. And the horrible power of these weapons, which has been amply
demonstrated in Japan and on Bikini and under Nevada and many times in
our imaginations, has led us fitfully in that hopeful direction.

By contrast, the various processes that lead to the end of nature have been    22
essentially beyond human thought. Only a few people knew that carbon
dioxide would warm up the world, for instance, and they were for a long time
unsuccessful in their efforts to alert the rest of us. Now it is too late — not too
late, as I shall come to explain, to ameliorate some of the changes and so perhaps to avoid the most gruesome of their consequences. But the scientists
agree that we have already pumped enough gas into the air so that a significant rise in temperature and a subsequent shift in weather are inevitable.

Just how inevitable we can see from the remedies that some scientists       23
have proposed to save us — not the remedies, like cutting fossil fuel use and
saving the rain forests, that will keep things from being any worse than they
need to be, but the solutions that might bring things back to "normal." The
most natural method anyone has suggested involves growing enormous
numbers of trees to take the carbon dioxide out of the air. Take, for argument's sake, a new coal-fired electric generating station that produces a thousand megawatts and operates at 38 percent thermal efficiency and 70 percent
availability. To counteract just the carbon dioxide generated by that plant, the
surrounding area to a radius of 24.7 kilometers would need to be covered
with American sycamore trees (a fast-growing species) planted at four-foot intervals and "harvested" every four years. It might be possible to achieve that
sort of growth rate — a government forestries expert told the Senate that with
genetic screening, spacing, thinning, pruning, weed control, fire and pest control, fertilization, and irrigation, net annual growth could be "very much
higher than at present." Even if it worked, though, would this tree plantation
be nature? A walk through an endless glade of evenly spaced sycamores, with
the weed-control chopper hovering overhead, and the irrigation pipes gurgling quietly below, represents a fundamental break with my idea of the wild
world.

Other proposals get even odder. One "futuristic idea" described in the    24
*New York Times* springs from the brain of Dr. Thomas Stix at Princeton: he
proposes the possibility of using a laser to "scrub" chlorofluorocarbons from
the earth's atmosphere before they have a chance to reach the ozone layer. Dr.
Stix calculates that an array of infrared lasers spaced around the world could
"blast apart" a million tons of chlorofluorocarbons a year — a procedure he
refers to as "atmospheric processing." Down at the University of Alabama,
Leon Y. Sadler, a chemical engineer, has suggested employing dozens of airplanes to carry ozone into the stratosphere (others have suggested firing a
continuous barrage of "bullets" of frozen ozone, which would melt in the
stratosphere). To deal with the warming problem, Columbia geochemist Wallace Broecker has considered a "fleet of several hundred jumbo jets" to ferry
35 million tons of sulfur dioxide into the stratosphere annually to reflect sunlight away from the earth. Other scientists recommend launching "giant or-

biting satellites made of thin films" that could cast shadows on the earth, counteracting the greenhouse effect with a sort of venetian-blind effect. Certain practical problems may hamper these various solutions; Dr. Broeker, for instance, admits that injecting large quantities of sulfur dioxide into the atmosphere would increase acid rain "and give the blue sky a whitish cast." Still, they just might work. And perhaps, as Dr. Broecker contends, a "rational society needs some sort of insurance policy on how to maintain a habitable planet." But even if they do work — even if the planet remains habitable — it will not be the same. The whitish afternoon sky blessed by the geometric edge of the satellite cloud will fade into a dusk crisscrossed by lasers. There is no way to reassemble nature — certainly not by following the suggestion of one researcher that, in order to increase the earth's reflectivity and thus cool its temperature, we should cover most of the oceans with a floating layer of white Styrofoam chips.

There are some people, perhaps many, to whom this rupture will mean little. A couple of years ago a group of executives went rafting down a river in British Columbia; after an accident killed five of them, one of the survivors told reporters that the party had regarded the river as "a sort of ersatz rollercoaster." Nature has become a hobby with us. One person enjoys the outdoors, another likes cooking, a third favors breaking into military computers over his phone line. The nature hobby boomed during the 1970s; now it is perhaps in slight decline (the number of people requesting permits to hike and camp in the rugged backcountry of the national parks has dropped by half since 1983, even as the number of drive-through visitors has continued to increase). We have become in rapid order a people whose conscious need for nature is superficial. . . .

Still, the passing of nature as we have known it, like the passing of any large idea, will have its recognizable effects, both immediately and over time. In 1893, when Frederick Jackson Turner announced to the American Historical Association that the frontier was closed, no one was aware that the frontier had been the defining force in American life. But in its absence it was understood. One reason we pay so little close attention to the separate natural world around us is that it has always been there and we presumed it always would. As it disappears, its primal importance will be clearer — in the same way that some people think they have put their parents out of their lives and learn differently only when the day comes to bury them.

| Questions to Start You Thinking | |
|---|---|

1. CONSIDERING MEANING: How does McKibben define "nature"? What does he say is the difference between the "meaning" or "idea" of nature and the physical character of nature?

2. IDENTIFYING WRITING STRATEGIES: How does McKibben use imagination to demonstrate the effects of humans on nature?

3. ANALYZING THE WRITER'S CHOICES: Reread paragraphs 23–24. Why does McKibben present the reader with examples of the various proposed remedies

for global warming? What is his attitude toward these kinds of remedies? How does he use these examples to support his argument that "there is no way to reassemble nature" (paragraph 24)?

4. EXPANDING VOCABULARY: What does McKibben mean by the word *postnatural* (paragraph 14)? What connotations does *post* bring to *nature*?

5. MAKING CONNECTIONS: What connection do you see between McKibben's discussion of altering nature and Melvin Konner's discussion of altering personality in "Out of the Darkness" (p. 615)?

**Journal Prompts**

1. Describe the scenery that surrounds you on a walk you take regularly. What elements are natural and what elements are man-made?

2. At the end of paragraph 2 McKibben asserts that soon, as a result of humans' continuous presence in nature, "the world outdoors will mean much the same thing as the world indoors, the hill the same thing as the house." Do you agree with this assertion?

**Suggestions for Writing**

1. Are you generally a pessimist or an optimist about the future of nature? Explain your position, arguing for why it is the more realistic attitude. Use examples from your own experiences to support your argument.

2. Do you agree with McKibben's critique of technological solutions to global warming and ozone depletion (paragraphs 23 and 24)? Why or why not? If you agree with McKibben, explain why. If you disagree, explain which proposal sounds most promising.

**Carol Kaesuk Yoon,** *born in 1963, received a B.S. in biology from Yale University and a Ph.D. in biology and evolutionary biology from Cornell University. She decided, however, that writing about science was much more rewarding than doing science and turned to journalism. She is now a regular contributor to the* New York Times *and also writes occasionally for the* Washington Post, *the* Los Angeles Times, *and* Science *magazine. Yoon is currently working on a book that describes the rainforest from the point of view of the creatures that live there. In "Drugs from Bugs," which was written for the Summer 1994 issue of* Garbage *magazine, Yoon describes the efforts of conservationists to harvest profitable medicines from the rainforest.*

# *Carol Kaesuk Yoon*   **Drugs from Bugs**

In northern Costa Rica on a warm, moonless night, two men stare into the glow of a black light reflecting off a sheet that flutters in the breeze. Attracted by the light, hundreds of brightly colored moths, beetles, and katydids descend from the darkness. A few dangle brightly from the surrounding tree branches, lit up like sparkling Christmas ornaments. The men grab excitedly at this one or that, turning the tiny beasts over in their hands. The insects are the gold these prospectors have come in search of, the treasure they believe may be the best hope for protecting the world's dwindling diversity of species. Among the finds this night is a regal moth, believed to contain chemicals that could yield valuable pharmaceuticals. The insect is deposited amongst the other living loot.

This same evening, nearly sixty other farmers, fisherman, housewives,   2
and students likewise scour the Costa Rican countryside, collecting all manner of known and unknown species: spectacular monkey pot trees; stilt-rooted Iriartea palms; dull brown moths as yet unnamed; one of the last red-eyed frogs known to inhabit Costa Rica.

These men and women are not driven by some esoteric scientific ques-   3
tion. Rather, they search in the hope that some species will carry the chemical building blocks that could yield drugs, perfumes, glues — any number of products valuable enough to protect the forests these species inhabit. The collectors aim, they say, to make the overflowing diversity of their nation's species its most profitable resource. And although no cure for cancer or AIDS has yet come from these forests and fields, the promise that Costa Rica's vast array of untapped species could produce such a billion-dollar drug has prompted international pharmaceutical companies to make million-dollar investments in this intensive species quest.

For conservationists, what fuels these efforts is the fear that "biodiversity"   4
— a newly popular term that describes all aspects of biological diversity, including all the world's species as well as their genes, interactions, behaviors, and even the ecosystems they comprise — is taking a fast and furious nosedive. Hard data on the number of species lost each year are impossible to come by. Many species remain undiscovered, and there are no reliable figures on the rates of habitat destruction. The best anyone can give is a rough estimate of extinction rates.

But even conservative estimates show the situation to be bleak.   5

Edward O. Wilson, an evolutionary biologist at Harvard University, de-   6
scribes the state of the state of knowledge of species extinctions in his acclaimed book *The Diversity of Life* (Norton, 1992). Due largely to logging and clearing for agriculture and human habitation, Dr. Wilson believes more than half of the world's tropical rainforests, thought to contain more than half of all the world's species, had been destroyed by 1989. Rainforests continue to be cleared at the rate of one football field per second, or an area the size of Florida each year.

Dr. Wilson reckons that this translates into 27,000 species of flora and   7
fauna that are driven to extinction each year, or 74 species lost each day. These figures do not include the uncalculated numbers of species thought to be lost each year due to overharvesting, pollution, and the havoc wreaked by invasive species. In his study of extinction rates published in *Science* ("Extinctions: A Paleontological Perspective," August 16, 1991), David Jablonski, a paleobiologist at the University of Chicago, figured the current die-off to be one of the greatest mass extinctions this planet has experienced.

### Biodiversity for Humans

Following years of warning the public of the aesthetic poverty of a planet    8
without jaguars or toucans, conservationists are changing their tune. Striking
an unexpectedly popular chord, they no longer ask what the public can do for
endangered species, but rather what such species might do for the public. Biodiversity, we are to understand, is a potential cornucopia of genetic material
that will produce precious drugs and food, as well as a source of money, jobs,
and better living. If biodiversity is going to do all that, of course, we've got to
keep it alive.

To protect the world's remaining habitats, conservationists are touting    9
the economic value of species known and unknown. In effect, they are attempting to market biodiversity to save it. Costa Rica is ahead of the pack in
a global bid to turn profits from the promise of its biodiversity, but the country is far from alone. As this new species-for-dollars movement catches fire,
additional nations announce national biological inventories, the most recent
additions being Mexico, Taiwan, India, and the United States. The most ambitious venture may be Systematics Agenda 2000, a global effort spearheaded
by the world's foremost systematists — experts in species discovery and identification. Their aim is to rally funds and scientists to discover and learn the
relationships of all — that's right, all — the world's species, seeking out those
organisms that could improve and sustain the quality of human life.

### Success: One in Ten Thousand

In the northwestern corner of Costa Rica, just below the Nicaraguan border,    10
lies Santa Rosa, the National Conservation Area, so far best developed in
Costa Rica for biological surveys. It provides a closeup of the inventory. Hundreds of tiny plastic bags hang from the wooden rafters under a tin roof. Between the deafening pings of rain hitting the rooftop, women at picnic tables
shout out descriptions of caterpillars in the bags and the plants the caterpillars are eating. Soon Felipe Chavarria drives up to show off the day's bounty:
a nest of vespid paper wasps and a bottle containing an eyelash viper — a
powerfully venomous snake that kills several Costa Ricans each year. He had
been searching for both species, as their venoms are potentially valuable
chemical sources.

Felipe is one of the species hunters with the National Biodiversity Insti-    11
tute, whose Spanish acronym is INBio. Questioned about their hunt, Chavarria and the others are cautious with their words and wary in their glances.
Because of the potential for making millions of dollars from even a single successful pharmaceutical, everything from the search for chemically rich species
to the nitty-gritty lab benchwork of isolating and testing the chemicals is
shrouded in secrecy.

Ana Sittenfeld, director of biodiversity prospecting at INBio, allows that    12
collectors often look for species known to carry biologically powerful chemicals, like venoms. But they also prospect for organisms whose interrelation-
ships with other organisms merely hint that they may carry useful chemicals.
For example, the search for anti-fungal agent might well begin with a plant
whose fallen leaves never sprout a mold during decomposition.

Once collected and identified, the most promising specimens are ground    13
up into "soups" and sent off to pharmaceutical companies such as Merck &
Co., where they're carefully screened for their ability, say, to kill fungi, bacteria, or viruses.

"Let's say Merck gets a positive result in an anti-fungal test," says Dr. Sit-    14
tenfeld. "Then the separation process starts. Which chemical compound
among the thousands in the specimen is responsible for the [anti-fungal] activity? That takes a year to determine, if you're lucky. Then you need to find
out if the compound is new or already on the market; how soluble it is;
whether it's nontoxic. Then you'll need to modify the structure, because it will
need lower toxicity or increased activity; then it will go into animal tests, then
clinical tests, and then be submitted for FDA approval."

The probability of discovering and developing a marketable natural com-    15
pound is about one in ten thousand. The whole process could easily take ten
years. But because profits from a new compound can be in the tens of millions annually, it's a chance many drug companies view as worth taking. In a
highly publicized deal, Merck paid $1 million to fund INBio's conservation
and research, in exchange for a first-chance look at the "soups" of an undis-
closed number of species. The deal, which was brokered in 1991, has not yet
produced results. But Merck and INBio are hoping that the arrangement may
yet culminate in a product.

There is some reason to believe the promise of such industry/conserva-    16
tionist alliances will be realized. As scientists explain, Nature's pharmacopoeia of plants, microbes, and animals already has a well-proven track
record for producing medicines. The painkiller codeine comes from the
opium poppy; digitoxin, a cardiac stimulant, is derived from common fox-
glove; ergonovine, which controls hemorrhaging and eases migraine
headaches, comes from a plant fungus known as smut-of-rye; the Pacific yew
tree is the source of taxol, an anti-cancer drug. In fact, today's 20 best-selling
drugs — worth some $6 billion a year — are derived from natural sources.

Agriculture has only begun to tap the benefits of biodiversity. During an    17
Andean expedition in 1962, Hugh Iltis, a botanist at the University of Wisconsin, picked up a "worthless weed." Subsequent study revealed that this
"weed" was a new species of wild tomato which, when crossed with cultivars,
dramatically increased their sweetness. "The genes from this one species have
been estimated to increase the value of the California tomato crop by $20
million a year," says Dr. Iltis.

Likewise, scientists say, many more plant and animal species could be    18
added wholesale to the short list of organisms that humans currently raise for
consumption. Edward O. Wilson estimates there are 30,000 species of plants
with edible parts. A mere 20 species currently provide 90% of the world's
food. Three species — maize, wheat, and rice — together account for more
than 50% of what we eat. When we do enjoy variety, scientists tell us, we can
thank biodiversity.

*Nowhere Are All Species Known*

As inventories get under way worldwide, INBio's trailblazing makes it clear    19
that efforts to take stock of the species in biodiverse countries face roadblocks.
To date, there is no place on Earth in which all the species are known.

Picture the problem of trying to discover all the species in even a few    20
square miles of a Costa Rican preserve. Costa Rica, though less than half the
size of the state of New York, is home to an estimated 5% of all the world's
species. In this wildness, hummingbirds fashion their nests on the dangling
threads of spiderwebs, beetles twinkle in the trees like polished dabs of silver,
butterflies masquerade as leaves, lizards walk on water, and snakes swim in
the sea.

Certain groups of animals and plants are already extremely well docu-    21
mented in Costa Rica, particularly those species which are beautiful (and
catchable) enough to make them the object of collectors. Institute Director
Rodrigo Gamez reports that the birds, mammals, fish, amphibians, and rep-
tiles of Costa Rica are essentially 100% collected and catalogued. "It was an
idea whose time had come," he says.

Perhaps so, but the hard part has just begun. Completing the inventory    22
means filing the gaping holes in the world's shockingly spotty knowledge of
its creatures and plants. Biologists say that a single handful of dirt from anywhere in the world will yield thousands of new species of bacteria, viruses,
and roundworms. While these creatures may be less aesthetically appealing
than a sapphire-throated hummingbird, in all likelihood they are more economically important. INBio is now searching for the species hardest to inventory but most likely to carry the stuff of discovery. Fungi, for example,
whose trailing rootlike systems weave together underground and may sprout
a mushroom only once in a human generation, make clear the obstacles in an
inventory of all biota.

It is the invisible world of microbes that has given us more than 3,000 an-    23
tibiotics, including the penicillin that has saved countless lives. Viruses and
bacteria comprise the backbone of the biotechnology industry. No life-saving
products have been derived from such "charismatic megafauna"[1] as snow
leopards and bald eagles, although they may symbolize conservation.

In Costa Rica, some 60 collectors are out scouring the countryside for new    24
species every day, sometimes 18 hours a day. Specimens are piling up. At last
count, INBio had amassed 1.3 million specimens of insects and 55,000 specimens of plants. Despite these large numbers, so far just 65,000 out of an estimated 225,000 insect species have been found and identified. Such
perseverance has allowed INBio to reap benefits unavailable to "one-shot" inventories, typically conducted in the tropics by visiting American or European
scientists whose short tenure leaves many species wholly unknown. Unlike
the rapid-assessment SWAT teams headed by the late biologists Alwyn Gen-

---

[1] **"charismatic megafauna"**: A term coined by Dennis Murphy, director of the Center
for Conservation Biology at Stanford University, to describe the kinds of mammals and
birds whose endangerment tends to attract public concern.

try and Ted Parker, who visited numerous areas in numerous countries to get the broad picture of what places were most biologically diverse INBio aims to know a few patches of forest as completely as possible.

Critics, however, say that INBio has done little more than amass a huge pile of unidentified animals and plants — a museum curator's nightmare. Others find flaws with the science underlying such burgeoning biological inventories, saying they are merely large-scale, disorganized collections run by nonexperts and doomed to fail. In Costa Rica, housewives and fisherman seek out new species, a botanist oversees the insect survey, and a virologist heads the National Biodiversity Institute — whose collections apparently contain everything but viruses.    25

But Dan Janzen, a visionary ecologist who has worked with the Costa Rican inventory since its inception five years ago, describes the coming changes to biodiversity studies as "a revolution," one that demands nonscientists collect species and conventional rules be set aside.    26

"Battle analogies aren't politically correct," Janzen says. "But we *are* in a war [to save species], and when you're at war you end up with doctors driving tanks."    27

In an assembly line setup in INBio's offices in San Jose, workers sort through the bugs and plants, attaching bar codes to specimens like so many grocery-store items. A small team of curators strive to unambiguously identify each species, a process which can take months, even years. Sometimes they enlist an outside expert to examine, say, the long-horned beetles collected thus far. Inventory director Jorge Jimenez acknowledges that the bulk of specimens remain unidentified. But he says it's a step in the process, and is hopeful that specialists will continue to visit to help.    28

Unfortunately, though, for many animals, plants, microbes, and fungi, there are no living experts who can sit down with a crate of specimens and even begin to identify them. Groups of unknown species, called orphans by systematics practitioners, are growing in number as experts are lost through retirement and death and not replaced by their museums and universities.    29

### Building Hope . . . and a Backlash?

Species identification is not the only problem plaguing conservation-for-profit efforts. Some economists warn that the rainforests may not produce the hoped-for profits. Saleable species may be too rare, and marketable drugs or chemicals too elusive to merit such a time-consuming, expensive search. Conservation may be profitable in theory only; they question whether in practice it is more profitable than more immediate alternatives, such as farming or grazing the same land.    30

One of the few researchers who has studied the economics of conservation is Michael Norton-Griffiths, research fellow at the Harvard Institute for International Development. The problem, he explains, is that even if conservation-friendly projects like eco-tourism or sales of natural products are somewhat profitable, it is often even more profitable to use the land in more destructive ventures. The so-called "cost of lost opportunities" — the money    31 *not* made by logging or farming — is borne by the local population, he observes — not by conservationists living in the United States. "If we're trying to sell conservation on the money that can be earned from it, we must be sure we're not selling [local] people the short end of the stick," he says.

Barbara Dugelby, a conservation biologist at Duke University, began studying extractive reserves — conserved forests from which products like chicle-tree latex, rubber, allspice, bromeliads, and rattan are harvested and sold — in the hopes that such enterprises might prevent rainforest destruction. Dr. Dugelby's up-close look at such reserves convinced her they are *not* the perfect solution for protecting rainforests. 32

Again the problem boils down to economics. All too often, Dr. Dugelby and colleagues have found, the valued species are too rare and too scattered to make hunting and gathering them a profitable venture. To support such projects the "crop" must grow in very high densities. "I don't want to build up false hopes," she says. "There may be a backlash because these extractive reserves don't work." 33

Even if Costa Rica's experience eventually proves that doubters are mistaken, others believe the tactic of touting biodiversity for its profits is ethically repellent. David Takacs, an environmental historian at Cornell University, says biologists typically describe their reasons for caring about biodiversity as tending toward the spiritual, not the economic. 34

"There is amongst conservation biologists a debate about which rationale to use to conserve biodiversity," says Dr. Takacs. "Some say whatever works is what you use. . . . Others say no, we have to choose our methods carefully lest we have unanticipated effects." 35

In the face of what scientists such as the University of Chicago's David Jablonski describe as a major mass extinction, those who would say whatever works may find ethical worries trivial. The reality is that conservation biologists of all persuasions are pressing ahead with ambitious species inventories, banking on marketing as they go. Nothing else rivals this new conservation tactic. By the decade's close, we should know whether encounters with the pharmaceutical industry will really protect the world's wild places. 36

The selling of conservation for profit is risky. If the tack were to fail, it could further damage the image of conservationists, who are already maligned as overly dramatic doomsayers. 37

For dedicated researchers, public persuasion is beside the point. Dr. Janzen, the University of Pennsylvania ecologist who has participated in the Costa Rican inventory since the beginning, reminds us that so few genes and crop plants and organisms are used in comparison with the very large quantity represented in a tropical wildland area. "It's as though we had the Library of Congress and we'd read ten books out of it. Am I raising false hopes to say, 'If you'd look at all the other stuff in the library you'd find things relevant to your lives, your industry'? I don't think so." 38

| | |
|---|---|
| **Questions to Start You Thinking** | 1. CONSIDERING MEANING: What is biodiversity? According to this article, how might "species-for-dollars" (paragraph 9) help maintain biodiversity? |

**Questions to Start You Thinking**

1. CONSIDERING MEANING: What is biodiversity? According to this article, how might "species-for-dollars" (paragraph 9) help maintain biodiversity?

2. IDENTIFYING WRITING STRATEGIES: What does Yoon identify as the causes and the possible effects of the new approach conservationists are taking toward preserving biodiversity?

3. ANALYZING THE WRITER'S CHOICES: Yoon seems to report fairly evenly the views of those on both sides of the "species-for-dollars" movement. Why do you think she takes this approach? Where in the article does her own opinion on the issue become apparent?

4. EXPANDING VOCABULARY: Define *esoteric* (paragraph 3), *acronym* (paragraph 11), *pharmacopoeia* (paragraph 16), *biotechnology*, and *charismatic* (paragraph 23). According to Yoon, why are conservationists often *maligned* as *doomsayers* (paragraph 37)?

5. MAKING CONNECTIONS: In what ways might critics of "species-for-dollars" conservation and of "new eugenics" (Robert Wright, "Mr. Clean Genes," p. 611) agree that there can be serious consequences when science becomes big business?

**Journal Prompts**

1. Recall a theory or formula that you have recently learned in a biology, chemistry, or other science course. Briefly speculate about the practical use for this theory or formula.

2. Do you think that conservationists are "overly dramatic doomsayers" (paragraph 37), or do you think they are justified in their concern over the loss of biodiversity? Explain your answer.

**Suggestions for Writing**

1. Would you be willing to pay more money for medical or cosmetic products derived from the rainforest if you knew that your money was helping preserve biodiversity? Why or why not? Would you (or do you) pay more for other environmentally correct products, such as recycled paper, "green" cotton, or polyester made from recycled plastic?

2. Write a code of ethics for use by the collectors and catalogers of new species. What rules of conduct should they follow in the collection, naming, and marketing of species? Should species-for-dollars be limited to medical purposes only, or could they be used for any other purposes as well, such as eugenics, food additives, cosmetics, or biological weapons?

**Gregg Easterbrook,** *born in 1953 in Buffalo, New York, attended Colorado College and Northwestern University and is now a contributing editor to* Newsweek *and the* Atlantic Monthly. *Besides writing editorials and essays, Easterbrook writes fiction, nonfiction, and plays. He is the author of the novel* This Magic Moment *(1987) and the nonfiction book* A Moment on the Earth: The Coming Age of Environmental Optimism *(1995). He is currently working on a play,* Abide for Me

*Many Days. In the following article, reprinted from the September 11, 1994, issue of the* New York Times Magazine, *Easterbrook argues that the worst environmental problems are caused not by the technologies of the developed world but rather by the poverty of the underdeveloped world.*

## *Gregg Easterbrook*   Forget PCBs. Radon. Alar: The World's Greatest Environmental Dangers Are Dung Smoke and Dirty Water

What environmental problems kill human beings in huge numbers today? Not ozone depletion or Alar. What kills them is dung smoke and diarrhea.

Throughout the world, many more people die each year from filthy air and dirty water than from asbestos, dioxin, electromagnetic radiation, nuclear wastes, PCBs, pesticide residues, and ultraviolet rays — the sorts of ecological issues that obsess Western environmentalists. Problems like dioxin and nuclear wastes are real enough and must be dealt with. But Western public consciousness and environmental groups continue to focus on such issues while all but ignoring millions of annual deaths from polluted air and water.

Dangerous air levels have become almost unknown in the West, but 1.3 billion people in the developing world live in zones of dangerously unsafe air. According to the World Health Organization, last year 4 million third-world children under the age of five died from acute respiratory disease, brought on in most cases by air pollution. This is about as many people of all ages who died of all causes that year in the United States and the European Union combined.

Urban air pollution is worse in Calcutta, Lagos, and Mexico City than in any Western metropolis, including Los Angeles. The developing world also has an insidious form of air pollution unknown in the West: rural smog. "Most of the four million annual child deaths from respiratory distress stem from children living in poorly ventilated huts where fuel wood, cow dung, or agricultural wastes are used for heating and cooking," says Gurinder Shahi, an official of the United Nations Development Program.

In the third world, polluted air is more than matched by polluted water. Some one billion people lack access to drinking water that meets the crudest safety standards. UNICEF reports that 3.8 million developing-world children under age five died last year from diarrheal diseases caused mostly by impure drinking water. In the West, diarrheal deaths are practically unknown; in the developing world, diarrhea kills far more people than cancer.

Most of Africa, the Indian subcontinent, and Latin America have no waste-water treatment facilities; raw human and industrial sewage is discharged directly into the same bodies of water used for drinking. Mothers draw for their children water of lower quality than the process effluent discharged from American factories. In India, ritual bathers enter the Ganges seeking spiritual purity while exposing their bodies to a wide range of toxicants and pathogens. In China, an estimated 25 billion tons of unfiltered industrial pollutants went directly into the waterways in 1991, which means there was more toxic water pollutions in that one country than in the whole of the Western world.

Yet such problems do not seem to be on the priority lists of Western environmentalists. "Things like African sewage are not sexy issues, so they always fall to the bottom of the agenda," says Deborah Moore, a staff scientist at the Environmental Defense Fund and one of the few Western environmentalists advocating a focus on basic third-world reform.

A large faction within the environmental movement concentrates on the comparatively minor ecological problems of developed nations in order to support the view that Western materialism is the root of all ecological malevolence. The low point of such thinking was reached at the Earth Summit in Rio de Janeiro in 1992. There, institutional environmental groups got the attention of the world and its heads of state, but what message did they choose to proclaim? That global warming is a horror. The sole environmental area in which the United States is the leading malefactor is carbon dioxide emission, which contributes to the greenhouse effect; in virtually every other ecological category, America is the world leader in progress.

To make Rio a fashionably negative event about Western guilt-tripping and America-bashing, the prospect of global warming was put above the urgent loss of lives in the third world from water and air pollution. Rio concluded with Western leaders' agreeing to devote billions of dollars to controlling global warming, while not lifting a finger for the 7.8 million poor children who die each year mainly from what they drink and breathe.

Eric Chivian is a psychiatrist on the faculty of Harvard Medical School. In the days of the arms race, he helped found International Physicians for the Prevention of Nuclear War, which in 1985 won the Nobel Peace Prize. When nuclear weapons began to be dismantled, Chivian enlarged his agenda to include pollution in the developing world. He has started a new program, the Project on Global Environmental Change and Health, and last year edited a powerful but little-noticed technical book, *Critical Condition: Human Health and the Environment.*

Chivian finds that he can hardly get anyone interested in his new group. "I've had great difficulty interesting environmental organizations in human health in poor countries," he says. "They all want to talk about forest loss and species diversity in the South" — the developing world — "but have much less interest in human health there."

Last year, notes Chivian, two teams of university researchers produced evidence that particulates — fine bits of soot and ash caused by incomplete combustion — were a much greater health threat than was previously realized. In the United States each year, particulates may account for 20,000 to 30,000 premature deaths due to respiratory failure. "Environmentalists in the

United States were disturbed by this finding," Chivian says. "But if these studies are right, then the particulate emergency is happening in the third world, not here. The problem is a thousand times worse for them than for us."

Under American law, particulates have long been closely regulated. Most developing nations do not regulate particulate emissions, even though the factories and vehicles in these countries employ the sort of inefficient engines likely to emit more soot. According to David Bates, a professor emeritus of medicine at the University of British Columbia, airborne particulate readings ten times higher than peak allowable American levels are common in the developing world. Within dwellings heated by wood or dung, particulates are higher still. A child's lungs are more sensitive than an adult's and, Bates points out, children in the developing world face heavy doses of air pollutants whether they live in the city or the country.

"If a developing-world child lives in a city," Bates says, "that child will be exposed to high levels of airborne lead from vehicle exhaust, since no third-world country is even close to mandating unleaded gasoline and catalytic converters." (Lead is a poison linked to I.Q. loss.) Since unleaded gasoline went on the market in the mid-1970s, ambient airborne lead levels in the United States have fallen 95 percent. During the same time, airborne lead levels have risen in developing-world cities where only leaded gasoline is burned. Lead is now so prevalent in Mexico City air that parents are advised to keep young children indoors as much as possible.

"The city child in the developing world will also be exposed to high levels of airborne sulfur and smog," Bates says. Poor nations lack the factory emissions controls found in the West, do not require catalytic converters on vehicles, and allow fuel stations to sell gasoline and diesel far too dirty to meet Western refinery standards. For example, in the Indian industrial city of Agra (home to the Taj Mahal), levels of airborne sulfur dioxide, which causes acid rain, are ten times higher than the maximum found in the United States.

"But at least the child in the developing-world city has electricity and propane as home energy, sparing constant indoor exposure to smoke," Bates continues. "In the country, the child is spared sulfur and lead in the air, but then gets the choking home air pollution from the wood or dung fire."

Robert S. Lawrence, director of health sciences for the Rockefeller Foundation in New York, draws a chart of developing-world home fuels. In it, a slope starts with dung and crop wastes, moves past wood, charcoal, kerosene, and propane, and ascends to electricity. "Through the early 1980s" Lawrence says, "many third-world countries were headed up the slope of cleaner fuels. In recent years, with the global economy stagnant, people are sliding back down the slope, from electricity back to propane, from fuel wood back to dung. Respiratory deaths are rising in concert."

Sliding down the slope from clean fuels isn't just a threat to human lungs. It threatens forests as well. Though environmental orthodoxy holds that third-world deforestation is caused by rapacious clear-cutters and ruthless cattle barons, penniless peasants seeking fuel wood may be the greatest threat to forests. Fuel wood consumption in the developing world rose 35 percent between 1975 and 1986, with replanting rare by peasants. Jodi Jacobson, director of the Health and Development Policy Project, an environmental organization, believes fuel wood supplies are becoming critical in Haiti, India, Nepal, Mexico, sub-Saharan Africa, and Thailand. A new saying among rural Indian women, Jacobson says, is "It's not what's in the pot but what's under the pot that worries you."

In many developing countries, women do the wood gathering, just as 19 they do most of the heavy labor. Gurinder Shahi, of the U.N. Development Program, estimates that in Nepal rural women spend five or six hours a day on foot searching for fuel wood and carrying it home. Such labors deny them the time for education and result in health damage to themselves and their children. In the high-altitude mountain areas of Nepal — places many people presume are pristine wonderlands — women, Bates notes, often suffer from a disease similar to anemia. The illness is caused by carbon monoxide in the bloodstream, a result of long-term exposure to crude energy sources like indoor cooking fires.

Western environmental thinking has great difficulty coming to terms with 20 such realities. That third-world economists would call propane and kerosene "clean fuels," and speak longingly of the day when their countries are wholly electrified like the West, horrifies Western environmentalists, or enviros, as they are known in Washington. According to ecological orthodoxy, fossil fuels are hideous and central electric generation promotes an aritficial greenhouse effect.

What developing nations need to free their populations from death by extreme air pollution is hydroelectric dams, advanced petroleum refining installations, high-efficiency power plants for the clean combustion of coal. But Western environmental lobbies oppose nearly all new central energy production facilities for the developing world, especially hydroelectric plants. Greenpeace, the Natural Resources Defense Council, the Sierra Club, and other major environmental advocacy groups are pressuring Washington, Tokyo, Paris, London, Bonn, and the World Bank not to support the Three Gorges and Xiaolangdi dams in China; the Narmada River dams in India; the Bío-Bío River dams in Chile, and power dams proposed for Malawi, Pakistan, and elsewhere. In most cases the campaigns have succeeded. The World Bank, for example, recently withdrew from the Narmada project.

The prinicpal objection to hydroelectric power is that reservoirs are 22 formed by inundating pristine areas, sometimes including the habitats of rare wildlife. This does happen, even though planned dams for the Yang-tze River in China and for the Narmada River Valley in India would also stop seasonal downstream flooding, which annually kills hundreds to thousands of people and destroys wildlife habitats.

Enviros correctly object to third-world hydropower initiatives having 23 budgets bloated by graft and involving displacement of peasants, which in developing nations always means more hardships. Yet they seem uninterested in the upside of such projects — mainly, huge amounts of zero-emission, zero-fossil-fuel energy for nations where runaway air polution is a daily threat to life. While passionately concerned about wildlife habitat losses from hydroelectric plants, enviros seem indifferent to the clear health benefits deriving from a reduction in indoor smoke.

Similarly, many enviros oppose oil field development in countries like     24
Ecuador, and are fighting the construction of new coal-fired power plants — even ones that employ advanced antipollution equipment — in China and elsewhere. Enviros contend that small-scale solar energy and "bio-gas" (dung fermented into methane, a clean fuel) are appropriate for the developing world. Often this is true. But how many Western enviros are willing to live at the limits of current solar technology? Today's solar converters can provide basic power requirements but they usually do not provide enough wattage for refrigeration, which is badly needed in developing countries. (About a quarter of third-world food production is lost to spoilage.)

One reason few environmentalists go solar is that it costs more than con-     25
ventional electricity from big generating stations. Prices for solar converters have been falling, but solar cell systems still cost four to five times as much per kilowatt-hour as fossil fuel systems, even ones with advanced pollution controls. And if small solar is too expensive for the Sierra Club set, why is it a great idea for peasants in Malawi?

Many enviros think the need for improved water purity can be dealt with     26
in small ways. Deborah Moore, of the Environmental Defense Fund, and groups like UNICEF have been pressuring development agencies to fund community-based water purity and sewage-control programs. As with small solar, there are many instances in which small water projects will provide the best returns. But in the expanding third-world cities where a billion of the world's poor reside, small is hardly the solution.

In Karachi, only a third of the homes have piped water. In Madras, only     27
about a third of dwellings connect to anything like a sewer system. In Kinshasa, there is no sewage system at all. The situation for numerous other third-world cities is the same. Often, the poor of developing cities must get safe drinking water from water sellers. The poorest of the world's poor therefore end up paying more for water than do the rich.

What is needed, Chivian says is "basic water infrastructure" — pipes, fil-     28
tration plants, waste-water treatment facilities, sometimes dams and aqueducts. Such big water-diversion projects, however, offend environmental orthodoxy.

Why are so many enviros paying more attention to greenhouse computer pro-     29
jections for the twenty-first century than they are to millions of children dying from impure water and air? When pressed, environmentalists say words like: "The human species is not imperiled; look at the incredible number of births in the developing world. We must concentrate on protecting species and habitats that are imperiled."

Population growth is the core environmental problem for most of the        30
world. But better environmental health, will help *slow* that growth, not expand it. "The technical literature is unanimous that when you improve basic
health, especially child and reproductive health, birth rates go down," Chivian says. "Many environmentalists don't understand this, but it is the essential fact of the issue. If you want species and habitats preserved, protecting
human health so that fertility rates decline will accomplish far more than
building walls around wildlife preserves."

In poor nations, women become pregnant many times to be confident of        31
having a few children survive till adulthood and provide for the parents' old
age. As education, women's rights, and childhood survival rates improve,
numbers of pregnancies decline. In the 1960s, the typical developing-world
woman gave birth to six live children; today the figure is four. Fertility rates
are declining in developing countries that have positive indexes for issues like
safe water and progress on the clean-energy slope. Fertility rates remain high
mainly in Africa and the Indian subcontinent, where deaths from dirty water
and dung smoke are concentrated.

Given the crisis in basic environmental needs among the world's disen-        32
franchised, Western environmentalists and governments would do well to
shift their focus from the ecological problems of the developed world. A dollar spent protecting the environment will accomplish ten times as much in
the third world as in the first.

Five years ago, Western environmental groups succeeded in drawing in-        33
ternational attention to the loss of tropical rainforests. Since then, deforestation rates have fallen. If Western environmentalists devoted as much energy
and concern to human health in the third world, progress might be seen there
as well.

**Questions to Start
You Thinking**

1. CONSIDERING MEANING: Why does Easterbrook believe that Western technology and materialism are not the environmental evils that mainstream environmentalists claim they are?

2. IDENTIFYING WRITING STRATEGIES: Where in the essay does Easterbrook write
   from reading and from conversation? In what ways does he use these voices
   to lend support to his argument?

3. ANALYZING THE WRITER'S CHOICES: To make his argument, Easterbrook contrasts
   "Western environmental thinking" (paragraph 20) with his own, more globally conscious evaluation of environmental priorities. What is the author's
   tone when he is presenting the opposition's views? Do you find it an effective argumentative approach? Why or why not?

4. EXPANDING VOCABULARY: Reread paragraphs 1 and 2, noting Easterbrook's
   choice of words. Why does he shift from common words, such as *dung smoke
   and diarrhea, filthy air and dirty water*, to scientific words, such as *dioxin, electromagnetic radiation, PCBs, and pesticide residues*? What is the effect of this
   shift? Find other places in the essay where the author juxtaposes common
   and scientific vocabulary for similar effects.

5. MAKING CONNECTIONS: How might Easterbrook react to the recent focus on preserving biodiversity, as discussed in Carol Kaesuk Yoon's "Drugs from Bugs" (p. 628)?

**Journal Prompts**

1. List the fuels your family uses or has used in the past to heat your house and to cook. What advantages and disadvantages do these fuels have over other fuels?

2. Were you surprised by any of Easterbrook's criticisms of the United States' environmental priorities? Explain your response.

**Suggestions for Writing**

1. Using your imagination as a resource, write an essay explaining what you would like to do to help resolve a global or local environmental problem. Explain both your general goals and your specific actions, anticipating the results of those actions. Will they have lasting benefits? Will they cause any harm?

2. Should we put more time, effort, and money into maintaining biodiversity and reversing global warming or into cleaning up the water and air in developing countries? Write an argumentative essay in which you take a stand on this issue, considering both the short- and long-term effects of your choice.

# A Writer's
# Research Manual

# Introduction:
# The Nature of Research

How were the Egyptian pyramids built?

What is the best treatment for AIDS today?

How was T. S. Eliot influenced by the metaphysical poets?

What steps can law enforcement take to help prevent domestic violence?

How much of an impact do strict death penalty laws have on crime reduction?

Why is baseball exempt from antitrust laws?

You may have asked yourself one or more of these questions. Perhaps you discussed the subject with your friends, asked a teacher about it, or read an article on it. In doing so, you were conducting informal research to satisfy your curiosity.

In your day-to-day life, you are often faced with making a decision that will determine what you are going to do. You may want to buy a CD player or a new automobile, to choose a college or an insurance policy, to decide whether to participate in an innovative medical procedure or go on an exciting vacation to an exotic destination. To be better informed about your decision, you pull together information from talking with friends, get facts from sales personnel, compare prices, read articles in magazines and newspapers, and listen to reports and commercials. You gather and weigh as much information as you can find. By doing so, you are conducting practical research. The more thorough your investigation, the better prepared you are to make a well-informed decision.

To do research is, in a sense, to venture into the unknown: to explore, to experiment, to discover, to constantly revise your thinking, to solve problems. Whether the object is to probe the mysterious recesses of the human brain or the far galaxies, the causes of earthquakes or the feasibility of using electric au-

645

tomobiles, research can be thrilling. That is why some people devote their entire lives to such investigation — in laboratories, in business, in libraries, in the field.

When one of your college professors assigns you a research paper due in a month or two, you may not be able to make any earthshaking discoveries. You won't be expected to unfold the secrets of the brain or the spiral nebula. Even so, you just might find yourself drawn into the excitement of research as you discover that research isn't merely pasting together information and opinions taken from other people; you use research to draw conclusions and arrive at your own fresh view. The key will be for you to start your investigation as professional researchers do: with a research question that truly interests you and that you really want to find out more about.

Naturally, in doing research and in writing about your discoveries, you'll find yourself taking certain steps ahead of others, just as you do in any composing task. Early on, you'll need to plan your time and block out the work to be done, but you won't follow any inflexible track laid down for you. The process isn't lockstep; it's often recursive: you can backtrack or jump ahead when it makes sense to do so. You might find, in the midst of writing, that you need to reorganize your outline. Or in rewriting, you might find you need more material on a certain point; in that case, back you go to the library or off to another interview. Like detective work, research sometimes will lead to an insurmountable obstacle. When stopped on one path, you can turn around, or go sideways, or set out in another direction altogether.

Whenever you are called upon to conduct research to come to a conclusion based on facts and expert opinions — be it in your personal life, for a college class, or on the job — this research manual will provide you with strategies and procedures for conducting efficient, effective research.

Chapter 28, "Conducting Library Research," will introduce you to the basics of dealing with a research assignment, developing your research question, investigating library sources, and taking notes. To help you find your own view and express it convincingly, our assignment for a library research investigation is fairly simple. If you take our advice, you will conduct a short investigation, not an extremely deep one. But you *will* learn how to do research in a library and how to use various useful sources to fulfill a purpose. Along the way we will introduce you to Maria Halloran, a student researcher, and observe the process she goes through as she develops her research question.

Chapter 29, "Conducting Field Research," will take you into the field, where you actively conduct your own primary research, using the skills of observation and conversation to find out something brand-new. You will learn what sources other than print sources are available and how to judge and use them. You will also meet Linda Hackler, a college student who used a combination of field and library research techniques to collect a wide range of sources to answer her research question.

Chapter 30, "Writing from Sources," helps you see how to manage the wealth of information you gather from your diverse sources. In this chapter we will show you how to synthesize the information in your sources to answer your research question and bring together your findings in a readable, trustworthy paper. Along the way you will share the experiences of our student researchers as they try to focus and organize all their notes and write coherent research papers that clearly communicate with readers and address their basic research questions. At the end, you will have the opportunity to read their papers: Maria Halloran's final paper using library research skills, "America's Obsession with Sports," and Linda Hackler's final paper using both library and field research sources, "America's Nightmare, Mexico's Dream: The Myth of the Hispanic Migrant Worker." You can also read another library research paper, "Female Identity in Kate Chopin's 'The Story of an Hour,'" by Chris Robinson. This paper is a literary analysis, as discussed in Chapter 12, "Writing about Literature." Unlike the sample student essay in Chapter 12, this paper uses literary critiques by professional writers and academic scholars as evidence to support the student's own ideas; these sources were uncovered through library research.

Chapter 31, "Documenting Sources," explains and illustrates the MLA and APA documentation styles you will use to indicate the sources of your information. Consult this chapter when type up the final draft of your paper.

The research skills you learn will prove invaluable in your future academic, professional, and personal life. We hope that you find the research manual helpful as you continue to conduct research in school and beyond.

# Chapter 28

# Conducting Library Research

All around us, information keeps exploding. From day to day, television, books, newspapers, and magazines shower us with facts and figures, statements and reports, views and opinions — some of them half-baked, some revealing and trustworthy. College requires you to sort through this massive burst of words, distinguishing between fact and opinion, between off-the-wall claims and sound expert interpretations. Researching a topic and composing a paper based on your findings help you gain such skills.

In Chapter 3, "Writing from Reading," if you did the main assignment, you read works by other writers and wrote a paper inspired by one of your readings. You may want to review that chapter now. Chapter 12, "Writing about Literature," expanded on these skills and showed you how to write a paper analyzing a literary work. When you wrote those papers, you gave credit to other writers in an informal way. That experience will prove good preparation for writing a research paper. This new task, though, will be different in the following ways.

You'll draw from more sources.

You'll use your sources as evidence to support your ideas, rather than as a subject to write about.

You'll do more interpreting, more evaluating, more piecing together, more throwing away of the unnecessary, more assimilating and synthesizing of ideas.

You'll learn to cite and list your sources in a form that scholars and professionals follow in writing research reports and articles.

This chapter will introduce you to the basic information you will need to carry out a research assignment. You will learn how to find a topic and develop it into a focused and answerable research question. When you are ready to begin answering your research question, you will find here the tools to get you started in your most accessible research source: the library. A virtual world of research awaits you on your library's bookshelves or in its computer databases. Armed with these basic skills and tools, you will find yourself prepared to set out and tackle even the most formidable of research tasks.

To be able to write a research paper is a useful skill. This kind of writing is essential not only in an academic community but also in business and the professions. Lawyers preparing legal briefs and arguments research previous cases that have a bearing on their own. Engineers rely on research studies when they write feasibility reports. Doctors synthesize discoveries from research to help them decide on treatment for patients. Business owners depend on market research to sell their products.

## Learning from Another Writer: One Student's Experience

To give you a sense of what one student encountered in fulfilling a typical research paper assignment, we will tell you a true story. It's about a student who began her investigation with curiosity and enthusiasm and, although she hit a few snags, continued searching diligently through various library resources until she had some answers to a question she sincerely wondered about. Her story will give you an idea of the typical research process.

Maria Halloran wasn't daunted to find herself taking English 102 that spring, even though it was a course many students dreaded. Its notorious requirement — a research paper — made some people register for it unhappily. But in high school Halloran had coped with more than one writing assignment that had taken her into the library, and she really enjoyed learning more about subjects of interest to her. Research in her experience hadn't been a cause for despair. Even so, the English 102 assignment presented challenges.

Halloran's professor had centered much of the reading for the composition course on the subject of popular culture in contemporary American society; the research paper, too, was to be on that general subject. Here is the assignment Halloran and her classmates were given:

> Write a paper of at least 1,500 words in which you use a variety of written sources to answer a question of interest to you. Your research question may be about one of the topics we have discussed in class, or it may address some other aspect of popular culture in the United States. The final paper is due in two months.

Although this assignment told Halloran quite a bit about what her professor expected her to accomplish in her paper, it left the choice of topic wide open. Two months seemed to be a short time to go from the broad subject of "popular culture" to a finished research paper on a focused question. But along the way, the instructor would confer individually with each student at each step of the process to follow the student's progress and offer advice.

As Halloran tried to decide on a topic for her research investigation, she thought back over some of the issues the class had discussed — violence in movies, the popularity of video games, the controversy over record labeling, the increasing obsession with TV talk shows. Halloran had grown up in the Philippines, so she viewed American culture differently from the way most of her classmates did. There was one aspect of popular culture that the class had not discussed that puzzled her — sports. Halloran had observed that people in the United States frequently talk about sports and refer to sports. She initially thought she would do her research on sports metaphors in public speeches, such as those used by politicians and newscasters; but she soon discovered that the scope of this subject was overwhelming and that copies of some of the speeches might be difficult to obtain. Next she considered investigating the phenomenon of sports celebrities, but she was not very interested in that angle.

Halloran regrouped, asked herself what she was most interested to learn about sports in America, and realized she wanted to know more about American attitudes toward sports. People aren't as enthusiastic about sports in the Philippines. Perhaps reading and reflecting on what other people said about American attitudes toward sports would help her to understand them better. She decided to do her research paper on the topic of Americans' preoccupation with sports.

Halloran made a preliminary search of her college library's catalog and of the *Readers' Guide to Periodical Literature* and did some preliminary reading about the great value Americans place on sports. She found one promising 1984 article in *U.S. News & World Report,* in which Richard Weinberg, professor of educational psychology at the University of Minnesota, defended the widespread interest in sports on the basis that "for young people, sports is an important self-esteem builder." But Halloran turned up very little recent material.

Because she was dealing with a contemporary phenomenon, she decided to concentrate her search in newspapers and magazines so that she would have up-to-date information. She expanded her search and began looking in other periodical guides and electronic databases. Finally she began to find some articles that intrigued her. For example, an article in the magazine *Sports Bulletin* apparently contradicted Weinberg's position; in it, Robert Lipsyte argued that fear of ridicule in playing sports was not good for building self-esteem. Looking through other issues of *Sports Bulletin,* she found other articles that made the further connection between sports and violence, crime, and suicide. Now Halloran began considering the negative effects of sports mania.

Then she read a comment in a *Chicago Tribune* article that amazed her: "There were 20 shootings after the Bulls' game Sunday night, four of which proved fatal. For any given weekend night in Chicago, that toll is high but not shocking." From her perspective, twenty shootings, four of which were fatal, were shocking. Halloran wondered just how prevalent the attitude displayed in this article was. She asked herself if we in America have now gone so over-board that we take sports violence casually.

Halloran was beginning to feel involved personally. This paper would be well worth writing! Her topic was also becoming more focused. Instead of just investigating Americans' fascination with sports, now Maria wanted to research the negative effects of our preoccupation with sports. Could she find out more about this outrageous situation? Could she find enough information to help her understand the American attitude toward sports better? Could she find other recent articles and some up-to-date statistics? Could she find books on this topic that would give her the in-depth analyses she needed? Could she find enough evidence to make some suggestions for changing the situation? If so, maybe the toil of shuffling note cards, outlining, and citing sources would be justified. She looked forward to the project with enthusiasm.

At this point, Halloran did some early freewriting. She started by stating her topic, as best she could, and then wrote for five minutes without stopping, setting down each thought as it occurred to her.

The negative effects of our preoccupation with sports. We don't care if fans get hurt. We don't care if kids get damaged. We just want the thrill. No cost is too high. Maybe the big business behind it is too powerful to stop now. Sports heroes with their endorsements, huge expensive stadiums, big salaries. Lots of money. Lots of power and prestige. It's like a cult. We'll do anything for it, and we want it to fill our lives with meaning. How did this happen? How did some simple games become our national religion? Wait a minute. Is this true? Is sports mania really part of our national identity? Part of who we are? Everywhere? Is America as a whole obsessed with sports?

Now Halloran had her research question. Although her freewriting turned up some interesting new angles that Halloran would have liked to pursue — the comparison of sports with a cult religion or the effect of big business on the culture of sports — she decided that these would take more time and resources than she had available. Instead, Halloran decided to focus on a more basic question, a question that she actually found more interesting: Is America obsessed with sports?

Because Maria Halloran's research question was focused and meaningful, it served as a good guide through the process of finding sources, gathering evidence, and writing her paper. In this chapter, we'll share with you some of the experiences Halloran had while conducting her research. We'll show you some of the library sources she consulted and some of the notes she took. Later, in Chapter 30, we'll show you how Halloran used her sources to write a convincing paper. Finally, at the end of Chapter 30, we'll let you see Halloran's final research paper, "America's Obsession with Sports."

# Learning by Writing

As a rule, in any composition course a research paper is your most complicated assignment. Some of our advice in this chapter may be old news to you. You may have learned in high school how to take research notes or how to make a working bibliography. At times, as we guide you through writing your paper, we'll pause to explain those special skills. Mastering them, if you haven't mastered them already, will speed you toward that triumphant day when you bang a final staple through your paper. But if at any moment you find us telling you more than you need to know, just skim that part and go on. Later, should you want to review that information, you can return to it.

## THE ASSIGNMENT: WRITING FROM LIBRARY RESEARCH

Find a topic that intrigues you, and develop a focused research question about it. Answering the question should require you to use one or more of the critical thinking skills you honed in Part Two of this book: analyzing, comparing and contrasting, taking a stand, evaluating, explaining causes and effects, proposing a solution, evaluating. Conduct whatever library research is necessary to answer your question, and synthesize the information you assemble to develop your own reasonable answer to the research question. Then write a paper in which you persuasively use a variety of source material to convey your conclusions. Assume that your audience is your instructor and your classmates. Here's how you proceed, in more or less this order:

1. Choose a general subject that you would like to investigate. (Your instructor may assign one or suggest some suitable possibilities.)
2. Do a little reading around in it, to see exactly what aspects of the subject most keenly interest you. Choose one of these as the topic for your research paper.
3. State, in the form of a question about your topic, what you think you want to find out. (This question may change as you read more; its purpose is to guide you in your research.)
4. Make a preliminary search to ascertain that library sources are available to answer your question. If necessary, revise your question.

5. Conduct library research to learn more about your topic and to find some possible answers to your question. As you develop an answer or answers to your research question, conduct more research to assemble the evidence you'll need to present your ideas persuasively.

6. Then in a paper of at least 1,500 words, set forth the conclusions you have drawn from your study. Give evidence from your research sources to support your ideas.

This paper, as you can see, will be more than a stack of facts. Reading and digesting the ideas of five to ten other writers is just the first step. In the process of writing your paper, you'll be called on as well to bring your own intelligence to bear on what you have read.

Among student research papers we have seen recently, the following were among the most informative.

After considering several possible solutions to the problem of America's national debt, a man came to the conclusion that the best solution would be a national lottery. He supported his proposal with evidence from his research into national lotteries held in other countries.

A woman researching the health problems of Vietnam veterans concluded that the ill effects of their exposure to Agent Orange would haunt them and their families well into the twenty-first century.

A Chinese-American student examined what he called "the myth of the model minority" — the perception in the United States that Asian immigrants generally succeed in spite of all obstacles — and found it to be little more than a justification for racism.

A woman, seeking causes for what she perceived as the decline of our national parks, concluded that underfunding and understaffing were paramount.

A Note on Schedules.    Along with the assignment to write a research paper, some instructors will suggest a schedule. Halloran's instructor blocked out the students' obligations like this:

February 21: Paper assigned

February 23: Three possible topics due [next class meeting]

February 28: Preliminary research question due [one week]

March 7: Working bibliography due (citations — on cards — of the sources you think will be useful) [one week]

March 21: Note cards due [two weeks]

March 28: Thesis statement (a one-sentence statement of what the paper will demonstrate) and preliminary outline due [one week]

April 11: First draft due [two weeks]

April 18: Completed revised paper due [one week]

If your instructor doesn't give you a series of deadlines, you'll be wise to set some for yourself. You can depend on this: a research paper will require more time than you expect. You'll find this huge job much more manageable if you break it into a series of small tasks. Writing the final draft, you'll need hours to revise, still more time to cite all your sources accurately, and not be forced to toss everything together in a desperate all-night siege. Then you'll need time to look it over and proofread it. A clear-cut schedule will help.

# *Generating Ideas*

How can we most effectively help long-term prisoners, on their release, to return to society?

Did Walt Disney make any admirable and original contributions to American art, or was he a mere imitator, a purveyor of slick schlock, as some of his critics have charged?

What should be done about acid rain on Lake Champlain?

What can be done to help the homeless in Dallas, Texas?

Should federal tax funds be spent for private education?

What is the media's role in defining Generation X?

If you already have a narrowly defined research question in mind, such as the preceding examples — congratulations. You can just skip to the research checklist on page 659. But if you don't have a question yet, read on.

## CHOOSING YOUR TERRITORY

To explore, you need a territory — a subject that interests you. Perhaps, as Maria Halloran found, your work in this very course or in another course will suggest an appropriate territory. Halloran wrote a paper suggested by a theme that ran through all the readings and discussions in her writing course. A psychology course might encourage you to investigate mental disorders; a sociology course, urban renewal; a geography course, tropical forests.

You'll have an easier time from the start if you can make your territory smaller than "mental disorders" or "urban renewal." "Schizophrenia" and "inner-city housing problems" are smaller, more readily explorable territories that will be more manageable as your research leads you to develop a more focused topic. But if you don't feel you can make your topic so narrow and definite at this point in the process, go ahead and start with a broad subject.

The following checklist may help you find a general subject. It sends you back once more to every writer's five basic resources.

**DISCOVERY**
**CHECKLIST**

## Choosing Your Territory

- Can you *recall* an experience from your work or leisure, from your travel or life as a student, that raises interesting questions or creates unusual associations in your mind?

- What have you *observed* recently — perhaps on your way to school or work today, or while running errands — that you could more thoroughly investigate with the aid of books and magazines?
- What have you recently *read*, whether for a course or for pleasure, that has left you still wondering? (You may want to review Chapter 3, "Writing from Reading.")
- In recent *conversation* with friends or in class discussions, have you encountered any new perspectives that you'd care to explore?
- Can you *imagine* a solution to a frustration, obstacle, or problem that plagues you?

## TAKING AN OVERVIEW

Before launching an expedition into a little-known territory, a smart explorer first makes a reconnaissance flight and takes an overview. Having seen the terrain, the explorer then chooses the very spot to set up camp: the point on the map that looks most promising. Research writers do something like that, too. Before committing themselves to a topic, they first look over a broader territory to see what parts of it look most attractive and then zero in on one small area that seems interesting.

How much time should you devote to your overview? Many students find that they can make such a reconnaissance flight in an evening or a few hours. How do you take an overview? You might begin by looking up your subject in an encyclopedia and reading the general articles about it — *inner cities* or *urban housing developments, schizophrenia* or *mental illness* or (still more general) *psychiatry.* You are probably a veteran reader of encyclopedias, but if you care for any tips on using both general encyclopedias and specialized ones, see the sections on your college library later in this chapter (p. 662). (When you write your paper, usually you'll find the information in a general encyclopedia too broad to use as a source, but at this stage it can help orient you within your subject.)

In your library's reference room, you might check the *Readers' Guide to Periodical Literature,* an index of recent articles in popular magazines. It will direct you to the latest information and opinion, classified by many subjects. You can also look in a newspaper index such as NewsBank, a computerized index now available in many libraries. Browsing in an introductory textbook, if any seems likely to help, is also a useful early step. For the general subjects we've been considering — urban renewal, mental illness, and tropical forests — you might go to a textbook in sociology or psychology or geography.

The point of this preliminary investigation is to help you find a narrow topic you want to learn and write about. When Maria Halloran began her preliminary investigation, she had only a large, vague subject in mind: Americans' attitudes toward sports. As she kept reading and thinking, she saw a smaller topic she wanted to concentrate on: the dangers of our preoccupation with sports.

## STATING YOUR QUESTION

Once you have zeroed in on part of a territory to explore, you can ask a definite question. Ask what you want to find out, and your task will leap into focus. Having begun with a broad, general interest in (let's say) social problems in large cities, you might then ask, "What happens to teenage runaways on the streets of Manhattan?" Or, if you have started with a general yen to know more about contemporary architecture, a definite question might be "Who in America today is good at designing sports arenas?" Keep in mind that the question you ask should be debatable and of interest to both you and your readers.

**Brainstorm.**    You might start with a brainstorming session. For fifteen or twenty minutes, let your thoughts revolve, and jot down whatever questions come to mind — even useless ones. Then, looking over your list, you may find one that appears promising. Your instructor also may have some suggestions, but you will probably be more motivated researching a question you select.

**Size Up Your Question.**    A workable question has to be narrow enough to allow a fruitful investigation in the library. Many interesting questions are too immense — the research they would require would take years, not the few weeks you have available: "How is the climate of the earth changing?" "Who are the world's best living storytellers?" "Why is there poverty?" "What's going on in outer space?" Restrict your thinking and your topic appropriately.

A question, however, can be too narrow or too insignificant. If you restrict your topic too far ("How did John F. Kennedy's maternal grandfather influence the decisions he made during his first month as president?"), it may be impossible to find relevant sources. A question may also be so narrow that it becomes uninteresting — avoid questions that can be answered with a simple yes or no or by stating a few statistics ("Are there more black students or white students in the freshman class this year?"). If a mere source or two could answer your research question, the resulting paper will be a thin summary, not a true research paper. Instead, ask a question that will lead you to a lot of meaty books and articles and into the heart of a lively controversy: "How does the ratio of black students to white students affect campus relations?" The best research questions are those about issues that other people take seriously and spend time arguing about. Not only will you find better sources if you focus on a significant, debatable issue, but your paper is more likely to be of real interest to both you and your readers.

A caution: If you pick a topic currently in the news, you may have trouble finding useful material — deep analysis, critical thought, ample historical background, intelligent controversy. For many current topics, the only printed sources may be recent newspapers and newsmagazines. The topic may be too new for anyone yet to have done a thought-provoking book or a really thorough magazine analysis about it. In this case, keep searching the periodical guides and electronic databases. If your search still doesn't yield any useful analysis or information about your research question, you may need to reconsider your topic.

**Hone Your Question.**   Try to make the wording of your question specific but simple: identify one thing to find out, not several. A question that reads "How do current art and music reflect the cultural revolution of the 1960s?" is too big. You could split such a question into two parts and then pick one of them: "How does contemporary art reflect the cultural revolution of the 1960s?" or "How does music . . .?" By qualifying the word *music,* you might further cut the question down to size: "How does rap music reflect the cultural revolution of the 1960s?" Focus on whatever you most keenly wish to learn, as Maria Halloran did.

A well-wrought question will help lead you into your research. Say the question is "What has caused a shortage of low-income housing in northeastern cities?" The wording of the question alone suggests subject headings that may be found in the library catalog or the *Readers' Guide* or NewsBank: *housing, housing shortage, low-income housing, urban housing.* If your question doesn't suggest such leads, try rewording to make it more concrete and specific.

Some writers find that having not only a *question* but also an *answer* in mind makes the research project easier to tackle. So, for example, if a writer's research question is "Why do people go into the nursing profession?" and he already has an inkling of the likely answer ("People go into nursing out of a strong commitment to caring and a feeling of personal responsibility"), then he might prefer to use the answer to focus the direction of his research. This will allow him to skip all the other possible answers (family background, financial rewards) and to focus on finding evidence that supports or disproves his theory. If you use an answer to your research question in this way, you are using a *working thesis* (see p. 707). At this stage, any answers you have are only tentative — you need to be flexible enough to change your answer or even your question if your research turns up something unexpected. Later, when you are writing your paper, you'll reexamine and revise your working thesis into a final thesis (see "Refining Your Thesis" in Chapter 30, p. 710).

Remember that a working thesis is meant to guide your research, not hinder it. If you find that you're not learning anything new, that you're just finding support for what you already thought was the case, then your working thesis has become too dominant and you're no longer conducting true research. Because of this possibility, many writers prefer to delay formulating a working thesis until they've already done a substantial part of their research — or they might even skip it altogether. Your approach will probably depend on your research assignment, on your instructor's expectations, and on your own work style.

Until you start working in the library, of course, you can't know for certain how fruitful your research question will be. If it doesn't lead you to any definite facts or reliable opinions, if it doesn't start you thinking critically, you'll need to reword it or throw it out and ask a new question. But at the very least, the question you first ask can give you a definite direction in which to start looking.

When you have tentatively stated your question, you can test it by asking these questions about it.

**RESEARCH CHECKLIST**

## Questioning Your Question

- Is the scope of your question appropriate — not too immense and not too narrow?
- Is your question answerable in the time you have? Within the word or page limits you have?
- Can you find sufficient timely information on your question in books and articles?
- Have you worded your question simply, so that you are seeking just one answer, not several?
- Have you worded your question concretely and specifically, so that you understand exactly what you are looking for?
- Is your question of real interest? Does it concern a real issue, about which there is some debate?
- Does your question interest you personally? Do you honestly crave to find the answers to it?

### MAKING A PRELIMINARY SEARCH

You can quickly see whether your question is likely to lead to an ample research paper by conducting a short, fast search that shouldn't take you more than an hour. Check the library catalog to see what books appear under the relevant subject headings. If possible, go into the stacks and look over the shelves. Take a quick check of magazine articles: consult the last annual *Readers' Guide* and an electronic database, looking under the subject headings closest to your special concern. Don't look up the articles yet; just see how many there are and whether their titles sound promising. If your subject is "the American obsession with sports," an article called "Daniel Dawes Honored with Birthday Cake for Fourteen Years as Coach" is probably going to be irrelevant.

This preliminary search has a simple purpose: to ascertain that you'll have enough material to do the job and enough time to do justice to the material. If the material available looks so skimpy that you won't have anything to choose from, and you'll need to force every crumb of it into your paper to get 1,500 words, you might better ask another question. If your first trip into the stacks reveals ten yards of books, alarm bells should start ringing. Instead of asking a question that only two books in your library address or one that a hundred articles address, pick a question that a dozen or twenty sources cover.

# Making a Working Bibliography

Before going on with your investigation, you need a working bibliography: a detailed list of books and articles you plan to consult. Don't worry about trying to write your final list of sources before you conduct your research. The working bibliography is a tool that will change and grow as you find new sources, eliminate others, and shift the focus of your research. It has two purposes: to guide you in your research by recording which sources you've examined and which you intend to examine and to help you document the final paper by recording detailed information about each source.

Your overview and preliminary search should have given you a good rough notion of where your most promising material lies. Now you need titles and information. Most writers find that a convenient and efficient way to compile such a working bibliography is on 4-by-6-inch note cards, one source to a card. Cards are handy to work with: you can arrange and shuffle them. Other writers keep track of everything in a notebook small enough to fit in a pocket. Still others use a computer database to keep track of bibliographical information. Whatever method you use, the more care you take in recording your tentative sources, the more time you'll save later, when at the end of your paper you compile a list of works you *actually* used and cited. At that point, you'll be grateful to find all the necessary information about titles, authors, dates, and page numbers at your fingertips. Otherwise, you'll have to make a frantic, time-consuming trip back to the library.

What should each source note in your working bibliography contain? Everything necessary to find the source later as well as to write the final list of sources to be placed at the end of your paper. Include the following *for books* (see Figure 28.1).

1. The library call number.
2. The author's full name, last name first.
3. The book's title, including its subtitle if it has one, underlined, or in italics if you are using a computer.
4. The publication information: place, publisher, and year of publication.

For *periodicals*, your source note does not need the library call number, but if your library classifies periodicals, the call number will be useful. You'll definitely need the following data (see Figure 28.2).

1. The author's full name.
2. The title of the article, in quotation marks, followed by the name of the publication, underlined or in italics.
3. For a scholarly journal, the volume number and, for certain journals, the issue number. (See Chapter 31 for details.)

GV                              BISSINGER
958.P4.7
B57
1990    Bissinger, H.G. _Friday Night_
            _Lights: A Town, a Team,_
            _and a Dream._
            Reading: Addison, 1990

        Concrete examples of football
        culture. Lots of quotations
        from coaches, etc.

FIGURE 28.1    A bibliography card for a book with one author, in MLA style

4. The date of the issue. (Form varies with the type of journal or magazine. See Chapter 31.)
5. The page numbers of the article. (A "+" indicates that the article covers more than one page, but not consecutive pages.)

For each source note, you may also want to include a brief annotation to
yourself on your impression of the usefulness of the work — "GREAT INFO!"
or "Maybe a few gems here" or "Probably not much use."

FIGURE 28.2    A bibliography source note recorded on a laptop computer for an
article in a monthly magazine, in MLA style

Full name of author

Date and issue
information

MALONEY                Last name of author

Maloney, Lawrence D. "Sports-Crazy Americans." US        Article title in quotation
News & World Report 13 Aug. 1984: 24.                    marks; publication name
                                                         underlined

                                                         Page numbers

You may list each item of information separately in your source note, but it will be wise at this time to put the information in the correct form for a final bibliography entry in your works cited list. This may seem like a lot of record keeping. But it will take you less time to jot down all this information in full now than to make future trips to the library to dig out something you have not recorded when you need it later.

## Finding Information: A Directory of Sources

Now that you have a narrowly defined research question and a working bibliography to guide you on your way, you are ready to plunge into the heart of the research process: reading sources and gathering information. The purpose of the following directory is to help you find promising sources on your topic. The next section of this chapter, "Working with Sources" (p. 679), will help you read those sources critically and take efficient notes. You will probably find it most useful to flip back and forth between these two sections.

The researcher today lives in a world on the cusp of change. A great deal of information is stored the way it has been for some centuries, on printed pages. But the tools for locating these pages and, increasingly, information itself are more and more often in electronic form. That means that the researcher needs to be at home in both the print and the electronic world.

When you enter a college library for your first research assignment, your initial impression may be very confusing. You may be overwhelmed by everything you see — books, periodicals, microfilm, government documents, videos, and computer terminals — and you may wonder how you can begin to access this wealth of materials. Libraries generally provide some help to get you started. Your library may offer tours, classes on how to use an on-line catalog, and brochures explaining the library's organization and services. Reference librarians are probably available to help you answer questions, from specifics such as "What is the GNP of Brazil?" to more general queries such as "Where can I find information on the Brazilian economy?" Before you start looking for sources for your paper, it pays to do a little research on the library itself. These basic questions about your library can start you off.

**RESEARCH CHECKLIST**

## Investigating Your Library

- Does the library have a pamphlet mapping the library's holdings and resources and explaining its services?
- Where is the reference desk and what hours is it open?
- If the catalog is computerized, is there a brochure explaining its use? Can you search the catalog from your computer at home or from the campus network?
- Where are periodicals kept and how are they arranged? Where are the indexes or computerized databases for locating articles by subject?

- If the library doesn't have a book or article that you need, can you order it through interlibrary loan?
- Are there quiet places to work on your research? Are there study carrels — usually small cubicles with desks in the stacks — that you can use while working on your research paper?

## SURVEYING THE REFERENCE SECTION

In any college library the reference collection contains an amazing array of resources. It can be both a good place to start a project, where you can quickly familiarize yourself with a topic, and a place to fine-tune your research by filling in the details of definitions, dates, statistics, or facts. If you are wondering what reference sources relate to your topic, you might want to look at the *Guide to Reference Books,* edited by Eugene P. Sheehy, a directory of sources arranged by discipline. Or you might simply start at the reference desk and ask the librarian what the reference collection offers on your general topic. Librarians know the library's collection thoroughly and keep up with new publications more effectively than any published guide can hope to do.

Certain basic reference books are worth knowing about for almost any research project. This brief introduction can get you started exploring the reference shelves.

Encyclopedias.   Back in high school when you had to do a research paper, chances are you went straight to an encyclopedia. (Sometimes you found articles in *two* encyclopedias, and that was all the research required.) An encyclopedia can still help you get an overview of your subject and may be especially valuable when you are first casting around for a topic. But when you start investigating more deeply, you will need to go to other sources as well.

General encyclopedias are written for readers who aren't specialists, who want an overview of a topic, or who want some fact they are missing. The *New Encyclopaedia Britannica* is the largest general encyclopedia on the shelves. Because the articles are written by experts, the information is authoritative, and bibliographies are included to point readers to the most important sources for further research. Other general encyclopedias, such as the *Encyclopedia Americana,* can also provide background material quickly. Encyclopedias generally have an index volume and cross-references to help you find what you need to know. The *Britannica* has two main sections, a *Micropaedia* of short articles on specific topics and a *Macropaedia* that covers broad topics in long articles. Some colleges have access to a computerized version of the *Britannica* in the library or on the campus network.

Specialized encyclopedias cover a field of study in much greater depth than general encyclopedias do. You might want to supplement your background reading by consulting one of these works, which often have useful bibliographies of related sources. Just to give you a notion of the variety of specialized encyclopedias, here is a sampling of titles:

*Dictionary of American History*
*Dictionary of the Middle Ages*
*Encylopedia of Human Biology*
*Encylopedia of Philosophy*
*Encyclopedia of Psychology*
*Encyclopedia of Religion*
*Encyclopedia of Sociology*
*Encyclopedia of the American Constitution*
*Encylopedia of World Art*
*Encyclopedia of World Cultures*
*McGraw-Hill Encyclopedia of Science and Technology*
*New Grove Dictionary of Music and Musicians*
*New Palgrave Dictionary of Money and Finance*

Some topics are too new or too controversial to be covered in encylopedias. One source that provides overviews of such topics is *CQ Researcher* (formerly called *Editorial Research Reports*). For each topic there are a background sketch, analysis, charts and statistics, a survey of viewpoints, and a bibliography of recommended sources. Current topics are covered in magazine-style format, with annual volumes published each year.

**Dictionaries.**    In addition to desk dictionaries like those most college students own, libraries have a variety of large and specialized dictionaries. You'll find dictionaries covering foreign languages, abbreviations, slang, and regionalisms as well as dictionaries for the specialized terminology in a particular field, such as *Black's Law Dictionary*, *Stedman's Medical Dictionary*, or the *Oxford Dictionary of Natural History*. Libraries often have unabridged dictionaries available on dictionary stands, where you can find the most obscure words currently in use and learn what they mean as well as how to pronounce them.

The largest dictionary in any language is the monumental *Oxford English Dictionary* (OED), now in its second edition. It fills a shelf or more, having twenty volumes in all, and is available in some libraries in a computerized version. It is primarily a historical dictionary that not only defines each word but tells how the word was used from its earliest appearance in the language to the present and gives many examples of its use through history. (See Figure 28.3 for a sample entry.) If you simply want a definition, you may find that this source gives you too much — information on the word *play*, for example, fills ten pages — but if you want to establish the significance of a key

**sla·pstick.** orig. *U.S.* Also **slap-stick.** [f. SLAP *v.*[1] + STICK *sb.*[1]] **1.** Two flat pieces of wood joined together at one end, used to produce a loud slapping noise; *spec.* such a device used in pantomime and low comedy to make a great noise with the pretence of dealing a heavy blow (see also quot. 1950). **1896** *N.Y. Dramatic News* 4 July 9/3 What a relief, truly, from the slap-sticks, rough-and-tumble comedy couples abounding in the variety ranks. **1907** *Weekly Budget* 19 Oct. 1/2 The special officer in the gallery, armed with a 'slap-stick', the customary weapon in American theatre galleries, made himself very officious amongst the small boys. **1925** M. W. DISHER *Clowns & Pantomimes* 13 What has caused the playgoers' sudden callousness? The slapstick. Towards the end of the seventeenth century Arlequin had introduced into England the double-lath of castigation, which made the maximum amount of noise with the minimum of injury. **1937** M. COVARRUBIAS *Island of Bali* iv. 77 Life-size scarecrows are erected, but soon the birds become familiar with them... Then watchmen circulate among the fields beating bamboo drums and cracking loud bamboo slapsticks. **1950** *Sun* (Baltimore) 10 Apr. 3/1 The 50-year-old clown..said that when he bent over another funnyman accidentally hit him with the wrong side of a slap-stick. He explained that a slap-stick contains a blank ·38-caliber cartridge on one side to make a bang.

**2. a.** *attrib.* passing into *adj.* Of or pertaining to a slapstick; of or reminiscent of knockabout comedy. **1906** *N.Y. Even. Post* 25 Oct. 10 It required all the untiring efforts of an industrious 'slap-stick' coterie..to keep the enthusiasm up to a respectable degree. **1914** *Photoplay* Sept. 91 (*heading*) Making slap-stick comedy.

**1923** *Weekly Dispatch* 4 Mar. 9 He likes good comedies.. but thinks the slapstick ones ridiculous. **1928** *Daily Sketch* 7 Aug. 4/3 The jokes..are rapier-like in their keenness, not the usual rolling-pin or slapstick form of humour. **1936** W. HOLTBY *South Riding* iv. v. 258 She took a one-and-threepenny ticket, sat in comfort, and watched a Mickey Mouse film, a slapstick comedy, and the tragedy of Greta Garbo acting Mata Hari. **1944** [see *POCHO]. **1962** A. NISBETT *Technique Sound Studio* x. 173 Decidedly unobvious effects, such as the cork-and-resin 'creak' or the hinged slapstick 'whip'. **1977** R. L. WOLFF *Gains & Losses* II. iv. 296 The prevailing tone of the book is highly satirical, with strong overtones of slapstick farce.

**b.** *absol.* Knockabout comedy or humour, farce, horseplay. **1926** *Amer. Speech* I. 437/2 *Slap-stick*, low comedy in its simplest form. Named from the double paddles formerly used by circus clowns to beat each other. **1930** *Publishers' Weekly* 25 Jan. 420/2 The slapstick of 1929 was often exciting. The Joan Lowell episode was regarded as exposing the gullibility of the critics... The popularity of 'The Specialist' made the whole book business look cockeyed. **1955** *Times* 6 June 9/1 A comic parson (Mr. Noel Howlett) is added for good measure, mainly to play on the piano while other people crawl under it. Even on the level of slapstick the farce seemed to keep in motion with some difficulty and raised but moderate laughter. **1967** M. KENYON *Whole Hog* xxv. 253 A contest which had promised..to be short and cruel, had become slapstick. **1976** *Oxf. Compan. Film* 640/1 As it developed in the decade 1910–20..slapstick depended on frenzied, often disorganized, motion that increased in tempo as visual gags proliferated.

FIGURE 28.3    Entry from the *Oxford English Dictionary*, 2nd ed.

word in your research, you'll find all the evidence you need here. One student, writing a paper on pollution in the environment, looked up the word *pollution* in the *OED* and as a result was able to reinvigorate the contemporary meaning of the word with earlier meanings of shame and sin. Anytime you ever want to unpack a word and demonstrate its multiple meanings or subtle changes in its interpretation over time, the *Oxford English Dictionary* will help.

**Handbooks and Companions.**    Between dictionaries and encyclopedias lies a species of reference book in which you will find concise surveys of terms and topics relating to a specific subject. The articles are generally longer than dictionary entries but more concise than those found in encyclopedias. These can be a great help in clearing up the puzzlements that a research project can generate. What is fabianism? What is the novel *Bleak House* about? What films have been made about angels? Which animals practice mimicry as a defense mechanism? Check with a reference librarian to see if there are specialized handbooks for your topic. The following list gives an idea of the variety available.

> *Blackwell Encyclopaedia of Political Thought*
> *Bloomsbury Guide to Women's Literature*
> *Brewer's Dictionary of Phrase and Fable*

*Dictionary of Afro-American Slavery*
*Dictionary of the Vietnam War*
*Halliwell's Filmgoer's Companion*
*Oxford Companion to Animal Behaviour*
*Oxford Companion to English Literature*

**Statistical Sources.**    For some research, numbers are an essential type of evidence. Many sources for statistics are available in the library. Perhaps the most useful single compilation is the *Statistical Abstract of the United States,* a small volume that contains hundreds of tables of numbers relating to population, social issues, economics, and so on. For public opinion statistics, consult the surveys conducted by the Gallup Poll, published in annual volumes and in a monthly magazine format. The federal government collects an extraordinary amount of statistical data and has recently been releasing much of the data on CD-ROM. If you need more detailed statistics than those available in the *Statistical Abstract,* see if your library has the *U.S. Census of Population and Housing* or *USA Counties* on CD-ROM. Two other popular sources of statistical information, especially for economic topics, are the *National Trade Data Bank* and the *National Economic Social and Environmental Data Bank,* put out by the Commerce Department, also on CD-ROM.

**Atlases and Gazetteers.**    If your research has a geographical angle, maps and atlases may come into play. In addition to atlases of countries, regions, and the world, there are atlases that cover history, natural resources, ethnic groups, and many other special topics. Gazetteers list place names and give basic information about them, including their location. The *Columbia Lippincott Gazetteer of the World* is one published gazetteer of note. The Geographic Name Server on the Internet gives the precise latitude and longitude of places that you can search for by name.

**Biographical Sources.**    If you want to know about someone's life and work, you have a rich array of sources. Directories that list basic information — degrees, work history, honors, address — for prominent people include *Who's Who in the United States, Who's Who in Politics,* and *American Men and Women of Science.* For more detailed biographical sketches, try *Contemporary Biography, Contemporary Authors,* or *Politics in America* for elected officials. Several biographical sources contain substantial entries of people who have died: prominent Americans are covered in *The Dictionary of American Biography,* British figures in *The Dictionary of National Biography,* and scientists from all countries and periods in *The Dictionary of Scientific Biography.* To help you locate biographical sources, you can use tools such as *Biography Index* and the *Biographical and Genealogical Master Index.*

## USING THE LIBRARY CATALOG

The library's catalog is a database containing information about the library's holdings of books, periodicals, videos, and so on. In the past, the database was kept on cards in wooden drawers. Now it is fairly common for the records to be searchable by computer. Whatever the form of access, the function is the same: to describe the materials owned by the library so that a library user can locate them by author, title, or subject.

Searching the Catalog.    When searching your library's catalog, first decide what kind of search you are doing. Are you looking for the works of a particular author? Are you searching for a particular title? Or do you simply want to know what is available on a topic? Some card catalogs file subject cards separately from author and title cards. Most computerized catalogs will ask you to specify what kind of search you are doing, either by making a menu choice or by typing in a command.

If you are searching by subject, you need to decide what to search under. When catalogers put a book into the database, they assign subject headings to it, using a list of standard terms used by many other libraries. The list most college libraries use is found in the *Library of Congress Subject Headings* (*LCSH*), a set of large red books that many libraries keep near the card catalog or computer terminals. (See Figure 28.4 for a sample entry.) If you are having trouble coming up with an effective term to search under, look in *LCSH*. You may be using different terminology than the catalogers did. For

---

FIGURE 28.4    Entries from the *Library of Congress Subject Headings*

---

```
Sports   (May Subd Geog)
    [GN454-GN455 (Ethnology)]
    [GV561-GV1198.995 (General)]
 UF  Field sports
     Pastimes
     Recreations
 BT  Recreation
 RT  Athletics
     Games
     Outdoor life
     Physical education and training
 SA  subdivision Sports under military
          services, e.g. United States.   Army
          —Sports; and under ethnic groups
 NT  Aeronautical sports
     Age and sports
     Aquatic sports
     Ball games
     Bullfights
     Discrimination in sports
```

example, rather than use the term "third world," catalogers use "developing countries" and because they are loath to change their terms, they continue to use "Afro-American" rather than "African American" and "motion pictures" rather than "movies."

Some computerized catalogs give you the additional option of using "free text" or "keyword" searches. You enter whatever term you want, and the computer gives you a list of every book for which that term is used in the title or subject heading. This is an easy way to find books on your topic, but keyword searches can also generate lots of irrelevant titles, especially if the term you enter is a common one.

You can narrow your search and make it more efficient by combining terms using the words "and" and "or." For example, if you're researching water conservation policies for lakes in Minnesota, you might be tempted to start by entering the word "water" — but in even a small library, that would probably generate a list of hundreds of books, including those on irrigation, on waterskiing, and on cooking with water chestnuts. If you search for "water and conservation," then you'll get information only on books that have both of those words in their titles or subject headings. Most likely, almost all of these books will be on water conservation (your general subject), but the list will still be quite long and will include works on conservation efforts along ocean shorelines and on rivers around the world. If you search for "water and conservation and Minnesota or lake," then you'll get information only on books that have the combinations "water/conservation/Minnesota" or "water/conservation/lake" in their entries. This list will probably be a few dozen books long and will contain mostly works of direct interest to you.

Search strategies like this work best if you're willing to play around with the terms a little. If you're getting more sources than you can use and many of them aren't relevant to your research, try adding a term with "and" or "or." If your search is turning up only a couple of sources or none, try changing the terms or omitting some of them. Remember, too, that your search will be more productive if you use the same terms that the catalogers used. Here's a good strategy: conduct a search using your own terms first. Then scan the entries, looking for relevant terms listed in the subject headings. Finally, conduct another search using these new terms listed in the subject headings.

Once you have done a search, you need to sort through your options. The information in each record or on each card can help. In addition to the call number or shelf location and the author and title, the record indicates where the work was published and when. A line of description includes how many pages the work contains, information that may help you decide whether it is going to be helpful. Often there are notes about the contents, and finally subject headings, which help clarify the scope of the work. (See Figures 28.5, 28.6, and 28.7 for examples of Library of Congress author, title, and subject cards.) Many computerized catalogs tell you if the book is on the shelf or not. Some computer catalogs even have a command for limiting a search by date of publication, a useful function if you need to stick to current information.

Library call number

Book title, author's name,
place of publication,
publisher, date of
publication

Number of pages,
illustrations (none), height
of book

The International
Standard Book Number

```
GV706.5    Umphlett, Wiley Lee, 1931-
.A44           American sport culture/
1985       by Wiley Lee Umphlett—1st ed.—
           Cranbury, NJ: Associated Uni-
           versity Presses, c1985.
             vi, 322 p.; 24 cm.
             ISBN 0-8387-5070-2: $34.50
             Includes bibliography.
             1. Sports—social aspects—
           United States-Addresses, es-
           says, lectures. I. Umphlett,
           Wiley, Lee.
                             83-45967
GV706.5.A441985    306´.483´0973
```

Special features

Subject headings

Library of Congress
Catalog Card Number

Dewey decimal number

FIGURE 28.5    A Library of Congress author card

Figure 28.8 illustrates a record from a computerized catalog. Though each system presents information slightly differently, the elements included generally are the same. Use these clues to help you choose your sources wisely.

**Finding Books on the Shelves.**    The call number that tells where a book is shelved may seem a random jumble of letters and numbers, but they are care-

FIGURE 28.6    A Library of Congress title card

```
        American sport culture

GV706.5    Umphlett, Wiley Lee, 1931-
.A44           American sport culture/
1985       by Wiley Lee Umphlett—1st ed.—
           Cranbury, NJ: Associated University Presses, c1985.
             vi, 322 p.; 24 cm.
             ISBN 0-8387-5070-2: $34.50
             Includes bibliography.
             1. Sports—social aspects—United States—
           Addresses, essays, lectures. I. Umphlett, Wiley,
           Lee.
                                    83-45967
        GV706.5.A441985             306´.483´0973
```

```
SPORTS—SOCIAL ASPECTS—UNITED STATES—ADDRESSES, ESSAYS
        LECTURES.
GV706.5   Umphlett, Wiley Lee, 1931-
.A44          American sport culture/
1985      by Wiley Lee Umphlett—1st ed.—
          Cranbury, NJ: Associated University Presses,
          c1985.
             vi, 322 p.; 24 cm.
             ISBN 0-8387-5070-2: $34.50
             Includes bibliography.
             1. Sports—social aspects—United States—
          Addresses, essays, lectures. I. Umphlett, Wiley,
          Lee.
                                        83-45967
          GV706.5.A441985               306´.483´0973
```

FIGURE 28.7    A Library of Congress subject card

fully chosen so that books on the same subject will end up next to each other on the shelves. College libraries generally use the classification system devised by the Library of Congress. If your library does, you'll find that call letters and numbers direct you to books grouped in subject areas. Others use the older and more familiar Dewey decimal system, which files books into large categories by number. Some large libraries have both, having changed from

FIGURE 28.8    On-line catalog display of an author entry

```
      Boston Public Library / Public Access Catalog Wed Feb 22, 1995
Friday night lights:   Bissinger, H.G.
            Author:   Bissinger, H.G.
             Title:   Friday night lights : a town, a team, and a dream /
                       H.G. Bissinger.
       Publication:   Reading, Mass. : Addison-Wesley Pub. Co., c1990.
Physical Description:   xiv, 357 p., [28] p. of plates : ill. ; 24 cm.
 Subject (Company):   Permian High School (Odessa, Tex.) — Football.
           Subject:   Football — Social aspects — Texas — Odessa.

     PF1: HELP  PF4: Back up  PF6: New Search  PF7: Reset
     PF9: Call Numbers  PF10: Format Toggle  PF11: Related Search
```

Dewey to the Library of Congress system some time in the past. In any case, it can be fruitful to reserve some of your research time for browsing, since you will almost certainly find some books on the shelf that are of interest next to the ones you found through the catalog. The two common classification systems are outlined here. You may notice that certain subjects aren't clearly included in either system — some fields, such as computer science, mass communications, and environmental studies, are newer than the classification systems themselves and so have had to be fit into other related areas.

LIBRARY OF CONGRESS CLASSIFICATION SYSTEM

| | |
|---|---|
| A | N |
| B | P |
| C–D | Q |
| E–F | R |
| G | S |
| H | T |
| J | U |
| K | V |
| L | Z |
| General Works | Music |
| Philosophy, Psychology, Religion | Fine Arts |
| Foreign History and Topography | Language and Literature |
| America | Science |
| Geography, Anthropology, Sports and Games | Medicine |
| Social Sciences | Agriculture and Forestry |
| Political Science | Engineering, Technology |
| Law | Military Science |
| Education | Naval Science |
| M | Bibliography and Library Science |

DEWEY DECIMAL CLASSIFICATION SYSTEM

| | |
|---|---|
| 000–099 | 500–599 |
| General Works | Natural Sciences |
| 100–199 | 600–699 |
| Philosophy | Applied Sciences |
| 200–299 | 700–799 |
| Religion | Fine and Decorative Arts |
| 300–399 | 800–899 |
| Social Sciences, Government, Customs | Literature |
| 400–499 | 900–999 |
| Language | History, Travel, Biography |

## USING PERIODICAL INDEXES, DATABASES, AND BIBLIOGRAPHIES

Sometimes students head straight to the catalog and try to find all of their research sources there. Frequently they are disappointed — the books are too old, or there is nothing listed on their specific topic. If this happens to you,

you may be looking in the wrong place. Often there is more information on certain topics — particularly current ones — published in the form of periodicals than in books. Periodicals are journals, magazines, newspapers, and other publications that are issued at regular intervals. Several indexes and databases exist to help you track down articles in periodicals. Another option is to use a bibliography (a list of sources on a particular topic) to lead you to relevant sources. Often you will find sources in bibliographies that you would never have thought to look up in a catalog.

**Periodical Indexes and Databases.**    An index is a guide to the material published within other works, sometimes within books but more often within periodicals. In a periodical index, you'll find every article for the periodicals and the period covered, listed alphabetically by author, title, and subject. The index will also include the source information you'll need to find each article, usually the periodical title, issue number, and page numbers. Indexes are available in print, on CD-ROM, and on-line. A database is a large index available only on CD-ROM or on-line. It usually includes more information on each article than an index does, such as a short summary. For computerized indexes and databases, whether on CD-ROM or on-line, you can use the same keyword search strategies as for computerized card catalogs (see p. 667).

Each index and database includes entries on a somewhat different collection of periodicals, so finding the right article is largely a matter of finding the right index or database. Before you start looking through an index or database, ask yourself these questions:

Is my subject covered in this index or database? Some indexes cover a very specific subject area in depth and others are more broadly focused.

Does it cover the time period I'm interested in? Most computerized indexes cover only recent publications — no earlier than 1980 — and so may not help if you are looking for anything older.

Does it cover articles written for an expert audience or a more general audience? Some indexes focus on highly technical research and scholarship; others lead to articles written for a nonspecialist audience.

Several common indexes can help you if you're looking for magazine or newspaper articles addressed to the general population. The *Readers' Guide to Periodical Literature* is this type of index and is available in print, on CD-ROM, and on-line. (See Figure 28.9 for a sample entry.) The printed version is a good choice if you are doing any historical work. Because it started publication in 1900, you can use older volumes to locate popular press coverage of events happening at any time in the twentieth century — for example, articles about the bombing of Pearl Harbor published days after it happened. The index to the *New York Times* can help you track down that newspaper's coverage of events. Since it goes back to 1851, it is great for historical research. Another popular index is *InfoTrac,* a computerized resource that emphasizes materials written for a fairly general audience (though one version, the *Expanded Academic Index,* includes scholarly journals). (See Figure 28.10 for a sample entry.)

**SPORTS**
> *See also*
> Athletes
> Coed sports
> College athletics
> Discrimination in sports
> Gymnastics
> Physical education and training
> Sex discrimination in sports
> Television broadcasting—Sports
> Track and field athletics
> Women—Sports
> > *See also* names of sports

Ahead of the game [workout tips for the weekend athlete]
M. Jannot. ii *Men's Health* v9 p42-9 Ap '94

**Accidents and injuries**
> *See also*
> Automobile racing—Accidents and injuries
> Football, Professional—Accidents and injuries
> Running—Accidents and injuries

The 10 most common sports injuries. M. Fuerst. il
*American Health* v13 p66-70 O '94

**FIGURE 28.9**   Entries from the *Readers' Guide to Periodical Literature*

Many libraries also subscribe to *NewsBank,* an index to newspapers that draws on more than five hundred local U.S. newspapers. (See Figure 28.11 for a sample entry.) Updated monthly, *NewsBank* is available both in print and on CD-ROM for computer searching. Your library may have an index to a local newspaper, which can help you track issues that have special importance in

**FIGURE 28.10**   Entry from *InfoTrac* index

```
InfoTrac * General Periodical Index  1992–Jan 1995


Heading: GELMAN, DAVID
   13.  I'm not a role model: the exploits of Michael Jordan and Charles Barkley
        have stirred a debate about just what pro athletes owe their fans. Are
        kids really that naive? by David Gelman il v121 Newsweek June 28 '93
        p56(2)
          69G0321                                                   71Z1586
        ABSTRACT / HEADINGS
   13.  I'm not a role model: the exploits of Michael Jordan and Charles Barkley
        have stirred a debate about just what pro athletes owe their fans. Are
        kids really that naive? by David Gelman il v121 Newsweek June 28 '93
        p56(2)
          69G0321                                                   71Z1586
        ABSTRACT / HEADINGS
ABSTRACT (6 lines)
  Barkley sparked a debate about the responsibility of professional athletes
for setting examples of appropriate conduct for young fans when he claimed he
was not a role model in a television commercial. The influence of celebrity
athletes on children is discussed.
  -END-
```

Nearly 20 million children under age of 14 participate in
nonschool-related sports teams, according to National
Youth Sports Coaches Association; despite their initial
enthusiasm, many children end up hating sports they used to
love largely because their coaches and parents turn
children's playing fields into battlefields; Rick Wolff, author
of book on parents and children's sports, says adults often
destroy children's passion for sports by overemphasizing
importance of winning; photos (M), N 18,C,1:3
  St John's University will drop nickname 'Redmen' in
deference to American Indian sensitivities, although name
originated with color of football uniforms (S), N 19,B,10:3
  William C Rhoden Sports of The Times column discusses
work of Garry Mendez in studying Sudden Cardiac Disease
among athletes; photo (M), N 23,B,13:1

FIGURE 28.11    Entry from the *New York Times Index*

your area. Some computerized indexes include abstracts or even the full text
of the articles which you can print out or download for later use.

If you are looking for articles that are aimed at a more specialized audience and provide more analysis than those found in popular magazines, try
the *Humanities Index,* the *Social Sciences Index,* the *General Science Index,* the
*Business Periodicals Index,* or *PAIS International,* an index focusing on public affairs. The computerized *Expanded Academic Index* provides the same kind of
coverage as the first three of these indexes. These tools index the most important scholarly journals in the fields covered, but they don't include obscure or
highly specialized publications. The articles you are likely to find in these indexes will be fairly long, include footnotes, and be based on and give detailed
information about research. These are the kinds of indexes you'll want to use
if you are looking for literary criticism, research on social issues, or scientific
or medical research which is only summarized or reported in the popular
press.

In addition are highly specialized indexes in each discipline that list
books, articles, dissertations, and other specialized materials. Many of the
items listed in these indexes are obscure and are available only in the largest
libraries. These indexes are good places to look if you are working on an in-depth project and have time to track down the items listed, either in a research
library or through interlibrary loan. The following specialized tools — and
dozens more — are available both in paper and as computerized databases.
A librarian can point you to a specialized index for your particular purpose.

*America: History and Life*

*Biological Abstracts* (*Biosis*)

*Index Medicus* (*Medline*)

*MLA International Bibliography*

*Psychological Abstracts* (*PsycINFO*)

**Bibliographies.**    Another way to find good research sources is to take advantage of the research other people have already done on your subject. Bibliographies are lists of sources on particular topics. Researchers compile them after completing their research, and they publish them so that other researchers (including you) won't have to duplicate their work. Bibliographies can give citations for a wide variety of materials — including not only books and articles but also films, manuscripts, letters, government documents, and pamphlets — and they will probably lead you to sources that you wouldn't otherwise find. Remember, though, that a bibliography is not a specialized version of your library catalog — not all of the sources will be available in your library or even available through interlibrary loan.

Sometimes you may be able to locate a book-length bibliography on your subject. For example, *Essential Shakespeare* is a bibliography that lists the best books and articles published on each of Shakespeare's works, a wonderful shortcut if you're looking for worthwhile criticism. To find a book-length bibliography in a computerized card catalog, add the word "bibliography" to a subject or keyword search (see p. 667). If you're lucky, such a bibliography will include annotations that describe and evaluate each source.

If there aren't any book-length bibliographies devoted to your subject, you can still take advantage of the work that other researchers have done. Every time you find a good book or article, look to see what sources the author draws on; chances are, at least some of these sources will be useful to you, too. An author may record his or her source information in several different places and formats. A full-length book may have a section labeled "Bibliography" at the back, or perhaps a section called "For Further Reading." If the author has quoted or referred to other works, there should be a list called "References" or "Works Cited" at the end. If the book or article uses footnotes or endnotes, be sure to check those too for possible leads.

How do you find books and articles based on their citations in bibliographies? If the citation gives an author, title, place, publisher, and date, you can search the book catalog by author or title. If a citation lists an author, an article title, the name of a journal, a volume, date, and pages, find out if your library subscribes to that journal and then look for the particular issue that has the article cited. Some citations are hybrids: they give an author and article title, but instead of journal information, the rest of the citation contains book information. Such a citation refers to an essay published in a collection of essays. In this case you would search the book catalog by the title of the collection, not by the author or title of the essay. Other bibliography citations are harder to interpret — they may refer to government documents, unpublished research reports, papers given at conferences, dissertations, or manuscripts. Some authors muddy the waters further by using abbreviations. If you are having trouble, a librarian can help you interpret a citation and figure out if the source is available in the library or through interlibrary loan. Once you start to use the clues provided in bibliographies and footnotes, those obscure rules you follow for citing sources in your own work begin to make more sense.

## EXPLORING THE INTERNET AND OTHER RESEARCH OPTIONS

The Internet. Many colleges and universities are part of a computer network that spans the globe. The Internet, as it is called, is a loosely organized system of connections, bridging computers from campus to campus, from government agency to corporation, from country to country, and from individual to individual — all on-line, that is, primarily across telephone lines. At each Internet site, computing professionals and interested amateurs can load information on the network for anyone to use and can communicate with people at other Internet sites by sending electronic mail, connecting to databases, or picking up files from the network on their own computer (called "downloading"). The Internet is an amazing information and communication resource, but it is also amazingly chaotic at first glance. Because no one oversees the whole operation, and no one imposes guidelines on what information is available and in what form, it is both a forum for free expression and something of a free-for-all.

What kind of information can you find on the Internet? Much of it is the same sort of information you can find in your library. The *CIA World Factbook,* the complete works of Shakespeare, the script of a Monty Python movie, and statistics from the U.S. Census Bureau are available over the network. Many journals are now bypassing the cost and delays of print technology and are publishing on the Internet — the *Bryn Mawr Classical Journal* and the *Journal of Postmodern Culture* are examples. You can find out what the weather is like in Poughkeepsie today or the latitude and longitude of Kankakee. You can pick up recipes and jokes and detailed genome data for *arabidopsis,* a plant used in genetic research. You can take part in discussion groups on medieval drama, on analysis of *Finnegans Wake,* and on *Star Trek.* In short, the Internet isn't a resource, it's a universe of resources.

How do you use the Internet? Your campus computing facility or library can help you find out how to get started. Generally, you need to set up a personal account at a site, with your own user name and password. Your user name and site are like a street address; your password is the key to your front door, the only way your personal files can be unlocked. Many books have been published that can help you learn what resources are available and how to get to them, but because each campus has its own way of organizing its computer resources and because the technology is constantly changing, faster than anyone's ability to catalog or map this terrain, you should also find out if classes or workshops or handouts are available locally.

There are three primary things you can do on the Internet.

*Communicate with other Internet users.* Electronic mail systems allow for sending messages to individuals anywhere on the Internet; there are also hundreds of discussion groups in which mail can be exchanged with a community of interested parties.

*Connect to remote computers.* You can, for example, connect to the Library of Congress and trace the progress of congressional legislation or read mathematics papers posted by the American Mathematical Society.

*Transfer files from a remote computer to your computer.* You can fetch the text of the Constitution, a computer program, or a graphic image from a computer elsewhere and have a copy on your hard drive for your own use.

Several tools make it relatively easy to navigate the Internet. Ask your computing staff what the local options are. If your campus is connected, you will, for example, have some sort of system for composing, sending, and receiving electronic mail. There is probably some kind of "news reader" program that helps you find news groups where discussion on a wide variety of issues takes place. Most Internet sites have a gopher, a menu-driven system for "burrowing" around the Internet; it even offers a way of searching by keywords all the other gophers in the world. The World Wide Web is a hypertext system that lets you click on a word and link to related documents. Web browsers, like Mosaic and Netscape, are programs that run these hypertext links, letting you bring up color images and sounds as well as texts.

Even with these tools, the Internet can be a confusing place, and often you will find the same or better information more quickly in your library. The *CIA World Factbook*, for example, can be found on the Internet, but far more detailed and informative country surveys can be found quite easily on the reference shelves. Much of what is on the network is outdated, inaccurate, or silly, but it offers a lot, and more every day, to the researcher who is patient, curious, and discerning.

Microforms.    Most libraries have some of their resources available on microfilm or microfiche. This technology puts a large amount of printed material — for example, two weeks of the *New York Times* — on a durable strip of film that fits into a small box or on a set of plastic sheets the size of index cards. Machines are used to read microfilm or microfiche and in many cases full-sized copies of pages can be printed out.

In addition to newspapers and magazines, many libraries have other primary source material in microform format. For example, the *American Culture Series* reproduces books and pamphlets published between 1493 and 1875 and includes a good subject index. It is one tool for examining colonial-era religious tracts or nineteenth-century abolitionist pamphlets without having to travel to a museum or rare books collection. The *American Women's Diaries* collection reproduces diaries kept by women living in New England and the South and pioneer women traveling west and provides rare firsthand glimpses of the past.

Government Documents.    The federal government is the most prolific publisher in the world and, in an effort to make information accessible to citizens all over the country, libraries in many locations serve as depositories for government publications. That is, they are sent a multitude of government publications and, in turn, make them available to the surrounding community. If your college library isn't a depository, there may be one nearby that serves that role. Large libraries often have collections of local and international documents as well.

When most people think of government documents they think of political information — congressional hearings, presidential papers, and reports from federal agencies — but government documents are not limited to governmental matters. In fact, the government has published something on practically any topic you can think of. The following sampling of government publication titles will give you an idea of what kinds of information you can find.

*Neurobiology of Seasonal Affective Disorder and Phototherapy*

*Ozone Depletion, the Greenhouse Effect, and Climate Change*

*Placement of School Children with Acquired Immune Deficiency*

*Policy Implications of U.S. Involvement in Bosnia*

*Remove Indians Westward* (*Committee on Indian Affairs, 1829*)

*Report of the Joint Committee on the Conduct of the War* (*on the Battle of Bull Run, 1863*)

*Small Business and the International Economy*

*Strengthening Support and Recruitment of Women and Minorities to Positions in Education Administration*

*Violence on Television*

There are several indexes to government documents, and some are computerized. Among them are the *Monthly Catalog of United States Government Documents*, the most complete index to federal documents, the *CIS Index*, which specializes in congressional documents and includes a handy legislative history index, and the *American Statistical Index*, a detailed index to statistics in government publications. Some large series, like the *Congressional Record*, which reports what happens in Congress each day during each session, have indexes of their own.

Many government publications are now being released on CD-ROM. These make information, particularly statistical data, easier to find than ever before. You can print out a detailed population profile of your hometown, including age groups, income, education level, and ethnic origins, using the *Census on CD-ROM*. You can find *Country Reports on Human Rights Practices*, *U.S. Industrial Outlook*, and *The Year in Trade* using the *National Trade Data Bank* (*NTDB*). The *National Economic Social and Environmental Data Bank* (*NESE*) covers small-business statistics, the cost of pollution abatement programs, regional and state business conditions, and a wealth of other economic data. Every year more and more databases like these are being released. If you plan to use government documents in your research, don't be shy about asking a librarian for help. The documents can be difficult to locate on the shelves, and since new computerized sources are coming out all the time, it's wise to get an expert on your side.

Pamphlets and Annual Reports.    When journalists need information, they typically get on the phone and make contacts, going directly to sources that can fill them in. You too can get pamphlets, brochures, reports, and annual reports by calling organizations or companies directly. The *Encyclopedia of Associations* is a useful guide to organizations, categorized by name and subject. For government agencies, try the *United States Government Manual.*

Your library may have already done some of the legwork for you. Many libraries maintain a vertical file in which you can find pamphlets organized by subject. Take information from such sources with a grain of salt — annual reports tend to paint a glowing picture of the companies they cover, and organizations advocating particular points of view will not hesitate to put their information in the most persuasive terms possible.

# Working with Sources

## EVALUATING SOURCES

When you go into a library not knowing how to proceed, you might poke around and think, "There's not much here — maybe I'd better change my topic." But once you learn about the tools of the trade, you may have the opposite feeling: "How can I possibly handle all of this information?" Remember that not every source you locate will be equally useful to you. Some sources are weakened by poor reasoning, some are invalidated by strong biases, and some are simply irrelevant to your specific research question. Part of the job of research is thinking critically about sources so that you can select the *best* evidence for your purposes. Before you spend time taking detailed notes on a source that may turn out to be untrustworthy or simply unimportant, take the time to preview it by asking yourself the following questions, a variation on the reporter's "five *W*'s and an *H*":

*Who?*  Who is the author, and what are his or her credentials? Is the author a recognized authority? With what institutions or organizations is he or she affiliated? If there is no author given, who is the sponsoring organization or publisher — for instance, is it a nationally respected newspaper rather than a supermarket tabloid? You want to make sure that any author you cite is reliable and trustworthy; if you are going to use this author's work to support a key point in your paper, you probably want to make sure he or she is an authority in the field.

See whether any credentials are given in the introduction or preface to a book or in a *blurb* (biographical note) at the beginning or end of a book or article. If you are still in doubt, you might check whether the author is listed in the library catalog or whether he or she is included in *Who's Who, Contemporary Authors,* or specialized reference works such as *American Men and Women of Science.* Inclusion in reference works such as these doesn't guarantee absolute trustworthiness, but you may be able to get an idea of the author's background. Ultimately, the best measure of someone's authority is whether his or her work meets the critical demands of other authorities. If your instructor knows the field, you might ask him or her about the author, or there might be someone else on campus who can answer your questions.

If your source is a weekly newsmagazine like *Time*, *Newsweek*, or *U.S. News & World Report*, the writer of an article is likely to be a reporter, not always a famous name, and probably not a world-renowned authority. Such magazines do, however, feature some articles by experts, and all such magazines have a good reputation for checking their facts carefully. They try to present a range of opinions, but be aware that they sometimes *select* facts to mirror the opinions of their editors. In a serious, reputable periodical of general interest, you can take the periodical's reputation as a yardstick for credibility of the authors.

If you get information from computer bulletin boards or certain electronic databases, determining the reliability of a writer may be a real problem because you may have trouble finding out what the center's credentials are. Remember that you need to apply the same evaluative criteria to electronic sources as to more traditional sources. If you can't find out anything about the author, you might e-mail him or her asking for a brief résumé relevant to the topic being discussed. If you can't find out anything about the writer, it is best not to use the information.

*What?* What does the text itself tell you about its reliability and usefulness? Is it carefully put together? Does it seem complete, and does it cite up-to-date references? If it has a thesis, is it convincing? What facts or evidence does it present, and is that evidence credible? (See pp. 118–19 for more ideas on testing evidence.) Does the argument or analysis seem convincing? If the book or article seems slipshod or leaves you with several important questions unanswered, you might do better to look for another source. Also, is the information directly relevant to your research question? Often researchers get sidetracked when they find a very persuasive book or article on a topic that is only slightly connected to the direction of their research.

*Where?* Where is the author coming from? Where are his or her allegiances? Is there a bias, either implicit or explicit? Do you need to look for a balancing viewpoint or approach? (Even scholars discussing what appear to be dry and factual data may have an ax to grind!) Just because the author has a strong bias does not mean that everything he or she has written is invalid. However, you will be better prepared to fend off attacks from those who want to challenge your analysis or argument if you recognize such biases early on.

The audience for whom something was written will also tell you something about the implicit biases of the piece. If you are reading a book, what does the name of the publisher tell you about the intended audience? Is this publisher known for publishing works in a specific field? with a specific political agenda? If you are reading a periodical, does it have a predictable point of view? *The Nation*, a magazine of commentary from a left-leaning political point of view, is likely to give you a different picture of the world from that found in the *National Review*, edited by conservative William F. Buckley, Jr.

How can you find out, if you don't already know, the general outlook of a periodical you are examining? Take a moment to skim through it, noting the following.

*Editorials.* In these, the editors, making no pretense of being impartial, set forth their views. In most magazines, editorials will be in a front section and may not even be signed, since the names of the editors are on the masthead, near the table of contents. If you can find an editorial commenting on a familiar issue, you can discover the bias of the magazine's editors.

*Featured columnists.* Usually the job of a columnist depends on his or her voicing opinions congenial to the magazine's editors and publishers. But this test isn't foolproof. Sometimes a dissenting columnist is hired to lend variety.

*Lead stories.* The lead story is usually the one placed most prominently in the issue; the cover of a magazine often reflects the lead story. If you don't have time to read the whole thing, skim the last paragraph, in which the writer often declares the overall message.

*Letters to the editor.* You can often deduce the level of schooling and intelligence of the letter writers, and this will tell you something about the magazine's readers. Political positions aren't always easy to decipher from letters to the editor since many magazines, such as *Time,* strive to offer space to a diversity of opinions.

*Advertisements.* Ads are usually a good guide to a magazine's audience. To whom are its editors trying to appeal? The many ads for office copiers, delivery services, hotels, and corporations in *Newsweek,* for instance, tell you that the magazine is trying to appeal to well-educated professionals.

**When?** When was the source published? Is the information in it still up to date, or at least still of importance? In most cases, you should strive to use the most current sources possible. In our fast-changing world, additional information and discoveries in most fields come out every year. If you cited five-year-old procedures for treating AIDS as if they were still used, for example, you'd be wrong. Use older materials only when their value has held up over time or if your research focuses on a particular period earlier than the recent past. If, for example, you see the same article cited over and over, it is probably still considered an important and valuable work, even if it was published in 1968.

**Why?** Why use this source rather than another? Are this text and the information it contains useful for your purposes as a writer? Does the source contain strong quotations or hard facts that would be effective in your final paper? Is it relevant, in terms of the subject matter and in the way it tackles it? For some papers it may be appropriate to use an article in a popular magazine, and for others you may need to cite the research findings published in the scholarly journal on which the magazine article was based. Remember that you're looking for the best possible sources for your particular paper. Always ask yourself not only "Will this do?" but "Would something else be better?"

*How?* How will using this source in your paper affect the future direction of your research? Does it contain information that challenges your assumptions about the topic? Does it present any strong evidence against your position for which you need to find counterevidence? Does it suggest a new direction that might be more interesting to pursue? Your research project will probably grow and change as you learn more about it. It's wise to check in with yourself now and again to make sure you're still headed in the right direction — whether it's the same old direction or a completely new one.

## CONSIDERING PRIMARY AND SECONDARY SOURCES

A *primary source* is a firsthand account written by an eyewitness or a participant. It contains raw data and immediate impressions. A *secondary source* is an analysis of the information contained in one or more primary sources. For example, primary sources for a large fire caused by a gas leak would include the statements of victims and witnesses, the article written by a journalist who was at the scene, and the report of the fire chief in charge of putting out the blaze. If another journalist used the first journalist's article as background for a story on industrial accidents, or if a historian used any of these sources in a book on urban life in the twentieth century, these would be secondary sources.

For most research papers, you will need to use both primary and secondary sources. Secondary sources aren't necessarily less trustworthy just because they are not firsthand reports. Eyewitnesses can be prejudiced, self-serving, or simply unable to know as much as a later writer who has synthesized many eyewitness accounts. In writing a history paper on the attitudes of American social workers toward World War I, you might quote a primary source: Jane Addams, founder of Chicago's Hull House, who was a pacifist. If you relied only on Addams's words, though, you might get the idea that social workers were unanimously opposed to the war effort. To put Addams's views into perspective, you'd also need secondary sources, which would show that most of her peers did not want to identify with her unpopular pacifism and publicly disagreed with her.

If, however, you find yourself repeatedly citing a fact or authority as it is quoted in someone else's analysis, you might be wise to go to the primary source of the information itself. For example, statistics are often used by those arguing both sides of an issue — often it's only the interpretation that differs. You might find it useful to go back to the original research (the publication of which is a primary source) to learn where the facts end and the interpretation begins.

**RESEARCH CHECKLIST**

## Maintaining Your Working Bibliography

- Have you made a source note for every book, part of a book, magazine article, and newspaper article you think will be useful for your topic?
- Have you recorded all the necessary information for each source? Is it in the same format that you will use to document your sources?
- Do you have sufficient sources to write a good research paper? If you have to discard some, will you still have enough?
- Are the sources up to date?
- Are the authors recognized experts in the field? Are the publications reliable?
- Is each source relevant to your research question?
- Have you made annotations to yourself about the probable usefulness of each source so that you can read the best ones first?
- Do you have both primary and secondary sources? Both books and articles? A range of opinions?

### TAKING NOTES

Now that you've developed a working bibliography, located some promising source material, and evaluated it to make sure it's reliable and useful, you're ready to begin taking notes. Your research notes are the tool you will use to transfer information from the original sources you find in the library to your research paper. In them, you should record every fact, idea, and quotation that you might eventually want to use. Make sure your notes are complete and accurate: if you sit down to draft your paper and find you've neglected to jot down that memorable phrase by the most authoritative expert in the field, you'll either have to trudge back to the library and look it up again (which is tedious) or write your paper without it (which can lead to a weaker paper). Remember, though, that your notes are where you start to analyze and synthesize your sources, turning them into the building blocks for your paper. If you copy down everything you read, exactly as it was written, you'll not only be wasting time, but you'll also be postponing the inevitable: if you want your paper to be a sound analysis or argument based on a variety of reliable sources (and not just a place to show off how many books you looked up), then sooner or later you're going to have to sit down and separate the useful nuggets in each source from all the rest. Your research notes are the best place to do that. A good research note includes three elements:

> An *identifier*, usually the last name of the author whose work you're citing, followed by the *page number or numbers* on which the information can be found. (You should already have a source note in your working bibliography for this source, with complete publication information. If not, make one now.)

> A *subject heading*, some key word or phrase you make up yourself to help you decide where in your paper the information will best fit.

> The *fact, idea, opinion, or quotation* you plan to use in your paper.

You'll need all these elements so that later, when it's time to incorporate your notes into your paper or develop your ideas from multiple sources, you'll have an accurate record of what you found in each source. You'll also know exactly where you found it, so you will be able to cite every source without difficulty. (For sample note cards, see Figures 28.12, 28.13, and 28.14. For an explanation of the type of information on each card, see pp. 687–90.)

What will you look for in the source? Facts, ideas, and opinions as well as examples and illustrations of the ideas you're pursuing along with evidence to support them — and to refute them. Avoid making the mistake of looking only for information that supports a preconceived notion. Research should be an opportunity to learn more about a topic, to answer an authentic question, not to collect evidence that tells you only what you want to know.

You've already looked over your source at least once to decide whether to take notes on it. Skim it again to be sure and to decide how extensively. Remember, though, that you can't always know the usefulness of a source in advance. Sometimes a likely article turns out to yield nothing much, and a book that seemed to be a juicy plum shrivels to a prune in your hands.

**Use a Sensible Format.**   Many writers find that using note cards or a word processing program works better than taking notes on sheets of notebook paper because when the time comes to organize the material you've gathered, you can shuffle and reshuffle cards or computerized notes to arrive at an order that makes most sense to you. If you use cards, roomy 4-by-6-inch or 5-by-8-inch cards will hold more than 3-by-5-inch cards. Even a meaty idea ought to fit on one card.

FIGURE 28.12   A sample note card giving a direct quotation from a source

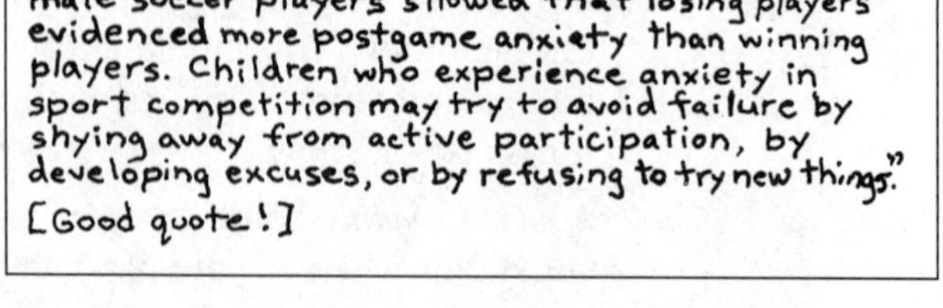

Children and sports                         Leonard 140
    "... [in organized sports] children may be subject to intense emotional stress caused by fear and anxiety, concern about physical safety, and doubts about performances and outcomes. This anxiety may emerge if children are ignored, chastised, or made to feel that they are no good. Scanlan and Passer's study of preadolescent male soccer players showed that losing players evidenced more postgame anxiety than winning players. Children who experience anxiety in sport competition may try to avoid failure by shying away from active participation, by developing excuses, or by refusing to try new things."
    [Good quote!]

PARAPHRASE IS ABOUT HALF THE LENGTH OF ORIGINAL PASSAGE.

NO INTERPRETING OR EVALUATION OF ORIGINAL PASSAGE IS INCLUDED.

Children and sports                    Leonard 140

Stress and anxiety on the playing field can result in children backing away from participating in sports because they fear rejection if they perform poorly. This anxiety and stress is a result of the child's fears of being hurt or not being good enough. A study by Scanlan and Passer showing that boys who lose in soccer have more anxiety after losing a game than boys who win confirm these findings.

ALTHOUGH EMPHASIS OF ORIGINAL IS MAINTAINED, WORDCHOICE AND ORDER HAVE BEEN REWORKED TO AVOID THE DANGER OF PLAGIARISM.

FIGURE 28.13   Paraphrasing the quotation from Leonard's book (Figure 28.12)

**Use One Card Per Idea.**   Putting two or more ideas on the same card will complicate your task when you reach the organizing and drafting stages. If you use a computer to take notes, separate your entries clearly so you can move them around easily later.

**Take Accurate Notes.**   Read the entire article or section of a book before beginning to take notes to help you avoid distorting the meaning. Put exact quotations in quotation marks, and take care not to quote something out of context or change the meaning. Double-check all statistics and lists.

**Take Thorough Notes.**   Many a writer has come to grief by setting down sketchy jottings and trusting memory to fill in the blanks. A good rule is to make your notes and citations full enough so that once they're written, you are totally independent of the source from which they came. That way you'll

**WRITING WITH A COMPUTER**

## Taking Notes on a Word Processor

Try taking notes on a word processor. For working in a library, nothing beats a laptop computer — if you are fortunate enough to have access to one. If you can't take a computer with you to the library, then try bringing a reasonable amount of materials to your computer. With your resources at hand, you can type in summaries or direct quotations, thus eliminating the need to recopy them later and lessening the chance of making mistakes. Don't fall into the trap of taking all notes as direct quotations: that will only postpone and fragment your thinking. Having a computer at hand as you are reading and collecting material should encourage you to compose your thoughts as they emerge and blend ideas as you go along.

SUBJECT HEADING

TERSE, EVEN
FRAGMENTARY, NOTES
CONVEY GIST OF
PASSAGE

> High school football                 Bissinger 44
>      experiences
>
> In the past, high school football players at
> Permian experienced (1) vomiting during
> practice; (2) playing games on broken
> ankles and hands; (3) shots of Novocain
> during halftime so that players with hip
> pointers and bad sprains could continue
> to play; (4) taking painkillers and
> Valium to continue playing.

IDENTIFIER: SOURCE AND
PAGE NUMBERS

MAIN POINTS CLEARLY
BROKEN OUT

FIGURE 28.14   Nutshelling, or summarizing, a paragraph

avoid having to rush back to the library in a panic trying to find again, in a book or periodical you returned weeks ago, some nugget of material you want to include in your paper.

**Photocopy Judiciously.**   Some research writers insist that the invention of photocopying has done away with the need to take notes. Indeed, judicious photocopying can save you time as you gather materials for your paper, but the key word here is *judicious*. Simply photocopying everything you read with the vague notion that some of it contains material valuable for your essay is likely in the end to waste money and to cost you more time rather than less. Much of the material won't be worth saving. Most important, you won't have digested and evaluated what was on the page; you will merely have copied it. Selecting what is essential, highlighting or transcribing it by hand, perhaps nutshelling or paraphrasing it (see pp. 688–90) helps make it yours. When you start drafting, digesting great bundles of photocopied material will take you much longer than working from carefully thought-out note cards.

If, however, you're using a source that doesn't circulate, such as a reference book always kept in the reference room, you may want to photocopy the relevant pages so that you can use them whenever and wherever it is convenient for you. If you are using an electronic source, you may prefer to get a hard copy of the material for easy reference. Just make sure that the name of the source and the page number appear on your copy so that you have the necessary information for a source note. If not, write the information on the photocopy. When you start organizing your notes, you may find it convenient to scissor out of a photocopied page what you're going to use and stick it onto a note card. Be sure to transfer the source information, too.

**Bristle While You Work.**   In reading the material you are collecting, looking at it a little sourly and suspiciously might be to your advantage because it helps you to remain critical. Mary-Claire van Leunen, author of *A Handbook for Scholars* (New York: Knopf, 1978), has advised researchers who must read much scholarly writing: "Do not smile sweetly as you read through pages of graceless, stilted, maundering bombast. Fume, fuss, be angry. Your anger will keep you up to the mark when you turn to writing yourself." This is also good advice for you as a student writer.

**Keep Evaluating.**    Decide whether the stuff is going to be greatly valuable, fairly valuable, or only a little bit valuable. Some note takers put a star at the top of any note they assign great value to, a question mark on a note that might or might not be useful. Later, when they're organizing their material, they can see what especially stands out and needs emphasis. Others write a notation to themselves at the bottom of the card.

**Know When to Stop.**    How many notes are enough? When you find that the sources you consult are mostly repeating what you've learned from previous sources — and aren't any more authoritative or credible — you have probably done enough reading and note taking.

## AVOIDING PLAGIARISM

You have an obligation to repay the researchers, scholars, and writers who came before you. That is why, in doing research, you cite your source materials so carefully, mentioning the names of all other writers you get information from. You do this not only for quotations you take but also for ideas, even though you have nutshelled or paraphrased them in your own words (see pp. 688–90). If a writer fails to acknowledge all sources or uses another writer's words without quotation marks, he or she has plagiarized, a very serious offense in the academic, business, and industrial communities. The writer is suspected of a rip-off, when he or she merely failed to make a debt clear. Chapter 31 offers information about how to cite and list sources so that, like any good scholar, you will know exactly how to pay your debts in full.

## QUOTING, PARAPHRASING, NUTSHELLING

When it comes time to draft your paper, you will incorporate your source material in a variety of ways: by quoting, transcribing the author's exact words; by paraphrasing, restating the author's ideas fully but in your own words; or by nutshelling, giving a brief summary of the author's main point. Your notes too, should be in these three forms — and the form you pick for any source should be your best guess as to the form you will use in the final paper.

There are two advantages to deciding whether to quote, paraphrase, or nutshell at the note-taking stage. First, it will save you time. A faithful transcription of a long quotation takes much longer than a quick nutshell, so if you know in advance that you intend to use only a nutshell, you might as well save yourself those extra minutes. Second, weighing each source carefully and deciding how to use it — even while you are in the midst of reading it — is part of reading critically. As we've tried to stress, research should be a dynamic process, with the researcher thinking critically about sources and their usefulness, not just taking the source material at face value and copying it word for word into the paper. You need to always be thinking about how you will use your sources — otherwise, they'll end up using you.

Of course, you won't always make the correct guess. Sometimes you will find, at the drafting stage, that the wonderful quotation that looked so persuasive back when you were taking notes is just run-of-the-mill rhetoric, and you may prefer to nutshell the author's significant ideas and use them as a single supporting point rather than as the focus of an entire paragraph. Still, it's almost always worth the effort to decide at the note-taking stage how you intend to use a particular source. How do you make the decision? Each method has advantages and disadvantages. Here are some things to consider.

**Quoting.**   Quoting needs to be done sparingly, and only when there is a good reason — to add support and authority to your assertions. Some writers of college research papers do much pointless quoting. Mary-Claire van Leunen in *A Handbook for Scholars* gives cogent advice:

> Quote only the quotable. Quote for color; quote for evidence. Otherwise, don't quote. When you are writing well, your sentences should join each other like rows of knitting, each sentence pulling up what went before it, each sentence supporting what comes after. Quotation introduces an alien pattern — someone else's diction, someone else's voice, someone else's links before and afterward. Even necessary quotations are difficult to knit smoothly into your structure.

That quotation, by the way, seems to us worth quoting. Its words are memorable, worth taking to heart.

If you intend to use a direct quotation, copy the quotation carefully onto a card, making sure to reproduce exactly the words, the spelling, the order, and the punctuation, even if they're unusual. Go back over what you've written to make sure that you've copied it correctly. *Put quotation marks around the material* so that when you come to include it in your paper, you'll remember that it's a direct quotation. You might also want to remind yourself in a bracketed note that you intend to use the author's words in a quotation. Maria Halloran extracted a lively quotation for the note card shown in Figure 28.12.

Sometimes it doesn't pay to transcribe a quotation word for word. Parts may fail to serve your purpose, such as transitions ("as the reader will recall from Chapter 14"), parenthetical remarks ("which slightly modifies the earlier view of Pflug"), and other information useless to you. If you take out one or more words, indicate the omission in your note by using an ellipsis mark (...).

**Paraphrasing.**   When paraphrasing, you restate an author's ideas in your own words. A good paraphrase retains the organization and emphasis of the original passage and often many of the details — so it isn't usually much shorter than the original. Why paraphrase? It is especially helpful when the language of another writer is not particularly vivid and memorable, but when you feel it necessary to walk your readers through the points made in the original source. (If you just want to convey the essence of the original passage, use nutshelling.) Remember, when you paraphrase you aren't judging or interpreting another writer's ideas — you are simply trying to restate them fairly and accurately. If Maria Halloran had chosen to paraphrase Bissinger, her note card might have looked like Figure 28.13.

When you paraphrase a passage, be careful not to hover so close to the author's own words that your paraphrase is merely an echo. If your source writes, "In staging an ancient Greek tragedy today, most directors do not mask the actors," and you write, "Most directors, in staging an ancient Greek play today, do not mask the actors," your version is too close to the original. Paraphrasing too close to the source is a form of plagiarism — you must express each thought in your own words. This would be a good paraphrase: "Few contemporary directors of Greek tragedy insist that their actors wear masks."

How do you write a good paraphrase? We suggest that you do the following.

1. Read the entire passage through a couple of times.
2. Either mentally or by marking the page lightly, divide the passage into its most important ideas or points. Three or four points for an average-length paragraph will make the task manageable.
3. Look away from the original source and restate the first idea in your own words.
4. After briefly reviewing the original passage, go on to the next idea and restate it in your own words. Continue in this way until you reach the end of the passage.
5. Go back and reread the entire original passage one more time, making sure you've conveyed its ideas faithfully. Revise your paraphrase if necessary.

Nutshelling.　　Sometimes even a paraphrase of another author's ideas will take more space than you want to spend on it or will cause more disruption to the flow of your own ideas than is necessary. Often it is sufficient to convey the main point of an original source "in a nutshell." Nutshelling, or summarizing, is a way to let your readers know the most important idea or ideas of a passage by restating those ideas in your own words. Obviously, this can save a lot of space — a page or more of detailed text can often be distilled into one or two succinct sentences. Be careful, though, that in reducing a long passage down to a brief nutshell you do not distort the original author's meaning or emphasis. Your goal should be to convey as faithfully as possible the meaning of the original. If Maria Halloran had put into nutshell form the essential ideas she wished to take from the paragraph in Bissinger's book, her note card might have looked like Figure 28.14.

How do you write a good nutshell? Try this approach.

1. Read the original passage a couple of times.
2. Without looking at it, state the gist of the passage, the point it makes, the main sense as you remember it.
3. Go back and reread the original passage one more time, making sure you've conveyed its ideas faithfully. Revise your nutshell if necessary.

## CONSIDERING OTHER SOURCES

Unless an assignment strictly confines you to library sources, which it might, no law forbids your using any promising nonlibrary materials in your research paper. To make a point, you can recall your own experiences, observations, conversations, or past reading. (For more information on using field research and integrating it into library research, see Chapter 29, "Conducting Field Research.") And why park your imagination outside the library? You might want to bring together sources not usually related. One fine research paper we have read, by a prelaw student, compared gambling laws in ancient Rome with gambling laws in present-day Atlantic City. Placing Rome and Atlantic City cheek to cheek took imagination.

**RESEARCH
CHECKLIST**

## Taking Notes

- Do you identify the source (by last name of author or an important word from the title) and the exact page for each research note? Does each note include a subject heading?
- Have you made a bibliography card or note for each new source you discovered during your reading?
- Does each note contain only one idea? Do you avoid lengthy notes?
- Do you retain the meaning of the original so that you are true to the source?
- Do you quote sparingly — only pithy, striking, short passages?
- When you quote, do you quote exactly? Do you use quotation marks around significant words or phrases as well as longer passages from the original sources? Do you use ellipsis marks as needed?
- Do you take most notes in your own words — summarizing or paraphrasing?
- Do you avoid paraphrasing too close to the source?

# Chapter 29

# Conducting Field Research

Finding material in a library is only one way to do research. If you enjoy meeting and talking with people and don't mind what news reporters call "legwork," you will relish the fun and satisfaction of obtaining ideas and information at first hand. Perhaps you will even investigate matters that few researchers have investigated before. Many rich, unprinted sources of ideas and information lie beyond library walls. This chapter will reveal a few of them. It will show you how to write a research paper not only by reading but also by observing, conversing with people, recalling, and imagining, or by combining several of these sources. In the future, researchers may be able to cite *you*.

The goal of field research is the same as that of library research: to gather the information you need to answer your research question and to marshall the evidence you need to present your conclusions persuasively in your research paper. The only difference is where you conduct the research. Far from being at odds with one another — either philosophically or practically — the two research techniques complement one another. In most cases, an assignment that calls for field research will also benefit from library research. You can use library research to collect background information before going out into the field. For example, before interviewing the manager of a recycling project in your community, you can use library research to find out how many tons of materials it processes annually, what the uses for recycled paper and plastic are, why recycling is a controversial issue in some areas, and so on. You can also use library research to follow up on a hunch you develop through field research. For example, if you're observing the playground behavior of seven-year-olds to learn more about how their games prepare them for the challenges of adulthood, you might start wondering if the concept of "sharing" is connected to a sense of morality. If you follow up this insight with a trip to the library, you'll find that there's quite a lot of professional literature on the subject.

Field research is often required in upper-level courses. For a term paper in the social sciences, business studies, or engineering, for example, you may be expected to interview people, gather statistics, or conduct a survey. But almost any paper will be enriched by the inclusion of authentic and persuasive field research sources. And you'll almost certainly learn more about your topic by going out into the field and developing firsthand knowledge of it.

Like library research, field research should be more than a squirreling-up of facts — or else you may end up with a great heap of rotting acorns and no nourishment. Field research (and kindly underline this sentence) has to be the sensitive, intelligent, and critical selection of *meaningful* ideas and information. As the chapter proceeds, we'll give you more specific suggestions for picking out what is meaningful from what isn't. Right now, it is sufficient to note that you can expect to change your initial hunches while at work in the field. Just as you do while conducting library research, you'll be exercising your critical thinking skills: sifting evidence, evaluating, drawing conclusions, revising and correcting your early thoughts, and forming clearer, more valid ideas. When you begin a project on identical twins, say, you might seek evidence not only in print sources but also through talking to twins to back up your hunch that identical twins are likely to enter the same line of work in later life. Perhaps, though, the evidence, based on interviews with several sets of twins, will refuse to march in the path you want it to follow. You might end up disproving your hunch and coming to a fresh realization: that some twins, perhaps, develop in independent directions.

## Learning from Another Writer: One Student's Experience

To show you how one student combined library research with field research, let us tell you the story of Linda Hackler. When conducting her research, Hackler tapped a variety of resources: library books and articles, personal observation, and interviews with knowledgeable people. In her final paper, she included information drawn from all these sources as support for her ideas.

When Bob Hooper, Hackler's English Composition II instructor, assigned the research project for the course, he suggested that students select a group of people they were interested in and research the answer to a question or problem related to that group. He urged them not to go into the project with preconceived ideas or to look only for evidence that would support their conclusions — instead, they should begin by being open-minded and should use the process of research itself to find the answers to their questions. Students were to present their conclusions in a persuasive paper that used both library and field research sources.

Professor Hooper reviewed with his class the five writer's resources that students were already familiar with from their work the preceding semester with Part One of this textbook: recall, observation, reading, conversation, and imagination. He pointed out that these resources were all still available to them and would aid them in their research projects, sometimes in new and more sophisticated ways. The class brainstormed together and found ways to use all these resources. *Recall* would be a good way to generate a research question — and would be a good resource to draw on for inspiration whenever they got stuck, as would *imagination*. The resource of *reading* was clearly necessary for any library research, but also for processing written sources of information gathered from field research, such as letters and questionnaires. The class's earlier practice with *observation* and *conversation* would give them a good foundation for the new field research techniques of site visits and interviews, respectively. Having armed his students with this arsenal of potential research techniques, Professor Hooper turned them loose with the additional advice that they pursue their research questions wherever they led them. "The point isn't to collect note cards," he said. "Your goal as a researcher is to find *answers* and *evidence*."

Because Hackler had grown up on an apple ranch in Oregon, she was familiar with Hispanic migrant workers. She was concerned because she thought they were the target of undue criticism from politicians and the media. She wondered if this criticism was unwarranted. In recalling her own observations, she found few similarities between the migrant workers she knew and the images of the workers portrayed in the media. Hackler believed that the Hispanic migrant workers were receiving the blame for something they did not do. She asked herself the question "Do Hispanics who come to the United States actually take jobs from Americans?"

Hackler realized that personal perceptions can be colored by an individual's limited experience and by preconceptions, so she went to the library to find out what objective experts had to say on the issue. There she found an article by Frank D. Bean and Rodolfo O. de la Garza that refuted the prevalent belief that illegal Hispanics are taking jobs that would otherwise go to non-Hispanic U.S. citizens. Their study supported her personal experience, so she looked further.

Hackler found other articles and books on myths about migrants, such as one that refuted the claim that they are lazy and poor workers. Hackler's research made her reflect on the hard workers she had known as she was growing up. She thought, "I was raised on an apple ranch in northeastern Oregon, where as a child and teenager I was expected to help with every phase of fruit production. In doing so, I was exposed to many migrant workers and their families, and I know firsthand the hard work required for them to earn a living." She decided to see if a fruit rancher with whom she was acquainted agreed with what she remembered and what she had found in her reading. Hackler arranged an interview and was pleased to discover that his position reinforced the research she had already done and that she could use what he said to strengthen her position in her research paper.

She continued her reading and arranged one other interview, this one with a Head Start teacher, Arla Kendall, who worked with migrant children and knew firsthand of their plight of poverty and underdevelopment. Kendall told Hackler that migrant workers have little education but that "they are the hardest workers and are very proud. They just need a chance."

From the notes that Hackler took from her own recall and observations, interviews, and reading, she now had the raw material for her paper. She just had to select the most convincing material and organize it so that her position would be persuasive to her readers. In this chapter, we'll show you some of the experiences Hackler had as she researched her paper. In Chapter 30, we'll show how she worked with the sources she collected to draft her paper, and finally we'll show you her completed paper. You can see how she integrated both field and library sources and used logic and imagination to reach the conclusion that it is a myth that Hispanic migrant workers threaten to take jobs from Americans and that their use of social services costs the U.S. taxpayers.

# Learning by Writing

## THE ASSIGNMENT: RESEARCHING A SUBCULTURE

Here is a typical *general* writing assignment for a field research paper, one that leaves up to you the task of finding a specific topic and developing a research question. Try to find a topic that, because you care about it, will elicit your desire to learn more and to write about what you have learned.

Consider some group of people in our society about whose lives and activities you would like deeper knowledge, similar to the Hispanic migrant workers that Linda Hackler chose to write about. The group you choose should be one whose members you would be able to engage in conversation — the homeless, amateur rock musicians, members of the Society of Friends, aspiring painters, women construction workers, model railroad buffs, hospital patients, people who live in a city that has casino gambling, or any other group of people that for any reason keenly interests you.

Find out more about the group by observing, by conversing with people, and by seeking other firsthand information — information that's not found in books but that you discover for yourself. You may want to begin your research with no particular goal in mind other than to learn more about the group. At some point, though, something you discover should spark a keener interest in one particular topic. You'll need to develop a research question about this topic that can serve as the beacon for your further research and for writing your paper. If you're having trouble finding a research question, sift through your initial impressions, looking for puzzles or problems that intrigue you. Is there some aspect of the behavior of this group or the individuals in it that's puzzling to you? Do you wonder about how the group got to be the way it is? how it might change in the coming months or years? Anything that you find interesting enough to research further — and that you have the resources to research satisfactorily — is a candidate for a good research question. (See p. 657 for more on the qualities of a good research question.)

In your continuing research — in which you will draw on both field and library sources — try to find an answer to your question, even if it's only tentative. Finally, present your findings and conclusions in a paper, supporting the points you make with evidence from your field and library sources. You will not need all the data you have gathered: focus and be selective. Write for an audience of your instructor and classmates, but to keep your paper fair and accurate, write it so that it might also be read by members of the group you have observed.

Among successful papers we have seen written from this assignment are the following.

> Using her own observations, a questionnaire she had devised, and a series of interviews, a woman set out to test the validity of an idea she had read: that the tradition of the family dinner was fast disappearing from middle-class life. She wrote this paper for a freshman English course centering on the theme "The Way We Live Now."

> A man studying child development, after observing two- and three-year-olds at a day-care center and keeping a log of his observations for three weeks, wrote about the ways the two groups of children differed from each other.

> In a sociology course, in an effort to find out what forces had driven homeless people to the streets and what was being done for them, a woman sought out and interviewed people in the helping professions who worked with street people in her city and also talked with some of the homeless people themselves.

> A man conducted a survey among his classmates to learn their reasons for choosing the college they attended. He sorted out their answers, emerging with a varied list and increased respect for his college's reputation.

## Generating Ideas

### CHOOSING YOUR TERRITORY AND DEVELOPING A QUESTION

Before you set out on your field research, you first have to decide on a subject you want to investigate — the later lives of identical twins, say, or airline pilots. Start by thinking about and casually looking into a group that appeals to you, and decide whether to persist in further investigation, as Linda Hackler did. Those trusty resources for writers discussed in Part One may prove their usefulness now. You might observe your subject in action and recall what you already know about it. You might talk with anyone familiar with it, do some reading about it in a library, and imagine yourself doing field research into it. The more you look into a subject, the more it is likely to interest you. Taking an overview of your subject area will enable you to start focusing in on a more specific area of interest, leading you to find a narrow topic — one that you want to learn more about and write about. (For more on taking an overview, see p. 656.)

**DISCOVERY CHECKLIST**

## Finding a Topic

- Is there a career you are considering but don't know much about? Talk to some people working in this field.
- Is there a local group you have become curious about through recent news reports (perhaps a group of immigrants or a religious group or a hobby club)?
- Is there a group of students (a club, an ethnic group, some athletes) on campus you'd like to know more about?
- Is there a nursing home nearby? A day-care center?
- Have you ever wondered why some people are so intense about an activity (fishing, poetry, exercise)?

Once you feel sure of your direction, state a research question — exactly what are you trying to find out? (How to word such a question is discussed on p. 657.) The research question is the central question to ask yourself and to keep living with: Do identical twins go into the same line of work when they become adults? Does an identical twin resent or relish having someone so much like himself or herself?

The following questions are other, smaller ones to help you confirm the direction for your research.

**DISCOVERY CHECKLIST**

## Weighing Possibilities

- What helpful background material on your topic did you find in the library?
- Where will you find more ideas and information about this subject? Whom might you consult for suggestions?
- What places should you visit?
- Whom should you talk with?
- How much time and effort is this investigation likely to take? Is your project reasonable?

You may not be able to answer the last question accurately until you start investigating, but make a rough guess. Set yourself a schedule, with deadlines for completing your research, for drafting, and for revising. For any project in which you interview people, an excellent rule of thumb is to allow fifty percent more time than you might reasonably think necessary. People may be out when you call or you may find that one interview doesn't supply all you need and that you'll have to do a follow-up. For a college paper, a field research project has to be humanly possible. Plan your work so that you will have everything completed satisfactorily — including drafting and revising the final paper — before the date the paper is due. If you begin with the intention of interviewing all the identical twins in your county, you might take a look at your deadline (and your course load) and then decide to limit your research to a sampling of, say, twenty individuals. Robert A. Day, author of *How to Write and Publish a Scientific Paper*, 4th ed. (Philadelphia: Oryx, 1994), offers this sound advice: "Don't start vast projects with half-vast ideas." Don't start half-vast projects, either.

### READING FOR BACKGROUND

Linda Hackler didn't plunge blindly into field research. Her thinking and reading gave her leads to follow up. Books such as Douglas Kent Hall's *The Border: Life on the Line* (New York: Abbeville Press, 1988) helped fill her in on the living conditions of Hispanic migrant workers. She also found a helpful article in *Harper's* on why Mexicans come to the United States. A useful question before you start to do field research is What helpful background material on your topic can you find first of all in your library? To be able to make the best of your limited time in the field, conducting interviews or making observations, you will want to gather enough background information to know what the relevant issues are. Read specific supplementary material that you think will be useful when you later go out into the field.

As you conduct your background research, take notes, recording source information carefully (see p. 683). Remember also that the library may continue to be a useful source to you during or after field research. You may need to return to confirm information that you gathered in the field, find additional sources presenting an opposing viewpoint or further substantiating your findings, or research an entirely new area that grew out of your field research.

## Using Field Research Techniques

### DIRECTING AN INTERVIEW

People in all walks of life are often willing, sometimes even eager, to talk to a college student writing a research paper. Many, you may find, will seem flattered by your attention. Interviews — conversations with a purpose — may prove to be your main source of material. Choose your interview subjects carefully. Whenever possible, try to arrange an interview with an expert in the field you are researching. Or if you are researching a particular group of people, interview a typical member of the group, someone who may or may not have any special knowledge of the field but is representative of the group. Linda Hackler chose to interview a fruit rancher who didn't have any special knowledge of the plight of migrant workers beyond his involvement with them, but she wanted to elicit the view of a typical employer of migrants.

Chapter 4, "Writing from Conversation," offers advice that may come in handy here:

1. Make sure your prospect is willing to be quoted in writing.
2. Plan an appointment for a day when the person will have enough time — if possible, an hour — to have a thorough talk with you.
3. Appear promptly, with carefully thought-out questions to ask.
4. Really listen. Let the person open up.
5. Be flexible and allow the interview to go in unanticipated directions.
6. If a question draws no response, don't persist and make a nuisance of yourself; just go on to the next question.
7. Make additional notes right after the interview to preserve anything you didn't have time to record during the interview.

Linda Hackler followed these guidelines in arranging her interviews. Despite the fruit rancher's initial reluctance to talk to her, after she assured him that she would use what he said anonymously she collected some exciting material from him. Her interviews with him and the Head Start teacher took forty-five minutes to an hour. Both of the people Hackler interviewed allowed her to tape-record the conversations, but some people will agree to be interviewed only on the condition that their voices not be recorded. If you want to use a tape recorder, remember to ask permission of the interviewee.

In an interview, be sure to take notes so that later when you reconstruct events in your paper, your memory of the interview will be accurate. Even if you use a tape recorder, you should take notes. This will allow you to distill the most important information as you interview. In addition to recording important points and quotations, you should record any telling details that might prove useful later — the interviewee's appearance, the setting, the mood, any notable gestures. All of these details will be useful as you work with your sources to write the paper.

For ease of note taking, we suggest you use a small journalistic notebook with a spiral at the top. Because you will be conducting an interview at the same time you're taking notes, use abbreviations as you take notes. At the end of the interview be sure to *confirm all direct quotations*.

For her own guidance, Hackler first made herself a list of questions she wanted to ask the fruit rancher and the Head Start teacher. She asked questions to reveal details from their experiences with and observations of the migrants. Hackler was careful to phrase her questions so that they would not elicit biased responses.

What is your relationship to Hispanic migrant workers? What is the extent of your experience with them?

What is your opinion of migrants? What kind of workers are they?

Why do they come to the United States?

Do you think most people view migrants as you do?

Should anything be done to help migrants?

Is there anything else you would like to add?

If you can't talk to an expert in person, your next best resource may be a telephone interview. Make a phone appointment for a time convenient for both you and your interviewee. A busy person whom you call during a working day may not be able to give you a half hour of conversation on the spur of a moment, and it is polite to ask for a time when you may call again. You will waste the person's time (and yours) if you try to wing your interview; have written questions in hand before you dial. Take notes.

Federal regulations, by the way, forbid recording an interview over the phone without notifying the person who is talking that you are recording his or her remarks and without using a recorder connector with a warning device that emits a beep signal every fifteen seconds.

## PREPARING A QUESTIONNAIRE

Questionnaires, as you know, are part of contemporary life. You probably filled one out the last time you applied for a job or for college. Many people, in our experience, enjoy having their knowledge tapped or their opinion solicited. Indeed, filling out a questionnaire has a gamelike appeal, as you can tell from the frequency with which self-quiz features appear in popular magazines and tabloid newspapers: "How Rigid Are You?" followed by a thirty-question quiz to score yourself. You may have responded to one in *People* or *Glamour* magazine.

As a rule, when researching a particular question, professional pollsters, opinion testers, and survey takers survey thousands of individuals, chosen to represent a certain segment of society or perhaps a broad range of the populace (diversified in geography, income, ethnic background, and education). Their purpose may be to inform manufacturers who are test-marketing new products or trying to identify a new market. It may be to help a politician in planning a campaign. Questionnaires are widely used because they deliver large stores of useful information quickly and efficiently.

None of the surveys you conduct for this course is going to be this extensive or thorough, and you should generally avoid deriving statistics from your questionnaire responses and generalizing about these figures as if they were unimpeachable "facts." It's one thing to say that "many of the students" who filled out a questionnaire on reading habits hadn't read a newspaper in the past month; it's another to claim that this is true of seventy-two percent of the student population at your school — especially when you gave questionnaires to only the twenty-two percent who attended the dining hall the day you were there and when half of *those* people just threw their questionnaires in the trash bins. A far more useful and reliable way for you to use questionnaires is to treat them as group interviews: assume that the information you collect from them is representative, use them to build your overall knowledge of the subject, and cull them for interesting or persuasive details or quotations. Use a questionnaire when you want to collect the same type of information from a large number of people, when you're more interested in what a group thinks as a whole than in what a particular individual has to say, or when an interview that would cover all the questions you're interested in is impossible or impractical.

Linda Hackler could have gathered more information for her research paper by surveying migrant workers. However, she did not have time to conduct such a survey before her research paper was due. Figure 29.1 shows what her questionnaire might have looked like. The questions call for short answers, easy to supply. This questionnaire asks for information revealing the migrant's personal history, family circumstances and background, income, edu-

FIGURE 29.1   Linda Hackler's questionnaire to Hispanic migrant workers

```
                        Questionnaire

   Interview number ____
   Age: ____
   Marital Status: Single ____   Married ____
                   Divorced ____   Widowed ____
   Number of dependents: ____
   Father's occupation: ____
   Mother's occupation: ____
   How old were you when you became a migrant
     farmworker? ____
   How long have you been a migrant farmworker? ____
   How many days a week do you do farmwork? ____
   How many hours a day do you work? ____
   How many months out of the year do you follow the crops? ____
   Do you hold another job? ____
   Have you ever done any other type of work? ____
   What is your weekly income? ____
   Where were you born? ____
   How long have you been in the United States? ____
   How much education have you had? ____
   What do you like to do when you are not working? ____
   What is your attitude toward your work? ____
   Why do you continue to do this type of work? ____
   What are your plans and hopes for your children? ____
   Do you want to return to your homeland? ____
```

cation, and attitudes toward family and work. To maintain the anonymity of the workers, Hackler would have given each questionnaire a number and not have asked for the respondent's name.

**Know Your Purpose.**    If you think you want to use a survey to gather information for your paper, ask yourself: What am I trying to discover with this questionnaire? Linda Hackler's questionnaire would deliver good results because it addresses the questions its author wanted answered and it is directed to the people able to answer them.

You will want to define the purpose of your questionnaire and then thoughtfully invent questions to fulfill it. If, for instance, you want to know how effective a day-care center is in the eyes of working mothers who entrust their children to it, you might ask questions like these: "Do your children report that they are happy there?" "Have you ever had reason to complain? If so, about what?"

**Keep It Simple.**    Any questionnaire you design has to be one that people are willing to answer. The main point to remember in writing a questionnaire is to make it easy and inviting to fill out. If you make it too complex and time-consuming, the recipient will throw it away. Ask questions that call for a check mark in a list of alternative answers, a simple yes or no, or one word or a few words. Ask yourself as you write each question what information you want to acquire with the question. Then read it over to be sure that it is not ambiguous and will elicit the response you are looking for. It's a good idea to ask for just one piece of information per question.

**Ask Open Questions When Appropriate.**    In addition to simple yes/no questions and multiple-choice questions, you might find it worthwhile to add to your questionnaire some "open questions," questions that call for short written responses. Although responses to these questions will be difficult to tally and you are likely to get a smaller number responding, the answers might supply you with something worth quoting or might suggest ideas for you to consider when you mull over the findings.

**Avoid Slanted Questions.**    Write unbiased questions that will solicit factual responses. Do not ask, "How religious are you?" Instead ask, "What is your religious affiliation?" and "How often do you attend religious services?" From the responses to the latter two questions, you could report actual numbers and draw logical inferences about the respondents.

**Make It Easy for People to Respond.**    Whenever possible, distribute your questionnaire to your interviewees at the end of your discussion. If not, assemble a group of people (at, say, an evening coffee for parents of children in a day-care center) and have them fill out your questionnaire on the spot. Facing the group, you can explain the purpose of your research, and to enlist their confidence you can invite questions and answer them. If you must mail your questionnaire to people, include a concise letter or note explaining what you are trying to do and what use you will make of the replies. You might say, "This questionnaire should take no more than ten minutes of your time to complete" or give some such estimate that will make the task look reasonable. To make it easy for the respondents, provide each with a stamped, self-addressed envelope. Some professional questioners offer a morsel of bait: a small check or a coupon good for a free jar of pickles. You might promise a copy of your finished paper or article, a brief report of the results, or a listing of each respondent's name in an acknowledgment.

Even with such enticements, professional poll takers and opinion testers find an acceptable response rate of fifty percent or higher difficult to achieve. That is why they often conduct surveys by telephone, with the phone caller filling in the questionnaire for the respondent. You might also use this technique, but better results will come if you distribute your questionnaire in person.

Tally Your Responses.    When you get back all your questionnaires, sit down and tally the results. It is easy enough to count short answers ("Republican," "Democrat"), but longer answers to open questions ("What is your goal in life?") will need to be summed up in paraphrase and then sorted into rough categories ("To grow rich," "To serve humanity," "To travel," "To save my soul"). By this means, you can count similar replies and accurately measure the extent of a pattern of responses.

## MAKING A FIELD TRIP

A visit to observe at first hand may well be essential in field research. In conducting her field research on Hispanic migrant workers, Linda Hackler visited a fruit farm, where she observed the migrant workers in action. In her paper, her observations confirmed the information that she gathered through inter-

**WRITING WITH A COMPUTER**

## Database and Spreadsheet Programs

Database and spreadsheet software can help you keep track of short responses to questionnaires and can perform statistical calculations. These programs are extremely powerful and time-saving tools that have become as nearly commonplace as word processors; in fact, the latest versions of many word processors have integrated database functions. They can save you hours of tallying with pencil and paper and assist in the creation of organized, attractive tables. But be aware that they also might require an investment of an hour or more to familiarize yourself with how they work. If you foresee number crunching as part of your professional future (and this task is a part of more jobs than you might think), you will be doing yourself a favor by spending the time needed to learn these applications now.

views: that migrant workers are dependable and hardworking. Her firsthand observations supplied authentic details from which her writing profited.

In making an observational visit, you may care to recall the suggestions we give in Chapter 2. You will need to make an appointment. As soon as you arrive, identify yourself and your business. Some receptionists will insist on identification. You might ask your instructor for a statement on college letterhead declaring that you are a bona fide student doing field research. Follow-up field trips may be necessary if, while you are writing, you find gaps in your research or if new ideas occur that you'll need to test by further observation.

You will want to take notes while conducting an observational visit, lest you forget any important details when it comes time to incorporate your ideas into your paper. In addition to jotting down any interesting facts you learn, record any telling details or sensory impressions.

You may also want to consider using a still camera or a videocamera. Even if you are only an amateur photographer, taking pictures in the field may greatly advance your research. Some photographs may serve as illustrations to include in your paper; others may help you remember details while you write. One student of architecture, making a survey of the best-designed buildings in her city, carried a 35mm camera and photographed each building she intended to describe. A student of sociology, looking into methods used to manage large crowds, found it effective to carry a videocamera to a football game. Later, watching a few crowd scenes in slow motion, he felt better able to write lively and accurate accounts of how police and stadium guards performed their jobs.

## INQUIRING BY LETTER

Is there a person whose knowledge or opinions you need but who lives too far away to interview? Write him or her a letter. Make it short and polite, send your questionnaire or ask a few pointed questions, and enclose a stamped, self-addressed envelope for a reply.

Large corporations, organizations such as the Red Cross and the National Wildlife Federation, branches of the military and the federal government, and elected officials are accustomed to getting such mail. In fact, many of them employ public relations officers whose duty is to answer you. Sometimes they will unexpectedly supply you with a bonus: free brochures, press releases, or other material that they think might interest you.

## USING TELEVISION AND RADIO PROGRAMS, FILMS, AND RECORDINGS

Intriguing possibilities for writing lie in the media. For a research paper about television, radio, movies, or contemporary theater or music, you may find yourself doing field research as original as if you went out and interviewed eighteen migrant workers. Because your material lies close at hand — in the case of television, it may be yours at the click of a remote control — our only advice to you is to get plenty of it. Watch (or listen to) a large amount of it and draw conclusions. Buy a stack of videotapes and use your VCR to keep track of what you discover and to review the information later.

Successful papers based on such research are legion. One student wrote a research paper on public service announcements, free airtime devoted to good causes (like accident prevention and saving whales), which all television channels are required by law to make available. Using her VCR, she recorded many such announcements and reviewed them several times. She classified the different causes being promoted and their different pitches or appeals, and she found unanticipated correlations between the causes given airtime and the presumed interests of a station's advertisers. Another student compared the news coverage of an election by three major networks and the Public Broadcasting System. She first videotaped a dozen televised newscasts and then made audio recordings of a dozen radio newscasts. Her main finding was that the networks seemed determined to cast the election into a more dramatic form — similar to a prizefight or a football game — than public broadcasting did, even though the outcome became clear very early.

For easy reference, the transcript or a tape of a broadcast or telecast may be available on request (or for a small charge) from a station or network; if the end credits do not proclaim that it is available, you can write or call to inquire.

## ATTENDING LECTURES AND CONFERENCES

Professionals in virtually every walk of life — and also special-interest groups — sometimes convene for a regional or national conference. Such conferences bring together doctors, lawyers, engineers, scientists, librarians, teachers, and assorted people bound together by some mutual concern. These meetings can be fertile sources of fresh ideas.

Often such conferences are open and free to students and the public, but to gain admission to others you might have to register and pay a fee. This drawback might discourage a casual researcher, but if your grade depends on material to be discussed at the conference or if you are thinking of a possible career in that profession, you might find it worthwhile to pay the fee. To attend a professional conference and to meet and talk with speakers and fellow attendees can be an excellent way to learn the language of a discipline. If you plan to be an ornithologist, start thinking and talking and writing like an ornithologist. Learn the vocabulary, the habits of mind. To steep yourself in the language of a specialized conference is one way to begin. You can take notes on the lectures, which are usually given by experts in the field, and thus get some firsthand live opinions. You may even be able to ask questions from the audience or corner a speaker or two later for informal talk. You might also want to record information about who attended the lecture or conference, the reaction of the audience, or any other background details that may prove useful in writing your paper.

In addition, you might obtain a copy of the proceedings of the conference — usually a set of all the lectures delivered, sometimes with accompanying commentary. Unfortunately, many proceedings are published months or even years after a conference (but looking in the library for proceedings of past conferences is another useful research technique).

College organizations frequently bring interesting speakers to campus — the science club might sponsor a nationally known marine biologist or the film club might bring in the producer of a successful television program. Check the schedules of events listed on bulletin boards and in your campus newspaper.

# Working with Sources

You'll need to scrutinize your field research sources just as carefully as you do your library sources. The trouble is, you can't really preview a field source to gauge its reliability and usefulness the same way you can a library source. What you *can* do is select sources that are likely to yield good information, work to stay on track while collecting information, and think critically about the information you've collected once you're back from the field. Just to remind yourself of the relevant issues, you may want to review the section "Working with Sources" in Chapter 28 (p. 679). What follows are a few more things to consider in the case of field research.

Be open to opposing viewpoints when you conduct field research. You may even want to seek them out, just to keep yourself honest. It's very easy to get caught up in the propaganda of a particular cause or viewpoint. Stop to consider the other side of the issue, and take the time to seek out sources that might tell you a completely different story from the one you've just been told. Also be open to unexpected angles. The wonderful thing about field research is that it's so rich — and so unpredictable. If you do it right, you usually won't know what's out there until you go and see. At the same time, try to stay focused on your research question. Unless you're willing to shift the course of your investigation, don't waste time pursuing little rivulets of information that, as enticing as they are, simply won't help you navigate the writing of your final paper.

Often, the first opportunity you have to consider whether a field source is credible, accurate, and useful is while you're in the process of collecting the information. The advantage is that you get the chance to judge for yourself whether an interviewee seems reliable and competent, whether the plant tour you've taken is really telling the whole story. The disadvantage is that you'll often find yourself wanting to go back to a source for further clarification. Sometimes this is impossible, as with questionnaires distributed on campus or filled out over the phone. But there's nothing wrong with asking for another interview or revisiting a site.

Once you've got your notes, you need to subject the information to the same scrutiny you would any piece of evidence. At this point, you may find it helpful to look back over the section "Testing Evidence" in the introduction to Part Two of "A Writer's Guide" (p. 118).

**DISCOVERY CHECKLIST**

## Evaluating Evidence

- Does your source seem biased or prejudiced? If so, is this bias or prejudice so strong that you have to discount some of the information?
- Have you compared different people's opinions or accounts? In general, the more viewpoints, the better.
- Does the information from your source agree with published accounts — in books, magazines, and newspapers? If not, can you think of a good reason why this would be so?
- Is any of your evidence hearsay, one person telling you the thoughts of another or telling you about comments or actions that he or she hasn't witnessed? If so, can you support or discount your source's view by comparing it with other evidence?
- If an interviewee or questionnaire respondent has told you about past events, has time possibly distorted his or her memory?
- If you have tried to question a random sampling of people, do you feel that they are truly representative? If you have tried to question everyone in a group, have you been thorough enough?

# Chapter 30

# Writing from Sources

## Planning, Drafting, and Developing

You began gathering material from library and field research sources with a question in mind. By now, if your research has been thorough and fruitful, you know the answer. The moment has come to weave together the material you have gathered. We can vouch for two time-proven methods.

**The Thesis Method.** Decide what your research has led you to believe. What does it all mean? Sum up that view in a sentence. That sentence is your thesis, the one main idea your paper will demonstrate. (For more advice on composing such a sentence, see p. 352.) You can then start planning and drafting, including only material that supports your thesis, concentrating from beginning to end on making that thesis clear.

**The Answer Method.** Some writers have an easier time if they plunge in and start writing without first trying to state any thesis at all. If you care to try this method, recall your original question and start writing with the purpose of answering it, lining up evidence as you go. You may discover what you want to say as you write. (Note that this method usually requires much revising. See p. 405.)

### EVALUATING YOUR MATERIAL

As you glance over the information you have collected, you must again analyze it critically. Do you have *enough* material to answer your research question? If not, you may need to get more. How much is enough? There's no hard-and-fast rule. But the larger the generalization you make from your investigation, the more supporting evidence you will need in support. Clearly, you cannot decide that all day-care centers in the state of Washington are safe, well-managed facilities if you have visited only five of them in Seattle. In a research project bounded by the limited time of a college course, you may need to trim your generalization: "The day-care centers *I visited in Seattle* impressed me by their safety and professional management" [emphasis ours].

About now, you will probably wish to sift through all the evidence you have collected. If you've been taking notes on cards, you can sort the cards into piles according to subject. If you've taken notes in a word processing program, you can group the notes right on the screen. The task of classifying your notes will be easy if you have used accurate, precise subject headings on each note. (See p. 683.) If you do not already have such headings, write one now on each card. But thinking will be the hardest part of sorting: you'll need to reread each note and reflect on it, imagining it as a piece of your finished paper.

In addition to sorting by subject, you may find it helpful to further categorize your notes according to their usefulness: * for excellent, essential material; OK for good but less important material; and X for irrelevant material. (But at this time don't discard any note because you may find a use for it when you start writing.)

How can you decide what is essential? *A useful note will plainly help answer your research question.* If that question was "How far advanced is Russian computer technology?" then a comment by a Norwegian engineer who was permitted to use a large computer at the Russian Academy of Sciences and who evaluated its performance would obviously be very valuable. Of lesser import might be an American tourist's recollection of seeing a large computer in Moscow being unloaded from a truck. Yet if for any reason the latter note seemed memorable, you should hang on to it, at least until writing a draft.

You aren't trying to impose your will on your material so that it proves only what you want to prove. Still, the rough rule we can offer for evaluating your material is this: *Does this note help you say what you now — after research and reflection — want to say?*

## MOVING FROM NOTES TO OUTLINE TO DRAFT

Source notes are only the raw material for the research material. If they are to end up in a readable, unified whole, they need to be put into the proper setting and to be carefully shaped and polished. Good, thoughtful notes can sometimes be copied verbatim from note card to first draft. But usually they will take rewriting to fit them in so they don't stand out like boulders in the stream of your prose. Moving from the nuggets of information in your notes to a smooth, persuasive analysis or argument is the most challenging part of the research process — and ironically the part on which we can give the least concrete advice. Every writer's habits of mind are different. Nonetheless, you'll probably find yourself cycling again and again through four basic activities: interpreting your sources, refining your thesis, organizing your ideas, and putting thoughts into the form of a draft. In the end, much of the verbiage in your notes probably won't need to go into your paper. Don't feel that your careful note taking was wasted effort though — your sifted notes are the by-products of a process that has carried you to the point where you know what you want to say and are able to say it effectively.

**Interpreting Your Sources.**    On their own, your source notes are only pieces of information. They need your careful analysis and interpretation to transform them into effective evidence. For her paper on America's obsession with sports, Maria Halloran may have found a reputable statistic indicating that seventy-four percent of the boys in a certain community play Little League baseball. But what does that number *mean?* Is it surprisingly high? Compared with what? And if it is high, does this fact mean that the town is "sports crazy"? Or does it mean that the promoters have done a good job selling their program? As a researcher and writer, you have to think critically about each fact and decide what it means in the context of your paper. Then you have to make sure that the fact itself is strong enough to bear the weight of the claim you're going to base on it. You may find that you need supplemental evidence to shore up an interesting but possibly ambiguous fact. Halloran, for instance, would have needed statistics on the enrollment in comparable activities in the same community to claim that the Little League enrollment was surprisingly high.

You'll also need to synthesize your sources and evidence, to weave them into a unified whole. If you've been guided throughout your research by a research question or a working thesis, you may find this synthesis fairly easy. You know what the question is; you know what the general answer is; you just need to let the pieces fall into place. Remember too that research questions and working theses change, often because during the research process the researcher unearths persuasive or interesting information that is somewhat at

**WRITING WITH A COMPUTER**

## Outlining on a Word Processor

Because of their ability to store, copy, and move information quickly and easily, word processors are well suited to the complex and recursive task of drafting a research paper. To help organize your ideas, you can write an outline in your word processor. By cutting and pasting parts of the outline, you can experiment with different organizations to find the one that's the clearest and most effective. The word processor also allows you to cut and paste chunks of material between documents. If you've taken notes on a computer (or if you've transcribed your best material) you can start to flesh out your paper by moving each piece of source information into the appropriate place in your outline. After doing this, you may realize that you don't have enough evidence to support certain claims, or you may decide to shift things around a bit so that your strongest evidence is in the most prominent position.

odds with the original direction of the research. In either case, it's important to stop a minute and ask yourself: Taken as a whole, what does all this information mean? What does it really tell me about my topic? What's the most important thing I've learned? What's the most important thing I can tell my readers?

Refining Your Thesis.    A thesis is a clear, precise statement of the point you want to make in your paper. It will help you, as a writer, decide what to say and how to say it. If your thesis is clear to your readers, it will help them interpret the information you present by letting them know in advance the scope of your paper and your general message. Most college papers — especially long, complex papers based on research and analysis — benefit greatly from having a clear thesis presented at the beginning.

Remember that explicitly stating your thesis, right out in the open, as the first or last sentence in your opening paragraph is only one option. Sometimes it is possible to craft your opening paragraph so that your readers know exactly what your thesis is even though you only imply it. Maria Halloran decided to include an explicit thesis statement in the opening paragraph of her paper "American's Obsession with Sports": "The national obsession with sports must end" (see p. 729). But her opening paragraph would also have been effective if she had omitted the thesis statement and ended with the question "Have we as a country gone so overboard on sports that we have learned to take casually whatever comes with this sports obsession, including violence?" Her readers would still have known her answer — her thesis. (Check with your instructor if you're unsure whether an implicit thesis statement will be acceptable.)

If you've been using a working thesis to guide your research, you should take the time to sharpen and refine it now before you start drafting. You may need to change it still further when you encounter unexpected twists in the process of writing, but a clear thesis will help guide you in organizing and expressing your ideas. If you haven't developed a thesis yet, now is the time to write one.

In your thesis, try to be precise and concrete, and don't claim more than you can demonstrate in your paper. If your paper is argumentative — that is, if you take a stand, propose a solution, or evaluate something — then you should make clear what your stand, solution, or appraisal is.

| TOPIC | Americans' attitudes toward sports |
|---|---|
| RESEARCH QUESTION | Is America obsessed with sports? |
| THESIS | The national obsession with sports must end. |

Organizing Your Ideas.    In organizing your research information, remember that, as is true of most other kinds of writing, some intuition is called for. It is not enough to relate the steps you took in answering your research question or to string the data together in chronological order. You aren't writing a memoir; you're reporting the significance of what you found out. Try putting your material together in various combinations until you arrive at an organization that seems engaging and clear. If you have trouble, review the patterns of organization in Part Two, "Thinking Critically," and in Chapter 16, "Strategies for Planning."

If your material seems not to want to shape up, you may find it helpful to plan the order of the ideas by writing an outline (see p. 358). You might arrange all your note cards in an order that makes sense. Then the stack of cards becomes your plan and as you write, turning over card after card, you follow it. Or you can make an informal outline on paper (see p. 358) or on the computer (p. 357). For such a complex writing task, you will probably find writing an outline helpful. That's what Maria Halloran did first.

Halloran made a rough preliminary listing of the points she planned to cover.

Introduction
American obsession with sports
Causes of the obsession
Arguments for sports
Arguments against sports
Conclusion

This early outline was general and tentative. Halloran flushed out her plan with specific information and even changed her plan as she drafted her ideas, but just preparing her rough outline proved stimulating: it made thoughts start to flow. She knew she wanted something gripping to start the essay off, and she needed specific examples of American sports mania. As she studied her preliminary outline, she realized that she needed to include arguments in favor of sports so that her paper would not be one-sided and to refute the ideas opposed to her own. Later she decided to drop the separate section on causes of the obsession and to integrate the material on causes into the other sections of the paper.

If you began with a clear, carefully worded research question (see p. 657), you will not have much difficulty selecting and organizing your evidence to answer it. But as we've said so often before, research questions often may change and re-form while you're at work at the library or in the field. When you begin organizing, don't be afraid to junk an original question that no longer works and to reorganize your material around a newly formed question. In the long run, you'll save both time and toil.

**Beginning to Draft.**    You'll probably benefit from a formal outline to guide your drafting. But remember that an outline is a skeleton to which you will add flesh (details). Use the outline as a suggested organizational plan and change the subdivisions or the order of the parts if you discover a better way.

When you look over your outline, compare each section with the notes you have on hand for it. If for a certain section you have no notes, or only a single note, your research has a gap, so go back to the library or into the field again.

When you are satisfied that your notes fall into some kind of order and you have material for every part of your outline, you can start to write. If things don't fall into perfect order, start writing anyway. Get something down on paper so that you will have something to revise. And remember that you don't have to start at the beginning; start wherever you feel most comfortable.

As you write, you should document all the ideas, facts, summaries, and paraphrases you've drawn from your reading or field research. Right after every such borrowing, you refer your readers to the exact source of your material. (In Chapter 31, we show you in detail how to cite your sources.) Although it takes a little extra time to cite your sources, it saves fuss when you're putting your paper into final form. And it prevents unintentional plagiarism (see p. 718).

Note in your draft, right after each borrowed item, the name of the author and the page of the book or article you took it from. If you are quoting a field research source, include the date of the interview or lecture and the name of the person speaking, if any. If you're using two or more works by the same author, you need one more detail to tell them apart: shorten the titles — the first word or phrase will do — and include the shortened title with the author's name.

**WRITING
WITH A
COMPUTER**

## Managing Source Material on Disk

The ability of a computer to help you juggle and rearrange is a great advantage when it comes to organizing and managing research material sources. By now, your library or field research will probably have generated an abundance of notes. If you have recorded your findings on a computer as you went along, your paper will be easier to organize now. If you still need to record your notes on a computer, now is the time to winnow the best of it so as not to have to type up everything.

When discarding electronically stored material, you don't have to permanently erase or destroy it. Just store the discards in a separate file. You can't tell — perhaps some of them might still come in handy. Floppy disks are relatively inexpensive and generally have more than enough room to store all your work from one paper.

> An assassin outrages us not only by his deed but also by offering an unacceptable reason for violence. Nearly as offensive as his act of wounding President Reagan was Hinckley's explanation that he fired in order to impress screen star Jodie Foster. (Szasz, "Intentionality," 5)

The title in parenthesis is short for "Intentionality and Insanity," the title of an article by Thomas Szasz, to distinguish it from another work by Szasz that the writer also cites: *The Myth of Mental Illness.*

When in writing a draft you include a direct quotation, you might as well save copying time. Just paste or tape in the whole note card bearing the quotation. Your draft may look sloppy, but who cares? Drafts usually are. You're going to recopy the quotation anyway when you type your final version. If your note is in a computer file, you can just copy the passage from the file and paste it right where you want in your draft file.

When you lay the quotation into place, add a few words to introduce it. A brief transition might go something like "A more negative view of standardized intelligence tests is that of Harry S. Baum, director of the Sooner Research Center." Then comes Baum's opinion, that IQ tests aren't very reliable. The transition announces why Baum will be quoted, to refute a previous quotation in favor of IQ tests. The transition, brief as it is, tells readers a little about Baum by including his professional title. Knowing that he is a recognized authority would probably make readers willing to accept his expert view. (For more suggestions on introducing ideas, see "Achieving Coherence," p. 380.)

If no transition occurs to you as you are placing a quotation or borrowed idea into your draft, don't sit around waiting for it. Make a marginal or mental note that you need a transition and keep writing while the spirit is moving you along. Later, when you rewrite, you can add connective tissue. Just remember to add it, though — a series of slapped-in summaries and quotations makes rough reading.

## INCORPORATING SOURCE MATERIAL

**Using Sources (Not Letting Sources Use You).**   Sometimes you can get drawn into discussing something that really doesn't have anything much to do with your investigation, perhaps because the material is interesting and you happen to have a heap of it. When a note has cost you time and toil, it's a great temptation to want to include it at all costs. Resist. Include only material that answers your research question. A note dragged in by force always sticks out like a pig in the belly of a boa constrictor.

Another common danger is for a writer to swagger in triumph over what he or she has discovered. Cultivate a certain detachment. Make no exorbitant claims for what you have discovered ("Thus I have shown that day-care centers deserve the trust of parents in the state of Washington"). You have probably not answered your research question for all time; you need not claim to be irrefutable. Norman Tallent, in his guidebook *Psychological Report Writing* (Englewood Cliffs: Prentice, 1976), quotes a professional reader of reports in the field of psychology: "I have seen some reports which affected me adversely because of a tendency to sound pompous with the implication 'This is the final word!' rather than 'This is an opinion intended to be helpful in understanding the whole.' "

Quoting, Paraphrasing, and Nutshelling.    Quoting is reproducing an author's exact words. Paraphrasing is restating an author's ideas in your own words. Nutshelling is extracting the essence of an author's meaning and stating it "in a nutshell." These methods of handling source material are also discussed in Chapter 28 (p. 649). Now you face a similar but different challenge: how to use these methods to incorporate your sources in your actual paper.

If to save time in the library, you made photocopies of long passages or you took too many notes as direct quotations, you now have to face the task of selecting from them, boiling them down, and weaving them into your paper. Nutshell and paraphrase are fine ways to avoid quoting excessively. Both methods translate another writer's ideas into your own words.

To illustrate once again how nutshelling and paraphrasing can serve you, let's first look at a passage from historian Barbara W. Tuchman. In *The Distant Mirror: The Calamitous 14th Century* (New York: Knopf, 1978), Tuchman sets

**WRITING WITH A COMPUTER**

## Shaping a Research Paper with a Word Processor

Fact: If you know how to use a word processor, shaping a research paper will be dramatically easier than if you do not. If you don't know how to use one, do yourself a tremendous favor by learning as soon as possible.

With a word processor, any material you've collected through research or generated on your own can be sorted and grouped on the screen — laid in the very place it should go. You can shift material around by "cutting and pasting," an aid to organizing long blocks of copy. You can easily discard material — and then bring it back again if you decide you need it after all. (Some writers create separate pages at the end of their computer files to store discarded material rather than erasing it permanently. Of course, the final draft should not include any of these leftovers.) You can save multiple copies of your paper (or parts of your paper) if you can't decide which version you think is more effective. Naming new versions of your paper according to the date can help you keep track of different drafts. And finally, with a word processor you can also easily add any stray material that may turn up late in the process of writing.

forth the effects of the famous plague the Black Death. In her foreword to her study, she admits that any historian dealing with the Middle Ages faces difficulties. For one, large gaps exist in the supply of recorded information.

ORIGINAL

A greater hazard, built into the very nature of recorded history, is overload of the negative: the disproportionate survival of the bad side — of evil, misery, contention, and harm. In history this is exactly the same as in the daily newspaper. The normal does not make news. History is made by the documents that survive, and these lean heavily on crisis and calamity, crime and misbehavior, because such things are the subject matter of the documentary process — of lawsuits, treaties, moralists' denunciations, literary satire, papal Bulls. No Pope ever issued a Bull to approve of something. Negative overload can be seen at work in the religious reformer Nicolas de Clamanges, who, in denouncing unfit and worldly prelates in 1401, said that in his anxiety for reform he would not discuss the good clerics because "they do not count beside the perverse men."

Disaster is rarely as pervasive as it seems from recorded accounts. The fact of being on the record makes it appear continuous and ubiquitous whereas it is more likely to have been sporadic both in time and place. Besides, persistence of the normal is usually greater than the effect of disturbance, as we know from our own times. After absorbing the news of today, one expects to face a world consisting entirely of strikes, crimes, power failures, broken water mains, stalled trains, school shutdowns, muggers, drug addicts, neo-Nazis, and rapists. The fact is that one can come home in the evening — on a lucky day — without having encountered more than one or two of these phenomena.

This passage in a nutshell, or summary, might become as follows:

NUTSHELL

```
Tuchman reminds us that history lays stress on misery and
misdeeds because these negative events attracted notice
in their time and so were reported in writing; just as in
a newspaper today, bad news predominates. But we should
remember that suffering and social upheaval didn't pre-
vail everywhere all the time.
```

As you can see, this nutshell merely abstracts from the original. Not everything in the original has been preserved: not Tuchman's thought about papal bulls, not the specific examples such as Nicolas de Clamanges and the modern neo-Nazis and rapists. But the gist — the summary of the main idea — echoes Tuchman faithfully.

Before you write a nutshell, or summary, an effective way to sense the gist of a passage is to carefully pare away examples, details, modifiers, offhand remarks, and nonessential points.

Here is the original quotation from Tuchman as one student marked it up on a photocopy, crossing out elements she decided to omit from her paraphrase:

> ~~A greater hazard,~~ built into the ~~very~~ nature of recorded history, is ~~overload of the negative:~~ the disproportionate survival of the bad side ~~of evil, misery, contention, and harm. In history~~ this is exactly the same as in the daily newspaper. ~~The normal does not make news. History is made by the~~ documents that survive, ~~and these~~ lean heavily on crisis and calamity, crime and misbehavior, because such things are the subject matter of the documentary process ~~of lawsuits, treaties, moralists' denunciations, literary satire, papal Bulls. No Pope ever issued a Bull to approve of something. Negative overload can be seen at work in the religious reformer Nicolas de Clamanges, who, in denouncing unfit and worldly prelates in 1401, said that in his anxiety for reform he would not discuss the good clerics because "they do not count beside the perverse men."~~
>
> Disaster is rarely as pervasive as it seems from recorded accounts. ~~The fact of being on the record makes it appear continuous and ubiquitous whereas~~ it is more likely to have been sporadic both in time and place. Besides, persistence of the normal is usually greater than the effect of disturbance, as we know from our own times. ~~After absorbing the news of today, one expects to face a world consisting entirely of strikes, crimes, power failures, broken water mains, stalled trains, school shutdowns, muggers, drug addicts, neo-Nazis, and rapists. The fact is that one can come home in the evening—on a lucky day—without having encountered more than one or two of these phenomena.~~

Rewording what was left, she wrote the following nutshell version:

NUTSHELL

```
History, like a daily newspaper, reports more bad than
good. Why?  Because the documents that have come down to
us tend to deal with upheavals and disturbances, which
are seldom as extensive and long-lasting as history books
might lead us to believe.
```

In filling her nutshell, you'll notice, the student couldn't simply omit the words she had deleted. The result would have been less readable and still long. She knew she couldn't use Tuchman's very words: that would be plagiarism. To make a good, honest, compact nutshell that would fit smoothly into her research paper, she had to condense the passage into her own words.

Now here is Tuchman's passage in paraphrase. The writer has put Tuchman's ideas into other words but retained her major points. Note that the writer gives Tuchman credit for the ideas.

PARAPHRASE

```
Tuchman points out that historians find some distortion
of the truth hard to avoid, for more documentation ex-
ists for crimes, suffering, and calamities than for the
events of ordinary life. As a result, history may over-
play the negative. The author reminds us that we are fa-
miliar with this process from our contemporary
newspapers, in which bad news is played up as being of
greater interest than good news. If we believed that
newspapers told all the truth, we would think ourselves
threatened at all times by technical failures, strikes,
crime, and violence--but we are threatened only some of
the time, and normal life goes on. The good, dull, ordi-
nary parts of our lives do not make the front page, and
praiseworthy things tend to be ignored. "No Pope," says
Tuchman, "ever issued a Bull to approve of something."
But in truth, social upheaval did not prevail as widely
as we might think from the surviving documents of me-
dieval life. Nor, the author observes, can we agree with
a critic of the church, Nicolas de Clamanges, in whose
view evildoers in the clergy mattered more than men of
goodwill.
```

In this reasonably complete and accurate paraphrase, about three-quarters the length of the original, most of Tuchman's points have been preserved and spelled out fully. Paraphrasing enables the writer to emphasize the ideas important to his or her research and makes readers more aware of them as support for the writer's thesis than if the whole passage had been quoted directly. But notice that Tuchman's remark about papal bulls has been kept a direct quotation because the statement is short and memorable, and it would be hard to improve on her words. In the paraphrase, the writer, you'll observe, doesn't interpret or evaluate Tuchman's ideas — she only passes them on.

When you use the information from a source in your paper, make sure that, like the writer of the nutshell and the paraphrase just given, you indicate your original source. You can pay due credit in a terse phrase — "Barbara W. Tuchman believes that ..." or "According to Barbara W. Tuchman ..." — and then give the page number in parentheses after the information you cite.

Often you paraphrase to emphasize one essential point. Here is an original passage from Evelyn Underhill's classic study *Mysticism*:

ORIGINAL

In the evidence given during the process for St. Teresa's beatification, Maria de San Francisco of Medina, one of her early nuns, stated that on entering the saint's cell whilst she was writing this same "Interior Castle" she found her [St. Teresa] so absorbed in contemplation as to be unaware of the external world. "If we made a noise close to her," said another, Maria del Nacimiento, "she neither ceased to write nor complained of being disturbed." Both these nuns, and also Ana de la Encarnacion, prioress of Granada, affirmed that she wrote with immense speed, never stopping to erase or to correct, being anxious, as she said, to write what the Lord had given her before she forgot it.

Suppose that the names of the witnesses do not matter but that the researcher wishes to emphasize, in fewer words, the celebrated mystic's writing habits. To bring out that point, the writer might paraphrase the passage (and quote it in part) like this:

PARAPHRASE WITH QUOTATION

Evelyn Underhill has recalled the testimony of those who saw St. Teresa at work on The Interior Castle. Oblivious to noise, the celebrated mystic appeared to write in a state of complete absorption, driving her pen "with immense speed, never stopping to erase or to correct, being anxious, as she said, to write what the Lord had given her before she forgot it."

Avoiding Plagiarism.    Here is a point we can't stress too strongly: when you paraphrase, never lift another writer's words or ideas without giving that writer due credit or without transforming them into words of your own. If you do use words or ideas without giving credit, you are plagiarizing. You have seen in this chapter examples of honest nutshelling and paraphrasing. Introducing them into a paper, a writer would clearly indicate that they belong to Barbara Tuchman (or some other originator). Now here are a few horrible examples: paraphrases of Barbara Tuchman's original passage (on p. 715) that lift, without thanks, her ideas and even her very words. Finding such gross borrowings in a paper, an instructor might hear the ringing of a burglar alarm. The first is an egregious example that lifts both thoughts and words.

PLAGIARIZED

Sometimes it's difficult for historians to learn the truth about the everyday lives of people from past societies because of the disproportionate survival of the bad

```
side of things. Historical documents, like today's news-
papers, tend to lean rather heavily on crisis, crime, and
misbehavior. Reading the newspaper could lead one to ex-
pect a world consisting entirely of strikes, crimes,
power failures, muggers, drug addicts, and rapists. In
fact, though, disaster is rarely so pervasive as recorded
accounts can make it seem.
```

What are the problems here? The phrase "the disproportionate survival of the bad side" is quoted directly from Tuchman's passage (line 2). The series "crisis, crime, and misbehavior" is too close to Tuchman's series "crisis and calamity, crime and misbehavior" (line 5); only the words "and calamity" have been omitted. The words "lead one to expect a world consisting entirely" is almost the same as the original "one expects to face a world consisting entirely" (lines 16–17). The phrase "strikes, crimes, power failures, muggers, drug addicts, and rapists" simply records — and in the same order — six of the ten examples Tuchman provides (lines 17–18). The last sentence in the plagiarized passage ("In fact, though, disaster is rarely so pervasive as recorded accounts can make it seem") is almost the same — and thus too close to the source — as the first sentence of Tuchman's second paragraph ("Disaster is rarely as pervasive as it seems from recorded accounts"). The student who wrote this attempted paraphrase failed to comprehend Tuchman's passage sufficiently to be able to put Tuchman's ideas in his or her own words.

The second example is a more subtle theft, lifting thoughts but not words.

### PLAGIARIZED

```
It's not always easy to determine the truth about the
everyday lives of people from past societies because bad
news gets recorded a lot more frequently than good news
does. Historical documents, like today's newspapers, tend
to pick up on malice and disaster and ignore flat normal-
ity. If I were to base my opinion of the world on what I
see on the seven o'clock news, I would expect to see
death and destruction around me all the time. Actually,
though, I rarely come up against true disaster.
```

By using the first-person pronoun *I*, this student suggests that Tuchman's ideas are his own. That is just as dishonest as quoting without using quotation marks, as reprehensible as not citing the source of ideas.

The next example fails to make clear which ideas belong to the writer and which belong to Tuchman (although none of them belong to the writer).

PLAGIARIZED

```
Barbara Tuchman explains that it can be difficult for
historians to learn about the everyday lives of people
who lived a long time ago because historical documents
tend to record only the bad news. Today's newspapers are
like that, too: disaster, malice, and confusion take up a
lot more room on the front page than happiness and seren-
ity. Just as the ins and outs of our everyday lives go
unreported, we can suspect that upheavals do not really
play so important a part in the making of history as they
seem to do.
```

After rightfully attributing the ideas in the first sentence to Tuchman, the student researcher makes a comparison to today's world in sentence 2. Then in sentence 3 she goes back to Tuchman's ideas without giving Tuchman credit. The placement of the last sentence suggests that this last idea is the student's whereas it is really Tuchman's.

**RESEARCH CHECKLIST**

## Avoiding Plagiarism

- Remember that taking notes is as much a process of understanding what you read as it is of writing.
- Carefully check each paraphrase or summary against the original. Be sure you have not misinterpreted or distorted the meaning of the original.
- When you quote from the original, be sure to quote exactly and use quotation marks. Place significant words from the original in quotation marks.
- Use an ellipsis mark ( ... ) to indicate where you have omitted something from the original, and use square brackets ([ ]) to indicate changes or additions you have made in a quotation. When you use these two conventions, take care not to distort the meaning of the original by your omissions or changes.
- Take pains to identify the author of any quotation, paraphrase, or summary. Credit by name the originator of any fact, idea, or quotation you use.
- Make sure you indicate where another writer's ideas stop and yours begin. (You might end your paraphrase with some clear phrase or phrases of transition: "— or so Tuchman affirms. In my own view. . . .")
- If at any place your paraphrase looks close to the exact words of the original, carefully rewrite it in your own words.

**EXERCISE**

## Paraphrasing

Study one of the following passages until you understand it thoroughly. Then using your own words, write a paraphrase of the passage. Compare and contrast your version with that of your classmates in your peer group. With their help, evaluate your own version: What are its strengths and weaknesses? Where should it be revised? In the future when you take notes from library or field research, be sure to avoid the problems that you identify in this group activity.

PASSAGE I

Within the next decades education will change more than it has changed since the modern school was created by the printed book over three hundred years ago. An economy in which knowledge is becoming the true capital and the premier wealth-producing resource makes new and stringent demands on the schools for educational performance and educational responsibility. A society dominated by knowledge workers makes even newer — and even more stringent — demands for social performance and social responsibility. Once again we will have to think through what an educated person is. At the same time, how we learn and how we teach are changing drastically and fast — the result, in part, of new theoretical understanding of the learning process, in part of new technology. Finally, many of the traditional disciplines of the schools are becoming sterile, if not obsolescent. We thus also face changes in *what* we learn and teach and, indeed, in what we mean by knowledge.

— Peter F. Drucker, *The New Realities*

PASSAGE 2

When I look to the future of humanity beyond the twenty-first century, I see on my list of things to come the extension of our inquisitiveness from the objective domain of science to the subjective domain of feeling and memory. Homo sapiens, the exploring animal, will not be content with merely physical exploration. Our curiosity will drive us to explore the dimensions of the mind as vigorously as we explore the dimensions of space and time. For every pioneer who explores a new asteroid or a new planet, there will be another pioneer who explores from the inside the minds of our fellow passengers on planet Earth. It is our nature to strive to explore everything, alive and dead, present and past and future. When once the technology exists to read and write memories from one mind into another, the age of mental exploration will begin in earnest. Instead of admiring the beauties of nature from the outside, we will look at nature directly through the eyes of the elephant, the eagle, and the whale. We will be able, through the magic of science, to feel in our own minds the pride of the peacock and the wrath of the lion. That magic is no greater than the magic that enables me to see the rocking horse through the eyes of the child who rode it sixty years ago.

— Freeman Dyson, *Infinite in All Directions*

## BEGINNING AND ENDING

Perhaps, as we have suggested, only after you have written the body of your paper will a good beginning and a concluding paragraph or paragraphs occur to you. The head and tail of your paper might then make clear your opinion of whatever you have found out. But that is not the only way to begin and end a research paper. Maria Halloran initially began her draft with a short summary of her conclusion from her research investigation:

```
America is obsessed with sports, and this national mania
is harmful to children. For their sake and the future of
our country, we should end the national obsession with
sports.
```

After reading over this introductory paragraph, she thought it probably wouldn't catch the interest of her readers and it might even alienate some who held the opposing point of view. As she drafted and revised her essay, she realized that to bring her readers around to her point of view, she needed to start out slowly and build to a strong finish. Both her opening paragraph and her paper as a whole follow this pattern. For her opening, she starts with a factual account of a real event, something her readers can hardly take issue with. Only after recounting the event and exploring its implications does she put forth her main idea (her thesis):

```
The national obsession with sports must end.
```

Although her message is clear, Maria Halloran's tone is not yet impassioned. She uses her paper to bombard her readers with evidence about the harmful effects of the U.S. sports mania and then, at the very end of the paper, issues the rousing call to action that she had originally thought to use as her opening:

```
For the sake of our children and the future of our coun-
try, isn't it time that we put the brakes on America's
sports mania? The youth of America have been sold a false
and harmful bill of goods. Let's stop such madness and
step off the carousel now. We owe that to the children of
America, and to ourselves.
```

Still another way to begin a research paper is to sum up the findings of other scholars. One research biologist, Edgar F. Warner, has reduced this kind of opening to a formula:

First, in one or two paragraphs, you review everything that has been said about your topic, naming the most prominent earlier commentators. Next you declare why all of them are wrong. Then you set forth your own claim, and you spend the rest of your paper supporting it.

That pattern may seem cut and dried, but it is clear and useful. It is a favorite technique among professional writers because it places the scholar's research and ideas into a historical and conceptual framework. If you browse in specialized journals in many fields — literary criticism, social studies, the sciences — you may be surprised how many articles begin and go on in that very way. Of course, you don't need to damn every earlier commentator. One or two other writers may be enough to argue with. Erika Wahr, a student writing on the American poet Charles Olson, starts her research paper by disputing two views of him:

> To Cid Corman, Charles Olson of Gloucester, Massachu-
> setts, is "the one dynamic and original epic poet twenti-
> eth-century America has produced" (116). To Allen Tate,
> Olson is "a loquacious charlatan" (McFinnery 92). In my
> opinion, the truth lies between these two extremes,
> nearer to Corman's view.

Whether or not you have stated your view in your beginning, you will certainly need to make it clear in your closing paragraph. A suggestion: before writing the last lines of your paper, read back over what you have written earlier. Then, without looking at your paper, try to put your view into writing. (For more suggestions on starting and finishing, see Chapters 17 and 19.)

## *Revising and Editing*

Looking over your evidence and your draft, you may possibly find your essay changing as Maria Halloran did. Don't be afraid to make a whole new interpretation, to shift the organization, to drop a section or add one.

When you look over your draft, here are a few points to inspect critically and try to improve.

**REVISION
CHECKLIST**

### Looking Over Your Results

- Have you honestly said something, not just heaped facts and statements by other writers that don't add up to anything? If your answer is no, a mere heap of meaningless stuff is all you've got, then you need to do some hard thinking and revising.
- Is your main idea or thesis clear?
- Have you included only evidence that makes a point? Do all your points support your main idea?
- Does each new idea or piece of information follow from the one before it? Can you see any stronger order in which to arrange things? Have you provided transitions to connect the parts?
- Have you ever yielded to the temptation to put in some fact or quotation just because it cost effort to obtain?
- Are your sources of information trustworthy? Do you have lingering doubts about something you read or anything anyone told you? (If so, whom might you consult to verify your information?)
- Do you need more evidence to back up any point? If so, where might you obtain it?

- Are the words that you quote truly memorable? Would you recall them if you hadn't written them down? Would any quotation be better paraphrased or summarized?
- Is the source of every quotation, every fact, every idea you have borrowed made unmistakably clear?
- Do you spend much space announcing what you are going to do or repeating what you demonstrated? (If you do, whittle down these passages or cut them out altogether.)

Once you have done all you can do by yourself to make your paper informative, tightly reasoned, and interesting to read, ask a classmate to read over your draft and give you reactions. When you set about the task of revising, you can start by backtracking at the trouble spots your peer editor has starred. If you need to improve connections between parts, try summarizing the previous section of your paper. By doing so, you remind your readers of what you have already said. This strategy can come in handy, especially in a long paper when, after a few pages, readers' memories may need refreshing and a summary of the argument so far will be welcome. Such a brief summary might go like this: "As we can infer from the previous examples, most Hispanic migrant workers are not in direct competition with native non-Hispanic American workers." This type of transition effectively points both back and forward. You might ask your peer editior to answer the following questions about your paper.

**FOR PEER**
**RESPONSE**

## Writing from Research

- What is your overall reaction to this paper?
- What do you understand the research question to be? Did the writer answer that question?
- What promises has the writer made that should be met in the paper? Did he or she meet them?
- What changes might you make to the introduction that would wake up a sleepy instructor drinking coffee at 3 A.M. and enlist his or her careful attention?
- What do you think about the conclusions the writer has drawn from his or her research? Do they seem fair and logical? Describe any problems you have with the writer's interpretation of the evidence.
- Look carefully at the concluding paragraph of the paper. Does it merely restate the introduction? Is it too abrupt or too hurried? What makes it effective?
- Is the organization logical and easy to follow? Are there any places where the essay becomes hard to follow? Star these.
- Do you know which information is from the student writer and which from the research sources? Star any facts, opinions, or questions that you think should be documented.
- Does the writer need all the quotations he or she has used? Point out any that puzzled you or that you thought were not well incorporated.

- Do you have any questions about the writer's evidence? Point out areas where the writer has not fully backed up his or her conclusions.
- Did the writer commit any logical fallacies (see Chapter 19)?
- How interested were you in continuing to read the paper? If you didn't have to, would you have kept on reading? Why or why not?

As you look over your draft, here are a few other points to inspect critically (and, if need be, to improve).

## DOCUMENTING SOURCES

A research paper calls on you to follow special rules in documenting your sources — in citing them as you write and in listing them at the end of your paper. At first, these rules may seem fiendishly fussy, but for good reason professional writers of research papers swear by them and follow them to a *T*. The rules will make sense if you imagine a world in which scholarly and professional writers could prepare their research papers in any old way they pleased. The result would be a new tower of Babel. Research papers go by the rules in order to be easily readable, easily set into type. The rules also ensure that all necessary information is there to enable any reader interested in the same subject to look up the original sources.

In humanities courses and the social sciences, most writers of research papers follow the style of the Modern Language Association (MLA) or the American Psychological Association (APA). Your instructor will probably suggest which style to observe; if you are not told, use MLA. The first time you prepare a research paper according to MLA or APA rules, you'll need extra time to look up just what to do in each situation. (For detailed information about documenting sources, see Chapter 31.)

Quotation Style.    One special manuscript convention for research papers is that for direct quotations. When you use a direct quotation from one of your sources, you must put quotation marks around the words you're using, and you must cite the author and page number. You may include the author's name either in the text of the essay — as in the following example — or in parentheses with the page number at the end of the quotation.

```
Johnson puts heavy emphasis on the importance of "giving
the child what she needs at the precise moment in her
life when it will do the most good" (23).
```

When you include a quotation longer than four typed lines, you set it off in your text by indenting the whole quotation one inch or ten spaces from the left margin if you're following MLA style, five spaces for APA style. You double-space the quotation, just as you do the rest of your paper. Don't place quotation marks around an indented quotation, and if the quotation is a paragraph or less, don't indent its first line. Following is an example, a critic's comment on Emily Dickinson's use of language:

```
Cynthia Griffin Wolff in her biography Emily Dickinson
comments on this nineteenth-century poet's incisive use
of language:
          Language, of course, was a far subtler weapon
          than a hammer. Dickinson's verbal maneuvers
          would increasingly reveal immense skill in
          avoiding a frontal attack; she preferred the
          silent knife of irony to the strident battering
          of loud complaint. She had never suffered fools
          gladly. The little girl who had written of a
          dull classmate, "He is the silliest creature
          that ever lived I think," grew into a woman who
          could deliver wrath and contempt with excruci-
          ating economy and cunning. Scarcely submissive,
          she had acquired the cool calculation of an as-
          sassin. (170-71)
```

**Works Cited.**   At the very end of a library research paper, you supply a list of all the sources you have cited: books, periodicals, and any other materials. Usually this list is the last thing you write. It will be easy to construct the list if, when you compiled your working bibliography, you included in each source note all the necessary information (as shown in Figures 28.1 and 28.2). If you did, you can now simply arrange the works you used in alphabetical order, and then type the information about each source, following the MLA or APA guidelines (see Chapter 31). The MLA specifies that you title your

---

**WRITING
WITH A
COMPUTER**

## Using Software to Document Sources

If you plan to use either footnotes or endnotes, most word processing programs will help you number and format these ancillary comments. Placing notes at the bottom of each page can be difficult on a conventional typewriter; a word processing program that does it for you will be particularly valuable if you plan to use this method.

Before the deadline for your paper approaches, spend an hour working with the footnote or endnote feature of the word processor you will use to prepare your final manuscript. Put together a four-page mock report with notes and practice editing and revising both the contents of your notes and their numbering.

list "Works Cited"; the APA, "References." Any leftover parts — notes for sources you haven't used after all — may now be sailed into the wastebasket or trashed on the computer. Resist the temptation to transcribe them, too, and impressively lengthen your list. Your list should include only the works you actually referred to in your paper.

## MANUSCRIPT FORM

Chapter 19 tells you the proper format for a final manuscript, whether typewritten or word processed. Its advice on proper formatting applies not only to research papers but to any other college papers you may write. Before you hand in your final revision, go over it one last time for typographical and mechanical errors. If you have written your paper on a word processor, it's an easy matter to correct all errors right on the screen before you print it. If you find any mistakes in a paper you have typewritten, don't despair. Your instructor knows how difficult and frustrating it would be to retype a whole page to fix one flyspeck error. Correct it neatly in ink. (How to be neat? See p. 421 and the proofreading symbols at the back of the book.)

# A Completed Library Research Paper

Maria Halloran's lack of understanding of the American preoccupation with sports and her consternation over the eruption of violence following a Chicago Bulls game led her to research the American obsession with sports.

---

**WRITING WITH A COMPUTER**

## Using Software to Edit and Proofread a Research Paper

Research papers, being rich in names and numbers, invite misspellings and other typographical errors. A great way to proofread your finished research paper, before you print it out, is to go to the bottom of the document you have been writing, scroll backward, and reread what you have written line by line. This technique prevents you from getting so interested in what you've written that you forget to notice mistakes. Instead, it keeps you looking at spelling, punctuation, and such mechanical matters, concentrating on one line at a time.

Applying the spell checker is another important step during the editing stage. However, be sure that you understand a spell checker's limitations; this tool cannot guarantee perfect spelling. Grammar checkers are even less reliable than programs that check spelling. Unless you are very familiar with a grammar checker, you shouldn't rely on one for help. (For more on spell checkers and grammar checkers, see p. 450 in Chapter 21.)

Today's high-resolution printers, particularly laser printers, produce attractive documents that resemble professionally typeset writing. Do not be fooled by the slick appearance that these tools can create. Even in the age of the computer, there is simply no substitute for attentive, thorough editing and proofreading.

Her completed paper is more than a compilation of facts, a string of quotations. Halloran sets forth a problem that troubled her, she provides evidence to support her concern, and she adds her own thoughts to the facts and ideas she gleaned from her research.

Halloran prefaced her paper with a formal *sentence outline*, with each heading stated as a complete sentence. (If your instructor asks for such an outline, see the advice on formal outlines on p. 361.)

Later in college and on her job after graduation, Maria found that the training she acquired as a researcher in her composition course proved valuable.

Although MLA guidelines do not require a title page, you may be asked to prepare one. A title page contains, on separate lines, centered and double-spaced, the title of the paper, the writer's name, the instructor's name, the course number, and the date.

America's Obsession with Sports

Maria Halloran

Professor Sylvia A. Holladay

English 102

April 18, 1994

Type "Outline," centered, one inch from the top. Double-space to the first line of text.

The thesis states the main idea of the paper.

This outline is in sentence form rather than in the shorter topic form. It is a skeleton of the research paper.

Halloran ii

Outline

Thesis: The national obsession with sports must end.

I. The American fervor for sports is running at an all-time high.

   A. Attitudes toward sports figures are overwhelmingly positive.

      1. The image of the sports hero remains untarnished despite unheroic behavior.

      2. The media perpetuate the sports hero myth despite a lack of good role models.

   B. Entire cities sometimes become obsessed with sports.

   C. Sports enthusiasts argue for the benefits of sports.

      1. Sports are fun.

      2. Sports provide exercise.

      3. Sports build character.

II. Critics warn of the harmful effects of organized sports on children.

   A. Sports can actually harm the self-esteem of children.

      1. Little League "cutting" makes children think they have failed.

      2. Ridicule of those who play Little League makes them think they are being rejected personally.

   B. Obsessed with sports, schools often fail to look out for children's best interests.

      1. Students are held back a year in school in order to mature for sports teams.

      2. The American school system is failing its students at the expense of sports.

Number all pages after the title page in the upper right corner, half an inch from the top. The writer's name appears before the page number. Number outline pages with small roman numerals (the title page is counted but is not numbered).

    3. Young people are misled into believing that they can become professional athletes.

C. Young athletes work at their game to the exclusion of academics.

    1. Many athletes get out of high school functionally illiterate.

    2. If they don't make it to the pros, they have nothing to fall back on.

Halloran 1

America's Obsession with Sports

On June 20, 1993, gunplay, violence, and vandalism erupted in Chicago as fans celebrated the Chicago Bulls' 99-98 victory over the Phoenix Suns for the National Basketball Association title. Several innocent bystanders were hit by flying bullets. The police were shot at or assaulted with bottles and bricks, and countless other people suffered minor injuries. Businesses and schools were looted and vandalized, and the damage done to 109 city buses was estimated at $150,000. A total of 682 people were arrested (Recktenwald and Gottesman 1, 6). But all over the country hardly any shock or condemnation was expressed over the outrageous behavior of the overzealous fans. Most of the media chose to minimize the shameful eruptions of violence as if they were just something to expect as part and parcel of a victory celebration. In a Chicago Tribune article following the Bulls' victory, William Recktenwald and Andrew Gottesman reported, "There were 20 shootings after the Bulls' game Sunday night, four of which proved fatal. For any given weekend night in Chicago, that toll is high but not shocking" (1). Not shocking? Have we as a country gone so overboard on sports that we have learned to take casually whatever comes with this sports obsession, including violence?  Violence is only one of the harmful effects of the American obsession with sports. This mania also has adverse effects on players' self-esteem and on the educational

If you have a title page and an outline, repeat the title on the first page of the text. Double-space to the first line of text.

Number text pages with arabic numerals in the upper right corner, preceded by writer's last name. Place half an inch from the top. Begin the text one inch from the top, and leave one-inch margins at the bottom and sides of the paper.

Citation of work by two or three authors gives the names of all authors. Halloran includes the page numbers for both pages that she cites from.

Authors' names introduce the quotation, so the parenthetical citation includes only the page number.

Use a comma before a quotation if the lead-in text is not a full sentence. Use a colon if the lead-in text is a full sentence.

Halloran 2

system. The national obsession over sports must
end.

Despite drug use, sexual assaults, and domestic violence by athletes, the American fervor for sports is running at an all-time high.
The image of sports heroes remains untarnished
despite such questionable behavior. Heavyweight boxing champion Mike Tyson was convicted
of rape charges, and Pete Rose had to leave
baseball because of his gambling (Sudo 2).
Former pro basketball player and Olympian
Michael Jordan also gambled heavily, but his
addiction has not adversely affected his reputation among sports fans. As one 12-year-old
fan in Lincoln, Nebraska, said in defense of
Jordan: "It was just something he did for fun,
not anything to harm anything" (qtd. in Gelman,
Springen, and Raghavan 56). The media have much
to do with the "selling" of these improper role
models, often making them into celebrities.
They are "a product of press agents and media-
hype who are sold to the public, rather than
being chosen by the public for their heroic
qualities" (Crepeau 79). The immature and sometimes illegal activities of sports "heroes"
have done little to diminish their standing
among those obsessed with sports.

Not only individuals, but even some cities
as a whole have become sports-crazy. Take
Odessa, Texas, for example. In a book titled
Friday Night Lights, Pulitzer Prize winning
writer H. G. Bissinger portrays the intense
football "win-at-any-cost" mentality of the
community. Football players with broken ankles

---

In the opening paragraph, Halloran recounts a real event and explains its implications before putting forth her thesis statement.

First section of body establishes the current problem of obsession with sports.

Place citations within text in parentheses before sentence. Use a period between entries.

Direct quotation for the exact words of a sports fan. The fan is a secondary source quoted in the article by Gelman, Springen, and Raghavan, so citation reads "qtd. in."

Quotation marks around an important word from source.

Transition to another aspect of the obsession.

Halloran 3

Halloran uses paraphrase and nutshell rather than direct quotation to discuss Bissinger's findings.

and hip pointers received painkillers so they could keep playing despite injuries (44). Permian High School spent more on medical supplies for the team than on educational materials for the entire English Department. Additionally, tens of thousands more dollars were spent chartering jets for games (145-46). As long as the team won, the coach was well liked, but when the team lost a game, "For Sale" signs appeared on his lawn the next morning (241). Bissinger says that although community pride resulted from the football team's success, Odessa "lost perspective on what a game should be" (qtd. in Herlinger 22). After the release of his book, Bissinger received innumerable threats of physical violence. Those threats, he said, were "an all-too-typical, and disturbing, indication of the increasingly unhealthy influence of sports on American life" (qtd. in Herlinger 23).

Sports enthusiasts argue that sports are beneficial. They claim not only that sports are fun and a superb way to exercise but also that children's experiences in sports can be an effective preparation for life. They argue that sports crystallize the meaning of hard work, self-discipline, teamwork, responsibility, goal setting, competition, fairness, and other positive values that build character. "For young people, sports is an important self-esteem builder," contends Richard Weinberg, professor of educational psychology at the University of Minnesota (qtd. in Maloney 24).

Title and credentials establish the source as an authority.

Halloran 4

Halloran uses transitional phrases to link discussion of opposing viewpoint with previous paragraphs.

Second section of essay identifies and provides evidence of the harmful effects of organized sports on children.

Halloran paraphrases valuable ideas that are not worth preserving in the source's original words.

Although these arguments may sound convincing, critics claim that sports can be harmful to children. Little League, for instance, uses a process of "cutting," whereby membership limits are based on quotas and physical ability. As a result of this elimination process, many children experience rejection. In such a sports setting, stress and anxiety on the playing field can result in children backing away from participating in sports because they fear rejection if they perform poorly (Leonard 140). Their self-esteem is damaged because they have been deemed unworthy of the team. At such a vulnerable age, they have failed to achieve the approval that matters most to them. Even those kids who do make the team are likely to have their self-esteem damaged. As sports columnist Robert Lipsyte explains, "Children know that when they're ridiculed for not catching a ball, they're being ridiculed for their bodies. I think this is much worse than being laughed at for reading badly or whatever. You're being totally rejected as a person." The rejection and ridicule often leave an indelible mark of unworthiness even on the children who participate.

In an obsession to win games, schools have sometimes failed to look out for children's best interests because sports are considered more important than studying. For instance, it was common in Texas for junior high school athletes to be "redshirted"--held back a grade-- to give the players more time to mature for high school competition (Maloney 24).

Halloran 5

H. G. Bissinger asserts that, indeed, "we are
turning out a generation of children who can't
read or write or make critical judgments," but
that "all of that takes a backseat to the great
god of high school football" (qtd. in Herlinger
23). Instead of making sure the young athletes
are trained to become functional citizens, parents and schools concentrate mainly on molding
kids to become professional athletes. Dr.
Robert Green, dean of the College of Urban Development at Michigan State, describes the
training process:

> When a kid as early as the sixth
> grade shows some potential in athlet-
> ics, a whole series of events, almost
> like a piece of machinery, goes into
> effect to start grooming that kid for
> the pros.
>
>     As he goes through the system and
> the better he gets, the kid sees he
> can get away with flunking tests, not
> handing in papers, skipping classes.
> Usually his coach will have enough
> clout so that very few teachers would
> dare fail that kid. (qtd. in Shapiro
> and Huff)

Also, young people are often given false
hope that if they work hard enough in sports,
they can play in the big leagues. But the odds
are stacked against them. Studies have shown
that only 1 high school athlete in 12,000 gets
the chance to become a pro (Maloney 24). The
American education system responsible for
preparing students for life after graduation

Quotation of more than
four typed lines is in-
dented ten spaces from
the left margin and is
double-spaced with no
quotation marks. Citation
of source is in parenthe-
ses following the end
punctuation of the
quotation.

Halloran interprets some
data in sentence form and
then presents the statis-
tics.

has been tainted by the sports fervor gripping
this country.

It's no wonder that many young athletes
work at their game to the exclusion of academics and everything else. The U.S. Department
of Education reports that "nearly 30% of senior
football and basketball players leave school
functionally illiterate" (Gordon 21). When
such athletes don't make the pros, they have
nothing to fall back on, and pent-up anger and
frustration may explode against society. One
expert observes that the federal prison system
is full of people with extraordinary athletic
ability, "but when they found they couldn't
make it, their energies were directed toward
anti-social behavior--crime, drugs, that kind
of thing" (qtd. in Shapiro and Huff).

Thomas Tutko, a San Jose State psychologist, summarizes the harmful effects of sports
obsession on youngsters:

Halloran uses direct quo-
tation rather than para-
phrase because of the
strong, effective language
in the original source.

> How many millions of youngsters are
> we sacrificing along the way so that
> 10 players can entertain us in a pro
> basketball game? I'm concerned with
> how many good athletes have been
> scarred by injury or burned out psy-
> chologically by the time they were 15
> because they were unable to meet the
> unsatiable needs of their parents,
> their coach, their fans or their own
> personal obsession; or are rejected
> and made to feel ashamed because of
> their limited athletic prowess.
> We'll tolerate almost anything in the

Halloran 7

name of winning--cruelty, insensitivity, drugs, cheating and lying.... Is
it any wonder the sports field is
overrun with neurotic behavior?
(qtd. in Maikovich 127)

Sports mania in the United States has created a legacy of violence and misplaced values.
Contrary to the popular view, sports are not
inherently beneficial for individuals. The negative effects of the sports fervor gripping the
nation has become harmful to children--affect-
ing their self-esteem, aspirations, and worldview. For the sake of our children and the
future of our country, isn't it time that we
put the brakes on America's sports mania? The
youth of America have been sold a false and
harmful bill of goods. Let's stop such madness
and step off the carousel now. We owe that to
the children of America and to ourselves.

An ellipsis mark indicates that something is omitted from the original.

Conclusion summarizes main points of essay and restates thesis.

Halloran 8

Works Cited

Book title with subtitle.

Bissinger, H. G. Friday Night Lights: A Town, a
    Team, and a Dream. Reading: Addison, 1990.

Chapter in an edited
book.

Crepeau, Richard C. "Where Have You Gone, Frank
    Merriwell? The Decline of the American
    Sports Hero." American Sports Culture. Ed.
    Wiley Lee Umphlett. Toronto: Associated
    Presses, 1985. 76-82.

Article in a weekly maga-
zine with three authors.

Gelman, David, Karen Springen, and Suadansan
    Raghavan. "I'm Not a Role Model." Newsweek
    28 June 1993: 56-57.

Gordon, Myles. "Making the Grade?" Scholastic
    Update 1 May 1992: 20-21.

Herlinger, Chris. "The Young Gods." Scholastic
    Update 1 May 1992: 22-23.

Works cited in text of paper are listed here alphabetically by authors' last
names. Type "Works
Cited," centered, one
inch from top. Double-
space to first entry and
double-space within and
between entries. Indent
second and following lines
of each entry five spaces.

Leonard, Wilbert Marcellus, II. A Sociological
    Perspective of Sport. 3rd ed. New York:
    Macmillan, 1988.

Lipsyte, Robert. "Peddling Sports Myths: A Dis-
    service to Young Readers." Children's Lit-
    erature in Education 11.1 (1980):12.
    Sports. Vol. 2. Boca Raton: SIRS, 1981.
    Art. 1.

Maikovich, Andrew J., ed. Sports Quotations.
    Jefferson, NC: McFarland, 1984.

Maloney, Lawrence D. "Sports-Crazy Americans."
    U.S. News & World Report 13 Aug. 1984: 23-
    24.

Newspaper article with
two authors. The "I+" in-
dicates that the article begins on page I and
continues, but not on
consecutive pages.

Recktenwald, William, and Andrew Gottesman.
    "Many Agree Violence Not as Bad as '92."
    Chicago Tribune 22 June 1993, souvenir
    ed., sec. 2: 1+.

Shapiro, Leonard, and Donald Huff. "The Games
    Always End." Washington Post 20 Mar.

1977:D1,D4. Sports. Vol. 1. Boca Raton:
SIRS, 1978. Art. 13.

Sudo, Phil. "America at Play." Scholastic Update 1 May 1992: 2-3.

| **Questions to Start** | *Meaning* |
| **You Thinking** | 1. What is Maria Halloran's thesis? |
| | 2. According to Halloran, what are the negative effects of sports? What are the positive effects of sports? |
| | *Writing Strategies* |
| | 1. Does Halloran provide sufficient support to convince you that the national obsession over sports must end? Are any of the points that she includes for support of her position not very convincing to you? |
| | 2. Is the example of violence following the Bulls' game effective in the introduction? How is that information related to her main point? |
| | 3. If you were Halloran's peer editor, what suggestions would you make for improving the paper? |

# A Completed Field and Library Research Paper

When Professor Bob Hooper gave Linda Hackler's class a research assignment to select a group of people they were interested in and to research the answer to a question or problem related to that group, Hackler searched for a subject she wanted to investigate, one she could spend several weeks reading and thinking about without getting bored or frustrated. She had grown up on an apple ranch in Oregon and was familiar with the plight of Hispanic migrant workers. The representation of migrant workers by the media was often different from what Hackler remembered about the migrant workers she knew. She wondered who was right, whose opinions were more accurate. Was her memory faulty? Were the media presenting a one-sided view? After Professor Hooper approved this subject as her topic for research investigation, Hackler formulated a research question: "Do migrants who come to the United States actually take jobs from Americans?"

Early in her investigation Hackler discovered that her question was still too broad: she could not adequately research and explain the situation of the Haitian migrants, the Mexican migrants, and all the other groups from Central America and the Caribbean. She decided to limit her search to the Mexican or Hispanic migrants because she was most familiar with and interested in that group. It was also the group that some of her classmates had seemed most prejudiced toward. Professor Hooper had told her class that each student would share the results of his or her research study with the entire class, so Hackler hoped that she could find some information that would help her classmates better understand Hispanic migrants.

At the college library Hackler found several books and articles with helpful information on her subject, but they all seemed lifeless and distant. She wanted something to give her paper more validity and more zip. Field research! That was the way she could make her paper not only more interesting but also more convincing. Hackler thought that the information she gathered in the field in conjunction with her use of library sources gave her paper just the spark it needed. As you read her paper, see if you agree. (For more on Linda Hackler's experiences writing this paper, see Chapter 29.)

Professor Hooper allowed the students to use either the MLA style or the APA style of documentation of sources. Hackler chose to use APA because it was appropriate for her sociological study. She prefaced her paper with a title page and a formal *sentence outline* (for advice on formal outlines, see p. 361), following the instructions of her instructor.

The experience of conducting field research and writing this paper proved beneficial in Linda Hackler's later work as a psychology major. In her major she found the training in conducting field research invaluable. Hackler was grateful for the opportunity this research project provided because "increasing one's reading and writing skills is beneficial in all walks of life," she said.

Hispanic Migrant Worker      1

The Myth of the Hispanic Migrant Worker
Linda Hackler
English 102
Professor Bob Hooper
October 29, 1993

Hispanic Migrant Worker    2

Outline

The thesis states the main idea of the paper.

In APA style, number all pages consecutively with arabic numerals in the upper right-hand corner, beginning with the title page. Each page is identified by 2 or 3 words from the title five spaces to the left of the page number.

Thesis: Hispanic migrant workers are misunderstood scapegoats for the economic problems that face our country.

I. Hispanic migrant workers are not taking jobs that would otherwise go to non-Hispanic U.S. citizens.

   A. Most Hispanic migrant workers, whether legal or illegal, are employed in work that most Americans are unwilling to perform.

      1. They often work for paltry remuneration.

      2. They do backbreaking labor.

   B. Hispanic migrant workers are good workers.

      1. They have a strong work ethic.

      2. They are often more willing to work than native workers.

II. Illegal Hispanic migrants do not drain U.S. social services.

   A. They do not use funds from U.S. social services extensively.

   B. They do not put a strain on U.S. schools.

      1. They quit school to work.

      2. They live a transitory life.

   C. Even illegal migrant workers pay taxes indirectly.

The Myth of the Hispanic Migrant Worker

They are labeled Latino, Chicano, Mexican, and sometimes less kindly as Wetback or Spic. However labeled, they are the fastest growing minority in the United States. They are also a vital, though much-maligned, segment of our economy and a necessary cog in the vast machinery of the U.S. workforce. Leading government and private sources agree that Hispanics will soon be the largest minority group in this country, and as such they are already blamed for a multitude of problems, including job losses for American workers and increased pressure on social and educational services. While there are some valid concerns behind these issues, much of the controversy is a simple matter of politics. Our politicians, as well as the general public, need a scapegoat for our country's economic problems, and Hispanic migrants are defenseless pawns in this political chess game. Politicians and the media have created a biased, misinformed view of Hispanic migrant workers that contributes to the myth that they are taking away jobs from Americans and draining funds from the American taxpayer.

With rising unemployment it is currently popular to voice the prevalent, but incorrect, belief that illegal Hispanic workers are taking jobs that would otherwise go to non-Hispanic U.S. citizens. This widely held view is simply untrue. In fact, sociologists Frank D. Bean and Rodolfo O. de la Garza (1993) reported that "the speculation that undocumented immigration leads to substantial negative impacts on the

---

**Thesis stated here.**

**Last sentence of opening paragraph reinforces the thesis and sets forth the two major divisions of the paper.**

**First section of essay presents the first aspect of the myth that Hackler wishes to debunk: that Hispanic migrant workers are taking jobs from Americans.**

employment and wages of natives has not been consistently borne out by research relevant to the issues" (p. 48).

The average Hispanic migrant, whether legal or illegal, is employed in work that most Americans are unwilling to perform. As Antonia, an illegal Hispanic domestic worker, explained to oral historian Ana Maria Corona (1993), most U.S. citizens are unwilling to work as a maid for $300 per month plus room and board; nor would most U.S. citizens follow the fruit and vegetable harvests in the hope of being allowed to do the backbreaking labor involved. Hispanic migrants are often employed in menial occupations such as domestic help and garment factory worker, jobs that in some cases might otherwise go unfilled. Cesar Cabrello, a Mexican-American who rose from the barrio to work at the University of Texas, related the common experience of many Hispanic migrant workers who

> look for jobs as maids or in the service industries--restaurants or doing gardening. If they cannot find work in these areas, they go out into the fields to do stoop labor, or into the canneries or construction sites. They take very menial jobs that many Americans don't want because the pay is too little and it's hard work. (Santoli, 1988, p. 289)

Many of these positions would otherwise remain vacant because of the low wages and the sometimes--and unfortunate--substandard working conditions.

---

Direct quotation adds support and authority to Hackler's assertions. When the author's name appears in the text, include the year in parentheses following the author's name. Put the page number preceded by "p." in parentheses after the quoted material but the period at end of the sentence.

Page numbers are given only for direct quotations or for paraphrases from long, complex works. This is a paraphrase from an uncomplicated work.

APA style prescribes past tense to describe past procedures, events, and results.

Direct quotation rather than paraphrase because of the strong, effective language in the original source.

In APA style, long quotations are displayed in double-spaced block, indented 5 spaces, with no quotation marks. Parenthetical citation follows last sentence punctuation; no additional period is needed after citation.

Hispanic Migrant Worker    5

It is often Hispanic migrants who accept these jobs and, in doing so, keep food on the table for many Americans. As Edwin P. Reubens, a professor of economics and a consultant on employment policy, suggested:

Title and credentials establish the source as an authority.

> The U.S. labor market is not homogeneous or perfectly competitive, but instead shows considerable segmentation. Even in the face of considerable unemployment, vacancies exist for workers with special skills in upper-bracket occupations, and for manual workers in low-level occupations. (p. 194)

Parenthetical citation contains only the page number because author's name appears before quotation in text.

Hispanic migrant workers fill these voids in the workforce, thereby creating a mutually beneficial arrangement that keeps many industries in full operation and keeps food on the table for migrant families.

To learn more about these workers, I spoke with an acquaintance who has been a fruit rancher in northeastern Oregon for over 40 years. During that time he has had direct contact with hundreds of Hispanic workers. He finds the ones whom he hires to be hardworking, dependable workers who seldom drink or cause trouble. Arla Kendall, migrant Head Start teacher for the past 5 years, agreed that most people "have the wrong view of migrant workers." She claimed that "they are the hardest workers and are very proud. They just need a chance" (personal communication, August 13, 1993). Kendall further maintained that Hispanic migrants are very family-oriented. One migrant family that she knows comes north every

Transitional phrase used to link field research with library research in previous paragraph.

In APA style, interviews and other personal communications are cited with dates of communication in parentheses but are not given in the reference list.

year in order to return to Mexico with enough
money to provide the barest of necessities as
well as a few things that they consider luxuries: refrigerator, range, and enough extra
money to buy electricity for their home. This
one nuclear family is the basis of support for
a larger, more extended family in Mexico.

Personal observation.

My personal observation of the day-to-day
work on the farm of my rancher acquaintance
confirms these beliefs. Many of the Hispanic
migrant workers at this particular fruit ranch
return year after year, proving themselves to
be dependable, hard workers. For these reasons, my source (who asked not to be named)
said that he prefers Hispanic workers to the
occasional Anglo who claims to be willing to
work but rarely stays to finish the job. In his
view, Anglos too often consider themselves
above the menial tasks required of the job and
often refuse to work in the fields alongside
Hispanic migrants unless they are given elevated status as tractor or truck drivers (personal communication, August 5, 1993).

To persuade the rancher to talk freely, Hackler had to guarantee his anonymity, and thus cites no name.

As we can infer from the previous examples, most Hispanic migrant workers are not in
direct competition with native non-Hispanic
Americans for jobs. Because the Hispanic migrant workers who come to the United States are
largely unskilled, most of the workers are "accustomed to heavy labor, eager for jobs, hardworking, reliable" (Reubens, 1983, p. 196).
Reubens further claimed that because the often
illegal migrant workers primarily fill jobs that
native workers do not want, the two groups of

Transition sentence sum-marizes and points for-ward.

Hispanic Migrant Worker   7

Hackler uses direct quotation for memorable words that support her main point.

workers neither compete with each other nor act to undercut wages or cause a decline in working conditions (p. 199). Additionally, "insofar as the alien workers are more hardworking than native workers, and more responsible, regular, and reliable, they tend to raise productivity, and therefore actually tend to reduce inflation and to promote exports" (p. 199).

The Hispanic work ethic was further illustrated by Douglas Kent Hall in his book The Border: Life on the Line (1988). Hall stated that many farmers and ranchers would perhaps rather hire locals but use migrant workers out of necessity. He observed that "the same problems with local workers . . . [are] echoed by employers everywhere . . . ; the relative ease and comfort of welfare [has] made [local] workers reluctant to take the hard jobs" (pp. 137-138). Furthermore, studies indicate that migrants are actually filling jobs in the garment industry, in restaurants, in agriculture, and in domestic housework that Americans "have been withdrawing from . . . for their own reasons, independent of the illegals and long before the latter came to take their place" (Reubens, 1983, p. 197). It is this Anglo reluctance that makes Hispanic migrants vital to our economy. Without their assistance, entire industries would be adversely affected, running a very real risk of downsizing or even the threat of closure.

An ellipsis mark indicates an omission of something from the original. Brackets indicate an added or altered word in a quotation.

Second part of paper presents the second aspect of the myth that Hackler is trying to debunk: that illegal Hispanic migrants drain U.S. social services.

Critics also contend that illegal migrant workers cost the U.S. taxpayer by placing a high demand on social services such as welfare

Hispanic Migrant Worker    8

and the public school system. Contrary to the
prevailing belief, most migrant Hispanic workers do not collect money or benefits from social
services. Bean and de la Garza (1993) explained that "analysts have found that undocumented aliens do not use those services
extensively and that their combined contributions to local, state, and national tax revenues approximately equals and often exceeds
the value of the social services they receive"
(p. 48). The fact is that because social welfare coverage throughout Latin America is generally "partial" at best (Ward, 1986, p. 4),
many Mexicans don't have access to sufficient
health care services, housing, or any kind of
welfare assistance to provide a healthier diet
(p. 132). Consequently, many Hispanics do not
have the U.S. mentality of expecting to be
cared for by the state. Furthermore, most migrant families are constantly moving, and their
undocumented status discourages many alien
workers from tapping into the U.S. social service network for fear of deportation (Atkin,
1993, p. 29).

        Critics also claim that Hispanic migrants
are putting a strain on our school systems.
However, most migrant workers have little formal schooling, and the children of migrant
workers often continue to suffer from this deprivation. One reason is that they have to
drop out of school to work. As Jose Luis
Urbina, an illegal migrant farmer, related, "I
was only allowed to finish grammar school. I am
the oldest in my family, of five sisters and two

Quotation marks around
an important word from
source.

Hackler paraphrases to
avoid quoting excessively.
Page number is given be-
cause the work is long
and complex.

boys. I had to stop going to school when I was twelve to work with my father to support the family" (Santoli, 1988, p. 272). Another reason is their transitory life. Migrant children are moved continuously, and schools are unable to sustain a consistent curriculum or high level of education for these highly transient children. And again, the illegal status of many migrant workers discourages them from enrolling their children in school.

While critics argue that migrants are abusing U.S. social service funds, illegal migrant workers do pay taxes, "in the form of excise taxes, sales taxes, and property taxes (included in rents)" (Reubens, 1983, p. 201). Additionally, as Reubens reported, even illegal Hispanic workers who use bogus social security cards pay into the system through income taxes withheld from their paychecks. While it is naive to think that illegal migrant workers do not create any demands on social services, the demand has been greatly exaggerated, contributing further to the misinformed view of Hispanic migrant workers as responsible for U.S. unemployment and the deficit problems of the U.S. government.

Conclusion summarizes main points of essay and restates thesis.

Hispanics do not come to the United States with the intention of taking jobs from Americans, nor in fact do they do so. The idea that Hispanic migrant workers are stealing jobs from U.S. citizens is a myth. Studies show that contrary to public opinion migrant workers fill a necessary void in the U.S. economy, and despite the prevailing opinion they do not drain

social service money to the degree that politicians and the media claim. I would challenge
anyone to live a migrant worker's life for a
single day. Only then could an American begin
to understand the sacrifices migrant workers
make in trying to provide the life-sustaining
necessities for their families. It is doubtful
that Hispanic workers would choose to leave
their homes and brave the dangers of crossing
the border if there were other avenues open to
them in Mexico. They are forced to come here
to provide for those who are dependent on them.
Migrant life is a hard life, but the migrant
workers who travel to the United States fill
necessary and vital jobs that wouldn't otherwise be filled.

Works cited in text of paper are listed here alphabetically by authors' last names. Type "References," centered, at top of page.

Article with two authors from a journal with continuous pagination.

Magazine article.

Book with one author.

Chapter in an edited book.

All interviews and personal communications are not given in the references list.

Hispanic Migrant Worker          11

References

Atkin, S. B. (1993). Voices from the fields. Boston: Little, Brown.

Bean, F. D., & de la Garza, R. O. (1993). Illegal aliens and the census count. Annual editions: Social problems, 20, 46-51.

Corona, A. M. (1993, April). Coming to America, to clean. Harper's, 286, 32-36.

Hall, D. K. (1988). The border: Life on the line. New York: Abbeville Press.

Reubens, E. P. (1983). Immigration problems, limited-visa programs, and other options. In P. G. Brown & H. Shue (Eds.), The border that joins: Mexican migrants and U.S. responsibility (pp. 187-222). Totowa, NJ: Rowman and Allanheld.

Santoli, A. (1988). New Americans: An oral history. New York: Ballantine.

Ward, P. (1986). Welfare politics in Mexico: Papering over the cracks. London: Allen and Unwin.

*Meaning*

1. What is Hackler's thesis?
2. What is a *scapegoat*? What is the origin of this word? What are some other scapegoats in contemporary society?

*Writing Strategies*

1. What types of evidence does Hackler use to support her thesis? Does her use of sources convince you to agree with her position?
2. How does Hackler integrate field research and library research? Does she integrate the information from these two types of sources effectively?
3. If you were Hackler's peer respondent, what would you point out to her as the strengths of her paper? What suggestions might you make for improving the paper?

# A Completed Literary Research Paper

The following is a literary research paper that Chris Robinson wrote for a composition class with a focus on literature. When Professor Whitney gave Robinson's class a research assignment to write a critical analysis with secondary sources on a work that they had read that semester, he was at a loss about where to begin. He considered some of the stories that he had enjoyed reading in class but was unable to come up with an interesting angle to analyze or a question that would benefit from further research.

Then Robinson remembered a discussion in his composition class about a short story by Kate Chopin, "The Story of an Hour" (p. 289). He had thoroughly enjoyed the story and remembered the heated discussion about the story. The issues raised by Chopin were intriguing to Robinson. He wondered what life was really like for Victorian women, why Chopin had written this story, and why some of his classmates had reacted so strongly to it. After rereading the story, conducting some preliminary research, and doing a little more thinking, he formulated a research question: "Why did Chopin write this story, and what was its impact on her society?" He realized that this was a two-pronged topic but decided that he would work on unifying it after he had done his research. As you read his paper, notice how he fuses these two aspects of his investigation to form a unified essay.

To guide the drafting of his paper, Chris Robinson prepared an outline of his paper. (Later he turned it in with the final draft of his paper.) Robinson compared each section of his outline with his research notes to make sure that he had enough sources to support each part of his paper. As he went through his notes, he discovered that the section on Chopin's commentary about the effect of marriage and love upon a woman's sense of self was lacking sufficient sources so he went back to the library and added an additional source to bolster this section. Here is the formal sentence outline, with each heading stated as a complete sentence, that Robinson prepared (for advice on formal outlines, see p. 361).

Outline

Thesis: Through the portrayal of Louise Mallard
in "The Story of an Hour," Kate Chopin sets
forth the universal theme of the importance of
a woman's individual identity.

I. Chopin portrays Louise Mallard as a traditional wife who changes into a New Woman who
   values individual freedom.
   A. One of Chopin's literary techniques is
      the names of the main character.
      1. Before her realization of freedom and
         personal identity, she is referred to
         as "Mrs. Mallard."
      2. After her awakening, she is called
         "Louise."
   B. Another technique is physical descrip-
      tion.
      1. Before her realization, she is sickly
         and vulnerable.
      2. After she changes, she is vibrant and
         victorious.
   C. The main techniques are actions and
      thoughts.
      1. Before gaining self-knowledge, she is
         passive and silent.
      2. After her self-understanding, she is
         free and fully alive.
II. Through Louise's realization, Chopin offers
    a commentary about the effect of marriage
    and love on a woman's sense of self, ideas
    against traditional beliefs of Victorian
    society.
    A. Chopin suggests that marriage can kill
       love.

Robinson ii

B. Chopin implies that freedom is a natural
   state that the institution of marriage
   upsets, yet such freedom is unrealistic
   for Victorian women.
C. Chopin suggests that life for the woman
   who dares to be different is difficult.

In researching and writing his paper, Robinson drew not only on the library research techniques described in this *Research Manual*, but also on the strategies for writing about literature that his class had been studying. (For more on writing about literature, see Chapter 12, p. 249)

Robinson's paper, according to his instructor's specifications, is in MLA style. Notice how Robinson cites his secondary research sources as well as his primary source "The Story of an Hour" in his essay.

Robinson 1

Chris Robinson

Professor MaryJane Whitney

English 101

March 23, 1995

Female Identity in Kate Chopin's

"The Story of an Hour"

In the nineteenth century males were clearly dominant and authoritarian, while females were subservient and passive. Slowly, women began to question their assigned role and responded to the battle between the sexes in a variety of new ways--withdrawal, revolt, and action to change society.

> Significantly, as the hope for a new future merged with revulsion against a contaminated past, and as the vision of a New Woman fused with horror at the traditional woman, much female-authored literature oscillated between extremes of exuberance and despair, between dreams of miraculous victory and nightmares of violent defeat. (Gilbert and Gubar 81)

Such are the characters in the fiction of Kate Chopin, American author of the late nineteenth century. In fact, literary critics Sandra Gilbert and Susan Gubar claim that this oscillation "is perhaps most brilliantly depicted in Kate Chopin's terse, O. Henry-like 'The Story of an Hour'" (81).

When Kate Chopin tried to publish "The Story of an Hour" in 1894, she met with resistance from various magazines, who found the story too radical and feminist for the times.

---

MLA guidelines do not require a title page. Instead, include the writer's name, instructor's name, course number, and date on separate, double-spaced lines one inch from the top of the first page flush with the left margin. Double-space to title.

Direct quotation from literary critics in opening paragraph lends credibility and provides background information. Indent quotations of more than four typed lines ten spaces and double-space with no quotation marks. Citation of source is in parentheses following the end punctuation of the quotation. Authors' names are included in citation following quotation because they are not given in text leading up to quotation.

Robinson 2

Robinson paraphrases to lead in to a memorable quotation.

R. W. Gilder, the editor of the popular magazine Century, rejected the story because he felt it was immoral. Gilder's opposition to Chopin's tale of a woman freed by her husband's apparent death is not surprising, since Gilder "had zealously guarded the feminine ideal of self-denying love, and was that very summer publishing editorials against women's suffrage as a threat to family and home" (Ewell 89).

To understand the radical nature of Chopin's message, readers must recognize the traditional Victorian society in which Chopin lived, a society in which gender roles were very traditionally defined. In the character of Louise Mallard, the author creates a woman who through the death of her husband comes to the profound realization of a new life and a self that she didn't know existed. But ironically, Chopin also shows Louise's feeling of independence to be a doomed fantasy, because in actuality such a vision of freedom outside of marriage was an unrealistic goal for nineteenth-century women. Through this narrative Chopin sets forth the universal theme of the importance of a women's individual identity outside of marriage, outside of her role as a man's wife.

The thesis states the main idea of the paper.

First section of essay analyzes Chopin's depiction of the evolution of Louise Mallard from a traditional wife to a woman who values individual freedom outside the confines of marriage.

Chopin portrays Louise Mallard as a typical nineteenth-century wife, fragile, feminine, and dependent, who changes into a self-assured, independent individual when she mistakenly thinks she is freed by her husband's death. One of Chopin's subtle techniques for this portrayal is the way she names the protagonist. Early in the story, the character is known as

Robinson 3

Transition identifying the source as a recognized authority leads in to a direct quotation, included for the strong, effective language in the original source. Name of the author is mentioned in the text, so the citation gives only the page number.

"Mrs. Mallard," a title that defines her as Brently's wife rather than her own person. Only after Mrs. Mallard realizes her freedom is she addressed as "Louise" by her sister Josephine. Critic Mary Papke notes that the reader comes to learn the difference between her "social self--Mrs. Mallard--and private female self--Louise" (74). Through the difference in how the heroine is addressed, Chopin clearly indicates Louise's awakening female identity. She has claimed an identity and a life for herself, a life beyond the confines of marriage.

Robinson uses transition word to indicate that he will list other examples.

Another effective technique Chopin uses to depict Mrs. Mallard/Louise is physical description. At the beginning of the story, Mrs. Mallard is very much the traditional Victorian ideal of a fragile, feminine being. The author describes her as a delicate creature who is likely to fall ill at any moment. For example, Josephine and Richard take great care to "break [the news of Mallard's death] to her as gently as possible" because she is believed to have "a heart trouble" (289). Another description of Mrs. Mallard's fragility occurs when, after she locks herself in her room and exposes herself to the cold air from the open window, Josephine begs her to "open the door--you will make yourself ill" (291). Other physical details portray her as passive. She sits with a "dull stare" (290) and "a suspension of intelligent thought" (290). In a particularly telling passage, Chopin describes Mrs. Mallard as "young, with a fair, calm face, whose lines [bespeak] repression and even a certain strength" (290).

Parenthetical references cite page numbers for both paraphrases and direct quotations in primary source, the short story.

Robinson uses narrative details from the plot of the story to support his analysis.

Robinson 4

This description suggests that she doesn't express her own desires and instead follows the
role prescribed for her by her society: that of
the stoic, silent wife.

While Chopin's early physical description
of Mrs. Mallard conforms to traditional notions
of the "weaker sex," the author gradually provides glimpses of Mrs. Mallard's newfound identity as she emerges from her shell and directly
challenges the prevailing notions of female
identity. Chopin provides physical details to
indicate the change that has occurred in
Louise: she is no longer passive or frightened.

> The vacant stare and the look of ter-
> ror that had followed it went from
> her eyes. They stayed keen and
> bright. Her pulses beat fast, and
> the coursing blood warmed and relaxed
> every inch of her body. (290)

She is fully alive and at ease for the
first time in her life because she is free, and
she is "drinking in a very elixir of life"
(291). There is "a feverish triumph" in her
eyes (291). As she descends the stairs at the
ironic ending, she carries herself like a "goddess of Victory" (291), suggesting that at that
moment she feels triumphant in her battle for
self.

The major evidence of the change in Louise
Mallard is in her actions and thoughts.
Through the shock of her grief Louise Mallard
experiences an awakening of her self and ultimately rejoices in her newfound female identity. Immediately after she hears of her

Transition summarizes
and points forward.
Robinson keeps emphasis
on analysis and interpre-
tation, not on plot of
story.

Robinson 5

husband's death, she experiences a "storm of
grief" (289), weeping "at once, with sudden
wild abandonment" (289). Then she enters the
first stage of self-discovery by locking herself
in her room alone. This act is her first moment
of stubborn self-assertion, as "she would have
no one follow her" (289). But at this stage,
she has not quite found her independent self.
She seems suspended, sitting "quite motionless"
except when a sob racks her, as a "child who
has cried itself to sleep continues to sob in
its dreams" (290). When she starts to feel
some "thing" or strange feeling, something "too
subtle and elusive to name," coming over her
(290), she waits for it "fearfully" (290). She
tries to "beat it back with her will" but finds
herself "as powerless as her two white slender
hands would have been" (290). Her response to
this newly discovered emotion is like that of a
child who is willful but has no power. According to literary critic Peggy Skaggs, her bewil-
derment and confusion over her emotions are
typical of Chopin's female characters, who often "seem to lack a clear concept of their own
roles and purpose in life, a constant groping
for such self-knowledge shaping their personalities and actions" (290). By allowing these
feelings merely to wash over her, Mrs. Mallard
indicates that she is still playing the passive
role of Brently's wife.

As these conflicting emotions overtake her,
however, Mrs. Mallard realizes the power that
she now holds because of her husband's death.
This "thing that was approaching to possess

Robinson combines his
own ideas with the critic's
comments and supporting
details from the story.

Robinson 6

her" (290) turns out to be a joyous realization
that she is free from her husband. Over and
over again, she says the words "Free, free,
free!" and feels a "monstrous joy" (290) that
she can live the rest of her life for herself.
She imagines the years "that would belong to
her absolutely" (290).

Through Louise's realization, Chopin offers a commentary about the effect of marriage
and love on a Victorian woman's sense of self.
First, she suggests that marriage can kill
love. The reader learns that Louise has loved
her husband only "sometimes" because he has often imposed his "private will" on her (290).
Even though she knows that Brently loved her,
she realizes that his kind intentions were
nonetheless cruel because they restricted her
independence and identity. She realizes that
love is not as strong a need as is "self-assertion, which she suddenly [recognizes] as the
strongest impulse of her being" (290). Literary critic Barbara Ewell writes of the recur-
rence of this theme in Chopin's work: "as
Chopin often insists, love is not a substitute
for selfhood; indeed, selfhood is love's pre-
condition" (89). Louise couldn't really love
her husband because she didn't have a sense of
her own identity; she didn't know herself.
Chopin seems to be saying that by squelching
individual identity, especially in women, marriage can squelch love. Love can flourish only
if both partners are free. This idea was quite
radical at the turn of the century.

*Transition sentence leads in to second section of essay, which claims that the story can be read as a commentary on the effect of marriage and love on a woman's sense of self.*

Robinson 7

Even further, Chopin suggests that freedom
is a natural thing, that the social institution
of marriage upsets. When Louise is having her
moment of revelation in her room, she communes
with nature, the blue sky and "the tops of
trees that were all aquiver with the new spring
life" (290). Her sister Josephine wants her to
shut the window, but Louise refuses because she
is "drinking in a very elixir of life through
that open window" (291). Women at this time
were usually confined to a domestic role, but
Louise wants a different role. The open window
and the natural images are symbolic of her desire to be free. As Ewell notes, Chopin's
story suggests that freedom is a "human right--
as natural as generation, spring, or even
death" (90). Through the ironic end of
Louise's short-lived vision of freedom, Chopin
suggests that freedom as an individual, freedom
outside of marriage, is unfortunately unrealistic for a nineteenth-century woman. When she
sees her husband alive, Louise dies of a heart
attack, an attack the doctor calls "joy that
kills" (291). The irony of the ending is that
she is not overjoyed at finding her husband
alive; rather, the "monstrous joy" she has felt
at experiencing her own freedom is actually the
source of her death. Now that she has found
herself, she can't go back to the inequality of
marriage, and the only way out is death.

Mary Papke argues that the conclusion of
the story both "informs and warns" that if an
individual changes but the world around her remains constant, then self-oblivion and death

Robinson paraphrases to
avoid quoting excessively.
He uses quotation marks
around important words
from the source.

Robinson 8

may result for a woman who dares to be different (76). Louise's family and friends, however, misinterpret the cause of her death, implying that Victorian society cannot comprehend the joy of a woman outside the confines of marriage. In fact, Chopin's readers at the time the story was first published may not have understood the irony of the ending. Elizabeth McMahan notes that "women in [Chopin's] day did not seek self-determination, did not question whether they had any identity outside of marriage" (34). The tragic ending of "The Story of an Hour" underscores the irony that only through her husband's death, and therefore the death of her marriage, can Louise see the possibilities in life for herself. When she realizes he is alive, she can be free only in death. As Emily Toth suggests, "The Story of an Hour" is "a criticism of the ideal of self-sacrifice that still haunted women at the end of the century" (252).

Chopin's fable of female self-assertion and identity was misunderstood and criticized in her time, but modern readers can find important messages in her story. Louise Mallard died, in a sense, because her society could not accept that a married woman could have a self outside of her role as wife. A similar situation brought tragedy to many women in the nineteenth century, and "The Story of an Hour" still carries an important warning for women today: find yourself before you marry.

Brackets indicate an added or altered word in a quotation.

Conclusion suggests that Chopin's story still resonates for contemporary women.

Robinson 9

## Works Cited

Chopin, Kate. "The Story of an Hour." The Bed-
    ford Guide for College Writers, with
    Reader, Research Manual, and Handbook. By
    X. J. Kennedy, Dorothy M. Kennedy, and
    Sylvia A. Holladay. Boston: Bedford, 1996.

Ewell, Barbara C. Kate Chopin. New York: Ungar,
    1986.

Gilbert, Sandra M., and Susan Gubar. The War of
    the Words. New Haven: Yale UP, 1988. Vol.
    1 of No Man's Land: The Place of the Woman
    Writer in the Twentieth Century. 3 vols.
    1988-89.

McMahan, Elizabeth. "Nature's Decoy: Kate
    Chopin's Presentation of Women and Mar-
    riage in Her Short Fiction." Turn of the
    Century Women 2.2 (1985): 32-35.

Papke, Mary E. "Chopin's Stories of Awakening."
    Approaches to Teaching Chopin's The Awak-
    ening. Ed. Bernard Koloski. New York: MLA,
    1988.

Skaggs, Peggy. Kate Chopin. Boston: Twayne,
    1985.

Toth, Emily. Kate Chopin. New York: Morrow,
    1990.

Works cited in text of paper are listed here alphabetically by authors' last names. Type "Works Cited," centered, one inch from top. Double-space to first entry and double-space within and between entries. Indent second and following lines of each entry five spaces.

Primary source is from a book by three authors.

Book by one author.

Multivolume work.

Journal article with pagination by issue.

Essay in an edited collection.

**Questions to Start
You Thinking**

*Meaning*

1. What did you learn about the role of Victorian women from reading Chris Robinson's essay?

2. According to Robinson, why did Kate Chopin write "The Story of an Hour"? How was it received by her society?

3. What does Robinson point out as the relevance of this story for modern women and men today? Do you agree with him?

4. What is his thesis?

*Writing Strategies*

6. How effectively does Robinson unify the two prongs of his original research question in his final research essay?

7. How does Robinson integrate information from the plot of the story with the information he gleaned from his research?

**Other Assignments**

Using your library and field sources, write a short research paper, under 2,000 words (Halloran's paper is 1,500 words; Hackler's is 1,750; Robinson's is 1,900), in which you give a rough survey of the state of knowledge on one of the following topics or on another that you and your instructor agree offers promising opportunities for research. Proceed as if you had chosen to work on the main assignment that is described on p. 653.

1. Investigate the career opportunities in a line of work that interests you. Include data from interviews conducted with people in the profession.

2. Write a paper discussing the progress being made in the prevention and cure of a disease or syndrome.

3. Discuss the treatment of drug abuse or the rehabilitation methods being used for substance abusers. Analyze the effectiveness of these methods.

4. Discuss the recent political or economic changes occurring in a European, Asian, or African country.

5. Write a comparison of the relative effectiveness of the present methods of disposing of nuclear wastes.

6. Survey the effects of banning smoking in public places.

7. Study the growth of telecommuting, the tendency of people to work in their own homes, keeping in touch by phone and computer modem with the main office.

8. Write a portrait of life in your town or neighborhood as it was in the past, using as sources articles in the local newspaper and interviews with senior citizens. Any photographs or other visual evidence you can gather might be valuable to include. Try to verify any testimony you receive by comparing it with old newspapers or by talking with a local historian.

9. Write a short history of your immediate family, drawing on interviews, photographs, scrapbooks, old letters, written but unpublished records, and any other sources.

10. Study the reasons students today give for going to college. Gather your information from actual interviews with and possibly a questionnaire of

students at your college. Try to contact a variety of types of students for your research.

11. Investigate a current trend you have noticed on television (collecting evidence by observing news programs, other programs, or commercials).

12. Write a survey of recent films of a certain kind (detective movies, horror movies, science fiction movies, comedies, love stories), making generalizations that you support with evidence from your own film watching.

**FOR GROUP LEARNING**

## Collaborating on a Research Assignment

To write a collaborative essay from library research is a complex job, and we recommend that you attempt it only if your writing group has already had some success in writing collaboratively. If you embark on such an endeavor, you will find that working as a research team can make your project advance with alacrity. After consulting with your instructor and getting a go-ahead, your group might develop a research paper following one of the assignments in this chapter.

You will need to fix a series of deadlines, parcel out the work, and meet faithfully according to a schedule. Everyone must do his or her share of the work. Here is a sample schedule that one group followed for an eight-week research project:

Week 1: Members individually seek a topic for the group project.

Week 2: The members of the group meet and agree on a topic: a research question. They choose a coordinator to keep the project moving, someone willing to make phone calls to keep in touch with people when necessary. They clear the topic with the instructor.

Weeks 3–4: Assisted by two people, the coordinator makes a preliminary search and compiles a tentative bibliography. The group members meet to divide up responsibilities: who will collect what material. Then, without further meetings, all members begin work.

Week 5: Each member continues his or her assigned portion of the research, reading and taking relevant notes.

Week 6: The group meets to evaluate the material and to see where any further information may be needed. Members collaborate on a rough plan or outline.

Week 7: Three writers divide up the outline and each writes part of a draft (if possible, with the aid of a word processor). The other group members read over the writing during this week and help solve any problems in it.

Week 8: All group members meet for one long evening session and carefully review the draft. All write comments and corrections on it. Then two fresh writers divide the criticized draft and type it up smoothly. One person in the group who is good at proofreading is designated to do that job for the group. The coordinator gives the whole paper another, final proofreading.

Obviously such a plan can succeed only if your group can work in a close, friendly, and responsible fashion. No one should enter into such an arrangement without first making sure he or she has enough unobstructed time to meet all assigned responsibilities — or else the whole project can bog down in an awful mess. But if it succeeds, as it probably will, your research will generate excitement. You'll know the pleasure of playing your part on a dynamic, functioning team. Many of you will do this type of writing on jobs in the future.

## *Applying What You Learn*

### SOME USES OF RESEARCH

In many courses beyond your English course you will be asked to write papers from research, both library research and field research. The more deeply you move into core requirements and specialized courses for your major, the more independent research and thinking you will do. At some colleges, a long research paper is required of all seniors to graduate. Beyond college, the demand for writing based on research is evident. Scholars explore issues that absorb and trouble them and the community of scholars to which they belong. In the business world, large companies often maintain their own specialized libraries since information and opinions are worth money, and decisions have to be based on them. If you should take an entry-level job in the headquarters of a large corporation, don't be surprised to be told, "We're opening a branch office in Sri Lanka, and Graham [the executive vice president] doesn't know a thing about the place. Can you write a report on it — customs, geography, climate, government, state of the economy, political stability, religion, lifestyle, and all that?" In a large city newspaper, reporters and feature writers continually do library research as well as field research, and the newspaper's library of clippings on subjects covered in the past (the "morgue") is in constant use.

As one of the ways they become prominent in their disciplines, academics and professionals in many fields — law, medicine, English, geography, sociology, art history, physics — write and publish papers in specialized journals and whole books based on research. Anthropologists and psychologists study how people live, archaeologists dig up evidence of how people lived in the past, biologists and students of the environment collect evidence about the behavior of species of wildlife — and all of them publish their findings so that other people can learn from them. In an exciting study of urban architecture, *Spaces: Dimensions of the Human Landscape* (New Haven: Yale UP, 1981), Barrie B. Greenbie draws connections between our notion of "self" — a personal universe bounded by the skin — and our sense of the kind of dwelling we feel at home in. In exploring this relationship (and the need to build dwellings that correspond to our psychic needs), Greenbie brings together sources in psychology, architecture, economics, and literature (the poetry of Emily Dickinson). This passage from the beginning of his book may give you a sense of his way of weaving together disparate materials:

> The psychoanalyst Carl Jung placed great emphasis on the house as a symbol of self, and many others have elaborated this idea.[1] Of course Jung considered "self" both in a social as well as individual sense, and in fact the concept of *self* has no meaning except in the context of *others*. Most of us share our houses with some sort of family group during most of our lives, and while parts of an adequately sized house may belong primarily to one or another individual, the boundaries of the home are usually those of a cluster of selves which form a domestic unit. Even people who by choice or circumstance live

alone express in their homes the images and traditions formed at one time in a family group.

The architects Kent C. Bloomer and Charles W. Moore view buildings as the projection into space of our awareness of our own bodies. Fundamental and obvious as this relationship might seem, it has been to a great extent ignored in contemporary architecture. Bloomer and Moore sum up the personal situation very well in their book, *Body, Memory, and Architecture:*

> One tell-tale sign remains, in modern America, of a world based not on a Cartesian abstraction, but on our sense of ourselves extended beyond the boundaries of our bodies to the world around: that is the single-family house, free-standing like ourselves, with a face and a back, a hearth (like a heart) and a chimney, an attic full of recollections of *up*, and a basement harboring implications of *down*.[2]

Many North American tract houses fit this characterization less adequately than they might. But whatever the deficiencies of domestic and other kinds of contemporary architecture may be, they are as nothing compared to the shortcomings of most urban design.... This book will focus on the hierarchical structures that extend from the "skin" of the family home to the street and beyond.

Notice that Greenbie uses endnote form (see p. 788) because the amount of information he has to put in his notes might have interrupted the flow of his prose. Endnote 1, for instance, reads:

> [1] Carl G. Jung, *Memories, Dreams, and Reflections* (London: Fontana Library Series, 1969). For an exceptionally good summary and elaboration, see Clare Cooper, "The House as Symbol of the Self," *Designing for Human Behavior*, ed. J. Lang et al. (Stroudsburg: Dowden, 1974).

In an example of effective field research, anthropologist E. Richard Sorenson reports his observations of children of the Fore, a tribal people in New Guinea who live by agriculture. He published his findings in "Cooperation and Freedom among the Fore in New Guinea" (in *Learning Non-Aggression: The Experience of Non-Literate Societies*, ed. Ashley Montagu [New York: Oxford UP, 1978]). Sorenson photographed growing children and their families in their daily activities. From the pictures and his notes, he formed several interesting generalizations about the Fore practices in childrearing.

> The core discovery was that young infants remained in almost continual bodily contact with their mother, her housemates, or her gardening associates. At first, mothers' laps were the center of activity, and infants occupied themselves there by nursing, sleeping, and playing with their own bodies or those of their caretakers. They were not put aside for the sake of other activities, as when food was being prepared or heavy loads were being carried. Remaining in close, uninterrupted physical contact with those around them, their basic needs, such as rest, nourishment, stimulation, and security, were continuously satisfied without obstacle....
> A second crucial thread running from infancy through childhood was the unrestricted manner in which exploratory activity and pursuit of interest were left to the initiative of the child. As the infant's awareness increased, his

interests broadened to the things his mother and other caretakers did and to the objects and materials they used. Then these youngsters began crawling out to explore things nearby that attracted their attention. By the time they were toddling their interests continually took them on short sorties to nearby objects and persons. As soon as they could walk well, the excursions extended to the entire hamlet and its gardens, and then beyond with other children. Developing without interference or supervision, this personal exploratory quest freely touched on whatever was around, even axes, knives, machetes, and fire [Figure 30.1].

Initially astonished by the ability of young children to manage so independently without being hurt, I eventually began to see how this capability also emerged from the infants' milieu of close human physical proximity and tactile interaction.... In continual physical touch with people engaged in daily pursuits, infants and toddlers began to learn the forms of behavior and

FIGURE 30.1   A generally practiced deference to the desires of the young in the choice of play objects permitted them to investigate and handle knives and other potentially harmful objects frequently. They were expected to make use of the tools and materials which belonged to their adult associates and were indulged in this expectation. As a result, use of knives was common, particularly for exploratory play.

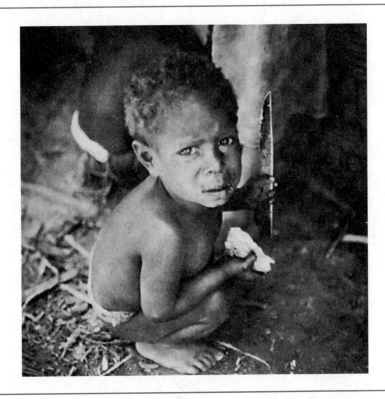

response characteristic of Fore life. . . . Competence with the tools of life developed quickly, and by the time they were able to walk, Fore youngsters could safely handle axes, knives, fire, and so on. . . .

At first I found it quite remarkable that toddlers did not recklessly thrust themselves into unappreciated dangers, the way our own children tend to do. Eventually I came to see that they had no reason to do so. From their earliest days, they enjoyed a benevolent sanctuary from which the world could be confidently viewed, tested, and appreciated. These human bases were neither demanding nor restrictive, so there was no need to escape or evade them in the manner so frequently seen in Western culture. Confidently, not furtively, the youngsters were able to extend their inquiry, widening their understanding as they chose. There was no need to play tricks or deceive in order to pursue life. Nor did they have to act out impulsively to break through subliminal fears induced by punishment or parental anxiety. Such children could safely move out on their own, unsupervised and unrestricted.

Most of us may never go on a field research expedition to New Guinea, but the techniques that Sorenson demonstrates — patiently collecting evidence, laying aside his own unwarranted assumptions, and finally making generalizations about the behavior patterns he observed — may serve for any investigation of the unfamiliar. You might try emulating Sorenson's accuracy, patience, and open-mindedness the next time you write a paper about people or a lifestyle different from your own.

# Chapter 31

# Documenting Sources:
# Using a Style Book

When writers use information from other sources — written or spoken — they *document* those sources. That is, in the text of their paper they cite the exact source (book or article with page number, person interviewed, television program) for every fact or idea, paraphrased or quoted, from their research. At the end of their paper, they list the sources cited. The purpose of citing and listing sources is twofold: (1) to give proper credit to the original writer or speaker and (2) to enable any interested reader to look up a source for further information. The mechanics of documentation may seem fussy, but the obligation to cite and list sources keeps research writers truthful and responsible.

Writers of college research papers most often follow the rules for citing sources from either of two handbooks, one compiled by the Modern Language Association (MLA), the other by the American Psychological Association (APA). The style of the MLA is generally observed in English composition, literature, history, foreign language courses, and other humanities. APA style usually prevails in the social sciences and business. If your research takes you into any scholarly or professional journals in those special areas, you will probably find all the articles following a recognizable style.

In other disciplines, other handbooks prescribe style: the *Scientific Style and Format: The CBE Style Manual for Authors, Editors, and Publishers* of the Council of Biology Editors (1994), for instance, is used in the biological sciences and medicine. You will need to familiarize yourself with it, or with other manuals, if you ever do much research writing in those or other disciplines.

You need not memorize any of the documentation styles. Instead, you should understand that you will use different styles in different disciplines, and you need to practice using at least one style to become accustomed to scholarly practices. For the purpose of the papers you write in your composition course, more than likely your instructor will ask you to use the MLA style. Maria Halloran's and Chris Robinson's papers in Chapter 30 illustrate the use of this style. Linda Hackler's paper is in APA style.

This chapter is here for handy reference. We try to tell you no more than you will need to know to write a freshman research paper. Knowing MLA style or APA style will be useful at these moments:

*In citing while you write* — at any time when you want to document, often on a note card or in your paper, exactly where you obtained a fact, statistic, idea, opinion, quotation, graph, or chart.

*In listing all your sources* — that is, in adding a final bibliography, a list entitled "Works Cited" or "References."

# Citing Sources: MLA Style

As you write, you need to indicate in the text of your paper or in a parenthetical reference what you borrowed and where you found it. For complete information about your source, readers can then turn to the end of your paper and refer to your list titled "Works Cited" (see p. 780). The *MLA Handbook for Writers of Research Papers*, 4th ed. (New York: MLA, 1995) has extensive and exact recommendations. If you want more detailed advice than that given here, you can purchase a copy of the *MLA Handbook* or see a copy in the reference room of your college library.

## CITING PRINTED SOURCES: NONFICTION BOOKS

To cite a book in the text of a paper, you usually place in parentheses the author's last name and the number of the page containing the information cited. You do this as close as possible to your mention of the information, as in the following examples.

### SINGLE AUTHOR

At least one critic maintains that Dean Rusk's exposure to Nazi power in Europe in the 1930s permanently influenced his attitude toward appeasement:

> In contrast to Acheson, who had attended Groton, Yale, and Harvard despite his family's genteel poverty, Rusk was sheer Horatio Alger stuff. He had grown up barefoot, the son of a tenant farmer in Georgia's Cherokee county, and

```
                    had worked his way through Davidson. . . .
                    Then came the moment that transformed his life
                    and his thinking. He won a Rhodes scholarship
                    to Oxford. More important, his exposure to Eu-
                    rope in the early 1930s, as the Nazis consoli-
                    dated their power in Germany, scarred his mind,
                    leading him to share Acheson's hostility to ap-
                    peasement in any form anywhere. (Karnow 194)
           One reason we admire Simone de Beauvoir is that "she
           lived the life she believed" (Morgan 58).
```

Notice that a direct quotation longer than four lines is indented one inch (or ten spaces) and needs no quotation marks to set it off from the text of your paper.

For the sake of readability and transition, you'll sometimes want to mention an author or authors in your text, putting only the page number in parentheses.

### TWO OR MORE AUTHORS

```
           Taylor and Wheeler present yet another view (25).
```

### MULTIPLE WORKS BY THE SAME AUTHOR

If you have used two or more works by the same author (or authors), you need to indicate with an abbreviated title which one you are citing in your text. In a paper that uses as sources two books by Iona and Peter Opie, *The Lore and Language of Schoolchildren* and *The Oxford Nursery Rhyme Book,* you would cite the first book as follows:

```
           The Opies found that the children they interviewed were
           more straightforward when asked about their "magic prac-
           tices" or their "ways of obtaining luck or averting ill-
           luck" than when asked about their "superstitions" (Lore
           210).
```

### A MULTIVOLUME WORK

For a work with multiple volumes, provide the author's name and the volume number followed by a colon and the page number.

```
           In ancient times, astrological predictions were sometimes
           used as a kind of black magic (Sarton 2: 319).
```

### ENTIRE WORK

If you refer to an entire work and include the title and the name of the author, a specific page reference is unnecessary.

In <u>The Story of My Boyhood and Youth</u>, John Muir details his boyhood in Scotland, his immigration to America, and the hardships of farm life.

### INDIRECT SOURCE

Whenever possible, cite the original source. If that source is unavailable to you (as often happens with published accounts of spoken remarks), use the abbreviation "qtd. in" (for "quoted in") before the secondary source you cite in parentheses.

> Zill says that, psychologically, children in stepfamilies most resemble children in single-parent families, even if they live in a two-parent household (qtd. in Derber 119).

## CITING PRINTED SOURCES: LITERATURE

### NOVEL OR SHORT STORY

> In A Tale of Two Cities, Dickens describes the aptly named Stryver, who "had a pushing way of shouldering himself (morally and physically) into companies and conversations, that argued well for his shouldering his way up in life" (110; bk. 2, ch. 4).

### MORE THAN ONE NOVEL OR SHORT STORY

When referring to more than one novel or short story in your paper, distinguish citations by using authors' names.

> The character Naomi spends money like water, buying a new kimono every month (Tanizaki 74; ch. 9). Dina's desires, however, are limited by her income. Early in White Horses she complains that her family cannot afford a new car (Hoffman 12; ch. 1).

### PLAY

For classic plays, leave out page numbers and include the act, scene, and line numbers, separating them with periods.

> Love, Iago says, "is merely a lust of the blood and a permission of the will" (Othello 1.3.326).

> In Equus, Dora says, "What the eye does not see, the heart does not grieve over, does it?" (1.7).

### POETRY

When you cite poetry, use the word "line" or "lines" in the first reference and cite only numbers in subsequent references, as in the following examples from William Wordsworth's "The World Is Too Much with Us." The first reference:

> "The world is too much with us; late and soon / Getting
> and spending, we lay waste our powers" (lines 1-2).

The subsequent reference:

> "Or hear old Triton blow his wreathed horn" (14).

### A WORK IN AN ANTHOLOGY

For works in an anthology, use the author of the selection, not the editor of the collection, in your text or in the parentheses.

> In the opening lines of Julio Marzan's "The Ingredient,"
> Vincent finds himself looking down upon his neighborhood
> from a rooftop and realizing that "there was a kind of
> beauty to the view" (145).

## CITING PRINTED SOURCES: REFERENCE BOOKS AND PERIODICALS

### ARTICLE IN A REFERENCE BOOK

In citing a one-page article from a work with entries arranged alphabetically, include the author's name in your text or in the parenthetical reference and omit the page number.

> Some intellectuals have offered unusual definitions of
> love, with one calling it the force that enables individ-
> uals to "understand the separateness of other people"
> (Havell).

If a reference article is long, give the page number.

> Gordon discusses Carver's "implosive" technique of ending
> stories just before epiphany (176).

If the article is unsigned, include a brief title in your text or in the parenthetical citation.

> She alienated many feminists with her portraits of women
> "who seemed to accept victimization" ("Didion").

### JOURNAL ARTICLE

If the author is named in the text, cite just the page number(s) in the parenthetical reference.

> Mueller notes that Arthur's quest "aims at a goal that
> is, suggestively, beyond the immediate context of the
> narrative" (751).

If the author is not named in the text, provide the name in the reference.

> Arthur's quest "aims at a goal that is, suggestively, be-
> yond the immediate context of the narrative" (Mueller
> 751).

### MAGAZINE OR NEWSPAPER ARTICLE

In citing a one-page magazine or newspaper article, include the author's name in your text or in a parenthetical reference. Do not include the page number, which will be noted in the list of works cited at the end of the paper.

> Vacuum-tube audio equipment is making a comeback, with
> aficionados praising the warmth and glow from the tubes,
> as well as the sound (Patton).

When citing articles longer than one page, provide the specific page number(s) in the parenthetical reference.

> Some less than perfect means have been used to measure
> television viewership, including a sensor that scans
> rooms for "hot bodies" (Larson 69).

When citing an anonymous magazine article, put the first few words of the title of the article in parentheses, beginning with the word by which it is alphabetized in the list of works cited.

> At least one former gang member has gone on to write
> about his experiences ("Other Side").

Omit the page number when citing a one-page article.

> Conservatives have attacked public television lately,
> with one calling <u>Sesame Street</u> "just another kids' show"
> (Carter).

THE BIBLE

```
The Bible speaks of the sacrifice God made to save the
world (John 3.16).
```

No entry is necessary in the list of works cited.


## CITING NONPRINT SOURCES

In both library and field research, some of your material will probably be drawn from nonprint sources: interviews, questionnaires, phone calls, tapes and recordings, personal letters, films, filmstrips, slide programs, videotapes, computer programs. You should document all your nonprint material as faithfully as you credit books, newspapers, and periodicals. Probably the easiest way to do that is to weave your mention of each source into the body of your paper.

```
Hearing Yeats read "The Song of the Old Mother" on tape
sheds new light on several lines in the poem.

On the H. L. Mencken recording, journalist Donald Howe
Kirkley, Sr., was able to persuade the veteran writer to
talk about his defeats as well as his triumphs.

Robert S. Boynton's article on The Atlantic Monthly
Online explored the recent achievements and popularity of
the new black intellectuals.
```

In your list of works cited you give complete information about each source. Transitions — phrases to introduce quotations, statistical tables, and other blocks of material — can also serve you well. (For weaving material in gracefully, see the suggestions in Chapter 30, p. 713.)


# Listing Sources: MLA Style

At the end of your paper, you will provide a list of the sources from which you have cited ideas or information in your text. If you indicated the work and page number on each of your source notes while doing your research, you will have little trouble compiling this list. For most English courses, you will follow the guidelines set forth by the Modern Language Association (MLA).

The list of sources is called "Works Cited," includes only those sources actually used in your paper, and is placed at the end of your paper. Center the title at the top of a new page. Double-space the list and alphabetize the entries by authors' last names, or, for works with no author, by title. When an entry exceeds one line, indent the second and subsequent lines one-half inch (or five spaces).

## LISTING PRINTED SOURCES: BOOKS

Notice that the information about each source is divided into three sections, each followed by a period: author or agency's name (if there is one), title, and publishing information. Give the author's name, last name first, and the title in full as they appear on the title page. (If a work has more than one author, all names after the first are given in normal order.) If the publisher lists more than one city, include just the first. Use just the first name of a publisher with multiple names: not Holt, Rinehart and Winston, but simply Holt. Omit initials too. For J. B. Lippincott Co., simply write Lippincott.

### SINGLE AUTHOR

Bolton, Ruthie. Gal: A True Life. New York: Harcourt,
     1994.

### TWO OR THREE AUTHORS

Majors, Richard G., and Janet M. Billson. Cool Pose: The
     Dilemmas of Black Manhood in America. New York: Lex-
     ington, 1992.

### FOUR OR MORE AUTHORS

Bercuson, David J., et al. Colonies: Canada to 1867.
     Toronto: Ryerson-McGraw, 1992.

### MULTIPLE WORKS BY THE SAME AUTHOR

List the works alphabetically by title.

Opie, Iona, and Peter Opie. The Lore and Language of
     Schoolchildren. Oxford: Clarendon-Oxford UP, 1960.

---, eds. The Oxford Nursery Rhyme Book. Oxford: Claren-
     don-Oxford UP, 1955.

### CORPORATE AUTHOR

American Red Cross. Lifesaving: Rescue and Water Safety.
     New York: Doubleday, 1984.

UNKNOWN AUTHOR

<u>Alcoholism and You</u>. Pearl Island: Okra, 1986.

EDITED BOOK

If your paper focuses on the work or its author, cite the author first.

Hardy, Thomas. <u>Tess of the D'Urbervilles</u>. Ed. Scott
    Elledge. 3rd ed. New York: Norton, 1991.

If your paper focuses on the editor or the edition used, cite the editor first.

Elledge, Scott, ed. <u>Tess of the D'Urbervilles</u>. By Thomas
    Hardy. 3rd ed. New York: Norton, 1991.

TRANSLATED WORK

Chekhov, Anton. <u>Love and Other Stories</u>. Trans. Constance
    Garnett. New York: Ecco, 1987.

If your paper focuses on the translation, cite the translator first.

Garnett, Constance, trans. <u>Love and Other Stories</u>. By An-
    ton Chekhov. New York: Ecco, 1987.

MULTIVOLUME WORK

<u>Out of Many: A History of the American People</u>. 2 vols.
    Englewood Cliffs: Prentice, 1994.

Ford, Boris, ed. <u>The Age of Shakespeare</u>. New York: Pen-
    guin, 1982. Vol. 2 of <u>The New Pelican Guide to Eng-
    lish Literature</u>. 8 vols. 1982-84.

REVISED EDITION

Eble, Kenneth E. <u>The Craft of Teaching</u>. 2nd ed. San Fran-
    cisco: Jossey, 1988.

Cuddon, J. A., ed. <u>A Dictionary of Literary Terms</u>. 3rd
    ed. Garden City: Doubleday, 1991.

BOOK IN A SERIES

```
Berlin, Jeffrey B., ed. Approaches to Teaching Mann's
        Death in Venice. Approaches to Teaching World Lit.
        43. New York: MLA, 1992.
```

## LISTING PRINTED SOURCES: PARTS OF BOOKS

When documenting parts of books give the author of the book first. The editor of the book should follow the title. Following the publication information give the page numbers of the selection.

CHAPTER OR SECTION IN A BOOK

```
Galbraith, John Kenneth. "The Military Power." The Nu-
        clear Crisis Reader. Ed. Gwyn Prins. New York: Vin-
        tage, 1984. 197-209.
```

ESSAY IN AN EDITED COLLECTION

```
Berthoff, Werner. "The Example of Billy Budd." Twentieth
        Century Interpretations of Billy Budd: A Collection
        of Critical Essays. Ed. Howard P. Vincent. Englewood
        Cliffs: Prentice, 1971. 58-60.
```

SHORT STORY, POEM, OR PLAY IN AN EDITED COLLECTION

```
Le Guin, Ursula K. "Nine Lives." The World Treasury of
        Science Fiction. Ed. Clifton Fadiman. Boston: Lit-
        tle, 1989. 572-94.
```

TWO OR MORE WORKS FROM THE SAME EDITED COLLECTION

The following examples show citations for articles in the collection *Growing Up Latino: Memoirs and Stories* as well as the citation for the collection itself.

```
Alvarez, Julia. "Daughter of Invention." Augenbraum and
        Stavans 3-15.
```

```
Augenbraum, Harold, and Ilan Stavans, eds. Growing Up
        Latino: Memoirs and Stories. Boston: Houghton, 1993.
```

```
Colón, Jesús. "Kipling and I." Augenbraum and Stavans
        155-58.
```

## LISTING PRINTED SOURCES: REFERENCE BOOKS

It is unnecessary to supply the editor, publisher, or place of publication for well-known references such as *Webster's, The Random House Dictionary, World Book Encyclopedia,* and *Encyclopaedia Britannica.* Omit volume and page numbers when citing an entry from a reference that is arranged alphabetically.

### SIGNED DICTIONARY ENTRY

```
Turner, V. W. "Divination." A Dictionary of the Social
     Sciences. Ed. Julius Gould and William L. Kolb. New
     York: Free, 1964.
```

### UNSIGNED DICTIONARY ENTRY

```
"Organize." Webster's Third New International Dictionary.
     1993 ed.
```

### SIGNED ENCYCLOPEDIA ARTICLE

```
Binder, Raymond C., et al. "Mathematical Aspects of Phys-
     ical Theories." Encyclopaedia Britannica: Macropae-
     dia. 15th ed. 1993.
```

### UNSIGNED ENCYCLOPEDIA ARTICLE

```
"Jellyfish." Encyclopaedia Britannica: Micropaedia. 1993
     ed.
```

## LISTING PRINTED SOURCES: PERIODICALS

### JOURNAL ARTICLE WITH SEPARATE PAGINATION

To list an article from a journal that paginates each issue of a volume separately, provide the volume number and issue number, separated by a period.

```
Fitzgerald, Kathryn R. "Rhetorical Implications of School
     Discourse for Writing Placement." Journal of Basic
     Writing 7.1 (1988): 61-72.
```

### JOURNAL ARTICLE WITH CONTINUOUS PAGINATION

In journals with continuous pagination, page numbers run continuously through all issues of a volume. To cite these journals, give the volume number, year, and page numbers.

Walker, Cheryl. "Feminist Literary Criticism and the Author." Critical Inquiry 16 (1990): 551-71.

### SIGNED MAGAZINE ARTICLE

Weschler, Lawrence. "Artist in Exile." New Yorker 5 Dec. 1994: 88-106.

If the article does not appear on consecutive pages, list the starting page number followed by +.

Lemley, Brad. "The Underground Architect." New Age Jan.-Feb. 1995: 66+.

### UNSIGNED MAGAZINE ARTICLE

"Other Side of Cool." Mother Jones May-June 1992: 19.

### SIGNED NEWSPAPER ARTICLE

Kolata, Gina. "Men and Women Use Brain Differently, Study Discovers." New York Times 16 Feb. 1995, natl. ed.: A1+.

Wilkie, Curtis. "Mississippi Flogging Debate Opens Old "Wounds." Boston Globe 21 Feb. 1995: 1.

### UNSIGNED NEWSPAPER ARTICLE

"US Seeks Broader NATO Ties for Russia." Boston Globe 21 Feb. 1995: 4.

### SIGNED EDITORIAL

Schrag, Peter. "When Government Goes on Autopilot." Editorial. New York Times 16 Feb. 1995, natl. ed.: A27.

### UNSIGNED EDITORIAL

"Budget Fudge." Editorial. Nation 27 Feb. 1995: 259-60.

### PUBLISHED INTERVIEW

Kallen, Ben. "Freeing Your Inner Artist." New Age Journal Feb. 1995: 53+.

LETTER TO THE EDITOR

```
Freeland, Edward P. Letter. Atlantic Feb. 1995: 10.
```

## LISTING OTHER PRINTED SOURCES

GOVERNMENT DOCUMENT

```
United States. Dept. of Health and Human Services. Mos-
    quito Control Measures in Gulf Coast States. Wash-
    ington: GPO, 1986.
```

PAMPHLET

```
Association of American Publishers. An Author's Primer to
    Word Processing. New York: Assn. of Amer. Publish-
    ers, 1983.
```

PERSONAL LETTER OR ELECTRONIC MAIL

```
Jones, Sam. Letter to the author. 3 May 1994.

Gilbert, Jenny. E-mail to the author. 15 Mar. 1995.
```

MATERIAL FOUND WITH A COMPUTER DATABASE

```
Edwards, Harry. "The Athlete as Role Model: Relic of
    America's Sports Past?" Sport Nov. 1994: 32. Info-
    Trac: Magazine Index Plus. CD-ROM. Information Ac-
    cess. Feb. 1995.
```

## LISTING NONPRINT SOURCES

COMPUTER SOFTWARE

```
Writer's Prologue. Vers. 3.3. Diskette. New York: St.
    Martin's, 1993.
```

MATERIAL ACCESSED THROUGH AN ON-LINE COMPUTER SERVICE

Cite the print information first; followed by the on-line information and the
date of access.

```
Boynton, Robert S. "The New Intellectuals." Atlantic
    Monthly Mar. 1995. Atlantic Monthly Online. Online.
    America Online. 3 Mar. 1995.
```

### MATERIAL ACCESSED THROUGH A COMPUTER NETWORK

Handle material accessed through computer networks as you do material accessed through on-line computer services.

> Washington, Booker T. Up from Slavery. Boston: Houghton,
> 1901. Online. Internet Wiretap. Internet. 6 Mar.
> 1995.

### AUDIOTAPE OR RECORDING

Begin with the name of the speaker, the writer, or the production director, depending on what you want to emphasize.

> Mencken, H. L. H. L. Mencken Speaking. Caedmon, 1960.

> Yeats, William Butler. "The Song of the Old Mother." The
> Poems of William Butler Yeats. Read by William But-
> ler Yeats, Siobhan McKenna, and Michael MacLiammoir.
> Audiotape. Spoken Arts, 1974.

### TELEVISION OR RADIO PROGRAM

> The Windsors: A Royal Family. PBS. WGBH, Boston. 12 Mar.
> 1995.

> "A Dangerous Man: Lawrence after Arabia." Perf. Ralph
> Fiennes and Siddig el Fadil. Great Performances.
> PBS. WNET, New York. 6 May 1992.

### FILM

> Knights of the Round Table. Dir. Richard Thorpe. MGM,
> 1953.

If you cite a person connected with the film, start with his or her name.

> Thorpe, Richard, dir. Knights of the Round Table. MGM,
> 1953.

### FILMSTRIP, SLIDE PROGRAM, VIDEOTAPE

> Wildlife Conservation. Sound filmstrip. Wildlife Research
> Group, 1986.

> A Midsummer Night's Dream. Dir. Peter Hall. Prof. Diana
> Rigg and David Warner. Videocassette. Drama Classics
> Video, 1968.

**A WORK OF ART**

Botticelli, Sandro. The Birth of Venus. Uffizi Gallery,
    Florence.

**SPEECH OR LECTURE**

Hurley, James. Address. Opening Gen. Sess. Amer. Bar
    Assn. Convention. Chicago, 17 Jan. 1987.

**BROADCAST INTERVIEW**

Edelman, Marian Wright. Interview. WBUR, Boston. 7 May
    1992.

**PERSONAL INTERVIEW**

Boyd, Dierdre. Personal interview. 5 Feb. 1994.

Ladner, John. Telephone interview. 20 Oct. 1995.

# Citing Sources: Endnotes

Some writers continue to prefer notes rather than simple parenthetical citations for documentation, especially when the citations need to be long.

If you use endnotes, you number your citations consecutively in the body
of your text, like this: [1]. You roll your typewriter platen up a notch or learn the
command in your word processing program for superscripts. Then, at the end
of your text, on a new page, you center the title "Notes," double-space, and
give the bibliographic information for each source, in sequence, with a corresponding number. Double-space the entire list, and indent the first line of

---

each entry one-half inch (or five spaces). Unless your instructor prefers otherwise, this method can eliminate the need for a "Works Cited" list since it contains the same publishing information, along with the specific page number for each citation. Only the form is slightly different.

A comma separates the authors' names from the title. For books, the publishing information is in parentheses, and the number of the page containing the borrowed information is not set off with a comma or any other punctuation.

For articles, the publication name is preceded by a comma and follows the form of the works cited list. The note for the first sentence of this paragraph would look like this (the example also shows how to cite a second or later edition of a book):

### FIRST REFERENCE TO A WORK

[1] Joseph Gibaldi, MLA Handbook for Writers of Research Papers, 4th ed. (New York: MLA, 1995) 183.

### SUBSEQUENT REFERENCES

If you cite the same work a second time, you use just the author's (or authors') last names and a page number.

[2] Gibaldi 181.

## PRINTED SOURCES: BOOKS

### REFERENCES TO MULTIPLE WORKS BY THE SAME AUTHOR

If you have consulted more than one work by the same author (or authors), give full documentation for each one the first time it is mentioned. In subsequent references, include an abbreviated title after the author's name. For instance, if you have previously referred to two books by Iona and Peter Opie, *The Lore and Language of Schoolchildren* and *The Oxford Nursery Rhyme Book,* a later citation might look like this:

[3] Opie and Opie, Lore 192.

### MULTIVOLUME WORK

When you cite a multivolume work, indicate which volume contains the pages from which you have borrowed.

[4] Francis James Child, ed., The English and Scottish Popular Ballads, vol. 2 (New York: Cooper Square, 1962) 373-76.

### WORK IN AN EDITED COLLECTION

5 Warner Berthoff, "The Example of Billy Budd," <u>Twentieth-Century Interpretations of Billy Budd: A Collection of Critical Essays</u>, ed. Howard P. Vincent (Englewood Cliffs: Prentice, 1971) 58-60.

## PRINTED SOURCES: PERIODICALS

### JOURNAL ARTICLE

6 Carol Cook, "'The Sign and Semblance of Her Honor': Reading Gender Difference in <u>Much Ado about Nothing</u>," <u>PMLA</u> 101 (1986): 200.

### NEWSPAPER OR MAGAZINE ARTICLE

7 Alan Cowell, "Attack on Austrian Gypsies Deepens Fear of Neo-Nazis," <u>New York Times</u> 21 Feb. 1995, natl. ed.: A1.

8 Robin Morgan, "The World without de Beauvoir," <u>Ms.</u> July 1986: 58.

## OTHER PRINTED SOURCES

### WORK WITH A CORPORATE AUTHOR

9 American Red Cross, <u>Lifesaving: Rescue and Water Safety</u> (New York: Doubleday, 1984) 181.

### GOVERNMENT DOCUMENT

10 United States, Dept. of Health and Human Services, <u>Mosquito Control Measures in Gulf Coast States</u> (Washington: GPO, 1986) 25.

### UNKNOWN AUTHOR

11 <u>Alcoholism and You</u> (Pearl Island: Okra, 1986) 3.

## NONPRINT SOURCES

### AUDIOTAPE OR RECORDING

12 H. L. Mencken, <u>H. L. Mencken Speaking</u>, Caedmon, 1960.

<sup>13</sup> William Butler Yeats, "The Song of the Old
Mother," The Poems of William Butler Yeats, read by
William Butler Yeats, Siobhan McKenna, and Michael
MacLiammoir, audiotape, Spoken Arts, 1974.

### FILMSTRIP, SLIDE PROGRAM, VIDEOTAPE

<sup>14</sup> Wildlife Conservation, sound filmstrip, Wildlife
Research Group, 1986.

### LECTURE

<sup>15</sup> Johndan Johnson-Eilola, "Accumulation and
Association: Economies of Text in Online Research
Spaces," address, Conf. on Coll. Composition and
Communication, Nashville, 19 Mar. 1994.

### PERSONAL LETTER OR ELECTRONIC MAIL

<sup>16</sup> Sam Jones, letter to the author, 3 May 1992.

<sup>17</sup> Jenny Gilbert, E-mail to the author, 15 Mar. 1995.

### PERSONAL INTERVIEW

<sup>18</sup> Helen Nearing, personal interview, 12 Nov. 1995.

<sup>19</sup> John Bowlby, telephone interview, 3 June 1993.

# Citing Sources: APA Style

The American Psychological Association (APA) details the style most commonly used in the social sciences in its *Publication Manual*, 4th ed. (Washington: APA, 1994). As in MLA style, APA citations are placed in parentheses in the body of the text.

## CITING PRINTED SOURCES

To cite a work in the APA style, you usually place in parentheses the author's last name and the year the source was published. Do this as close as possible to your mention of the information you have borrowed. Give a page number in parentheses only for a direct quotation from the source.

### SINGLE AUTHOR NOT CITED IN TEXT

A number of experts now believe that cognitive development begins much earlier than Piaget had thought (Gelman,
1978).

#### AUTHOR CITED IN TEXT

If the author's name appears in the body of the text, give only the date in parentheses.

```
As Gelman (1978) points out, a number of experts now be-
lieve that cognitive development begins much earlier than
Piaget had thought.
```

If you are citing ideas from a long work, you can refer to a specific page so your readers can easily find the reference. Use the abbrevation "p." (or "pp.").

```
Dean Rusk's exposure to Nazi power in Europe in the 1930s
seems to have permanently influenced his attitude toward
appeasement (Karnow, 1991, p. 194).
```

When the author's name appears in the text, put the page number in parentheses after the cited material.

Karnow (1991) maintains that Dean Rusk's exposure to Nazi power in Europe in the 1930s "scarred his mind" (p. 194).

### QUOTATION FORMAT

If you quote more than forty words from your source, indent the whole quotation five spaces. Put the author's name, the publication year, and the page number in parentheses following the quotation with no additional period.

At least one critic maintains that Dean Rusk's exposure to Nazi power in Europe in the 1930s permanently influenced his attitude toward appeasement:

> Then came the moment that transformed his life and his thinking. He won a Rhodes scholarship to Oxford. More important, his exposure to Europe in the early 1930s, as the Nazis consolidated their power in Germany, scarred his mind, leading him to share Acheson's hostility to appeasement in any form anywhere. (Karnow, 1991, p. 194)

### TWO AUTHORS

Refer to coauthors by their last names, in the order in which they appear in the book or article you cite. Join the names by "and" if you mention them in the body of your text, by an ampersand ("&") in parentheses.

Ex-mental patients released from institutions but given no follow-up care will almost surely fail to cope with the stresses of living on their own (Bassuk & Gerson, 1978).

Bassuk and Gerson (1978) hold out little hope for ex-mental patients who are released from institutions but are given no follow-up care.

### THREE TO FIVE AUTHORS

When a book or article you cite has three to five authors, include all the last names in your first reference only. In referring to the same source again, use the first author's name only, followed by "et al." (for "and others"), whether in text or in parentheses.

In one study, the IQs of adopted children were found to correlate more closely with the IQs of their biological

mothers than with those of their adoptive mothers (Horn,
Loehlin, & Wellerman, 1975).

### SIX OR MORE AUTHORS

For six or more authors, use "et al." even in the first reference.

Later studies have challenged the genetic view advanced
by Wesson et al. (1978) by citing, among other things,
selective placement on the part of adoption agencies.

### CORPORATE AUTHOR

There are three signs of oxygen deprivation (American Red
Cross, 1984).

### GOVERNMENT DOCUMENT

In the first citation in your text, identify the document by originating agency,
followed by its abbreviation (if any) and year of publication (and page number, if appropriate).

Clearly, it is of paramount importance to stop the spread
of mosquito-borne diseases (Department of Health and Human Services [DHHS], 1986, p. 25).

In later citations use just the abbreviation for the agency and the date:
(DHHS, 1986).

### UNKNOWN AUTHOR

When you cite an anonymous work, identify it with a short title and a date.

There are questions people can ask themselves if they
suspect their drinking has gotten out of hand
(Alcoholism, 1986).

### MULTIPLE WORKS BY THE SAME AUTHOR

One nuclear energy proponent for years has insisted on
the importance of tight controls for the industry (Weinberg, 1972). . . . He goes so far as to call on utility
companies to insure each reactor with their own funds
(Weinberg, 1977).

When citing two or more sources written by the same author in the same year, arrange the titles alphabetically in the reference list (see p. 133) and identify each with a lowercase letter placed after the date (1976a, 1976b, 1976c, and so on). Identify them the same way in your text.

```
Those who advocate the "genesis strategy" would have the
world store up food in preparation for future climatic
changes (Schneider, 1976b).
```

## CITING OTHER SOURCES

### PERSONAL COMMUNICATIONS

Personal communications — including personal interviews, letters, memos, and electronic mail — are not given in the reference list in APA style. But in the text of your paper, you should include the initials and surname of your communicator, with the date of the communication.

```
C. G. Sherwood (personal communication, September 29,
1986) has specific suggestions about the market in Bel-
gium.
```

```
It is important to keep in mind the cultural differences
between countries, especially the differences between the
United States and Belgium (C. G. Sherwood, personal com-
munication, September 29, 1986).
```

# Listing Sources: APA Style

If you're using APA guidelines, each entry should contain most of the same information given in an MLA citation, but the format is slightly different. In the APA style, the list of works cited is called "References" and appears at the end of the text. For entries that run past the first line, indent subsequent lines five spaces.

Organize your list alphabetically by authors' last names. The year appears immediately following the authors' names, in parentheses. In the titles of books and articles, capitalize only the first word, proper names, and the word following a colon. Underline book titles, but use no quotation marks or underlining for article titles. Underline journal names and capitalize all important words. For the authors' first and middle names, only initials are used. Note that APA style uses a more complete name for a publisher (including "Press") than does MLA style.

## LISTING PRINTED SOURCES: BOOKS

### SINGLE AUTHOR

Karnow, S. (1991). <u>Vietnam: A history.</u> New York: Viking.

### TWO OR MORE AUTHORS

Abelson, R., & Friquegnon, M. (1982). <u>Ethics for modern life.</u> New York: St. Martin's Press.

### CORPORATE AUTHOR

American Red Cross. (1984). <u>Lifesaving: Rescue and water safety.</u> New York: Doubleday.

### UNKNOWN AUTHOR

<u>Alcoholism and you.</u> (1986). Pearl Island: Okra Press.

### MULTIPLE WORKS BY THE SAME AUTHOR

Arrange the titles by date, the earliest first.

Terkel, S. (1988). <u>The great divide: Second thoughts on the American dream.</u> New York: Pantheon Books.

Terkel, S. (1992). <u>Race: How blacks and whites think and feel about the American obsession.</u> New York: New Press.

### MULTIPLE WORKS BY THE SAME AUTHOR, PUBLISHED DURING THE SAME YEAR

Arrange the titles alphabetically and identify their order with lowercase letters beginning with "a."

Schneider, S. H. (1976a). <u>Climate change and the world predicament: A case study for interdisciplinary re-search.</u> Boulder, CO: National Center for Atmospheric Research.

Schneider, S. H. (1976b). <u>The genesis strategy: Climate and global survival.</u> New York: Plenum Press.

CHAPTER OR SECTION OF A BOOK

Galbraith, J. K. (1984). The military power. In Gwyn
        Prins (Ed.), The nuclear crisis reader (pp. 197-
        209). New York: Vintage Books.

WORK IN AN EDITED COLLECTION

Lewontin, R. C. (1976). Race and intelligence. In N. J.
        Block & G. Dworkin (Eds.), The IQ controversy (pp.
        78-92). New York: Pantheon Books.

EDITED BOOK

Schneir, M. (Ed.). (1994). Feminism in our time: Essen-
        tial writings, World War II to the present. New
        York: Vintage Books.

TRANSLATED WORK

Ishinomori, I. (1988). Japan inc.: Introduction to Japan-
        ese economics (B. Schneiner, Trans.). Berkeley: Uni-
        versity of California Press. (Original work
        published 1986.)

REVISED EDITION

Koch, H. W. (Ed.). (1984) The origins of the First World
        War: Great power rivalry and German war aims (2nd
        ed.). New York: St. Martin's Press.

## LISTING PRINTED SOURCES: PERIODICALS

ARTICLE FROM A JOURNAL PAGINATED BY ISSUE

Meyer, D. S. (1992). Star wars, Star Wars, and American
        political culture. Journal of Popular Culture,
        26(2), 99-115.

ARTICLE FROM A JOURNAL PAGINATED BY VOLUME

Gelman, R. (1978). Cognitive development. Annual Review
        of Psychology, 29, 297-332.

MAGAZINE ARTICLE

Laycock, G. (1991, September-October). Good times are
        killing the Keys. Audubon, 93, 38-49.

### SIGNED NEWSPAPER ARTICLE

Brody, J. E. (1995, February 21). Health factor in veg-
    etables still elusive. The New York Times, p. C1.

### UNSIGNED NEWSPAPER ARTICLE

Stimulation seen to hurt babies' sleeping habits. (1995,
    February 21). Boston Globe, p. 13.

### LETTER TO THE EDITOR

Beeman, R. H. (1994, September). Time travel [Letter to
    the editor]. Scientific American, 271, 10.

## LISTING OTHER PRINTED SOURCES

### GOVERNMENT DOCUMENT

Start with the name of the department and then give the date of publication,
the title (and author, if any), identifying number, and publisher.

Department of Health and Human Services. (1986). Mosquito
    control measures in Gulf Coast states (DHHS Publica-
    tion No. F 82-06000). Washington, DC: U.S. Govern-
    ment Printing Office.

### MATERIAL FOUND WITH AN INFORMATION SERVICE OR COMPUTER DATABASE

Rocco, P. L. (1991). Lithium and suicidal behavior in
    bipolar patients. Medical Science Research, 19, 910-
    916. (PsycLIT Accession No. 78- 34111)

## LISTING NONPRINT SOURCES

### RECORDING

Mencken, H. L. (1960). H. L. Mencken speaking (Record No.
    TC 1082). New York: Caedmon.

### VIDEOTAPE, AUDIOTAPE, SLIDE PROGRAM

Burns, K. (Producer). (1992). Empire of the air [Video-
    tape].

The location of the distributor, if it is known, appears at the end of the citation.

#### TELEVISION OR RADIO PROGRAM

```
Braithwaite, D., & Jimenez, S. (1995). Murder, rape and
     DNA. In: P. Aspell (Executive Producer), Nova.
     Boston: WGBH.
```

#### FILM OR FILMSTRIP

```
Wildlife Research Group (Producer). (1986). Wildlife
     conservation [Sound filmstrip].
```

#### COMPUTER SOFTWARE

```
Microsoft Excel (Version 4.0) [Computer software].
     (1992). Redmond, WA: Microsoft Corporation.
```

#### MATERIAL ACCESSED THROUGH A COMPUTER NETWORK OR SERVICE

```
Boynton, R. S. (1994, March 3). The new intellectuals [3
     parts]. The Atlantic Monthly Online: [On-line ser-
     ial]. Available American Online: Directory: The At-
     lantic Monthly Online: Main Menu: Newsstand: Folder:
     The Atlantic Monthly 40-99669: File: The New Intel-
     lectuals: Article: The New Intellectuals Parts 1-3.
```

#### PERSONAL INTERVIEW

The newest APA guidelines suggest omitting personal interviews from the reference list because they do not provide recoverable data. You would of course mention such sources in the text of your paper (see p. 795).

## A Note on the Number System of Documentation

The MLA style is an example of the *author/page* approach to in-text citation; the APA style is an example of the *author/date* approach. A third common approach to in-text citation that you may encounter in your reading, and that you may be required to use in your writing, is the *number system*. This approach, which is often employed in the sciences and technologies, assigns a number to each source in a reference list. As each source is referred to in the text, the number is cited:

```
Females dominate males in spotted hyena clans (1).
```

Depending on the writer's preference or the guidelines prescribed, the number may appear in parentheses: (1); brackets: [2]; as superscript: [3]; or underlined in parentheses: (4).

In the sciences and technologies, where articles and books frequently have multiple authors, the number system is less cumbersome than the author/page or author/date system. It allows a writer to cite multiple sources with minimal disruption to a sentence:

```
Monogamous behavior among spectral tarsiers (2, 3) and
tree shrews (6, 7, 12) has been well documented.
```

As you can see, the number system is also less immediately informative than the author/page or author/date system. The writer generally cites whole works, not pages within works, and rarely quotes directly. Still, number system citations can be more specific and informative, if necessary:

```
Sagan writes that "when Velikovsky is original he is very
likely wrong" (8, p. 95).
```

In the number system, in-text citations are keyed to a numbered list of references that is included at the end of the paper. The list is organized either alphabetically according to author or according to the order in which the works were cited in the text of the paper. In either case, if a source is referred to more than once in the text, the same reference number is cited each time. The list of references is given a title such as "References Cited" or "Literature Cited."

Here are a few sample entries from a references cited list using the number system.

**BOOK**

```
1. Kruuk, H. The spotted hyena. Chicago: Univ. of Chicago
   Press; 1972.
```

**PART OF A BOOK**

```
2. Niemitz, C. Outline of the behavior of Tarsius ban-
   canus. In: Doyle, G.; Martin, R. D., eds. The study of
   prosimian behavior. New York: Academic Press; 1979:pp.
   631-660.
```

**JOURNAL ARTICLE**

```
3. Tilson, R. L.; Tenaza, R. R. Monogamy and duetting in
   an old world monkey. Nat. 263:320-321; 1976.
```

These samples follow the recommendations of the *CBE Style Manual* of the Council of Biology Editors. Note that the title of the journal *Nature* has been abbreviated in the third reference. Because many scientific journals have lengthy titles, some style guides in the sciences require that the journal titles in the references cited list be abbreviated according to the recommendations of the *American National Standard for Abbreviations of Titles and Periodicals.*

Although there are style manuals for every branch of science and technology, and variations in style among different publications within every branch, the basic features of the number system — in-text numbers and a numbered reference list — stay the same. If you are assigned a paper using the number system, be sure to ask your instructor to specify the style sheet or manual guidelines you are expected to follow.

# A Writer's Handbook

# Handbook Contents

# Introduction: Grammar, or The Way Words Work

Reprinted by permission: Tribune Media Services

One way to view grammar is as a set of rules for using language, like chalk-drawn lines that writers and speakers of English must toe. This approach is *prescriptive*: there are right and wrong ways to use the English language.

An alternative is a *descriptive* approach: **grammar** is that study of language concerned with the regular, systematic, and predictable ways in which words work together. How do speakers of English create sentences? How do they understand each other's sentences? In the last fifty years grammarians haven't been laying down strict rules so much as they have been listening, observing, and trying to describe the way language is used.

Every speaker of English, even a child, commands a grammatical system of tremendous complexity. Take the sentence "A bear is occupying a telephone booth while a tourist impatiently waits in line." In theory, there are nineteen billion different ways to state the idea in that sentence.[1] (Another is "A tourist fumes while he waits for a bear to finish yakking on a pay phone.") How do we understand a unique sentence like that one? For we do understand it, even though we have never heard it before — not in those very same words, not in the very same order.

To begin with, we recognize familiar words and we know their meanings. Just as significantly, we recognize grammatical structures. As we read or hear the sentence, we know that it contains a familiar pattern of *syntax,* or word order. This meaningful order helps the sentence make sense to us.

Ordinarily we aren't even conscious of such an order, for we don't need to think about it; but it is there. To notice it, all we need do is rearrange the words of our sentence:

> Telephone a impatiently line in waits tourist bear a occupying is a booth while.

The result is nonsense: it defies English grammar. The would-be sentence doesn't follow familiar rules or meet our expectations of order.

Hundreds of times a day, with wonderful efficiency, we perform tasks of understanding and of sentence construction more complex than any computer can even try. (Were artificial intelligence equally far advanced, a computer could not only scan books but make sense of them for you, and it could put words together to write your papers.) Indeed, linguist Noam Chomsky has suggested that the human brain probably contains some kind of language-grasping structure. Built into us before birth, it enables us to understand what we hear (whether that is English, Chinese, or Swahili) and equips us to put together our own sentences. Certainly some kind of language-grasping ability is part of our makeup. For we can understand and create sentences even as toddlers, before we know anything about "grammar."

Why, then, think about grammar in college? Isn't it entirely possible to write well without contemplating grammar at all? Yes. If your innate sense of grammar is reliable, you can write clearly and logically and forcefully without knowing a predicate nominative from a handsaw. Many of the writers featured in current magazines and newspapers would be hard pressed to name all the parts of speech they use. Most successful writers, though, have been practicing for so many years that grammar has become second nature to them. Few students we know have a built-in sense so infallible. Those who speak English as a second language must work especially hard to develop a sense of English grammar. When you doubt a word or a construction, a glance in a handbook can clear up your confusion and restore your confidence — just as referring to a dictionary can help your spelling.

---

[1] Richard Ohmann, "Grammar and Meaning," *American Heritage Dictionary* (Boston: Houghton, 1979), pp. xxxi–xxxii.

Besides helping us solve problems and bolstering our self-confidence, the study of grammar can be unexpectedly satisfying. Some students enjoy knowing, for instance, exactly why it makes more sense to say "Our soccer team is better than any other" than to say "Our soccer team is better than any." (For a grammatical reason, see p. H-104.) After all, to write without knowledge of grammar is a little like driving a car without caring what goes on under the hood. Most of the time, you can drive around without knowing a thing except how to steer and brake and tromp on the gas; but at times you may thank your stars you know how a carburetor works and, when it won't work, what to do about it.

More complex than a car, the English language provides subtler challenges. For one thing, merely following accepted practices doesn't guarantee good writing. The so-called grammatical conventions you'll find in this handbook are not mechanical specifications, but accepted ways in which skilled writers and speakers put words together to convey meaning efficiently and clearly. They come from observations of what educated, accomplished users of English actually do — how they utilize the language to communicate their ideas successfully. The amateur writer can learn by following their example, just as an amateur athlete, artist, or even auto mechanic can learn by watching the professionals. Knowing how the English language works, and how its parts get along together, is of enormous value to you as a writer. Once you understand what goes on under the hood, so to speak, you will have a keener sense of words and of why at times they won't go — so that when you write, you drive smoothly to your destination.

This handbook is divided into six chapters: "Basic Grammar," "Grammatical Sentences," "Effective Sentences," "Word Choice," "Punctuation," and "Mechanics." At times your instructor may refer you directly to a section in the handbook, but more often you will probably find yourself looking up information to answer your own questions. With practice, you will be able to find the answers to your questions on your own. To get you started, we want to alert you to a number of quick and easy ways to find information in this book. The most obvious way is to use the *table of contents* at the beginning of the handbook (p. H-2). If you were looking for help with quotation marks, for instance, you would first look under the chapter titled "Punctuation." By scanning the list of topics, you would quickly find the section and page number you needed (section 29, "Quotation Marks," p. H-165). Another quick way to find information is the alphabetically arranged *index* located at the back of the book. Here you will find all of the key terms used in the handbook followed by the exact page that you should turn to. If you are having trouble deciding whether you have used a particular word correctly (for example, should it be *accept* or *except?*), try turning to the alphabetically arranged *Glossary of Troublemakers* (pp. H-206–H-215) for a list of words and phrases whose usage commonly troubles student writers. Here you will find a brief description of a word's correct usage as well as a cross-reference to a fuller explanation if there is one elsewhere in the handbook. For those of you who are speakers of English as a second language, near the back of the book is an *ESL index* listing all the ESL boxes in the handbook.

If you want to use this handbook for self-study, you will find ample help throughout. Numerous sets of exercises are located in each section of the handbook. Most of the exercise sets begin with five lettered sentences, followed by five to fifteen numbered sentences. To test yourself on a particular skill, simply try your hand at answering the lettered exercise sentences and then turn to the ***Answers for Lettered Exercises*** at the back of the handbook (pp. H-216–H-222).

We hope that you find the handbook a useful tool both in and out of the classroom. With time and practice, you will be able to quickly find the answers to the questions that arise as you are writing for your composition class, major, and beyond.

## Chapter 32

# Basic Grammar

## 1. *Parts of Speech*

Grammar deals with the elements that make up sentences. These elements may be single words or whole phrases and clauses. Let's look first at the simplest building blocks of sentences: words.

We sort words into eight classes: the *parts of speech.* We tell them apart by their functions (the jobs they do in sentences), by their forms, and by their meanings. Like most classifications, the parts of speech are a convenience: it is easier to refer to "an adjective modifying a noun" than "that word there that tells something about that thing." Here is a quick review of the celebrated eight.

**1a.** Nouns

A *noun* names. A *common noun* names a general class of person (*clergyman, believer*), place (*town, dormitory*), thing (*car, dog*), or concept (*freedom, industrialization*). A *proper noun* names a specific person, place, thing, or concept: *Billy Graham, Milwaukee, Cadillac, New Deal.*

**1b.** Pronouns

A *pronoun* stands in place of a noun. Without pronouns, most writing would be top-heavy with repeated nouns. Imagine writing an essay on Martin Luther King, Jr., in which you had to say "Martin Luther King, Jr." or "the clergyman and civil rights leader" every time you mentioned your subject. Instead, you can handily use *personal pronouns* (*he* and *him*) and the *possessive pronoun* (*his*).

There are nine types of pronouns.

1. *Personal pronouns* (*I, you, it*) stand for nouns that name persons or things. "Mark awoke slowly, but suddenly *he* bolted from the bed."

2. *Possessive pronouns* (*his, our/ours*) are a form of personal pronoun showing ownership. They are used in place of nouns or as adjectives modifying nouns. "*His* trophy is on the left; *hers* is on the right."

3. *Intensive pronouns* (*yourself, themselves*) emphasize a noun or another pronoun. "Michael Jackson *himself* opened the door."

4. *Relative pronouns* (*who, that, which*) start a subordinate clause (see p. H-31) that functions as an adjective modifying a noun or pronoun in another clause. "The gift *that* you give them ought to be handsome."

5. *Reflexive pronouns* have the same form as intensive pronouns but are used as objects referring back to subjects. "She helped *herself*."

---

### Pronouns

|  | SINGULAR | PLURAL |
|---|---|---|
| **PERSONAL PRONOUNS** | | |
| *First person* | I, me | we, us |
| *Second person* | you | you |
| *Third person* | he, she, it, him, her | they, them |
| | | |
| **POSSESSIVE PRONOUNS** | | |
| *First person* | my, mine | our, ours |
| *Second person* | your, yours | your, yours |
| *Third person* | his, her, hers, its | their, theirs |
| | | |
| **INTENSIVE AND REFLEXIVE PRONOUNS** | | |
| *First person* | myself | ourselves |
| *Second person* | yourself | yourselves |
| *Third person* | himself, herself, itself | themselves |

**RELATIVE PRONOUNS**
that, what, whatever, which, who, whoever, whom, whomever, whose

**INTERROGATIVE PRONOUNS**
what, which, who, whom, whose

**INDEFINITE PRONOUNS**
all, another, any, anybody, anyone, anything, both, each, either, everybody, everyone, everything, few, many, neither, nobody, none, no one, nothing, one, several, some, somebody, someone, something

**DEMONSTRATIVE PRONOUNS**
such, that, these, this, those

**RECIPROCAL PRONOUNS**
each other, one another

6. *Interrogative pronouns* (*who, what*) ask or introduce questions. "*What* did you give them?"

7. *Indefinite pronouns* (*any, no one*) stand for persons or things not specified. "*No one* ran because of the rain."

8. *Demonstrative pronouns* (*this, those*) point to nouns. "*That's* the man, officer!"

9. *Reciprocal pronouns* (*each other, one another*) express relationship between two or more nouns or other pronouns. "Joe and Donna looked at *each other* with complete understanding."

**EXERCISE 1–1**

## Identifying Nouns and Pronouns

Underline the nouns and pronouns in the following sentences. Identify each noun as common or proper. Identify the type of each pronoun (personal, possessive, relative, and so on). Answers for the lettered sentences appear in the back of the book. Example:

Little Boy Blue, come blow your horn.

Little Boy Blue [proper noun], come blow your [possessive pronoun] horn [common noun].

a. If Karen sells two paintings, her husband will be delighted.
b. The price seems high, but Tanya herself makes only a small profit.
c. The bulk of the money that she earns pays for her tuition.
d. Lewis wants to sell his Corvette to someone who appreciates it.
e. He could not restrain himself from talking to anyone who would listen.

1. Which band would you yourself prefer to see — U2 or Pearl Jam?
2. Is that the man to whom you gave your phone number?
3. I heard that Linda plans to buy herself the first dress that fits her.
4. Why don't you give her the old Calvin Kleins that don't fit you anymore?
5. The members of the task force congratulated one another for meeting the deadline.

## 1c.   Verbs

A *verb* shows action ("The cow *jumped* over the moon") or a state of being ("The cow *is* brown," "The cow *felt* frisky").

Verbs like *is* or *felt* often show a state of being by linking the sentence's subject with another word that renames or describes the subject, as in the last two examples. Such verbs are called *linking verbs.* (See also 5a.)

A verb that shows action is called *transitive* when it has a direct object.

      VT     DO
Jim *hit* the *ball* hard.

         VT        DO
*Does* she *resemble* her *mother*?

A transitive verb must have an object to complete its meaning. You can't write just *Jim hit* or *Does she resemble?* But if a verb is complete in itself and needs no object, we call it **intransitive.**

The surgeon *paused.*

Sally *lives* on Boilermaker Street.

Look up a verb in your dictionary and you will find it classified *vt* (for "verb, transitive") or *vi* (for "verb, intransitive"). Many verbs can work either way.

The bus *stopped.* [Intransitive]

The driver *stopped* the bus. [Transitive]

Not all verbs consist of just one word. The **main verb** in a sentence identifies the central action (*hit, stopped*). We can show variations on this action by adding **helping verbs,** such as *do, can, have,* or *will.* The main verb with its helping verbs is the **complete verb** or **verb phrase.**

HV    MV
Alan *did* not *hit* the ball.

┌─ HV ─┐  MV
The bus *will have stopped* six times before we reach Main Street.

---

### Helping Verbs

There are twenty-three helping verbs in English. Fourteen of them can also function as main verbs:

be, is, am, are, was, were, being, been
do, does, did
have, has, had

The other nine can function only as helping verbs, never as main verbs:

can, could, should, would, may, might, must, shall, will

---

EXERCISE 1–2

## Identifying Verbs

Underline the verbs in the following sentences. Identify each one as transitive (vt), intransitive (vi), linking (lv), or helping (hv). Answers for the lettered sentences appear in the back of the book. Example:

Marie released the ball too early and it rolled into the gutter.

VT                        VI
Marie released the ball too early and it rolled into the gutter.

a. When Jorge goes to Providence, Jim will accompany him.
b. Sylvia prefers television shows that are educational.
c. Never give yellow roses to a friend: they symbolize infidelity.
d. The president should have spent more time on our proposal.
e. Harry dreams of becoming a famous novelist, but he rarely reads fiction.

1. People watched helplessly as the fire destroyed their homes and neighborhood.
2. Louise introduced herself to Leon while he was walking his dog.
3. Ian is the musician whose band she likes so much.
4. Woodpeckers must have a padded lining inside their skulls.
5. If Hitler had become an artist as he had wished, perhaps the course of history would be very different.

## 1d. Adjectives

An *adjective* describes, or modifies, a noun or a pronoun. In doing so it often answers the question Which? or What kind? Usually an adjective is a single word.

War is a *primitive* activity.

*Young* men kill other *young* men.

The *small brown* cow let out a *lackluster* moo.

**Articles.**   In the preceding examples, some grammarians would classify *the* and *a* as adjectives. Others would call them by a special name: *articles. The* is called the *definite article* because it indicates one particular item.

I need to borrow *the* car.

*A* and *an* are the *indefinite articles* because they indicate any old whatever-it-is.

I need to borrow *a* car.

## 1e. Adverbs

An *adverb* modifies a verb, an adjective, or another adverb.

The cow bawled *loudly.* [The adverb *loudly* modifies the verb *bawled.*]

The cow bawled *very loudly indeed.* [Three adverbs in a row: *loudly* modifies the verb *bawled,* while *very* and *indeed* modify the adverb *loudly.*]

Adverbs often flesh out thoughts by showing how, when, or where an action happens.

The cow *quickly* [how] galloped *outside* [where] and *immediately* [when] kicked the farmer.

**EXERCISE 1–3**

## Identifying Adjectives and Adverbs

Underline and identify the adjectives, definite articles, indefinite articles, and adverbs in the following sentences. For each adverb, draw an arrow to the word it modifies and mark that word as a verb, adjective, or adverb. Answers for the lettered sentences appear in the back of the book. Example:

> The opera was too long, but Judith sang beautifully.

>            ADV  ADJ             V     ADV
> The opera was <u>too long</u>, but Judith sang <u>beautifully</u>.

a. After a mild winter, the environmental experts greatly fear a drought.
b. James's young cousins are incredibly mature for their years.
c. The wildly handsome Jake often made wise women act foolishly.
d. She had a very difficult message to relate, so she chose her words carefully.
e. We were absolutely delighted to get tickets to the lovely play.

1. The character of Mercutio is not bad; the actor just played him badly.
2. The part of Juliet, in contrast, was remarkably well acted.
3. With someone so young in the role of Juliet, Romeo probably should have been younger.
4. The tragic end invariably makes me sad.
5. In an ethnically and economically divided world the play will always have a strong appeal.

## 1f.   Prepositions

A *preposition* is a transitional word, usually short, that leads into a phrase. The preposition and its object (a noun or pronoun), plus any modifiers, form a *prepositional phrase*: *in the bar, under a rickety table, with you.*

A prepositional phrase can function as an adjective or an adverb. When it modifies a noun or pronoun, a prepositional phrase is called an *adjective phrase.*

> I want a room *with a view.* [The adjective phrase *with a view* modifies the noun *room.*]

> Everybody *in Hillsdale* knows Big Jake. [The adjective phrase *in Hillsdale* modifies the pronoun *Everybody.*]

When it modifies a verb, an adjective, or an adverb, a prepositional phrase is called an *adverb phrase.*

> Jarvis, the play reviewer, always leaves *after the first act.* [The adverb phrase *after the first act* modifies the verb *leaves.*]

> Alice is miserable *without you.* [The adverb phrase *without you* modifies the adjective *miserable.*]

> Ken works far *from home.* [The adverb phrase *from home* modifies the adverb *far.*]

There are dozens of prepositions in English. The chart includes the most common ones. Notice that some prepositions consist of more than one word. Also, some prepositions occasionally play other roles: *since*, for example, can be a preposition (*I've known him since childhood*), or an adverb (*He has since left town*), or a subordinating conjunction (*Let's go, since there's nothing to do here*).

## Common Prepositions

| | | | | |
|---|---|---|---|---|
| about | below | except for | on | to |
| above | beneath | for | onto | toward |
| according to | beside | from | opposite | under |
| across | besides | in | out | underneath |
| after | between | in addition to | outside | unlike |
| against | beyond | inside | over | until |
| along | but (except) | in spite of | past | up |
| among | by | instead of | plus | upon |
| around | concerning | into | regarding | with |
| as | considering | like | since | within |
| at | despite | near | than | without |
| because of | down | next to | through | |
| before | during | of | throughout | |
| behind | except | off | till | |

**EXERCISE 1–4**

## Identifying Prepositional Phrases

Underline each prepositional phrase in the following sentences, and identify it as an adjective or adverb phrase. Circle the preposition. Answers for the lettered sentences appear in the back of the book. Example:

In the distance, you can see the tornado.

(In) the <u>distance</u>, you can see the tornado. [Adverb phrase]

a. Rarely has anyone ever behaved so rudely to me.
b. The bright light in the sky was a supernova.
c. Ann warned us before the meeting that her proposal might cause trouble.
d. She presented her sculpture strictly according to the rules.
e. My belief is that all but a few troublemakers will be reasonable once they understand the new rules.

1. The politicians at City Hall would welcome a chance to intervene.
2. Napoleon's soldiers were decimated by the Russian winter.
3. Luis wants to go to the arcade.
4. From his seat beyond the foul pole he can hardly see the batter.
5. We drove to a house at the edge of a lake.

## 1g. Conjunctions

A *conjunction* links words or groups of words and connects them in sense.

A *coordinating conjunction* is a one-syllable word that joins elements with equal or near-equal importance: "Jack *and* Jill," "Sink *or* swim."

A word used to make one clause dependent on, or subordinate to, another is called a *subordinating conjunction*. (See 3e–3g.)

*Before* we left the party, six people had fainted.

They passed out *because* Roger had spiked the punch.

I heard *that* they went looking for him the next day.

---

**ESL GUIDELINES**

### In, On, At — Prepositions of Location and Time

The prepositions *in, on,* and *at* are frequently used to express location.

Maria lives *in* the United States.

Elaine lives *at* a swanky address *on* Fifth Avenue.

- *In* means "within" or "inside of" a place, including geographical areas, such as cities, states, countries, and continents.

    I packed my books *in* my knapsack.

    I left my bags *in* the train station.

    My cousins live *in* Canada, but my uncle lives *in* Texas.

    Brazil is *in* South America.

- Whereas *in* emphasizes *location* only, *at* is often used to refer to a place when a specific *activity* is implied: *at the store* (to shop), *at the office* (to work), *at the theater* (to see a play), and so on.

    Angelo parked his bicycle *in* the bike rack.

    He left the bicycle there while he was *at* school, and then he rode it home.

- *On* means "on the surface of" or "on top of" something and is used with floors of buildings and planets. It is also used to indicate a location *beside* a lake, river, ocean, or other body of water.

    The service department is *on* the fourth floor.

    Mardi Gras in New Orleans is the greatest free show *on* earth.

    The raft floated *on* calm water.

We have a cabin *on* Lake Michigan.

- *In, on,* and *at* can all be used in addresses. *In* is used to identify a general location, such as a city or neighborhood. *On* is used to identify a specific street. *At* is used to give an exact address.

    We live *in* Boston.

    We live *on* Medway Street.

    We live *at* 20 Medway Street.

- *In* and *at* can both be used with the verb *arrive*. *In* indicates a large place, such as a city, state, country, or continent. *At* indicates a smaller place, such as a specific building or address. (*To* is never used with *arrive*.)

    Joel's plane arrives *in* Alaska tomorrow; he will arrive *in* Fairbanks the day after that.

    Anya arrived *in* Asia yesterday.

    She will arrive *at* the airport soon.

The prepositions *in, on,* and *at* are also used in many time expressions.

- *In* indicates the span of time during which something occurs or a time in the future; it is also used in the expressions *in a minute* (meaning "shortly") and *in time* (meaning "soon enough"). *In* is also used with seasons, months, and periods of the day.

    He needs to read this book *in* the next three days. [During the next three days]

    I'll see you *in* two weeks. [Two weeks from now]

    We'll be leaving *in a minute;* I hope to get there *in time* to see the first act.

    My birthday is *in* April.

    We usually exercise *in* the morning.

- *On* is used with the days of the week, with the word *weekend,* and in the expression *on time* (meaning "punctually").

    Let's have lunch *on* Friday.

    The train arrived in the station *on time.*

    I like to travel *on weekends.*

- *At* is used in reference to a specific time on the clock as well as a specific time of the day (*at night, at dawn, at twilight*).

    We'll meet again next Monday *at* 2:15 P.M.

    The office is cleaned *at night.*

---

### Coordinating Conjunctions

and, but, for, nor, or, so, yet

### Common Subordinating Conjunctions

| | | | |
|---|---|---|---|
| after | even if | since | when |
| although | even though | so | whenever |
| as | how | so that | where |
| as if | if | than | wherever |
| as soon as | in order that | that | while |
| as though | once | though | why |
| because | provided that | unless | |
| before | rather than | until | |

### Correlative Conjunctions

| | | |
|---|---|---|
| as . . . as | just as . . . so | not only . . . but also |
| both . . . and | neither . . . nor | whether . . . or |
| either . . . or | not . . . but | |

### Common Conjunctive Adverbs

| | | | |
|---|---|---|---|
| accordingly | furthermore | moreover | then |
| also | hence | nevertheless | thereafter |
| anyway | however | next | therefore |
| as | incidentally | nonetheless | thus |
| besides | indeed | now | undoubtedly |
| certainly | instead | otherwise | |
| consequently | likewise | similarly | |
| finally | meanwhile | still | |

---

Some conjunctions consist of paired words, such as *either . . . or,* that appear separately but work together to join elements of a sentence. Such a pair is called a ***correlative conjunction.***

*Not only* for her money *but also* for her cooking, Augustus courted Serena.

*Neither* his friends *nor* hers thought the marriage would last.

When you use a correlative conjunction, remember to complete the pair.

INCOMPLETE    *Not only* was Robert saving money for his college tuition, he was saving for a new car.

REVISED    *Not only* was Robert saving money for his college tuition, *but* he was *also* saving for a new car.

Certain adverbs also can function as conjunctions. Called ***conjunctive adverbs,*** these linking words connect independent clauses and show a relationship between two ideas, such as addition (*also, besides*), comparison (*likewise, similarly*), contrast (*instead, however*), emphasis (*namely, certainly*), cause and effect (*thus, therefore*), or time (*finally, subsequently*).

> Armando is a serious student; *therefore,* he studies every day.

## 1h.   Interjections

An ***interjection*** inserts an outburst of feeling at the beginning, middle, or end of a sentence.

> I'd go, but, *oh,* I don't want to.

> *Ow!* What torture it was to read that essay!

> There are pigeons on the grass, *alas.*

An entire phrase can work as an interjection.

> Who *the dickens* are you?

> What *in the world* is my term paper doing in the wastebasket?

**EXERCISE 1–5**

## Identifying Conjunctions and Interjections

Underline and identify the conjunctions and interjections in the following sentences. Mark each conjunction as coordinating, subordinating, or correlative. Answers for the lettered sentences appear in the back of the book. Example:

> Do we have to eat liver and onions again, for heaven's sake?

>           COORD CONJ             INTERJ
> Do we have to eat liver <u>and</u> onions again, <u>for heaven's sake?</u>

  a. Oh, well, the team will do better when Smoots gets back in the game.
  b. According to Polonius and many others, neither borrowing nor lending is wise.
  c. Steve and Matt could not decide whether to leave town or work on their apartment over vacation.
  d. Holy mackerel, what a big fish!
  e. Although time and tide wait for no man, Juan is taking hours to launch his boat.

  1. I'll dive in if you will, but, oh, that water's cold!
  2. Neither Larry's father nor Kevin's is tall, yet both boys grew up to be over six feet tall.
  3. How in the world are you and Elwood going to patch up your differences if neither of you will talk to the other?

4. Even though he seemed both weakened and depressed in the hospital, in a few weeks he had regained his strength.
5. Athens and the other Greek city-states were bitter rivals; nevertheless, they put aside their differences in the face of the Persian threat.

**EXERCISE 1–6**

## Identifying Parts of Speech

Identify the part of speech of each underlined word in the following passages. Answers for the lettered words appear in the back of the book. Example:

> We live by our imaginations, by our admirations, by our sentiments.
>
> — Ralph Waldo Emerson, "Illusions," in *The Conduct of Life*
>
> We: pronoun; live: verb; our: pronoun; sentiments: noun

A. It is a mellow day, very a. gentle b. The ash has lost its leaves and when c. I went out to get the mail and d. stopped to look up e. at it 1., I rejoiced 2. to think that soon everything 3. here will be honed down to structure. It is all a rich farewell 4. now to leaves, to color. I think of 5. the trees and how simply 6. they let go, let fall the riches of a season, how without 7. grief (it seems) they can 8. let go and go deep 9. into their 10. roots for renewal and sleep.

— May Sarton, *Journal of a Solitude*, October 6, 1977

B. The other day a. I rowed in my boat a free, even b. lovely young lady, and as c. I plied the oars, she d. sat in the e. stern, and there was nothing 1. but 2. she between 3. me and the sky. So might all our 4. lives be picturesque 5. if 6. they were free enough, but mean relations and prejudices intervene 7. to shut out the sky, and we never 8. see a man as simple and distinct as the man-weathercock 9. on 10. a steeple.

— *The Journals of Henry David Thoreau*, 1840

# 2. *Sentence Structure*

## PARTS OF SENTENCES

Every sentence has two basic parts: a subject and a predicate. The *subject* names something — a person, an object, an idea, a situation. The *predicate* makes an assertion about the subject. Any word group that is missing either of these elements is not a complete sentence.

Both subject and predicate may consist of either one word or a group of words. A one-word subject is always a noun or pronoun; a one-word predicate is always a verb.

> ### Sentence Parts at a Glance
>
> The *subject* of a sentence identifies some person, place, thing, activity, or idea.
> The *predicate* of a sentence makes an assertion about the subject.
> An *object* is the target or recipient of the action described by a verb.
> A *complement* renames or describes a subject or object.
>
> For basic sentence patterns, see page H-00.

SUBJ   PRED
Birds fly.

Many subjects and most predicates contain other elements as well, such as modifiers, objects, and complements. A modifier (such as an adjective or adverb) provides more information about the subject or some part of the predicate. A *direct* or *indirect object*, which always appears in the predicate, is the target or recipient of the action indicated by the verb. A *complement*, which also appears in the predicate, renames or describes the sentence's subject or object.

Let's look more closely at subjects, predicates, objects, and complements. Then we can explore the various ways of combining these elements in sentences.

## 2a. Subject

The *subject* of a sentence identifies some person, place, thing, activity, or idea. Often the subject is the agent of the action identified by the predicate ("*Jill* hit the ball"). Sometimes the subject is the receiver of the action of the predicate ("The *ball* was hit by Jill"; "*Baseball* came up for discussion"). Because the subject names something, it almost always is (or includes) a noun or pronoun. That noun or pronoun is the *simple subject.*

*Queen Elizabeth* waved to the crowd.

*I* waved back.

Often a subject includes additional nouns or pronouns, modifiers, or both. A subject that consists of two or more nouns or pronouns linked by a conjunction is called a *compound subject.*

*The Queen and I* exchanged waves.

*My mother, my father, and my sister* just stood and stared.

The *complete subject* consists of the simple or compound subject plus any words that modify it.

*The imposing, world-famous Queen* smiled at me.

*Prince Charles on her left and Princess Anne on her right* didn't notice me.

Occasionally a subject is a phrase or clause that contains no nouns at all.

*Whether or not to smile back* was the question.

In a command, the subject is understood to be *you,* even though the word does not appear in the sentence.

Don't [*you*] stand so close to me.

## 2b. Predicate

The *predicate* of a sentence makes an assertion about the subject. This assertion can involve an action ("Birds *fly*"), a relationship ("Birds *have* feathers"), or a state of being ("Birds *are* cold-blooded"). The *simple predicate* consists of the main verb plus any helping verbs that accompany it (*will fly, should have flown*). (For a full list of helping verbs, see 1c.) The *complete predicate* consists of the verb plus any other words that help it make its assertion, such as modifiers, objects, and complements.

Geese normally *can fly* more gracefully than chickens. [Simple predicate]

Geese *normally can fly more gracefully than chickens.* [Complete predicate]

Hiram *showed* me a goose that bites. [Simple predicate]

Hiram *showed me a goose that bites.* [Complete predicate]

In many sentences, the subject appears between two parts of the predicate.

When I visited his farm, Hiram *showed* me a goose that bites. [Simple predicate]

*When I visited his farm,* Hiram *showed me a goose that bites.* [Complete predicate]

You can tell that the opening clause *When I visited his farm* is part of the predicate because it modifies the verb (*showed*), not the subject (*Hiram*).

Just as a sentence may have a compound subject, a sentence may also have a compound predicate.

The child *screamed, cried, and kicked* until he got his way. [Simple compound predicate]

The child *screamed, cried, and kicked until he got his way.* [Complete compound predicate]

The receiver *intercepted* the pass *and ran* for a touchdown. [Simple compound predicate]

The receiver *intercepted the pass and ran for a touchdown.* [Complete compound predicate]

EXERCISE 2–1

# Identifying Subjects and Predicates

Identify each simple subject (SS), complete subject (CS), simple predicate
(SP), and complete predicate (CP) in the following sentences. Answers for the
lettered sentences appear in the back of the book. Example:

Does your brother George really dye his hair?

Does your brother George really dye his hair?

a. Several coyotes have been seen recently in this area.
b. War, that curse of the human race, has plagued civilization throughout history.
c. Even after he became deaf, the composer Beethoven continued to write music.
d. One cup of coffee in the morning keeps me awake all day.
e. John Updike's mother, who had been a writer herself, always encouraged
   her son's literary aspirations.

1. Until the 1850s, the city now known as San Francisco was a tiny outpost
   with few human inhabitants.
2. San Francisco, like many California cities, was given its name by Spanish
   missionaries.
3. The Golden Gate Bridge was named after the harbor entrance, long known
   as the Golden Gate.
4. The introduction of the telegraph enabled San Franciscans to find out when
   a ship was approaching the city.
5. It was the Gold Rush that brought a flood of easterners and other outsiders
   to northern California.
6. Today people still flock to California, but few expect to get rich by finding
   gold.
7. During the 1989 World Series, an earthquake hit the San Francisco area and
   caused millions of dollars of damage.
8. Buildings burned, roads buckled, and bridges collapsed.
9. Frightened people called for help, ran into the streets, and cried when they
   saw the devastation.
10. Immediately after the earthquake the number of visitors to San Francisco
    decreased; however, the slump in tourism did not last long.

## 2c.  Objects

An *object* is the target or recipient of the action of a verb. Whereas the subject
of a sentence does something, the object has something done to it or for it.
Objects, like subjects, usually are (or include) nouns or pronouns.

Some geese bite *people*.

A sentence can have two types of objects: direct and indirect. A ***direct object***
completes the action performed by the subject or asserted about the subject;

it is the verb's target. (Not all verbs take direct objects. Those that do are called *transitive verbs*; see 1c.)

> She sells *seashells* by the seashore.

> Birds have *feathers*.

> Give me *your tired, your poor....*

An *indirect object* names a person or other entity that is affected by the subject's action. Usually an indirect object is the recipient of the direct object, via the action indicated by the verb. Only certain transitive verbs take indirect objects. Among them are *ask, bring, buy, get, lend, offer, pay, promise, sell, show, tell,* and *write.*

> She sells *the tourists* seashells.

> Give *me* your tired, your poor....

As you can see, the word *to* is implied before an indirect object. "She sells seashells [*to*] *the tourists,*" "Give your tired, your poor *to me....* "

## 2d. Complements

A *complement* renames or describes a subject or object. It consists of a word or group of words in the predicate that completes the assertion in a sentence.

A complement that renames or describes the subject of a sentence is called a *subject complement.* It always follows a linking verb such as *be, am, were, seem, feel* (see 1c, 5a). A subject complement can be a noun, an adjective, or a group of words that functions as a noun or adjective.

> S        SC
> That *dog* looks *friendly.* [Describes]

> ┌─ S ─┐        ┌──────── SC ────────┐
> *Manute Bol* must be *the tallest basketball player in the NBA.* [Renames]

A complement that renames or describes a direct object is called an *object complement.* Like a subject complement, an object complement can be a noun, an adjective, or a group of words that functions as a noun or adjective.

> DO ┌──── OC ────┐
> Leroy calls *Julie the hostess with the mostest.* [Renames]

> ┌─ DO ─┐  OC
> This new computer will keep *Professor Mutt happy.* [Describes]

Sentence Patterns

With a subject, a verb, an object or two, a complement or two, and some modifiers, you can build virtually any English sentence. As complex as our language is, most sentences that we recognize as grammatical follow one of five patterns. Sometimes the order of the ingredients changes, and sometimes

---

**ESL GUIDELINES**

## Indirect Objects and Prepositions

These two sentences mean the same thing:

> I sent the president a letter.

> I sent a letter to the president.

In the first sentence, the phrase *the president* is the **indirect object**: it receives the direct object (*a letter*), which was acted upon (*sent*) by the subject of the sentence (*I*). In the second sentence, the same idea is expressed by using a **prepositional phrase** beginning with *to*. (see 3a.)

- Some verbs can either have an indirect object or use the preposition *to*: *give, send, lend, offer, owe, pay, sell, show, teach,* and *tell*. Some verbs can use either an indirect object or the preposition *for*: *bake, build, buy, cook, find, get,* and *make*.

  > I paid *the travel agent* one hundred dollars.

  > I paid one hundred dollars *to the travel agent*.

  > Margarita cooked *her family* some chicken.

  > Margarita cooked some chicken *for her family*.

- Some verbs cannot have an indirect object; they must use a preposition. The following verbs must use the preposition *to*: *describe, demonstrate, explain, introduce,* and *suggest*.

  | INCORRECT | Please explain me indirect objects. |
  |---|---|
  | CORRECT | Please explain indirect objects *to me*. |

- The following verbs must use the preposition *for*: *answer* and *prepare*.

  | INCORRECT | He prepared me the nonalcoholic punch. |
  |---|---|
  | CORRECT | He prepared the nonalcoholic punch *for me*. |

- Some verbs must have an indirect object; they cannot use a preposition. The following verbs must have an indirect object: *ask* and *cost*.

  | INCORRECT | Sasha asked a question to her. |
  |---|---|
  | CORRECT | Sasha asked her a question. |

the pattern is obscured by modifying words and phrases. Here are the five basic sentence patterns, with examples. (Only simple subjects, verbs, objects, and complements are marked.)

1. *subject/verb*

       S   V
The *king lives.*

          S       V
The former *king* now *lives* in a cottage on the palace grounds.

       V      S
Long *live* the *king!*

2. *subject/verb/subject complement*

       S   V   SC
This *plum tastes ripe.*

                 S      V     V    V   SC
When this plum was picked, *it* probably *would* not *have tasted ripe.*

       SC   V      S    V
How *ripe does* this *plum taste* to you?

3. *subject/verb/direct object*

   S     V          DO
*I photographed* the *sheriff.*

   S  V             V       DO
*I did* not, however, *photograph* the *deputy.*

     V  S  V    V      DO
*Would I have photographed Sheriff Brown* if he were a kinder man?

4. *subject/verb/indirect object/direct object*

     S    V  IO    DO
*Charlene asked you* a *question.*

    V   IO           DO
*Ask me* no more *questions* than you wish to hear answered. [The subject of the verb *Ask* is *you,* understood.]

     V     S    V  IO    DO
*Didn't Charlene ask you* a *question?*

5. *subject/verb/direct object/object complement*

     S    V   DO         OC
The *judges rated Hugo* the best *skater.*

S    V   V   DO        OC

Last year's *judges had rated Hugo* second *best* of all the skaters.

V       S    V  DO  OC

Will the *judges rate Hugo first* again next year?

**EXERCISE 2–2**

## Identifying Objects and Complements

Underline and identify the subject complements (SC), indirect objects (IO), direct objects (DO), and object complements (OC) wherever they appear in the following sentences. Mark the whole complement or object, not just its key noun or pronoun. Answers for the lettered sentences appear in the back of the book. Example:

Venus, the goddess of love, considered Adonis her equal.

                                               DO     OC

Venus, the goddess of love, considered <u>Adonis</u> <u>her equal</u>.

a. You are an educated person; how can you believe such a story?
b. King Lear gave his daughters his kingdom.
c. Elizabeth, a cynical observer, believes that the president is an evasive man.
d. Holography is an interesting art, but it requires expensive equipment.
e. Many people call Chicago the windy city.

1. The outfielder's agent negotiated him a new contract.
2. The scorers named Shaquille O'Neal most valuable player in last week's game.
3. Her uncle left Maria a fortune.
4. The Empire State Building was once the tallest building in the world.
5. My friend Alicia calls her yellow Volkswagen "Buttercup."

# 3. *Phrases and Clauses*

Grammar deals not only with single words but also with groups of words known as phrases and clauses. A *phrase* consists of two or more related words that work together: *my uncle Zeke, in the attic, will have been*. Words that do not work together do not make up a phrase: *Zeke uncle my, in attic the, been have will*.

Notice that a phrase doesn't make complete sense the way a sentence does. Useful as it may be, it is lacking. It may lack a subject (*will have been*), a verb (*my uncle Zeke*), or both (*in the attic*).

A *clause* too is a group of related words that work together. However, it has more going for it than a phrase: it contains both a subject and a verb. Clauses come in two forms: main and subordinate. A *main clause* needs only end punctuation to make it a complete sentence.

           S        V
        *Uncle Zeke likes* solitude.

A *subordinate clause* contains a subject and a verb, but it cannot stand alone; it depends on a main clause to help it make sense.

           S    V
        *who plays* the oboe

Only in combination with a main clause does a subordinate clause work in a sentence.

        Uncle Zeke, *who plays the oboe*, likes solitude.

## TYPES OF PHRASES

Phrases, being incomplete by themselves, are versatile. They can function as nouns, verbs, adjectives, or adverbs. Every compound subject or object is a phrase by definition: *Zeke and Jake, my father and I.* So is every verb that consists of more than one word: *will have played, sang and danced.* Other types of phrases can play varied roles in sentences.

        *Playing the oboe* is Uncle Zeke's favorite pastime. [Noun phrase — subject]

        He really enjoys *making music.* [Noun phrase — object]

        Uncle Zeke plays an oboe *custom-made for him.* [Adjective phrase modifying *oboe*]

        My music teacher says he plays *like a professional.* [Adverb phrase modifying *plays*]

To determine whether a phrase functions as a noun, an adjective, or an adverb in a sentence, you can ask yourself what question the phrase answers. If it answers the question Who? or What?, it is a noun phrase. If it answers the question What kind?, it is an adjective phrase. If it answers the question When? or Where? or How?, it is usually an adverb phrase.

We can name phrases by the roles they play in a sentence: noun phrase, adjective phrase, adverb phrase. We can also name them by their form: prepositional phrase, verbal phrase, absolute phrase, appositive phrase. Because the form of a phrase determines the roles it can play, our discussion of phrases will classify them by form.

**3a.**  Prepositional Phrases

What do the following sentences have in common?

        Doesn't Lew have other friends besides Pat?

        Over the next sand dune lies the ocean.

        To understand his comments you must read between the lines.

Each sentence contains a ***prepositional phrase***, so named because it starts with a preposition: *besides Pat, Over the next sand dune, between the lines.* (See the prepositions chart in 1f.)

Prepositional phrases are a common and very useful sentence ingredient. Most often, they function as adjectives or adverbs. When a prepositional phrase does the work of an adjective — that is, when it modifies a noun — it is an ***adjective phrase.***

> Joyce wanted to live in a city *without smokestacks.* [Adjective phrase modifying *city*]

> Tyrone is a man *of honor.* [Adjective phrase modifying *man*]

When a prepositional phrase does the work of an adverb — that is, when it modifies a verb, an adjective, or another adverb — it is an ***adverb phrase.***

> She writes *with vigor.* [Adverb phrase modifying the verb *writes*]

> Jake feels indebted *to his coach.* [Adverb phrase modifying the adjective *indebted*]

> Mr. Francis phoned early *in the morning.* [Adverb phrase modifying the adverb *early*]

Some prepositional phrases function as nouns; they are ***noun phrases.***

> *Over the river and through the woods* is the long way to Grandmother's house.

## 3b.   Verbal Phrases

A ***verbal*** is a form of a verb that cannot function as a simple predicate in a sentence. Verbals include infinitives (*to live, to dream*), present participles (*falling, dancing*), and past participles (*lived, fallen*).

A verbal and its modifiers, if any, constitute a ***verbal phrase.*** The three types of verbal phrases are infinitive phrases (*to live alone, to dream vividly*); participial phrases (*falling behind, written in stone*); and gerund phrases (*smoking in the boys' room, slow dancing*). Verbal phrases (and verbals) can operate as nouns, adjectives, and adverbs.

### Infinitive Phrases

An ***infinitive phrase*** consists of the infinitive form of a verb preceded by *to* (*to quit*) plus any modifiers or objects (*to quit suddenly; to quit the job*). Infinitive phrases function as nouns, adjectives, and adverbs.

> *To err* is human. [Noun phrase used as subject]

> Their goal is *to stop the pipeline project.* [Noun phrase used as subject complement]

> Jennifer is the candidate *to watch.* [Adjective phrase modifying *candidate*]

Melvin lives *to eat.* [Adverb phrase modifying *lives*]

He is too fat *to play tennis.* [Adverb phrase modifying *fat*]

---

### Phrases at a Glance

A *prepositional phrase* contains a preposition and its object(s) and any modifiers: "*In the old mansion* we found a stack *of books* hidden *behind the fireplace.*" (3a)

A *verbal phrase* consists of a verbal and its modifiers: "All she wanted was *to attend college someday*" [*infinitive phrase*]; "*Swimming in cold water,* we hardly noticed that the air temperature was 101 degrees" [*participial phrase*]; "*Combing the dog's hair* took at least thirty minutes every other day" [*gerund phrase*]. (3b)

An *absolute phrase* does not modify any one word in a sentence but modifies the entire sentence. It usually consists of a noun followed by a participial phrase: "*The 12:30 bus having already passed,* Arturo waited in the hot sun for the next one." (3c)

An *appositive phrase* is a group of words that adds information about a subject or object by identifying it in a different way: "Magali, *a student from France,* learned colloquial English by living with an American family." (3d)

---

An infinitive phrase is easy to distinguish from a prepositional phrase starting with *to:* in an infinitive phrase, *to* is followed first by a verb (*to row*) and only then by an object, if any (*to row a boat*). In a prepositional phrase, *to* is followed directly by its object, a noun or pronoun (*to me, to the lighthouse, to the boat*).

### Participial Phrases

A *participial phrase* is an adjective phrase that opens with the present or past participle of a verb. Here are examples of the infinitive and participial forms of a few common verbs:

| INFINITIVE | PRESENT PARTICIPLE | PAST PARTICIPLE |
|---|---|---|
| (to) find | finding | found |
| (to) fly | flying | flown |
| (to) go | going | gone |
| (to) see | seeing | seen |
| (to) walk | walking | walked |

All participial phrases share two characteristics: they start with participles, and they function as adjectives.

*Leading the pack,* Michael sprinted into the final straightaway. [Modifies *Michael*]

He made the most of the few seconds *remaining in his race.* [Modifies *seconds*]

*Worn out by the intensity of his effort,* Michael fell. [Modifies *Michael*]

### Gerund Phrases

A *gerund phrase* is a noun phrase that begins with the present participle of a verb. It can serve as the subject of a sentence, a direct object, a subject complement, or the object of a preposition.

*Giving blood* is a valuable public service. [Subject]

Audrey loves *performing in plays.* [Direct object]

Phil's job is *making doughnuts.* [Subject complement]

My mother is nervous about *traveling by herself.* [Object of a preposition]

## 3c. Absolute Phrases

An *absolute phrase* usually consists of a noun followed by a participle. It does not modify any one word; rather, it modifies an entire clause or sentence. It can appear anywhere in the sentence.

The stallion pawed the ground, *nostrils flaring, chestnut mane and tail swirling in the wind.*

*Nostrils flaring, chestnut mane and tail swirling in the wind,* the stallion pawed the ground.

## 3d. Appositive Phrases

An appositive is a word that adds to what we know about a subject or object simply by identifying it in a different way ("my dog *Rover,*" "Harvey's brother *Fred*"). An *appositive phrase* is a group of words that provides the same kind of amplification.

Bess, *the landlord's daughter,* had long black hair.

I walked across the field, *a golden sea of wheat flecked with daisies,* to the stone wall.

---

 **ESL GUIDELINES**

## Using Participles, Infinitives, and Gerunds

A *verbal* is a form that does not function as the main verb in a sentence. Verbals can function as adjectives, adverbs, and nouns. There are three types of verbals: *participles,* *gerunds,* and *infinitives.*

### Using Participles
- **Participles** end in either *-ing* (the present participle) or *-ed* or *-d* (the past participle).
- When used as an adjective, the *-ing* form expresses cause, and the *-ed* and *-d* forms express effect or result.

  The movie was *terrifying to the children*. [The movie caused terror]

  The children were *terrified by the movie*. [The movie resulted in terrified children]

### Using Verbs with Gerunds and Infinitives
- A *gerund* is a form of a verb ending in *-ing* that functions as a noun (*going, playing*). An **infinitive** is the base form of the verb preceded by *to* (*to go, to play*). Some verbs are followed by gerunds while other verbs are followed by infinitives.
- Verbs that are followed by infinitives include *decide, expect, pretend, refuse,* and *want*.

  My mother decided *to eat* at McDonald's for dinner.

- Verbs that are followed by gerunds include *appreciate, avoid, consider, discuss, enjoy, finish, imagine, practice,* and *suggest*.

  My family enjoys *going* to the beach.

- Some verbs, including *continue, like, love, hate, remember, forget, start,* and *stop,* can be followed by either a gerund or an infinitive.

  I like *going* to the museum.

  I like *to go* to the movies.

NOTE: Some verbs, such as *stop, remember,* and *forget,* have significantly different meanings according to whether they are followed by a gerund or an infinitive.

  I stopped *smoking*. [I don't smoke anymore.]

  I stopped *to smoke*. [I stopped so that I could smoke.]

- Be careful to distinguish between *used to* (meaning "did in the past") and *be used to* or *get used to* (meaning "be or become accustomed to"). *Used to* is followed by the basic form of the verb; *be used to* or *get used to* is followed by a gerund.

  I *used to live* in Rio, but now I live in New York. [I lived in Rio in the past.]

  I *am used to living* in the United States. [I am accustomed to living in the United States.]

  I *got used to living* in the United States. [I became accustomed to living in the United States.]

## Identifying Phrases

Underline and identify the prepositional, verbal (infinitive, participial, and gerund), absolute, and appositive phrases in the following sentences. For each prepositional and verbal phrase, also identify its role in the sentence (noun, adjective, adverb). Answers for the lettered sentences appear in the back of the book. Example:

The hero of the movie *Robocop* is half human, half machine.

The hero of the movie *Robocop* is half human, half machine. [Prepositional phrase, adjective]

a. Traveling cross-country has always held a romantic appeal.
b. The fellow in the beret is a fourth-generation Californian.
c. The Rolls-Royce, its silver hood ornament gleaming in the morning sun, stood waiting.
d. The Confederacy, gone with the wind, remains a cherished southern memory.
e. The North, Civil War victor, is less nostalgic.

1. I heard their astonishing news through the grapevine.
2. Looking out on the morning rain, Carole used to feel uninspired.
3. Raymond's Las Vegas escapade gave playing blackjack a bad name.
4. Elsa didn't want to get on the plane, but Rick insisted.
5. One of the great victories of modern science has been eradicating smallpox.
6. The money stolen from Gene's wallet would have paid his rent.
7. Alexander, King Philip's son, conquered a vast empire.
8. Your loud music having interrupted my concentration, I can't finish my essay right now.
9. Plagued by guilt, he returned to the scene of the crime.
10. Steve's dream is to ride his motorcycle across the country.

## TYPES OF CLAUSES

The main difference between a clause and a phrase is that a clause has both a subject and a verb. Some clauses, indeed, can stand alone as complete sentences. They are called **main clauses** (or **independent clauses**).

My *sister has* a friend.

The *flowers were* beautiful.

Clauses that cannot stand alone are called **subordinate clauses** (or **dependent clauses**).

*who comes* from Lebanon

that *Dan gave* Nicola

A subordinate clause begins with a subordinate word, either a subordinating conjunction (H-14) or a relative pronoun (H-8), and must be linked with a main clause for its meaning to be entirely clear.

My sister has a friend *who comes from Lebanon.*

The flowers *that Dan gave Nicola* were beautiful.

Subordinate clauses, like phrases, are versatile: they can function as nouns, adjectives, and adverbs. A clause that answers the question What? or Who? is a noun clause. One that answers the question What kind? or Which one? is an adjective clause. One that answers the question When? or How? or Where? is usually an adverb clause.

## 3e.     Noun Clauses

A subordinate clause that serves as a sentence subject, object, or complement is called a **noun clause.** Usually a noun clause begins with a subordinating conjunction: *how, when, where, whether, why* or with a relative pronoun: *what, who, whom, whoever, whomever,* or *that.*

*What I believe* is none of their business. [Noun clause as subject]

James doesn't know *whom he should blame.* [Noun clause as direct object]

---

### Subordinate Clauses at a Glance

A *noun clause* serves as a sentence subject, object, or complement. It answers the question What? or Who? (3e)

An *adjective clause* serves as an adjective by modifying a noun or pronoun. It answers the question What kind? or Which one? (3f)

An *adverb clause* plays the role of an adverb, modifying a verb, an adjective, or another adverb. It answers the question When? or How? or Where? (3g)

---

In both of these examples, the relative pronoun that opens the subordinate clause (*What, whom*) is followed by the subject and verb of the clause. In both cases, the pronoun serves as the direct object within the subordinate clause.

          DO  S  V
*What I believe* is none of their business.

                    DO   S     V
James doesn't know *whom he should blame.*

Sometimes, however, the relative pronoun that opens the subordinate clause also serves as the subject of the clause.

S   V
James doesn't know *who did it.* [Noun clause as direct object]

S       V
Sarah gave *whoever walked* through the door a coupon for a free meal. [Noun clause as indirect object]

## 3f. Adjective Clauses

Subordinate clauses can serve as adjectives modifying nouns or pronouns. Usually an adjective clause is introduced by one of the relative pronouns: *who, which,* or *that.* Sometimes the relative pronoun is implied: "I got the letter [*that*] you sent me." You can tell an adjective clause from a noun clause by its function in a sentence.

I like people *who are optimistic.* [Adjective clause modifying *people*]

I plan to major in psychology, *which I have always found fascinating.* [Adjective clause modifying *psychology*]

Science is a tide *that can only rise.* — Jonathan Schell [Adjective clause modifying *tide*]

## 3g. Adverb Clauses

An adverb clause plays the role of an adverb in a sentence, modifying a verb, an adjective, or another adverb.

Larry left *before I could explain my mistake.* [Adverb clause modifying the verb *left*]

He was sure *that I had insulted him.* [Adverb clause modifying the adjective *sure*]

He loses his temper faster *than most people do.* [Adverb clause modifying the adverb *faster*]

Generally, subordinate clauses acting as adverbs are introduced by one of the common subordinating conjunctions, such as the following:

| after | before | than | until | wherever |
| although | if | that | when | while |
| as | since | though | whenever | why |
| because | so that | unless | where | |

(For a complete list of subordinating conjunctions, see 1g.) As with adjective clauses, the subordinating conjunction in an adverb clause sometimes is implied rather than stated: "You paint so well [*that*] you could be a professional."

**EXERCISE 3–2**

## Identifying Clauses

Underline the subordinate clauses in the following sentences, and identify each one as a noun, an adjective, or an adverb clause. Answers for the lettered sentences appear in the back of the book. Example:

> The man whose toe Susan had stepped on yelped in pain.

> The man <u>whose toe Susan had stepped on</u> yelped in pain. [Adjective clause]

a. My grandfather was a rolling stone; wherever he lived at the moment was his home.
b. While we were still arguing about its value, the statue was removed from the gallery.
c. The shirt that I took to the cleaners came back with a ripped sleeve.
d. Ann did so badly on the exam that she may fail the course.
e. He won't know what hit him.

1. Although many had tried, none could pull the sword from the stone.
2. The man who was so charming has been arrested for fraud.
3. Sailing, which is Charlie's favorite summer pastime, has been banned in Rock Harbor.
4. There before them lay more gold than they had ever seen.
5. Blame John's death on the cocaine he refused to give up.

**ESL GUIDELINES**

## Adjective Clauses and Relative Pronouns

Be sure to use relative pronouns (*who, which, that*) correctly in sentences with adjective clauses.

- Do not omit the relative pronoun when it is the subject within the adjective clause.

    INCORRECT   The woman *gave us directions to the museum* told us not to miss the Picasso exhibit.

    CORRECT   The woman *who gave us directions to the museum* told us not to miss the Picasso exhibit. [*Who* is the subject of the adjective clause.]

- In speech and informal writing, you can imply (not state) a relative pronoun when it is the object of a verb or preposition within the adjective clause. In formal writing, you should use the relative pronoun.

    FORMAL   Jose forgot to return the book *that I gave him.* [*That* is the object of *gave.*]

    INFORMAL   Jose forgot to return the book *I gave him.* [The relative pronoun *that* is implied.]

    FORMAL   This is the box *in which we found the jewelry.* [*Which* is the object of the preposition *in.*]

INFORMAL   This is the box *we found the jewelry in.* [The relative pronoun *which* is implied.]

NOTE:  The preposition moves to the end of the sentence when the relative pronoun is omitted. The preposition must not be left out, even when the relative pronoun is omitted.

- *Whose* is the only possessive form of a relative pronoun. It is used with persons, animals, and things. No other form may be used as a possessive introducing an adjective clause.

    INCORRECT   I sat on a chair *that its* legs were wobbly.

    CORRECT     I sat on a chair *whose* legs were wobbly.

NOTE:  If you are not sure how to use a relative pronoun, try rephrasing the sentence more simply.

I sat on a chair *that had wobbly legs* [or *with wobbly legs*].

# 4. *Types of Sentences*

What is a *sentence*? There is more than one answer. In conversation, the single word *Where?* can be a sentence. But in striving to write clear, readable prose, you will find it useful to think of a sentence as the expression of a complete thought containing at least one *main clause*. (See pp. H-31–H-35 on types of clause.) Sentences come in four varieties according to their structure.

## 4a.  Simple Sentences

Any sentence that contains only one main clause is a *simple sentence*, even if it includes modifiers, objects, complements, and any number of phrases in addition to its subject and verb.

Even amateur stargazers can easily locate the Big Dipper in the night sky.

George Washington exhibited courage and leadership during a crucial period in our country's history.

Fred and Sandy have already applied for summer jobs.

The spectators laughed and cried at the same time.

Notice in the last two examples that a simple sentence may have a compound subject (*Fred and Sandy*) or a compound verb (*laughed and cried*). Still, it remains a simple sentence, for it contains only one main clause. Sometimes the subject of a simple sentence is not stated but is clearly understood. In the command "Run!," the understood subject is *you*.

## 4b.   Compound Sentences

A *compound sentence* consists of two or more main clauses joined by a coordinating conjunction such as *and, but,* or *for* or by a semicolon. Sometimes the semicolon is followed by a conjunctive adverb such as *however, nevertheless,* or *therefore.* (For complete lists of coordinating conjunctions and conjunctive adverbs, see 1g.)

MAIN CLAUSE
────────MAIN CLAUSE──────┐  ┌─────────┐
I would like to accompany you, but I can't.

MAIN CLAUSE   MAIN CLAUSE
Two's company; three's a crowd.

─────── MAIN CLAUSE ───────┐       ┌──────── MAIN
Henry Kissinger was born in Europe; therefore, he cannot be a candidate for
CLAUSE ──────────────────────┘
the presidency of the United States.

## 4c.   Complex Sentences

A *complex sentence* consists of one main clause and one or more subordinate clauses.

MAIN              SUBORDINATE
── CLAUSE ──┐ ┌── CLAUSE ──┐
I will be at the airport when you arrive.

SUBORDINATE                     MAIN
── CLAUSE ──────┐ ┌───── CLAUSE ─────┐
Since Amy bought a computer, she has been out of circulation.

SUBORDINATE                 MAIN
──────── CLAUSE────────┐ ┌─ CLAUSE ─┐ ┌──────── SUBORDINATE
Because George has to travel widely, he is grateful whenever his far-flung ac-
CLAUSE ─────────────────────────────┘
quaintances invite him to a home-cooked meal.

In some sentences, the relative pronoun linking the subordinate clause to the main clause is implied rather than stated.

MAIN        SUBORDINATE
CLAUSE ┌── CLAUSE ──┐
I know [that] you saw us.

## 4d.   Compound-Complex Sentences

As its name implies, a *compound-complex sentence* shares the attributes of both a compound sentence (it contains two or more main clauses) and a complex sentence (it contains at least one subordinate clause).

SUBORDINATE   MAIN
CLAUSE        CLAUSE        MAIN

Where politics is concerned, Michael seems indifferent and Joanne seems

CLAUSE

ill informed.

MAIN   SUBORDINATE  SUBORDINATE   MAIN
CLAUSE   CLAUSE   CLAUSE   CLAUSE

I'd gladly wait until you're ready; but if I do, I'll miss the boat.

**EXERCISE 4–1**

## Identifying Sentence Types

Identify each of the following sentences as simple, compound, complex, or compound-complex. Don't just pin labels on them: briefly explain the elements that make you classify each sentence as you do. Answers for the lettered sentences appear in the back of the book. Example:

> If a bullfrog had wings, he wouldn't bump his tail so much, but he'd have a hard time swimming.

SUBORDINATE   MAIN
CLAUSE        CLAUSE        MAIN

If a bullfrog had wings, he wouldn't bump his tail so much, but he'd have

CLAUSE

a hard time swimming. [Compound-complex]

a. Not only women but also men and children benefit from society's increasing resistance to sex-role stereotypes.
b. To become a doctor, you know how hard you must study.
c. Biology is interesting, but I prefer botany as it is taught in our department.
d. Do you prefer bacon and eggs or cereal and toast for breakfast this morning?
e. Most people believe that poverty begets poverty; however, recent studies have shown that, more often than not, when children from welfare families reach adulthood, they achieve economic independence.

1. Geraldine believes that the sexual revolution, without compensating women for their losses, has robbed them of all the advantages automatically bestowed by old-fashioned marriage.
2. Just before the earthquake, the animals became agitated.
3. Do you want to join us, or are you just going to lie there like a slug?
4. Since Jennifer moved to the city, her attendance at concerts, plays, and museum shows has increased markedly; and she dines out at least once a week.
5. As a boy, Mike couldn't wait to qualify for the Little League team; a few weeks after joining, he wanted only to quit.
6. Executives who promote incompetent workers can drive a corporation to the brink of disaster.
7. In the Virgin Islands the sun shines every day, the temperature drops to a comfortable level every night, and the breeze rustles through the palm trees at all hours.
8. Because of the flood, traffic was rerouted and flights were delayed.

9. At some point in the long and surprisingly complex history of popular music, rock 'n' roll acquired its present identity as the music of youth and rebellion.

10. If a man makes a better mousetrap, the world will beat a path to his door.
— Ralph Waldo Emerson

## Chapter 33

# Grammatical Sentences

## 5. *Verbs*

Most verbs show action (*swim, fight, eat, hide, pay, sleep, win*). Some verbs indicate a state of being by linking the subject of a sentence with a word that renames or describes it; they are called *linking verbs* (*is, become, seem*). A few verbs work with a main verb to give more information about its action; they are called *helping verbs* or *auxiliary verbs* (*have, must, can*).

### VERB FORMS

**5a.** Use a linking verb to connect the subject of a sentence with a subject complement.

A *linking verb* indicates what the subject of a sentence *is* or *is like*. Some common linking verbs are *be, appear, feel,* and *grow*. A linking verb creates a sort of equation, either positive or negative, between the subject and its complement (see 2d). The subject complement can be a noun, a pronoun, or an adjective.

      LV         SC

Julia will *make* a good *doctor*. [Noun]

**H-39**

LV      SC
George *is* not the *one*. [Pronoun]

LV     SC
London weather *seems foggy*. [Adjective]

A verb may be a linking verb in some sentences and not in others.

I often *grow* sleepy after lunch. [Linking verb with subject complement *sleepy*]

I often *grow* tomatoes in my garden. [Transitive verb with direct object *tomatoes*]

If you pay attention to what the verb means, you can usually tell whether it is functioning as a linking verb.

---

### Common Linking Verbs

Some linking verbs tell what a noun is, was, or will be.

> *be, become, remain*
> *grow*: The sky *is growing* dark.
> *make*: One plus two *makes* three.
> *prove*: His warning *proved* accurate.
> *turn*: The weather *turned* cold.

Some linking verbs tell what a noun might be.

> *appear, seem, look*

Most verbs of the senses can operate as linking verbs.

> *feel, smell, sound, taste*

---

## 5b. Use helping verbs to add information about the main verb.

A *helping* or *auxiliary verb* can add essential information about a main verb's action or state of being. Adding a helping verb to a simple verb (*go, shoot, be*) allows you to express a wide variety of tenses and moods (*am going, did shoot, would have been*). (See 5g–5l and 5n–5p.)

All the forms of *be, do,* and *have* can function as helping verbs. The other helping verbs are *can, could, may, might, must, shall, should, will,* and *would.* These last nine can function only as helping verbs, never as main verbs.

A main verb plus one or more helping verbs is called a *verb phrase.* The parts of a verb phrase need not appear together but may be separated by other words.

I probably *am going* to France this summer.

You *should* not *have shot* that pigeon.

This change *may* well *have been* seriously *contemplated* by the governor even before the election.

## 5c. Use the correct principal parts of the verb.

The **principal parts** are the forms the verb can take — alone or with helping verbs — to indicate the full range of times when an action or state of being does, did, or will occur. Verbs have three principal parts: the infinitive, the past tense, and the past participle.

The **infinitive** is the simple or dictionary form of the verb (*go, sing, laugh*) or the simple form preceded by *to* (*to go, to sing, to laugh*). (See 3b.)

The **past tense** signals that the verb's action is completed (*went, sang, laughed*).

The **past participle** is combined with helping verbs to indicate action occurring at various times in the past or future (*have gone, had sung, will have laughed*). It is also used with forms of *be* to make the passive voice. (See 5m.)

In addition to the three principal parts, all verbs have a present participle, the *-ing* form of the verb (*going, walking*). The present participle is used to make the progressive tenses. (See 5k and 5l.) It also can modify nouns and pronouns ("the *leaking* bottle"); and, as a gerund, it can function as a noun ("*Sleeping all day* pleases me"). (See 3b.)

## 5d. Use *-d* or *-ed* to form the past tense and past participle of regular verbs.

Most verbs in English are *regular verbs*: they form the past tense and past participle in a standard, predictable way. Regular verbs that end in *-e* add *-d* to the infinitive; those that do not end in *-e* add *-ed.*

| INFINITIVE | PAST TENSE | PAST PARTICIPLES |
|------------|------------|------------------|
| (to) smile | smiled | smiled |
| (to) act | acted | acted |
| (to) please | pleased | pleased |
| (to) trick | tricked | tricked |

## 5e. Use the correct forms for the past tense and past participle of irregular verbs.

The English language has at least two hundred *irregular verbs,* which form their past tense and past participle in some other way than by adding *-d* or *-ed.* Most irregular verbs are familiar to native English speakers and pose no problem, although they can be a torment to people trying to learn the language. The following chart of principal parts lists just the most troublesome irregular verbs.

## Principal Parts of Common Irregular Verbs

| INFINITIVE | PAST TENSE | PAST PARTICIPLE |
|---|---|---|
| be | was | been |
| become | became | become |
| begin | began | begun |
| blow | blew | blown |
| break | broke | broken |
| bring | brought | brought |
| burst | burst | burst |
| catch | caught | caught |
| choose | chose | chosen |
| come | came | come |
| do | did | done |
| draw | drew | drawn |
| drink | drank | drunk |
| drive | drove | driven |
| eat | ate | eaten |
| fall | fell | fallen |
| fight | fought | fought |
| freeze | froze | frozen |
| get | got | got, gotten |
| give | gave | given |
| go | went | gone |
| grow | grew | grown |
| have | had | had |
| hear | heard | heard |
| hide | hid | hidden |
| know | knew | known |
| lay | laid | laid` |
| lead | led | led |
| let | let | let |
| lie | lay | lain |
| make | made | made |
| raise | raised | raised |
| ride | rode | ridden |
| ring | rang | rung |
| rise | rose | risen |
| run | ran | run |
| say | said | said |
| see | saw | seen |
| set | set | set |
| sit | sat | sat |
| sing | sang | sung |
| slay | slew | slain |
| slide | slid | slid |
| speak | spoke | spoken |
| spin | spun | spun |
| stand | stood | stood |
| steal | stole | stolen |

---

### Principal Parts of Common Irregular Verbs *(continued)*

| INFINITIVE | PAST TENSE | PAST PARTICIPLE |
|---|---|---|
| swim | swam | swum |
| swing | swung | swung |
| teach | taught | taught |
| tear | tore | torn |
| think | thought | thought |
| throw | threw | thrown |
| wake | woke, waked | woken, waked |
| write | wrote | written |

For the appropriate form of any irregular verb not on this list, consult your dictionary. (Some dictionaries list principal parts for all verbs, some just for irregular verbs.)

---

**5f.** Use the correct forms of the principal parts of *lie* and *lay* and *sit* and *set*.

Among the most troublesome verbs in English are *lie* and *lay*. If you have difficulty choosing between them, you can forever eliminate confusion by taking two easy steps. The first is to memorize the principal parts and present participles of both verbs (see the chart on pp. H-43–44).

The second step in deciding whether to use *lie* or *lay* is to fix in memory that *lie*, in all its forms, is intransitive. *Lie* never takes a direct object: "The island *lies* due east," "Jed *has lain* on the floor all day." *Lay*, on the other hand, is a transitive verb. It always requires an object: "*Lay* that pistol down."

The same distinction exists between *sit* and *set*. Usually, *sit* is intransitive: "He *sits* on the stairs." *Set*, on the other hand, almost always takes an object: "He *sets* the bottle on the counter." There are, however, a few easily memorized exceptions. The sun *sets*. A hen *sets*. Gelatin *sets*. You *sit* on a horse. You can *sit* yourself down at a table that *sits* twelve.

---

### Principal Parts and Present Participles of *Lie* and *Lay*, *Sit* and *Set*

*lie*: recline

| PRESENT TENSE | | PAST TENSE | |
|---|---|---|---|
| I lie | we lie | I lay | we lay |
| you lie | you lie | you lay | you lay |
| he/she/it lies | they lie | he/she/it lay | they lay |

PAST PARTICIPLE
lain      (We have *lain* in the sun long enough.)

PRESENT PARTICIPLE
lying     (At ten o'clock he was still *lying* in bed.)

Principal Parts and Present Participles of *Lie* and *Lay*, *Sit* and *Set* *(continued)*

*lay*: put in place, deposit

| PRESENT TENSE | | PAST TENSE | |
|---|---|---|---|
| I lay | we lay | I laid | we laid |
| you lay | you lay | you laid | you laid |
| he/she/it lays | they lay | he/she/it laid | they laid |

PAST PARTICIPLE

laid  (Having *laid* his clothes on the bed, Mark jumped into the shower.)

PRESENT PARTICIPLE

laying  (*Laying* her cards on the table, Lola cried, "Gin!")

*sit*: be seated

| PRESENT TENSE | | PAST TENSE | |
|---|---|---|---|
| I sit | we sit | I sat | we sat |
| you sit | you sit | you sat | you sat |
| he/she/it sits | they sit | he/she/it sat | they sat |

PAST PARTICIPLE

sat  (I have *sat* here long enough.)

PRESENT PARTICIPLE

sitting  (Why are you *sitting* on that rickety bench?)

*set*: place

| PRESENT TENSE | | PAST TENSE | |
|---|---|---|---|
| I set | we set | I set | we set |
| you set | you set | you set | you set |
| he/she/it sets | they set | he/she/it set | they set |

PAST PARTICIPLE

set  (Paul has *set* the table for eight.)

PRESENT PARTICIPLE

setting  (Jerry has been *setting* pins at the Bowl-a-drome.)

EXERCISE 5–1

## Using Irregular Verb Forms

Underline each incorrectly used irregular verb in the following sentences and substitute the verb's correct form. Some sentences may be correct. Answers for the lettered sentences appear in the back of the book. Example:

Lie your books on the windowsill near the spot where the flowers are setting.

<u>Lay</u> your books on the windowsill near the spot where the flowers are <u>sitting</u>.

a. When Joe's mother catched him laying around the house during school hours, she throwed him out.

b. We woke soon after the sun rose, and then we swam to the raft.

c. He lay his cards triumphantly on the table but soon found that he was not setting in a lucky chair after all.
d. Wendy knew how much Roger had drank, but she gone with him anyway.
e. If I had knew that he'd stole the money, he'd never have lain a foot inside this door.

1. Why don't you lay down for a while after you have lain a fire in the fireplace?
2. My computer screen has froze and everyone who could fix it has went home.
3. I thought I had bought the right amount of groceries for tonight's birthday dinner, but now I doubt that all of it will be eaten.
4. Frank throwed a rock through the window and then teared down the curtains climbing inside.
5. That raccoon has ate all the pies you lay on the porch to cool.

## TENSES

The *tense* of a verb is the *time* when its action did, does, or will occur. With the *simple tenses* we can indicate whether the verb's action took place in the past, takes place in the present, or will take place in the future. The *perfect tenses* enable us to narrow the timing even further, specifying that the action was or will be completed by the time of some other action. With the *progressive tenses* we can indicate that the verb's action did, does, or will continue.

**5g.** Use the simple present tense for an action that takes place once, recurrently, or continuously in the present.

The simple present tense is the infinitive form of a regular verb plus *-s* or *-es* for the third-person singular.

| | |
|---|---|
| I like, I go | we like, we go |
| you like, you go | you like, you go |
| he/she/it likes, he/she/it goes | they like, they go |

Notice that some irregular verbs, such as *go*, form their simple present tense following the same rules as regular verbs. Other irregular verbs, such as *be* and *have*, are special cases for which you should learn the correct forms.

| | |
|---|---|
| I am, I have | we are, we have |
| you are, you have | you are, you have |
| he/she/it is, he/she/it has | he/she/it is, he/she/it has |

You can use the simple present tense for an action that is happening right now ("I *welcome* this news"), an action that happens repeatedly in the present ("Judy *goes* to church every Sunday"), or an ongoing present action ("Wesley *likes* ice cream"). In some cases, if you want to ask a question or intensify the action, use the helping verb *do* or *does* before the infinitive form of the main verb.

I *do think* you should take the job.

*Does* Andy *want* it?

Besides present action, you can use the simple present for future action: "Football season *starts* Wednesday."

Use the simple present for a general truth, even if the rest of the sentence is in a different tense:

Columbus proved in 1492 that the world *is* round.

Mr. Hammond will argue that people *are* basically good.

---

## Verb Tenses at a Glance

Note: the examples show first person only.

| SIMPLE TENSES | REGULAR | IRREGULAR |
|---|---|---|
| *Present* | *Past* | *Future* |
| I cook | I cooked | I will cook |
| I see | I saw | I will see |

| PERFECT TENSES | | |
|---|---|---|
| *Present perfect* | *Past perfect* | *Future perfect* |
| I have cooked | I had cooked | I will have cooked |
| I have seen | I had seen | I will have seen |

| PROGRESSIVE TENSES | REGULAR | IRREGULAR |
|---|---|---|
| *Present progressive* | *Past progressive* | *Future progressive* |
| I am cooking | I was cooking | I will be cooking |
| I am seeing | I was seeing | I will be seeing |

| *Present perfect progressive* | *Past perfect progressive* | *Future perfect progressive* |
|---|---|---|
| I have been cooking | I had been cooking | I will have been cooking |
| I have been seeing | I had been seeing | I will have been seeing |

---

**5h.**    Use the simple past tense for actions already completed.

Indicate the simple past tense with the verb's past tense form. Regular verbs form the past tense by adding *-d* or *-ed* to the infinitive; the past tense of irregular verbs must be memorized. (See 5e.)

Jack *enjoyed* the party. [Regular verb]

Suzie *went* home early. [Irregular verb]

In the past tense, you can use the helping verb *did* (past tense of *do*) to ask a question or intensify the action. Use *did* with the infinitive form of the main verb for both regular and irregular verbs.

You can use the helping verb *did* (past tense of *do*) to ask a question or intensify the action. Use *did* with the infinitive form of the main verb for both regular and irregular verbs.

| | | |
|---|---|---|
| I went. | I did go. | Why did I go? |
| You saw. | You did see. | What did you see? |
| She ran. | She did run. | Where did she run? |

NOTE: In some cases, spoken language may interfere with written language, causing problems with forming the past tense. Although speakers may not always pronounce the *-d* or *-ed* ending clearly, standard written English requires that you add the *-d* or *-ed* on all regular past tense verbs.

> NONSTANDARD   I *use* to wear weird clothes when I was a child.
>
> STANDARD      I *used* to wear weird clothes when I was a child.

**5i.** Use the simple future tense for actions that are expected to happen but have not happened yet.

> George *will arrive* in time for dinner.

> *Will* you please *show* him where to park?

To form the simple future tense, add *will* to the infinitive form of the verb.

| | |
|---|---|
| I will go | we will go |
| you will go | you will go |
| he/she/it will go | they will go |

You can also use *shall* to inject a tone of determination: "We *shall overcome!*" or in polite questions: "Shall we dance?"

Although the present tense can indicate future action ("We *go* on vacation next Monday"), most actions that have not yet taken place are expressed in the simple future tense ("Surely it *will snow* tomorrow").

**5j.** Use the perfect tenses for an action completed at the time of another action.

The present perfect, past perfect, and future perfect tenses consist of a form of the helping verb *have* plus the past participle. The tense of *have* indicates the tense of the whole verb phrase.

The action of a **present perfect** verb was completed before the sentence is uttered. Its helping verb is in the present tense: *have* or *has.*

> I *have* never *been* to Spain, but I *have been* to Oklahoma.

> Mr. Grimaldi *has gone* home for the day.

> *Have* you *seen* John Sayles's new film?

You can use the present perfect tense either for an action completed before some other action ("I *have washed* my hands of the whole affair but I am watching from a safe distance") or for an action begun in the past and still going on ("Max *has worked* in this office for twelve years").

The action of a **past perfect** verb was completed before some other action in the past. Its helping verb is in the past tense: *had.*

> The concert *had ended* by the time we found a parking space.

Until I met her, I *had* not *pictured* Jenna as a redhead.

*Had* you *wanted* to clean the house before Mother arrived?

The action of a ***future perfect*** verb will be completed by some point (specified or implied) in the future. Its helping verb is in the future tense: *will have.*

The builders *will have finished* the house by June.

When you get the Dutch Blue, *will* you *have collected* every stamp you need?

The store *will* not *have closed* by the time we get there.

**5k.**    Use the simple progressive tenses for an action in progress.

The present progressive, past progressive, and future progressive tenses consist of a form of the helping verb *be* plus the present participle (which is formed by adding *-ing* to the infinitive). The tense of *be* determines the tense of the whole verb phrase.

The ***present progressive*** expresses an action that is taking place now. Its helping verb is in the present tense: *am, is,* or *are.*

I *am thinking* of a word that starts with *R.*

*Is* Joe *babysitting* while Marie *is* off *visiting* her sister?

You can also express future action with the present progressive of *go* plus an infinitive phrase:

I *am going to read* Tolstoy's *War and Peace* someday.

*Are* you *going to sign up* for Professor Blaine's course on the sixties?

The ***past progressive*** expresses an action that took place continuously at some time in the past, whether or not that action is still going on. Its helping verb is in the past tense: *was* or *were.*

The old men *were sitting* on the porch when we passed.

Lucy *was planning* to take the weekend off.

The ***future progressive*** expresses an action that will take place continuously at some time in the future. Its helping verb is in the future tense: *will be.*

They *will be answering* the phones while she is gone.

*Will* we *be dining* out every night on our vacation?

**ESL GUIDELINES**

# The Simple Tenses

**Present Tense**: base form of the verb (+ -*s* or -*es* for *he, she, it*)

- Use the simple present tense to express general statements of fact or habitual activities or customs. Although it is called "present," this tense is really *general* or "timeless."

    You *make* wonderful coffee.

    Henry *goes* to the movies every Sunday afternoon.

- To form negatives and questions, use *do* or *does* + base form.

    Henry *does not* (*doesn't*) *go* to the movies during the week.

    *Do* you still *make* wonderful coffee?

**Past Tense**: base form + -*d* or -*ed* for regular verbs (for irregular verbs, see 5e.)

- Use the simple past tense to express an action that occurred at a specific time in the past. The specific time may be stated or implied.

    The package *arrived* yesterday.

    They *went* to San Juan for spring break.

- To form negatives and questions, use *did* + base form.

    They *did not* (*didn't*) *go* to Fort Lauderdale.

    *Did* the package *arrive* yesterday?

**Future Tense**: *will* or *be going to* + base form

- Use the simple future tense to express an action that will take place in the future. Also use *will* to imply promises and predictions.

    The students *will study* hard for their exam.

    The students *are going to study* hard for their exam.

    We *will help* you move. [Promise]

    Computers *will* soon *replace* most typewriters. [Prediction]

- To form negatives and questions, use *will* + base form.

    Jose *will not* (*won't*) *graduate* this year.

    *Will* computers *replace* typewriters?

NOTE: Use the simple present, not the future, to express future meaning in clauses beginning with *before, after*, or *when*.

INCORRECT   When my mother *will get* home from work, we will make dinner.

CORRECT     When my mother *gets* home from work, we will make dinner.

Use the simple present to show a future action when other words in the sentence make the future meaning clear.

The bus *departs* in five minutes.

We *leave* for Chicago in the morning and *return* next Wednesday.

 **ESL GUIDELINES**

## The Perfect Tenses

**Present Perfect Tense:** *has* or *have* + past participle (-*ed* or -*en* form for regular verbs; for irregular verbs, see 5e.)

• Use the present perfect tense when an action took place at some unspecified time in the past. The action may have occurred repeatedly.

I *have traveled* to many countries.

The dog *has bitten* my aunt twice.

• Use the present perfect tense with *for* and *since* to indicate that an action began in the past, is occurring now, and will probably continue.

I *have gone* to school with Jim and Susan since fifth grade.

Jenny *has lived* next door to the Kramers for twelve years.

**Past Perfect Tense:** *had* + past participle

• Use the past perfect tense to indicate an action was completed in the past before some other past action.

Josef *had smoked* for many years before he decided to quit.

We got rid of the dog because he *had bitten* my aunt twice.

• Particularly in speech or informal writing, the simple past may be used instead of the past perfect when the relationship between actions is made clear by a conjunction such as *when, before, after,* or *until.*

Observers *saw* the plane catch fire *before* it landed.

**Future Perfect Tense:** *will* + *have* + past participle

• Use the future perfect tense when an action will take place before some time in the future.

The package *will have* already *arrived* by the time we get home from work.

By June, the students *will have studied* ten chapters.

**51.**   Use the perfect progressive tenses for a continuing action that began in the past.

Use the present perfect progressive, the past perfect progressive, or the future perfect progressive tense for an action that started in the past and did, does, or will continue.

ESL
GUIDELINES

### The Simple Progressive Tenses

**Present Progressive Tense:** present tense of *be* + present participle (*-ing* form)

- Use the present progressive tense when an action began in the past, is happening now, and will end at some time in the future.

  The students *are studying* for their exam.

  My sister *is living* with us until she graduates from college.

- You can also use the present progressive tense to show a future action when other words in the sentence make the future meaning clear.

  Maria *is flying* to Pittsburgh on July 8.

NOTE: Linking verbs (such as *be, seem, look*), verbs that express an emotional or mental state (such as *trust, like, guess, realize*), and verbs without action (such as *belong, have, need*) are not generally used in the present progressive tense. For these verbs, use the present tense to express a continuous state.

     INCORRECT    I think I *am liking* you very much.

     CORRECT      I think I *like* you very much.

**Past Progressive Tense:** *was* or *were* + present participle

- Use the past progressive tense when an action began and continued at a specific time in the past.

  Maria *was watching* the news when I arrived.

  The students *were studying* for their exam all day.

**Future Progressive Tense:** *will be* + present participle; or present tense of *be* + *going to be* + present participle

- Use the future progressive tense when an action will begin and will continue in the future.

  Hans *will be wearing* blue jeans to the party.

  The students *are going to be studying* until midnight.

The *present perfect progressive* indicates an action that started in the past and is continuing in the present. Form it by adding the present perfect of *be* (*has been* or *have been*) to the present participle (the *-ing* form) of the main verb.

All morning Fred *has been singing* the blues about his neighbor's wild parties.

*Have* you *been reading* Janine's postcards from England?

The *past perfect progressive* expresses a continuing action that was completed before another past action. Form it by adding the past perfect of *be* (*had been*) to the present participle of the main verb.

By the time Dave finally arrived, I *had been waiting* for twenty minutes.

The *future perfect progressive* expresses an action that is expected to continue into the future beyond some other future action. Form it by adding the future perfect of *be* (*will have been*) to the present participle of the main verb.

---

**ESL GUIDELINES**

## The Perfect Progressive Tenses

**Present Perfect Progressive Tense:** *have* or *has been* + present participle (*-ing* form)

- Use the present perfect progressive tense when an action began at some time in the past and has continued to the present. The words *for* and *since* are often used in sentences with this tense.

    She *has been answering* questions all day.

    The students *have been studying* for a long time.

**Past Perfect Progressive Tense:** *had been* + present participle

- Use the past perfect progressive tense when an action began and continued in the past and then was completed before some other past action.

    We *had been studying* for three hours before we took a break.

    Miguel *had been ringing* the bell for five minutes when we got home.

**Future Perfect Progressive Tense:** *will have been* + present participle

- Use the future perfect progressive tense when an action will continue in the future for a specific amount of time and then end before another future action.

    The students *will have been studying* for twenty-four hours by the time they take the exam tomorrow.

    The captain *will have been sailing* for ten days when she arrives in Jamaica.

By 1997 Joanne *will have been attending* school longer than anyone else I know.

Studying tenses can improve your writing by making you aware of the variety of verb forms at your disposal and by giving you practice at using them effectively. An important thing to remember about verb tenses is to avoid changing from one to another without reason. (See 11a.).

**EXERCISE 5–2**

## Identifying Verb Tenses

Underline each verb or verb phrase and identify its tense in the following sentences. Answers for the lettered sentences appear in the back of the book. Example:

> John is living in Hinsdale, but he prefers Joliet.

> John is living [present progressive] in Hinsdale, but he prefers [simple present] Joliet.

a. Yesterday Joan broke her leg because she was skiing too fast.
b. Bill sleeps for nine hours every night; even so, he is always yawning.
c. Until last weekend, Josh had never seen a whale, except on those nature specials the public television station runs.
d. The upcoming tour represents the first time the band will have performed together since they split up.
e. I have heard that if you spend the night alone on the summit of Mount Snowdon, you will climb down either mad or a poet.

1. After they had burned the dead on funeral pyres, the Greeks turned back to the siege of Troy.
2. As of December 1, Ira and Sandy will have been going together for three years.
3. I was thinking about all the fun we've had since we met in third grade.
4. Dan will have embarked on his career by the time his brother starts college.
5. She will be working in her study if you need her.
6. By the time they have counted the last votes, you will have heard so much about the candidates that you won't be looking forward to an election campaign for a long time.
7. Have you been hoping that Carlos will come to your party?
8. I know that he will not yet have returned from Chicago.
9. His parents had been expecting him home any day until they heard that he was still waiting for the bus.
10. Probably he is sitting in the depot right now, unless he has switched to the train.

# VOICE

Intelligent students read challenging books.

Challenging books are read by intelligent students.

These two statements convey similar information, but their emphasis is different. In the first sentence, the subject (*students*) performs the verb's action (*read*); in the second sentence, the subject (*books*) receives the verb's action (*are read*). One sentence states its idea directly, the other indirectly. We say that the first sentence is in the *active voice* and the second is in the *passive voice*.

**5m.** Use the active voice rather than the passive voice.

Verbs in the **active voice** consist of principal parts and helping verbs. Verbs in the **passive voice** consist of the past participle preceded by a form of *be* ("you

---

**ESL GUIDELINES**

### The Passive Voice

**Passive Voice**: form of *be* + past participle (*-ed* or *-en* form for regular verbs; for irregular forms, see 5e.)

- In a passive voice sentence, the grammatical subject *receives* the action of the verb instead of performing it.

   ACTIVE   The university *awarded* Hamid a scholarship. [The subject (*university*) performs the action of *awarding*.]

   PASSIVE   Hamid *was awarded* a scholarship by the university. [The subject (*Hamid*) receives the action.]

- Often the identity of the action's performer is not important or is understood, and the *by* phrase is omitted.

   PASSIVE   Automobiles are built in Detroit. [It is understood that they are built *by people*.]

- When forming the passive, be careful to use the appropriate tenses of *be* to maintain the tense of the original active sentence.

   ACTIVE   Bongo the clown *entertains* children. [Present tense]

   PASSIVE   Children *are entertained* by Bongo the clown. [Present tense]

   ACTIVE   Bongo the clown *entertained* the children. [Past tense]

   PASSIVE   The children *were entertained* by Bongo the clown. [Past tense]

NOTE: Intransitive verbs are not used in the passive voice (see 1c).

   INCORRECT   The plane *was arrived*.

   CORRECT    The plane *arrived*.

NOTE: The future progressive and future perfect progressive tenses are not used in the passive voice.

   INCORRECT   The novel *will be being read* by John.

   CORRECT    John *will be reading* the novel.

are given," "I *was given*," "she *will be given*"). Most writers prefer the active to the passive voice because it is clearer and simpler, requires fewer words, and identifies the actor and the action more explicitly.

ACTIVE VOICE   *Sergeants give* orders. *Privates obey* them.

Some writers use a verb in the passive voice when the active voice would be more effective. Normally the subject of a sentence is the focus of the readers' attention. If that subject does not perform the verb's action but instead receives the action, readers may wonder: What did the writer mean to emphasize? Just what is the point?

PASSIVE VOICE   *Orders are given* by sergeants. *They are obeyed* by privates.

Other writers misuse the passive voice to try to lend pomp to a humble truth (or would-be truth). The nervous student, trying to impress the professor, says, "Your help is greatly appreciated by me." When the airplane needs repairs, the flight attendant tells the passengers, "Slight technical difficulties are being experienced."

Some writers use the passive voice deliberately to obscure the truth — a contradiction of the very purpose of writing. One of the witnesses in the congressional Iran-Contra hearings tried to dodge a key question by replying, "Whether full knowledge had been attained by us at that time is uncertain." If he had answered in the active voice — "I don't know whether we knew everything then or not" — his listeners easily would have recognized an evasion.

You do not need to eliminate the passive voice entirely from your writing. In some contexts the performer of the verb's action in a sentence is unknown or irrelevant. With a passive voice verb, you can simply omit the performer, as in "Many fortunes were lost in the stock market crash of 1929" or "The passive voice is often misused." It's a good idea, though, as you comb through a rough draft, to substitute the active voice for the passive unless you have a good reason for using the passive.

EXERCISE 5–3

## Using Active and Passive Voice Verbs

Revise the following passage, changing the passive voice to the active voice in each sentence, unless you can justify keeping the passive. Example:

The Galápagos Islands were reached by many species of animals in ancient times.

Many species of animals *reached* the Galápagos Islands in ancient times.

The unique creatures of the Galápagos Islands have been studied by many scientists. The islands were explored by Charles Darwin in 1835. His observations led to the theory of evolution, which he explained in his book *The Origin of Species*. Thirteen species of finches on the islands were discovered by Darwin, all descended from a common stock; even today this great variety of species can be seen by visitors to the islands. Each island species has evolved by adapting to local conditions. A twig is used by the wood-pecker finch to probe trees for grubs. Algae on the ocean floor is fed on by the marine iguana. Salt water can be drunk by the Galápagos cormorant, thanks to a salt-extracting gland. Because of the tameness of these animals, they can be studied by visitors at close range.

## MOOD

Still another characteristic of verbs is mood. Every verb is in one of three *moods*: the *indicative,* the *imperative,* or the *subjunctive.* The indicative mood is the most common. The imperative mood and subjunctive mood add valu-able versatility to the English language.

**5n.** Use the indicative mood to state a fact, to ask a question, or to express an opinion.

The vast majority of verbs in English are in the indicative mood.

| | |
|---|---|
| FACT | Pat *left* home two months ago. |
| QUESTION | *Will* she *find* happiness as a belly dancer? |
| OPINION | I *think* not. |

**5o.** Use the imperative mood to make a request or to give a command or direction.

The understood but usually unstated subject of a verb in the imperative mood is *you.* The verb's form is the infinitive.

| | |
|---|---|
| REQUEST | Please *be* there before noon. [*You* please be there....] |
| COMMAND | *Hurry!* [*You* hurry!] |
| DIRECTION | To reach my house, *drive* east on State Street. [... *you* drive east....] |

**5p.** Use the subjunctive mood to express a wish, a requirement, a suggestion, or a condition contrary to fact.

The subjunctive mood is used in a subordinate clause to suggest uncertainty: the action expressed by the verb may or may not actually take place as speci-fied. In any clause opening with *that* and expressing a requirement, the verb is in the subjunctive mood and its form is the infinitive.

Professor Avery requires that every student *deliver* his or her work promptly.

She asked that we *be* on time for all meetings.

When you use the subjunctive mood to describe a condition that is con-trary to fact, use *were* if the verb is *be;* for other verbs, use the simple past tense.

Wishes, whether present or past, follow the same rules.

> If I *were* rich, I would be happy.

> If I *had* a million dollars, I would be happy.

> Elissa wishes that Ted *were* more goal-oriented.

> Elissa wished that Ted *knew* what he wanted to do.

For a condition that was contrary to fact at some point in the past, use the past perfect tense.

> If I *had been* awake, I would have seen the meteor showers.

> If Jessie *had known* you were coming, she would have cleaned her room.

Although use of the subjunctive mood has grown scarcer over the years, it still sounds crude to write "If I *was* you...." If you ever feel that the sub-

---

**ESL GUIDELINES**

## Conditionals

**Conditional sentences** usually contain an *if* clause, which states the condition, and a result clause.

- When the condition is true or possibly true in the present or future, use the present tense in the *if* clause and the present or future tense in the result clause. The future tense is not used in the *if* clause.

  > If Jane *prepares* her composition early, she usually *writes* very well.

  > If Maria *saves* enough money, she *will buy* some new software.

- When the condition is not true in the present, for most verbs use the past tense in the *if* clause; for the verb *be*, use *were*. Use *would, could,* or *might* + infinitive form in the result clause.

  > If Carlos *had* a computer, he *would need* a monitor, too.

  > If Claudia *were* here, she *could do* it herself.

- When the condition was not true in the past, use the perfect past tense in the *if* clause. If the possible result was in the past, use *would have, could have,* or *might have* + past participle (*-ed* or *-en* form) in the result clause. If the possible result is in the present, use *would, could,* or *might* + infinitive form in the result clause.

  > If Claudia *had saved* enough money last month, she *could have bought* new software. [Result in the past.]

  > If Annie *had finished* law school, she *might be* a successful lawyer now. [Result in the present.]

junctive mood makes a sentence sound stilted, you can rewrite it, substituting an infinitive phrase.

> Professor Avery requires every student *to deliver* his or her work promptly.

**EXERCISE 5–4**

## Using the Correct Mood of Verbs

Find and correct any errors in mood of verbs in the following sentences. Identify the mood of the incorrect verb as well as of its correct replacement. Some sentences may be correct. Answers for the lettered sentences appear in the back of the book. Example:

> If a wish was a horse, then a beggar could ride.

> If a wish *were* a horse, then a beggar could ride. [Incorrect *was*, indicative; correct *were*, subjunctive]

a. When Janet cooks, she insists that Tom washes the dishes.
b. If John believe that of me, I no longer wish to be his friend.
c. If I was a licensed plumber, I could install the washing machine myself.
d. The IRS recommends that tax forms are filled out as soon as they become available.
e. If that man do not go away, call the police.

1. The government requires that each citizen supports the war effort.
2. You are at my house at six or we'll leave you behind.
3. I would feel more comfortable about leaving if someone was watching my things.
4. Courtesy demands that Jill returns your call.
5. I will forgive her if she apologize.

# 6. *Subject-Verb Agreement*

What does it mean for a subject and a verb to agree? Practically speaking, it means that their forms are in accord: plural subjects take plural verbs, third-person subjects take third-person verbs, and so forth. Creating agreement in a sentence is like making sure that all the instruments in a song are playing in the same key. When your subjects and verbs agree, you prevent a discord that could distract readers from your message.

**6a.** A verb agrees with its subject in person and number.

Subject and verb agree in person (first, second, or third):

> *I write* my research papers on a typewriter. [Subject and verb in first person.]

> *Jim writes* his research papers on a word processor. [Subject and verb in third person.]

Subject and verb agree in number (singular or plural):

*Susan has enjoyed* college. [Subject and verb singular.]

*She and Jim have enjoyed* their vacation. [Subject and verb plural.]

The present tense of most verbs is the infinitive form, with no added ending except in the third-person singular. (See 5g–5l.)

| | |
|---|---|
| I enjoy | we enjoy |
| you enjoy | you enjoy |
| he/she/it enjoys | they enjoy |

Forms of the verb *be* vary from this rule.

| | |
|---|---|
| I am | we are |
| you are | you are |
| he/she/it is | they are |

**6b.** A verb agrees with its subject, not with any words that intervene.

My *favorite* of O. Henry's short stories *is* "The Gift of the Magi."

*Dollars,* once the dominant currency in international trade, *have fallen* behind the yen.

A singular subject linked to another noun or pronoun by a prepositional phrase such as *along with, as well as,* or *in addition to* remains a singular subject and takes a singular verb.

My cousin *James* as well as his wife and son *plans* to vote for the Democratic candidate.

**6c.** Subjects joined by *and* usually take a plural verb.

Two or more nouns or pronouns linked by *and* constitute a *compound subject.* (See 2a.) In most cases, a compound subject counts as plural and takes a plural verb.

*"Howl" and "Gerontion" are* Barry's favorite poems.

*Sugar, salt, and fat* adversely *affect* people's health.

However, for phrases like *each man and woman* or *every dog and cat,* where the subjects are considered individually, use a singular verb.

*Each man and woman* in the room *has* a different story to tell.

Use a singular verb for two singular subjects that refer to the same thing.

*Lime juice and soda quenches* your thirst.

**6d.**   With subjects joined by *or* or *nor*, the verb agrees with the part of the subject nearest to it.

>   Either they or *Max is* guilty.

>   Neither Sally nor *I am* willing to face the truth.

Subjects containing *not... but* follow this rule also.

>   Not we but *George knows* the whole story.

>   You can remedy the awkwardness of such constructions by rephrasing the offending sentences.

>   Either they are guilty or Max is.

>   Sally and I are unwilling to face the truth.

>   We do not know the whole story, but George does.

**6e.**   Most collective nouns take singular verbs.

What do you do when the number of a subject is not obvious? Collective nouns, such as *committee, congregation, family, group, jury,* and *trio,* represent more than one person. When a collective noun refers to a group of people acting in unison, use a singular verb.

>   The *jury finds* the defendant guilty.

>   My *family upholds* traditional values.

When the members act individually, use a plural verb.

>   The *jury do* not yet *agree* on a verdict.

>   Alice's *family* rarely *eat* together.

>   If you feel that using a plural verb with a collective subject results in an awkward sentence, reword the subject so that it refers to members of the group individually. (Also see 9e.)

>   The *jurors do* not yet *agree* on a verdict.

>   The *members* of Alice's family rarely *eat* together.

**6f.**   Most indefinite pronouns take a third-person singular verb.

The indefinite pronouns *each, either, neither, anyone, anybody, anything, everyone, everybody, everything, one, no one, nobody, nothing, someone, somebody,* and *something* are considered singular and take a third-person singular verb.

>   *Someone is bothering* me.

>   Even when one of these subjects is followed by a phrase containing a noun or pronoun of a different person or number, use a singular verb.

**ESL GUIDELINES**

## Count Nouns and Articles

Nouns that refer to items that can be counted are called *count* (or *countable*) nouns. Count nouns can be made plural.

> *table, chair, egg*    two *tables*, several *chairs*, a dozen *eggs*

- Singular count nouns must be preceded by a *determiner.* The class of words called determiners includes *articles* (*a, an, the*), *possessives* (*John's, your, his, my,* and so on), *demonstratives* (*this, that, these, those*), *numbers* (*three, the third,* and so on), and *indefinite quantity words* (*no, some, many,* and so on).

> *a* dog, *the* football, *one* reason, *the first* page, *no* chance

- The choice between using an indefinite article (*a, an*) or the definite article (*the*) before a singular count noun depends on context and meaning. Use the indefinite article when the noun is unspecific or when you are introducing something not previously known to the reader or you the writer.

> She likes to have *a* milkshake every day. [Any milkshake, not a specific one]

> I saw *a* dog in my backyard this morning. [The dog is not known to the reader or writer.]

- Use the definite article when a noun is mentioned for the second time.

> She likes to have *a* milkshake every day. *The* milkshake must be cold.

> I saw *a* dog in my backyard this morning. *The* dog was black.

- Use the definite article before a specific count noun mentioned the first time when the reader or listener is given enough information to identify what is referred to, usually in a phrase or clause after the noun.

> *The* young woman wearing blue is my sister. [*Wearing blue* identifies the particular woman.]

- Use the definite article before a singular count noun to make a generalization.

> *The* dog has been humans' favorite pet for centuries. [All dogs]

- Use the definite article before some geographical names.

> *Collectives:* the United States, the United Kingdom
> *Groups of islands:* the Bahamas, the Canary Islands
> *Large bodies of water (except lakes):* the Atlantic Ocean, the Dead Sea
> *Mountain ranges:* the Rocky Mountains, the Himalayas

- When plural count nouns are used to name a general group, they are not preceded by an article. When they are used to name a definite or specific group they must be preceded by *the* or another determiner.

> *Horses* don't eat meat, and neither do *cows.*

> Hal is feeding *the horses* in the barn, and he has already fed *his cows.*

*Each* of you *is* here to stay.

*One* of the pandas *seems* dangerously ill.

**6g.** The indefinite pronouns *all, any,* and *some* use a singular or plural verb depending on their meaning.

I have no explanation. *Is any* needed?

*Any* of the changes that really needed to be made *have* been made already.

---

**ESL GUIDELINES**

## Noncount Nouns and Articles

Nouns that cannot be counted are called ***noncount*** (or ***uncountable***) nouns. Noncount nouns cannot be made plural.

INCORRECT   I need to learn more *grammars.*

CORRECT   I need to learn more *grammar.*

- Common categories of noncount nouns include types of ***food*** (*cheese, meat, bread, broccoli,* and so on), ***solids*** (*dirt, salt, chalk*), ***liquids*** (*milk, juice, gasoline*), ***gases*** (*methane, hydrogen, air*), and ***abstract ideas*** including emotions (*democracy, gravity, love, jealousy*).
- Another category of noncount nouns is ***mass*** nouns, which usually represent a large group of countable nouns, such as *furniture, equipment, luggage, mail,* and *clothing.*
- The only way to count noncountable nouns is to use a countable noun with them; these countable nouns usually indicate a quantity or a container.

  one *piece* of furniture

  two *quarts* of water

  an *example* of jealousy

- Noncount nouns are never preceded by an indefinite article; they are often preceded by *some.*

  INCORRECT   She gave us *a* good advice.

  CORRECT   She gave us good advice.

  CORRECT   She gave us *some* good advice.

- When noncount nouns are *general* in meaning, no article is required, but when the context makes them specific (usually in a phrase or a clause after the noun), the definite article is used.

  GENERAL   Deliver us from *evil.*

  SPECIFIC   The *evil* that humans do lives after them.

*All is* lost.

*All* of the bananas *are gone.*

*Some* of the blame *is* mine.

*Some* of us *are* Democrats.

*None* — like *all, any,* and *some* — takes a singular or a plural verb, depending on the sense in which the pronoun is used. (See also 9d, 9f.)

*None* of you *is* exempt.

*None* of his wives *were* blond.

### 6h. In a subordinate clause with a relative pronoun as the subject, the verb agrees with the antecedent.

When you are writing a subordinate clause that modifies a noun, the subject may be a relative pronoun: *who, which,* or *that.* To determine the person and number of the verb in the clause, look back at the pronoun's antecedent, the word to which the pronoun refers. (See 9a–9f.) The antecedent is usually (but not always) the noun closest to the relative pronoun.

I have a friend *who studies* day and night. [The antecedent of *who* is the third-person singular noun *friend.* Therefore the verb in the subordinate clause is third-person singular, *studies.*]

Unfortunately, I bought one of the two hundred recently manufactured cars *that have* defective upholstery. [The antecedent of *that* is *cars,* so the verb is third-person plural, *have.*]

This is the only one of the mayor's new ideas *that has* any worth. [Here *one,* not *ideas,* is the antecedent of *that.* Thus the verb in the subordinate clause is third-person singular, *has,* not *have.*]

### 6i. A verb agrees with its subject even when the subject follows the verb.

A writer need not necessarily place the subject of a sentence before the verb. In some sentences, an introductory phrase or a word such as *there* or *here* changes the ordinary subject-verb order. If a sentence opens with such a phrase or word, look for the subject after the verb. Remember that verbs agree with subjects and that *here* and *there* are never subjects.

Here *is* a *riddle* for you.

There *are* forty *people* in my law class.

Under the bridge *were* a broken-down *boat and* a worn *tire.*

**6j.** A linking verb agrees with its subject, not its subject complement.

In some sentences, a form of the verb *be* is used to link two or more nouns ("Matthew *is* the composer"). The linking verb's subject is the noun that precedes it. Nouns that follow the linking verb are subject complements. (See 2d.) Take care to make a linking verb agree with the subject of the sentence, not with the subject complement.

> *Jim is* a gentleman and a scholar.

> Amy's *parents are* her most enthusiastic audience.

**6k.** When the subject is a title, use a singular verb.

> When I was younger, *James and the Giant Peach* by Roald Dahl *was* my favorite book.

> "Memories" sung by Barbra Streisand *is* my favorite song.

**6l.** Singular nouns that end in *-s* take singular verbs.

Some nouns look plural even though they refer to a singular subject: *news, measles, logistics, mathematics, physics, electronics, economics.* Such nouns take singular verbs.

> The *news is* that *economics has become* one of the most popular majors.

---

**EXERCISE 6–1**

## Making Subjects and Verbs Agree

Find and correct any errors of subject-verb agreement in the following sentences. Some sentences may be correct. Answers for the lettered sentences appear in the back of the book. Example:

> Addressing the audience tonight is the nominees for club president.

> Addressing the audience tonight *are* the nominees for club president.

a. Our foreign policy in Cuba, Nicaragua, El Salvador, and Panama have not been as successful as most Americans had hoped.
b. The large amount of metal and chlorine in our water makes it taste funny.
c. I read about a couple who is offering to trade their baby for a brand-new Chevrolet.
d. A shave, a haircut, and a new suit has turned Bill into a different person.
e. Neither the guerrillas nor the government are willing to negotiate.

1. Each of us, including Alice, want this to be a successful party.

2. The police force, after the recent rash of burglaries, have added more patrols in this neighborhood.
3. More disturbing than John's speech was the gestures that accompanied it.
4. One of Korea's most fascinating cities are Kyongju.
5. Nearly everybody who traveled by air during the last six weeks was aware of increased security precautions.
6. The bad news about interest rates have been widely publicized.
7. Most of the class believed that both the private sector and the government was taking appropriate action on homelessness.
8. Jane Austen, along with George Eliot and Charles Dickens, are still popular today.
9. Ron Wood is not the only member of the Rolling Stones who have played in the band Faces.
10. Beside the cottage was a small barn and a well.

# 7. *Pronoun Case*

As you know, pronouns come in distinctive forms. The first-person pronoun can be *I*, or it can be *me, my, mine, we, us, our,* or *ours.* Which form do you pick? It depends on what job you want the pronoun to do. Filling these jobs may sound easy, but now and again every writer has a hard time hiring the pronoun that is properly qualified.

To choose correctly, it may help you to know the three *cases* used to classify pronouns. Depending on a pronoun's function in a sentence, we say that it is in the **subjective case,** the **objective case,** or the **possessive case.**

Some pronouns change form when they change case and some do not. The personal pronouns *I, he, she, we,* and *they* and the relative pronoun *who* have different forms in the subjective, objective, and possessive cases. Other pronouns, such as *you, it, that,* and *which,* have only two forms: the plain case (which serves as both subjective and objective) and the possessive case.

We can pin the labels *subjective, objective,* and *possessive* on nouns as well as on pronouns. Like the pronouns *you, it, that,* and *which,* nouns shift out of their plain form only in the possessive case (*teacher's* pet, the *Joneses'* poodle).

Beware, when you are not sure which case to choose, of the temptation to fall back on a reflexive pronoun (*myself, himself*). Reflexive pronouns have limited, specific uses in writing (see 1b). They do not take the place of subjective or objective pronouns. If you catch yourself writing, "You can return the form to John or *myself*" or "John and *myself* are in charge," replace the reflexive pronoun with one that is grammatically correct: "You can return the form to John or *me*"; "John and *I* are in charge."

**7a.**  Use the subjective case for the subject of a sentence or clause.

*I* ate the granola.

*Who* cares?

---

## Pronoun Cases

| SUBJECTIVE | OBJECTIVE | POSSESSIVE |
|---|---|---|
| I | me | my, mine |
| you | you | your, yours |
| he, she, it | him, her, it | his, her, hers, its |
| we | us | our, ours |
| you | you | your, yours |
| they | them | their, theirs |
| who | whom | whose |

### Subjective Pronouns

I, you, he, she, it, we, they, who, whoever, that, which

### Objective Pronouns

me, you, him, her, it, us, them, whom, whomever, that, which

### Possessive Pronouns

my, mine, our, ours, his, her, hers, its, your, yours, their, theirs

---

Mark recalled that *she* played jai alai.

Election officials are the people *who* count.

Sometimes a compound subject will lead a writer astray: "Jed and *me* ate the granola." *Me*, an objective pronoun, is the wrong one for this job. Use the subjective form, *I*, instead: "Jed and *I* ate the granola."

A pronoun serving as subject for a verb is subjective even when the verb isn't written but is only implied:

Jed is hungrier than *I* [am].

Don't be fooled by a pronoun that appears immediately after a verb, as if it were a direct object, but that functions as the subject of a clause. The pronoun's case is determined by its role in the sentence, not its position.

The judge didn't believe *I* hadn't been the driver.

We were happy to interview *whoever* was running. [Subject of *was running*]

**7b.**  Use the subjective case for a subject complement.

A pronoun can function as a subject complement after a linking verb such as *is*, *seems*, or *appears*. (See 2d for more on subject complements, 5a for more on linking verbs.) Because it plays essentially the same role as the subject, the pronoun's case is subjective.

The phantom graffiti artist couldn't have been *he*. It was *I*.

**7c.** Use the subjective case for an appositive to a subject or subject complement.

A pronoun placed in apposition to a subject or subject complement is like an identical twin to the noun it stands beside. It has the same meaning and the same case. (See also 3d.)

The class *officers* — Jed and *she* — announced a granola breakfast.

**7d.** Use the objective case for a direct object, an indirect object, the object of a preposition, or a subject of an infinitive.

The custard pies hit *him* and *me*. [Direct object]

Mona threw *us* towels. [Indirect object]

Mona threw towels to *him* and *us*. [Object of a preposition]

We always expect *him* to win. [Subject of an infinitive]

**7e.** Use the objective case for an appositive to a direct or indirect object or the object of a preposition.

Mona helped *us* all — Mrs. Van Dumont, *him*, and *me*. [*Him* and *me* are in apposition to the direct object *us*.]

Binks gave his favorite *students*, Tom and *her*, an approving nod. [*Her* is in apposition to the indirect object *students*.]

Yelling, the persistent pie flingers ran after *us* — Mrs. Van Dumont, Mona, *him*, and *me*. [*Him* and *me* are in apposition to *us*, the object of the preposition *after*.]

**7f.** Use the possessive case to show ownership.

Possessive pronouns can function as adjectives or as nouns. The pronouns *my, your, his, her, its, our,* and *their* function as adjectives by modifying nouns or pronouns.

*Their* apartment is bigger than *our* house.

*My* new bike is having *its* first road test today.

Notice that the possessive pronoun *its* does not contain an apostrophe. *It's* with an apostrophe is not a possessive pronoun, but a contraction for *it is*, as in "*It's* a beautiful day." If you want to write about the day and *its* beauty, be sure to omit the apostrophe.

The possessive pronouns *mine, yours, his, hers, ours,* and *theirs* can discharge the whole range of noun duties. These pronouns can serve as subjects,

subject complements, direct objects, indirect objects, or objects of prepositions.

> *Yours* is the last vote we need. [Subject]

> This day is *ours.* [Subject complement]

> Don't take your car; take *mine.* [Direct object]

> If we're honoring requests in chronological order, give *hers* top priority. [In-direct object]

> Give her request priority over *theirs.* [Object of a preposition]

## 7g. Use the possessive case to modify a gerund.

A possessive pronoun (or a possessive noun) is the appropriate escort for a
gerund, a form of verb that functions as a noun: *griping, being, drinking.* (See
3b.) As a noun, a gerund requires an adjective, not another noun, for a modifier.

> Mary is tired of *his griping.* [The possessive pronoun *his* modifies the gerund *griping.*]

> I can stand *their being* late every morning, but not *his drinking* on the job. [The possessive pronoun *their* modifies the gerund *being;* the possessive pronoun *his* modifies the gerund *drinking.*]

Gerunds can cause confusion when you edit your writing because they
look exactly like participles. (See 5c.) Whereas a gerund functions as a noun,
a participle often functions as an adjective modifying a noun or pronoun.

> Mary heard *him griping* about work. [The participle *griping* modifies the direct object *him.*]

If you are not sure whether to use a possessive or an objective pronoun
with a word ending in *-ing,* look closely at your sentence. Which word — the
pronoun or the *-ing* word — is the object of your main verb? That word functions as a noun; the other word modifies it.

> Mr. Phipps remembered *them* smoking in the boys' room.

> Mr. Phipps remembered *their* smoking in the boys' room.

In the first sentence, Mr. Phipps's memory is of *them,* those naughty students.
*Them* is the object of the verb, so *smoking* is a participle modifying *them.* In the
second sentence, Mr. Phipps remembers *smoking,* that nasty habit. The gerund
*smoking* is the object of the verb, so the possessive pronoun *their* is the right
choice to modify it.

In everyday speech, the rules about pronoun case apply less rigidly.
Someone who correctly asks in conversation, "To whom are you referring?" is

likely to sound pretentious. You are within your rights to reply, as did the comic-strip character Pogo Possum, "Youm, that's whom!" Say, if you like, "It's *me*," but write "It is *I*." Say, if you wish, "*Who* did he ask to the party?" but write "*Whom* did he ask?"

EXERCISE 7–I

## Using Pronouns Correctly

Replace any pronouns that are used incorrectly in the following sentences. (Consider all these examples as written — not spoken — English, and so apply the rules strictly.) Explain why each pronoun was incorrect. Some sentences may be correct. Answers for the lettered sentences appear in the back of the book. Example:

In the photograph, that's him at the age of seven.

In the photograph, that's *he* at the age of seven. [*He* is a subject complement.]

a. She can run faster than me.
b. Mrs. Van Dumont awarded the prize to Mona and I.
c. Judy laughed at both of us — she and I.
d. I am sure that I overheard that rude man speaking of we.
e. Jerry, myself, and the pizza chef regard you and she as the very people who we wish to get acquainted with.

1. I like to watch them swimming in the hotel pool.
2. Lee and me would be delighted to serenade whomever will listen.
3. The waiters and us busboys are highly trustworthy.
4. The neighbors were driven berserk by him singing.
5. Strictly platonic affairs suit us — Biff, the Flipper, and me.
6. Dean Fitts and them, who I suspect of being the pie throwers, flung crusty missiles at Stan, he, and myself.
7. Have you guessed the identity of the person of who I am speaking?
8. I didn't appreciate you laughing at her and I.
9. They — Jerry and her — are the troublemakers.
10. It was him asking about the clock that started me suspecting him.
11. Juliana isn't as old-fashioned in her views as them.
12. The Jeffersons invited Martha and I over for dinner.
13. There is a lack of communication among you and he and Dean.
14. The counterattack was launched by Dusty and myself.
15. Whomever this anonymous letter writer is, I resent him lying about Jules and me and the cabbages.

# 8. *Pronoun Reference*

Look hard at just about any piece of writing — this discussion, if you like — and you'll find that practically every pronoun in it points to some noun. This is the main use of pronouns: to refer in a brief, convenient form to some *an-*

*tecedent* that has already been named. A pronoun usually has a noun or another pronoun as its antecedent. Often the antecedent is the subject or object of the same clause in which the pronoun appears.

> Josie hit the *ball* after *its* first bounce.

> Smashing into *Greg,* the ball knocked off *his* glasses.

The antecedent also can appear in a different clause or even a different sentence from the pronoun.

> *Josie* hit the *ball* when *it* bounced back to *her.*

> The *ball* smashed into *Greg. It* knocked off *his* glasses.

A pronoun as well as a noun can be an antecedent.

> My *dog* hid in the closet when *she* had *her* puppies. [*Dog* is the antecedent of *she; she* is the antecedent of *her.*]

**EDITING CHECKLIST**

### Making Pronoun Reference Clear

- Do all pronouns have named, not just implied, antecedents? (8a)
- Is the meaning of the pronoun *it, this, that,* or *which* always clear? (8b)
- Where there is more than one noun preceding a pronoun, is the identity of the antecedent clear? (8c)
- Is every pronoun close enough to its antecedent to make the relationship clear? (8d)

**8a.** Name the pronoun's antecedent — don't just imply it.

In editing, in combing over what you write, be sure you have identified clearly the antecedent of each pronoun. A writer who leaves a key idea unsaid is likely to confuse readers.

> VAGUE    Ted wanted a Norwegian canoe because he'd heard that *they* produce the lightest canoes afloat.

What does *they* refer to? Not to *Norwegian,* which is an adjective; the antecedent of a pronoun has to be a noun or pronoun. We may guess that this writer has in mind Norwegian canoe builders, but no such noun has been mentioned. To make the sentence work, the writer must supply an antecedent for *they.*

> CLEAR    Ted wanted a Norwegian canoe because he'd heard that Norway produces [*or* Norwegians produce] the lightest canoes afloat.

Watch out for possessive nouns. They won't work as antecedents.

> VAGUE    On William's canoe *he* painted a skull and bones. (For all we know, *he* might be some joker named Fred.)

> CLEAR    On his canoe William painted a skull and bones.

**8b.**    Give the pronoun *it, this, that,* or *which* a clear antecedent.

Vagueness arises, thick as fog, whenever *it, this, that,* or *which* points to something a writer assumes he or she has said but indeed hasn't. Is the reference of a pronoun fuzzy? Might a reader get lost in the fog? Often the best way out of the fog is to substitute a specific noun or phrase for the pronoun.

VAGUE    I was an only child, and *it* was hard.

CLEAR    I was an only child, and *my solitary life* was hard.

VAGUE    Ruth majored in economics and applied for a job in a broker's office, *which* caused her father to exult. Still, *it* was not what she desired.

CLEAR    Ruth majored in economics and applied for a job in a broker's office, *decisions* that pleased her father. Still, *a career in finance* was not what she desired.

**8c.**    Make the pronoun's antecedent clear.

Confusion strikes if the antecedent of a pronoun is ambiguous — that is, if the pronoun seems to point in two or more directions. In such a puzzling situation, there's no lack of antecedent; the trouble is that more than one antecedent looks possible. Baffled, the reader wonders which the writer means.

CONFUSING    Rob shouted to Jim to take off his burning sweater.

Whose sweater does *his* mean — Jim's or Rob's? Simply changing a pronoun won't clear up the confusion. The writer needs to revise the sentence drastically enough to move the two antecedents out of each other's way.

CLEAR    "Help, Rob!" Jim shouted. "My sweater's on fire! Take it off!"

CLEAR    "Jim!" shouted Rob. "Your sweater's on fire! Take it off!"

CLEAR    Flames were shooting from Jim's sweater. Rob shouted to Jim to take it off.

As you can tell from that first fogbound sentence, pronouns referring to nouns of the same gender are particular offenders. How would you straighten out this grammatical tangle?

CONFUSING    Linda welcomed Lee-Ann's move into the apartment next door. Little did she dream that soon she would be secretly dating her husband.

Let meaning show the way. If you had written these sentences, you would know which person is the sneak. One way to clarify the antecedents of *she* and *her* is to add more information.

CLEAR    In welcoming Lee-Ann to the apartment next door, Linda didn't dream that soon her own husband would be secretly dating her former sorority sister.

Instead of *her own husband,* you can identify that philanderer by name if you have previously identified him as Linda's husband: "Ned would be secretly dating...." (Grammatical tangles are easier than human tangles to straighten out.)

**8d.**   Place the pronoun close to its antecedent to keep the relationship clear.

Watch out for distractions that slip in between noun and pronoun. If, before your readers come to a pronoun in your sentence, they meet other nouns — interesting nouns — that might look like antecedents, they may become bewildered.

> CONFUSING   Harper steered his dinghy alongside the polished mahogany cabin cruiser that the drug smugglers had left anchored under an overhanging willow in the tiny harbor and eased it to a stop.

What did Harper ease to a stop? By the time readers reach the end of the sentence, they are likely to have forgotten. To avoid confusion, keep the pronoun and its antecedent reasonably close together.

> CLEAR   Harper steered his dinghy into the tiny harbor and eased it to a stop alongside the polished mahogany cabin cruiser that the drug smugglers had left anchored under an overhanging willow.

Never force your readers to stop and think, "What does that pronoun stand for?" You, the writer, have to do this thinking for them.

**EXERCISE 8–1**

## Making Pronoun Reference Clear

Revise each sentence or group of sentences so that any pronoun needing an antecedent clearly points to one. Possible revisions for the lettered sentences appear in the back of the book. Example:

> If your dog tries to bite your guest, tie him up in the yard.

> If your dog tries to bite your guest, tie the dog up in the yard.

a. When computers cost the same as television sets, every American will own one.
b. After Sarah's meeting with her newspaper's editor, she reported that she wasn't sure if she agreed with her position on freedom of speech.
c. I cannot give you my observations on the behavioral differences between apes and human beings because I've never seen any.
d. Swaying gently in his parachute, floating lazily to earth, Edgar felt pure joy. It had been the finest thing he'd ever tried, and he was all for it.
e. Glancing down, Edgar saw the cactus loom and the rattlesnake coil, which promised an uncertain landing.

1. Marsha didn't know Russian and had allergies, but this didn't stop her from summering on a Ukrainian wheat farm.
2. The delicacy of the statue's carving, which obviously dates from a period when sculptors were highly respected, is what makes it valuable.
3. The delegates from western and third world nations found that they place greater emphasis on the community than on the individual. This is something that affects all aspects of culture and politics.
4. Dr. Wright told Yukio that his condition was deteriorating rapidly and that he would soon be too ill to practice medicine.
5. Beachcombing, picking up shells, bottles, and driftwood, I found one containing a yellowed message dated 1792. "Why," he pleaded, "has no one answered the message I launched in 1789?"

# 9. *Pronoun-Antecedent Agreement*

A pronoun's job is to fill in for a noun, much as an actor's double fills in for the actor. Pronouns are a short, convenient way for writers to avoid repeating the same noun over and over. The noun that a pronoun stands for is called its *antecedent.*

> The sheriff drew a six-shooter; he fired twice.

This action-packed sentence unfolds in a familiar order. First comes a noun (*sheriff*) and then a pronoun (*he*) that refers back to it. *Sheriff* is the antecedent of *he.*

Just as verbs need to agree with their subjects, pronouns need to agree with the nouns they stand for. A successful writer takes care not to shift number, person, or gender in mid-sentence ("The *sheriff* and the *outlaw* drew *their* six-shooters; *he* fired twice"). Rather, the writer starts each sentence with nouns clearly in mind and picks appropriate pronouns to refer to them.

## 9a. Pronouns agree with their antecedents in person and number.

A pronoun matches its antecedent in person (first, second, or third) and in number (singular or plural), even when a string of intervening words separates the pronoun and its antecedent. (See the pronoun chart in 1b.)

> FAULTY   All *campers* should bring *your* knapsacks.

Here, noun and pronoun disagree in person: *campers* is third person, but *your* is second person.

> FAULTY   Every *camper* should bring *their* knapsack.

Here, noun and pronoun disagree in number: *camper* is singular, but *their* is plural.

REVISED  All *campers* should bring *their* knapsacks.

REVISED  Every *camper* should bring *his or her* knapsack. (See also 9f.)

EDITING
CHECKLIST

## Making Pronouns Agree with Their Antecedents

- Do pronouns agree with their antecedents in number (singular or plural)? (9a)
- Do pronouns agree with their antecedents in person (first, second, or third)? (9a)
- Do pronouns agree with their antecedents in gender (masculine, feminine, or neuter)? (9f)

**9b.** Most antecedents joined by *and* require a plural pronoun.

What if the subject of your sentence is two nouns (or a noun and a pronoun) connected by *and*? Such a *compound subject* is plural; use a plural pronoun to refer to it.

*George,* who has been here before, *and Susan,* who hasn't, should bring *their* knapsacks.

However, if the nouns in a *compound subject* refer to the same person or thing, they make up a singular antecedent. In that case, the pronoun too is singular.

The *owner and founder* of this camp carries *his* own knapsack everywhere.

**9c.** A pronoun agrees with the closest part of an antecedent joined by *or* or *nor*.

If your subject is two or more nouns (or a combination of nouns and pronouns) connected by *or* or *nor*, look closely at the subject's parts. Are they all singular? If so, your pronoun should be singular.

Neither *Joy nor Jean* remembered *her* knapsack last year.

If *Sam, Arthur, or Max* shows up, tell *him* I'm looking for *him.*

If the part of the subject closest to the pronoun is plural, the pronoun should be plural.

Neither *Joy nor her sisters* remembered *their* knapsacks last year.

If you see *Sam, Arthur, or their friends,* tell *them* I'm looking for *them.*

**9d.**   An antecedent that is an indefinite pronoun takes a singular pronoun.

An indefinite pronoun is one that does not refer to any specific person, place, or thing: *anybody, each, either.* (For a complete list, see the pronoun chart in 1b.) Indefinite pronouns are usually singular in meaning, so a pronoun referring to one of them is also singular.

> *Either* of the boys can do it, as long as *he's* on time.

> Warn *anybody* who's still in *her* swimsuit that a uniform is required for dinner.

Sometimes the meaning of an indefinite pronoun is plural. To avoid awkwardness, avoid using such a pronoun as an antecedent.

> Tell *everyone* in Cabin B that I'm looking for *him.*

This sentence works better if it is phrased differently.

> Tell *all the campers* in Cabin B that I'm looking for *them.*

(See also 6f, 9f.)

**9e.**   Most collective nouns used as antecedents require singular pronouns.

A collective noun is a singular word for a group of people or items: *army, band, committee, jury.* When the members of such a group act as a unit, use a singular pronoun to refer to them.

> The *cast* for the camp play will be posted as soon as our theater counselor chooses *it.*

When the group members act individually, use a plural pronoun.

> The *cast* will go *their* separate ways when summer ends.

(See also 6e.)

**9f.**   A pronoun agrees with its antecedent in gender.

> If *one of your parents* brings you to camp, invite *him* to stay for lunch.

While technically correct (the singular pronoun *he* is used to refer to the singular antecedent *one*), this sentence overlooks the fact that some parents are male, some female. To make sure the pronoun refers to both, a writer has two choices. (See 22a, 22c, 22d.)

If *one of your parents* brings you to camp, invite *him or her* to stay for lunch.

If your *parents* bring you to camp, invite *them* to stay for lunch.

EXERCISE 9–1

## Making Pronouns and Antecedents Agree

If any nouns and pronouns disagree in number, person, or gender in the following sentences, substitute pronouns that agree with the nouns. If you prefer, strengthen any sentence by rewriting it. Some sentences may be correct. Possible revisions for the lettered sentences appear in the back of the book. Example:

A cat expects people to feed them often.

A *cat* expects people to feed *it* often.

*Cats* expect people to feed *them* often.

a. All students are urged to complete your registration on time.
b. When a baby doesn't know their own mother, they may have been born with some kind of vision deficiency.
c. Each member of the sorority has to make his own bed.
d. If you don't like the songs the choir sings, don't join them.
e. Young people should know how to protect oneself against AIDS.

1. Many architects find work their greatest pleasure.
2. Neither Melissa nor James has received their application form yet.
3. He is the kind of man who gets their fun out of just sipping one's beer and watching his Saturday games on TV.
4. Many a mother has mourned the loss of their child.
5. When one enjoys one's work, it's easy to spend all your spare time thinking about it.

EXERCISE 9–2

## Making Pronouns and Antecedents Agree

Revise the following passage so that all nouns and pronouns agree in number, person, or gender. If you prefer, strengthen any sentence by rewriting it. Some sentences may be correct. Example:

Ken, a physics major, and Elaine, who is studying chemistry, work hard at her job.

Ken, a physics major, and Elaine, who is studying chemistry, work hard at their jobs.

It isn't easy juggling the responsibilities of school and work. All working students know how difficult it is to keep his eyes open in class after an exhausting day at his job. Ken Tucker, a student at Boston College, and Elaine Vierra, a student at Northeastern University, agree that she doesn't know how she finds the time to balance her responsibilities. With most of their time spent at work or in class, neither Ken nor Elaine has much time to devote to their friends. Ken, a quarterback with Boston College, complains that he is often unable to join his team as they celebrate their victories after the game. Elaine adds that if any of her old friends comes to visit, she does not have much time to spend with her. Neither Ken, Elaine, nor their working friends see his student life as ideal and advise all those entering college to budget her time and finances carefully.

# 10. *Adjectives and Adverbs*

An *adjective* is a word that modifies a noun or pronoun. (See 1d.) A phrase also can function as an adjective. (See 3a, 3b, 3f.) An adjective's job is to provide information about the person, place, object, or idea named by the noun or pronoun. The adjective typically answers the question Which? or What kind?

> Karen bought a *small red* car.

> The radios *on sale* are an *excellent* value.

An *adverb* is a word (or a phrase) that modifies a verb, an adjective, or another adverb. (See 1e, 3a, 3b, 3g.) An adverb typically answers the question How? or When? or Where? Sometimes it answers the question Why?

> Karen bought her car *quickly.*

> The radios arrived *yesterday;* Max put them *in the electronics department.*

> Karen needed her new car *to commute to school.*

The most common problems that writers have with adjectives and adverbs involve mixing them up: sending an adjective to do an adverb's job or vice versa.

**10a.** Use an adverb, not an adjective, to modify a verb, adjective, or another adverb.

> FAULTY    Karen bought her car *quick.*
> FAULTY    It's *awful* hot today.

Although an informal speaker might be able to get away with these sentences, a writer cannot. *Quick* and *awful* are adjectives, so they can modify only nouns or pronouns. To modify the verb *bought* we need the adverb *quickly;* to modify the adjective *hot* we need the adverb *awfully.*

> REVISED    Karen bought her car *quickly.*
> REVISED    It's *awfully* hot today.

---

## Adjectives and Adverbs at a Glance

**ADJECTIVES**
1. Typically answer the question *Which?* or *What kind?*
2. Modify nouns or pronouns

**ADVERBS**
3. Answer the question *How? When? Where?* or sometimes *Why?*
4. Modify verbs, adjectives, and other adverbs

---

**ESL GUIDELINES**

# The Definite Article *(the)*

- Use the definite article, *the,* with a specific count or noncount noun when both the writer and the reader know the identity of what is referred to or when the noun has been mentioned before. (See p. H-62 for examples of count and noncount nouns.)

  Did you feed *the* baby? [Both the reader and the writer know which baby is referred to.]

  *The* coffee tastes strong today. [Both the reader and the writer know which coffee is referred to.]

  She got a huge box in the mail. *The* box contained oranges from Florida. [*The* is used the second time the noun (*box*) is mentioned.]

- Use the definite article, *the,* before specific count or noncount nouns when the reader is given enough information to identify what is being referred to.

  *The* furniture in my apartment is old and faded. [Specific furniture]

  *The* young woman wearing blue is my sister. [Specific young woman]

- Use the definite article, *the,* before a singular count noun to make a generality.

  *The* dog has been humans' favorite pet for centuries. [*The dog* here refers to all dogs.]

- Use the definite article before some geographical names.

  *Collectives:* the United States, the United Kingdom

  *Groups of Islands:* the Bahamas, the Canary Islands

  *Large Bodies of Water* (except lakes): the Atlantic Ocean, the Dead Sea, the Monongahela River, the Gulf of Mexico

  *Mountain Ranges:* the Rockies, the Himalaya Mountains

**10b.** Use an adjective, not an adverb, as a subject complement or object complement.

If we write, "Her old car looked awful," *awful* is a *subject complement*: it follows a linking verb and modifies the subject, *car*. (See 2d, 5a.)

FAULTY   Her old car looked *awfully*.

REVISED   Her old car looked *awful*.

An *object complement* is a word that renames a direct object or completes the sentence's description of it. (See 2d.) Object complements can be adjectives or nouns, but never adverbs.

Early to bed and early to rise makes a man *healthy, wealthy,* and *wise.* [Adjectives modifying the direct object *man*]

When you are not sure whether you're dealing with an object complement or an adverb, look closely at the word's role in the sentence. If it modifies a noun, it is an object complement and therefore should be an adjective.

The coach called the referee *stupid* and *blind.* [*Stupid* and *blind* are adjectives modifying the direct object *referee.*]

If it modifies a verb, you want an adverb instead.

---

**ESL GUIDELINES**

## The Indefinite Article (*a, an*)

- Use the indefinite article, *a* or *an*, with a nonspecific, singular count noun when it is not known to the reader or to either the reader or the writer. (See p. H-62 for examples of count nouns.)

    My brother has *an* antique car. [The car's identity is unknown to the reader.]

    I saw *a* dog in my back yard this morning. [The dog's identity is unknown to both the reader and writer.]

- Use the indefinite article (*a, an*) when the noun is mentioned for the first time. Use the definite article (*the*) when the noun is mentioned again.

    I saw *a* car that I would love to buy. *The* car was red and had a leather interior.

- Use *some* or no article instead of *a* or *an* with noncount nouns or plural nouns used in a general sense. (See p. H-62 for examples of noncount nouns.)

    INCORRECT   I am going to buy *a* furniture for my apartment.

    CORRECT   I am going to buy *some* furniture for my apartment.

    CORRECT   I am going to buy furniture for my apartment.

In fact, though, the ref had called the play *correctly*. [*Correctly* is an adverb modifying the verb *called*.]

## 10c. Use *good* as an adjective and *well* as an adverb.

A common adjective-adverb mix-up occurs when writers confuse *good* and *well* as subject complements. *Good* is almost always an adjective; *well* is almost always an adverb.

This sandwich tastes *good*. [The adjective *good* is a subject complement following the linking verb *tastes* and modifying the noun *sandwich*.]

Heloise's skin healed *well* after surgery. [The adverb *well* modifies the verb *healed*.]

Only if the verb is a linking verb (see 5a) can you safely follow it with *good*. Other kinds of verbs do not take subject complements. Instead, they need adverbs to modify them.

FAULTY   That painting came out *good*.

REVISED   That painting came out *well*.

Complications arise when we write or speak about health. It is perfectly correct to say *I feel good*, using the adjective *good* as a subject complement after the linking verb *feel*. However, generations of confusion have nudged the adverb *well* into the adjective category, too. A nurse may speak of "a well baby"; and greeting cards urge patients to "get well" — meaning, "become healthy." Just as *healthy* is an adjective here, so is *well*.

What, then, is the best answer when someone asks, "How do you feel?" If you want to duck the issue, reply, "Fine!" Otherwise, in speech either *good* or *well* is acceptable; in writing, use *good*.

## 10d. Form comparatives and superlatives of most adjectives with *-er* and *-est* and of most adverbs with *more* and *most*.

Comparatives and superlatives are special adjective and adverb forms that allow us to describe one thing in relation to another. You can put most adjectives into their comparative form by adding *-er* and into their superlative form by adding *-est*.

The budget deficit is *larger* than the trade deficit.

This year's trade deficit is the *largest* ever.

We usually form the comparative and superlative of long adjectives with *more* and *most* rather than with *-er* and *-est*, to keep them from becoming cumbersome.

Our national debt is *enormous*.

It may become *more enormous* over the next few years.

For short adverbs that do not end in *-ly*, usually add *-er* and *-est* in the comparative and superlative forms. With all other adverbs, use *more* and *most*. (Also see 10f.)

Spending *faster* than one earns will plunge a person into debt *sooner* than any other way I know.

**ESL GUIDELINES**

## Cumulative Adjectives

*Cumulative adjectives* are two or more adjectives used directly before a noun and not separated by commas or the word *and* (see 25d). They usually have a specific order of placement before a noun. Use the following chart as a guideline for writing sentences with adjectives, but keep in mind that the order can be varied.

1. Articles or determiners
   *a, an, the, some, this, these, his, my, two, several*

2. Evaluative adjectives
   *beautiful, wonderful, hardworking, distasteful*

3. Size or dimension
   *big, small, huge, obese, petite, six-foot*

4. Length or shape
   *long, short, round, square, oblong, oval*

5. Age
   *old, young, new, fresh, ancient*

6. Color
   *red, pink, aquamarine, orange*

7. Nation or place of origin
   *American, Japanese, European, Bostonian, Floridian*

8. Religion
   *Protestant, Muslim, Hindu, Buddhist, Catholic*

9. Matter or substance
   *wood, gold, cotton, plastic, pine, metal*

10. Noun used as an adjective
    *telephone* (as in *telephone operator*), *computer* (as in *computer software*)

Cumulative adjectives do not require commas when used in a series.

She is an *attractive older French* woman.

His *expressive large brown* eyes moved me.

The *more indiscriminately* we import foreign goods, the *more rapidly* the trade deficit grows.

It grows *fastest* and *most uncontrollably* when exports are down.

For negative comparisons, use *less* and *least* for both adjectives and adverbs.

Michael's speech was *less interesting* than Louie's.

Paulette spoke *less interestingly* than Michael.

Bud's speech was the *least interesting* of all.

The comparative and superlative forms of irregular adjectives and adverbs (such as *bad* and *badly*) are also irregular and should be used with special care.

Tom's golf is *bad,* but no *worse* than George's.

Tom plays golf *badly,* but no *worse* than George does.

| Comparison of Irregular Adjectives and Adverbs | | | |
| --- | --- | --- | --- |
| | POSITIVE | COMPARATIVE | SUPERLATIVE |
| ADJECTIVES | good | better | best |
| | bad | worse | worst |
| | little | less, littler | least, littlest |
| | many, some, much | more | most |
| ADVERBS | well | better | best |
| | badly | worse | worst |
| | little | less | least |

**10e.** Omit *more* and *most* with an adjective or adverb that is already comparative or superlative.

Some words become comparative or superlative when we tack on -*er* or -*est.* Others, such as *top, favorite,* and *unique,* mark whatever they modify as one of a kind by definition. Neither category requires further assistance to make its point. To say "a *more worse* fate" or "my *most favorite* movie" is redundant — "a *worse* fate" or "my *favorite* movie" does the job.

FAULTY   Lisa is *more uniquely* qualified for the job than any other candidate.

REVISED   Lisa is *better* qualified for the job than any other candidate.

REVISED   Lisa is *uniquely* qualified for the job.

**10f.** Use the comparative form of an adjective or adverb to compare two people or things, the superlative form to compare more than two.

No matter how fantastic, wonderful, and terrific something is, we can call it the *best* only when we compare it with more than one other thing. Any comparison between two things uses the comparative form, (*better*), not the superlative.

> FAULTY    Their chocolate and vanilla are both good, but I like the chocolate *best.*

**ESL GUIDELINES**

## Negatives

You can make a sentence negative by using either *not* or another negative adverb.

- With *not*: subject + helping verb + *not* + main verb

    Regina has *not* driven across the country before.

    Jerry did *not* go to the concert.

    They will *not* call again.

- For questions: helping verb + *n't* (contraction for *not*) + subject + main verb

    *Hasn't* Regina driven across the country before?

    *Didn't* Jerry go to the concert?

    *Won't* [for *Will not*] they call again?

Negative adverbs besides *not* include **seldom, rarely, never, hardly, hardly ever,** and **almost never.**

- With a negative adverb: subject + negative adverb + main verb; *or* subject + helping verb + negative adverb + main verb

    My son *seldom* watches TV.

    John may *never* see them again.

    Maxine is *rarely* in a bad mood.

- With a negative adverb at the beginning of a clause: negative adverb + helping verb + subject + verb

    *Not only* does Emma play tennis well, but she also excels in golf.

    *Never* before have I been so happy.

    *Seldom* have I experienced the satisfaction I felt when we finished the design project.

REVISED   Their chocolate and vanilla are both good, but I like the chocolate *better.*

FAULTY   Of his two dogs, he treats Bonzo *most affectionately.*

REVISED   Of his two dogs, he treats Bonzo *more affectionately.*

EXERCISE 10–1

## Using Adjectives and Adverbs Correctly

Find and correct any improperly used adjectives and adverbs in the following sentences. Some sentences may be correct. Answers for the lettered sentences appear in the back of the book. Example:

> Nobody on our team pitches as good as Jesse.
>
> Nobody on our team pitches as *well* as Jesse.

a. Which of your two brothers is the oldest?
b. I can't speak German as good as I'd like to.
c. Using adjectives correct is tricky, but using adverbs correct is trickiest.
d. Among spring's greatest joys are the birds that sing so sweet every morning.
e. Reiko talks a lot about Scott, but she spends all her time with Todd, so she must like Todd the most.

1. Hank's science project didn't work out as bad as he had feared.
2. They carved an ice sculpture more bigger than anyone had ever seen.
3. Food tastes well when you're awful hungry.
4. After Luke's dog bit a skunk, the house didn't smell very good.
5. Would Snow White and her prince have lived happier ever after with the Seven Dwarfs out of the picture?
6. It's more better to hope for victory than to expect defeat.
7. Which dwarf in the Disney film is funnier: Sleepy, Dopey, or Doc?
8. Lucy's most favorite Disney film is *Dumbo.*
9. Her father, Tim, says that the excitingest filmmaker today is not Martin Scorsese but Quentin Tarantino.
10. Tim considered *Duck Soup* better than *A Day at the Races,* and he liked the middle film in the *Star Wars* trilogy the least.

# 11. *Shifts*

When you look at a scene, you view it from a particular position in time and space. If you go to your favorite spot at the beach at dawn, at noon, at twilight, and at midnight, the scene will appear different each time. If you look at the scene standing on a sand dune, lying flat on the sand, or swimming in the surf, it will appear different from each location. Your perspective or point of view determines the details of the scene.

Similarly, when you perceive a subject in a sentence, you may consider it from various positions. If the time or the actor changes, your writing should reflect the change. However, writers sometimes shift point of view unconsciously or unnecessarily, causing ambiguity and confusion for readers. Such shifts are evident in grammatical inconsistencies.

## 11a. Maintain consistency in verb tense.

When you write a paragraph or an essay, keep the verbs in the same tense unless the time changes.

| INCONSISTENT | Football *is* a favorite spectator sport in my hometown. When the quarterback *threw* for a touchdown, everyone in the bleachers *stood* up and *cheered*. |
| CONSISTENT | Football *is* a favorite spectator sport in my hometown. When the quarterback *throws* for a touchdown, everyone in the bleachers *stands* up and *cheers*. [All verbs are present tense.] |
| INCONSISTENT | The driver *yelled* at us to get off the bus, so I *ask* him why and he *tells* me it *is* none of my business. |
| CONSISTENT | The driver *yells* at us to get off the bus, so I *ask* him why and he *tells* me it *is* none of my business. [All verbs are present tense.] |
| CONSISTENT | The driver *yelled* at us to get off the bus, so I *asked* him why and he *told* me it *was* none of my business. [All verbs are past tense.] |

## 11b. If the time changes, change the verb tense.

*Tense* indicates time. Shifts in tense should indicate an actual change in time. If you are writing about something that occurred in the past, use past tense verbs. If you are writing about something that occurs in the present, use present tense verbs. If the time shifts, change the verb tense.

> I *do* not *like* the new television programs this year. The situation comedies *are* too realistic to be amusing, the adventure shows *don't have* much action, and the courtroom dramas *drag* on and on. Last year the television programs *were* different. The sitcoms *were* hilarious, the adventure shows *were* action-packed, and the courtroom dramas *were* fast-paced. I *prefer* reruns of last year's programs to new episodes of this year's choices.

The time and the verb tense change appropriately from present (*do like, are, do have, drag*) to past (*were, were, were, were*) back to present (*prefer*), indicating contrast between this year's *present* programming and last year's *past* programming and ending with *present* opinion.

NOTE: When writing papers about literature, the accepted practice is to use present tense verbs to summarize what happens in a story, poem, or play. When discussing other aspects of a work, use present tense for present time, past tense for past, and future tense for future.

> John Steinbeck *wrote* "The Chrysanthemums" in 1937. [Past tense for past time.]

In "The Chrysanthemums," John Steinbeck *describes* the Salinas Valley as "a closed pot" cut off from the world by fog.

## 11c. Maintain consistency in the voice of verbs.

In most writing, active voice is preferable to passive voice (see 5m). Shifting unnecessarily from active to passive voice causes confusion for readers.

INCONSISTENT   My roommates and I *sit* up late many nights talking about our problems. Grades, teachers, jobs, money, and dates *are discussed* at length.

CONSISTENT   My roommates and I *sit* up late many nights talking about our problems. We *discuss* grades, teachers, jobs, money, and dates at length.

## 11d. Maintain consistency in person.

Person indicates the perspective from which an essay is written. First person (*I, we*) establishes a personal, informal relationship with readers. Second person (*you*) is also informal and personal, bringing the readers into the writing. Third person (*he, she, it, they*) is more formal and objective than the other two persons. (See 7.) In a formal scientific report, first person and second person are seldom appropriate. In a personal essay, using *he, she,* or *one* to refer to yourself sounds stilted. Choose the person appropriate for your purpose and stick to it.

INCONSISTENT   In *my* composition class is a divorced woman returning to school after fifteen years of raising her children. Watching her, *you* can tell she is uncertain about her decision to enter college.

CONSISTENT   In *my* composition class is a divorced woman returning to school after fifteen years of raising her children. Watching her, *I* can tell she is uncertain about her decision to enter college.

INCONSISTENT   Today college *students* need transportation, but *you* need a job to pay for the insurance and the gasoline.

CONSISTENT   Today college *students* need transportation, but *they* need jobs to pay for the insurance and the gasoline.

INCONSISTENT   *Anyone* can go skydiving if *you* have the guts.

CONSISTENT   *Anyone* can go skydiving if *he or she* has the guts.

## 11e. Maintain consistency in the mood of verbs.

Closely related to shift in person is shift in the mood of the verb, usually from the indicative to the imperative. (See 5n–5p.)

INCONSISTENT   Counselors *advised* the students to register early to choose the best professors. Also *pay* tuition on time to avoid being dropped from classes. [Shift from indicative to imperative.]

| CONSISTENT | Counselors *advised* the students to register early to choose the best professors. They also *advised* them to pay their tuition on time to avoid being dropped from classes. [Both verbs in indicative.] |
|---|---|

## 11f.  Maintain consistency in level of language.

Attempting to impress readers, writers sometimes inappropriately use inflated language or slip into slang or a too informal tone. The level of language should be appropriate to your purpose and your audience throughout an essay.

If you are writing a personal essay, use informal language.

| INCONSISTENT | I felt like a typical tourist. I carried an expensive camera with lots of gadgets I didn't quite know how to operate, and I had brought as much film as I could carry. But I was in a quandary because there was such a plethora of picturesque tableaus to record for posterity. |
|---|---|

The sudden shift to formal language is inappropriate. The writer could end the passage simply: *But there was so much beautiful scenery all around that I just couldn't decide where to start.*

If you are writing an academic essay, use formal language.

| INCONSISTENT | Puccini's final work *Turandot* is set in a China of legends, riddles, and fantasy. Brimming with beautiful melodies masterfully orchestrated — including the famed tenor aria "Nessum dorma" — this opera is music drama at its most spectacular. Man, I dig this gig! |
|---|---|

The shift from formal language to slang is unnecessary. The last sentence can be cut without weakening the rest of the paragraph.

---

**EXERCISE 11–1**

## Maintaining Grammatical Consistency

Revise the following sentences to eliminate shifts in verb tense, voice, mood, person, and level of language. Possible revisions for the lettered sentences appear in the back of the book. Example:

> I needed the job at the restaurant, so I tried to tolerate the insults of my boss, but a person can take only so much.

> I needed the job at the restaurant, so I tried to tolerate the insults of my boss, but I could take only so much.

a. Sometimes late at night, I hear stereos booming from passing cars. The vibrations are so great you can feel your house shake.
b. Dr. Jamison is an erudite professor who cracks jokes in class.
c. The audience listened intently to the lecture, but the message was not understood.

d. It was in the Near East that people first began to grow crops and city-states were established.
e. Most of the people in my psychology class are very interesting, and you can get into some exciting discussions with them.

1. Scientists can no longer evade the social, political, and ethical consequences of what they did in the laboratory.
2. To have good government, citizens must become informed on the issues. Also, be sure to vote.
3. Good writing is essential to success in many professions, especially in business, where ideas must be communicated in down-to-earth lingo.
4. Our legal system made it extremely difficult to prove a bribe. If the charges are not proven to the satisfaction of a jury or a judge, then we jump to the conclusion that the absence of a conviction demonstrates the innocence of the subject.
5. Before Morris K. Udall, Democrat from Arizona, resigns his seat in the U.S. House of Representatives, he helped preserve hundreds of acres of wilderness.
6. When Washington, D.C., was redesigned in the early twentieth century, many critics objected that the Mall would separate the government center from the residential city, and time has proved them dead right.
7. Anyone can learn another language if you have the time and the patience.
8. The immigration officer asked how long we planned to stay, so I show him my letter of acceptance from Tulane.
9. Many people do not like the accelerating pace of modern life. In the last century, people have time to relax with their friends and families instead of rushing back and forth to work.
10. Archaeologists spent many months studying the site of the African city of Zimbabwe and many artifacts were uncovered.

# 12. *Sentence Fragments*

A ***complete sentence*** is one that has both a subject and a predicate and can stand alone. (See 2a, 2b.) A ***fragment*** lacks a subject or a predicate or both or for some other reason fails to express a complete thought. We all use fragments in everyday speech, where their context and the way they are said make them understandable and therefore acceptable.

That bicycle over there.

Good job.

Not if I can help it.

In writing, fragments like these fail to communicate complete, coherent ideas. Notice how much more effective they are when we turn them into complete sentences.

I'd like to buy that bicycle over there.

You did a good job sanding the floor.

Nobody will steal my seat if I can help it.

Some writers purposefully use fragments. For example, advertisers are fond of them because short, emphatic fragments command attention, like a series of quick jabs to the head.

Seafood special. Every Tuesday night. All you can eat. Specially priced at $6.95. For seafood lovers.

Professional writers use fragments, too, especially in journals, descriptions, and fiction — often to good effect, as in this passage from the beginning of Vladimir Nabokov's novel *Lolita*:

Lolita, light of my life, fire of my loins. My sin, my soul. Lo-lee-ta: the tip of the tongue taking a trip of three steps down the palate to tap, at three, on the teeth. Lo. Lee. Ta.

In your college writing, though, it is good practice to express your ideas in complete sentences. Writing a paper or a report is a more formal, less experimental activity than writing fiction. Besides, complete sentences usually convey more information than fragments — a big advantage in expository writing. Sprinkling fragments through your work, unless you do so with great skill and style, tends to make readers wonder if you can tell a piece of thought from a whole thought completely thought through.

If you sometimes write fragments without recognizing them, learn to edit your work. Luckily, fragments are fairly easy to correct. Often you can attach a fragment to a neighboring sentence with a comma, a dash, or a colon. Sometimes you can combine two thoughts without adding any punctuation at all.

**EDITING CHECKLIST**

### Recognizing Sentence Fragments

- Does the sentence have a subject? (See 2a.)
- Does the sentence have a complete verb? (See 2b.)
- If the sentence contains a subordinate clause, does it contain a complete main clause too? (See 3e–3g.)

**12a.**   If a fragment is a phrase, link it to an adjoining sentence or make it a complete sentence.

A freestanding phrase is a fragment because it lacks a subject or a verb or both. You have two choices for revising a fragment if it is a phrase: (1) link it to an adjoining sentence using punctuation such as a comma or a colon or (2) add a subject or a verb to the phrase to make it a complete sentence.

FRAGMENT   Malcolm has two goals in life. *Wealth and power.*

FRAGMENT   Schmidt ended his stories as he mixed his martinis. *With a twist.*

FRAGMENT    *To stamp out the union.* That was the bosses' plan.

FRAGMENT    The students taking the final exam in the auditorium.

*Wealth and power* is a phrase rather than a sentence because it has no verb. *With a twist* has neither a subject nor a verb. *To stamp out the union* has a verbal, which cannot be used as the main verb of a sentence, and it has no subject. *Taking* is not a complete verb: it is a participle and requires a helping verb to make it complete. You can make each of these phrases express a complete thought by linking it with a neighboring sentence or by adding the missing element. In each case there are several ways to complete the thought. Here is one set of possibilities:

REVISED    Malcolm has two goals in life: wealth and power. [A colon links *wealth and power* to *goals*.]

REVISED    Schmidt ended his stories as he mixed his martinis, with a twist. [The prepositional phrase *with a twist* is connected to the main clause with a comma.]

REVISED    To stamp out the union was the bosses' plan. [The infinitive phrase *To stamp out the union* becomes the subject of the sentence.]

REVISED    The students were taking the final exam in the auditorium. [The helping verb *were* completes the verb and thus makes a sentence.]

REVISED    The students taking the final exam in the auditorium were interrupted by the fire alarm. [The predicate *were interrupted by the fire alarm* completes the sentence.]

EDITING
CHECKLIST

## Correcting Sentence Fragments

- Is the fragment a phrase? If so, link it to an adjoining sentence. (12a)
- Is the fragment a clause? If so, link it to an adjoining sentence or eliminate its subordinating conjunction. (12b)
- Does the fragment use *being* or another participle as its verb? If so, either change the participle to a main verb or link the fragment to an adjoining sentence. (12c)
- Is the fragment part of a compound predicate? If so, link it to the other part of the predicate. (12d)

**12b.**    If a fragment is a subordinate clause, link it to an adjoining sentence or eliminate the subordinating conjunction.

Some fragments are missing neither subject nor verb. Instead, they are subordinate clauses, unable to express complete thoughts unless linked with main clauses. (See 3e–3g, 4c.) As you examine your writing for sentence fragments, be on the lookout for *subordinating conjunctions*. (Some of the most common subordinating conjunctions are *although, because, if, since, unless, until*, and *while*; for a complete list, see 1g.) When you find a subordinating conjunction at the start or in the middle of a word group that looks like a sentence, that word group may be a subordinate clause and not a sentence at all.

FRAGMENT   The new law will stem the tide of inflation. *If it passes.*

FRAGMENT   Wealth doesn't guarantee happiness. *Whereas poverty does guarantee unhappiness.*

FRAGMENT   George loves winter in the mountains. *Because he is an avid skier.*

If you find that you have treated a subordinate clause as if it were a complete sentence, you can correct the problem in one of two ways: (1) you can combine the fragment with a main clause nearby or (2) you can make the subordinate clause into a complete sentence by dropping the subordinating conjunction.

REVISED   The new law will stem the tide of inflation, if it passes.

REVISED   Wealth doesn't guarantee happiness, whereas poverty does guarantee unhappiness.

REVISED   George loves winter in the mountains. He is an avid skier.

A sentence is not necessarily a fragment just because it opens with a subordinating conjunction. Some perfectly legitimate complex or compound-complex sentences have their conjunctions up front instead of in the middle. (See 4c, 4d.)

*If* you leave early, say good-bye.

*Because* of rain, the game was canceled.

**12c.** If a fragment has a participle but no other verb, change the participle to a main verb or link the fragment to an adjoining sentence.

A participle (the *-ing* form of the verb, such as *being, writing, looking*) can serve as the main verb in a sentence only when it is accompanied by a form of *be* ("Jeffrey *is working* harder than usual"). When a writer mistakenly uses a participle alone as a main verb, the result is a fragment.

FRAGMENT   *Sally being the first athlete on the team to compete in a national contest.* She received many congratulatory telegrams.

FRAGMENT   Jon was used to the pressure of deadlines. *Having worked the night shift at the daily newspaper.*

One solution is to combine the fragment with an adjoining sentence.

REVISED   Being the first athlete on the team to compete in a national contest, Sally received many congratulatory telegrams.

REVISED   Jon was used to the pressure of deadlines, having worked the night shift at the daily newspaper.

Another solution is to turn the fragment into a complete sentence by choosing a form of the verb other than the participle.

REVISED    Sally *was* the first athlete on the team to compete in a national contest. She received many congratulatory telegrams.

REVISED    Jon was used to the pressure of deadlines. He *had worked* the night shift at the daily newspaper.

**12d.** If a fragment is part of a compound predicate, link it with the complete sentence containing the rest of the predicate.

FRAGMENT    In spite of a pulled muscle, Jeremy ran the race. *And won.*

A fragment such as *And won* sounds satisfyingly punchy. Still, it cannot stand on its own. *Ran . . . and won* is a compound predicate — two verbs with the same subject. You can create a complete sentence by linking the verbs.

REVISED    In spite of a pulled muscle, Jeremy *ran* the race *and won.*

If you want to keep more emphasis on the second verb, you can turn the fragment into a full clause by adding punctuation and another subject.

REVISED    In spite of a pulled muscle, Jeremy ran the race — and *he* won.

(For a review of the rules about punctuating linked phrases and clauses, see 18a.)

EXERCISE 12–1

## Eliminating Fragments

Find and eliminate any fragments in the following examples. Some sentences may be correct. Possible revisions for the lettered sentences appear in the back of the book. Example:

Bryan hates parsnips. And loathes squash.

Bryan hates parsnips and loathes squash.

a. Polly and Jim plan to see the new Woody Allen movie. Which was reviewed in last Sunday's *New York Times.*
b. For democracy to function at all, two elements are crucial. An educated populace and a firm collective belief in people's ability to chart their own course.
c. Scholastic achievement is important to Alex. Being the first person in his family ever to attend college.
d. Does our society rob children of their childhood? By making them aware too soon of adult ills?
e. No one would ever forget that night. The half-empty lifeboats. The useless flares. The band playing hymns as the ship slid under.

1. If the German people had known Hitler's real plans. Would they have made him führer?
2. Lisa advocated sleeping no more than four hours a night. Until she started nodding through her classes.
3. You must take his stories as others do. With a pinch of salt.

4. Jack seemed well qualified for a career in the air force. Except for his tendency to get airsick.
5. Illness often accompanies stress. Catching a cold after the death of a loved one, for example.
6. None of the board members objected to Butch's proposal at the time. Only afterward, when they realized its implications.
7. Michael had a beautiful southern accent. Having lived many years in Georgia.
8. Richard III supposedly had the young princes murdered. No one has ever found out what really happened to them.
9. They met. They talked. They fought. They reached agreement.
10. Pat and Chris are determined to marry each other. Even if their families do not approve.

**EXERCISE 12–2**

## Eliminating Fragments

Rewrite the following paragraph, eliminating all fragments. Explain why you made each change. Example:

Little league baseball damaged my self-esteem. And turned me off to organized sports forever.

Little league baseball damaged my self-esteem, and turned me off to organized sports forever.

When I was about eleven years old. I played on a Little League baseball team. Played, that is, when I wasn't sitting on the bench. Which was most of the time. I got into the lineup only because the rules said every kid had to get a chance at bat. A rule my coach didn't like. Because he wanted our team to win every game. I rarely got to play in the field. Only when a shortage of players made my presence there necessary. Then always right field. Unless there were a lot of lefties coming up to bat on the opposing team. Believe me when I say that for me Little League baseball was no fun.

# 13. *Comma Splices and Fused Sentences*

Splice two ropes, or two strips of movie film, and you join them into one. Splice two main clauses by putting only a comma between them, however, and you get an ungainly construction called a *comma splice.* (See p. H-31 on main clauses.) Here, for instance, are two perfectly good main clauses, each separate, each able to stand on its own as a sentence:

The detective wriggled on his belly toward the campfire. The drunken smugglers didn't notice him.

Now let's splice those sentences with a comma.

COMMA SPLICE   The detective wriggled on his belly toward the campfire, the drunken smugglers didn't notice him.

The resulting comma splice makes for difficult reading.

Even more confusing than a comma splice is a *fused* (or *run- on*) *sentence:* two main clauses joined without any punctuation.

> FUSED SENTENCE   The detective wriggled on his belly toward the campfire the drunken smugglers didn't notice him.

Lacking clues from the writer, a reader cannot tell where to pause. To understand the sentence, he or she must halt and reread.

Even writers who know better can fall at times into fusing and comma splicing. Temptation may overwhelm them when, having written one sentence, they want to add some further thought. Either they simply jam the two thoughts together or they push in a comma, like a thumbtack, to stick on the second thought.

Here are five simple ways to eliminate both comma splices and fused sentences. Your choice depends on the length and complexity of your main clauses and the effect you want to achieve.

EDITING
CHECKLIST

### Revising Comma Splices and Fused Sentences
- Can you make each main clause a separate sentence? (13a)
- Can you link the two main clauses with a comma or a coordinating conjunction? (13b; 1g)
- Can you link the two main clauses with a semicolon or, if appropriate, a colon? (13c)
- Can you subordinate one clause to the other? (13d)
- Can you link the two main clauses with a semicolon, a conjunctive adverb, or a comma? (13e)

**13a.**   Write separate complete sentences to correct a comma splice or a fused sentence.

> COMMA SPLICE    Sigmund Freud has been called an enemy of sexual repression, the truth is that he is not a friend of free love.

> FUSED SENTENCE    Sigmund Freud has been called an enemy of sexual repression the truth is that he is not a friend of free love.

Neither sentence yields its meaning without a struggle. To point readers in the right direction, separate the clauses.

> REVISED   Sigmund Freud has been called an enemy of sexual repression. The truth is that he is not a friend of free love.

**13b.**   Use a comma and a coordinating conjunction to correct a comma splice or a fused sentence.

Is it always incorrect to join two main clauses with a comma? No. If both clauses are of roughly equal weight, you can use a comma to link them — as long as you add a coordinating conjunction (*and, but, for, nor, or, so, yet*) after the comma.

COMMA SPLICE    Hurricane winds hit ninety miles an hour, they tore the roof from every house on Paradise Drive.

REVISED    Hurricane winds hit ninety miles an hour, *and* they tore the roof from every house on Paradise Drive.

## 13c. Use a semicolon or a colon to correct a comma splice or a fused sentence.

A semicolon can keep two thoughts connected while giving full emphasis to each one.

COMMA SPLICE    Hurricane winds hit ninety miles an hour, they tore the roof from every house on Paradise Drive.

REVISED    Hurricane winds hit ninety miles an hour; they tore the roof from every house on Paradise Drive.

If the second thought clearly illustrates or explains the first, add it on with a colon.

REVISED    The hurricane caused extensive damage: it tore the roof from every house on Paradise Drive.

Remember that the only punctuation powerful enough to link two main clauses single-handedly is a semicolon, a colon, or a period. A lone comma won't do the job.

## 13d. Use subordination to correct a comma splice or a fused sentence.

If one main clause is more important than the other, or if you want to give it more importance, you can subordinate the less important clause to it. Using subordination helps your reader more than simply dividing a fused sentence or comma splice into two sentences does. When you make one clause subordinate, you throw weight on the main clause. In effect, you show your reader how one idea relates to another — you decide which matters more.

FUSED SENTENCE    Hurricane winds hit ninety miles an hour they tore the roof from every house on Paradise Drive.

REVISED    *When hurricane winds hit ninety miles an hour,* they tore the roof from every house on Paradise Drive.

REVISED    Hurricane winds hit ninety miles an hour, *tearing the roof from every house on Paradise Drive.*

For a rundown of different ways to use subordination, see 3e–3g and 18d–18f.

## 13e. Use a conjunctive adverb with a semicolon and a comma to correct a comma splice or a fused sentence.

A writer who is sharp enough to beware of fused sentences and comma splices but who still wants to cram more than one clause into a sentence may join two clauses with a *conjunctive adverb*. Some common conjunctive adverbs are *also, besides, consequently, even so, finally, furthermore, however, indeed, moreover, nevertheless,* and *therefore.* (See 1g.) These transitional words and phrases can be a useful way of linking clauses — but only if used with the right punctuation.

> COMMA SPLICE   Sigmund Freud has been called an enemy of sexual repression, however the truth is that he is not a friend of free love.

The writer might consider a comma plus the conjunctive adverb *however* glue enough to combine the two main clauses; but that cheap fish glue won't hold. Stronger binding is called for.

> REVISED   Sigmund Freud has been called an enemy of sexual repression; however, the truth is that he is not a friend of free love.

A writer who fuses and comma splices sentences is like a man trying to join two boards. If he comma splices, he tries to put them together with only one nail; if he fuses, he puts them together with no nail at all. But most thoughts, to hang together, need plenty of hammering.

EXCEPTION: Certain very short, similar main clauses can be joined with a comma. Only if you now feel sure that you can tell a comma splice or a fused sentence when you see one, read on: here comes a fine point. We hate to admit it, lest it complicate life, but once in a great while you'll see a competent writer joining main clauses with nothing but a comma between them.

> Jill runs by day, Tom walks by night.

> I came, I saw, I conquered.

Commas are not obligatory with short, similar clauses. If you find this issue confusing, you can stick with semicolons to join all main clauses, short or long.

> Jill runs by day; Tom walks by night.

> I came; I saw; I conquered.

EXERCISE 13–1

## Revising Comma Splices and Fused Sentences

In the following examples, correct each comma splice or fused sentence in two ways and decide which way you believe works best. Be creative — don't correct every one in the same way. Some sentences may be correct as written. Possible revisions for the lettered sentences appear in the back of the book. Example:

> The castle looked eerie from a distance, it filled us with nameless fear as we approached.

1. The castle looked eerie from a distance; it filled us with nameless fear as we approached.
2. The castle, which looked eerie from a distance, filled us with nameless fear as we approached.

a. Everyone had heard alarming rumors in the village about strange goings-on, we hesitated to believe them.

b. Bats flew about our ears as the carriage pulled up under a stone archway an assistant stood waiting to lead us to our host.

c. We followed the scientist down a flight of wet stone steps at last he stopped before a huge oak door.

d. From a jangling keyring Dr. Frankenstein selected a heavy key, he twisted it in the lock.

e. The huge door gave a groan it swung open on a dimly lighted laboratory.

1. Our guide turned, with a lopsided smile, silently he motioned us into the room.

2. Before us on a dissecting table lay a form with closed eyes to behold it sent a quick chill down my spine.

3. With glittering eyes the scientist strode to the table, he lifted a white-gloved hand.

4. The form lying before us seemed an obscenely large baby in disbelief I had to rub my eyes.

5. It resembled no human child instead it seemed constructed of rubber or clay.

6. With a hoarse cry Frankenstein flung a power switch, blue streamers of static electricity crackled about the table, the creature gave a grunt and opened smoldering eyes.

7. "I've won!" exclaimed the scientist in triumph he circled the room doing a demented Irish reel.

8. The creature's right hand strained, the heavy steel manacle imprisoning his wrist groaned in torment.

9. Like a staple wrenched from a document, the manacle yielded.

10. The creature sat upright and tugged at the shackles binding his ankles, Frankenstein uttered a piercing scream.

**EXERCISE 13–2**

## Revising Comma Splices and Fused Sentences

Revise the following passage, using subordination, a conjunctive adverb, a semicolon, or a colon to correct each comma splice or fused sentence. You may also write separate complete sentences. Some sentences may be correct. Example:

Ancient Rome is an ambiguous political symbol, it has come to represent freedom and slavery, dictatorship and democracy, law and cruelty.

Ancient Rome is an ambiguous political symbol: it has come to represent freedom and slavery, dictatorship and democracy, law and cruelty.

The classical world of Greece and Rome is the foundation of Western art and thought, it has also provided the modern world with much of its political imagery. In the eighteenth century, French revolutionaries believed they were restoring the democracies of ancient Athens and of republican Rome, they modeled themselves on those ancient Roman heroes who had resisted the authority of kings. In the United States, Jefferson and the founding fathers established a new system of government that revived the terminology and symbols of ancient Rome, the United States was to be represented by a Roman eagle, and a *Senate* was to meet in a *Capitol*, a word derived from the early meeting place of the ancient Roman Senate on the Capitoline hill. Both the American and the French revolutionaries saw the Roman republic as the model for their new democratic states, however, in the early nineteenth century, a dictator like Napoleon was more interested in the imperial phase of Roman power. Napoleon advertised himself as the new Caesar, he believed he was destined to restore Roman peace and unity to Europe. Although Napoleon failed in his bid to revive the Roman empire, the myth of a powerful centralized state endured, it influenced the political imagery and ideology of the totalitarian governments of the twentieth century. The use of Roman political symbols by governments from all shades of the ideological spectrum is significant in itself, it indicates the powerful grip that Rome still exerts on the Western imagination.

**EXERCISE 13–3**

## Revising Comma Splices and Fused Sentences

Write six fused sentences and comma splices. Then trade papers with a classmate and revise each other's deliberate errors. You may want to revise each sentence in several ways and then confer with your partner to decide which revision works best.

## Chapter 34

# Effective Sentences

## 14. *Misplaced and Dangling Modifiers*

The purpose of a modifier is to give readers additional information. To do so, the modifier must be linked clearly to whatever it is meant to modify. If you wrote, "We saw a stone wall around a house on a grassy hill, beautiful and distant," your readers would be hard put to figure out whether *beautiful* and *distant* modify *wall, house,* or *hill.* When you finish writing, double-check your modifiers — especially prepositional phrases and subordinate clauses — to make sure each one is in the right place.

### 14a.   Keep modifiers close to what they modify.

*Misplaced modifiers* — phrases and clauses that wander away from what they modify — produce results that are more likely to amuse your readers than inform them. To avoid confusion, place your modifiers as close as possible to whatever they modify.

MISPLACED  She offered handcrafted toys to all the orphans in colorful packages. [Does the phrase *in colorful packages* modify *toys* or *orphans?*]

CLEAR  She offered handcrafted toys in colorful packages to all the orphans.

MISPLACED  Today's assignment is to remove the dishes from the crates that got chipped. [Does the clause *that got chipped* modify *dishes* or *crates?*]

CLEAR      Today's assignment is to remove from the crates the dishes that got chipped.

Sometimes when you move a misplaced modifier to a better place, an additional change or two will help you to clarify the sentence.

MISPLACED   Jim offered cream and sugar to his guests in their coffee.

CLEAR      Jim offered his guests cream and sugar in their coffee. [When *guests* is made an indirect object, *to* is cut.]

## 14b. Place each modifier so that it clearly modifies only one thing.

A *squinting modifier* is one that looks two ways, leaving the reader uncertain whether it modifies the word before it or the word after it. Don't let your modifiers squint. Make sure each modifies only one element in a sentence. A good tactic is to place your modifier close to the word or phrase it modifies and away from any others that might cause confusion.

SQUINTING   The best-seller that appealed to Mary *tremendously* bored Max.

CLEAR      The best-seller that *tremendously* appealed to Mary bored Max.

CLEAR      The best-seller that appealed to Mary bored Max *tremendously*.

**EXERCISE 14-1**

## Placing Modifiers

Revise the following sentences, which contain modifiers that are misplaced or squinting. Possible revisions for the lettered sentences appear in the back of the book. Example:

Miranda placed the book on the table that was overdue at the library.

Miranda placed on the table the book that was overdue at the library.

a. The team that lost miserably remained silent on the trip home.
b. Complete the writing assignment in the textbook that follows Chapter 2.
c. Those who make mistakes frequently learn valuable lessons.
d. The managers presented bouquets of roses to every employee with long stems.
e. A person who snacks often gets fat.

1. Leo hid the stolen diamonds as soon as he heard the police siren under the driver's seat.
2. How can Jeannie keep that house looking so elegant at such an advanced age?
3. The United Nations voted to extend aid to the victims of the earthquake in Kobe, Japan, which they can ill afford.

4. Don't ask one of the boys to carry the groceries out to the car when there are so few.

5. Dorothy hobbled over to observe the snake with a limp.

## 14c. Have something in the sentence for each modifier to modify.

Generally we assume that a modifying phrase that appears at the start of a sentence will modify the subject of the main clause to follow. If we encounter a modifying phrase midway through a sentence, we assume that it modifies something just before or (less often) after it.

*Feeling sick to his stomach, Jason* went to bed.

*An early bird by nature, Felix* began at eight o'clock.

*Alice, while sympathetic,* was not inclined to help.

Occasionally a writer will slip up by allowing a modifying phrase to dangle. A ***dangling modifier*** is one that, on close inspection, is found to be shirking its job: it doesn't modify anything in its sentence.

DANGLING   *Noticing a slight pain behind his eyes,* an aspirin seemed like a good idea. [The introductory phrase cannot be said to modify *aspirin.* In fact, it doesn't modify anything.]

DANGLING   *To do a good job,* the right tools were needed.

To correct a dangling modifier, recast the sentence. First, figure out what noun, pronoun, or noun phrase the modifier is meant to modify and then make that word or phrase the subject of the main clause.

CLEAR   *Noticing a slight pain behind his eyes, he* decided to take an aspirin.

CLEAR   *To do a good job, the plumber* needed the right tools.

**EDITING CHECKLIST**

## Correcting Dangling Modifiers

• What noun, pronoun, or noun phrase is the dangling modifier meant to modify? Make that word or phrase the subject of the main clause.
• Can you turn the dangling modifier into a clause that includes the missing noun or pronoun?

Another way to correct a dangling modifier is to turn the dangler into a clause that includes the missing noun or pronoun.

DANGLING   Her progress, *although talented,* has been slowed by poor work habits.

CLEAR   *Although she is talented,* her progress has been slowed by poor work habits.

Sometimes a bit of rewriting will clarify what the modifier modifies and improve the sentence as well.

CLEAR   *Although talented, she* has been handicapped by poor work habits.

EXERCISE 14–2   ### Revising Dangling Modifiers

Revise any sentences that contain dangling modifiers. Some sentences may be correct. Possible revisions for the lettered sentences appear in the back of the book. Example:

> Angry at her poor showing, geology would never be Joan's favorite class.
>
> Angry at her poor showing, Joan knew that geology would never be her favorite class.

a. After working for six hours, the job was done.
b. Unable to fall asleep, a warm bath relaxes you.
c. To compete in the Olympics, talent, training, and dedication are needed.
d. It's common, feeling lonely, to want to talk to someone.
e. Having worried all morning, relief flooded over him when his missing son returned.

1. Once gripped by the urge to sail, it never leaves you.
2. Further information can be obtained by calling the specified number.
3. Passing the service station, the bank will appear on your right.
4. Having created strict ethical standards, there should be some willingness on Congress's part to live up to them.
5. Recalling Ben Franklin's advice, "hanging together" became the club members' new policy.
6. Short-tempered and irritable, his paintings reveal a passionate love of humanity.
7. To get the job, his portfolio had to be meticulously assembled.
8. Pressing hard on the brakes, the car spun into a hedge.
9. Showing a lack of design experience, the architect advised the student to take her model back to the drawing board.
10. When deep in concentration, interruptions are unwelcome.

# 15. *Incomplete Sentences*

A fragment fails to qualify as a sentence because it lacks a subject or a predicate or both (see 12). However, a sentence can contain these two essentials and still miss the mark. If it lacks some other key element — a crucial word or phrase — the sentence is *incomplete*. Often the problem is carelessness: the writer sets down too few words to cover a whole idea. The resulting incomplete sentence is likely to lose readers. Like a bridge open to the public, it invites us to cross; but it has unexpected gaps that we topple through.

Incomplete sentences catch writers most often in two writing situations: comparisons and the abbreviated type of parallel structure called elliptical constructions.

## COMPARISONS

**15a.** Make your comparisons clear by stating fully what you are comparing with what.

> INCOMPLETE   Roscoe loves spending time with a computer more than Diane.

What is the writer of this sentence trying to tell us? Does Roscoe prefer the company of a keyboard to the company of his friend? Or, of these two people, is Roscoe (and not Diane) the computer addict? We can't be sure, because the writer has not completed the comparison. Adding a word would solve the problem.

> REVISED   Roscoe loves spending time with a computer more than Diane *does*.

> REVISED   Roscoe loves spending time with a computer more than *with* Diane.

In editing what you write, double-check your comparisons to be sure they are complete.

> INCOMPLETE   Miami has more newcomers from Havana than New York.
>
> REVISED   Miami has more newcomers from Havana than New York *has*.
>
> REVISED   Miami has more newcomers from Havana than *from* New York.

**15b.** When you start to draw a comparison, finish it.

The unfinished comparison is a favorite trick of advertisers — "Our product is better!" — because it dodges the question "Better than what?" A sharp writer (or shopper) knows that any item being compared must be compared *with* something else.

> INCOMPLETE   Scottish tweeds are warmer.
>
> REVISED   Scottish tweeds are warmer *than any other fabric you can buy*.

**15c.** Be sure the things you compare are of the same kind.

The saying "You can't compare apples and oranges" makes a useful grammatical point. A sentence that draws a comparison should assure its readers that the items involved are similar enough for comparison to be appropriate. When you compare two things, be sure the terms of the comparison are clear and logical.

> INCOMPLETE   The engine of a Ford truck is heavier than a Piper Cub airplane.

What is being compared? Truck and airplane? Or engine and engine? If we consider, we can guess: since a truck engine is unlikely to outweigh an airplane, the writer must mean to compare engines. Readers, however, should not have to make the effort to complete a writer's incomplete thought.

> REVISED  The engine of a Ford truck is heavier than *that of* a Piper Cub airplane.

> REVISED  A Ford truck's engine is heavier than a *Piper Cub's.*

In this last example, parallel structure (*Ford truck's* and *Piper Cub's*) helps to make the comparison concise as well as clear. (See 17a and 17c for more on parallel structure.)

## 15d. To compare an item with others of its kind, use *any other.*

A comparison using *any* shows how something relates to a group without belonging to the group.

> Alaska is larger than *any* country in Central America.

> Bluefish has as much protein as *any* meat.

A comparison using *any other* shows how one member of a group relates to other members of the same group.

> Death Valley is drier than *any other* place in the United States.

> Bluefish has as distinctive a flavor as *any other* fish.

**EXERCISE 15–1**

## Completing Comparisons

Revise the following sentences by adding needed words to any comparisons that are incomplete. (There may be more than one way to complete some comparisons.) Some sentences may be correct. Possible revisions for the lettered sentences appear in the back of the book. Example:

> I hate hot weather more than you.

> I hate hot weather more than you *do.*

> I hate hot weather more than I *hate* you.

a. She plays the *Moonlight Sonata* more brilliantly than any pianist her age.
b. Driving a sports car means more to Jake than his professors.
c. People who go to college aren't necessarily smarter, but they will always have an advantage at job interviews.
d. I don't have as much trouble getting along with Michelle as Karin.
e. Annapolis, Maryland, has more colonial brick houses than any city in the United States.

1. The crime rate in the United States is higher than Canada.

2. A more sensible system of running the schools would be to appoint a school board.
3. A hen lays fewer eggs than any turtle.
4. The town meeting form of government doesn't function as efficiently as a mayor.
5. Sex is closer to prayer than a meal of Chicken McNuggets.

## ELLIPTICAL CONSTRUCTIONS

A well-known poem by Robert Frost begins:

> Some say the world will end in fire, some say in ice.

When Frost wrote that sentence, he avoided needless repetition by implying certain words rather than stating them. The result is more concise and more effective than a complete version of the same sentence would be:

> Some say the world will end in fire, some say the world will end in ice.

This common writer's tactic — leaving out (for the sake of concision) an unnecessary word — produces an *elliptical construction.* Readers can easily fill in the words that, although not written, are clearly understood. Elliptical constructions can create confusion, however, if the writer gives readers too little information to fill in those missing words accurately.

**15e.** When you eliminate repetition, keep all words that are essential for clarity.

An elliptical construction saves repeating what a reader already knows. But whenever you use this strategy, make sure to omit only words that are stated elsewhere in the sentence. Otherwise, your reader may fill the gap incorrectly.

> INCOMPLETE   How can I date her, seeing that she is a senior, I a mere freshman?

This elliptical construction won't work. A reader supplying the missing verb in the last part of the sentence would get "I *is* a mere freshman." Although the writer means *am,* *is* is the verb already stated.

> REVISED   How can I date her, seeing that she is a senior and I *am* a mere freshman?

Leaving out a necessary preposition also can produce a faulty elliptical construction.

> INCOMPLETE   The train neither goes nor returns from Middletown.

Without a *to* after *goes,* readers are likely to fill in an extra *from* to complete the verb's action. Write instead:

> REVISED   The train neither goes *to* nor returns from Middletown.

**15f.**  In a compound predicate, leave out only verb forms that have already been stated.

Compound predicates are especially prone to incomplete elliptical constructions. Writing in haste, we accidentally omit part of a verb that is needed for the sentence to make sense. When you write a sentence with a compound predicate, check your verbs most carefully if they are in different tenses. Be sure that no necessary part is missing.

INCOMPLETE  The committee never has and never will vote to raise taxes.

REVISED  The committee never has *voted* and never will vote to raise taxes.

**15g.**  If you mix comparisons using *as* and *than,* include both words.

To contrast two things that are different, we normally use the comparative form of an adjective followed by *than: better than, more than, fewer than.* To show a similarity between two things that are alike, we normally use the simple form of an adjective sandwiched between *as* and *as: as good as, as many as, as few as.* Often we can combine two *than* comparisons or two *as* comparisons into an elliptical construction.

The White House is smaller [than] and newer than Buckingham Palace.

Some corporate executives live in homes as large [as] and as grand as the White House.

If you want to combine a *than* comparison with an *as* comparison, however, an elliptical construction won't work.

INCOMPLETE  The White House is smaller but just as beautiful as Buckingham Palace.

REVISED  The White House is smaller *than* but just *as* beautiful *as* Buckingham Palace.

INCOMPLETE  Some corporate executives live in homes as large and no less grand than the White House.

REVISED  Some corporate executives live in homes *as* large *as* and no less grand *than* the White House.

EXERCISE 15–2

## Completing Sentences

Revise the following sentences by adding needed words to any constructions that are incomplete. (There may be more than one way to complete some constructions.) Some sentences may be correct. Possible revisions for the lettered sentences appear in the back of the book. Example:

President Kennedy should have but didn't see the perils of invading Cuba.

President Kennedy should have *seen* but didn't see the perils of invading Cuba.

a. Eighteenth-century China was as civilized and in many respects more sophisticated than the Western world.
b. Pembroke was never contacted, much less involved with, the election committee.
c. I haven't yet but soon will finish my term paper.
d. Ron likes his popcorn with butter, Linda with parmesan cheese.
e. George Washington always has been and will be regarded as the father of his country.

1. You have traveled to exotic Tahiti; Maureen to Asbury Park, N.J.
2. The mayor refuses to negotiate or even talk to the civic association.
3. Building a new sewage treatment plant would be no more costly and just as effective as modifying the existing one.
4. You'll be able to tell Jon from the rest of the team — Jon wears white Reeboks, the others black high-tops.
5. Erosion has and always will reshape the shoreline.

# 16. *Mixed Constructions and Faulty Predication*

Sometimes a sentence contains all the necessary parts and still doesn't work. Reading it, we feel uneasy, although we may not know why. The problem is a discord between two or more parts of the sentence: the writer has combined phrases or clauses that don't fit together (a *mixed construction*) or mismatched a verb and its subject, object, or modifier (*faulty predication*). The resulting tangle looks like a sentence at first glance, but it fails to make sense.

## 16a.   Link phrases and clauses logically.

A *mixed construction* results when a writer connects phrases or clauses (or both) that don't work together as a sentence.

MIXED   In her efforts to solve the tax problem only caused the mayor additional difficulties.

The prepositional phrase *In her efforts to solve the tax problem* is a modifier; it cannot function as the subject of a sentence. The writer, however, has used this phrase as a noun — the subject of the verb *caused*. To untangle the mixed construction, the writer has two choices: (1) rewrite the phrase so that it works as a noun or (2) use the phrase as a modifier rather than as the sentence's subject.

REVISED   Her efforts to solve the tax problem only caused the mayor additional difficulties. [With *in* gone, *efforts* becomes the subject of the sentence.]

REVISED   In her efforts to solve the tax problem, the mayor created additional difficulties. [The prepositional phrase now modifies the verb *created*.]

To avoid mixed constructions, check the links that join your phrases and clauses — especially prepositions and conjunctions. A sentence, like a chain, is only as strong as its weakest link.

> MIXED   Jack, although he was picked up by the police, but was not charged with anything.

Using both *although* and *but* gives this sentence one link too many. We can unmix the construction in two ways.

> REVISED   Jack was picked up by the police but was not charged with anything.

> REVISED   Although he was picked up by the police, Jack was not charged with anything.

## 16b.   Relate the parts of a sentence logically.

*Faulty predication* refers to a skewed relationship between a verb and some other part of a sentence.

> FAULTY   *The temperature of water freezes at 32 degrees Fahrenheit.*

At first glance, that sentence looks all right. It contains both subject and predicate. It expresses a complete thought. What is wrong with it? The writer has slipped into faulty predication by mismatching the subject and verb. The sentence tells us that *temperature freezes,* when science and common sense tell us it is *water* that freezes. To correct this error, the writer must find a subject and verb that fit each other.

> REVISED   *Water freezes at 32 degrees Fahrenheit.*

Faulty predication also can result from a mismatch between a verb and its direct object.

> FAULTY   Rising costs *diminish college* for many students.

Costs don't *diminish college.* To correct this predication error, the writer must change the sentence so its direct object follows logically from its verb.

> REVISED   Rising costs *diminish the number of students who can attend college.*

Subtler predication errors result when a writer uses a linking verb to forge a false connection between the subject and a subject complement.

> FAULTY   *Industrial waste* has become *an important modern priority.*

Is it really *waste* that has become a *priority?* Or, rather, is it *working to solve the problems caused by careless disposal of industrial waste?* A writer who says all that, though, risks wordiness. Why not just replace *priority* with a closer match for *waste?*

> REVISED   *Industrial waste* has become *a modern menace.*

Predication errors tend to plague writers who are too fond of the passive voice. Mismatches between a verb and its subject, object, or another part of the sentence are easier to avoid (and to spot during editing) when the verb is active than when it is passive. To improve your sentences, cast them in the active voice whenever possible. (See 5m.)

FAULTY   The idea of giving thanks for a good harvest *was not done* first by the Pilgrims.

REVISED   The idea of giving thanks for a good harvest *did not originate* with the Pilgrims.

## 16c.  Avoid starting a definition with *when* or *where.*

Many inexperienced writers slip into predication errors when they define terms. A definition, like any other phrase or clause, needs to fit grammatically with the rest of the sentence.

FAULTY   Dyslexia is when you have a reading disorder.

REVISED   Dyslexia is a reading disorder.

FAULTY   A lay-up is where a player drives in close to the basket and then makes a usually one-handed, banked shot.

REVISED   To shoot a lay-up, a player drives in close to the basket and then makes a usually one-handed, banked shot.

## 16d.  Avoid using *the reason is because* . . .

Anytime you start an explanation with *the reason is,* what follows *is* should be a subject complement: an adjective, a noun, or a noun clause. (See 2d.) *Because* is a conjunction; it cannot function as a noun or adjective.

FAULTY   *The reason* Gerard hesitates *is because* no one supported him two years ago.

REVISED   *The reason* Gerard hesitates *is simple*: no one supported him two years ago.

REVISED   *The reason* Gerard hesitates *is that no one supported him two years ago.*

REVISED   *The reason* Gerard hesitates *is his lack of support two years ago.*

EXERCISE 16–1

## Correcting Mixed Constructions and Faulty Predication

Correct any mixed constructions and faulty predication you find in the following sentences. Possible revisions for the lettered sentences appear in the back of the book. Example:

"Coming about" is when a sailboat makes a turn into the wind.

"Coming about" is a sailboat's turn into the wind.

a. The characteristics of a balanced budget call for careful planning.
b. Television, although it is entertaining, but it turns viewers into passive zombies.
c. In one sizzling blast, the destruction of the enemy space fleet was instantly wiped out.
d. Financial aid searches for able students and decides to pay their college costs.
e. One good reason for financial aid is because it enables capable lower-income students to attend college.

1. Déjà vu is where you feel that you have already lived through the moment you are experiencing.
2. Despite hundreds of years of abusing the environment, but we continue our reckless ways.
3. The damp weather swelled Joe's arthritis.
4. Getting a job can improve a person's status symbols in the community.
5. One theory for the sudden extinction of the dinosaurs is because the earth was hit by a giant comet.
6. Life's saddest moments are experienced by the loss of a loved one.
7. One solution to urban decay is when old neighborhoods are revitalized rather than torn down.
8. Addiction to crack cocaine has become a national crusade.
9. Market research demonstrates to a manufacturer the consumers using its products.
10. American cars try to look flashier than foreign cars.

# 17. *Parallel Structure*

An important tool for any writer is *parallel structure,* or parallelism. You use this tool when you create a series of words, phrases, clauses, or sentences with the same grammatical form. The pattern created by the series — its parallel structure — emphasizes the similarities or differences among the items, which may be things, qualities, actions, or ideas.

My favorite foods are roast beef, deep-dish apple pie, and linguine with clam sauce.

Louise is charming, witty, intelligent, and talented.

Jeff likes to swim, ride, and run.

Dave likes movies that scare him and books that make him laugh.

Each series is a perfect parallel construction, composed of equivalent words: nouns in the first example, adjectives in the second, verbs in the third, and adjective clauses in the fourth.

**17a.** In a series linked by a coordinating conjunction, keep all elements in the same grammatical form.

Whenever you connect items with a coordinating conjunction (*and, but, for, or nor, so* and *yet*), you cue your readers to expect a parallel structure. Whether your series consists of single words, phrases, or clauses, its parts should balance one another.

> AWKWARD    The puppies are *tiny, clumsily bumping* into each other, *and cute.*

Two elements in this series are parallel one-word adjectives (*tiny, cute*) but the third is a verb phrase (*clumsily bumping*). The writer can improve this awkward sentence by making the series consistent.

---

**ESL GUIDELINES**

## Mixed Constructions, Faulty Predication, and Subject Errors

*Mixed constructions* result when phrases or clauses are joined even though they do not logically go together. Combine clauses with either a coordinator (*and, but, so,* and so on) or a subordinator (*although, because,* and so on). Never use both a coordinator and a subordinator to join two clauses.

> INCORRECT    *Although* baseball is called "the national pastime" of the United States, *but* football is probably more popular.
>
> CORRECT    *Although* baseball is called "the national pastime" of the United States, football is probably more popular.
>
> CORRECT    Baseball is called "the national pastime" of the United States, *but* football is probably more popular.

*Faulty predication* results when a verb and its subject, object, or modifier do not match. Do not use a noun as both the subject of the sentence and the object of a preposition.

> INCORRECT    *In my neighborhood has* several good restaurants.
>
> CORRECT    *My neighborhood has* several good restaurants.
>
> CORRECT    *In my neighborhood, there are* several good restaurants.

Avoid also these common errors that may occur with the subject of a clause.

- Do not omit *it* used as a subject. A subject is required in all English sentences except imperatives.

> INCORRECT    *Is* interesting to visit museums.
>
> CORRECT    *It is* interesting to visit museums.

- Do not repeat the subject of a sentence with a pronoun.

> INCORRECT    *My brother-in-law, he* is a successful investor.
>
> CORRECT    *My brother-in-law* is a successful investor.

PARALLEL    The puppies are *tiny, clumsy, and cute.*

Don't mix verb forms in a series. Avoid, for instance, pairing a gerund and an infinitive.

AWKWARD    Switzerland is a good place for a winter vacation if you like *skiing and to skate.*

PARALLEL    Switzerland is a good place for a winter vacation if you like *skiing and skating.*

PARALLEL    Switzerland is a good place for a winter vacation if you like *to ski and to skate.*

In a series of phrases or clauses, be sure that all elements in the series are similar in form, even if they are not similar in length.

AWKWARD    The fight in the bar happens after the two lovers have their scene together but before the car chase. [The clause starting with *after* is not parallel to the phrase starting with *before.*]

PARALLEL    The fight in the bar happens after the love scene but before the car chase.

AWKWARD    You can take the key, or don't forget to leave it under the mat. [The declarative clause starting with *You can* is not parallel to the imperative clause starting with *don't forget.*]

PARALLEL    You can take the key, or you can leave it under the mat.

 **EDITING
CHECKLIST**

## Keeping Parallel Structure

- Are all the elements in a series in the same grammatical form? (17a–17c)
- Are the elements in a comparison parallel in form? (17c)
- Are articles, conjunctions, or prepositions between elements in a series repeated rather than mixed? (17d)
- In a series of clauses, are lead-in words repeated? (17e)

**17b.**    In a series linked by correlative conjunctions, keep all elements in the same grammatical form.

When you use a correlative conjunction (*either . . . or, neither . . . nor, not only . . . but also*), follow each part of the conjunction with a similarly structured word, phrase, or clause.

AWKWARD    I'm looking forward *to either attending* Saturday's wrestling match *or to seeing* it on closed-circuit TV. [Parallel structure is violated because *to* precedes the first part of the correlative conjunction (*to either*) but follows the second part (*or to*).]

PARALLEL    I'm looking forward *either to attending* Saturday's wrestling match *or to seeing* it on closed-circuit television.

AWKWARD    Take my advice: try *neither to be first nor last* in the lunch line.

[Parallel structure is violated because *to be* follows the first part of the correlative conjunction but not the second part.]

PARALLEL    Take my advice: try to be *neither first nor last* in the lunch line.

## 17c.    Make the elements in a comparison parallel in form.

A comparative word such as *than* or *as* cues the reader to expect a parallel structure. This makes logical sense: to be compared, two things must resemble each other, and parallel structure emphasizes this resemblance. (See also 15g.)

AWKWARD    Philip likes *fishing* better than *to sail.*

PARALLEL    Philip likes *fishing* better than *sailing.*

PARALLEL    Philip likes *to fish* better than *to sail.*

AWKWARD    *Maintaining* railway lines is as important to our public transportation system as *to buy* new trains.

PARALLEL    *Maintaining* railway lines is as important to our public transportation system as *buying* new trains.

## 17d.    Reinforce parallel structure by repeating rather than mixing articles, conjunctions, or prepositions.

When you write a series involving articles, conjunctions, or prepositions, be consistent. Try to repeat rather than to vary the word that begins each phrase or clause.

"The time has come," the Walrus said,
"To talk of many things:
Of shoes — and ships — and sealing-wax —
Of cabbages — and — kings — "

In this famous rhyme from *Through the Looking-Glass,* Lewis Carroll builds a beautiful parallel structure on three *of*'s and three *and*'s, each followed by a noun. The repetition of preposition and conjunction makes clear the equivalence of the nouns.

Sometimes the same lead-in word won't work for all elements in a series. In such cases you may be able to preserve a parallel structure by changing the order of the elements to minimize variation.

AWKWARD    The new school building is large but not very comfortable, and expensive but unattractive.

PARALLEL    The new school building is large and expensive, but uncomfortable and unattractive.

**17e.** In a series of clauses, repeat lead-in words to emphasize parallel structure.

Parallel structures are especially useful in complex sentences expressing equivalent ideas. Whenever you write a sentence containing a series of long, potentially confusing clauses, try to precede each clause with *that, who, when, where,* or some other connective, repeating the same connective every time. To do so not only helps you to keep your thoughts in order as you write but helps readers to follow them with ease.

> No one in this country needs a government that aids big business at the expense of farmers and laborers; that ravages the environment in the name of progress; that slashes budgets of health and education; that turns its back on the unemployed, the illiterate, the mentally ill, the destitute; that constantly swaggers and rattles its sabers; that spends billions piling up missiles it would be insane to use.

Repeating an opening phrase can accomplish the same goal in a series of parallel sentences, as the following graceful example shows.

> The Russian dramatist is one who, walking through a cemetery, does not see the flowers on the graves. The American dramatist is one who, walking through a cemetery, does not see the graves under the flowers.

EXERCISE I7–I

## Making Sentences Parallel

Revise the following sentences by substituting parallel structures for awkward ones. Possible revisions for the lettered sentences appear in the back of the book. Example:

> Not only are you wasting your time but also mine.

> You are wasting not only your time but also mine.

a. Linda loves to watch soccer and tennis and playing squash.
b. Better than starting from scratch would be to build on what already has been done.
c. Her apartment needed fresh paint, a new rug was a necessity, and Mary Lou wished she had a neater roommate and that she had chosen quieter friends.
d. All my brothers are blond and athletes.
e. For breakfast the waiter brought scrambled eggs, which I like, and kippers, although I don't like them.

1. The United States must start either focusing more attention on education or we must accept a future as a second-rate power.
2. Not only were they homeless but sick as well.
3. The best teachers are kind, firm, are smart, and have a sense of humor.
4. Students can write either a term paper or give a presentation.

5. The twentieth century was not an age of progress, but violence and brutality on a scale unknown since ancient times.
6. Melrose would rather carry his battle to the Supreme Court than he would be willing to give up without a fight.
7. My landlady is tidy, generous, easygoing, and a talker.
8. Are problem novels for the young really good for children or merely exploit them by making life appear more burdensome, chaotic, more wretched, and evil than it really is?
9. When you first start out, running halfway around the track is as big a challenge as to complete several circuits.
10. Her excuses were the difficulty of the task, the instructions were awkwardly worded, and having only four hours to complete the assignment.
11. In my drama class so far we've read a Shakespearean tragedy, another by Marlowe, and one of Webster's.
12. When you are broke and unemployed and your friends have deserted you, while you have nowhere to sleep but under a bridge, then and only then should you call this number.
13. Giving is better than to receive.
14. Not only should we accept Marinda's kind offer, but thank her for making it.
15. How often Reuben has done this kind of work is less important than the quality of his output.

# 18. *Coordination and Subordination*

A good piece of writing is greater than the sum of its parts. Links between sentences help readers to see how one thought relates to another and to share the writer's overview of the topic.

When you write, you can use coordination and subordination to bring out the relationships between your ideas. Coordination clarifies the connection between thoughts of equal importance; subordination shows how one thought affects another. These two techniques will help you produce sentences, paragraphs, and essays that function as a coherent whole.

**18a.** Coordinate clauses or sentences that are related in theme and equal in importance.

The car skidded for a hundred yards. It crashed into a brick wall.

These two clauses make equally significant statements about the same subject, a car accident. Because the writer has indicated no link between the sentences, we can only guess that the crash followed from the skid; we cannot be sure.

Suppose we join the two with a conjunction.

The car skidded for a hundred yards, and it crashed into a brick wall.

Now the sequence is clear: first the car skidded, then it crashed. That's coordination.

Another way to coordinate the two clauses is to combine them into a single sentence with a compound verb. The second main clause, losing its subject, becomes a phrase.

The car skidded for a hundred yards and crashed into a brick wall.

Now the connection is so clear we can almost hear screeching brakes and crunching metal.

Once you decide to coordinate two clauses, there are three ways you can do it: with a conjunction, with a conjunctive adverb, or with punctuation.

1. Join two main clauses with a coordinating conjunction (*and, but, for, or, nor, so,* or *yet*).

| | |
|---|---|
| UNCOORDINATED | George does not want to be placed on your mailing list. He does not want a salesperson to call him. |
| COORDINATED | George does not want to be placed on your mailing list, nor does he want a salesperson to call him. |
| COORDINATED | George does not want to be placed on your mailing list or called by a salesperson. |

2. Join two main clauses with a semicolon and a conjunctive adverb such as *furthermore, however, moreover,* or *therefore.* (See 1g.)

| | |
|---|---|
| UNCOORDINATED | The guerrillas did not observe the truce. They never intended to. |
| COORDINATED | The guerrillas did not observe the truce; furthermore, they never intended to. |

3. Join two main clauses with a semicolon or a colon. (For details on when to use which punctuation mark, see 26 and 27.)

| | |
|---|---|
| UNCOORDINATED | The government favors negotiations. The guerrillas prefer to fight. |
| COORDINATED | The government favors negotiations; the guerrillas prefer to fight. |
| UNCOORDINATED | The guerrillas have two advantages. They know the terrain, and the people support them. |
| COORDINATED | The guerrillas have two advantages: they know the terrain, and the people support them. |

**EDITING
CHECKLIST**

## Coordinating and Subordinating

- Are all coordinated clauses related in theme and equal in importance? (18a)
- Are all coordinated clauses clearly and logically related? (18b)
- Do all coordinated clauses work together to make a coherent point? (18c)
- Is subordination used to link a less important idea to a more important idea? (18d)
- Is the main idea always expressed in the main clause? (18e)

**18b.** Coordinate clauses only if they are clearly and logically related.

Whenever you hitch together two sentences, make sure they get along. Will the relationship between them be evident to your readers? Have you chosen a coordinating conjunction, conjunctive adverb, or punctuation mark that accurately reflects this relationship?

> FAULTY    The sportscasters were surprised by Easy Goer's failure to win the Kentucky Derby, but it rained on Derby day.

The writer has not included enough information for the reader to see why these two clauses are connected.

> COORDINATED    The sportscasters were surprised by Easy Goer's failure to win the Kentucky Derby; *however, he runs poorly on a muddy track,* and it rained on Derby day.

Another route to faulty coordination is a poorly chosen link between clauses.

> FAULTY    The sportscasters all expected Easy Goer to win the Kentucky Derby, and Sunday Silence beat him.

The conjunction *and* implies that both clauses reflect the same assumptions. This is not the case, so the writer should choose a conjunction that expresses difference.

> COORDINATED    The sportscasters all expected Easy Goer to win the Kentucky Derby, *but* Sunday Silence beat him.

**18c.** Coordinate clauses only if they work together to make a coherent point.

When a writer strings together several clauses in a row, often the result is excessive coordination. Trying to pack too much information into a single sentence can make readers dizzy, unable to pick out which points really matter.

> EXCESSIVE    Easy Goer was the Kentucky Derby favorite, and all the sportscasters expected him to win, but he runs poorly on a muddy track, and it rained on Derby day, so Sunday Silence beat him.

What are the main points in this passage? Each key idea deserves its own sentence so that readers will recognize it as important.

> REVISED    Easy Goer was the Kentucky Derby favorite, and all the sportscasters expected him to win. However, he runs poorly on a muddy track, and it rained on Derby day; so Sunday Silence beat him.

Excessive coordination also tends to result when a writer uses the same conjunction repeatedly.

EXCESSIVE  Phil was out of the house all day, so he didn't know about the rain, so he went ahead and bet on Easy Goer, so he lost twenty bucks, so now he wants to borrow money from me.

REVISED  Phil was out of the house all day, so he didn't know about the rain. He went ahead and bet on Easy Goer, and he lost twenty bucks. Now he wants to borrow money from me.

One solution to excessive coordination is subordination: making one clause dependent on another instead of giving both clauses equal weight. (See 18d.)

EXERCISE 18–1

## Using Coordination

Revise the following sentences, adding coordination where appropriate and removing faulty or excessive coordination. Possible revisions for the lettered sentences appear in the back of the book. Example:

The wind was rising, and leaves tossed on the trees, and the air seemed to crackle with electricity, and we knew that a thunderstorm was on the way.

The wind was rising, leaves tossed on the trees, and the air seemed to crackle with electricity. We knew that a thunderstorm was on the way.

a. Congress is expected to pass the biotechnology bill. The president already has said he will veto it.
b. Mortgage rates have dropped. Home buying is likely to increase in the near future.
c. The earth trembled. The long-dreaded cataclysm had begun.
d. I left the house in a hurry and ran to the bank so I could cash a check to buy lunch, but it was the bank's anniversary, and the staff was busy serving coffee and cake, so by the time I left, after chatting and eating for twenty minutes, I wasn't hungry anymore.
e. The U.S. Postal Service handles millions of pieces of mail every day. It is the largest postal service in the world.

1. The rebels may take the capital in a week. They may not be able to hold it.
2. If you want to take Spanish this semester, you have only one choice. You must sign up for the 8 A.M. course.
3. Peterson's Market has raised its prices. Last week tuna fish cost $.89 a can. Now it's up to $1.09.
4. Joe starts the morning with a cup of coffee, which wakes him up, and then at lunch he eats a chocolate bar, so that the sugar and caffeine will bring up his energy level.
5. The *Hindenburg* drifted peacefully over New York City. It exploded just before landing.

## 18d. Subordinate less important ideas to more important ideas.

Subordination is one of the most useful of all writing strategies. By subordinating a less important clause to a more important one, you show your readers that one fact or idea follows from another or affects another. You stress what counts, thereby encouraging your readers to share your viewpoint — an important goal, whatever you are writing.

When you have two sentences that contain ideas in need of connecting, you can subordinate one to the other in any of the following three ways.

1. Turn the less important idea into a subordinate clause by introducing it with a subordinating conjunction such as *although, because, if,* or *when.* (See 1g for a list of subordinating conjunctions.)

> Jason has a keen sense of humor. He has an obnoxious, braying laugh.

From that pair of sentences, readers don't know what to feel about Jason. Is he likable or repellent? The writer needs to decide which trait matters more and to emphasize it.

> *Although Jason has a keen sense of humor,* he has an obnoxious, braying laugh.

The revision makes Jason's sense of humor less important than his annoying hee-haw. The less important idea is stated as a subordinate clause opening with *Although,* the more important idea as the main clause.

The writer could reverse the meaning by combining the two ideas the other way around:

> *Although Jason has an obnoxious, braying laugh,* he has a keen sense of humor.

That version makes Jason sound fun to be with, despite his mannerism.

Which of Jason's traits to emphasize is up to the writer. What matters is that, in both combined versions of the original two separate sentences, the writer takes a clear stand by making one sentence a main clause and the other a subordinate clause.

2. Turn the less important idea into a subordinate clause by introducing it with a relative pronoun such as *who, which,* or *that.* (See 1b for a list of relative pronouns.)

> Jason, *who has an obnoxious, braying laugh,* has a keen sense of humor.

> Jason, *whose sense of humor is keen,* has an obnoxious, braying laugh.

3. Turn the less important idea into a phrase.

> Jason, *a keen humorist,* has an obnoxious, braying laugh.

> *Despite his obnoxious, braying laugh,* Jason has a keen sense of humor.

## 18e.  Express the more important idea in the main clause.

Sometimes a writer accidentally subordinates a more important idea to a less important idea and turns the sentence's meaning upside down.

> FAULTY          Although the Algonquin Round Table lives on in spirit, the
> SUBORDINATION   writers who created it are nearly all dead now.

This sentence is factually accurate. Does the writer, however, really want to stress death over life? This is the effect of putting *are nearly all dead* in the main clause and *lives on* in the subordinate clause. Recognizing a case of faulty subordination, the writer can reverse the two clauses.

> REVISED    Although the writers who created it are nearly all dead now, the Algonquin Round Table lives on in spirit.

## 18f.   Limit the number of subordinate clauses in a sentence.

The cause of excessive subordination is usually that a writer has tried to cram too much information into one sentence. The result is a string of ideas in which readers may not be able to pick out what matters.

> EXCESSIVE SUBORDINATION    Debate over the Strategic Defense Initiative (SDI), which was originally proposed as a space-based defensive shield that would protect America from enemy attack, but which critics have suggested amounts to creating a first-strike capability in space, has to some extent focused on the wrong question because it concentrates on the plan's technological flaws and thus fails to consider adequately whether SDI would in fact lower or increase the odds of nuclear war.

In revising this sentence, the writer needs to decide which are the main points and turn each one into a main clause. Lesser points can remain as subordinate clauses, arranged so that each of them gets an appropriate amount of emphasis.

> REVISED    Debate over the Strategic Defense Initiative (SDI) has to some extent focused on the wrong question. The plan was originally proposed as a space-based defensive shield that would protect America from enemy attack; but critics have suggested that it amounts to creating a first-strike capability in space. However, most arguments about SDI have concentrated on its technological flaws and thus have failed to consider adequately whether SDI would in fact lower or increase the odds of nuclear war.

---

EXERCISE 18–2 | ## Using Subordination

Revise the following sentences, adding subordination where appropriate and removing faulty or excessive subordination. Possible revisions for the lettered sentences appear in the back of the book. Example:

Some playwrights like to work with performing theater companies. It is helpful to hear a script read aloud by actors.

Some playwrights like to work with performing theater companies because it is helpful to hear a script read aloud by actors.

a. Although we occasionally hear horror stories about fruits and vegetables being unsafe to eat because they were sprayed with toxic chemicals or were grown in contaminated soil, the fact remains that, given their high nutritional value, these fresh foods are generally much better for us than processed foods.

b. English has become an international language. Its grammar is filled with exceptions to the rules.

c. Some television cartoon shows have become cult classics. This has happened years after they went off the air. Examples include *Rocky and Bullwinkle* and *Speedracer.*

d. At the end of Verdi's opera *La Traviata*, Alfredo has to see his beloved Violetta again. He knows she is dying and all he can say is good-bye.

e. Violetta gives away her money. She bids adieu to her faithful servant. After that she dies in her lover's arms.

1. Cape Cod is a peninsula in Massachusetts. It juts into the Atlantic Ocean south of Boston. The Cape marks the northern turning point of the Gulf Stream.

2. The developer had hoped the condominiums would sell quickly. Sales were sluggish.

3. Tourists love Italy. Italy has a wonderful climate, beautiful towns and cities, and a rich history.

4. Although bank customers have not yet begun to shift their money out of savings accounts, the interest rate on NOW accounts has gone up.

5. I usually have more fun at a concert with Rico than with Morey. Rico loves music. Morey merely tolerates it.

---

**EXERCISE 18–3**

## Using Coordination and Subordination

Revise the following passage, adding coordination and subordination where appropriate and removing faulty or excessive subordination. Example:

> The car plays an essential but destructive role in American consumer society. It requires the maximum consumption of resources and energy. It contributes to the disintegration of community.

> The car plays an essential but destructive role in American consumer society: it not only requires the maximum consumption of resources and energy but also contributes to the disintegration of community.

The invention of the automobile transformed society in one profound way. It offered everyone unlimited freedom of movement. It is true that the car has allowed the population greater mobility, and the cost to the landscape and the environment has been devastating. The reliance on the car has created sprawling suburbs, miles of ugly strip malls and acres of parking lots, and it has destroyed farmland, wetland, and wildlife habitat, while it continues to pollute the environment, poisoning the air we breathe, and discouraging walking, a traditional fat-burning activity, thus contributing directly to our personal health problems. In addition to ecological damage, the obsessive reliance on the automobile has had serious social consequences and has accentuated social and racial polarization, separating the suburban middle classes from the urban poor and has also intensified the social isolation of the individual. The car owner spends a great deal of his or her time alone in the car, driving to and from shopping and living zones, so with shopping malls far from the centers of towns and cities, consumers no longer patronize town centers and thus contribute to the destruction of traditional American community life. The car is here to stay. We must find a way to limit its destructive power.

# 19. *Sentence Variety*

Just as the special-effects experts in movies use the unexpected to shock or to please, writers may combine sentence elements in unexpected ways to achieve special effects. Writers use some patterns more than others to express ideas directly and efficiently, but sometimes they vary the normal expectations in sentences to emphasize ideas and surprise readers.

## 19a.  Normal Sentences

In a *normal sentence*, a writer puts the subject before the verb at the beginning of the main clause. This pattern is the most common in English because it expresses ideas in the most straightforward manner.

> Most college *students* today *are* not interested in reading.

> *Franklin sighed* because he was frustrated over his inability to solve the quadratic equation.

## 19b.  Inverted Sentences

In an *inverted sentence*, a writer inverts or reverses the subject-verb order to emphasize an idea in the predicate.

> NORMAL    My peers are uninterested in reading.
> INVERTED  How uninterested in reading are my peers!

## 19c.  Balanced Sentences

In a *balanced sentence*, a writer purposefully repeats key words and uses parallel sentence patterns to emphasize ideas.

> In studying the heavens, we are debarred from all senses except sight. *We cannot* touch the sun, *or* travel to it: *we cannot* walk around the moon, *or* apply a foot-rule to the Pleiades.

## 19d.  Cumulative Sentences

In a *cumulative sentence*, a writer piles details at the end of a sentence to help readers visualize a scene or understand an idea.

They came walking out in heavily brocaded yellow and black costumes, the familiar "toreador" suit, heavy with gold embroidery, cape, jacket, shirt and collar, knee breeches, pink stockings, and low pumps.

— Ernest Hemingway, "Bull Fighting a Tragedy"

## 19e.  Periodic Sentences

The positions of emphasis in a sentence are the beginning and the end. In a **periodic sentence,** a writer suspends the main clause for a climactic ending, emphasizing an idea by withholding it until the end.

Leaning back in his chair, shaking his head slowly back and forth, frustrated over his inability to solve the quadratic equation, Franklin scowled.

**EXERCISE 19–1**

### Increasing Sentence Variety

Revise the following passage, adding sentence variety to create interest, emphasize important ideas, and strengthen coherence.

We are terrified of death. We do not think of it, and we don't speak of life. We don't mourn in public. We don't know how to console a grieving friend. In fact, we have eliminated or suppressed all the traditional rituals surrounding death.

The Victorians coped with death differently. Their funerals were elaborate. The yards of black crepe around the hearse, hired professional mourners, and its solemn procession leading to an ornate tomb is now only a distant memory. They wore mourning jewelry. They had a complicated dress code for the grieving process. It governed what mourners wore, and it governed how long they wore it. Many of these Victorian rituals may seem excessive or even morbid to us today. The rituals served a psychological purpose in helping the living deal with loss.

**EXERCISE 19–2**

### Generating Varied Sentences

Try your hand — either alone or with classmates — at composing each of these types of sentences: a normal sentence, an inverted sentence, a balanced sentence, a cumulative sentence, and a periodic sentence.

## Chapter 35

# Word Choice

## 20. *Appropriateness*

When you talk to people face to face, you can gauge how they are reacting to what you say. Often their responses guide your tone of voice and your choice of words: if your listener chuckles at your humor, you go on being humorous; if your listener frowns, you cut the comedy and speak more seriously.

When you write, you cannot gauge your readers' reactions as easily because you cannot see them. To know whether your comments will be successful, you must imagine yourself in a reader's place. Although you may consider your readers from time to time as you gather material and as you write, you probably focus most closely on their responses when you reread your writing to determine how to revise.

### 20a. Choose a tone appropriate for your topic and audience.

Like a speaker, a writer may come across as warm and friendly or cool and aloof, furious or merely annoyed, playful or grimly serious. This attitude is the *tone* of the piece of writing, and, like the tone of the speaking voice, it strongly influences the audience's response. A tone that seems right to a reader comes when you have written with an awareness of and concern for how the reader may react. If you ignore or are unaware of your reader, then your tone will be inappropriate. For instance, taking a humorous approach to a disease such as cancer or AIDS probably would yield an inappropriate tone. The reader, not finding the topic funny, is likely to reject what you say.

To help you convey your tone, you may use sentence length, level of language, vocabulary, and other elements of style. You may choose formal or informal language, colorful or bland words, coolly objective words, or words loaded with emotional connotations ("You pig!" "You angel!").

## 20b.   Choose a level of formality appropriate for your tone.

Being aware of the tone you want to convey to your audience helps you choose words that are neither too formal nor too informal. By *formal* language, we mean the impersonal language of educated persons, usually written. In general, formal language is marked by relatively long and complex sentences and by a large, often esoteric, vocabulary. It doesn't use contractions (such as *doesn't*), and the writer's attitude toward the topic is serious.

*Informal* language more closely resembles ordinary conversation. Its sentences tend to be relatively short and simple. Informal language is marked by common words and may include contractions, slang, and references to everyday objects and activities (cheeseburgers, T-shirts, car repair). It may address the reader as *you,* and the writer may use *I.*

The right language for most college essays lies somewhere between formal and informal. If your topic and your tone are serious (say, for an expository paper on the United Nations), then your language is likely to lean toward formality. If your topic is not weighty and your tone is light and humorous (say, for a narrative paper about giving your dog a bath), then your language can be informal.

**EXERCISE 20–1**

### Choosing an Appropriate Tone and Level of Formality

Revise the following passages to ensure that both the tone and the level of formality are appropriate for the topic and audience. Example:

> I'm sending you this letter because I want you to meet with me and give me some info about the job you do.

> I'm writing to inquire about the possibility of an interview.

1. Dear Senator Crowley:
       I think you've got to vote for the new environmental law, so I'm writing this letter. We're messing up forests and wetlands — maybe for good. Let's do something now for everybody who's born after us.
   Thanks,
   Glenn Turner

2. The new Holocaust Museum in Washington, D.C., is a great museum dedicated to a real bad time in history. It's real hard not to get bummed out by the stuff on show. Take it from me, it's an experience you'll never forget.

3. Dear Elaine,
       I am so pleased that you plan on attending the homecoming dance with me on Friday. It promises to be a gala event and I am confident that we will enjoy ourselves immensely. I understand a local recording act by the name of "Acid Bunny" will be providing the musical entertainment. Please call me at your earliest convenience to let me know when I should pick you up.
   Sincerely,
   Bill

## 20c.    Choose common words instead of jargon.

Whatever your tone and your level of formality, certain types of language are best avoided when you write an essay. *Jargon* is the name given to the specialized vocabulary used by people in a particular field. Nearly every academic, professional, and even recreational field — music, carpentry, the law, computer programming, sports — has its own jargon. In baseball, pitcher Dennis Eckersley says that when he faces a dangerous batter, he thinks: "If I throw him *the heater,* maybe he *juices it out* on me" (emphasis added). Translation: "If I throw him a fastball, he might hit a home run."[1]

To a specialist addressing other specialists, jargon is convenient and necessary. Without technical terms, after all, two surgeons could hardly discuss a patient's anatomy. To an outsider, though, such terms may be incomprehensible. If your writing is meant (as it should be) to communicate information to your readers and not to make them feel excluded or confused, you should avoid unnecessary jargon.

Commonly, we apply the name *jargon* to any private, pretentious, or needlessly specialized language. Jargon can include not only words but ways of using words. Some politicians and bureaucrats like to make nouns into verbs by tacking on suffixes like *-ize.*

| | |
|---|---|
| JARGON | Let us *prioritize* our objectives. |
| CLEAR | Let us *assign priorities to* our objectives. |
| CLEAR | Let us *rank* our objectives *in order of urgency.* |
| JARGON | The government intends to *privatize* federal landholdings. |
| CLEAR | The government intends to *sell* federal landholdings *to private buyers.* |

Although *privatize* implies merely "convert to private ownership," usually its real meaning is "sell off" — as might occur, say, were a national park to be auctioned to developers. *Privatize* thus also can be called a *euphemism,* which is any pleasant term that masks an unpleasant meaning (see 20c).

Besides confusing readers, jargon is likely to mislead them. Recently, high technology has made verbs of the familiar nouns *access, boot,* and *format.* Other terms that have entered the popular vocabulary include *interface, x amount of, database,* and *parameters.* Such terms are useful to explain technical processes; but when thoughtlessly applied to nontechnical ideas, they can obscure meaning.

| | |
|---|---|
| JARGON | A democracy needs the electorate's *input.* |
| CLEAR | A democracy needs the electorate *to vote and to express its views to elected officials.* |

Here's how to shun needless jargon.

1. Beware of choosing any trendy new word when a perfectly good old word will do.

[1] Quoted by Mike Whiteford, *How to Talk Baseball* (New York: Dembner, 1983) 51.

2. Before using a word ending in *-ize, -wise,* or *-ism,* count to ten. This will give you time either to think of a clearer alternative or to be sure that none exists.
3. Avoid the jargon of a special discipline — say, psychology or fly-fishing — unless you are writing of psychological or fly-fishing matters and you know for sure that your reader, too, is familiar with them. If you're writing for an audience of general readers about some field in which you are an expert — if, for instance, you're explaining the fundamentals of hang gliding — define any specialized terms. Even if you're addressing fellow hang-gliding experts, use plain words and you'll rarely go wrong.

**EXERCISE 20–2**

## Avoiding Jargon

Revise the following sentences to eliminate the jargon. If you see a need to change a sentence extensively, go ahead. If you can't tell what a sentence means, decide what it might mean and rewrite it so that its meaning is clear. Possible revisions for the lettered sentences appear in the back of the book. Example:

> The proximity of Mr. Fitton's knife to Mr. Schering's arm produced a violation of the integrity of the skin.

> Mr. Fitton's knife cut Mr. Schering's arm.

a. The driver education course prepares the student for the skills of handling a vehicle on the highway transportation system.
b. We of the State Department have carefully contexted the riots in Lebanon intelligencewise, and after full and thorough database utilization, find them abnormalling rapidly.
c. Certain antinuclearistic and pacifistic/prejudicial factions have been picketing the missile conference in hopes of immobilizing these vital peacekeeping deliberations.
d. In the heart area, Mr. Pitt is a prime candidate-elect for intervention of a multiple bypass nature.
e. Within the parameters of your insurance company's financial authorization, he can either be regimed dietwise or be bypass prognosticated.

1. The study will examine the negative ramifications of toxic nonbiodegradable manufactured waste products.
2. Engaging in a conversational situation with God permits an individual to maximally interface with God.
3. The deer hunters number-balanced the ecological infrastructure by quietizing x amount of the deer populace.
4. "I am very grateful that we have education up where it is, high on the educational agenda of this country." — Secretary of Education T. H. Bell, in a speech, June 1983
5. A noninterventionist policy has been adopted by the government with respect to the situation in Bosnia.

## 20d. Use euphemisms sparingly.

Euphemisms are plain truths dressed in attractive words, sometimes hard facts stated gently and pleasantly. To say that someone *passed away* instead of *died* is a common euphemism — useful and humane, perhaps, in breaking terrible news to an anxious family. In such shock-absorbing language, an army that retreats *makes a strategic withdrawal;* a poor old man becomes a *disadvantaged senior citizen.* But euphemisms aren't always oversized words. If you call someone *slim* who you think *underweight* or *skinny,* you use a euphemism, though it has only one syllable.

Because they can bathe glum truths in a kindly glow, euphemisms are beloved by advertisers — like the *mortician (undertaker)* who offered *pre-need arrangements.* Euphemisms also can make ordinary things sound more impressive. Some acne medications treat not *pimples* but *blemishes.* In Madison, Wisconsin, a theater renamed its candy counter the *patron assistance center.*

Euphemisms may serve grimmer purposes. During World War II, Jewish prisoners sent to Nazi extermination camps carried papers stamped *Rückkehr Unerwünscht* (Return Unwanted). In 1984, the Doublespeak Award of the National Council of Teachers of English went to the U.S. State Department for its announcement that it would no longer use the word *killing* in its official reports but would substitute *unlawful or arbitrary deprivation of life.*

Even if you aren't prone to using euphemisms in your own writing, be aware of them when you read, especially when collecting evidence from biased sources and official spokespersons.

**EXERCISE 20–3**

### Avoiding Euphemisms

Revise the following sentences to turn euphemisms into plainer words. Possible revisions for the lettered sentences appear in the back of the book. Example:

> I am temporarily between jobs, so I am currently experiencing a negative cash flow.

> I'm out of work and therefore in debt.

a. After the Rodney King trial, Los Angeles was engulfed in a riot, during which many innocent people passed away.
b. The ship sank because of loss of hull integrity.
c. The new K27 missile will effectively depopulate the cities of any aggressor nation.
d. In our town, sanitation engineers must wear professional apparel when making their rounds.
e. Freddie the Rocker has boarded a first-class flight for the great all-night discotheque in the sky.

1. Our security forces have judiciously thinned an excessive number of political dissidents.

2. The soldiers were victims of friendly fire during a strategic withdrawal.
3. To bridge the projected shortfall between collections and expenditures in next year's budget, the governor advocates some form of revenue enhancement.
4. Saturday's weather forecast calls for extended periods of shower activity.
5. We anticipate a downturn in economic vitality.

## 20e. Avoid slang in formal writing.

Poet Carl Sandburg once said, "Slang is language that takes off its coat, spits on its hands, and gets to work." Clearly, Sandburg approved. Probably even the purists among us will concede that slang, especially when new, can be colorful ("She's not playing with a full deck"), playful ("He's wicked cute!"), and apt (*ice* for diamonds, a *stiff* for a corpse).

The trouble with most slang, however, is that it quickly comes to seem quaint, even incomprehensible. We don't hear anyone say *groovy* anymore except on reruns of *The Brady Bunch*. *Bad vibes*, ubiquitous in the 1960s, today wear spiderwebs. Even the lately minted *bummer* and *grody to the max* already seem as old and wrinkled as the Jazz Age's favorite exclamation of glee, *twenty-three skidoo!*

In the classroom and out of it, your writing communicates your thoughts. To be understood, your best bet is to stick to Standard English. Most slang is less than clever. The newest of it, apt though it may seem, like any fad is in danger of being quickly tossed aside in favor of something newer still. Seek words that are usual but exact, not the latest thing, and your writing will stay young longer.

**EXERCISE 20–4**

## Avoiding Slang

Revise the following sentences to replace slang with Standard English. Possible revisions for the lettered sentences appear in the back of the book. Example:

I can see that something is bugging you, so you may as well lay it on me.

I can see that something is bothering you, so you may as well tell me about it.

a. Judy doesn't dig the way Paul's been coming on to her.
b. If large animals do not clear out of the combat zone, the army's policy is to waste them.
c. Judge Lehman's reversal of the *Smith v. Jones* verdict shows that his lights are on but nobody's home.
d. Anybody who's checked out the plays of Sophocles finds them totally awesome.
e. If he can make bail, he'll probably split.

1. The insider trading thing on Wall Street has turned out to be a major scam.
2. Blue-collar criminals get nailed; white-collar criminals walk.

3. This dude got so hung up about his final exam that his shrink told him just to chill.
4. They got busted by the coach after they dissed the other team.
5. He could draw five to ten in the slammer.

# 21. *Exact Words*

What would you think if you read in a newspaper that a certain leading citizen is a *pillow of the community?* How would you react to a foreign dignitary's statement that he has no children because his wife is *inconceivable?* Good writing — that is, effective written communication — depends on more than good grammar. Just as important are knowing what words and phrases mean and using them precisely.

**21a.** Choose words for their connotations as well as their denotations.

The **denotation** of a word is its basic meaning — its dictionary definition. *Stone,* for instance, has the same denotation as *rock. Excited, agitated,* and *exhilarated* all denote a similar state of physical and emotional arousal. When you look up a word in a dictionary or thesaurus, the synonyms you find have been selected for their shared denotation.

The **connotations** of a word are the shades of meaning that set it apart from its synonyms. We say *Phil's house is a stone's throw from mine,* not *a rock's throw.* You might be *agitated* by the prospect of exams next week, but *exhilarated* by your plans for a vacation afterward. When you choose one out of several synonyms listed in a dictionary or thesaurus, you base your choice on connotation.

Paying attention to connotation helps a writer to say exactly what he or she intends, instead of almost but not quite.

IMPRECISE    Advertisers have given light beer a macho image by showing football players *sipping* the product with *enthusiasm.*

REVISED    Advertisers have given light beer a macho image by showing football players *guzzling* the product with *gusto.*

IMPRECISE    The cat's eyes *shone* as she *pursued* the mouse.

REVISED    The cat's eyes *glittered* as she *stalked* the mouse.

**21b.** Avoid clichés.

A **cliché** is a trite expression, worn out from too much use. It may have glinted once, like a coin fresh from the mint, but now it is dull and flat from years of passing from hand to hand. If a story begins, "It was a dark and stormy night," and introduces a *tall, dark,* and *handsome* man and a woman who is *a vision of loveliness,* then its author is obviously using worn coins.

A cliché isn't just any old dull expression: it is one whose writer mistakenly assumes is bright. "Let's run this up the flagpole and see if anyone salutes," proposes the executive, while his or her colleagues yawn at the effort to sound clever. Stale, too, is the suggestion to put an idea *on the back burner*. Clichés abound when writers and speakers try hard to sound vigorous and colorful but don't trouble to invent anything vigorous, colorful, and new.

George Orwell once complained about prose made up of phrases "tacked together like the sections of a prefabricated henhouse." If you read newspapers, you are familiar with such ready-made constructions. A strike is usually settled after *a marathon bargaining session* that *narrowly averts a walkout,* often *at the eleventh hour.* Fires customarily *race* and *gut.* Some writers use clichés to exaggerate, giving a statement more force than they feel. The writer to whom everything is *fantastic* or *terrific* arouses a reader's suspicion that it isn't.

No writer can entirely avoid clichés or avoid echoing colorful expressions first used by someone else. You need not ban from your writing all proverbs ("It takes a thief to catch a thief"), well-worked quotations from Shakespeare ("Neither a borrower nor a lender be"), and other faintly dusty wares from the storehouse of our language. "Looking for a needle in a haystack" may be a time-worn phrase, yet who can put that idea any more memorably?

Nor should you fear that every familiar expression is a cliché. *Just in time, more or less, sooner or later* — these are old, familiar expressions, to be sure; but they are not clichés, for they don't try to be vivid or figurative. Inevitably, we all rely on them.

When editing your writing, you will usually recognize any really annoying cliché you'll want to eradicate. If you feel a sudden guilty desire to surround an expression with quotation marks, as if to apologize for it —

> In his campaign speeches for his fourteenth term, Senator Pratt shows that he cannot "cut the mustard" any longer.

— then strike it out. Think again: what do you want to say? Recast your idea more clearly, more exactly.

> At age seventy-seven, Senator Pratt no longer can hold a crowd with an impassioned, hour-long speech, as he could when he first ran for Congress.

By what other means can you spot a cliché? One way is to show your papers to friends, asking them to look for anything trite. As you go on in college, your awareness of clichés will grow with reading. The more you read, the easier it is to recognize a cliché on sight, for you will have met it often before.

Meanwhile, here is a list of a few clichés still in occasional circulation. If any is a favorite of yours, try replacing it with something more vivid and original.

| | |
|---|---|
| Achilles' heel | an astronomical sum |
| acid test | beyond a shadow of a doubt |
| add insult to injury | born with a silver spoon in one's |
| apple of one's eye | mouth |
| as American as apple pie | |

bosom companions, bosom
   buddies
burn one's bridges
burn the midnight oil
busy as a beaver (or a bee)
But that's another story.
come hell or high water
cool as a cucumber
cream of the crop
cut like a knife
dead as a doornail
do your own thing
dressed fit to kill
eager beaver
easy as falling off a log
easy as taking candy from a baby
a face that would stop a clock
feeling on top of the world
few and far between
fine and dandy
fly in the ointment
from (or since) time immemorial
golden years
greased lightning
hands-on learning experience
hard as a rock
high as a kite
holler bloody murder
honest as the day is long
In conclusion, I would like
   to say . . .
in my wildest dreams
last but not least
little did I dream
make a long story short
natural inclination

neat as a pin
nutty as a fruitcake
old as the hills
on the ball
on the brink of disaster
over and above the call of
   duty
pay through the nose
piece of cake
point with pride
proud as a peacock
pull the wool over someone's
   eyes
salad days
sell like hotcakes
a sheepish grin
since the dawn of time
skating on thin ice
a skeleton in the closet
slow as molasses
smell a rat
a sneaking suspicion
stab me in the back
stack the deck
stagger the imagination
stick out like a sore thumb
sweet as honey
That's the way the ball
   bounces.
through thick and thin
time-honored
tip of the iceberg
too little and too late
tried but true
You could have knocked me over
   with a feather.

## 21c.   Use idioms in their correct form.

Every language contains *idioms*, or *idiomatic expressions:* phrases that, through long use, have become standard even though their construction may defy logic or grammar. Idioms can be difficult for a native speaker of English to explain to someone just learning the language. They sound natural, however, to those who have heard them since childhood.

Many idiomatic expressions require us to choose the right preposition. We say we live *in* the city, but vacation *at* the seashore, even though we might be hard pressed to explain why we use *in* in one phrase and *at* in the other. To pause *for* a minute is not the same as to pause *in* a minute. We work *up* a sweat while working *out* in the gym. We argue *with* someone, but *about* something. We can also argue *for* or *against* it.

For some idioms we must know which article to use before a noun — or whether to use any article at all. We can be *in motion,* but we have to be *in the swim.* We're occasionally in *a tight spot* but never in *a trouble.* Certain idioms vary from country to country: in Britain, a patient has an operation *in hospital*; in America, *in the hospital.* Idioms can involve choosing the right verb with the right noun: we *seize* an opportunity, but we *catch* a plane. We *break* a law but *explode* a theory.

Sometimes even the best writers draw a blank when they confront a common idiomatic expression. Is *compared with* or *compared to* the right phrase? Should you say *agree to, agree on,* or *agree with*? *Disgusted at* or *disgusted with*? *Smile about, smile at, smile on,* or *smile over*?

Depending on what you mean, sometimes one alternative is correct, sometimes another. When you're at work on a paper, the dictionary can help you choose. Look up *agree* in *The American Heritage Dictionary,* for instance, and you will find *agree to, agree with, agree about, agree on,* and *agree that* illustrated with sentence examples that make clear just where and when each combination is appropriate. You can then pick the idiom that belongs in the sentence you are working on. In the long run, though, you learn to use idioms accurately in your writing by reading the work of careful writers, by absorbing what they do, and by doing likewise.

**EXERCISE 21–1**

## Selecting Words

Revise the following passage to replace inappropriate connotations, clichés, and faulty idioms. Example:

> The Mayan city of Uxmal is a common tourist attraction. The ruins have stood alone in the jungle since time immemorial.

> The Mayan city of Uxmal is a popular tourist attraction. The ruins have stood alone in the jungle since ancient times.

We spent the first day of our holiday in Mexico arguing around what we wanted to see on our second day. We finally agreed to a day trip out to some Mayan ruins. The next day we arrived on the Mayan city of Uxmal, which is as old as the hills. It really is a sight for sore eyes, smack dab in a jungle stretching as far as the eye can see, with many buildings still covered in plants and iguanas moving quickly over the decayed buildings. The view from the top of the "Soothsayer's Temple" was good, although we noticed storm clouds gathering in the distance. The rain held up until we got off of the pyramid, but we drove back to the hotel in a lot of rain. After a day of sightseeing, we were so hungry that we could have eaten a horse, so we had a good meal before we turned in.

# 22. *Bias-Free Language*

The words we use reveal our attitudes — our likes and dislikes, our preferences and prejudices. Favorable or unfavorable connotations help us to express how we feel. A *brat* is quite different from a *little angel*, a *childish prank* from an *act of vandalism*, a *jalopy* from a *limousine*.

Language with unfavorable connotations has the power to insult or hurt someone. Thoughtful writers attempt to avoid harmful bias in language. They respect their readers and don't want to insult them or make them angry. They realize that discriminatory language can impede communication. According to Rosalie Maggio, "Ordinary people have chosen to replace linguistic pejoration and disrespect with words that grant full humanity and equality to all of us."[2] You may not be able to eliminate discrimination from society, but you can eliminate discriminatory language in your writing. Be on the lookout for words that insult or stereotype individuals or groups by gender, age, race, ethnic origin, sexual preference, or religion.

Accept your inability to change the English language overnight, single-handedly. As more people come to regard themselves as equals, the language will increasingly reflect the reality. Meanwhile, in your writing, try to be fair to all individuals without succumbing either to clumsiness or to grammatical error.

**22a.**    To eliminate sexist language, use alternatives that make no reference to gender.

Among the prime targets of American feminists in the 1960s and 1970s was the male bias built into the English language. Why, they asked, do we talk about *prehistoric man, manpower,* and *the brotherhood of man,* when by *man* we mean the entire human race? Why do we focus attention on the gender of an accomplished woman by calling her a *poetess* or a *lady doctor*? Why does a letter to a corporation have to begin "Gentlemen:"?

Early efforts to provide alternatives to sexist language often led to awkward, even ungrammatical solutions. To substitute "Everyone prefers their own customs" for "Everyone prefers *his* own customs" is to replace sexism with bad grammar. "Everyone prefers his or her [*or* his/her] own customs" is correct, but sometimes clumsy. Even clumsier is "Was it George or Jane who submitted his or her [his/her] resignation?" *Chairperson, policeperson, businessperson, spokesperson,* and *congressperson* do not flow easily from tongue or pen; and some people object to *chairwoman, policewoman,* and similar words because they call attention to gender where gender ought not to matter. *Male nurse* or *female supervisor* elicits the same objection.

---

[2] *The Dictionary of Bias-Free Usage: A Guide to Nondiscriminatory Language* (Oryx, 1991) vii.

Some writers try to eliminate sexual bias by alternating between the masculine and feminine genders every few sentences. Dr. Benjamin Spock, when referring to babies in recent revisions of his well-known *Baby and Child Care*, uses *he* and *she* in roughly equal numbers. Some readers find this approach refreshing. Why should we, after all, think of every baby as a boy, every parent as a woman? Other readers find such gender switches confusing.

Well-meaning attempts to invent or borrow neutral third-person pronouns (*thon asks* instead of *he asks* or *she asks*, for instance) have not gained general acceptance. How then can we as sensitive writers minimize the sexist constraints that the English language places in our path? Although there are no hard-and-fast rules, no perfect solutions, we can be aware of the potholes and try to steer around them as smoothly as possible.

## 22b.  Avoid terms that include or imply *man*.

We all know from experience that the most obvious way to neuter *man* or a word starting with *man* is to substitute *human*. The result, however, is often clumsy.

> SEXIST    Mankind has always been obsessed with man's inhumanity to man.
>
> NONSEXIST  Humankind has always been obsessed with humans' inhumanity to other humans.

Adding *hu-* to *man* alleviates sexism but weighs down the sentence. When you run into this problem, think for a moment. Usually you can find a more graceful solution.

> REVISED   Human beings have always been obsessed with people's cruelty to one another.

Similarly, when you face a word that ends with *-man*, you need not simply replace that ending with *-person*. Take a different approach: think about what the word means and find a synonym that is truly neutral.

> SEXIST    Did you leave a note for the mailman?
>
> REVISED   Did you leave a note for the mail carrier?

The same tactic works for designations with a male and a female ending, such as *steward* and *stewardess*.

> SEXIST    Ask your steward [or stewardess] for a pillow.
>
> REVISED   Ask your airline attendant for a pillow.

## 22c.  Use plural instead of singular.

Another way to avoid sexist language is to use the plural rather than the singular (*they* and *their* rather than *he* and *his*). This strategy sometimes has the additional benefit of avoiding an unintentional stereotype, which is always a danger when writers let a single individual stand for a large and diverse group.

| | |
|---|---|
| SEXIST | Today's student values his education. |
| REVISED | Today's students value their education. |
| STEREOTYPE | The Englishman drives on the left-hand side of the road. |
| REVISED | English people drive on the left-hand side of the road. |

## 22d.  Where possible, omit words that denote gender.

If you find yourself using words that denote gender, stop and ask yourself if the words are really necessary. You can make your language more bias-free by ommitting pronouns and other words that needlessly indicate gender.

| | |
|---|---|
| SEXIST | For optimal results, there must be rapport between a stockbroker and his client, a teacher and her student, a doctor and his patient. |
| REVISED | For optimal results, there must be rapport between stockbroker and client, teacher and student, doctor and patient. |
| SEXIST | My uncle is a male nurse and my aunt is a woman doctor. |
| REVISED | My uncle is a nurse and my aunt is a doctor. |

You should also be careful to treat men and women equally in terms of description or title.

| | |
|---|---|
| SEXIST | I now pronounce you man and wife. |
| REVISED | I now pronounce you husband and wife. |
| SEXIST | Please call Mr. Pease, Mr. Mankodi, and Susan Brillantes into the conference room. |
| REVISED | Please call Mr. Pease, Mr. Mankodi, and Ms. Brillantes into the conference room. |

## 22e.  Avoid condescending labels.

A responsible writer does not call women *chicks, coeds, babes, woman drivers,* or any other names that imply that they are not to be taken seriously. Nor should an employee ever be referred to as a *girl* or *boy.* Avoid any terms that put down individuals or groups because of age (*old goat, the grannies*); race or ethnic background (*Indian giver, Chinaman's chance*); or disability (*amputee, handicapped*).

| | |
|---|---|
| CONDESCENDING | The girls in the office bought President Schmutz a birthday cake. |
| REVISED | The secretaries bought President Schmutz a birthday cake. |
| CONDESCENDING | My neighbor is just an old fogy. |
| REVISED | My neighbor has old-fashioned ideas. |

CONDESCENDING I heard that the cripple who lives around the corner won the lottery.

REVISED I heard that the disabled person who lives around the corner won the lottery.

When describing any group, try to use the label or term that the members of that group prefer. While the preferred label is sometimes difficult to determine, the extra effort will be appreciated.

POSSIBLY OFFENSIVE Alice is interested in learning about Oriental culture.

REVISED Alice is interested in learning about Asian culture.

POSSIBLY OFFENSIVE Many of the Hispanics at our school speak Spanish at home.

REVISED Many of the Latino students at our school speak Spanish at home.

## 22f. Avoid implied stereotypes.

Sometimes a negative stereotype is linked to a title or designation indirectly. Aside from a few obvious exceptions such as *mothers* and *fathers*, never assume that all the members of a group are of the same gender.

STEREOTYPE Pilots have little time to spend with their wives and children.

REVISED Pilots have little time to spend with their families.

Sometimes we debase individuals or groups by assigning a stereotypical descriptor to them. Be alert for these widespread biases. Stereotypes that seem positive should also be avoided if they assume that all people of a certain group share a certain characteristic.

STEREOTYPE Roberto isn't very good at paying his rent on time, which doesn't surprise me because he is from Mexico.

REVISED Roberto isn't very good at paying his rent on time.

STEREOTYPE I assume Ben will do very well in medical school because both of his parents are Jewish.

REVISED I assume Ben will do very well in medical school.

## 22g. Use *Ms.* for a woman with no other known title.

*Ms.* is a wonderfully useful form of address. Comparable to *Mr.* for a man, it is easier to use than either *Miss* or *Mrs.* for someone whose marital status you don't know. Now that many married women are keeping their original last names, either professionally or in all areas of their lives, *Ms.* is often the best choice even for someone whose marital status you do know. However, if the woman to whom you are writing holds a doctorate, a professional office, or some other position that comes with a title, use that title rather than *Ms.*

Ms. Jane Doe, Editor. Dear Ms. Doe:
Professor Jane Doe, Department of English. Dear Professor Doe:
Senator Jane Doe, Washington, D.C. Dear Senator Doe:

**EXERCISE 22–1**

### Avoiding Bias

Revise the following sentences to eliminate bias words. Possible revisions for the lettered sentences appear in the back of the book. Example:

> A fireman needs to check his equipment regularly.

> Firefighters need to check their equipment regularly.

a. My cousin volunteered as a candy striper at the old folks' home.
b. The television crew conducted a series of man-on-the street interviews on the new tax proposal.
c. Whether the president of the United States is a Democrat or a Republican, he will always be a symbol of the nation.
d. The senator was highly regarded by voters in her district even though she was a spinster.
e. Simon drinks like an Irishman.

1. Dick drives a Porshe because he likes the way she handles on the road. He gets pretty upset at the little old ladies who slow down traffic.
2. Like most Asian Americans, Soon Li excels at music and mathematics.
3. The new doctors on our staff include Dr. Scalia, Anna Baniski, and Dr. Throckmorton.
4. Our school's extensive athletic program will be of particular interest to Black applicants.
5. The diligent researcher will always find the sources he seeks.

## 23. *Wordiness*

Writers who try to impress their audience by offering few ideas in many words rarely fool anyone but themselves. Concision takes more effort than wordiness, but it pays off in clarity. (For more on how to unpad your prose, see "Cutting and Whittling," p. 411.)

The following list contains common words and phrases that take up more room than they deserve. Each has a shorter substitute. If this list contains some of your favorite expressions, don't worry. Not even the best professional writer is perfectly terse. Still, being aware of verbal shortcuts may help you avoid rambling. The checklist can be useful for self-editing, particularly if you ever face a strict word limit. When you write an article for a college newspaper where space is tight, or a laboratory report that you must squeeze into a standard worksheet, or an assignment limited to six hundred words, use this list to pare your prose to the bone.

CHECKLIST OF WINDY WORDS AND PHRASES

| WORDY VERSION | CONCISE VERSION |
|---|---|
| adequate enough | adequate |
| a period of a week | a week |
| approximately | about |
| area of, field of | [Omit.] |
| arrive at an agreement, conclude an agreement | agree |
| as a result of | because |
| as far as . . . is concerned | about |
| as to whether | whether |
| as you are already well aware | as you know |
| at an earlier point in time | before, earlier |
| at a later moment | after, later |
| join together | join |
| kind of, sort of, type of | [Omit.] |
| large in size, large-sized | large |
| a large number of | many |
| lend assistance to | assist, aid, help |
| main essentials | essentials |
| make contact with | call, talk with |
| members of the opposition | opponents |
| merge together | merge |
| numerous | many |
| numerous and sundry | many different |
| on the occasion of | on |
| on a daily basis | daily |
| other alternatives | alternatives |
| past experience, past history | experience, history |
| persons of the female gender | women |
| persons of the homosexual persuasion | homosexuals, gays, lesbians |
| persons of the Methodist faith | Methodists |
| pertaining to | about, on |
| plan ahead for the future | plan |
| prior to | before |
| put an end to, terminate | end |
| rarely ever, seldom ever | rarely, seldom |
| strongly urge | urge |
| sufficient amount of | enough |
| the reason why | the reason |
| refer to by the name of | call, name |
| refer back to | refer to |
| remarks of a humorous nature, remarks on the humorous side | humorous remarks |
| render completely inoperative | break, smash, destroy |
| repeat again | repeat |
| resemble in appearance | look like |
| respective, respectively | [Omit.] |
| returning back | returning |

| | |
|---|---|
| similar to | like |
| subsequent to | after |
| subsequently | later, then |
| sufficient number (or amount) of | enough |
| true facts | facts, truth |
| until such time | until |
| utilize, make use of | use |
| very | [Omit unless you very much need it.] |
| wastage | waste |
| way in which | way |
| whether or not | whether |

EXERCISE 23–1

## Eliminating Wordiness

Revise the following passage to eliminate wordiness. Example:

> At this point in time, a debate pertaining to freedom of speech is raging across our campuses.

> A debate about freedom of speech is raging across our campuses.

The media in recent times have become obsessed with the conflict on campuses across the nation between freedom of speech and the attempt to protect minorities from verbal abuse. Very innocent remarks or remarks of a humorous nature, sometimes taken out of context, have got a large number of students into trouble for the violation of college speech codes. Numerous students have become very vocal in attacking these "politically correct" speech codes and defending the right to free speech. But is the campaign against the politically correct really pertaining to freedom of speech, or is it itself a way in which to silence debate? Due to the fact that the phrase "politically correct" has become associated with liberal social causes and sensitivity to minority feelings, it now carries a very extraordinary stigma in the eyes of conservatives. It has become a kind of condemnation against which no defense is possible. To accuse someone of being politically correct is to refute their ideas before hearing their argument. The attempt to silence the members of the opposition is a dangerous sign of our times and suggests that we are indeed in the midst of a cultural war.

**Chapter 36**

# Punctuation

## 24. *End Punctuation*

Three marks can signal the end of a sentence: the period, the exclamation point, and the question mark.

**24a.** Use a period to end a declarative sentence, a directive, or an indirect question.

Most English sentences are *declarative,* meaning simply that they make a statement. No matter what its topic, a declarative sentence properly ends with a period.

> Most people on earth are malnourished.

> The Cadillac rounded the corner on two wheels and careened into a newsstand.

A period is also used after a *directive,* a statement telling someone to do something.

> Please send a check or money order with your application.

> Put down your weapons and come out with your hands up.

Some readers are surprised to find a period, not a question mark, at the end of an *indirect question*. But an indirect question is really a kind of declarative sentence: it states that a question was asked or is being asked. Therefore, a period is the right way to end it.

The counselor asked Marcia why she rarely gets to class on time.

I wonder why George didn't show up.

If those sentences were written as *direct questions,* they would require a question mark.

The counselor asked, "Marcia, why do you rarely get to class on time?"

Why, I wonder, didn't George show up?

## 24b. Use a period after most abbreviations.

A period within a sentence shows that what precedes it has been shortened.

Dr. Hooke's plane arrived in Washington, D.C., at 8:00 P.M.

The names of most organizations (YMCA, PTA), countries (USA, UK), and people (JFK, FDR) are abbreviated without periods. Other abbreviations, such as those for academic degrees and designations of time, use periods. (See 32e.)

When an abbreviation that uses periods falls at the end of a sentence, follow it with just one period, not two.

Jim hopes to do graduate work at UCLA after receiving his B.A.

## 24c. Use a question mark to end a direct question.

How many angels can dance on the head of a pin?

The question mark comes at the end of the question even if the question is part of a longer declarative sentence. (See 29a for advice about punctuating indirect quotations and questions.)

"What'll I do now?" Marjorie wailed.

Only if the question is rewritten into indirect form does it end in a period.

Marjorie, wailing, wanted to know what she should do now.

You can use a question mark, also, to indicate doubt about the accuracy of a number or date.

Aristophanes, born in 450 (?) B.C., became the master comic playwright of Greece's Golden Age.

Usually, however, the same purpose can be accomplished more gracefully in words:

Aristophanes, born around 450 B.C., became the master comic playwright of Greece's Golden Age.

In formal writing, avoid using a question mark to express irony or sarcasm: *her generous (?) gift*. If your doubts are worth including, state them directly: *her meager but highly publicized gift*.

**24d.** Use an exclamation point to end an interjection or an urgent command.

An exclamation point signals strong, even violent, emotion. It can end any sentence that requires unusually strong emphasis.

We've struck an iceberg! We're sinking! I can't believe it! This is horrible!

It may mark the short, emphatic structure known as an *interjection*. (See 1h.)

Oh, no! Fire!

Or it may indicate an urgent directive.

Hurry up! Help me!

Because most essays appeal to readers' reason more than to their passions, you will rarely need this punctuation mark in expository writing. In newspaper parlance, exclamation points are *astonishers*. Although they can grab a reader's attention, they cannot hold it. Tossing in an exclamation point, as if it were a firecracker, is no substitute for carefully selected emphatic words and syntax.

**EXERCISE 24–1**

## Using End Punctuation

Where appropriate, correct the end punctuation and internal periods in the following sentences. Give reasons for any changes you make. Some sentences may be correct. Answers for the lettered sentences appear in the back of the book. Example:

Mr. Keung asked if George could manage to get to the church on time?

Mr. Keung asked if George could manage to get to the church on time.

a. Unlike Gerald Ford and L.B.J., who came to the vice-presidency from Congress, George Bush won that office after heading the C.I.A..
b. The population of California is much greater than that of Nevada!
c. Why don't you meet us after the game.
d. "When will the world end," my four-year-old nephew asked in a quavering voice?

e. Yes! The Republicans are worried about the gender gap! They fear that women in increasing numbers will vote for the Democrats! How can the Republicans fight back!

1. If you're not happy in your dorm, why don't you switch to another.
2. "Help, help. It's a murder. Call the police," cried Jim.
3. Petra asked the doctor how else she could have caught the flu?
4. "Does it make sense to you?" he asked, "that the thief took the money but left the credit cards?"
5. In the history of the Cape Cod Community Players (C.C.C.P.), only one managing director has had an MA in theater.
6. "Oh, my God — that's the largest Chihuahua I've ever seen."
7. I didn't ask Sylvia, "Will you go to the meeting?" I told her, "You *will* go to the meeting!"
8. How do you expect me to learn the Latin names of fifty plants in an hour.
9. "Why is the sky blue" is a question that any physicist can answer.
10. So where are all those baby iguanas, anyway!

# 25. *The Comma*

Speech without pauses would be hard to listen to. Likewise, writing without commas would make hard reading. Like a split-second pause in conversation, a *comma* helps your readers to catch the train of your thought. It keeps them, time and again, from stumbling over a solid block of words. A comma can direct readers' attention, pointing them to what you want them to notice. And a well-placed comma can prevent misreading: it keeps your audience from drawing an inaccurate conclusion about what you are trying to tell them.

Consider the following sentence:

Lyman paints fences and bowls.

From this statement, we can deduce that Lyman is a painter who works with both a large and a small brush. But add commas before and after *fences* and the portrait changes:

Lyman paints, fences, and bowls.

Now our man wields a paintbrush, a sword, and a bowling ball. What the reader learns about Lyman's activities depends on how the writer punctuates the sentence. Carefully placed commas prevent misreading and ensure that readers meet the real Lyman.

**25a.** Use a comma with a coordinating conjunction to join two main clauses.

The joint between main clauses has two parts: a coordinating conjunction (*and, but, for, or, nor, so,* or *yet*) and a comma. The comma comes after the first clause, right before the conjunction.

The chocolate pie whooshed through the air, and it landed in Lyman's face.

The pie whooshed with deadly aim, but the agile Lyman ducked.

If your clauses are short and parallel in structure, you may omit the comma.

Spring passed and summer came.

They urged but I refused.

Or you may keep the comma. It can lend your words a speechlike ring, throwing a bit of emphasis on your second clause.

Spring passed, and summer came.

They urged, but I refused.

CAUTION: Don't use a comma with a coordinating conjunction that links two phrases or that links a phrase and a clause.

FAULTY   The mustangs galloped, and cavorted across the plain.

REVISED   The mustangs galloped and cavorted across the plain.

**EDITING CHECKLIST**

## Using the Comma Where Required

- Are two main clauses joined with a coordinating conjunction and a comma? (25a)
- Is there a comma after each introductory clause, phrase, or word? (25b)
- Are items in a series separated by commas? (25c)
- Is there a comma or commas between adjectives that are separate and equal modifiers of the same noun (coordinate adjectives)? (25d)
- Is there a comma before and after each nonrestrictive phrase or clause? (25e)

See 25f–25m for other uses of the comma.

**25b.**   Use a comma after an introductory clause, phrase, or word.

*Weeping,* Lydia stumbled down the stairs.

*Before that,* Arthur saw her reading an old love letter.

*If he knew who the writer was,* he didn't tell.

Placed after any such opening word, phrase, or subordinate clause, a comma tells your reader: "Enough preliminaries — now the main clause starts." (See 3 for a quick refresher on phrases and clauses.)

EXCEPTION: You need not use a comma after a single introductory word or a short phrase or clause if there is no danger of misreading.

*Sooner or later* Lydia will tell us the whole story.

## Using Commas

Add any necessary commas to the following sentences, and remove any commas that do not belong. Some sentences may be correct. Answers for the lettered sentences appear in the back of the book. Example:

> Your dog may have sharp teeth but my lawyer can bite harder.

> Your dog may have sharp teeth, but my lawyer can bite harder.

a. When Verity gets to Paris I hope she'll drop me a line.
b. Beethoven's deafness kept him from hearing his own music yet he continued to compose.
c. Adrian plans to apply for a grant, and if her application is accepted, she intends to spend a year in Venezuela.
d. The cherries are overripe for picking has been delayed.
e. Antonio expected Minnesota to be cold, but was unprepared for the frigid temperatures of his first winter there.

1. During the summer of the great soybean failure Larry took little interest in national affairs.
2. Unaware of the world he slept and grew within his mother's womb.
3. While across the nation farmers were begging for mortgages he swam without a care.
4. Neither the mounting agricultural crisis, nor any other current events, disturbed his tranquillity.
5. In fact you might have called him irresponsible.

**25c.** Use a comma between items in a series.

When you list three or more items, whether they are nouns, verbs, adjectives, adverbs, or entire phrases or clauses, separate them with commas.

> Country ham, sweet corn, tacos, bratwurst, and Indian pudding weighted Aunt Gertrude's table.

> Joel prefers music that shakes, rattles, and rolls.

> In one afternoon, we rode a Mississippi riverboat, climbed the Matterhorn, voyaged beneath the sea, and flew on a rocket through space.

Notice that no comma *follows* the final item in the series.

NOTE: Some writers (especially Britons and journalists) omit the comma *before* the final item in the series. This custom has no noticeable advantage. It has the disadvantages of throwing off the rhythm of a sentence and, in some cases, obscuring the writer's meaning. Using the comma in such a case is never wrong; omitting it can create confusion.

> I was met at the station by my cousins, brother and sister.

Who are these people? Are they a brother-and-sister pair who are the writer's cousins or a group consisting of the writer's cousins, her brother, and her sister? If they are in fact more than two people, a comma would clear up the confusion.

> I was met at the station by my cousins, brother, and sister.

**25d.** Use a comma between coordinate adjectives, but not between cumulative adjectives.

Adjectives that function independently of each other, even though they modify the same noun, are called *coordinate adjectives.* Set them off with commas.

> Ruth was a clear, vibrant, persuasive speaker.

> Life is nasty, brutish, and short.

CAUTION: Don't use a comma after the final adjective before a noun.

> FAULTY   My economics professor was a wonderful, brilliant, caring, teacher.

> REVISED   My economics professor was a wonderful, brilliant, caring teacher.

To check whether adjectives are coordinate, apply two tests. Can you rearrange the adjectives without distorting the meaning of the sentence? (*Ruth was a persuasive, vibrant, clear speaker.*) Can you insert *and* between them? (*Life is nasty and brutish and short.*)

If the answer to both questions is yes, the adjectives are coordinate. Removing any one of them would not greatly affect the others' impact. Use commas between them to show that they are separate and equal.

NOTE: If you choose to link coordinate adjectives with *and* or another conjunction, omit the commas.

> New York City is huge and dirty and beautiful.

*Cumulative adjectives* work together to create a single unified picture of the noun they modify. Remove any one of them and you change the picture. No commas separate cumulative adjectives.

> Ruth has two small white poodles.

> Who's afraid of the big bad wolf?

If you rearrange cumulative adjectives or insert *and* between them, the effect of the sentence is distorted (*two white small poodles; the big and bad wolf*).

---

EXERCISE 25–2 | **Using Commas**

Add any necessary commas to the following sentences, remove any commas that do not belong, and change any punctuation that is incorrect. Some sentences may be correct. Answers for the lettered sentences appear in the back of the book. Example:

Mel has been a faithful hardworking consistent pain in the neck.

Mel has been a faithful, hardworking, consistent pain in the neck.

a. Mrs. Carver looks like a sweet, little, old lady, but she plays a wicked electric guitar.
b. Her bass player, her drummer and her keyboard player all live at the same rest home.
c. They practice individually in the afternoon, rehearse together at night and play at the home's Saturday night dances.
d. The Rest Home Rebels have to rehearse quietly, and cautiously, to keep from disturbing the other residents.
e. Mrs. Carver has two Fender guitars, a Stratocaster and a Telecaster, and she also has an acoustic twelve-string Gibson.

1. When she breaks a string, she doesn't want her elderly crew to have to grab the guitar change the string and hand it back to her, before the song ends.
2. The Rest Home Rebels' favorite bands are U-2, the Talking Heads and Lester Lanin and his orchestra.
3. They watch a lot of MTV because it is fast-paced colorful exciting and informative and it has more variety than soap operas.
4. Just once, Mrs. Carver wants to play in a really, huge, sold-out, arena.
5. She hopes to borrow the rest home's big, white, van to take herself her band and their equipment to a major, professional, downtown, recording studio.

## 25e.   Use commas to set off a nonrestrictive phrase or clause.

A *nonrestrictive modifier* adds a fact that, while perhaps interesting and valuable, isn't essential. You could leave it out of the sentence and still make good sense. When a word in your sentence is modified by a nonrestrictive phrase or clause, set off the modifier with commas before and after it.

Potts Alley, *which runs north from Chestnut Street,* is too narrow and crowded for cars to get through.

At the end of the alley, *where the street fair book sale was held last summer,* a getaway car waited.

A *restrictive modifier* is essential. Omit it and you significantly change the meaning of both the modified word and the sentence. Such a modifier is called *restrictive* because it limits what it modifies: we are talking about this specific place, person, action, or whatever, and no other. Because a restrictive modifier is part of the identity of whatever it modifies, no commas set it off from the rest of the sentence.

They picked the alley *that runs north from Chestnut Street* because it is close to the highway.

Anyone *who robs my house* will regret it.

Leave out the modifier in that last sentence — write instead *Anyone will regret it* — and you change the meaning of your subject from potential robbers to all humankind.

Here are two more examples to help you tell a nonrestrictive modifier, which you set off with commas, from a restrictive modifier, which you don't.

Germans, who smoke, live to be 120.

Germans who smoke live to be 120.

See what a difference a couple of commas make? The first sentence declares that all Germans smoke, but they nevertheless live to old age. The second sentence singles out smokers from the rest of the population and declares that they reach age 120.

NOTE: Use *that* to introduce (or to recognize) a restrictive phrase or clause. Use *which* to introduce (or to recognize) a nonrestrictive phrase or clause.

The food *that I love best* is chocolate.

Chocolate, *which I love*, is not on my diet.

**25f.** Use commas to set off nonrestrictive appositives.

An *appositive* is a noun or noun phrase that renames or amplifies the noun it follows. (See 3d.) Like the modifiers discussed in 25e, an appositive can be either restrictive or nonrestrictive. If it is nonrestrictive — if the sentence still makes sense when the appositive is omitted or changed — then set it off with commas before and after.

My third ex-husband, *Hugo*, will be glad to meet you.

We are bringing dessert, *a blueberry pie*, to follow your wonderful dinner.

Hugo created the recipe for his latest cookbook, *Pies! Surprise!*

If the appositive is restrictive — if you can't take it out or change it without changing your meaning — then include it without commas.

Of all the men I've been married to, my ex-husband *Hugo* is the best cook.

His cookbook *Pies! Surprise!* is selling better than his beef, wine, and fruit cookbooks.

**EXERCISE 25–3** | **Using Commas**

Add any necessary commas to the following sentences, and remove any commas that do not belong. You may have to draw your own conclusions about what the writer meant to say. Some sentences may be correct. Possible revisions for the lettered sentences appear in the back of the book. Example:

Jay and his wife the former Laura McCready were high school sweethearts.

Jay and his wife, the former Laura McCready, were high school sweethearts.

a. The aye-aye which is a member of the lemur family is threatened with extinction.
b. The party, a dismal occasion ended earlier than we had expected.
c. Secretary Stern warned that the concessions, that the West was prepared to make, would be withdrawn if not matched by the East.
d. Although both of Don's children are blond, his daughter Sharon has darker hair than his son Jake.
e. Herbal tea which has no caffeine makes a better after-dinner drink than coffee.

1. The colony, that the English established at Roanoke disappeared mysteriously.
2. If the base commanders had checked their gun room where powder is stored, they would have found several hundred pounds missing.
3. Brazil's tropical rain forests which help produce the air we breathe all over the world, are being cut down at an alarming rate.
4. Senator Edward Kennedy's late brothers, Joe and Jack, were older than his third brother, Bobby.
5. Excavations have revealed that Paris which was a thriving Roman town developed on the Île de la Cité an island in the Seine.

## 25g.  Use commas to set off conjunctive adverbs.

A key function of the comma, as you probably have noticed, is to insert material into a sentence. To perform this service, commas work in pairs. When you drop a conjunctive adverb such as *furthermore, however,* or *nevertheless* into the midst of a clause, set it off with commas before and after it. (See 1g for a full list of conjunctive adverbs.)

Using lead paint in homes has been illegal, *however,* since 1973.

Builders, *indeed,* gave it up some twenty years earlier.

## 25h.  Use commas to set off parenthetical expressions.

Use a pair of commas around any parenthetical expression — that is, a transitional expression (*for example, as a result, in contrast*) or any kind of aside from you to your readers.

Professional home inspectors, *for this reason,* are often asked to test for lead paint.

The idea, *of course,* is to protect small children who might eat flaking paint.

The Cosmic Construction Company never used lead paint, *or so their spokesperson says,* even when it was legal.

**25i.** Use commas to set off a phrase or clause expressing contrast.

> It was Rudolph, *not Dasher*, who had a red nose.

> EXCEPTION: Short contrasting phrases beginning with *but* need not be set off by commas.

> It was not Dasher but Rudolph who had a red nose.

**25j.** Use commas to set off an absolute phrase.

An *absolute phrase* modifies an entire clause rather than a single word. (See 3c.) The link between an absolute phrase and the rest of the sentence is a comma, or two commas if the phrase falls in mid-sentence.

> *Our worst fears drawing us together*, we huddled over the telegram.

> Luke, *his knife being the sharpest*, slit the envelope.

---

EXERCISE 25–4 | **Using Commas**

Add any necessary commas to the following sentences, remove any commas that do not belong, and change any punctuation that is incorrect. Answers for the lettered sentences appear in the back of the book. Example:

> The screenwriter unlike the director believes the film should be shown unedited.

> The screenwriter, unlike the director, believes the film should be shown unedited.

a. I want to warn you however that we are experiencing some problems with our public address system.
b. Our speaker, listed in your program as a professor, tells us that on the contrary she is a teaching assistant.
c. The discussion that followed was not so much a debate, as a free-for-all.
d. Alex insisted that predestination not free will shapes human destiny.
e. Shirley on the other hand, who looks so calm, passionately defended the role of choice.

1. Believing Cortés to be a god the Aztecs at first did not resist the invasion.
2. The car rolled down the hill, a problem Bill should have anticipated when he left it in gear and crashed into a telephone pole.
3. This attic apartment its windows notwithstanding, is very hot in summer.
4. The orchard smelled fruity and felt squishy underfoot; hundreds of apples having fallen from the trees.
5. The essay suggested that it is the environment not heredity that has the greater influence on character.

**25k.** Use commas to set off a direct quotation from your own words, and vice versa.

When you briefly quote someone, distinguish the source's words from yours with commas (and, of course, quotation marks). When you insert an explanation into a quotation (such as *he said*), set that off with commas.

> Shakespeare wrote, "Some are born great, some achieve greatness, and some have greatness thrust upon them."

> "The best thing that can come with success," commented the actress Liv Ullmann, "is the knowledge that it is nothing to long for."

Notice that the comma always comes *before* the quotation marks. (For more on how to use other punctuation with quotation marks, see 29h and 29i.)

EXCEPTION: Do not use a comma with a very short quotation or one introduced by *that*.

> Don't tell me "yes" if you mean "maybe."

> Jules said that "Nothing ventured, nothing gained" is his motto.

Don't use a comma with any quotation that is run into your own sentence and that reads as part of your sentence. Often such quotations are introduced by linking verbs.

> Her favorite statement at age three was "I can do it myself."

> It was Shakespeare who originated the expression "my salad days, when I was green in judgment."

**25l.** Use commas around *yes* and *no*, mild interjections, tag questions, and the name or title of someone directly addressed.

| | |
|---|---|
| YES AND NO | *Yes*, I would like to own a Rolls-Royce, but, *no*, I didn't place an order for one. |
| INTERJECTION | *Well*, don't blame it on me. |
| TAG QUESTION | It would be fun to drive down Main Street in a Silver Cloud, *wouldn't it?* |
| DIRECT ADDRESS | Drive us home, *James*. |

**25m.** Use commas to set off dates, states, countries, and addresses.

> On June 6, 1969, Ned Shaw was born.

> East Rutherford, New Jersey, seemed like Paris, France, to him.

Shortly after his tenth birthday his family moved to 11 Maple Street, Middletown, Ohio.

NOTE: Do not use a comma between a state and a zip code: *Bedford, MA 01730*.

**EXERCISE 25–5**

## Using Commas

Add any necessary commas to the following sentences, remove any commas that do not belong, and change any punctuation that is incorrect. Some sentences may be correct. Answers for the lettered sentences appear in the back of the book. Example:

> When Alexander Graham Bell said "Mr. Watson come here, I want you" the telephone entered history.

> When Alexander Graham Bell said, "Mr. Watson, come here, I want you," the telephone entered history.

a. On October 2 1969 the future discoverer of antigravity tablets was born.
b. Corwin P. Grant entered the world while his parents were driving to a hospital in Costa Mesa California.
c. The car radio was playing that old song "Be My Baby."
d. Today ladies and gentlemen Corwin enjoys worldwide renown.
e. Schoolchildren from Augusta Maine to Azuza California can recite his famous comment "It was my natural levity that led me to overcome gravity."

1. Yes I was born on April 14 1973 in Bombay India.
2. Move downstage Gary, for Pete's sake or you'll run into Mrs. Clackett.
3. Vicki my precious, when you say, "great" or "terrific," look as though you mean it.
4. Perhaps you have forgotten darling that sometimes you make mistakes, too.
5. Well Dotty, it only makes sense that when you say, "Sardines!," you should go off to get the sardines.

**25n.**  Do not use a comma to separate a subject from its verb or a verb from its object.

FAULTY   The slim athlete driving the purple Jaguar, was the Reverend Mr. Fuld. [Subject separated from verb.]

REVISED  The slim athlete driving the purple Jaguar was the Reverend Mr. Fuld.

FAULTY   The new president should not have given his campaign manager, such a prestigious appointment. [Verb separated from direct object.]

REVISED  The new president should not have given his campaign manager such a prestigious appointment.

**25o.** Do not use a comma between words or phrases joined by correlative or coordinating conjunctions.

Be careful not to divide a compound subject or predicate unnecessarily with a comma.

FAULTY   Neither Peter Pan, nor the fairy Tinkerbell, saw the pirates sneaking toward their hideout. [Compound subject.]

REVISED   Neither Peter Pan nor the fairy Tinkerbell saw the pirates sneaking toward their hideout.

FAULTY   The chickens clucked, and pecked, and flapped their wings. [Compound predicate.]

REVISED   The chickens clucked and pecked and flapped their wings.

**25p.** Do not use a comma before the first or after the last item in a series.

FAULTY   We had to see, my mother's doctor, my father's lawyer, and my dog's veterinarian, in one afternoon.

REVISED   We had to see my mother's doctor, my father's lawyer, and my dog's veterinarian in one afternoon.

**25q.** Do not use a comma to set off a restrictive word, phrase, or clause.

A restrictive modifier is essential to the definition or identification of whatever it modifies; a nonrestrictive modifier is not. If you are not sure whether an element in your sentence is restrictive, review 25e.

FAULTY   The fireworks, that I saw on Sunday, were the best ones I've ever seen.

REVISED   The fireworks that I saw on Sunday were the best ones I've ever seen.

**25r.** Do not use commas to set off indirect quotations.

When *that* introduces a quotation, the quotation is an indirect one and requires neither a comma nor quotation marks.

FAULTY   He told us that, we shouldn't have done it.

FAULTY   He told us that, "You shouldn't have done it."

REVISED   He told us that we shouldn't have done it.

This sentence also would be correct if it were recast as a direct quotation, with a comma and quotation marks.

REVISED   He told us, "You shouldn't have done it."

**EDITING CHECKLIST**

## Recognizing Misused Commas

- Have you used a comma between adjectives that depend on each other (cumulative adjectives)? (25d)
- Have you used a comma to separate a subject from its verb or a verb from its object? (25n)
- Have you used a comma between words or phrases joined by a coordinating conjunction? (25o)
- Have you divided a compound subject or predicate unnecessarily with a comma? (25o)
- Have you used a comma before the first or after the last item in a series? (25p)
- Have you used a comma to set off a restrictive word, phrase, or clause? (25q)
- Have you used a comma to set off an indirect quotation? (25r)

If the answer to any of these questions is yes, the comma is used incorrectly.

**EXERCISE 25–6**

## Comma Review

Revise the following passage, adding any necessary commas, removing any commas that do not belong, and changing any punctuation that is incorrect. Example:

> Everyone knows the myth of Atlantis the island, that sank beneath the waves.

> Everyone knows the myth of Atlantis, the island that sank beneath the waves.

> Like many old legends, the myth of Atlantis may be a distant memory of a historical event — the volcanic eruption of Thera a Greek island in 1628 B.C.E. Thera which is located in the eastern Mediterranean had trading connections with Crete the center of Minoan civilization. The Minoans had created one of the most sophisticated, affluent and influential civilizations in the world. Minoan influence and trade reached, Egypt, Cyprus and the Levant and the people of Thera where the eruption occurred also had important trading links with the Minoans. With plenty of warning of the coming explosion the inhabitants of Thera fled the island never to return. The eruption of Thera, resulted in the decline of Minoan civilization or so it is believed because of the tidal waves that damaged Minoan ports. The fame of Minoan power however endured. The civilization that dominated the Mediterranean became legendary and out of these myths developed the story of Atlantis the sophisticated wealthy and powerful island that sank beneath the sea.

# 26. *The Semicolon*

A semicolon is a sort of compromise between a comma and a period: it creates a stop without ending a sentence.

**26a.** Use a semicolon to join two main clauses not joined by a coordinating conjunction.

Suppose, having written one statement, you want to add another. You could start a new sentence, but let's say that both statements are closely related in sense. You decide to keep them both in a single sentence.

Shooting clay pigeons was my mother's favorite sport; she would smash them for hours at a time.

A semicolon is a good substitute for a period when you don't want to bring your readers to a complete stop.

By the yard life is hard; by the inch it's a cinch.

I never travel without my diary; one should always have something sensational to read in the train.

Remember that usually when you join two statements with a coordinating conjunction (*and, but, for, or, nor, so, yet*), no semicolon is called for — just use a comma. (For exceptions to this general rule, see 26d.)

 **EDITING CHECKLIST**

### Using the Semicolon

- Does a semicolon join two main clauses not joined with a coordinating conjunction? (26a)
- Does a semicolon join two main clauses that are linked by a conjunctive adverb? (26b)
- Do semicolons separate items in a series that contain internal punctuation or that are long and complex? (26c)
- Do semicolons separate main clauses that contain internal punctuation or that are long and complex? (26d)
- Does a comma, not a semicolon, separate a phrase or subordinate clause from the rest of the sentence? (26d)

**26b.** Use a semicolon to join two main clauses that are linked by a conjunctive adverb.

When the second of two statements begins with (or includes) a conjunctive adverb, you can join it to the first statement with a semicolon. Common conjunctive adverbs include *also, consequently, however, indeed, nevertheless, still, therefore,* and *thus.* (For a complete list, see 1g.)

Bert is a stand-out player; *indeed,* he's the one hope of our team.

We yearned to attend the concert; tickets, *however,* were hard to come by.

Note in the second sentence that the conjunctive adverb falls within the second main clause. No matter where the conjunctive adverb appears, the semicolon is placed between the two clauses.

**26c.** Use a semicolon to separate items in a series that contain internal punctuation or that are long and complex.

The semicolon is especially useful for setting off one group of items from another. More powerful than a comma, it divides a series of series.

The auctioneer sold clocks, watches, and cameras; freezers of steaks and tons of bean sprouts; motorcycles, cars, speedboats, canoes, and cabin cruisers; and rare coins, curious stamps, and precious stones.

If the writer had used commas in place of semicolons in that sentence, the divisions would have been harder to notice.

Commas are not the only internal punctuation that warrants the extra force of semicolons between items.

> The auctioneer sold clocks and watches (with or without hands); freezers of steaks and tons of bean sprouts; trucks and motorcycles (some of which had working engines); and dozens of smaller items.

**26d.** Use a semicolon to separate main clauses that are long and complex or that contain internal punctuation.

The semicolon also separates the clauses in a long sentence of two or more clauses, at least one of which contains internal punctuation.

> Though we had grown up together, laughing and playing like brother and sister, I had never regarded Spike as a possible lover; and his abrupt proposal took me by surprise.

In that sentence, an important break between clauses needs a mark stronger than a comma to give it impact. A semicolon is appropriate, even though it stands before a coordinating conjunction — where, ordinarily, a comma would suffice.

You can see the difference between a compound sentence joined with a comma and one joined with a semicolon in these examples:

> Captain Bob planned the hog-riding contest for Thursday, but it rained.

> Captain Bob, that old cynic, planned the hog-riding contest for Thursday despite a ban by the city council; but it rained.

You would not be wrong if you kept the original comma between clauses in the second sentence. The sentence is easier to read, however, with a semicolon at its main intersection.

A semicolon can do the same job for clauses that contain internal punctuation other than commas.

> Captain Bob — that cynical crowd assembler — planned the hog-riding contest for Thursday (although the city council had banned such events); but it rained.

You also can use a semicolon with a coordinating conjunction to link clauses that have no internal punctuation but that are long and complex.

> The powers behind Her Majesty's secret service occasionally deem it advisable to terminate the infiltrations of an enemy agent by ending his life; and in such cases they generally call on James Bond.

**26e.** Use a comma, not a semicolon, to separate a phrase or subordinate clause from the rest of a sentence.

Remember that a semicolon has the force of a period; its job is to create a strong pause in a sentence, especially between main clauses. When your purpose is simply to add a phrase to a clause, use a comma, not a semicolon.

FAULTY    The road is long; winding through many towns.

REVISED    The road is long, winding through many towns.

Similarly, use a comma, not a semicolon, to join a subordinate clause to a main clause.

FAULTY    Columbus sailed unknowingly toward the New World; while Ferdinand and Isabella waited for news from China.

REVISED    Columbus sailed unknowingly toward the New World, while Ferdinand and Isabella waited for news from China.

**EXERCISE 26–1**

## Using Semicolons

Add any necessary semicolons to the following sentences, and change any that are incorrectly used. Some sentences may be correct. Answers for the lettered sentences appear in the back of the book. Example:

If you knew all the facts; you would see that I am right.

If you knew all the facts, you would see that I am right.

a. Gasoline prices almost always rise at the start of the tourist season, this year will be no exception.
b. I disagree with your point, however I appreciate your reasons for stating it.
c. The garden is a spectacular display of fountains and gargoyles, beds of lilies, zinnias, and hollyhocks, bushes shaped like animals, climbing roses, wisteria, and ivy, and lawns as wide as golf greens.
d. Janet has not had much money this term; but she hopes to get a part-time job this summer.
e. Dr. Elliott's intervention in the dispute was well intentioned, nevertheless it was unfortunate.

1. When they opened the tomb they found crystal cups, onyx bowls, and alabaster dishes, cloaks, sandals, and jewelry, and gold and silver coins from the first century B.C.E.
2. If that shyster deceives you once, shame on him, if he deceives you twice, shame on you.
3. A Newfoundland dog is huge and furry; much like a Saint Bernard.
4. Senator Omaguchi favors increasing state aid to small businesses, he believes however that such a bill cannot pass this year.
5. The east coast of Britain is fairly flat, the west is more rugged and mountainous.
6. The town council voted to approve the affordable housing project, a decision that may, over time, lead to a tax increase.
7. If the residents and tourists of Athens were willing to leave their automobiles outside the city, air pollution would not threaten the caryatids on the Acropolis, but the impracticality of banning cars has forced authorities to move those stone maidens to a museum.
8. The resolution must pass by a two-thirds majority, otherwise it fails, and its supporters must reintroduce it next year.

9. The teachers on the School Committee are hoping the contract amendment will pass; for they are its primary supporters.
10. Soon there were widespread desertions. The soldiers had had enough of war.

# 27. *The Colon*

A colon introduces a further thought, one added to throw light on a first. In using it, a writer declares: "What follows will clarify what I've just said."

> Her Majesty's navy has three traditions: rum, sodomy, and the lash.
> — Winston Churchill

Some writers use a capital letter to start any complete sentence that follows a colon; others prefer a lowercase letter. Both habits are acceptable; but whichever you choose, be consistent. A *phrase* that follows a colon always begins with a lowercase letter.

**27a.** Use a colon between two main clauses if the second exemplifies, explains, or summarizes the first.

Like a semicolon, a colon can join two sentences into one. The chief difference is this: a semicolon says merely that two main clauses are related; a colon says that the second clause gives an example or explanation of the point made in the first clause. You can think of a colon as an abbreviation for *that is* or *for example*.

> Mayor Curley was famed as a silver-tongued orator: it is said that, with a few well-chosen words, he could extract campaign contributions from a mob intent on seeing him hanged.

> She tried everything: she scoured the library, made dozens of phone calls, wrote letters, even consulted a lawyer.

**27b.** Use a colon to introduce a list or a series.

A colon can introduce a word, a phrase, or a series as well as a second main clause. Sometimes the introduction is made stronger by *as follows* or *the following*.

> The dance steps are as follows: forward, back, turn, and glide.

> Engrave the following truth upon your memory: a colon is always constructed of two dots.

When a colon introduces a series of words or phrases, it often means *such as* or *for instance*. A list of examples after a colon need not include *and* before the last item unless all possible examples have been stated.

On a Saturday night many different kinds of people crowd our downtown area: gamblers, drifters, bored senior citizens, college students out for a good time.

## 27c.  Use a colon to introduce an appositive.

An *appositive* is a noun or noun phrase that renames another noun. A colon can introduce an appositive when the colon is preceded by an independent clause.

I have discovered the key to the future: plastics.

## 27d.  Use a colon to introduce a long or comma-filled quotation.

Sometimes you can't conveniently introduce a quoted passage with a comma. Perhaps the quotation is too long or heavily punctuated; perhaps your prefatory remarks demand a longer pause than a comma provides. In either case, use a colon.

God told Adam and Eve: "Be fruitful, and multiply, and replenish the earth, and subdue it."

## 27e.  Use a colon when convention calls for it.

| AFTER A SALUTATION | Dear Professor James:<br>Dear Sir or Madam: |
| --- | --- |
| BIBLICAL CITATIONS | Genesis 4:7 [The book of Genesis, chapter four, seventh verse.] |
| BOOK TITLES<br>AND SUBTITLES | *In the Beginning: Creation Stories from around the World*<br>*Convergences: Essays on Art and Literature* |
| SOURCE REFERENCES | Welty, Eudora. *The Eye of the Story: Selected Essays and Reviews.* New York: Random, 1978. |
| TIME OF DAY | 2:02 P.M. |

## 27f.  Use a colon only at the end of a main clause.

In a sentence, a colon always follows a clause, never a phrase. Avoid using a colon between a verb and its object, between a preposition and its object, and before a list introduced by *such as*. Any time you are in doubt about whether to use a colon, first make sure that the preceding statement is a complete sentence. Then you will not litter your writing with unnecessary colons.

FAULTY   My mother and father are: Jill and Jim.

REVISED   My mother and father are Jill and Jim.

FAULTY   Many great inventors have changed our lives, such as: Edison, Marconi, and Hymie Glutz.

REVISED   Many great inventors have changed our lives, such as Edison, Marconi, and Hymie Glutz. *Or* Many great inventors have changed our lives: Edison, Marconi, Hymie Glutz.

Use either *such as* or a colon. You don't need both.

EXERCISE 27–I

## Using Colons

Add, remove, or replace colons wherever appropriate in the following sentences. Where necessary, revise the sentences further to support your changes in punctuation. Some sentences may be correct. Possible revisions for the lettered sentences appear in the back of the book. Example:

Yum-Yum Burger has franchises in the following cities; New York, Chicago, Miami, San Francisco, and Seattle.

Yum-Yum Burger has franchises in the following cities: New York, Chicago, Miami, San Francisco, and Seattle.

a. The Continuing Education Program offers courses in: building and construction management, engineering, and design.
b. The interview ended with a test of skills, taking dictation, operating the switchboard, proofreading documents, and typing a sample letter.
c. The sample letter began, "Dear Mr. Rasheed, Please accept our apologies for the late shipment."
d. Constance quoted Proverbs 8, 18: "Riches and honor are with me."
e. A book that profoundly impressed me was Kurt Vonnegut's *Cat's Cradle* (New York, Dell, 1963).

1. The following rhyme was written in the eighteenth century for the collar of the king's dog at Kew Gardens, London, "I AM his Highness Dog at Kew;/Pray, tell me Sir, whose Dog are you?"
2. If you go to the beach this summer, remember these three rules: wear plenty of sunscreen, eat plenty of fruit to replace lost fluids, and avoid exposure during the hottest hours of the day.
3. These are my dreams, to ride in a horse-drawn sleigh, to fly in a small plane, to gallop down a beach on horseback, and to cross the ocean in a sailboat.
4. In the case of *Bowers v. Hardwick*, the Supreme Court decided that: citizens had no right to sexual privacy.
5. Paris at night presents an array of characters; sidewalk artists, jugglers, and dancers; rap musicians and one-man bands; hippies, bohemians, and amazed tourists.
6. He ended his speech with a quotation from Homer's *Iliad*, "Whoever obeys the gods, to him they particularly listen."
7. To get onto Route 6: take Bay Lane to Old Stage Road, turn right, and go straight to the end.
8. Professor Bligh's book is called *Management, A Networking Approach*.
9. George handed Cynthia a note, "Meet me after class under the big clock on Main Street."
10. Rosa expected to arrive at 4.10, but she didn't get there until 4.20.

# 28. *The Apostrophe*

Use apostrophes for three purposes: to show possession, to indicate an omission, and to add an ending to a number, letter, or abbreviation.

**28a.**  To make a singular noun possessive, add –'s.

The *plumber's* wrench left grease stains on *Harry's* shirt.

Even when your singular noun ends with the sound of *s*, form its possessive case by adding -'s.

*Felix's* roommate enjoys reading *Henry James's* novels.

Some writers find it awkward to add -'s to nouns that already end in an -s, especially those of two syllables or more. You may, if you wish, form such a possessive by adding only an apostrophe.

The Egyptian king *Cheops'* death occurred more than two thousand years before *Socrates'*.

**28b.**  To make a plural noun ending in -s possessive, add an apostrophe.

A *stockbrokers'* meeting combines *foxes'* cunning with the noisy chaos of a *boys'* locker room.

**28c.**  To make a plural noun not ending in -s possessive, add -'s.

Nouns such as *men, mice, geese,* and *alumni* form the possessive case the same way as singular nouns: with -'s.

What effect has the *women's* liberation movement had on *children's* literature?

**28d.**  To show joint possession by two people or groups, add an apostrophe or -'s to the second noun of the pair.

I left my *mother and father's* house with our *friends and neighbors'* good wishes.

If the two members of a noun pair possess a set of things individually, add an apostrophe or -'s to each noun.

*Men's* and *women's* marathon records are improving steadily.

**28e.**  To make a compound noun possessive, add an apostrophe or -'s to the last word in the compound.

A compound noun consists of more than one word (*commander in chief, sons-in-law*); it may be either singular or plural. (See 37a–5 for plurals of compound words.)

The *commander in chief's* duties will end on July 1.

Esther does not approve of her *sons-in-law's* professions, but she is glad to see her daughters happily married.

**28f.** To make an indefinite pronoun possessive, add *-'s.*

Indefinite pronouns such as *anyone, nobody,* and *another* are usually singular in meaning, so they form the possessive case the same way as singular nouns: with *-'s.* (See 28a.)

What caused the accident is *anybody's* guess; but it appears to be *no one's* fault.

**28g.** To indicate the possessive of a personal pronoun, use its possessive case.

The personal pronouns — *I, me, he, she, it, him, her, we, us, they, them,* and *who* — are irregular; each has its own possessive form. No possessive personal pronoun contains an apostrophe. If you are ever tempted to make a personal pronoun possessive by adding an apostrophe or *-'s,* resist the temptation.

NOTE: If you learn nothing else this year, learn when to write *its* (no apostrophe) and when to write *it's* (with an apostrophe). *Its* is always a possessive pronoun.

I retreated when the Murphys' German shepherd bared *its* fangs.

*It's* is always a contraction.

*It's* [It is] not our fault.

*It's* [It has] been a memorable evening.

---

### Possessive Case of Personal Pronouns

| PERSONAL PRONOUN | POSSESSIVE CASE |
|---|---|
| I | my, mine |
| you | your, yours (*not* your's) |
| he | his |
| she | her, hers (*not* her's) |
| it | its (*not* it's) |
| we | our, ours (*not* our's) |
| they | their, theirs (*not* their's) |
| who | whose (*not* who's) |

---

**28h.** Use an apostrophe to indicate an omission in a contraction.

*They're* [They are] too sophisticated for me.

*I've* [I have] learned my lesson.

Pat *didn't* [did not] finish her assignment.

*Bill's* [Bill has] been in jail for a week.

Americans grow up admiring the Spirit of '76 [1776].

It's nearly eight *o'clock* [of the clock].

When you are presented to the Queen, say "Your Majesty"; after that, say "*Ma'am*" [Madam].

**28i.**   Use an apostrophe to form the plural of an abbreviation and of a letter, word, or number mentioned as a word.

ABBREVIATION   Do we need I.D.'s at YMCA's outside our hometown?

LETTER   How many *n*'s are there in *Cincinnati?*

WORD   Try replacing all the *should*'s in that sentence with *could*'s.

NUMBER   Cut out two *3*'s to sew on Larry's shirt.

NOTE: A letter, word, or number named as a word is usually italicized (underlined).

EXCEPTION: To refer to the years in a decade, simply add -*s* without an apostrophe.

The 1980s differed greatly from the 1970s.

---

### Apostrophes and Plural Nouns

Using apostrophes with plural nouns may cause confusion for writers because both plural nouns and possessive nouns often end with -*s*. To avoid confusion in your writing, remember that *plural* means more than one (two *dogs*, six *friends*), but *possessive* means ownership (the *dogs'* biscuits, my *friends'* cars). If you can substitute the word *of* instead of the -*s* and apostrophe (the biscuits *of* the dog, the cars *of* my friends) you need the plural possessive with an apostrophe after the -*s*. If you cannot substitute *of*, you need the simple plural with no apostrophe (the *dogs* are well fed, my *friends* have no *money for gas*).

---

EXERCISE 28–1

### Using the Apostrophe

Correct any errors in the use of the apostrophe in the following sentences. Some sentences may be correct. Answers for the lettered sentences appear in the back of the book. Example:

Youd better put on you're new shoes.

You'd better put on your new shoes.

a.  Its not easy to be old in our society.
b.  I dont understand the Jameses's objections to our plans for a block party.

   c. Its not fair that you're roommate wont help with the cleaning.
   d. Is this collection of 50's records your's or your roommates?
   e. Alas, Brian got two Ds on his report card.

1. Joe and Chucks' fathers were both in the class of 53.
2. They're going to finish their term papers as soon as the party ends.
3. It was a strange coincidence that all three womens' cars broke down after they had picked up their mothers-in-law.
4. Dont forget to dot you're *is* and cross you're *ts*.
5. Mario and Shelley's son is marrying the editor's in chief's daughter.
6. The Hendersons' never change: their always whining about Mr. Scobee farming land thats rightfully their's.
7. Its hard to join a womens' basketball team because so few of them exist.
8. I had'nt expected to hear Janice' voice again.
9. Don't give the Murphy's dog it's biscuit until it's sitting up.
10. Isnt' it the mother and fathers' job to teach kid's to mind their *ps* and *qs*?

# 29. *Quotation Marks*

Quotation marks always come in pairs: one at the start and one at the finish of a quoted passage. In the United States, the double quotation mark (") is preferred over the single one (') for most uses. Use quotation marks to set off a quoted or highlighted word or words from the rest of your text.

> "Injustice anywhere is a threat to justice everywhere," wrote Martin Luther King, Jr.

**29a.** Use quotation marks around direct quotations from another writer or speaker.

You can enrich the content, language, and authority of your writing by occasionally quoting a source whose ideas support your own. When you do this, you owe credit to the quoted person. If you use his or her exact words, enclose them in quotation marks.

> The Arab concept of community is reflected in Egyptian leader Anwar el-Sadat's comment "A man's village is his peace of mind."

> Minnesota-born songwriter Bob Dylan told an interviewer, "When I was growing up in Hibbing, home was a place to run away from."

(See 33j for correct capitalization with quotation marks.)

In an indirect quotation, you report someone else's idea without using his or her exact words. Do not enclose an indirect quotation in quotation marks. Do, however, name your source; and stay as close as you can to what the source actually said.

> Anwar el-Sadat asserted that a person's community provides a sense of well-being.

(For punctuation of direct and indirect questions, see 24a, 24c, and 25r.)

**29b.** Use single quotation marks around a quotation inside another quotation.

Sometimes a source you are quoting quotes someone else or puts a word or words in quotation marks. When that happens, use single quotation marks around the internal quotation (even if your source used double ones), and put double quotation marks around the larger passage that you are quoting.

> "My favorite advice from Socrates, 'Know thyself and fear all women,' " said Dr. Blatz, "has been getting me into trouble lately."

**29c.** Indent a quotation of more than four lines, instead of using quotation marks.

Suppose you are writing an essay about Soviet dissidents living in the United States. You might include a paragraph like this:

---

**ESL GUIDELINES**

## Direct and Indirect Quotations

Avoid the problems that arise when a direct quotation (someone else's exact words) is changed into an indirect quotation (when you report someone else's idea without using his or her exact words). Be sure to change the punctuation and capitalization.

| | |
|---|---|
| DIRECT QUOTATION | Sasha said, "Dallas is in Texas." |
| INDIRECT QUOTATION | Sasha said that Dallas is in Texas. |

- In addition to the punctuation and capitalization, you may need to change the verb tense.

| | |
|---|---|
| DIRECT QUOTATION | Pascal said, "The assignment is on Chinua Achebe, the Nigerian writer." |
| INDIRECT QUOTATION | Pascal said that the assignment was on Chinua Achebe, the Nigerian writer. |

- If the direct quotation is a question, you must change the word order in the indirect quotation.

| | |
|---|---|
| DIRECT QUOTATION | Jean asked, "How far is it to Boston?" |
| INDIRECT QUOTATION | Jean asked how far it was to Boston. |

NOTE: Use a period, not a question mark, with questions in indirect quotations.

- Very often, you must change pronouns when using an indirect quotation.

| | |
|---|---|
| DIRECT QUOTATION | Antonio said, "I think you are mistaken." |
| INDIRECT QUOTATION | Antonio said that he thought I was mistaken. |

In a June 1978 commencement address at Harvard University, Alexander Solzhenitsyn commented:

> I have spent all my life under a Communist regime, and I will tell you that a society without any objective legal scale is a terrible one indeed. But a society with no other scale but the legal one is not quite worthy of man either.

Merely by indenting the quoted passage, you have shown that it is a direct quotation. You need not frame it with quotation marks. Simply double-space above and below the passage, indent it ten spaces from the left margin, and double-space the quoted lines.

Follow the same practice if your quoted material is a poem of more than three lines.

> Phillis Wheatley, the outstanding black poet of colonial America, expresses a sense that she is condemned to write in obscurity and be forgotten:
>
>> No costly marble shall be reared,
>>> No Mausoleum's pride--
>> Nor chiselled stone be raised to tell
>>> That I have lived and died.

Notice that not only the source's words but her punctuation, capitalization, indentation, and line breaks are quoted exactly. (See also 33j.)

**29d.** In dialogue, use quotation marks around a speaker's words, and mark each change of speaker with a new paragraph.

Randolph gazed at Ellen and uttered a heartfelt sigh. "What extraordinary beauty."

"They are lovely," she replied, staring at the roses, "aren't they?"

**29e.** Use quotation marks around the titles of a speech, an article in a newspaper or magazine, a short story, a poem shorter than book length, a chapter in a book, a song, and an episode of a television or radio program.

The article "An Updike Retrospective" praises "Solitaire" as the best story in John Updike's collection *Museums and Women*.

In Chapter 5, "Expatriates," Schwartz discusses Eliot's famous poem "The Love Song of J. Alfred Prufrock."

My favorite episode of *The Brady Bunch* is the one in which they sing "Sunshine Day" at the variety show audition.

(Most other types of titles are underlined. See 35a.)

## 29f. Avoid using quotation marks to indicate slang or to be witty.

Quotation marks should not be used around slang or would-be witticisms. By "quoting" them, you make them stand out like the nose of W. C. Fields; and your discomfort in using them becomes painfully obvious.

> INADVISABLE　Liza looked like a born "loser," but Jerry was "hard up" for companionship.
>
> REVISED　　　Liza looked like a born loser, but Jerry was hard up for companionship.

Stick your neck out. If you really want to use those words, just go ahead.

Some writers assume that, by placing a word in quotation marks, they wax witty and ironic.

> INADVISABLE　By the time I finished all my chores, my long-awaited "day off" was over.
>
> REVISED　　　By the time I finished all my chores, my long-awaited day off was over.

No quotation marks are needed after *so-called* and other words with similar meaning.

> FAULTY　Call me "a dreamer," but I believe we can win.
>
> REVISED　Call me a dreamer, but I believe we can win.

## 29g. Put commas and periods inside quotation marks.

A comma or a period always comes before quotation marks, even if it is not part of the quotation.

> We pleaded and pleaded, "Keep off the grass," in hope of preserving the lawn.

(Also see 25k.)

## 29h. Put semicolons and colons outside quotation marks.

> We said, "Keep off the grass"; they still tromped onward.

## 29i. Put other punctuation inside or outside quotation marks depending on its function in the sentence.

Parentheses that are part of the quotation go inside the quotation marks. Parentheses that are your own, not part of the quotation, go outside the quotation marks.

We said, "Keep off the grass (unless it's artificial turf)."

They tromped onward (although we had said, "Keep off the grass") all the way to the road.

If a question mark, exclamation point, or dash is part of the quotation, place it inside the quotation marks.

She hollered, "Fire!"

"Marjorie?" he called. "I thought you — "

If any of these marks is not part of the quoted passage, place it after the closing quotation marks.

Who hollered "Fire"?

"Marjorie" — he paused for breath — "we'd better go."

As these examples show, don't close a sentence with two end punctuation marks, one inside and one outside the quotation marks. If the quoted passage ends with a dash, exclamation point, question mark, or period, you need not add any further end punctuation. If the quoted passage falls within a question asked by you, however, it should finish with a question mark, even if that means cutting other end punctuation (*Who hollered "Fire"?*).

---

**EXERCISE 29–1**

## Using Quotation Marks

Add quotation marks wherever they are needed in the following sentences, and correct any other errors. Answers for the lettered sentences appear in the back of the book. Example:

How do you say This is a holdup in Spanish? Etta asked the Sundance Kid.

"How do you say 'This is a holdup' in Spanish?" Etta asked the Sundance Kid.

a. Don't think about it, advised Jason; it will only make you unhappy.
b. Do you want to dance, Joan asked, or shall we have a drink?
c. In her story The Wide Net, Eudora Welty wrote, The excursion is the same when you go looking for your sorrow as when you go looking for your joy.
d. Who's supposed to say the line Tennis, anyone? asked the director.
e. Robert Burns's poem To a Mouse opens: Wee, sleekit, cow'rin, tim'rous beastie, / O, what a panic's in thy breastie!

1. How now! a rat? exclaimed Hamlet when Polonius stirred behind the curtain.
2. This so-called "art," spluttered the senator, is the symptom of a morally diseased society.
3. Irving Berlin wrote God Bless America, which some people think should replace The Star-Spangled Banner as our national anthem.

4. The legend that Marie Antoinette said let them eat cake! about her starving subjects is simply not true.
5. Dame Edith Sitwell wrote, Rhythm was described by Schopenhauer as melody deprived of its pitch.

# 30. *The Dash*

A **dash** is a horizontal line used to separate parts of a sentence — a more dramatic substitute for a comma, semicolon, or colon. To type a dash, hit your hyphen key twice. When using a pen, make your dashes good and long, so that readers can tell them from hyphens.

**30a.** Use a dash to indicate a sudden break in thought or shift in tone.

The dash signals that a surprise is in store: a shift in viewpoint, perhaps, or an unfinished statement.

Ivan doesn't care which team wins — he bet on both.

I didn't even pay much attention to my parents' accented and ungrammatical speech — at least not at home.

**30b.** Use a dash to introduce an explanation, an illustration, or a series.

When you want the kind of preparatory pause that a colon provides, but without the formality of a colon, try a dash.

My advice to you is simple — stop complaining.

You can use a dash to introduce an appositive (a noun or noun phrase that renames the noun it follows) if the appositive needs drama or contains commas.

Elliott still cherishes the pastimes of the '60s — sex, drugs, and rock 'n' roll.

Longfellow wrote about three young sisters — grave Alice, laughing Allegra, and Edith with golden hair — in "The Children's Hour."

**30c.** Use dashes to set off an emphatic aside or parenthetical element from the rest of a sentence.

It was as hot — and I mean *hot* — as a seven-dollar pistol on Fourth of July in Death Valley.

If I went through anguish in botany and economics — for different reasons — gymnasium work was even worse.

Dashes set off a phrase or clause with more punch than commas or parentheses can provide. (Compare commas, 25, and parentheses, 31a–31b.)

**30d.**  Avoid overusing dashes.

Like a physical gesture of emphasis — a jab of a pointing finger — the dash becomes meaningless if used too often. Use it only when a comma, a colon, or parentheses don't seem strong enough.

> EXCESSIVE   Algy's grandmother — a sweet old lady — asked him to pick up some things at the store — milk, eggs, apples, and cheese.

> REVISED   Algy's grandmother, a sweet old lady, asked him to pick up some things at the store: milk, eggs, apples, and cheese.

**EXERCISE 30–1**

### Using the Dash

Add, remove, or replace dashes wherever appropriate in the following sentences. Some sentences may be correct. Possible answers for the lettered sentences appear in the back of the book. Example:

> Stanton had all the identifying marks, boating shoes, yellow slicker, sunblock, and an anchor, of a sailor.

> Stanton had all the identifying marks — boating shoes, yellow slicker, sunblock, and an anchor — of a sailor.

a. I enjoy going hiking with my friend John — whom I've known for fifteen years.
b. Pedro's new boat is spectacular: a regular seagoing Ferrari.
c. The Thompsons devote their weekends to their favorite pastime, eating bags of potato chips and cookies beside the warm glow of the television.
d. We were running the rapids when — WHAM!
e. "A rock!" I cried. "Anthony, I'm afraid we're"

1. The sport of fishing — or at least some people call it a sport — is boring, dirty — and tiring.
2. Ancient Egypt had just the right geographic features, a warm climate, a fertile soil along the Nile, and a protective periphery of desert, to allow the development of civilization.
3. At that time, three states in the Sunbelt, Florida, California, and Arizona, were the fastest growing in the nation.
4. The refugees have been forced to build a village if you can call it that out of boxes, rusting cars, and planks.
5. LuLu was ecstatic when she saw her grades, all A's!

# 31. *Parentheses, Brackets, and the Ellipsis Mark*

Like quotation marks, parentheses (singular, *parenthesis*) work in pairs. So do brackets. Both sets of marks usually surround bits of information added to make a statement perfectly clear. An ellipsis mark is a trio of periods inserted to show that some bit of information has been cut.

# PARENTHESES

**31a.**  Use parentheses to set off interruptions that are useful but not essential.

> FDR (as people called Franklin D. Roosevelt) won four presidential elections.

> In fact, he occupied the White House for so many years (1933 to mid-1945) that babies became teenagers without having known any other president.

The material within the parentheses may be helpful, but it isn't essential. Were the writer to omit it altogether, the sentence would still make good sense. Use parentheses when adding in mid-sentence a qualifying word or phrase, a helpful date, or a brief explanation — words that, in conversation, you might introduce in a changed tone of voice.

**31b.**  Use parentheses around letters or numbers indicating items in a series.

> Archimedes asserted that, given (1) a lever long enough, (2) a fulcrum, and (3) a place to stand, he could move the earth.

You need not put parentheses around numbers or letters in a list that you set off from the text by indentation.

EXERCISE 31–1

## Using Parentheses

Add, remove, or replace parentheses wherever appropriate in the following sentences. Some sentences may be correct. Possible answers for the lettered sentences appear in the back of the book. Example:

> The Islamic fundamentalist Ayatollah Khomeini — 1903–1989 — was described as having led Iran forward into the fifteenth century.

> The Islamic fundamentalist Ayatollah Khomeini (1903–1989) was described as having led Iran forward into the fifteenth century.

a. In *The Last Crusade*, archaeologist Indiana Jones, who took his name from the family dog, joins his father in a quest for the Holy Grail.
b. Our cafeteria serves the four basic food groups: white — milk, bread, and mashed potatoes — brown — mystery meat and gravy — green — overcooked vegetables and underwashed lettuce — and orange — squash, carrots, and tomato sauce.
c. The hijackers will release the hostages only if the government, 1, frees all political prisoners and, 2, allows the hijackers to leave the country unharmed.
d. When Phil said he works with whales (as well as other marine mammals) for the Whale Stranding Network, Lisa thought he meant that his group lures whales onto beaches.
e. Actually, the Whale Stranding Network, WSN, rescues whales that have stranded themselves.

1. The new pear-shaped bottles will hold 200 milliliters, 6.8 fluid ounces, of lotion.
2. The letter from Agatha — not her real name — told a heart-wrenching story of abandonment and abuse.
3. Al's policeman clown was a fantastic success (even his mother was fooled).
4. World War I, or "The Great War," as it was once called, destroyed the old European order forever.
5. The Internet is a mine of fascinating, and sometimes useless, information.

## BRACKETS

Brackets, those open-ended typographical boxes, work in pairs like parentheses. They serve a special purpose: they mark changes in quoted material.

**31c.**    Use brackets to add information or to make changes within a direct quotation.

A quotation must be quoted exactly. If you need to add or alter a word or a phrase in a quotation from another writer, place brackets around your changes. When is it appropriate to make such a change? Most often the need arises when you weave into your own prose a piece of someone else's, and you want to get rid of dangling threads.

Suppose you are writing about James McGuire's being named chairman of the board of directors of General Motors. In your source, the actual words are these: "A radio bulletin first brought the humble professor of philosophy the astounding news." But in your paper, you want readers to know the professor's identity. So you add that information, in brackets.

"A radio bulletin first brought the humble professor of philosophy [James McGuire] the astounding news."

Be careful never to alter a quoted statement any more than you have to. Every time you consider an alteration, ask yourself: do I really need this word-for-word quotation, or should I paraphrase?

**31d.**    Use brackets around *sic* to indicate an error in a direct quotation.

When you faithfully quote a statement that contains an error and you don't want your reader to blame you for it, follow the error with a bracketed *sic* (Latin for "so" or "so the writer says").

"President Ronald Reagan foresaw a yearly growth of 29,000,000,000 [*sic*] in the American populace."

Of course, any statement as incorrect as that one is not worth quoting. Usually you're better off paraphrasing an error-riddled passage than pointing out its weaknesses. The writer who uses *sic* is like someone who goes around with a mean dog, siccing it on fellow writers. Never unleash your dog unless your target truly deserves a bite.

# THE ELLIPSIS MARK

**31e.** Use the ellipsis mark to signal that you have omitted part of a quotation.

Occasionally, in quoting a passage of prose, you will want to cite just those parts that relate to your topic. It's all right to make judicious cuts in a quotation, as long as you acknowledge them. To do this, use the *ellipsis mark*: three periods with a space before and after each one (. . .).

Let's say you are writing an essay, "Today's Children: Counselors on Marital Affairs." One of your sources is Marie Winn's book *Children without Childhood*, in which you find this passage:

> Consider the demise of sexual innocence among children. We know that the casual integration of children into adult society in the Middle Ages included few sexual prohibitions. Today's nine- and ten-year-olds watch pornographic movies on cable TV, casually discourse about oral sex and sadomasochism, and not infrequently find themselves involved in their own parents' complicated sex lives, if not as actual observers or participants, at least as advisers, friendly commentators, and intermediaries.

You want to quote Winn's last sentence, but it has too much detail for your purposes. You might shorten it by omitting two of its parts.

> Today's nine- and ten-year-olds . . . not infrequently find themselves involved in their own parents' complicated sex lives, . . . at least as advisers, friendly commentators, and intermediaries.

If you want to include parts of two or more sentences, use a period plus the ellipsis mark — four periods altogether. The period that ends the first sentence appears in its usual place, followed by the three spaced periods that signal the omission.

> Consider the demise of sexual innocence among children. . . . Today's nine- and ten-year-olds [and the rest].

**31f.** Avoid using the ellipsis mark at the beginning or end of a quotation.

Even though the book *Children without Childhood* keeps on going after the quoted passage, you don't need an ellipsis mark at the end of your quotation. Nor do you ever need to begin a quotation with three dots. Save the ellipsis mark for words or sentences you omit *inside* whatever you quote.

Anytime you decide to alter a quotation, with an ellipsis mark or with brackets, pause to ask yourself whether the quoted material is still necessary and still effective as changed. A passage full of ellipsis marks starts to look like Swiss cheese. If you plan to cut more than one or two sections from a quotation, think about paraphrasing instead.

**EXERCISE 31–2**

# Using Brackets and the Ellipsis Mark

The following are two hypothetical passages from original essays. Each one is followed by a set of quotations. Adapt or paraphrase each quotation, using brackets and ellipsis marks, and splice it into the essay passage.

*1. ESSAY PASSAGE*

Has evil lost its capacity to frighten us? Today's teenagers use words like *wicked, bad,* and *evil* not to condemn another person's behavior or style but to show that they approve of it. Perhaps the declining power of organized religion has allowed us to stop worrying about evil. Perhaps the media's coverage of war, genocide, and murder has made us feel impotent against it. Perhaps the worldwide spread of nuclear weapons has made evil too huge and uncontrollable for our imaginations to grapple with.

QUOTATIONS

a. It was as though in those last minutes he was summing up the lessons that this long course in human wickedness had taught us — the lesson of the fearsome, word-and-thought-defying *banality of evil.*
— Philosopher Hannah Arendt,
writing about the Nazi leader Adolf Eichmann

b. I am not a pessimist; to perceive evil where it exists is, in my opinion, a form of optimism.
— Filmmaker Roberto Rossellini

c. The world has achieved brilliance without conscience. Ours is a world of nuclear giants and ethical infants.
— General Omar Bradley

*2. ESSAY PASSAGE*

Every human life is touched by the natural world. Before the modern industrial era, most people recognized the earth as the giver and supporter of existence. Nowadays, with the power of technology, we can (if we choose) destroy many of the complex balances of nature. With such power comes responsibility. We are no longer merely nature's children, but nature's parents as well.

QUOTATIONS

a. A land ethic for tomorrow should be as honest as Thoreau's *Walden,* and as comprehensive as the sensitive science of ecology. It should stress the oneness of our resources and the live-and-help-live logic of the great chain of life. If, in our haste to "progress," the economics of ecology are disregarded by citizens and policymakers alike, the result will be an ugly America.
— Former Secretary of the Interior Stewart Lee Udall

b. The overwhelming importance of the atmosphere means that there are no longer any frontiers to defend against pollution, attack, or propaganda. It means, further, that only by a deep patriotic devotion to one's country can there be a hope of the kind of protection of the whole planet, which is necessary for the survival of the people of other countries.
— Anthropologist Margaret Mead

c.  The survival of our wildlife is a matter of grave concern to all of us in Africa. These wild creatures amid the wild places they inhabit are not only important as a source of wonder and inspiration but are an integral part of our natural resources and of our future livelihood and well-being.

— Former President of Tanzania Julius Nyerere

   d.  [Religion] is a force in itself and it calls for the integration of lands and peoples in harmonious unity. The lands wait for those who can discern their rhythms. The peculiar genius of each continent, each river valley, the rugged mountains, the placid lakes, all call for relief from the constant burden of exploitation.

— Native American leader Vine Deloria, Jr., a Standing Rock Sioux

**EXERCISE 31–3**

## Punctuation Review

Punctuate each of the following sentences correctly, changing punctuation and capitalization if necessary. Example:

> The English language, is all around us we speak it read it and hear it constantly.

> The English language is all around us; we speak it, read it, and hear it constantly.

The English language, that we speak today, has a long history. During the fifth century C.E. Germanic tribes emigrated to Britain from Denmark, Germany and Holland and they brought their languages with them. These languages the ancestors of modern English were closely related and formed the basis for the language that we speak today. The Viking invasions which began in 793 C.E. also influenced the development of Old English however it was the Norman invasion of 1066 that had the greatest impact on the language. The Normans brought French and Latin words into Britain, and contributed to the evolution of the next linguistic phase Middle English. The most famous writer of this Middle English period is of course Geoffrey Chaucer. Chaucer's achievement was widely acknowledged at the time and by subsequent generations. In the seventeenth century the poet Dryden wrote, " ... He must have been a Man of a most wonderful comprehensive Nature, because, as it has been truly observed of him, he has taken into the compass of his *Canterbury Tales* the various Manners and Humours (as we now call them) of the whole *English* Nation" ...

In the late sixteenth century emerged the greatest writer in the English language William Shakespeare. Shakespeare, was the first to demonstrate the flexibility of the language and its great range of expression. It was also during this time that British colonists began carrying English to distant parts of the world. In America words from Native American languages were absorbed and as the British Empire expanded so did English vocabulary. By the late nineteenth century English speakers, were using words from languages as different as: Algonquian and Hindi as well as from almost every European language French, German, Dutch, Danish Yiddish, Swedish, Italian and Spanish. As Ralph Waldo Emerson wrote "The English language is the sea which receives tributaries from every region under heaven".

The English language is always changing like the world itself it is in a constant state of flux. In the late twentieth century English is no longer the language of the British Empire and its colonies. As Salman Rushdie writes:

> "English, no longer an English language, now grows from many roots; and those whom it once colonized are carving out large territories within the language for themselves. The Empire is striking back."

In India there are now more speakers of English than there are in Britain about seventy million according to some estimates. Some writers have compared the state of modern English in the former colonies to the vitality of the language during Shakespeares' time. Whereas the grammar police patrol British and American English, other forms of English: such as Indian, Caribbean and African English are developing relatively unrestrained. Anthony Burgess has commented with admiration that "It (Indian English) is not pure English, but it's like the English of Shakespeare, Joyce, and Kipling — gloriously impure." The language will continue to change under the influence of many factors cultural, technological and historical far from its original, island home.

## Chapter 37

# Mechanics

## 32. *Abbreviations*

Abbreviations are a form of shorthand that enables a writer to include certain necessary information in capsule form. In your writing, limit abbreviations to those that are common enough for readers to recognize and understand without pausing. When a reader has to stop and ask, "What does this mean?," your writing loses impact.

If ever you're unsure about whether to abbreviate a word, remember: when in doubt, spell it out.

**32a.** Use abbreviations for some titles with proper names.

Abbreviate the following titles:

> Mr. and Mrs. Hubert Collins    Dr. Martin Luther King, Jr.
> Ms. Martha Reading    St. Matthew

Write out other titles in full:

> General Douglas MacArthur    Senator Nancy L. Kassebaum
> President George Bush    Professor Shirley Fixler

Titles that are unfamiliar to readers of English, such as *M.* (for the French *Monsieur*) or *Sr.* (for the Spanish *Señor*), should be spelled out.

Spell out most titles that appear without proper names.

FAULTY    Fred is studying to be a dr.

REVISED    Fred is studying to be a doctor.

H-178

When an abbreviated title (such as an academic degree) follows a proper name, set it off from the name and from the rest of the sentence with commas.

Alice Martin, C.P.A., is the accountant for Charlotte Cordera, Ph.D., and John Hoechst, Jr., Esq.

Lucy Chen, M.D., and James Filbert, D.D.S., have moved their offices to the Millard Building.

An academic degree that appears without a proper name can be abbreviated, but it is not set off with commas.

My brother has a B.A. in economics.

Avoid repeating different forms of the same title before and after a proper name. You can properly refer to a doctor of dental surgery as either *Dr. Jane Doe* or *Jane Doe, D.D.S.*, but not as *Dr. Jane Doe, D.D.S.*

## 32b.   Use *a.m., p.m.,* B.C., A.D., and *$* with numbers.

9:05 a.m.     3:45 p.m.
2000 B.C.     A.D. 1066

The words we use to pinpoint years and times are so commonly abbreviated that many English speakers have forgotten what the letters stand for. In case you are curious: *a.m.* means *ante meridiem,* Latin for "before noon"; *p.m.* means *post meridiem,* "after noon." A.D. is *anno domini,* Latin for "in the year of the Lord" — that is, since the official year of Jesus' birth. B.C. stands for "before Christ." You may also run into alternative designations such as B.P., "before present," and B.C.E., "before the common era." If you think your readers may not know what an abbreviation stands for, spell it out or add an explanation.

The ruins date from 1200 B.P. (before present).

For exact prices that include cents and for amounts in the millions, use a dollar sign with numbers (*$17.95, $10.52, $3.5 billion*).

Avoid using an abbreviation together with a word or words that mean the same thing: write *$1 million,* not *$1 million dollars.* Write *9:05 a.m.* or *9:05 in the morning,* not *9:05 a.m. in the morning.*

## 32c.   Avoid abbreviating names of months, days of the week, units of measurement, or parts of literary works.

Many references that can be abbreviated in footnotes or citations should be spelled out when they appear in the body of an essay.

NAMES OF MONTHS AND DAYS OF THE WEEK

FAULTY    After their meeting on 9/3, they did not see each other again until Fri., Dec. 12.

REVISED   After their meeting on September 3 [*or* the third of September], they did not see each other again until Friday, December 12.

UNITS OF MEASUREMENT

FAULTY    It would take 10,000 lb. of concrete to build a causeway 25 ft. × 58 in. [*or* 25′ × 58″].

REVISED   It would take 10,000 pounds of concrete to build a causeway 25 feet by 58 inches.

EXERCISE 32–1

## Using Abbreviations

Substitute abbreviations for words and vice versa wherever appropriate in the following sentences. Correct any incorrectly used abbreviations. Answers for the lettered sentences appear in the back of the book. Example:

> My history teacher, Doctor Lembas, got her doctor of philosophy degree at the University of Southwest Florida.

> My history teacher, Dr. Lembas, got her Ph.D. at the University of Southwest Florida.

a. Built for the Paris Exposition of 1889, the Eiffel Tower contains 15 million lb. of pig iron, protected by 37 T of paint.
b. Fri., 7/14, 1989, was the Eiffel Tower's 100th anniversary.
c. M. Eiffel would be pleased that Pres. Mitterrand et al. now accept his controversial "iron giraffe" as a national landmark.
d. In some Parisian tourist traps, a cup of coffee costs as much as 5 dollars.
e. France is a member of NATO, but the French historically have mistrusted some of their fellow NATO members, e.g., the U.K.

1. Sen. Puffin and Prof. Kite will be among the honored speakers at our next symposium in Alabama.
2. When the Senate considered whether the U.S. should aid the famine victims, Sens. Kerry, Kennedy, and Biden requested an authorization of $1.2 million dollars.
3. When John Fitzgerald Kennedy picked Lyndon Baines Johnson for VP, Democrats never guessed that three yrs later JFK would be dead and LBJ would be in the White House.
4. At 8:20 p.m. this evening we heard that Dr. Reginald Styx, M.D., had stumbled upon relics dating to 1400 B.C.
5. Has the annual operating budget for N.A.T.O. ever been less than $1 billion dollars?

PARTS OF LITERARY WORKS

FAULTY   Von Bargen's reply appears in vol. 2, ch. 12, p. 187.

REVISED   Von Bargen's reply appears in volume 2, chapter 12, page 187.

FAULTY   Leona first speaks in act 1, sc. 2.

REVISED   Leona first speaks in act 1, scene 2 [*or* the second scene of act 1].

## 32d. Use the full English version of most Latin abbreviations.

Unless you are writing for an audience of ancient Romans, translate Latin abbreviations into English and spell them out whenever possible.

COMMON LATIN ABBREVIATIONS

| ABBREVIATION | LATIN | ENGLISH |
|---|---|---|
| et al. | *et alia* | and others, and other people, and the others (people) |
| etc. | *et cetera* | and so forth, and others, and the rest (things) |
| i.e. | *id est* | that is |
| e.g. | *exempli gratia* | for example, such as |

Latin abbreviations are acceptable, however, for source citations and for comments in parentheses and brackets. (See also 31d.)

## 32e. Use abbreviations for familiar organizations, corporations, and people.

Most sets of initials that are read as letters do not require periods between the letters (CIA, JFK, UCLA). You will not be wrong if you insert periods (C.I.A., J.F.K., U.C.L.A.), as long as you are consistent.

A set of initials that is pronounced as a word is called an **acronym** (NATO, AIDS, UNICEF) and never has periods between letters.

To avoid misunderstanding, write out an organization's full name the first time you mention it, followed by its initials in parentheses. Then, in later references, you can rely on initials alone. (With very familiar initials, such as FBI, CBS, and YMCA, you need not give the full name.)

## 32f. Avoid abbreviations for countries.

When you mention the United States or another country, give its full name, unless the name is repeated so often that it would weigh down your paragraph.

The president will return to the United States [*not* U.S.] on Tuesday from a trip to the United Kingdom [*not* U.K.].

EXCEPTION: Although it is not advisable to use *U.S.* as a noun, you can use it as an adjective: *U.S. Senate, U.S. foreign policy.* For other countries, find an alternative: *British ambassador.*

---

### Capitalization at a Glance
Capitalize the following.

**PROPER NAMES AND ADJECTIVES MADE FROM THEM**
Marie Curie     Cranberry Island     Smithsonian Institution
a Freudian reading

**RANK OR TITLE BEFORE A PROPER NAME**
Ms. Olson     Professor Harvey

**FAMILY RELATIONSHIP ONLY WHEN IT SUBSTITUTES FOR OR IS PART OF A PROPER NAME**
Grandma Jones     Father Time

**RELIGIONS, THEIR FOLLOWERS, AND DEITIES**
Islam     Orthodox Jew     Buddha

**PLACES, REGIONS, AND GEOGRAPHIC FEATURES**
Palo Alto     the Berkshire Mountains

**DAYS OF THE WEEK, MONTHS, AND HOLIDAYS**
Wednesday     July     Labor Day

**HISTORICAL EVENTS, PERIODS, AND DOCUMENTS**
the Boston Tea Party     the Middle Ages     the Constitution

**SCHOOLS, COLLEGES, UNIVERSITIES, AND SPECIFIC COURSES**
Temple University     Introduction to Clinical Psychology

**FIRST, LAST, AND MAIN WORDS IN TITLES OF PAPERS, BOOKS, ARTICLES, WORKS OF ART, TELEVISION SHOWS, POEMS, AND PERFORMANCES.**
*The Decline and Fall of the Roman Empire*

**THE FIRST LETTER OF A QUOTED SENTENCE**
She called out, "Come in! The water's not cold."

---

# 33. *Capital Letters*

The main thing to remember about capital letters is to use them only with good reason. If you think a word will work in lowercase letters, you're probably right.

**33a.**  Capitalize proper names and adjectives made from proper names.

Proper names designate individuals, places, organizations and institutions, brand names, and certain other distinctive things.

| | |
|---|---|
| Miles Standish | University of Iowa |
| Belgium | a Volkswagen |
| United Nations | a Xerox machine |

Any proper name can have an adjective as well as a noun form. The adjective form too is capitalized.

Australian beer          a Renaissance man
Shakespearean comedy     Machiavellian tactics

**33b.** Capitalize a title or rank before a proper name.

Now in her second term, Senator Wilimczyk serves on two important committees.

In his lecture, Professor Jones went on and on about fossil evidence.

In formal writing, titles that do not come before proper names are not capitalized.

Ten senators voted against the missile research appropriation.

Jones is the department's only full professor.

EXCEPTION: The abbreviation for the full name of an academic or professional degree is capitalized, whether or not it accompanies a proper name. The informal name of a degree is not capitalized.

Dora E. McLean, M.D., also holds a B.A. in music.

Dora holds a bachelor's degree in music.

**33c.** Capitalize a family relationship only when it is part of a proper name or when it substitutes for a proper name.

Do you know the song about Mother Machree?

I've invited Mother to visit next weekend.

I'd like you to meet my aunt, Emily Smith.

**33d.** Capitalize the names of religions, their deities, and their followers.

Christianity     Muslims      Jehovah     Krishna
Islam          Methodists    Allah       the Holy Spirit

**33e.** Capitalize proper names of places, regions, and geographic features.

Los Angeles    the Black Hills    the Atlantic Ocean
Death Valley    Big Sur         the Philippines

Do not capitalize *north, south, east,* or *west* unless it is part of a proper name (*West Virginia, South Orange*) or refers to formal geographic locations.

Drive south to Chicago and then east to Cleveland.

Jim, who has always lived in the South, likes to read about the mysterious East.

A common noun such as *street, avenue, boulevard, park, lake,* or *hill* is capitalized when part of a proper name.

| | |
|---|---|
| Meinecke Avenue | Hamilton Park |
| Sunset Boulevard | Lake Michigan |

**33f.**  Capitalize days of the week, names of months, and holidays, but not seasons or academic terms.

By the Monday after Passover I have to choose between the January study plan and junior year abroad.

At Easter we'll be halfway through the spring term.

**33g.**  Capitalize historical events, periods, and documents.

| | |
|---|---|
| Black Monday | Magna Carta |
| the Civil War | Declaration of Independence |
| the Holocaust | Atomic Energy Act |
| the Bronze Age | |
| the Roaring Twenties | |

**33h.**  Capitalize the names of schools and colleges, department names, and course titles.

West End School, Central High School [*but* elementary school, high school]

Reed College, Arizona State University [*but* the college, a university]

Department of Geography [*but* geography department, departmental meeting]

Feminist Perspectives in Nineteenth-Century Literature [*but* literature course]

**33i.**  Capitalize the first, last, and main words in titles.

When you write the title of a paper, book, article, work of art, television show, poem, or performance, capitalize the first and last words and all main words in between. Do not capitalize articles, conjunctions, or prepositions unless they come first or last in the title or follow a colon.

| | |
|---|---|
| ESSAY | "Once More to the Lake" |
| NOVEL | *Of Mice and Men* |
| VOLUME OF POETRY | *Poems after Martial* |
| POEM | "A Valediction: Of Weeping" |
| BALLET | *Swan Lake* |

(For advice about using quotation marks and italics for titles, see 29e and 35a.)

**33j.**    Capitalize the first letter of a quoted sentence.

Oscar Wilde wrote, "The only way to get rid of a temptation is to yield to it."

Only the first word of a quoted sentence is capitalized, even when you break the sentence with words of your own.

"The only way to get rid of a temptation," wrote Oscar Wilde, "is to yield to it."

If you quote more than one sentence, start each one with a capital letter.

"Art should never try to be popular," said Wilde. "The public should try to make itself artistic."

(For advice about punctuating quotations, see 29g–29i.)

If the beginning of the quoted passage blends in with your sentence, use lowercase for the first word of the quotation.

Oscar Wilde wrote that "the only way to get rid of a temptation is to yield to it."

EXERCISE 33–1

## Using Capitalization

Correct any capitalization errors you find in the following sentences. Some sentences may be correct. Answers for the lettered sentences appear in the back of the book. Example:

"The quality of mercy," says Portia in Shakespeare's *The Merchant Of Venice*, "Is not strained."

"The quality of mercy," says Portia in Shakespeare's *The Merchant of Venice*, "is not strained."

a. At our Family Reunion, I met my Cousin Sam for the first time, and also my father's brother George.
b. I already knew from dad that his brother had moved to Australia years ago to explore the great barrier reef.
c. At the reunion, uncle George told me that he had always wanted to be a Marine Biologist.
d. He had spent the Summer after his Sophomore year of college in Woods Hole, Massachusetts, on cape cod.
e. At the Woods Hole oceanographic institution he studied Horseshoe Crabs.

1. "These crabs look like armored tanks," he told me. "They have populated the Northeast for millions of years."
2. "I'm writing a book," he said, "Entitled *Horseshoe Crabs are Good Luck*."
3. I had heard that uncle George was estranged from his Mother, a Roman catholic, after he married an Atheist.
4. She told George that God created many religions so that people would not become Atheists.

5. When my Uncle announced that he was moving to a Continent thousands of miles Southwest of the United States, his Mother gave him a bible to take along.

6. My Aunt, Linda McCallum, received her Doctorate from one of the State Universities in California.

7. After graduation she worked there as Registrar and lived in the San Bernardino valley.

8. She has pursued her interest in Hispanic Studies by traveling to South America from her home in Northeastern Australia.

9. She uses her maiden name — Linda McCallum, Ph.D. — for her nonprofit business, Hands across the Sea.

10. After dinner we all toasted grandmother's Ninetieth Birthday and sang "For She's A Jolly Good Fellow."

# 34. *Numbers*

When do you write out a number (*twenty-seven*) and when do you use figures for it (*27*)? Unless your essay relies on statistics, you'll want in most cases to use words. Figures are most appropriate in contexts where readers are used to seeing them, such as times and dates (*11:05 P.M. on March 15*).

**34a.** In general, write out a number that consists of one or two words and use figures for longer numbers.

Short names of numbers are easily read (*ten, six hundred*); longer ones take more thought (*two thousand four hundred eighty-seven*). So for numbers of more than a word or two, use figures.

> More than two hundred suckers paid twenty-five dollars apiece for that cheap plastic novelty item.

> A frog's tongue has 970,580 taste buds, one-sixth as many as a human being's.

EXCEPTION: For multiples of a million or more, you can use a figure plus a word.

> The earth is 93 million miles from the sun.

> The Pentagon has requested a $3.4 billion increase.

**34b.** Use figures for most addresses, dates, decimals, fractions, parts of literary works, percentages, exact prices, scores, statistics, and times.

Using figures is mainly a matter of convenience. If you think words will be easier for your readers to follow, you can always write out a number.

NOTE: Any number that precedes *o'clock* should be in words, not figures.

(For pointers on writing the plurals of figures [*6's, 1960s*], see 28i.)

---

### Figures at a Glance

| | |
|---|---|
| ADDRESSES | 4 East 74th Street; also, One Copley Place; 5 Fifth Avenue |
| DATES | May 20, 1992; 450 B.C.; also, Fourth of July |
| DECIMALS | 98.6° Fahrenheit; .57 acre |
| FRACTIONS | 3½ years ago; 1¾ miles; also, half a loaf; three-fourths of voters surveyed |
| PARTS OF LITERARY WORKS | volume 2, chapter 5, page 37; act 1, scene 2 (*or* act I, scene ii) |
| PERCENTAGES | 25 percent; 99.9 percent |
| EXACT PRICES | $1.99; $200,000; also, $5 million; ten cents; a dollar |
| SCORES | a 114-111 victory; a final score of 5 to 3 |
| STATISTICS | men in the 25–30 age group; odds of 5 to 1 (*or* 5–1 odds); height 5'7"; also, three out of four doctors |
| TIMES | 2:29 P.M.; 10:15 tomorrow morning; also, three o'clock, half past four |

---

**34c.** Use words or figures consistently for numbers in the same category throughout a passage.

Switching back and forth between words and figures for numbers can be distracting to readers. Choose whichever form suits like numbers in your passage and use that form consistently for all numbers in the same category.

> Ten years ago, only 25 percent of the land in town was developed; now, all but 15 percent is occupied by buildings.

> Of the 276 representatives who voted, 97 supported a 25 percent raise, while 179 supported an amendment that would implement a 30 percent raise over five years.

**34d.** Write out a number that begins a sentence.

Readers recognize a new sentence by its initial capital; however, you can't capitalize a figure. When a number starts a sentence, either write it out or move it deeper into the sentence. If a number starting a sentence is followed by other numbers in the same category, write them out, too, unless to do so would make the sentence excessively awkward.

> Five percent of the frogs in our aquarium ate sixty-two percent of the flies.

> Ten thousand people packed an arena built for 8,550.

## Using Numbers

Correct any inappropriate uses of numbers in the following sentences. Some sentences may be correct. Answers for the lettered sentences appear in the back of the book. Example:

> As Feinberg notes on page 197, a delay of 3 minutes cost the researchers 5 years' worth of work.

> As Feinberg notes on page 197, a delay of three minutes cost the researchers five years' worth of work.

a. Wasn't it the 3 Musketeers whose motto was "One for all and all for one"?
b. In the 1970s, there were about ninety-two million ducks in America, but in the last 4 years their number has dropped to barely sixty-nine million.
c. Of the 3 pyramids built at Giza, Egypt, between two thousand five hundred and eighty and two thousand four hundred and ninety B.C.E., the largest pyramid is four hundred and fifty feet high.
d. Forty days and 40 nights would seem like 40 years if you were sailing on an ark with two of every kind of animal.
e. I doubt that I'll ever bowl a perfect 300, but I hope to break 250 if it takes me till I'm eighty.

1. If the murder took place at approximately six-twenty P.M. and the suspect was $^1/_2$ a mile away at the time, he could not possibly have committed the crime.
2. A program to help save the sea otter transferred more than eighty animals to a new colony over the course of 2 years; however, all but 34 otters swam back home again.
3. 1 percent or less of the estimated fifteen to twenty billion pounds of plastic discarded annually in the United States is recycled.
4. The 1983 Little League World Series saw the Roosters beat the Dusters ninety-four to four before a throng of seven thousand five hundred and fifty.
5. In act two, scene nine of Shakespeare's *The Merchant of Venice*, Portia's 2nd suitor fails to guess which of 3 caskets contains her portrait.
6. *Fourscore* means 4 times 20; a *fortnight* means 2 weeks; and a *brace* is two of anything.
7. 50 years ago, traveling from New York City to San Francisco took approximately 15 hours by plane, 50 hours by train, and almost 100 hours by car.
8. The little cottage we bought for fifty-five thousand dollars in the nineteen-seventies may sell for $2,000,000 today.
9. At 7 'o clock this morning the temperature was already ninety-seven degrees Fahrenheit.
10. Angelica finished volume one of Proust's *Remembrance of Things Past*, but by the time she got to page forty of volume two, she had forgotten the beginning and had to start over.

# 35. *Italics*

*Italic type — as in this line — slants to the right.* Slightly harder to read than perpendicular type, it is usually saved for emphasis or for special use of a word or phrase. In handwriting or typewriting, indicate italics by underlining.

**35a.** Italicize the titles of magazines, newspapers, and long literary works (books, pamphlets, plays); the titles of films; the titles of paintings and other works of art; the titles of long musical works (operas, symphonies); the titles of record albums; and the names of television and radio programs.

> We read the story "Araby" in James Joyce's book *Dubliners*.

> The Broadway musical *My Fair Lady* was based on Shaw's play *Pygmalion*.

> Pete read reviews in the *Washington Post* and *Newsweek* magazine of the Cleveland Philharmonic's recording of Beethoven's *Pastoral* Symphony.

> I saw a *Melrose Place* episode that featured cuts from R.E.M.'s album *Monster*.

The names of the Bible (King James Version, Revised Standard Version), the books of the Bible (Genesis, Matthew), and other sacred books (the Koran, the Rig-Veda) are not italicized.
(For titles that are put in quotation marks, see 29e.)

**35b.** Italicize the names of ships, boats, trains, airplanes, and spacecraft.

> The launching of the Venus probe *Magellan* was a heartening success after the *Challenger* disaster.

> The *Concorde* combines the elegance of an ocean liner like the *Queen Mary* with the convenience of high-speed air travel.

**35c.** Italicize a word or phrase from a foreign language if it is not in everyday use.

> Gandhi taught the principles of *satya* and *ahimsa:* truth and nonviolence.

> Although there is no one-word English equivalent for the French *chez,* we can translate *chez Bob* simply as "at Bob's."

Foreign words that are familiar to most American readers need not be italicized. (Check your dictionary to see which words are considered familiar.)

> After being declared passé several years ago, détente is making a reappearance in East-West politics.

> I prefer provolone to mozzarella.

## Italics at a Glance

### TITLES

**MAGAZINES AND NEWSPAPERS**
*Ms.*      the *London Times*

**LONG LITERARY WORKS**
*Heart of Darkness* (a novel)     *The Less Deceived* (a collection of poems)

**FILMS**
*Notorious*     *Black Orpheus*

**PAINTINGS AND OTHER WORKS OF ART**
*Four Dancers* (a painting)     *The Thinker* (a sculpture)

**LONG MUSICAL WORKS**
*Aïda*     Handel's *Messiah*

**RECORD ALBUMS**
*Sticky Fingers*

**TELEVISION AND RADIO PROGRAMS**
*I Love Lucy*     *All Things Considered*

### OTHER WORDS AND PHRASES

**NAMES OF SPECIFIC VEHICLES AND SPACECRAFT**
the *Orient Express*     the *Challenger*

**A WORD OR PHRASE FROM A FOREIGN LANGUAGE IF IT IS NOT IN EVERYDAY USE**
The Finnish sauna ritual uses a *vihta,* a brush made of fresh birch branches tied together.

**A LETTER, NUMBER, WORD, OR PHRASE WHEN YOU DEFINE IT OR REFER TO IT AS A WORD**
There were two *5's* on the door, and she guessed that a *4* had fallen off between them.

What do you think *fiery* is referring to in the second line?

NOTE:  See 29e for titles that need to be placed in quotation marks.

When you give a synonym or a translation — a definition that is just one or two words long — italicize the word being defined and put the definition in quotation marks.

The word *orthodoxy* means "conformity."

*Trois, drei,* and *tres* are all words for "three."

**35d.** Italicize a word when you define it.

> The rhythmic, wavelike motion of the walls of the alimentary canal is called *peristalsis.*

**35e.** Italicize a letter, number, word, or phrase used as a word.

> George Bernard Shaw pointed out that *fish* could be spelled *ghoti:* *gh* as in *tough,* *o* as in *women,* and *ti* as in *fiction.*

> Watching the big red *8* on a basketball player's jersey, I recalled the scarlet letter *A* worn by Hester Prynne.

> Psychologists now prefer the term *unconscious* to *subconscious.*

**35f.** Use italics sparingly for emphasis.

When you absolutely *must* stress a point, use italics; but watch out. Frequent italics can make your writing look hysterical. In most cases, the structure of your sentence, not a typographical gimmick, should give emphasis where emphasis is due.

> He suggested putting the package *under* the mailbox, not *into* the mailbox.

> People committed to saving whales, sea otters, and baby seals may not be aware that *forty thousand children per day* die of starvation or malnutrition.

**EXERCISE 35–1**

## Using Italics

Add or remove italics as needed in the following sentences. Some sentences may be correct. Answers for the lettered sentences appear in the back of the book. Example:

> Hiram could not *believe* that his parents had seen *the Beatles'* legendary performance at Shea Stadium.

> Hiram could not believe that his parents had seen the Beatles' legendary performance at Shea Stadium.

a. Hiram's favorite Beatles album is "Sergeant Pepper's Lonely Hearts Club Band," but his father prefers "Magical Mystery Tour."
b. Hiram named his rowboat the "Yellow Submarine."
c. He was disappointed when I told him that the play *Long Day's Journey into Night* is *definitely not* a staged version of the movie "A Hard Day's Night."
d. I had to show him the article "Eugene O'Neill's Journey into Night" in "People" magazine to convince him.
e. We ate *spaghetti* and *tortellini* in the new Italian restaurant.

1. Is "avocado" Spanish for "lawyer"?
2. During this year's *First Night* celebrations, we heard Verdi's Requiem and Monteverdi's Orfeo.

3. You can pick out some of the best basketball players in the *NBA* by the 33 on their jerseys.
4. It was fun watching the passengers on the Europa trying to dance to *Blue Moon* in the midst of a storm.
5. In one episode of the sitcom "Seinfeld," Kramer gets a job as an underwear model.
6. *Eye* in France is *oeil*, while *eyes* is *yeux*.
7. "Deux yeux bleus" means "two blue eyes" in French.
8. Jan can never remember whether Cincinnati has three n's and one t or two n's and two t's.
9. My favorite comic bit in "The Pirates of Penzance" is Major General Stanley's confusion between "orphan" and "often."
10. In Tom Stoppard's play "The Real Thing," the character Henry accuses Bach of copying a *cantata* from a popular song by *Procol Harum.*

# 36. *The Hyphen*

The hyphen, that Scotch-tape mark of punctuation, is used to join words and to connect parts of words. You will find it indispensable for the following purposes.

## 36a. Use hyphens in compound words that require them.

Compound words in the English language take three forms:

1. Two or more words combined into one (*crossroads, salesperson*)
2. Two or more words that remain separate but function as one (*gas station, high school*)
3. Two or more words linked by hyphens (*sister-in-law, window-shop*)

Compound nouns and verbs fall into these categories more by custom than by rule. When you're not sure which way to write a compound, refer to your dictionary. If the compound is not listed in your dictionary, write it as two words.

Use a hyphen in a compound word containing one or more elements beginning with a capital letter.

Bill says that, as a *neo-Marxist* living in an *A-frame* house, it would be politically incorrect for him to wear a Mickey Mouse *T-shirt.*

Bubba doesn't mind being labeled a *pre-Neanderthal*, but he'll break anyone's neck who calls him *anti-American.*

There are exceptions to this rule: *unchristian,* for one. If you think a compound word looks odd with a hyphen, check your dictionary.

**36b.** Use a hyphen in a compound adjective preceding a noun but not following a noun.

> Jerome, a devotee of *twentieth-century* music, has no interest in the classic symphonies of the *eighteenth century*.

> I'd like living in an *out-of-the-way* place better if it weren't so far *out of the way*.

In a series of hyphenated adjectives with the same second word, you can omit that word (but not the hyphen) in all but the last adjective of the series.

> Julia is a lover of eighteenth-, nineteenth-, and twentieth-century music.

The adverb *well*, when coupled with an adjective, follows the same hyphenation rules as if it were an adjective.

> It is *well known* that Tony has a *well-equipped* kitchen, although his is not as *well equipped* as the hotel's.

Do *not* use a hyphen to link an adverb ending in *-ly* with an adjective.

> FAULTY    The sun hung like a newly-minted penny in a freshly-washed sky.

> REVISED   The sun hung like a newly minted penny in a freshly washed sky.

**36c.** Use a hyphen after the prefixes *all-*, *ex-*, and *self-* and before the suffix *-elect*.

> Lucille's *ex-husband* is studying *self-hypnosis*.

> This *all-important* debate pits Senator Browning against the *president-elect*.

Note that these prefixes and suffixes also can function as parts of words that are not hyphenated (*exit, selfish*). Whenever you are unsure whether to use a hyphen, check a dictionary.

**36d.** Use a hyphen in most cases if an added prefix or suffix creates a double vowel, triple consonant, or ambiguous pronunciation.

It is also acceptable to omit the hyphen in the case of a double *e*: *reeducate*.

> The contractor told us that his *pre-estimate* did not cover any *pre-existing* flaws in the building.

> The recreation department favors the *re-creation* of a summer activities program.

**36e.** Use a hyphen in spelled-out fractions and compound whole numbers from twenty-one to ninety-nine.

> When her sister gave Leslie's age as six and *three-quarters*, Leslie corrected her: "I'm six and *five-sixths*!"

The fifth graders learned that *forty-four* rounds down to forty while *forty-five* rounds up to fifty.

**36f.** Use a hyphen to indicate inclusive numbers.

The section covering the years 1975–1980 is found on pages 20–27.

**36g.** Use a hyphen to break a word between syllables at the end of a line.

Words are divided as they are pronounced, by syllables. Break a hyphenated compound at its hyphen and a nonhyphenated compound between the words that make it up. For a noncompound word, saying it out loud usually will give you a good idea where to break it; if you still are not sure, check your dictionary.

| | |
|---|---|
| FAULTY | Bubba hates to be called an-<br>ti-American. |
| REVISED | Bubba hates to be called anti-<br>American. |
| FAULTY | Francis will not be home until dinn-<br>er. |
| REVISED | Francis will not be home until din-<br>ner. |

Don't split a one-syllable word, even if keeping it intact makes your line come out a bit too short or too long.

| | |
|---|---|
| FAULTY | I'm completely drench-<br>ed. |
| REVISED | I'm completely drenched. |
| FAULTY | Arnold is a tower of stren-<br>gth. |
| REVISED | Arnold is a tower of<br>strength. |

Don't split a word after a one-letter syllable or before a one- or two-letter syllable.

| | |
|---|---|
| FAULTY | What's that up the road a-<br>head? |
| REVISED | What's that up the road<br>ahead? |
| FAULTY | I am proud to be an Americ-<br>an. |
| REVISED | I am proud to be an Ameri-<br>can. |

Don't split a word after a segment that looks like a whole word, even if a dictionary puts a syllable break there.

| | |
|---|---|
| CONFUSING | The lusty sailor aimed his sex-<br>tant at the stars. |
| CLEAR | The lusty sailor aimed his<br>sextant at the stars. |
| CONFUSING | He is addicted to her-<br>oin. |
| CLEAR | He is addicted to heroin. |

**EXERCISE 36–1**

## Using Hyphens

Add necessary hyphens and remove incorrectly used hyphens in the following sentences. Some sentences may be correct. Answers for the lettered sentences appear in the back of the book. Example:

Carlos presented Isabel with a beautifully-wrought silver necklace.

Carlos presented Isabel with a beautifully wrought silver necklace.

a. Do nonAmericans share our view of ourselves as a freedom loving people?
b. The dealer told George the two vases are within nine-tenths of an inch of being a perfect match.
c. Patrick Henry's words reecho down through the ages: "Give me liberty or give me death!"
d. Our sociology textbook is well-written and presents some well researched information.
e. The weather forecast calls for showers followed by suns-
hine.

1. The town council voted to extend domestic partnership benefits to all happily-unmarried couples.
2. Henry's exact height is six feet, four and a half inches.
3. As Joyce walked away, a voice behind her called, "You-
're under arrest!"
4. The site of Troy will be reexcavated and all the archaeological evidence re-
examined.
5. Critics applauded the fast moving plot and fully realized characters.
6. As part of his recovery from hand surgery, Chuck has learned to crossstitch.
7. Batman fended off the Joker's surprise attack with a powerful right hook to the jaw.
8. Despite his plummeting approval ratings, the president elect refused to succumb to selfpity.
9. The guerrillas insist that being anticapitalist doesn't mean they are proCuba.
10. The downpour that sent everyone running for shelter end-
ed as quickly as it had started.

# 37. *Spelling*

English spelling so often defies the rules that many speakers of the language wonder if, indeed, there *are* rules. You probably learned to spell — as most of us did — mainly by memorizing. By now you remember that there's a *b* in *doubt* but not in *spout*, a *k* in *knife* but not in *nine*. You know that the same sound can have several spellings, as in *here, ear, pier, sneer,* and *weird*. You are resigned to the fact that *ou* is pronounced differently in *four, round, ought,* and *double*. Still, like most people, you may have trouble with the spelling of certain words.

How many times have you heard someone say "ath-uh-lete" for *athlete*, "gov-er-ment" for *government*, or "nuc-yu-lar" for *nuclear*? Get the pronunciation right and you realize that the spelling has to be *arctic* (not *artic*), *mischievous* (not *mischievious*), *perform* (not *preform*), *surprise* (not *suprise*), *replenish* (not *replentish*), *similar* (not *similiar*).

The trouble is that careful pronunciation is only sometimes a reliable guide to English spelling. Knowing how to pronounce *psychology, whistle, light, gauge,* and *rhythm* doesn't help you spell them. How, then, are you to cope?

## 37a.    Follow spelling rules.

Fortunately, there are a few rules for spelling English words that work most of the time. Learning them, and some of their exceptions, will give you a sturdy foundation on which to build.

---

### Commonly Confused Homonyms

**accept** (v., receive willingly); **except** (prep., other than)

Mimi could *accept* all of Lefty's gifts *except* his ring.

**affect** (v., influence); **effect** (n., result)

If the new rules *affect* us, what will be their *effect*?

**allusion** (n., reference); **illusion** (n., fantasy)

Any *allusion* to Norman's mother may revive his *illusion* that she is upstairs, alive, in her rocking chair.

**capital** (adj., uppercase; n., seat of government); **capitol** (n., government building)

The *Capitol* building in Washington, D.C. (our nation's *capital*), is spelled with a *capital* C.

---

### Commonly Confused Homonyms *(continued)*

**cite** (v., refer to); **sight** (n., vision or tourist attraction); **site** (n., place)

Did you *cite* Mother as your authority on which *sites* feature the most interesting *sights?*

**complement** (v., complete; n., counterpart); **compliment** (v. or n., praise)

For Lee to say that Sheila's beauty *complements* her intelligence may or may not be a *compliment.*

**desert** (v., abandon); **dessert** (n., end-of-meal sweet)

Don't *desert* us by leaving before *dessert.*

**elicit** (v., bring out); **illicit** (adj., illegal)

By going undercover, Sonny should *elicit* some offers of *illicit* drugs.

**formally** (adv., officially); **formerly** (adv., in the past)

Jane and John Doe-Smith, *formerly* Jane Doe and John Smith, sent cards *formally* announcing their marriage.

**led** (v., past tense of *lead*); **lead** (n., a metal)

Gil's heart was heavy as *lead* when he *led* the mourners to the grave.

**principal** (n. or adj., chief); **principle** (n., rule)

The *principal* problem is convincing the media that our school *principal* is a person of high *principles.*

**stationary** (adj., motionless); **stationery** (n., writing paper)

Hubert's *stationery* shop stood *stationary* for twenty years until a flood swept it down the river.

**their** (pron., belonging to them); **there** (adv., in that place); **they're** (contraction of *they are*)

Sue said *they're* going over *there* to visit *their* aunt.

**to** (prep., toward); **too** (adv., also or excessively); **two** (n. or adj., numeral: one more than one)

Let's not take *two* cars *to* town — that's *too* many unless Lucille and Harry are coming *too.*

**who's** (contraction of *who is*); **whose** (pron., belonging to whom)

*Who's* going to tell me *whose* dog this is?

**your** (pron., belonging to you); **you're** (contraction of *you are*)

*You're* not getting *your* own way this time!

### EI or IE?

The best way to remember which words are spelled *ei* and which ones *ie* is to recall this familiar jingle:

*I* before *e* except after *c*,
Or when sounded like *a*, as in *neighbor* and *weigh*.

*Niece, believe, field, receive, receipt, ceiling, beige,* and *freight* are just a few of the words you'll be able to spell easily once you learn that rule. Then memorize a few of the exceptions:

| | | | | |
|---|---|---|---|---|
| counterfeit | foreign | kaleidoscope | protein | seize |
| either | forfeit | leisure | science | weird |
| financier | height | neither | seismograph | |

Also among the rule breakers are words in which *cien* is pronounced "shen"; *ancient, efficient, conscience, prescience.*

### Homonyms

Words that sound the same, or almost the same, but are spelled differently are called **homonyms.** Here are some of the most commonly confused homonyms, briefly identified, with examples of how to use them. (Also see the Glossary of Troublemakers at the end of the *Handbook.*)

### Plurals

1. To form the plural of most common nouns, add *-s.* If a noun ends in *-ch, -sh, -s,* or *-x,* form its plural by adding *-es.*

| | |
|---|---|
| attack, attacks | umbrella, umbrellas |
| ridge, ridges | zone, zones |
| boss, bosses | trellis, trellises |
| sandwich, sandwiches | crash, crashes |
| tax, taxes | Betamax, Betamaxes |

2. To form the plural of a common noun ending in *-o*, add *-s* if the *-o* follows a vowel and *-es* if it follows a consonant.

| | |
|---|---|
| radio, radios | video, videos |
| hero, heroes | potato, potatoes |

3. To form the plural of a common noun ending in *-y*, change the *y* to *i* and add *-es* if the *y* follows a consonant. Add only *-s* if the *y* follows a vowel.

| | |
|---|---|
| baby, babies | sissy, sissies |
| fly, flies | wallaby, wallabies |
| toy, toys | monkey, monkeys |
| guy, guys | day, days |

4. To form the plural of a proper noun, add *-s* or *-es* without changing the noun's ending.

Proper nouns follow the same rules as common nouns, with one exception: a proper noun never changes its spelling in the plural form.

Mary Jane, Mary Janes         Dr. Maddox, the Maddoxes
Mr. Curry, the Currys          Saturday, Saturdays
Professor Jones, the Joneses

5. To form the plural of a compound noun, add -s or -es to the chief word, or to the last word if all the words are equal in weight.

brother-in-law, brothers-in-law      actor-manager, actor-managers
aide-de-camp, aides-de-camp          tractor-trailer, tractor-trailers

6. Memorize the plural forms of nouns that diverge from these rules. Certain nouns have special plurals. Here are a few:

alumna, alumnae          man, men
alumnus, alumni          medium, media
child, children          mouse, mice
half, halves             self, selves
goose, geese             tooth, teeth
leaf, leaves             woman, women

## Suffixes

The -s added to a word to make it plural is one type of *suffix,* or tail section. Suffixes allow the same root word to do a variety of jobs, by giving it different forms for different functions. Keeping a few basic rules in mind will help you to use suffixes successfully.

1. Drop a silent *e* before a suffix that begins with a vowel.

move, mover, moved, moving
argue, arguer, argued, arguing
accrue, accruing, accrual

EXCEPTION: If the *e* has an essential function, keep it before adding a suffix that begins with a vowel. In *singe,* for instance, the *e* changes the word's pronunciation from "sing" to "sinj." If you dropped the *e* in *singeing,* it would become *singing.*

singe, singed, singeing
tiptoe, tiptoed, tiptoeing

2. Keep a silent *e* before a suffix that begins with a consonant.

move, movement
hope, hopeless

EXCEPTION: In a word ending in a silent *e* preceded by a vowel, sometimes (but not always) drop the *e.*

argue, argument
true, truly

3.  Change a final *y* to *i* before a suffix if the *y* follows a consonant but not if the *y* follows a vowel.

> cry, crier, cried
> joy, joyous, joyful
> happy, happiest, happily
> hurry, hurried
> pray, prayed, prayer

EXCEPTION: Keep the *y* whenever the suffix is *-ing*.

> hurry, hurrying
> pray, praying

Drop a final *y* before the suffix *-ize*.

> deputy, deputize
> memory, memorize

4.  Double the final consonant of a one-syllable word before a suffix if (1) the suffix starts with a vowel *and* (2) the final consonant follows a single vowel.

> sit, sitter, sitting
> flop, flopped, floppy
> rob, robbed, robbery

Don't double the final consonant if it follows two vowels or another consonant.

> fail, failed, failure
> stack, stacking, stackable

Don't double the final consonant if the suffix starts with a consonant.

> top, topless
> cap, capful

5.  Double the final consonant of a word with two or more syllables if (1) the suffix starts with a vowel *and* (2) the final consonant follows a single vowel *and* (3) the last syllable of the stem is accented once the suffix is added.

> commit, committed, committing
> rebut, rebuttal
> regret, regretted, regrettable

Don't double the final consonant if it follows more than one vowel —

> avail, available
> repeat, repeating

or if it follows another consonant —

> accent, accented
> depend, dependence

or the suffix starts with a consonant —

commit, commitment
jewel, jewelry

or, when the suffix is added, the final syllable of the stem is unaccented.

confer, conference (*but* conferred)
travel, traveler

### Prefixes

The main point to remember when writing a word with a *prefix* (or nose section) is that the prefix usually does not alter the spelling of the root word it precedes.

dis + appear = disappear
dis + satisfied = dissatisfied
mis + step = misstep
mis + understand = misunderstand
with + hold = withhold
un + necessary = unnecessary

(For guidelines on when to use a hyphen to attach a prefix, see 36c and 36d.)

## 37b. Develop spelling skills.

Besides becoming familiar with the rules in this chapter, you can use several other tactics to teach yourself to be a better speller.

1. ***Use mnemonic devices.*** To make unusual spellings stick in your memory, invent associations. *Weird* behaves *weirdly*. Would you rather study *ancient science* or be an *efficient financier*? Using such *mnemonic devices* (tricks to aid memory) may help you not only with *ie* and *ei* but with whatever troublesome spelling you are determined to remember. Rise ag*ain*, Brit*ain*! One *d* in *dish*, one in *radish*. Why isn't *mathe*matics like *athle*tics? You write a let*ter* on station*ery*. Any silly phrase or sentence will do, as long as it brings tricky spellings to mind.

2. ***Keep a record of words you misspell.*** Buy yourself a little notebook in which to enter words that invariably trip you up. Each time you proofread a paper you have written and each time you receive one back from your instructor, write down any words you have misspelled. Then practice pronouncing, writing, and spelling them out loud until you have mastered them.

3. ***Check any questionable spelling by referring to your dictionary.*** Keep a dictionary at your elbow as you write. In matters of spelling, that good-as-gold book is your best friend. Use it to check words as you come up with them and to double-check them as you proofread and edit your work.

4. ***Learn commonly misspelled words.*** To save you the trouble of looking up every spelling bugbear, here is a list of words frequently misspelled. This list will serve to review our whole discussion of spelling, for it contains the trickiest words we've mentioned. Check-mark those that give you trouble —

but don't stop there. Spend a few minutes each day going over them. Pronounce each one carefully or have a friend read the list to you. Spell every troublesome word out loud; write it ten times. Your spelling will improve rapidly.

Everybody has at least ten or twenty bugbears. Shoot down yours.

### COMMONLY MISSPELLED WORDS

| | | |
|---|---|---|
| absence | appreciate | cemetery |
| abundance | appropriate | certain |
| academic | arctic | changeable |
| acceptable | arrest | changing |
| accessible | argument | characteristic |
| accidentally | ascend | chief |
| accommodate | assassinate | choose (present tense) |
| accustom | assistance | chose (past tense) |
| achievement | association | climbed |
| acknowledgment | athlete | column |
| acquaintance | athletics | coming |
| acquire | attach | commitment |
| acquitted | attendance | committed |
| across | attractive | committee |
| address | audible | comparative |
| advertisement | audience | competent |
| advice | average | competition |
| advise | awkward | complement |
| aggravate | balloon | compliment |
| aggressive | barbarous | conceive |
| aging | beginning | condemn |
| allege | believe | congratulate |
| alleviate | beneficial | connoisseur |
| all right | benefited | conscience |
| all together (all in one | borne (carried) | conscientious |
|   group) | boundary | consistent |
| a lot | breath (noun) | controlled |
| already | breathe (verb) | controversy |
| although | Britain | corollary |
| altogether (entirely) | buoyant | corps (a group) |
| amateur | bureaucracy | corpse (a body) |
| analogous | business | criticism |
| analysis | cafeteria | criticize |
| analyze | calendar | cruise |
| annual | candidate | curiosity |
| antecedent | capital | curious |
| anxiety | capitol (a building) | deceive |
| apology | careful | decision |
| apparatus | casualties | defendant |
| apparent | category | deficient |
| appetite | causal | definite |
| appearance | ceiling | deity |

| | | |
|---|---|---|
| dependent | exercise | imitation |
| descendant | exhaust | immediately |
| describe | existence | incidentally |
| description | experience | incredible |
| desirable | explanation | indefinite |
| despair | extremely | independence |
| desperate | familiar | indispensable |
| detach | fascinate | infinite |
| develop | February | influential |
| develops | fiery | inoculate |
| development | finally | intelligence |
| device (noun) | financial | intentionally |
| devise (verb) | foreign | interest |
| diaphragm | foremost | interpret |
| diary | foresee | interrupt |
| difference | foreword (a preface) | irrelevant |
| dilemma | forfeit | irresistible |
| dining | forth | irritable |
| disappear | forty | island |
| disappoint | forward | its (possessive) |
| disastrous | fourth (number four) | it's (it is, it has) |
| discipline | frantically | jealousy |
| discussion | fraternities | judgment |
| disease | friend | knowledge |
| disparate | fulfill | laboratory |
| dissatisfied | fulfillment | led (past tense of *lead*) |
| dissipate | gaiety | library |
| divide | gauge | license |
| divine | genealogy | lightning |
| doesn't | generally | literature |
| dominant | genuine | loneliness |
| don't | government | loose (adjective) |
| drawer | grammar | lose (verb) |
| drunkenness | grief | lying |
| ecstasy | grievous | magazine |
| efficiency | guarantee | maintenance |
| eighth | guard | marriage |
| either | guidance | mathematics |
| eligible | harass | medicine |
| embarrass | height | miniature |
| emphasize | heroes | mischievous |
| entirety | hoping | misspell |
| environment | humorous | misstep |
| equipped | hurriedly | muscle |
| equivalent | hurrying | mysterious |
| especially | hygiene | necessary |
| exaggerate | hypocrisy | neither |
| exceed | illiterate | nickel |
| excel | illogical | niece |
| excellence | imaginary | ninety |

ninth
noticeable
notorious
nuclear
nucleus
numerous
obstacle
occasion
occasionally
occur
occurred
occurrence
official
omission
omit
omitted
opinion
opportunity
originally
outrageous
overrun
paid
pamphlet
panicky
parallel
particularly
pastime
peaceable
perceive
perform
performance
perhaps
permanent
permissible
persistence
personnel
persuade
physical
picnic
playwright
possession
possibly
practically
precede
predominant
preferred
prejudice
preparation
prevalent
primitive

principal (adj., main;
    n., head of a school)
principle (a rule or
    standard)
privilege
probably
procedure
proceed
professor
prominent
pronounce
pronunciation
propeller
psychology
psychological
pursue
quantity
questionnaire
quiet
quizzes
realize
rebelled
recede
receipt
receive
recipe
recommend
reference
referring
regrettable
relevance
relief
relieve
religious
remembrance
reminisce
reminiscence
renown
repetition
replenish
representative
resistance
restaurant
review
rhythm
rhythmic
ridiculous
roommate
sacrifice
sacrilegious

safety
scarcely
scarcity
schedule
secretary
seize
separate
sergeant
shining
siege
similar
sincerely
sophomore
source
specifically
specimen
sponsor
stationary (in one
    place)
stationery (writing
    material)
strategy
strength
strenuous
stretch
succeed
successful
suddenness
superintendent
supersede
suppress
surprise
suspicious
synonymous
technical
technique
temperature
tendency
therefore
thorough
thoroughbred
though
thought
throughout
tragedy
transferred
traveler
traveling
truly
twelfth

tyranny              valuable            wholly
unanimous            vengeance           who's (who is)
undoubtedly          vicious             whose (possessive of
unnecessary          view                    *who*)
unnoticed            villain             withhold
until                warrant             woman
useful               weather             women
usually              Wednesday           writing
vacancy              weird               yacht
vacuum               whether

**EXERCISE 37–1**

## Spelling

Edit the following passage to correct misspelled words.

There are alians living among us, who are commited to enslaveing the human race.

There are aliens living among us, who are committed to enslaving the human race.

They are mysterios beings of devious inteligence who qietly govern our lives. They are all around us, in our homes and our streets. When you come home exausted after a disasterous day at work, they are there waiting for you, and if you do not feed them immediatly, there behavior becomes barberous: now begins the theatrical nibbling of plants and other iritable antics devised to harrass you until you finally either lose your mind or open the can of tuna fish. They will flaunt their power before your very eyes by tormenting flys, or assasinating moths. Their senses are tuned to a world beyond human perception. Strange, explosive sprints into ajoining rooms suggest involvment with the imaginery Olympics, while imperceptable air currents on the ceiling will keep them amused indefinitly. They have a passion for shredding favorite chairs and enjoy decorating with fur balls. Despite thier destructive habits, we need fear no personal injury, for they look on us compasionately as thier pets.

# A Glossary of Troublemakers

*Usage* refers to the way in which writers customarily use certain words and phrases. It includes matters of accepted practice or convention. To incorporate appropriate usage in your writing, you can observe (as dictionary makers carefully do) the practices followed by a majority of admirable writers.

This glossary lists words and phrases whose usage troubles student writers. Not every possible problem is listed — only some that frequently puzzle students. This brief list is meant to help you pinpoint a few sources of difficulty and wipe them out. Look it over; refer to it when you don't remember the preferred usage. It may clear up a few problems for you.

For advice on getting rid of long-winded expressions (*in the field of, in regards to*), see page H–138. For advice on spelling, see Chapter 37.

**a, an**   Use *an* only before a word beginning with a vowel sound. "*An* asp can eat *an* egg *an* hour." (Note that some words, such as *hour* and *honest*, open with a vowel sound even though spelled with an *h*.)

**above**   Using *above* or *below* to refer back or forward in an essay is awkward and may not be accurate. Less awkward alternatives: "the *preceding* argument," "in the *following* discussion," "on the *next* page."

**accept, except**   *Accept* is a verb meaning "to receive willingly"; *except* is usually a preposition meaning "not including." "This motel *accepts* all children *except* infants under two." Sometimes *except* is a verb, meaning "to exempt." "The rate of $20 per person *excepts* children under twelve."

**adverse, averse**   *Adverse* means "unfavorable or antagonistic" and is used to modify things, not people.

*Averse* means "reluctant or strongly opposed" and is followed by *to*. "Because of the *adverse* winds, the captain is *averse* to setting sail."

**advice, advise**   *Advice* is a noun, *advise* a verb. When someone *advises* you, you receive *advice*.

**affect, effect**   Most of the time, the verb *affect* means "to act on" or "to influence." "Too much beer can *affect* your speech." *Affect* can also mean "to put on airs." "He *affected* an Oxford accent." *Effect*, a noun, means "a result": "Too much beer has a numbing *effect*." But *effect* is also a verb, meaning "to bring about." "Beer *effected* his downfall."

**aggravate**   Although in speech people often use *aggravate* to mean "to annoy," in formal writing use *aggravate* to mean "to make worse." "The noise of the jackhammers *aggravated* her headache."

**agree to, agree with, agree on** *Agree to* means "to consent to"; *agree with*, "to be in accord." "I agreed to attend the New Age lecture, but I didn't *agree with* the speaker's views." *Agree on* means "to come to or have an understanding about." "Chuck and I finally *agreed on* a compromise: the children would go to camp, but not overnight."

**ain't** Don't use *ain't* in writing; it is nonstandard English for *am not*, *is not* (*isn't*), and *are not* (*aren't*).

**allusion, illusion** An *allusion* is a reference to history, literature, music, science, or some other area of knowledge. In the statement "Two by two we hurried aboard Flight 937 as though the waters of the flood lapped at our heels," the writer makes an allusion to the biblical story of Noah's ark. An *illusion* is a misleading appearance ("an optical illusion") or a mistaken assumption. "He labors under the *illusion* that he's Romeo" (to give an example with an allusion in it).

**a lot** Many people mistakenly write the colloquial expression *a lot* as one word: *alot*. Use *a lot* if you must; but in writing, *much* or *a large amount* is preferable. See also *lots, lots of, a lot of.*

**already, all ready** *Already* means "by now"; *all ready* means "set to go." "At last our picnic was *all ready*, but *already* it was night."

**altogether, all together** *Altogether* means "entirely." "He is *altogether* mistaken." *All together* means "in unison" or "assembled." "Now *all together* — heave!" "Inspector Trent gathered the suspects *all together* in the drawing room."

**among, between** *Between* refers to two persons or things; *among*, to more than two. "Some disagreement *between* the two superpowers was inevitable. Still, there was general harmony *among* the five nations represented at the conference."

**amoral, immoral** *Amoral* means "neither moral nor immoral" or "not involved with moral distinctions or judgments." "Some people think children are *amoral* and should not be held accountable for their actions." *Immoral* means "violating moral principles, morally wrong." "Stealing from the poor is *immoral.*"

**amount, number** Use *amount* to refer to quantities that cannot be counted or to bulk; use *number* to re-

fer to countable, separate items. "The *number* of people you want to serve determines the *amount* of ice cream you'll need."

**an, a** See *a, an*.

**and/or** Usually use either *and* or *or* alone. "Tim *and* Elaine will come to the party." "Tim *or* Elaine will come to the party." If you mean three distinct options, write, "Tim *or* Elaine, *or both*, will come to the party, depending on whether they can find a babysitter."

**ante-, anti-** The prefix *ante-* means "preceding." An *antechamber* is a small room that leads to a larger one; *antebellum* means "before the Civil War." *Anti-* most often means "opposing": *antidepressant*. It needs a hyphen in front of *i* (*anti-inflationary*) or in front of a capital letter (*anti-Marxist*).

**anxious, eager** Although the meanings of these two words overlap to some extent, in writing reserve *anxious* for situations involving anxiety or worry. *Eager* denotes joyous anticipation. "We are *eager* to see him, but we're *anxious* about his failing health."

**anybody, any body** When *anybody* is used as an indefinite pronoun, write it as one word: "*Anybody* in his or her right mind abhors murder." (*Anybody* is singular; therefore it is wrong to say "Anybody in *their* right mind." See 22 for acceptable alternatives.) *Any body*, written as two words, is the adjective *any* modifying the noun *body*. "Name *any body* of water in Australia."

**anyone, any one** *Anyone* is an indefinite pronoun written as one word. "Does *anyone* want dessert?" The phrase *any one* consists of the pronoun *one* modified by the adjective *any* and is used to single out something in a group: "Pick *any one* of the pies — they're all good."

**anyplace** *Anyplace* is colloquial for *anywhere* and should not be used in formal writing.

**anyways, anywheres** These are nonstandard forms of *anyway* and *anywhere* and should not be used in writing.

**apt** Usually, *apt* means "likely." "That film is *apt* to bore you." "Jack's big feet make him *apt* to trip." *Apt* can also mean "fitting" and "quick to learn": "an apt nickname," "an apt student of French." See also *liable, likely*.

**as** Sometimes using the subordinating conjunction *as* can make a sentence ambiguous. "*As* we were climbing the mountain, we put on heavy sweaters." Does *as* here mean "because" or "while"? Whenever using *as* would be confusing, use a more specific term instead, such as *because* or *while*.

**as, like** Use *as, as if,* or *as though* rather than *like* to introduce clauses of comparison. "Dan's compositions are tuneful, *as* [not *like*] music ought to be." "Jeffrey behaves *as if* [not *like*] he were ill." *Like,* because it is a preposition, can introduce a phrase but not a clause. "My brother looks *like* me." "Henrietta runs *like* a duck."

**as to** Usually this expression sounds stilted. Use *about* instead. "He complained *about* [not *as to*] the cockroaches."

**at** See *where . . . at, where . . . to.*

**averse** See *adverse, averse.*

**bad, badly** *Bad* is an adjective; *badly* is an adverb. They are commonly misused after linking verbs (*be, appear, become, grow, seem, prove*) and verbs of the senses (*feel, look, smell, sound, taste*). Following a linking verb, use the adjective form. "I feel *bad* that we missed the plane." "The egg smells *bad.*" (See 10a, 10b.) The adverb form is used to modify a verb or an adjective. "They played so *badly* they lost to the last-place team." "It was a *badly* needed victory that saved the cellar-dwellers from elimination."

**being as, being that** "*Being as* I was ignorant of the facts, I kept still" is a nonstandard way to say "*Because* I was ignorant" or "*Not knowing* the facts."

**beside, besides** *Beside* is a preposition meaning "next to." "Sheldon enjoyed sitting *beside* the guest of honor." *Besides* is an adverb meaning "in addition." "*Besides,* he has a sense of humor." *Besides* is also a preposition meaning "other than." "Something *besides* shyness caused his embarrassment."

**between, among** See *among, between.*

**between you and I** The preposition *between* always takes the objective case. "Between *you* and *me* [not *I*], that story about the dog's eating Joe's money sounds suspicious." "Between *us* [not *we*], what's going on between Chris and *her* [not *she*] is unfathomable."

**bi-, semi-** These prefixes are often confused. *Bi-* means "two." *Semi-* means "half of." Thus, *semiauto-* *matic* means "partly automatic," and *semiannual* means "happening every half year." *Biaxial* means "having two axes." Although sometimes people also use *bi-* to mean "happening twice in," avoid that use because it can be confusing (for example, it's difficult to know whether the person using *biweekly* means "twice a week" or "every two weeks").

**but that, but what** "I don't know *but what* [or *but that*] you're right" is a wordy, imprecise way of saying "Maybe you're right" or "I believe you're right."

**can, may** Use *can* to indicate ability. "Jake *can* bench-press 650 pounds." *May* involves permission. "*May* I bench-press today?" "You *may*, if you *can.*"

**capital, capitol** A *capital* is a city that is the center of government for a state or country. *Capital* can also mean "wealth." A *capitol* is a building in which legislators meet. "Who knows what the *capital* of Finland is?" "The renovated *capitol* is a popular tourist attraction."

**censor, censure** *Censor* as a verb means "to evaluate and remove objectionable material." As a noun, it means "someone who censors." "All mail was *censored* before it left the country." *Censure* as a verb means "to find fault with, criticize." As a noun, it means "disapproval." "The governor's extreme actions were met with public *censure.*"

**center around** Say "Class discussion *centered on* [or *revolved around*] her paper." In this sense, the verb *center* means "to have one main concern" — the way a circle has a central point. (Thus, to say a discussion centers *around* anything is a murky metaphor.)

**cite, sight, site** *Cite,* a verb, means "to quote from or refer to." *Sight* as a verb means "to see or glimpse"; as a noun it means "a view, a spectacle." "When the police officer *sighted* my terrier running across the playground, she *cited* the leash laws and told me I'd be fined." *Site,* a noun, means "location." "Standing at the *site* of his childhood home, he wept tears of nostalgia. He was a pitiful *sight.*"

**climatic, climactic** *Climatic,* from *climate,* refers to meteorological conditions. Saying "climatic conditions," however, is wordy — you can usually substitute "the climate": "*Climatic* conditions are [or "The *climate* is"] changing because of the hole in the ozone." *Climactic,* from *climax,* refers to the culmination of a progression of events. "In the *climactic* scene the hero drives his car off the pier."

**compare, contrast**   *Compare* has two main meanings. The first, "to liken or represent as similar," is followed by *to*. "She *compared* her room *to* a jail cell." "He *compared* me *to* a summer's day." In its second meaning, *compare* means "to analyze for similarities and differences" and is generally followed by *with*. "The speaker *compared* the American educational system *with* the Japanese system."
*Contrast* also has two main meanings. As a transitive verb, taking an object, it means "to compare or analyze to emphasize differences" and is generally followed by *with*. "The speaker *contrasted* the social emphasis of the Japanese primary grades *with* the academic emphasis of ours." As an intransitive verb, *contrast* means "to exhibit differences when compared." "The matted tangle of Sidney's fur *contrasted* sharply *with* its usual healthy sleekness."

**complement, compliment**   *Compliment* is a verb meaning "to praise" or a noun meaning "praise." "The professor *complimented* Sarah on her perceptiveness." *Complement* is a verb meaning "to complete or reinforce." "Jennifer's experiences as a practice teacher *complemented* what she learned in her education class."

**continual, continuous**   *Continual* means "often repeated." "Mike was in *continual* conflict with his neighbors." *Continuous* means "uninterrupted." "Lisa's *continuous* chatter made it impossible for Debbie to concentrate on her reading."

**could care less**   This is nonstandard English for *couldn't care less* and should not be used in writing. "The cat *couldn't* [not *could*] *care less* about which brand of cat food you buy."

**could of**   *Could of* is colloquial for *could have* and should not be used in writing.

**couple of**   Write "a *couple of* drinks" when you mean two. For more than two, say "a *few* [or *several*] drinks."

**criteria, criterion**   *Criteria* is the plural of *criterion*, which means "a standard or requirement on which a judgment or decision is based." "The main *criteria* for this job are attention to detail and good typing skills."

**data**   *Data* is a plural noun. Write "The data *are*" and "*these* data." The singular form of *data* is *datum* — rarely used because it sounds musty. Instead, use *fact*, *figure*, or *statistic*.

**different from, different than**   *Different from* is usually the correct form to use. "How is good poetry *different from* prose?" Use *different than* when a whole clause follows. "Violin lessons with Mr. James were *different than* I had imagined."

**disinterested, uninterested**   *Disinterested* means "impartial, fair, objective." "The defendant hoped for a *disinterested* judge." *Uninterested* means "indifferent." "Suzanne was *uninterested* in world news."

**don't, doesn't**   *Don't* is the contraction for *do not*, and *doesn't* is the contraction for *does not*. "They *don't* want to get dressed up for the ceremony." "The cat *doesn't* [not *don't*] like to be combed."

**due to**   *Due* is an adjective and must modify a noun or pronoun; it can't modify a verb or an adjective. Begin a sentence with *due to* and you invite trouble: "*Due to rain*, the game was postponed." Write instead, "*Because of rain*." *Due to* works after the verb *be*. "His fall was *due to* a banana peel." There, *due* modifies the noun *fall*.

**due to the fact that**   A windy expression for *because*.

**eager, anxious**   See *anxious, eager*.

**effect, affect**   See *affect, effect*.

**either**   Use *either* when referring to one of two things. "Both internships sound great; I'd be happy with *either*." When referring to one of three or more things, use *any one* or *any*. "*Any one* of our four trained counselors will be able to help you."

**elicit, illicit**   *Elicit*, a verb, means "to bring or draw out." *Illicit*, an adjective, means "unlawful" or "not permissible." "Try as he might, Gus could not *elicit* details from Bob about his *illicit* nighttime activities."

**emigrant, immigrant**   An *emigrant* has left a country or region; an *immigrant* has moved into a country or region. The verb forms reflect the same distinction: *emigrate from*, *immigrate to*. "Even in the United States, *immigrants* often hold the lowest-paying positions." "Anders *emigrated* from Norway."

**eminent, imminent**   *Eminent* means "distinguished or outstanding"; *imminent* means "about to happen." "The *eminent* novelists shyly announced their *imminent* marriage."

**enormity, enormousness, enormous**   *Enormity* means "monstrous evil"; *enormousness* means "vastness or immensity"; and *enormous* means "vast or huge." "The *enormity* of the convicted woman's crimes baffled her acquaintances." "The *enormousness* of the lake impressed them."

**enthuse**    Good writers shun this verb. Instead of "The salesman *enthused* about the product," write, "The salesman *was enthusiastic* about the product."

**et cetera, etc.**    Replace *et cetera* (or its abbreviation, *etc.*) with exact words, and you will sharpen your writing. Even translating the Latin expression into English is an improvement: *and other things*. Rather than announcing an athletic meet to feature "high-jumping, shot-putting, *etc.*," you could say, "high-jumping, shot-putting, and other field events."

**everybody, every body**    When used as an indefinite pronoun, *everybody* is one word. "Why is *everybody* on the boys' team waving his arms?" Keep in mind that *everybody* is singular. It is a mistake to write, "Why is *everybody* waving *their* arms?" (See 9d and 22a for acceptable alternatives.) *Every body* written as two words refers to separate, individual bodies. "After the massacre, they buried *every body* in *its* [not *their*] own grave."

**everyone, every one**    Used as an indefinite pronoun, *everyone* is one word. "*Everyone* has *his or her* own ideas." Remember that *everyone* is singular. Therefore it is wrong to write, "*Everyone* has *their* own ideas." (See 9d and 22a for acceptable alternatives.) *Every one* written as two words refers to individual, distinct items. "I studied *every one* of the assigned exercises."

**except, accept**    See *accept, except.*

**expect**    In writing, avoid the informal use of *expect* to mean "suppose, assume, or think." "I *suppose* [not *expect*] you've heard that half the class flunked."

**fact that**    This is an expression that, nearly always, you can do without. "*The fact that* he was puny went unnoticed" is wordy; write, "That he was puny went unnoticed." "Because [not *Because of the fact that*] it snowed, the game was canceled."

**famous, infamous**    Do something that attracts wide notice and you become celebrated, or *famous*: "Marcia dreamed of growing up to be a *famous* inventor." But if your deeds are detestable, you may instead become notorious, or *infamous*, like Bluebeard, the *infamous* wife killer.

**farther, further**    In your writing, use *farther* to refer to literal distance. "Chicago is *farther* from Nome than from New York." When you wish to denote additional degree, time, or quantity, use *further*: "Sally's idea requires *further* discussion."

**fewer, less**    *Less* refers to general quantity or bulk; *fewer*, to separate, countable items. "Eat *less* pizza." "Salad has *fewer* calories."

**field**    In a statement such as "He took courses *in the field of* economics," leave out *the field of* and save words.

**firstly**    The recommended usage is *first* (and *second*, not *secondly*; *third*, not *thirdly*; and so on)

**flaunt, flout**    To *flaunt* is to show off. "She *flaunted* her wealth by buying much more than she needed." To *flout* is to defy. "George *flouted* the law by refusing to register for the draft."

**former, latter**    *Former* means "first of two"; *latter*, "second of two." They are an acceptable but heavy-handed pair, best done without. Too often, they oblige your reader to backtrack. Nine times out of ten, your writing will be clearer if you simply name again the persons or things you mean. Instead of writing, "The *former* great artist is the master of the flowing line, while the *latter* is the master of color," write, "Picasso is the master of the flowing line, while Matisse is the master of color."

**further, farther**    See *farther, further.*

**get, got**    *Get* has many meanings, especially in slang and colloquial use. Some, such as the following, are not appropriate in formal writing:

"To start, begin": "Let's start [not *get*] painting."

"To stir the emotions": "His frequent interruptions finally started annoying [not *getting to*] me."

"To harm, punish, or take revenge on": "She's going to take revenge on [not *get*] him." Or better, be even more specific about what you mean. "She's going to spread rumors about him to ruin his reputation."

**good, well**    To modify a verb, use the adverb *well*, not the adjective *good*. "Jan dives *well* [not *good*]." Linking verbs (*be, appear, become, grow, seem, prove*) and verbs of the senses (such as *feel, look, smell, sound, taste*) call for the adjective *good*. "The paint job looks *good*." *Well* is an adjective used only to refer to health. "She looks *well*" means that she seems to be in good health. "She looks *good*" means that her appearance is attractive. (See 10b, 10c.)

**hanged, hung**   Both words are the past tense of the verb *hang*. *Hanged* refers to an execution. "The murderer was *hanged* at dawn." For all other situations, use *hung*. "Jane *hung* her wash on the clothesline to dry."

**have got to**   In formal writing, avoid using the phrase *have got to* to mean "have to" or "must." "I *must* [not *have got to*] phone them right away."

**he, she, he or she**   Using *he* as a matter of course to refer to an indefinite person is considered sexist; so is using *she* with reference to traditionally female occupations or pastimes. However, peppering your writing with the phrase *he or she* can seem wordy and awkward. For alternatives, see 22.

**herself**   See -*self, -selves*.

**himself**   See -*self, -selves*.

**hopefully**   *Hopefully* means "with hope." "The children turned *hopefully* toward the door, expecting Santa Claus." In writing, avoid *hopefully* when you mean "it is to be hoped" or "let us hope." "*I hope* [not *Hopefully*] the posse will arrive soon."

**if, whether**   Use *whether*, not *if*, in indirect questions and to introduce alternatives. "Father asked me *whether* [not *if*] I was planning to sleep all morning." "I'm so confused I don't know *whether* [not *if*] it's day or night."

**illicit**   See *elicit, illicit*.

**illusion, allusion**   See *allusion, illusion*.

**imminent**   See *eminent, imminent*.

**immoral**   See *amoral, immoral*.

**imply, infer**   *Imply* means "to suggest"; *infer* means "to draw a conclusion." "Maria *implied* that she was too busy to see Tom. As their conversation proceeded, Tom *inferred* that Maria had lost interest in him."

**in, into**   *In* refers to a location or condition; *into* refers to the direction of movement or change. "The hero burst *into* the room and found the heroine *in* another man's arms." "Hiroko decided to go *into* banking."

**individual**   Don't use *individual* for *person*. "What kind of *person* [not *individual*] would do that?" Save

the word to mean "one" as opposed to "many": "an *individual* thinker in a conforming crowd."

**infer, imply**   See *imply, infer*.

**ingenious, ingenuous**   *Ingenious* means "clever." "The *ingenious* inventor caught the mouse unharmed." *Ingenuous* has two related meanings: "naive, unsophisticated" and "frank, candid." "Little Lord Fauntleroy's *ingenuous* remarks touched even his ill-tempered grandfather."

**in regards to**   Write *in regard to, regarding*, or *about*.

**inside of, outside of**   As prepositions, *inside* and *outside* do not require *of*. "The students were more interested in what was going on *outside* [not *outside of*] the building than in what was happening *inside* [not *inside of*] the classroom." Do not use *inside of* to refer colloquially to time or *outside of* to mean "except." "I'll finish the assignment *within* [not *inside of*] two hours." "He told no one *except* [not *outside of*] a few friends."

**irregardless**   *Irregardless* is a double negative. Use *regardless*.

**is because**   See *reason is because*.

**is when, is where**   Using these expressions results in errors in predication. "Obesity *is when* a person is greatly overweight." "Biology *is where* students dissect frogs." *When* refers to a point in time, but *obesity* is not a point in time; *where* refers to a place, but *biology* is not a place. Write instead, "Obesity is the condition of extreme overweight." "Biology is a laboratory course in which students dissect frogs." (See 16b.)

**its, it's**   *Its* is a possessive pronoun, never in need of an apostrophe. *It's* is a contraction for *it is*. "Every new experience has *its* bad moments. Still, *it's* exciting to explore the unknown."

**it's me, it is I**   Although *it's me* is widely used in speech, don't use it in formal writing. Write "It is I," which is grammatically correct. The same applies to other personal pronouns. "It was *he* [not *him*] who started the mutiny." (See 7.)

**kind of, sort of, type of**   When you use *kind, sort*, or *type* — singular words — make sure that the sentence construction is singular. "That *type* of show *offends* me." "Those *types* of shows *offend* me." In speech, *kind of* and *sort of* are used as qualifiers. "He is *sort of* fat." Avoid them in writing. "He is *rather* [or *somewhat* or *slightly*; not *sort of*] fat."

**latter, former**  See *former, latter.*

**lay, lie**  The verb *lay*, meaning "to put or place," takes an object. *Lie*, meaning "to rest or recline," does not. Their principal parts are *lay, laid, laid*, and *lie, lay, lain.* "*Lay* that pistol down." "*Lie* on the bed until your headache goes away." (See 5f.)

**leave, let**  *Leave* means "to go away." *Let* means "to permit." "I'll *leave* on a jet plane." "*Let* the child run — she needs the exercise."

**lend, loan**  Although *lend* and *loan* are used interchangeably in speech, avoid using *loan* as a verb. "Can you *lend* (not *loan*) me some money?"

**less, fewer**  See *fewer, less.*

**let, leave**  See *leave, let.*

**liable, likely**  Use *likely* to mean "plausible" or "having the potential." "Jake is *likely* [not *liable*] to win." Save *liable* for "legally obligated" or "susceptible." "A stunt man is *liable* to injury."

**lie, lay**  See *lay, lie.*

**like, as**  See *as, like.*

**likely, liable**  See *liable, likely.*

**literally**  Don't sling *literally* around for emphasis. It means "strictly according to the meaning of a word (or words)"; if you are speaking figuratively, it will wreck your credibility. "Professor Gray *literally* flew down the hall to the chairman's office" means that Gray traveled on wings. "Rick was *literally* stoned out of his mind" means that someone drove Rick insane by pelting him with mineral specimens. Save *literally* to mean that, by everything holy, you're reporting a fact. "Chemical wastes travel on the winds, and it *literally* rains poison."

**loan, lend**  See *lend, loan.*

**loath, loathe**  *Loath* is an adjective meaning "reluctant." *Loathe* is a verb meaning "to detest." "We were *loath* to say good-bye." "We *loathed* our impending separation."

**loose, lose**  *Loose*, an adjective, most commonly means "not fastened" or "poorly fastened." *Lose*, a verb, means "to misplace" or "to not win." "I have to be careful not to *lose* this button — it's so *loose.*"

**lots, lots of, a lot of**  Use these expressions only in informal speech. In formal writing, use *many* or *much.* See also *a lot.*

**mankind**  This term is considered sexist by many people. Use *humanity, humankind, the human race,* or *people* instead.

**may, can**  See *can, may.*

**media, medium**  *Media* is the plural of *medium* and most commonly refers to the various forms of public communication. "Some argue that of all the *media*, television is the worst for children because it leaves so little to the imagination."

**might of**  *Might of* is colloquial for *might have* and should not be used in writing.

**most**  Do not use *most* when you mean "almost" or "nearly." "*Almost* [not *Most*] all of the students felt that Professor Chartrand should have received tenure."

**must of**  *Must of* is colloquial for *must have* and should not be used in writing.

**myself**  See *-self, -selves.*

**not all that**  *Not all that* is colloquial for *not very*; do not use it in formal writing. "The movie was *not very* [not *not all that*] exciting."

**number, amount**  See *amount, number.*

**of**  See *could of, might of, must of, should of.*

**off of**  *Of* is unnecessary with *off.* Use *off* alone, or use *from*: "Cartoon heroes are forever falling *off* [or *from*] cliffs."

**O.K., o.k., okay**  In formal writing, do not use any of these expressions. *All right* and *I agree* are possible substitutes.

**one**  Like a balloon, *one*, meaning "a person," tends to inflate. One *one* can lead to another. "When *one* is in college, *one* learns to make up *one's* mind for *oneself.*" Avoid this pompous usage. Whenever possible, substitute *people* or a more specific plural noun. "When *students* are in college, *they* learn to make up their minds for *themselves.*" Also see *you* and 22c.

**ourselves**  See *-self, -selves.*

**outside of, inside of**  See *inside of, outside of.*

**percent, per cent, percentage**  When you specify a number, write *percent* (also written *per cent*). "Eight *percent* of the listeners responded to the offer." The only time to use *percentage*, meaning "part," is with an adjective, when you mention no number. "A high *percentage* [or *a large percentage*] of listeners responded." *A large number* or *a large proportion* sounds better yet, and we urge you to strike *percentage* from your vocabulary.

**per se**  Translate this Latin expression into English and you'll sound less stiff. Write "Getting a good education is important *in itself* [or *by itself*; not *per se*]."

**phenomenon, phenomena**  *Phenomena* is plural for *phenomenon*, which means "an observable fact or occurrence." "I've read about many mysterious supernatural *phenomena*." "Clairvoyance is the strangest *phenomenon* of all."

**pore over, pour over**  *Pore over* a book and you study it intently; *pour over* a book and you get it wet.

**precede, proceed**  *Precede* means "to go before or ahead of"; *proceed* means "to go forward." "The fire drill *proceeded* smoothly; the children *preceded* the teachers into the safety of the yard."

**principal, principle**  *Principal* means "chief," whether used as an adjective or as a noun. "Marijuana is the *principal* cash crop of Colombia." "Our high school *principal* frowns on pot." Referring to money, *principal* means "capital." "Investors in marijuana earn as much as 850 percent interest on their *principal*." *Principle*, a noun, means *rule* or *standard*. "Let's apply the *principle* of equality in hiring."

**proved, proven**  Although both forms can be used as past participles, *proved* is recommended. Use *proven* as an adjective. "They had *proved* their skill in match after match." "Try this *proven* cough remedy: lemon, honey, whiskey, and hot water blended into a toddy."

**quote, quotation**  *Quote* is a verb meaning "to cite, to use the words of." *Quotation* is a noun meaning "something that is quoted." "The *quotation* [not *quote*] next to her yearbook picture fits her perfectly."

**raise, rise**  *Raise*, meaning "to cause to move upward," is a transitive verb and takes an object. *Rise*, meaning "to move up (on its own)" is intransitive and does not take an object: "I *rose* from my seat and *raised* my arm, but the instructor still didn't see me."

**rarely ever**  *Rarely* by itself is strong enough. "George *rarely* [not *rarely ever*] eats dinner with his family."

**real, really**  *Real* is an adjective, *really* an adverb. Do not use *real* to modify a verb or another adjective, and avoid overusing either word. "*The Ambassadors* is a *really* [not *real*] fine novel." Even better: "*The Ambassadors* is a fine novel."

**reason is because, reason . . . is**  *Reason . . . is* requires a clause beginning with *that*. Using *because* is nonstandard. "The *reason* I can't come *is that* [not *is because*] I have the flu." But *reason . . . is* is a wordy construction that can usually be rephrased more succinctly. It is simpler and more direct to write, "I can't come because I have the flu."

**respectfully, respectively**  *Respectfully* means "with respect, showing respect." *Respectively* means "each in turn" or "in the order given." "They stopped talking and stood *respectfully* as the prime minister walked by." "Joan, Michael, and Alfonso majored in history, sociology, and economics, *respectively*."

**rise**  See *raise, rise*.

**seldom ever**  Let *seldom* stand by itself. "Martha *seldom* [not *seldom ever*] attends church."

**-self, -selves**  Don't use a pronoun ending in *-self* or *-selves* in place of *her, him, me, them, us,* or *you*. "Nobody volunteered but Jim and *me* [not *myself*]." Use the *-self* pronouns to refer back to a noun or another pronoun and to lend emphasis. "*We* did it *ourselves*." "Sarah *herself* is a noted musician." (See 7b.)

**semi-**  See *bi-, semi-*.

**sensual, sensuous**  Both words have to do with stimulation of the senses, but *sensual* has more blatantly carnal overtones. "Gluttony and lust were the *sensual* millionaire's favorite sins." *Sensuous* pleasures are more aesthetic. "The *sensuous* beauty of the music stirred his soul."

**set, sit**  *Set*, meaning "to put or place," is a transitive verb and takes an object. *Sit*, meaning "to be seated," is intransitive and does not take an object. "At the security point we were asked to *set* our jewelry and metal objects on the counter and *sit* down." (See also 5f.)

**shall, will; should, would**  The helping verb *shall* formerly was used with first-person pronouns. It is still used to express determination ("We *shall* overcome"; "They *shall* not give in") or to ask consent ("*Shall* I let the cat out?"). Otherwise *will* is commonly used with all three persons. "I *will* enter medical school in the fall." "They *will* accept the bid if the terms are clear." *Should* is a helping verb that expresses obligation; *would*, a helping verb that expresses a hypothetical condition. "I *should* wash the dishes before I watch TV." "He *would* learn to speak English if you *would* give him a chance."

**should of**   *Should of* is colloquial for *should have* and should not be used in writing.

**sight**   See *cite, sight, site.*

**since**   Sometimes using *since* can make a sentence ambiguous. "*Since* the babysitter left, the children have been watching television." Does *since* here mean "because" or "from the time that"? If using *since* might be confusing to your readers, use an unambiguous term (*because, ever since*).

**sit**   See *set, sit.*

**site**   See *cite, sight, site.*

**sort of**   See *kind of, sort of, type of.*

**stationary, stationery**   *Stationary,* an adjective, means "fixed, unmoving." "The fireplace remained *stationary* though the wind blew down the house." *Stationery* is paper for letter writing. To spell it right, remember that *letter* also contains *-er.*

**suppose to**   Write *supposed to.* "He was *supposed to* appear for dinner at eight o'clock."

**sure**   *Sure* is an adjective, *surely* an adverb. Do not use *sure* to modify a verb or another adjective. If by *sure* you mean "certainly," write *certainly* or *surely* instead. "He *surely* [not *sure*] is crazy about cars."

**than, then**   *Than* is a conjunction used in comparisons; *then* is an adverb indicating time. "Marlene is brainier *than* her sister." "First crack six eggs; *then* beat them."

**that, which**   Which pronoun should open a clause — *that* or *which*? If the clause adds to its sentence an idea that, however interesting, could be left out, then the clause is nonrestrictive and should begin with *which* and be separated from the rest of the sentence with commas. "The vampire, *which* had been hovering nearby, leaped for Sarah's throat."

If the clause is essential to your meaning, it is restrictive and should begin with *that* and should not have commas around it. "The vampire *that* Mel brought from Transylvania leaped for Sarah's throat." The clause indicates not just any old vampire but one in particular. (See 25e.)

Don't use *which* to refer vaguely to an entire clause. Instead of "Jack was an expert drummer in high school, *which* won him a college scholarship," write: "Jack's skill as a drummer won him . . . ." (See 8b.)

**themselves**   See *-self, -selves.*

**then, than**   See *than, then.*

**there, their, they're**   *There* is an adverb indicating place. *Their* is a possessive pronoun. *They're* is a contraction of *they are.* "After playing tennis *there* for three hours, Lamont and Laura went to change *their* clothes because *they're* going out to dinner."

**to, too, two**   *To* is a preposition. *Too* is an adverb meaning "also" or "in excess." *Two* is a number. "Janet wanted to go *too,* but she feared she was still *too* sick to travel in the car for *two* days. Instead, she went *to* bed."

**toward, towards**   *Toward* is preferred in the United States, *towards* in Britain.

**try and**   Use *try to.* "I'll *try to* [not *try and*] attend the opening performance of your play."

**type of**   See *kind of, sort of, type of.*

**uninterested, disinterested**   See *disinterested, uninterested.*

**unique**   Nothing can be *more unique, less unique, really unique, very unique,* or *somewhat unique. Unique* means "one of a kind."

**use to**   Write *used to.* "Jeffrey *used to* have a beard, but now he is clean-shaven."

**wait for, wait on**   Write *wait for* when you mean "await." *Wait on* means "to serve." "While *waiting for* his friends, George decided to *wait on* one more customer."

**well, good**   See *good, well.*

**where at, where to**   The colloquial use of *at* or *to* after *where* is redundant. Write "*Where* were you?" not "Where were you *at*?" "I know *where* she was rushing [not *rushing to*]."

**where, that**   Although speakers sometimes use *where* instead of *that,* you should not do so in writing. "I heard on the news *that* [not *where*] it got hot enough to fry eggs on car hoods."

**whether**   See *if, whether.*

**which, that**   See *that, which.*

**who, which, that, whose**   *Who* refers to people, *which* to things and ideas. "Was it Pogo *who* said, 'We have met the enemy and he is us'?" "The blouse, *which* was lime green embroidered with silver, accented her dark skin and eyes." *That* refers to things but can also be used for a class of people. "The team *that* puts in the most overtime will get a bonus." Using *of which* can be cumbersome; use *whose* even to refer to things. "The mountain, *whose* snowy peaks were famous world over, was covered in a dismal fog." See also *that, which.*

**who, whom**    *Who* is used as a subject, *whom* as an object. In *"Whom* do I see?" *Whom* is the object of *see.* In *"Who* goes there?" *Who* is the subject of "goes." (See also 7a, 7d.)

**who's, whose**    *Who's* is a contraction for *who is* or *who has.* "*Who's* going with Phil?" *Whose* is a possessive pronoun. "Bill is a conservative politician *whose* ideas are unlikely to change."

**will, shall**    See *shall, will.*

**would, should**    See *should, would.*

**would of**    *Would of* is colloquial for *would have* and should not be used in writing.

**you**    *You,* meaning "a person," occurs often in conversation. "When you go to college you have to work hard." In writing, use *one* or a specific, preferably plural noun. "When *students* go to college *they* have to work hard." But see *one* for some cautions. And see 22c.

**your, you're**    *Your* is a possessive pronoun; *you're* is the contraction for *you are.* "*You're* lying! It was *your* handwriting on the envelope."

**yourself, yourselves**    See *-self, -selves.*

# Answers for Lettered Exercises

Throughout *The Bedford Guide for College Writers, Fourth Edition*, revisions have consistently focused on the needs of the students within the classroom and as working adults. A Writer's Handbook has been thoroughly updated with the same concerns in mind. New to this edition is the incorporation of connected discourse exercises and more advice, teaching cues, and information for ESL students. We think you will find the handbook to be a pragmatic and accurate reference guide to "the way words work."

### EXERCISE 1–1   IDENTIFYING NOUNS AND PRONOUNS (p. H-9)

**a.** Proper noun: Karen; common nouns: paintings, husband; possessive pronoun: her;   **b.** Proper noun: Tanya; common nouns: price, profit; intensive pronoun: herself;   **c.** Common nouns: bulk, money, tuition; relative pronoun: that; personal pronoun: she; possessive pronoun: her;   **d.** Proper nouns: Lewis, Corvette; possessive pronoun: his; indefinite pronoun: someone; relative pronoun: who; personal pronoun: it;   **e.** Personal pronoun: He; reflexive pronoun: himself; indefinite pronoun: anyone; relative pronoun: who

### EXERCISE 1–2   IDENTIFYING VERBS (p. H-10)

**a.** Transitive: accompany; intransitive: goes; helping: will;   **b.** Transitive: prefers; linking: are;   **c.** Transitive: give, symbolize;   **d.** Transitive: spent; helping: should have;   **e.** Transitive: reads; intransitive: dreams

### EXERCISE 1–3   IDENTIFYING ADJECTIVES AND ADVERBS (p. H-12)

**a.** Adjectives: mild, environmental; indefinite article: a; definite article: the; adverb: greatly, modifying verb fear;   **b.** Adjectives: young, mature; adverb: incredibly, modifying adjective mature;   **c.** Adjectives: handsome, wise; definite article: The; adverbs: wildly, modifying adjective handsome; often, modifying verb made; foolishly, modifying verb act;   **d.** Adjective: difficult; indefinite article: a; adverbs: very, modifying adjective difficult; carefully, modifying verb chose;   **e.** Adjectives: delighted, lovely; definite article: the; adverb: absolutely, modifying adjective delighted

### EXERCISE 1–4   IDENTIFYING PREPOSITIONAL PHRASES (p. H-13)

**a.** To me, preposition to; adverb phrase;   **b.** In the sky, preposition in; adjective phrase;   **c.** Before the meeting, preposition before; adverb phrase;   **d.** According to the rules, preposition according to; adverb phrase;   **e.** But a few troublemakers, preposition but; adjective phrase

### EXERCISE 1–5   IDENTIFYING CONJUNCTIONS AND INTERJECTIONS (p. H-17)

**a.** Conjunction: when (subordinating); interjection: Oh, well;   **b.** Conjunctions: and (coordinating), neither . . . nor (correlative);   **c.** Conjunctions: and (coordinating), whether . . . or (correlative);   **d.** Interjection: Holy mackerel;   **e.** Conjunctions: Although (subordinating), and (coordinating)

### EXERCISE 1–6   IDENTIFYING PARTS OF SPEECH (p. H-18)

**A. a.** adverb;   **b.** adjective;   **c.** subordinating conjunction;   **d.** coordinating conjunction;   **e.** adverb;   **B. a.** noun;   **b.** adverb;   **c.** subordinating conjunction;   **d.** pronoun;   **e.** adjective (article)

### EXERCISE 2–1   IDENTIFYING SUBJECTS AND PREDICATES (p. H-21)

**a.** Simple subject: coyotes; complete subject: Several coyotes; simple predicate: have been seen; complete predicate; have been seen recently in this area;   **b.** Simple subject: War; complete subject: War, that curse of the human race; simple predicate: has plagued; complete predicate: has plagued civilization throughout history;   **c.** Simple subject: composer; complete subject: the composer Beethoven; simple predicate: continued; complete predicate: Even after he became deaf . . . continued to write music;   **d.** Simple subject: cup; complete subject: One cup of coffee in the morning; simple predicate: keeps; complete predicate: keeps me awake all day; **e.** Simple subject: mother; complete subject: John Updike's mother, who was a writer herself; simple predicate: encouraged; complete predicate: encouraged her son's literary aspirations

## EXERCISE 2–2   IDENTIFYING OBJECTS AND COMPLEMENTS (p. H-25)

**a.** Subject complement: an educated person; direct object: such a story;   **b.** Direct object: his kingdom; indirect object: his daughters;   **c.** Subject complement: an evasive man;   **d.** Subject complement: an interesting art; direct object: expensive equipment;   **e.** Direct object: Chicago; object complement: the windy city

## EXERCISE 3–1   IDENTIFYING PHRASES (p. H-31)

**a.** Traveling cross-country: gerund phrase, noun;   **b.** in the beret: prepositional phrase, adjective;   **c.** its silver hood ornament gleaming in the morning sun: absolute phrase; gleaming in the morning sun: participial phrase, adjective; in the morning sun: prepositional phrase, adverb;   **d.** gone with the wind: participial phrase, adjective;   **e.** Civil War victor: appositive phrase

## EXERCISE 3–2   IDENTIFYING CLAUSES (p. H-35)

**a.** wherever he lived at the moment: noun clause; **b.** While we were still arguing about its value: adverb clause; **c.** that I took to the cleaners: adjective clause;   **d.** that she may fail the course: adverb clause;   **e.** what hit him: noun clause

## EXERCISE 4–1   IDENTIFYING SENTENCE TYPES (p. H-37)

**a.** Simple sentence. Compound subject: Not only women but also men and children; verb: benefit;   **b.** Complex sentence. Infinitive phrase: To become a doctor; main clause: you know; subordinate clause: how hard you must study; **c.** Compound-complex sentence. Main clauses: Biology is interesting; I prefer botany; subordinate clause: as it is taught in our department;   **d.** Simple sentence. Subject: you; verb: do prefer; compound direct object: bacon and eggs or cereal and toast;   **e.** Compound-complex sentence. Main clauses: Most people believe; recent studies have shown; subordinate clauses: that poverty begets poverty; that they achieve economic independence; when children from welfare families reach adulthood

## EXERCISE 5–1   USING IRREGULAR VERB FORMS (p. H-42)

**a.** When Joe's mother *caught* him *lying* around the house during school hours, she *threw* him out.
**b.** Correct
**c.** He *laid* his cards triumphantly on the table but soon found that he was not *sitting* in a lucky chair after all.
**d.** Wendy knew how much Roger had *drunk*, but she *went* with him anyway.
**e.** If I had *known* that he'd *stolen* the money, he'd never have *laid* a foot inside this door.

## EXERCISE 5–2   IDENTIFYING VERB TENSES (p. H-53)

**a.** broke: simple past; was skiing: past progressive; **b.** sleeps: simple present; is yawning: present progressive;

**c.** had seen: past perfect; runs: simple present;   **d.** represents: simple present; will have performed: future perfect; split: simple past;   **e.** have heard: present perfect; spend: simple present; will climb: simple future

## EXERCISE 5–4   USING THE CORRECT MOOD OF VERBS (p. H-58)

**a.** When Janet cooks, she insists that Tom *wash* the dishes. (Incorrect *washes*, indicative; correct *wash*, subjunctive)
**b.** If John *believes* that of me, I no longer wish to be his friend. (Incorrect *believe*, subjunctive; correct *believes*, indicative)
**c.** If I *were* a licensed plumber, I could install the washing machine myself. (Incorrect *was*, indicative; correct *were*, subjunctive)
**d.** The IRS recommends that tax forms *be* filled out as soon as they become available. (Incorrect *are*, indicative; correct *be*, subjunctive)
**e.** If that man *does* not go away, call the police. (Incorrect *do*, subjunctive; correct *does*, indicative)

## EXERCISE 6–1   MAKING SUBJECTS AND VERBS AGREE (p. H-64)

**a.** Our foreign policy in Cuba, Nicaragua, El Salvador, and Panama *has* not been as successful as most Americans had hoped.
**b.** Correct
**c.** I read about a couple who *are* offering to trade their baby for a brand-new Chevrolet.
**d.** A shave, a haircut, and a new suit *have* turned Bill in a different person.
**e.** Neither the guerrillas nor the government *is* willing to negotiate.

## EXERCISE 7–1   USING PRONOUNS CORRECTLY (p. H-69)

**a.** She can run faster than *I*. (*I* is the subject of the implied verb *can run*.)
**b.** Mrs. Van Dumont awarded the prize to Mona and *me*. (*Me* is an object of the preposition *to*.)
**c.** Jud laughed at both of us — *her* and *me*. (*Her* and *me* are appositives to *us*, the object of the preposition.)
**d.** I am sure that I overheard that rude man speaking of *us*. (*Us* is the object of the preposition *of*.)
**e.** Jerry, the pizza chef, and *I* regard you and *her* as the very people *whom* we wish to get acquainted with. (*I* is a subject of the verb *regard*; *her* is a direct object of the verb *regard*; *whom* is the object of the preposition *with*.)

## EXERCISE 8–1   MAKING PRONOUN REFERENCE CLEAR (p. H-72)

*Suggested revisions:*

**a.** Every American will own a computer when it costs the same as a television set.
**b.** After meeting with her newspaper's editor, Sarah reported that she wasn't sure if the editor agreed with her position on freedom of speech.

c. Never having seen any apes, I cannot give you my observations on the social differences between them and human beings.

d. Swaying gently in his parachute, floating lazily to earth, Edgar felt pure joy. The jump had been the finest thing he'd ever tried, and he was all for this new sport.

e. Glancing down, Edgar saw the cactus loom and heard the rattlesnake hiss, obstacles that promised an uncertain landing.

### EXERCISE 9–1 MAKING PRONOUNS AND ANTECEDENTS AGREE (p. H-76)

*Suggested revisions:*

a. All students are urged to complete *their* registration on time.

b. *Babies* who don't know *their* own mothers may have been born with some kind of vision deficiency.

c. Each member of the sorority has to make *her* own bed.

d. If you don't like the songs the choir sings, don't join *it.*

e. Young people should know how to protect *themselves* against AIDS.

### EXERCISE 10–1 USING ADJECTIVES AND ADVERBS CORRECTLY (p. H-84)

a. Change *oldest* to *older;* b. Change *good* to *well;*
c. Change *correct* to *correctly* (in both places); change *trickiest* to *trickier;* d. Change *sweet* to *sweetly;* e. Change *the most* to *more*

### EXERCISE 11–1 MAINTAINING GRAMMATICAL CONSISTENCY (p. H-87)

*Suggested revisions:*

a. Sometimes late at night, I hear stereos booming from passing cars. The vibrations are so great *I* can feel *my* house shake.

b. Dr. Jamison is an erudite professor who *tells amusing anecdotes in class.* (Formal) *Or* Dr. Jamison is a *comical* teacher who cracks jokes in class. (Informal)

c. The audience listened intently to the lecture but *did not understand* the message.

d. It was in the Near East that people first began to grow crops and *establish* city-states.

e. Most of the people in my psychology class are very interesting, and *I* can get into some exciting discussions with them.

### EXERCISE 12–1 ELIMINATING FRAGMENTS (p. H-92)

*Suggested revisions:*

a. Polly and Jim plan to see the new Woody Allen movie, which was reviewed in last Sunday's *New York Times.*

b. For democracy to function at all, two elements are crucial: an educated populace and a firm collective belief in people's ability to chart their own course.

c. Scholastic achievement is important to Alex, being the first person in his family ever to attend college.

d. Does our society rob children of their childhood by making them aware too soon of adult ills?

e. No one would ever forget that night: the half-empty lifeboats, the useless flares, and the band playing hymns as the ship slid under.

### EXERCISE 13–1 REVISING COMMA SPLICES AND FUSED SENTENCES (p. H-96)

*Suggested revisions:*

a. Everyone had heard alarming rumors in the village about strange goings-on. We hesitated to believe them.
Although everyone had heard alarming rumors in the village about strange goings-on, we hesitated to believe them.

b. Bats flew about our ears as the carriage pulled up under a stone archway. An assistant stood waiting to lead us to our host.
Bats flew about our ears as the carriage pulled up under a stone archway, where an assistant stood waiting to lead us to our host.

c. We followed the scientist down a flight of wet stone steps. At last he stopped before a huge oak door.
We followed the scientist down a flight of wet stone steps, until at last he stopped before a huge oak door.

d. From a jangling keyring Dr. Frankenstein selected a heavy key; he twisted it in the lock.
From a jangling keyring Dr. Frankenstein selected a heavy key, which he twisted in the lock.

e. The huge door gave a groan and swung open on a dimly lighted laboratory.
The huge door gave a groan; it swung open on a dimly lighted laboratory.

### EXERCISE 14–1 PLACING MODIFIERS (p. H-100)

*Suggested revisions:*

a. After they lost miserably, the team remained silent on the trip home. *Or* After they lost, the team remained miserably silent on the trip home.

b. Complete the writing assignment that follows Chapter 2 in the textbook.

c. Those who frequently make mistakes learn valuable lessons. *Or* Frequently those who make mistakes learn valuable lessons.

d. The managers presented bouquets of roses with long stems to every employee.

e. A person who often snacks gets fat. *Or* Often a person who snacks gets fat.

### EXERCISE 14–2 REVISING DANGLING MODIFIERS (p. H-102)

*Suggested revisions:*

a. After working for six hours, they finished the job. *Or* After they worked for six hours, the job was done.

b. When you are unable to fall asleep, a warm bath relaxes you.

c. To complete in the Olympics, you need talent, training, and dedication.

d. It's common for a person feeling lonely to want to talk to someone.

e. Having worried all morning, he felt relief flood over him when his missing son returned.

## EXERCISE 15–1    COMPLETING COMPARISONS (p. H-104)

*Suggested revisions:*

a. She plays the *Moonlight Sonata* more brilliantly than any *other* pianist her age.

b. Driving a sports car means more to Jake than *it does to* his professors. *Or* Driving a sports car means more to Jake than his professors *do*.

c. People who go to college aren't necessarily smarter *than those who don't*, but they will always have an advantage at job interviews.

d. I don't have as much trouble getting along with Michelle as *I do with* Karin. *Or* I don't have as much trouble getting along with Michelle as Karin *does*.

e. Annapolis, Maryland, has more colonial brick houses than any *other* city in the United States.

## EXERCISE 15–2    COMPLETING SENTENCES (p. H-106)

a. Eighteenth-century China was as civilized *as* and in many respects more sophisticated than the Western world.

b. Pembroke was never contacted *by*, much less involved with, the election committee.

c. I haven't yet *finished* but soon will finish my term paper.

d. Ron likes his popcorn with butter; Linda *likes hers* with parmesan cheese.

e. Correct

## EXERCISE 16–1    CORRECTING MIXED CONSTRUCTIONS AND FAULTY PREDICATION (p. H-109)

*Suggested revisions:*

a. A balanced budget calls for careful planning.

b. Although television is entertaining, it turns viewers into passive zombies.

c. In one sizzling blast, the enemy space fleet was instantly wiped out.

d. A college's financial aid staff searches for able students and decides to pay their costs.

e. One good reason for financial aid is that it enables capable lower-income students to attend college.

## EXERCISE 17–1    MAKING SENTENCES PARALLEL (p. H-114)

*Suggested revisions:*

a. Linda loves to watch soccer and tennis and to play squash.

b. Better than starting from scratch would be building on what already has been done.

c. Her apartment needed fresh paint and a new rug, and Mary Lou wished she had a neater roommate and quieter friends.

d. All my brothers are blond and athletic.

e. For breakfast the waiter brought scrambled eggs, which I like, and kippers, which I don't like.

## EXERCISE 18–1    USING COORDINATION (p. H-118)

*Suggested revisions:*

a. Congress is expected to pass the biotechnology bill, but the president already has said he will veto it.

b. Mortgage rates have dropped, so home buying is likely to increase in the near future.

c. The earth trembled; the long-dreaded cataclysm had begun.

d. I left the house in a hurry and ran to the bank so I could cash a check to buy lunch. But, it was the bank's anniversary, and the staff was busy serving coffee and cake. By the time I left, after chatting and eating for twenty minutes, I wasn't hungry anymore.

e. The U.S. Postal Service handles millions of pieces of mail every day; it is the largest postal service in the world.

## EXERCISE 18–2    USING SUBORDINATION (p. H-120)

*Suggested revisions:*

a. We occasionally hear horror stories about fruits and vegetables being unsafe to eat because they were sprayed with toxic chemicals or were grown in contaminated soil. The fact remains that, given their high nutritional value, these fresh foods are generally much better for us than processed foods.

b. English has become an international language although its grammar is filled with exceptions to the rules.

c. Some television cartoon shows, such as *Rocky and Bullwinkle* and *Speedracer,* have become cult classics years after they went off the air.

d. At the end of Verdi's opera *La Traviata,* Alfredo has to see his beloved Violetta again, even though he knows she is dying and all he can say is good-bye.

e. After giving away her money and bidding adieu to her faithful servant, Violetta dies in her lover's arms.

## EXERCISE 20–2    AVOIDING JARGON (p. H-127)

*Suggested revisions:*

a. The driver education course teaches the student how to drive.

b. We the State Department staff have investigated the riots in Lebanon, and all our data indicate that they are rapidly becoming worse.

c. Antinuclear protesters have been picketing the missile conference in hopes of stalling the negotiations.

d. I recommend multiple bypass heart surgery for Mr. Pitt.

e. If your insurance company will pay for it, he can be scheduled for bypass surgery; if not, he should go on a strict diet.

EXERCISE 20–3    AVOIDING EUPHEMISMS (p. H-128)

*Suggested revisions:*

a. After the Rodney King trial, Los Angeles was engulfed in a riot, during which many innocent people died.
b. The ship sank because of a hole in the hull.
c. The new K27 missile will kill everyone in the cities of any nation that attacks us.
d. In our town, trash collectors must wear uniforms at work.
e. Freddie the Rocker is dead.

EXERCISE 20–4    AVOIDING SLANG (p. H-129)

*Suggested revisions:*

a. Judy doesn't like Paul's sexual advances.
b. If large animals don't leave the combat zone, the army's policy is to kill them.
c. Judge Lehman's reversal of the *Smith v. Jones* verdict shows that he cannot think clearly.
d. Anyone familiar with the plays of Sophocles finds them very impressive.
e. If he can get the money to pay his bail, he'll probably flee.

EXERCISE 22–1    AVOIDING BIAS (p. H-138)

*Suggested revisions:*

a. My cousin volunteered as an aide at the retirement home.
b. The television crew interviewed a number of average passersby about the new tax proposal.
c. Whether the president of the United States is a Democrat or a Republican, he or she will always be a symbol of the nation.
d. The senator was highly regarded by voters in her district.
e. Simon drinks quite a bit.

EXERCISE 24–1    USING END PUNCTUATION (p. H-143)

a. Unlike Gerald Ford and LBJ, who came to the vice-presidency from Congress, President Bush won that office after heading the CIA.
b. The population of California is much greater than that of Nevada.
c. Why don't you meet us after the game?
d. "When will the world end?" my four-year-old nephew asked in a quavering voice.
e. Yes, the Republicans are worried about the gender gap. They fear that women in increasing numbers will vote for the Democrats. How can the Republicans fight back?

EXERCISE 25–1    USING COMMAS (p. H-146)

a. When Verity gets to Paris, I hope she'll drop me a line.
b. Beethoven's deafness kept him from hearing his own music, yet he continued to compose.
c. Correct
d. The cherries are overripe, for picking has been delayed.
e. Antonio expected Minnesota to be cold but was unprepared for the frigid temperatures of his first winter there.

EXERCISE 25–2    USING COMMAS (p. H-147)

a. Mrs. Carver looks like a sweet little old lady, but she plays a wicked electric guitar.
b. Her bass player, her drummer, and her keyboard player all live at the same rest home.
c. They practice individually in the afternoon, rehearse together at night, and play at the home's Saturday night dances.
d. The Rest Home Rebels have to rehearse quietly and cautiously to keep from disturbing the other residents.
e. Correct

EXERCISE 25–3    USING COMMAS (p. H-149)

*Suggested revisions:*

a. The aye-aye, which is a member of the lemur family, is threatened with extinction.
b. The party, a dismal occasion, ended earlier than we had expected.
c. Secretary Stern warned that the concessions that the West was prepared to make would be withdrawn if not matched by the East.
d. Although both of Don's children are blond, his daughter, Sharon, has darker hair than his son, Jake.
e. Herbal tea, which has no caffeine, makes a better after-dinner drink than coffee.

EXERCISE 25–4    USING COMMAS (p. H-151)

a. I want to warn you, however, that we are experiencing some problems with our public address system.
b. Our speaker, listed in your program as a professor, tells us that, on the contrary, she is a teaching assistant.
c. The discussion that followed was not so much a debate as a free-for-all.
d. Alex insisted that predestination, not free will, shapes human destiny.
e. Shirley, on the other hand, who looks so calm, passionately defended the role of choice.

EXERCISE 25–5    USING COMMAS (p. H-153)

a. On October 2, 1969, the future discoverer of antigravity tablets was born.
b. Corwin P. Grant entered the world while his parents were driving to a hospital in Costa Mesa, California.
c. Correct
d. Today, ladies and gentlemen, Corwin enjoys worldwide renown.
e. Schoolchildren from Augusta, Maine, to Azuza, California, can recite his famous comment "It was my natural levity that led me to overcome gravity."

EXERCISE 26–1    USING SEMICOLONS (p. H-158)

a. Gasoline prices almost always rise at the start of the tourist season; this year will be no exception.

b. I disagree with your point; however, I appreciate your reasons for stating it.

c. The garden is a spectacular display of fountains and gargoyles; beds of lilies, zinnias, and hollyhocks; bushes shaped like animals; climbing roses, wisteria, and ivy; and lawns as wide as golf greens.

d. Janet has not had much money this term, but she hopes to get a part-time job this summer.

e. Dr. Elliott's intervention in the dispute was well intentioned; nevertheless, it was unfortunate.

## EXERCISE 27–1   USING COLONS (p. H-161)

*Suggested revisions:*

a. The Continuing Education Program offers courses in building and construction management, engineering, and design.

b. The interview ended with a test of skills: taking dictation, operating the switchboard, proofreading documents, and typing a sample letter.

c. The sample letter began, "Dear Mr. Rasheed: Please accept our apologies for the late shipment."

d. Constance quoted Proverbs 8:18: "Riches and honor are with me."

e. A book that profoundly impressed me was Kurt Vonnegut's *Cat's Cradle* (New York: Dell, 1963).

## EXERCISE 28–1   USING THE APOSTROPHE (p. H-164)

a. It's not easy to be old in our society.

b. I don't understand the Jameses' objections to our plans for a block party.

c. It's not fair that your roommate won't help with the cleaning.

d. Is this collection of '50s records yours or your roommate's?

e. Alas, Brian got two D's on his report card.

## EXERCISE 29–1   USING QUOTATION MARKS (p. H-169)

a. "Don't think about it," advised Jason; "it will only make you unhappy."

b. "Do you want to dance," Joan asked, "or shall we have a drink?"

c. In her story "The Wide Net," Eudora Welty wrote, "The excursion is the same when you go looking for your sorrow as when you go looking for your joy."

d. "Who's supposed to say the line 'Tennis, anyone?' " asked the director.

e. Robert Burns's poem "To a Mouse" opens: "Wee, sleekit, cow'rin, tim'rous beastie,/O, what a panic's in thy breastie!"

## EXERCISE 30–1   USING THE DASH (p. H-171)

*Suggested revisions:*

a. I enjoy going hiking with my friend John, whom I've known for fifteen years.

b. Pedro's new boat is spectacular — a regular seagoing Ferrari.

c. The Thompsons devote their weekends to their favorite pastime — eating bags of potato chips and cookies beside the warm glow of the television.

d. Correct

e. "A rock!" I cried. "Anthony, I'm afraid we're —"

## EXERCISE 31–1   USING PARENTHESES (p. H-172)

*Suggested revisions:*

a. In *The Last Crusade*, archaeologist Indiana Jones (who took his name from the family dog) joins his father in a quest for the Holy Grail.

b. Our cafeteria serves the four basic food groups: white (milk, bread, and mashed potatoes), brown (mystery meat and gravy), green (overcooked vegetables and underwashed lettuce), and orange (squash, carrots, and tomato sauce).

c. The hijackers will release the hostages only if the government (1) frees all political prisoners and (2) allows the hijackers to leave the country unharmed.

d. Correct

e. Actually, the Whale Stranding Network (WSN) rescues whales that have stranded themselves.

## EXERCISE 32–1   USING ABBREVIATIONS (p. H-182)

a. Built for the Paris Exposition of 1889, the Eiffel Tower contains 15 million pounds of pig iron, protected by 37 tons of paint.

b. Friday, July 14, 1989, was the Eiffel Tower's hundredth anniversary.

c. Monsieur Eiffel would be pleased that President Mitterrand and others now accept his controversial "iron giraffe" as a national landmark.

d. In some Parisian tourist traps, a cup of coffee costs as much as $5.

e. France is a member of the North Atlantic Treaty Organization (NATO), but the French historically have mistrusted some of their fellow NATO members, such as the United Kingdom.

## EXERCISE 33–1   USING CAPITALIZATION (p. H-185)

a. At our family reunion, I met my cousin Sam for the first time, and also my father's brother George.

b. I already knew from Dad that his brother had moved to Australia years ago to explore the Great Barrier Reef.

c. At the reunion, Uncle George told me that he had always wanted to be a marine biologist.

d. He had spent the summer after his sophomore year of college in Woods Hole, Massachusetts, on Cape Cod.

e. At the Woods Hole Oceanographic Institution he studied horseshoe crabs.

EXERCISE 34–1   USING NUMBERS (p. H-188)

a. Wasn't it the Three Musketeers whose motto was "One for all and all for one"?

b. In the 1970s, there were about 92 million ducks in America, but in the last four years their number has dropped to barely 69 million.

c. Of the three pyramids built at Giza, Egypt, between 2580 and 2490 B.C.E., the largest pyramid is 450 feet high.

d. Forty days and forty nights would seem like forty years if you were sailing on an ark with two of every kind of animal.

e. Correct

EXERCISE 35–1   USING ITALICS (p. H-191)

a. Hiram's favorite Beatles album is *Sergeant Pepper's Lonely Hearts Club Band*, but his father prefers *Magical Mystery Tour.*

b. Hiram named his rowboat the *Yellow Submarine.*

c. He was disappointed when I told him that the play *Long Day's Journey into Night* is definitely not a staged version of the movie *A Hard Day's Night.*

d. I had to show him the article "Eugene O'Neill's Journey into Night" in *People* magazine to convince him.

e. We ate spaghetti and tortellini in the new Italian restaurant.

EXERCISE 36–1   USING HYPHENS (p. H-195)

a. Do non-Americans share our view of ourselves as a freedom-loving people?

b. The dealer told George the two vases are within nine-tenths of an inch of being a perfect match.

c. Patrick Henry's words re-echo down through the ages: "Give me liberty or give me death!"

d. Our sociology textbook is well written and presents some well-researched information.

e. The weather forecast calls for showers followed by sunshine.

# ACKNOWLEDGMENTS

Michael Dorris. "Crazy Horse Malt Liquor." From *Paper Trail* by Michael Dorris. Copyright © 1994 by Michael Dorris. Reprinted by permission of HarperCollins Publishers, Inc.

Peter Drucker. From *The New Realities.* Copyright 1989 by HarperCollins Publishers.

Freeman Dyson. From *Infinite in All Directions.* Copyright © 1988 by HarperCollins Publishers.

Gerald Early. "Black like . . . Shirley Temple." Copyright © 1992 by *Harper's Magazine.* All rights reserved. Reproduced from the February issue by special permission.

Gregg Easterbrook. "Forget PCB's. Radon. Alar." From the September 11, 1994 issue of *New York Times Magazine.* Reprinted by permission of the author.

David L. Evans. "The Wrong Examples." From *Newsweek,* March 1, 1993. Reprinted by permission of the author.

Kurt W. Fischer and Arlyne Lazerson. From *Human Development* by Kurt W. Fischer and Arlyne Lazerson. Copyright © 1984 by W. H. Freeman and Company. Reprinted by permission.

Robert Frost. "Putting in the Seed," "The Road Not Taken," and "Stopping by Woods on a Snowy Evening." From *The Poetry of Robert Frost* edited by Edward Connery Lathem. Copyright 1916, © 1969 by Holt, Rinehart and Winston. Copyright © 1944 by Robert Frost, Henry Holt and Company, Inc., Publisher.

Melina Gerosa. "Jodie Loses Her Cool." © Copyright 1995 by the Meredith Coporation. All rights reserved. Reprinted with permission from *Ladies' Home Journal* Magazine.

Ellen Goodman. "The New Hollywood Male." © 1994 by The Boston Globe Newspaper Co./Washington Post Writers Group. Reprinted with permission.

Stephen Jay Gould. "The Geometer of Race." Copyright © 1994 by The Walt Disney Co. Reprinted with permission of *Discover Magazine.*

Stephen Jay Gould. Excerpt from "Sex and Size" reprinted from *The Flamingo's Smile: Reflections in Natural History* by Stephen Jay Gould, with the permission of W. W. Norton & Company, Inc. Copyright © 1985 by Stephen Jay Gould.

Barrie B. Greenbie. From *Spaces: Dimensions of the Human Landscape* by Barrie Greenbie. Copyright © 1981 by Barrie B. Greenbie. Reprinted by permission of the publisher, Yale University Press.

Meg Greenfield. "Wish You Were Here." From *Newsweek,* August 30, 1993. © 1993 by Newsweek, Inc. All rights reserved. Reprinted by permission.

Garrett Hardin. Reprinted with permission from *Naked Emperors: Essays of a Taboo Stalker* by Garrett Hardin. Copyright © 1982 by William Kaufmann, Inc., Menlo Park, CA 94025. All rights reserved.

Joy Harjo. "Three Generations of Native American Women's Birth Experiences." Reprinted by permission of *Ms.* Magazine, © 1991.

Mary Harris "Mother" Jones. From *The Autobiography of Mother Jones* published by Charles H. Kerr, Chicago, 1980.

Christina Hoff Sommers. "The Backlash Myth: The Truth about How Women Are Doing in the Workplace." Simon & Schuster.

Richard J. Herrnstein and Charles Murray. "Jobs and Intelligence." Reprinted with the permission of The Free Press, an imprint of Simon & Schuster, Inc., from *The Bell Curve: Intelligence and Class Structure in American Life* by Richard J. Herrnstein and Charles Murray. Copyright © 1994 by Richard J. Herrnstein and Charles Murray.

Shirley Jackson. "The Lottery" From *The Lottery* by Shirley Jackson. Copyright © 1948, 1949 by Shirley Jackson. Copyright renewed © 1976, 1977 by Laurence Hyman, Barry Hyman, Mrs. Sarah Webster and Mrs. Joanne Schnurer. Reprinted by permission of Farrar, Straus & Giroux, Inc.

Carol Kaesuk Yoon. "Drugs from Bugs." Reprinted with permission from the Summer 1994 issue of *Garbage,* the *Independent Environmental Quarterly.*

Jamaica Kincaid. Excerpt from *A Small Place* by Jamaica Kincaid. Copyright © 1988 by Jamaica Kincaid. Reprinted by permission of Farrar, Straus & Giroux, Inc.

Stephen King. "Why We Crave Horror Movies." Reprinted with permission. © Stephen King. All rights reserved.

Melvin Konner. "Out of the Darkness." From the Good Health column in the October 2, 1994 issue of *The New York Times Magazine.* Copyright © 1994 by The New York Times Company. Reprinted by permission.

Elisabeth Kübler-Ross. From *On Death and Dying* by Elisabeth Kübler-Ross. Copyright © 1969 by Elisabeth Kübler-Ross. Reprinted with the permission of the Macmillan Publishing Company.

Charles R. Lawrence, III. "Limiting Racist Speech." From *The Chronicle of Higher Education,* October 25, 1989. Reprinted by permission of the author.

Primo Levi. "You who live safe." From *If This Is a Man (Survival in Auschwitz)* by Primo Levi, translated by Stuart Woolfe, translation copyright © 1959 by Orion Press, Inc., © 1958 by Guilio Einaudi editore S.p.A. Used by permission of Viking Penguin, a division of Penguin Books USA, Inc.

William McKibben. "The End of Nature." From *The End of Nature* by William McKibben. Copyright © 1989 by William McKibben. Reprinted by permission of Random House, Inc.

Charles C. Mann and Mark L. Plummer. "The Butterfly Problem." © 1992 by Charles C. Mann and Mark L. Plummer, as originally published in *The Atlantic,* January 1992. Reprinted with permission.

Lydia Minatoya. "Transformation." From *Talking to High Monks in the Snow* by Lydia Minatoya. Copyright © 1992 by Lydia Minatoya. Reprinted by permission of HarperCollins Publishers, Inc.

Jessica Mitford. "Behind the Formaldehyde Curtain." Retitled from "The American Way of Death." Reprinted by permission of Jessica Mitford. All rights reserved. Copyright © 1963, 1978 by Jessica Mitford.

N. Scott Momaday. From "To the Singing, to the Drums." Reprinted with permission of *Natural History,* (2/75). Copyright 1975 by the American Museum of Natural History.

Toni Morrison. "On the Backs of Blacks." From *Time,* Fall 1993. Copyright © 1993 by Toni Morrison. Reprinted by permission of International Creative Management, Inc.

Steve Olson. "The Year of the Blue-Collar Guy." From *Newsweek,* November 6, 1989. Reprinted by permission of the author.

Judith Ortiz Cofer. "The Myth of the Latin American Woman: I Just Met a Girl Named Maria." From *The Latin Deli: Prose and Poetry* by Judith Ortiz Cofer. Published by The Unversity of Georgia Press, 1993. © 1993 by Judith Ortiz Cofer.

Noel Perrin. "A Part-Time Marriage." From the About Men column in the September 9, 1984 issue of *The New York Times Magazine.* Reprinted by permission. Copyright © 1984 by The New York Times Company. Reprinted by permission.

Sylvia Plath. From "Northampton" in *The Journals of Sylvia Plath,* edited by Ted Hughes and Frances McCullough. Copyright © 1982 by Ted Hughes and Frances McCullough. Reprinted by permission of Doubleday, a division on Bantam, Doubleday, Dell Publishing Group, Inc.

Katha Pollitt. "The Future is Coed." From the August 22/29, 1994 issue of *The Nation*. Reprinted with permission from *The Nation* magazine. © 1994 The Nation Company, L.P.

Emily Prager. "Our Barbies, Ourselves." Retitled from "Major Barbie." Originally published in *INTERVIEW* Magazine, Brant Publications, December 1991. Reprinted by permission.

Anna Quindlen. "Evan's Two Moms." From the February 5, 1992 issue of *The New York Times*. Copyright © 1992 by The New York Times Company. Reprinted by permission.

Howell Raines. From an interview with Franklin McCain in *My Soul is Rested*. Copyright © 1977 by Howell Raines. Reprinted by permission of the Putnam Publishing Group.

Elayne Rapping. "In Praise of Roseanne." From *The Progressive*, July 14, 1994, pages 36-8. Reprinted with permission of *The Progressive*, 409 East Main Street, Madison, WI 53703.

Mary Ann Raywid. From "Power to Jargon, for Jargon is Power," *Journal of Teacher Education*, September/October 1978, p. 95. Reprinted by permission.

Wilbert Rideau. "Why Prisons Don't Work." From *Time*, March 21, 1994. © 1994 by Time, Inc. Reprinted by permission.

Edwin Arlington Robinson. "Richard Cory." From *The Children of the Night* by Edwin Arlington Robinson. New York: Charles Scribner's Sons, 1897.

Susanna Rodell. "Do You Work? Are You Guilty?" From the May 8, 1994 issue of *The New York Times*. Copyright © 1994 by The New York Times Company. Reprinted by permission.

Richard Rodriguez. "Does America Still Exist?" Copyright © 1984 by Richard Rodriguez. Reprinted by permission of Georges Borchardt, Inc. for the author.

Alex Ross. "Generation Exit." From the April 25, 1994 issue of *The New Yorker*.

Scott Russell Sanders. "The Men We Carry in Our Minds." Copyright © 1984 by Scott Russell Sanders. First appeared in *Milkweed Chronicle*; reprinted by permission of the author and Virginia Kidd. Literary Agent.

Richard Sorenson. Text excerpt and figure from *Learning Non-Aggression: The Experience of Non-Literature Societies* by Ashley Montagu. Copyright © 1978 by Ashley Montagu. Reprinted by permission of Oxford University Press, Inc.

Gary Soto. "Black Hair." From *Living up the Street*. Published by Dell, 1992. Copyright 1985 by Gary Soto. Reprinted by permission of the author.

Brent Staples. "Black Men and Public Space." From *Harper's*, December 1987. Reprinted by permission of the author.

Andrew Sullivan. "Wouldn't Normally Do." From *The New Republic*, February 21, 1994. Reprinted by permission of *The New Republic*, © 1994 by The New Republic, Inc.

Ann Swidler. From *Habits of the Heart: Individualism and Commitment in American Life* by Robert N. Bellah, Richard Madsen, William M. Sullivan, Ann Swidler, and Steven M. Tipton. Copyright © 1985 by the Regents of the University of California. Reprinted by permission of the University of California Press.

Amy Tan. "Mother Tongue." Copyright © 1990 by Amy Tan. As first appeared in *The Threepenny Review*. Reprinted by permission of Amy Tan and the Sandra Dijkstra Literary Agency.

Deborah Tannen. "Women and Men Talking on the Job." From pages 32–36 and 39–41 from *Talking from 9 to 5* by Deborah Tannen. Copyright © 1994 by Deborah Tannen, PhD. Reprinted by permission of William Morrow and Company, Inc.

James Thurber. "The Case for the Daydreamer." From *Let Your Mind Alone*, published by HarperCollins. Copyright © 1937 by James Thurber. Copyright © 1965 by Rosemary A. Thurber.

Barbara W. Tuchman. From *A Distant Mirror: The Calamitous Fourteenth Century* by Barbara W. Tuchman. Copyright © 1978 by Barbara W. Tuchman. Reprinted by permission of Alfred A. Knopf, Inc.

John Updike. Excerpt from "Venezuela for Visitors." From *Hugging the Shore: Essays and Criticsm* by John Updike. Copyright © 1983 by John Updike. Alfred A. Knopf, Inc., Publisher.

Charles Van Riper. Excerpt from *A Career in Speech Pathology*. © 1979 by Allyn and Bacon, p. 29. Reprinted/adapted by permission of the author.

Nicholas Wade. "How Men and Women Think." From the June 12, 1994 issue of *The New York Times Magazine*. Copyright © 1994 by The New York Times Company. Reprinted by permission.

Bruce Weigl. "Song of Napalm." From *Song of Napalm*, Atlantic Monthly Press, 1988. Reprinted by permission of the author.

Gerald Weissmann. "Foucault and the Bag Lady." From *The Woods Hole Cantata: Essays on Science and Society* by Gerald Weissmann. © 1985 by Gerald Weissmann, M.D. Reprinted by permission of the author and the Watkins/Loomis Agency.

E. B. White. "Once More to the Lake." From Essays of E. B. White. Copyright 1944 by E. B. White. Reprinted by permission of HarperCollins Publishers.

Patricia Williams. "Hate Radio." Reprinted by permission of *Ms.* Magazine, © 1994.

Robert Wright. "Mr. Clean Genes." From *The New Republic*, October 24, 1994. Reprinted by permission of *The New Republic*, © 1994 by The New Republic, Inc.

Philip Zaleski. From "The Superstars of Heart Research." *Boston Magazine*, December 1982. Copyright © 1982 by Philip Zaleski. Reprinted by permission of the author.

*Art and Photograph Credits*

*Page 461:* Photo "Mary and Morris Shaving, 1966" by Ruth Orkin. © 1974 by Ruth Orkin. Reprinted by permission of Mary Engel and the Estate of Ruth Orkin.

*Page 489:* Photo "Laughing" from the tryptych "Living, Loving, Laughing." © 1988 by Martin M. Stone.

*Page 513:* Photo by Ulli Steltzer from page 82 of *The New Americans*. Published by NewSage Press, 1988. © 1988 by Ulli Steltzer.

*Page 541:* Photo "Executives in Corridor" by Michael Krasowitz. Reprinted by permission of FPG International.

*Page 576:* Photo from *Star Trek*. Reprinted courtesy of Photofest.

*Page 603:* Photo "Worker Spraying Bean Field" by Richard Steven Street. From *Organizing for Our Lives: New Voices from Rural Communities* by Richard Steven Street. Published by NewSage Press, 1992.

*Figure 28.3:* Entry from *The Oxford English Dictionary*, 2nd. ed. © 1989 by Oxford University Press. Reprinted by permission.

*Figure 28.9:* *Reader's Guide to Periodical Literature*, entries under "Sports" from January 1995, Volume 94, No. 11, page 289. Copyright © 1995 by the H. W. Wilson Company. Material reproduced with the permission of the publisher.

"Shoe" cartoon. Reprinted by permission of Tribune Media Services.

# Index

*Use these standard proofreading marks when making minor corrections in your final draft. If extensive revision is necessary, type or print out a clean copy.*

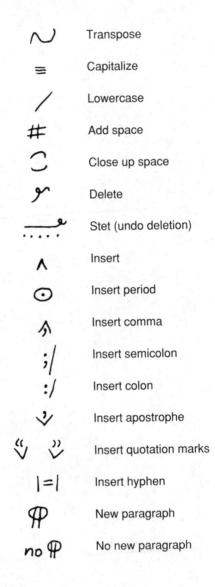

| | |
|---|---|
| ∽ | Transpose |
| ≡ | Capitalize |
| / | Lowercase |
| # | Add space |
| ⌒ | Close up space |
| ℐ | Delete |
| ⟶ℯ | Stet (undo deletion) |
| ∧ | Insert |
| ⊙ | Insert period |
| ⋏ | Insert comma |
| ;/ | Insert semicolon |
| :/ | Insert colon |
| ∨ | Insert apostrophe |
| ⟪∨ ⟫∨ | Insert quotation marks |
| \|=\| | Insert hyphen |
| ¶ | New paragraph |
| no ¶ | No new paragraph |

## CORRECTION SYMBOLS

*Many Instructors use these abbreviations and symbols to mark errors in student papers. Refer to this chart to find out what they mean.*

**Boldface numbers refer to sections of the handbook.**

| | | | |
|---|---|---|---|
| abbr | faulty abbreviation **32** | om | omitted word **15** |
| ad | misuse of adverb or adjective **10** | p | error in punctuation **24–31** |
| agr | faulty agreement **6, 9** | ^ | comma **25** |
| appr | inappropriate language **20, 22** | no , | no comma **25n–r** |
| awk | awkward | ; | semicolon **26** |
| cap | capital letter **33** | : | colon **27** |
| case | error in case **7** | ˅ | apostrophe **28** |
| coord | faulty coordination **18** | " " | quotation marks **29** |
| cs | comma splice **13** | . ? ! | period, question mark, exclamation point **24** |
| dm | dangling modifier **14** | – ( ) [ ] . . . | dash, parentheses, brackets, ellipsis **30–31** |
| exact | inexact language **21** | par, ¶ | new paragraph |
| frag | sentence fragment **12** | pass | ineffective passive **5m** |
| fs | fused sentence **13** | ref | error in pronoun reference **8** |
| gl | see glossary of trouble-makers | rev | revise |
| gr | grammar **1–4** | sp | misspelled word **37** |
| hyph | error in use of hyphen **36** | sub | faulty subordination **18** |
| inc | incomplete construction **15** | t | error in verb tense **5c, g–l** |
| irreg | error in irregular verb **5e** | v | voice **5m** |
| ital | italics (underlining) **35** | vb | error in verb form **5** |
| lc | use lowercase letter **33** | w | wordy **23** |
| mixed | mixed construction **16** | // | faulty parallelism **17** |
| mm | misplaced modifier **14a–b** | ^ | insert |
| mood | error in mood **5n–p** | x | obvious error |
| ms | manuscript form pp.420–22 | # | insert space |
| nonst | nonstandard usage **20, 21** | ⌒ | close up space |
| num | error in use of numbers **34** | | |

# A GUIDE TO THE HANDBOOK